W9-CTJ-416

PSYCHOLOGY

PSYCHOLOGY

FIFTH EDITION

Lester A. Lefton

University of South Carolina

ALLYN AND BACON

Boston   London   Toronto   Sydney   Tokyo   Singapore

Vice President and Publisher: Susan Badger
Developmental Editor: Elizabeth Brooks
Editorial Assistant: Laura L. Ellingson
Production Administrator: Susan McIntyre
Cover Administrator: Linda Dickinson
Composition Buyer: Linda Cox
Manufacturing Buyer: Megan Cochran
Design and Art Development: Deborah Schneck
Illustrators: Rolin Graphics, Wayne Clark, Lyrl Ahern
Photo Research: Laurel Anderson/Photosynthesis

Copyright 1994, 1991, 1985, 1982, 1979 by Allyn and Bacon
A Division of Paramount Publishing
160 Gould Street
Needham Heights, MA 02194

All rights reserved. No part of the material protected by this copyright notice may be reproduced or utilized in any form or by any means, electronic or mechanical, including photocopying, recording, or by any information storage and retrieval system, without the written permission of the copyright owner.

Library of Congress Cataloging-in-Publication Data

Lefton, Lester A., 1946–
    Psychology / Lester A. Lefton. — 5th ed.
        p.   cm.
    Includes bibliographical references and indexes.
    ISBN 0-205-15248-1
    1. Psychology.   I. Title.
BF121.L424 1994
150—dc20   93-27969
                                         CIP

Printed in the United States of America

10 9 8 7 6 5 4 3   98 97 96 95 94

*For Linda, a woman of beauty, courage, strength, and
sensitivity; my wife, partner, and friend.*

Contents

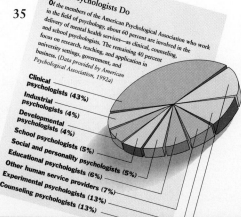

FIGURE 1.1
What Psychologists Do
Of the members of the American Psychological Association who work in the field of psychology, about 60 percent are involved in the delivery of mental health services—as clinical, counseling, and school psychologists. The remaining 40 percent focus on research, teaching, and application in university settings, government, and business. (Data provided by American Psychological Association, 1992a)

Clinical psychologists (43%)
Industrial psychologists (4%)
Developmental psychologists (4%)
School psychologists (5%)
Social and personality psychologists (5%)
Educational psychologists (6%)
Other human service providers (7%)
Experimental psychologists (13%)
Counseling psychologists (13%)

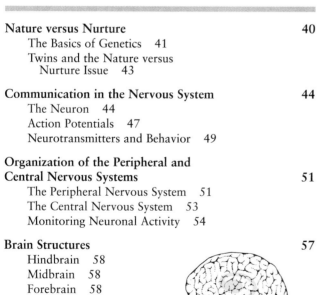

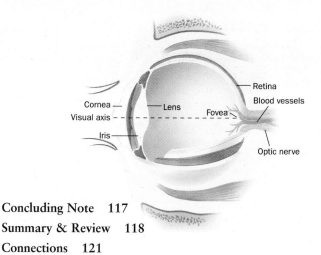

3 Sensation and Perception 74

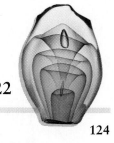

4 States of Consciousness 122

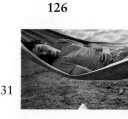

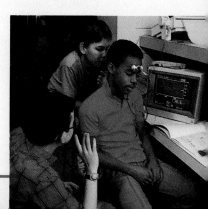

5 Learning 156

Pavlov Measuring Salivation

Pavlov attached a tube to a dog's salivary gland, which had been surgically moved to the outside of the dog's cheek to allow easy collection of saliva. He then measured the number of drops of saliva that naturally occurred when a bell was sounded.

Next, he measured the number of drops of saliva that occurred when a bell was sounded along with the presentation of food.

He found that, after repeated presentations of the bell followed by food, the dog's saliva increased as soon as the bell was sounded, indicating that it had learned to associate the food and the bell.

6 Memory 202

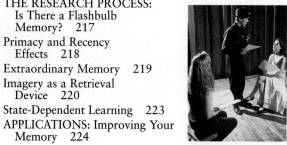

7 Cognitive Psychology 242

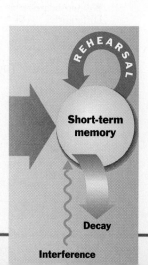

8 Child Development 276

9 Adolescence and Adulthood 314

12 Personality and Its Assessment 424

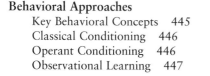

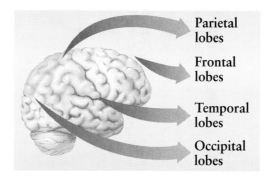

13 Stress and Health Psychology 466

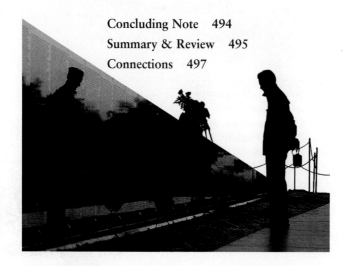

14 Psychological Disorders 498

15 Approaches to Treatment 534

16 The Social World 572

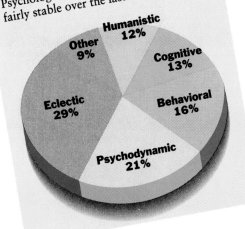

The primary orientation of clinical psychologists who belong to the American Psychological Association has remained fairly stable over the last decade.

Humanistic 12% · Cognitive 13% · Other 9% · Eclectic 29% · Behavioral 16% · Psychodynamic 21%

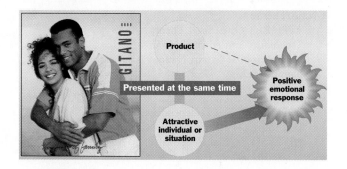

17 Social Interactions 606

Module A: Scientific and Statistical Methods 642

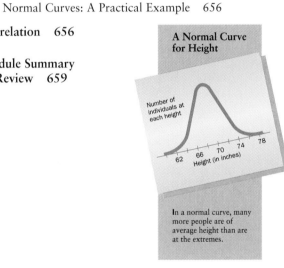

A Normal Curve for Height

Number of individuals at each height

62   66   70   74   78
Height (in inches)

In a normal curve, many more people are of average height than are at the extremes.

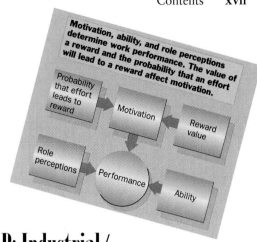

Motivation, ability, and role perceptions determine work performance. The value of a reward and the probability that an effort will lead to a reward affect motivation.

Probability that effort leads to reward

Motivation

Reward value

Role perceptions

Performance

Ability

Module B: Industrial/ Organizational Psychology 661

Preface

Writing this text was both an adventure and a challenge. Four strategic goals guided my work on *Psychology*, Fifth Edition. My first goal was *to make psychology understandable* by presenting the principles and methodology of psychology in a straightforward and accessible manner. My second goal was *to stress the critical thinking process* of discovering what is true, and building on current facts and theories. My third goal was *to enrich the student's understanding of the applications of psychology* in everyday life and to show the integration of science and application; I feel strongly that science and application flow from one another, each dependent on the other. My fourth goal was *to provide a cohesive narrative* that presents the student with a unitary and clear view of the field, connecting concepts from chapter to chapter.

A New Edition: Organization, Content, and Diversity

The previous edition of *Psychology* was very well received by both students and instructors. They liked its clarity and appreciated its balance of research and application. They applauded its pedagogical structure, particularly the highly praised Building Tables and Connections Tables. But, for all of its strengths, I wanted to keep the text attuned to the needs of students and professors of the 90s.

My plan for the fifth edition focused on six specific areas: diversity, research, critical thinking, ethics, application, and students. First, I wanted to stress *diversity* and sensitivity to culture and gender; I was particularly interested in showing that psychologists must consider the wide range of participants in research. To make reasonable generalizations about human behavior they must consider ethnic, cultural, age, and gender issues. Second, I wanted to show that *research* is a cornerstone of psychology; the revision of *Psychology* reflects an increased emphasis on the role of research in psychology. To this end, I especially wanted to focus on *critical thinking* as a key to good scientific thought and research, my third goal. Fourth, I wanted to highlight *ethics* in research. Ethics with animals and human subjects has been brought to the forefront of psychology and the new edition reflects this concern. Fifth, I wanted to focus on how *applications* grow from research. Last, I wanted to ensure that *student interest* and understanding continued to take a prominent role in my writing. To help accomplish this goal, I planned to use a more personal voice in my writing and share my personal point of view more often.

To achieve my goals, I enlisted the aid of colleagues, friends, and students who read both the previous edition of the book and new drafts. The publisher sought the help of instructors throughout the country. Psychologists read the manuscript with an eye to accuracy, current trends, sensitivity to gender and diversity issues, pedagogy, and general student interest.

These reviews were extremely helpful. I was buried for months in reams of letters, manuscripts, articles, faxes, and phone calls. The result is a new edition with a spirited and elegant design; an especially clear, organized writing style; and a direct personal approach to student learning. In addition, the following specific changes have been made.

Reorganization. The overall table of contents is organized in a new, more logical manner, starting with the basics of psychology (biology, perception, and learning) and moving to the more applied, clinical, and socially relevant chapters. Yet, every chapter is written so that it can stand alone and be read in any sequence. Every chapter has been rewritten with the aim of providing a more structured approach, with a smoother, more cohesive flow of information. The internal structure of each chapter attempts to match the way teachers present material; we talked with hundreds of psychology teachers to determine the most logical and sought after structure.

Content. This new edition covers the core concepts of psychology in addition to emerging, high-interest topics. The traditional areas of learning, memory, and perception are presented fully and clearly. Current data and theories that impact on behavior from the biological sciences are presented. The applied fields are similarly represented with complete coverage of topics such as child development, gender differences, performance appraisal, and testing issues. New topics such as brief therapy, codependence, and substance abuse are covered, as well as brain plasticity, sexual dysfunctions, and Alzheimer's disease. These high-interest topics are presented in an integrated manner by bringing science and application together and showing how they flow directly from traditional psychology. The content of the text reflects the current status of psychological science without being trendy or neglecting the classics.

Diversity. This new edition has an emphasis on diversity and is sensitive to issues such as culture, ethnicity, gender, and age. Psychologists now recognize the important role of culture and gender in psychological phenomena. This makes our research more difficult but it also makes the outcomes of our work more relevant. I have attempted to integrate diversity throughout the book, with a special focus on high interest topics that have both application and basic research in them. These special sections are called "Diversity."

Pedagogical Features

A primary aim of *Psychology*, Fifth Edition, is to make psychology both understandable and interesting for students. Eight major pedagogical features have been integrated into *Psychology* to stimulate student involvement and critical thinking about issues, theories, and data.

Focus. Throughout the text short review sections called "Focus" ask students to pause, review, question, and think about what they have just learned. These are critical thinking questions and do not simply test rote memory. These sections are nonintrusive and conveniently placed; they include page references to show where topics are discussed. Answers to these questions are available for instructors.

Critical Thinking. Learning about psychology means learning about the thinking process. Developing critical thinking skills is a major theme in chapter 1 and throughout the book. In addition, special sections called "The Research

Process" show students how psychologists use (and sometimes abuse) the scientific method.

Diversity. A key theme of this edition is to introduce students to the diversity of people and their backgrounds and to show how diversity factors must be taken into consideration when viewing psychological data. This means looking at issues such as gender, ethnicity, age, and social class from a critical thinking point of view. Diversity issues are featured in special "Diversity" sections in most chapters and are integrated throughout the book.

Applications. Featuring interesting topics such as solving sleep problems, managing children's behavior, and improving memory, special "Applications" sections focus on how psychology can be applied to everyday life. Applications are a regular theme in the text, and these sections highlight especially interesting examples and place them in context.

Building Tables. Presenting major theories and concepts in a way that shows the development of ideas is a major structural and pedagogical element in this text. Pioneered in previous editions, "Building Tables" have been visually enhanced and expanded. As one set of concepts is mastered, a new set is added on. These tables allow for comparisons and contrasts, while providing a means for integrating concepts. They are also an excellent aid for study and review.

Key Terms. Key terms are boldfaced in the text and defined in the margins, as well as in the end-of-book glossary, with a pronunciation guide where appropriate. In addition, the key terms are listed with page references within the chapter summary to help students review the main concepts.

Summary & Review. Every chapter has a well-structured chapter summary, organized by section headings with page references to relevant portions of the text. The review is organized in a question and answer format with key terms integrated into the summary.

Connections. At the end of each chapter is a connections table that provides cross-references for major, high-interest topics. Students can use connections tables to learn more about various areas of interest and also to see the interrelated nature of psychology.

Supplements for Students

Keeping Pace Plus. *Keeping Pace Plus: A Success Guide for Psychology* is an active reading study guide. Now in its fifth edition, this carefully structured study guide helps students participate actively in learning about psychology. It contains book-specific exercises, learning objectives, review sections, and practice test questions. The new edition includes a language enrichment section for students who need help with vocabulary. With page-referenced reviews, *Keeping Pace Plus* guarantees learning for students who use it.

Studying Psychology. A brief how-to manual, *Studying Psychology: A Manual for Success* is designed to help students develop the skills to master psychology more effectively. With down-to-earth techniques and ideas, this booklet helps students develop effective strategies for studying, listening, dealing with lectures, and preparing for examinations.

Critical Thinking. Developed by James Bell, this booklet focuses on helping students evaluate psychological information. The focus of this valuable book is to show students how to evaluate research evidence systematically and improve their critical thinking skills.

World of Psychology. A brief series of current articles taken from *The Washington Post, World of Psychology* focuses on diversity. High-interest, topical, and provocative, these articles can be used to encourage critical thinking. The readings are cross-referenced to related topics in the text.

Psychology and Culture. Walter Lonner and Roy Malpass have developed an entry-level, broad based book of readings that serve as an introduction to the role of culture and ethnicity in human behavior. It features original articles by experts in the field and an extensive introductory overview that sketches conceptual and methodological issues.

SoundGuide. This cassette tape is an audio study guide for the text and helps students review, rehearse, and take practice tests. For use in portable tape players and automobiles, this study aid facilitates another mode of studying, active learning, and thinking about psychology.

Annotated Instructor's Edition and Supplements for Instructors

An Annotated Instructor's Edition is provided to encourage student involvement and understanding. It includes an instructor's section bound into the front of the book and detailed annotations in the margin of each chapter with teaching suggestions, examples, demonstrations, visual aids, and learning objectives. In addition to the *Annotated Instructor's Edition,* a wide array of supplementary materials is available, including an instructor's resource manual filled with activities, handouts, and a wide array of additional teaching aids; a superb set of transparencies; a lengthy computer-ready test item file; *PsychScience,* an interactive, computer simulation of real-life experiments; CNN videos, plus superb video discs with video segments and graphics; and an extensive videotape library. All of these supplements, and more, are keyed to the *Annotated Instructor's Edition.*

Acknowledgments

The cast of characters who helped me prepare this textbook is extraordinary; some are psychologists, some are students, some are professional textbook developers. I am especially appreciative of the help that instructors and students have given me. They have corrected mistakes, focused my vision, and encouraged me to consider the special needs of diverse populations of students and instructors. A number of these reviewers were colleagues of mine at the University of South Carolina whom

I prevailed on regularly for guidance. I especially thank Ernest Furchtgott who gave me line-by-line comments on the entire book. I also thank Sandra Kelly, Jay Coleman, Jim Appel, Tom Carferty, and Dave Clement who provided chapter commentaries. Faculty at other institutions ranging from research institutions to teaching-oriented community colleges, helped me focus my ideas, pointed me in new research directions, and queried my logic. They met in focus groups, talked with me individually, and wrote lengthy reviews of each chapter. In immeasurable ways, these reviewers helped make this book better. I thank each of them:

Spencer Adams
Salt Lake Community College

Bob Ahlering
Central Missouri State University

George Alliger
SUNY-Albany

Galen Bodenhausen
Michigan State University

John Best
Eastern Illinois University

Kathleen Bey
Palm Beach Community College

Edward Caldwell
West Virginia University

Robert B. Cameron
Fairmont State College

Michael Bernard Casey
Virginia Polytechnic Institute and State University

George A. Cicala
University of Delaware

Patrick Conley
University of Illinois-Chicago

Joan Cook
County College of Morris

Verne Cox
University of Texas-Arlington

Patrick De Boli
Nassau Community College

Jadwiga Dolzycki
Tennessee Tech

Margaret E. Donnelly
Pace University

Jane Fillmore
Utah Valley Community College

Dashiel Geyen
University of Houston-Downtown

Drusilla Glascoe
Salt Lake Community College

Howard Harris
Bronx Community College

Richard J. Harris
Kansas State University

Larry Hochhaus
Oklahoma State University

Charles A. Homra
Murray State University

James J. Johnson
Illinois State University

Arthur D. Kemp
Central Missouri State

Walter J. Lonner
Western Washington University

Duane Martin
University of Texas-Arlington

Linda Musun Miller
University of Arkansas at Little Rock

James Moore, Jr.
Marshall University

Glenda G. Nichols
Tarrant County Junior College

Ronald D. Pearse
Fairmont State College

Janet Proctor
Purdue University

Peter J. Rowe
College of Charleston

K. Elaine Royal
Middle Tennessee State University

Mike Scoles
University of Central Arkansas

Harold I. Siegel
Rutgers University

Gene Smith
Western Illinois University

Janet Sniezak
University of Illinois-Urbana/Champaign

Donald M. Stanley
North Harris College

Frank Vattano
Colorado State University

Charles Weichert
San Antonio College

I would also like to acknowledge and thank the reviewers of previous editions who helped me build the firm foundation on which this book stands. They include the following individuals:

Lewis Aiken
Pepperdine University

Georgia Babladelis
California State University

Jean Badry
Indiana University-South Bend

Lew Barker
Baylor University

Brian Bate
Cuyahoga Community College-Western Campus

William Beatty
North Dakota State University

Hal Beck
Appalachian State University

George Bishop
National University of Singapore

Richard Bowen
Loyola University of Chicago

Jay Braun
Arizona State University

Brian Burnie
George Brown College

John Caruso
Southeastern Massachusetts University

Lawrence Casler
SUNY-Geneseo

Kathleen Chen
Rochester Institute of Technology

James Corwin
University of New Orleans

Winifred Curtis
Community College of Rhode Island

Donald Devers
Northern Virginia Community College

Terry Devietti
Central Western University

Thornton Dozier
Michigan State University

Cheryl Dreut
SUNY-Fredonia

Leslie Fisher
Cleveland State University

Linda Flickinger
St. Clair Community College

Leonard Flynn
Framingham State College

Mark Garrison
Kentucky State University

James Grosch
SUNY-Geneseo

Ernest Gurman
University of Southern Mississippi

Michael Gurtman
University of Wisconsin-Parkside

Jane Halpert
DePaul University

Joy Hammersla
Seattle Pacific University

Charles Hinderliter
University of Pittsburgh

Morton Hoffman
Metropolitan State University

Peter Holland
University of Pittsburgh

Kermit Hoyenga
Western Illinois University

William Kalberer
California State University-Chico

Dennis Karpowitz
University of Kansas

Jane Kelly
Hinds Community College

Harold Kiess
Framingham State College

Jack Kirshenbaum
Fullerton Community College

James Knight
Humboldt State University

Wayne Lesko
Marymount University

Robert Levy
Indiana State University

Ted Lewandoski
Delaware County Community College

Marjorie Lewis
Illinois State University

Sal Macias
University of South Carolina-Sumter

Sheldon Malev
Westchester Community College

Cynthia Margolin
San Jose State College

Richard Maslow
Delta College

James Matiya
Moraine Valley Community College

Robert Meyer
University of Louisville

David Townsend
Montclair State University

Jerry Mikosz
Moraine Valley Community College

Benjamin Wallace
Cleveland State University

Harvey Pines
Canisius College

William Wallace
Marshall University

Edward Pollak
West Chester State College

Andrea Wesley
University of Southern Mississippi

Christopher Rhoades
Hilbert College

Richard Wesp
Elmira College

James Roll
William Rainey Harper College

David Whitsett
University of Northern Iowa

Paul Salmon
University of Louisville

John Williams
Westchester Community College

Robert Shaw
Texas Southmost College

Kevin Williams
Rensselaer Polytechnic Institute

Dirk Steiner
Louisiana State University

Patrick Williams
Wharton County Junior College

Michael Stevenson
Ball State University

Joe Rae Zuckerman
Los Angeles Harbor College

Warren Street
Central Western University

The students who read the chapters in this book are my greatest friends and my most important audience. For the past ten years, students in my classroom and in classrooms all over the country have read chapters of this text—both previous editions and drafts of new chapters. They provided criticism and help, and pointed out areas that needed to be strengthened. I am in their debt.

I also thank Marcia Gardner, my administrative assistant, who makes my life easier by attending to details, keeping up with my correspondence, and facilitating my work flow. Marcia keeps me on an even keel, and her hard work provides me the time needed to write this text. My thanks also go to Ian Birnie who helped with library research and a seemingly endless number of details, and to Jodi Helton who worked with me to coordinate permissions, a tedious task. I am also grateful to Mark Garrison from Kentucky State University, who prepared the instructor's section, the annotations, and the instructor's resource manual; to Jan Simons of Central Iowa Psychological Services, for writing a superb test bank; and to Andrew Ryan, Jr., Laura Valvatne, and Joyce Bishop for their work on the study guide.

My friends at Allyn and Bacon are an incredibly creative team. Many worked behind the scenes and had limited contact with me directly, but I know of their involvement, and I am appreciative. I thank the sales force and their experienced managers who gathered information from instructors and students, and Dana Hayes and Laura Ellingson who coordinated reviews and contacted instructors. The marketing team, especially Joyce Nilsen, Lou Kennedy, and Sandi Kirshner, has helped immeasurably in gathering information and helping me set the agenda for the text. The design of the text is exciting, and I thank Debbie Schneck for her work; I also appreciate the striking cover which was designed by Linda Dickinson.

Production is among the most time-consuming and exacting of the steps in putting a textbook together, and every page of the text shows the superb work of Elaine Ober, Judy Fiske, and especially production editor Susan McIntyre. With a fine eye for detail, Susan managed the specialized elements in this complicated text. Susan was flexible and responded to dozens of last-minute changes needed to keep the book current despite a breakneck schedule and many technical challenges.

The editorial team at Allyn and Bacon is the best in textbook publishing. I have had the benefit of over a decade of guidance and expertise from top-notch developmental and acquisition editors such as Allen Workman, Sandi Kirshner, and Bill Barke. At various points in the production and development of this book they have had crucial input. I especially thank Sandi and Bill, respectively Vice President and President of Allyn and Bacon, for their continued confidence in me and this project.

On a day-to-day basis, Elizabeth Brooks and Susan Badger were the people who made this book happen. They worked with me to ensure the quality, thematic integrity, and overall direction of the text. Elizabeth Brooks was the developmental editor who worked with me line by line to make certain that every thought was precise. Beth challenged, prodded, and provided advice. Her skill, knowledge, and sound judgment are reflected on every page of text, and I cannot thank her enough.

Every creative team has to have a leader; Allyn and Bacon has the best psychology editor in the business—Vice President and Publisher Susan Badger. Susan has keen judgment and terrific insight into what psychologists and students want in a text. Susan commits herself to every detail, and her ideas and creativity are unmatched. She sets the standard for editors. I thank her.

Last, I dedicate this text to my wife, Linda, a woman of great beauty, courage, strength, and sensitivity. Linda is my wife, my partner, and my friend; this book would not exist without her active involvement in my life.

To the Student

Be Actively Involved in Learning

Here are some important study tips that will reduce your stress level and increase your effectiveness as a student.

▶ Be actively involved in the learning process.

▶ Make new information meaningful by linking your existing life experiences and knowledge (what you already know) to new information (what you are learning for the first time).

▶ Take responsibility for your own learning.

One way to really improve your studying and be an active learner is to use the SQ3R system which reminds learners to *survey, question, read, recite,* and *review* when reading textbooks (Robinson, 1970). SQ3R has been used effectively and successfully by college students since 1941—it is a tried-and-true active reading and study method, which is why it is the reading strategy most recommended by psychology teachers. I have modified the original SQ3R method slightly to SQ3R *plus: survey, question, read, recite, review*—plus, *write and reflect*. To be effective learners, use the SQ3R *plus* system when studying psychology—it means putting a little psychology to work.

To start you with SQ3R *plus*, follow these steps: Before you begin studying, **survey:**

▶ Quickly read the *outline* at the beginning of the chapter and the chapter's opening paragraphs; this will provide a brief *overview* of the chapter.

▶ Scan *topic headings* and examine the "Focus" questions that appear throughout the chapter; this will further refine your overview of the chapter goals.

▶ Look at the *photos, art work, tables, and graphs*—these will help you get a more concrete idea of what you will be studying.

▶ Take time to scan the *tables,* especially the "building tables"—these will give you a preview of concepts that you will want to compare and contrast as you read, so that you can learn the similarities and differences among theories presented in a chapter.

▶ Pay attention to other special features, such as print styles, the use of color in the text, and summaries.

▶ You also may want to plan a study break at the end of each major section in the chapter.

Next, **question.** Ask yourself questions about the material to be studied. Examine the "Focus" questions that appear every few pages. This will increase your involvement, interest, and concentration because for each question you ask, you will have the goal of finding an answer.

Third, **read.** Read the text and answer the questions that you asked yourself. Focus on making the material you are reading personally relevant.

Fourth, **recite.** *Recite* means saying things from memory, but being an active learner means putting thoughts in your own schematic conceptions and words.

Fifth, **review.** Double check your accuracy and understanding of the material to be learned. Try to pull together key terms and concepts.

Plus, **write and reflect.** When you write a summary of key points, you increase the quality and quantity of your own learning. When you *reflect* on your learning, you are not only an active learner, but also a critical thinker—a person able to make good use of newly learned information.

Psychology as a Career

For those who would like to read more about psychology as a profession and potential career, the American and Canadian Psychological Associations publish several books and booklets that provide further information. Your school's psychology department or counseling center may have copies of them. Or you may write to the APA or CPA at the addresses given in the membership section below. The APA publishes the following items:

Is Psychology the Major for You? This 137-page volume is oriented toward students who wish to make a career of psychology. It tells you what careers are available, how to find a job, how to utilize career counseling, and how to survive as a new employee.

Preparing for Graduate Study in Psychology: NOT for Seniors Only! This 96-page source book discusses how to plan the steps needed for graduate school, with an emphasis on students who do not have the "credentials" yet. It provides help on acquiring recommendations, writing resumes, practicing interviews and the like.

Graduate Study in Psychology and Associated Fields. This book is a comprehensive guide (over 600 pages) to graduate programs in the United States and Canada. It indicates which schools offer which specialties and discusses admission requirements, housing facilities, financial assistance, tuition, and so on.

Careers in Psychology. This brief (28-page) pamphlet describes the fields of and careers in psychology. Single copies are free to students.

The Canadian Psychological Association publishes the *Graduate Guide: Description of Graduate Psychology Programs in Canadian Universities.*

Memberships

You can join a national organization as a student affiliate. APA's annual fee for students is $25, for which you get (1) discounts on books published by APA, (2) lower prices on APA journal subscriptions, (3) the *APA Monitor* (the organization's monthly newspaper), and (4) the *American Psychologist* (its official journal) at no extra cost. Write to 750 First Street, N.E., Washington, D.C. 20002.

The Canadian Psychological Association's student membership is only $10, for which you receive news in the field and journals. Write to Vincent Road, Old Chelsea, Quebec JOX 2NO.

Text Credits

Figures, Tables, and Quotations: Chapter 2: QUOTE p. 41—From Watson, J. B. (1930). *Behaviorism,* Second Edition. New York: W. W. Norton & Company, Inc. Reprinted by permission.

Chapter 3: FIG. 3.1, p. 78—From Held, R., & Hein, A. (1963). Movement produced stimulation in the development of visually guided behavior. *Journal of Comparative and Physiological Psychology, 56,* pp. 872–876. Copyright © 1963 by the American Psychological Association. Reprinted by permission. FIG. 3.3, p. 81—Neural interconnections figure from Dowling, J. E., & Boycott, B. B. (1966). *Proceedings of the Royal Society* (London), Series B, *166,* pp. 80–111. Reprinted by permission. FIG. 3.5, p. 83—From Pirenne, M. H. (1967). *Vision and the eye,* p. 32. London: Chapman & Hall, Ltd. Reprinted by permission. FIG. 3.9, p. 86—From Hubel, D. H., & Wiesel, T. N. (1962). Receptive fields, binocular interaction, and functional architecture in the cat's visual cortex. *Journal of Physiology, 160,* pp. 106–164. Reprinted by permission. FIG. 3.10, p. 87—From Noton, David, & Stark, Lawrence. Eye movements and visual perception, p. 34. Copyright © 1971 by *Scientific American,* Inc. All rights reserved. Reprinted by permission. FIG. 3.13, p. 89—Reprinted from *Vision Research, 4,* MacNichol, Edward F. Jr., Retinal mechanisms of color vision, pp. 119–133. Copyright 1964, with kind permission from Pergamon Press Ltd., Headington Hill Hall, Oxford 0X3 0BW, UK. FIG. 3.15, p. 99—From Beck, Jacob (1966). Effects of orientation and of shape similarity on perceptual grouping. *Perception and Psychophysics, 1,* pp. 300–302. Reprinted by permission of Psychonomic Society, Inc.

Chapter 4: FIG. 4.1, p. 130—From *Some must watch while some must sleep,* by William C. Dement. Copyright © 1972 by William C. Dement. Used by permission of the Stanford Alumni Association and William C. Dement. FIG. 4.2, p. 131—From Roffwarg, H. P., Muzio, and Dement (1966). Ontogenetic development of human sleep-dream cycle. *Science, 152,* pp. 604–609. Copyright 1966 by the AAAS. Reprinted by permission. FIG. 4.4, p. 144—From Ray, Oakley, & Ksir, Charles (1983). *Drugs, society, & human behavior,* ed. 6, p. 194. St. Louis, MO: Mosby-Year Book, Inc. Reprinted by permission. TABLE 4.1, p. 145—From Ray, Oakley, & Ksir, Charles (1983). *Drugs, society, & human behavior,* ed. 6, p. 192. St. Louis, MO: Mosby-Year Book, Inc. Reprinted by permission.

Chapter 6: FIG. 6.8, p. 221—From Kosslyn, Stephen. M. (1975). Information representation in visual images. *Cognitive Psychology, 55,* pp. 162–170. Reprinted by permission. FIG. 6.9, p. 222—From Shepard, R. N., & Metzler, J. (1971). Mental rotation of three-dimensional objects. *Science, 171,* pp. 701–703. Copyright 1971 by the AAAS. Reprinted by permission. QUOTE p. 223—From Bower, G. H. (1981). Mood and memory. *American Psychologist, 36,* p. 129. Copyright 1981 by the American Psychological Association. Reprinted by permission. TABLE 6.1, p. 228—From Hall, J. F. (1982).

An invitation to learning and memory, p. 153. Boston: Allyn & Bacon. Reprinted by permission.

Chapter 7: FIG. 7.8, p. 264—From Moskowitz, Breyne A. The acquisition of language. Copyright © 1978 by *Scientific American,* Inc. All rights reserved. Reprinted by permission. FIG. 7.10, p. 270—From Premack, David (1971). Language in chimpanzees? *Science, 172,* pp. 808–822. Copyright 1971 by the AAAS. Reprinted by permission.

Chapter 8: FIG. 8.2, p. 285—Adapted from Fantz, Robert L. The origin of form and perception, p. 72. Copyright © 1961 by *Scientific American,* Inc. Photo by David Linton. All rights reserved. Adapted by permission. FOLDOUT pp. 292a–292b—From Clarke-Stewart, A., Friedman, S., & Koch, J. *Child development: A topical approach,* p. 191. Copyright © 1985 by John Wiley & Sons, Inc. Reprinted by permission from John Wiley & Sons, Inc. FIG. 8.3, p. 289—From Frankenberg, W. K., & Dobbs, J. B. (1967). The Denver Developmental Screening Tests. *Journal of Pediatrics, 71,* p. 191. St. Louis, MO: Mosby-Year Book, Inc. Reprinted by permission. QUOTE p. 291—From Piaget, Jean (1963, Autumn). The attainment of invariants and reversible operations in the development of thinking. *Social Research, 30* (3), p. 283. Reprinted by permission. FIG. 8.4, p. 293—From Fox, N., Kagan, J., & Weiskopf, S. (1979). The growth of memory during infancy. *Genetic Psychology Monograms, 99,* pp. 91–130. Reprinted with permission of the Helen Dwight Reid Educational Foundation. Published by Heldref Publications, 1319 Eighteenth St., N. W., Washington, D. C. 20036-1802. Copyright © 1979.

Chapter 9: TABLE 9.2, p. 331—Reprinted with the permission of Macmillan Publishing Company from *The journey of adulthood* by Helen L. Bee. Copyright © 1987 by Macmillan Publishing Company.

Chapter 10: QUOTE p. 353—From Rodin, Judith (1981). Current status of the internal-external hypothesis for obesity. *American Psychologist, 36* (2), pp. 129–148. FIG. 10.6, p. 370—From Lazarus, R. S., & Alfert, E. (1964). Short-circuiting of threat by experimentally altering cognitive appraisal. *Journal of Abnormal and Social Psychology, 69,* pp. 195–205. Copyright 1964 by the American Psychological Association. Reprinted by permission. TABLE 10.2, p. 375—From Frijda, Nico H. (1988). The laws of emotion. *American Psychologist, 43,* pp. 349–358. Copyright 1988 by the American Psychological Association. Reprinted by permission. FIG. 10.8, p. 376—Figure from *Emotion: A psychoevolutionary synthesis* by Robert Plutchik. Copyright © 1980 by Individual Dynamics, Inc. Reprinted by permission of HarperCollins Publishers Inc. FIG. 10.11, p. 385—From Hebb, Donald O. (1972). *Textbook of psychology,* Third Edition, p. 199. Reprinted by permission of Mary Hebb.

Chapter 11: TABLE 11.4, p. 411—Adapted from Sattler, Jerome M. (1992). *Assessment of children,* revised and updated, 3rd Edition, 1992, p. 79. San Diego: Sattler. Reprinted by permission. FIG. 11.7, p. 413—Bouchard, T. J., Jr., & McGue, M. (1981). Familial studies of intelligence: A review. *Science, 212,* pp. 1055–1058. Copyright 1981 by the AAAS. Reprinted by permission. QUOTE p. 417—From *Mental retardation:*

Definition, classification, and symptoms of supports, 1992, p. 5. Reprinted by permission of the American Association on Mental Retardation.

Chapter 12: TABLE 12.2, p. 457—From the *Minnesota Multiphasic Personality Inventory.* Copyright © the University of Minnesota 1942, 1943 (renewed 1970). MMPI scale names reproduced by permission of the publisher. QUOTE p. 458—From Aiken, Lewis R. *Psychological testing and assessment,* 6th ed., p. 390. Copyright © 1988 by Allyn & Bacon. Reprinted by permission of Allyn & Bacon. TABLE 12.3, p. 460—From Cohen, R. J., Montague, P., Nathanson, L. S., & Swerdik, M. E. (1988). *Psychological testing.* Mountainview, CA: Mayfield Publishing. Reprinted by permission.

Chapter 13: FIG. 13.4, p. 475—Figure from Selye, H. (1978). *The stress of life,* 2E. Copyright 1978. Reprinted with permission of McGraw-Hill, Inc. TABLE 13.1, p. 476—Reprinted with permission from Holmes, T. H., & Rahe, R. H. (1967). Social readjustment rating scale. *Journal of Psychosomatic Research,* Vol. II. Pergamon Press, Ltd., Oxford, England. TABLE 13.3, p. 481—From Meyer, Robert. G., & Salmon, Paul. *Abnormal psychology,* 2nd ed., p. 333. Copyright 1988 by Allyn & Bacon. Reprinted by permission. FOLDOUT pp. 486a–486b—From Roper College Track™. The Roper Organization, 1991-92. Reprinted by permission.

Chapter 14: QUOTE p. 509—From Melville, J. (1977). *Phobias and compulsions,* p. 22. London: Penguin Books. Reprinted by permission of the Peters, Fraser & Dunlop Group Ltd. FIG. 14.2, p. 523—From Snowden, L. R., & Cheung, F. K. (1990). Use of inpatient health services by members of ethnic minority groups. *American Psychologist, 45,* pp. 347–355. Copyright 1990 by the American Psychological Association. Reprinted by permission. FIG. 14.3, p. 527—From Tsaung, M. T., & Vandermey, R. (1980). *Genes and the mind.* Reprinted by permission of Oxford University Press, Oxford, England.

Chapter 15: FIG. 15.1, p. 537—Norcross, J. C., Prochaska, J. O., & Gallagher, K. M. (1989). Clinical psychologists in the 1980's: 2. Theory, research, and practice. *The Clinical Psychologist, 42,* pp. 45–52. Reprinted by permission. TABLE 15.2, p. 539—Adapted from Mahrer, A. R., & Nadler, W. P. (1986). Good moments in psychotherapy: A preliminary review, a list, and some promising research avenues. *Journal of Consulting and Clinical Psychology, 54,* pp. 10–15. Copyright 1986 by the American Psychological Association. Reprinted by permission. QUOTE p. 540—From Freud, Sigmund. An introduction to psychoanalysis. In J. Riviere (Ed.), *A general introduction to psychoanalysis.* New York: Liveright Publishers, 1963. (Original work published 1920.) FIG. 15.3, p. 550—Reprinted from *Behavior Research and Therapy, 2,* Ayllon, T., & Azrin, N. H. Modification of symptomatic verbal behavior of mental patients, pp. 87–97. Copyright 1964, with kind permission from Pergamon Press Ltd., Headington Hill Hall, Oxford 0X3 0BW, UK. FIG. 15.4, p. 551—From Ayllon, T., & Azrin, N. H. (1965). The measurement and reinforcement of behavior of psychotics. *Journal of the Experimental Analysis of Behavior, 8,* pp. 357–383. Copyright 1965

by the Society for the Experimental Analysis of Behavior, Inc. Reprinted by permission. TABLE 15.4, p. 555—From the book, *A guide to rational living* by Albert Ellis, Ph.D., & Robert A. Harper, Ph.D. © 1989, 1961. Used by permission of the publisher, Prentice-Hall/a Division of Simon & Schuster, Englewood Cliffs, NJ.

Chapter 16: FIG. 16.8, p. 599—From Milgram, S. (1963). Behavioral study of obedience. *Journal of Abnormal and Social Psychology, 67,* pp. 371–378. Copyright 1963 by Alexandra Milgram. Adapted by permission.

Chapter 17: FIG. 17.1, p. 609—From Anderson, C. A., & Anderson, D. C. (1984). Ambient temperature and violent crime: Tests of the linear and curvilinear hypotheses. *Journal of Personality and Social Psychology, 46,* pp. 91–97. Copyright 1984 by the American Psychological Association. Reprinted by permission. FIG. 17.3, p. 613—From Altman, I., & Vinsel, A. M. (1977). Personal space: An analysis of E. T. Hall's proxemics framework. In I. Altman, A. Rapoport, & J. F. Wohlwill (Eds.), *Human behavior and environment: advances in theory and research.* Vol. 2. New York: Plenum Press. Reprinted by permission. TABLE 17.2, p. 636—From Hendrick, C., & Hendrick, S. (1986). A theory and method of love. *Journal of Personality and Social Psychology, 50,* pp. 392–402. Copyright 1986 by the American Psychological Association. Reprinted by permission.

Module B: FIG. B1, p. 666—From Lawler, E. F., & Porter, L. W. (1967). Antecedent attitudes of effective managerial performance. *Organizational Behavior and Human Performance, 2,* pp. 122–142. Reprinted by permission of Academic Press. FIG. B2, p. 668—From Locke, E. A., & Schweiger, D. M. (1979). Participation in decision-making: One more look. In B. M. Staw (Ed.), *Research in organizational behavior, 1.* Greenwich, CT: JAI Press. Reprinted by permission.

Photo Credits

Chapter 1: Opener, Courtesy of Carol Grigg/Trillium Press; p. 5, L. Migdale/Stock Boston; p. 19, A. Reininger/Contact Press/Woodfin Camp & Associates; p. 21, Steve Winter/Black Star; p. 27, AT&T Archives; p. 29, Stephen Marks; p. 30, B. Daemmrich/Stock Boston; p. 33, P. Ward/Stock Boston; p. 35, Steve Winter/Black Star.

Chapter 2: Opener, Harvey Littleton/Don Wheeler Photographers, Inc.; p. 42 (left), CNRI Science Library/Photo Researchers, Inc.; p. 42 (right), C. Melloan/Tony Stone Worldwide, Ltd.; p. 43, L. T. Rhodes/TSW-Click, Chicago; p. 46, Biophoto Associates/Photo Researchers; p. 52, R. Morsch/The Stock Market; p. 56 (top left), Superstock; p. 56 (top right), New York Hospital/Peter Arnold; p. 56 (bottom), Courtesy of Drs. Michael E. Phelps & John Mazziotta, UCLA School of Medicine; p. 57, A. Glauberman/Photo Researchers, Inc.; p. 69, M. Gouveneur/Liaison; p. 71, C. Melloan/Tony Stone Worldwide, Ltd.

Chapter 3: Opener, Lucas Samaras/Whitney Museum of America; p. 81, J. L. Weber/Peter Arnold, Inc.; p. 86, CNN; p. 88, Douglas Faulkner/Photo Researchers, Inc.; p. 91, T. Farmer/Tony Stone Worldwide, Ltd.; p. 92, Superstock; p. 97, T. Eiler/Stock Boston; p. 98, Baron Wolman/Woodfin Camp & Associates, Inc.; p. 98a, Allyn & Bacon; p. 98b (top), Kevin Schafer/Peter Arnold, Inc.; p. 98b (bottom), Carol Purcell/Photo Researchers, Inc.; p. 101, T. Svensson/Stock Market; p. 106, B. Hryenwych/Stock Boston; p. 108, Omikron/Photo Researchers, Inc.; p. 111, Momatuik-Eastcott/Woodfin Camp & Associates; p. 114, A. Reininger/Woodfin Camp & Associates; p. 116, Herbert Migdoll/Rainbow; p. 118, Superstock.

Chapter 4: Opener, Courtesy of Corning Museum of Glass/Dominick Labino; p. 125, Stephen Marks; p. 127, J. Nettis/Stock Boston; p. 130, R. Morsch/The Stock Market; p. 133, M. Furman/Stock Market; p. 135, J. Corwin/Stock Boston; p. 138, B. Daemmrich/Stock Boston; p. 140, A. Reininger/Woodfin Camp & Associates; p. 144, M. Richards/PhotoEdit; p. 146, A. Glauberman/Photo Researchers, Inc.; p. 149, M. Ferri/The Stock Market; p. 150, R. Morsch/The Stock Market; p. 151, Tannenbaum/Sygma; p. 153, R. Morsch/The Stock Market.

Chapter 5: Opener, Rafael Ferrer/Nancy Hoffman Gallery; p. 162, CNN; p. 165, Stan Wayman/Photo Researchers, Inc.; p. 172, Woodfin Camp & Associates; p. 174, Stock Boston; p. 177, J. Brown/Offshoot Stock; p. 178 (top left), Brian Smith; p. 178 (top right), Omikron/Photo Researchers, Inc.; p. 178 (bottom left), Kevin Horan/Stock Boston; p. 178 (bottom right), Jim Pickerell; p. 179 Associated Press/Wide World Photos; p. 188, Jim Pickerell; p. 192, Stephen Marks; p. 194, R. Kopstein/Monkmeyer Press; p. 196, R. Pastey/Stock Boston; p. 199, Jim Pickerell.

Chapter 6: Opener, Robert Frerck/Odyssey; p. 207 (left, middle, right), Stephen Marks; p. 209, Peter Menzel/Stock Boston; p. 211, Brian Smith; p. 215 (left), D. Woods/The Stock Market; p. 215 (right), A. Hvhkihn/Woodfin Camp & Associates; p. 217, Wide World Photos; p. 219, R. Sandler/The Picture Group; p. 225, Brian Smith; p. 231, CNN; p. 232, David Dempster; p. 239, Brian Smith.

Chapter 7: Opener, Robert Arneson/University Art Museum, Berkeley; p. 244, M. Miller/Photo Researchers, Inc.; p. 251, Brylak/Liaison; p. 255, Stephen Marks; p. 256, R. Das/Monkmeyer Press; p. 258, Courtesy of Lotus Corporation; p. 260 (top), George Dillon/Stock Boston; p. 260 (bottom), Laima Druskis/Stock Boston; p. 262, S. Rutherford/Black Star; p. 266 (top), Corron/Monkmeyer Press; p. 266 (bottom), B. Gallery/Stock Boston; p. 271, CNN; p. 273, Courtesy of Lotus Corporation; p. 276, Robert Frerck/Odyssey.

Chapter 8: Opener, Science Library/Photo Researchers, Inc.; p. 282 (top), Petit Format-Nestle/Photo Researchers, Inc.; p. 282 (middle), Petit Format-Nestle/Photo Researchers, Inc.; p. 282 (bottom), J. Stevenson/Science Library/Photo Researchers, Inc.; p. 285, Courtesy of Dr. David Linton; p. 286, Enrico Ferorelli; p. 291, The Bettman Archive; p. 292a (top left), Charles Gupton/Stock Boston; p. 292a (top right), Spencer Grant/Stock Boston; p. 292a (bottom left), Michael Heron/Woodfin Camp & Associates; p. 292a (bottom right, above), Laura Dwight/Peter Arnold, Inc.; p. 292a (bottom right, below), Barbara Alper/Stock Boston; p. 292b (top left), FourByFive/Superstock; p. 292b (top right), Laura Dwight/Peter Arnold, Inc.; p. 292b (middle left), James Sugar/Black Star; p. 292b (middle right), Laura Dwight/Peter Arnold, Inc.; p. 292b (bottom left) Andy Cox/Tony Stone Worldwide, Ltd.; p. 292b (bottom right), Richard Hutchings/Photo Researchers, Inc.; p. 293 (top & bottom), D. Goodwin/Monkmeyer Press; p. 298, B. Daemmrich/Stock Boston; p. 304, O. Franken/Stock Boston; p. 305, David Young-Wolff/PhotoEdit; p. 309, Stephen Marks; p. 311, B. Daemmrich/Stock Boston.

Chapter 9: Opener, Alison Saar, Collection of Daniel Jacobs & Derek Mason, The D&D Studio-NY; p. 317, H. Rainer/Offshoot Stock; p. 319, Stephen Marks; p. 321, Renato Rotolo/The Gamma Liaison Network; p. 324 (top), Jeffrey W. Myers/Stock Boston; p. 324 (middle), Stephen Marks; p. 324 (bottom), Courtesy of Martin Marietta Corporation; p. 327, R. Nelson/Black Star; p. 332, R. Schleipman/Offshoot Stock; p. 334, CNN; p. 336, Peter Menzel/Stock Boston; p. 388, Charles Gupton/The Stock Market; p. 341, Stephen Marks; p. 343, C. Gupton/The Stock Market; p. 345, Peter Menzel/Stock Boston.

Chapter 10: Opener, Peter Voulos, Scripps College/Collection of Mr. & Mrs. Fred Marer; p. 351, W. Sallaz/Duomo Photography; p. 353, Courtesy of Dr. Miller; p. 354, Arizona Historical Society Library; p. 355 (left), Culver Pictures; p. 355 (right), G. Marrineau/Black Star; p. 357, Superstock; p. 361, Tom Hutchins/Black Star; p. 362, Duomo Photography; p. 366, Stephen Marks, p. 373 (top left), Stephen Marks, p. 373 (bottom left), K. Reininger/Black Star; p. 373 (right), Stephen Marks; p. 380, Mike Abramsom/Woodfin Camp & Associates; p. 382, M. Rogers/Tony Stone Worldwide, Ltd., p. 384, Courtesy of Dr. Paul Eckhart; p. 387, Tom Hutchins/Black Star.

Chapter 11: Opener, Ron Nagle/Collection of Daniel Jacobs & Derek Mason, The D&D Studio-NY; p. 393, F. Baldwin/Photo Researchers, Inc.; p. 397 (bottom), Jim Pickerell; p. 404, CNN; p. 407, Lew Merrim/Monkmeyer Press; p. 411 (left), Jim Pickerell; p. 411 (top right), Jim Pickerell; p. 411 (bottom right), Brian Smith; p. 413, Porterfield-Chickering/Photo Researchers; p. 414, S. Grant/Liaison; p. 415, CNN; p. 418, Mario Ruiz/Picture Group; p. 419, Jim Pickerell; p. 421, Jim Pickerell.

Chapter 12: Opener, Suzanne Page; p. 430, A. Canavesio/Photo Researchers, Inc.; p. 433, Ulrike Welsch; p. 437, Stephen Marks; p. 442, P. Silva/Picture Group; p. 447, Richard Hutchings/Photo Researchers, Inc.; p. 451, B. Aron/Photo Edit; p. 461, Ulrike Welsch.

Chapter 13: Opener, Hank Murta Adams/Collection of John McCall/Austin, Texas; p. 472, D. Young-Wolfe/PhotoEdit; p. 473, L. Kolvoord/The Image Works; p. 474, M. Gibson/Stock Market; p. 475, Courtesy of Hans Selye; p. 477, David Dempster/Offshoot Stock; p. 480, R. Crandall/The Picture Group; p. 482, P. Chauvel/Sygma; p. 485, H. Morgan/Rainbow; p. 486a (top), Lawrence Migdale/Tony Stone Worldwide, Ltd.; p. 486a (middle), Reuters/Bettmann; p. 486b (top), David Young-Wolf/PhotoEdit; p. 486b (bottom), Bruce Ayres/Tony Stone Worldwide, Ltd.; p. 490, Stephen Marks; p. 495, David Dempster/Offshoot Stock.

Chapter 14: Opener, AMHN/Superstock; p. 501, C. Ursillo/ Photo Researchers, Inc.; p. 502, Northwind Photo Archives; p. 507, David Dempster/Offshoot Stock; p. 510, C. Mellon/Tony Stone Worldwide, Ltd.; p. 517, R. Crandall/Picture Group; p. 520, CNN; p. 521, Bob Daemmrich; p. 525, Monkmeyer Press Photo; p. 527, Courtesy of the Genain Estate; p. 528, NIH/Photo Researchers, Inc.

Chapter 15: Opener, Orlando Agudelo-Botero; p. 537, B. Daemmrich/Tony Stone Worldwide, Ltd.; p. 541, Mary Evans Picture Library; p. 551, Stephen Marks; p. 553, W. Spunbarg/Photo Edit; p. 562, Mary Kate Denny/PhotoEdit; p. 563, L. Migdale/Photo Researchers, Inc.; p. 564, James Wilson/ Woodfin Camp & Associates; p. 571, R. Crandall/The Picture Group.

Chapter 16: Opener, Wayne & Donna Higby, Alfred Station, NY; p. 576, Courtesy of Gitano; p. 582, Wide World Photos; p. 583, Gamma Liaison; p. 585 (left), D. Austen/Stock Boston; p. 585 (right), C. Schwartz/The Image Bank; p. 587, D. Luria/ Photo Researchers, Inc.; p. 590, J. Nemerofsky/Picture Group; p. 591, D. Grossman/Photo Researchers, Inc.; p. 598 (left), Neil Farrin/Tony Stone Worldwide, Ltd.; p. 598 (right), Sylvan Grandadam/Photo Researchers, Inc.; p. 603, N. Farrin/Tony Stone Worldwide, Ltd.

Chapter 17: Opener, Superstock; p. 609, Woodfin Camp & Associates; p. 613, B. Barnes/PhotoEdit; p. 615, B. Barnes/ PhotoEdit; p. 616, Stephen Marks; p. 619, J. Greenberg/Photo Researchers, Inc.; p. 621, C. Wolinsky/Stock Boston; p. 625, M. Richards/PhotoEdit; p. 627, A. Stein/Photo Researchers, Inc.; p. 628, R. Nelson/The Picture Group; p. 631, G. Chan/ Photo Researchers, Inc.; p. 633, John Curtis/Offshoot Stock; p. 633, David Dempster/Offshoot Stock; p. 636, Superstock; p. 639, D. Luria/Photo Researchers, Inc.

PSYCHOLOGY

1

What Is Psychology?

In 1993, a bomb exploded in the parking garage of New York's World Trade Center, killing 6 people and injuring more than 1,000. Thousands of frightened workers had to be evacuated through smoke-filled stairways. Many expected to die and left the building so frightened that they swore never to return. The economic cost of the bombing was in the billions of dollars, but the toll of disasters is counted in more than dollars and cents. Lives change in ways that few people who have been untouched by such disasters can understand. Our country faces disasters nearly every year; Hurricanes Hugo and Andrew, the San Francisco earthquake, the recent flooding along the Mississippi and Missouri rivers, and the forest fires in California are just a few examples. The psychological aftermath is seen in the kinds of symptoms that usually appear during a war. Victims wake up at night in terror; parents lash out at children; people suffer from flashbacks and bouts of depression; they may experience short-term memory losses. Children are among the most vulnerable. In Florida, many months after Hurricane Andrew, thousands were still dealing with life in tent cities, lost possessions, illness, and stress. Both city dwellers and farmers were hard hit after the flooding in the Midwest; after a lifetime of work, thousands lost their possessions and security.

The average person responds to a war or natural disaster with stress and depression. Helping people recognize that fact is one of the first tasks for professionals at the scene. In addition, school psychologists train teachers, guidance counselors, and parents to recognize emotional problems. Psychologists, psychiatrists, and social workers do crisis intervention work and counseling. For example, in New York City, officials opened 24-hour emergency response centers, where psychologists helped people deal with their immediate symptoms and manage the days and weeks that followed the bombing. Later in this chapter, we will learn more about how people in the field of psychology can help.

Of course, professionals are not the only ones who help. After a natural disaster, thousands of people come to offer assistance: the old and the young, the wealthy and the poor. Farmers, carpenters, and plumbers from South Carolina left for Florida even before Hurricane Andrew had hit land; they remembered the help they had received just three short years before, following Hurricane Hugo. After floods, fires, winds, and drought, donations typically come from all over the nation—in the form of money, clothing, food, medical supplies, and services. In the face of disaster, people's humanity shines.

What determines whether people will choose to help or not? Are people more likely to help in some situations than in others? Why do people donate millions to help hurricane victims but often ignore the homeless in their hometowns? Psychologists who study helping behavior say it depends on a number of factors, including anonymity, embarrassment, and the number of observers present. We will examine helping behavior in more detail in chapter 17.

Psychologists also study human development from birth to death. They seek answers to questions such as: What are the things that motivate people to work? Why do some siblings often turn out to be so different from one another? How can we best cope with feelings of depression and anxiety? What is the best way to teach people new behavior? How does memory work? How does the brain affect behavior?

The focus of psychology is people's behavior and mental processes. Psychologists try to understand how biology and the physical and social world influence people's day-to-day behavior and interactions. Psychology helps us understand ourselves.

Defining Psychology

What exactly is psychology? It is difficult to provide a definition of psychology that includes all its elements. We begin with a broad definition. **Psychology** is the science of behavior and mental processes. Lets expand on this simple definition: Because psychology is a *science,* psychologists use scientific principles, carefully defined methods, and precise procedures to present an organized body of knowledge and to make inferences (discussed later in the chapter). As a science, psychology is committed to:

▶ *Objectivity*—evaluating research and theory on their own merits, without preconceived ideas.

▶ *Accuracy*—gathering data from the laboratory and the real world in precise ways.

▶ *Healthy skepticism*—cautious viewing of data, hypotheses, and theory until results are repeated and verified.

Psychology: The science of behavior and mental processes.

Scope of Psychology

Psychologists observe most aspects of human functioning—overt actions, mental processes, emotional responses, and physiological reactions.

Theory: A collection of inter-related ideas and facts put forward to explain and predict behavior and mental processes.

▶ *Overt actions* are directly observable and measurable movements or the results of such movements. Walking, talking, playing, kissing, gestures, and expressions are examples of overt actions. Products of overt actions might be the term papers you write, the mess in your bedroom, or your finely tuned body if you exercise regularly.

▶ *Mental processes* include thoughts, ideas, and reasoning processes.

▶ *Emotional responses* include anger, regret, lust, happiness, and depression.

▶ *Physiological reactions* are closely associated with emotional responses and include an increased heart rate when you are excited, biochemical changes when light stimulates your eyes, and high blood pressure and ulcers in response to stress.

Goals of Psychology

The goals of psychology are to *describe* the basic components of behavior, to *explain* them, to *predict* them, and, potentially, to *manage* them. That is, psychologists describe and explain behavior to predict behavior and help people manage it. Therefore, some psychologists do basic research to uncover, explore, and understand the principles of behavior. They measure and describe behavior in a scientific way, using verifiable observations and carefully controlled research methods.

Because behavior and mental processes are not always directly observable, psychologists must sometimes infer the thought processes, emotions, and motivations behind the actions they observe. From their research, psychologists develop theories to explain, predict, and help manage behavior. A **theory** is a collection of interrelated ideas and facts put forward to explain and predict behavior and mental processes. For example, a theory of why people choose to help might put together related facts about personality, gender differences, cultural differences, and demographics. Such a theory would explain and predict behavior on the basis of special circumstances.

Every modern school of thought attempts to explain how people learn.

FOCUS

▶ Name a specific research problem that psychology addresses. Identify a situation in which psychology can be used to solve a real-life problem.   p. 4

▶ Why are description and explanation fundamental to psychological inquiry?   p. 5

▶ Why might thought be considered a type of behavior?   p. 5

Predicting behavior is important; it enables psychologists to help people anticipate situations and learn how to express their feelings in manageable and reasonable ways. For example, because excessive stress can cause anxiety, depression, and even heart attacks, psychologists use theories about stress to devise therapies to help people handle it more effectively.

A general goal of the discipline of psychology is to combine science, the application of science, and professional practice into one organized endeavor (Stricker, 1992; Strickland, 1988). In sum, psychology is a problem-solving science rooted in research and scientific principles. For most psychologists, the work is an adventure and an exploration into understanding human behavior and mental processes.

Past and Present Schools of Psychological Thought

Psychologists subscribe to many different perspectives in trying to analyze human behavior. These perspectives, which have been developed over time, serve to orient researchers and provide them with a frame of reference. A specific approach to the study of behavior is a *school of psychological thought*. This section discusses the development of schools of psychological thought (summarized in Table 1.1). Table

TABLE 1.1

Schools of Psychological Thought

STRUCTURALISM	FUNCTIONALISM	GESTALT	PSYCHOANALYSIS
Wilhelm Wundt	Functions of the mind	Max Wertheimer	Unconscious mental processes

Structure of the mind	William James	The total experience	Sigmund Freud

1.2 on pages 8–11 presents a timeline of key events in the history of psychology. You will see that the study of behavior and mental processes has had a roller-coaster history, with each school emphasizing a different topic.

The Early Traditions

Structuralism—The Contents of Consciousness. Wilhelm Wundt (1832–1920) developed the first widely accepted school of thought. In 1879, he founded the first psychological laboratory, in Leipzig, Germany. Its focus was the study of mental life (Leahey, 1992). Before Wundt, the field of psychology did not exist; psychological questions were in the domains of philosophy, medicine, and theology. One of Wundt's major contributions was teaching his students to use the scientific method when asking psychological questions (Benjamin et al., 1992).

Edward B. Titchener (1867–1927), an Englishman, popularized Wundt's ideas, along with his own, in the United States and the rest of the English-speaking world. What Wundt, Titchener, and others developed was **structuralism**—the school of psychological thought that considered immediate, conscious experience the proper subject matter of psychology. Instead of looking at the broad range of behavior and mental processes that psychologists consider today, the structuralists tried to observe only the inner workings of the mind to find the elements of conscious experience.

Titchener used the technique of **introspection,** or *self-examination*—the description and analysis by a person of what he or she is thinking and feeling—to discover the elements of conscious experience. Wundt and Titchener also conducted some of the first experiments in psychology. For example, they studied the speed of thought by observing reaction times for simple tasks.

By today's standards, the structuralists focused too narrowly on individuals' conscious experiences. Understanding one person's conscious experiences tells us

Structuralism: The school of psychological thought that considered immediate, conscious experience the proper subject matter of psychology.

Introspection: The description and analysis by a person of what he or she is thinking and feeling. Also known as *self-examination.*

TABLE 1.1 *cont.*

Schools of Psychological Thought

BEHAVIORISM	HUMANISTIC	COGNITIVE	BIOLOGICAL
B. F. Skinner	*Free will and self-actualization*	Albert Bandura	*Basic biological structures and mechanisms*
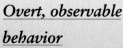 *Overt, observable behavior*	 Abraham Maslow	 *Thought processes*	 Michael Gazzaniga

TABLE 1.2

Key Events in the History of Psychology

1883 G. Stanley Hall establishes the first American psychology laboratory, at Johns Hopkins University.

1879 Wilhelm Wundt founds the first psychology laboratory, in Leipzig, Germany.

1887 G. Stanley Hall establishes the first professional journal of psychology in the United States (*American Journal of Psychology*).

little about another's. Thus, the structuralists' results allowed for few generalizations and the school made little progress in describing the nature of the mind.

Functionalism—How Does the Mind Work? Before long, a new school—functionalism—developed, bringing with it a new way of thinking about behavior. An outgrowth of structuralism, **functionalism** was the school of psychological thought that tried to discover how and why the mind *functions* and the mind's relation to consciousness. It also sought to understand how people adapted to their environment.

With William James (1842–1910) at its head, functionalism was the first truly American psychology. James, a physician and professor of anatomy at Harvard University, argued that knowing only the contents of consciousness (structuralism) was too limited. A psychologist had to know also how the contents functioned and worked together. Through such knowledge, the psychologist could understand how the mind (consciousness) guided behavior.

In 1890, James published *Principles of Psychology*, in which he described the mind as a dynamic set of continuously evolving elements. In this work, he coined the phrase *stream of consciousness*, describing the mind as a river, always flowing, never remaining still.

James broadened the scope of structuralism by studying animals, by applying psychology in practical areas such as education, and by experimenting on overt behavior, not just mental processes. James's ideas influenced the life and writing of another American psychologist, G. Stanley Hall (1844–1924). Hall was the first person to receive a doctorate in psychology, the founder of the American Psychological Association, and an organizer and promoter of psychology in the United States.

Functionalists continued to use introspection as a technique—for them psychology was still the study of consciousness. For many of the new emerging schools

Functionalism: The school of psychological thought (an outgrowth of structuralism) that was concerned with how and why the conscious mind works; its main aim was to know how the contents of consciousness functioned and worked together.

TABLE 1.2 *cont.*

Key Events in the History of Psychology

1890 William James publishes the widely used *Principles of Psychology*.

1892 The American Psychological Association is founded by G. Stanley Hall, its first president.

1894 Margaret Floy Washburn becomes the first woman to receive a PhD in psychology.

of psychology, however, this technique was too limiting. The early schools of psychological thought were soon replaced by different conceptualizations: Gestalt psychology, psychoanalysis, behaviorism, and humanistic and cognitive approaches.

Gestalt Psychology—Examining Wholes. While some psychologists were grappling with structuralism and functionalism, others were developing very different approaches. One such approach was **Gestalt psychology** (*Gestalt* means configuration)—the school of psychological thought that argued that it is necessary to study a person's total experience, not just parts of the mind or behavior. Gestalt psychologists such as Max Wertheimer and Kurt Koffka suggested that conscious experience is more than simply the sum of its parts. Arguing that the mind organizes the elements of experience into something unique, Gestalt psychologists analyzed the world in terms of perceptual frameworks. They proposed that people form simple sensory elements into patterns through which they interpret the world. By analyzing the whole experience—the patterns of a person's perceptions and thoughts—one could understand the mind and its workings.

Eventually, Gestalt psychology became a major influence in many areas of psychology—for example, in therapy. A Gestalt-oriented therapist dealing with a problem member of a family might call in the rest of the family to see how the "part" (the person with the problem) could be better understood in the context of the "whole" (the family configuration). However, as broad as its influence was, Gestalt psychology seemed somewhat mystical and never achieved as wide a following as did psychoanalysis.

Psychoanalysis—Probing the Unconscious. One of the first researchers to develop a theory about emotional disturbance was Sigmund Freud (1856–1939). Freud, a physician interested in helping people overcome anxiety, focused on the

Gestalt psychology: [gesh-TALT] The school of psychological thought that argued that behavior cannot be studied in parts but must be viewed as a whole; the focus was on the unity of perception and thinking.

> ## TABLE 1.2 *cont.*
>
> ### Key Events in the History of Psychology
>
>
>
> **1898** Edward L. Thorndike conducts the first experiments on animal learning.
>
> **1900** Sigmund Freud introduces his psychoanalytic theory in *The Interpretation of Dreams.*
>
>
>
>
>
> **1901** Gilbert Haven Jones becomes the first African-American holder of a PhD to teach psychology in the United States.

causes and treatment of emotional disturbances. Working from the premise that unconscious mental processes direct daily behavior, he developed techniques to explore those unconscious processes, including free association and dream interpretation. He emphasized that childhood experiences influence future adult behaviors and that sexual energy fuels day-to-day behavior.

Freud created the **psychoanalytic approach,** or *psychoanalysis*—the school of psychological thought that assumes that psychological maladjustment is a consequence of anxiety resulting from unresolved conflicts and forces of which a person may be unaware. The psychoanalytic perspective has undergone many changes since Freud devised it. At times, in fact, it seems only loosely connected to Freud's basic ideas. Its overall focus remains similar, however. When it was introduced in the United States, most psychologists ignored it, but by the 1920s its influence had grown so broad that it threatened to eclipse research-based laboratory psychology (Hornstein, 1992). Chapter 12 discusses Freud's theory of personality, and chapter 15 discusses psychoanalysis as the therapeutic technique derived from his theory.

Psychological Schools Grow Broader

Behaviorism—Observable Behavior. Despite their differences in focus, the structuralists, functionalists, Gestaltists, and psychoanalysts were all concerned with the functioning of the mind. They were all interested in private perception and conscious or unconscious activity. However, in the early 20th century, American psychology moved from studying the contents of the mind to studying overt behavior. At the forefront of that movement was John B. Watson (1878–1958), the founder of **behaviorism**—the school of psychological thought that rejects the study of the contents of consciousness and focuses on describing and measuring only what is observable directly or through assessment instruments.

Psychoanalytic approach: [SIE-ko-an-uh-LIT-ick] The school of psychological thought developed by Freud, who was interested in how personality develops. His approach focused on the unconscious and on how it directs day-to-day behavior. Also known as *psychoanalysis*.

Behaviorism: The school of psychological thought that rejects the study of the contents of consciousness and focuses on describing and measuring only what is observable directly or through assessment instruments.

TABLE 1.2 *cont.*

Key Events in the History of Psychology

1905 Alfred Binet and Theodore Simon devise the first intelligence test.

1906 Ivan Pavlov begins to publish his classic studies of animal learning.

1913 John B. Watson champions psychology as the science of behavior.

Watson was an upstart—clever, brash, and defiant. Trained as a functionalist, he argued that there is no reasonable, objective way to study the human mind. He contended that behavior, not the private contents of the mind, is the proper subject matter of psychology. According to Watson, psychologists should study only activities that can be objectively observed and measured; prediction and control should be the theoretical goal of psychology. This contention was a major break with previous psychological thought. It rejected the work of Wundt and most other early psychologists and argued that psychologists should put the study of consciousness behind them.

After Watson, other American researchers extended and developed behaviorism. Among them was Harvard psychologist B. F. Skinner (1904–1990), who attempted to explain the causes of behavior by cataloging and describing the relations among events in the environment (*stimuli*) and a person's or animal's reactions (*responses*). Skinner's behaviorism led the way for thousands of research studies on conditioning and human behavior, a special focus on stimuli and responses, and the controlling of behavior through learning principles.

The behaviorists focus on how observable responses are learned, modified, and forgotten. They usually emphasize how current behavior is acquired or modified rather than dealing with inherited characteristics or early childhood experiences. One of their fundamental assumptions is that disordered behavior can be replaced with appropriate, worthwhile behavior through traditional learning techniques (described in chapter 5).

Early behaviorists took a stern, unbending view of the scope of psychology by refusing to study mental phenomena. Nonbehaviorists of their time argued that not all behavior can be explained by stimuli and responses. They focused instead on such topics as creativity, the origins of thought, and the expression of love. Behaviorists today are beginning again to study a wide range of human behavior, including mental phenomena—especially thought processes.

Humanistic Psychology—Free Will. Another school of thought that figures into the landscape of modern psychology is **humanistic psychology**—the school of psychological thought that emphasizes the uniqueness of the human experience and the idea that human beings have free will to determine their destiny. It arose in response to psychoanalytic and behavioral views. Humanistic psychologists see people as inherently good and as striving to fulfill themselves; they believe that psychoanalytical theorists see people as fraught with inner conflict and that behaviorists are too narrowly focused on stimulus-response relations. Humanists focus on individual uniqueness and decision-making ability and assume that inner psychic forces contribute positively to establishing and maintaining a normal lifestyle.

Humanistic psychologists assert that human beings are conscious, creative, and born with an innate desire to fulfill themselves. They say that psychologists must examine human behavior individually. Proponents of the humanistic view, such as Abraham Maslow and Carl Rogers (whom we will study in chapter 12), believe that human beings have a desire for **self-actualization**—the fulfillment of their human potential—and for creating their own perceptions and choosing their own experience of reality (Andrews, 1989).

Cognitive Psychology—Thinking Again. Many psychologists realized that strict behaviorism had limitations; they reacted particularly against its narrow focus on observable behavior. As an outgrowth of behaviorism (and a reaction to it), they created **cognitive psychology**—the school of psychological thought that focuses on the mental processes and activities involved in perception, memory, learning, and thinking. It includes the mental processes involved in behavior—for example, how people solve problems and appraise threatening situations. Cognitive psychology is sometimes seen as antibehaviorist, but it is not. It simply views the strict behavioral approach as missing a key component—mental processes. Cognitive psychology encompasses both symbolic thought processes and the physiological processes that underlie thought.

The cognitive perspective asserts that human beings engage in behaviors, both worthwhile and maladjusted, because of ideas and thoughts. Cognitive psychologists may be clinicians working with maladjusted clients to help them achieve more realistic ideas about the world so that they can change their behavior to adjust to it more effectively. Cognitive psychologists may also be researchers who study artificial intelligence, memory, perception, and the mental processes underlying all thought.

Because cognitive psychology spans many psychological fields and research traditions, it is hard to identify a single person who can be called its leader. However, psychologists Albert Bandura, Albert Ellis, Aaron Beck, George Miller, and Richard Lazarus have each taken prominent roles.

Biological Perspective—Predispositions. Increasingly, researchers are turning to biology to explain some human behavior. The **biological perspective,** or *neuroscience perspective,* is the school of psychological thought that examines psychological issues based on how heredity and biological structures affect mental processes and behavior, focusing on how physical mechanisms affect emotions, feelings, thoughts, desires, and sensory experiences. Researchers with a biological perspective might study genetic abnormalities, central nervous system problems, brain damage, or hormonal changes, for example. Researchers Michael Gazzaniga, Seymour Kety, Irving Gottesman, and Robert Plomin are often cited as leaders of the biological perspective.

The biological perspective is especially important in studies of sensation and perception, memory, and some types of maladjustment. It is pivotal in examining

---

Humanistic psychology: The school of psychological thought that emphasizes the uniqueness of the human experience and the idea that human beings have free will to determine their destiny.

Self-actualization: The process by which individuals strive to fulfill themselves.

Cognitive psychology: The school of psychological thought that focuses on the mental processes and activities involved in perception, memory, learning, and thinking.

Biological perspective: The school of psychological thought that examines psychological issues based on how heredity and biological structures affect mental processes and behavior, focusing on how physical mechanisms affect emotions, feelings, thoughts, desires, and sensory experiences. Also known as the *neuroscience perspective.*

abnormal behavior such as schizophrenia, which is linked in part to genetics, and alcoholism, which in many cases has biological underpinnings.

Eclecticism—The Best of Everything

Psychologists realize that a complex relationship exists among the factors that affect both overt behavior and mental processes. Therefore, most American psychologists involved in applied psychology, especially clinical and counseling psychology, are eclectic in their perspective. **Eclecticism** is a combination of theories, facts, or techniques. In clinical and counseling psychology, it is the use of a variety of approaches to evaluate data, theories, and therapies.

Eclecticism allows a researcher or practitioner to view a problem from several orientations. For example, consider depression, the disabling mood disorder that affects 10 to 20 percent of men and women in America at some time in their lives (chapter 14 discusses depression at length). From a biological perspective, people become depressed because of changes in brain chemistry. From a behavioral point of view, people learn to be depressed and sad because of faulty reward systems in their environment. From a psychoanalytic perspective, people become depressed because their early childhood experiences caused them to form a negative outlook on life. From a humanistic perspective, depression is often caused by people choosing inaction because of poor role models. From a cognitive perspective, depression is made worse by the interpretations (thoughts) an individual adopts about a situation. An eclectic practitioner recognizes the complex nature of depression and acknowledges each of the possible contributions; the practitioner evaluates the person, the depression, and the context in which the person is depressed. The wide range of psychologists' orientations is often reflected in their careers, considered next.

FOCUS

▶ Identify the key assumptions underlying each school of psychological thought.   pp. 7–13

▶ How would the biological, behavioral, and cognitive schools of thought view depression?   pp. 10–12

Careers in Psychology

Psychologists study nearly every aspect of life, not only to understand how people behave but also to help them lead happier, healthier, more productive lives. Some people mistakenly assume that psychologists primarily assist those suffering from debilitating mental disorders, such as schizophrenia and severe depression; but only a portion do this kind of work.

Psychologists also help well-adjusted people to lead more exciting, fulfilling lives by providing services such as career counseling and assisting with community projects. Psychologists seek to provide people with interpersonal skills and knowledge about self-help techniques. Some psychologists practice psychology; others teach or do research. Most are involved in a combination of activities.

Psychologists are professionals who study behavior and use behavioral principles in scientific research or in applied settings for the treatment of emotional problems. Most have advanced degrees, usually PhDs (doctorates of philosophy). Many psychologists also train for an additional year or two in a specialized area such as mental health, physiology, or child development.

The oldest and largest professional organization for psychologists is the American Psychological Association (APA). Founded in 1892, its purpose is to advance

Eclecticism: [ek-LECK-ti-sizm] A combination of theories, facts, or techniques. In clinical and counseling psychology, eclecticism is the practice of using whatever therapeutic techniques are appropriate for an individual client rather than relying exclusively on the techniques of one school of psychology.

Psychologists: Individuals with advanced training who study behavior and use behavioral principles in scientific research or in applied settings for the treatment of emotional problems.

psychology as a science, a profession, and a means of promoting human welfare. Today, the APA has more than 68,000 members, with the majority holding doctoral degrees from accredited universities. In addition, there are more than 25,000 student affiliates. The APA disseminates a large number of research publications, which serve as a primary means for many psychologists to present their research to other professionals.

The APA is not the sole voice of psychology. Many specialty groups have emerged over the years. For example, organizations consisting mainly of developmental, behavioral, cognitive, or neuroscience psychologists have been formed. In 1989, the American Psychological Society (APS) was founded; it has a large membership of psychologists with academic interests and focuses on scientific research rather than on practice or applied interests. Two of its goals are to preserve the scientific base of psychology and to promote public understanding of psychology as a science.

Differences among Practitioners

People often confuse clinical psychologists, psychiatrists, and psychoanalysts. All are mental health practitioners who help people with serious emotional and behavior problems, but each looks at behavior differently. **Clinical psychologists** usually have a PhD in psychology and view behavior and emotions from a psychological perspective. In contrast, **psychiatrists** are physicians (medical doctors) who specialize in the treatment of disturbed behavior. Patients who see psychiatrists often have both physical and emotional problems. Because of their medical training, psychiatrists can prescribe drugs and can admit patients for hospitalization. Clinical psychologists and psychiatrists often see a similar mix of clients and often work together as part of a mental health team. Most psychologists and psychiatrists support collaborative efforts. However, a friendly rivalry exists between the two disciplines because of their sometimes very different points of view.

Clinical psychologists generally have more extensive training than psychiatrists in assessment, research, and psychological treatment of emotional problems. Their nonmedical perspective gives them different roles in hospital settings and allows them to view patients differently from psychiatrists (Kingsbury, 1987). Psychiatrists use a medical approach, which often involves making assumptions about behavior—for example, that abnormal behavior is diseaselike in nature—that psychologists do not make.

Psychoanalysts are usually psychiatrists; they have training in the technique of psychoanalysis and use it in treating people with emotional problems. As we saw earlier, psychoanalysis was originated by Freud and includes the study of unconscious motivation and dream analysis. It often requires a course of daily therapy sessions; the patient's treatment may last several years. In the past, psychoanalysts had to be physicians. In 1988, however, psychoanalytic institutes began to accept nonphysicians into their training programs. Thus, all practitioners may treat similar clients, but the individual training and assumptions may vary, and this may be reflected in their choice of treatment.

Choosing Psychology as a Career

Psychology is a diverse and exciting field. It attracts many college students who like the idea of understanding human behavior and helping others. Every year, almost all of the approximately 3,000 recipients of PhDs in psychology accept jobs directly related to their training. There are slightly more than 100,000 psychologists in the United States. If you are considering the field of psychology or a related field, there

Clinical psychologists: Mental health practitioners who view behavior and mental processes from a psychological perspective and who use their knowledge to treat persons with serious emotional or behavioral problems or to do research into the causes of behavior.

Psychiatrists: Physicians (medical doctors) who have completed a residency specializing in the study of behavior and the treatment of patients with emotional and physical disorders.

Psychoanalysts: Psychiatrists or occasionally nonmedical practitioners who have studied the technique of psychoanalysis and use it in treating people with emotional problems.

is good news. Unemployment among psychologists is low, and new psychologists continue to find employment in areas related to their graduate training. Most experts agree that employment opportunities will continue to improve.

Training is the key to employment opportunities. A psychologist who (1) obtains a PhD in clinical psychology from an accredited university, (2) does an internship in a state hospital, and (3) becomes licensed will have a wide variety of job opportunities available in both the private and the public sectors. Individuals with master's degrees can function in a variety of settings, and even those with bachelor's degrees can play an important role in delivering psychological services. Salaries, responsibilities, and working conditions tend to be commensurate with level of training in the discipline.

As indicated in Figure 1.1, about 60 percent of the members of the APA who work in the field of psychology deliver human services. Of this number, about 40 percent work in clinics, community mental health centers, health maintenance organizations, veterans' hospitals, public hospitals, and public and private mental health hospitals. The remainder are private practitioners who maintain offices and work in public and private school settings (American Psychological Association, 1992a; Pion, Bramblett, & Wicherski, 1987).

Psychologists with PhDs provide more than 50 million hours annually to 4 to 10 million people (Howard et al., 1986). Most of the psychologists employed by

FIGURE 1.1

What Psychologists Do

Of the members of the American Psychological Association who work in the field of psychology, about 60 percent are involved in the delivery of mental health services—as clinical, counseling, and school psychologists. The remaining 40 percent focus on research, teaching, and application in university settings, government, and business. (*Data provided by American Psychological Association, 1992a*)

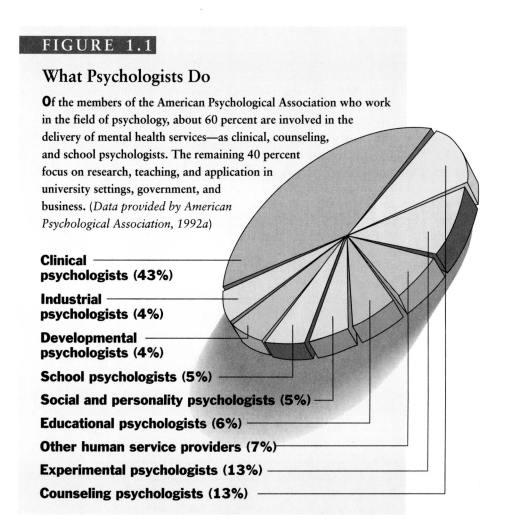

Clinical psychologists (43%)

Industrial psychologists (4%)

Developmental psychologists (4%)

School psychologists (5%)

Social and personality psychologists (5%)

Educational psychologists (6%)

Other human service providers (7%)

Experimental psychologists (13%)

Counseling psychologists (13%)

hospitals spend their time in the direct delivery of human services, including individual and group therapy. About 5 percent of psychologists are employed by business, government, and industry. About 30 percent of the APA's members are employed by universities, nearly half of them in psychology departments. University psychologists spend most of their time researching and teaching.

Hidden No Longer: Women and Ethnic Minorities

A helping profession with deep scientific roots, psychology is attracting an increasing number of women and members of ethnic minorities. For example, the number of women in graduate training programs has doubled in the last 20 years and the number of full-time faculty who are women has grown to 27 percent (Kohout, Wicherski, & Cooney, 1992). Data suggest that this trend is likely to continue (Russo & Denmark, 1987). Although proportionately more women than men are entering psychology, women are also more likely than men to be employed part-time.

The first women psychologists received training similar to their male colleagues but were much less likely to achieve professional status equivalent to that of men (Furumoto & Scarborough, 1986). But today research by women is at the forefront of scientific inquiry. Among the important women in this field are Mavis Hetherington, who has studied the impact of divorce on children; Judith Rodin, who has done important work on eating and eating disorders; Elizabeth Loftus, who has studied the ability of eyewitnesses to remember accurately; and Sandra Scarr, who studies intelligence. Women are presidents of national, regional, and local psychological organizations, and their thoughts and work often dominate psychological journals (Russo & Denmark, 1987).

The number of members of ethnic minorities who become psychologists is small—currently about 8.5 percent—but is slowly growing (Kohout & Pion, 1990). Data show that African Americans receive about 3 percent of the PhDs in psychology; Hispanic Americans also earn 3 percent of the PhDs (Smith & Davidson, 1992). In the early part of this century, there was sharp discrimination against members of minority groups. Still, many African Americans overcame the odds; they received PhDs, published scientific research, and made lasting contributions to the discipline. Gilbert Haven Jones was the first African-American holder of a PhD to teach psychology in the United States. Albert S. Beckham was a clinician who published studies in the 1930s of socioeconomic status and adolescence among minority groups. Add Inez Prosser and Howard H. Long to the distinguished list of early psychologists who published in the 1930s. Francis C. Sumner (1895–1954), who chaired the psychology department at Howard University, is considered the father of African-American psychology. Kenneth Clark, former president of the American Psychological Association, achieved national prominence for his work on the harmful effects of segregation. The works of Mamie Phipps Clark on self-esteem and racial identification with her husband Kenneth Clark have become classics.

There is less documentation about the role of Hispanic Americans in the history of psychology. Yet we know that a number of prominent Hispanic-American psychologists have focused on a variety of psychological issues. Manuel Barrera has done important work in community psychology, especially on social support systems. R. Díaz-Guerrero has examined cultural and personality variables in Hispanic Americans. Jorge Sanchez conducted exemplary research on the role of education in minority achievement, biased test scores, and intelligence testing.

Psychology is strengthened by understanding rather than avoidance of the range of people's abilities. Research and theory become more complete when the multicultural nature of human beings is explored. On a practical level, the helping professions are enhanced when practitioners understand their clients. The variety of psychologists, of their research interests, and of their socioeconomic and ethnic background is now contributing to a greater recognition of diversity among people—and this diversity is a strength that psychologists today not only recognize but celebrate.

One Psychologist's Career

My career in psychology began in the 10th grade, when I conducted a survey of sexual attitudes at my high school. First, I passed out questionnaires to the juniors and seniors (who were to respond anonymously). Then I spent days collating and summarizing the data. I found the data fascinating (and was relieved to find that I was about as advanced as my peers), although I did not yet understand how to make sense out of them.

In college, I majored in psychology and was particularly interested in clinical psychology. I took courses in traditional experimental psychology—learning, physiology, perception—but especially enjoyed abnormal psychology, child development, and personality. In addition to attending classes, I worked in a treatment center for emotionally disturbed children. The work was hard and emotionally demanding, and the pay was not particularly good. Later, as a laboratory assistant, I collected and analyzed data for a psychologist doing research in vision. I loved hunting for answers to scientific questions, speculating about new ideas, designing research questions, and collecting data.

My graduate studies included research in perception, and I studied information processing in vision. In graduate school, my intellectual skills were sharpened, my knowledge base was expanded, and my interests were focused and refined. After earning my PhD, I became an assistant professor at the University of South Carolina. My research in cognitive psychology involved studying perceptual phenomena such as eye movements. Today, I teach, do research in cognitive psychology, and write psychology textbooks. My goal is to share my excitement for psychology in the classroom, in my textbooks, and in professional journals.

Over time, my interests changed. At first, I was interested in the delivery of mental health services to children. Later, I focused on applied research issues concerning sensation and perception, such as eye movements among learning disabled readers. But my primary focus remains in basic research issues. My change in orientation reflects the three major areas in which psychologists work: applied research, human services, and experimental psychology.

What Psychologists Do

Applied research, human services, and experimental psychology have much in common. Actually, human services is a subfield of applied research, but it comprises such a large proportion of psychologists that it is generally viewed as a separate field of psychology. All psychologists consider research and theory to be the cornerstone of their approach. A human services provider may also do research, and a researcher who works in a university may also provide human services to the university or the community at large. For example, a human services psychologist may help an alcoholic patient by applying learning principles discovered in an experimental laboratory. Similarly, problems discovered by therapists challenge researchers to investigate causes in the laboratory. This cross-fertilization is stimulating. Let's look at each of these areas.

Applied Research. Applied psychologists do research and then use that research to solve practical problems. Many use psychological principles in businesses, government, and institutions, such as hospitals.

▶ *Engineering psychologists* (sometimes called *human factors psychologists*) use psychological principles to help people handle machines efficiently (for example, by designing an easy-to-use automated bank teller).

▶ *Educational psychologists* focus on such topics as how learning occurs in the classroom, how intelligence affects performance, and the relationship between personality and learning.

▶ *Forensic psychologists* deal with legal issues, including courts and correctional systems. They often evaluate whether inmates are ready for parole or whether a rehabilitation program is achieving its goals.

▶ *Health psychologists* determine how lifestyle changes can improve health. They devise techniques for helping people avoid medical and psychological problems.

▶ *Behavioral medicine psychologists* help people who suffer from chronic physical problems such as back pain and migraine headaches.

▶ *Sports psychologists* are in an emerging field that focuses on brain-behavior interactions, the role of sports in healthful lifestyles, and the motivation and preparation of athletes.

▶ *Industrial/organizational psychologists* help employers evaluate employees. They also focus on personnel selection, employee motivation, employee training, work behavior, incentives, and work appraisals. They apply psychological research and theory to organizational problems such as productivity, turnover, absenteeism, and management-labor relations. Working in personnel offices and in other departments at universities and businesses, they also evaluate organizational programs. Industrial/organizational psychologists are discussed in greater detail in Module B, at the end of the text.

Human Services. Many applied psychologists use behavioral principles to teach people to cope with life more effectively. They try to help people solve problems and to promote well-being. Within the human services area are the subfields of clinical, counseling, community, and school psychology.

▶ *Clinical psychologists* help clients with behavior problems such as anger, shyness, depression, and marital discord. They work either in private practice or at hospitals, mental institutions, or social service agencies. They administer psychological tests, interview potential clients, and use psychological methods to treat emotional problems. Many universities employ psychologists to help students and staff handle the pressures of academic life.

Clinical psychology resulted from the work of Lightner Witmer (1867–1956), a charter member of the APA, who called for the establishment of a field within psychology that would focus on helping people (McReynolds, 1987). Witmer established the first psychological clinic, at the University of Pennsylvania, and coined the term *clinical psychologist*. The field of clinical psychology grew in the next 80 years, especially after World War II, when its training began to focus on professional practice and human service needs (Strickland, 1988).

▶ *Counseling psychologists,* like clinical psychologists, work with people who have behavior problems. They also help people handle career planning, marriage and family problems, and parenting problems.

Counseling psychology emerged in the 1940s, and at first the problems presented by its clients were less serious than those presented by the clients of clinical psychologists. However, since the 1980s, the problems have become more serious and counseling psychologists have increasingly used psychotherapy and other therapies that were previously used exclusively by clinical psychologists. According to many practitioners and researchers, counseling and clinical psychology are converging (Fitzgerald & Osipow, 1986).

Counseling psychologists may work for public agencies such as mental health centers, hospitals, and universities. Many work in college or university counseling centers, where they help students adjust to the academic atmosphere and provide vocational and educational guidance. Like clinical psychologists, many counseling psychologists research the causes and treatment of maladjustment.

Community psychologists help individuals and communities face a variety of challenges, often by forming support groups.

▶ *Community psychologists* strengthen existing social support networks and stimulate the formation of new networks to meet a variety of challenges (L. R. Gonzales et al., 1983). Their goals are to help individuals and their neighborhoods or communities to grow, develop, and plan for the future. Community psychology emerged in response to the widespread desire for an action-oriented approach to individual and social adjustment, and one of its key elements is community involvement to effect social change. For example, community psychologists have been instrumental in organizing social support groups that help AIDS patients and their families handle the stress and loss of self-esteem produced by this catastrophic illness. They work in mental health agencies, state governments, and private organizations.

▶ *School psychologists* help students, teachers, parents, and others to understand one another and accomplish mutually agreed upon goals. School psychology began in 1896 at the University of Pennsylvania in a clinic founded to study and treat children considered morally or mentally defective. Both G. Stanley Hall and Lightner Witmer were crucial in promoting psychological interventions and techniques in schools (T. K. Fagan, 1992).

There are more than 30,000 school psychologists, most of whom work in educational systems. They administer and interpret tests, help teachers with classroom-related problems, and influence school policies and procedures (Bardon, 1983). They establish communication among parents, teachers, administrators, and other psychologists at the school. They also provide information to teachers and parents about students' progress and advise them how to help students achieve more.

Experimental Psychology. Experimental psychologists try to identify and understand the basic elements of behavior and mental processes. Theirs is an approach, not a specific field. That is, experimental psychologists use a set of *techniques;* experimental psychology does not define the topics they examine. For example, applied psychologists may be involved in experimental research and experimental psychologists may teach in university settings as well as do research. However, experimental psychologists focus on understanding basic research issues,

FOCUS

▶ Careers in psychology are diverse and plentiful; differentiate the major vocational choices available for psychologists. pp. 18–20

▶ Identify the focus of applied research, human services, and experimental psychology. pp. 18–20

▶ What makes experimental psychologists different from applied psychologists? pp. 18–20

whereas applied psychologists may use experimental techniques to improve a specific situation, help a mental health practitioner, or work with an employer.

Experimental psychology covers many areas of interest, some of which overlap with fields outside psychology. Experimental psychologists may be interested, for example, in visual perception, in how people learn language or solve problems, or in how hormones influence behavior.

▶ *Developmental psychologists* focus on the emotional, physical, and intellectual changes that take place throughout people's lives.

▶ *Social psychologists* study how people affect an individual's behavior and thoughts and how people interact with one another. They may examine attitude formation, aggressive versus helping behavior, and the formation of intimate relationships.

▶ *Cognitive psychologists* focus on thought processes, especially the relationships among learning, memory, and perception. They may, for example, examine how organisms process and interpret information on the basis of some internal representation in memory.

▶ *Physiological psychologists* (sometimes called *neuropsychologists*) try to understand the relationship between the brain and its mechanisms and behavior. They may examine drugs, hormones, and even brain transplants.

Ethics in Psychological Research

If you ever have the opportunity to tour a psychologist's laboratory, do so. Even better, if you have the chance to assist a psychologist in research, take advantage of it. Although psychologists use some of the same techniques as other scientists, they refine these techniques to deal with the uncertainties of human behavior. Some psychologists study behavior by first observing it in animals and then generalizing the principles to human behavior. Research with animals, especially human beings, is extensive, and researchers must pay special attention to ethical considerations. *Ethics* in research is the rules of conduct that investigators use to guide their research; these rules concern the treatment of animals, the rights of human beings, and the responsibilities of investigators.

Research with Animals

Why are animals used in research? Using animals in research studies allows experimenters to isolate simple aspects of behavior and to eliminate the complex distractions and variables that arise in studies involving human beings. Their use also enables researchers to conduct studies that could not ethically be conducted with human beings. For example, it would be unethical to deprive human infants of visual

Research with animals is only a small part of psychological research, but it is invaluable for exploring key issues such as attachment.

stimulation to investigate the effects of visual restriction. Furthermore, because most animals have shorter life spans than human beings, experimenters can observe and control their life history, can perform autopsies to obtain information, and can study several generations in a short time. Research with animals has helped psychologists understand many aspects of human behavior, including eating, learning, perception, and motivation (Baldwin, 1993).

Some people object to the use of animals in research, but there are no known realistic alternatives at present (Gallup & Suarez, 1985). For example, experiments on laboratory rats reveal much about the addictive properties of cocaine and its adverse effects on behavior. Similar experiments on human beings would be unethical. In addition, many people with incurable diseases, such as multiple sclerosis and Alzheimer's disease, hope for a cure through animal research and experimentation (Feeney, 1987). Most researchers are sensitive to the needs of animals (Novak & Suomi, 1988), and the American Psychological Association has strict ethical guidelines for animal research.

Research on animals is only a small part (about 7 percent) of all the research published in psychological journals (Dewsbury, 1991; N. E. Miller, 1985). Nonetheless, animal testing and research is a complicated and sometimes emotional issue. Today, most psychologists believe the benefits far outweigh the costs when ethical guidelines are carefully followed.

Human Participants

While animal research is an important component of the psychological landscape, psychologists more often work with **human participants,** or *subjects*—individuals who participate in experiments and whose behavior is observed for research data collection. In such research, psychologists investigate many of the same processes they do with animals, as well as design experiments specifically for human subjects. A psychologist who wishes to test whether an enhanced environment makes organisms smarter may use both animals and human subjects. The researcher may first

Human participants: Individuals who participate in experiments and whose behavior is observed for research data collection. Also known as *subjects*.

Informed consent: The signature of human participants on a document that indicates they understand the nature of their participation in the upcoming research and have been fully informed about the general nature of the research, its goals, and its methods.

Debriefing: The process of providing the participants in a study, at the end of the project, with information about the exact nature of the research, its hypothesis, and its methods.

Experiment: A procedure in which a researcher systematically manipulates some variables to describe objectively the relationship between the variables of concern and the resulting behavior; well-designed experiments permit inferences about cause and effect and test hypotheses.

train one rat to run complicated mazes while leaving its littermate in a barren environment. Several months later, the researcher, in examining the two animals, may discover that the brain cells of the maze-running rat are larger and have more internal connections. Along the same lines, the psychologist may test whether a decline in IQ scores shown by some nursing home residents can be halted or reversed by the enrichment of their environment with classes and special activities.

The American Psychological Association (1992b) has strict ethical guidelines for research with human participants: Participants cannot be coerced to do things that are harmful to themselves, that would have negative effects, or that would violate standards of decency. The investigator is responsible for ensuring the ethical treatment of the participants, and the participants are free to decline to participate or to withdraw at any time without penalty. In addition, any information gained in an experimental situation is considered strictly confidential.

Before a study begins, human participants must also give the researcher their **informed consent**—their signature on a document that indicates they understand the nature of their participation in the research and have been fully informed about the general nature of the research, its goals, and its methods. At the end of the project, the participants must go through **debriefing**—the process of providing the participants with information about the exact nature of the research, its hypotheses, and its methods. Debriefing preserves both the validity of the responses and ethical considerations.

Deception in Psychological Research

Is it ever acceptable to deceive human participants in psychological research? Imagine a situation where a researcher tricks a person into believing that she is causing another person pain. Is this acceptable? Is it acceptable for a researcher to change a human participant's views of social or political issues just to see if the researcher can do so? The answer to both of these situations is generally no. Researchers must not use deception unless the study has important scientific, educational, or applied value. And even then, two key conditions must be met: informed consent and debriefing.

Many psychologists believe deception is unacceptable under any circumstances. They assert that it undermines the public's belief in the integrity of scientists and that its cost outweighs its potential benefits. Today, most psychologists do not conduct research in which there is deception; those who do are especially careful to use rigorous informed consent procedures and extensive debriefing to minimize potentially harmful effects. Whenever deception must be used, psychologists go to extraordinary lengths to protect the well-being, rights, and dignity of the participants; anything less is considered a violation of American Psychological Association guidelines. Most research with human participants is done within the context of the controlled experiment, our next topic.

The Controlled Experiment

The typical research process is usually systematic and begins with a specific question. It is in the form of an **experiment**—a procedure in which a researcher systematically manipulates and observes elements of a situation in order to answer a question. For example, if a researcher wants to determine the relationship between an animal's eating behavior and weight, the researcher could systematically vary (manipulate) how much the animal ate and then weigh (observe) the animal each day.

Correlation Is Not Causation

Only controlled laboratory experiments permit researchers to make *cause-and-effect statements*—inferences about the causes of behavior. This is a key point: *Correlated events are not necessarily causally related*. Two events are *correlated* when the increased presence (or absence) of a particular situation is regularly associated with a high (or low) presence of another situation, event, or situational feature. For example, a researcher who finds that children from broken homes have more emotional problems and commit more crimes than other children can state that there is a correlation. However, the researcher cannot conclude that broken homes cause emotional problems or crime. (See Figure 1.2.) By contrast, events are causally related when one event makes another event occur—when one event or situation is contingent on another.

When psychologists suggest that one situation causes another, they have to be sure that several specific conditions are met. They pay close attention to how the data are collected and to whether the results of the study are repeatable in additional experiments. To make meaningful causal inferences, psychologists must create situations in which they can limit the likelihood of obtaining a result that is simply a chance occurrence or due to other irrelevant factors. Only by using carefully formulated experiments can psychologists make sound interpretations of their results and cautiously extend them to other (sometimes therapeutic) situations. Experiments have specific components and requirements, which are discussed next.

> **Variable:** A condition or a characteristic of a situation or person that is subject to change (that varies) across situations or individuals.

Variables, Hypotheses, and Experimental and Control Groups

Variables. A **variable** is a condition or a characteristic of a situation or person that is subject to change (that varies) either within or across situations or individuals. Researchers manipulate variables in order to measure how the changes in them

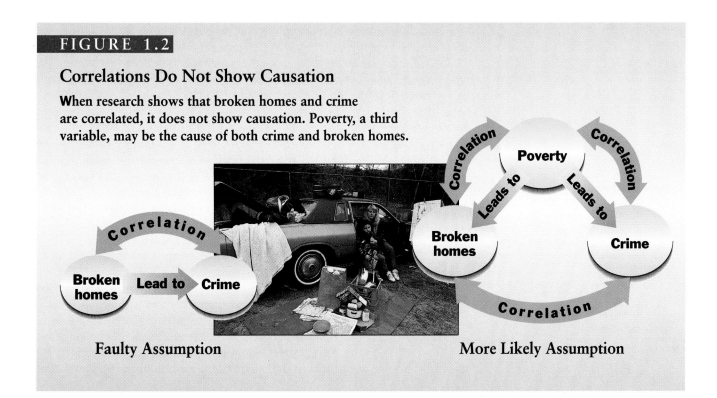

FIGURE 1.2

Correlations Do Not Show Causation

When research shows that broken homes and crime are correlated, it does not show causation. Poverty, a third variable, may be the cause of both crime and broken homes.

Faulty Assumption   **More Likely Assumption**

affect other variables. There are two types of variables in any experiment: independent variables and dependent variables. The **independent variable** is the variable in a controlled experiment that is directly and purposefully manipulated by the experimenter to see how the variables under study will be affected. The **dependent variable** is the variable that is expected to change because of the manipulation of the independent variable. For example, one characteristic of a situation that might change is temperature, and a change in temperature might affect behavior. A researcher might therefore raise the temperature in a room to determine if a person's activity level is increased or decreased by the change.

To visualize how variables come into play, imagine a simple experiment intended to determine the effects of sleep loss on behavior. The independent (manipulated) variable might be the number of hours college students are allowed to sleep. The dependent variable could be the students' reaction to a stimulus—for example, how quickly they push a button when a light is flashed. The participants in the study might be a large group of college students who normally sleep about 7 hours per night.

Hypotheses. A **hypothesis** is a tentative statement or idea expressing a causal relationship between two events or variables that are to be evaluated in a research study. The hypothesis of a sleep experiment might be that students deprived of sleep will react more slowly to a stimulus than will students allowed to sleep their regular 7 hours. Suppose the subjects sleep in the laboratory on 4 successive nights and are tested each morning on a reaction time task. The subjects sleep 7 hours on each of three nights but only 4 hours on the fourth. If the response times after the first three nights are constant, the researcher can infer that any slowing of reaction time on the fourth test (following the night of 4 hours of sleep) is the result of depriving the subjects of sleep.

If all other factors are held equal, any observed differences in reaction time can be attributed to the number of hours of sleep. That is, changes in the independent variable (numbers of hours of sleep) will produce changes in the dependent variable (reaction time). Also, if the results show that students deprived of sleep respond on the reaction time task a half second slower than they did after normal sleep, the researcher could feel justified in concluding that sleep deprivation acts to slow down reaction time. The experiment would have affirmed the researcher's tentative idea.

Experimental and Control Groups. Researchers must determine whether it is actually the changes in the manipulated variable (and not some unknown extraneous factor) that cause a change in the dependent variable. One way to do this is to set up at the start of the experiment at least two groups of subjects who are identical in important ways. The attributes they must have in common will depend on what the experimenter is testing. For example, because reflexes slow down as a person grows older, the researcher in a sleep experiment would want to ensure that the two groups were composed of subjects of the same or nearly the same age.

Once the subjects are known to be identical on important attributes, they are assigned randomly to either the experimental or the control group. *Random assignment* means that the subjects are assigned by chance rather than on the basis of any particular characteristic, preference, or situation that might have even a remote possibility of influencing the outcome. The **experimental group** is the group of subjects for whom the independent variable is manipulated. The

Independent variable: The variable in a controlled experiment that is directly and purposefully manipulated by the experimenter to see how the variables under study will be affected.

Dependent variable: The variable in a controlled experiment that is expected to change because of the manipulation of the independent variable.

Hypothesis: A tentative statement or idea expressing a causal relationship between two events or variables that are to be evaluated in a research study.

Experimental group: In an experiment, the group of subjects for whom the independent variable is manipulated and who receive the treatment under investigation.

control group is the comparison group—the group of subjects tested on the dependent variable in the same way as the experimental group but for whom the independent variable is not manipulated. In the reaction time experiment, the students who sleep a full 7 hours on all 4 nights are the control group. Those who are allowed to sleep only 4 hours on the last night are the experimental group. By comparing the reaction times (the dependent variable) for the experimental and control groups, the researcher can determine whether the independent variable is responsible for any differences in the dependent variable between the groups.

If the researcher is confident that all the subjects responded with the same reaction time before the experiment—that is, that the two groups are truly comparable—then the person can conclude that sleep deprivation is the cause of the experimental group's decreased performance. Without comparable groups, the effect of the independent variable is not clear, and few real conclusions can be drawn from the data.

Operational Definitions, Sample Size, and Significant Differences

Operational Definitions. A key component of successful scientific research is that all terms used in describing the variables and the experimental procedure must be given operational definitions. An **operational definition** is the set of methods or procedures used to define a variable. When a researcher manipulates an organism's state of hunger, the concept *hunger* must be defined in terms of the procedures necessary to produce hunger. For example, a researcher might be interested in the effects of hunger (the independent variable) on exploratory behavior (the dependent variable) in mice. The researcher might deprive mice of food for 6, 10, 12, or 24 hours and might record the exploratory behavior of the mice before and during each of the conditions of food deprivation. The researcher might operationally define hunger in terms of the number of hours of food deprivation and exploratory behavior in terms of the number of times the mice walked farther than 2 feet down a path.

Sample Size. Another important factor in an experiment is the size and representativeness of the sample. A **sample** is a group of subjects who are assumed to be representative of the population about which an inference is being made. For example, a researcher studying schizophrenia has to put together a sample of people with that disorder. A psychiatrist who wishes to discover whether murderers have low levels of the neurotransmitter serotonin in their brains would have more luck finding a relevant sample at a maximum security penitentiary than at a garden club.

The number of subjects in a sample is very important. If an effect is obtained consistently with a large enough number of subjects, the researcher can reasonably rule out individual differences and chance as causes. The assumption is that a large sample better represents the population to which the researcher wishes to generalize the results.

Significant Differences. Researchers want to be sure that the differences they find are significant. For psychologists, a **significant difference** is the statistically determined likelihood that a behavior has not occurred because of chance alone. For example, when one therapy technique appears to be more effective than another, the researcher wants to be sure that the first technique is significantly different from the second and that the difference is enough to be important. The results are significantly different only if they could not be due to chance, due to one or two subjects, or due to a unique set of subjects. Such conclusions can come only from experiments. If experimental results are not statistically significant, they could have occurred by chance, so they are not considered to have proved or disproved the hypothesis.

Control group: In an experiment, the comparison group—the group of subjects tested on the dependent variable in the same way as the experimental group but for whom the independent variable is not manipulated.

Operational definition: The set of methods or procedures used to define a variable.

Sample: A group of subjects or participants who are assumed to be representative of the population about which an inference is being made.

Significant difference: The statistically determined likelihood that a behavior has not occurred because of chance alone.

Successful Experiments Avoid Pitfalls

Good experiments often involve several experimental groups, each tested under different conditions. Another study of the effects of sleep deprivation might involve a control group and five experimental groups. The subjects in each of the experimental groups might be deprived of sleep for a different length of time (sleep deprivation operationally defined in terms of number of hours of sleep lost from the normal number of hours slept). In this way, the researcher can examine the effects of several different periods of sleep deprivation on reaction time.

In a well-designed experiment, the experimenter also looks closely at the nature of the independent variable. Are there actual values for the independent variable above or below which results will differ markedly? For example, the researcher might find that a 1-hour period of sleep deprivation has no effect, that a 2-hour period of deprivation produces only a modest effect, and that every additional hour of deprivation markedly slows reaction time. These results would show that reaction time is dependent on the duration of sleep deprivation. The use of several experimental groups yields better understanding of how the independent variable (sleep deprivation) affects the dependent variable (reaction time).

Expectancy Effects. Frequently, things turn out just the way a researcher expects. Researchers are aware that their expectations about results might influence their findings, particularly regarding human behavior. They may unwittingly create a situation that leads to specific prophesied results—a **self-fulfilling prophecy.** For example, teachers may develop expectations about students' performance early in the year, and students usually confirm those expectations, even when the expectations do not reflect the students' potential ability (Jussim, 1989). In these instances, the students' performance has fulfilled the teachers' prophecies, regardless of other factors.

To avoid self-fulfilling prophecies, researchers often use a **double-blind technique**—a research technique in which neither the experimenter nor the subjects know who is in the control or the experimental group. In this situation, someone who is not connected with the research project keeps track of which subjects are assigned to which group. The double-blind technique minimizes the effect that a researcher's subtle cues might have on subjects. (In a single-blind experiment, the researcher knows who is in the experimental group and who is in the control group but the subjects do not know who is assigned to which group or whether they are being presented with a manipulated variable.)

Researchers also try to make sure their studies do not lead to specific results by minimizing the demand characteristics of studies. The **demand characteristics** are the elements of a study situation that might clue a subject as to the purpose of the study and might thereby elicit specific behavior from the subject. Subjects who think they know the real purpose of a study may try to behave "appropriately" and in so doing may distort the results. Some techniques that minimize the impact of demand characteristics are the use of computers to decrease interaction with people (subjects are less likely to want to act appropriately for a computer), of unobtrusive measures (such as tape recording rather than note taking), and of deception (concealing the real purpose of the study) until the end of the research session.

Even when demand characteristics are minimized and a double-blind procedure is used, participants often behave differently when they are in a research study. This finding is known as the **Hawthorne effect,** after some early research studies at the Hawthorne industrial plant that showed that people behave differently (usually better) when they know they are being observed. Researchers therefore attempt to make subjects feel comfortable and natural and to create experimental situations that min-

Self-fulfilling prophecy: The unwitting creation by a researcher of a situation that leads to specific prophesied results.

Double-blind technique: A research technique in which neither the experimenter nor the subjects know who is in the control or the experimental group.

Demand characteristics: The elements of a study situation that might clue a subject as to the purpose of the study and might thereby elicit specific behavior from the subject.

Hawthorne effect: The finding, based on early research studies at the Hawthorne industrial plant, that people behave differently (usually better) when they know they are being observed.

The Hawthorne studies alerted researchers to some of the potential problems inherent in the way experiments are designed.

imize the effects of participation. They often do not collect data until after subjects have adapted to the experimental situation and have become less excited about their participation in the research study.

Avoiding Gender and Racial Bias. We just saw that one way to avoid bias is have a large enough sample of participants who accurately reflect the population. However, researchers must also be careful to avoid subtle biases that influence results, such as gender and racial bias. At any stage of the research endeavor, an experimenter can influence the results and their interpretation by making assumptions about people, their tendencies, and how they might be affected by the variable under study. Such assumptions often include whether to report or not report a finding such as a gender difference or racial difference among participants. The issue of gender and cultural bias is examined further in the Diversity box on page 28.

FOCUS

▶ What are the implications of a study that is poorly conducted or that has a flawed methodology?   pp. 23–27

▶ Identify two elements in designing an experiment that are especially important to making generalizations about the results.   p. 25

▶ Why is it important for psychologists to consider the cultural context in which behavior occurs?   p. 28

Alternative Methods of Psychological Inquiry

Experiments are not the only way to collect data about human behavior. Techniques providing information other than about cause-and-effect relations also are important. These techniques include questionnaires, interviews, naturalistic observation, and case studies.

Questionnaires

A **questionnaire,** or *survey,* is usually a printed form with questions, often given to a large group of people. It is used by researchers to gather a large amount of information from many people in a short time. A questionnaire being used to learn the typical characteristics of psychology students might be sent to students enrolled in an introductory psychology course. It might ask each student to list age, sex, height,

Questionnaire: A printed form with questions, usually given to a large group of people; used by researchers to gather a substantial amount of data in a short time. Also known as a *survey.*

Avoiding Gender and Cultural Bias

When research studies are used to draw conclusions and make generalizations about people, it is important to understand that enormous differences exist among both individuals and groups of people. The young and the old may behave differently under similar conditions; research done only on men may yield different results from research done only on women. To a great extent, researchers have become especially sensitive to issues of human diversity. *Human diversity* is the basic individuality of human beings. People are not all alike and do not all behave in the same way, even when in the same situation.

To do effective research, draw meaningful conclusions, and make generalizations that may be wide-ranging, researchers must recognize and test for elements of diversity, even within one society, such as the United States. A society is made up of individuals from many different cultures, races, religions, and so on. Each subgroup has developed its own style of living, which may vary considerably from that of the majority culture (Snowden, 1987) and may lead to marked ethnic-related differences in day-to-day behavior and in mental health (Snowden & Cheung, 1990). Psychologists say that a group is culturally diverse if it has differences in race, ethnicity, language, nationality, age, and religion within a community, organization, or nation.

Race is a person's ancestry and descent; race is genetically determined. Ethnicity refers to peoples' common traits, background, and allegiances, which are often cultural, religious, or language based; ethnicity is learned from family, friends, and experiences. Families of African-American, Hispanic-American, and Asian-American descent bring to the American experience a wealth of different world views and different ways of bringing up children, based on their unique heritages. The extent of racial and ethnic diversity in the United States is growing rapidly; in the 1980s, the non-Hispanic population grew by less than 8 percent, but the Hispanic-American population grew by 39 percent.

Culture reflects a person's racial background, religious values, and concern for the arts, music, and scholarly interests. Culture is the unwritten social and psychological dictionary that each of us has learned and through which we interpret ourselves and others (Landrine, Klonoff, & Brown-Collins, 1992). Various cultural vantage points shape behavior, values, and even mental health. For example, Asian-American families have strongly held views about respect for elders and the continuity of the family. Asian-American culture, like any culture, helps its group members interpret what they have seen, felt, and experienced; it offers guidelines for interpretation of the world.

Closely tied to culture is a person's class. Although the U.S. class structure is not as rigid as in the last century or in some non-Western countries, people in the United States do fall into several socioeconomic classes. The classes are fuzzy and overlap one another, but they include the poor, the disadvantaged, the educated, and the middle class. In different socioeconomic classes (which include different races and cultures), people may view the world differently and behave differently primarily because of their socioeconomic status. A research study that is not sensitive to such variables may confuse the causes of its results.

Psychologists know that for both biological and learned reasons women often react differently from men in psychological situations. It becomes easy to see that the gender of the population in a research study is

weight, previous courses taken, grades in high school, SAT scores, number of brothers and sisters, and parents' financial status. There might also be questions regarding sexual relations, career goals, and personal preferences in TV shows, clothing styles, and music.

One aim of surveys is to discover relationships among variables. For example, a questionnaire designed to assess aggressiveness might ask respondents to list their gender, the number of fights they have had in the past, their feelings of anger, and the sports they enjoy. The researcher analyzing the results might check to see whether men and women tend to differ in aggressive behaviors.

The strength of the questionnaire is that it has the potential to gather a large amount of information in a short time. Its weaknesses are that it is impersonal, it generally gathers only the information asked by the questions, it limits the subjects'

crucial. For example, research on morality shows that women in general see moral situations differently from men; research on communication styles, aggression, and love shows sharp differences between men and women. Further, we know that more than half of the people seen by mental health practitioners are women, but this may be because men with mental health problems are less likely to seek therapy. These differences must be explored to find their causes.

The exceptional and the elderly are two other groups who shape research results in unique ways. The exceptional include individuals diagnosed as having mental retardation, learning disabilities, or physical disabilities. They often require a special sensitivity on the part of professionals to their unique needs. In addition, the elderly are a growing percentage of the general population. More than 30 million Americans are 65 or older. Psychologists are developing programs that focus on the special needs of the exceptional and the elderly for social support, physical and psychological therapy, and continuing education.

The differing perspectives on day-to-day behavior that special groups bring to the fabric of our society have not always been appreciated, understood, or even recognized in research

or theory. For example, we now take Freud to task for developing a personality theory that is seen as clearly sexist. (We will be studying and evaluating Freud's theory in chapter 12.) In his day, however, considerations of sexism were unheard of. Further, mi-

Researchers must take cultural differences into account when studying all aspects of behavior, including learning.

norities and special groups such as the exceptional and elderly were rarely—if ever—included in research studies intended to represent the general population. Today, psychologists seek to study all types of people to make valid conclusions based on scientific evidence. They see cultural diversity as an asset for both theorists and practitioners; however, they also recognize that they must research, learn about, and theorize about this diversity to help individuals optimize their potential (Betancourt & López, 1993). It is crucial to realize, though, that *there are usually more differences within a group than between groups*—for example, there are more differences among Asian Americans than between Asian Americans and some other ethnic group (Zuckerman, 1990).

Individual circumstances exist, and people's unique experiences make glib generalizations impossible. It is true that individuals and special populations often act just as the majority population does, but with a slightly different twist or variation. Here is the key point to remember as you read this book: While people are very much alike and share many common, even universal, experiences and behaviors, every individual is unique; and each person's behavior reflects diverse life experiences.

range of responses, it cannot prevent respondents from leaving some questions unanswered or from being untruthful in their responses, and it does not provide a structure from which cause-and-effect relationships can be inferred (although correlations may be found).

Interviews

An **interview** is typically a face-to-face meeting in which a researcher (interviewer) asks an individual a series of standardized questions. The subject's responses are usually tape recorded or written by the interviewer. The advantage of an interview over a questionnaire is that it allows for a wider range of responses. An interviewer who notes an exaggerated response, for example, might decide to ask related questions

Interview: A series of open-ended questions used to gather detailed information about a person.

Brief questionnaires or surveys can help researchers quickly gather a great deal of information.

and thus explore more fully an area that seems important to the subject. The interview technique is time-consuming, however, and no cause-and-effect relationships can be inferred.

Naturalistic Observation

A seemingly simple way to find out about behavior is to observe it. However, when people are told that they are going to be observed, they tend to become self-conscious and alter their natural behavior. Therefore, psychologists use the technique of **naturalistic observation**—careful and objective observation of events from a distance without observer intervention. The intent is to see how people or animals behave in their natural settings.

A psychologist conducting research on persuasion might act like a browsing shopper at car lots, furniture stores, and appliance centers to discover how salespeople convince customers to buy expensive products. For example, the researcher might observe that one particularly successful car salesperson tends to show budget-minded customers the most expensive automobiles first. Mid-priced models then seem more affordable by comparison. The researcher might also watch a salesperson through a one-way mirror of the kind used to detect thefts in supermarkets.

The strength of naturalistic observation is that the data collected are largely uncontaminated by the researcher's presence or the laboratory setting. The weakness is that the behavior the psychologist might wish to examine is not always exhibited. For example, sometimes animals do not show mating behavior; or groups of people might not act persuasively or become aggressive. Naturalistic observation is also very time-consuming.

Naturalistic observers take their data where and how they find them. They cannot manipulate the environment because that might alter the behavior they are observing. Because variables cannot be manipulated, data from naturalistic observation, like those from questionnaires and interviews, do not permit cause-and-effect conclusions.

Case Studies

The **case study** is a method of interviewing subjects to gain information about their background, including data on such things as childhood, family, education, and social and sexual interactions. The information in a case study describes in detail a specific person's responses to the world and can be used to determine a method of treatment.

The case study's strength is that it provides complete information. A weakness is that the information describes only one individual and that person's unique problem. Because one person's behavior may be like that of others or unique, researchers

Naturalistic observation: Careful and objective observation of events from a distance, without observer intervention.

Case study: A method of interviewing subjects to gain information about their background, including data on such things as childhood, family, education, and social and sexual interactions.

cannot generalize from one individual to an entire population. They must be cautious even when generalizing from a large number of case studies.

Combining Techniques

Researchers often use several techniques, either at different times or in combination. When I was an undergraduate in a course on research methods, a group of us tried to examine how hitchhikers' attire affects success at getting rides. We posed as hitchhikers and alternated our clothing from grubby to moderately pleasant to dressy. One of us hid behind a sign and counted the number of cars passing by, the number of drivers who stopped to inquire where we were going, and the number of drivers who provided a ride (not many).

Our experiment had many flaws, but it attempted to use the experimental method; that is, it manipulated an independent variable—type of clothes. It also used naturalistic observation—hiding behind the sign and counting. The mixing of methods is not only acceptable but often desirable; sometimes it is the only way certain types of research can be conducted. See Figure 1.3 for a summary of the major approaches to data collection. The Research Process box on page 32 describes how you can use critical thinking to evaluate all types of research.

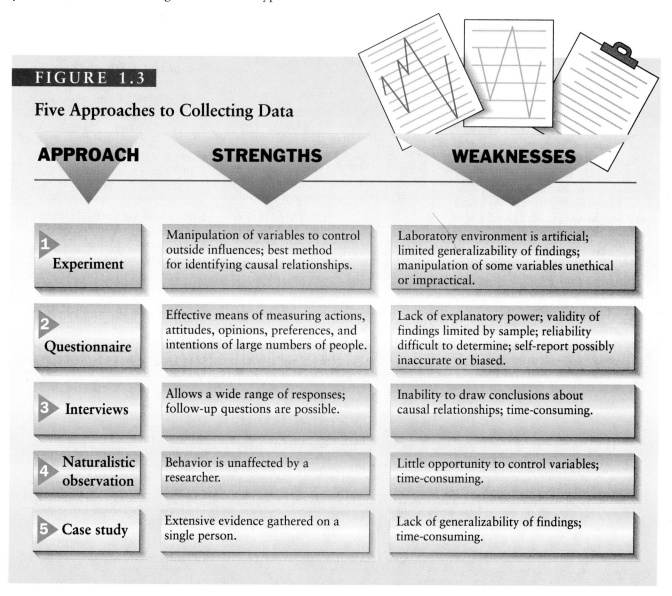

FIGURE 1.3

Five Approaches to Collecting Data

APPROACH	STRENGTHS	WEAKNESSES
1 **Experiment**	Manipulation of variables to control outside influences; best method for identifying causal relationships.	Laboratory environment is artificial; limited generalizability of findings; manipulation of some variables unethical or impractical.
2 **Questionnaire**	Effective means of measuring actions, attitudes, opinions, preferences, and intentions of large numbers of people.	Lack of explanatory power; validity of findings limited by sample; reliability difficult to determine; self-report possibly inaccurate or biased.
3 **Interviews**	Allows a wide range of responses; follow-up questions are possible.	Inability to draw conclusions about causal relationships; time-consuming.
4 **Naturalistic observation**	Behavior is unaffected by a researcher.	Little opportunity to control variables; time-consuming.
5 **Case study**	Extensive evidence gathered on a single person.	Lack of generalizability of findings; time-consuming.

THE RESEARCH PROCESS

Thinking Critically and Evaluating Research

Psychologists, like all scientists, are trained to think, to evaluate research critically, and to put their results into a meaningful framework. Whatever the method used to ask and answer research questions, researchers think critically about the questions, the methods, and the results. Psychologists follow a traditional approach to evaluating research. To benefit from this textbook, you may find it helpful to use the same critical thinking skills and framework in order to follow their logic, to understand their approach, and to evaluate their research.

Critical thinking involves evaluating evidence, sifting through choices, assessing outcomes, and deciding whether conclusions make sense. When you think critically, you are being evaluative. You are not accepting glib generalizations; instead you are determining the relevancy of facts and looking for biases and imbalances, as well as for objectivity and testable, repeatable results. A critical thinker identifies central issues and is careful not to reach cause-and-effect conclusions from correlations.

When you think critically about research, you become a detective sorting through facts. You look objectively at the facts, question the hypotheses and conclusions, avoid oversimplifications, and consider all of the arguments, objections, and counterarguments. You revise your opinions when the data and conclusions call for revisions. Whenever you have to evaluate a research study in this text, in the popular press, or in a psychological publication, you will find it helpful to focus on five research criteria: purpose, methodology, subjects, repeatability, and conclusions.

▶ *Purpose.* What is the purpose of this research? What is the researcher trying to test, demonstrate, or prove? Has the problem been clearly defined? Is the researcher qualified to conduct this research?

▶ *Methodology.* Is the methodology appropriate? Is it carefully executed? Is the method of investigation used (for example, case study, survey, experiment) the most appropriate one for the topic? Has the method been used properly? Is there a control group? Have the variables been carefully (operationally) defined? Has the researcher followed ethical guidelines?

▶ *Subjects.* Was the sample of subjects properly chosen and carefully described? How was the sample selected? Does the sample accurately reflect the characteristics of the population of individuals about which the researcher would like to make generalizations? Will any generalizations be possible from this study?

▶ *Repeatability.* Can the results be repeated? Has the researcher shown the same finding more than once? Have other investigators made similar findings? Are the results clear and unambiguous—that is, not open to criticism based on poor methodology? What additional evidence will be necessary for a psychologist to support the conclusions?

▶ *Conclusions.* Are the conclusions, implications, and applications suggested by the study logical? Are they supported by the researcher's data? Has the researcher gone beyond the data, drawing conclusions that might fit a predisposed view rather than conclusions that follow logically from the facts of the study? What implications do the data have for psychology as a science and as a profession and potentially for you as an individual? Has the researcher considered alternative explanations?

Goals of This Book: Psychology's Central Issues

This book will introduce you to the basic theories and principles of psychology. Some of what you learn may help you resolve everyday problems. For example, how does your life history affect your future development? How much do your thoughts about yourself and others determine what you will do tomorrow? How can an understanding of personality and motivation help you interact with other people? How can the principles of memory be applied to improving your skills and grades?

Some of the specific information may help you to cope with difficult situations. For example, an understanding of personality and motivation may help some indi-

Think back to the sleep deprivation experiment described earlier. Use the five criteria to evaluate this research. The subjects were college students deprived of sleep and tested on a reaction time task.

Was the purpose of the study clear? The purpose was to assess the effect of sleep loss on reaction time.

Was the methodology appropriate? The method involved depriving subjects of sleep after they had grown used to sleeping in a controlled environment; subjects were tested each morning. The task was carefully operationally defined.

What about the subjects? Since the subjects were college students who were in good health, reasonable generalizations from their reaction times to the reaction times of other similarly aged people might be possible.

What about repeatability? If the results obtained were found with several groups of subjects, and if the results were consistent within each of those groups, the repeatability of the results would seem assured.

Last, what about conclusions? Limited conclusions can be drawn from such a research study. There was only one age group—college students. There were no controls on other factors in the students' environment, such as work loads, school

pressure, energy expenditures, and history of sleep loss. A simple conclusion about sleep deprivation could be drawn: In controlled research studies of college students, sleep deprivation tends to slow down reaction time. However, not much more could be said, and no generalizations could be applied to, say, children, older adults, or the chronically mentally ill. The results of the study do not contradict common sense, but they add little to our overall understanding of reaction times.

A key to thinking critically about research is to be evaluative, to question all aspects of the study. Think about the advantages as well as the limitations of the research method. When a television commercial tells you that 9 out of 10 doctors recommend Brand X, think critically about that claim. What kind of doctors, for what kind of ailment, for patients of what age, and for what extent of usage?

As you read this text, evaluate research findings. I will present the research to you in ways that allow you to critically evaluate it and to draw

All researchers, regardless of the method they use, are trained to think critically about the question, method, procedures, results, and implications of their research.

your own conclusions. In addition, from time to time in each chapter I will ask you some "focus questions." These questions will suggest new ideas and perspectives for you to consider as you evaluate the research studies presented. These are not the only places in the text where you should use your critical thinking skills, but they are places where you can be especially evaluative.

viduals deal with underachieving children. Knowledge about depression and its causes will help others cope with rejection in dating. Understanding the origins, symptoms, and treatment of illness may help families deal with feelings about a beloved grandmother with Alzheimer's disease.

Psychologists address all of these issues and many more. In the following chapters, you will explore psychological topics such as the effects of drugs on behavior, mental disorders and forms of therapy, the processes of perception and memory, and the physical, mental, and social development of human beings from birth through death.

It is evident that psychology, with its great diversity and its many specialities, is wide-ranging. But with all of its breadth, certain key issues and ideas emerge over and over again and are presented regularly in this text:

▶ The scientific method is a mainstay of psychological research.

▶ Psychology is an ever-changing science based on empirical observation.

▶ Psychological theories are diverse, are always expanding, and must be considered in the context of the time at which they are initiated.

▶ The relative contribution of heredity versus environment (nature versus nurture) is frequently questioned by psychologists.

▶ People continue to develop throughout their lives, and this is evident in the various fields of psychology.

▶ Such aspects of human behavior as personality and intelligence must be considered within an environmental context.

▶ Thought (cognition) is becoming an increasingly important topic in the study of behavior; human beings are competent and thoughtful and are able to decide their future.

▶ Many disorders previously thought to be caused solely by psychological conditions are now known to have a biological component.

▶ People's behavior reflects not only their genetic heritage but their ethnicity, class, culture, race, gender, and age. Human diversity—individual differences and the wide range of human behaviors—is an exciting aspect of psychology.

Concluding Note

Psychology is a stimulating, challenging, and diverse discipline. Its terminology may be unfamiliar, and its theories may be new to you. However, understanding psychology can be rewarding and worthwhile. Psychologists from various fields and perspectives are often both scientists and practitioners. As scientists, they gather basic information about behavior and mental processes; as practitioners, they apply their findings in various disciplines, including law. For example, psychologists influence legal decisions, serve on the faculties of law schools, and are even cited in legal case books.

Psychology is also applied in public service sectors to help formulate public policy. Psychologists do research and serve as consultants on issues that affect the quality of life for people everywhere. They are especially interested in the elderly, health and nursing care, education and learning, and mental health issues. Psychologists do both laboratory and field-based research to investigate, for example, the effects of day care on emotional development, of aging on intelligence, of preparation courses on intelligence tests and the SAT, of drugs such as cocaine on memory, and of therapy on mental disorders.

You are faced with a future of challenges. To succeed in college, you must take responsibility for your own learning. Make and follow a study schedule. Observe yourself as a learner to determine what study methods and learning arrangements work best, and make adjustments when the learning process is not working effectively. Being a competent student does not come naturally or easily for most people. It takes self-discipline, realistic scheduling, and a true desire to learn. Becoming a confident and competent learner takes time and practice, so go easy on yourself if you make mistakes or don't quite live up to your expectations of yourself. The important thing to remember is that almost anyone who wants to be a successful student can be one. In the end, the day-by-day progress you make will lead you to your goals.

I sincerely hope you enjoy your experience with *Psychology*. I hope this book will provide you with a fundamental understanding of the principles of human behavior and mental process and with some effective problem-solving tools you can use for the rest of your life.

Summary & Review

Defining Psychology

What is psychology and what do psychologists study?

Psychology is the science of behavior and mental processes. Psychologists observe numerous aspects of human functioning including overt actions, mental activity, emotional, and physiological reactions. *Overt actions* are any directly observable and measurable movements, or the results of such movements. *Mental processes* include thoughts, ideas, and reasoning processes. *Emotional responses* include feelings such as anger, regret, and happiness. *Physiological reactions* include an increased heart rate when you are excited or biochemical changes when light stimulates your eyes.   p. 5

Identify four key goals of psychologists.

Psychologists attempt to *describe* the basic components of behavior, to *explain* them, to *predict* them, and, potentially, to *manage* them.   p. 5

KEY TERMS: *psychology*, p. 4; *theory*, p. 5

Past and Present Schools of Psychological Thought

Describe the early schools of psychology.

Psychology became a field of study in the mid-1800s. *Structuralism*, led by Wundt, focused on the contents of consciousness and was the first true school of psychology. *Functionalism*, led by James and others, emphasized how and why the mind works. *Gestalt psychology*, in contrast to structuralism and functionalism, focused on perceptual processes; the early Gestalt psychologists studied phenomena such as figure–ground relationships. *Psychoanalysis*, developed by Freud, was both a theory of personality and a treatment procedure to help people cope with their problems; it centered around the mo-

tivation of individuals and their unconscious desires and needs as determinants of behavior.   pp. 7–10

Describe behaviorist, humanistic, cognitive, and biological psychology.

Watson led the *behaviorist* movement and argued that the proper subject of psychological study was observable behavior. *Humanistic psychology* arose in response to the psychoanalytic and behavioral views and stresses free will and *self-actualization*. *Cognitive psychology* focuses on perception, memory, learning, and thinking and asserts that human beings engage in both worthwhile and maladjusted behaviors because of ideas and thoughts. The *biological perspective* examines how heredity and biological structures affect mental processes and behavior. pp. 10–12

KEY TERMS: *structuralism*, p. 7; *introspection*, p. 7; *functionalism*, p. 8; *Gestalt psychology*, p. 9; *psychoanalytic approach*, p. 10; *behaviorism*, p. 10; *humanistic psychology*, p. 12; *self-actualization*, p. 12; *cognitive psychology*, p. 12; *biological perspective*, p. 12; *eclecticism*, p. 13.

Careers in Psychology

Distinguish between psychologists and psychiatrists.

A *psychologist* has a graduate degree in psychology (typically a PhD), and studies behavioral principles; a *psychiatrist* is a medical doctor who has specialized in the treatment of disordered behavior. A master's degree or a doctorate in psychology requires years of study, but opens doors to many fields of endeavor such as private practice, mental health centers, or working in schools. Opportunities for individuals with bachelor's degrees are more limited but still varied

and include mental health centers and state hospitals.   pp. 13–14

In what fields do the majority of psychologists work?

About 60 percent of psychologists in the American Psychological Association are in human service fields such as clinical, counseling, community, and school psychology. Most of the remaining 40 percent work in universities, business, and government doing research, teaching, and evaluation of programs. Psychology is attracting an increasing number of women, with the number of women in graduate training programs doubling in the last 20 years.   pp. 14–16

What are the three main fields of psychology and what do they have in common?

The three main fields of psychology —applied research, human services, and experimental psychology—all consider research and theory to be the cornerstone of the psychological approach. Applied researchers use research to solve everyday practical problems. Human service psychologists focus on helping individuals solve problems and promote their well-being. Experimental psychologists usually focus on teaching and research.   pp. 17–20

KEY TERMS: *psychologists*, p. 13; *clinical psychologists*, p. 14; *psychiatrists*, p.14; *psychoanalysts*, p. 14.

continued

Summary & Review

Ethics in Psychological Research

Describe the ethical considerations in psychological research.

Human participants cannot be coerced to do things that are harmful to themselves, that would have negative effects, or that would violate standards of decency. In addition, any information gained in an experimental situation is considered strictly confidential. Human participants must give *informed consent* to a researcher and be *debriefed* following the experiment to explain the true nature of the research. In general, researchers must not use deception unless the study has highly important scientific, educational, or applied value. Animal research constitutes only a small portion (about 7 percent) of psychological research, and the American Psychological Association has strict ethical guidelines for such research.   pp. 20–22

KEY TERMS: *human participants*, p. 21; *informed consent*, p. 22; *debriefing*, p. 22.

The Controlled Experiment

Describe the controlled experiment and indicate its key components.

An *experiment* is any procedure in which a researcher systematically strives to discover and describe the relationship between variables. Only the controlled experiment allows for cause-and-effect statements. A *variable* is a characteristic of a situation or person that is subject to change (that varies) either within or across situations or individuals. The *independent variable* is directly and purposefully manipulated by the experimenter. The *dependent variable* is expected to change because of manipulations of the independent variable.   pp. 22–24

How do researchers define variables and how do they ensure objectivity?

An *operational definition* is the set of procedures used to define a variable. To ensure objectivity, researchers attempt to minimize *self-fulfilling prophecies* with carefully controlled situations that might include the *double-blind technique,* in which neither researcher nor subject knows who is assigned to the *experimental* or *control* group.   pp. 25–26

When is a group considered culturally diverse?

Psychologists say that a group is culturally diverse if it has differences in race, ethnicity, language, nationality, age, and religion within a community, organization, or nation.   p. 28

KEY TERMS: *experiment*, p. 22; *variable*, p. 23; *independent variable*, p. 24; *dependent variable*, p. 24; *hypothesis*, p. 24; *experimental group*, p.24; *control group*, p. 25; *operational definition*, p. 25; *sample*, p. 25; *significant difference*, p. 25; *self-fulfilling prophecy,* p. 26; *double-blind technique,* p. 26; *demand characteristics,* p. 26; *Hawthorne effect,* p. 26.

Alternative Methods of Psychological Inquiry

Describe questionnaires, interviews, naturalistic observation, and case studies.

A *questionnaire* or survey is used by researchers to gather a large amount of information from many people in a short time. An *interview* is usually a face-to-face meeting in which a researcher (interviewer) asks an individual a series of standardized questions. In *naturalistic observation* psychologists observe from a distance how people or animals behave in their natural settings. By contrast, *case study* methods involve interviewing subjects to gain information about their background, including data on such things as childhood, family, education, and social and sexual interactions.   pp. 27–31

What is critical thinking?

Critical thinking involves evaluating evidence, sifting through choices, assessing outcomes, and deciding whether conclusions make sense. Critical thinkers focus on five basic research criteria: purpose, methodology, subjects, repeatability, and conclusions. pp. 32–33

KEY TERMS: *questionnaire*, p. 27; *interview*, p. 29; *naturalistic observation*, p. 30; *case study*, p. 30

CONNECTIONS

If you are interested in...

2

The Biological Bases of Behavior

Oscar award winner Patty Duke, who starred in *The Miracle Worker* and *The Patty Duke Show,* lived a double life. As a star, she was glamorous and talented. But in her personal life, starting in her late teen years, Patty Duke suffered the devastating and complex effects of bipolar disorder. Not accurately diagnosed and treated until she was 35, Duke experienced periods during which she felt euphoric, creative, and energetic. She was also often angry and acted impulsively. Within days of her highs, she would descend into periods of depression and extreme sadness.

The course of Patty Duke's illness is not uncommon. People who suffer from bipolar disorder often go through hospitalizations, suicide attempts, panic attacks, crushing depressions, and extraordinary highs. The disorder plays havoc with patients' lives and is often misdiagnosed. This is especially unfortunate because good treatments are available for bipolar disorder. The drug lithium carbonate has been remarkably successful in the treatment of this disorder. The once manic Patty Duke no longer suffers from wild, frenetic mood swings.

Research on mood disorders will be discussed in detail later in this book. However, Patty Duke's problems highlight an important point: Some problems may be solely emotional, but others may be caused by a person's malfunctioning biological systems. This idea challenges the long-held view of many psychologists that the various forms of mood disorders are unique to each person and must be dealt with through intensive talking therapy. New research findings show that chemicals in the brain may hold the key to mood disorders, including depression. Researchers will continue to explore this idea and eventually will either confirm, deny, or modify the proposition that mood problems such as depression have a strong biological base and need to be treated with long-term medication (Greenberg et al., 1992).

Biology plays a crucial role in shaping our behavior. Many behavioral, psychological, and physical disorders stem from biological factors. A child who acts out in class may have a neurological problem. A person with severe depression may have a chemical imbalance. Men and women may view and operate in the world differently because they have differing brain organization. Researchers are working to answer such questions as: Can people intentionally control their own physiological processes? What is the relationship between biological and psychological mechanisms? Can diet affect day-to-day behavior?

Our biological heritage is important; however, a complex interplay exists between biology and experience, between inherited traits and encounters in the world—that is, between nature and nurture. **Nature** is a person's inherited characteristics, determined by genetics; **nurture** is a person's experiences in the environment. For example, you can lift weights for years trying to build up physical strength, but your capabilities are limited by your inherited body structure. Similarly, people try to maximize their intellectual skills through education; yet not everyone can become a brain surgeon. Also, a person's inherited traits may not become evident in behavior unless the environment supports and encourages them. Thus, people with special talents must be given opportunities to express and develop them. If Mozart had not had access to musical instruments, his talent might have remained untapped.

In this chapter, we examine the issue of nature versus nurture and then focus on the biological processes that underlie all human behavior and mental processes. Beginning with genetics and neurons (the building blocks of behavior), we follow with the structure and functioning of the brain. We look at how scientists study brain activity and how various chemical substances affect our behavior.

Nature versus Nurture

My father always insisted I was a born athlete and he argued that my sister was the scholar in the family (she began reading at a very early age). He reasoned that each of his children was born as *either* an athlete or a scholar. My father's beliefs about my sister and me illustrates a major question in psychology: What is the relationship between biological mechanisms and environmental mechanisms—nature versus nurture? The debate over what determines our abilities and behavior is a debate over the relative contributions of biological and environmental variables. How much of what we are depends on the genes we inherit from our parents? How much is related to the environment in which we are raised?

Our genetic heritage is unaffected by day-to-day experiences. However, over tens of thousands of years, humans have evolved a highly organized brain that allows learning to affect our behavior. Our brain acts as a library of information. Each new enriching experience affects our later behavior. Some who consider nurture more important than nature suggest that people are not limited by their genetic

Nature: An individual's genetically inherited characteristics.

Nurture: An individual's experiences in the environment.

heritage, because experience, training, and hard work can stretch their potential to amazing lengths. John B. Watson, a pioneer in the field of behaviorism (which we will examine further in chapter 5), wrote:

> Give me a dozen healthy infants, well-formed, and my own specialized world to bring them up in and I'll guarantee to take any one at random and train him to become any type of specialist I might select—doctor, lawyer, artist, merchant-chief and, yes, even beggar man and thief, regardless of his talents, penchants, tendencies, abilities, vocations, and race of his ancestors. (1924, p. 104)

It is clear that biological makeup affects intelligence. But can the environment interact with and modify biological makeup, as Watson suggested? Valid answers to this question must take into account the idea that both nature and nurture affect the expression of traits such as intelligence. Further, the surrounding environment must make it possible for an inherited trait to be expressed in behavior. Last, the complex and constantly changing relationship between biology and environment affects behaviors directly. The truth is that genetic traits provide the framework for behavior; within that framework, experiences ultimately shape what we feel, think, and do. Let's take a closer look at the key factors that shape our day-to-day behavior.

The Basics of Genetics

Genetics is the study of *heredity*—the biological transmission of traits and characteristics from parents to offspring. Biologists examine such things as how blue eyes, brown hair, height, and blood pressure are transmitted from one generation to the next. Behavioral traits such as temperament and intelligence and disorders such as depression also have a genetic basis; this is why psychologists are especially interested in heredity. A new field—*behavioral genetics*—has thus emerged; its focus is on the relationship of genetics to behavior.

    Uniqueness of Human Beings. With the exception of identical twins (discussed on p. 43), every human being is genetically unique. Although each of us shares traits with our brothers, sisters, and parents, none of us is identical to them or to anyone else. This occurs because a large number of genes determine characteristics.

    Each human cell normally contains 23 pairs of chromosomes (46 chromosomes total). **Chromosomes** come in pairs and are strands of deoxyribonucleic acid (DNA) in the nuclei of cells that carry genetic information in their basic functional units—genes. **Genes** are the units of heredity transmission carried in chromosomes and consisting of DNA and protein. They line up on the chromosomes in the nucleus (center) of a cell and control various aspects of a person's body structure, including eye color, hair color, height, and perhaps basic intellectual abilities. Traits are determined by pairs of genes, which are located in corresponding positions on the chromosome pairs. These corresponding genes both influence the same trait, but they often carry a different form of the genetic code for that trait; and one of the genes may be dominant over the other. Different, alternative forms of the gene that occupy the same genetic locus on the chromosomes are called **alleles.** Each allele of a chromosome has a corresponding allele on the corresponding chromosome of the chromosome pair. Most behavioral characteristics are the result of a number of genes.

    Sperm and ova each contain half of the final pairings of genes. The first 22 pairs of chromosomes are the same in both males and females. The 23rd pair differs.

Genetics: The study of heredity, the biological transmission of traits and characteristics from parents to offspring.

Chromosomes: Strands of DNA in the nuclei of cells that occur in pairs and carry genetic information.

Genes: The units of heredity transmission carried in chromosomes and consisting of DNA and protein.

Allele: Each member of a pair of genes that occupies the same genetic locus on a chromosome

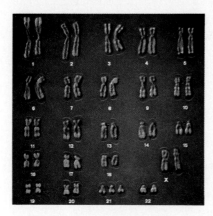

Down syndrome, a genetic defect that occurs when every cell in the body has more than exactly two copies of chromosome number 21, causes mental retardation.

This pair of chromosomes determines a person's sex. In females, the 23rd pair contains two X chromosomes; in males, it contains one X and one Y chromosome. At the moment of conception, a sperm and an ovum, each containing half of each pair of the parent's chromosomes, combine to form a new organism; and the chromosomes join to form new pairs. There are 8,388,608 possible recombinations of the 23 pairs of chromosomes, with 70,368,744,000,000 possible combinations of genes. You can see that the chance of any two individuals being exactly alike is exceedingly slim.

Genetic Defects. One goal of genetic research is to prevent *genetic defects*—genetically transmitted diseases and behavioral abnormalities. When a person is born with the genetic defect of too few or too many chromosomes, the result is usually dramatic.

Down syndrome is a human genetic defect in which more than two whole chromosomes are present for the 21st pair. It occurs when every cell in the body has more than exactly two copies of chromosome number 21. There may be an entire extra copy, or a piece of one chromosome number 21 may break off and be joined to another chromosome. This genetic accident occurs in 1 out of every 660 live births. Most people with Down syndrome have distinct physical features: a short, stocky build, flattened face, and almond-shaped eyes. Many are born with problems such as heart defects, eye problems, and respiratory disorders. People with Down syndrome also have some degree of mental retardation.

Phenylketonuria (PKU) is a human genetic disorder in which the presence of a particular recessive gene prevents an individual from processing the amino acid phenylalanine. Unless the disorder is detected soon after birth and the newborn is put on a diet containing low levels of phenylalanine, PKU can cause irreparable mental retardation. Accordingly, in the United States, all newborns are given a PKU test. In this case, manipulating the physical environment (through diet) can help control the harmful consequences of the genetic disorder.

Down syndrome: A human genetic defect in which more than two whole chromosomes are present for the 21st pair; usually accompanied by characteristic physical abnormalities and mental retardation.

Phenylketonuria (PKU): [fee-nil-key-ton-NYEW-ree-uh] A human genetic disorder that prevents an individual from processing the amino acid phenylalanine.

Mapping the Genome. In an exciting research revolution that has been taking place since the 1980s, biological researchers have been trying to map the specific traits associated with specific chromosomes. That is, they have been trying to map the human *genome*—the DNA blueprint of heritable traits contained in every cell of the body.

They have been modestly successful in this effort. More than 3,400 of the estimated 100,000 human genes have been mapped. Researchers have mapped the exact location of markers for muscular dystrophy, Huntington's disease, some cancers, and some psychological disorders, such as schizophrenia. As McClearn asserts, "The focus of research has shifted from demonstrating the existence of genetic influence to exploring its details" (McClearn et al., 1991, p. 222).

By understanding the basic biological mechanisms and their relationship to behavior, psychologists can better predict the situations in which maladjustment and some specific behavior disorders might occur. Yet this raises some interesting ethical dilemmas: What if a particular chromosomal pattern is associated with aggressiveness? Would it be desirable or ethical to screen newborn infants to identify people at risk of becoming criminals? Could this information be used to terminate pregnancies? Medical ethicists and psychologists argue that such screening cannot and should not be used for such purposes. Ethical considerations and legislation to guard people's rights must be high on the agenda of researchers who do such research.

Twins and the Nature versus Nurture Issue

In addition to studying the impact of biological mechanisms, researchers balance the study of behavior and mental processes by examining the contributions of the environment. One of the best ways psychologists have found to do so is to use studies of twins to assess the contributions of nature and nurture. Twins make good subjects for these experiments because they begin life in the same uterine environment and share the same nutrition and other prenatal influences. **Fraternal twins** are double births that occur when two sperm fertilize two ova (eggs) and the two resulting zygotes (fertilized eggs) implant themselves in the uterus and grow alongside each other. The genes of the twins are not identical, so the siblings are only as geneticallysimilar as other brothers and sisters. Only about 12 sets of fraternal twins occur in every 1,000 births. **Identical twins** are double births that occur when one zygote splits into two identical cells, which then separate and develop independently. The multiplication of these cells proceeds normally, and the cells become two genetically identical organisms. Only 4 sets of identical twins occur in every 1,000 births.

Identical twins occur when one zygote separates into two identical cells. Their genetic makeup is identical. Research with twins, particularly identical twins, is useful in exploring the debate over the influence of nature versus nurture.

What have twin studies revealed about human behavior? In one study, researchers at the University of Louisville School of Medicine followed 450 sets of twins (half identical and half fraternal) from infancy through adolescence. The study assessed intelligence as well as home and family variables that might influence intellectual development. By adolescence, identical twins had very similar IQs, although not identical levels of intellectual achievement. In contrast, the IQs of fraternal twins were no more similar than those of nontwin siblings. The most important conclusion of the Louisville twins study was that although such environmental variables as family interactions strongly influenced IQ, genetics affected IQ test scores more than environment did (R. S. Wilson, 1983). We will study more about heredity and intelligence in chapter 11.

Twins' genetic factors (nature) are fixed; but if the twins are reared apart, their environments (nurture) are different—that is, they grow up with different families and homes. By comparing psychological characteristics of identical twins reared apart, researchers can assess the extent to which environment affects behavior, perhaps unraveling the nature-nurture fabric a bit more. Researchers have concluded that significant psychological similarities between identical twins are probably due to biological variables and significant differences are probably due to environmental variables.

There are striking similarities in identical twins, even in those reared apart all of their lives. For example, the Minnesota adoption studies show that young adopted children are similar intellectually and have similar personalities to other children in their adoptive family. This suggests that family environment exerts a great influence on young children. However, by adolescence, there is greater variation. Teenagers raised in the same family resemble one another intellectually only if

Fraternal twins: Double births resulting from the release of two ova that are fertilized by two sperm; fraternal twins are no more or less genetically similar than nontwin siblings.

Identical twins: Double births resulting from the splitting of a zygote into two identical cells, which then separate and develop independently; identical twins have exactly the same genetic makeup.

FOCUS

▶ What is the fundamental distinction between nature and nurture? pp. 40–41

▶ Twins make good subjects in the study of nature versus nurture because they allow researchers to make what fundamental assumption? p. 43

▶ What information do adoption studies provide that makes them so crucial to the study of the nature-nurture issue? pp. 43–44

they have common genes (Scarr & Weinberg, 1983). Experts such as Plomin (1989) and Bouchard (Bouchard et al., 1990) assert that even though environmental influences on intelligence are strong, heredity exerts a stronger influence (Turkheimer, 1991).

Endowed with a fixed genetic heritage, a biology sensitive to change, and a brain sensitive to experience, human beings have the capacity to experience the world in unique ways, to develop new technologies, and, with each new generation, to better the general human condition. Love for other people, a desire to do good, and the ability to develop high levels of creativity, communication, and technology all reflect human genetic endowment and years of learning. Genetic makeup is the foundation on which all behaviors are built.

Nervous System

Communication in the Nervous System

Before we can fully understand the nature and diversity of human behavior, we must first examine the structure of the human body. The nervous system underlies all of our behavior; it is the communication system that enables us to engage in complex activities. The nervous system acts like a busy air traffic control center—sending, receiving, processing, interpreting, and storing vital information. Many psychologists study how electrical and chemical signals in the brain represent and process information. By studying how the components work together and how they are integrated, they learn a great deal about the complexity of human behavior.

The **nervous system** is the structures and organs that act as the communication system for the body, allowing all behavior and mental processes to take place. The nervous system consists of two divisions—the *central nervous system* (consisting of the brain and spinal cord) and the *peripheral nervous system* (consisting of all the other parts); they allow the brain to communicate with the rest of the body. Before we examine the two divisions, we need to understand how communication proceeds within the system as a whole. The nervous system is composed of hundreds of billions of cells, each of which receives information from thousands of other cells. The most elementary unit in the nervous system is the neuron, the building block of the entire system.

The Neuron

Nervous system: The structures and organs that act as the communication system for the body, allowing all behavior and mental processes to take place.

Neuron: [NEW-ron] The basic unit (a single cell) of the nervous system, comprising dendrites, which receive neural signals; a cell body, which generates electrical signals; and an axon, which transmits neural signals. Also known as a *nerve cell.*

The basic unit (a single cell) of the nervous system is the **neuron,** or *nerve cell.* There are billions of neurons throughout the body (over 100 billion in the brain alone), differing in shape, size, and function. Some neurons operate quickly, some relatively slowly. Some neurons are large; others are especially small. Often, neurons are grouped together in bundles; the bundles of fibers are called *nerves* if they exist in the peripheral nervous system and *tracts* if they are in the central nervous system.

Although all of the neurons in your body are alive, they are not all especially active at once. Nonetheless, they are on alert, ready to convey information and signals to some part of the nervous system. Neurons fire in two directions: (1) to the brain and spinal cord from the sense organs and muscles, and (2) from the brain and spinal cord to the sense organs and muscles, with messages for initiating new behavior. Each direction of the two-way neuronal firing has a name: **Afferent neurons** are neurons that send messages to the spinal cord and brain; **efferent neurons** are neurons that send messages from the brain and spinal cord to other structures in the body. (See Figure 2.1.)

> **Afferent neurons:** Neurons that send messages to the spinal cord and brain.
>
> **Efferent neurons:** Neurons that send messages from the brain and spinal cord to other structures in the body

Types of Neurons. There are three types of neurons: sensory neurons, motor neurons, and interneurons. *Sensory neurons* convey information inward from the sensory organs to the brain and spinal cord. *Motor neurons* carry information from the brain and spinal cord to the muscles and glands. *Interneurons* connect neurons together and combine activities of sensory and motor neurons; there are many more interneurons than sensory or motor neurons, and they form the network that allows the neurons to interact with one another. The millions of neurons that work together

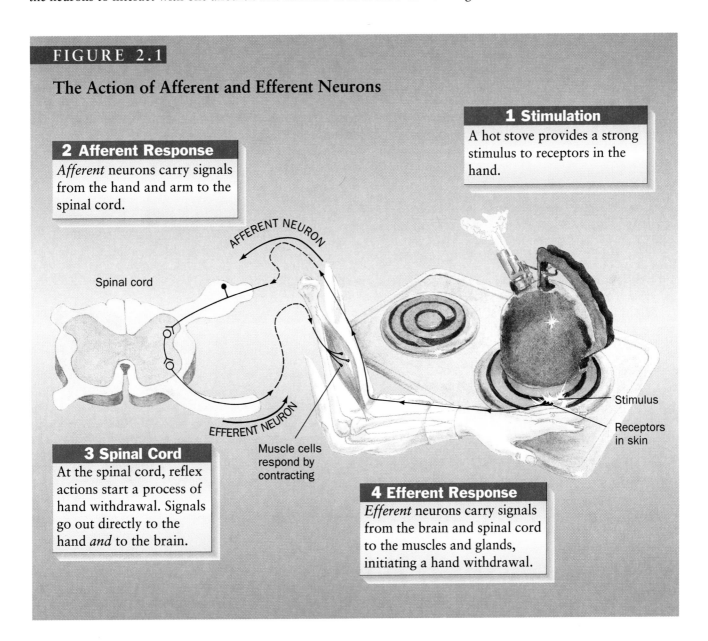

FIGURE 2.1

The Action of Afferent and Efferent Neurons

1 Stimulation
A hot stove provides a strong stimulus to receptors in the hand.

2 Afferent Response
Afferent neurons carry signals from the hand and arm to the spinal cord.

AFFERENT NEURON

Spinal cord

EFFERENT NEURON

Stimulus

Receptors in skin

3 Spinal Cord
At the spinal cord, reflex actions start a process of hand withdrawal. Signals go out directly to the hand *and* to the brain.

Muscle cells respond by contracting

4 Efferent Response
Efferent neurons carry signals from the brain and spinal cord to the muscles and glands, initiating a hand withdrawal.

Synapse: [SIN-apps] The juncture of the axon terminals of one neuron and the receptor site of another including the microscopically small space between them.

are surrounded by *glial cells,* which nourish the neurons and help hold them in place. Glial cells are small—and 10 times more numerous than sensory, motor, or interneurons. They help insulate the brain from toxins, and they are the basis of the *myelin sheath*—the covering of the neurons. Many neurons, especially the longer ones, are *myelinated*—covered with a thin white substance (the myelin sheath) that allows for fast conduction of signals.

Parts of a Neuron. Typically, a neuron is composed of dendrites, a cell body (containing a nucleus), an axon, and axon terminals (see Figure 2.2). *Dendrites* (from the Greek word for "tree" because of their treelike appearance) are thin, widely branching fibers that get narrower as they spread away from the cell body. They receive signals from neighboring neurons and carry them to the cell body. At the *cell body,* the signals are transformed and continue to travel along the long, slim *axon* to the *axon terminal* (the end point of the neuron). Like dendrites, axons have branches.

Neuronal Synapses. For almost all neurons, the axon terminals of one neuron are very close to the receptor site (the dendrites, cell body, or axon) of another neuron. The juncture and microscopically small space between the axon terminals of one neuron and the receptor site of another is a **synapse** (see Figure 2.3). The signal from one neuron may leap across the synapse to another neuron. You can think of many neurons strung together in a long chain as a relay team sending signals, conveying information, or initiating some action in a cell, muscle, or gland. Each neuron receives information from about 1,000 neighboring neurons and may synapse on (transmit information to) as many as 1,000 to 10,000 other neurons.

FIGURE 2.2

The Basic Components of a Neuron

(A) Neurons appear in many forms, but all possess the basic structures shown here: a cell body, an axon (with axon terminals), and dendrites.
(B) Actual human neurons, greatly magnified.

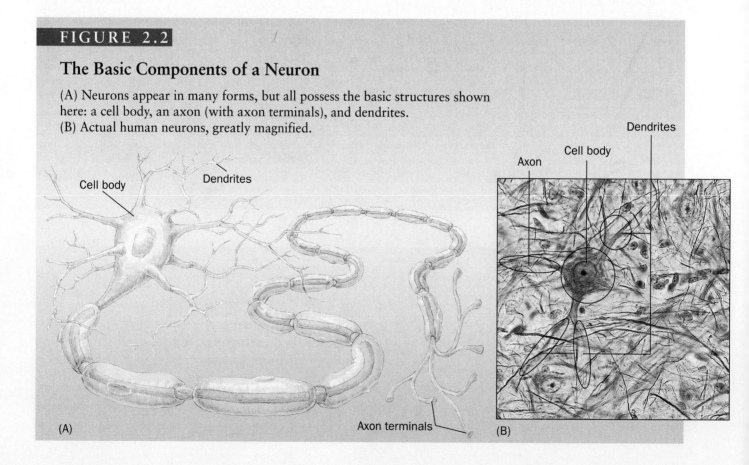

Action Potentials

How do neurons communicate with one another? Each year, scientists learn more about the nature of the neural impulse and about how information moves from cell to cell across synapses. The process, which involves both electrical and chemical changes, is sometimes termed *electrochemical.* Two types of electrochemical processes take place. The first involves activity within a cell; the second involves transmitter substances (chemicals) released from the axons of one cell and acting on the cell body or dendrites of another cell.

Electrochemical Processes. Understanding the electrochemical processes within a cell is essential to understanding the role of the neuron in behavior. A widely accepted explanation of electrochemical processes is the following: An extremely thin—less than 0.00001 millimeter thick—membrane surrounds every cell (neuron); and there are channels, or gates, through which electrically charged ions and small particles can pass. Normally, the neuron is in a resting state, which is negatively charged inside and positively charged outside. This resting state is maintained by the cell membrane. The difference in electrical charge is a state of *polarization*; that is, the internal state of the neuron (negatively charged) differs from its outside state (positively charged).

When the neuron has been stimulated (its resting state has been disturbed) to the point where it reaches a *threshold* (a level of stimulation intensity below which nothing happens), it is said to be *depolarized.* At this point, the sodium gates of the cell membrane open. A rapid reversal of electrical polarity occurs when positively charged sodium ions move through the membrane into the neuron and positively charged ions simultaneously leave the neuron, thereby disturbing the resting level. We say that an action potential has been generated (see Figure 2.4). The **action potential,** or *spike discharge,* is an all-or-none electrical current sent down the axon of a neuron, initiated by a rapid reversal of the electrical balance of the cell membrane. This is an especially active process.

FIGURE 2.3

The Synapse

The synapse is very small. Chemicals released by the axon terminal cross the synapse to stimulate the cell body or dendrites of another neuron.

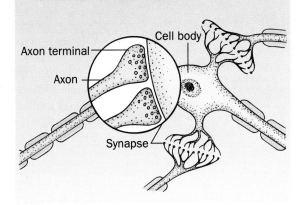

Action potential: An all-or-none electrical current sent down the axon of a neuron, initiated by a rapid reversal of the electrical balance of the cell membrane. Also known as a *spike discharge.*

FIGURE 2.4

Generation of an Action Potential

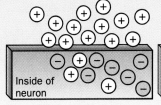

1. When the neuron is at rest, the inside is negatively charged relative to the outside

2. When the neuron is stimulated, positively charged particles enter

3. After a brief period, other particles are pushed outside the neuron

4. The neuron is then returned to its initial resting state

All-or-none: The principle by which a neuron will fire either at full strength or not at all.

Refractory period: The recovery period of a neuron after it fires, during which time it cannot fire again; this period allows the neuron to reestablish electrical balance with its surroundings.

Neurotransmitters: [NEW-roh-TRANS-mitt-erz] Chemicals that reside in the axon terminal within synaptic vesicles and that, when released, move across the synaptic space and bind to the dendrites of the next cell.

A neuron does not necessarily fire every time it is stimulated. If the level of polarization across the cell membrane has not been disturbed enough to generate the action potential—has not reached a threshold—the cell will not fire. Cells that are highly stimulated are more likely to fire than cells that are less stimulated. When neurons fire, they generate action potentials (spikes) in an **all-or-none** fashion—that is, the firing of the neuron, like the firing of a gun, occurs at either full strength or not at all. Action potentials occur in 2 to 4 milliseconds; generally, neurons cannot fire more than 500 times per second. After each firing, the neuron needs time to recover, generally just a few thousandths of a second; the time needed for recovery is called the **refractory period.** During this period, action potentials are much less likely to occur.

Neurotransmitters. When an action potential moves down to the end of an axon, it initiates the release of **neurotransmitters**—chemicals that reside in the axon terminal within synaptic vesicles (small storage structures in the axon terminal) (Dunant & Israel, 1985). The neurotransmitter is released into the synapse, moves across the synaptic space, and binds itself to a receptor site on the dendrites of the next cell, thereby conveying information to the next neuron (see Figure 2.5). We will examine the types and the various effects of neurotransmitters in just a few paragraphs. Sometimes the neurotransmitters cause the receptor sites to fire more easily, sometimes less easily. A change in the membrane potential of a neuron due to the release of neurotransmitters is called a *postsynaptic potential (PSP),* discussed next.

Excitatory and Inhibitory Postsynaptic Potentials. There are two kinds of postsynaptic potentials, and they cause opposite effects. *Excitatory PSPs* make it easier for the cell to fire; *inhibitory PSPs* make it harder for the cell to fire. Because thousands of neurons may synapse onto a single cell, a single neuron can receive

FIGURE 2.5

Major Steps in Neuronal Transmission

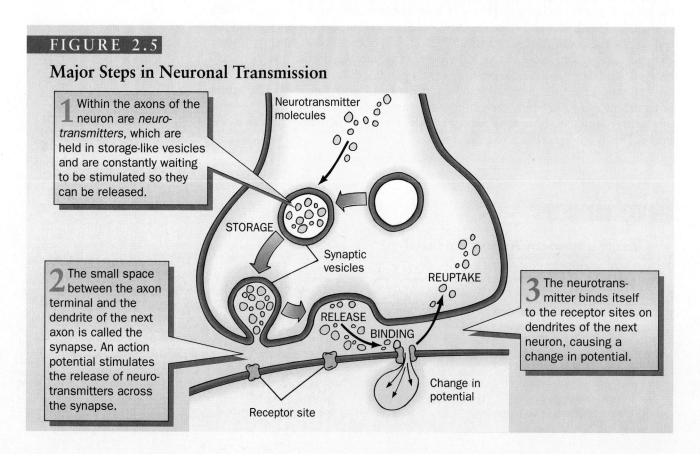

1 Within the axons of the neuron are *neurotransmitters*, which are held in storage-like vesicles and are constantly waiting to be stimulated so they can be released.

2 The small space between the axon terminal and the dendrite of the next axon is called the synapse. An action potential stimulates the release of neurotransmitters across the synapse.

3 The neurotransmitter binds itself to the receptor sites on dendrites of the next neuron, causing a change in potential.

Neurotransmitter molecules

STORAGE

Synaptic vesicles

REUPTAKE

RELEASE

BINDING

Change in potential

Receptor site

both excitatory and inhibitory PSPs. If it receives more excitatory ones, another action potential is likely to be generated. If it receives more inhibitory ones, further excitation along the nerve pathway may be ended. Some neurotransmitters are involved in blocking pain; others facilitate sensory experiences such as pain. Some may be excitatory in some situations and inhibitory in others. For example, when the neurotransmitter acetylcholine attaches itself to muscle cells, it has an excitatory effect; in some areas of the brain not related to the excitation of muscles, it can have an inhibitory effect. The effects of a neurotransmitter are determined by the receptor onto which it binds itself.

Neurotransmitters and Behavior

The array of neurotransmitters is dazzling; at least 50 have been studied in depth. One of them, gamma-amino-butyric acid (GABA), is involved in virtually every behavior, including anxiety states. Another important neurotransmitter, serotonin, is located throughout the brain and is especially important in sleep (McGinty & Szymusiak, 1988). The most well known neurotransmitter, however, is acetylcholine, which is found in neurons throughout the brain and spinal cord. Acetylcholine is crucial to exciting the skeletal muscles, which allow us to move. It is also important in such day-to-day functions as memory, learning, and sexual behavior. Memory disorders such as Alzheimer's disease (discussed in chapter 9) may be related to an inability to produce acetylcholine. Table 2.1 describes five key neurotransmitters and their effects.

Research on Neurotransmitters. Neuropeptides are chains of amino acids that act as neurotransmitters. Endorphins, one type of neuropeptide, are mimicked by the actions of the narcotic morphine. Endorphins act to inhibit certain synaptic transmissions, particularly those involving pain. (We will examine pain, endorphins, and pain management in more detail in chapter 4.) The study of neurotransmitters may hold the key to our understanding of drug addiction. Many addictive drugs affect neurotransmitter actions; this effect helps explain the addictive nature of the drugs themselves. The study of neurotransmitters may also help us find drugs that will effectively block the powerfully addictive drugs, such as cocaine.

At first, researchers thought that only one neurotransmitter existed in each neuron and that it acted on only one type of receptor. Today, researchers know that a

---

TABLE 2.1 *Five Key Neurotransmitters*

Neurotransmitter	Location	Effects
Acetylcholine	Brain, spinal cord, autonomic nervous system, target organs of the parasympathetic system	Excitation in brain and autonomic nervous system; excitation or inhibition in target organs
Norepinephrine	Brain, spinal cord, target organs of sympathetic system	Inhibition in brain; excitation or inhibition in target organs
Dopamine	Brain	Inhibition
Serotonin	Brain, spinal cord	Inhibition
GABA	Brain, spinal cord	Inhibition

Neuromodulators: [NEW-roh-MOD-u-lay-torz] Chemical substances that function to increase or decrease the sensitivity of widely distributed neurons to the specific effects of neurotransmitters.

Agonists: Chemicals that mimic the actions of a neurotransmitter, usually by occupying receptor sites.

Antagonists: Chemicals that oppose the actions of a neurotransmitter, usually by preventing the neurotransmitter from occupying a receptor site.

neuron can hold more than one neurotransmitter, which may act on more than one receptor. Some neurotransmitters (especially neuropeptides) are released into the bloodstream, so their effects are far-reaching. Researchers now think of such neurotransmitters as **neuromodulators**—chemical substances that function to increase or decrease the sensitivity of widely distributed neurons to the specific effects of neurotransmitters. A neuropeptide released into the bloodstream, for example, affects not only a single cell's immediate ion transfer but whole classes or groups of cells.

Although scientists have known about the existence of neurotransmitters for a long time, only recently have they realized their significance in the study of human behavior. For example, researchers have found that serotonin affects motivation and mood (e.g., Young et al., 1985) and that schizophrenia is associated with increased levels of activity in neural circuits that use certain neurotransmitters. In addition, they have found that people with Parkinson's disease, whose symptoms include weakness and uncontrollable shaking, have low levels of the neurotransmitter dopamine. When they give these people drugs that have the same effects as dopamine (such as L-dopa), many of their symptoms are alleviated. Although it is unlikely that one neurotransmitter alone can cause a disorder such as schizophrenia or Parkinson's disease, a single neurotransmitter may play an important role in the onset or maintenance of such an illness.

Psychopharmacology. The study of how drugs affect behavior is called *psychopharmacology.* Researchers study many abusive drugs to learn the physiological mechanisms that cause behavioral reactions. Research has shown that many common drugs alter the amount of neurotransmitter released at synapses; other research has demonstrated that drugs alter the way neurotransmitters operate. Thus, for example, a drug may change behavior by changing the speed or efficiency with which electrochemical information is transferred from one cell to the next. Chemicals can also be used to mimic the actions of a neurotransmitter; such chemicals are called **agonists.** When an agonist is administered, it is as if the neurotransmitter itself has been released. Other chemicals, called **antagonists,** oppose the actions of a neurotransmitter. When an antagonist is administered, a cell's receptor site is blocked and the neurotransmitter cannot have its usual effect. Schizophrenia, a disabling mental disorder, is often treated with antagonists. Cells that normally respond to dopamine are blocked from doing so by being exposed to certain drugs that act as antagonists, and symptoms of the disorder are thereby alleviated. Dopamine in relation to schizophrenia will be discussed in more detail in chapter 14. Some drugs block the reabsorption of a neurotransmitter from a receptor site (the process of reabsorption is called *reuptake*). This blocking of reuptake is useful in the treatment of depression.

When neurons fire, information is transferred from the sense organs to the brain and from the brain to the muscular system and the glands. If psychologists knew precisely how this transfer occurred, they could more successfully predict and manage the behavior of people with neurological damage, mood disorders, or epilepsy. However, the firing of neurons and the release of neurotransmitters and neuromodulators do not in themselves completely explain the biological bases of human behavior. The firing of individual neurons is an incomplete picture because it is the brain as a whole that receives, interprets, and acts on neuronal impulses.

FOCUS

▶ What are the essential components of an action potential? pp. 47–49

▶ What is the difference between excitatory and inhibitory postsynaptic potentials? pp. 48–49

▶ Distinguish between a neurotransmitter and a neuromodulator. pp. 49–50

Organization of the Peripheral and Central Nervous Systems

The nervous system, and especially the brain, controls behavior on a second-by-second basis. Psychologists must therefore understand the organization and functions of the nervous system and its mutually dependent systems and divisions. Recall that the nervous system is made up of the peripheral nervous system and the central nervous system. The peripheral nervous system connects the central nervous system to the rest of the body; the central nervous system is composed of the brain and spinal cord. Let's examine them both in detail.

The Peripheral Nervous System

The **peripheral nervous system** is the part of the nervous system that carries information to and from the spinal cord and the brain through spinal nerves attached to the spinal cord and by a system of 12 cranial nerves, which carry signals directly to and from the brain. The peripheral nervous system contains all nerves that are not in the central nervous system; its nerves focus on the *periphery,* or outer parts, of the body. Its two major systems are the somatic nervous system and the autonomic nervous system.

The Somatic Nervous System. The **somatic nervous system** is the part of the peripheral nervous system that responds to external senses and acts on the outside world. Generally considered under voluntary control, it is involved in perceptual processing (processing sensory information) and controlling movement and muscles. It consists of both sensory and motor neurons and carries information from the sense organs to the brain and from the brain and spinal cord to the consciously controlled muscles. It is the somatic system that allows you to take off your jacket in the warm afternoon sun and that facilitates a quick sprint to class before the instructor starts a lecture.

The Autonomic Nervous System. The **autonomic nervous system** is the part of the peripheral nervous system that controls the vital processes of the body, such as the heart rate, digestive processes, blood pressure, and regulation of internal organs. In contrast to the somatic nervous system, it operates continuously and involuntarily and focuses on the utilization and conservation of energy resources (although the technique of biofeedback, discussed in chapter 4, has sometimes proven to be effective in bringing some of these processes under voluntary control). The system is called autonomic because many of its subsystems are self-regulating. It is made up of two divisions: the sympathetic nervous system and the parasympathetic nervous system, which work together in controlling the activities of the muscles and glands. (See Figure 2.6 on page 52.)

The **sympathetic nervous system** is the part of the autonomic nervous system that responds to emergency situations. Its activities are easy to observe and measure. Activation results in a sharp increase in heart rate and blood pressure, slowing of the digestive processes, dilation of the pupils, and general

Peripheral nervous system: [puh-RIF-er-al] The part of the nervous system that carries information to and from the central nervous system through a network of spinal and cranial nerves.

Somatic nervous system: [so-MAT-ick] The part of the peripheral nervous system that carries information to skeletal muscles and thereby affects bodily movement; this part of the nervous system controls voluntary, conscious sensory and motor functions.

Autonomic nervous system: [au-toe-NOM-ick] The part of the peripheral nervous system that controls the vital and automatic processes of the body, such as the heart rate, digestive processes, blood pressure, and regulation of internal organs.

Sympathetic nervous system: The part of the autonomic nervous system that responds to emergency situations; active only occasionally, it calls up bodily resources as needed for major energy expenditures.

FIGURE 2.6

The Two Divisions of the Autonomic Nervous System

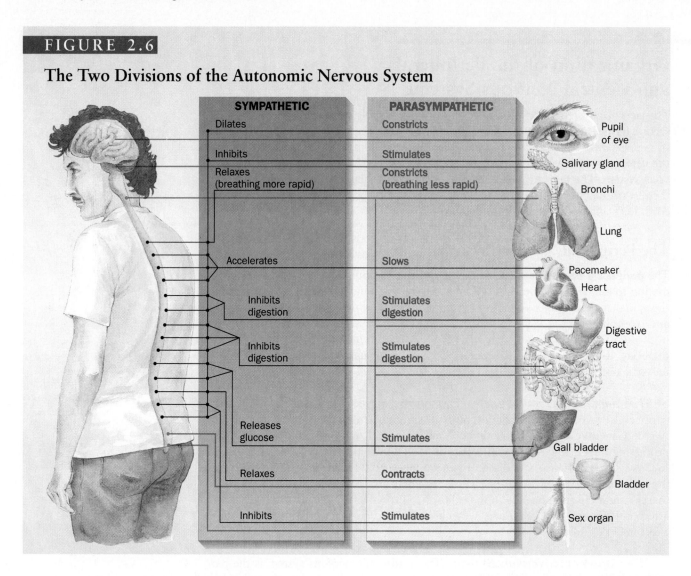

SYMPATHETIC	PARASYMPATHETIC	
Dilates	Constricts	Pupil of eye
Inhibits	Stimulates	Salivary gland
Relaxes (breathing more rapid)	Constricts (breathing less rapid)	Bronchi / Lung
Accelerates	Slows	Pacemaker / Heart
Inhibits digestion	Stimulates digestion	Digestive tract
Inhibits digestion	Stimulates digestion	
Releases glucose	Stimulates	Gall bladder
Relaxes	Contracts	Bladder
Inhibits	Stimulates	Sex organ

preparation for an emergency—sometimes called the fight-or-flight reflex. These changes are usually accompanied by an increased flow of epinephrine (adrenaline), a substance released by the adrenal gland (to be discussed later). The sympathetic nervous system makes your heart pound when your car narrowly misses hitting an oncoming car.

The **parasympathetic nervous system,** which is active most of the time, is the part

Parasympathetic nervous system: [PAIR-uh-sim-puh-THET-ick] The part of the peripheral nervous system that controls the ongoing maintenance processes of the body, such as the heart rate, digestive processes, and blood pressure.

The sympathetic nervous system is responsible for the body's general preparation for an emergency, known as the fight-or-flight response.

of the peripheral nervous system that controls the normal operations of the body, such as digestion, blood pressure, and heart rate. This system calms everything down and moves the heartbeat back to normal after an emergency. In other words, it keeps the body running smoothly. Parasympathetic activity does not show sharp changes on a minute-by-minute basis.

When the sympathetic nervous system is active and the organism is in a fight-or-flight posture, the somatic nervous system is also active. For example, when a large, growling dog chases a runner, the runner's adrenal gland is stimulated; the burst of energy produced by epinephrine affects the somatic system, making the runner's muscles respond strongly and rapidly. Thus, changes in the autonomic nervous system produce rapid changes in the organism; these changes are usually seen in stress reactions and in emotional behavior (discussed in detail in chapters 10 and 13). Even simple responses, such as blushing from embarrassment, are regulated by the autonomic nervous system. Blushing may occur when a speaker realizes his behavior is being observed and he has made a blunder, looks foolish, or is being scrutinized carefully; it occurs automatically.

The Central Nervous System

The **central nervous system** is one of the two major parts of the nervous system, consisting of the brain and the spinal cord. It serves as the main processing system for most information in the body (see Figure 2.7 on page 54). Recognizing that the **brain** plays a central role in controlling behavior, psychologists and physiologists are continually trying to understand it better. Some researchers study the brains of people who have died of tumors, brain diseases, and trauma (injury) to the brain, hoping to correlate the type of brain damage with the loss of specific abilities, such as seeing, reading, and writing. Others observe the behavioral effects of lesions (damage) to different areas of animals' brains. Still others study brain-behavior relationships by watching both animals and children as they interact with their environment and solve problems. Some brain damage occurs through accidents, strokes, and brain tumors; observing the behaviors and mental processes of individuals with known damage provides further information.

Although our understanding of the brain's functions is far from complete, we know that the brain operates through many mutually dependent systems and subsystems to affect and control behavior. Millions of brain cells are involved in the performance of even simple activities. When we walk, for example, the visual areas of the brain are active and our sight guides us, the brain's motor areas help make our legs move, and the cerebellum helps us keep our balance. It is the central nervous system communicating with the muscles and glands, under the control of the brain, that allows all these things to happen. The brain is the control center, but it receives most of its information from the spinal cord, the main communication line to the rest of the body and the cranial nerves.

The **spinal cord** receives signals from the sensory organs, muscles, and glands and relays the signals to the brain. Some behaviors do not involve the brain directly. Among them are *spinal reflexes*—actions that are controlled almost solely by the spinal cord and a system of neurons that create a reflexive response. The knee jerk, elicited by a tap on the tendon below the kneecap, is a spinal reflex. It links a sensory input (the tap) to a motor response (the knee jerk) without passing through the brain. Most signals eventually make their way up the spinal cord to the brain for further analysis, but the initial knee jerk happens at the level of the spinal cord, before the brain has had time to register and act on the tap.

The spinal cord's importance cannot be overstated. When a person's spinal cord is severed, the information exchange between the brain and the muscles and glands

Central nervous system: One of the two major parts of the nervous system, consisting of the brain and spinal cord.

Brain: The part of the central nervous system that regulates, monitors, processes, and guides other nervous system activity; located in the skull.

Spinal cord: The portion of the central nervous system that is contained within the spinal column and that transmits and receives signals from the senses to the brain, controls reflexive responses, and conveys signals from the brain to the muscles and glands

FIGURE 2.7

The Basic Divisions of the Nervous System

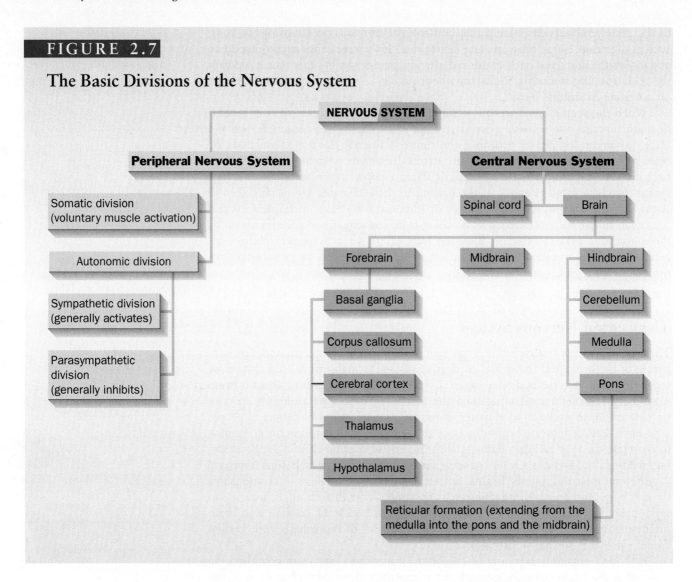

below the point of damage is halted. Spinal reflexes still operate, and knee jerk responses are evident. However, individuals who suffer spinal cord damage lose voluntary control over muscles in the parts of their bodies below the injury. This shows that the spinal cord serves a key communication function between the brain and the rest of the body; it is the chief trunk line for neuronal activity.

Monitoring Neuronal Activity

Though nonliving brains can be dissected easily, scientists are more interested in exploring the functions and interconnections of the active central nervous system, a more difficult task. Much of what scientists now know about the electrical activity in the nervous system comes from laboratory studies of abnormalities in brain structure and function. In conducting such studies, scientists use several basic procedures to measure the activity of the nervous system.

One measuring technique is *single unit recording,* which involves placing a thin wire, needle, or glass tube containing an electrolyte solution in or next to a single neuron to measure its electrical activity. Because neurons fire extremely rapidly, the data are often fed into a computer, which averages the number of times the cell fires in 1 second or 1 minute. This recording technique is usually performed on the neurons of cats, rats, and monkeys.

Another technique, *electroencephalography,* measures electrical activity in the nervous systems of both human beings and animals. It produces a record of brain-wave activity—an **electroencephalogram (EEG).** (*Electro* means "electrical," *encephalon* means "brain," and *gram* means "record".) A small electrode placed on a subject's scalp records the activity of thousands of cells beneath the skull to produce the EEG. EEGs, which are generally computer analyzed, are used for a variety of purposes, including the assessment of brain damage, epilepsy, tumors, and other abnormalities. When brain waves that are normally synchronized become erratic, this is usually evidence of an abnormality requiring further investigation and analysis.

In normal, healthy human beings, EEGs show a variety of characteristic brain-wave patterns, depending on the subject's level and kind of mental activity. We usually describe brain waves in terms of their *frequency* and *amplitude*—that is, the number of waves in a unit of time and the relative height or size of the waves (see Figure 2.8).

If people are awake, relaxed, and not engaged in active thinking, their EEGs show *alpha waves,* which occur at a rate of 8 to 12 cycles per second and are of moderate amplitude. When people are excited, their brain waves change dramatically from alpha waves to *beta waves* and *gamma waves*—high-frequency and low-amplitude waves. At different times during sleep, people show patterns of high-frequency and low-frequency waves.

Three significant new techniques for measuring the activity of the nervous system have emerged: CAT scans, MRI scans, and PET scans. *CAT* (computerized axial tomography) *scans* are computer-assisted X-ray procedures used to visualize the brain (or any area of the body) in three dimensions—essentially a computerized series of X-rays that show photographic slices of part of the brain or body. They are especially helpful in locating specific lesions and tumors in the brain. *MRI* (magnetic resonance imaging) *scans,* are similar to CAT scans but do not use radiation and produce greater clarity and resolution.

Electroencephalogram (EEG): [eel-ECK-tro-en-SEFF-uh-low-gram] A record of electrical brain-wave patterns obtained through electrodes placed on the scalp.

FIGURE 2.8

The EEG in Different States of Awareness

Characteristic electrical activity patterns in the EEGs of healthy humans in different states of excitation. High frequency is indicated by the occurrence of a large number of waves within a single period of time.

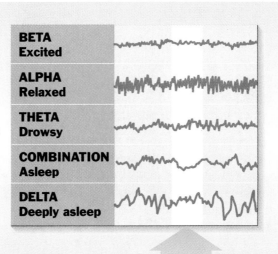

BETA Excited

ALPHA Relaxed

THETA Drowsy

COMBINATION Asleep

DELTA Deeply asleep

1 second

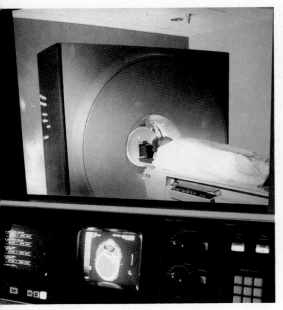

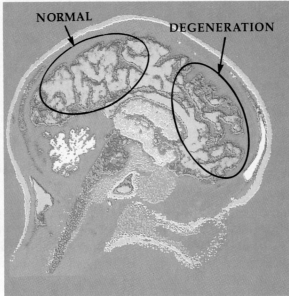

CAT scans (left) are computer-assisted X-rays that allow researchers to view the brain (or any other part of the body) in three dimensions. MRI scans (right) are similar to CAT scans, but do not use radiation and produce higher clarity and resolution. This MRI scan reveals degeneration of the frontal lobe, a possible sign of Alzheimer's disease.

PET (positron emission tomography) *scans,* which use radiochemical procedures, enable researchers to watch the metabolic changes taking place in an organism. PET scans may eventually allow researchers to watch the actual functioning of the brain, to observe how the brain modifies itself as mental activity occurs, and to predict human behavior from brain functioning. PET scans are relatively new to brain scientists. Their potential has yet to be fully unleashed, but researchers are using them to study a wide range of psychological disorders (Rubin et al., 1992).

PET scans use radiochemical procedures that allow researchers to watch metabolic changes taking place in an organism. Its potential as a tool in brain research is exciting, although not yet fully realized. In this scan, areas of high activity are indicated by reds and yellows.

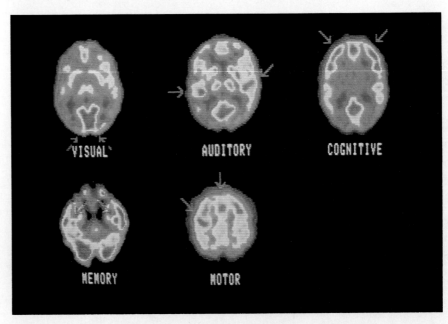

CAT, MRI, and PET scans are making the examination of brain tissue and its processes easier and more precise, thereby providing more information about the brain and its workings. For example, researchers are now able to show that small brain lesions are common in elderly people and are a natural part of aging. Further, they are establishing a tentative link among brain lesions, illness, neurochemistry, and depression (Nemeroff et al., 1988). Lawyers are using brain imaging as part of their defense in some criminal trials. For example, an attorney may assert that PET scans show damage to the client's brain that traditional neurological tests could not find. In one California case, a diagnosis of a mental disorder, confirmed through a PET scan, kept a man from going to the gas chamber.

FOCUS

▶ Distinguish between the essential activities of the sympathetic and the parasympathetic nervous systems. pp. 51–53

▶ Identify the differences between single unit recording and the EEG. pp. 54–55

▶ What kinds of evidence do PET scans provide that make them potentially so important? pp. 56–57

Brain Structures

There is no doubt that the brain is the body's central computing, processing, and storage mechanism—a mechanism intimately involved in day-to-day and minute-by-minute behavior. Our understanding of the brain and its relationship to behavior comes about in part through the study of *neuroanatomy*—the structures of the nervous system—using a wide range of techniques. Neuroanatomists who study behavior often use ablation as a principal technique. In *ablation*, a portion of an animal's brain is removed, and the animal is studied to determine which behaviors have been disrupted. Today, in addition to ablation, neuroanatomists use electrical recording techniques such as EEGs, CAT and PET scans, and neurochemical techniques.

We know a lot about the structure and functions of the brain, but we still have a great deal to learn. The human brain weighs about 3 pounds and is composed of two large *cerebral hemispheres,* one on the left side and one on the right. A large, thick structure, the *corpus callosum,* connects the two hemispheres and permits the transfer of information between them. Besides being divided into right and left halves, the brain can be roughly divided into areas with special functions. Some parts are specialized for visual activities; others are involved in hearing, sleeping, breathing, eating, and a number of other important functions. Some brain activities are localized. Most speech and language activity, for example, can be pinpointed to a specific area, usually on the left side of the brain. Other activities may occur in both hemispheres. Visual activity, for example, occurs in the visual cortex, which occupies both sides of the brain. Psychologists disagree on the extent to which functions are localized within the brain.

In examining the brain, we begin where the spinal cord and the brain meet. Many structures and functions deep within the brain are responsible for basic bodily processes, such as breathing, sleeping, and eating. As we move higher up through the brain, we see more complicated structures and functions. Organizationally, we divide the brain into three sections: the hindbrain, the midbrain, and the forebrain (which includes the cortex). (See the illustrations on pages 64a & b, which show the major sections of the human brain.) Structures in the hindbrain and midbrain are often assumed to be organizationally more primitive than those in the forebrain and are responsible for more basic, reflexive actions. Structures in the lower portions of

The human brain weighs about three pounds and is composed of two large cerebral hemispheres which are joined by the corpus callosum.

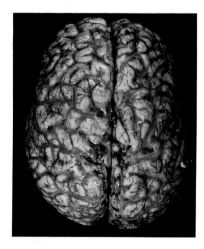

the forebrain are organizationally somewhat more complex and involve higher mental functions. Of still higher functioning is the cortex, which covers the cerebral hemispheres and serves as the basis for thought processing—one of the most advanced abilities of humans.

Hindbrain

The four main structures of the hindbrain receive afferent signals from other parts of the brain and from the spinal cord; they interpret the signals and either relay the information to more complex parts of the brain or cause the body to act. The *hindbrain* consists of the cerebellum, the medulla, the reticular formation, and the pons. The *cerebellum*, a large structure attached to the back surface of the brain stem, influences balance, coordination, and movement. It allows you to do such things as walk in a straight line, type accurately on a keyboard, and coordinate the many movements involved in dancing. The cerebellum may also be involved in a number of cognitive (thinking) operations, although this role is not clearly established (Leiner, Leiner, & Dow, 1986). See the illustrations on pages 64a & b.

The *medulla,* through which many afferent and efferent signals pass, lies just above the spinal cord and controls heartbeat and breathing. Within the medulla and extending out into the cortex is a latticelike network of nerve cells, the *reticular formation,* which directly controls a person's state of arousal, waking, and sleeping, as well as responsive bodily functions; damage to it can result in coma and death. The reticular formation extends into and through the pons and the midbrain, with projections toward the cortex (see the illustrations on page 64b). The *pons* provides a link between the cerebellum and the rest of the brain; and like the medulla, portions of the pons affect sleep and dreaming.

Midbrain

The *midbrain* consists of nuclei (collections of cell bodies) that receive afferent signals from other parts of the brain and from the spinal cord, interpret the signals, and either relay the information to a more complex part of the brain or cause the body to act at once. One portion of the midbrain is involved in smoothness of movement and another in reflexive movements. Movements of the eyeball in its socket, for example, are controlled by the *superior colliculus,* a structure in the midbrain. The reticular formation system continues in the midbrain and is important in the regulation of attention, as well as sleep and arousal.

Forebrain

The forebrain is the largest and most complicated of the brain structures because of its many related parts: the thalamus and hypothalamus, the limbic system, the basal ganglia and corpus callosum, and the cortex.

Thalamus and Hypothalamus. The *thalamus* acts primarily as a routing station to send information to other parts of the brain, although it probably also performs some interpretive functions (see Figure 2.9). Nearly all sensory information proceeds through the thalamus before going to other areas of the brain. The *hypothalamus* has numerous connections with the rest of the forebrain and the midbrain and affects many complex behaviors, such as eating, drinking, and sexual activity. It plays a crucial role in the regulation of food intake; disturbances in the hypothalamus often produce sharp changes in eating and drinking behavior. We will examine these topics in more detail in chapter 10.

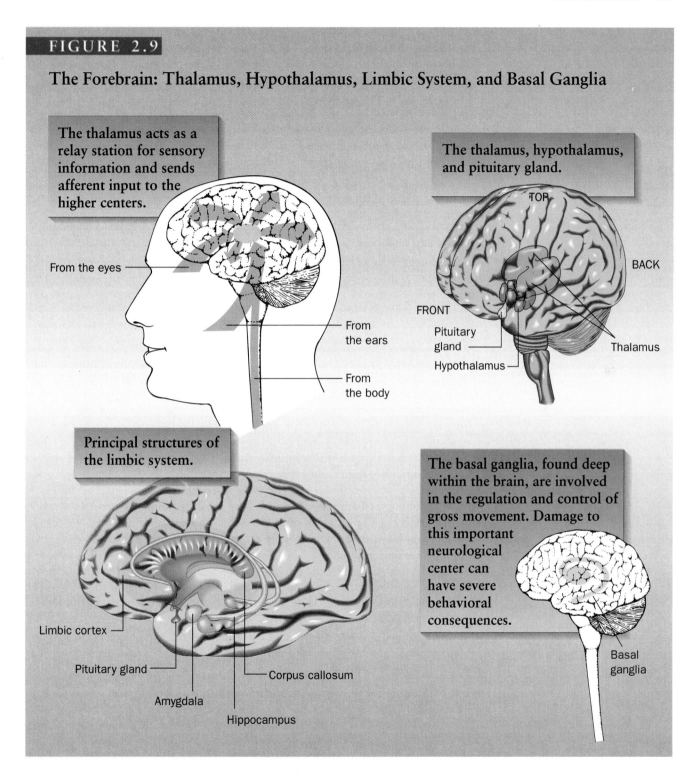

FIGURE 2.9

The Forebrain: Thalamus, Hypothalamus, Limbic System, and Basal Ganglia

The thalamus acts as a relay station for sensory information and sends afferent input to the higher centers.

From the eyes

From the ears

From the body

The thalamus, hypothalamus, and pituitary gland.

TOP

FRONT

BACK

Pituitary gland

Hypothalamus

Thalamus

Principal structures of the limbic system.

Limbic cortex

Pituitary gland

Amygdala

Hippocampus

Corpus callosum

The basal ganglia, found deep within the brain, are involved in the regulation and control of gross movement. Damage to this important neurological center can have severe behavioral consequences.

Basal ganglia

Limbic System. One of the most complex and least understood structures of the brain is the *limbic system*. This system is an interconnected group of structures (including parts of the cortex, thalamus, and hypothalamus) involved in emotional behavior, memory, social behavior, and brain disorders such as epilepsy. Within the limbic system are the hippocampus and the amygdala. In human beings, the *hippocampus* is involved in memory functions. The *amygdala* is involved in the control of some emotional behaviors. Stimulation of the amygdala in animals produces attack responses, and surgical removal of the amygdala in human beings was once a radical way of treating people who were extremely violent. Stimulation of several areas of the limbic system in rats also produces very pleasurable sensations. Olds and Milner (1954) discovered that rats, when given small doses of electric current in some of the limbic areas as rewards for bar pressing, chose bar pressing over eating, even after having been deprived of food for long periods. The researchers called the areas of the brain being stimulated *pleasure centers.*

The Basal Ganglia and Corpus Callosum. The *basal ganglia* are a series of nuclei located deep in the brain to the left and right of the thalamus (refer back to Figure 2.9 on page 59). They control movements and posture and are also associated with Parkinson's disease. Parts of the basal ganglia influence muscle tone and initiate commands to the cerebellum and to higher brain centers. The *corpus callosum* connects and conveys information between the cerebral hemispheres; damage to it results in essentially two separate brains. The corpus callosum is described in detail in the Research Process box on page 62.

Cortex. We divide the brain into two major portions, referred to as the left and right *cerebral hemispheres* (see the Research Process box for a detailed discussion of brain specialization). The exterior covering of the hemispheres, called the *cortex* (or neocortex), is about 2 millimeters thick and consists of six thin layers of cells. It is *convoluted,* or furrowed. These **convolutions,** folds in the tissue, have the effect of creating more surface area within a small space. The overall surface area of the cortex is about 1.5 square feet. A highly developed cortex is evident in human beings, but not all mammals show such specialization. The cortex plays a special role in behavior because it is intimately involved in thought.

A traditional way to divide the cortex is to consider it as a series of lobes, or areas, each with characteristic structures. The most prominent structures are two deep fissures (very deep furrows or folds)—the *lateral fissure* and the *central fissure*—that divide the lobes. These easily recognizable fissures are like deep ravines that run among the convolutions, separating the various lobes. The *frontal lobe* is in front of the central fissure; the *parietal lobe* is behind it. Below the lateral fissure and the parietal lobe is the *temporal lobe,* and at the back of the head, next to the parietal and temporal lobes, is the *occipital lobe.* Figure 2.10 describes each lobe and its primary functions.

Plasticity and Change

Do our brains stay the same from birth to death, or can they change through experience or simply through the passage of time? The basic structure of brain organization is established well before birth and does not change in any substantial way after birth; but details of its structure and functions, particularly in the cerebral cortex, are subject to continued growth and development (Kalil, 1989). Psychologists say that the brain is still *malleable* (teachable) during the formative years. Within limits, the nervous system can be modified and fine-tuned by experience—and this experience can be acquired over a protracted period (Shatz, 1992).

Experience with some specific stimuli reinforces the development of neural structures. Aoki and Siekevitz (1988) liken the developing brain to a highway system that evolves with use. Less traveled roads are abandoned, but popular ones are broadened and new ones are added when needed. When neural structures are used, reused, and constantly updated, they become faster and more easily accessed. Dur-

Convolutions: Characteristic folds in tissues of the cerebral hemispheres and overlying cortex in human beings.

FIGURE 2.10

The Cortex

The cortex is the exterior covering of the cerebral hemispheres. It plays a special role in behavior because of its intimate involvement in thought.

The cortex is comprised of four major lobes and the association cortex.

	LOCATION	FUNCTION
Frontal lobe	In front of the central fissure;	Involved with memory
	contains: (1) Motor cortex and	Concerned with movement
	(2) Broca's area	Involved in speech and language production
Parietal lobe	Behind frontal lobe	Associated with activities involved in the sense of touch and body position
Temporal lobe	Below lateral fissure and parietal lobe	Involved with speech, hearing, and some visual information processing
Occipital lobe	Back of head, next to parietal and temporal lobes	Responsible for visual sense
Association cortex	Areas between parietal, temporal, and occipital lobes	Believed to be involved in complex behaviors that involve thinking and sensory processes

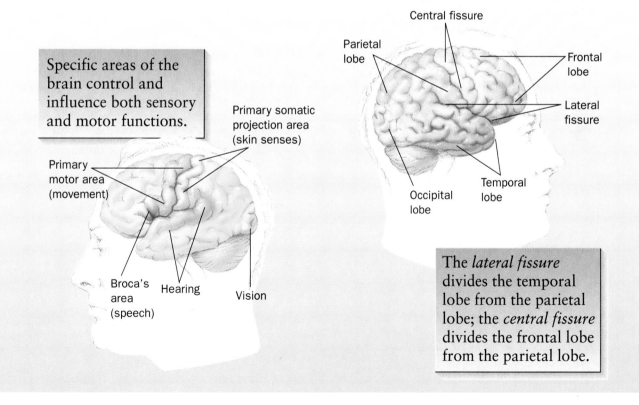

Specific areas of the brain control and influence both sensory and motor functions.

Primary somatic projection area (skin senses)

Primary motor area (movement)

Broca's area (speech)   Hearing   Vision

Central fissure

Parietal lobe   Frontal lobe

Lateral fissure

Occipital lobe   Temporal lobe

The *lateral fissure* divides the temporal lobe from the parietal lobe; the *central fissure* divides the frontal lobe from the parietal lobe.

ing early fetal and infant development the neural links, connections, and interconnections are embellished. Such elaboration and refinement is greater when organisms are placed in complex, super-enriched (e.g., visually stimulating) environments (Chang, Isaacs, & Greenough, 1991).

THE RESEARCH PROCESS

Brain Specialization—The Left and Right of Things

The brain's control over other structures of the body is continually evident. We see this easily when people take psychoactive drugs (drugs that affect the nervous system, especially the brain). When a person takes a drug, which affects brain firing and neurotransmitters (in the brain), this change makes the person feel different. The person responds to the feeling, and further brain changes take place. In other words, the brain affects behavior *and* behavior affects the brain.

Are there specific places in the brain that control specific behaviors and thoughts? Does one side of the brain have more control than the other side? Lavach (1991) says yes, suggesting that brain dominance might even affect your choice of occupation, and certainly your world view. Let's explore the evidence.

Early Research on the Cortex. If a cubic centimeter of cortex were removed, how would it affect the ability to think, smell, or see? Although scientists began mapping the brain hundreds of years ago, and we currently know much about the structure of the brain, research into brain functions did not begin until the 1930s. Early researchers asked: What happens to visual perception if the cortex of the brain is removed? In 1936, Heinrich Kluver (1897– 1979) removed the visual cortex in monkeys and discovered that not all visual functions were impaired. This showed that although the cortex is important to vision, it is not the only structure involved.

There is no doubt that the cortex is a crucial part of the brain, but it is only part of a highly complicated structure. By studying victims of accidents, strokes, and brain tumors and observing their behaviors and mental processes, researchers have learned a great deal more about the brain. Some of the most exciting work comes from studies that examine differences between the two hemispheres.

Splitting the Brain. Studies of brain structure show that different areas of the brain are responsible for different functions. Roger Sperry and Michael Gazzaniga have been at the forefront of research in brain organization. Gazzaniga asserts that the human brain has a modular organization—that it is divided into discrete units that interact to produce mental activity (Gazzaniga, 1989).

Studies by Sperry (1985) and Gazzaniga (1983) show that in most human beings one cerebral hemisphere, usually the left, is specialized for processing speech and language; the other, usually the right, appears better able to handle spatial tasks and musical and artistic endeavors. Some of the evidence comes from studies monitoring brain-wave activity in normal subjects exposed to different kinds of stimuli. For example, when normal subjects are asked to look at or think about letters or perhaps to rehearse a speech, some characteristic brain-wave activity can be detected on the left side of the brain. When they are asked to do creative tasks or are told to reorganize some spatial pattern, brain-wave activity is apparent on the right side of the brain. Still, studies of brain waves do not yield clear or thoroughly convincing evidence of brain function or brain structure.

What happens to behavior and mental processes when connections between the left and right sides of the brain are cut and communication between them ceases? A number of important studies have involved **split-brain patients**—often, people who have uncontrollable, life-threatening epilepsy who have undergone an operation to sever the *corpus callosum* (the band of fibers that connects the left and right hemispheres of the brain) in order to prevent seizures from spreading across the hemispheres. Special testing revealed that there was little or no perceptual or cognitive interaction between the hemispheres, and the patients seemed to have two distinct, independent brains, each with its own abilities. Studies of split-brain patients are invaluable to scientists seeking to understand how the brain works and how the left and right sides function together.

Each cerebral hemisphere is neurologically connected to the opposite side of the body; thus, the left hemisphere normally controls the right side of the body. Split-brain patients are unable to use the speech and language capabilities of the left cerebral hemisphere to describe activities carried out by the right one. When stimulus information is presented exclusively to their left hemisphere, they can describe the stimulus, match it, and deal with it in essentially normal ways. However, when the same stimulus is presented to their right cerebral hemisphere, they can perform the matching tasks (saying that two items are identical) but are unable to verbally describe the stimuli (a left hemisphere task). For example, using simple tests, investigators have found that a split-brain subject holding a pencil in the left hand behind a screen cannot describe it. However, the subject can easily perform a visual matching task if the pencil is switched to the right hand. By studying the two separate hemispheres, researchers are discovering the characteristic functions of each. (See Figure 2.11.)

Studies of split-brain patients do show localization of specific functions, but not every behavior is trace-

FIGURE 2.11

The Effects of Severing the Corpus Callosum

Researchers have developed devices that allow words or pictures to be flashed briefly on a screen that stimulates only one cerebral hemisphere. In individuals whose *corpus callosum* has been severed, images stimulate only the left (language-oriented) cerebral hemisphere. Individuals can name the object *and* select it with their right hand from behind a screen. When the image stimulates only the right cerebral hemisphere, they cannot name it, but they can select it from among a series of objects with their left hand. This shows the key role of the corpus callosum in transferring information between the hemispheres.

able to a single structure in the central nervous system. Most behaviors involve the combined work of several areas. Although there seem to be some specifically left-brain and right-brain activities (see, for example, Koenig, Reiss, & Kosslyn, 1990) which may have developed early in life (McManus & Bryden, 1991), the two halves of our brain work together; although we have localization of functions, we have a unified conscious experience (Gevins & Illes, 1990). We will examine this topic in more detail in chapter 4.

There is no doubt that lateralization and specificity of functions exist. There is also no doubt that the study of brain functions and the work of Sperry and Gazzaniga have been influential in developing our understanding of brain specificity. For example, studies show that people with a strong right-brain dominance, who are generally left-handed, may develop differently from right-handers, and this may affect a number of important events in their lives (Coren & Halpern, 1991). Unfortunately, the popular press and television newscasters oversimplify the specificity of functions, and in some cases trivialize them, to account for school problems, marital problems, artistic abilities, and even baseball batting averages. The extent of hemispheric specialization is yet to be determined, and most scientists and critical thinkers maintain a healthy skepticism about the existence of "two minds" in one (e.g., Hines, 1991; Hellige, 1993).

Split-brain patients: Persons whose *corpus callosum*—which normally connects the two cerebral hemispheres—has been surgically severed.

Changes in the brain occur not only in young organisms but in aging ones as well. As human beings grow older, their central nervous systems function differently, sometimes not as well as before. There are decreases in the number of receptors and cells, for example. In addition, some learning tasks become more difficult for aging animals and human beings. Recent work has attempted to identify drugs that facilitate simple learning. For example, nimodipine helped aging rabbits learn simple responses as well as young rabbits do. The drug, used to improve blood flow in stroke patients, may help learning by blocking calcium transmission to areas of the brain involved in memory. Nimodipine is only one of a large number of drugs that are effective in treating age-related learning problems (Deyo, Straube, & Disterhoft, 1989) or potentially restoring brain functions after brain damage (LeVere et al., 1989).

Work on drug enhancement of learning is speculative and exciting; finding specific proteins, drugs, and new treatments that alter brain functioning may be a key to our overall understanding of brain development and its effects on behavior. This understanding is especially important in cases of neural diseases such as Alzheimer's or trauma to the nervous system. Can damage done to the nervous system be repaired? Injury to the brain early in an organism's life is especially damaging, but the extent and permanence of the damage depend on the nature of the injury, the age at which it takes place, and the presence of several helping factors, such as the availability of an enriched environment (Kolb, 1989).

Neurotransplants

The idea of replacing body parts is no longer science fiction; we routinely do liver transplants, and heart transplants are making serious headway. But can you take a portion of a brain and move it to another organism? Researchers are focusing on this question in an effort to help patients with brain disorders such as epilepsy and Parkinson's disease. The research is complicated and not clear-cut; it also has serious ethical implications.

Can tissue that is transplanted from one organism to another survive and develop normally? Research shows the answer depends on the site where the tissue is transplanted. Some sites prove to be good locations; others are less successful at fostering normal growth. Transplantation is most likely to be successful where cells are clearly organized (Raisman, Morris, & Zhou, 1987). In a series of studies, researchers Fine (1986) and Mikhailova et al. (1991) successfully grafted (attached) brain tissue to the central nervous system of rats and other organisms and were able to observe behavior changes associated with the graft.

Yet animal research, however successful, is not the same as research with human beings. People with Parkinson's disease (in which brain tissue no longer secretes sufficient levels of dopamine, causing muscular rigidity and tremors) have been treated with implants of healthy fetal brain tissue with positive results (Bekhtereva et al., 1990). The implants survive, grow naturally, and secrete dopamine; and the patients' condition improves (Lindvall, 1991; Lindvall et al., 1990).

Someday, neurotransplants may open a world of therapeutic possibilities. Victims of head injuries, brain diseases, and birth defects could all benefit. Research with human beings poses ethical problems, however.

FOCUS

► Why is the corpus callosum so essential to effective communication in the brain? p. 60

► How does the overall structure of the cortex help researchers evaluate brain function? p. 60

► What is the *potential* function of convolutions of the cortex? p. 60

► What evidence suggests that the left hemisphere and the right hemisphere of the brain can operate independently? p. 62

THE HINDBRAIN AND THE MIDBRAIN*

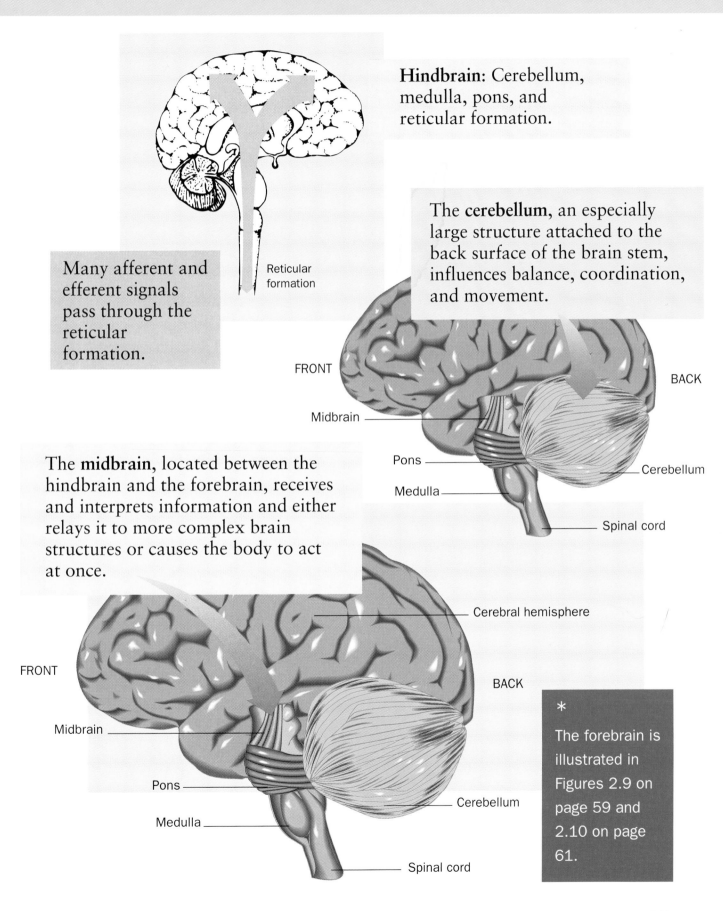

Hindbrain: Cerebellum, medulla, pons, and reticular formation.

Reticular formation

Many afferent and efferent signals pass through the reticular formation.

The **cerebellum**, an especially large structure attached to the back surface of the brain stem, influences balance, coordination, and movement.

FRONT

BACK

Midbrain

Pons

Medulla

Cerebellum

Spinal cord

The **midbrain**, located between the hindbrain and the forebrain, receives and interprets information and either relays it to more complex brain structures or causes the body to act at once.

Cerebral hemisphere

FRONT

BACK

Midbrain

Pons

Medulla

Cerebellum

Spinal cord

*
The forebrain is illustrated in Figures 2.9 on page 59 and 2.10 on page 61.

Should the medical and psychological community be allowed to create a more perfect human being? There are surgical risks; the techniques are dangerous and as yet unproven. Physicians and researchers must establish procedures for choosing the best candidates for such experimentation. And what about the source of the transplanted tissue? Implants that have been successful have come from human fetal tissue. Researchers and ethicists alike are unsure under what, if any, conditions fetal tissue should be made available. One possibility that skirts some of the ethical issues is the use of a patient's own dopamine-producing healthy tissue. This procedure is being explored with some success (Madrazo et al., 1987).

Hormones and Glands

In 1978, Dan White fatally shot both San Francisco mayor George Moscone and city supervisor Harvey Milk. In court, White's attorney successfully argued that a diet of junk food had jumbled his client's brain and reduced his capacity for moral behavior. White spent only 3 years in prison for committing the double homicide. Although the "Twinkie defense" is no longer a legal defense in California, White's lawyer capitalized on the fact that a person's body chemistry—even an imbalance in blood-sugar levels—can have a dramatic impact on behavior. In fact, body chemistry, hormones, and learned experiences can work together to influence a person. But does this render us unaccountable for our own actions, as Dan White's lawyer claimed?

Combinations of factors are usually the answer to many complex psychological questions, but research shows that some abilities and behaviors have a direct hormonal link. For example, in a paper presented at a scientific meeting in 1988, psychologist Doreen Kimura reported that when a woman experiences low estrogen levels during and immediately after menstruation, she excels at spatial tasks but performs less well on motor tasks. The differences are small and do not occur with all women. This work is in its early stages, but it is interesting because of the links shown between hormones and behavior and because of the differences observed between men and women. The links are mediated by the endocrine glands and show the complexity of the relationship of behavior, body structures, and the hormones and other substances that flow through our bodies.

Endocrine Glands

Many of our behaviors are affected by the secretions of *glands*—groups of cells that form a structure and secrete a substance. Psychologists are particularly interested in the **endocrine glands**—ductless glands—that secrete hormones directly into the bloodstream. (See Figure 2.12 on page 66 for the location of several endocrine glands.) **Hormones**—endocrine gland chemicals that regulate the activities of specific organs or cells—travel through the bloodstream to target organs containing cells that respond specifically to particular hormones. Although researchers do not know the extent to which hormones control people's behavior, there is no doubt that the glandular system is interconnected. Each hormone affects behavior and eventually other glands. A disorder in the thyroid, for example, affects not only the metabolic rate but also the pituitary gland, which in turn affects other behaviors. The glands, the hormones, and the target organs interact; the brain initiates the release of hormones, which affect the target organs, which in turn affect behavior, which in turn affects the brain, and so on. The Diversity box on page 68 explores the question of whether gender differences are caused by hormones.

Endocrine glands: [END-oh-krin] Ductless glands that secrete hormones directly into the bloodstream.

Hormones: Endocrine gland chemicals that regulate the activities of specific organs or cells.

Lift page to see illustrations on pages 64a & b.

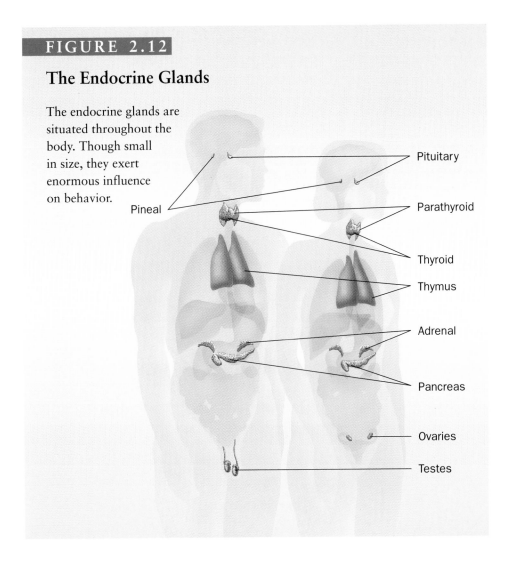

FIGURE 2.12

The Endocrine Glands

The endocrine glands are situated throughout the body. Though small in size, they exert enormous influence on behavior.

Pineal

Pituitary

Parathyroid

Thyroid

Thymus

Adrenal

Pancreas

Ovaries

Testes

Sexual Behavior. In newborn animals, hormones have an irreversible effect on behavior—they set specific behavior patterns in motion by permanently affecting brain development. In human adults, sexual behavior is to some extent under hormonal control. One study, for example, showed a significant correlation between married couples' hormone levels and frequency of intercourse (Persky, 1978). Hormones such as testosterone and estrogen, whose release is affected by the pituitary gland, the adrenal gland, the testes, and the ovaries, is certainly involved in the desire for sexual activity.

Pituitary Gland. The most important endocrine gland is the pituitary gland, which is referred to as the body's master gland because it regulates the actions of other endocrine glands (see Figure 2.13). A major function of the pituitary gland is the control of growth hormones.

The pituitary gland is divided into two lobes, the anterior and the posterior. Secretions from the lobes produce direct changes in bodily functions (e.g., growth) and affect other glands. The *anterior lobe* produces three types of hormones: hormones that stimulate the thyroid and adrenal glands, each of which controls specific

The Human Brain

▶ The human brain is divided into three major sections:

THE HINDBRAIN
THE MIDBRAIN
THE FOREBRAIN

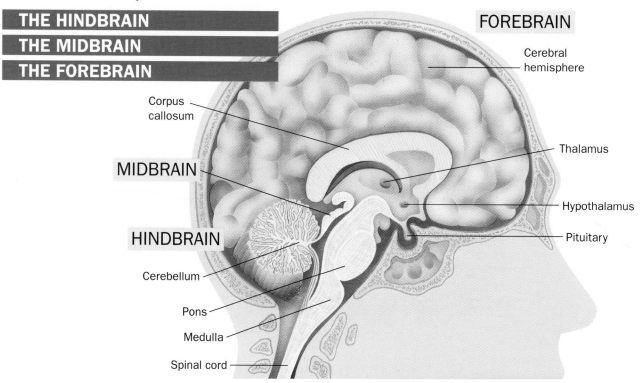

FOREBRAIN
Cerebral hemisphere
Thalamus
Hypothalamus
Pituitary

Corpus callosum

MIDBRAIN

HINDBRAIN

Cerebellum

Pons

Medulla

Spinal cord

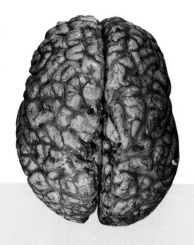

The human brain weighs about 3 pounds and is composed of two large cerebral hemispheres, which are joined by the corpus callosum.

INFORMATION FLOWS TO THE BRAIN:

1 By a system of 12 cranial nerves that send neuronal impulses directly to an appropriate location in the brain.

2 By afferent neuronal impulses that make their way up the spinal cord and through the reticular formation from the muscles and glands.

3 By cross-connections within the brain. One structure of the brain sends vital information to other structures during and after information processing.

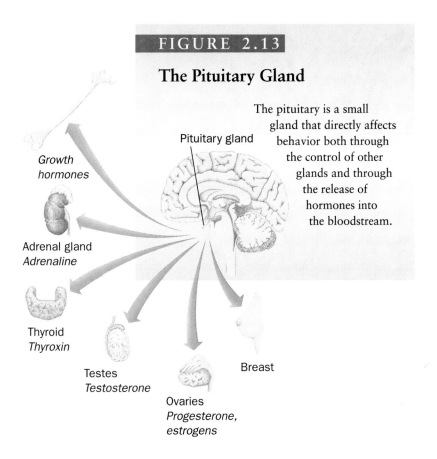

FIGURE 2.13

The Pituitary Gland

Pituitary gland

The pituitary is a small gland that directly affects behavior both through the control of other glands and through the release of hormones into the bloodstream.

Growth hormones

Adrenal gland
Adrenaline

Thyroid
Thyroxin

Testes
Testosterone

Ovaries
Progesterone, estrogens

Breast

behaviors; growth hormones (called somatotrophins), which control the body's development; and sex hormones (called gonadotrophins), which are involved in sexual behavior.

A person's psychological state influences the secretions from the anterior pituitary; for example, viewing sexually explicit films can raise the level of gonadotrophins (LaFerla, Anderson, & Schalch, 1978).

The *posterior lobe* of the pituitary gland stores and secretes two major hormones, antidiuretic hormone (ADH) and oxytocin. ADH acts on the kidneys to increase fluid absorption and decrease the amount of urine produced by the body. Oxytocin stimulates uterine contractions in pregnant women and causes labor to begin. It also helps nursing mothers release milk.

FOCUS

▶ What evidence has led researchers to conclude that hormonal differences in development affect behavior in adulthood? p. 68

▶ Why are researchers justified in concluding that the pituitary is the master gland? pp. 66–67

▶ What are the implications of the conclusions researchers have reached about gender differences in intellectual ability? p. 68

Pancreas. Another endocrine gland, the *pancreas*, is involved in regulating the body's sugar levels. Sugar in the blood determines a person's energy level. When blood sugar is high, people are energetic; when it is low, they feel weak and tired. Cells in the pancreas—the islets of Langerhans—control the production of **insulin**—the pancreatic hormone that facilitates the transport of sugar to the body

Insulin: A hormone produced by the pancreas that facilitates the transport of sugar from the blood into body cells, where it is metabolized.

Are Gender Differences Caused by Hormones?

In some circles, it is popular to believe that men and women are essentially the same; however, research shows some important biological and behavioral differences. In recent years, research on gender differences in brain organization has created a volatile debate.

Let's look at some facts. During pregnancy, sex hormones are present and help create sexual differentiation; they are also thought to create permanent changes in brain development that become evident in later behavior. Research shows that, on average, men do better than women on some spatial tasks, especially the mental rotation of objects (Linn & Petersen, 1985). Across a number of research studies, men do better, on average, in mathematical reasoning and in some motor tasks, such as guiding projectiles through space (Halpern, 1986).

By contrast, women do better than men at some perceptual tasks—for example, the rapid matching of items. They have greater verbal fluency than men and outperform men in some arithmetic calculations (Hyde, Fennema, & Lamon, 1990). They also do better than men at reading emotions from photographs.

Women and men perform tasks differently. Women tend to use both sides of the brain in cognitive tasks such as spelling, for example, while men use primarily the left side. Women also listen with both ears equally, whereas men favor the right ear. Not all of the gender differences appear at all ages and at all phases of learning. Gender differences in problem solving, for example, tend to favor women in elementary school and men after puberty (Hyde, Fennema, & Lamon, 1990).

The gender differences in various mental and performance abilities described here are minimal; there is no dramatic difference between men and women on any one task. However, researchers have observed subtle, yet potentially important, differences.

What causes gender differences? Are they a result of our biology, or do they reflect the way we are raised? At birth, our 3- to 4-pound brains are remarkably alike. Kimura (1992) asserts that differing patterns of abilities probably reflect different hormonal influences and structural asymmetries. In males, male hormones predominate; they may affect the size and function of brain structures such as the hypothalamus. For example, when newborn rats are administered large doses of male hormones, their brains develop dif-

ferently from when they are administered large doses of female hormones; and this difference alters their behavioral abilities permanently.

Of course, making the leap to human beings is difficult because ethics precludes the manipulation of hormone levels of newborns. However, researchers have been able to measure the abilities of human adults and simultaneously measure their levels of the hormone testosterone. Testosterone is evident in all human beings, although men show significantly higher levels than women. Valerie Shute measured the levels in men and women and found that women with high levels of testosterone perform better on spatial tasks than women with low levels; in men, the reverse was true. Her conclusion was that testosterone levels in men and women affect performance (Shute et al., 1983).

But are gender differences also influenced by the way we are raised? The answer to this question is certainly yes. There may exist gender differences that are biologically based, but our culture emphasizes and encourages them. Traditionally, boys have been encouraged to participate in physically rough-and-tumble sports; girls have been encouraged to take part in domestic, genteel activities. Traditionally, men have been the providers—the wage earners, the problem solvers. Today,

---

Diabetes mellitus: A condition in which too little insulin is produced, causing sugar to be insufficiently transported into body cells.

Hypoglycemia: [hi-po-gly-SEE-me-uh] Very low blood sugar levels resulting from the overproduction of insulin.

cells, where it is metabolized. Two insulin-related problems are diabetes and hypoglycemia. **Diabetes mellitus** is a condition in which an insufficient amount of insulin is produced, causing sugar to be inefficiently transported out of the bloodstream to the cells and thus allowing too much sugar to accumulate in the blood. If the pancreas errs in the opposite direction, the result is **hypoglycemia**—very low blood sugar levels caused by the overproduction of insulin. Hypoglycemic patients have little energy and often feel faint. The condition can usually be controlled through diet, with careful monitoring of the daily consumption of calories and types of food.

While there are genetic differences between men and women, society also greatly influences behavior. However, there tend to be more differences among women as a group than between men and women.

politics, and even economics play in shaping the study of gender differences (Riger, 1992). Psychologist Sandra Lipsitz Bem (1993) asserts that many of our traditionally held gender stereotypes are embedded in our culture and social institutions and they perpetuate a society that values males more than females. In chapter 9, we'll see that many of the differences, especially mathematical differences, between males and females are exceedingly small, and the extent of those differences is shrinking each year.

Most important is the fact that *there are usually more differences within a group than between groups.* For example, there are more differences among women than between women and men (see chapter 1, pp. 28–29). This idea is especially important when one considers the applicability of data. It becomes impossible to generalize results to all people if the data are taken only from a small sample of women or men.

however, men and women are sharing roles and responsibilities; in raising children, parents are showing a much greater understanding that boys and girls should have equal opportunities.

The results are evident in behavior. Differencesthathave long been apparent between men and women are disappearing; access to and enrollment in courses where problem solving is encouraged—for example, physics—no longer disproportionately favor boys. Researchers are becoming more sensitive to bias in reporting and to the roles that culture,

While genetics lays the foundation for our development, our hormones affect the process further. Ultimately, how we are raised by our parents, schools, and society shapes our adult abilities. Nature lays the foundation for behavior, and nurture shapes and modifies it. The gender differences in abilities lie not only within our genes but within our society.

Adrenal Gland. The *adrenal gland,* which is also involved in behavior, is located adjacent to the kidneys and is divided into two parts. The *adrenal medulla* produces epinephrine (adrenaline), a substance that dramatically alters energy levels and greatly affects a person's reactions to stress through stimulation of the sympathetic nervous system. Imagine you are being chased through a dark alley. The release of epinephrine causes your heart to pound and gives you a burst of energy to help you outdistance your pursuer. The *adrenal cortex* secretes several hormones, one of which is involved in growth and development and others of which are involved in cardiovascular functions.

Concluding Note

This chapter shows a wide range of human behaviors that are greatly influenced by genetics, hormones, and bodily structures. The release of epinephrine affects behavior; damage to the spinal cord is devastating; even the food we eat has physiological effects on day-to-day behaviors. Kagan and Snidman (1991b) have shown that infants exhibit stable, long-lasting, and probably inborn temperamental differences, such as reticence and shyness. The researchers suggest that some temperamental behaviors and emotions are predisposed. They also note, however, that people can change their behaviors, monitor their moods, and be affected by more than just their biology. We humans are adaptable.

Recall the problem of Patty Duke and bipolar disorder at the beginning of this chapter. Many years ago I believed that mood disorders were solely emotional; on the basis of new research, I now believe (along with most of my colleagues) that such disorders are partly biological and partly emotional. Just as some people are prone to shyness, some are prone to depression. Both shyness and depression can be affected by a wealth of experiences in the environment. What makes psychology so exciting is that we can examine a person's fixed nature and the day-to-day events that affect behavior—a person's heredity and environment.

Summary & Review

Nature versus Nurture

What is genetics and why do psychologists study it?

Genetics is the study of *heredity*—the biological transmission of traits and characteristics from parents to offspring. Each person receives traits from both parents through the transmission of *genes*. Each person's heredity is unique because each parent has a unique genetic makeup. Psychologists generally assert that human behavior is influenced by both *nature* (heredity) and *nurture* (environment). Psychologists study the biological bases of behavior to understand how these two variables interact.   pp. 41–42

How are inherited characteristics transmitted and why do psychologists study twins?

The inherited potential of people is carried by *chromosomes*. Each chromosome contains thousands of genes, which are made up of DNA. Genes are the basic unit of heredity. The 23rd pair of chromosomes determines the gender of fetuses. *Identical twins* share exactly the same genetic heritage; they come from one ovum and one sperm and are always the same sex. *Fraternal twins* are produced by two ova and two sperm and therefore can be both males, both females, or one male and one female. They share the genetic characteristics of normal siblings. Twins allow researchers to separate the effects of nature versus nurture on developmental processes. p. 43

KEY TERMS: *nature*, p. 40; *nurture*, p. 40; *genetics*, p. 41; *chromosomes*, p. 41; *genes*, p. 41; *allele*, p. 41; *Down syndrome*, p. 42;

phenylketonuria (PKU), p. 42; *fraternal twins*, p. 43; *identical twins*, p. 43.

Communication in the Nervous System

Describe the basic structure of the neuron.

The basic unit of the nervous system, the *neuron*, is made up of *dendrites*, a *cell body*, an *axon*, and *axon terminals*. The space between the axon terminals and the dendrite of another neuron is the *synapse*.   p. 44

Describe the action potential.

The *action potential* is caused by the stimulation of the cell body. If there is enough activity at the cell body, a spike discharge occurs (with a rapid reversal of cell membrane polarity). The neuron fires in an *all-or-none* manner and has a *refractory period*, during which it cannot fire. The action potential propagates down the long slim axon and stimulates the release of chemicals, called *neurotransmitters*, that reside in the axon terminal and synaptic vesicles. The neurotransmitters move across the synaptic space and bind themselves to receptor sites on the dendrites of the next cell, thereby conveying information to the next neuron. pp. 47–49

What is psychopharmacology?

Psychopharmacology is the study of how drugs affect behavior. Research often focuses on *agonists* and *antagonists*. An agonist is a chemical that mimics the action of a neurotransmitter, usually by occupying receptor sites. An antagonist is a chemical that opposes the action of a neurotransmitter, usually by blocking a neuro-

transmitter from occupying a receptor site.   p. 50

KEY TERMS: *nervous system*, p. 44; *neuron*, p. 44; *afferent neurons*, p. 45; *efferent neurons*, p. 45; *synapse*, p. 46; *action potential*, p. 47; *all-or-none*, p. 48; *refractory period*, p. 48; *neurotransmitters*, p. 48; *neuromodulator*, p. 50; *agonists*, p. 50; *antagonists*, p. 50.

Organization of the Peripheral and Central Nervous Systems

What is the overall organization of the nervous system?

The nervous system is composed of two subsystems: the central and the peripheral nervous systems. *The central nervous system* consists of the brain and spinal cord. The *peripheral nervous system* carries information to and from the *spinal cord* and *brain* through spinal and cranial nerves. The peripheral nervous system is further divided into the *somatic* and *autonomic nervous systems*. The autonomic nervous system is made up of two divisions: the *sympathetic* and the *parasympathetic nervous systems*, each having different functions. pp. 51–53

continued

Summary & Review

Describe several techniques for measuring electrical activity in the nervous system.

One technique for measuring the electrical activity that takes place in the nervous system is the *electroencephalogram (EEG).* The resulting records of brain-wave patterns can be used to assess neurological disorders and the types of electrical activity that occur during thought, sleep, and other behaviors. *Single unit recording,* another technique, records activity from single cells by placing an electrode within or next to single cells. Three significant new techniques for measuring the activity of the nervous system have been developed. *CAT (computerized axial tomography) scans* are computer assisted X-ray procedures. *MRI (magnetic resonance imaging) scans* are similar to CAT scans but do not use radiation. *PET (positron emission tomography) scans* use radiochemical procedures and allow researchers to watch metabolic changes taking place.   pp. 54–57

KEY TERMS: *peripheral nervous system,* p. 51; *somatic nervous system,* p. 51; *autonomic nervous system,* p. 51; *sympathetic nervous system,* p. 51; *parasympathetic nervous system,* p. 52; *central nervous system,* p. 53; *brain,* p. 53; *spinal cord,* p. 53; *electroencephalogram,* p. 55.

Brain Structures

Describe the overall structure of the brain.

The brain is divided into three sections: hindbrain, midbrain, and forebrain (which includes the cortex). The hindbrain consists of four main structures: the cerebellum, the medulla, the reticular formation, and the pons. The midbrain is made up of nuclei that receive afferent signals from other parts of the brain and from the spinal cord, interpret them, and either relay the information to other parts of the brain or cause the body to act at once. The forebrain is the largest and most complicated of the brain structures; it is composed of the thalamus and hypothalamus, the limbic system, the basal ganglia and corpus callosum, and the cortex. pp. 57–61

Describe the overall structure of the cerebral hemispheres.

The normal cerebral hemisphere is neurologically connected to the opposite side of the body. In laboratory studies of *split-brain patients,* the patients are unable to use the speech and language capabilities of the left cerebral hemisphere to describe ac-

tivities carried out by the right one. The most prominent structures of the cortex are the two deep fissures—the lateral fissure and the central fissure—that divide the lobes.   pp. 60–61

What is brain lateralization?

Research shows that in most human beings, one cerebral hemisphere—usually the left—is specialized for processing speech and language; the other—usually the right—appears better able to handle spatial tasks and musical and artistic endeavors. pp. 62–63

KEY TERMS: *convolutions,* p. 60; *split-brain patients,* p. 63.

Hormones and Glands

What is the endocrine system?

The endocrine system is a series of ductless glands that affect behavior by secreting *hormones* into the bloodstream. Each gland controls a different aspect of behavior, but all are related in one way or another to the pituitary gland. The pituitary gland is appropriately referred to as the master gland because of its central role in regulating hormones; another important gland is the *pancreas,* which is involved in regulating the body's sugar levels.   pp. 65–69

CONNECTIONS

If you are interested in...

Brain structures and how they affect behavior, see ...

CHAPTER 4, pp. 143–144

The extent to which alcohol affects higher brain functions and behavior.

CHAPTER 9, pp. 340–341

The profound effect of Alzheimer's disease on memory.

CHAPTER 15, pp. 564–565

The effects of electroconvulsive shock therapy on memory and behavior in a person suffering from depression.

The nature versus nurture controversy, see ...

CHAPTER 4, pp. 148–149

The impact of a person's genetic heritage on the likelihood that he or she will become an alcoholic.

CHAPTER 7, pp. 269–272

How the study of communication in apes is helping resolve the issue of nature versus nurture.

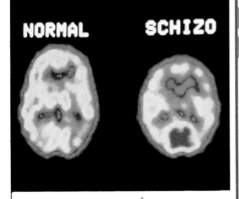

CHAPTER 14, pp. 526–529

The extent to which a person's home environment can increase the likelihood of developing schizophrenia.

Communication between brain structures and the nervous system, see ...

CHAPTER 3, pp. 77, 84–87

How the eyes communicate information to the brain that allows us to perceive the world.

CHAPTER 10, pp. 379–381

How emotional responses affect us and, in turn, affect emotion.

CHAPTER 13, pp. 471–474

How our bodies' reaction to stressful situations is often arousal, followed by eventual exhaustion.

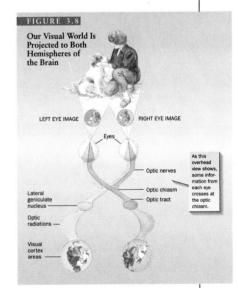

FIGURE 3.8

Our Visual World Is Projected to Both Hemispheres of the Brain

LEFT EYE IMAGE
RIGHT EYE IMAGE

Eyes

Optic nerves

Optic chiasm

Lateral geniculate nucleus

Optic tract

Optic radiations

Visual cortex areas

As this overhead view shows, some information from each eye crosses at the optic chiasm.

3

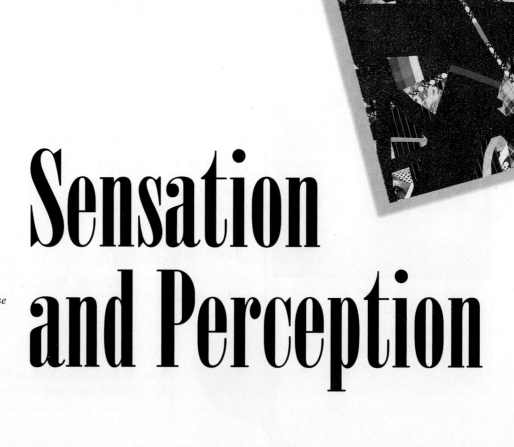

Sensation and Perception

A complete waste of money! That is what researchers claim about subliminal audio self-help tapes. Over the last 40 years, magazine, radio, and television advertisements have sold tapes and records that have hidden, or subliminal, messages that can supposedly affect your behavior in positive ways. Such tapes promise help with weight loss, self-esteem, and addictions. Makers of the tapes claim that a message hidden in the tape, when played over and over (even while you are asleep), will teach you new ideas, provide a positive attitude, and influence your life in a positive way.

Tape makers assert that if an auditory stimulus is presented so quickly or at such a low intensity or volume that you cannot consciously perceive it, it affects your behavior. Modern studies of subliminal perception (*subliminal* means "below the threshold of awareness") show, however, that subliminal self-help tapes do not work. When the tapes have been analyzed, researchers have found that human beings cannot discriminate between self-help tapes with and without "hidden" messages. Moreover, some of the hidden-message tapes do not even contain the messages.

Subliminal perception, however, does exist. Later in this chapter, we will see that subliminal perception studies show there is perception without awareness, but its effects are subtle and do not exist on self-help tapes.

Although subliminal self-help tapes may not work, we know that people's view of the world is affected by a wide array of strong, and sometimes subtle, events in the environment. Architects use the laws of perception to affect our view of their work. Spacious atriums create an open look; massive granite walls provide a sense of stability. Theater lighting experts know that a soft pink light makes older people look younger; they also know that sharp contrasts in lighting make for startling and dramatic effects. Similarly, painters use light, shadow, and texture to creature exciting effects.

Our perceptions of the world depend on a variety of important variables. Consider what happens when you try to read program notes in a darkened theater. The text and photographs are visible, but both are viewed with difficulty and with a loss of detail and visual clarity. Wearing sunglasses indoors would affect your perceptual experience in much the same way. Similarly, your hearing may be impaired for a few hours after a rock concert. Tasting the delicacy of a wine may be nearly impossible after eating very spicy food. Our perception of the visual, auditory, and taste environment depends not only on light, sound, and food but also on intervening environmental events such as dimming of the lights and eating hot tamales.

What Is a Perceptual Experience?

Whenever you are exposed to a stimulus in the environment, it initiates an electrochemical change in the receptors in your body. That change in turn initiates the processes of sensation and perception. Psychologists study sensation and perception because what people sense and perceive determines how they will understand and interpret the world. This interpretation depends on a combination of stimulation, past experiences, and current interpretations.

Sensation and Perception: Definitions

Traditionally, sensation and perception have been studied together as closely related fields. **Sensation** is the process of stimulating the sense organ receptor cells and relaying their initial information to higher centers for further processing. **Perception** is the process by which an organism selects and interprets sensory input so it acquires meaning. Thus, sensation provides the stimulus for further perceptual processing. For example, when light strikes the eyeball and initiates electrochemical processes, we experience sensation. But our interpretation of the pattern of light and its resulting neural representation as an image is part of perception.

Today, perceptual psychologists generally acknowledge that a strict distinction between sensation and perception is unnecessary. We now think in terms of *perceptual systems*—the sets of structures, functions, and operations by means of which people perceive the world around them. Perception is not merely the firing of a single group of neurons; it involves sets of neurons and previous experience, as well as stimulation that occurs at our eyes or ears. Psychologists are especially aware that perceptual systems interact. Thus, as researchers gather more sophisticated information about sensation and perception, the boundaries between the two begin to fade.

Sensory and perceptual processes rely so closely on each other that many researchers think about the two processes together as perception. For them, *percep-

Sensation: The process of stimulating the sense organ receptor cells and relaying their initial information to higher centers for further processing.

Perception: The process by which an organism interprets sensory input so it acquires meaning.

tion is the entire process by which an organism acquires and interprets sensory input (which has been converted into electrochemical energy) so it acquires organization, form, and meaning. It is through perception that people explore the world and discover its rules (E. J. Gibson, 1988). This complex process involves the nervous system and one or more of the perceptual or sensory systems: vision, hearing, taste, smell, or touch.

Although perceptual systems are different, they share common processes. In each case, an environmental stimulus creates an initial stimulation. Receptor cells translate that form of energy into neuronal impulses, and the impulses are then sent to specific areas of the brain for further processing.

Psychologists who study such relationships are using **psychophysics**—the study of the relationship between physical stimuli and people's conscious experience of them. Psychophysical studies attempt to relate the physical dimension of stimuli to psychological experience. In doing so, they reveal that environmental stimuli are rich with information and cues. These studies show that human beings (and animals for that matter) gather information and interpret it in an active, constructive manner. They also show that past experiences affect our interpretation and shape our perceptions.

Interacting Perceptual Systems

A fast-paced indoor racquetball game provides an exhilarating example of the interaction of perceptual systems. Your opponent's ball ricochets off the front wall and whizzes overhead. By the loud smack on the wall behind you, you know instantly that the ball has rebounded too fast to be intercepted at the back of the court. You run to the front of the court, turn, and swat the ball, sending it flying into the left corner. Your opponent raises his racquet in response but is too slow, and the ball thumps into his chest. As you play, you must coordinate your hearing, eyesight, motor systems, sense of balance, and posture in order to react effectively to the speeding ball as it bounces off the walls and floor of the court.

Your actions are based on a mixture of perceptual information. Researchers who study the active integration of perceptual systems find that for the systems to develop fully, they must have varied experiences as well as a way to exchange information about the world. In a classic study of visual and motor coordination in kittens, Held and Hein (1963) demonstrated the need for the perceptual systems to act together. Pairs of kittens were placed in a circular enclosure, and one of each pair was equipped with a harness and collar that let it move actively as it explored the environment. The other kitten was restrained so that it perceived the visual world only in response to the movements of the first kitten (see Figure 3.1 on page 78). Active, voluntary movement initiated by the first kitten caused identical but not self-initiated movement by the second kitten. After observing many pairs of kittens, Held and Hein noted that only the kittens who were allowed to initiate voluntary movements were later able to make good visually guided motor movements; the others had deficits in their perceptual abilities.

Studies of human beings also show that both varied sensory experiences and interaction among different systems are necessary for perception to develop properly. Von Senden (1932) reported case histories of people who were born with cataracts (which cloud vision) and had them removed in adulthood. These individuals, seeing clearly for the first time as adults, had several deficiencies. For example, they were unable to recognize simple forms presented in a different color or a different context. People need varied sensory and perceptual experiences early in life for normal perceptual experiences to occur in adulthood. The consequences of deprivation of and isolation from combined perceptual experiences are debilitating. The effects of limited stimulation have been followed up with animal and human subjects in studies of restricted environmental stimulation.

Psychophysics: [SIE-co-FIZ-icks] The study of the relationship between physical stimuli and people's conscious experience of them.

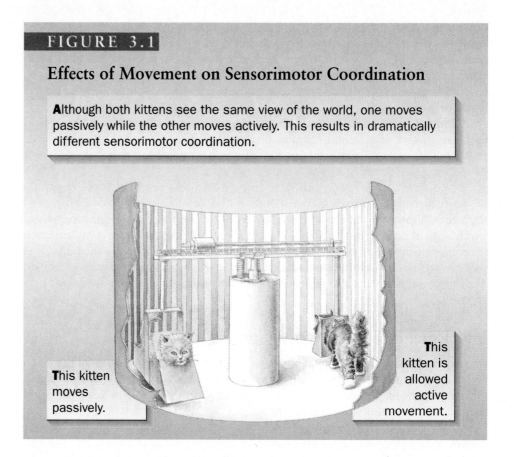

FIGURE 3.1

Effects of Movement on Sensorimotor Coordination

Although both kittens see the same view of the world, one moves passively while the other moves actively. This results in dramatically different sensorimotor coordination.

This kitten moves passively.

This kitten is allowed active movement.

Restricted Environmental Stimulation

Throughout the ages, mystics of all kinds have claimed to obtain special trance states by purposely limiting their sensory experiences—taking vows of silence, adhering to austere lifestyles, meditating while sitting as still as stone for hours, and so on. In 1954, neurophysiologist John Lilly enlisted modern technology to find out what would happen if the brain were deprived of all sensory input. He constructed an isolation tank that excluded all light and sound and was filled with heavily salted water, which allows for easy floating. In this artificial sea, deprived of all external stimuli, Lilly experienced dreams, reveries, hallucinations, and other altered states.

The benefits of sensory restriction (deprivation)—isolation from sights, sounds, smells, tastes, and feeling—have been exaggerated, but such restriction can have profound effects on animals and humans. Heron studied the effects of sensory restriction by confining college students to a comfortable but dull room. To limit their auditory experiences, they heard only the continuous hum of an air conditioner; they wore translucent plastic visors to limit their vision; and they wore tubes lined with cotton around their hands and arms to limit their skin's sensory input. The results were dramatic. Within a few hours, the subjects' performance on tests of mental ability was impaired. The students became bored and irritable, and many said they saw "images" (Bexton, Heron, & Scott, 1954).

Several fascinating follow-up studies placed subjects in identical conditions *except* that the subjects were told that their deprivation would serve as an aid to meditation. How do you think this information affected their response to sensory deprivation? The subjects did not hallucinate or become irritable; in fact, their mental ability actually improved (Lilly, 1956; Zuckerman, 1969). These studies suggest that people do not necessarily become bored because of lack of stimulation. Rather, when people *feel* their situation is monotonous, they become bored. Given the opportunity to relax in a quiet place for a long time, many people meditate; they find such "deprivation" relaxing. Such findings indicate the need for caution in interpreting data from sensory deprivation studies involving human beings, particularly because subjects approach these situations with powerful expectations (recall the effects of self-fulfilling prophecies mentioned in chapter 1).

Sensory restriction has proven to have positive effects with some people (Harrison & Barabasz, 1991). The profound relaxation that occurs in an extreme sensory restricted environment can be highly effective in modifying some existing habits, such as smoking, and in treating such problems as obesity and insomnia (Suedfeld, 1990) and addictions (Borrie, 1991). Men, older individuals, and people with religious backgrounds may be more likely to benefit than others, and some people may be adversely affected. Further, previous experience with sensory restriction may produce a cumulative effect; that is, each time a person undergoes the restriction, it may have a greater effect. In general, the benefits of restricted environmental stimulation are probably underestimated (Suedfeld, 1990).

FOCUS

▶ Why have modern researchers viewed perception as a unitary rather than a two-step (sensation followed by perception) process?   pp. 76–77

▶ What fundamental assumption does a researcher make when depriving an organism of sensory experience and then measuring behavior?   pp. 78–79

The Visual System

Imagine that you are in a house at night when the power goes out and you are left in total darkness. You hear creaking sounds but have no idea where they are coming from. You stub your toe on the coffee table, then frantically grope along the walls until you reach the kitchen, where you fumble through the drawers in search of a flashlight.

Human beings derive more information in sight than through any other sense. By some estimates, the eyes contain 70 percent of all the body's sense receptors. Although eyes respond to pressure, the appropriate stimulus for vision is **electromagnetic radiation**—the entire spectrum of waves initiated by charged particles. The electromagnetic spectrum includes visible light, gamma rays, X-rays, ultraviolet rays, infrared rays, radar waves, broadcast bands, and AC circuits (see Figure 3.2 on page 80). **Light** is the very small portion of those wavelengths that is visible to the eye. It may come directly from a source or be reflected from an object.

The Structure of the Eye

Figure 3.3 on page 81 shows the major structures of the human eye. Light first passes through the *cornea*—a small, transparent bulge covering over both the *pupil* (the dark opening in the center of the eye) and the pigmented *iris*. The iris either constricts to make the pupil smaller or dilates to make it larger. Behind the pupil is the *lens,* which is about 4 millimeters thick. Together, the cornea, the pupil, the iris, and the lens form images in much the same way as a camera shutter and camera lens do. The *retina,* which lines the back of the eye, is like the film in a camera: It captures an image. Constriction of the iris makes the pupil smaller, improving the quality of the image on the retina and increasing the depth of focus—the distance of the visual field that is in sharp focus. This action also helps control the amount of light entering the eye.

Electromagnetic radiation: [Ee-LEK-tro-mag-NET-ick] The entire spectrum of waves initiated by charged particles.

Light: The portion of the electromagnetic spectrum visible to the eye.

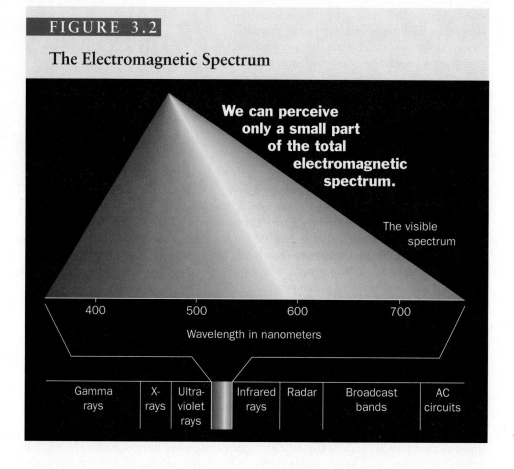

FIGURE 3.2

The Electromagnetic Spectrum

We can perceive only a small part of the total electromagnetic spectrum.

The visible spectrum

400   500   600   700

Wavelength in nanometers

| Gamma rays | X-rays | Ultra-violet rays | | Infrared rays | Radar | Broadcast bands | AC circuits |

When people's eyeballs are not perfectly shaped, how is their vision affected (see Figure 3.4 on page 82)? Some people are **myopic,** or *nearsighted*—able to see things that are close to them but having trouble seeing objects at a distance. Others are **hyperopic,** or *farsighted*—having trouble seeing things up close but able to see objects at a distance. Near- and farsightedness occur because the image that is cast on the back of the eye is not focused well.

The *retina* consists of 10 layers of cells. Of these, the most important are the **photoreceptors** (the light-sensitive cells), the bipolar cells, and the ganglion cells. After light passes through several layers of other kinds of cells, it strikes the photoreceptor layer, which consists of *rods* (rod-shaped receptors) and *cones* (cone-shaped receptors); these receptors will be described in detail later. In this layer, the light breaks down *photopigments* (light-sensitive chemicals), which causes an electrochemical change in the rods and cones; and the electrical energy is transferred to the next major layer, the *bipolar cells*. The process by which the perceptual system analyzes stimuli and converts them into electrical impulses is **transduction,** or *coding*.

Each eye contains more than 120 million rods and 6 million cones. These millions of photoreceptors do not have individual pathways to the higher visual centers in the brain. Instead, through the process of *convergence*, neural electrochemical signals from rods come together onto a single bipolar cell. At the same time, hundreds of cones synapse and converge onto other bipolar cells.

Myopic: [my-OP-ick] Able to see things that are close but having trouble seeing objects at a distance. Also known as *nearsighted*.

Hyperopic: [HY-per-OP-ick] Having trouble seeing things that are nearby but able to see objects at a distance. Also known as *farsighted*.

Photoreceptors: The light-sensitive cells in the retina: rods and cones.

Transduction: The process by which the perceptual system analyzes stimuli and converts them into electrical impulses. Also known as *coding*.

FIGURE 3.3

The Main Structures of the Eye

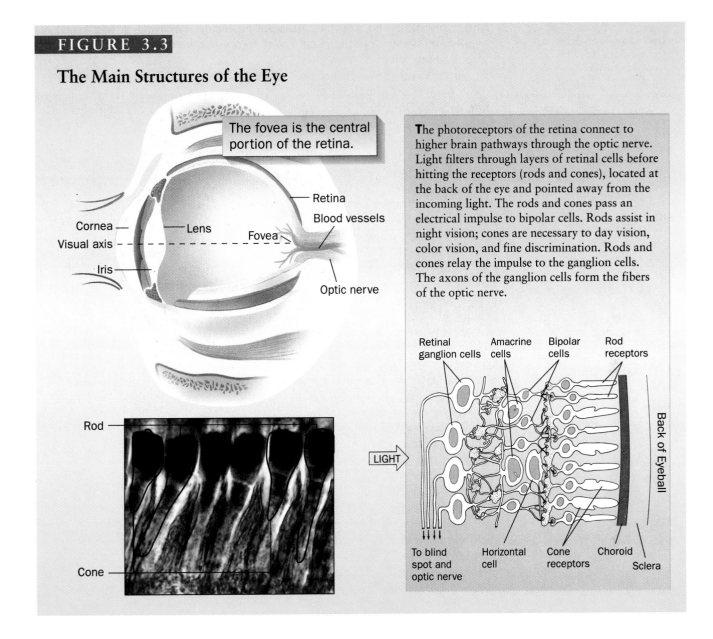

The fovea is the central portion of the retina.

Cornea

Lens

Visual axis

Iris

Retina

Blood vessels

Fovea

Optic nerve

The photoreceptors of the retina connect to higher brain pathways through the optic nerve. Light filters through layers of retinal cells before hitting the receptors (rods and cones), located at the back of the eye and pointed away from the incoming light. The rods and cones pass an electrical impulse to bipolar cells. Rods assist in night vision; cones are necessary to day vision, color vision, and fine discrimination. Rods and cones relay the impulse to the ganglion cells. The axons of the ganglion cells form the fibers of the optic nerve.

Rod

Cone

Retinal ganglion cells

Amacrine cells

Bipolar cells

Rod receptors

Back of Eyeball

LIGHT

To blind spot and optic nerve

Horizontal cell

Cone receptors

Choroid

Sclera

From the bipolar cells, electrochemical energy is transferred to the *ganglion cell layer.* A number of bipolar cells synapse and converge onto each ganglion cell (there are about 1 million ganglion cells). The axons of the ganglion cells make up the *optic nerve,* where information that was initially received by the rods and cones is carried via higher pathways in the nervous system. Still further coding takes place at the brain's **visual cortex,** or *striate cortex.* The visual cortex is the most important layer of the brain's occipital lobe; it is the location at which signals from the lateral geniculate body are processed and visual information receives complex analysis.

Rods and Cones. The *duplicity theory of vision,* which is now universally accepted, asserts that there are two separate receptor systems in the retina. It also states that rods and cones are structurally different and are used to accomplish different tasks. Cones are tightly packed in the center of the retina, or *fovea,* and are used for day vision, color vision, and fine discrimination. Rods (and some cones) are found on the rest of the retina (the periphery) and are used predominantly for night vision

Visual cortex: The first and most important layer of the brain's occipital lobe, which receives information from the lateral geniculate nucleus. Also known as the *striate cortex.*

Dark adaptation: Increased sensitivity to light in a dark environment. When a person moves from a light environment to a dark one, chemicals in the photoreceptors regenerate and return to their inactive pre-light-adapted state, which results in an increase in sensitivity.

(see Figure 3.5). The fact that cones are especially important in fine visual discrimination is shown in the visual acuity tests you take when you apply for a driver's license. A *visual acuity test* measures the resolution capacity of the visual system—the ability to see fine details. This ability is principally mediated by cones. You do best on these tests in a well-lit room (cones operate at high light levels) and when the test is presented to your central (foveal) vision (again, more cones are in the center of the retina than in any other place).

If you go from a well-lit lobby into a dark theater, you will experience a brief period of low light sensitivity, during which you will be unable to distinguish empty seats. Within 30 minutes, you will have almost fully adapted to the dark and will be far more light-sensitive. Our eyes are always in some state of light or dark adaptation. Rods and cones are sensitive to light, but in a well-lit room they are less sensitive than they are after having been in the dark. **Dark adaptation** is the increase in sensitivity that occurs when the illumination level changes from high to low. It is the process by which chemicals in the photoreceptors (rods and cones) regenerate and return to their inactive state and by which the light sensitivity of the visual system increases. Of course, after leaving a

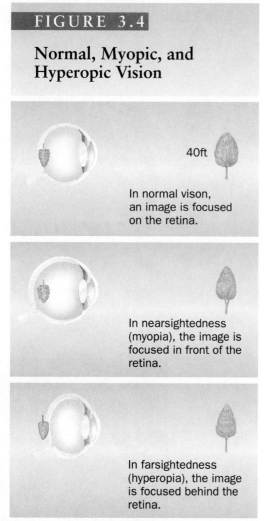

FIGURE 3.4

Normal, Myopic, and Hyperopic Vision

40ft

In normal vison, an image is focused on the retina.

In nearsightedness (myopia), the image is focused in front of the retina.

In farsightedness (hyperopia), the image is focused behind the retina.

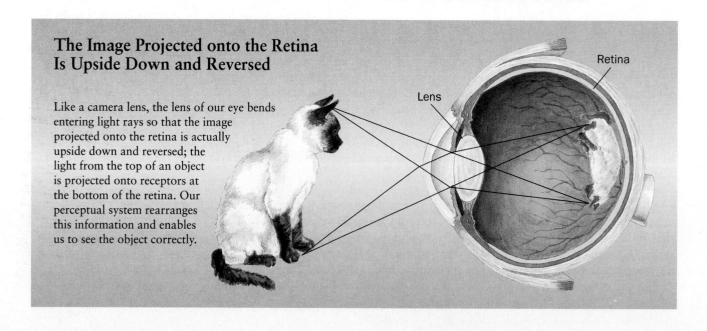

The Image Projected onto the Retina Is Upside Down and Reversed

Like a camera lens, the lens of our eye bends entering light rays so that the image projected onto the retina is actually upside down and reversed; the light from the top of an object is projected onto receptors at the bottom of the retina. Our perceptual system rearranges this information and enables us to see the object correctly.

Lens

Retina

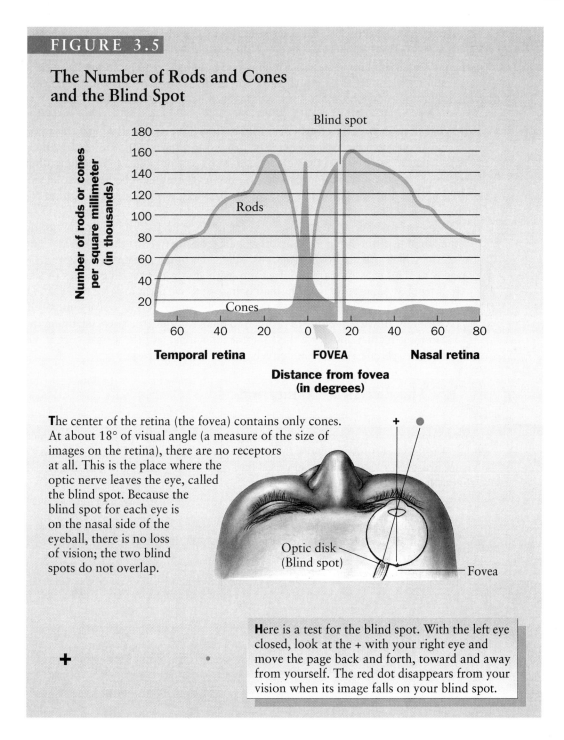

FIGURE 3.5

The Number of Rods and Cones and the Blind Spot

The center of the retina (the fovea) contains only cones. At about 18° of visual angle (a measure of the size of images on the retina), there are no receptors at all. This is the place where the optic nerve leaves the eye, called the blind spot. Because the blind spot for each eye is on the nasal side of the eyeball, there is no loss of vision; the two blind spots do not overlap.

Here is a test for the blind spot. With the left eye closed, look at the + with your right eye and move the page back and forth, toward and away from yourself. The red dot disappears from your vision when its image falls on your blind spot.

dark theater and returning to the afternoon sunlight, you must squint or shade your eyes until they become adapted to the light.

Figure 3.6 on page 84 shows a dark adaptation curve. The first part of the curve is determined by cones, the second part by rods. The data for such curves are obtained from experiments with subjects who possess only rods or cones. Typically, a subject is first shown bright light for 2 minutes. The light is then turned off, and the subject waits in total darkness for 1 minute. Next, a very dim test spot of light is turned on for half a second and the subject is asked if he or she sees it. Usually, the subject will report seeing the test spot only after several successive presentations, because dark

FIGURE 3.6

A Dark Adaptation Curve

The dashed line represents a typical overall dark adaptation curve.

Rods only

Cones only

Intensity of light to produce vision

0   10   20   30   40

Time in the dark (minutes)

The two solid lines represent separate dark adaptation for rods and cones. The process of light and dark adaptation occurs continually as people's eyes are exposed to different light intensities. Most of the dark adaptation takes place in the first 10 minutes.

Optic chiasm: [KI-azm] The point at which optic nerve fibers from the nasal and temporal sides of the eye cross over and project to the other side of the brain.

adaptation occurs gradually. The speed at which the photochemicals in the rods and cones regenerate determines the shape of the two parts of the curve. This is why, when you are driving along a road at night, you may have trouble seeing clearly for a few minutes after a car drives toward you with its high beams on; the photochemicals in the rods take some time to regenerate to their dark-adapted state.

Higher Pathways. As electrical impulses leave the retina through the optic nerve, they proceed to higher centers of the brain (see Figure 3.7). Knowledge about the way visual structures are connected to the brain not only aids psychologists but also enables physicians to diagnose many conditions, including whether a stroke victim with poor vision has a blood clot that is obstructing circulation in the right hemisphere of the brain.

Each eye is connected to both sides of the brain, with half of its impulses going to the left side of the brain and the other half crossing over to the right side. The point at which the crossover occurs is called the **optic chiasm** (see Figures 3.7 and 3.8). This crossover of impulses allows the brain to process two sets of signals from an image and helps human beings perceive form in three dimensions. If the optic nerves are severed at the optic chiasm, vision is sharply impaired. Normally, however, impulses proceed to higher brain structures, including the lateral geniculate nucleus, the superior colliculus, and the striate cortex. Of course, people are seldom actively aware of the process.

The Electrical Connection

Vision and other perceptual processes are electrochemical in nature. When receptors in the perceptual systems are stimulated, the information is coded and sent to the brain for interpretation and further analysis. Exciting research with a visual prosthesis—a device to help the blind see—is now under way, with positive early results (Bak et al., 1990).

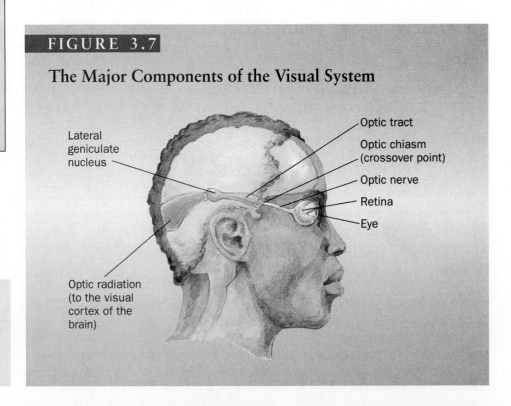

FIGURE 3.7

The Major Components of the Visual System

Lateral geniculate nucleus

Optic tract

Optic chiasm (crossover point)

Optic nerve

Retina

Eye

Optic radiation (to the visual cortex of the brain)

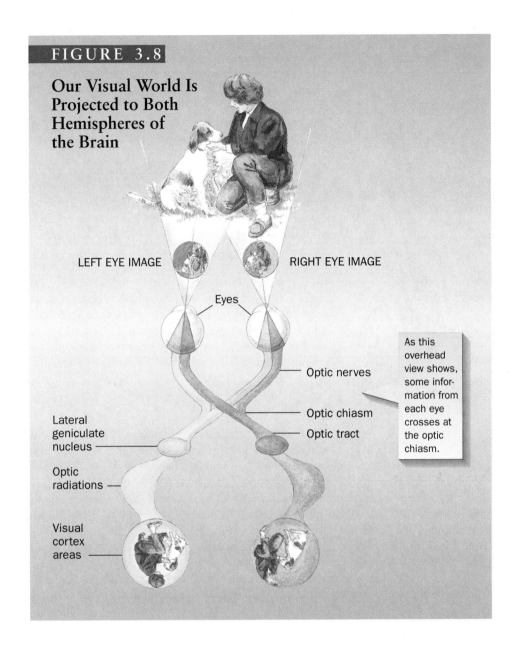

FIGURE 3.8

Our Visual World Is Projected to Both Hemispheres of the Brain

LEFT EYE IMAGE

RIGHT EYE IMAGE

Eyes

Optic nerves

Optic chiasm

Optic tract

As this overhead view shows, some information from each eye crosses at the optic chiasm.

Lateral geniculate nucleus

Optic radiations

Visual cortex areas

Much of our knowledge about how the brain processes electrochemical signals comes from studies of receptive fields. **Receptive fields** are the areas of the retina that, when stimulated, produce a change in the firing of cells in the visual system (see Figure 3.9 on page 86). For example, specific cells will fire, or become active, if a vertical line is presented to the retina but not if a horizontal line is presented. David Hubel and Torsten Wiesel (1962) found cells in the receptive fields that are sensitive to the position, length, movement, color, or intensity of a line. They characterized the cells as simple, complex, or hypercomplex. *Simple cells* respond to the shape and size of lights that stimulate the receptive field. *Complex cells* respond most vigorously to the movement of light in one direction. *Hypercomplex cells* are the most specific; they respond only to a line of the correct length and orientation that moves in the proper direction.

Hubel and Wiesel further learned that cells, especially those in the center of the visual cortex, are organized in columns; thus, lines with a single orientation or width

Receptive fields: The areas of the retina that, when stimulated, produce a change in the firing of cells in the visual system.

FIGURE 3.9

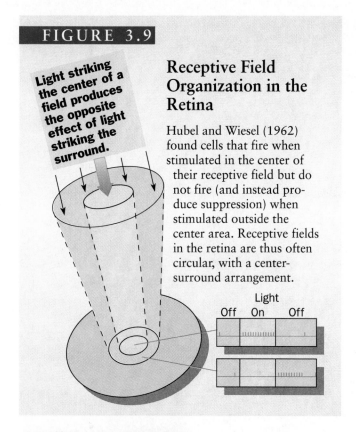

Light striking the center of a field produces the opposite effect of light striking the surround.

Light
Off   On   Off

Receptive Field Organization in the Retina

Hubel and Wiesel (1962) found cells that fire when stimulated in the center of their receptive field but do not fire (and instead produce suppression) when stimulated outside the center area. Receptive fields in the retina are thus often circular, with a center-surround arrangement.

stimulate cells that cut across several, or even all, layers of the visual cortex. Coding becomes more complex as electrical information proceeds through the visual system to higher centers (Burr, Morrone, & Spinelli, 1989). The work of Hubel and Wiesel, which has been supported by other noted researchers (e.g., DeValois, Thorell, & Albrecht, 1985), earned them a Nobel prize in 1981.

Hirsch and Spinelli (1971) conducted a series of experiments in which they controlled the visual experiences of newborn kittens. The kittens wore goggles that let them perceive either vertical lines or horizontal lines. When the goggles were later removed, kittens raised with only horizontal experiences bumped into chair legs (vertical) but could leap into a chair seat (horizontal); kittens raised with only vertical experiences had problems with horizontal surfaces (Blakemore & Cooper, 1970). Such studies indicate that although most of the connections in the visual system are present in newborns, the proper functioning of the system is sensitive to and depends on experience.

Eye Movements

Your eyes are constantly in motion. They search for familiar faces in a crowded classroom, scan a page of headlines and articles in a newspaper, and follow a baseball hit high into right field for a home run. Research on eye movements reveals what people are looking at, how long they look at it, and perhaps where they will look next. It also helps psychologists understand some visual problems, such as reading disabilities. Zangwill and Blakemore (1972) studied the eye movements of a man who had difficulty reading. They found that he was moving his eyes from right to left across the page, rather than in the usual left-to-right direction. We know that eye movements depend on the context in which they are measured. The eye movements of a reader are different from those of a keyboard operator, even when both are examining the same material, because the text viewed by the keyboard operator is not processed for meaning the way it is by a reader (Inhoff, Morris, & Calabrese, 1986).

Rapid movements of the eyes from one point to another, called **saccades,** are the most common type of eye movement. These are the voluntary movements people make when reading, driving, or looking for an object. The eye can make only four or five saccades in a second. The movement of the eye takes only about 20 to 50 milliseconds, but there is a delay of about 200 to 250 milliseconds before the next movement can be made (C. M. Harris et al., 1988). We use eye fixations to form representations of the visual world, probably by integrating successive glances into memory (Irwin, Brown, & Sun, 1988). This requires that observers move their eyes, pay attention to key elements of a visual scene, and exert eye movement control in a careful, systematic manner (Rayner & Pollatsek, 1992).

Eye movements have been used to determine the *perceptual span*—the size of the region a person sees when fixating, or staring; for example, it is the number of letters you see when you fixate at a specific point on this page. Research shows that people use information gathered in both central (foveal) vision and peripheral vision (noncentral regions of the eye) to determine the location of their next eye movements; this ultimately affects the size of the perceptual span (Pollatsek, Rayner, &

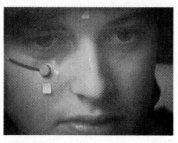

Researchers are studying the relationship of eye movements and task performance. The frequency and duration of eye blinks, monitored by electrodes, can determine when and how well a person is learning. (Photo courtesy of CNN.)

Saccades: [sack-ADZ] Rapid movements of the eyes from one point to another.

FIGURE 3.10

Scan Paths Are Highly Individual

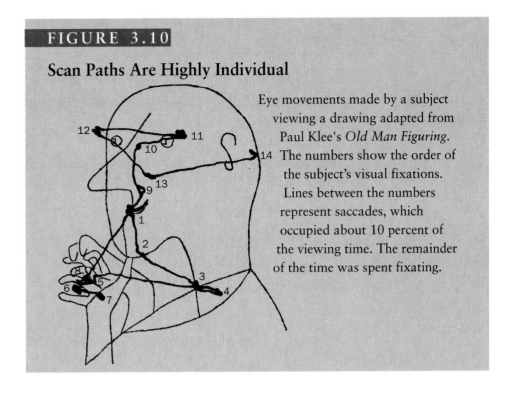

Eye movements made by a subject viewing a drawing adapted from Paul Klee's *Old Man Figuring*. The numbers show the order of the subject's visual fixations. Lines between the numbers represent saccades, which occupied about 10 percent of the viewing time. The remainder of the time was spent fixating.

Balota, 1986; Rayner & Fisher, 1987). We also know that people tend to direct their gaze to a point just to the left of center of words when they are reading. This site (left of center) may help them make inferences about the rest of the word (McConkie et al., 1988). A key assertion of this line of research is that eye movements can tell researchers a great deal about cognitive processes in general, reading in particular (Rayner, 1993), and, as is shown next, the perception of scenes and pictures.

In a study of eye movements and perception, Noton and Stark (1971) presented subjects with a series of pictures and told them they would have to identify the pictures later in different groupings. The researchers recorded the subjects' eye movements during the learning period and in subsequent testing. Each subject fixated on the same area and followed identical scan paths for a specific picture in both phases of the experiment. The researchers suggested that in perceiving and recognizing forms, people use a characteristic pattern of eye movement—a pattern that follows a fixed path from one feature to the next (see Figure 3.10). Noton and Stark concluded that eye movements are important to the way the brain stores information and that there are significant individual differences among scan paths. Yet eye movement research shows more similarities across cultures than between individuals; in cross-cultural research, Western, Middle Eastern, and East Asian cultures show similar eye movement patterns (Abed, 1991.)

Color Vision

Think of all the different shades of blue (navy blue, sky blue, baby blue, royal blue, turquoise, aqua). If you are like most people, you have no trouble discriminating among a wide range of colors. Color depends on the wavelength of light particles that stimulate the photoreceptors. It has three psychological dimensions: *hue, brightness,* and *saturation.* These dimensions correspond to three physical properties of light: *wavelength, intensity,* and *purity.*

Hue: The psychological property of light referred to as color, determined by the wavelength reflected from an object.

Brightness: The lightness or darkness of reflected light, determined in large part by a light's intensity.

Saturation: The depth of hue of reflected light, as determined by the homogeneity of the wavelengths contained in the light. Also known as *purity*.

Trichromatic theory: [try-kroe-MAT-ick] The visual theory, stated by Young and Helmholtz, that all colors can be made by mixing three basic colors: red, green, and blue. Also known as the *Young-Helmholtz theory*.

When people speak of the color of an object, they are referring to its **hue**—whether the light reflected from the object looks red, blue, orange, or some other color. *Hue* is a psychological term, because objects themselves do not possess color. Rather, people's perception of color is determined by how their eyes and brain interpret reflected wavelengths. In the visible spectrum, a different hue is associated with each wavelength. Light with a wavelength of 400 nanometers looks blue; light with a wavelength of 700 nanometers looks red.

The second psychological dimension of color is **brightness**—how light or dark the hue of an object appears. It is affected by three variables: (1) The greater the intensity of reflected light, the brighter the object. (2) The longer the wavelength of reflected light, the less bright the object. (3) The nearer the wavelengths are to being in the 500 to 600 nanometer range, the more sensitive the photoreceptors (see Figure 3.11). This is why school buses and fire engines are usually painted yellow—they are more visible to motorists.

The third psychological dimension of color is **saturation,** or *purity*—saturation is the depth and richness of hue of reflected light, determined by the purity of the wavelengths contained in the light. Few objects reflect light that is totally pure. Usually they reflect a mixture of wavelengths. Pure, saturated light has a narrow band of wavelengths and, thus, a narrow range of perceived color. A saturated red light with no blue, yellow, or white in it, for example, appears as a very deep red. Unsaturated colors are produced by a wider band of wavelengths. Unsaturated red light can appear to be light pink or dark red, or it can look muddy because its wider range of wavelengths makes it less pure. (See Figure 3.12.)

Theories of Color Vision. How does the brain code and process color? Two 19th century scientists, Thomas Young and Hermann Von Helmholtz, working independently, proposed that different types of cones provide the basis for color coding in the visual system. *Color coding* is the ability to discriminate among colors on the basis of differences in wavelength. According to the **trichromatic theory,** or *Young-Helmholtz theory,* all colors can be made by mixing three basic colors: red, green, and blue. (*Trichromatic* means "three colors"; *tri* means "three" and *chroma* means "color.") All cones are assumed to respond to all wavelengths that stimulate them;

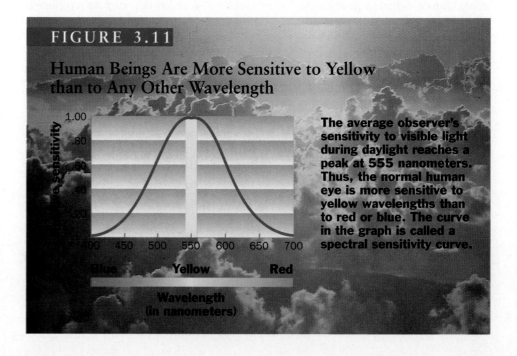

FIGURE 3.11

Human Beings Are More Sensitive to Yellow than to Any Other Wavelength

The average observer's sensitivity to visible light during daylight reaches a peak at 555 nanometers. Thus, the normal human eye is more sensitive to yellow wavelengths than to red or blue. The curve in the graph is called a spectral sensitivity curve.

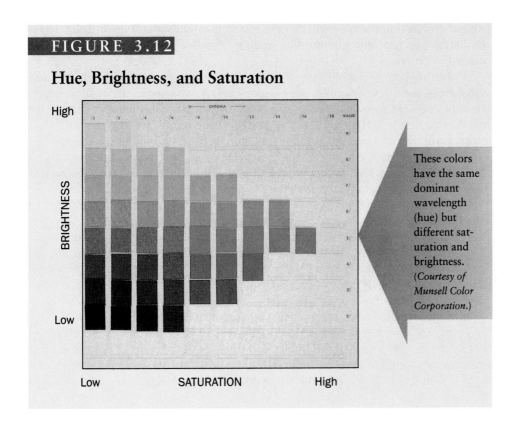

FIGURE 3.12

Hue, Brightness, and Saturation

These colors have the same dominant wavelength (hue) but different saturation and brightness. (*Courtesy of Munsell Color Corporation.*)

but each type of cone—red, green, or blue—responds maximally to the red, green, or blue wavelength (see Figure 3.13). The combined neural output of the three types of cones provides the information that enables a person to distinguish color. If the neural output of one type of cone is sufficiently greater than that of the others, a

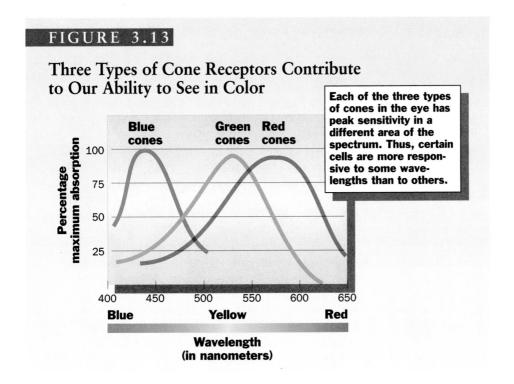

FIGURE 3.13

Three Types of Cone Receptors Contribute to Our Ability to See in Color

Each of the three types of cones in the eye has peak sensitivity in a different area of the spectrum. Thus, certain cells are more responsive to some wavelengths than to others.

person's perception of color will be determined mainly by that type of color receptor. Because each person's neurons are unique, it is likely that each of us sees color somewhat differently.

Unfortunately, the trichromatic theory does not explain some specific visual phenomena well. For example, it does not explain why some colors look deeper when placed next to other colors (color contrast). It does not explain why people asked to name the basic colors nearly always name more than three. Further, the trichromatic theory does not explain well studies of **color blindness**—the inability to perceive different hues. For example, when people have color deficiencies, they often cannot discriminate colors successfully in two areas of the visual spectrum. In 1887, to solve some of the problems left unsolved by the trichromatic theory, Ewald Herring proposed another theory of color vision—the **opponent-process theory.** This theory assumes that there are six primary colors to which people respond and that there are three types of receptors: red-green, blue-yellow, and black-white. Every receptor fires in response to all wavelengths; but in each pair of receptors, one fires maximally to one wavelength. Maximum firing to red, for example, is accompanied by a low rate of firing to green. Opponent-process theory explains color contrast and color blindness better than the trichromatic theory.

Both the trichromatic theory and the opponent-process theory have received support from research (e.g., Hurvich & Jameson, 1974). Studies of the chemistry and absorptive properties of the retina show three classes of cones. Thus, the trichromatic theory seems to describe accurately the coding at the retina (Marks, Dobell, & MacNichol, 1964). Support for the opponent-process theory comes from microelectrode studies of the lateral geniculate nucleus in monkeys. (The lateral geniculate nucleus is one of the major visual projection areas in the visual system of both human beings and monkeys.) Cells in this nucleus respond differently to various wavelengths. When the eye is stimulated with light of a wavelength between 400 and 500 nanometers, some cells in the lateral geniculate nucleus decrease their rate of firing. If the eye is stimulated with a longer wavelength light, the firing rate increases (DeValois & Jacobs, 1968). This change is predicted by the opponent-process theory. Exactly how color information is transferred from the retina to the lateral geniculate nucleus remains to be discovered. Some of the data that helped test the trichromatic and opponent-process theories came from people with abnormal color vision.

Color Blindness. In 1794, John Dalton, formulator of the atomic theory of matter, believed he had figured out why he couldn't distinguish his red stockings from his green ones. He reasoned that something blue in his eyeball absorbed red light and prevented him from seeing red. Dalton was not the first person to suffer from red-green color blindness, but he was the first to describe it scientifically.

Most human beings have normal color vision and are considered **trichromats**—people requiring only the three primary colors to see any color. A very few people (fewer than 1 percent) do not see any color. These people, known as **monochromats,** are totally color-blind and cannot discriminate among wavelengths, often because they lack cone receptors in their retinas (Boynton, 1988). The lack of a specific color-absorbing pigment or chemical in the cones makes accurate color discriminations impossible. Fortunately, most people with color deficiencies (about 8 percent of men and 1 percent of women) are only partially color-deficient (Nathans, 1989). **Dichromats**—people who can distinguish only two of the three basic hues—have deficiencies in either the red-green or the blue-yellow area. About 2 percent of men cannot discriminate between reds and greens (Wyszecki & Stiles, 1967). What does the world look like to a person who is a dichromat? People with color deficiencies see all the colors in a range of the electromagnetic spectrum as the same. For example,

Color blindness: The inability to perceive different hues.

Opponent-process theory: The theory, proposed by Ewald Herring, that color is coded by stimulation of one of three pairs of receptors; each pair of receptors is assumed to operate in an antagonistic way so that stimulation by one wavelength produces excitation in one pair, and inhibition to its antagonistic pair.

Trichromats: [TRY-kroe-MATZ] People who experience color vision in the most common way and who require only the three primary colors to see any color.

Monochromats: [MON-o-kroe-MATZ] People whose retinas contain only rods and who therefore cannot perceive any color.

Dichromats: [DIE-kroe-MATZ] People who can distinguish only two of the three basic hues.

Color blindness, the inability to see certain colors, is a hereditary condition in which the proteins of one or more cones either do not function or are inadequate in number. The balloons on the right are shown as they might appear to a dichromat with a red-green deficiency.

to a person with a blue deficiency, all greens, blues, and violets look the same; a person with a red-green deficiency may see red, green, and yellow as yellow. Many color-blind individuals have distorted color responses in several areas of the electromagnetic spectrum; that is, they have trouble with several colors.

The precise role of genetics in color blindness is not clear, but we know that it is transmitted genetically from mothers to their male offspring. The high number of men who are color-blind, compared to women, is due to the way the genetic information is coded and passed on to each generation. The genetic transmission occurs on the 23rd pair of chromosomes and results from inherited alterations in the genes on the X chromosomes that are responsible for cone pigments (Nathans, 1989).

FOCUS

► What is the evidence for the duplicity theory of vision? pp. 81–82

► What do receptive fields in the retina tell researchers about the perceptual process?   pp. 85–86

► What is the evidence in support of the trichromatic and opponent-process theories of color?   pp. 88–90

Visual Perception

The electrochemical processes that stimulate vision and the subsequent changes that take place in the pathways that lead to higher visual centers are crucial parts of the perceptual process. However, many perceptual experiences involve past events in addition to current stimulation. Integrating our previous experiences with new events makes our perceptual encounters more meaningful. For example, it is only with experience that we know that an object stays the same size and shape when it is moved away from our immediate vision. In the next section, we will look at a range of visual perceptual phenomena that depend especially on the integration of past experience with current experiences.

At close range Seurat's paintings would appear unintelligible; the forms and objects gain definition when seen as a whole from a distance.

Perception of Form: Constancy

Everyday experience shows that people fill in missing information. For example, if your friend is wearing dark sunglasses that conceal most of her face, you will probably still recognize her. Similarly, impressionist artists count on people's ability to infer a complete object from dots of paint on canvas, and cartoonists use exaggerated features to portray well-known people. Understanding how human beings perceive form and space helps architects to design buildings and designers to create furniture and clothes. Perception of form involves the interpretation of stimuli of different sizes, shapes, and depths to create a unit. Two important activities in form perception are recognizing forms at a distance and recognizing forms that appear to have changed size or shape.

Size Constancy. People can generally judge the size of an object, even if the size of its image on the retina changes. For example, you can estimate the height of a 6-foot man from 50 feet away, with a small image on the retina, as well as from only 5 feet away, with a much larger image on the retina. **Size constancy** is the ability of the perceptual system to recognize that an object remains constant in size regardless of its distance from the observer or the size of its image on the retina.

Three variables determine a person's ability to maintain size constancy: (1) previous experience with the true size of objects, (2) the distance between the object and the person, and (3) the presence of surrounding objects (Day & McKenzie, 1977). As an object is moved farther away, the size of its image on the retina decreases and its perceived distance increases. These two processes always work together. Moreover, as an object is moved away, its perceived size does not change in relation to that of stationary objects. This is why knowing the size of surrounding objects helps people determine the moved object's distance as well as its actual size. (See illustrations on pages 98a & b.)

Researchers have studied how experience helps people establish and maintain size constancy. T. G. R. Bower (1966) trained 50- to 60-day-old infants to look toward a specific object by reinforcing their direction of gaze (the reinforcement was by an adult saying "peek-a-boo"). He then placed other objects of different sizes at various distances from the infants so that the sizes of their retinal images varied. Finally, he arranged the objects so that the small ones were close to the infants and the large ones were farther away, causing the sizes of retinal images to be the same. In all these situations, the infants showed size constancy. They turned their heads only toward the original reinforced object, not toward the other objects that produced images of the same size on the retina. It is clear that infants attain size constancy by the age of 6 months and probably as early as 4 months (McKenzie, Tootell, & Day, 1980; Luger, Bower, & Wishart, 1983).

Hollywood special effects artists used the brain's tendency to judge an object's size by comparing it with surrounding objects to convince moviegoers that a 6-inch clay model of an ape was the giant King Kong. However, size constancy can also work to a filmmaker's disadvantage. In the early days of Hollywood, a Western was made that attempted to be humorous by starring a cast of dwarfs. The sheriff, the bad guys, and the heroine were all of diminutive stature. However, because the director also downsized all the props and settings (for example, using Shetland ponies for the horses), the characters appeared normal-sized, and the movie lost its potential.

Shape Constancy. Another important aspect of form perception is **shape constancy**—the ability to recognize a shape despite changes in the angle or position from which it is viewed. For example, even though you usually see trees perpendicular to the ground, you can recognize a tree when it has been chopped down and is

Size constancy: The ability of the perceptual system to know that an object remains constant in size regardless of its distance from the observer or the size of its image on the retina.

Shape constancy: The ability to recognize a shape despite changes in the orientation or angle from which it is viewed.

lying on the ground. Similarly, an ice cream cone looks circular when you view it from above; yet you perceive it as an ice cream cone even when you view it from the side, where it appears more triangular than circular.

Depth Perception

For centuries, Zen landscape artists have used the principles of perception to create seemingly expansive, rugged gardens out of tiny plots of land. The gardeners place smaller, less detailed, and darker objects (such as round stones and smooth-barked shrubs) at the rear of the garden and light-colored, well-textured objects (such as craggy rocks and rough-barked trees) near the front to create the illusion of depth. They also make a tapering trail that winds back to the rear of the garden, where it disappears behind a rock or tree, leading the viewer to assume it continues for some distance.

Although the Zen landscape artist can fool the eye, you judge the distance of objects every day when you drive a car, catch a ball, or take a picture. You estimate your distance from the object and the distance between that object and another one. Closely associated with these two tasks is the ability to see in three dimensions— that is, in terms of height, width, and depth. Both *monocular* (one-eyed) *cues* and *binocular* (two-eyed) *cues* are used in depth perception. Binocular cues predominate at close distances, and monocular cues are used for distant scenes and two-dimensional fields of view, such as paintings.

Monocular Depth Cues. Depth cues that do not depend on the use of both eyes are **monocular depth cues** (see the illustrations on pages 98a & b). Two important monocular depth cues deal with the effects of motion on perception. The first, *motion parallax,* occurs when a moving observer stares at a fixed point. The objects behind that point appear to move in the same direction as the observer; the objects in front of the point appear to move in the opposite direction. For example, if you stare at a fence while riding in a moving car, the trees behind the fence rails seem to move in the same direction as the car (forward) and the bushes in front of the rails seem to move in the opposite direction (backward). Motion parallax also affects the speed at which objects appear to move. Objects at a greater distance from the moving observer appear to move more slowly than objects that are closer.

The second monocular depth cue derived from movement is the *kinetic depth effect.* Objects that look flat when they are stationary appear to be three-dimensional when set in motion. When two-dimensional projections—such as pictures of squares, cubes, or rods shown on a computer screen—are rotated, they appear to have three dimensions.

Other monocular depth cues come from the stimulus itself; they are often seen in photographs and paintings. For example, larger or taller objects are usually perceived to be closer than smaller ones, particularly in relation to surrounding objects. In addition, *linear perspective* affects perception; this is based on the principle that distant objects appear to be closer together than nearer objects. Two parallel lines in a painting will appear to converge as they recede into the distance (see the illustration on page 98a).

Another monocular cue for depth is *interposition.* When one object blocks out part of another, the first appears to be closer. A fourth monocular cue is *texture.* Surfaces that have little texture or detail seem to be in the distance. Artists often use the clues of *highlighting* and *shadowing.* Highlighted (light) objects appear close; shadowed (dark) objects appear to be farther away. In addition, the perceptual system picks up other information from shadowing, including the curvature of surfaces (Cavanagh & Leclerc, 1989).

Monocular depth cues: [mah-NAHK-you-ler] Depth cues that do not require the use of two eyes.

Still another monocular depth cue is *atmospheric perspective,* which relates to the wavelengths themselves. Distant mountains often look blue, for example, because long (red) wavelengths are more easily scattered as they pass through the air, allowing more short (blue) wavelengths to reach our eyes. Leonardo da Vinci used this phenomenon in his paintings; he even developed an equation for how much blue pigment should be mixed with the normal color of an object so it would appear as close or as far away as he wished. Michelangelo's angels seem to float off the ceiling of the Sistine Chapel because he used color so effectively to portray depth.

The preceding monocular depth cues are derived from the stimulus. The depth cue of accommodation, however, is not. If a person looks from one object to another one at a different distance, the lenses of the eye will accommodate—that is, change shape to adapt to the depth of focus. This cue is available from each eye separately. **Accommodation** is the change in the shape of the lens that enables the observer to keep an object in focus on the retina when the object is moved or when the choice of objects for focus changes. It is controlled by muscles attached to the lens, which provide information about the shape of the lens to the higher processing systems in the brain.

Binocular Depth Cues. Most people, even infants, use **binocular depth cues** as well as monocular depth cues. One important binocular depth cue is **retinal disparity**—the slight difference in the visual image projected on each retina. Retinal disparity occurs because the eyes are physically separated (by the bridge of the nose), causing them to see an object from slightly different angles.

To see how retinal disparity works, hold a finger up in front of some distant object. Examine the object first with one eye and then with the other eye. The finger will appear in different positions relative to the object. The closer the objects are to the eyes, the farther apart their images on the retinas will be—and the greater the retinal disparity. Objects at a great distance produce little retinal disparity.

Another binocular depth cue is **convergence**—the movement of the eyes toward each other in order to keep information at corresponding points on the retina as an object moves closer to the observer. Like accommodation, convergence is controlled by muscles in the eye that convey information to the brain and thus provide a potent physiological depth cue for stimuli close to observers. Beyond 20 or 30 feet, the eyes are aimed pretty much in parallel, and the effect of this cue diminishes.

Illusions

Have you ever seen water ahead on the road, only to find it has disappeared a moment later as you drive by? You most likely have seen railroad tracks that appear to converge in the distance. When the normal visual process and depth cues seem to break down, we experience an optical illusion. An **illusion** is a perception of a physical stimulus that differs from the commonly expected appearance; many consider it a misperception of stimulation.

A common illusion is the *Müller-Lyer illusion,* in which two equal-length lines with arrows attached to their ends appear to be of different lengths. A similar illusion is the *Ponzo illusion* (sometimes called the railroad illusion), in which two horizontal lines of the same length, surrounded by slanted lines, appear to be of different lengths. (See Figure 3.14 for examples of these illusions and three others.) A natural illusion is the *moon illusion.* Although the actual size of the moon and the size of its image on the retina do not change, the moon appears about 30 percent larger when it is over the horizon than when it is overhead. The moon illusion is quite striking. In just a few minutes, the size of the moon appears to change from quite large to quite small. The moon illusion is even experienced in drawings, photographs, and paintings (Coren & Aks, 1990).

Accommodation: The change in the shape of the lens of the eye to keep an object in focus on the retina when the object moves closer to or farther away from the observer.

Binocular depth cues: Any visual cues for depth perception that require the use of both eyes.

Retinal disparity: The slight difference in the visual image projected on each retina.

Convergence: The movement of the eyes toward each other to keep information at corresponding points on the retina as an object moves closer to the observer.

Illusion: A perception of a physical stimulus that differs from normal expectations about its appearance.

FIGURE 3.14

Five Well-Known Illusions

In the Müller-Lyer and Ponzo illusions, lines of equal length appear different in length. The Müller-Lyer illusions show how the arrows usually represent "near corners" and "far corners." In the Zollner illusion, the short lines make the longer ones seem not parallel, even though they are. In the Wundt illusion, the center horizontal lines are parallel, even though they appear bent. In the Poggendorf illusion, the line disappears behind a solid and reappears in a position that seems wrong.

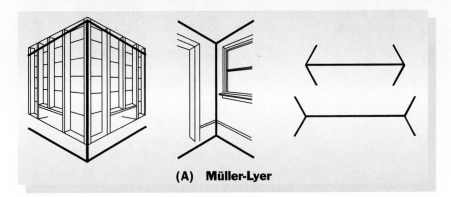

(A) Müller-Lyer

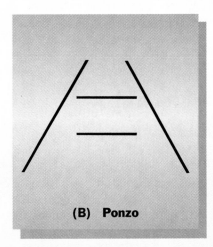

(B) Ponzo

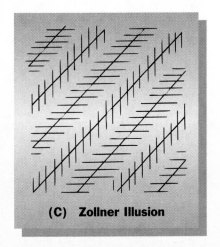

(C) Zollner Illusion

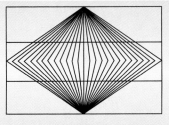

(D) Wundt Illusion

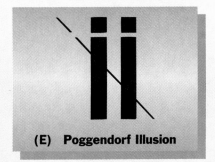

(E) Poggendorf Illusion

Three Well-Known Illusions

Two ambiguous figures. (A) shows a rabbit facing toward the right or a duck facing toward the left. (B) shows either an old woman in profile or a young woman whose head is turned slightly away.

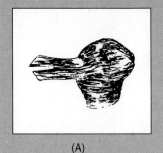

(A)   (B)

A drawing in which figure and ground can be reversed. You can see either two faces against a white background or a goblet against a dark background.

How do visual illusions work? No completely satisfactory explanations have been found. Recent theories account for them in terms of the backgrounds against which the objects are seen. These explanations are based on the observer's previous experiences and on well-developed perceptual constancies. (The Diversity box explores how cultural experiences affect the experience of illusions.)

The moon illusion, for example, is explained by the fact that, when seen overhead, the moon has a featureless background, whereas at the horizon objects are close to it. Objects in the landscape provide cues about distance through a number of means that change the observer's perception of the size of the moon (Restle, 1970; Baird, Wagner, & Fuld, 1990). To see how the moon illusion depends on landscape cues, try this: When the moon is at the horizon, bend over and look at it from between your legs. Since that position screens out some of the horizon cues, the magnitude of the illusion will be reduced.

The Ponzo illusion is similarly accounted for by the linear perspective provided by the slanted background lines. The Müller-Lyer illusion occurs because of the angle and shape of the arrows attached to the ends of the lines. Lines angled inward are often interpreted as far corners—those that are most distant from the observer. Lines angled outward are commonly interpreted as near corners—those that are closest to the observer. Therefore, lines with far-corner angles attached to them appear longer because their length is judged in a context of distance.

These are not the only ways of explaining illusions. Some researchers assert that people see the moon as a different size on the horizon than overhead because they judge it

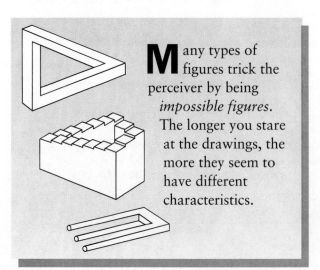

Many types of figures trick the perceiver by being *impossible figures.* The longer you stare at the drawings, the more they seem to have different characteristics.

DIVERSITY

Cross-Cultural Research on Illusions

A wonderful advertisement a number of years ago featured a 12-year-old African-American boy eating a thick deli sandwich. The caption: "You don't have to be Jewish to like Levy's rye bread." You also don't have to be Russian to appreciate Tchaikovsky; nor do you have to be from Ireland to like U2. Yet there is no doubt that artists bring to their work a nationalistic tone. George Gershwin's *Rhapsody in Blue* sounds distinctly American, as does jazz from New Orleans.

Each person brings a lifetime of experiences to the perceptual experience. This becomes especially clear as a result of research conducted cross-culturally; this research is exciting and illuminating but unfortunately limited in its extent. Cross-cultural research on illusions, for example, shows that the Müller-Lyer and Ponzo illusions are perceived differently by different cultures. Leibowitz (1971) conducted a series of studies on the Ponzo (railroad) illusion using both American subjects and subjects from Guam, where there were no railroads and perspective cues are far less prevalent than in the United States. Leibowitz had his participants judge the size of the Ponzo illusion drawn with straight lines; they also judged the illusion in photographs. He found that the size of the illusion increased for American students as he added more pictorial depth cues. Students from Guam showed few differences when more pictorial cues were added. Other differences also existed; for example, the students from Guam viewed depth differently from their American counterparts. The different cultures viewed the world in dissimilar ways.

Other illusions have been investigated with different cultural groups. For example, Pedersen and Wheeler (1983) compared the reactions of two groups of Navajos to the Müller-Lyer illusion. One group lived in rectangular houses, where the individuals had extensive experience with corners, angles, and oblique lines. The other group lived in traditional Navajo round houses, where early experiences included far fewer encounters with corners and angles. The researchers found that those who lived in angular houses were more susceptible to the Müller-Lyer illusion, which depends on angles. Some researchers say such illusions depend on the *carpenter effect,* because in Western culture carpenters use lines, angles, and geometry to build houses.

Although there is no systematic scientific research on the topic, musicians have long known that a person's experiences with Western music make 12-tone music and Indian and Asian melodies sound unfamiliar and dissonant. Our experience of music, like our experience of illusions, depends on early experiences. Research shows that people's visual and auditory perceptions are culturally dependent. Deregowski (1980) asserts that there is a dearth of non-Western studies—regrettably little evidence from other parts of the world and a distressingly modest number of studies from remote areas. He concludes in his review of studies of language, pictures, smell, and illusions that there exist cross-cultural differences that reflect people's cultures. Individuals from other cultures do not initially see illusions and some features of depth; but when key characteristics of pictures and scenes are pointed out, they often exclaim, "Oh, now I see it!" Yet their initial experiences often show a lack of the recognition that Western cultures have. For psychologists to develop truly comprehensive theories of perception, cross-cultural differences must be incorporated into them.

Illusions are not universal. For example, a Navajo living in a traditional round house such as this might not be susceptible to the Müller-Lyer illusion.

At odd angles and depths, the surfaces of this room are arranged so that these two people *appear* to be of different heights. In reality, they are the same height. This is the Ames room illusion.

like they judge other moving objects that pass through space. Because the moon does not get closer to them, they assume it is moving away. Objects that move away get smaller; hence the illusion of a change in the size of the moon (Reed, 1984). This explanation focuses on constancies but also takes account of movement, space, and the atmosphere.

Gestalt Laws of Organization

Gestalt psychologists (see page 9) suggest that conscious experience is more than the sum of its parts. They argue that the mind organizes the elements of experience to form something unique; they thus view the world in terms of perceptual frameworks. Analyzed as a whole experience, the patterns of a person's perceptions make sense. Gestalt psychologists—including Max Wertheimer, Kurt Koffka, and Wolfgang Köhler—greatly influenced early theories of form perception. These psychologists assumed (wrongly) that human perceptual processes reflect brain organization and that they could learn about the workings of the brain solely by studying perception. They focused their perceptual studies on the ways in which people experience form and organization. The early Gestaltists believed people organize each complex visual field into a coherent whole rather than seeing individual, unrelated elements. That is, they believed we see groups of elements, not fragmented parts. According to this idea, called the **law of Prägnanz,** items or stimuli that can be grouped together and seen as a whole, or a form, will be seen that way. Figure 3.15 (bottom left) shows a series of 16 dots that people tend to see as a square.

The law of Prägnanz as an organizing idea was based on principles of organization for the perception of figures, especially on contours, which help define figure-ground relationships. Gestalt psychologists focused on the nature of *figure-ground relationships,* contending that the *figures* (the main objects of sensory attention—the foregrounds) are perceived as distinct from the *grounds* (the backgrounds) on which they are presented. Gestalt psychologists developed the following series of laws (the first three of which are illustrated at the top of Figure 3.15) for predicting which areas of an ambiguous pattern would be seen as the figure (foreground) and which as the ground (background) (Hochberg, 1974, 1979):

▶ The *law of proximity:* Elements close to one another in space or time will be perceived as groups.

▶ The *law of similarity:* Similar items will be perceived in groups.

Law of Prägnanz: The Gestalt principle that when items or stimuli *can* be grouped together and seen as a whole, they *will* be.

FIGURE 3.15

Gestalt principles focus on organizing elements into the coherent wholes by which human beings perceive the world.

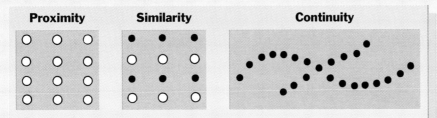

| Proximity | Similarity | Continuity |

According to the Gestalt law of proximity, the circles in the left panel appear to be arranged in vertical columns because items that are close together tend to be perceived as a unit. According to the Gestalt law of similarity, the filled and empty circles in the middle panel appear to be arranged in horizontal rows because similar items tend to be perceived in groups. According to the Gestalt law of continuity, an observer will predict where the next item should occur in the arrangement on the right because the group of items projects into space.

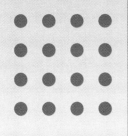

The law of Prägnanz: Items or stimuli that *can* be grouped together as a whole *will* be. These 16 dots are typically perceived as a square.

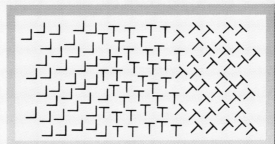

In a study asking people to divide these lines into two groups, Beck (1966) found that subjects generally placed the boundary between the upright and tilted *T*s rather than between the backward *L*s and upright *T*s. Beck argued that this result supports the Prägnanz principle.

▶ The *law of continuity:* A string of items will indicate where the next item in the string will be found.

▶ *Common fate principles:* Items that move or change together will be seen as a whole.

▶ The *law of closure:* Parts of a figure that are not presented will be filled in by the perceptual system.

J. Beck (1966) conducted a well-known study that examined Gestalt principles (see Figure 3.15, bottom right). However, Beck's work also showed that the principles are vague. They apply whether subjects choose orientation or shape to break up the figure, but they do not explain why orientation predominated in Beck's study.

Lift page to see illustrations on pages 98a & b.

Depth Perception

▶ **T**he ability to see in three dimensions—height, width, and depth—depends on both monocular and binocular depth cues.

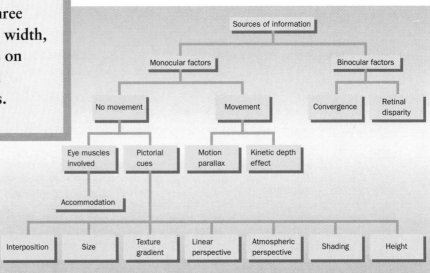

Sources of information
- **Monocular factors**
  - **No movement**
    - **Eye muscles involved**
      - Accommodation
    - **Pictorial cues**
  - **Movement**
    - **Motion parallax**
    - **Kinetic depth effect**
- **Binocular factors**
  - **Convergence**
  - **Retinal disparity**

Interposition | Size | Texture gradient | Linear perspective | Atmospheric perspective | Shading | Height

▶ **M**onocular cues such as linear perspective and interposition create the illusion of depth in art.

▶ **A** binocular cue such as convergence provides direct information to the brain, helping us interpret the world in three dimensions.

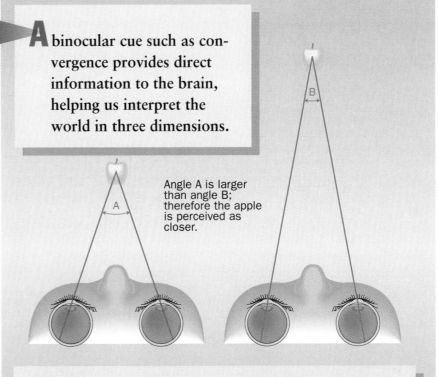

Angle A is larger than angle B; therefore the apple is perceived as closer.

When the eyes converge on a nearby object, the angle between them is greater than when they converge on a distant object. The brain uses this information in establishing both depth and distance.

Perceptual Constancies

SIZE CONSTANCY

Size constancy is the perceptual system's ability to recognize that an object remains the same size regardless of its distance from an observer or the size of its image on the retina.

The size of the image on the retina gets larger or smaller as you move closer to or farther away from an object. But thanks to *size constancy*, you still perceive the object as being the same size.

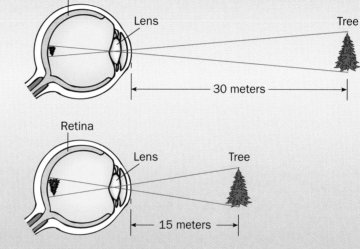

Retina
Lens
Tree
30 meters

Retina
Lens
Tree
15 meters

SHAPE CONSTANCY

A door is a door is a door . . . whether open, shut, or viewed at an angle.

Shape constancy is the perceptual system's ability to recognize a shape despite changes in the angle or position from which it is viewed.

Gestalt laws are not always obeyed; nor are they consistent with our current knowledge of brain organization. Nevertheless, these early investigations continue to influence perceptual psychologists.

Hearing

Listening to a Beethoven symphony is delightful and intriguing, but it is difficult because so much is going on at once. With more than 20 instruments playing, the listener must process many sounds, rhythms, and intensities simultaneously. Not all hearing is this difficult, but it is still a complex process. As in seeing, hearing involves converting physical stimuli into a psychological experience.

For example, suppose that a tuning fork is struck or a stereo system booms out a bass note. In both cases, sound waves are being created and air is being moved. The movement of the air and the accompanying changes in air pressure (physical stimuli) cause the eardrum to move back and forth rapidly. The movement of the eardrum triggers a series of electromechanical and electrochemical changes that are psychologically experienced as sound.

Sound

When any object is set in motion—be it a tuning fork, the reed of a clarinet, or a person's vocal cords—its vibrations cause sound waves. You can place your hand in front of a stereo speaker (or over your throat) and feel the displacement of sound

FIGURE 3.16

The Frequency and Amplitude of Sound Waves

A person's psychological experience of sound depends on the frequency and amplitude of sound waves.

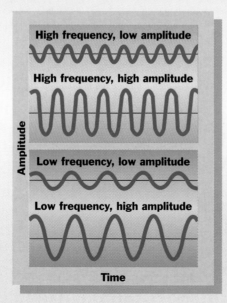

High frequency, low amplitude

High frequency, high amplitude

Low frequency, low amplitude

Low frequency, high amplitude

Amplitude

Time

High-frequency sound waves have a large number of complete cycles per second and a high pitch; they can be of low amplitude (sound soft), or high amplitude (sound loud).

Low-frequency sound waves have a small number of complete cycles per second and a low pitch; they can be of low amplitude (sound soft), or high amplitude (sound loud).

waves when the volume is turned up. **Sound** is the psychological experience that occurs when there are changes in air pressure that take place at the receptive organ for hearing and that vary in frequency and amplitude. Sound is often thought of in terms of two psychological aspects, pitch and loudness, which correspond to two physical attributes, frequency and amplitude. **Frequency** is the number of times a complete change in air pressure occurs during a given unit of time. Within 1 second, for example, there may be 50 complete changes (50 cycles per second) or 10,000 complete changes (10,000 cycles per second). Frequency determines the **pitch,** or tone, of a sound; pitch is the psychological experience that corresponds with the frequency of an auditory stimulus. High-pitched tones usually have high frequencies. Frequency is usually measured in hertz (Hz); 1 Hz equals 1 cycle per second. When a piano hammer strikes a short string on a piano (at the right), the string vibrates at a high frequency and sounds high in pitch; when a long string (at the far left) is struck, it vibrates less frequently and sounds low in pitch.

Amplitude, or *intensity,* is the total energy of a sound wave, which determines the loudness of a sound. High-amplitude sound waves have more energy than low-amplitude waves; they apply greater force to the ear (see Figure 3.16). Amplitude is measured in *decibels.* Every increase of 20 decibels corresponds to a tenfold increase in intensity. (Decibels are measured on a logarithmic scale, which means that increases are exponential, not linear; thus, the increases in sound intensity measured in decibels are quite steep.) As Figure 3.17 shows, normal conversation occurs at about 60 decibels and painful sounds occur at about 120 decibels.

Amplitude and frequency are not correlated. A low-frequency sound can be very loud or very soft; that is, it can have either high or low amplitude. Middle C on a piano, for example, can be loud or soft. The frequency (pitch) of the sound stays the same—it is still middle C; only its amplitude (loudness) varies. Our psychological

Sound: A psychological term describing changes in pressure through a medium; the psychological experience that occurs when there are changes in air pressure that take place at the receptive organ for hearing and that vary in frequency and amplitude.

Frequency: In sound waves, a measure of the number of complete pressure waves per unit of time, expressed in hertz (Hz), or cycles per second.

Pitch: The psychological experience that corresponds roughly with the frequency of an auditory stimulus. Also known as *tone.*

Amplitude: The total energy of a sound wave, which determines the loudness of a sound. Also known as *intensity.*

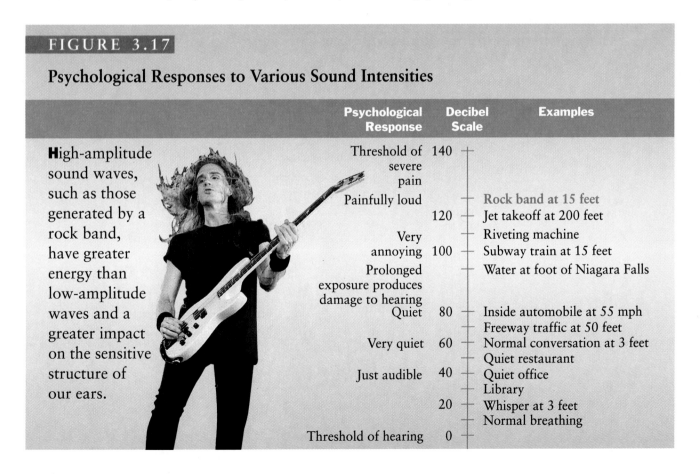

FIGURE 3.17

Psychological Responses to Various Sound Intensities

High-amplitude sound waves, such as those generated by a rock band, have greater energy than low-amplitude waves and a greater impact on the sensitive structure of our ears.

Psychological Response	Decibel Scale	Examples
Threshold of severe pain	140	
Painfully loud		Rock band at 15 feet
	120	Jet takeoff at 200 feet
Very annoying		Riveting machine
	100	Subway train at 15 feet
Prolonged exposure produces damage to hearing		Water at foot of Niagara Falls
Quiet	80	Inside automobile at 55 mph
		Freeway traffic at 50 feet
Very quiet	60	Normal conversation at 3 feet
		Quiet restaurant
Just audible	40	Quiet office
		Library
	20	Whisper at 3 feet
		Normal breathing
Threshold of hearing	0	

perception of loudness depends on other factors, such as background noise and whether we are paying attention to the sound. Another psychological dimension, *timbre*, is the quality of a sound—the different mixture of amplitudes and frequencies that make up the sound. Our perception of all these qualities depends on the physical structure of our ears.

Structure of the Ear

The ear is the receptive organ for *audition,* or hearing. It translates physical stimuli (sound waves) into electrical impulses that the brain can interpret. The ear has three major parts: the outer ear, the middle ear, and the inner ear. The tissue on the outside of the head is part of the outer ear. The eardrum (*tympanic membrane*) is the boundary between the outer and middle ear. When sound waves enter the ear, they produce changes in the pressure of the air on the eardrum. The eardrum responds to these changes by vibrating.

The middle ear is quite small. Within it, tiny bones known as *ossicles* help convert the large forces striking the eardrum into a small force. Two small muscles are attached to the ossicles; these muscles contract involuntarily in response to loud vocalizations and especially when they are exposed to an annoyingly loud noise. They help protect us from the damaging effects of a loud noise that could overstimulate the delicate mechanisms of the inner ear (Borg & Counter, 1989). Ultimately, the ossicles stimulate the *basilar membrane,* which runs down the middle of the *cochlea,* a spiral tube in the inner ear. Figure 3.18 shows the major structures of the middle and inner ear, and Figure 3.19 shows the basilar membrane.

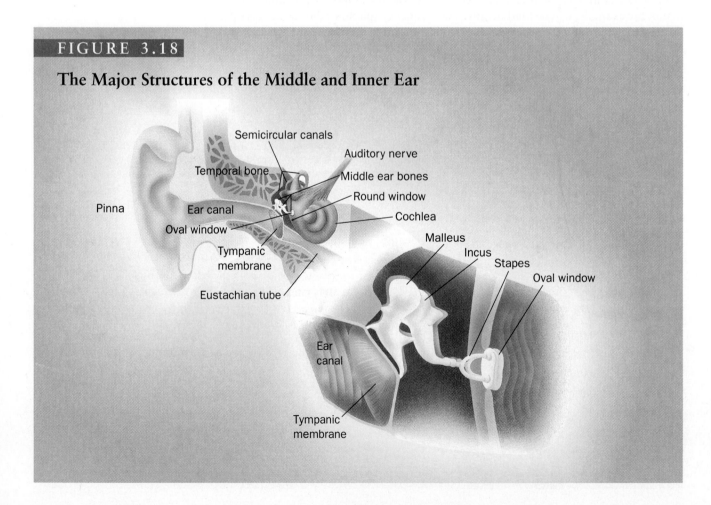

FIGURE 3.18

The Major Structures of the Middle and Inner Ear

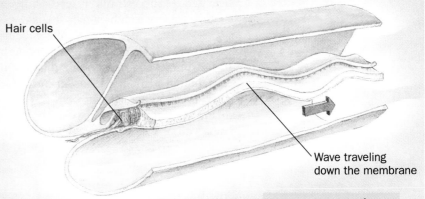

FIGURE 3.19

The Basilar Membrane

The cochlea is unwound and cut open to reveal the basilar membrane, which is covered with thousands of hair cells.

Hair cells

Wave traveling down the membrane

Pressure waves in the fluid filling the cochlea cause oscillations to travel in waves down the basilar membrane, stimulating the hair cells.

In the cochlea, which is shaped like a snail's shell and comprises three chambers, sound waves of different frequencies stimulate different areas of the basilar membrane. These areas, in turn, stimulate hair cells, which bring about the initial electrical coding of sound waves. These cells are remarkably sensitive. Hudspeth (1983), for example, found that hair cells respond when they are displaced as little as 100 picometers (trillionths of a meter). These cells are responsible for the transduction of mechanical energy into electrochemical energy.

Electrical impulses make their way through the brain's auditory nervous system in much the same way that visual information proceeds through the visual nervous system. The electrochemical neuronal impulses proceed through the auditory nerve to the midbrain and finally to the auditory cortex. Studies of single cells in the auditory areas of the brain show that some cells are more responsive to certain frequencies than to others. Katsuki (1961) found cells that are maximally sensitive to certain narrow frequency ranges; if a frequency is outside that range, the cells might not fire at all. This finding is analogous to the findings reported by Hubel and Wiesel, who discovered receptive visual fields in which proper stimulation brought about dramatic changes in the firing of a cell.

Theories of Hearing

Most theories of hearing fall into two major classes: place theories and frequency theories. *Place theories* claim that the analysis of sound occurs in the basilar membrane, with different frequencies and intensities affecting different parts (places) of the membrane. They assert that each sound wave causes a traveling wave on the basilar membrane, which in turn causes changes in the basilar membrane's displacement. The hair cells on the basilar membrane are displaced by the traveling wave, and the displacement of individual hair cells triggers specific information about pitch.

By contrast, *frequency theories* maintain that the analysis of pitch and intensity occurs at higher centers (levels) of processing (perhaps in the auditory area of the cortex) and that the basilar membrane merely transfers information to those centers. These theories suggest that the entire basilar membrane is stimulated and its overall rate of responding is transferred to the auditory nerve and beyond, where analysis takes place.

Like theories that attempt to explain color vision, both place theories and frequency theories present theoretical problems. And neither one explains all the data about pitch and loudness. For example, the hair cells do not act independently (as place theories suggest) but instead act together (as frequency theories suggest). Further, the rate at which hair cells fire is not fast enough to keep up with sound waves (e.g., 1,000 cycles per second), as frequency theories suggest.

To get around the difficulties, modern researchers have developed theories of auditory information processing that attempt to explain pitch in terms both of specific action in parts of the basilar membrane and of complex frequency analyses at higher levels. Theories that seem at odds with one another can work together to explain pitch and loudness when the best parts of them are combined. (Does this remind you of the debate between the trichromatic and the opponent-process theories of color coding?)

Sound Localization

Although not as well tuned as many animals, human beings have amazingly efficient sound localization (direction-determining) abilities. Two key concepts in sound localization are interaural time differences and interaural intensity differences. Because you have two ears, a sound made from the left of your head will arrive at the left ear before the right. Thus, you have an *interaural time difference*. In addition, the sound will reach the two ears at different intensities. A sound to the left will be slightly more intense to the left ear than the right; thus, there is an *interaural intensity difference*. These two pieces of information are analyzed in the brain at nuclei that are especially sensitive to time and intensity differences between the ears.

Some potential ambiguities, however, exist in sound localization. What happens when the sound source is just in front of you, and thus is equidistant from your two ears? It turns out that head and body movements help resolve the source of a sound. You rotate your head or move your body when you are unsure of the source of a sound. In addition, the external ear has ridges and folds that bounce sounds around just a bit. This creates slight delays that help you localize sounds. Last, sight and past experiences with sounds aid in the task of localizing sounds in space. Konishi (1993) has been investigating the interaction of these variables in an attempt to determine how the brain combines signals into a single spatial perception.

Hearing Impairments

Not everyone has perfect hearing. About 13 million people in the United States have hearing impairments, ranging from minor hearing loss to total deafness. Older individuals are one group of people who suffer from such impairments, and they are often discriminated against because of their problem. The causes of the impairments are various; and they lead to varying degrees of conduction deafness, sensorineural deafness, or a combination of the two.

Conduction deafness: Deafness resulting from interference with the transmission of sound to the neural mechanism of the inner ear.

Sensorineural deafness: Deafness resulting from damage to the cochlea, the auditory nerve, or higher auditory processing centers.

Conduction deafness is deafness resulting from interference with the transmission of sound to the neural mechanism of the inner ear. The interference may be caused by something temporary, such as a head cold or a buildup of wax in the outer ear canal. Or it may be caused by something far more serious, such as hardening of the tympanic membrane, destruction of the tiny bones (ossicles) within the ear, or diseases that create pressure in the middle ear. If the person can be aided in transmitting the sound past the point of the conduction problem, hearing can be improved.

Sensorineural deafness is deafness resulting from damage to the cochlea, the auditory nerve, or higher auditory processing centers. The most common cause of this type of deafness is ongoing exposure to very high intensity sound, such as that of rock bands or jet planes. Listening to even moderately loud music for longer than 15 minutes a day can cause permanent damage.

Hearing impairments can create special problems for children. Too many schoolchildren have been diagnosed as having low intelligence and have been labeled as stupid by their classmates when they actually only suffer from hearing losses. Sometimes, children with partial hearing do not even realize that they are missing much of what is said to them. Older people, too, are more likely to have hearing impairments, particularly for sounds in the high-frequency range. Because normal speech involves primarily the lower frequencies (between 1,000 and 5,000 Hz), such impairment generally causes few major difficulties.

Hearing is measured by an *audiometer,* which presents sounds of different frequencies through a headphone; and results are presented as an *audiogram,* a graph showing hearing sensitivity at selected frequencies. The patient's audiogram is compared with that of an adult with no known hearing loss.

One simple way to assess and diagnose hearing impairment is to test a person's recognition of spoken words. In a typical test of this sort, a person listens to a tape recording of speech sounds that are standardized in terms of loudness and pitch. Performance is based on the number of words the subject can repeat correctly at various intensity levels. This test is often administered by nonmedical personnel, who then refer individuals who may have hearing problems to a physician.

You can easily see that hearing and vision have many similarities in their perceptual mechanisms. In both perceptual systems, physical energy is transduced into electrochemical energy. Coding takes place at several locations in the brain, and people can have impairments in either visual or auditory abilities.

Attention

Have you ever tried to study hard and listen to music at the same time? Have you found your attention wandering? Did melodies or words start to interrupt your studying? Research on attention shows that human beings constantly extract signals from the world around them. Although they receive many different messages at once, they can watch, listen, and pay attention only to a selected message.

Selective Attention

Because people can pay attention to only one or two things at a time, psychologists sometimes call the study of attention the study of *selective attention*. Early in its study, researchers discovered the *cocktail party phenomenon,* wherein people can hear their names being spoken across a crowded and noisy room. An associated phenomenon inhibits our ability to remember names when we are being introduced to someone. People often fail to catch the name of someone they are introduced to because they are too preoccupied with thinking of something to say or with appraising the new person.

Perceptual psychologists are concerned with the complex processes involved in extracting information from the environment. They hope to answer the question: Which stimuli do people choose to listen to? They focus on the *allocation* of a person's attention. In selective-listening experiments, subjects wearing a pair of headphones receive different messages simultaneously in each ear. Their task is often to shadow, or repeat, a message heard in one ear. Typically, they report that they are able to listen to a speaker in *either* the left or the right ear and can provide information about the content and quality of that speaker's voice.

Of the several theories about how people are able to attend selectively, the two described here are the filter theory and the attenuation theory. The *filter theory* states that human beings possess a limited capacity to process information and that perceptual filters must choose between information presented to the left ear and information presented to the right ear. The *attenuation theory* states that all the information is analyzed but that intervening factors inhibit (attenuate) attention, so only selected information reaches the highest centers of processing.

Hundreds of selective-listening studies have examined the claims of filter versus attenuation theory (e.g., Cherry, 1953; Treisman, 1969). Regardless of whether people filter or attenuate information, selective-attention studies show that human beings must select one of the available stimuli (Duncan, 1980). It is impossible, for example, to pay attention to four lectures at once. A listener can extract information from only one speaker at a time. Admittedly, you can do more than one task at a time—for example, you can drive a car and listen to the radio—but you cannot use the same channel (such as vision) for several tasks simultaneously. You cannot drive a car, read a book, and inspect photographs at the same time.

Clearly, both the auditory and visual systems have limited capacities. People have limited ability to divide their attention between tasks and must allocate their perceptual resources for greatest efficiency. How can we do this? Can we prime, or pre-cue, ourselves to focus our attention in important ways? Can we structure our world to make the most of our perceptual abilities?

While it is easy to be caught up in the atmosphere of excitement generated by the sights and sounds of a three-ring circus, we can only attend carefully to one event at a time.

Subliminal Perception

At the beginning of this chapter, I raised the issue of audio self-help tapes and subliminal perception. Let's explore the issue in more detail. If a visual or auditory stimulus is presented so quickly or at such a low intensity or volume that you cannot consciously perceive it, can it affect your behavior? As we noted at the beginning of the chapter, **subliminal perception** is perception below the threshold of awareness.

Modern studies of this type of perception began in the 1950s with an innovative advertising ploy. A marketing executive superimposed messages on a regular movie; they said such things as "Buy popcorn." According to some advertising agents, movie theaters could induce audiences to buy more popcorn by flashing advertisements on the screen at speeds too fast to be consciously observed. Many psychologists dismissed the popcorn marketing campaign as nonsense, but it created a stir.

According to Goleman (1985), subliminal perception is possible. In fact, many cognitive scientists take unconscious perception for granted and build theories around it (e.g., Kihlstrom, Barnhardt, & Tataryn, 1992). However, subliminal perception has had a controversial history. Many of the early (1960s) studies lacked control groups and did not specify the variables being manipulated. Some presented stimuli for durations in which several words might easily be seen by one subject and no words by another. Other studies presented "dirty," or taboo, words to see if they affected responses more than neutral or emotionally uncharged words did. Of course, some subjects were embarrassed to repeat the noxious words to the experimenter (often a person of the opposite sex) and denied having seen them.

To avoid some of these methodological problems, later experiments presented subjects with both threatening and neutral words for very brief durations. The sub-

Subliminal perception: Perception below the threshold of awareness.

jects responded by repeating the words or by pressing a button as soon as they saw each word. In these experiments, threatening words had to be presented for a longer time or at a greater intensity level than nonthreatening words in order to be identified.

The presentation of a threatening message—for example, a dirty word—may raise the perceptual threshold above normal levels, making it harder for the subject to perceive subsequent subliminal words. Some researchers suggest that the unconscious or some other personality variable acts as a censor. For example, Silverman (1983) asserts that if an aggressive or sexual message is presented subliminally to subjects, it will affect their subsequent behavior—that unconscious processes are at work. More recently, Balay and Shevrin (1988) suggest that a stage beyond the sensory or perceptual stages affects the perceptual process. They maintain that subliminal perception can be explained in terms of such nonperceptual variables as motivation, previous experience, and unconscious or critical censoring processes that influence perceptual thresholds.

In some controlled situations, subliminal stimuli probably can influence behavior (e.g., Krosnick et al., 1992; Merikle & Reingold, 1990). In the real world, however, we are constantly faced with many competing sensory stimuli. Therefore, what grabs our attention depends on many variables, such as importance, prominence, and interest. Should we fear either mind control by advertisers or other unsolicited outside stimuli? The answer is probably no. Can backward speech in rock music interpreted and understood? Again, the answer is no (Begg, Needham, & Bookbinder, 1993). In the end, subliminal perception, and any learning that results from it, is subtle and greatly affected by such nonperceptual variables as motivation, previous experience, personality, and other learned behaviors (Greenwald, 1992). However, most psychologists argue that more research is needed to determine exactly what is taking place when subliminal perception occurs and to what degree, if any, subliminal stimuli can influence us (Erdelyi, 1992). For example, whether a person has had a previous experience with a visual, auditory, or taste event affects later experiences.

FOCUS

▶ Explain how monocular and binocular depth cues help people see depth. pp. 93–94

▶ Identify the differences between *conduction deafness* and *sensorineural deafness*. p. 104

▶ What evidence exists to show that when a person receives more than one incoming message at the same time, the person can attend to only one? pp. 105–106

▶ What was a major research design problem with early subliminal perception experiments? pp. 106–107

Taste and Smell

Try the following experiment. Cut a fresh onion in half and inhale its odor while holding a piece of raw potato in your mouth. Now chew the potato. Does the potato taste like an onion? This experiment demonstrates that taste and smell are closely linked. Food contains substances that act as stimuli for both taste and smell.

There is one taste most people have a special fondness for: sweetness. Babies prefer sweet foods; so do our great-grandmothers. But researchers know that a sweet tooth reflects a craving for more than the taste of sugar. People with a sweet tooth crave candy, cake, ice cream, and sometimes liquor. Our bodies perceive the sweetness and learn that it is associated with many foods that are high in carbohydrates and fat. Carbohydrates act almost as sedatives. So our cravings for some substances—our desire to taste or smell or eat or drink them—are affected by a number of variables, including the composition of the food, its smells, what it ultimately does to us, and our previous experiences with it.

Taste

I remember the first time I was in a cheese store. My father was supposed to buy some cheese and crackers because company was coming for dinner. The store owner allowed me to sample a variety of cheeses: Swiss, blue, cheddar, Gruyère, Gorgonzola, and Brie. The cheddar was too sharp, the blue cheese tasted bitter, and the Swiss was bland in comparison. We finally decided on a large slice of Brie; it was soft and creamy, with a slightly sweet, mild flavor. I was overwhelmed by the quantity of cheeses and their different tastes and smells.

Taste is a chemical sense; food placed in the mouth is partially dissolved in saliva and stimulates the *taste buds,* the primary receptors for taste stimuli (see Figure 3.20). When substances contact the taste buds, we experience taste. The taste buds are found on small bumps on the tongue—papillae. Each hill-like papilla is separated from the next by a trenchlike moat; on the wall of this moat are located the taste buds, which can be seen only under a microscope. Each taste bud (human beings have about 10,000 of them) consists of several *taste cells.* These cells last only about 10 days and are constantly being renewed.

Although psychologists do not know exactly how many tastes there are, most agree that there are four basic ones: sweet, sour, salty, and bitter. Most foods contain more than one primary taste; veal parmigiana, for example, offers a complicated stimulus to the tongue and also stimulates the sense of smell (described in the following section). All taste cells are sensitive to all taste stimuli, but some cells are more sensitive to some stimuli than to others. (In this regard, they are much like the cones in the retina, which are sensitive to all wavelengths but are especially sensitive to a specific range of wavelengths.) By isolating stimuli that initiate only one taste sensation, psychologists have found that some regions of the tongue seem to be more

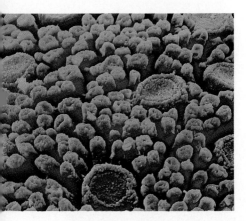

The surface of the human tongue. The taste buds have been highlighted in purple.

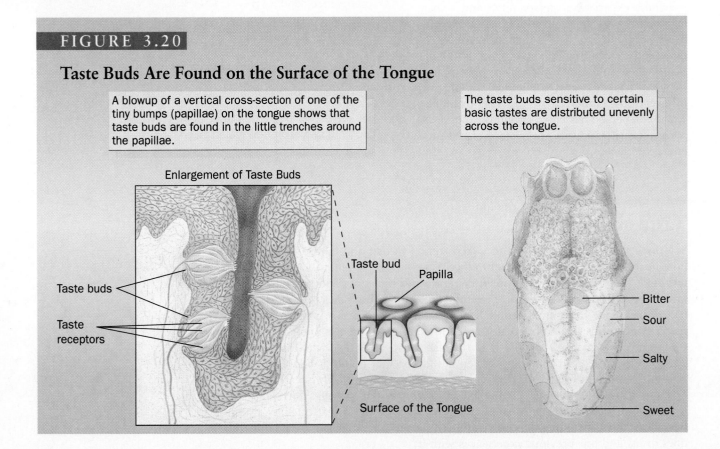

FIGURE 3.20

Taste Buds Are Found on the Surface of the Tongue

A blowup of a vertical cross-section of one of the tiny bumps (papillae) on the tongue shows that taste buds are found in the little trenches around the papillae.

The taste buds sensitive to certain basic tastes are distributed unevenly across the tongue.

Enlargement of Taste Buds

Taste buds

Taste receptors

Taste bud

Papilla

Surface of the Tongue

Bitter

Sour

Salty

Sweet

sensitive to particular taste stimuli than others. The tip of the tongue, for example, is more sensitive to sweet tastes than the back of the tongue, and the sides are especially sensitive to sour tastes (see Figure 3.20).

The taste of a particular food depends not only on its chemical makeup but also on our past experiences with this or similar foods, on how much saliva is being mixed into the food as we chew, and on how long we chew the food. A food that is chewed well has a strong taste. A food that rests on the tongue for a long time will lose its ability to stimulate; *sensory adaptation* will occur. A food that loses its texture by being mashed up, blended, or mixed with other foods has less taste and is less appealing to most adults. Thus, a taste experience, much like our other perceptual experiences, depends not only on a sensory event but also on past experience and other sensory and perceptual variables.

Smell

Like the sense of taste, **olfaction**—the sense of smell—is a chemical sense. That is, the stimulus for smell is a chemical in the air. The olfactory system in human beings is remarkably sensitive and can recognize a smell from as few as 40 or 50 molecules of a chemical. For the sensation of smell to occur, chemicals must move toward the receptor cells located on the walls of the nasal passage. This happens when we breathe them in through our nostrils or take them in through the back of the throat when we chew and swallow. When a chemical substance in the air moves past the receptor cells, it is partially absorbed into the mucus that covers the cells, thereby initiating the process of smell.

For human beings to perceive smell, information must be sent to the brain. At the top of the nasal cavity is the *olfactory epithelium,* which contains the olfactory rods—the nerve fibers that process odors and transmit information about smell to the brain (see Figure 3.21). There can be as many as 30 million olfactory rods in each nostril, making the olfactory system very sensitive. This fact is dramatically illustrated by perfume manufacturers.

Olfaction: [ole-FAK-shun] The sense of smell.

FIGURE 3.21

The Olfactory System

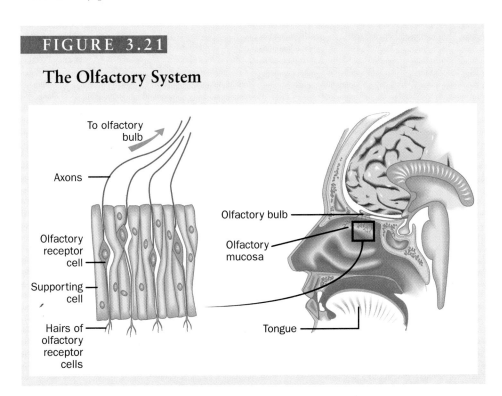

Smell and Communication

Animals secrete *pheromones* (pronounced FER-uh-moans)—scented chemical substances that are detected by other animals. Pheromones act as a means of communication. In fact, scents released by one animal may influence the physiology of another animal.

Pheromones are widely recognized as initiators of sexual activity among animals. For example, female silkworms release a pheromone that can attract a male silkworm from miles away. Similarly, when female hamsters are sexually receptive, they emit a highly odorous substance that attracts males (Montgomery-St. Laurent, Fullenkamp, & Fischer, 1988); mice are similarly equipped (Coppola & O'Connell, 1988).

Many animals emit pheromones to elicit specific behavioral reactions; others, notably dogs, use scents from their feces and urine simply to maintain their territories and identify one another. Beavers attempt to keep strangers out of their territory by depositing foul-smelling substances

emitted by sacs near the anus. Reindeer have scent glands between their toes that leave a trail for the rest of the herd. Communication through pheromones is found throughout the animal world. But do human beings share this ability?

Early Ideas. Though people have always said that a kind of "chemistry" exists between close friends, few really believed that one person's secretions might alter another person's behavior. It was generally believed that human beings do not communicate through smell. However, ground-breaking research in the 1970s began to change psychologists' thinking about smell and communication. McClintock (1971) found that the menstrual periods of women living in a college dormitory who were either roommates or close friends became roughly *synchronous*. That is, after they had lived together for several months, their menstrual cycles began and ended at about the same time. McClintock and others began to question whether the synchronization of the menstrual cycles was due to some type of chemical message.

Research Evidence. In the mid-1980s, two studies stirred up the pheromone debate. These studies were conducted by two scientists, Cutler and Preti, and they focused on a specific issue: Could chemical signals from other people—both men and women—alter women's menstrual cycles? They sought to test McClintock's idea that synchronization of the menstrual cycles was caused by some type of chemical message—pheromones. They used a fascinating technique. They swabbed underarm secretions on the lips of women to see whether these chemicals would affect their menstrual cycles.

In the first study, underarm secretions from a group of men were gathered on swabs that they wore under their armpits (Cutler et al., 1986). The secretions were then swabbed on the upper lips of seven women whose menstrual cycles were either short (under 26 days) or long (over 33 days). The female subjects were told that they were receiving a "natural fragrance" that had been injected into alcohol. The study was double-blind—neither the subjects nor the experimenter knew which of the sub-

Perfume manufacturers know that making a perfume is complex. They may combine hundreds of scents to make one new perfume; dozens of perfumes have the same basic scent and vary only slightly. The manufacturer's task is to generate a perfume that has a distinctive top note—the first impact of a smell. If the substance that creates a smell is not chemically pure, it will be followed by a middle and an end note. The middle note follows after the top note fades away, and the end note is long-lasting; it remains long after the top and middle notes have disappeared.

Theories of smell involve both the stimulus for smell and the structure of the receptor system. Some theories posit a few basic smells; others suggest many—including flowery, foul, fruity, resinous, spicy, and burnt. Psychologists have not agreed on a single classification system for smells; nor do they completely understand how odors affect the receptor cells. Research into the coding of smell is intense, and physiological psychologists make headway each year. Another area in which important progress has been made is whether and how odors affect human behavior. We consider this issue in the Research Process box above.

jects were receiving the underarm secretions and which were receiving the control substance (which was nothing other than alcohol).

Within 3 months, the menstrual cycles of the experimental subjects became similar, approaching the norm of 29.5 days. The researchers did another study, also double-blind, with secretions from other women (Preti et al., 1986). As in the first study, women were swabbed on the upper lip with either underarm secretions or alcohol. The results were comparable. The times of menstruation became similar and approached the norm. The secretions affected the women's menstrual cycles; pheromones were causing the change.

One Problem, One Strength. A problem with the Cutler and Preti studies is that the researchers used a limited number of subjects. The first study used 15 subjects and the second 19. Because of this, the researchers were cautious in making generalizations. However, the studies were well designed. Their results were highly regarded because the studies were double-blind, used an experimental method with control groups, and produced results that were statistically significant.

Implications. The Cutler and Preti studies suggest that the smell of other human beings affects physiological processes in women. They also indicate that pheromones emitted by a man may alter a woman's menstrual cycle. The data imply that women who live with men may have more regular cycles, and thus may be more fertile, than those who live alone (see Cutler et al., 1986).

Although other people's physiological processes may affect us, the evidence that smell affects human behavior is still suggestive. The effects of pheromones in animals is profound, but the role of pheromones in human beings remains controversial. Nevertheless, perfume makers have been sent into a frenzy of activity trying to formulate a perfume with pheromone-like capabilities. Is it reasonable for perfume makers to assert that perfumes, like pheromones, can attract members of the opposite sex? Probably not. Pheromones probably are not as powerful in human beings as they are in animals because so many other environmental stimuli affect human behavior, attitudes, and interpersonal relations.

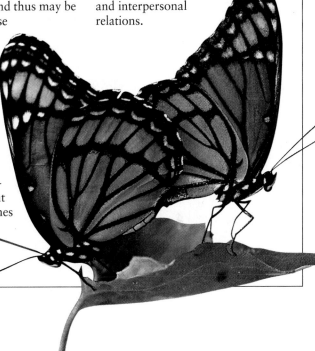

The Skin Senses

Our skin, an organ of our body, contains a wide range of receptors that convey information about touch, pressure, warmth, cold, and pain. In each case, a stimulus is converted into neural energy and then the brain interprets that neural energy as a psychological experience. Skin receptors ultimately send information to the somatosensory cortex of the brain.

Touch

The skin acts as the housing for our *sense of touch*—our *tactile system*. It is more than just a binding that holds us together. The skin of an adult human being measures roughly 2 square yards and comprises three layers: the epidermis, the dermis, and the hypodermis. The top layer, the *epidermis* (*epi* means "outer," among other things), consists primarily of dead cells and varies in thickness. On the face it is thin; on the elbows and heels of the feet it is quite thick. The epidermis is constantly regenerating; in fact, every 28 days or so, all of its cells are replaced. The layer underneath the epidermis—the *dermis*—contains live cells as well as a supply of nerve endings, blood, hair cells, and oil-producing (sebaceous) glands. The dermis and epidermis are resilient, flexible, and quite thick, which protects the body against quick changes in temperature and pressure. The epidermis in particular guards against pain from small scratches and bumps. The deepest layer—the *hypodermis* (*hypo* means "under")—is a thick, insulating cushion.

Specialized receptors are responsible for relaying information about the *skin senses*—pain, touch, and temperature (warmth and cold). The receptors for each of these senses vary in shape, size, number, and distribution. For example, the body has many more cold receptors than heat receptors; it has more pain receptors behind the knee than on the top of the nose. In the most sensitive areas of the hand, there are as many as 1,300 receptors per square inch.

The skin sense receptors appear to interact with one another; sometimes one sensation seems to combine with or change to another. Thus, increasing pressure can become pain. Similarly, an itch seems to result from a low-level irritation of nerve endings in the skin; however, a tickle can be caused by the same stimulus and produce a reflexlike response. Further, we are far more sensitive to pressure in some parts of our bodies than in other parts (compare your fingers to your thigh); the more sensitive areas have more receptors than do the less sensitive areas. (See Figure 3.22.)

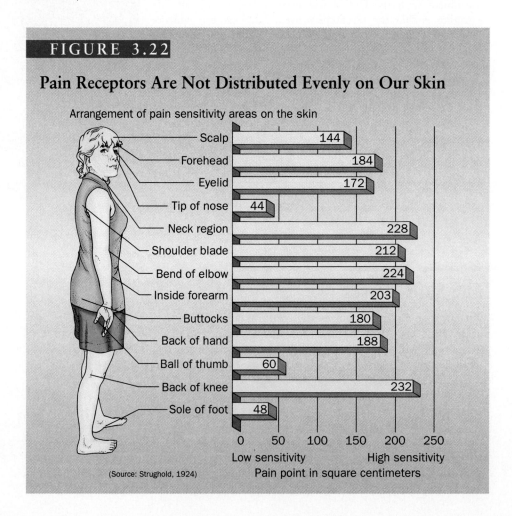

FIGURE 3.22

Pain Receptors Are Not Distributed Evenly on Our Skin

Arrangement of pain sensitivity areas on the skin

Area	Pain point (sq. cm)
Scalp	144
Forehead	184
Eyelid	172
Tip of nose	44
Neck region	228
Shoulder blade	212
Bend of elbow	224
Inside forearm	203
Buttocks	180
Back of hand	188
Ball of thumb	60
Back of knee	232
Sole of foot	48

Low sensitivity — High sensitivity
Pain point in square centimeters

(Source: Strughold, 1924)

Many of our determinations of how something feels are relative. When we say a stimulus is cold, we mean it is cold compared to normal skin temperature. When we say an object is warm, we mean it feels warmer than normal skin temperature. When we feel a child's head with the back of our palm and say the child has a fever, we are comparing normal skin temperature to a sick child's elevated skin temperature (and we wouldn't make such a determination immediately after coming in from a 20-degree outdoors temperature).

Pain

Generally, people look forward to sensory experiences: new smells, sights, tastes, and sounds. One exception is pain; pain is a perceptual experience with particular negative qualities (Fernandez & Turk, 1992). Pain is the most common symptom found in medical settings; nevertheless, it is adaptive and necessary. In rare cases, children have been born without the ability to feel pain, which places them in constant danger. Their encounters with caustic substances, violent collisions, and deep cuts elicit no painful cautions to avoid such experiences. Further, they do not recognize serious conditions that would send most of us to the doctor for attention— for example, broken bones, deep burns, and the sharp pains that signal appendicitis.

Studying pain is difficult because it can be elicited in so many ways. Stomach pains may be caused by hunger or the flu, for example, toothaches by a cavity or an abscess, and headaches by stress or eye strain. Myriad kinds of pain exist, including sunburn pain, pain from terminal cancer, labor pains, pain from frostbite, and even pain when a limb is lost as a result of trauma or surgery. Psychologists use several kinds of stimuli to study pain. Among them are chemicals, extreme heat and cold, and electrical shock (Flor & Turk, 1989). Most researchers believe the receptors for pain are free nerve endings located throughout the body.

Some areas of the body are more sensitive to pain than others. For example, the sole of the foot and the ball of the thumb are less sensitive than the back of the knee and the neck. Also, though an individual's pain threshold remains fairly constant, different individuals possess different sensitivities to pain. Some people have a low threshold for pain; they will report a comparatively low-level stimulus as being painful. Others have fairly high pain thresholds. However, the perception of pain is psychological, and much depends on a person's previous experience and attitude. For example, athletes often report not feeling the pain of an injury until after the competition has ended. What allows pain suppression? How does the body process, interpret, and stop pain? Gate control theory may offer an answer.

Gate Control Theory. One explanation of how the body processes pain is the Melzack-Wall gate control theory (Melzack & Wall, 1970). The theory is complex, taking into account the sizes of nerve fibers, their level of development, and the interplay of excitatory and inhibitory cells that can diminish painful sensations. The theory contends that when a signal that might normally indicate a painful stimulus is sent to the brain, it goes through a series of gates. These gates can be opened or closed either fully or partially. How far they open determines how much of the original pain signal gets through. A chemical called substance P (P stands for pain), which is released by the sensory nerve fibers, transmits pain impulses across the gates. Specific research support for gate control theory is sparse, although a variety of drugs, as well as electrical stimulation and acupuncture needles, are thought to close the gates partially or fully, making the original painful stimulus less potent.

Many people who suffer chronic, unrelieved pain have sought help from acupuncture. Initially developed in China thousands of years ago, *acupuncture* is a technique in which long, slender needles are inserted into the body at specific locations in order to relieve particular kinds of pain at particular locations. Controlled

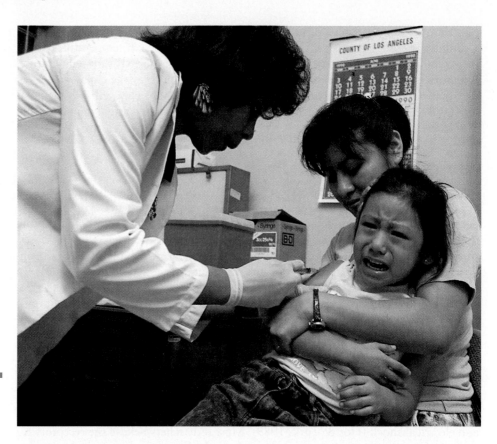

Pain is a decidedly negative perceptual experience, but it is adaptive and necessary.

studies of acupuncture have yielded varying results. The National Institutes of Health has reported that acupuncture is no more effective than sugar pills; a few studies, however, have suggested that it helps with mild back pain (Price et al., 1984). Controlled research on the results of acupuncture is still inconclusive.

Endorphins. There have been some exciting breakthroughs in research on pain receptors and the nature of pain. Consider, for example, the study of endorphins. **Endorphins** (from *endogenous,* meaning "naturally occurring," and *morphine,* an opiate—a painkiller usually derived from opium) are painkillers that are naturally produced in the brain and pituitary gland. There are many kinds of endorphins, and many help regulate several bodily functions, including the control of blood pressure and body temperature (Bloom, 1981). Endorphins also can produce euphoria and a sense of well-being in the way that morphine does, but to an even greater extent. Stress, anticipated pain, and athletic activities bring about an increased endorphin level. During and after running, runners often report feeling "high," a sensation many believe is directly related to their increased endorphin level.

Endorphins bind themselves to receptor sites in the brain and spinal cord, thereby preventing pain signals from going to higher levels of the nervous system. Naturally produced endorphins include some that increase tolerance to pain and others that actually reduce pain. *Enkephalin,* for example, is an innate brain endorphin that blocks pain signals (Snyder, 1980). Physicians prescribe synthetic endorphins or endorphinlike substances, such as morphine, to block pain.

Pain Management. Usually the pain resulting from a headache, toothache, or small cut is temporary and can be alleviated with a simple pain medication such as aspirin. For millions of people, however, aspirin is not enough. For those who suffer from constant pain caused by back injury, arthritis, or cancer, drug treatment

Endorphins: [en-DOR-finz] Painkillers produced naturally in the brain and pituitary gland.

either is not effective, is dangerous because of the high dosages required, or is not prescribed because of fear of addiction—a fear that is often overstated in the case of pain relief (Melzack, 1990). Further, each type of pain may require a different treatment (Flor & Turk, 1989).

New technologies are emerging to help people manage pain. Solomon Snyder, a leader in pain research, reasons that something must happen at the site of an injury to trigger endorphin production. What if a drug could stop the whole pain perception process at the actual place where an injury occurs? Solomon, Innis, and Manning are studying the receptor sites in skin tissue and observing how chemicals bind to them (Bishop, 1986). They hope to find compounds that will stop the entire pain perception process, even before endorphin production starts. The compounds they discover may not be total pain relievers; but in combination with other pain medications, such as aspirin, they may be very effective.

Practitioners who deal with pain recognize that it can have both physical and psychological sources. Although pain may initially arise from physical complaints, it can continue even after the physical cause abates because it provides other benefits to the sufferer (Fernandez & Turk, 1992). For example, pain may provide the sufferer with attention, which is reinforcing; or pain may provide a distraction from other problems. Treatment focuses on helping people cope with pain regardless of its origins.

Hypnosis (which will be examined in more detail in chapter 4) has been used to treat patients who suffer pain. They may be instructed to focus on other aspects of their lives and may be told that after the hypnotic session their pain will be more bearable. Hilgard and Morgan (1975) suggest that two-thirds of patients who are considered highly susceptible to suggestion can experience some relief of pain through hypnosis.

Anxiety and worry can make pain worse. People who suffer from migraine headaches, for example, often make their condition worse by becoming fearful—and therefore tense—when they feel a headache coming on. Researchers find that biofeedback training, which teaches people how to relax and cope more effectively, can help those who suffer from chronic pain and migraine headaches gain some relief (Nuechterlein & Holroyd, 1980). (Biofeedback will be discussed further in chapter 4.) Other treatments, closely related to biofeedback, are cognitive coping strategies (discussed in chapters 13 and 15). A poor or hopeless attitude can make pain worse. Cognitive coping strategies teach patients to have a better attitude about their pain. Patients learn to talk to themselves in positive ways, to divert attention to pleasant images, and to take an active role in managing their pain and transcending the experience.

Kinesthesis and Vestibular Sense

If you are a dancer or an athlete, you rely mightily on your body to provide you with information about hand, arm, and leg movements. You try to keep your balance, be graceful, and move about with coordinated skill. Two of the sensory systems that allow for skilled, accurate, and smooth movement are often ignored, but vitally important—the kinesthetic and vestibular systems.

Kinesthesis is the awareness aroused by movements of the muscles, tendons, and joints. It is what allows you to touch your finger to your nose with your eyes closed, leap over hurdles during a track and field event, dance without stepping on your partner's feet, and so on. The study of kinesthesis provides information about bodily movements. The movements of muscles around your eye, for example, help let you know how far away objects are. Kinesthesia and your other internal sensations

Kinesthesis: [kin-iss-THEE-sis] The awareness aroused by movements of the muscles, tendons, and joints.

The kinesthetic and vestibular systems allow for skilled, accurate, and smooth movement by providing information about bodily movements, bodily orientation, and postural adjustment.

(such as stomach upset) are *proprioceptive cues* (kinesthesia is sometimes called proprioception)—sensory cues coming from within your body and providing information about bodily movements and internal sensations.

The **vestibular sense** is the sense of bodily orientation and postural adjustment. It helps us keep our balance and sense of equilibrium. The structures essential to these functions are in the ear. Vestibular sacs and semicircular canals, which are associated with the body wall of the cochlea, provide information about the orientations of the head and body relative to the eye movement and posture systems (Parker, 1980). The vestibular sense allows you to walk on a balance beam without falling off, to know which way is up after diving into the water, and to sense that you are turning a corner on a ride, even when your eyes are closed.

Rapid movements of the head bring about changes in the semicircular canals. These changes induce eye movements to help compensate for head changes and changes in bodily orientation. They may also be accompanied by physical sensations ranging from pleasant dizziness to unbearable motion sickness. Studies of the vestibular sense help scientists understand what happens to people during space travel and under conditions of weightlessness.

Extrasensory Perception

Vision, hearing, taste, smell, touch, and even pain are all part of the normal sensory experience of human beings. Some people, however, claim there are other perceptual experiences that not all normal human beings recognize as such. People have been fascinated by *extrasensory perception (ESP)* for hundreds of years. The British Society for the Study of Psychic Phenomena has investigated reports of ESP since the 19th century. Early experimenters tested for extrasensory perception by asking sub-

Vestibular sense: [ves-TIB-you-ler] The sense of bodily orientation and postural adjustment.

jects to guess the symbols on what are now called ESP cards, each marked with a star, a cross, a circle, a square, or a set of wavy lines. One of the most consistently successful guessers once guessed 25 cards in a row, an event with the odds of nearly 300 quadrillion to 1 of happening by chance.

ESP includes telepathy, clairvoyance, precognition, and psychokinesis. *Telepathy* is the transfer of thought from one person to another. *Clairvoyance* is the ability to recognize objects or events, such as the contents of a message in a sealed envelope, that are not present to normal sensory receptors. *Precognition* is unexplained knowledge about future events, such as knowing when the phone is about to ring. *Psychokinesis* is the ability to move objects by using only one's mental powers.

Support for the existence of ESP is generally weak and has not been repeated very often. Moreover, ESP phenomena such as bending a spoon through mental manipulation and "reading people's minds" are not affected by experimental manipulations in the way that other perceptual events are. In addition, the National Research Council has denounced the scientific merit of most of these experiments. None of these criticisms means that ESP does not exist, and active research using scientific methods continues. New techniques include the use of sophisticated electronic detection devices, and attempts to relate ESP phenomena to traditional psychology are under way. However, psychologists see so much trickery and falsification of data and so many design errors in experiments on this subject that they remain skeptical.

FOCUS

▶ What is the evidence that behavior in animals is directly affected by pheromones?   pp. 110–111

▶ Why is the study of pain so complicated?   pp. 113–114

▶ What evidence exists to support the idea that athletes experience a "high" when they exercise?   p. 114

Concluding Note

The perceptual process is so complex that it is easy to see that subliminal television messages are, at best, marketing hype. Sensory messages are analyzed at many levels of the perceptual system, from initial electrochemical changes to complex processing based on previous experience. As a baby boomer in my 40s, I have had to buy a special pair of reading glasses to wear at my computer screen; this has highlighted for me the vulnerability of our perceptual system. The perceptual system is so complex that we need to keep the front end—the input—clear and accurate if we are to achieve accurate perceptual experiences.

Our perceptual experience is affected not only by input but by our visual system itself, for example, initial degradation due to a misshapen eyeball. In addition, our environment shapes our perceptions of the world. Our experiences with various tastes affect how we perceive the flavor of a new fruit. Past experiences with pain shape our expectations for future experiences. Our experiences with music determine how we will perceive new pieces performed by an orchestra; for example, growing up with Western music, most up us find that the music of the East takes a while to get used to. Our perceptual experience is just that—an experience. Perception is a psychological phenomenon determined not only by stimulation, receptors, and electrochemical changes but also by our previous experiences. We place our perceptual experiences within a context that makes them meaningful. This context is part of our consciousness (discussed in the next chapter) and is affected by learning (the topic of chapter 5).

Summary & Review

What Is a Perceptual Experience?

What is perception?

Perception is the process through which people attach meaning to sensory stimuli by means of complex processing mechanisms. Each perceptual system operates in a similar way; although all are different, they share common processes. pp. 76–77

What are the findings of studies of sensory deprivation and sensory restriction?

Studies of sensory deprivation have shown that an organism's early experience is important in the development and proper functioning of its perceptual systems. The profound relaxation that occurs in an extreme sensory restricted environment can be effective in helping to modify some behaviors, including smoking. pp. 78–79

KEY TERMS: *sensation*, p. 76; *perception*, p. 76; *psychophysics*, p. 77.

The Visual System

What are the main structures of the eye?

The main structures of the eye are the cornea, pupil, iris, lens, and retina. The retina is made up of 10 layers, of which the most important are the *photoreceptors*, the bipolar cells, and the ganglion cells. The axons of the ganglion cells make up the optic nerve. pp. 79–81

What is the duplicity theory of vision?

The *duplicity theory* of vision states that rods and cones are structurally unique and are used to accomplish different tasks. It asserts the two classes of receptors have special functions and operate differently, for example, cones being specialized for color, day vision, and fine acuity and rods being specialized for low light levels but lacking color abilities and fine acuity abilities. pp. 81–84

What are receptive fields?

Receptive fields are areas on the retina that, when stimulated, produce changes in the firing of cells in the visual system. Retinal cells and cells at the lateral geniculate nucleus and the striate cortex have receptive fields, some of which are highly specialized, for example, for motion or color. pp. 85–86

What are the three main characteristics of color? Briefly describe two theories of color vision.

The three main psychological characteristics of color are *hue*, *brightness*, and *saturation*. They correspond to the three physical characteristics of light: wavelength, intensity, and purity. Young and Helmholtz's *trichromatic theory* of color vision states that all colors can be made by mixing three basic colors and that the retina has three types of cones. Herring's *opponent-process theory* states that color is coded by a series of receptors that respond either positively or negatively to different wavelengths of light. pp. 87–91

KEY TERMS: *electromagnetic radiation*, p. 79; *light*, p. 79; *myopic*, p. 80; *hyperopic*, p. 80; *photoreceptors*, p. 80; *transduction*, p. 80; *visual cortex*, p. 81; *dark adaptation*, p. 82; *optic chiasm*, p. 84; *receptive fields*, p. 85; *saccades*, p. 86; *hue*, p. 88; *brightness*, p. 88; *saturation*, p. 88; *trichromatic theory*, p. 88; *color blindness*, p. 90; *opponent-process theory*, p. 90; *trichromats*, p. 90; *monochromats*, p. 90; *dichromats*, p. 90.

Visual Perception

What are some monocular and binocular cues for depth perception, and what is size constancy?

The *monocular* cues for depth perception include motion parallax, the kinetic depth effect, linear perspective, interposition, highlighting and shadowing, atmospheric perspective, and accommodation. The two primary binocular cues are *retinal disparity* and *convergence*. *Size constancy* is the ability of the perceptual system to recognize that an object remains constant in size regardless of its distance from the viewer or the size of the retinal image. pp. 91–94

What is a perceptual illusion?

An *illusion* is a perception of a physical stimulus that differs from the way people normally expect it to appear. pp. 94–98

What Gestalt law is used as an organizing idea for perception?

According to the *law of Prägnanz*, stimuli that can be grouped together and seen as a whole, or as a form, will be seen that way. Using the law of Prägnanz as an organizing idea, Gestalt psychologists developed principles of organization for the perception of figures, especially figure-ground relationships.   pp. 98–100

KEY TERMS: *size constancy*, p. 92; *shape constancy*, p. 92; *monocular depth cues*, p. 93; *accommodation*, p. 94; *binocular depth cues*, p. 94; *retinal disparity*, p. 94; *convergence*, p. 94; *illusion*, p. 94; *law of Prägnanz*, p. 98.

Hearing

What is sound?

Sound refers to changes in pressure passing through a gaseous, liquid, or solid medium—usually air. The *frequency* and *amplitude* of a sound wave principally determine in large part how a sound will be experienced by a listener.   p. 100

Describe the anatomy of the ear and how sound waves are processed.

The ear has three main parts: the outer ear, the middle ear, and the inner ear. The eardrum (tympanic membrane) is the boundary between the outer ear and the middle ear. Tiny bones in the middle ear (ossicles) stimulate the basilar membrane in the cochlea, a tube in the inner ear. Place theories of hearing claim that the analysis of sound takes place in the inner ear; frequency theories claim that the analysis of pitch and intensity takes place at higher centers (levels) of processing. p. 102–104

What is the difference between conduction and nerve deafness?

Conduction deafness results from interference in the delivery of sound to the neural mechanism of the inner ear, and *sensorineural deafness* results from damage to the cochlea, the auditory nerve, or higher auditory processing centers.   p. 104

KEY TERMS: *sound*, p. 101; *frequency*, p. 101; *pitch*, p. 101; *amplitude*, p. 101; *conduction deafness*, p. 104; *sensorineural deafness*, p. 104.

Attention

What is the cocktail party phenomenon?

The cocktail party phenomenon is the finding that people can hear their name being spoken across a crowded and otherwise noisy room. It is a basic finding of selective attention studies, which show that people have limited-capacity attentional abilities. p. 105

What is subliminal perception and does it exist?

If a visual or auditory stimulus is presented so quickly or at such a low volume that you cannot consciously perceive it, we say that it is presented subliminally. Research on *subliminal perception* is controversial, and many researchers maintain that it can be explained in terms of such nonperceptual variables as motivation, previous experience, and unconscious or critical censoring processes.   pp. 106–107

KEY TERM: *subliminal perception*, p. 106.

Taste and Smell

Describe the anatomy of the tongue and how it allows for taste.

The tongue contains thousands of bumps, or papillae, each of which is separated from the next by a "moat." The taste buds are located on the walls of the moats. Each taste bud consists of many taste cells. All taste cells are sensitive to all taste stimuli, but certain cells are more sensitive to some stimuli than to others.   pp. 107–109

How do we perceive smell and what substances allow smells to act as communication agents?

For smell to occur, chemicals must move toward the receptor cells located on the walls of the nasal passage. When a chemical substance in the air moves past these receptor cells, it is partially absorbed into the mucus that covers the cells, thereby initiating the process of smell. The olfactory epithelium contains the olfactory rods—the nerve fibers that process odors and enable us to perceive smell. Pheromones are scented chemical substances secreted by animals that act as communicating agents.   pp. 109–111

KEY TERM: *olfaction*, p. 109.

continued

Summary & Review

The Skin Senses

Describe the anatomy of the skin.

The skin is made up of three layers. The top layer is called the epidermis. The layer underneath the epidermis is called the dermis. The deepest layer, called the hypodermis, is a thick insulating cushion. The skin sense receptors appear to interact with one another; sometimes one sensation seems to combine with or change to another.   pp. 111–113

What is the most prominent theory of pain?

A widely accepted explanation of how the body processes pain is the Melzack-Wall gate control theory. It suggests that when a signal that might normally indicate a painful stimulus is sent to the brain, it goes through a series of gates. These gates can be opened or closed, and how far they open determines how much pain signal gets through. This theory helps account for the fact that certain areas of the body are more sensitive to pain than others.   pp. 113–114

What are endorphins?

Endorphins are painkillers that are naturally produced in the brain and pituitary gland. They help regulate several bodily functions, including the control of blood pressure and body temperature. Stress, anticipated pain, and athletic activities bring about an increased endorphin level. p. 114

What is kinesthesis?

Kinesthesis is the awareness aroused by movements of the muscles, tendons, and joints. One kinesthetic sense is the *vestibular sense*—the sense of bodily orientation and postural adjustment; it helps us keep our balance and sense of equilibrium. pp. 115–116

KEY TERMS: *endorphins,* p. 114; *kinesthesis,* p. 115; *vestibular sense,* p. 116.

Extrasensory Perception

What is ESP?

ESP includes telepathy, clairvoyance, precognition, and psychokinesis. Research support for the existence of ESP is generally weak. Psychologists remain skeptical about ESP because they see so much trickery and falsification of data, as well as design errors. pp. 116–117

CONNECTIONS

If you are interested in...

4

States of Consciousness

A wonderful Broadway show, *Fiddler on the Roof* (later made into a movie), used a dream sequence to great advantage. The father, Tevye, wants to convince his wife, Golde, that a prearranged wedding for his young daughter, with an unappealing but wealthy butcher, must be called off. Tevye tells Golde he dreamed that her long-dead grandmother came all the way from heaven to tell him that the impending marriage must be averted. Golde, who is superstitious, believes that the dream and its contents are real and ominous and that they portend the future. She agrees with Tevye to call off the marriage and allow their daughter to marry her true love, the poor tailor.

Dream sequences have long been used in literature, theater, ballet, and movies. Joseph dreams of climbing the ladder to heaven in the Bible, little Clara dreams of sugar plum fairies in the Nutcracker ballet, and dreamlike flashbacks are central to such classics as *The Wizard of Oz* and *Alice in Wonderland*. Dream sequences are used so often as a literary device because artists and authors see the dream as a vehicle to express a person's wishes and desires. In a dream, people lose control of their behavior. Time and space become distorted; auditory and visual stimuli can become bizarre. Of course, not all dreams are nightmares or fantasies; many are boring, routine replays of daily activities.

Psychologists are especially interested in dreams because they represent a different form of consciousness from routine day-to-day awareness. Studying dreams may not unlock our unconscious, primal motivations, or even the basics of the nature of consciousness. However, by studying dreams and sleep and how we move from one conscious state to another, we learn more about ourselves.

Consciousness

Human beings are aware (conscious) of the messages the brain is constantly receiving and sending. The word *conscious* has a checkered history in psychology. Early psychologists, such as Wilhelm Wundt, studied the content of consciousness; later psychologists, such as William James, studied how consciousness operates. However, in the 1920s behaviorists, such as John B. Watson, argued that consciousness should be eliminated as a subject of psychological study because it is not a physical structure to be examined, probed, or diagrammed. As the behavioral approach came to dominate American psychology, the study of consciousness and thought was all but forgotten. Only in the 1960s and 1970s, as cognitive psychology emerged, was consciousness discussed again. The tide has clearly turned; today, consciousness is a topic of both scientific and popular interest.

Defining Consciousness

Almost all psychologists agree that a person who is conscious is aware of the environment; for example, we are conscious when we listen to a lecture. However, consciousness also refers to inner awareness—knowledge of our own thoughts, feelings, and memories.

When early psychologists studied the mind and its contents, they were studying consciousness. Wundt and his students in the late 1880s had subjects report the contents of their consciousness while sitting still, while working, and while falling asleep. At the turn of the century, Sigmund Freud (whom we will study in more depth later) wrote that deep within a person's consciousness are needs, wishes, and desires that influence feeling and behavior. According to Freud, people have different levels of consciousness—conscious thoughts that they are aware of as well as unconscious thoughts of which they are unaware.

Today, cognitive psychologists assert that people are aware of certain mental processes and unaware of others. For example, when you first learn to play tennis, your movements are often uncoordinated. But with practice you learn to move more automatically. In fact, as a ball approaches, you automatically (unconsciously) approach it. Cognitive psychologists generally do not speak about the unconscious but instead refer to controlled (deliberate) versus automatic processes. All of these psychologists—the early structuralists, Freud, and even today's cognitive researchers—acknowledge that different levels of consciousness exist.

Each view of conscious behavior depends on a person's orientation to psychology. Rather than taking a specific view, let us take a generally agreed-upon view and define **consciousness** as the general state of being aware of and responsive to events in the environment and to our own mental processes. Consciousness can range from alert attention to dreaming, hypnosis, or drug-induced states. We say that a person who is in a state of consciousness that is different from the usual waking state is in an **altered state of consciousness.** Consciousness is a process, not a thing. Consciousness and the ongoing biological processes in our bodies are closely linked; our biological processes influence how incoming stimuli affect us and our degree of awareness about the world. Thus, as Crick and Koch (1992) argue, perceiving the world and being conscious are constructive processes that take into account new stimulation, past experience, and an active brain that is attempting to make sense of the world. A person who does not pay attention or is not alert is not as conscious as one who is vigilant and alert.

Being conscious involves an awareness of both the environment and our own thoughts, feelings, and memories.

The idea of a continuum of awareness guides many researchers who believe that consciousness is made up of several levels of awareness, from alertness to total unresponsiveness. Researchers who favor this view suggest, for example, that a person who is drinking heavily enters, temporarily, a lower (deeper) *level* in the range of conscious levels—that of intoxication. Other researchers believe that distinctly different conscious *states* explain specific behaviors and attention patterns. Researchers who favor the latter interpretation believe a heavy drinker has entered a totally different state of consciousness. The issue of levels versus states is far from resolved.

Theories of Consciousness

As in other areas of psychology, theory guides research in the study of consciousness and its altered states. Several researchers have proposed biologically based theories of consciousness. Julian Jaynes (1976) suggests that understanding the evolution of the human brain is the key to understanding altered states. He believes consciousness originates in differences in the function and physiology of the two hemispheres of the brain. Thus, when one of the two structures of the brain is operating, one specific level of consciousness will be activated; when the other structure is operating, another level will be activated.

Robert Ornstein (1977) suggests that two modes of consciousness exist, each controlled by one side of the brain: the active-verbal-rational mode (called the active mode) and the receptive-spatial-intuitive-holistic mode (called the receptive mode). Ornstein believes evolution has made the active mode automatic: Human beings limit their awareness automatically in order to shut out experiences, events, and stimuli that do not directly relate to their ability to survive. When people need to gain perspective and judgment about what they are doing, they expand their normal awareness by using the receptive mode. According to Ornstein, techniques such as meditation, biofeedback, hypnosis, and even the use of some specific drugs can help people learn to use the receptive mode to balance the active mode.

Consciousness: The general state of being aware of and responsive to events in the environment and to our own mental processes.

Altered state of consciousness: A pattern of functioning that is dramatically different from that of ordinary awareness and responsiveness.

Ornstein and his collaborator, David Galin, support many of their ideas with laboratory data showing that the brain is divided and specialized in significant ways. They point out that the left-dominated and right-dominated modes of consciousness operate in a complementary and alternating fashion, one working while the other is inhibited (Galin, 1974; Ornstein, 1976). In Ornstein's (1977) model, intellectual activities take place in the active, or left-dominated, mode; and intuitive activities take place in the receptive, or right-dominated, mode. The integration of these two modes underlies the highest human accomplishments. Although the existence of two physiological modes of operation in the brain lends support to Ornstein's ideas, many researchers are skeptical of his theory (Zaidel, 1983). They argue that the structure of the brain does not necessarily explain its function and that no data exist to show how the brain actually operates.

One of the newest explainers of consciousness is Daniel Dennett (1991). In his best-selling book, *Consciousness Explained,* he asserts that human beings possess many sources of information, which, after processing, editing, and the passage of time, taken together, create a conscious experience. He argues that the brain creates multiple drafts (copies) of experiences, which are constantly being reanalyzed. According to Dennett, the brain develops a sense of consciousness as well as a sense of self (which is made up of multiple copies of past experiences) through this constant updating and reanalysis of experience. The theory is as yet untested and not widely accepted; however, it takes a new path in bringing together perceptual, physiological, and historical information from one individual to explain consciousness.

Regardless of the theory that explains it, being conscious means being aware; and because we are aware, we can tell researchers about our experiences. Psychologists can also study our consciousness by measuring some specific physiological functions. In the remainder of this chapter, we will focus on a wide array of states of consciousness. Some of these states are desirable and normal; others alter human behavior in negative ways. We begin with a state of awareness with which all of us are familiar—sleep.

FOCUS

► What are the key characteristics of a definition of consciousness? pp. 124–125

► Explain the theory that two modes of consciousness exist, each controlled by one side of the brain. pp. 125–126

Sleep

In January 1964, at age 17, Randy Gardner made history. He set a world's record by staying awake for more than 260 hours—just short of 11 days. A science fair near his San Diego home was the location of his experiment. He enlisted two friends to help keep him awake, and he took no stimulants—not even coffee.

After 6 days, a local physician came to supervise his progress, much to the relief of Gardner's parents. Although he did not suffer any serious physical symptoms, there were marked psychological effects. On day 2, he had trouble focusing his eyes. On day 3, there were mood changes. On day 4, he was irritable and uncooperative; he also began to see images. By day 6, Gardner had speech difficulties and memory lapses. By day 9, his thoughts and speech were incoherent. On day 10, blurred vision became more of a problem and he was regularly forgetting things. Mornings were his most difficult time, but at no time did he behave in a socially deviant manner.

One of the most interesting aspects of Randy Gardner's adventure is what happened to his sleep after his deprivation. Sleep researcher William Dement followed

Gardner's sleep, mental health, physical recovery, and electroencephalogram results for days afterward to see how his subject recovered, what happened to his sleep patterns, and whether he made up for lost sleep. Dement found that for the 3 nights following his deprivation, Gardner slept an extra 6.5 hours; and on the 4th night, he slept an extra 2.5 hours (Gulevich, Dement, & Johnson, 1966; Johnson, Slye, & Dement, 1965).

Following Randy Gardner's sleep loss and his subsequent recovery is part of the history of the study of sleep. Early researchers, such as Dement, began to realize that sleep and wakefulness follow specific patterns, which can be tracked and predicted. They noted that as you move through the day, your general awareness—responsiveness, thought processes, and physiological responses—changes. On first waking, you may not be fully aware and responsive. You move sluggishly, slow to realize that the coffee is perking and your toast is burning. Later, at a job or in class, you are probably very alert. But as the day wears on, you find your awareness decreasing; and in the evening, you may fall asleep in front of the television. Research on sleep is one part of the larger puzzle of human awareness, human consciousness, and altered states of being.

The Sleep-Wakefulness Cycle: Circadian Rhythms

In the casinos of Las Vegas, it is difficult to tell night from day. There are no windows, activity is at fever pitch 24 hours a day, and there are few clocks. People never seem to sleep; it is as if there is no day or night. Nevertheless, people do sleep; unlike Randy Gardner, they give in to their bodily urge to rejuvenate themselves. Our bodies tell us we are tired even if there is no clock on the wall to remind us.

We are not at the mercy of light and darkness to control our activities. We seem instead to have a biological clock ticking within us to control our sleep-wakefulness cycle. This clock seems to run in about a 24-hour cycle; thus, the term *circadian* was born—from the Latin *circa diem* ("about a day"). Circadian rhythms are internally generated and help control our body rhythms, sleep patterns, and body temperature. When time cues (clocks, windows, temperature changes as the sun goes down) are removed from the environment, an interesting event occurs—our circadian rhythm

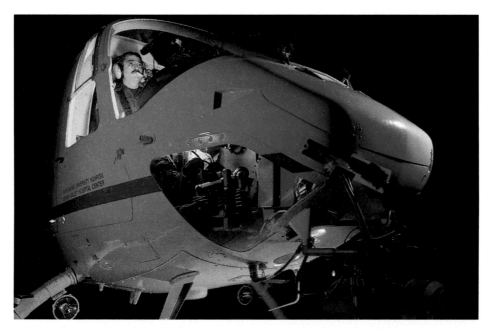

Approximately 7 million Americans work at night. Workers whose schedules are not regular, such as those who work swing shifts, may become less attentive and efficient due to sleep deprviation. In some cases, this is potentially dangerous, and employers need to be aware of and try to minimize the danger to employees and the general public.

runs a bit slow. When human beings are placed in artificially lit environments and allowed to sleep, eat, and read whenever they want to, they sleep a constant amount of time; but each "day" they go to sleep a bit later (Foster, 1993). This is because the full sleep-wakefulness cycle runs about 24.5 to 25.5 hours. Body temperature and other bodily functions tend to follow a similar circadian rhythm.

Because we have daylight, clocks, and arbitrary schedules, our circadian rhythms do not alone control sleep and wakefulness. You can see the impact of circadian rhythms when your routine is thrown off by your having to work through the night, then sleep, then rise, and so forth—your body's clock may not match your work clock. This interruption becomes especially apparent if you are an airline pilot, a surgeon, or a firefighter—one of the approximately 7 million Americans who work at night (Czeisler et al., 1990). When you put in long hours that stretch through the night and into the dawn, and when these hours are not regular, you become less attentive, think less clearly, and may even fall asleep from time to time. Thus, employers, workers, and consumers need to be aware of the potential decreased efficiency of night workers, who often vary their schedules, such as airline pilots and medical interns.

Consider the air traveler's dilemma—jet lag. If you travel from, say, New York City to London, England, the trip will take about six hours. If you leave at 9:00 P.M., you will arrive in London 6 hours later, at 3:00 A.M.—at least as far as your body is concerned. You will be exhausted. But local time is only 9:00 P.M. People meeting you may want to chat and catch up on gossip or business. You stay up till midnight; but according to your body, it is 3 hours later, 6:00 A.M. You go to bed and sleep 7 hours, but your body thinks it is the middle of the day. You experience jet lag as exhaustion and disorientation. You may want to sleep during the day and stay up at night. If you suffer jet lag or if you work long, irregular shifts, your work performance may not be at its peak. We have learned this through studying sleep, the sleep-wakefulness cycle, and sleep deprivation.

Sleep: A Restorative Process

Sleep is a natural state of consciousness experienced by everyone. **Sleep** is a nonwaking state of consciousness characterized by general unresponsiveness to the environment and general physical immobility. Some psychologists think sleep allows the body to recover from the day's expenditure of energy; they see it as a restorative process. Others perceive sleep as a holdover from a type of hibernation. They believe an organism conserves energy during sleep, when its expenditure would be inefficient (night is not a good time for animals to catch or produce food). Still other sees sleep as a time when the brain recovers from exhaustion and overload. They believe sleep has little effect on basic physiological processes in the rest of the body. Horne (1988) asserts that sleep can be divided into two major types: core and optional. *Core sleep* repairs the effects of waking wear and tear on cerebral functions; it is thus restorative. *Optional sleep* fills the time from the end of core sleep till waking. These views of sleep—as physical restoration, hibernation, brain restoration, and core repairs—guide researchers' investigations into sleep patterns.

Why do some people need more sleep than others? Everyone needs some amount of sleep. Most of us require about 8 hours, but some people can function with only 4 or 5 hours and others need as many as 9 or 10. Young teenagers tend to sleep longer than college students, and elderly people tend to sleep less than young people. Most young adults (65 percent) sleep between 6.5 and 8.5 hours a night, and about 95 percent sleep between 5.5 and 9.5 hours (Horne, 1988).

Do you think people who are active and energetic require more sleep than those who are less active? Surprisingly, this is not always the case. Bedridden hospital

Sleep: A nonwaking state of consciousness characterized by general unresponsiveness to the environment and general physical immobility

patients, for example, sleep about the same amount of time as people who are on their feet all day. The amount of sleep a person needs is physiologically determined and depends greatly on sleep cycles.

Sleep Cycles and Stages: REM and NREM Sleep

Our sleep-wakefulness cycle is repetitive, determined in part by circadian rhythms, work schedules, and a host of other events. When early sleep researchers such as Nathaniel Kleitman and William Dement studied the sleep-wakefulness cycle, they found stages within sleep that could be characterized through **electroencephalo-grams** (EEGs—records of electrical brain patterns) and by eye movements that occur during sleep. Researchers working in sleep laboratories study the EEG patterns that occur in the brain during sleep by attaching electrodes to a subject's scalp and fore-head and monitoring the person's brain waves throughout the night. New portable devices allow the recording of brain waves throughout the day as well (Broughton, 1991).

Recordings of the brain waves of sleeping subjects have revealed that, during an 8-hour period, people typically progress through five full cycles of sleep, with each cycle having four NREM stages (see Figure 4.1 on page 130) and the REM stage. A full sleep cycle lasts approximately 90 minutes. We characterize the first four stages as **no rapid eye movement (NREM) sleep.** The fifth stage is **rapid eye movement (REM) sleep**—a stage of sleep characterized by high-frequency, low-voltage brain-wave activity, rapid and systematic eye movements, and dreams. When people first fall asleep, they are in stage 1; their sleep is light, and they can be awakened easily. Within the next 30 to 40 minutes, they pass through stages 2, 3, and 4. Stage 4 is very deep sleep; when subjects leave that stage, they pass again through stage 3 and then 2 (both are described in the following paragraph).

People experience REM sleep for the first time after they have left stage 4 sleep and have passed again through stage 3 and then stage 2. Thus, the longer they sleep (and the more sleep cycles they go through), the more REM sleep they experience (Agnew & Webb, 1973). Figure 4.1 shows the distinctive brain-wave patterns of wakefulness, the four stages of NREM sleep, and REM sleep in a normal adult. The waking pattern exhibits a fast, regular rhythm. In stage 1, sleep is light; the brain waves are of low amplitude (height) but are relatively fast, with mixed frequencies. Sleepers in stage 1 can be awakened easily. Stage 2 sleep shows low-amplitude, non-rhythmic activity combined with special patterns called sleep spindles and K complexes. A *sleep spindle* is a rhythmic burst of brain waves that wax and wane for 1 or 2 seconds. A *K complex* is a higher-amplitude burst of activity seen in the last third of stage 2. Sleep spindles and K complexes appear only during NREM sleep. Sleepers in stage 2 are in deeper sleep than in stage 1 but can still be easily awakened.

Stage 3 sleep is a transitional stage between stages 2 and 4, with slower but higher-amplitude activity than at stage 2. Stage 4 sleep, the deepest sleep stage, has even higher-amplitude brain-wave traces, called *delta waves*. During this stage, people breathe deeply and have slowed heart rate and lowered blood pressure. Stage 4 sleep has two well-documented behavioral characteristics. First, subjects are difficult to awaken. Subjects awakened from stage 4 sleep often appear confused and disturbed and take several seconds to rouse themselves fully. Second, subjects in this stage generally do not dream, although they may report some vague mental activity.

In contrast, subjects who are awakened during REM sleep (which occurs after stage 4) can report in great detail the imagery and activity characteristic of a dream state. Because REM sleep is considered necessary for normal physiological functioning and behavior, it might be expected to be a deep sleep; however, it is an active

Electroencephalogram (EEG): [eel-ECK-tro-en-SEFF-uh-low-gram] The record of an organisms electrical brain patterns, obtained by placing electrodes on a subject's scalp.

NREM (no rapid eye movement) sleep: Four distinct stages of sleep during which no rapid eye movements occur.

REM (rapid eye movement) sleep: A stage of sleep characterized by high-frequency, low-voltage brain-wave activity, rapid and systematic eye movements, and dreams.

FIGURE 4.1

EEG Activity during Sleep

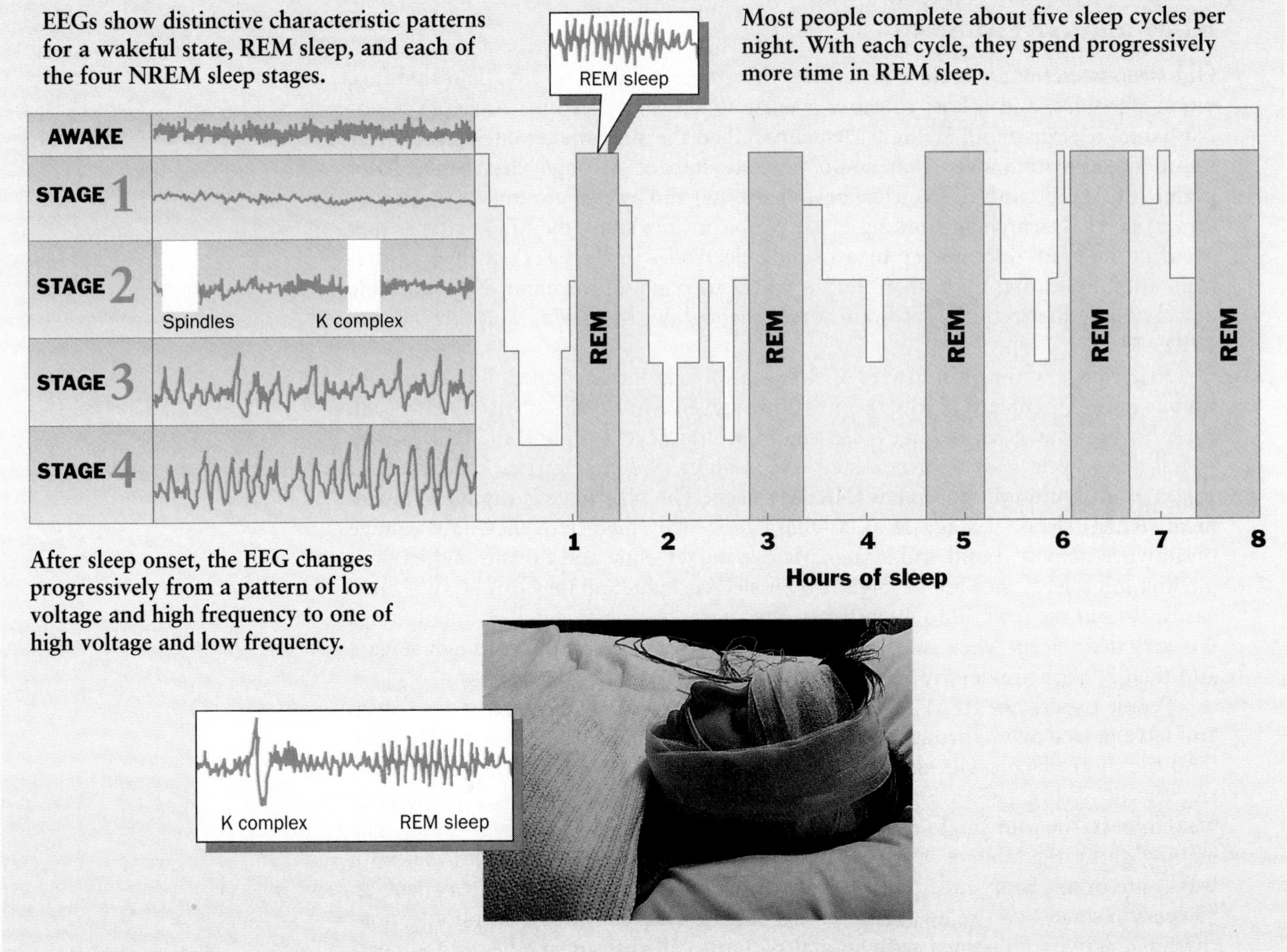

EEGs show distinctive characteristic patterns for a wakeful state, REM sleep, and each of the four NREM sleep stages.

Most people complete about five sleep cycles per night. With each cycle, they spend progressively more time in REM sleep.

REM sleep

AWAKE

STAGE 1

STAGE 2

Spindles   K complex

STAGE 3

STAGE 4

REM REM REM REM REM

1   2   3   4   5   6   7   8

Hours of sleep

After sleep onset, the EEG changes progressively from a pattern of low voltage and high frequency to one of high voltage and low frequency.

K complex   REM sleep

sleep, during which the brain-wave activity resembles that of an aware person. For this reason, it is often called *paradoxical sleep*. In REM sleep, subjects seem agitated; their eyes move and their heart rate and breathing are variable. Subjects are difficult to awaken during REM sleep.

The bottom pattern in Figure 4.1 describes an EEG transition from NREM stage 2 sleep to REM sleep. The first part of the tracing shows a clear K complex, indicating stage 2 sleep; the last part shows waves characteristic of REM sleep. During periods of sleep in which the high-frequency, low-amplitude waves are apparent, subjects experience rapid eye movements and typically report dreaming. Researchers can identify the stage in which an individual is sleeping by watching an EEG recording. If delta waves are present, the subject is in stage 4 sleep. To confirm this, an experimenter may awaken the subject and ask whether the person was dreaming.

Sleep cycles develop from before birth and continue to change into adulthood. Initially, fetuses show no eye movements. Later, they show eye, facial, and bodily

FIGURE 4.2

Changes in Sleep Patterns over a Lifetime

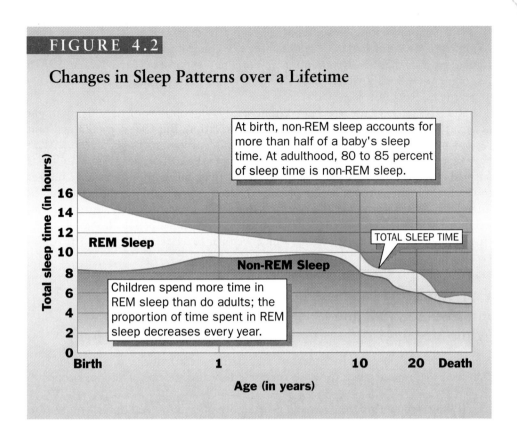

At birth, non-REM sleep accounts for more than half of a baby's sleep time. At adulthood, 80 to 85 percent of sleep time is non-REM sleep.

REM Sleep

TOTAL SLEEP TIME

Non-REM Sleep

Children spend more time in REM sleep than do adults; the proportion of time spent in REM sleep decreases every year.

Total sleep time (in hours)

Birth   1   10   20   Death

Age (in years)

movements. Newborns spend about half their sleep time in REM sleep. From age 1 to age 10, the proportion of REM sleep to stage 4 sleep decreases dramatically; in later adulthood, there is increased fragmentation of sleep patterns (see Figure 4.2).

Sleep Deprivation: Doing without REM

The need for sleep is painfully obvious to anyone who has been deprived of it. Just ask Randy Gardner, who went without sleep for close to 11 days. When people who normally sleep 8 hours miss a few hours on a particular night, they may be tired the following day but can function quite well. However, when people lose a couple hours of sleep for several nights in a row, they usually look tired, feel lethargic, and are irritable.

Researchers have investigated what happens to people who are totally or partially deprived of sleep for various amounts of time. The research is generally conducted on laboratory subjects who sleep in a sleep laboratory, where their brain-wave activity and eye movements are recorded for several nights. One study deprived subjects of all sleep for 205 hours (8.5 days). Researchers found that on the nights immediately after the experiment, subjects spent a greater-than-normal amount of time in REM and stage 4 sleep and the least amount of time in stage 1 and 2 sleep—the lightest stages of sleep (Kales et al., 1970; Webb & Agnew, 1975). Similar results were obtained in a study in which subjects were partially deprived of REM sleep. They reported feeling sleepy and spent more time in REM sleep on a subsequent night (Dement, Greenberg, & Klein, 1966). According to Horne (1988), only about 30 percent of lost sleep needs to be recovered, mostly stage 4 sleep and REM sleep.

What happens to subjects who are regularly deprived of REM sleep? They become anxious and irritable, report difficulty concentrating, and do worse than normal on tests that involve attention and original responses (May & Kline, 1987). As soon as they are allowed to have REM sleep again, the psychological changes disappear (e.g., Roehrs et al., 1989).

Some researchers used to believe that serious disruptions of personality might occur as a result of prolonged REM sleep deprivation. But today it is known that serious maladjustments do not occur with sleep deprivation (Bonnet, 1980). With the exception of brain function effects, especially in the cortex, sleep deprivation has surprisingly few effects on the rest of the body. Even more important, any changes in cerebral functions that do take place with sleep deprivation are quickly reversed after later sleep (Horne, 1988). We saw this in the case of Randy Gardner, who exhibited normal sleep patterns after his deprivation. Some people, however, suffer from altered states of sleep patterns, which we refer to as sleep disorders. The Applications box examines sleep disorders in greater depth.

Can You Tell Time or Improve Your Memory While Sleeping?

Since everybody sleeps, it is natural to wonder if we can put this time to good use. Can we program ourselves to wake at certain times or to learn while we sleep?

Telling Time. Can you awaken every morning at a predetermined time? Can you tell time even in your sleep? Psychologists doubt it; they believe some external cue, such as chirping birds or sunlight, usually helps people wake up. In a research study to assess if subjects had the ability to wake themselves at a predetermined time, electroencephalographic readings were made of the sleeping subjects (Zepelin, 1986). No subject was consistently able to wake up at a predetermined time, although some subjects could wake up at the proper time some of the time. The researchers found that subjects were able to awaken themselves most easily when they were in REM sleep. The cyclical occurrence of REM sleep may have helped. Being in REM sleep probably facilitated the ability to recall the intention to wake—and perhaps even the act of waking itself.

Sleep and Memory. Have you ever seen ads for "learn while you sleep" programs? Does this technique actually work? Most research shows that claims for learning during sleep are false at worst and exaggerated at best (Aarons, 1976; Bierman & Winter, 1989). Researchers examining the subjects who listened to tapes while they slept found that learning did not occur. Sleep can, however, aid memory and learning in a different way.

Research in the 1920s showed that sleeping before a test is better than being involved in other kinds of activities. In a now classic study, Jenkins and Dallenbach (1924) had two subjects learn lists of nonsense syllables and recall them either immediately after presentation or up to 8 hours later. During the period between learning and recall, the subjects either slept or engaged in normal waking activities. The performance of the subject who slept during the delay period was better than that of the subject who stayed awake; the waking subject's intervening activity affected his memory.

In a study by Benson and Feinberg (1977), subjects learned to pair lists of words either in the morning just after sleep or at night just before sleep. The subjects were tested on their recall after 8, 16, or 24 hours. Those who learned the lists in the

APPLICATIONS

Sleep Disorders

Do you have trouble falling asleep, snore loudly, sleepwalk, or fall asleep at inappropriate times, such as when driving a car? You may have a sleep disorder. People who fall asleep suddenly and unexpectedly have a disorder known as *narcolepsy*. Narcolepsy is probably a symptom of an autonomic nervous system disturbance and lowered arousal but may also reflect neurochemical problems (Mamelak, 1991).

Another sleep disorder, *sleep apnea,* causes airflow to stop for at least 15 seconds, so the person ceases breathing. People with this disorder often have as many as 100 apnea episodes in a night; during the day, they are exceedingly sleepy and sometimes have memory losses. People with severe apnea may have work-related accidents and severe headaches, and they may fall asleep during the day. Drug therapy and some minor surgical techniques for creating better airflow have been used to treat those with sleep apnea. Monitoring equipment for prolonged breathing pauses has also been used to wake the sleeper (Sheridan, 1985). Males are more likely than females to suffer from sleep apnea (Ingbar & Gee, 1985); and sleep apnea is a major hypothesis for explaining sudden infant death syndrome (SIDS), in which infants die suddenly during sleep for no obvious reason. Alcohol and other cen-

tral nervous system depressant drugs often contribute to sleep apnea in adults.

Insomnia, a prolonged inability to sleep, is a common sleep disorder, often caused by anxiety or depression; 1 in 10 people report suffering from it. Sleep disturbances and insomnia are especially common among older adults (Prinz et al., 1990). Insomniacs tend to be listless and tired during the day and may use sleeping pills

or other drugs to induce sleep at night. Ironically, researchers have found that these drugs do not induce natural sleep; instead, they reduce the proportion of REM sleep (Webb & Agnew, 1975). (Recall that the body's normal response to sleep deprivation is to *increase* REM sleep.) Researchers such as Dement have found that lack of REM sleep may alter normal behavior; accordingly, people with chronic insomnia should

not regularly use drugs that force sleep. Various researchers have proposed behavioral methods that do not rely on drugs to help solve the problem (e.g., Woolfolk & McNulty, 1983); among these methods are relaxation training and self-hypnosis. Vitiello (1989) asserts that diet affects sleep by affecting sympathetic nervous system activity, which may stimulate people in the middle of the night. Research on diet and insomnia is still in its early stages. But since diet affects mood and sleepiness, this idea does have experimental support.

Night terrors, another sleep disorder, consist of panic attacks that occur within an hour after a person falls asleep. Sitting up abruptly in a state of sheer panic, a person with a night terror may scream, breathe quickly, and be in a total state of fright. Night terrors are especially common in young children between the ages of 3 and 8. They usually disappear as a child grows older and do not seem to be a symptom of any psychological disorder. The cause of night terrors is not fully established, but they may be due to electrochemical processes overloading during NREM sleep.

Sleep disorders probably have several origins and will require the development of a research methodology, a theory, and a set of treatment plans that reflect the complexity of the problem. To date, no single approach has been considered universally successful.

morning and were tested at night did worse than those who learned the material at night and were tested in the morning. Moreover, after 24 hours, when all the subjects had had an equal amount of sleep and waking activity, those who had learned the pairings just before sleeping still showed better recall. The researchers concluded that sleep not only insulates subjects from interfering activity but also provides a period during which information can be consolidated. Studies such as this show that sleep is an important aid to memory, although psychologists do not yet know exactly how it works. A good night's sleep will not guarantee either learning or excellent memory, but lack of it surely will impair performance.

Insomnia: Prolonged inability to sleep.

Dreams

Why do some people rarely remember their dreams while other people can recall theirs in vivid detail? Do our dreams have hidden meanings and mysterious symbols to be uncovered? Sometimes lifelike, sometimes chaotic, and sometimes incoherent, dreams may replay a person's life history or may venture into the unknown. Dreams have long occupied an important place in psychology, but only since the 1950s have they come under close scientific scrutiny. Dream research is difficult to conduct; in addition, the data from dream research are always memories of past events, and they are sometimes difficult to quantify and verify (Koulack, 1991).

What Is a Dream?

A **dream** is a state of consciousness that occurs largely during REM sleep and is usually accompanied by vivid visual imagery, although the imagery may also be tactile or auditory. During a dream, there is an increase in heart rate, the appearance of rapid eye movements, a characteristic brain-wave pattern, and a lack of bodily movements. Although dreams occur most often in REM sleep, they can also occur during NREM sleep; during NREM sleep, they tend to be less visual and more thought-oriented. Dreams during REM sleep are intensely visual, may be action-oriented, and are more likely to be emotional than are NREM dreams.

Most people dream four or five times a night, and their dreams last from a few seconds to several minutes. The first dream of a typical night occurs 90 minutes after a person has fallen asleep and lasts for 10 minutes. With about four dreams per night and 365 days per year, a person dreams more than 100,000 dreams in a lifetime. However, people remember only a few dreams. Usually, they recall a dream because they woke in the middle of it or because a specific dream had powerful imagery.

Content of Dreams

Sometimes, the content of a dream is related to day-to-day events, to a desire a person wishes to fulfill, or to reliving an unpleasant experience. Sometimes, a person experiences the same dream or a sequence of related dreams over and over again. Most dreams are commonplace, focusing on events related to people with whom we come into contact frequently—family, friends, or coworkers. Common dream themes include sex, aggressive incidents, and misfortunes. Sounds and other sensations from the environment that do not awaken a sleeper are often incorporated into a dream. For example, when a researcher sprayed water on the hands of sleepers, 42 percent of those who did not awaken later reported dreaming about swimming pools, baths, or rain (Dement & Wolpert, 1958).

Dreams are mostly visual, and they occur mostly in color. Dement and Kleitman (1957) found that the patterns of rapid eye movements were related to the visual imagery of subjects' dreams. When a subject dreamed about climbing a series of ladders, eye movements were vertical; when a subject dreamed about two people throwing tomatoes at each other, eye movements were horizontal. Not surprisingly, blind individuals, especially those who lost their sight before age 5, tend to have dream imagery that is mostly auditory.

Sometimes, people report that they are aware of dreaming while the dream is going on; this type of dream is a **lucid dream.** Most people have had a lucid dream at one time or another. When people have experienced a lucid dream, they often report that they were inside and outside the dream at the same time. For some people, this is upsetting; and they may awaken from the dream. The Diversity box on page 136 explores sleeping and dreaming in other cultures.

Dream: A state of consciousness that occurs largely during REM sleep and is usually accompanied by vivid visual, tactile, and auditory imagery.

Lucid dream: A dream in which people are aware of their dreaming while it is happening.

Dream Theories

Some psychologists assume that dreams express desires and thoughts that may be unacceptable to the conscious mind. Therapists who interpret and analyze dreams assume that dreams represent some element of a person that is seeking expression. The suggested meaning of a dream depends on the psychologist's orientation. Some psychologists see much symbolism in dreams and assert that the content of a dream hides the dream's true meaning. Other psychologists find dreams meaningless. Two who made much of the meaning of dreams are Freud and Jung; both wrote extensively on the meaning of dreams, and yet there is little or no scientific support for their theories of dreams. Other psychologists focus on the physiological aspects of dreaming. (See Figure 4.3.)

Freudian Theory. Sigmund Freud described dreams as "the royal road to the unconscious." For Freud, a dream expressed desires, wishes, and unfulfilled needs that exist in the unconscious. In his book *The Interpretation of Dreams* (1900/1953), Freud spoke about the manifest and the latent content of dreams. The **manifest content** of a dream is its overt story line, characters, and setting—the obvious, clearly discernible events of the dream. The **latent content** of a dream is its deeper meaning, usually involving symbolism, hidden content, and repressed or obscured ideas and wishes—often uncomfortable ones. We will see in chapters 12 and 15 that Freud used dreams extensively in his theory of personality and in his treatment approach. Freudian psychoanalysts use dream analysis as a therapeutic tool in the treatment of emotional disturbance. Many contemporary therapists use patients' dreams to understand current problems and may see the dreams themselves only as a jumping-off point.

Jungian Theory. Carl G. Jung (1875–1961) was trained in Freudian approaches to therapy and personality analysis, and he too considered the dream a crucial way to understand human nature. However, Jung, more than Freud, focused on the meaning of dreams and took for granted the idea that a dream was nature's way of communicating with the unconscious. Each thing a person dreams has a meaning, so dreams are the language through which an individual expresses the deepest feelings in an uncensored form. The dream gives visual expression to instinct. Jungian

Manifest content: The overt story line, characters, and setting of a dream—the obvious, clearly discernible events of the dream.

Latent content: The deeper meaning of a dream, usually involving symbolism, hidden content, and repressed or obscured ideas and wishes.

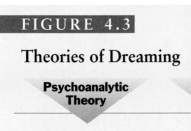

FIGURE 4.3

Theories of Dreaming

Psychoanalytic Theory	Jungian Theory	Physiological Model
Psychoanalytic theorists such as Freud view dreams as expressions of desires, wishes, and unfulfilled needs that exist in the unconscious.	Jungian theorists see dreams not only as expressions of needs and desires but as a reflection of people's collective unconscious.	Physiological models of dreaming focus on combining neural signals that are randomly generated and on making sense out of often random events.

Sleep and Dreaming in Three Hispanic Cultures

Sleep literature that focuses on the physiology of sleep and dreams is vast, but it includes little cross-cultural information. However, a study of sleep habits of the elderly in three Hispanic cultures offers some interesting data and insights.

George Domino (1986) asked 562 individuals from Mexico, Spain, and Venezuela, as well as additional non-Hispanic U.S. citizens, to fill out a sleep questionnaire. All of the participants in the study were over age 50, were natives of their country, were city dwellers, were in good health, and were at similar occupational levels. The questionnaire included such statements as "I am a very light sleeper"; the possible responses were "usually," "often," "sometimes," "not usually," and "never." The results were analyzed for each culture and for a number of different groups of questions.

There were several key findings. For example, when participants rated their feelings about dreams (such as in response to "my dreams

are unpleasant"), important cultural differences showed up. Both the Mexican and Venezuelan participants reported greater negative emotions associated with their dreams. One particularly noteworthy finding was that there were no important differences in the number of dreams recalled by the three Hispanic groups; however, the number recalled by U.S. participants was significantly higher.

It would be difficult to make sweeping conclusions about Hispanic culture, dreams, and cultural differences from the results of this study; but Domino offers a few conclusions and implications. First, he asserts that all three Hispanic groups are less likely to recall dreams than their non-Hispanic U.S. counterparts, because, in general, the Hispanic groups are slightly more passive in their coping styles and don't care about the meaning of dreams. This is quite a generalization, but Domino says it explains his data. He also points out that death, sleep, and dreams are often closely related in Hispanic cultures; and dreaming is often seen

as an omen. Thus, Hispanic people do not want to remember dreams that might carry bad omens. Domino found another important cultural difference as well. Among working people, siesta time in Mexico is looked on as a pleasant time; in the United States, taking a nap in midday is considered frivolous. Thus, Hispanic cultures view sleep as necessary and even positive; by contrast, people in the United States often see sleep as a necessary evil, with its enjoyment being a vice not to be condoned.

Of course, some of the differences found by Domino may be due to architectural differences in housing designs, to the sharing of sleeping quarters, and to other building and sleeping arrangements. Nevertheless, cultural differences in living styles are important and are reflected in day-to-day behavior and sleep patterns. Our physiology may be the same, but the culture in which we live biases our view of the world, our sleep patterns, and even how we view what we dream.

FOCUS

▶ What evidence suggests that sleep disorders have serious implications for day-to-day behavior? p. 133

▶ Why should people not take pills or alcohol to induce sleep? p. 133

▶ What evidence supports the assertion that people dream in the middle of the night? p. 134

therapy focuses on dream analysis as an approach to understanding the human condition. We will consider Jung's focus on dreams and the collective unconscious of humankind in more detail in our study of personality in chapter 12.

Activation-Synthesis Theory. Is it possible that dreams have no underlying meaning at all? Two researchers from Harvard Medical School, Allan Hobson and Robert McCarley (1977), believe dreams have a physiological basis. They argue that during periods of REM sleep, the parts of the brain responsible for long-term memory, vision, audition, and perhaps even emotion are spontaneously *activated* (stimulated) from cells in the hindbrain, especially the pons. The cortex tries to *synthesize,* or make sense out of, the messages. Because this activity is not organized by any external stimuli, the resulting dream is often fragmented and incoherent (Hobson, 1989). Activation-synthesis theory is supported by researchers who assert that, during sleep, the brain (especially the cortex) scans previous memories, refreshes old storage mechanisms, and maintains the active memory. However, other researchers point out that dreamlike activity occurs even when cells in the pons are not active. This controversial theory is still being actively researched.

Controlling Consciousness: Biofeedback, Hypnosis, and Meditation

Can you learn to control your own consciousness? Can you manipulate your mental states to achieve certain bodily reactions? Research and anecdotal data suggest that you can. People have long been taught to relax and breathe deeply when they are in pain—for example, during childbirth. Marathons have been won through intense concentration that allowed contestants to endure especially difficult physical circumstances. Laboratory research also shows that people can bring some otherwise autonomic bodily states (see chapter 2), such as blood pressure, under conscious control through a technique called biofeedback.

Biofeedback

Imagine a special clinic where people are taught to treat themselves for headaches, nearsightedness, high blood pressure, and stress-related illnesses. By learning to influence consciously what are normally involuntary reactions, patients might be able to cure themselves. Such a psychological-medical clinic may exist in the future if biofeedback proves to be the healing tool some researchers predict it will be.

Physicians and psychologists once assumed that most biological functions, especially those involving the autonomic nervous system, could not be voluntarily controlled except through drugs or surgery. Since the 1960s, however, studies have explored the extent to which subjects can learn to control these functions. What has been studied is the use of **biofeedback**—the general technique by which individuals can monitor and learn to control the involuntary activity of the body's organs and functions. A well-known psychologist, Neal E. Miller, was one of the first researchers to train rats to control certain glandular responses. Miller (1969) suggested that the same techniques could be used to help human beings manage their bodies and behavior. Since then, studies have shown that people can manipulate the electrical activity of their bodies by changing their level of excitation.

A relaxed person viewing alpha waves on a monitor, for example, can change those alpha waves to high-frequency waves by becoming more alert and by paying attention. Similarly, a subject whose heart rate is displayed on a monitor can watch the rate decrease as the person relaxes, thereby learning about the physiological states that allow the body to work easily and efficiently. The person can learn which behaviors relax the heart and lower blood pressure and, in time, can learn to control heart rate and blood pressure by reproducing behaviors associated with reduced heart rate.

Some researchers, among them Drennen and Holden (1984), contend that biofeedback training is not effective; other researchers point out that the effects can be obtained without real feedback (Plotkin, 1980). Some are skeptical about the long-term effectiveness of biofeedback. Others have used biofeedback successfully to treat people with stress-related symptoms, hyperactivity, stuttering, depression,

Biofeedback: The general technique by which individuals can monitor and learn to control the involuntary activity of some of the body's organs and functions.

Through biofeedback, people attempt to bring normally involuntary functions under conscious control.

nearsightedness, and learning disabilities. For example, Dietvorst (1978) successfully used biofeedback to help victims of recent heart attacks reduce their anxiety and fear of the future. He trained subjects to decrease their level of arousal, and thus their level of anxiety, by monitoring one measure of their autonomic activity—hand temperature.

Although a number of laboratory studies have demonstrated biofeedback's effectiveness in helping people manage a wide range of physiological problems, only carefully controlled research will answer persistent questions about its usefulness. For example, under what conditions, with what kinds of problems, and with what types of clients is biofeedback effective (Middaugh, 1990)? Methodological issues, such as those described in chapter 1 (the Hawthorne effect, for example), make this a challenging research area.

Hypnosis

"You are falling asleep. Your eyelids are becoming heavy. The strain on your eyes is becoming greater and greater. Your muscles are relaxing. You are feeling sleepier and sleepier. You are feeling very relaxed."

These instructions are typical of those used in *hypnotic induction*—the process used in hypnosis. **Hypnosis** is an altered state of consciousness brought about by procedures that induce a trance. The generally accepted view of hypnosis is that hypnotized individuals are in a semimystical state of consciousness and no longer have control over their behavior. They are aware of their surroundings and are conscious, but their level of awareness and responses to others are altered. A person's willingness to follow unconventional instructions given by the hypnotist, such as to make funny noises, is called *hypnotic susceptibility* or *suggestibility*. Most people can be hypnotized to some extent (Hilgard, 1965). Children between 7 and 14 are the most susceptible; those who daydream are also especially susceptible (Hoyt et al., 1989).

Effects of Hypnosis. People who have been hypnotized report that they know they have been hypnotized and are aware of their surroundings. Some report being in a special, almost mystical state; and most report a sense of time distortion (K. S. Bowers, 1979). One time distortion effect of hypnosis is **age regression**—the ability to report details about an experience that took place many years earlier or to act and feel like a child. Because few studies that report age regression during hypnosis have been controlled for accuracy of recall, the authenticity of age regression has been questioned (Nash, 1987). *Heightened memory* is another effect of hypnosis. Evidence indicates that hypnosis helps subjects recall information (e.g., McConkey & Kinoshita, 1988). However, techniques that do not involve hypnosis may work just as well for this purpose.

In a study by Putnam (1979), hypnotized and nonhypnotized subjects were asked to recall events they had seen earlier on a videotape. Hypnotized subjects

Hypnosis: An altered state of consciousness brought about by procedures that induce a trance.

Age regression: The ability, sometimes induced by hypnosis, to "return" to an earlier time in one's life and to report events that occurred at that time.

made more errors when answering leading questions than did nonhypnotized subjects. Putnam suggests that hypnotized subjects not only make more errors (misrecollection) but also mistakenly believe that their memories are accurate (McConkey & Kinoshita, 1988). Results from such studies have led researchers to question the use of hypnosis in courtroom settings; in fact, some states do not allow the testimony of hypnotized subjects as evidence (Sanders & Simmons, 1983; M. C. Smith, 1983).

Hypnosis is also used for pain reduction. In a case reported by E. F. Siegel (1979), hypnosis successfully reduced lower-leg pain in a woman who had undergone an above-the-knee amputation. (The phenomenon of pain in a part of the body that no longer exists is called *phantom pain;* it occurs in some amputees.) Hypnosis has also been used to reduce pain from heat, pressure, and childbirth (Harmon, Hynan, & Tyre, 1990). Few studies of pain management, however, are conducted with adequate experimental rigor. Critics of hypnosis note that most patients show signs of pain even when hypnotized. Also, in many cases, analgesic drugs (pain relievers) are used along with the hypnotism. Some researchers (especially Barber, considered next) challenge the ability of hypnosis to reduce pain, reasoning that relaxation and a subject's positive attitude and lowered anxiety account for reported reductions in pain.

Challenges to Hypnosis. Theodore Xenophon Barber, one of the major skeptics of traditional theories of hypnotism, contends that the concepts of hypnosis and the hypnotic trance are meaningless and misleading. According to Barber, behaviors of hypnotized subjects are no different from behaviors of subjects willing to think about and imagine themes suggested to them. If subjects' attitudes toward a situation lead them to expect certain effects, those effects will be more likely to occur. Barber's approach is called the *cognitive-behavioral viewpoint* (Barber, Spanos, & Chaves, 1974).

Barber's studies show that subjects given task-motivating instructions perform similarly to subjects undergoing hypnotic induction. Typically, more than half of the subjects in experimental groups showed responsiveness to task suggestions, in contrast to 16 percent in the control groups, which were given no special instructions. From the results, Barber has concluded that task-motivating instructions are almost as effective as hypnotic induction procedures in increasing subjects' responsiveness to task suggestions.

Barber's studies have received support from other research. Salzberg and DePiano (1980), for example, found that hypnosis did not facilitate performance any more than task-motivating instructions did. In fact, they argued that, for cognitive tasks, task-motivating instructions are more effective than hypnosis. The evidence showing that hypnosislike effects can be achieved in various ways (e.g., Bryant & McConkey, 1989) does not mean that psychologists must discard the concept or use of hypnosis. It simply means they should reconsider traditional assumptions.

Hypnosis continues to be widely used as an aid in psychotherapy. Most clients report that it is a pleasant experience. Therapists assert that in some cases it can (1) help focus a client's energy on a specific topic, (2) aid memory, and (3) help a child cope with the aftereffects of child abuse. Many therapists use hypnosis to help patients relax, enhance their memory, reduce stress and anxiety, lose weight, and stop smoking (e.g., Somer, 1990). Some psychologists assert that hypnosis can be a formidable aid to help athletes concentrate (Morgan, 1992). Research into the process and effects of hypnosis continues, with an emphasis on defining critical variables in hypnosis itself and in the subjects who are the most and the least easily hypnotized (e.g., Nilsson, 1990) and on ascertaining potential negative effects (e.g., Owens et al., 1989).

Meditation: A state of consciousness induced by a variety of techniques and characterized by concentration, restriction of sensory stimuli, and deep relaxation to produce a sense of detachment.

Psychologists who are skeptical about hypnosis may have the same attitude toward another altered state of consciousness, meditation.

Meditation

Meditation has become an important daily routine for a colleague of mine. Previously, searing migraines, stomach pains, and high blood pressure had afflicted her during stressful periods. Despite prescription drugs and frequent visits to the doctor, she had found little relief. Then, at a stress management clinic, she discovered how to ease her tensions through meditation. Now, instead of taking a pill, she meditates at the onset of a headache.

Meditation is a state of consciousness induced by a variety of techniques and characterized by concentration, restriction of incoming stimuli, and deep relaxation to produce a sense of detachment. It has been used for centuries to alter consciousness and help relieve health problems. Practitioners report that it can reduce anxiety, tension headaches, backaches, asthma, and the need for sleep. It can also increase self-awareness and feelings of inner peace (West, 1980, 1982).

We distinguish between two major types of meditation: *mindfulness* and *concentrative*. Both forms of meditation uses different techniques to induce an altered state of awareness (Delmonte, 1983). Both direct the focus of attention away from the outside world through intense concentration (Schuman, 1980). The forms of meditation now practiced in the Western world derive from the Eastern religions of Buddhism and Hinduism and are considered mindfulness approaches. One mindfulness approach, *Zen,* is especially popular among people interested in healing and nutritional approaches to health. People using *Zen Buddhist* techniques concentrate on their breathing and count their breaths, with the aim of focusing attention on a specific visual stimulus.

Yoga uses physical and mental exercises to alleviate stress.

Concentrative meditation has been commercially exploited and for some has acquired a bad reputation. Both yoga and transcendental meditation are considered concentrative meditation. People using *yoga* focus their attention by gazing at a fixed stimulus. Yoga also involves special physical and breathing exercises, with the aim of controlling autonomic physiological processes such as heart rate and blood pressure; it may also require a special seating position. *Transcendental meditation (TM)* uses techniques similar to those of yoga; its practitioners may repeat a phrase, known as a mantra, over and over to themselves, although they do not have to meditate while in a specific posture.

Supporters of meditation claim that it is a unique state, capable of causing profound physiological and psychological changes. They argue that mindfulness meditation produces a different mode of cognitive processing, by training people to maintain awareness of ongoing events and increasing attention. But a study comparing the physiological responses of meditators with those of hypnotized subjects found them to be nearly identical (Holmes, 1984). Experimental studies also show that individuals trained to simply relax and concentrate have been able to achieve bodily states similar to those of meditators (Fenwick et al., 1977).

Although most theories that explain the nature and effects of meditation rely on concepts that are not scientifically measurable or observable, some controlled studies have been done. The data from these studies have shown that meditators can alter physiological responses, including oxygen consumption, brain-wave activity, and sleep patterns (Pagano et al., 1976). Such evidence encourages some scientists to continue to investigate meditation for relieving tension, anxiety, and arousal.

FOCUS

▶ What underlying assumption do biofeedback practitioners make when they treat various disorders?   pp. 137–138

▶ What is the fundamental difference between the traditional view of hypnosis and the cognitive-behavioral view of hypnosis?   pp. 138–139

Altering Consciousness with Drugs

In 1993, physicians wrote more than 2 billion prescriptions for drugs. Of those, almost 50 million were written for the tranquilizer diazepam (Valium). At least one-third of all U.S. citizens between the ages of 18 and 74 regularly use some kind of consciousness-altering drug that changes both brain activity and daily behavior. There is no doubt that the United States is a drug-using culture. We use drugs to help us wake up in the morning, to get us through stresses in the day, and to help us sleep. Drugs may be legal or illegal; they may be used responsibly or abused with tragic consequences.

A **drug** is any chemical substance that alters normal biological processes. Many widely used drugs are both psychoactive and addictive. A **psychoactive drug** is a drug that alters behavior, thought, or emotions by altering biochemical reactions in the nervous system, thereby affecting consciousness. An **addictive drug** is a drug that causes a compulsive physiological need and that, when withheld, produces withdrawal symptoms (discussed in the next section). Addictive drugs also usually produce tolerance (also discussed in the next section).

In studying drug (or substance) use and abuse, we have to consider the drug itself, its properties, and the context of its use. For example, not all people respond in the same way to the same drug, and one person may respond differently on different occasions. Two important questions we need to ask are the following: Does the drug produce dependence? Are there adverse reactions to the drug for the user, other people, or society (Newcomb & Bentler, 1989)?

There is no single explanation for substance use and abuse. Societal factors, individual family situations, medical problems, and genetic heritage are all potentially part of a person's reasons for using or abusing drugs. The use versus abuse issue becomes more sharply delineated when we look at children who have to sort out the conflicting messages our society delivers. Newcomb and Bentler (1989) argue, "Adolescents are quite adept at spotting hypocrisy and may have difficulty understanding a policy of 'saying no to drugs' when suggested by a society that clearly says 'yes' to the smorgasbord of drugs that are legal as well as the range of illicit drugs that are widely available and used" (p. 242).

Who Are the Substance Abusers?

Most **substance abusers**—people who overuse and rely on drugs to deal with their stress and anxiety—turn to alcohol and other readily available drugs such as cocaine and marijuana, but substance abuse is not confined to these drugs. Psychologists are

Drug: Any chemical substance that alters normal biological processes.

Psychoactive drug: [SIE-koh-AK-tiv] A drug that alters behavior, thought, or emotions by altering biochemical reactions in the nervous system, thereby affecting consciousness.

Addictive drug: A drug that causes a compulsive physiological need and that, when withheld, produces withdrawal symptoms.

Substance abusers: People who overuse drugs and rely on them to deal with stress and anxiety.

seeing a growing number of people abusing such legal drugs as tranquilizers and diet pills, as well as such illegal drugs as amphetamines and heroin. A person is a substance abuser if all three of the following statements apply:

▶ The person has used the abused substance for at least a month.

▶ The use has caused legal difficulties or social or vocational problems.

▶ There is recurrent use in hazardous situations such as driving a car.

Substance abuse can lead to psychological dependence, pathological use, or both. **Psychological dependence** is a compelling desire to use a drug, along with an inability to inhibit that desire. *Pathological use* is out-of-control episodes of use, such as an alcohol binge. Most drugs produce a physiological reaction when they are no longer administered; in general, this reaction is called *dependence*. Without the drug, a dependent person suffers from **withdrawal symptoms**—a variety of physiological reactions that occur when an addictive drug is no longer administered to an addict. The reactions may include headaches, nausea, and an intense craving for the absent drug.

In addition, addictive drugs usually produce **tolerance**—a progressive insensitivity to repeated use of a specific drug in the same dosage and at the same frequency of use. Tolerance forces an addict to use increasing amounts of the drug or to use the drug at an increased frequency to achieve the same effect. For example, alcoholics must consume larger and larger amounts of alcohol to become drunk. Most addictive drugs produce both withdrawal symptoms and tolerance.

Each time people take a psychoactive drug, they change their ability to function normally. Specifically, psychoactive drugs change behavior by altering a person's physiology and normal state of consciousness. Some drugs increase alertness and performance; others relax people and relieve high levels of arousal and tension. Some produce physical and psychological dependence. All psychoactive drugs alter a person's thoughts and moods; they are all considered consciousness-altering.

Illicit drug use dropped for most, but not all, groups during the late 1980s, except for cocaine. This is probably in response to national media campaigns, school- and community-based drug programs, and interventions in the workplace. But drug abuse is still a major problem, with millions of people using illicit drugs on a regular basis.

Why Do People Abuse Drugs?

Drug abuse is based on many physiological and psychological factors. Some people are likely to develop a substance abuse problem for physiological and genetic reasons; others are victims of the numerous emotional problems caused by stress, poverty, boredom, loneliness, or anxiety. Sadly, many people believe alcohol and drugs provide a quick fix for these problems. People may turn to drugs to relax, be sociable, forget their worries, feel confident, or lose weight. Parental drug use, peer drug use, poor self-esteem, stressful life changes, divorce, and social isolation have all been implicated. Our society and its materialistic values also contribute to the problem.

Determining the causes of drug abuse is complicated by the definition of addiction. We can define addictive drugs by saying that they are habit forming (reinforcing) or that such drugs produce a physiological dependence, for example, dependence on alcohol or barbiturates. These two processes are not independent, however; physiological processes may lead to addictive reinforcement patterns. Many drugs that affect the brain differently all share the property of being addictive—alcohol and cocaine are two examples. Researchers today are attempting to develop models that account for psychological variables such as cravings, physio-

Psychological dependence: A compelling desire to use a drug, along with an inability to inhibit that desire.

Withdrawal symptoms: A variety of physiological reactions that occur when an addictive drug is no longer administered to an addict.

Tolerance: A progressive insensitivity to repeated use of a specific drug in the same dosage and at the same frequency of use.

logical variables such as changes in brain structures and firing patterns, and social variables such as family support and therapy to develop drug policies.

Most researchers argue that no single explanation can account for drug use and abuse (Marlatt et al., 1988). No two substance abusers have identical abuse patterns. Some people use only one drug—for example, alcohol. Others are *polydrug abusers,* taking several drugs; a heroin addict, for example, might also take amphetamines. When amphetamines are difficult to obtain, the person might switch to barbiturates. Some researchers assert that many people are addiction-prone (Sutker & Allain, 1988). Others note that addicts are often ambivalent about whether they want to give up the drug (Bradley, 1990). Still other researchers assert that later addictive behaviors can be predicted from antisocial childhood behavior (Nathan, 1988; Shedler & Block, 1990).

Let's take a closer look at some of the most commonly used drugs and their consciousness-altering properties. We begin with alcohol, the source of one of the most complicated and widespread drug problems in the United States today.

Alcohol

The students at my daughter's high school wore black arm bands to show they mourned the death of their sophomore friend Mark Smoak. At 15 years of age, with a learner's permit to drive, Mark Smoak crashed into a telephone pole on a poorly lit street just 2 miles from his home. It was later learned that his blood alcohol level was exceedingly high. That a high school student crashed his car, killed himself, and maybe even seriously injured a friend in the front seat is a tale that is told all over America, every year in every community.

Alcohol consumption in the United States has been at an all-time high for more than a decade. According to the U.S. Department of Health and Human Services, about 80 percent of urban U.S. adults report having used alcohol at some time; it is estimated that 10 million people in the United States over age 18 are problem drinkers or alcoholics (defined and discussed shortly). In a recent survey, about one-fourth of 8th-grade students and more than one-third of 10th-grade students reported having had five or more drinks on at least one occasion during the previous 2 weeks (Landers, 1988).

Alcohol is classified as a **sedative-hypnotic**—a class of drugs that relax and calm people and that, in higher doses, induce sleep. Alcohol is the most widely used sedative-hypnotic. Because it is easily available, relatively inexpensive, and socially accepted, addiction to the drug is easy to establish and maintain. In fact, most Americans consider some alcohol consumption appropriate; they often consume alcoholic beverages before, during, and after dinner, at weddings and funerals, at religious events, and during sports events.

Effects of Alcohol. Alcohol is a depressant that decreases inhibitions and thus increases some behaviors that are normally under tight control. For example, it may diminish people's social inhibitions and make them less likely to restrain their aggressive impulses (Steele & Josephs, 1990). The physiological effects of alcohol vary, depending on the amount of alcohol in the bloodstream and the gender and weight of the user (see Figure 4.4 on page 144). After equal amounts of alcohol consumption, women have higher blood alcohol levels than men do, even allowing for differences in body weight (Frezza et al., 1990). Table 4.1 on page 145 shows various blood alcohol levels and the behavior associated with them.

With increasing amounts of alcohol in the bloodstream, people typically exhibit progressively slowed behavior; often, they exhibit severe motor disturbances, such as staggering. A blood alcohol level of greater than 0.10 percent (0.1 milligrams of alcohol per 100 milliliters of blood) usually indicates that the person has consumed

Sedative-hypnotic: A class of drugs that relax and calm people and that, in higher doses, induce sleep.

FIGURE 4.4

Relationships between Alcohol Consumption and Blood Alcohol Level, by Gender and Weight

Blood Alcohol Level
(in milligrams of alcohol per 100 milliliters of blood)

Alcohol (in ounces)	Beverage Intake in 1 Hour	Male			Female		
		100 lbs.	150 lbs.	200 lbs.	100 lbs.	150 lbs.	200 lbs.
1/2	1 oz. spirits* 1 glass wine 1 can beer	.037	.025	.019	.045	.03	.022
1	2 oz. spirits 2 glasses wine 2 cans beer	.075	.050	.037	.090	.06	.045
2	4 oz. spirits 4 glasses wine 4 cans beer	.150	.100	.070	.180	.12	.090
3	6 oz. spirits 6 glasses wine 6 cans beer	.220	.150	.110	.270	.18	.130
4	8 oz. spirits 8 glasses wine 8 cans beer	.300	.200	.150	.360	.24	.180
5	10 oz. spirits 10 glasses wine 10 cans beer	.370	.250	.180	.450	.30	.220

*All spirits are assumed to be 100 proof.

too much alcohol to function responsibly. In most states, a 0.10 percent blood alcohol level legally defines intoxication; police officers may arrest drivers who have this level of blood alcohol.

The nervous system becomes less sensitive to, or accommodates, alcohol with increased usage. After months or years of drinking, drug tolerance develops, and a person has to consume ever-increasing amounts of alcohol to achieve the same effect. Thus, when not in an alcoholic state, a heavy drinker develops anxiety, cravings, and other withdrawal symptoms (Levin, 1990).

Problem Drinkers versus Alcoholics. Alcohol-related problems are medical, social, or psychological problems associated with alcohol use. A person who shows an alcohol-related problem such as missing work occasionally because of hangovers, spending a paycheck to buy drinks for friends, or losing a driver's license because of drunk driving is exhibiting alcohol abuse. Alcohol-related problems caused by chronic (repeated) usage of alcohol may include liver deterioration, memory loss, and significant mood swings (Nace, 1987).

A person with alcohol-related problems who also has a physiological and psychological need to consume alcohol and to experience its effects is an **alcoholic.** All alcoholics are problem drinkers, but not all problem drinkers are alcoholics. With-

Alcoholic: A problem drinker who also has both a physiological and a psychological need to consume alcohol and to experience its effects.

TABLE 4.1

Behavioral Effects of Various Blood Alcohol Levels

Blood Alcohol Level (in milligrams of alcohol per milliliter of blood)	Behavioral Effects
.05	Lowered alertness, impaired judgment, release of inhibitions, good feelings
.10	Slowed reaction times and impaired motor function, less caution
.15	Large, consistent increases in reaction time
.20	Marked depression in sensory and motor capability, decidedly intoxicated behavior
.25	Severe motor disturbance and impairment of sensory perceptions
.30	In a stupor but still conscious—no comprehension of events in the environment
.35	Surgical anesthesia; lethal dose for about 1 percent of the population
.40	Lethal dose for about 50 percent of the population

out alcohol, alcoholics develop physiological withdrawal symptoms. In addition, they often develop tolerance; a single drink or even a few will not affect them. See Table 4.2 on page 146 for a list of some of the warning signals of alcoholism.

Social and Medical Problems. From both a medical and a psychological standpoint, alcohol abuse is one of the greatest social problems in the United States. Among the homeless, alcohol abuse is widespread; between 30 and 40 percent of the homeless have alcohol problems (McCarty et al., 1991). Drunkenness is the biggest law enforcement problem today, accounting for millions of arrests each year. The Department of Transportation has estimated that alcohol was involved in more than 39,000 automobile deaths in 1993. Although the number of deaths caused by alcohol-related accidents has decreased in the last few years, the number in the next 3 years will exceed the death toll of the Vietnam War (Turrisi & Jaccard, 1991). In addition, people involved in violent crimes and suicide are often found to have been drinking.

Although alcoholism is seen as a social disease because of its devastating social consequences, it is also a medical problem. Biomedical researchers look for the effects of alcohol on the brain, as well as anything about the brains of alcoholics that may predispose them to alcoholism. Researchers know that chronic excessive drinking is associated with loss of brain tissue, liver malfunctions, and impaired cognitive and motor abilities (e.g., Ellis & Oscar-Berman, 1989).

Treatment Programs. For some alcoholics, psychological and medical treatment is successful. The most widely known program is Alcoholics Anonymous, which helps individuals abstain from alcohol by providing a therapeutic and emotionally nurturing environment. Treatment programs make abstinence their goal. The fundamental assumptions, based on the difficulty alcoholics have controlling

The liver at the top is normal. Excessive alcohol consumption has caused the middle liver to be fatty and unhealthy and the bottom liver to be cirrhotic.

TABLE 4.2 *Warning Signals of Alcoholism*

Following are some of the warning signals that alcoholism is developing:

You drink more than you used to and tend to gulp your drinks.

You try to have a few extra drinks before or after drinking with others.

You have begun to drink alone.

You are noticeably drunk on important occasions.

You drink the "morning after" to overcome the effects of previous drinking.

You drink to relieve feelings of boredom, depression, anxiety, or inadequacy.

You have begun to drink at certain times, to get through difficult situations, or when you have problems.

You have weekend drinking bouts and Monday hangovers.

You are beginning to lose control of your drinking; you drink more than you planned and get drunk when you did not want to.

You promise to drink less but do not.

You often regret what you have said or done while drinking.

You are beginning to feel guilty about your drinking.

You are sensitive when others mention your drinking.

You have begun to deny your drinking or lie about it.

You have memory blackouts or pass out while drinking.

Your drinking is affecting your relationship with friends or family.

You have lost time at work or school because of drinking.

You are beginning to stay away from people who do not drink.

---

their drinking, are that an alcoholic is an alcoholic forever and that alcoholism should be considered diseaselike in nature—and incurable (Peele, 1984).

Some practitioners, on the other hand, believe that limited, nonproblem drinking should be the goal of treatment programs (Vaillant & Milofsky, 1982). This view assumes that alcohol abuse is a learned behavior and can therefore be unlearned. It also assumes that abstinence is an unattainable goal. Those who prefer controlled use claim that alcohol abuse is merely a symptom of a larger underlying problem, such as poor self-esteem or family instability (Sobell & Sobell, 1982). However, most researchers hold that controlled drinking is not a reliable answer for most alcoholics, although it might be a reasonable alternative for young, heavy drinkers who are not yet alcoholics (Nathan & Skinstad, 1987; Rosenberg, 1993).

Family therapy is generally considered an important part of treatment for alcoholism because the alcohol problem of one family member becomes a problem for the entire family. A multimodal treatment approach (one involving many modes of treatment) is often the best plan; the objective is to combine individual or group therapy with Alcoholics Anonymous or some other self-help group (Levin, 1990). Few systematic, carefully controlled studies of alcoholism and procedures for its treatment exist. Some researchers are investigating the use of drugs and behavioral therapies to control alcohol intake (e.g., Weins & Menustik, 1983; G. T. Wilson, 1987). Others are studying detoxification centers and halfway houses as treatments for alcoholics. Still others are trying to determine who is at risk (who is likely to become an alcoholic), in the hope that early intervention can prevent alcoholism (e.g., Hawkins, Catalano, & Miller, 1992). The Research Process box on page 148 examines who is at risk for alcoholism.

Barbiturates and Tranquilizers

Like alcohol, most barbiturates and tranquilizers are considered to be in the sedative-hypnotic class of drugs. They relax and calm individuals; and when taken in higher doses, they often induce sleep. *Barbiturates* decrease the excitability of neurons throughout the nervous system. They calm the individual by depressing the central nervous system. Their use as sedatives, however, has diminished; they have largely been replaced by another class of drugs—tranquilizers.

Tranquilizers are a group of drugs (technically benzodiazepines) that also sedate, calm, and relax people. With a somewhat lower potential for abuse and for depressing the central nervous system than sedative-hypnotics, they are sometimes called *minor tranquilizers*. Valium and Librium are two of the most widely used tranquilizers prescribed by physicians for relief of mild stress. Such drugs have been widely abused by all segments of society because of their availability.

Opiates: Heroin

Opiates are a class of drugs with sedative properties that are addictive and produce tolerance; heroin is an opiate, a derivative of opium, and is widely abused. Heroin dulls the senses, relieves pain, tranquilizes, and induces euphoria. Like many other addictive drugs, heroin is considered reinforcing biologically; many researchers assert it is this reinforcing property that keeps people addicted (Wise & Bozarth, 1987).

In the past, a number of opiates have been used for everything from relieving children's crying to reducing pain from headaches, surgery, childbirth, and menstruation. Today, most opiates are illegal; but heroin and other opiates (such as morphine, which is illegal when not prescribed by a physician) are readily available from drug dealers. The high cost of these drugs has led many addicts to engage in crime to support their habits.

Heroin can be smoked or eaten, but typically it is injected into a vein. Heroin addicts tend to be young, poor, and undereducated. Most become addicts as a result of peer pressure and a desire for upward mobility among their peers. Estimates of the number of heroin addicts range dramatically from 0.5 million to 13 million. Heroin addicts often use other drugs in combination with heroin; among them are alcohol, barbiturates, amphetamines, and cocaine (the last two drugs will be described in a later section). This polydrug use makes it difficult to classify heroin users as addicts of one drug or another. Moreover, even when classification is possible, treatment is complicated by the medical, psychological, and social problems associated with using many drugs simultaneously.

The major physiological effect of heroin is impaired functioning of the respiratory system. Other effects are some detrimental changes in the heart, arteries, and veins, as well as possible constipation and loss of appetite. Few heroin addicts die of overdoses. A lethal dose of the drug would be much larger than that injected even by heavy users. More often than not, heroin addicts die from taking a mixture of drugs (such as heroin and alcohol) or from disease—especially AIDS, contracted from nonsterile needles and other paraphernalia used in injecting the substance into the bloodstream. Some lawmakers are advocating community programs for distributing sterile needles to drug users to prevent the spread of AIDS. But, as you might expect, such programs are extremely controversial.

The only major successful treatment program for heroin addiction is methadone maintenance. Like heroin, methadone is an addicting drug and must be consumed daily or withdrawal symptoms will occur. Unlike heroin, however, methadone does

THE RESEARCH PROCESS

Who Is at Risk for Alcoholism?

Are some people more likely than others to become alcoholics? The answer is yes, according to researchers who study the biological side of alcoholism. Researchers assert that genetics, blood and brain chemistry, and some specific brain structures predispose some people to alcoholism.

Correlational Studies. Some of the most interesting research on alcoholism comes from studies that focus on *high-risk* individuals—people who seem more at risk for a disorder. (For example, the culturally disadvantaged and the economically poor are at high risk for substance abuse because often they live in urban environments that expose them to substance abuse, alcoholism, and crime.) Who is at high risk for alcoholism? Children of alcoholics are more likely to be alcoholics, even if they are raised by nonalcoholic adoptive parents. The correlations suggest that the physiology of alcoholics and their children predispose the children to alcoholism.

Experimental Research. Studies show that alcoholics, more than non-alcoholics, tend to respond with physiological arousal to stress and other aversive stimulation. Finn and Pihl (1987), two McGill University researchers, decided to test the hypothesis that men with extensive family histories of alcoholism are more reactive physiologically to aversive stimulation than are control subjects. Further, they attempted to see whether alcohol reduces physiological responses more for men with a family history of alcoholism than for control subjects. Their overall aim was to find out whether certain people are at high risk for alcoholism.

They divided men into three groups on the basis of family history: high, moderate, and low risk for alcoholism. The high-risk subjects had alcoholic fathers and grandfathers and at least one other male alcoholic in the family. The moderate-risk subjects had one alcoholic parent and no other close alcoholic relative. The low-risk subjects had no identifiable alcoholics in the present or the two previous generations of their family.

Finn and Pihl investigated two physiological responses—heart rate and blood volume—of subjects who knew that they were going to receive mild electrical shocks. Anticipation of a shock induces a physiological response in nearly everybody; the question to be answered was whether the responses were more pronounced in high-risk subjects. To add another dimension to the experiment, the researchers gave some subjects a moderate amount of alcohol (the amount was adjusted for body weight) to bring the blood alcohol to a level of 0.07. Would the high-risk subjects show a greater physiological reaction to the impending shock than the low-risk subjects? Would alcohol consumption affect the responses of the high-risk subjects more than those of the low-risk subjects?

Results. The results showed that sober high-risk subjects were more cardiovascularly reactive than sober moderate-risk subjects—that is, their heart rates increased quickly compared to moderate-risk subjects. In addition, alcohol consumption led to a reduction in physiological response in the high-risk group only. In the

---

not produce euphoria or tolerance in the user, and daily dosages do not need to be increased. Because methadone blocks the effects of heroin, a normal injection of heroin has no effect on individuals on methadone maintenance. As a result, many methadone treatment patients (there are about 100,000) who might be tempted to use heroin to achieve a high do not do so. Moreover, because methadone is legal, many of the patients are able to hold jobs to support themselves and stay out of jail. Research suggests that methadone treatment combined with psychotherapy and behavior modification techniques to reduce illicit drug use may be far more effective than methadone by itself (Stitzer, 1988). Unfortunately, there are methadone treatment programs that do not focus on treatment; they simply prescribe methadone and have been seen as unscrupulous money making machines that feed an ongoing habit. Thus, methadone treatment programs are seen by many as controversial, and potentially unethical.

Marijuana

Consciousness-altering drugs that affect moods, thoughts, memory, and perception are called *psychedelics* (hallucinogens). Perhaps the most widely used of these drugs

moderate- and low-risk groups, alcohol consumption increased physiological responses.

Conclusions and Implications.

According to Finn and Pihl, a different pattern of alcohol sensitivity may show up when a strict criterion that requires multi-generational alcoholism versus a one-generation-alcoholic-father criterion is used to select high-risk subjects. Men at high genetic risk for alcoholism in stressful situations show a consistent reduction in physiological responses when they consume alcohol. This finding suggests a genetic predisposition to being calmed by alcohol when faced with stressful or aversive stimulation. The researchers assert that a high-risk label should be assigned to an individual only if two prior generations have been considered. They were able to show a difference between the high-risk (two generations) and the moderate-risk (one generation) subjects when comparing them to control low-risk subjects. Other researchers (Pickens et al., 1991) lend support to the inheritance factor in alcoholism—especially among young men (McGue, Pickens, &

Svikis, 1992). That inheritance is involved in alcoholism is clear; how it interacts with the environment, parental influences (Chassin et al., 1993),

and especially thought processes (Goldman et al., 1991), is the future challenge for researchers (Hawkins, Catalano, & Miller, 1992).

A Matter of Ethics.

Place a man who is genetically at high risk for alcoholism in a stressful situation, provide that man with alcohol, and the reinforcing effects of stress reduction are likely to make alcohol a highly prized and rewarding substance. Some questions still remain, however. For example, are there high-risk, higher-risk, and extremely-high-risk individuals? Are there other measures of reactivity that might be more sensitive? The research continues; the Finn and Pihl study is just one of hundreds examining the genetic and other risk factors for alcoholism.

Although drug researchers realize the importance of their mission, they also are sensitive to the ethical problems inherent in doing drug research with human beings. Psychologists have ethical guidelines for participants in human research, and asking people who are at risk for alcoholism to drink puts them at risk. Today, psychologists insist that research with human participants provide safeguards, treatments, and a thorough risk-benefit analysis for participants (Koocher, 1991).

---

is marijuana. Because of its widespread use (nearly 20 percent of the adult population has tried it), we will examine it in detail.

The marijuana that is used is the dried leaves and flowering tops of the *cannabis sativa* plant, the active ingredient of which is *tetrahydrocannabinol (THC)*. Marijuana can be ingested (eaten), but in the United States it is most commonly smoked. Smoking marijuana is inefficient, however; 20 to 80 percent of the THC is lost in the smoke.

In the 1800s, marijuana was used in the United States as a pain reliever for everything from toothaches to childbirth. Not until the early 20th century did people begin to fear the potential hazards of its use. The 1930s witnessed the passage of strict laws prohibiting its possession or sale. Marijuana was virtually forgotten until it was rediscovered by young people in the 1960s. Since then, it has become one of the most widely used illegal drugs in the United States. More than 20 million adults have used marijuana; nearly 10 percent of high school seniors use it daily, and 50 percent have tried it (U.S. Department of Health and Human Services, 1988).

People smoke marijuana to alter their consciousness, to alleviate depression, or just as a distraction. Most users report a sense of elation and well-being; others assert that it induces psychoses. Some users report other adverse reactions, such as

Smoking marijuana interferes with mental processes and the ability to perform simple psychomotor tasks.

sleeplessness, bad dreams, and nausea. Marijuana's effects are felt about 1 minute after smoking, begin to diminish within an hour, and disappear almost completely after 3 to 5 hours—although traces of THC can be detected in the body for weeks.

Individuals under the influence of marijuana demonstrate impaired performance on simple intellectual and psychomotor tasks. They become less task-oriented and have slower reaction times. Marijuana also interferes with memory. Little is known about how marijuana affects fetal development and reproductive abilities, and little is known about its long-term effects on those who use it from early adolescence until middle age. Marijuana has been widely used only since the late 1960s; it will take a couple generations before we know all of its long-term effects.

Although researchers agree that marijuana is not physiologically addictive, many argue that it produces psychological dependence. People use and become dependent on marijuana for a variety of reasons. One is that it is more easily available than such substances as barbiturates and cocaine. Another is the relief of tension that marijuana users experience. Further, most people believe the drug has few, if any, long-lasting side effects.

Despite considerable social acceptance of marijuana use in the United States, its sale and possession are still against the law in most states. In several states, the decriminalization of marijuana has meant that possession is treated as a civil violation instead of a crime. There are no arrests, jail sentences, or trials, but its use is still illegal. For the most part, laws against the sale and possession of marijuana have been ineffective, and the drug is widely available across the United States in both urban and rural areas. Legalization is considered a good idea by some experts, although few legislators take the idea seriously.

Amphetamines and Cocaine

Amphetamines and cocaine are considered psychostimulants and are highly addictive. A **psychostimulant** is a drug that increases alertness, reduces fatigue, and elevates mood when taken in low to moderate doses. *Amphetamines* are a chemical group of drugs that act on the central nervous system to increase excitability, depress appetite,. and increase alertness and talkativeness. They also increase blood pressure and heart rate. After long-term use, individuals have cravings for the drug and experience exhaustion, lethargy, and depression without it.

Cocaine is a central nervous system stimulant and an anesthetic. It acts on brain neurotransmitters such as norepinephrine (noradrenaline) and dopamine. It also

Psychostimulant: A drug that in low to moderate doses increases alertness, reduces fatigue, and elevates mood.

Cocaine and crack are highly addictive, yet are widely used despite the fact that their usage leads to an alarming range of dangerous consequences.

stimulates sympathetic activity in the peripheral nervous system, causing dilation of the pupils; increases in heart rate, blood pressure, and blood sugar; and decreased appetite.

The drug produces an exceptional euphoria—a light-headed feeling, a sense of alertness, increased energy, sexual arousal, and sometimes a sense of infallibility—but this euphoria is short-lived. People who use cocaine report feeling a sense of new confidence and self-worth.

Cocaine can be sniffed (snorted), smoked, or injected. Sniffing is the most popular method. Once inhaled, the drug is absorbed into the tiny blood vessels that line the nose. Within 5 minutes, the user starts to feel the effects; the peak effect is in 15 minutes and may last 20 to 30 minutes. The processed and smokable form of cocaine, *crack*, delivers an unusually large dose and induces euphoria in a matter of seconds. Cocaine can also be injected, since it is soluble in water. However, because of concerns about contracting AIDS through infected needles, intravenous injections are less common than they used to be (Washton, 1989).

Cocaine is widely abused. At least 15 percent of high school seniors have used it at least once. Crack is readily available, especially in schools. Admissions to cocaine treatment centers have increased sharply, as have deaths associated with cocaine abuse.

Why is cocaine use so prevalent in our society? First, cocaine acts as a powerful reward. For example, animals will work incessantly, even to the point of exhaustion, to obtain it. Second, cocaine produces tolerance and potent urges and cravings. A cocaine high is pleasurable but also brief; users wish to repeat the sensation. When the cocaine wears off, it is replaced by unpleasant feelings (known as *crashing*). These feelings can be alleviated only through more cocaine. Third, in our pleasure-now, pay-later society, instant gratification through drug use seems appropriate to some people (Washton, 1989).

What are some of the problems of cocaine use? At a minimum, the drug is addictive and produces irritability and eating and sleeping disturbances. It also seems to precipitate other disturbances, such as panic attacks. Further, cocaine can produce serious mental disorders, including paranoia, agitation, and suicidal behavior. Overdosing causes physical problems such as heart attacks, hemorrhages, and heat stroke. Complications associated with cocaine administration include nose sores, lung damage, infection at injection sites, and AIDS. The use of cocaine during pregnancy may result in premature birth, malformations of the fetus, and spontaneous abortions.

FOCUS

▶ What are the defining characteristics of a substance abuser? pp. 141–142

▶ How can we test the hypothesis that alcoholism may have genetic components? pp. 148–149

▶ What evidence did researchers find to suggest a genetic predisposition to alcoholism among some of their subjects? pp. 148–149

▶ What are the principal risks of cocaine use? pp. 150–152

Treatment for cocaine addiction first requires getting the addict into therapy (which is difficult because addicts feel invulnerable), providing a structured program, and making sure the addict refrains from all mood-altering addictive drugs, including alcohol. Blocking the pleasure centers with a drug such as methadone is not realistic because cocaine (unlike heroin) works through almost all of the major neurotransmitter systems. Even if such a drug could be found, it would probably make the person listless. Because a drug treatment for cocaine addiction is so hard to achieve, a great burden is placed on psychological therapy. Treatment usually includes education, family involvement, group and individual therapy, a focus on abstinence, and long-term follow-up; it is time-intensive and expensive (Hall, Havassy & Wasserman, 1991).

See Table 4.3 for a summary of the effects of commonly abused drugs.

TABLE 4.3   *Commonly Abused Drugs*

Types of Drugs	Drugs	Effects of Drugs	Tolerance?	Physiological Dependence?
Sedative-hypnotics	Alcohol	Reduces tension	yes	yes
	Barbiturates (e.g., Seconal)	Reduce tension; induce sleep	yes	yes
	Tranquilizers (e.g.,Valium)	Alleviate tension; induce relaxation	yes	yes
Narcotics	Opium Morphine Heroin	Alleviates pain and tension; achieves a high	yes	yes
Psychedelics	Marijuana	Changes mood and perception	no	no
Psychostimulants	Amphetamines	Increase excitability, alertness, talkativeness; decrease appetite	yes	yes
	Cocaine	Increases alertness, decreases fatigue, stimulates sexual arousal	yes	yes

Note: Even though a drug may not produce physiological dependence, it may produce a psychological need that compels repeated use.

Concluding Note

The study of consciousness is complex because it brings together physiology, learning, and motivation. Psychologists attempt to use their knowledge of learning, meditation, biofeedback, and drug treatment to help people better their lives. This often means helping people who are self-destructive, for example, substance abusers. Drug usage in our society is at exceedingly high levels, despite the fact that we all know the dangers involved.

The study of consciousness helps researchers define key issues, develop research methods, and develop techniques to help people lead more fulfilling lives. Drug treatments and techniques to help people sleep are one obvious venue. In addition, new data and theories in hypnosis, biofeedback, and medita-tion are being developed. Researchers are mapping the brain and relating it to consciousness and behavior with various models and theories. We know that all our behavior ultimately has a biological basis, so understanding the relationship between biology and behavior is extremely important. It may hold the key to comprehending why drugs such as cocaine are so reinforcing, why quitting cigarette smoking is so difficult, or why fighting alcoholism is so arduous. By studying these diverse topics, researchers can better understand the physiology, motivation, actions, and results of people's behavior. Armed with knowledge about consciousness, psychologists can develop therapeutic techniques to improve the human condition.

Summary & Review

Consciousness

What are consciousness and altered states of consciousness?

Consciousness is a general awareness of and responsiveness to the environment. It can range from alert attention to dreaming, hypnosis, or drug-induced states. We define an *altered state of consciousness* as a pattern of functioning that is dramatically different from that of ordinary awareness and responsiveness. pp. 124–125

KEY TERMS: *consciousness*, p. 125; *altered state of consciousness*, p. 125.

Sleep

What are circadian rhythms?

A biological clock ticks within us to control our sleep-wakefulness cycle; circadian rhythms are these internally generated bodily rhythms. When time cues such as daylight and the clock on the wall are removed from the environment, our circadian rhythm runs a bit slow. pp. 127–128

What is the pattern of sleep stages?

Recordings of the brain waves of sleeping subjects have revealed five distinct cycles of sleep. Each cycle has four *no rapid eye movement (NREM)* stages and one *rapid eye movement (REM)* stage. During REM sleep, rapid and systematic eye movements occur. A full sleep cycle lasts about 90 minutes, so five complete sleep cycles occur in an average night's sleep. Subjects deprived of REM sleep tend to catch up on REM sleep on subsequent nights. pp. 129–132

Identify two sleep disorders.

If you snore loudly, sleepwalk, or fall asleep at inappropriate times you may have a sleep disorder. People who fall asleep suddenly and unexpectedly have a disorder known as *narcolepsy*. Narcolepsy is probably a symptom of an autonomic nervous system disturbance and lowered arousal but may also reflect neurochemical problems. Another sleep disorder—*insomnia*—is a prolonged inability to sleep and is often caused by anxiety or depression.   p. 133

KEY TERMS: *sleep*, p. 128; *electroencephalogram*, p. 129; *NREM sleep*, p. 129; *REM sleep*, p. 129; *insomnia*, p. 133.

continued

Summary & Review

Dreams

What are dreams and how often do they occur?

A *dream* is a state of consciousness that occurs largely during REM sleep and is usually accompanied by vivid visual imagery, although the imagery may be tactile or auditory. Most people dream four or five times a night. The first dream of a typical night occurs 90 minutes after a person has fallen asleep and lasts for approximately 10 minutes.   p. 134

What is the content of a dream?

Most dreams are commonplace, focusing events related to people whom we come into contact with frequently—family, friends, or coworkers. The *manifest content* of a dream is its overt story line, characters, settings. The *latent content* of a dream is its deeper meaning, usually involving symbolism, hidden content, and repressed or obscured ideas and wishes.   p. 134

KEY TERMS: *dream,* p. 134; *lucid dream,* p. 134; *manifest content,* p. 135; *latent content,* p. 135.

Controlling Consciousness

What is biofeedback?

Biofeedback is the general technique by which individuals can monitor and learn to control the involuntary activity of some bodily organs and functions. A number of laboratory studies have demonstrated biofeedback's effectiveness in helping people manage a wide range of physiological problems such as headaches and high blood pressure, but only carefully controlled research will answer persistent questions about its usefulness. pp. 137–138

What are hypnosis and meditation?

Hypnosis is an altered state of consciousness brought about by a procedure that may induce a trance. Hypnosis can produce special effects such as *age regression,* heightened memory, and pain reduction. Physical states produced by *meditation* resemble those achieved by individuals trained to relax and concentrate. Those who practice meditation claim that it induces inner peace and tranquillity.   pp. 138–141

KEY TERMS: *biofeedback,* p. 137; *hypnosis,* p. 138; *age regression,* p. 138; *meditation,* p. 140.

Altering Consciousness with Drugs

What are the characteristics of a substance abuser?

Substance abusers have used drugs for at least one month, experienced legal difficulties or social or vocational problems due to drug use, and used the drug in hazardous situations. Most researchers agree that no single explanation can account for drug use and abuse.   pp. 141–143

Who is an alcoholic?

An *alcoholic* is a person with alcohol-related problems who also has a physiological and psychological need to consume alcoholic products and experience their effects. Without alcohol, alcoholics develop physiological *withdrawal symptoms.* In addition, they often develop *tolerance,* whereby a single drink or even a few will not affect them. All alcoholics are problem drinkers, but not all problem drinkers are alcoholics. pp. 144–145

How much alcohol is necessary to influence behavior?

Alcohol affects behavior in proportion to its level in the bloodstream and the sex and weight of the user. A person with a blood alcohol level of 0.10 percent or more is generally considered intoxicated; if driving, the person can be arrested. pp. 143–144

Distinguish among barbiturates, tranquilizers, and heroin.

Barbiturates and tranquilizers are in the class of drugs that relax and calm individuals and, when taken in higher doses, they can induce sleep. Barbiturates are considered to produce a deeper relaxation than tranquilizers. Heroin is an opiate, a distinctly different class of drug. It has become a social problem in part because addicts commit crimes to obtain the drug. Heroin addiction has been successfully treated with methadone, which blocks heroin's effects. Although addictive, methadone is legal and does not produce euphoria; methadone programs are not without critics, however, due to the lack of programs to help addicts become totally drug free.   pp. 147–148

What is a psychostimulant?

A *psychostimulant* is a drug that increases alertness, reduces fatigue, and elevates mood when taken in low to moderate doses. Cocaine is such a drug. It is widely abused in our society, and treatment for cocaine addiction is difficult.   pp. 150–152

KEY TERMS: *drug,* p. 141; *psychoactive drug,* p. 141; *addictive drug,* p. 141; *substance abusers,* p. 141; *psychological dependence,* p. 142; *withdrawal symptoms,* p. 142; *tolerance,* p. 142; *sedative-hypnotics,* p. 143; *alcoholic,* p. 144; *psychostimulants,* p. 150.

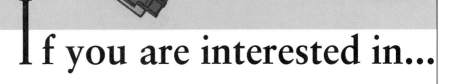

CONNECTIONS

I f you are interested in...

Sleep and dreaming, see ...

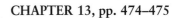

CHAPTER 12, p. 436

How some personality theorists use dreams as an important part of their personality theories.

CHAPTER 13, pp. 474–475

How stress affects the normal rhythm of sleep and dreams.

CHAPTER 14, p. 519

The impact of depression on normal sleep.

CHAPTER 15, p. 541

Why Freud's interpretation of dreams is used as a therapeutic technique by many practitioners.

Consciousness, see ...

CHAPTER 13, pp. 471–472, 474–475

How everyday awareness is affected in adverse ways by stressors in the environment.

CHAPTER 13, pp. 474–477

How biological underpinnings of normal everyday awareness depend on normal consciousness.

CHAPTER 15, pp. 540–541

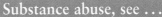

How treatment procedures of maladjustment sometimes rely on the notion of an *unconscious* to direct day-to-day behavior.

Substance abuse, see ...

CHAPTER 8, pp. 282–283

How drug use by pregnant women affects their unborn children.

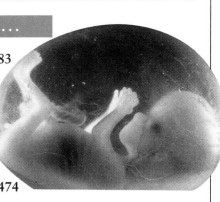

CHAPTER 13, pp. 469–474

Why people turn to substances such as alcohol to help relieve stress.

CHAPTER 16, pp. 575–579, 583

How people's attitudes about lifestyles, including substance use and abuse, are influenced by parents and peers.

5

Learning

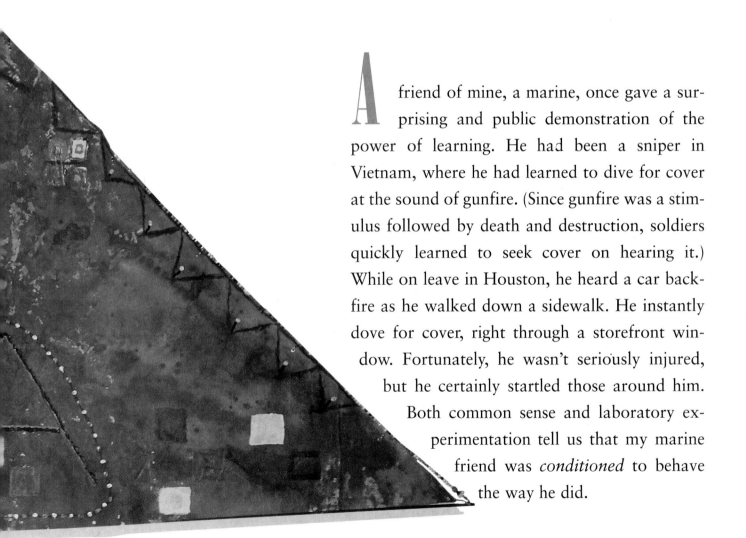

A friend of mine, a marine, once gave a surprising and public demonstration of the power of learning. He had been a sniper in Vietnam, where he had learned to dive for cover at the sound of gunfire. (Since gunfire was a stimulus followed by death and destruction, soldiers quickly learned to seek cover on hearing it.) While on leave in Houston, he heard a car backfire as he walked down a sidewalk. He instantly dove for cover, right through a storefront window. Fortunately, he wasn't seriously injured, but he certainly startled those around him. Both common sense and laboratory experimentation tell us that my marine friend was *conditioned* to behave the way he did.

Like the marine, we learn a great deal in our lives, including how to protect ourselves from danger. Learning also explains many of our day-to-day behaviors. Consider, for example, Patrick's behavior. While walking across campus to his psychology class, Patrick wonders how he can get Cathy to notice him. He has made a strategic move to attract her attention by wearing his blue argyle sweater. The sweater became his favorite after several female friends complimented him on it. As Patrick climbs the carpeted stairs to class, he passes Ray, an upperclassman he admires. Noticing that Ray has his jacket collar up, Patrick flips his own collar up as he reaches for the metal knob on the classroom door. He touches the knob and, expecting a shock, instantly jerks back his hand. Patrick has been shocked often by touching this particular doorknob, but not today. He solves the mystery when he remembers that he is wearing sneakers instead of his leather-soled loafers.

By the time we reach adulthood, experience has taught us a large number of simple, predictable associations. We know, for example, that a long day at the beach may result in a painful sunburn and that a gas station should be our next stop when the fuel gauge reads empty. We have also learned sophisticated, complicated processes, such as how to drive a car and how to appreciate music ranging from Bach to Sting. Some people learn socially deviant behaviors, such as stealing and drug abuse.

In general, we say that learning is the process by which we acquire new knowledge. Psychologists define **learning** as a relatively permanent change in an organism that occurs as a result of experiences in the environment. This change is often seen in overt behavior. The definition of *learning* has three important parts:

▶ experience in the environment

▶ change in the organism, and

▶ permanence.

First, in order for learning to occur, the organism must experience something in the environment. (Patrick observed that Ray was wearing his jacket collar up.) Second, some measurable change in the organism must be evident. (Patrick flipped up his own jacket collar.) Third, the change must be relatively permanent. (Weeks after seeing Ray, Patrick may still be wearing upturned collars.)

Because the internal processes of learning cannot be seen, psychologists study the results of learning, including such overt behavior as solving an algebra problem or throwing a ball. To do so, they may measure physiological changes, such as brain-wave activity, heartbeat, and temperature.

Behavior is always being modified; new experiences affect learning, and what is learned may be forgotten. An organism's motivation, abilities, and physiological state influence its ability to learn. For example, if you are tired, learning the material in this chapter will be especially difficult. Also, practice and repeated experiences ensure that you will remember and will easily exhibit newly acquired learning, information, and skills. When learning has occurred, some process within you has changed, and a physiological change has occurred as well.

The factors that affect learning are often studied in animal behavior because the genetic heritage of animals is easy to control and manipulate and because an animal's history and environmental experiences can be known. Although some psychologists claim that different processes underlie animal and human learning, most believe—and experiments show—that the processes are similar. Differences become apparent and important when complex behaviors are being evaluated and experiments require the use of language.

As you read this chapter, keep in mind what Patrick did. You will see how his actions illustrate the three basic learning processes that are the subject of this chapter: classical conditioning, operant conditioning, and cognitive learning.

Learning: A relatively permanent change in an organism that occurs as a result of experiences in the environment.

Pavlovian, or Classical, Conditioning Theory

When Patrick jerked his hand back from a doorknob in anticipation of a shock, his reaction was elicited by the presence of the doorknob. In the past, Patrick had been shocked when he touched this particular doorknob. Now he reacts in a reflexive manner when he touches it, whether it shocks him or not. He learned this relationship through a process known as classical conditioning.

In a general sense, psychologists use the term *conditioning* to mean learning. But **conditioning** is a systematic procedure through which associations and responses to specific stimuli are learned. It is one of the simplest forms of learning. For example, consider what generally happens when a man dressed in black enters a scene on television. We suspect that something evil will soon happen because black clothing is usually worn by villains, and we become alarmed or fearful. We have been conditioned to feel that way. In the terminology used by psychologists, the black-clothed villain is the *stimulus,* and alarm or fear is the *response.*

When psychologists first studied conditioning, they found relationships between specific stimuli and responses. Each time a certain stimulus occurs, the same reflexive response, or behavior, follows. For example, the presence of food in the mouth leads to salivation; a tap on the knee leads to a knee jerk; a bright light in the eye leads to contraction of the pupil and eye blinking.

A **reflex** is an involuntary, automatic behavior in response to stimuli that occurs without prior learning; such behaviors usually show little variability from instance to instance. Conditioned behaviors, in contrast, are learned. Many people have learned the response of fear to the stimulus of sitting in a dentist's chair, since they associate the chair with drilling and pain. An object by itself (a neutral stimulus) does not elicit fear, but an object associated with pain becomes a stimulus that can elicit fear. This is an example of *conditioning.*

Conditioned behaviors may occur so automatically that they appear to be reflexive; remembering Patrick's jerking his hand away from the doorknob. Like reflexes, conditioned behaviors are involuntary; but unlike reflexes, they are learned. In classical conditioning (to be defined shortly), previously neutral stimuli such as chairs, lights, and buzzers become associated with specific events and lead to responses such as fear, eye blinks, and nervousness.

In 1927, Ivan Pavlov (1849–1936), a Russian physiologist, summarized a now-famous series of experiments in which he uncovered a basic principle of learning—conditioning. His research began quite by accident in a series of studies on how saliva and gastric secretions work on the digestive processes of dogs. He knew it is normal for dogs to salivate when they eat—salivation is a reflexive behavior that aids digestion—but the dogs were salivating *before* they tasted food. Pavlov reasoned that this might be happening because the dogs had learned to associate the trainers, who brought them food, with the food itself. Anxious to know more about this basic form of learning, Pavlov abandoned his medical research and redirected his efforts into teaching dogs to salivate to a new stimulus, such as a bell.

What Pavlov discovered was **classical conditioning,** or *Pavlovian conditioning,* in which an originally neutral stimulus, by repeated pairing with a stimulus that naturally elicits a response, comes to elicit a similar or even identical response. The process occurs in this way: When a neutral stimulus (such as a bell, buzzer, or light) is associated with a stimulus that normally brings about a response (such as food), the neutral stimulus over time will bring about the same response as the normal stimulus. Pavlov termed the stimulus that normally produces a response (for example,

Conditioning: A systematic procedure through which associations and responses to specific stimuli are learned.

Reflexes: Involuntary, automatic behaviors in response to stimuli, which occur without prior learning and usually show little variability from instance to instance.

Classical conditioning: A conditioning process in which an originally neutral stimulus, by repeated pairing with a stimulus that normally elicits a response, comes to elicit a similar or even identical response. Also known as *Pavlovian conditioning.*

Unconditioned stimulus: A stimulus that normally produces an involuntary, measurable response.

Unconditioned response: The unlearned or involuntary response to an unconditioned stimulus.

Conditioned stimulus: A neutral stimulus that, through repeated association with an unconditioned stimulus, becomes capable of eliciting a conditioned response.

Conditioned response: The response elicited by a conditioned stimulus.

food) an **unconditioned stimulus;** he termed the response to this stimulus (for example, salivating) an **unconditioned response.** The unconditioned response occurs involuntarily, without learning, in response to the unconditioned stimulus.

Pavlov started with a relatively simple experiment—teaching dogs to salivate in response to a bell. First, he surgically altered the location of the dog's salivary gland to make the output accessible. Then he attached tubes to the salivary gland to measure the amount of saliva produced by the food—the unconditioned stimulus. Then, he introduced a bell—the new stimulus (see Figure 5.1). He called the bell a *neutral stimulus,* because the sound of a bell is not necessarily related to salivation. Pavlov measured the amount of saliva the dogs produced when a bell was rung by itself; the amount was negligible. He then began the conditioning process by ringing the bell and immediately placing food in the dogs' mouths. After he did this several times, the dogs salivated in response to the sound of the bell alone. Pavlov reasoned that the dogs had learned that the bell meant food was coming. He termed the bell, which elicited salivation as a result of learning, a **conditioned stimulus**—a neutral stimulus that, through repeated association with an unconditioned stimulus, becomes capable of eliciting a conditioned response. He termed the salivation—the learned response to the sound of the bell—a **conditioned response** (the response elicited by a conditioned stimulus). From his experiments, Pavlov discovered that the conditioned stimulus (the bell) brought about a similar but somewhat weaker response than the unconditioned stimulus (the food). The process of Pavlovian conditioning is outlined in Figure 5.2.

FIGURE 5.1

Pavlov Measuring Salivation

Pavlov attached a tube to a dog's salivary gland, which had been surgically moved to the outside of the dog's cheek to allow easy collection of saliva. He then measured the number of drops of saliva that naturally occurred when a bell was sounded.

Next, he measured the number of drops of saliva that occurred when a bell was sounded along with the presentation of food.

He found that, after repeated presentations of the bell followed by food, the dog's saliva increased as soon as the bell was sounded, indicating that it had learned to associate the food and the bell.

FIGURE 5.2

The Three Stages of Classical Conditioning

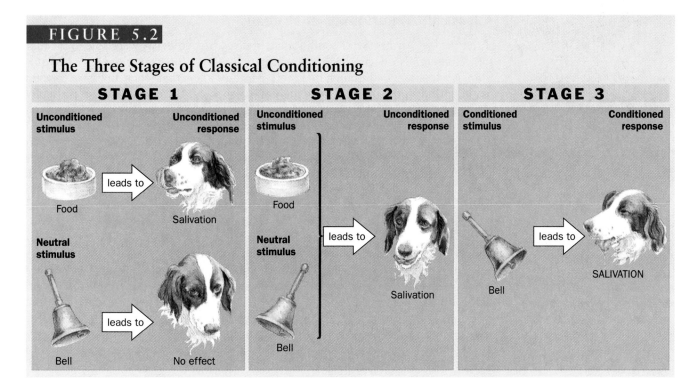

The key characteristic of classical conditioning is the use of an originally neutral stimulus (here a bell) to elicit a response (here salivation) through repeated pairing of the neutral stimulus with an unconditioned stimulus that elicits the response naturally (here food). On the first few trials of pairings, conditioning is unlikely to occur. With additional trials, there is a greater likelihood that conditioning will occur. After dozens or even hundreds of pairings, the neutral stimulus will yield a conditioned response. We generally refer to this process as an *acquisition process;* we say that an organism has acquired a response. Figure 5.3 shows a typical acquisition curve.

Classical conditioning occurs regularly in the everyday world. Your cat or dog may be conditioned to the whirring of an electric can opener, which sends it running for food. Similarly, when we enter a dentist's office, our heart rate may increase and we may begin to exhibit nervous behaviors because of the learned associations we have developed. When classical conditioning occurs, behavior changes.

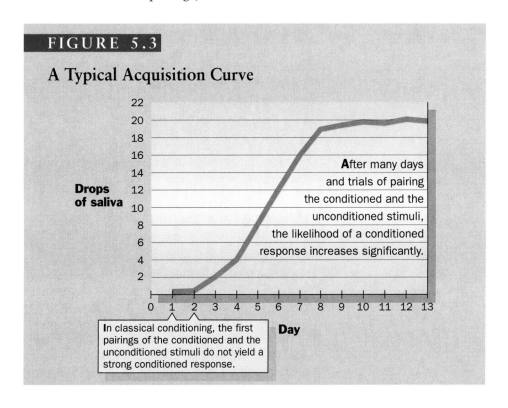

FIGURE 5.3

A Typical Acquisition Curve

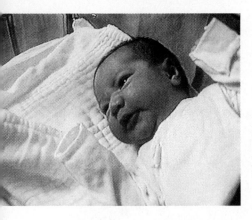

Classical conditioning appears to play a role in one of the earliest skills learned by newborns—the ability to recognize their mothers using their sense of smell. (Photo courtesy of CNN.)

Classical Conditioning in Humans

After Pavlov's success with conditioning in dogs, psychologists were able to see that conditioning also occurs in human beings. In 1931, for example, D. P. Marquis showed classical conditioning in infants. Marquis knew that when an object touches an infant's lips, the infant immediately starts sucking, because the object is usually the nipple of a breast or bottle, from which the infant gets milk. The nipple, an unconditioned stimulus, elicits sucking, an unconditioned response. After repeated pairings of a sound or light with a nipple, infants were conditioned to suck when only the sound or light was presented.

Sucking is one of many reflexive behaviors in human beings, and hence it is one of many responses that can be conditioned. Newborns show reflexive responses to loud noises, for example. (We examine newborns' reflexes in chapter 8.) A loud noise naturally elicits a startle response—an outstretching of the arms and legs associated with changes in heart rate, blood pressure, and breathing. Any responses of this sort can be elicited through conditioning procedures.

All kinds of neutral stimuli can become conditioned stimuli that elicit either pleasant or defensive reactions. A puff of air delivered to the eye, for example, produces the unconditioned response of an eye blink. When a light or buzzer is paired with puffs of air to the eye, it will eventually elicit the eye blink by itself. This effect can be produced in many animals, as well as in human adults and infants.

Some psychologists believe both pleasant and unpleasant emotional responses can be classically conditioned. Consider the following: If a child who is playing with a favorite toy is repeatedly frightened by a sudden loud noise, the child may be conditioned to be afraid each time he or she sees the toy. This type of relationship was explored in 1920 by John B. Watson and Rosalie Raynor in a famous experiment with an 11-month-old infant named Albert. The infant was given a series of toys to play with, including a live white rat. One day, as Albert reached for the rat, the experimenters made a sudden loud noise that frightened the child. After repeated pairing of the noise and the rat, Albert learned the relationship. The rat served as a conditioned stimulus and the loud noise as the unconditioned stimulus; presentation of the rat evoked an unconditioned response of fear on each subsequent presentation.

An example of a pleasant emotional response comes from the beer commercial that applies conditioning principles by featuring beautiful people enjoying their favorite beer while frolicking on a warm, sunny beach or socializing in a cozy ski chalet. The producers hope that when viewers associate the beer (a neutral stimulus) with an unconditioned stimulus that naturally elicits a positive emotional response (the pleasant scene), the beer will elicit a positive response. In other words, they hope to condition people to feel good whenever they think about this beer. The powerful role of classical conditioning in advertising has been supported by experimental studies with adults in the laboratory (Stuart, Shimp, & Engle, 1987).

Higher-Order Conditioning

After a neutral stimulus becomes a conditioned stimulus, it is likely to elicit the conditioned response whenever it is presented. Moreover, there also exists **higher-order conditioning**—the process by which another neutral stimulus takes on conditioned properties through pairing with the conditioned stimulus. Thus, higher-order conditioning permits increasingly remote associations, which can result in a complex network of conditioned stimuli and responses. At least two factors determine the extent of higher-order conditioning: (1) the similarity between the higher-order stimulus and the original conditioned stimulus and (2) the frequency and consistency with which the two conditioned stimuli are paired (Rescorla, 1978).

Higher-order conditioning: The process by which a neutral stimulus takes on conditioned properties through pairing with a conditioned stimulus.

Suppose a light is paired with mild electric shocks to a dog. On seeing the light, the dog exhibits fear; the light has thus become a conditioned stimulus that elicits a set of fear responses. If a bell is now paired with or presented just before the light, the new stimulus (the bell) can also take on properties of the conditioned stimulus (the light). After repeated pairings, the dog will learn to associate the two events (the light and the bell), and either event by itself will elicit a fear response. When a third stimulus—say, an experimenter wearing a white lab coat—is introduced, the dog may learn to associate the experimenter with the bell or light. After enough trials, the dog may have conditioned fear responses to each of the three stimuli: the light, the bell, and the experimenter (Pavlov, 1927; Rescorla, 1977).

Higher-order conditioning is common in our daily lives. For example, a driver who has received several expensive speeding tickets from the highway patrol may reflexively slow down whenever she sees a patrol car to avoid receiving another ticket. If the same driver repeatedly observes a highway patrol car parked inconspicuously on a particular stretch of road, she may start slowing down whenever she drives that stretch of road, whether or not she sees a patrol car. The stretch of road becomes another stimulus that induces the driver to ease up on the gas pedal. Even the model of the car that the highway patrol uses may elicit the response. You can see that successful pairing of conditioned and unconditioned stimuli—that is, successful classical conditioning—involves many key variables.

FOCUS

▶ Identify the fundamental difference between a reflex and a conditioned behavior.   p. 156

▶ Distinguish between a conditioned and an unconditioned response.   pp. 157–158

▶ Provide an example of how higher-order conditioning occurs in your life.   pp. 159–160

Key Variables in Classical Conditioning

Classical conditioning is not a simple process. How loud does the buzzer have to be? How long does the bell have to ring? How sinister must the movie's scary music be? How many times must someone sit in a dentist's chair to become afraid of dentists? How strong does the pain have to be? How would a driver react to the sight of a highway patrolman if his only encounter with one had occurred when his car had broken down on a cold, stormy night and he had been aided by a patrolman? As with other psychological phenomena, situational variables affect when, if, and under what conditions classical conditioning will occur. Some of the most important variables in classical conditioning are the strength, timing, and frequency of the unconditioned stimulus. When these variables are optimal, conditioning occurs easily.

Strength, Timing, and Frequency

Strength of the Unconditioned Stimulus. A puff of air delivered to the eye will easily elicit a conditioned response, but only if the puff of air (the unconditioned stimulus) is sufficiently strong. Research shows that when the unconditioned stimulus is strong and elicits a quick and regular reflexive (unconditioned) response, conditioning of the neutral stimulus is likely to occur. On the other hand, when the unconditioned stimulus is weak, it is unlikely to elicit an unconditioned response, and conditioning of the neutral stimulus is unlikely to occur. Thus, pairing a neutral stimulus with a weak unconditioned stimulus will not reliably lead to conditioning.

Timing of the Unconditioned Stimulus. For conditioning to occur, an unconditioned stimulus must usually be paired with a conditioned stimulus close enough in time for the two to become associated; we say that they must be temporally contiguous. (In Pavlov's experiment, conditioning would not have occurred if the bell and the food had been presented an hour apart.) The two stimuli may be presented together or may be separated by a brief interval. The actual time between the onset of the two stimuli varies from one study to another and depends on many variables, including the type of conditioned response sought. Some types of conditioning can occur with fairly long delays, but a general guideline for achieving a strong conditioned response is that the conditioned stimulus should occur about half a second before the unconditioned stimulus and overlap with it, particularly for reflexes such as the eye blink.

Frequency of Pairings. Occasional or rare pairings of a neutral stimulus with an unconditioned stimulus at close intervals does not result in conditioning; generally speaking, frequent pairings and pairings that establish a relationship between the unconditioned and conditioned stimulus are usually necessary. If, for example, food and the sound of a bell are paired on every trial, a dog is conditioned more quickly than if the stimuli are paired on every other trial. The frequency of the natural occurrence of the unconditioned stimulus is also important. If the unconditioned stimulus does not occur frequently but is always associated with the conditioned stimulus, more rapid conditioning is likely, because one stimulus predicts the other (Rescorla, 1988). Once the conditioned response has reached its maximum strength, additional pairings of the stimuli do not increase the likelihood of a conditioned response. There are exceptions to this general rule, and specific one-time pairings can produce learning.

Predictability

A key determining factor in whether conditioning will occur is the predictability of the association of the unconditioned and conditioned stimuli. Closeness in time and a regular frequency of pairings promote conditioning, but these are not enough. Predictability facilitates, and turns out to be a central factor in, conditioning (Rescorla, 1988).

Pavlov thought classical conditioning was based on timing. However, research now shows that if the unconditioned stimulus (such as the food) can be predicted by the conditioned stimulus (such as the bell), then conditioning is rapidly achieved. Conditioning is achieved not because of the number of times the two events have occurred but rather because of the reliability with which the conditioned stimulus predicts the unconditioned stimulus. Pavlov's dogs learned that bells were good predictors of food; the conditioned stimulus (bells) reliably predicted the unconditioned one (food), so conditioning was quickly achieved.

In Rescorla's (1988) view, what is learned in conditioning is the predictability of events—bells predicting food, light predicting eye blinks, dentist chairs predicting pain. Predictability is one of the key elements in classical conditioning; but without other contextual cues, it usually is not enough (Papini & Bitterman, 1990). The predictability of events, however, becomes especially important in learned behaviors, such as the food aversions considered next.

Taste Aversion Challenges the Principles of Learning

My daughter Sarah has hated mustard ever since her sixth birthday party. After her friends and their mothers left the party, we sat down for ham sandwiches with lettuce and mustard. Two hours later, she was ill—fever, vomiting, chills, and swollen glands. It was the flu. But as far as Sarah was concerned, it was the mustard that had made her sick; 14 years later, she still refuses to eat mustard.

This association of mustard and nausea is an example of a conditioned taste aversion. In a famous experiment, John Garcia gave animals some specific foods or liquids to eat or drink and then induced nausea (usually by injecting a drug or by providing irradiated water to drink). He found that after only one pairing of a food or drink (the conditioned stimulus) and the drug or irradiated water (the unconditioned stimulus), the animals avoided the food or drink that preceded the nausea (see, e.g., Garcia & Koelling, 1971; Linberg et al., 1982).

Two aspects of Garcia's work startled the research community. First, Garcia showed that a conditioned taste aversion could be obtained even if the nausea was induced several hours after the food or drink had been consumed. This contradicted the previously held assumption that the time interval between the unconditioned stimulus and the conditioned stimulus had to be short, especially if conditioning was to occur quickly.

Garcia also proved that not all stimuli can serve as conditioned stimuli. He tried to pair bells and lights with nausea to produce an aversion in rats, but he was unable to do so. This led him to conclude, "Strong aversions to the smell or taste of food can develop even when illness is delayed for hours after consumption [but] avoidance reactions do not develop for visual, auditory, or tactile stimuli associated with food" (Garcia & Koelling, 1971, p. 461). Garcia had disproved two accepted principles of learning.

The Garcia Effect. Conditioned taste aversion, sometimes called the *Garcia effect,* has adaptive value. In one trial or instance, animals learn to avoid foods that make them sick by associating the smells of poisonous foods with the foods themselves. This clearly has survival value. Conditioned taste aversion is unaffected by intervening events during the delay between the taste and the illness (Holder et al., 1989). Human beings quickly learn to associate rancid smells with the illness caused by spoiled food. Anyone who has suffered from food poisoning will attest to the lasting memory of the food or meal that caused it!

Conditioned taste aversion has practical uses. Coyotes and wolves often attack sheep and lambs, destroying entire flocks. Garcia laced lamb meat with a substance that causes a short-term illness and put the food on the outskirts of sheep ranchers' fenced-in areas. Coyotes who ate the lamb became sick and developed a lamb aversion. After this experience, they approached the sheep as if ready to attack, but they nearly always backed off (see, e.g., Garcia et al., 1976). By using conditioned taste aversion, Garcia deterred coyotes from eating sheep.

Learning, Weight Loss, and Cancer. Cancer patients often undergo chemotherapy; an unfortunate side effect of the therapy is vomiting and nausea. The patients often lose weight and their appetite during their treatment. Is it possible that they lose weight because of a conditioned taste aversion? According to researcher Ilene Bernstein (1988), some cancer patients become

Conditioned taste aversion, or the Garcia effect, has been used successfully to deter coyotes from attacking sheep.

conditioned to avoid food. They often check into a hospital, have a meal, are given chemotherapy, become sick, and then avoid the food that preceded the therapy. Bernstein conducted research with children and adults who were going to receive chemotherapy. Her research showed that patients given foods before therapy developed specific aversions to those foods; control groups who were not given those foods before their therapy did not develop aversions to them. Bovbjerg et al. (1992) found similar results.

Patients develop the food aversions even when they know it is the chemotherapy that induces the nausea. Bernstein suggests an intervention based on learning theory: Patients could be given a "scapegoat" food just before chemotherapy, so any conditioned aversion that develops will be to a nutritionally unimportant food rather than to nutritious foods. When Bernstein (1988) tried this procedure, results were successful.

Extinction and Spontaneous Recovery

Some conditioned responses last for a long time; others disappear quickly. Much depends on whether the conditioned response can still predict the unconditioned one. Consider the following: What would have happened to Pavlov's dogs if he had rung the bell each day but never followed the bell with food? What would happen if you went to the dentist every day for 2 months, but the dentist only brushed your teeth with a pleasant-tasting toothpaste and never drilled?

If a researcher continues Pavlov's experiment by presenting the conditioned stimulus (bell) but no unconditioned stimulus (food), the likelihood of a conditioned response decreases with every trial; it undergoes extinction. In classical conditioning, **extinction** is the process through which withholding the unconditioned stimulus gradually reduces the probability (and often the strength) of a conditioned response. Imagine a study in which a puff of air is associated with a buzzer that consistently elicits the conditioned eye-blink response. If the unconditioned stimulus (the puff of air) is no longer delivered in association with the buzzer, the likelihood that the buzzer will continue to elicit the eye-blink response decreases over time (see Figure 5.4). When presentation of the buzzer alone no longer elicits the conditioned response, we say that the response has been extinguished.

An extinguished conditioned response can recur, especially after a rest period; this phenomenon is termed **spontaneous recovery.** For example, when a dog has been conditioned to salivate in response to the sound of a bell and then experiences a long series of trials in which food is not paired with the bell, the dog makes few or no responses to the bell. The behavior has been extinguished. If the dog is placed in the experimental situation again after a rest period of 20 minutes, its salivary response to the bell will recur

Extinction: [Egg-STINCK-shun] In classical conditioning, the process of reducing the likelihood of a conditioned response to a conditioned stimulus by withholding the unconditioned stimulus.

Spontaneous recovery: The recurrence of an extinguished conditioned response following a rest period.

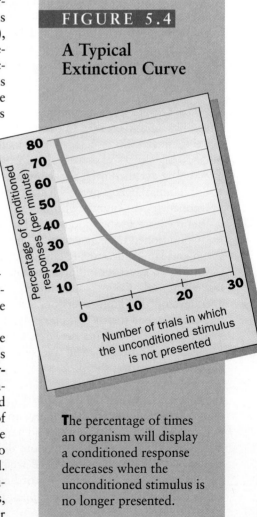

FIGURE 5.4

A Typical Extinction Curve

Percentage of conditioned responses (per minute)

Number of trials in which the unconditioned stimulus is not presented

The percentage of times an organism will display a conditioned response decreases when the unconditioned stimulus is no longer presented.

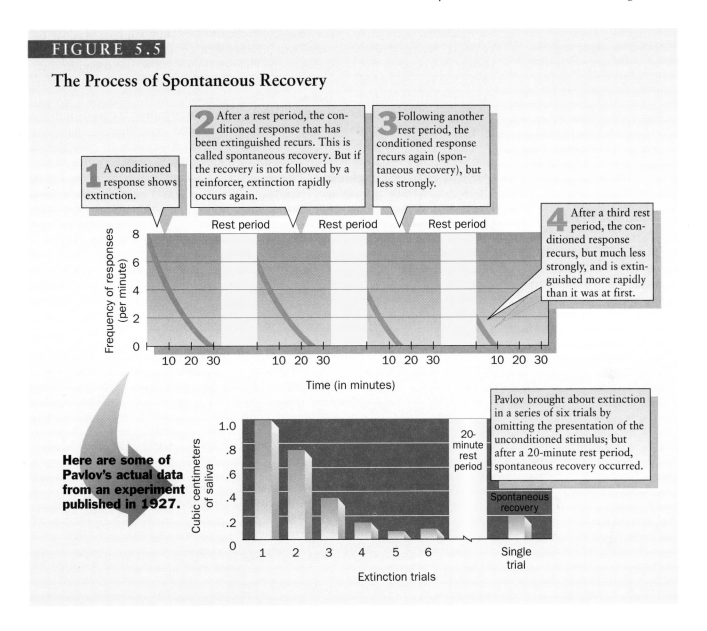

FIGURE 5.5

The Process of Spontaneous Recovery

1 A conditioned response shows extinction.

2 After a rest period, the conditioned response that has been extinguished recurs. This is called spontaneous recovery. But if the recovery is not followed by a reinforcer, extinction rapidly occurs again.

3 Following another rest period, the conditioned response recurs again (spontaneous recovery), but less strongly.

4 After a third rest period, the conditioned response recurs, but much less strongly, and is extinguished more rapidly than it was at first.

Here are some of Pavlov's actual data from an experiment published in 1927.

Pavlov brought about extinction in a series of six trials by omitting the presentation of the unconditioned stimulus; but after a 20-minute rest period, spontaneous recovery occurred.

briefly (although less strongly than before). This behavior shows that the effects of extinction are not permanent and that the learned association is not totally forgotten (see Figure 5.5).

Stimulus Generalization and Stimulus Discrimination

Imagine that a 3-year-old child pulls a cat's tail and receives a painful scratch. It would not be surprising if the child developed a fear of that cat, or even of all cats. The child might even develop a fear of dogs and other four-legged animals. Adults may respond in the same way to similar stimuli, a phenomenon that psychologists call stimulus generalization.

Stimulus generalization is the occurrence of a conditioned response to a stimulus that is similar but not identical to the original conditioned stimulus. The extent to which an organism responds to a stimulus similar to the original one depends on how alike the two stimuli are. If, for example, a loud tone is the conditioned stimulus

Stimulus generalization: The occurrence of a conditioned response to a stimulus that is similar but not identical to the original conditioned stimulus.

Stimulus discrimination: The process by which an organism learns to respond only to a specific reinforced stimulus.

for an eye-blink response, somewhat lower but similar tones will also produce the response. A totally dissimilar tone will produce little or no response. Likewise, the marine described at the beginning of the chapter responded to the sound of a car backfiring because it was similar to the sound of gunfire. See Figure 5.6 for another example of stimulus generalization.

Stimulus discrimination is the process by which an organism learns to respond only to a specific reinforced stimulus. Pavlov showed that animals that have learned to differentiate between pairs of stimuli display frustration or even aggression when discrimination is made difficult or impossible. He trained a dog to discriminate between a circle and an ellipse and then changed the shape of the ellipse on successive trials to look more and more like the circle. Eventually, the animal was unable to discriminate between the shapes; it randomly chose one or the other and also became aggressive.

Human beings exhibit similar disorganization in behavior when placed in situations in which they feel compelled to make a response but do not know how to respond correctly. In such situations, where discrimination becomes impossible, behavior can become stereotyped and limited in scope; people may choose either not to respond to the stimulus or to respond always in the same way (Lundin, 1961; Maier & Klee, 1941). Often, therapists must teach maladjusted people to learn to be more flexible in their responses to difficult situations.

Table 5.1 summarizes four important concepts in classical conditioning: extinction, spontaneous recovery, stimulus generalization, and stimulus discrimination.

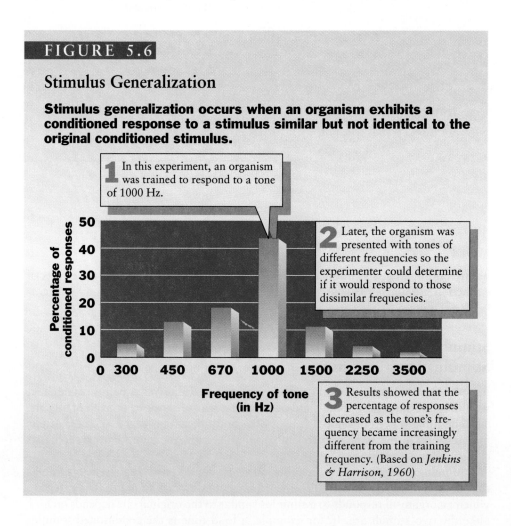

FIGURE 5.6

Stimulus Generalization

Stimulus generalization occurs when an organism exhibits a conditioned response to a stimulus similar but not identical to the original conditioned stimulus.

1 In this experiment, an organism was trained to respond to a tone of 1000 Hz.

2 Later, the organism was presented with tones of different frequencies so the experimenter could determine if it would respond to those dissimilar frequencies.

3 Results showed that the percentage of responses decreased as the tone's frequency became increasingly different from the training frequency. (Based on *Jenkins & Harrison, 1960*)

TABLE 5.1   *Four Important Concepts in Classical Conditioning*

Property	Definition	Example
Extinction	The process of reducing the probability of a conditioned response by withholding the unconditioned stimulus (the reinforcer).	An infant conditioned by the stroking of its lips to suck in response to a light is no longer given the unconditioned stimulus of stroking the lips; the infant stops sucking in response to the conditioned stimulus.
Spontaneous recovery	The recurrence of an extinguished conditioned response following a rest period.	A dog's conditioned salivary response has been extinguished. After a rest period, the dog again salivates in response to the conditioned stimulus, though less than it did before.
Stimulus generalization	The occurrence of a conditioned response to stimuli that are similar but not identical to the original conditioned stimulus.	A dog conditioned to salivate in response to a high-pitched tone also salivates in response to a lower-pitched tone.
Stimulus discrimination	The process by which an organism learns to respond only to a specific reinforced stimulus.	A goat is conditioned to salivate only in response to lights of high intensity, not in response to lights of low intensity.

Conditioning Physical Symptoms

Think of Patrick's hand on the doorknob, the marine's reaction to a loud noise, and a person's fear of the dentist chair. You can see that classical conditioning explains a wide range of human behaviors, including some of our physical responses to the world, such as heart rate acceleration and changes in blood pressure.

Substances such as pollen, dust, animal dander, and mold initiate an allergic reaction in many people. Cat fur, for example, may naturally elicit an allergic reaction, such as an inability to breathe, in asthmatics. Asthma attacks, like other behaviors, can be conditioned to occur. If cat fur is *always* found in Lindsay's house (a regular pairing), classical conditioning theory predicts that an asthmatic individual entering Lindsay's house would have an allergic reaction. (A conditioned stimulus, the house, predicts an unconditioned response, the allergic reaction.) Researchers have shown that people with severe allergies can have an allergic reaction merely from seeing a cat (or entering Lindsay's house), regardless of the presence of cat fur.

Even the body's immune system can be conditioned. Normally, our bodies release antibodies to fight disease when toxic substances appear in the blood. This is an involuntary activity that is independent of the nervous system. In a striking series of studies, animals were classically conditioned in a way that altered their immune responses (Ader, Cohen, & Bovbjerg, 1982). The experimenters paired a sweet-tasting solution with a drug that produced illness and, as a side effect, also suppressed the immune response. The animals quickly learned to avoid the sweet-tasting substance that seemed to predict illness. When later presented with the sweet-tasting substance alone, they showed a

FOCUS

▶ How do the variables of strength, timing, and frequency affect learning? pp. 160–161

▶ What evidence led Garcia to conclude that taste aversion can occur in one trial or one instance? What other examples of learning could occur in one trial or one instance? p. 162

▶ What happens to the conditioned response if a researcher in a Pavlovian experiment presents the conditioned stimulus but no unconditioned stimulus? p. 164

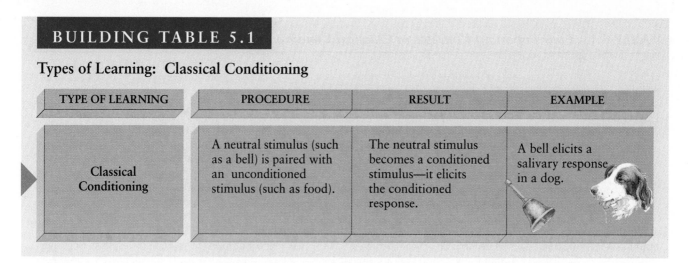

BUILDING TABLE 5.1

Types of Learning: Classical Conditioning

TYPE OF LEARNING	PROCEDURE	RESULT	EXAMPLE
Classical Conditioning	A neutral stimulus (such as a bell) is paired with an unconditioned stimulus (such as food).	The neutral stimulus becomes a conditioned stimulus—it elicits the conditioned response.	A bell elicits a salivary response in a dog.

reduction in immune system antibodies. The experimenters had classically conditioned an immune system response that was previously thought not to be under nervous system control. This is a striking finding.

New research also shows that drug users condition themselves. When heroin addicts inject heroin, their bodies produce an antiopiate substance to protect them from an overdose; this is a natural response. Siegel (1988) has shown that if the addict always injects the drug in the same room, the place itself may serve to initiate an antiopiate response, without the heroin ever actually being administered. Therefore, the location of a user's heroin administration can serve as a conditioned stimulus for the antiopiate response. When this happens, an addict may develop withdrawal symptoms, which in turn may create an even greater "need" for the drug. The stimulus for the increased use may have been merely the location of the drug consumption.

Building Table 5.1 summarizes some of the key elements of classical conditioning. Classical conditioning explains a wide range of phenomena, but not all of our behaviors are the result of such associations. Most complex behaviors result from another form of learning, *operant conditioning*, which is discussed next.

Operant Conditioning

Let's return to Patrick, the student described at the beginning of the chapter. Patrick was wearing a blue argyle sweater, which had become his favorite sweater after he had received several compliments on it. Patrick's decision to wear that particular sweater, unlike his jerking away from an electric shock, is a nonreflexive behavior and cannot be attributed to classical conditioning. Rather, Patrick's wearing of the blue sweater was reinforced through operant conditioning.

Pioneers: B. F. Skinner and E. L. Thorndike

The process by which Patrick was conditioned to wear his sweater was described in the 1930s by B. F. Skinner (1904–1990), who challenged and began to change the way psychologists think about conditioning and learning. In fact, Skinner questioned whether Pavlovian (classical) conditioning should be studied at all. Like Pavlov, Skinner focused only on an organism's observable behavior. Thought processes, consciousness, brain-behavior relationships, and the mind were not considered the proper subject matter of psychology. Skinner's early work was in the tradition of such strict behaviorists as Watson, although ultimately Skinner modified some of his most extreme positions. His 1938 book, *The Behavior of Organisms,* continues to have an impact on studies of conditioning.

According to Skinner, many behaviors are acquired and maintained through operant conditioning, not through Pavlov's classical conditioning. Skinner used the term *operant conditioning* because the organism *operates* on the environment, with every action followed by a specific event, or consequence. **Operant conditioning,** or *instrumental conditioning,* is a conditioning procedure in which an increase or decrease in the likelihood that a behavior will recur is affected by the delivery of a rewarding or punishing event as a consequence of the behavior. The conditioned behavior is usually voluntary, not reflexlike as in classical conditioning. Consider what happens when a boss rewards and encourages her overworked employees by giving them unexpected cash bonuses. If the bonuses improve morale and induce the employees to work harder, then the employer's conditioning efforts have been successful. In turn, the employees could condition the boss's behavior by rewarding her bonus paying with further increases in productivity, thereby encouraging her to continue paying bonuses.

In the laboratory, researchers have studied similar sequences of behaviors followed by rewards. One of the most famous experiments was conducted by the American psychologist E. L. Thorndike (1874–1949), who pioneered the study of operant conditioning during the 1890s and first reported his work in 1898. Thorndike placed hungry cats in boxes and put food outside the boxes. The cats could escape from the boxes and get food by hitting a lever that opened a door in each box. The cats quickly performed the behavior Thorndike was trying to condition (hitting the lever), because doing so (at first by accident and then deliberately) gave them access to food. Because the response (hitting the lever) was important (instrumental) in obtaining the reward, Thorndike used the term *instrumental conditioning* to describe the process and called the behaviors *instrumental behaviors.*

Although Skinner spoke of operant conditioning and Thorndike of instrumental conditioning, the two terms are often used interchangeably. What is important is that both Skinner and Thorndike acknowledged that first the behavior is *emitted* (displayed), and then a consequence (for example, a reward) follows. This is unlike classical (Pavlovian) conditioning, in which first there is a change in the environment (for example, bells and food are paired) and then the conditioned behavior (usually a reflexive response) is *elicited* (see Figure 5.7).

In operant conditioning, such as in Thorndike's experiment with cats, an organism emits a behavior and then a consequence follows. The type of consequence that follows the behavior is a crucial component of the conditioning, because it determines whether the behavior is likely to recur. Principally, the consequence can be a reinforcer or a punisher. As in classical conditioning, a reward acts as a *reinforcer,* increasing the likelihood that the behavior targeted for conditioning will recur; in Thorndike's experiment, food was the reinforcer for hitting the lever. A *punisher,* on the other hand, decreases the likelihood that the targeted behavior will recur. If an electric shock is delivered to a cat's paws each time the cat touches a lever, the cat quickly learns not to touch the lever. Parents use reinforcers and punishers when they link the behavior of their teenagers to the use of the family car. A teenager on a date is more likely to return home at an appropriate hour if doing so will ensure use of the car again. (We will discuss punishment and its consequences in more detail later in this chapter.)

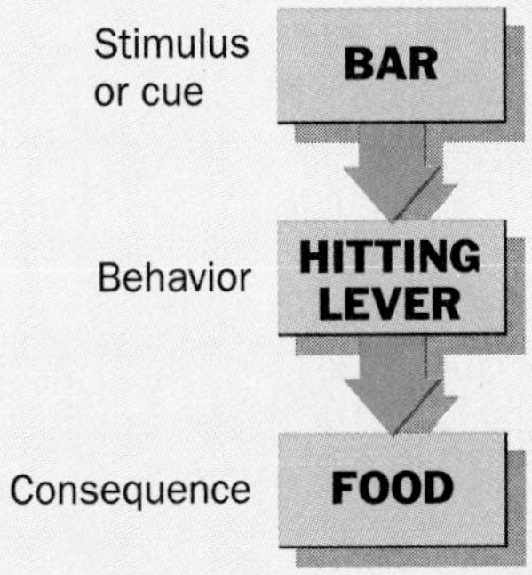

B. F. Skinner—The Man and His Ideas. Skinner is arguably the most influential psychologist the United States has ever produced. Although he spent his career

FIGURE 5.7

The Process of Instrumental (Operant) Conditioning

Instrumental (operant) conditioning is different from classical conditioning in that the behavior to be conditioned (such as hitting a lever) is reinforced or punished *after* it occurs.

Operant conditioning: [OP-er-ant] A conditioning procedure in which the probability that an organism will emit a response is increased or decreased by the subsequent delivery of a reinforcer or punisher. Also known as *instrumental conditioning.*

Skinner box: Named (by others) for its developer, B. F. Skinner, a box that contains a responding mechanism (usually a lever) capable of delivering a consequence, often a reinforcer, to an organism.

studying animals, his writings are all about people. His theories about using principles of operant conditioning to design a utopian society brought him lasting fame.

Burrhus Frederic Skinner was more an engineer than a theorist. Determining the best time to get up in the morning, inventing a better hearing aid, designing a comfortable enclosed crib for his daughters—these were the kinds of tasks he found most rewarding. Skinner's thinking classified him as a behaviorist. He believed that we are what we do—that there is no "self," only a collection of possible behaviors. Skinner was also a determinist. In his view, our actions are more a result of past experiences than genetics. But he took the phrase *a result of* very literally. According to Skinner, our environment determines completely what we do. We control our actions about as much as a rock in an avalanche controls its resting place.

Skinner was born March 20, 1904, near Scranton, Pennsylvania. He wanted to be a writer but had little success. After turning to psychology and getting his PhD from Harvard in 1931 Skinner taught at the University of Minnesota in the 1930s and at Indiana University in the 1940s. He returned to Harvard in 1947 and remained there through the rest of his career.

In his later years, Skinner didn't enjoy the theater because his hearing was poor. He didn't dine out because his taste buds had dulled. And he gave up piano because of his failing eyesight. "I'm in good health from the neck down," he said, half-joking. But death didn't scare him, he insisted. "My only fear is that I won't finish the papers I'm writing." Skinner died in August 1990 at 86 years of age.

The Skinner Box and Shaping

Much of the research on operant conditioning has used an apparatus that most psychologists call a Skinner box—even though Skinner never approved of the idea of naming it after him. A **Skinner box** is a box that contains a mechanism for delivering a consequence whenever the animal in the box makes a readily identifiable response that the experimenter has decided to reinforce or punish. In experiments that involve rewards, the delivery mechanism is often a small lever or bar in the side of the box; whenever the animal presses it, the behavior is rewarded. Punishment often takes the form of electric shocks delivered through a grid on the floor of the box.

In a traditional operant conditioning experiment, a rat that has been deprived of food is placed in a Skinner box. The rat moves around the box, often seeking to escape; eventually, it stumbles on the lever and presses it. Immediately following that action, the experimenter delivers a pellet of food into a cup. The rat moves about some more and happens to press the lever again; another pellet of food is delivered. After a few trials, the rat learns that pressing the lever brings food. A hungry rat will learn to press the lever many times in rapid succession to obtain food.

In the Skinner box, behavior is punished or rewarded after an animal makes a response.

Counting the lever presses or measuring the salivary responses is a tedious but necessary part of studying conditioning. To make the measuring easier, psychologists developed a practical and simple device, a *cumulative recorder* (see Figure 5.8). This device was essential for the early progress made in animal-learning laboratories. Today, psychologists use computerized devices to quantify behavior such as bar pressing and to track the progress an organism makes in learning a response. Teaching an organism a complex response takes many trials because most organisms need to be taught in small steps, through *shaping*.

Shaping is the process of reinforcing behavior that approximates (comes close to) a desired behavior. To teach a hungry rat to press a bar in a Skinner box, for example, a researcher begins by giving the rat a pellet of food each time it enters the side of the box on which the bar is located. Once this behavior is established, the rat receives food only when it touches the wall where the bar is located. It then receives food only when it approaches the lever, and so on, until it receives food only when it actually presses the bar. At each stage, the reinforced behavior (entering the half of the box nearest the lever, touching the wall that houses the lever, and so on) more closely approximates the desired behavior (pressing the lever). The sequence of obtaining increasingly closer approximations of the desired behavior is sometimes called the *method of successive approximations*; it means approximately the same thing as *shaping*.

Shaping is effective for teaching animals new behaviors; for example, shaping is used to train a dog to sit on command. This generally is done by pairing food with

Shaping: The gradual training of an organism to give the proper responses by selectively reinforcing behaviors as they approach the desired response.

FIGURE 5.8

A Cumulative Recorder Tracing an Organism's Response Activity

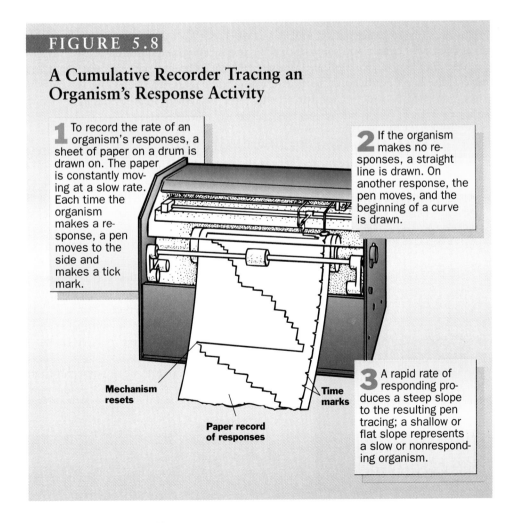

1 To record the rate of an organism's responses, a sheet of paper on a drum is drawn on. The paper is constantly moving at a slow rate. Each time the organism makes a response, a pen moves to the side and makes a tick mark.

2 If the organism makes no responses, a straight line is drawn. On another response, the pen moves, and the beginning of a curve is drawn.

3 A rapid rate of responding produces a steep slope to the resulting pen tracing; a shallow or flat slope represents a slow or nonresponding organism.

Mechanism resets

Time marks

Paper record of responses

Reinforcer: Any event that increases the probability of a recurrence of the response that preceded it.

Positive reinforcement: Presentation of a rewarding or pleasant stimulus after a particular response to increase the likelihood that the response will recur.

a push on the dog's rear while verbally commanding "Sit!" With reinforcement following the sitting, the dog begins to sit with less and less pressure applied to its rear; eventually, the dog sits on command. Shaping is also helpful in teaching people new behaviors. For example, were you taught how to play baseball? If so, first you were taught how to hold the bat correctly, then how to swing it, then how to make contact with the ball, and finally how to hit the ball for a base hit.

Teaching new behaviors with operant conditioning is time-consuming and often must be done in several stages, especially if the behaviors are complex. For example, a father who wants his son to make his bed neatly will at first reinforce *all* of the child's attempts at bed making, even if the results are sloppy. Over successive weeks, the father will reinforce only the better attempts, until finally he reinforces only neat bed making. Patience is important because it is essential to reinforce all steps toward the desired behavior, no matter how small (Fischer & Gochros, 1975). Shaping embodies a central aspect of behaviorism—that reinforced behaviors recur. Skinner is the individual most responsible for advancing that notion; we attribute to him the idea that a variety of procedures can redirect the natural flow of behavior; among the most important is reinforcement (R. Epstein, 1991).

Reinforcement

To really understand operant conditioning, you need to study the basic principles of reinforcement. To psychologists, a **reinforcer** is any event that increases the probability of a recurrence of the response that preceded it. Thus, a behavior followed by a desirable event is likely to recur. Examples of reinforcement in our lives abound. A person works hard in a factory and is rewarded with high pay; a student studies long hours for an examination and is rewarded with a top grade; sales agents call on hundreds of clients and sell lots of their products; young children behave appropriately and receive affection and praise from their parents. The specific behaviors of working hard, studying a great deal, calling on clients, and behaving for parents are established because of reinforcement. Such behaviors can be taught by using either or both of two kinds of reinforcers: positive and negative.

Positive Reinforcement. Most people have used positive reinforcement at one time or another. **Positive reinforcement** is the presentation of a rewarding or pleasant stimulus after a particular response, to increase the likelihood that the response will recur. When you are teaching your dog tricks, you reward it with a biscuit or a pat on the head. When a parent is toilet-training a 2-year-old, the parent often applauds when the child successfully completes a bowel movement; the applause is a reinforcer. The dog and the child continue the behaviors because they have been rewarded with something that is important or desired; their behaviors have been positively reinforced.

Some reinforcers are more powerful than others, and a reinforcer for one person may

His father's praise and attention act as reinforcers for this young boy's involvement in baseball.

not have reinforcing value for another. A smile from an approving parent may be a powerful reinforcer for a 2-year-old; high grades may be the most effective reinforcer for a student; money may be effective for one adult, position or status for another. At many corporations, bonuses for effective performance may include color televisions, cassette tape recorders, or trips to Hawaii.

Negative Reinforcement. Whereas positive reinforcement increases the probability of a response through delivery of a reward, **negative reinforcement** increases the probability of a response through removal of an unpleasant, aversive, or noxious stimulus. Negative reinforcement is still reinforcement, because it strengthens or increases the likelihood of a response; it is called "negative" because, instead of adding a positive experience, it removes a negative one. For example, suppose a rat is placed in a Skinner box with an electrified grid that delivers a shock every 50 seconds, and the rat can escape the shock by pressing a bar. The behavior to be conditioned is bar pressing; the reinforcement is termination of the painful stimulus. In this case, negative reinforcement—termination of the painful stimulus—increases the probability of the response (bar pressing) because that is the way to turn off the unpleasant stimulus.

> **Negative reinforcement:** Removal of an aversive stimulus after a particular response to increase the likelihood that the response will recur.

Noxious or unpleasant stimuli are often used in animal studies of escape and avoidance. In *escape conditioning,* a rat in a Skinner box receives a shock just strong enough to cause it to thrash around until it bumps against a bar, thereby stopping the shock. In just a few trials, the rat learns to press the bar to escape being shocked, to bring an unpleasant situation to an end. In *avoidance conditioning,* the same apparatus is used, but a buzzer or some other cue precedes the shock by a few seconds. In this case, the rat learns that when it is presented with a stimulus or cue such as a buzzer, it should press the bar to avoid the shock—to prevent it from occurring. Pressing the bar allows the rat to avoid the unpleasant experience.

Avoidance conditioning generally involves escape conditioning as well. First the animal learns how to escape the shock by pressing the bar. Then it learns how to avoid the shock by pressing the bar when it hears the buzzer that signals the oncoming shock. In avoidance conditioning, the organism learns to respond in such a way that the noxious stimulus is never delivered. For example, to avoid receiving a bad grade on an English quiz, a student may study before an examination. And when an adult develops an irrational fear of airplanes, the person may avoid airplane travel. If the person can get to where he or she needs to go by some other means, the person may never unlearn the fear of planes. Thus, avoidance conditioning can explain adaptive behaviors such as studying before an exam, and it can also explain why some people maintain irrational fears.

Most children master both escape and avoidance conditioning at an early age. Appropriate signals from a disapproving parent often elicit an avoidance response so punishment will not follow; for example, just knowing the possible effects of an automobile accident will make most cautious adults wear seatbelts. Both positive and negative reinforcements *increase* the likelihood that an organism will repeat a behavior. If the reinforcement is strong enough, is delivered often enough, and is important enough to the organism, it can help maintain behaviors for long periods.

The Nature of Reinforcers. The precise nature of reinforcers is a murky issue. Early researchers recognized that events that satisfy biological needs are powerful reinforcers. Later researchers added events that decrease a person's various needs—for example, conversation that relieves boredom, sounds that relieve sensory deprivation, and money that relieves housing congestion. Then, in the 1960s, researchers acknowledged that an array of events can be reinforcers: *Probable behaviors*— behaviors likely to happen, including biological behaviors such as eating and social behaviors such as playing tennis, writing letters, or talking—can reinforce less probable or unlikely behaviors (such as cleaning closets, studying calculus, or pressing levers). Researchers call this idea the *Premack principle,* after David Premack, whose influential writings and research fostered it (Premack, 1962, 1965). Parents employ the Premack principle when they tell their children that they can go outside to play *after* they clean up their rooms.

The Premack principle and its refinements focus on the problem of determining what is a good reinforcer. Therapists and learning theorists know, for example, that something that acts as a reinforcer for one person may not do so for another, and something that acts as a reinforcer on one day may not do so for the same person on the next day. Therefore, they are very careful about determining what events in a client's life—or a rodent's environment—act as reinforcers. If someone were to offer you a reinforcer for some extraordinary activity on your part, what would be the most effective reinforcer? Do reinforcers change with a person's age and experiences, or do they depend on how often the person has been reinforced? Today, researchers are trying to find out ahead of time what reinforcers will work in practical settings such as the home and the workplace (Timberlake & Farmer-Dougan, 1991).

A reinforcer that is known to be successful may work only in specific situations. The delivery of food pellets to a hungry rat that has just pressed a lever increases the likelihood that the rat will press the lever again. But this reinforcer works only if the rat is hungry; for a rat that has just eaten, food pellets are not reinforcing.

Psychologists studying learning and conditioning create the conditions for reinforcement by depriving animals of food or water before an experiment. In doing so, they motivate the animals and allow the delivery of food to take on reinforcing properties. In most experiments, the organism is motivated in some way. Chapter 10 discusses the role of an organism's needs, desires, and physiological state in determining what can be used as a reinforcer.

A **primary reinforcer** is a reinforcer (something that increases the likelihood of a response) that has survival value for the organism—for example, food, water, or the termination of pain; its value does not have to be learned. Food can be a primary reinforcer for a hungry rat, water for a thirsty one. A **secondary reinforcer** is a neutral stimulus (such as money or grades) that initially has no intrinsic value for the organism but that when linked with a primary reinforcer can become rewarding. Many human pleasures are secondary reinforcers that have acquired value—for example, leather coats that keep people no warmer than cloth ones and sports cars that take people around town no faster than four-door sedans.

Secondary reinforcers are generally used to modify human behavior. Approving nods, unlimited use of the family car, and job promotions are secondary reinforcers that act to establish and maintain a wide spectrum of behavior. People will work long hours when the rewards are significant. Salespeople may work 72-hour weeks to reach their sales objectives. This may happen when a manager, using basic psychology, offers them bonuses for increasing their sales by a specific percentage during a slow month. The manager may reason that increasing the amount of the reinforcer (money) may promote better performance (higher sales). Research shows that increasing or decreasing the amount of a reinforcer can significantly alter an organism's behavior.

Superstitious Behaviors. Because reinforcement plays a key role in learning new behaviors, parents and educators try to reinforce children and students on a regular basis. However, what happens when a person or animal is unintentionally rewarded for a behavior—when a reward has nothing to do with the behavior that immediately preceded it? Under this condition, people and animals may develop **superstitious behavior**—behavior learned through coincidental association with

Primary reinforcer: Any stimulus or event that follows a particular response and that, by its mere delivery (if pleasant) or removal (if unpleasant), acts naturally (without learning) to increase the likelihood that the response will recur.

Secondary reinforcer: A neutral stimulus that has no intrinsic value to an organism but that acquires reinforcement value through repeated pairing with a reinforcing stimulus.

Superstitious behavior: Behavior learned through coincidental association with reinforcement.

For centuries people have tried to influence the events affecting their lives. The belief that repeating a certain random action such as lighting joss sticks may elicit a positive outcome is known as superstition.

reinforcement. For example, a baseball player may try to extend his hitting streak by always using the same "lucky" bat. A student may study at the same table in the library because she earned an A after studying there for the last exam. A number of superstitious behaviors—including fear responses to the number 13, black cats, and walking under ladders—are centuries old and have strong cultural associations. These behaviors generally arise from a purely random consequence that occurred immediately after the behavior. Thus, a person who happens to wear the same pair of shoes in three bicycle races and wins the races may come to believe there is a causal relationship between wearing that pair of shoes and winning a bicycle race.

Animals can learn superstitious behaviors even in a Skinner box. For example, on trials in which a pigeon learns the bar-pressing response, it may turn its head to the right before pressing the bar and receiving reinforcement. Although the reinforcement actually is contingent only on pressing the bar, to the pigeon it may seem that both the head turning *and* the bar pressing are necessary (Skinner, 1948). Therefore, the pigeon will continue to turn its head to the right before pressing the bar.

Punishment

You already know that the consequences of an action—whether reward or punishment—affect behavior. Clearly, rewards can establish new behaviors and maintain them for long periods. How effective is punishment in manipulating behavior? **Punishment** is the process of presenting an undesirable or noxious stimulus, or the removal of a positive desirable stimulus, to decrease the probability that a particular preceding response will recur. Punishment, unlike reinforcement, decreases the probability of a particular response. As such, it is one of the most commonly used techniques for teaching children and pets to control their behavior. For example, when a dog growls at visitors, its owner chastises it or chains it to a post. When children write on the walls with crayons, their parents may scold them harshly or make them scrub the walls clean. In both cases, people indicate displeasure by the delivery of an action in order to suppress an undesirable behavior.

Researchers use the same technique to decrease the probability that a behavior will recur. They deliver a noxious or unpleasant stimulus, such as a mild electric shock, when an organism displays an undesirable behavior. If an animal is punished for a specific behavior, the probability that it will continue to perform that behavior decreases.

Another form of punishment involves removal of a pleasant stimulus. For example, if a teenager stays out past her curfew, she may be grounded for a week. A child

Punishment: The process of presenting an undesirable or noxious stimulus or removing a desirable stimulus to decrease the probability that a particular preceding response will recur.

Primary punisher: Any stimulus or event that follows a particular response and that by its delivery or removal acts naturally (without learning) to decrease the likelihood that the response will recur.

Secondary punisher: A neutral stimulus with no intrinsic value to the organism that acquires punishment value through repeated pairing with a punishing stimulus.

may be forbidden to watch television if he misbehaves. One effective punishment is the *time-out,* in which a person is removed from an environment containing positive events or reinforcers. For example, a child who hits and kicks may be put in a room in which there are no toys, television, or people.

Thus, punishment can involve either adding a noxious event, such as a scolding, or subtracting a positive event, such as television watching. In both cases, the aim is to decrease the likelihood of a behavior (see Table 5.2 for a summary of the effects of adding or subtracting a reinforcer or punisher).

The Nature of Punishers. Just as reinforcers are used for reinforcement, *punishers* are used for punishment. They can be primary or secondary. A **primary punisher** is a stimulus that is naturally painful to an organism; two examples are an electric shock to an animal and a spanking to a child. A **secondary punisher** is a neutral stimulus that takes on punishing qualities; examples are a verbal no, a frown, and indifference. Secondary punishers can be effective means of controlling behavior, especially when used in combination with reinforcers for desired behaviors.

TABLE 5.2

Effects of Reinforcement and Punishment

ADDITION OF A STIMULUS	SUBTRACTION OR WITH-HOLDING OF A STIMULUS	EFFECT
Positive reinforcement Delivery of food, money, or some other reward 	**Negative reinforcement** Removal of shock or some other aversive stimulus 	Establishes or increases a specific behavior
Punishment Delivery of electric shock, a slap on the hand, or some other aversive stimulus 	**Punishment** Removal of automobile, television, or some other pleasant stimulus 	Suppresses or decreases a specific behavior

Punishment Plus Reinforcement. Some psychologists (e.g., Appel & Peterson, 1965) argue that punishment by itself is not an effective way to control or eliminate behavior. Punishment can suppress simple behavior patterns; but once the punishment ceases, animals and human beings often return to their previous behavior. To be effective, punishment must be continuous and the desired alternative behavior should be reinforced. Therefore, those who study children in classrooms urge the combination of punishment for antisocial behavior and reinforcement for prosocial, worthwhile behaviors. A combination of private reprimands for disruptive behaviors and praise for good behaviors is often the most effective method for controlling classroom behavior.

Limitations of Punishment. A serious limitation of punishment as a behavior-shaping device is that it suppresses only existing behaviors. It cannot be used to establish new, desired behaviors. Punishment also has serious social consequences (Azrin & Holtz, 1966). If parents use excessive punishment to control a child's behavior, for example, the child may try to escape from the home so that punishment cannot be delivered. Further, children who receive frequent physical punishments demonstrate increased levels of aggression when away from the punisher. Punishment may control the child's behavior while the parents are nearby, but it may also alienate the child from the parents. Further, if punishment is ineffectively or inconsistently delivered, it may lead to learned helplessness, in which a person or animal feels powerless to control the punishment and stops making any response at all. We discuss learned helplessness in detail in chapter 16.

As indicated, punishment can lead to aggression and other antisocial behaviors. Research shows that children will imitate aggression; thus, parents who punish children physically are likely to have children who are physically aggressive (Mischel &

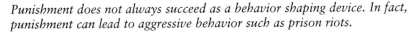

Punishment does not always succeed as a behavior shaping device. In fact, punishment can lead to aggressive behavior such as prison riots.

FOCUS

▶ What is the fundamental difference between positive reinforcement and negative reinforcement? Give an example of each.   pp. 174–175

▶ Explain why the type of reinforcer that follows a behavior is crucial to whether the behavior will be repeated. pp. 175–177

▶ What evidence is there that probable behaviors can reinforce less probable or unlikely behaviors (the Premack principle)?   pp. 175–177

▶ Distinguish between primary reinforcers and secondary reinforcers.   p. 176

▶ How could a child's undesirable behavior be shaped to a desired behavior?   pp. 179–180

Grusec, 1966). In addition, a child or institutionalized person may strike out at the person who administers punishment in an attempt to eliminate the source of punishment, sometimes inflicting serious injury.

Punishment can also bring about generalized aggression. For example, if two rats in a Skinner box both receive painful shocks, they will strike out at each other. Similarly, punished individuals are often hostile and aggressive toward other members of their group. This is especially true for prison inmates, whose hostility is well recognized, and even for class bullies, who are often the most strictly disciplined by their parents or teachers.

Skinner (1988) believed that punishment in schools is unnecessary and harmful. He advocated nonpunitive techniques that might involve developing strong bonds between students and teachers and reinforcing school activities at home (Comer, 1988). In general, procedures that lead to a perception of control are much more likely to lead to nonoccurrence of the undesired behavior, even when the punishing agent (often mom or dad) is not around.

Key Variables in Operant Conditioning

As with classical conditioning, many variables affect operant conditioning. Most important are the strength, timing, and frequency of consequences (either reinforcement or punishment).

Strength, Timing, and Frequency

Strength of Consequences. Studies comparing productivity with varying amounts of reinforcement show that the greater the reward, the harder, longer, and faster a person will work to complete a task (see Figure 5.9). For example, if you were a gardener, the more money you received for mowing lawns, the more lawns you would want to mow. Similarly, the stronger the punishment, the more quickly and longer the behavior can be suppressed. If you receive a heavy fine for speeding, you probably will start to obey the speed limit.

The strength of a consequence can be measured in terms of either time or degree. For example, the length of time a child stays in a time-out room without positive reinforcements affects how soon and for how long an unacceptable behavior will be suppressed. Thus, theoretically, a 2-minute stay would not be as effective as a 10-minute stay. Likewise, a tentative "Please do not do that, sweetie" is not as effective as a firm "Don't do that again."

Punishment, whatever its form, is best delivered in moderation; too much may be as ineffective as too little. If too much punishment is delivered, it may cause panic, decrease the likelihood of an appropriate response, or even elicit behavior that is contrary to the punisher's goals.

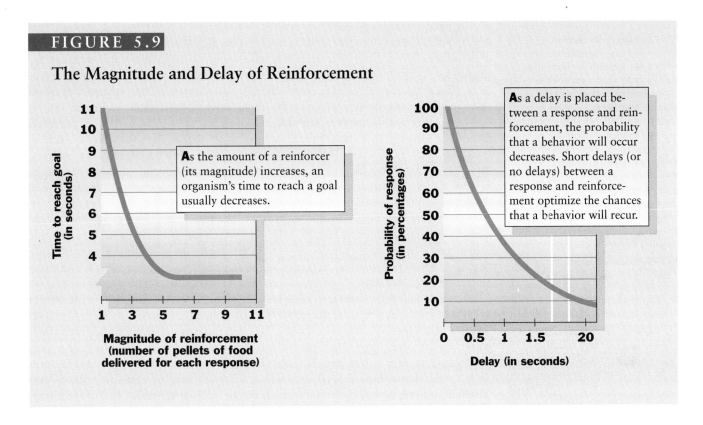

FIGURE 5.9

The Magnitude and Delay of Reinforcement

As the amount of a reinforcer (its magnitude) increases, an organism's time to reach a goal usually decreases.

As a delay is placed between a response and reinforcement, the probability that a behavior will occur decreases. Short delays (or no delays) between a response and reinforcement optimize the chances that a behavior will recur.

Magnitude of reinforcement (number of pellets of food delivered for each response)

Delay (in seconds)

Timing of Consequences. Just as the interval between presenting the conditioned stimulus and the unconditioned stimulus is important in classical conditioning, the interval between a desired behavior and the delivery of the consequence (reward or punishment) is important in operant conditioning. Generally, the shorter the interval, the greater the likelihood that the behavior will be learned (again, see Figure 5.9).

Frequency of Consequences. How often do people need to be reinforced? Is a paycheck once a month sufficient? Will people work better if they receive reinforcement regularly or if they receive it at unpredictable times? Until now, we have assumed that a consequence follows each response.

What if people are reinforced only some of the time, not continually? When a researcher varies the frequency with which an organism is to be reinforced, the researcher is said to manipulate the *schedule of reinforcement*—the pattern of presentation of the reinforcer over time. The simplest and easiest reinforcement pattern is *continuous reinforcement*—reinforcement for every occurrence of the targeted behavior. However, most researchers, or parents for that matter, do not reinforce a behavior every time it occurs; rather, they reinforce occasionally or intermittently. What causes the occurrence of reinforcement? Schedules of reinforcement generally are based either on intervals of time or on frequency of response. Some schedules establish a behavior quickly; however, quickly established behaviors are more quickly extinguished than are behaviors that are slower to be established. (We discuss extinction further in a few paragraphs.) Researchers have devised four basic schedules of reinforcement; two are *interval schedules* (which deal with time periods), and two are *ratio schedules* (which deal with work output).

The interval schedules can be either fixed or variable. Imagine that a rat in a Skinner box is being trained to press a bar in order to obtain food. If the experiment

Fixed-interval schedule: A reinforcement schedule in which a reinforcer (reward) is delivered after a specified interval of time, provided that the required response has occurred at least once after the interval.

Variable-interval schedule: A reinforcement schedule in which a reinforcer (reward) is delivered after predetermined but varying intervals of time, provided that the required response has occurred at least once after each interval.

Fixed-ratio schedule: A reinforcement schedule in which a reinforcer (reward) is delivered after a specified number of responses has occurred.

Variable-ratio schedule: A reinforcement schedule in which a reinforcer (reward) is delivered after a predetermined but variable number of responses has occurred.

is on a **fixed-interval schedule,** the reward will follow the first required response that occurs after a specified interval of time. That is, the rat will be given a reinforcer if it presses the bar at least once after a specified interval, regardless of how much the rat works. As Figure 5.10 shows, a fixed-interval schedule produces a scalloped pattern. Just after reinforcement, both animals and human beings typically respond slowly; just before the reinforcer is due, there is an increase in performance.

Under a **variable-interval schedule,** the reinforcer is delivered after predetermined but varying amounts of time, as long as an appropriate response is made at least once after each interval. The organism may be reinforced if it makes a response after 40 seconds, after 60 seconds, and then after 25 seconds. For example, if grades are posted at various unpredictable intervals during a semester, you probably will check the bulletin board at a fairly steady rate.

Rats reinforced on a variable-interval schedule work at a slow, steady rate, without showing the scalloped effect of those on a fixed-interval schedule. The work rate is relatively slow, because the delivery of the reinforcer is tied to time intervals rather than to output. Nevertheless, rats on a variable-interval schedule have a better overall rate of response than those on a fixed-interval schedule.

Ratio schedules, which can also be either fixed or variable, deal with output instead of time. In a **fixed-ratio schedule,** the subject is reinforced for a specified number of responses (amount of work). For example, a rat in a Skinner box might be reinforced after every 10th bar press. In this case, the rat will work at a fast, steady, regular rate. It has learned that hard work brings the delivery of a reinforcer on a regular basis. Figure 5.10 shows that the work rate of a rat on a fixed-ratio schedule is much higher than that of a rat on an interval schedule. In the same way, a teenager who is paid by the job (for the amount of work completed) to mow lawns will probably mow more lawns than one who is paid by the hour.

Variable-ratio schedules can achieve very high rates of response. In contrast to a fixed-ratio schedule, a **variable-ratio schedule** reinforces the subject for a prede-

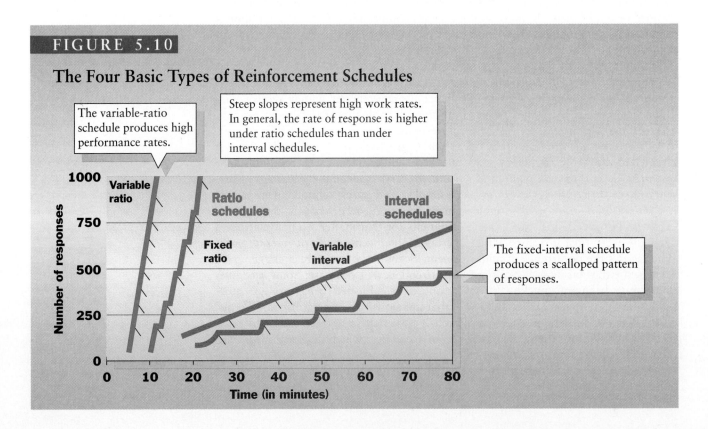

FIGURE 5.10

The Four Basic Types of Reinforcement Schedules

The variable-ratio schedule produces high performance rates.

Steep slopes represent high work rates. In general, the rate of response is higher under ratio schedules than under interval schedules.

The fixed-interval schedule produces a scalloped pattern of responses.

termined but variable number of responses (amount of work). Thus, a rat learns that hard work produces a reinforcer, but it cannot predict when the reinforcer will be delivered. Therefore, the rat's best bet is to work at an even, steady, high rate, thereby generating the highest available rate of response. Sales agents for insurance companies know that the more prospects they approach, the more insurance they will sell. They may not know who will buy, but they do know that a greater number of selling opportunities will result in more sales. Similarly, gamblers pour quarters into slot machines because they never know when they will be reinforced with a jackpot.

An efficient way to teach a response is to have an organism learn the response on a fixed-ratio schedule, and then to introduce a variable-ratio schedule. For example, a rat can be reinforced initially on every trial so it will learn the proper response quickly. It can then be reinforced after every other trial, then after every fifth trial, and then after a variable number of trials. Once the rat has learned the desired response, very high response rates can be obtained even with infrequent reinforcers.

When an experimenter implements a *variable*-ratio or a *variable*-interval schedule, the frequency for each ratio or the length of each interval is predetermined, though it will not appear so in the view of the subject. Table 5.3 lists the four basic reinforcement schedules and their effects. These schedules can easily be combined for maximum effect, depending on the targeted behavior.

Using Schedules of Consequences. The study of reinforcement has many practical implications. Psychologists use the principles of reinforcement to study such frequently asked questions as: How can I change my little brother's rotten attitude? How can I get more work out of my employees? How do I learn to say no? How do I get my dog to stop biting my ankles?

To get your brother to shape up, you can shape his behavior. Each time he acts in a way you like, however slight the action, reward him with praise or affection. When he acts poorly, withhold attention or rewards and ignore him. Continue this pattern for a few weeks; and as he becomes more pleasant, show him more attention. Remember, reinforced behaviors tend to recur.

Most workers get paid a fixed amount each week. They are on a fixed-interval schedule—regardless of their output, they get their paycheck. One way to increase productivity is to place workers on a fixed-ratio schedule. A worker who is paid by

TABLE 5.3   *Schedules of Reinforcement*

Schedule	Description	Effect
Fixed-interval	Reinforcement is given for the first response after a fixed time.	Response rate drops right after reinforcement but increases near the end of the interval.
Variable-interval	Reinforcement is given for the first response after a predetermined but variable interval.	Response rate is slow and steady.
Fixed-ratio	Reinforcement is given after a fixed number of responses.	Response rate is fast, steady, and regular.
Variable-ratio	Reinforcement is given after a predetermined variable number of responses.	Response rate is even, steady, and high.

the piece, by the report, by the page, or by the widget is going to produce more pieces, reports, pages, or widgets than one who is paid by the hour and whose productivity therefore does not make a difference. Automobile salespeople, who are known for their persistence, work on a commission basis; their pay is linked to their ability to close a sale. Research in both the laboratory and the business world shows that when pay is linked to output, people generally work harder.

Stimulus Generalization and Stimulus Discrimination

Stimulus generalization and *stimulus discrimination* occur in operant conditioning much as they do in classical conditioning. The difference is that in operant conditioning the reinforcement is delivered only after the animal correctly discriminates between the stimuli. For example, suppose an animal in a laboratory is shown either a vertical or a horizontal line and is given two keys to press—one if the line is vertical, the other if the line is horizontal. The animal is reinforced for correct responses. The animal will usually make errors at first; but after repeated presentations of the vertical and horizontal lines, with reinforcements given only for correct responses, discrimination will occur. Stimulus discrimination can also be established with colors, tones, and more complex stimuli.

The processes of stimulus generalization and discrimination are evident daily. Children often make mistakes by overgeneralizing. For example, a baby who knows that cats have four legs and a tail may call all four-legged animals cats. With experience and the help, guidance, and reinforcement of parents, the child will learn to discriminate between dogs and cats, using body size, shape, fur, and sounds. Similarly, you may once have been indifferent to all Chinese food; but after several experiences, you probably have learned to discriminate among the various dishes. Perhaps you recognize that you especially like the Hunan dishes and don't care for the Szechuan dishes.

Extinction and Spontaneous Recovery

In operant conditioning, if a reinforcer or punisher is no longer delivered—that is, if a consequence does not follow an instrumentally conditioned behavior—the behavior either will not be well established or, if it is already established, will undergo extinction (see Figure 5.11). **Extinction,** in operant conditioning, is the process by which the probability of an organism's emitting a conditioned response is reduced when reinforcement no longer follows the response. Suppose, for example, that a pigeon is trained to peck a key whenever it hears a high-pitched tone. Pecking in response to a high-pitched tone brings reinforcement, but pecking in response to a low-pitched tone does not. If the reinforcement process ceases entirely, the pigeon will eventually stop working. If the pigeon has been on a variable-ratio schedule and thus expects to work for long periods before reinforcement occurs, it will probably work for a very long time before stopping. If it is on a fixed-interval schedule and thus expects reinforcement within a short time, it will stop pecking after just a few unreinforced trials.

One way to measure the extent of conditioning is to measure how resistant a response is to extinction. *Resistance to extinction* is a measure of how long it takes, or how many trials are necessary, to achieve extinction. Consider a pigeon that is trained to peck when it hears a high-pitched tone and that is rewarded each time it pecks correctly. The pigeon is tested for 30 minutes a day for 60 days. On the 61st day it is not reinforced for its correct behavior. For the first few minutes, the pigeon continues to work normally. But soon its work rate decreases; and by the end of the 30-minute session, it is not pecking at all. When the pigeon is presented with a tone

Extinction: In operant conditioning, the process by which the probability of an organism's emitting a conditioned response is reduced when reinforcement no longer follows the response.

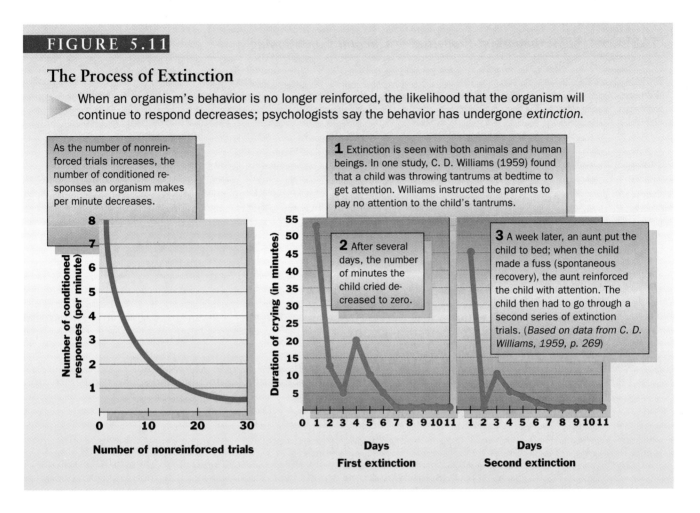

FIGURE 5.11

The Process of Extinction

> When an organism's behavior is no longer reinforced, the likelihood that the organism will continue to respond decreases; psychologists say the behavior has undergone *extinction*.

As the number of nonreinforced trials increases, the number of conditioned responses an organism makes per minute decreases.

Number of conditioned responses (per minute)

Number of nonreinforced trials

1 Extinction is seen with both animals and human beings. In one study, C. D. Williams (1959) found that a child was throwing tantrums at bedtime to get attention. Williams instructed the parents to pay no attention to the child's tantrums.

2 After several days, the number of minutes the child cried decreased to zero.

3 A week later, an aunt put the child to bed; when the child made a fuss (spontaneous recovery), the aunt reinforced the child with attention. The child then had to go through a second series of extinction trials. (*Based on data from C. D. Williams, 1959, p. 269*)

Duration of crying (in minutes)

Days
First extinction

Days
Second extinction

the next day, it again responds with pecking but receives no reinforcer. Within a short time, the pecking behavior is extinguished.

Note that the decrease in response is not always immediately apparent. When a reinforcer is withheld, organisms sometimes work harder—showing an initial increase in performance. In such cases, the curve depicting the extinction process shows a small initial increase in performance, followed by a decrease (Allen, Turner, & Everett, 1970).

As in classical conditioning, *spontaneous recovery* also occurs in operant conditioning. If an organism's conditioned behavior has undergone extinction and the organism is given a rest period and then retested, the organism will show spontaneous recovery of the behavior. If the organism is put through this sequence several times, its work rate in each session will decrease. After one rest period, the organism's work rate will almost equal what it was when the conditioned response was reinforced. However, after a dozen or so rest periods (with no reinforcements), the organism may make only one or two responses; the level of spontaneous recovery will have decreased markedly. Eventually, the behavior will disappear completely.

People also show spontaneous recovery. When you answer a question in class, reinforcement usually follows. The instructor praises you for your intelligence or berates you for your ignorance. However, if the instructor stops reinforcing correct answers or does not call on you when you raise your hand, you will probably stop responding (your behavior will be extinguished). After a vacation, you may start raising your hand again (spontaneous recovery), but you will quickly stop if your behavior again is not reinforced. (Instructors learn early in their careers that if they

TABLE 5.4   *Four Important Properties of Operant Conditioning*

Property	Definition	Example
Stimulus generalization	The process by which an organism learns to respond to stimuli that are similar but not identical to the original conditioned stimulus.	A cat presses a bar when presented with either an ellipse or a circle.
Stimulus discrimination	The process by which an organism learns to respond only to a specific reinforced stimulus.	A pigeon presses a key only in response to red lights, not to blue or green ones.
Extinction	The process of reducing the probability of a conditioned response by withholding the reinforcer after the response.	A rat trained to press a bar stops pressing when it is no longer reinforced.
Spontaneous recovery	The recurrence of an extinguished conditioned response following a rest period.	A rat's continued bar-pressing behavior has undergone extinction; after a rest period, the rat again presses the bar.

want to have lively classes, they need to reinforce not just correct answers but also attempts at correct answers. In doing so, they help shape, or manage, their students' behavior.

Table 5.4 summarizes four important properties of operant conditioning: stimulus generalization, stimulus discrimination, extinction, and spontaneous recovery.

Intrinsically Motivated Behavior

Psychologists have shown that reinforcement is effective in establishing and maintaining behavior. But some behaviors are intrinsically rewarding—they are pleasurable in themselves. People are likely to repeat intrinsically motivated behaviors for their own sake—for example, they might work on craft projects for the feeling of satisfaction they bring. They are likely to perform extrinsically motivated behavior, such as working for a paycheck, only for the sake of the external reinforcement. Interestingly, if reinforcement is offered for intrinsically motivated behavior, performance may actually decrease. Imagine, for example, that a man performs charity work because it makes him feel good. Paying the man could cause him to lose interest in the work because it no longer offers the intrinsic reward of selfless behavior. A student pianist may lose her desire to practice when her teacher enters her in a competition; practice sessions become ordeals, and the student may wish to stop playing altogether.

All people are motivated intrinsically. The question is: Why are some people intrinsically motivated to do crossword puzzles and others to climb mountains? One explanation is that, as children, human beings are conditioned to feel pleasure, or achieve intrinsic reinforcement, for specific behaviors. Someone who likes crossword puzzles may have been reinforced for accomplishing challenging intellectual tasks; someone who prefers mountaineering may have been reinforced for performing physically demanding feats. (In chapter 10, we will examine the conditions under which intrinsically motivated behavior occurs.) The Research Process box on page 188 examines some of the hidden costs of rewards.

Electrical Brain Stimulation

Until the 1950s, researchers assumed that reinforcers were effective because they satisfied some need or drive in an organism. Then James Olds (1955, 1969) found an apparent exception to this assumption. He discovered that rats find electrical stimulation of specific areas of the brain to be rewarding.

Olds implanted electrodes in the hypothalamus of rats and attached the electrodes to a stimulator that provided a small voltage. The stimulator was activated only when the rats pressed a lever in a Skinner box. Olds found that the rats pressed the lever thousands of times in order to continue the self-stimulation. In one study, they pressed it at a rate of 1,920 times per hour (Olds & Milner, 1954). Rats even crossed an electrified grid to obtain this reward. Animals who were rewarded with brain stimulation performed better in a maze, running faster with fewer errors. And hungry rats often chose self-stimulation over food.

Stimulation of specific areas of the brain initiates different drives and activities. In some cases, it reinforces behaviors such as bar pressing; in others, it increases eating, drinking, or sexual behavior. Psychologists are still not sure how electrical stimulation reinforces a behavior such as lever pressing; but they do know that certain neurotransmitters play an important role. For example, when specific neurotransmitters, such as dopamine, are increased after bar pressing, a rat is far more likely to continue bar pressing (P. M. Milner, 1991; White & Milner, 1992). The area of the brain stimulated (initially thought to be the medial forebrain bundle but now recognized to include large parts of the limbic system), the state of the organism, its particular physiological needs, and the levels of various brain neurotransmitters are all important. A hungry rat, for example, will self-stimulate faster than a rat that is not hungry. In addition, a hungry rat will generally choose electrical brain stimulation over food but will not starve to death by always making this choice.

Behavioral Regulation

Behavioral regulation theorists assume that people and animals make choices and that they will choose, if possible, activities that seem optimal to them. Rats, for example, will spend their time eating, drinking, and running on a wheel—activities they find pleasurable. An experiment by Bernstein and Ebbesen (1978) showed that human beings readjust their activities in a systematic manner. The researchers paid subjects to live in an isolated room 24 hours a day, 7 days a week, for several weeks. The room had all the usual amenities of a home—bed, tables, shower, books, cooking utensils, and so forth. The experimenters observed the subjects through a one-way mirror and recorded their *baseline activity*—the frequency of specific behaviors when no restrictions are placed on the subjects. The researchers found, for example, that one subject spent nearly twice as much baseline time knitting as studying. The experimenters used the subject's baseline to determine the reinforcing event—in this case, knitting.

The experimenters then imposed a contingency. In the case of the subject who liked to knit, they insisted that she study for a specific amount of time before she could knit. If she studied only as much as she did before, she would be able to knit for much less time. As a consequence, the subject altered her behavior so she could knit more. She began to study for longer periods of time, eventually more than doubling the time she spent studying.

The techniques of self-regulation are based on simple learning principles. Here is an illustration. People with Type I diabetes require insulin shots each day. People with Type II diabetes (90 percent of the diabetic population) do not require shots each day but are often obese, must take medication daily, and must follow a strict diet. Both groups show poor adherence to their self-care regime: 80 percent use unhygienic techniques, 58 percent administer wrong doses of insulin, 75 percent do not eat the prescribed food, and 77 percent test their urine incorrectly (Wing et al., 1986).

THE RESEARCH PROCESS

The Hidden Cost of Rewards

A child may love playing checkers, doing simple crossword puzzles, or coloring in a coloring book. But offer her a dime for doing these things and she may no longer want to play. This effect has been called the hidden cost of offering a reward. Why does it occur? Why do some activities seem like fun and others seem like work? Are there things psychologists can do to make activities fun? What are the critical variables?

In general, psychologists find that some activities are intrinsically fun—people like to do them for their own reward. Others, however, are not nearly as much fun; and people need to be motivated to perform them, either with reinforcers or with threats of punishment. Psychologists talk about *intrinsic* and *extrinsic* motivation—whether things are done for fun or for rewards. They have found

that intrinsically motivated activities are less likely to occur if a reward is offered for them.

Hypotheses Are Formed. On the basis of the fundamental findings about intrinsic and extrinsic motivation, some schools have experimented with a grade-free system. But two researchers from Hebrew University of Jerusalem, Butler and Nisan (1986), have found that in some cases rewards encourage learning and performance, although they may decrease creativity. The researchers wanted to know if performance feedback would affect children's willingness to do tasks and how well they did these tasks. They hypothesized that if there is a hidden cost of reward, the feedback should interfere with the students' performance.

Methods of Study. Butler and Nisan asked sixth-grade children to

play two word games that involved constructing words from the letters of a longer word. There were two tasks. The first focused on the quantity of words constructed. The second involved more creative thinking; the children were asked to use the first and last letter of the longer word as the first and last letter of still another word. Both tasks were repeated each day over a three-day period.

The children were divided into three feedback groups. The first group received *written comments* at the end of a session—for example: "The words you wrote were correct,

---

Researchers who wish to help diabetics can put some basic psychological principles to work. According to Wing et al. (1986), if diabetics are to regulate themselves carefully, they must self-observe, self-evaluate, and then self-reinforce. The researchers assert that when clients *self-observe* the target behavior, they are better able to *self-evaluate* their progress. After evaluating their progress, it is crucial that they achieve *reinforcement* for adhering to their medical regimen. When these procedures are followed, adherence to the medical regimen improves.

Behavioral regulation has a number of other practical applications. For example, members of Weight Watchers might be told to keep track of when and what they eat, when they have the urge to eat, and what feelings or events precede those urges. The organizers seek to help people identify the events that lead to eating so they can control it. The aim is to help people think clearly, regulate themselves, and thus manage their lives better. This decision process and the focus on thinking is clearly seen in studies of cognitive learning, considered next.

Building Table 5.2 summarizes the key points comparing classical and operant conditioning.

FOCUS

▶ Why are partial reinforcement schedules more effective than other reward schedules?   pp. 181–183

▶ What is the evidence that an intrinsically motivated behavior will diminish in frequency when external events reinforce it?   pp. 186–187

▶ In doing human and animal research on learning, researchers often record baseline activity. Why is such evidence important?   p. 187

but you did not write many words." The second group were given *numerical grades* on their performance. The third group were given *no feedback* on their performance. Butler and Nisan asked all the students to fill out an attitude questionnaire at the end of the third session in order to help the researchers assess how the students felt about the tasks. The questions included: How interesting were the tasks? and How many more would you like to receive? The three groups—*comments, numerical grade,* and *no feedback*—were each tested in three sessions. The variables being measured were the total number of words generated and the number of words generated using the first and last letter from a longer word.

Study Results. The results of the study showed that in the *no feedback* group the number of words for both tasks decreased from the first to the last session; the students became bored with the task. The *comments* students improved their overall performance on both tasks from the first to the last session. Providing *numerical grades* improved performance on the first task (quantity of words) but decreased performance on the quality task (creative thinking).

Conclusions and Implications. Contrary to the general finding that a reward sometimes decreases performance, the results of the Butler-Nisan study show that rewards improve performance on easier tasks. On harder tasks, if feedback is in the form of written comments rather than grades, it also improves performance.

The implications of this experiment are important. School grades may motivate learners, but on tasks that involve creativity they may decrease motivation. The researchers asked students how they felt about both sets of tasks. Generally speaking, students liked getting feedback and preferred written comments to grades. However, they would rather get grades than no feedback at all.

Linney and Seidman (1989) assert, "Now more than ever schools need to examine ways to optimize the learning potential of students and facilitate the creation of learning environments that are best matched to their developmental and sociocultural needs" (p. 339). The hidden cost of reward does not have to exist. School systems that provide interesting tasks are more likely to have motivated students; feedback other than grades can be important in enhancing students' creativity. But most important, learning is facilitated when a task continues to be perceived as challenging and when feedback is given to students who show progress.

BUILDING TABLE 5.2

Types of Learning: Classical Conditioning and Operant Conditioning

TYPE OF LEARNING	PROCEDURE	RESULT	EXAMPLE
Classical Conditioning	A neutral stimulus (such as a bell) is paired with an unconditioned stimulus (such as food).	The neutral stimulus becomes a conditioned stimulus—it elicits the conditioned response.	A bell elicits a salivary response in a dog.
Operant Conditioning	A behavior is followed by a consequence of reinforcement or punishment.	The behavior increases or decreases in frequency.	A rat will press a bar 20 times per hour to achieve a reward or avoid punishment.

Cognitive Learning

"Enough!" shouted Patrick after four grueling hours of trying to program his personal computer. Errors were rampant in his program, and they all resulted from the same basic problem; but he didn't know what the problem was. After dozens of trial-and-error manipulations, Patrick turned off the computer and went on to study for his history exam. Then, while staring at a page in the text, he saw a difficult phrase that was set off by commas; he thought about it and suddenly realized his programming mistake. His program's if-then statements were missing a necessary comma. After he placed the missing comma in all the statements, the program ran flawlessly.

Patrick solved his problem by thinking. His learning was not a matter of simple conditioning of a simple response with a simple reinforcer. Learning researchers have actively focused on learning that involves reinforcement. Conditioning evidence in studies by Pavlov, Thorndike, and Skinner requires a reinforcer if behavior is to be maintained. Much of the learning literature has focused on stimuli and responses and their relationship, timing, and frequency. But is a reinforcer always necessary for learning? Can a person learn new behaviors just by thinking or using the imagination? These questions are problematic for traditional learning researchers but not for cognitive psychologists or learning researchers with a cognitive emphasis on learning.

Thinking about a problem allows you to solve the problem and makes other behaviors possible; this thinking becomes crucial to learning and problem solving (Skinner, 1989). The emphasis of cognitive research, evident even in early learning studies, will be shown over and over again as we examine such areas of psychology as motivation, maladjustment, and therapy. Some of the most famous psychologists of the early part of the century examined learning when reinforcement was not evident and behavior was not shown. Their early studies focused on insight and latent learning. Some of the studies gave birth to modern studies of cognitive mapping. Recent research has focused on generative learning and observational learning. Still other cognitive research has focused on problem solving, creativity, and concept formation (which will be covered in chapter 7). All of this work makes us realize that there are different views of what is learned and how learning takes place.

Insight

When you discover a relationship between a series of events, you may say that you had an *insight*. Insights are usually not taught to people but rather are discovered after a series of events has occurred. Like Patrick's discovery of his missing comma, many types of learning involve sustained thought and insight.

Discovering the causes of insight was the goal of researchers working with animals during World War I. Wolfgang Köhler, a Gestalt researcher, showed that chimps developed insights into methods of retrieving food that was beyond their reach. The chimps discovered that they could pile boxes on top of one another to reach food or attach poles together, making a long stick, to grab the bananas. They were never reinforced for the specific behavior, but they learned how to get their food through insight. Once a chimp learns how to pile boxes, or once Patrick realizes his comma error, the insight is not forgotten. The insight occurs through thought, without direct reinforcement. Once it occurs, no further instruction, investigation, or training is necessary. The role of insight is often overlooked in studies of learning; however, it is an essential element in problem solving, a topic that will be discussed in chapter 7

Latent Learning

After a person has an insight, learns a task, or solves a problem (or elements of a problem), the new learning is not necessarily evident. Researchers in the 1920s placed hungry rats in mazes and recorded how many trials it took the rats to reach a "goal"—the spot where food was hidden. It took many days and many trials, but the hungry rats learned the mazes well. Other hungry rats were put into the mazes but were not reinforced with food on reaching the same goal; instead, they were merely removed from the maze. A third group of hungry rats, like the second group, was not reinforced; but after 10 days, these rats were given food on reaching the goal. Surprisingly, in one day, the rats in the third group were reaching the goal with few errors. During the first 10 days of maze running, they must have been learning something but not showing it. After being given a reward, they had a reason to reach the goal quickly.

Researchers such as E. C. Tolman (1886–1959)argued that this was **latent learning**—learning that is not demonstrated when it occurs. Tolman showed that when a rat is given a reason (such as food) to show learning, the behavior will be evident. In other words, a rat—or a person—without motivation may not show learning, even if it exists. Tolman's work with rats led him to propose the idea that animals and human beings develop (or generate) a kind of mental map of their world, which allows them to navigate a maze, or even a city street. His early work laid the foundation for more modern studies of latent learning (e.g., Chamizo & Mackintosh, 1989) and of generative learning, learning to learn, and cognitive maps. We consider each in turn.

Generative Learning

Modern cognitive psychology is changing the way in which educational psychologists think about learning that occurs in school. In addition to realizing that people organize new information in neural structures resembling maps, most cognitive psychologists are suggesting that each individual also places a unique meaning on information being learned. People use existing individual cognitive maps to interpret new information. These psychologists see learning as a *generative process*—that is, the learner generates (constructs) meaning by building relationships between familiar and unfamiliar events (Wittrock, 1987). According to this model, when we are exposed to new information or experiences, we perceive them according to our own previous experiences. We then interpret them (generate meaning about them) in ways that are consistent with our prior learning experiences and with our memories of those experiences. In other words, we access existing ideas and link new ideas and experiences to them. As a result, we alter our brain structures. These modified structures are then encoded in our memory and can be accessed later to interpret more new information. The *generative learning model* asserts that learning with comprehension occurs when a person actively links previously learned ideas to new information. Learning is thus seen as a generative, or constructive, process—a process of constantly remodeling and building on existing knowledge.

According to the generative learning model, classroom learning is not so much a matter of engaging in activities that receive external reinforcement from the teacher or even of receiving thoughts that are transferred from the teacher to the learner. Rather, it is the result of an active process in which the learner plays a critical role in generating meaning and learning. This is because no one other than the learner can build relationships between what is already known by the learner and what the person is currently learning. As a result, what a person actually learns is unique to the person. The Applications box on page 192 explores ways to enhance our potential as learners.

Latent learning: Learning that occurs in the absence of any direct reinforcement and that is not necessarily demonstrated in any observable behavior, though it has the potential to be exhibited.

APPLICATIONS

Learning to Learn

Most college seniors believe they are much better students now than they were as first-year students. What makes the difference? How do students learn to learn better? Today, educators and cognitive researchers are focusing on how information is learned, as opposed to what is learned. To learn new information, students generate hypotheses, make interpretations, make predictions, and revise earlier ideas. They are active learners (Wittrock, 1987).

Human beings learn how to learn; they learn special strategies for special topics, and they devise general rules that depend on their goals (McKeachie, 1988). The techniques for learning foreign languages differ from those needed to learn mathematics. Are there general cognitive techniques that students can use to learn better? McKeachie, Pintrich, and Lin (1985) have argued that lack of effective learning strategies is a major cause of low achievement by university students. They conducted a study to see whether grades would improve overall when rote learning, repetition, and memorization were replaced by more efficient cognitive strategies.

To help students become better learners, McKeachie, Pintrich, and Lin developed a course on learning to learn; it provided practical suggestions for studying and a theoretical basis for understanding learning. It made students aware of the processes used in learning and remembering. This awareness (thinking about thinking, learning about learning) is called *metacognition*. Learning-skills practice, development of motivation,

and development of a positive attitude were also included. Among specific topics were learning from lectures, learning from textbooks, test taking, self-monitoring, reduction of test anxiety, discovering personal learning styles, and learning through such traditional strategies as SQ3R plus (Survey, Question, Read, Recite, Review, *plus* write and reflect). The course focused on learning in general, not on specific courses such as history or chemistry. The goal was to develop generalized strategies to facilitate learning.

The voluntary learning-to-learn course attracted 180 students. They were tested at the beginning and end of the sem-

ester, and their test scores were compared with those of control groups enrolled in other psychology classes. Various measures were used to assess whether the course had any impact on SAT scores, reading test scores, anxiety test scores, and especially academic grades.

The results showed that the learning-to-learn students made gains in a number of areas, including grades and motivation. In later semesters, the students continued to improve. This straightforward study tells an

important story about psychology in general and about learning psychology in particular. First, it shows that psychologists are engaged in activities that help people, not just in esoteric laboratory studies. Second, it shows a shift in emphasis from studies of learning specific facts or of specific stimuli and responses to studies of learning strategies. Third, it shows that research into thought processes can lead to more effective thought and, subsequently, to high levels of motivation. Last, this simple study shows that people can be taught to be more efficient learners.

McKeachie, Pintrich, and Lin argued: "The cognitive approach has generated a richer, deeper analysis of what goes on in learning and memory, increasing our understanding and improving our ability to facilitate retrieval and use of learning. . . . We need to be aware of several kinds of outcomes— not just *how much knowledge* was learned, but *what kinds of learning* took place" (p. 602). Students can better grasp history, chemistry, or economics if they understand *how* to go about studying these topics. Law, psychology, and medicine require different learning strategies. After we learn how to learn, the differences become obvious; indeed, some researchers think of creativity as a metacognitive process involving thinking about our own thoughts (Pesut, 1990). Individuals can learn to learn, reason, and make better choices across a variety of domains (Larrick, Morgan, & Nisbett, 1990).

Cognitive Maps

Some people are easily disoriented when visiting a new city, while others seem to possess an internal map. These internal maps are sometimes called *cognitive maps*— cognitive representations that enable people to navigate from a starting point to an unseen destination. How are these cognitive routes perceived and learned?

Travel routes can be learned through simple associations: This street leads to that street, that street leads to the pizza parlor, and then you go left. But researcher Gary Allen (1987) asserted that learning routes also involves perceptual and cognitive influences, not just rote memorization of turns and signs. He devised a series of studies to demonstrate this.

Slides depicting an actual walk through an urban neighborhood were shown in sequential order to a group of subjects; the same slides were shown in random order to a second group. All subjects were then asked to make judgments about the distance from the beginning of the walk to a variety of specific locations. Amazingly, the subjects who viewed the random presentations made judgments that were almost as good as those of the subjects who saw the sequential walk. How did they do it?

Allen contended that the subjects formed a cognitive map by using visual information from some slides that overlapped with information in other slides. From this overlap they pieced together a map of the neighborhood. (Without the overlap among the scenes, the pictures would have appeared to show a random walk through different neighborhoods.) The random-walk subjects tried to mentally place the slides in order by paying particular attention to parts of the visual world they had seen in previous slides. In Allen's words, they attempted to impose "order on a collage of perceptual information" (p. 277).

Allen's research showed that human beings pay attention to important landmarks in determining routes and that not all landmarks are equally useful. The value of various types of landmarks is learned during childhood. In one study, Allen and his colleagues discovered that young children do not value landmarks the same way adults do. As they gain experience, children are more likely to pick landmarks that lead to choices. Human beings also tend to divide portions of a route into segments and learn the map of those segments (Allen, 1981). Allen made a strong case for perceptual and cognitive influences on learning routes. His research suggests that people learn routes by integrating segments of routes and landmarks into cognitive maps. Human beings are active processors of information, and that helps them form cognitive maps.

The Theory of Observational Learning

Let's return to Patrick, whose walk to his psychology class was described at the beginning of the chapter. On seeing Ray wearing his jacket collar turned up, Patrick flipped his own collar up to imitate his role model. Patrick learned to change his behavior through observation.

A truly comprehensive learning theory of behavior must be able to explain how people learn behaviors that are not taught. Although Patrick learned to turn his collar up, he was not taught to do so. As another example, everyone knows that smoking cigarettes is unhealthy. Smokers regularly try to stop smoking; and for most people, the first experience with smoking is unpleasant. Nonetheless, 12-year-olds light up anyway. They inhale the smoke, cough for several minutes, and feel nauseated. There is no doubt that it is a punishing experience for them, but they try again. Over time, they master the technique of inhaling and, in their view, look "cool" with a cigarette. That's the key to the whole situation: The 12-year-olds observed other people with cigarettes, thought they looked cool, wanted to look cool themselves, and therefore imitated the smoking behavior.

Such situations present a problem for traditional learning theorists, whose theories require the concept of reinforcement and give it a central role. There is little reinforcement in establishing smoking behavior; instead, there is punishment (coughing and nausea). Nonetheless, the behavior recurs. To explain this type of

Observational learning theory:
The theory that organisms learn new responses by observing the behavior of a model and then imitating it. Also known as *social learning theory*.

learning, Stanford University psychologist Albert Bandura has contended that the principles of classical and operant conditioning are just two ways in which people learn. Another way is by observing other people:

> Although it is generally assumed that social behavior is learned and modified through direct reward and punishment of instrumental responses, informal observation and laboratory study of the social learning process reveal that new responses may be rapidly acquired and existing behavior and attitudes exhibited by models. (Bandura, Ross, & Ross, 1963, p. 527)

During the past 30 years, Bandura's ideas, expressed through observational learning theory, or *social learning theory*, have expanded the range of behaviors that can be explained by learning theory (Woodward, 1982). **Observational learning theory** is the theory that suggests organisms learn new responses by observing the behavior of a model and then imitating it. Observational learning theory focuses on the role of thought in establishing and maintaining behavior. Bandura and his colleagues conducted important research to confirm their idea that people can learn by observing and then imitating the behavior of others (Bandura, 1969, 1977b; Bandura, Ross, & Ross, 1963). In their early studies, they showed a group of children some films with aggressive content, in which an adult punched an inflated doll; they showed another group of children some films that had neither aggressive nor passive content. They then compared the play behavior of both groups. The researchers found that the children who had viewed aggressive films tended to be aggressive afterward, whereas the other children showed no change in behavior (Bandura, Ross, & Ross, 1963; Bandura & Walters, 1963). Bandura's research and many subsequent studies have shown that observing aggression creates aggression in children, but children do not imitate aggressiveness when the person they observe being aggressive is punished for the aggressive behavior.

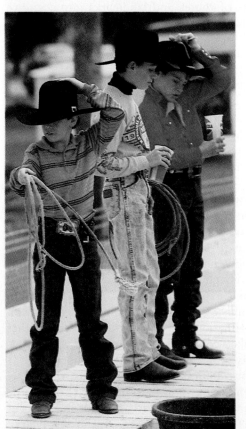

Everyday experience also shows that people imitate the behavior of others, especially those whom they hold in high esteem. Children emulating Rambo dress in army fatigues, carry toy machine guns, and pretend to launch missiles. You may buy a particular brand of soap or shampoo because your favorite television star claims to use it. Scores of young girls became interested in gymnastics after watching Olympic star Mary Lou Retton and in track events after watching Florence Griffith Joyner. Unfortunately, not all observational learning is positive. Alcohol and other drug use often begins when children and teenagers imitate people they admire.

These boys have learned to mimic traits of the adults around them simply by observing ongoing behavior mannerisms in their community.

Laboratory studies of observational learning show that people can learn new behaviors by merely observing them, without being reinforced. For example, in a study by Bernal and Berger (1976), subjects watched a film of other subjects being conditioned to produce an eye-blink response. The filmed subjects had a puff of air delivered to their eyelids; this stimulus was paired with a tone. After a number of trials, the filmed subjects showed an eye-blink response to the tone alone. The subjects who watched the film also developed an eye blink in response to a tone. Other studies show that cats also learn by observing. John et al. (1968) found that cats can learn to avoid receiving a shock through a grid floor by watching other cats successfully avoid the shocks by performing a task. People who stutter can decrease their stuttering by watching others do so (Martin & Haroldson, 1977). Even children who fear animals can learn to be less fearful by watching other children interact with animals (Bandura & Menlove, 1968).

A key point to remember is that if a person observes an action that is not reinforced, but rather is punished, the person will not imitate that action—at least not right away. Children who observe aggression that is punished do not immediately behave aggressively; nevertheless, they may learn aggressive responses that might become evident in the future. Learning may take place through observation, but performance of specific learning may depend on a specific setting and a person's perceived expectations about the effect of exhibiting the learned behaviors.

Key Variables in Observational Learning

Observational learning theory has three important elements. One is the *type and power of the model* employed. Nurturing, warm, and caring models, for example, are more likely to be imitated than indifferent, angry ones; dominant parents are more likely to be imitated than passive ones. In a classroom, children are more likely to imitate peers whom they see as powerful and dominant.

Another element is the *learner's personality and degree of independence*. Dependent children are more likely to imitate models than are independent children. Generally, the less self-confidence a person has, the more likely the person is to imitate a model.

A third factor is the *situation*. People are more likely to imitate others when there is uncertainty about correct behavior. A teenager going on a first date, for example, takes cues about dress from peers and imitates their behavior. A person who has never before been exposed to death but who loses someone close may not know what to say or how to express feelings. Watching other people express their grief provides a model for behavior. But not everyone learns well, and there are sharp differences in how people learn. There is even evidence that men and women learn differently, as is shown in the Diversity box on page 196.

Building Table 5.3 on page 197 compares the three major types of learning discussed in this chapter: classical conditioning, operant conditioning, and observational learning.

FOCUS

► What is the evidence that students who are taught how to learn make gains in a number of areas, including grades and motivation?   p. 192

► Observational learning theorists make what fundamental assumptions about reinforcement in the learning process? pp. 193–194

► For a behavior to be learned through observational learning, who would make the best type of model? pp. 194–195

DIVERSITY

Do Men and Women Learn Differently?

Psychologists have been assessing the cognitive learning styles of human beings for decades; in doing so, they have found that males and females *seem* to learn differently. As boys and girls, children are taught different behavior on the playground and in the home, and these behaviors affect the way they learn—at least according to some experts. In general, psychologists argue that boys are more independent and aggressive than girls; girls, by contrast, are more cooperative than boys. In general, boys are taught to win, whereas girls are encouraged to enjoy the game and the process of playing. These cultural styles affect learning in the classroom. As children, boys both in the classroom and on the playground have traditionally been taught to prevail, whereas girls have been taught to get along, communicate, and cooperate (Kohn, 1992). As a consequence, women tend to learn in cooperative learning situations, whereas men tend to learn independently.

Research on the role of learning styles shows some important differences between men and women. In a study of test preparation strategies of college students, Speth and Brown (1990) found that men and women vary in how they prepare for multiple-choice versus essay examinations. The women described multiple-choice tests as more problematic and challenging than did the men. This probably reflects the different approaches to acquiring knowledge, including a task orientation on the part of men, according to Magolda

(1990). Magolda found that men viewed learning more as an active, task-oriented process than did women. Magolda also found that men enjoyed the challenge more than the process of learning. Furthermore, according to Crawford and MacLeod (1990), men take a more active participatory role in classrooms than do women; and this role facilitates learning. Yet, gender differences in learning styles tend to be small, to be focused on a narrow range of abilities, and to emerge when a particular

type of processing is encouraged by test developers, teachers, or employers (Dweck, 1986; Meyers-Levy & Maheswaran, 1991).

Women also view morality differently from men (morality will be explored in more detail in chapter 8) and see learning, workplace issues, and relationships differently. These differences show up in the workplace, where men are more likely than women to focus on winning at all costs. Differences also appear in relationships. Family responsibilities are viewed from sharply different vantage points, as is the raising of children. Well-practiced learning styles encourage children's learning and

morality from a sometimes distinctly male or female point of view.

Today, entire curricula are being designed around the idea that gender differences in learning exist. Using research by Belenky et al. (1986), faculty at Ohio's Ursuline College are organizing the first-year curriculum of their female students around the idea that women work better in groups, in cooperative efforts, with connections among their ideas, and with a greater emphasis on critical thinking. Critical thinking, which focuses on integrating ideas rather than memorizing information, is the core of the school's approach. It builds on the research finding that women take advantage of cooperative learning and focus on developing their own voice (point of view) in evaluating research findings. (Keep in mind, though, that more differences exist among women than between men and women.)

Some feminist scholars assert that an approach that teaches women differently from men only reinforces differences between men and women and encourages sexism. Psychologists know that men and women have different approaches in many areas of life—child care and the workplace are two obvious examples. However, there exists no evidence that they are born this way. Evidence does exist that men and women are raised in a culture that exhibits gender differences, lauds those differences, and reinforces those differences. It is not surprising that men and women learn about the world differently, that they develop a distinctly different world view, and that this world view affects their learning style.

BUILDING TABLE 5.3

Types of Learning: Classical Conditioning, Operant Conditioning, and Observational Learning

TYPE OF LEARNING	PROCEDURE	RESULT	EXAMPLE
Classical Conditioning	A neutral stimulus (such as a bell) is paired with an unconditioned stimulus (such as food).	The neutral stimulus becomes a conditioned stimulus—it elicits the conditioned response.	A bell elicits a salivary response in a dog.
Operant Conditioning	A behavior is followed by a consequence of reinforcement or punishment.	The behavior increases or decreases in frequency.	A rat will press a bar 20 times per hour to achieve a reward or avoid punishment.
Observational Learning	An observer attends to a model to learn a behavior.	The observer learns a sequence of behaviors and becomes able to perform them at will.	After watching television violence, children are more likely to show aggressive behaviors.

Concluding Note

More than any other field, learning has played a central role in the development of psychology. It has served as a core element in most theories of maladjustment, therapy, and thinking. For many psychologists, learning *is* psychology; for most, however, it at least plays a key role. The early emphasis in learning was on classical conditioning; a later emphasis was on operant conditioning. Today, cognitive approaches to understanding learning are gaining an ever more important role in learning theory. Traditional views of insight, latent learning, and generative learning are being rethought.

Even die-hard learning researchers who have been doing work on operant conditioning for years acknowledge that some learning takes place through thought processes involving observation. Observational learning theorists are not interested in replacing traditional learning theory; rather, they want observational learning to stand alongside classical and operant conditioning as another way of explaining human learning and behavior. Psychologists are concluding that observational learning in combination with classical and operant conditioning can account for nearly all learned behavior.

Bandura's explanation of learning through observation has closed a large gap in psychologists' understanding of the role of thought in learning, but it has also raised questions. Psychologists must identify the variables involved in observational learning and understand what people think about the events they observe. They need to be sensitive to diversity issues: Why do men and women learn differently? Do older people learn the same way younger people do? Are there ways to optimize the learning process for minorities?

Summary & Review

Pavlovian, or Classical, Conditioning Theory

What is learning?

Learning is a relatively permanent and stable change in an organism that usually, but not always, can be seen in behavior; it occurs as a result of experience in the environment. By contrast, *Reflexes* occur involuntarily, quickly, and *without learning* in response to a stimulus.   p. 158

Describe the process of classical conditioning.

Classical conditioning involves the pairing of a neutral stimulus (for example, a bell) with an *unconditioned stimulus* (for example, food) so that the *unconditioned response* (for example, salivation) becomes a *conditioned response*. In higher-order conditioning, a second neutral stimulus takes on reinforcing properties by being associated with the *conditioned stimulus*. For *conditioning* to occur, the unconditioned stimulus and the conditioned stimulus must be presented in rapid sequence, and the conditioned stimulus must predict the occurrence of the unconditioned stimulus.   pp. 159–164

KEY TERMS: *learning*, p. 158; *conditioning*, p. 159; *reflexes*, p. 159; *classical conditioning*, p. 159; *unconditioned stimulus*, p. 160; *unconditioned response*, p. 160; *conditioned stimulus*, p. 160; *conditioned response*, p. 160; *higher-order conditioning*, p. 162.

Key Variables in Classical Conditioning

What are the most important variables in classical conditioning?

The most important variables in classical conditioning are the strength, timing, and frequency of the unconditioned stimulus. When these variables are optimal, the conditioned stimulus will predict the likelihood of an unconditioned stimulus.   pp. 163–164

What is the key finding in studies of conditioned taste aversion?

Conditioned taste aversion, or the Garcia effect, shows that after only one pairing of a food or drink (the conditioned stimulus) and a nausea-inducing substance (the unconditioned stimulus), organisms avoid the food or drink that preceded the nausea. Conditioned taste aversion can be obtained even if the nausea was induced several hours after the food or drink had been consumed; this is important because previously learning theorists had always assumed that closeness in time between the two events was essential.   pp. 165–166

Describe extinction and spontaneous recovery.

Extinction is the process of reducing the likelihood of a conditioned response by withholding (not pairing) the unconditioned and conditioned stimulus. *Spontaneous recovery* is the recurrence of a conditioned response following a rest period after extinction, showing that previously learned associations are not totally forgotten.   pp. 166–167

What are stimulus generalization and stimulus discrimination?

Stimulus generalization is the occurrence of a conditioned response to stimuli similar to, but not the same as, the training stimulus. By contrast, *stimulus discrimination* is the process by which an organism learns to respond only to a specific reinforced stimulus.   pp. 167–168

KEY TERMS: *extinction*, p. 166; *spontaneous recovery*, p. 166; *stimulus generalization*, p. 167; *stimulus discrimination*, p. 168.

Operant Conditioning

What occurs in operant conditioning?

In *operant conditioning*, an organism emits, or shows, a particular behavior, which is then followed by a consequence (reward or punishment). The process often occurs through shaping; *shaping* is the process of reinforcing behavior that approximates a desired behavior. A key component of operant conditioning is reinforcement.   pp. 170–174

What is a reinforcer?

A *reinforcer* is any consequence that increases the probability that the response that preceded it will recur. *Positive reinforcement* increases the probability that a desired response will occur by introducing a rewarding or pleasant stimulus. *Negative reinforcement* increases the probability that a desired behavior will occur by removing an aversive stimulus. pp. 174–176

Distinguish between primary and secondary reinforcers.

Primary reinforcers have survival value for the organism; their value does not have to be learned. *Secondary reinforcers* are neutral stimuli that initially have no intrinsic value for the organism, but that when paired with a primary reinforcer, become rewards.   pp. 176–177

continued

Summary & Review

KEY TERMS: *operant conditioning,* p. 171; *Skinner box,* p. 172; *shaping,* p. 173; *reinforcer,* p. 174; *positive reinforcement,* p. 174; *negative reinforcement,* p. 175; *primary reinforcer,* p. 176; *secondary reinforcer,* p. 176; *superstitious behavior,* 176; *punishment,* p. 177; *primary punisher,* p. 178; *secondary punisher,* p. 178.

Key Variables in Operant Conditioning

Identify the key variables in operant conditioning.

The most important variables affecting operant conditioning are the strength, timing, and frequency of consequences. Strong consequences delivered quickly produce high work rates. However, consequences do not have to be continuous. Studies of schedules of consequences, especially of reinforcement, have shown that consequences can be intermittent. Interval schedules provide reinforcement after fixed or variable time periods; ratio schedules provide reinforcement after fixed or variable amounts of work. *Variable ratio schedules* produce the highest rates of work, while *fixed interval schedules* induce the slowest work rates. pp. 180–184

What are extrinsic and intrinsic motivation, and what do behavioral regulation theorists assume about behavior?

Psychologists have shown that reinforcement (extrinsic motivation) is effective in establishing and maintaining behavior. But some behaviors are intrinsically motivated; they are performed because they are pleasurable in themselves. Behavioral regulation theorists assume that organisms have choices and that if possible, they will engage in the activities that seem optimal to them. If they are prevented from performing a desired activity, they will readjust their activities. pp. 184–189

KEY TERMS: *fixed-interval schedule,* p. 182; *variable-interval schedule,* p. 182; *fixed-ratio schedule,* p. 182; *variable ratio schedule,* p. 182; *extinction,* p. 184.

Cognitive Learning

What are cognitive learning, insight, and latent learning?

Cognitive learning psychologists focus on thinking processes and thought that helps process, establish, and maintain learning. Some of the early studies focused on insight and latent learning. When you discover a relationship between a series of events, psychologists say that you have had an insight. *Latent learning* is learning that occurs in the absence of any direct reinforcement and that is not necessarily demonstrated in any observable behavior, though it has occurred and has the potential of being exhibited. pp. 190–191

What is observational learning theory?

Observational learning theory suggests organisms learn new responses by observing the behavior of a model and then imitating it; it is also called *social learning theory*. Observational learning theory has expanded the range of behaviors that can be explained by learning theory and focuses on the role of thought in establishing and maintaining behavior. pp. 193–195

Identify three key elements of social learning theory.

Some of the key elements of social learning theory are the type and power of the model, the learner's own personality and degree of independence, and the situations in which people find themselves. p. 195

KEY TERMS: *latent learning,* p. 191; *observational learning theory,* p. 194.

CONNECTIONS

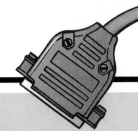

I f you are interested in...

Classical conditioning, see ...

CHAPTER 12, p. 445

Why behavioral theories of personality depend on the idea that predictability in the environment determines personality.

CHAPTER 13, pp. 483–488

How a person's physical responses to the stresses in his or her life can be conditioned and reversed. ▶

CHAPTER 15, pp. 551–553

How treatment for phobias relies on reconditioning of individuals.

Operant conditioning, see ...

CHAPTER 7, p. 268

How conditioning has played a crucial role in the development of theories of how people learn language.

CHAPTER 10, pp. 370–372 ▶

The impact of providing reinforcement to people when they already find a behavior rewarding.

CHAPTER 16, p. 575

When, and under what conditions, attitudes such as prejudice are shaped by a parent's use of reinforcement.

Cognitive learning, see ...

CHAPTER 7, pp. 252–261

How people develop reasoning processes and gain insight into problem-solving tasks.

CHAPTER 12, pp. 447

Why behavior that is observed, imitated, and then reinforced becomes part of an individual's personality. ▶

CHAPTER 17, pp. 621–622

How aggression researchers have used observational learning theory to show that watching television violence has a deleterious influence on children's behavior.

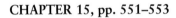

6

Memory

We were just back from our honeymoon. My wife, Linda, and I were living in a one-room studio apartment. We were awaiting married student housing at the University of Rochester, where I was to attend graduate school. I clearly remember hearing a radio announcer, his voice charged with excitement, telling listeners that Neil Armstrong in Apollo 11 had just landed on the moon. Linda and I sat on the edge of an oversized single bed in a room crammed with boxes; we were trying to tune in an old black and white television without much success; the room was stuffy and hot.

Those images recalled from events that happened more than 20 years ago are vivid. But I often have to make a concerted effort to remember how to get to a destination I have driven to just the day before.

Psychologists have long recognized that recalling well-learned facts can sometimes be difficult. Even though something has been *learned,* it may not always be *remembered.* You may easily remember the Pledge of Allegiance, for example, but forget the chemical formula for sugar. That's because learning and memory are different. From chapter 5, recall that *learning* is a relatively permanent change in the organism that occurs as a result of experience; this change is often, but not always, seen in overt behavior. **Memory** is the ability to remember past events, images, ideas, or previously learned information or skills; memory is also the storage system that allows us to retain and retrieve previously learned information.

Early memory studies focused on how quickly people learned lists of nonsense words and how long they remembered them or how quickly they forgot them. Later studies focused on variables that affected retention and forgetting—for example, the organization of material. Current research is focusing on how people code information and use memory aids, imagery, and other learning cues to retrieve information from memory. It is also examining the biological basis of memory. Researchers use different tasks to examine subjects' memory because they know that various memory tasks require different knowledge (Richardson-Klavehn & Bjork, 1988).

As we saw in chapter 5, psychologists studying learning and memory usually use performance (such as the score on an SAT test) to infer that an organism (such as a student) can maintain previously learned information or skills. In animals, physical performance is the only indication of memory, since the communication skills of animals are limited. However, human beings can demonstrate memory in verbal and written performance. This chapter examines the complex learning in human beings that leads to memory.

Approaches to Memory

It would be wonderful to have a perfect memory, right? Not necessarily. Soviet psychologist A. R. Luria studied a man who possessed a memory far surpassing that of normal humans. Shereshevskii, better known as S, could repeat back strings of 70 digits or letters and recite entire conversations verbatim. Even years after hearing a list, S could repeat it, backward or forward. But his remarkable memory also proved an intellectual hindrance. S had to devise ways to forget lists—for example, by writing down the words and then burning the paper. He found it difficult to carry on a simple conversation because a single word triggered a flood of memories, causing him to lose the gist of what was being said.

Few individuals have a memory like S's. Most people learn things through the processes discussed in chapter 5. And their acquisition of some knowledge does not mean they can call it forth at will. Learning can be either forgotten or retained. What variables determine what is remembered and what is forgotten? Under what conditions is memory enhanced? When are people likely to forget?

As in most areas of psychological investigation, various approaches have been developed to help researchers understand the workings of the topic under study. In the area of memory, two main views dominate: the modal model and parallel distributed processing. The *modal model* asserts the existence of a three-stage process, with various activities taking place in each stage. It is called the modal model because it represents a number of different (but highly similar) models of memory. *Parallel distributed processing,* which grew out of the modal model, asserts the exis-

Memory: The ability to remember past events, images, ideas, or previously learned information or skills; the storage system that allows for retention and retrieval of learned information.

tence of a multi-stage, multi-process action that focuses on the distribution of mental effort and action to store and retrieve memories.

The Modal Model: Focus on Information Processing

For many years, researchers thought of the brain as a huge map with certain areas that code vision, others that code auditory events, and still others that code, analyze, and store memory. Their research goal was to discover the spatial layout of the brain and to see how the brain operates. Today, we know that the brain is not that simple.

In the 1960s and 1970s, researchers began to compare the brain to a computer with complex interconnections and processing abilities. They compared memory in human beings to information processed by computers, with analogies made to computer encoding, storage, and retrieval (these three terms are defined later in the chapter). Human brains, of course, are not computers; nor do they work exactly the way computers do. They make mistakes and are affected by biological, environmental, and interpersonal events. Nevertheless, enough similarities exist between human brains and computers for psychologists to discuss learning and memory in terms of information processing.

The most basic form of the modal model uses the information-processing approach. Information processing refers to an analysis of how environmental stimulation is acted on so that it acquires meaning. The *information-processing approach* refers to the sequence of steps or stages through which this process occurs (Massaro and Cowan, 1993). The information-processing approach typically describes three stages—sensory memory, short-term memory, and long-term memory. It assumes that each stage is separate, though related, and that each is analyzable by scientific methods. *Sensory memory*, sometimes called the sensory register, is the mechanism by which information is entered. When we do word processing on a computer, when we listen to a rock band, when we touch a piece of silk, we start the memory process by entering information. After the information is entered, we store it for a short time in *short-term memory*, just as a computer keeps our work in temporary random access memory—and if the electricity goes off before we store our information, we lose it. In the same way, if we read a definition but do not process it adequately, we quickly lose its meaning. Our storage mechanism, short-term memory, is fragile; it requires repetition, further coding, and transfer of information to a final resting place. In a computer, we store our information for long periods on a floppy or hard disk. In the brain, we store our information in *long-term memory*, from which we can recall, retrieve, and reconstruct previous experiences.

In general, the three-stage modal model has served psychologists well. It has organized their thinking and provided a structure they can attempt to examine. However, it is by no means the only model to do so. Another important model is parallel distributed processing.

Parallel Distributed Processing

Many researchers grew to believe that the connections within the brain are so sophisticated that a simple three-step model was inadequate. *Parallel distributed processing (PDP)* is an alternative. It suggests that many operations take place simultaneously and at many locations within the brain: a number of PDP theories have been offered, but they share these common characteristics.

PDP is appealing because of the analogy to the way so many operations take place in the world. At telephone companies, thousands of calls arrive at switching

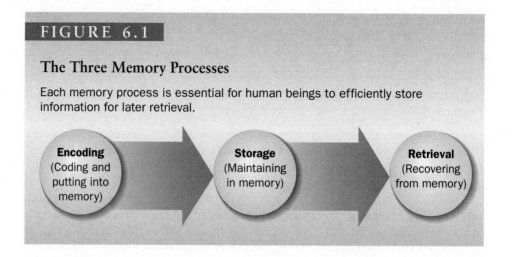

FIGURE 6.1

The Three Memory Processes

Each memory process is essential for human beings to efficiently store information for later retrieval.

Encoding (Coding and putting into memory) → **Storage** (Maintaining in memory) → **Retrieval** (Recovering from memory)

stations simultaneously. At airline offices, hundreds of requests for information about flights are made simultaneously from all around the world. As we listen to a symphony, we hear dozens of instruments simultaneously. PDP models assert that we can process and store many events simultaneously.

PDP models are models not only of memory but also of perception and learning. They take the information-processing modal model a step further. Researchers using positron emission tomography techniques (described in chapter 2) are trying to study the location, extent, and time course of processing in the brain as it occurs. PDP models, which focus on the biological basis of memory, are difficult to characterize in traditional terms, are hard to test experimentally, and have not achieved as wide an acceptance as has the traditional modal model. Nevertheless, PDP in its various forms has influenced the way psychologists think about memory and has even affected conceptions about the modal model.

As we begin to examine the process and structures of memory, try thinking of information stored in the brain as books stored in a library. Books can be checked out and new ones added—many at a time. Similarly, the books can deteriorate with age, be misplaced, or be difficult to locate. Books that are used frequently are the easiest to find—you know exactly where to look. Sometimes, you may reorganize the books, storing them differently. (We will use the library analogy again later in this chapter.)

To better understand how the various approaches view sensory memory, short-term memory, and long-term memory, researchers have focused on the brain's encoding, storage, and retrieval of information.

Three Key Processes: Encoding, Storage, and Retrieval

In virtually every model of memory that has been offered, rejected, or modified, researchers seem to agree that three processes must be examined: encoding, storage, and retrieval (see Figure 6.1). These processes are the organizing themes around which many psychologists focus their theories.

Encoding is the process of organizing information so the nervous system can process it. It can be visual or auditory or can include taste, touch, temperature or other sensory information. The conversion of an experience into electrochemical energy is the first step in establishing a memory. **Storage** is the process of maintaining information in memory. The storage may be for a few seconds or for many years. **Retrieval** is the process by which stored information is recovered from memory.

Encoding: The process by which information is put into memory, through transduction of an experience into electro-chemical energy for neural representations.

Storage: The process of maintaining information in memory.

Retrieval: The process by which stored information is recovered from memory.

Recalling your social security number, remembering the details of a phone call, and recalling the names of the Beastie Boys band members are all retrieval tasks.

Each of the three stages in memory—sensory memory, short-term memory, and long-term memory—focuses on encoding, storage, and retrieval to a different extent. Sensory memory provides initial encoding of information and instantaneous, fleeting, temporary storage and retrieval; the focus is on encoding. Later, short-term memory provides encoding and temporary storage for about 30 seconds; the focus is on initial processes, especially storage (see Figure 6.2 for an overview of the information-processing model and the processes that will be discussed as this chapter

FIGURE 6.2

The Information-Processing Approach

When information enters the memory-processing system, it proceeds from sensory memory to short-term memory and then to long-term memory.

At each stage, decay or interference may be operative.

Sensory memory: The mechanism that performs initial encoding and brief storage of stimuli. Also known as the *sensory register.*

unfolds). Long-term memory may preserve information for a lifetime; the focus for researchers is often on retrieval. Let's now examine the three processes—encoding, storage, and retrieval—and how they relate to the stages of memory.

Sensory Memory: Focus on Encoding

As George Sperling demonstrated in the early 1960s, **sensory memory,** or the *sensory register,* is the mechanism that performs initial encoding and provides brief storage of stimuli from which human beings can retrieve information. Sperling (1960) briefly presented visual arrays of letters to subjects and found they were able to recall more than 3 items out of 12 from just a 50-millisecond presentation (see Figure 6.3). From his studies and others that followed, researchers claimed the existence of a brief (250-millisecond, or 0.25-second), rapidly decaying sensory memory. *Decay* refers to the loss of information from memory as a result of the passage of time and disuse. The brief image of a stimulus appears the way lightning does on a dark evening; the lightning flashes, and you retain a brief continuing image of it. Although some researchers have challenged the existence and the physiological basis of sensory memory (Sakitt & Long, 1979), most researchers still hold that it is the first stage of encoding.

Sensory memory transforms a visual, auditory, or chemical stimulus (such as an odor) into a form the brain can interpret. Consider the visual system. The initial coding usually contains information in a picturelike representation. Sensory memory establishes the visual stimulus in an electrical or neural form and stores it for 0.25 second with little interpretation, in an almost photographic manner. This visual sen-

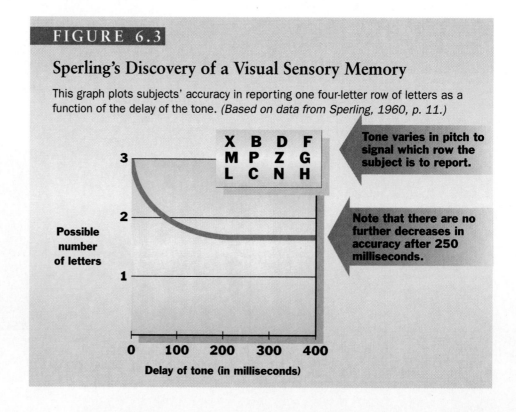

FIGURE 6.3

Sperling's Discovery of a Visual Sensory Memory

This graph plots subjects' accuracy in reporting one four-letter row of letters as a function of the delay of the tone. *(Based on data from Sperling, 1960, p. 11.)*

Tone varies in pitch to signal which row the subject is to report.

Note that there are no further decreases in accuracy after 250 milliseconds.

Possible number of letters

Delay of tone (in milliseconds)

Sensory memory holds visual images, such as this moving pen light, for a fraction of a second.

sory memory is sometimes called an *icon,* and the storage mechanism is called *iconic storage.* The storage mechanism for the auditory system is called *echoic storage;* it stores an auditory representation for about 3 seconds.

Sensory memory is temporary and fragile. Once information is established, it must be transferred elsewhere for additional encoding and storage or it will be lost. For example, when you look up a phone number in a telephone book, it is established in the visual sensory memory; but unless you quickly transfer it to short-term memory by repeating it over and over to yourself, you will forget it. Building Table 6.1 summarizes key processes in sensory memory.

FOCUS

▶ What are the fundamental assumptions of the information-processing approach?   p. 205

▶ Why do researchers who focus on parallel distributed processing find the information-processing approach unsatisfactory ?   pp. 205–206

▶ What is the evidence to suggest that sensory memory is temporary and fragile?   pp. 208–209

BUILDING TABLE 6.1

Key Processes in Sensory Memory

STAGE	ENCODING	STORAGE	DURATION	RETRIEVAL	FORGETTING
Sensory Memory	Visual or auditory (iconic or echoic memory).	Brief, fragile, and temporary.	Visual: 250 milliseconds; auditory: less than 4 seconds.	Information extracted from stimulus presentation and transferred to working or short-term memory.	Rapid decay of information; interference possible if a new stimulus is presented.

Short-Term Memory: Focus on Storage

After sensory memory, stimuli either decay and are lost or are transferred to a second stage—short-term memory. **Short-term memory** is the memory storage system that temporarily holds current or recently attended information for immediate or short-term use. In short-term memory, information is further encoded, then stored or maintained for about 30 seconds. It is here that active processing takes place. A person may decide that a specific piece of information is important; if it is complicated or lengthy, it will need to be actively repeated or rehearsed. **Rehearsal** is the process of repeatedly verbalizing, thinking about, or otherwise acting on information in order to keep the information in memory. Generally, researchers agree that the more rehearsal, the greater a person's memory for the item to be recalled; also, not all items are recalled equally well.

To understand how encoding works in short-term memory, imagine a waiter who is given a lengthy and complex order. When the order is in short-term memory, it is unlikely that the waiter will remember it after about 2 minutes. Thus, he might repeat the order over and over, rehearsing it until he is able to write it down or give it to the chef. Because of the limitations of short-term memory, rehearsal of information is crucial for encoding and keeping the information active.

The Discovery of Short-Term Memory

Researchers had been studying memory and retrieval for decades, but it was not until 1959 that Lloyd and Margaret Peterson presented evidence for the existence of short-term memory. The Petersons asked subjects to recall a three-consonant sequence, such as *xbd*, after varying time intervals. During a time that ranged from no delay to 18 seconds, the subjects were required to count backwards by threes. The aim of counting backwards was to prevent the subjects from repeating or rehearsing the sequence. The Petersons wanted to examine recall when rehearsal was not possible. Figure 6.4 presents their results. As the interval between presentation and recall increased, accuracy of recall decreased. The Petersons interpreted this result as evidence for the existence of short-term memory.

The storage of information in sensory memory is temporary; the information is either lost through decay or transferred to the second stage—short-term memory. In short-term memory, semipermanent storage

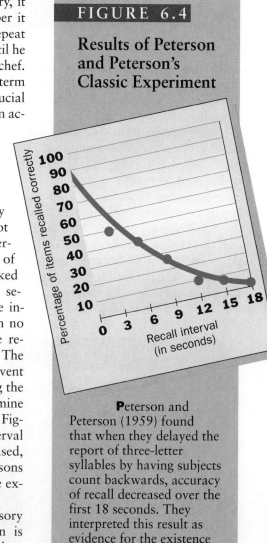

FIGURE 6.4

Results of Peterson and Peterson's Classic Experiment

Peterson and Peterson (1959) found that when they delayed the report of three-letter syllables by having subjects count backwards, accuracy of recall decreased over the first 18 seconds. They interpreted this result as evidence for the existence of short-term memory.

Short-term memory: The memory storage system that temporarily holds current or recently acquired information for immediate or short-term use.

Rehearsal: The process of repeatedly verbalizing, thinking about, or otherwise acting on information in order to keep the information in memory.

exists; information is actively processed—further encoded and stored for a bit longer (about 20 to 30 seconds). At this stage, people rehearse important information to make sure they will remember it; if they do not rehearse, the information will be lost. Thousands of research studies have been done on the components and characteristics of storage in short-term memory. They focus on the importance of duration, capacity, and rehearsal.

Duration. The Petersons' experiment, like many others that followed, showed that information contained in short-term memory is available for no more than 30 seconds. After that, it must be transferred to and stored in long-term memory or it will be lost. (Of course, it could be maintained indefinitely if a person were to rehearse it over and over again until recall was necessary.)

Capacity. In 1956, George Miller argued that human beings can retain about seven (plus or minus two) items in short-term memory. Subsequent research has confirmed that claim. The brief and limited number of items that can be easily reproduced after presentation in short-term memory is the **memory span.** It usually contains one or two single **chunks**—manageable and meaningful units of information. A chunk can be a letter, a group of numbers and words, or even sentences organized in a familiar way for easy encoding, storage, and retrieval. Many people remember their social security number in three chunks and their telephone number in two chunks. Chunks can be made up of groupings based on meaning, past events, associations, perception, rhythm (for example, the rhythm of how you say your phone number), or some arbitrary strategy devised by a learner to help encode large amounts of data (Schweickert & Boruff, 1986). Determining what is a chunk is sometimes difficult because what is perceptually or cognitively grouped together for one individual may be different for other individuals.

Rehearsal. As noted earlier, *rehearsal* is the process of repeatedly verbalizing, thinking about, or otherwise acting on information to be remembered. People will

Memory span: The brief and limited number of items that can be easily reproduced after presentation in short-term memory, usually confined to a chunk of information.

Chunks: Manageable and meaningful units of information that allow for groupings to be easily encoded, stored, and retrieved.

Lengthy material, such as a script, must be rehearsed repeatedly in order to pass beyond short-term memory.

quickly forget a list of meaningless letters or symbols, such as *xbdfmpg,* unless they use rehearsal to maintain the list in short-term memory. Actively rehearsed items can be maintained in short-term memory almost indefinitely. In general, however, the information entered in short-term memory either is transferred to long-term memory or is lost.

There are two types of rehearsal: maintenance and elaborative. **Maintenance rehearsal** is the repetitive review of information with little or no interpretation. This shallow form of rehearsal involves the physical stimulus, not its underlying meaning. It goes on principally in short-term memory—for example, when we repeat a phone number to be recalled. **Elaborative rehearsal** involves repetition in which the stimulus may be associated with other events and be further processed. This type of rehearsal in short-term memory allows information to be transferred into long-term memory. Elaborative rehearsal is especially evident in encoding information within long-term memory. Maintenance rehearsal alone is usually not sufficient for information to be transferred into long-term memory and permanently stored.

Short-Term Memory as Working Memory

Alan Baddeley and Graham Hitch (1974) thought of short-term memory as a **working memory,** in which several substructures operate to maintain information while it is being processed. One subsystem may encode and rehearse auditory information; another may be a visual-spatial scratchpad or blackboard that stores information for a brief time and then is erased so new information can be stored; this occurs over and over. Baddeley and Hitch demonstrated the several components of working memory by having subjects recall digits while doing some other type of reasoning task. They showed that people have limited capacities. If one mental task is demanding, performance on the other will suffer.

Baddeley and Hitch's introduction of a working memory expanded the concept of short-term memory, focusing on its complexity and on how single tasks analyze only single components of a multi-stage system. Psychologists often concentrate on those single tasks, trying to understand each of the components in encoding, storage, and retrieval. However, this conception of working memory goes beyond individual stages and describes the active integration of both conscious processes (such as repetition) and unconscious processes (processes of which a person is unaware). Repetition or practice turns out to be an important component of developing some type of working memory (Carlson, Sullivan, & Schneider, 1989).

Baddeley and other researchers argue that within working memory is a central processing mechanism, like an executive, that controls the work flow; and the distinction between short-term memory and long-term memory is blurred (Cowan, 1988). This notion of an executive suggests that people can control the processing flow of information and adjust it when necessary. (See Figure 6.5 for a comparison of the traditional view of short-term memory with the current view of short-term memory as a working memory.) Other researchers suggest that the traditional view of short-term memory (the modal model) and even the broader view of working memory are still too limiting. For example, a theory invoking both neurophysiology and attention asserts that localization of

Maintenance rehearsal: The repetitive review of information (usually in short-term memory) with little or no interpretation.

Elaborative rehearsal: Rehearsal involving repetition (often in long-term memory) in which the stimulus may be associated with other events and be further processed.

Working memory: A new conception of short-term memory that focuses on the central processing capacities of this type of memory and views it as a holding place for information while other information is being processed and directed for further processing.

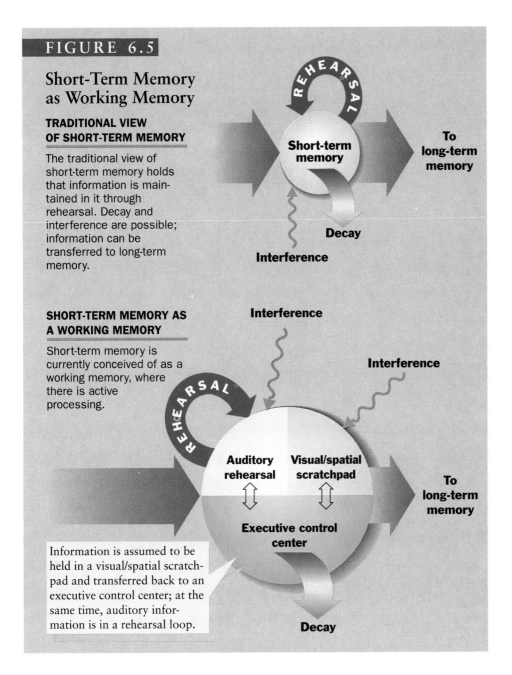

FIGURE 6.5

Short-Term Memory as Working Memory

TRADITIONAL VIEW OF SHORT-TERM MEMORY

The traditional view of short-term memory holds that information is maintained in it through rehearsal. Decay and interference are possible; information can be transferred to long-term memory.

REHEARSAL

Short-term memory

To long-term memory

Decay

Interference

SHORT-TERM MEMORY AS A WORKING MEMORY

Short-term memory is currently conceived of as a working memory, where there is active processing.

Interference

Interference

REHEARSAL

Auditory rehearsal

Visual/spatial scratchpad

Executive control center

To long-term memory

Information is assumed to be held in a visual/spatial scratchpad and transferred back to an executive control center; at the same time, auditory information is in a rehearsal loop.

Decay

brain functions plays an important role (Schneider & Detweiler, 1987). Other researchers are examining the possibility that animals have a working memory (Green & Stanton, 1989). These newer theories do not discount theories about sensory, short-term, and long-term memory. Rather, they refocus, refine, and elaborate on them; and many tend to center on parallel distributed processing. Building Table 6.2 on page 214 summarizes key processes in the first two stages of memory.

FOCUS

► How did the Petersons' experiment show that short-term memory exists?   pp. 210–211

► Provide three examples of information you have chunked to facilitate recall.   p. 211

► In what way is working memory a broader conception than short-term memory?   pp. 212–213

BUILDING TABLE 6.2

Key Processes in the First Two Stages of Memory

STAGE	ENCODING	STORAGE	DURATION	RETRIEVAL	FORGETTING
Sensory Memory	Visual or auditory (iconic or echoic memory).	Brief, fragile, and temporary.	Visual: 250 milliseconds; auditory: less than 4 seconds.	Information extracted from stimulus presentation and transferred to working or short-term memory.	Rapid decay of information; interference possible if a new stimulus is presented.
Short-Term Memory	Visual and auditory; auditory encoding is especially important.	Repetitive rehearsal maintains information in storage, perhaps on a visual/auditory scratchpad where further encoding can take place.	Less than 20 seconds, no more than 30 seconds; depends on specific task and stimuli.	Maintenance and elaborative rehearsal can keep information available for retrieval; retrieval is enhanced through elaboration and further encoding.	Interference and decay are operative; new stimulation causes rapid loss of information unless information is especially important.

Long-Term Memory: Focus on Retrieval

Information such as names, faces, dates, places, smells, and events—both important and trivial—can be found in a relatively permanent form in **long-term memory.** The duration of information in long-term memory is indefinite; much of it lasts a lifetime. The capacity for long-term memory is seemingly infinite; the more information we acquire, the easier it is to acquire information. Using the library analogy again, we can say that long-term memory includes all the books in the library's permanent collection.

The information that is typically encoded and stored in long-term memory either is important (a friend's birthday, for example) or is used frequently (your telephone number, for example). Maintaining information in long-term memory often involves rehearsal or repetition, but sometimes an important event is immediately etched into long-term memory (Schmidt, 1991).

Several types of information are stored in long-term memory. For example, a person may remember the words to a Springsteen song, the meaning of the word *sanguine,* and how to operate a compact disc player. Each of these types of information seems to be stored and called on in a different way. Psychologists therefore split long-term memory into two types: procedural and declarative.

Procedural memory is memory for the perceptual, motor, and cognitive skills or habits required to complete a task (see Figure 6.6). Learning how to drive an automobile, wash dishes, or swim involves a series of steps that include perceptual, motor, and cognitive skills—and thus procedural memory. Acquiring such skills is usually time-consuming and difficult at first; but once the skills are learned, they are relatively permanent. The encoding and retrieval of procedural information are indi-

Long-term memory: The memory storage system that keeps a relatively permanent record of information.

Procedural memory: Memory for the perceptual, motor, and cognitive skills required to complete a task.

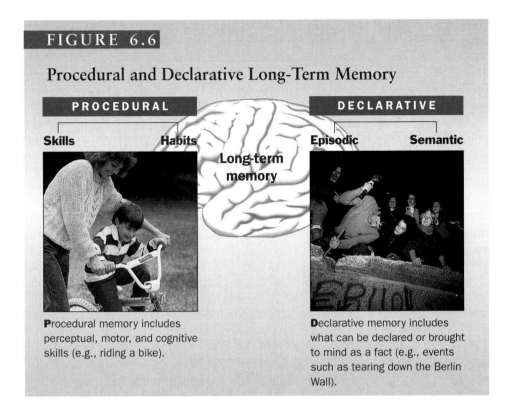

FIGURE 6.6

Procedural and Declarative Long-Term Memory

Procedural memory includes perceptual, motor, and cognitive skills (e.g., riding a bike).

Declarative memory includes what can be declared or brought to mind as a fact (e.g., events such as tearing down the Berlin Wall).

rect; the pieces of information are not stored together and must be assembled (Richardson-Klavehn & Bjork, 1988).

Declarative memory is memory for specific facts (see Figure 6.6), such as Bill Clinton was elected President in 1992 or Neil Armstrong was accompanied to the moon by Edwin Aldrin and Michael Collins. The memory is established quickly, and the information is more likely to be forgotten over time than is the information in procedural memory. It is easier to examine declarative memory than procedural memory, since people can quickly relate a specific fact but have more trouble explaining how to do something such as swimming. We consider declarative memory in more detail next.

Declarative Memory as Episodic and Semantic Memory

In 1972, Endel Tulving suggested that there are two kinds of declarative long-term memory: episodic and semantic. **Episodic memory** is memory for specific events, objects, and situations. It might include what you had for breakfast, the movie you saw last night, or what you did on vacation last summer. Studies of memory for events long past show that people remember them well, especially events involving themselves. Episodic memory is often specific; a person can describe when something happened, where it happened, and the circumstances surrounding it.

When researchers have examined people's ability to remember real-world events (rather than artificially created laboratory events), the results have shown that people have amazingly good memory. These studies often are referred to as *autobiographical memory studies* because they often examine people's memory for their own past (Conway, 1991). People can accurately recognize a person, situation, or event years later (Nelson, 1993). Studies of autobiographical memory suggest that long-term memory is especially durable and fairly easy to access if a helpful retrieval

Declarative memory: Memory for specific facts.

Episodic memory: [ep-ih-SAH-dick] Memory for specific events, objects, and situations.

Semantic memory: Memory for ideas, rules, and general concepts about the world.

cue is available. The more clearly and sharply defined memory cues are, the more often a memory has been recalled or reconstructed, the more vivid the memories are and the less likely it is that a person will experience retrieval failures (Friedman, 1993). (We will look into this issue later in this chapter when we examine forgetting.) The Research Process box examines another type of memory, *flashbulb memory*, that is related to episodic memory.

Semantic memory is memory of ideas, rules, and general concepts about the world. It is based on a set of generalizations about previous events, experiences, and learned knowledge. It is not time-specific; it refers to knowledge that may have been gathered over days or weeks, and it continues to be modified and expanded over a lifetime (Bahrick & Hall, 1991). Semantic memory develops earlier in childhood than episodic memory (Tulving, 1993).

Semantic memory seems to be stored at different levels of memory, like sections or floors of a library; so a person needing information must go to different levels to access it. At superficial levels of processing, the immediate sensory cues are interpreted. At deeper levels, the cues are encoded and categorized according to the kind of information they give and the meanings for each cue. At still deeper levels, the meanings are analyzed and synthesized. For example, is the following sentence true or false? "U.S. astronauts Armstrong, Collins, and Aldrin were the first to land on the moon and did so on July 20, 1969, at 4:18 P.M. eastern standard time." You would need to access several classes of information, including interrelations among times, dates, people, and historical events—which may be complex. The time and effort you will need in order to respond will depend in part on the number of levels of processing required (Tilley & Warren, 1983) and the complexity of the information. We will examine the levels-of-processing idea more fully in the next section.

Levels of Processing

Does the human brain process some information at a deeper, more complex level than other information? Do thinking processes depend on the depth of storage? From the 1940s on, researchers have tried to distinguish between short-term and long-term memory. But during the 1970s, a new approach to explaining memory encoding and retrieval, the *levels-of-processing approach,* changed the course of research and thinking.

Researchers Craik and Lockhart (1972) argued that a person can process a stimulus in different ways, to different extents, and at different levels. For example, a person presented with the computer screen display "Cast your vote for Smith, the candidate of distinction" will analyze the display on several levels, in several ways. The lines and angles of the display will be encoded at one level, the words will be encoded for basic meaning and categorized at another level, and the meaning of the display will be analyzed, stored, and encoded at still another, deeper level.

Cognitive psychologists began to equate the level of processing with the degree of semantic analysis. When the level of processing becomes more complex, the code goes deeper in memory. Thus, the memory for the lines and angles of the computer screen (sensory memory) may be fleeting and short-lived, the memory for the words themselves may be longer (short-term memory), and the memory for the content of the words (semantic components of long-term memory) may be long-lasting. According to Craik and Lockhart, encoding in various memory levels involves different operations, and memory features are stored in different ways and for different durations.

The levels-of-processing approach generated an enormous amount of research. It explained why some information is retained for long periods while other information is quickly forgotten. It was consistent with an information-processing structural analysis and explained the varying decay rates of memory stages. It showed

THE RESEARCH PROCESS

Is There a Flashbulb Memory?

Where were you when you learned that the Persian Gulf war had started? That the space shuttle *Challenger* had exploded? How did you hear about the events? What were you doing? What were your first thoughts?

People vividly remember the circumstances in which they learned of major personal and public events. This phenomenon is often called *flashbulb memory,* and among the first to research it were Brown and Kulik (1977). They argued that there is a special type of memory for events that possess a critical level of surprise and what they called *consequentiality.* Most people believe they have flashbulb memories, and the Brown and Kulik work generated an avalanche of debate and research.

Theories. Two basic theories explain flashbulb memory. The first focuses on emotion, the second on rehearsal. The emotion approach, sometimes called the *now-print theory,* suggests that recall is facilitated when extraordinary cognitive information overactivates the limbic system (the brain's emotion center). In addition, information associated with strong emotions may be talked about more, and the rehearsal of information facilitates its recall. The second theory concerns rehearsal and reconstruction. This *reconstructive-script theory* focuses on people telling and retelling the story and gradually filling in, or reconstructing, their story to match a standard story format.

Research. To determine which of the two approaches was correct, J. N. Bohannon (1988) of the Virginia Polytechnic Institute conducted a study of 279 subjects and their memories of the *Challenger* disaster. Subjects were tested at 2 weeks and then at 8

months following the explosion. They were asked to estimate both their emotions on hearing the news (to test the now-print theory) and the number of times they had retold the story (to test the reconstructive-script theory). Each subject's memory was assessed on three basic tasks: (1) free recall of the story, (2) probed recall of the story (recall when given hints), and (3) probed recall of specific facts about the accident itself.

Results. The study's results were dramatic. Subjects who rated themselves as more shocked by the shuttle accident remembered more details, were more confident of their answers, and had more complete stories at both testing times than did subjects who rated themselves as less shocked. These results, which focus on emotion, support the now-print approach. However, the reconstructive-script theory was also supported. This theory suggests that subjects organize their memory and fill in the details. The study's results showed that free recall at 8 months was just as good as within 2 weeks

of the explosion, but accurate responses to questions asking for specific details declined over testing times. With short delays, either factor (emotion or rehearsal) is sufficient to generate flashbulb memories. But after a delay of 8 months, *both* are required.

Conclusions. Simple emotional responses without rehearsal, according to Bohannon (1988), produce good short-term recall only. In the same manner, rehearsed information that does not have a strong emotional component results in superior short-lived memory. Bohannon claims that flashbulb memory is maintained over time *only* "if the flashbulb event was important enough to get the person to repeatedly rehearse the information by telling others" (p. 195). When the experience of learning about an event is especially significant, and when it is repeatedly rehearsed, both the circumstances and the event have a high probability of being remembered in detail.

Is flashbulb memory a special kind of memory? McCloskey, Wible, and Cohen (1988) argue that "There is no qualitative distinction . . . between memories for learning about shocking, important events, and memories for learning about expected, trivial events" (p. 181). They assert that flashbulb memory is ordinary memory with no special characteristics. Bohannon's findings on flashbulb memories and the role of emotion and rehearsal in maintaining them are consistent with McCloskey, Wible, and Cohen's argument. Such memories may be vivid, but they must be about emotional events and must be rehearsed. According to Weaver (1993), what makes flashbulb memories special is the undue confidence those who recall them have in their accuracy. The research suggests that there is no special location or encoding mechanism responsible for them.

Primacy effect: The more accurate recall of items that were presented first.

Recency effect: The more accurate recall of items presented last.

that when people are asked to encode information in only one way, they do not encode it in other ways. Thus, when people are not asked to encode words for meaning, they can recall very few of them. This helps explain why some problems tend to be solved in only one way.

However, not every researcher was enamored of the levels-of-processing approach. The concept was impossible to define, Craik and Lockhart's finding could be achieved in a number of ways, and some researchers did not obtain the same results. Refinements were suggested; they focused on how memory codes are established, how they are elaborated on or made distinctive, and how recall of codes takes place. The initial levels-of-processing theory dealt primarily with establishing codes in memory. Later research focused on how those codes were used in recall.

The landmark levels-of-processing research of the early 1970s still shapes the way cognitive researchers think about memory and thought. The traditional distinction short-term and long-term memory suggested a structural difference in memory stores. The levels-of-processing approach, however, stated that the way information is encoded may determine how it is stored, processed, and recalled.

Primacy and Recency Effects

Long-term memory studies have brought forth some interesting findings about retrieval and have generated hundreds of research studies focusing on what are called primacy and recency effects. In a typical experiment, a subject may be asked to study 30 or 40 words, with a word presented every 2 seconds. A few seconds later, the subject is asked to recall the words, so the researcher can determine whether the information was transferred from short-term to long-term memory. Such experiments typically show an overall recall rate of 20 percent. However, recall is higher for words at the beginning of a list of words than for those at the middle, a phenomenon termed the **primacy effect.** This effect occurs when no information is stored in short-term memory; at the moment a new task is assigned, the subject's attention to new stimuli is at its peak. Recall is even higher for words at the end of a list, a phenomenon termed the **recency effect.** This is due to the active rehearsal of the information in short-term memory and its subsequent encoding into long-term memory. See Figure 6.7 for a graph showing the recall rate for items in various posi-

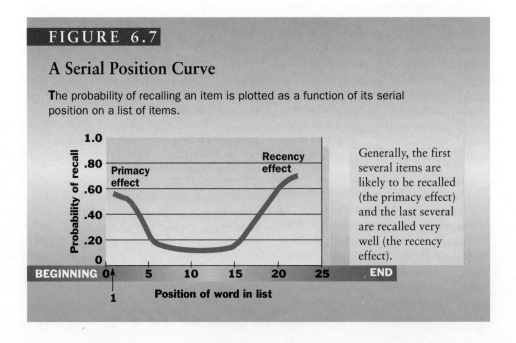

FIGURE 6.7

A Serial Position Curve

The probability of recalling an item is plotted as a function of its serial position on a list of items.

Generally, the first several items are likely to be recalled (the primacy effect) and the last several are recalled very well (the recency effect).

According to the primacy and recency effects, the first and last speakers will be remembered best and will have the greatest impact on listeners.

tions of a list of words. It is called a *serial position curve* and presents the accuracy or speed of recall as a function of the item position in a list or series of presented items.

Campaign managers attempt to capitalize on the primacy and recency effects in their candidates' speeches. For example, they urge their candidates to speak both very early in the campaign and very late, just before people vote. If several candidates are to speak back-to-back, campaign managers will try to schedule their candidates either first or last. Primacy effects suggest that attention is at its peak at the beginning; recency effects suggest that speaking last will be effective because other speakers won't interfere with the transfer of information from short-term to long-term memory.

Extraordinary Memory

As noted earlier, nearly perfect recall is rare. But is it possible for an average person to develop a remarkable memory? We saw earlier that the memory span for most adults is limited to one or two chunks each containing seven items, plus or minus two items. Recent research shows, however, that with practice and special use of chunking strategies, memory span can be increased greatly. One study increased the memory span to 79 digits (Ericsson, Chase, & Faloon, 1980), another to 106 digits (Staszewski, 1987). The subjects in these experiments developed strategies for effective, efficient encoding and efficient retrieval of meaningful chunks of information; the process was effortful, deliberate, and effective. The subjects were using exceptionally efficient retrieval structures.

Attempting to increase digit span is a time-consuming process. In the two studies just discussed, the time needed was 20 months in the first case and 5 years in the second—and the results did not carry over to other study materials. But exceptional memory skills can be seen in other research domains. For example, Staszewski (1988) presented research on "lightning mental calculators"—individuals who can solve complex arithmetic problems (such as 54,917 x 63) with remarkable speed and accuracy. The key to such achievement is steady practice, efficient use of memory, and extensive knowledge of numerical relationships. A person can't train to be a lightning mental calculator without extensive daily and weekly practice. Nor can a

Imagery: A cognitive process in which a mental picture of a sensory event is created.

person learn to calculate calendar date problems (for example, what day of the week was July 27, 1946?) without extensive practice and considerable knowledge of day, date, and calendar rules (Howe & Smith, 1988).

Imagery as a Retrieval Device

People use perceptual imagery every day as a long-term memory retrieval aid. In **imagery,** people create, recreate, or conjure up a mental picture of a sensory or perceptual experience to be remembered. They constantly invoke images to recall things they did, said, read, or saw. People's imagery systems can be activated by visual, auditory, or olfactory stimuli or by other images. Even a lack of sensory stimulation can produce vivid imagery. Imagery helps you answer such questions as: Which is darker, a pea or a Christmas tree? Which is bigger, a tennis ball or an orange? Does the person you met last night have brown eyes or blue?

Measuring Imagery. More than 50 years ago, Gestalt psychologists, who were interested in form perception, recognized the importance of imagery. That importance is being acknowledged once again. The difficulty for psychologists today is to devise techniques and experimental manipulations to measure imagery. One technique, used extensively by Stephen Kosslyn of Harvard University, was to ask subjects to imagine objects of various sizes—for example, an animal such as a rabbit next to either an elephant or a fly. In a 1975 study by Kosslyn, subjects reported that when they imagined a fly, plenty of room remained in their mental image for a rabbit. However, when they imagined an elephant, it took up most of the space. One particularly interesting result was that the subjects required more time and found it harder to see the rabbit's nose when the rabbit was next to an elephant than when it was next to a fly, because the nose appeared to be extremely small in the first instance (see Figure 6.8).

In another series of experiments, Kosslyn (1978) asked subjects first to imagine an object at a distance and then to imagine that they were moving toward the object. The subjects were next asked if the object seemed larger to them than before and whether it overflowed their mental visual field so they could no longer see all of it. The subjects were instructed to stop mentally walking at the point at which the object seemed to overflow the visual field. By having the subjects estimate the size of the object and the distance at which the images seemed to overflow the visual field, Kosslyn was able to estimate the size of a visual image that people can imagine.

Using this mental walk technique, Kosslyn found a limited image space. Larger objects tended to overflow at greater imagined distances than smaller objects did. Kosslyn also learned that images overflowed in all directions at about the same size. Perhaps the most important finding from Kosslyn's research is that images possess spatial properties. Although they are mental, not physical, phenomena, they have photographlike edges—points beyond which visual information ceases to be represented (Kosslyn, 1987). People can construct mental images, transform them, and interpret what they look like (Finke, Pinker, & Farah, 1989). For example, you can use your mental imagery ability to decide whether your new station wagon will fit into your single-car garage or to count the number of windows in your new apartment; and you can do so in three dimensions, regardless of the angle from which you view these objects (Roth & Kosslyn, 1988). Imagery has been used in a wide variety of studies to measure the nature and speed of thought (see, for example, Figure 6.9 on page 222).

Imagery as a Memory Aid. Imagery is an important perceptual memory aid. In fact, a growing body of evidence suggests that it is a means of preserving perceptual information that might otherwise decay. According to Paivio (1971), a per-

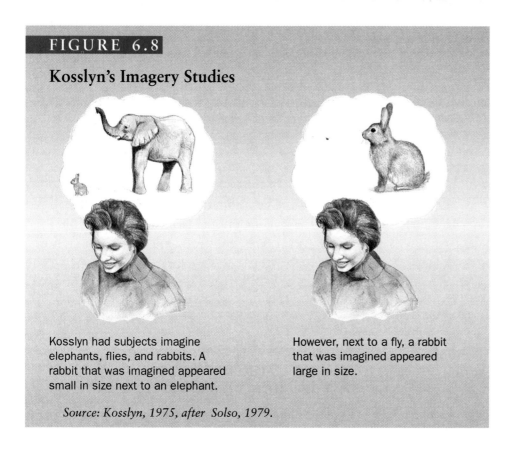

FIGURE 6.8

Kosslyn's Imagery Studies

Kosslyn had subjects imagine elephants, flies, and rabbits. A rabbit that was imagined appeared small in size next to an elephant.

However, next to a fly, a rabbit that was imagined appeared large in size.

Source: Kosslyn, 1975, after Solso, 1979.

son told to remember two words may form an image combining those words. Someone told to remember the words *house* and *hamburger,* for example, might form an image of a house made of hamburgers or of a hamburger on top of a house. When the person is later presented with the word *house,* the word *hamburger* will come to mind. Paivio suggests that words paired in this way are conceptually linked, with the crucial factor being the image.

How images facilitate recall and recognition is not yet fully understood, but one possibility is that an image could add another code to semantic memory. Thus, with two codes, semantic and imaginal, a person has two ways to access previously learned information. Some researchers argue that imagery, verbal encoding mechanisms, and semantic memory operate together to encode and to aid in retrieval (Marschark et al., 1987).

Eidetic Imagery. In the 1960s, while Paivio was trying to make the study of imagery respectable to behavioral colleagues, other researchers were investigating a different kind of imagery: photographlike imagery. If everyone could maintain a photographlike image of each glimpse of the world, how easy learning and memory would be. Although many people say they have photographic memories, no one reports having an image of everything ever seen. Most reports of photographic memory are normal vivid imagery. However, Haber (1969, 1979) showed that some children do have a special kind of photographlike imagery, called eidetic imagery. *Eidetic imagery,* which is found in fewer than 4 percent of school-age children, is vivid, long-lasting, and complete.

Haber's basic procedure was to place a picture on an easel for about 30 seconds, instruct children to move their eyes so they would see all the details in the picture, and then remove the picture. As the subjects continued to look at the blank white

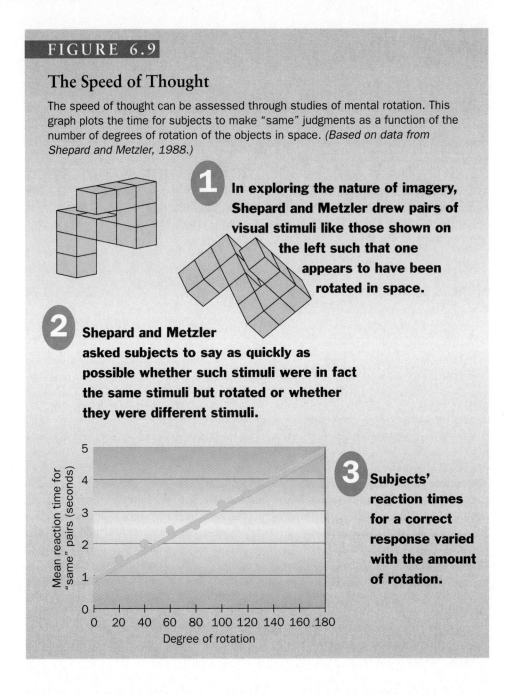

FIGURE 6.9

The Speed of Thought

The speed of thought can be assessed through studies of mental rotation. This graph plots the time for subjects to make "same" judgments as a function of the number of degrees of rotation of the objects in space. *(Based on data from Shepard and Metzler, 1988.)*

1 In exploring the nature of imagery, Shepard and Metzler drew pairs of visual stimuli like those shown on the left such that one appears to have been rotated in space.

2 Shepard and Metzler asked subjects to say as quickly as possible whether such stimuli were in fact the same stimuli but rotated or whether they were different stimuli.

3 Subjects' reaction times for a correct response varied with the amount of rotation.

easel, they were asked about the nature of their imagery. Children who were eventually termed *eidetic* reported that their images lasted from a half minute to a full minute. Their imagery was so vivid that they could describe even tiny details of the pictures. If the picture showed a cat with a striped tail, for example, they could report how many stripes were on the tail. A few eidetic children were even able to develop three-dimensional images. Children who could not remember parts of a picture said they had not looked at those parts long enough. And when they were told to move their image from the easel to another surface, they said that it fell off the edge of the easel. Young adults with eidetic capabilities have been identified by Japanese researchers (Matsuoka et al., 1987).

State-Dependent Learning

The distinguished psychologist Gordon Bower used the following example to describe a phenomenon known as *state-dependent learning* (Bower, 1981, p. 129):

> When I was a kid I saw the movie *City Lights* in which Charlie Chaplin plays the little tramp. In one very funny sequence, Charlie saves a drunk from leaping to his death. The drunk turns out to be a millionaire who befriends Charlie, and the two spend the evening together drinking and carousing. The next day, when sober, the millionaire does not recognize Charlie and even snubs him. Later the millionaire gets drunk again, and when he spots Charlie treats him as his long-lost companion. So the two of them spend another evening together carousing and drinking and then stagger back to the millionaire's mansion to sleep. In the morning, of course, the sober millionaire again does not recognize Charlie, treats him as an intruder, and has the butler kick him out by the seat of his pants. The scene ends with the little tramp telling the camera his opinion of high society and the evils of drunkenness.

The millionaire remembers Charlie only when he is intoxicated, the same state in which he originally met him. Psychologists find that information learned while a person is in a particular physiological state is recalled most accurately when the person is again in that physiological state. This phenomenon, known as **state-dependent learning,** is associated with such states as those involving drugs, time of day (Holloway, 1977), mental illness (Weingartner, 1977), and shock therapy (discussed in chapter 15) (Robbins & Meyer, 1970).

In a typical study of state-dependent learning, Weingartner and colleagues (1976) had four groups of subjects learn lists of high- and low-imagery words. To induce intoxication, all subjects except those in the control group drank vodka and fruit juice. The control group learned and recalled while sober, a second group learned and recalled while intoxicated, a third group learned while sober and recalled while intoxicated, and a fourth group learned while intoxicated and recalled while sober. The results showed that subjects recalled the lists best when they were in the same state in which they had learned the lists.

Several theories attempt to explain state-dependent learning. A widely accepted explanation focuses on how altered or drugged states affect the storage process. According to this view, part of learning involves the encoding of stimuli in specific ways at the time of learning; to access the stored information, a person must evoke the same context in which the encoding occurred. When you study for an examination with music in the background but are tested in quiet conditions, is your recall not as good? The answer to this question is as yet unresolved, but studies of state-dependent learning may hold the key; and recent studies of mood-dependent memory suggest that the answer may be yes (Eich & Metcalfe, 1989).

The Applications box on page 224 suggests how you can use the information presented in this chapter to help improve your memory.

FOCUS

▶ What evidence supports episodic memory? Semantic memory?   pp. 215–216

▶ What is the underlying assumption of the levels-of-processing approach to memory?   pp. 216–218

▶ What evidence did researchers use to conclude that flashbulb memories are not unique?   p. 217

▶ What fundamental assumption have memory researchers taken from studies of short-term memory and applied to help people improve their memory?   pp. 224–225

State-dependent learning: The tendency to recall information learned in a particular physiological state most accurately when one is again in that physiological state.

Improving Your Memory

Several techniques can improve memory. Here are some of the most powerful ones; they move from simple strategies to more complex overall approaches. Try using them to learn this chapter's concepts.

Rehearse, Rehearse, Rehearse.

If you want to remember something, there is no substitute for rehearsal (pp. 211–212). Maintenance rehearsal, in which you simply memorize words without giving any meaning to them, will facilitate recognition or rote recall if you do not have to remember the words for very long. However, if you really want to remember ideas for a long time, you need to understand them; and this requires the use of elaborative rehearsal. With elaborative rehearsal, you generate meaning as you repeat and think about the information you are learning.

Practice over Time.

You can benefit from practice if you review your class notes soon after class or write a summary of an article soon after reading it. However, when you plan to study, distributing practice and rehearsal over time becomes important. Distributing practice means studying a particular subject for a relatively short time every day or every other day, instead of trying to cram all your studying into one long session. If you stick with a schedule for doing schoolwork so that you can avoid cramming, you can make use of the distributed practice principle. In doing so, you will increase the amount of material you learn and remember within the same total amount of time.

Plan on Relearning.

Memory studies show that most forgetting occurs right after we have learned something. They also show that if we go back and relearn (rehearse again) the same material, we learn it more quickly and forget less of it. Whenever you return to one of the subjects you are studying, go back and review what you already studied before you move forward to learn more. In this way, you will be making use of the relearning principle.

Take Advantage of Primacy and Recency Effects.

Research concerning the primacy and recency effects (pp. 218–219) show that we are most likely to remember information at the beginning and at the end of a study session or lecture. So instead of forcing yourself to endure long, drawn-out study sessions, take a short (5- to 10-minute) break after you have studied for 20 to 30 minutes. Taking such breaks will enhance your learning and memory because it will increase the number of times that the primacy and recency effects can influence you. It will also allow you to lessen the interference effects of proactive and retroactive inhibition (unless your breaks are also cognitively demanding).

Focus to Prevent Interference.

You can facilitate memory storage by doing whatever you can to avoid unnecessary interference. For example, when you are studying, focus on one course or one learning task at a time. If you are studying for a big Shakespeare test, stick with that subject until you feel confident you have learned it.

Make Use of Chunking.

Chunking allows us to increase the capacity of our working memory (p. 211). For instance, consider the word *psychoneuroendocrinology*. This long word refers to the field of psychology ("psycho...ology") that investigates the influence of hormones ("endocrin") on the nervous system ("neuro"). What if you had to learn to say this word so you could spell it on an essay exam? How would you do it with the limited capacity of short-term memory? The answer is that you would use chunking. To remember the word, you would break it into small chunks: *psycho-neuro-endocrin-ology*. Another way to chunk material is to group ideas

Forgetting—The Loss of Memory

Quick! Name your first-grade teacher. Your social security number. Where you went on your last vacation. In general, your memory serves you amazingly well. Nevertheless, at times you may have trouble recalling the name of someone you know well, where you read an interesting article, or the phone number of a close friend. Have you ever begun an examination only to have your mind suddenly go blank?

There are many causes of forgetting, including not rehearsing information well enough and not using it for a long time. Forgetting also occurs because of interfer-

together in organized ways. For example, list some factors that increase recall as one chunk of things to remember and some factors that contribute to forgetting as another chunk.

Use Mnemonics. If you transform information that is abstract, difficult, or still unlearned into information that is personally meaningful, it will be easier to remember. Using mnemonics, allows you to combine seemingly unrelated items into an organized format, rhyme, or jingle so you can easily remember all of the items. For example, as a child you may have learned the notes of the treble-clef musical scale EGBDF by using the mnemonic jingle "*Every Good Boy Does Fine.*" The more you can relate unfamiliar information that you want to recall to familiar information that you already know, the easier it will be for you to learn and remember it.

Use Mediation. Mediation is a bridging technique that allows you to link two items to be remembered with a third item (or image) that ties them together and serves as a cue for retrieval. Cermak (1975) uses the names John and Tillie as an example. John reminds someone of a bathroom, which can be associated with the image of tiles, which sounds and is spelled somewhat like Tillie.

Therefore, remembering a tiled bathroom helps the person remember the names John and Tillie.

Make Use of the von Restorff Effect. If one item in a group of things to be learned stands out because it differs from the other items, it will be easier to learn and remember; this is known as the *von Restorff effect.* You can make use of this effect by deliberately making an idea you want to remember stand out. Do this by using a colored highlighter on printing in your notes, by exaggerating the meaning of the idea you want to remember, by making the idea seem funny or bizarre in your mind, or by emphasizing the distinctiveness of the idea in your mind as you think about it.

Review in Different Contexts and Modalities. The place where you learned something can be an important retrieval cue. For example, when you see a familiar bank teller in a gymnasium, you may not be able to remember the person. Try to review and rehearse in different settings. Also, try learning and studying through more than one sensory modality. For example, if you heard (auditory) a lecture, write down (tactile-kinesthetic and visual) what you heard. If you have been developing mnemonics on paper, try saying them out loud. If you have been outlining

a chapter aloud, write down or draw a map of the key ideas.

Prepare the Environment. Because there is so much to learn and remember, you can facilitate the task if you prepare your environment (A. S. Brown, 1989). Limit the number of opportunities for people to grab your attention. Study in a quiet place where there are few people.

Avoid visual clutter in your study area; it is a distraction from the task at hand. Limit the number of tasks you are working on so as to focus your attention and thus stay tuned in to one task. Finish the tasks that you start so they will not take further attention. Keep a notebook handy to jot down ideas, insights, and potential mnemonics.

ence from newly learned information or previously learned information, because the information is unpleasant, or because of physiological problems. Moreover, forgetting occurs in both short- and long-term memory. We study forgetting because it teaches us a great deal about memory.

Early Studies

Some of the first experimenters in psychology studied learning, memory, and forgetting. Sometimes, the tasks they created involved paper and pencil; but more often they merely involved a subject, the experimenter, and some information to be learned. Computers were unheard of, and techniques that psychologists use today would not have made sense.

Relearning. Through the technique of *relearning,* Hermann Ebbinghaus (1850–1909) studied how well people learn stored information. Ebbinghaus earnestly believed that the contents of consciousness could be studied by scientific principles. He tried to quantify how quickly subjects could learn, relearn, and forget information. Ebbinghaus was the first person to investigate memory scientifically and systematically, which made his technique as important as his findings.

In his early studies, Ebbinghaus was both researcher and subject. He assigned himself the task of learning lists of letters in order of presentation. First, he strung together groups of three letters to make nonsense syllables such as *nak, dib, mip,* and *daf.* He then recorded how many times he had to present the lists to himself before he could remember them perfectly. Ebbinghaus found that when the lists were short, learning was nearly perfect in one or two trials. When they contained more than seven items, however, he had to present them over and over for accurate recall.

Later, Ebbinghaus did learning experiments with other subjects. He had them learn lists of words and then, after varying amounts of time, measured how quickly they relearned the original list. If subjects relearned the list quickly, Ebbinghaus concluded that they still had some memory of it. He called this learning technique the *saving method* because what was initially learned was not totally forgotten. (See Figure 6.10 for Ebbinghaus's "forgetting curve.")

Practice. Following Ebbinghaus's lead, from the 1930s through the 1960s many researchers investigated the best ways for people to learn new material and relearn forgotten skills. In one study in 1966, Baddeley and Longman wanted to learn which of two types of practice resulted in more optimal learning and retention: intensive practice at one time (massed practice) or practice over several intervals (distributed practice.) To answer this question, they taught postal workers to touch-type.

The subjects were divided into four groups. One group practiced typing 1 hour a day, the second practiced 2 hours a day, the third practiced 1 hour twice a day,

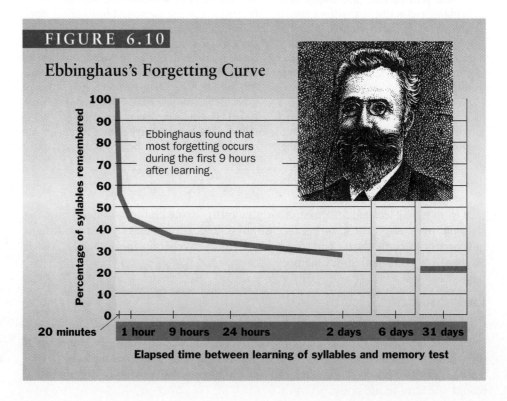

FIGURE 6.10

Ebbinghaus's Forgetting Curve

Ebbinghaus found that most forgetting occurs during the first 9 hours after learning.

Percentage of syllables remembered

100 90 80 70 60 50 40 30 20 10 0

20 minutes   1 hour   9 hours   24 hours   2 days   6 days   31 days

Elapsed time between learning of syllables and memory test

and the fourth practiced 2 hours twice a day. Thus, the subjects used either massed practice or distributed practice. The dependent variable was how well they typed— that is, the number of accurate keystrokes per minute. A typing test showed that after an equal number of hours of practice, distributed practice was more effective. From this experiment and others, researchers have learned that the effectiveness of distributed practice depends on several variables, including the method, order, and speed of presentation. Distributed practice is especially effective in perceptual motor skills, where eye-hand coordination is important.

In the 1970s, researchers began to study the best way to present information to be learned. (This interest paralleled the innovations being carried out in public schools, including open classrooms, the new math, and cooperative learning.) They found, for example, that if one item in a list differs from the others (say, one plant name in a list with nine animal names), the one different item is learned more easily. This phenomenon is called the *von Restorff effect*.

Measures of Retention

Psychologists study retention by measuring people's ability to relearn information through several techniques: recall, recognition, reconstruction, and pictorial memory. The most widely investigated techniques have been recall and recognition. *Recall* is remembering the details of a situation or idea and placing them together in a meaningful framework (usually without any cues or aids). Asking someone to name the craft that exploded with U.S. astronauts aboard is a test of recall. *Recognition* is remembering whether one has seen a stimulus before—whether the stimulus is familiar. Asking someone whether Neil Armstrong landed on the moon in 1969 is a test of recognition. *Reconstruction* is the procedure of restoring a disrupted event to its original order. This is often aided by *pictorial memory*.

Recall. In recall tasks, subjects have to remember previously presented information. (Essay exams require you to recall information.) In experiments, the information usually comprises strings (or lists) of digits or letters. A typical study might ask subjects to remember 10 nonsense syllables, each of which is presented on a screen every half second. They would then have to repeat the list at the end of the 5-second presentation period.

Three widely used recall tasks are free recall, serial recall, and paired associate tasks. In *free recall tasks,* subjects are to recall items in any order, much as you might recall the items on a grocery list. *Serial recall tasks* are more difficult; the items must be recalled in the order in which they were presented, just as you would recall a telephone number. In *paired associate tasks,* subjects are given a cue to help them recall the second half of a pair of items. In the learning phase of a study, the experimenter might pair the words *tree* and *shoe*. In the testing phase, subjects would be presented with the word *tree* and would have to respond with the correct answer, *shoe*. Table 6.1 on page 228 lists typical tasks and objectives used in testing the three main types of recall.

Recognition. In a multiple-choice test, you are asked to recognize relevant information. Psychologists have found that recognition tasks can help them measure differences in memory ability better than recall tasks can. That's because although someone may recognize a previously studied fact, the person may be unable to recall the associated details contained in the fact. Asked to name the capital of Maine, you would probably have a better chance of answering correctly if you were given four names to choose from: Columbus, Annapolis, Helena, or Augusta.

TABLE 6.1   *Three Types of Recall Tasks and Objectives*

Type of Task	Objective
Free Recall *Ghoul* *Vanquish* *Painless*	Subject learns the items in any order.
Serial Recall *GIP, MAG, DEC, LIG*	Subject learns the items in the order in which they were presented; often, items are nonsense syllables.
Paired Associate Recall *GIP/MAG* *Hall/Pencil*	Subject learns to associate the second item of the pair with the first. Items are either words or nonsense syllables.

Reconstruction. Here's a test of your memory: What did Neil Armstrong say when he first landed on the moon (his "one small step for a man" statement)? Few of us can recall Armstrong's words exactly, but most can probably recognize them or reconstruct them approximately. Researchers have shown that people often "construct" memories of past events; the constructions are close approximations but not exact memories. For example, you might construct the gist of Armstrong's speech by saying that Armstrong said something about man's first steps on the moon being important for all mankind. (Just for the record, his exact words were: "That's one small step for a man, one giant leap for mankind.")

In 1932, English psychologist Sir Frederick Bartlett reported that when college students tried to recall stories they had just read, they changed them in interesting ways. They shortened and simplified details, a process called *leveling;* they focused on or emphasized certain details, a process called *sharpening;* and they altered facts to make the stories fit their own views of the world, a process called *assimilation.* In other words, the students constructed memories that distorted the events to some degree.

Contemporary explanations of this *reconstructive memory* have centered on the constructive nature of the memory process and on how people develop a **schema**—a conceptual framework that organizes information and makes sense of the world. Because we cannot remember *all* the details of an event or situation, we keep key facts and lose minor details. By developing schemas, we group together key pieces of information. In general, we try to fit the entire memory into some framework that will be available for later recall. For example, my schema for life in the United States during 1969, the year the first U.S. astronauts landed on the moon, might include memories of such events as watching Walter Cronkite's news reports, listening to the Beatles, my honeymoon trip, and reading about urban unrest.

Pictorial Memory. Related to reconstruction is the study of *pictorial memory,* in which researchers test how well people can remember visual images. The results of these studies show that people are amazingly good at recognizing pictures they have previously seen. In fact, Haber (1979) found that subjects can recognize thousands of pictures with almost 100 percent accuracy.

In 1970, Standing, Conezio, and Haber showed subjects thousands of slides, each for a few seconds. They then presented pairs of slides, only one of which the subjects had seen before, and asked the subjects to identify which of the pair they had seen. The subjects recognized the previously seen slides with greater than 95 percent accuracy. More recent studies have repeated the results of Standing and his col-

Schema: [SKEEM-uh] A conceptual framework that organizes information and makes sense of the world by laying out a structure in which events can be encoded.

leagues, and researchers have developed other approaches as well. They suggest that pictorial information may be encoded, stored, and retrieved differently from other information; this is why pictorial memory is so good (Intraub, 1980; Intraub & Nicklos, 1985; Standing, 1973).

Reasons for Memory Loss

Data can be lost from both short- and long-term memory. Two concepts, decay and interference, help explain the loss (see Figure 6.11).

Decay of Information. **Decay** is the loss of information from memory as a result of the passage of time and disuse. In decay theory, unimportant events fade from memory, and details become lost, confused, or fuzzy. Another way to look at decay theory is this: Memory exists in the brain in a physiological form known as a *memory trace.* With the passage of time and a lack of active use, the trace disintegrates, fades, and is lost.

Decay theory was popular for many years but is not widely accepted today. Many early studies did not consider several important variables that affect memory processes, among them the rate and mode of stimulus presentation. Although decay does form a small part of the final explanation of forgetting, it is probably less important than other factors, such as interference.

Interference in Memory. **Interference** is the suppression or confusion of one bit of information with another that was received either earlier or later. In interference theory, the limited capacity of short-term memory makes it susceptible to interference from, or confusion among, other learned items. That is, when competing information is stored in short-term memory, the crowding that results affects a person's memory for particular items. For example, if someone looks up a telephone number and is then given another number to remember, the second number will

Decay: The loss of information from memory as a result of the passage of time and disuse.

Interference: The suppression or confusion of one bit of information with another that was received either earlier or later.

FIGURE 6.11

The Interaction of Short- and Long-Term Memory

The transfer of information from short-term memory to long-term memory is crucial for later accurate recall and is subject to decay and interference in both short- and long-term memory.

REHEARSAL

Short-term memory

Long-term memory

Decay

Decay

Interference

Interference

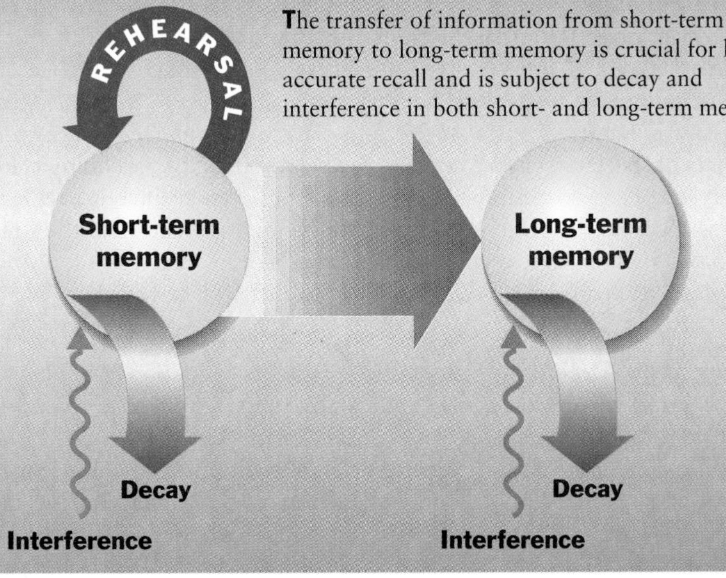

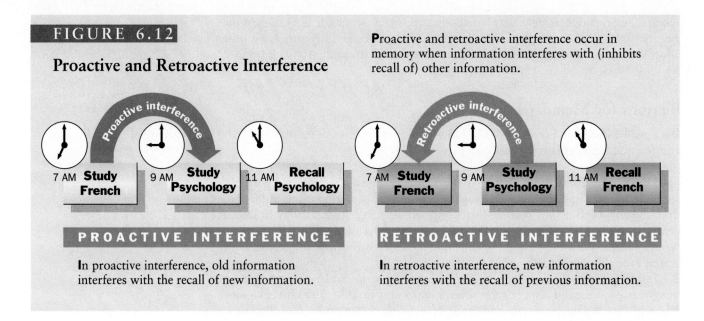

FIGURE 6.12

Proactive and Retroactive Interference

Proactive and retroactive interference occur in memory when information interferes with (inhibits recall of) other information.

Proactive interference

| 7 AM **Study French** | 9 AM **Study Psychology** | 11 AM **Recall Psychology** |

Retroactive interference

| 7 AM **Study French** | 9 AM **Study Psychology** | 11 AM **Recall French** |

PROACTIVE INTERFERENCE

R E T R O A C T I V E   I N T E R F E R E N C E

In proactive interference, old information interferes with the recall of new information.

In retroactive interference, new information interferes with the recall of previous information.

probably interfere with the ability to remember the first one. Moreover, interference in memory is more likely to occur when a person is presented with a great deal of new information. (In this text, you are being provided with a great deal of new information. Organizing your studying into coherent chunks will help you avoid confusing the information you are trying to enter into long-term memory.)

Research on interference theory shows that the extent and nature of a person's experiences both before and after learning are important. For example, a subject given a list of nonsense syllables may recall 75 percent of the items correctly. However, if the subject was given 20 similar lists to learn earlier, the number of items correctly recalled would be lower; the previous lists would interfere with recall. If the subject was given additional lists to learn, recall would be even lower. Psychologists call these interference effects proactive and retroactive interference (or inhibition). **Proactive interference,** or *proactive inhibition,* is the decrease in accurate recall as a result of previous information interfering with the recall. **Retroactive interference,** or *retroactive inhibition,* is the decrease in accurate recall of information as a result of the subsequent presentation of different information. (See Figure 6.12 for an illustration of both types of interference.) Proactive and retroactive interference help explain recall failures in long-term memory.

Here is an illustration of proactive and retroactive interference: Suppose you attend a series of speeches, each 5 minutes long. According to psychological research on proactive and retroactive interference, you will be most likely to remember the first and last speeches. There will be no proactive interference with the first speech and no retroactive interference with the last speech. Your memory of all the middle speeches will suffer from both proactive and retroactive interference.

Interference in Attention. Interference has long been a potent explanatory factor in memory and perception studies. For many years, it was used to explain what is called the Stroop effect (Stroop, 1935). The Stroop test is a procedure in which people are asked to name colors that are printed in an ink color different from the color being named. For example, the word *red* may be printed in blue ink. Most people find it difficult to attend to the ink color alone when they are asked to name the color in which the word is printed (the Stroop effect). This is because of an

Proactive interference: [pro-AK-tiv] The decrease in accurate recall of particular information as a result of previous information interfering with its recall. Also known as *proactive inhibition.*

Retroactive interference: [RET-ro-AK-tiv] The decrease in accurate recall of information as a result of the subsequent presentation of different information. Also known as *retroactive inhibition.*

assumed automatic tendency to read the word, which produces interference. This explanation has been popular, but it is being modified in favor of attentional strategies (rather than interference) determining the Stroop effect (MacLeod, 1991).

Retrieval Failure. Some contemporary researchers assert that every memory is retained and available but that some memories are less accessible than others. Think of the library analogy; all the books in the library are there, but some cannot be found (perhaps because they are misshelved), making retrieval difficult or impossible.

Research on retrieval failure focuses on how people encode information and on the cues that act to help in retrieval. If you are given a cue for retrieval and the originally stored information contains that cue, retrieval is easier, faster, and more accurate. The value of a specific retrieval cue depends on how well it compares with the original memory code; this notion is referred to as the *encoding specificity hypothesis.* The more clearly and sharply your memory cues are defined, the better your recall will be and the less likely you will be to experience retrieval failures. To increase your access to information stored in memory, you should match the test situation to the original learning situation as much as possible.

Motivated Forgetting and Amnesia. Freud (1933) was the first to formally suggest the idea of *motivated forgetting*—that unwanted or unpleasant events might be lost in memory simply because people want to forget them. He stated that such loss occurs through repression—the burying of unpleasant ideas in the unconscious, where they remain inaccessible. Most researchers agree that motivated forgetting probably exists in some form. But they have found it hard to measure and difficult to demonstrate experimentally, though anecdotal clinical evidence abounds. A related phenomenon, amnesia, can be examined in the laboratory.

Television soap operas frequently portray people with amnesia, but in fact the condition is relatively rare. **Amnesia** is the inability to remember events, usually because of physiological trauma (such as a blow to the head). Typically, it involves loss of memory for all events within a specific period. There are two basic kinds of amnesia: retrograde and anterograde.

Retrograde amnesia is the inability to remember events that preceded a traumatizing event. The loss of memory can cover the period just before the event or a period of several years before it. Recovery tends to be gradual, with earlier events remembered before more recent ones.

Anterograde amnesia is the inability to remember events that occur after an injury or brain damage. People suffering from anterograde amnesia are stuck in the lives they lived before being injured; new events are often completely forgotten. For example, if the onset of the amnesia occurred in 1993, the sufferer may be able to remember clearly events in 1992 or earlier but have a difficult time recalling what he or she did only half an hour ago. The victim may meet someone for the hundredth time, yet think he or she is being introduced to a perfect stranger.

In studying patients with brain damage or those who have undergone surgery for major epileptic attacks, researchers have found that the region of the brain called the *hippocampus* may be responsible for the

Some memory loss is the result of brain damage. An auto accident left this woman unable to recognize faces, even the familiar face of Ronald Reagan. (Photo courtesy of CNN.)

Amnesia: The inability to remember events from the past, usually because of physiological trauma; typically involves loss of memory for all events within a specific period.

Retrograde amnesia: [RET-ro-grade] Loss of memory for events and experiences occurring in a period preceding the amnesia-causing event.

Anterograde amnesia: Loss of memory for events and experiences occurring after the amnesia-causing event.

transfer of new information to permanent memory. Milner showed that if certain regions of the brain are damaged or removed, people can remember old information but not new information (B. Milner, 1966; Milner, Corkin, & Teuber, 1968). The ability to remember remote events seems to depend on brain mechanisms that are separate and distinct from those required for new learning of recent events (Shimamura & Squire, 1986). These studies do not conclusively confirm the existence of separate places or processes in the brain for different types of amnesia or memory, but they are suggestive. Moreover, new research on learning and memory of emotional responses by Kim and Fanselow (1992) supports the idea that memory is not a single process. The ability to remember remote events is particularly important in studies of eyewitness testimony, in which people try to remember real-life past events.

Eyewitness Testimony

We saw earlier that, in Bartlett's laboratory, subjects sometimes constructed and altered their memories. The constructive nature of memory can have serious consequences for real-life situations, especially for eyewitness testimony. If someone sees an accident or crime, for example, can the witness accurately report the facts of the situation to the police or the courts? The answer is yes and no. The police and the courts have generally accepted *eyewitness testimony* as some of the best evidence that can be presented. They are hearing from people who saw the crime, have no bias or grudge, and are sworn to tell the truth. But do they?

Some studies show that eyewitnesses often recall events incorrectly and identify the wrong people as being involved in the events (Bekerian & Bowers, 1983; Loftus, 1979). In fact, eyewitnesses of the same event often report seeing different things. Langman and Cockburn (1975) recorded the 1968 eyewitness testimony of people who reported seeing Sirhan Sirhan shoot Senator Robert F. Kennedy (brother of President John F. Kennedy). Even though many of the eyewitnesses were standing next to one another, they reported seeing different things. In addition, identification of a criminal, even in a lineup, is prone to significant mistakes (Navon, 1990), although techniques have been developed to improve lineup accuracy (Sporer, 1993; Wells, 1993).

To complicate the matter, eyewitnesses often enhance their memories over time (recall Bartlett's theory of assimilation). Harvard law

Both field-based research and laboratory simulations are needed in order to determine the accuracy of eyewitness recollections.

professor Alan Dershowitz (1986) asserts that the memories of witnesses—particularly those with a stake in the eventual outcome—tend to get better with the passage of time. Dershowitz calls this process memory enhancement and argues that it occurs when people fit their hazy memories into a coherent theory and pattern of other results.

A witness's initial recollections of a crime may be vague, for example. However, as a trial approaches, the person is coached and rehearsed and tends to remember better, with more clarity and less ambiguity. According to Dershowitz (1986), what begins as a hazy recollection becomes crystal clear. The result in the courtroom, however, may be slightly inaccurate, seriously biased, or largely untrue testimony; that is, it may be constructed testimony. Ironically, the more detailed a witness is (even about irrelevant details), the more credible that witness is assumed to be, even if the witness recalled things inaccurately (Bell & Loftus, 1989). Whether the memory is weakened, clouded, or confused or whether retrieval processes are impaired is still not clear (Zaragoza & McCloskey, 1989). As Loftus and Hoffman (1989, p. 103) argue, "That people come to accept misinformation and adopt it faithfully as their own is an important phenomenon in its own right."

Loftus (1991, 1993) has been asking recently if recall of other events—for example, being sexually abused as a child—is due to memory enhancement or outright overinflation of facts. With her data from laboratory situations, she has extrapolated her findings to other such situations—and has caused a furor among professionals who treat sexually abused victims. These professionals assert that their clients' claims, often from many years before, are accurate, vivid, and truthful. Research shows that children and adults can be lead and have their memories enhanced (Lindsay, 1993), but Ceci and Bruck (1993) argue that adults and even very young children are capable of accurately recalling events that occurred early in their lives.

Despite strong evidence of errors in eyewitness testimony, two researchers from the University of British Columbia believe that eyewitness testimony is accurate and that it is the laboratory studies of eyewitness testimony that may be inaccurate. Yuille and Cutshall (1986) argue that laboratory studies generally use simulated events, films of events, television presentations, and slide shows to study eyewitness testimony—and that this is not the same as actually seeing a crime or accident. They further state that real events are well remembered and that researchers who study eyewitness testimony should do fieldwork before making further claims. This idea is being echoed by other prominent memory researchers (e.g., Klatzky, 1991). Studying real-life everyday memories may turn out to be crucial to the study of learning and memory and to be a necessary adjunct to traditional laboratory studies (Ceci & Bronfenbrenner, 1991; Yuille, 1993).

Generalizing from field-based situations is difficult because of numerous uncontrolled variables; generalizing from laboratory situations is difficult because of their artificial nature (Banaji & Crowder, 1989). Today, researchers are insisting on both. Before the issue is resolved, however, more field-based research and further laboratory simulation studies are needed (Tulving, 1991).

Building Table 6.3 on page 234 summarizes key processes in the three stages of memory.

FOCUS

▶ Why is distributed practice more effective than massed practice for learning?   pp. 224–225

▶ The fact that recall and recognition tap different processes reflects what view held by memory researchers? p. 227

▶ How do interference explanations of forgetting explain errors in retrieval?   pp. 229–231

BUILDING TABLE 6.3

Key Processes in the Stages of Memory

STAGE	ENCODING	STORAGE	DURATION	RETRIEVAL	FORGETTING
Sensory Memory	Visual or auditory (iconic or echoic memory).	Brief, fragile, and temporary.	Visual: 250 milliseconds; auditory: less than 4 seconds.	Information extracted from stimulus presentation and transferred to working or short-term memory.	Rapid decay of information; interference possible if a new stimulus is presented.
Short-Term Memory	Visual and auditory; auditory encoding is especially important.	Repetitive rehearsal maintains information in storage, perhaps on a visual/auditory scratchpad where further encoding can take place.	Less than 20 seconds, no more than 30 seconds; depends on specific task and stimuli.	Maintenance and elaborative rehearsal can keep information available for retrieval; retrieval is enhanced through elaboration and further encoding.	Interference and decay are operative; new stimulation causes rapid loss of information unless information is especially important.
Long-Term Memory	Salient or important information processed through short-term memory is transferred into long-term memory through elaborative rehearsal.	Storage is organized on logical and semantic lines for rapid recall. People organize information by categories, events, and other structures that aid retrieval.	Indefinite; many events will be recalled with great detail for a lifetime.	Retrieval is aided by cues and careful organization; errors in retrieval can be introduced; long-term memory is fallible.	Both decay and interference contribute to retrieval failure.

The Physiology of Memory

We have explored the structure, function, and operation of memory and forgetting. We also need to know what memories are and where they are found in the brain. Memories are stored in electrochemical form in the brain. Many psychologists who study the biological bases of behavior now believe that most, if not all, memories are retained in some manner. Today, researchers are exploring the neurobiological basis of memory. How does the brain store memories? Where are memories stored? Are memory traces localized or distributed?

Consolidation Theory and Coding

Memories are not physical things; rather, they are made up of unique groupings of neurons in the brain. Using this fact, Canadian psychologist Donald Hebb (1904–1985) presented in 1949 one of the major psychological and physiological theories of memory. Hebb suggested that when groups of neurons are stimulated, they form patterns of neural activity. If a specific group of neurons fires frequently, a reverberating and regular neural circuit is established. This evolution of a temporary neural circuit into a more permanent circuit is known as **consolidation.**

According to Hebb, consolidation serves as the basis of short-term memory and permits the coding (also known as encoding) of information into long-term memory. If Hebb is correct, when people first sense a new stimulus, only temporary changes in neurons take place; with repetition, consolidation occurs and the temporary circuit becomes a permanent one.

Many psychologists believe that the consolidation process provides the key to understanding both learning and memory—that individual differences in ability to learn or remember may be due to differing abilities to consolidate new information properly. Confirmation of this notion comes from studies using electroconvulsive shock therapy (discussed in chapter 15) to disrupt consolidation, which results in impaired memory both in human beings and in animals. Further support comes from studies showing that recent memories are more susceptible to amnesic loss than are older memories (P. M. Milner, 1989).

The consolidation process may even play a role in the physiological development of the brain. Researchers have compared the brains of animals raised in enriched environments with the brains of animals raised in deprived environments. In enriched environments, toys and other objects are available for the animals to play with and to learn from. The brains of animals raised in such environments have more elaborate networks of nerve cells, with more dendrites and more synapses with other neurons (Chang, Isaacs, & Greenough, 1991). This means that when a neuron is stimulated over and over again, it is enriched; and it may branch out and become more easily accessible. Such elaboration is greater when organisms are placed in complex, super-enriched visual or auditory environments.

If a neuron is stimulated, the biochemical processes that are involved make it more likely to respond again later; further, the number of dendrites of that cell increases because of previous stimulation (Lynch & Baudry, 1984). This suggests that biochemical actions and repeated use may make learning and remembering easier, a conception that fits perfectly with Hebb's suggestions. In addition, clear evidence exists that specific protein synthesis occurs just after learning and that long-term memory depends on this synthesis (Matthies, 1989). Psychologists now generally accept the idea that the structure of synapses changes after learning, and especially after repeated learning experiences. As Hebb said (1949, p. 62): "Some memories are both instantaneously established and permanent. To account for the permanence, some structural change seems necessary."

Consolidation theory has been refined, extended, and supported by research. For example, we know that a single neuron has many synaptic sites on its dendrites. Alkon (1989) has shown that there is extensive interaction among those sites and with the sites of other neurons. He argues that the spread of electrical and chemical activity from one site to another—without activity or firing of the neurons—seems to be critical for initiating memory storage. He asserts that, on a given neuron, a huge number of different incoming signals can be received and stored. Alkon has been developing mathematical and computer models to simulate neuronal encoding for memory and to study animal memory. This exciting work extends Hebb's ideas one step further.

Work on the physiology of memory has expanded into other fronts. For example, Schacter (1992) asserts that many traditional memory tasks can be assessed using a neuroscience perspective. He argues that what researchers need to do to extend their work is to study traditional memory tasks within another domain—for example, to present words visually and test them auditorially or to present words to one hemisphere and test them from the other. This approach, according to Schacter, is proving fruitful but is still in its infancy.

Consolidation: [kon-SOL-ih-DAY-shun] The evolution of a temporary neural circuit into a more permanent circuit.

Location of Memory in the Brain: A General History

Where exactly is memory located? The search for memory—that is, the memory trace—is long-standing. Early researchers, such as Penfield (1958), looked for a single place in the brain; later researchers discovered that memory resides in many areas. Some areas might involve every type of memory; others might be used for only one type of memory, such as visual or auditory memory. In addition, because of the many steps and the many sensorimotor features involved, procedural (perceptual, motor, and cognitive) information is probably stored in many more locations than is declarative (factual) information. For example, when you load a videocassette into your VCR, you must coordinate your eye and hand to insert the cassette; and you probably listen and feel (kinesthesis) to sense when the cassette has been inserted far enough. This relatively simple procedure thus requires a great number of neural connections.

Milner (1966) reported the case of a brain-damaged adult whose short-term memory was intact but who was unable to form new long-term memories. As long as the subject was able to rehearse information and keep it in short-term memory, his recall performance was normal. However, as soon as he could no longer rehearse and had to use long-term memory, his recall was poor. Milner's data provide neurological support for a distinction between short- and long-term memory. They also focus researchers' attention on the action of specific brain centers and cells and on how cells might change through time and experience.

Researchers have also sought to determine if memory traces are localized or distributed throughout the brain. For example, Thompson (1991) asserts that the hippocampus, which has long been known to be an important brain structure for memory, plays an important role for certain kinds of memory. But other structures, including the cerebellum, are also important (see Kim & Fanselow, 1992; Akshoomoff & Courchesne, 1992). Further, Thompson asserts that procedural memories may be relatively localized but declarative memories are more widely distributed. Such ideas are a long way from being resolved with data from human beings.

Until recently, psychologists concentrated on how cells and synapses changed in response to environmental changes, such as deprivation of sound or light. Now, however, researchers use a variety of techniques to investigate the physiological basis of memory (Zola-Morgan, Squire, & Mishkin 1982). For example, McGaugh (1990) contends that *hormones* (chemicals in the bloodstream) may affect the way in which memories are stored. He points out that newly established memories are particularly sensitive to chemical and electrical stimulation of the brain. Other researchers are attempting to arrange computer models of the neural networks of the brain (often parallel distributed processing models). Their attempts are fascinating but often limited in scope to related groups of brain cells (Sejnowski, Koch, & Churchland, 1988). Also, such work doesn't explain many kinds of learning and memory phenomena, such as state-dependent learning, memory for remote events, or extraordinary memory. The theories that follow from such research help explain a limited range of psychological information about memory (Watkins, 1990).

Where Does Memory Reside? The Penfield Studies

Early researchers tried in vain to determine exactly where memory resides in the brain. They hoped to find the location of the memory trace (sometimes called the engram). Although the goal was not achieved, the research took some important and fascinating turns. Wilder Penfield, a surgeon, was one of the principal players in the memory trace hunt.

During brain surgery on patients suffering from epilepsy, Penfield and his colleagues were able to explore the cortex with electrodes. The electrodes were used to stimulate specific cortical neurons. The patients received only local anesthetic, because the brain contains no pain receptors; and they were therefore conscious during surgery. When Penfield stimulated the temporal lobe cortex (on either the left or the right side), patients reported seeing images—coherent perceptions of experiences. They also reported visual and auditory perceptions that included speech and music. Familiar and unfamiliar experiences were often intermixed with unrealistic and even strange circumstances (Penfield, 1958; Penfield & Jasper, 1954; Penfield & Mathieson, 1974; Penfield & Milner, 1958; Penfield & Perot, 1963).

Penfield interpreted these reports as true perceptions of past events. His patients were reporting memories elicited by the stimulation (Squire, 1987). Penfield concluded that temporal lobe stimulation triggered the memory retrievals. The concept that specific brain locations stored specific memories that could be accessed through stimulation was revolutionary.

The initial excitement over Penfield's claim soon dissipated, however. Penfield's patients may not have been retrieving memories at all. Even Penfield acknowledged that the reported memories were dreamlike. Experiences were said to seem familiar but were not necessarily specific past occurrences. Further, stimulation of different brain sites often brought about the same perception. In addition, removal of specific sites (because of the surgery) failed to destroy the memory for the experience (Squire, 1987).

More recent research using similar techniques has shown that patients report mental images when the brain is stimulated with small electrical charges, and they are more likely to report these images with greater stimulation or repeated stimulation. However, when the same site is stimulated repeatedly, different mental images are reported! No consistent mental image has been associated with specific anatomical locations (see Halgren et al., 1978). One study found that reports of visual effects occurred only when stimulation of the cortex was great enough to spread to visual areas of the brain (Gloor et al., 1982). Perceptual experiences seemed to be reported only when structures deep within the brain, in the limbic system, were also stimulated. (Remember that Penfield searched only through the temporal cortex.)

Penfield's conclusion that the temporal lobe holds the memory trace has been contested for several reasons. First, destruction of tissue at these locations did not destroy the memory. Second, nearly half the reported visual images occurred when stimulation spread from the cortex to other areas of the brain. Third, structures in other parts of the brain, especially the limbic system, seem to be involved in producing mental images.

Nonetheless, Penfield's work was a landmark. It gave impetus to additional speculation, research, controversy, and excitement. However, subsequent work showed that many brain areas other than the cortex are involved in memory, especially the limbic system. No single area holds the memory trace. As is often the case with scientific research, although Penfield's conclusions were wrong, his work was significant.

FOCUS

► Explain how consolidation plays a role in the development of the brains of animals, and discuss the implications for human beings.   p. 235

► What initial evidence led Penfield to hypothesize that the location of memory could be found?   pp. 236–237

► What was Penfield's conclusion about the location of memory? Was he correct?   pp. 236–237

Concluding Note

Educational (or instructional) psychologists focus their attention on instruction and academic learning and know a lot about what it takes for a person to learn in school. Three characteristics that they stress for effective studying and memory are the following:

▶ Be actively involved in the learning and memory process.

▶ Make new information meaningful by linking your existing life experiences and knowledge (what you already know) to new information (what you are learning for the first time).

▶ Take responsibility for your own learning.

These characteristics are important to memory for several reasons. The first characteristic, *active learning* or *active participation,* means that you interact with new information so that it becomes alive and challenging. Instead of passively yawning over lifeless facts that refuse to stay in your mind even long enough for you to pass a test, you make the facts appear to be alive and important by wrestling and dancing with them and really getting to know them. By simply using your own thoughts, asking and answering your own questions, and organizing information in ways that make sense to you, you become an active learner. When you are an active learner, the facts become more than facts—they become mean-

ingful and stay with you. This suggests the second characteristic of effective learning.

To *generate personal meaning* out of new material (so it becomes relevant to your life and needs), you must find ways to connect yourself, your knowledge, and your life experiences to the material you are studying. People have a natural tendency to do this. But by knowing that learning and memory are enhanced when you create personal meaning, you will be more likely in the future to do it intentionally. When you can relate new information to your own life by connecting it to your past or present, to problems you need to solve, or to events in the world, you make it important; and you are much more likely to understand it, remember it, and use it.

The third characteristic of effective study and memory is *taking responsibility.* No one can do your learning for you. You do not learn much just by being present in class and skimming over printed words on a page. To learn and remember means to change, and to change, you must experience things for yourself. Teachers (and textbooks) can present ideas and try to make them interesting; but only you can learn those ideas for yourself, and only you can make them meaningful to your life. For this reason, it is important to take responsibility not only for how you go about learning and remembering but also for how you will shape and mold the ideas presented to you.

Summary & Review

Approaches to Memory

What is memory?

Memory is the ability to remember past events or previously learned information or skills; it also refers to the storage system that allows retention and retrieval of information. pp. 204–208

What is the information-processing approach and what are the three processes it describes?

The *information-processing approach* assumes that each stage of learning and memory is separate, although related, and analyzable by scientific methods. *Encoding* involves organizing information so that the nervous system can process it. *Storage* is the process of maintaining information in memory for a few seconds or for many years. *Retrieval* is the process by which stored information is recovered from memory. p. 206–208

KEY TERMS: *memory*, p. 204; *encoding*, p. 206; *storage*, p. 206; *retrieval*, p. 206.

Sensory Memory

What is sensory memory?

Sensory memory is the mechanism that performs initial encoding and brief storage from which human beings can retrieve information. The visual sensory memory is sometimes called the *icon*, and the storage mechanism is *iconic storage*. The storage mechanism for the auditory system is *echoic storage*. Once information is established in sensory memory, it must be transferred elsewhere for additional encoding or it will be lost. pp. 208–209

KEY TERM: *sensory memory*, p. 208.

Short-Term Memory

What is short-term memory?

Short-term memory is the memory storage system that temporarily holds current or recently acquired information for immediate or short-term use. The duration of information maintained in it is about 30 seconds and its capacity is limited to approximately nine to five items. In short-term memory, active processing takes place, including rehearsal and the transfer to long-term memory. p. 210

What is a person's memory span?

The brief and limited number of items that can be reproduced easily after presentation is called the *memory span*. The immediate memory span usually contains a single *chunk*—a manageable and meaningful unit of information. p. 211

What is rehearsal in short-term memory?

Rehearsal is the process of repeatedly verbalizing, thinking about, or otherwise acting on information to be remembered. *Maintenance rehearsal* is the repetitive review of information with little or no interpretation; this shallow form of rehearsal involves the physical stimulus, not its underlying meaning. *Elaborative rehearsal* involves repetition in which the stimulus may be associated with other events and be further processed; this type of rehearsal is more typical in long-term memory than in short-term memory. pp. 211–212

What is working memory?

Working memory is a new and broader conception of short-term memory that focuses on the central capacities of memory. Working memory is seen as a scratchpad, a holding place for information while other information is being analyzed and directed for further processing; this allows for more than one type of information to be processed simultaneously. pp. 212–213

KEY TERMS: *short-term memory*, p. 210; *rehearsal*, p. 210; *memory span*, p. 211; *chunks*, p. 211; *maintenance rehearsal*, p. 212; *elaborative rehearsal*, p. 212; *working memory*, p. 212.

Long-Term Memory

What is long-term memory?

Long-term memory is the memory storage system that keeps a relatively permanent record of information. It is divided into two types: procedural and declarative. *Procedural memory* is memory for the perceptual, motor, and cognitive skills necessary to complete a task; *declarative memory* is memory for specific facts. Declarative memory is further subdivided into *episodic memory*, memory for specific events, objects, and situations, and *semantic memory*, memory for ideas, rules, and general concepts about the world. pp. 214–216

What are primacy and recency effects in memory?

A *primacy effect* refers to the more accurate recall items presented first; a *recency effect* refers to the tendency to more accurately recall items presented last. pp. 218–219

continued

Summary & Review

What is imagery?

Imagery is a cognitive process in which a mental picture is created of a sensory event. People's imagery systems can be activated by visual, auditory, or olfactory stimuli. Even a lack of sensory stimulation can produce vivid imagery. This imagery can be measured; one researcher using a mental walk technique found a limited image space.   pp. 220–222

What are the findings of studies of state-dependent learning?

State-dependent learning is the tendency to recall information learned in a particular physiological state, such as being inebriated, most accurately when one is again in that physiological state.   p. 223

KEY TERMS: *long-term memory,* p. 214; *procedural memory,* p. 214; *declarative memory,* p. 215; *episodic memory,* p. 215; *semantic memory,* p. 216; *primacy effect,* p. 218; *recency effect,* p. 218; *imagery,* p. 220; *state-dependent learning,* p. 223.

Forgetting—The Loss of Memory

What are recall, recognition, and reconstructive memory?

Recall is remembering the details of a situation or idea and placing them together in a meaningful framework (usually without any cues or aids). *Recognition* is remembering whether one has seen a stimulus before—whether the stimulus is familiar. *Reconstructive memory* focuses on the constructive nature of the memory process and how people develop a *schema*—a conceptual framework that organizes information and makes sense of the world.   pp. 224–229

Why is information lost from short-term memory?

According to *interference theory,* the limited capacity of short-term memory makes it susceptible to interference or confusion. *Proactive interference* is the decrease in accurate recall as a result of previous presentation of material. *Retroactive interference* is the decrease in accurate recall as a result of subsequent presentation of material to be learned. pp. 229–230

What are two types of amnesia?

Amnesia is the inability to remember events from the past, usually because of physiological trauma (such as a blow to the head). *Retrograde amnesia* is the inability to remember events that preceded a traumatizing event; *anterograde amnesia* is the inability to remember events that occur after an injury or brain damage. pp. 231–232

KEY TERMS: *schema,* p. 228; *decay,* p. 229; *interference,* p. 229; *proactive interference,* p. 230; *retroactive interference,* p. 230; *amnesia,* p. 231; *retrograde amnesia,* p. 231; *anterograde amnesia,* p. 231.

The Physiology of Memory

What is consolidation in studies of memory?

Consolidation is the evolution of a temporary neural circuit into a more permanent circuit. If a neuron is stimulated, the biochemical processes involved make it more likely to respond later compared to nonstimulated neurons; further, the number of dendrites in the neuron increases because of previous stimulation. pp. 234–235

Can stimulation of the cortex generate recall from memory?

When Penfield stimulated the temporal lobe cortex, patients reported seeing images—coherent perceptions of experiences. More recent research shows, however, that no consistent mental images are associated with specific anatomical locations. Further research has proven that no single area holds the memory trace. pp. 234–235

KEY TERMS: *consolidation,* p. 235.

CONNECTIONS

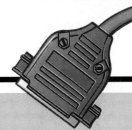

If you are interested in...

The role of memory in everyday life, see ...

CHAPTER 3, pp. 98–100

How Gestalt psychologists developed theories of perception based on past experiences.

CHAPTER 4, p. 150

The effects of drug use on long-term memory. ▼

CHAPTER 12, pp. 427, 429

How personality theorists such as Freud suggested that everyday memories are buried deep within the unconscious.

Forgetting, see ...

CHAPTER 9, pp. 340–341 ▶

How Alzheimer's disease has such a profound effect on people's ability to remember past events.

CHAPTER 15, pp. 540–543

Why certain personality approaches to treatment rely on the ability to recall events that were forgotten and perhaps dismissed to the unconscious.

The biological basis of memory, see ...

CHAPTER 2, p. 60

How psychobiologists study the biochemical bases of behavior, including memory, to understand the role of biology in memory.

CHAPTER 10, pp. 379–382

How theories of emotion depend, in part, on a person's memory for past events and the subsequent interpretation of new events. ▶

CHAPTER 15, pp. 564–565

How electroconvulsive shock therapy, used to treat people who have been seriously depressed, wipes out many past memories.

7

Cognitive Psychology

George Koltanowski was a master chess player in the 1950s. He once played 50 opponents at once while blindfolded—with a limit of 10 seconds per move—and won 43 of the games. He was never permitted to view the board, the pieces, or the opponent, but rather was told his opponent's moves by a third person. This amazing ability is a testament to his extraordinary memory.

Chess was one of the first games that human beings played against a computer. It was a logical choice: Chess has a finite number of rules, there is a clear playing field (the chessboard), the game is extremely complex (so the computer doesn't always win), and the rules are rational. Human beings often lose to computers. When I play computer chess, I usually lose, even at low difficulty levels.

Nevertheless, through playing computer chess and studying the computer's responses, I have learned a great deal. One thing I have learned is that I usually have not looked at all the alternatives before making a move. My computerized chess game allows me to see first-, second-, and third-choice moves. This allows me to trace the logic of the computer program—which is exactly what psychologists attempt to do when they study thought, reasoning, and language. They try to "see" inside the human brain by devising tasks that will reveal human logic and reasoning. They try to map human strategies and listen to human speech with the aim of getting a glimpse inside the mind.

Thought and language are separate but closely related concepts. Thoughts are usually expressed in language. Language gives human beings a unique vehicle for planning for the future and analyzing the past. This chapter covers cognition (thought)—especially that related to learning, perceiving, remembering, and using information—and language (the symbolic system people use to communicate their thoughts verbally).

Cognitive Psychology: An Overview

How are a tiger and a domestic cat similar? Who is the U.S. Secretary of State? How do you make an omelet? Answering each of these questions requires a different mental procedure. To answer the first question, you probably drew mental images of both felines and then compared the images. In answering the second question, you may simply have known the right name or called forth a list of cabinet members and chosen from the list. The third question may have required you to mentally walk through the procedure of preparing an omelet and describe each step out loud. The thinking you used to answer all the questions required the use of knowledge, language, and images.

Cognitive psychology is the study of the overlapping fields of learning, memory, perception, and thought with a special focus on encoding, analysis, recall, reconstruction, elaboration, and memory. The word *cognition* means "to know"; cognitive psychologists are interested primarily in mental processes that influence our acquisition and use of knowledge as well as our ability to reason. *Reasoning* is the process by which we generate and evaluate situations and reach conclusions. Thus, it is an intimate part of cognitive psychology. Cognitive psychologists study thinking; cognitive researchers assume that mental processes exist, that we are active processors, and that we can study cognitive processes through time and accuracy measures (Ashcraft, 1989).

Cognitive psychology has had a roller coaster history, which began in the late 1800s. As we saw in chapter 1, at the dawn of the study of psychology, the main areas of study were mental processes, thought, and the internal working of the mind. In the 1920s, behaviorism became mainstream psychology, and there was little reference to cognitive processes. Discussion and research of such "mentalistic" topics were avoided. Then, in the 1960s, with the introduction of high-

Cognitive psychology: The study of the overlapping fields of learning, memory perception, and thought that emphasizes encoding, storage, analysis, recall, reconstruction, elaboration, and memory of events.

For this little girl, buttoning her overalls is an effortful task, but eventually she will be able to do it almost automatically.

speed computers, the brain began to be compared to a computer; and research in thought began again. Researchers now examine such questions as: How do we read? How do we know that a robin has wings? Today, cognitive psychology is a dominant force in psychological study; it affects the way psychologists study language, thought, problem solving, and maladjustment.

Cognitive researchers are interested in controlled versus automatic processes. *Controlled processes* require a great deal of effort and attention; *automatic processes* take little effort and happen without conscious awareness—although certain physiological changes accompany both processes (Strayer & Kramer, 1990). Most complex tasks begin as controlled processes; after hundreds of repetitions, they become automatic and easy, requiring little or no attention. Contemporary cognitive psychologists want to find out how once-difficult tasks such as reading, driving a car, and word processing become automatic.

Closely associated with controlled and automatic processes is the role of *attention*. Limited mental resources must be divided up so memory can be utilized efficiently. Once something is stored in memory, cognitive researchers want to know how we make inferences from our knowledge and how we *represent knowledge*. Even the monitoring of our own awareness, a process called *metacognition*, has become a focus for cognitive researchers.

This chapter concentrates on a series of cognitive topics that show the breadth of cognitive psychology—the diversity of thought processes being examined and the subjects emerging in the 1990s. We begin with the study of concept formation, which is crucial for decision making.

Concept Formation

Each day, people make decisions, solve problems, and behave logically; the steps in decision making and problem solving are complicated but orderly. The reasoning process itself is conceived of by many researchers as an orderly process taking place in discrete steps, with one set of ideas leading to another (Rips, 1990). To follow this process, we need to understand complex forms of reasoning—to recognize that every decision involves our ability to form, manipulate, transform, and relate concepts. **Concepts** are the mental categories we use to classify events and objects with respect to common properties. The study of *concept formation* is the examination of the way people organize and classify events and objects, usually in order to solve problems. How do you plan a winning strategy in a game of chess? How do you decide whether you are for or against the death penalty?

By helping people organize their thinking, concepts make events in the world more meaningful. People develop progressively more complex concepts throughout life. Infants learn the difference between parents and strangers very early. Within a year, they can discriminate among objects, colors, and people; and they comprehend such simple concepts as animals and flowers. By age 2 they can verbalize these differences.

Much of what we teach young children involves classification, because this is the key to organizing and understanding our complex world (see Figure 7.1 on page 246). Think back to your early school years and to television shows such as "Sesame Street." You were taught to classify the range of colors; farm animals (and their sounds); shapes such as triangles, circles, and squares; and the letters in the alphabet. You learned to organize the people in your house—mother, father, sister, brother—into a group called a *family*. The process of concept formation is lifelong and always changing. It involves separating dissimilar events and finding

Concepts: Classifications of objects or ideas that distinguish them from others on the basis of some common properties or features.

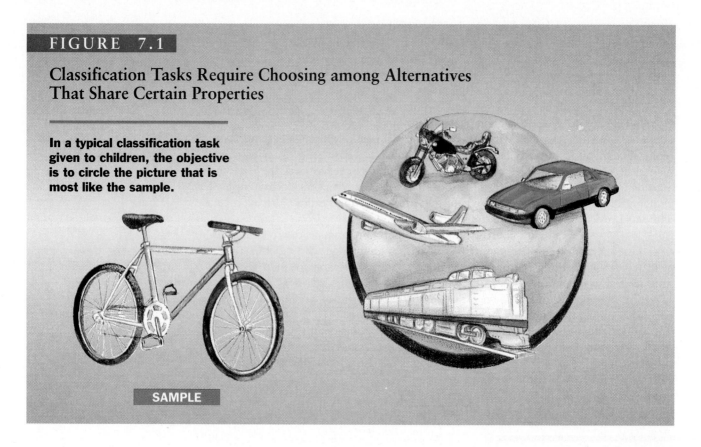

FIGURE 7.1

Classification Tasks Require Choosing among Alternatives That Share Certain Properties

In a typical classification task given to children, the objective is to circle the picture that is most like the sample.

SAMPLE

commonalities (Medin, 1989). But what is the best way to study the processes by which children and adults classify and organize information?

Studying Concept Formation

To study concept formation in a carefully controlled environment, psychologists design laboratory studies in which the subject's objective is to form a concept using a wide range of tasks. Suppose you were the subject in a laboratory experiment. You might be asked to make judgments such as: Is a bicycle a toy or a vehicle? Is aqua more blue or more green?

Here is a common task used in laboratory investigations of concept formation: An experimenter presents you with objects (stimuli) of different shapes, sizes, and colors and tells you that something about the objects makes them similar. You are asked to identify this characteristic. Each time the researcher presents a stimulus, you ask whether it has the property (characteristic) being targeted; and the experimenter answers yes or no. Suppose, for example, the first stimulus is a large red triangle. The experimenter tells you that it is a **positive instance** (a stimulus that is an example of the concept under study). You now know that the concept may be largeness, redness, or triangularity. The second stimulus is a small red triangle; the experimenter says that this too is a positive instance. You now know that size is not important. The third stimulus is a large blue triangle; it too is a positive instance. You surmise that the relevant property is triangularity. When, on the fourth trial, the stimulus is a large blue circle and the experimenter says it is a **negative instance** (a stimulus that is not an example of the concept), you can say with conviction that triangularity is the concept. (See Figure 7.2.)

There are two broad variations in the procedure for studying concept forma-

Positive instance: A stimulus that is an example of the concept under study.

Negative instance: A stimulus that is not an example of the concept under study.

tion: the reception method and the selection method. In the *reception method,* the researcher presents subjects with a series of instances—the task being to classify each as a positive or negative instance. Subjects are told after each trial whether their response was correct. For example, a researcher might show a subject 30 objects, 1 at a time. After 10 or 20 correct responses, the researcher can be certain that the subject has learned the concept.

In the *selection method,* the researcher presents all the possible instances at once (see Figure 7.3). Usually, the experimenter designates one of the stimuli (instances) as a positive instance at the outset. After guessing what the concept is, the subject chooses a second stimulus and asks whether it is a positive instance. After learning whether the second is positive or negative, the subject picks a third, a fourth, and a fifth instance. This less-structured procedure allows the experimenter to examine the hypotheses or strategies that a subject uses in forming a concept.

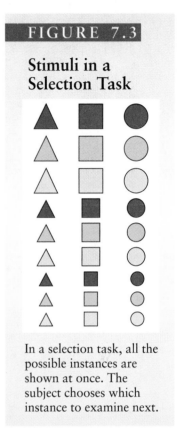

FIGURE 7.2

Stimuli in a Concept-Formation Task

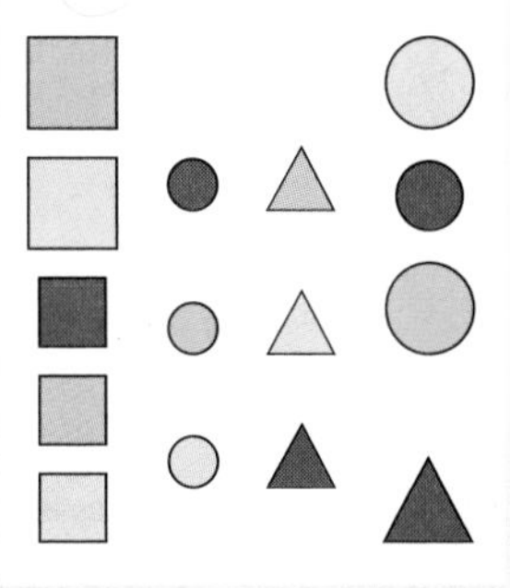

In a concept-formation task, the subject is asked to classify objects of various shapes, sizes, and colors.

FIGURE 7.3

Stimuli in a Selection Task

In a selection task, all the possible instances are shown at once. The subject chooses which instance to examine next.

Concept Formation Theories

As in other areas of psychology, theory has guided research. Over the past 50 years, theories of concept formation have changed substantially—from mediation theory to hypothesis-testing theory.

Mediation Theory. Can people form concepts about situations without much effort, simply by absorbing new ideas? If so, then concept formation is merely the association of certain stimuli and responses. According to **mediation theory,** people discover relations between previously unconnected things; they use bridging thought processes to connect a stimulus (for example, a German shepherd) to a concept response (a dog). Mediation theory thus suggests that a link exists between specific instances of a category and the general category. This theory was very popular in the 1950s and 1960s, but it has been replaced by the more sophisticated hypothesis-testing theory.

Hypothesis-Testing Theory. The hypothesis-testing theory views concept formation as an active process. It assumes that people acquire new information by generating hypotheses about stimuli, testing those hypotheses, discarding old hypotheses if necessary, and making an inference about the stimuli.

Levine (1975) identified three hypothesis-testing strategies in adults: hypothesis checking, dimension checking, and global focusing. In *hypothesis checking,* an unsophisticated strategy that resembles gambling, subjects test one hypothesis at a time. In *dimension checking,* subjects test a hypothesis about a single dimension or feature. In *global focusing,* the most consistently efficient strategy, subjects keep all possible hypotheses in mind but focus on one at a time, ruling out alternatives as they are given feedback. To be an efficient global focuser, a person has to be actively involved in seeking solutions and in forming concepts.

Another type of hypothesis-testing strategy, but not necessarily the most efficient, is **conservative focusing**—the successive elimination of possible solutions. It works

Mediation theory: The theory that people can create or discover a connection between previously unconnected things.

Conservative focusing: A hypothesis-testing strategy that involves the elimination of alternative possibilities from a narrow range of options.

FOCUS

► Identify three key assumptions that cognitive psychologists make about thought.   pp. 244–245

► Distinguish between a positive and a negative instance in concept formation. How might a researcher use them to trace thought processes?   pp. 246–247

► In concept formation, what is the fundamental difference between mediation theory and hypothesis-testing theory? pp. 247–248

for a limited range of concepts. If you are asked to determine which of many dimensions is the relevant one from a visual stimulus, you might try to determine if the relevant dimension has angles in it rather than curves; after this determination, you might try to eliminate another possibility—on each trial you try to eliminate as many dimensions as possible. By narrowing choices in this way, you can determine the relevant dimension or concept most efficiently. Of course, this entire process is part of reasoning and decision making, the topic we'll consider next.

Reasoning and Decision Making

We are generally unaware of our cognitive processes; we don't usually think about thinking. And yet we are thinking all the time—sorting through choices, deciding where to go, what to do, and when to do it. In general, *thinking* refers to reasoning, decision making, and problem solving (Galotti, 1989). As we saw earlier, **reasoning** is the process by which we generate and evaluate situations and reach conclusions. The procedure we use to reach a valid conclusion is **logic.** We can think about reasoning and logic as proceeding in an ordered way. Alternatively, we can think of reasoning and logic as a process in which ideas and beliefs are continuously updated in a loose, unstructured way (Rips, 1990).

To help us understand reasoning, researchers have focused on the tasks involved in decision making. **Decision making** is the assessment of and choosing among alternatives. We make decisions that involve the probability of some event occurring (will my friends want to go on this trip with me?) and those that involve expected value (how important is *this* trip, rather than some other one?). Our decisions vary from the trivial to the complex: what to eat for breakfast, which courses to take in a semester, and what career to pursue. The trivial decisions are usually made quickly, without much effort, and usually unconsciously. The complicated ones require conscious, deliberate thought and effort. Sometimes, our reasoning, thought, and decision making are logical. But at other times, we are not sure how things will work out or whether our reasoning is valid.

Psychologists have devised many approaches for looking at the thought processes of individuals. We examine three: (1) formal reasoning, or syllogisms—situations for which there is a single correct answer; (2) logical decision making; and (3) situations in which the answer or decision is less certain and which therefore involve estimating probabilities.

Syllogisms: Formal Reasoning

One of the traditional ways to study thinking, reasoning, and decision-making processes is to provide subjects with deduction tasks such as syllogisms. A *syllogism* is a sequence of statements, or premises (usually two), followed by a conclusion. The task is to decide (deduce) whether the conclusion is warranted. The assumption in logic is that the *premises* are true.

By asking subjects to describe their thinking and decision-making processes

Reasoning: The process by which we generate and evaluate situations and reach conclusions.

Logic: The procedure we use to reach a valid conclusion.

Decision making: The assessment of and choosing among alternatives.

while they contemplate syllogisms, a psychologist can trace people's cognitive processes. The psychologist can analyze each decision in the process and thus follow the subject's thoughts. People are not especially good at solving abstract syllogisms; more concrete ones are easier to follow. Consider the following syllogism.

> Premise 1: All poodles are dogs.
>
> Premise 2: All dogs are animals.
>
> Conclusion: All poodles are animals.

Is the conclusion a logical statement? Do the two premises allow you to conclude that poodles are animals? In the preceding example, it is easy to see that the conclusion is accurate. Because logic assumes that the premises are true, you can devise a syllogism where the conclusion validly follows from the premises but is really false—because the premises are false. For example, if you changed Premise 1 to "all flowers are dogs," you could logically come to the valid (but false) conclusion that "all flowers are animals."

You can learn how to use logic and how to be a better critical thinker and decision maker. One way is to be skeptical about the premises on which the conclusion is based. A second way is to systematically evaluate premises for truth. A third way is to think the way a detective does, using logical decision-making skills to eliminate the possibilities one by one.

Logical Decision Making

When making a decision, we are often faced with outcomes that have positive and negative attributes. On the simplest level, we need to add up the positive attributes of the alternatives and then make a decision. For example, when I buy a bicycle, I have to consider its cost, weight, appearance, intended use, and safety, as well as my preference for a specific brand. I must weigh the relative importance of each of these factors to me. If you were buying the bicycle, you might consider different factors, and you would give each one a different weight in terms of its importance to you.

A decision-making approach in which some factors take on more importance than others is called a *compensatory model*. In the bicycle example, you might do the following:

1. Assign a relative importance to each of the several factors you have chosen (weight, cost, and appearance, for example).
2. Evaluate the factors of each bicycle you have been considering.
3. Determine which bicycle has the greatest overall positive score, according to your assessment.

A problem with compensatory models is that a good value on one attribute sometimes cannot compensate for a poor value on another (Payne, Bettman, & Johnson, 1992). Accordingly, another approach to decision making involves ruling out alternatives that do not meet minimum criteria. For example, if you are interested in purchasing a mountain bike, you need not consider a high-performance racing bike. If you cannot spend more than $250 for the bicycle, you can rule out all the higher-priced models. This approach, called *elimination by aspects,* is generally a fast and efficient way to make decisions. It is logical, and it helps people reduce the uncertainties about a pending decision.

Uncertainty: Estimating Probabilities

How do we decide what to wear, where to go, or how to answer a question on the SAT? How do we decide when something is bigger, longer, or more difficult? Many

Sexist Language Affects Our Thoughts

When the pilot episode for "Star Trek: The Next Generation" aired in 1987, thousands of faithful viewers of the old "Star Trek" were surprised to hear Captain Jean-Luc Picard announce the mission of the Enterprise: "To boldly go where no one has gone before." Captain James T. Kirk, of the original series, had always said: "To boldly go where no *man* has gone before."

Over the last three decades, psychologists have become particularly aware of the role of language in shaping people's conceptual structures and problem-solving abilities. If you have a concept that all nurses are women, then when a man walks into your hospital room wearing a white lab coat, you assume he is a doctor. Your concept of who fights fires—firemen—is likely to include the idea that only men fight fires. In general, we know that the English language has evolved in such a way that words define every role as male, except for roles that tradition-

ally have been played by women (nurses, teachers) (Bem, 1993). Walk down any street where work is being done on sidewalks or telephone poles and you are likely to see the warning sign: Men Working. Today, you are as likely to see women climbing telephone poles as you are men. However, the sign still reads: *Men Working.*

Our concepts of the world first form in childhood, as we hear stories from parents and teachers. They tell us of pioneers who traveled to the West with their wives, children, and farm animals. We know from fairy tales that it is the king who rules the castle. Children and adults learn that the law was written so as to be acceptable to a reasonable man (lawyers even call it the *reasonable man standard*). Language with a sexist bias expresses stereotypes and expectations about men and women. Thus, a *virile* person is usually a man; and masculine traits are usually positive (for example, *successful, strong, independent,* and *courageous*). Women have traditionally been de-

scribed as *soft, sexy,* and *passive.* When strong or courageous words are applied to women, it is often in the context of incongruity—for example, "She thinks like a man."

That women are thought of as sexy and men as successful or that women are thought of as weak and men as strong is important to psychologists who study concept formation, problem solving, and language—the main topics of this chapter—because such concepts set an attitude and approach on the part of men and women to a whole range of behaviors. Bem (1993) asserts that we perceive the world from a male point of view and assume that this is the preferred value system. Men in business have been assumed to be task-oriented and problem solvers. Women, by contrast, have been assumed to be people-oriented rather than problem-oriented. There exist men and women who fit such stereotypes; this is not surprising since they were raised in environments where the stereotypes were nurtured.

Research supports the idea that men and women are perceived and

decisions are based on formal logic, some on carefully tested hypotheses, and some on educated guesses. Making an educated guess implies being educated (knowing something) on the basis of past experiences. When you see rainclouds, for example, you guess—but you cannot be 100 percent sure—it will rain. The likelihood of rain is expressed as a percentage—that is, as a probability.

Psychological factors, especially previous events, affect how people estimate probabilities. Consider a study by Tversky and Kahneman (1973). Subjects were given the names of 40 famous people—20 men and 20 women. In one case, the subjects read a list in which the men were more famous than the women; in another, the subjects read a list in which the women were more famous than the men. After reading their respective lists, the subjects were asked if the list contained more names of men or more names of women. The subjects who read the list with more famous men said there were more men on the list; those who read the list with more famous women said there were more women on the list. The critical variable affecting the results was the subjects' familiarity with the names of the famous people. In other words, the fact that one gender on the list was more famous affected the subjects' perceptions.

People make probability estimates of all types of behaviors and events. In elec-

treated differently. Frable (1989) found that if people believe in gender-specific abilities, they are likely to use that belief in making decisions. Frable found that people with strong gender-typed ideas were especially likely to pay attention to the gender of a job applicant and then to devalue the interview performance of women. McDonaugh (1992) found that interviewers not only devalue the résumés of women in general but devalue even more the résumés of women who are African American or who are not beautiful. Thus, gender stereotyping is complicated by racial and physical stereotyping.

While stereotypes continue to exist in the 1990s—especially with television reruns reinforcing them—women and men are becoming increasingly androgynous and are recognizing their insensitivities (Hale et al., 1990). (*Androgyny* is the state of possessing both male and female characteristics.) Today, people are more open to those who express androgynous characteristics—for example, men who cook and women who are engineers. Even more im-

portantly, people are becoming more sensitive to how language shapes their concept of the world and their problem-solving abilities. McMinn and colleagues (1990) found that those who used gender-neutral lan-

---

The term fireman *has given way to the gender-neutral term* firefighter *as more women have entered the field.*

guage in writing were also likely to use gender-neutral language in conversation; however, he also found that it is difficult to change the use of sexist language (McMinn et al., 1991). Further, avoiding sexist language is just a beginning; sexism and the behavior that follows from it are deeply embedded in our thoughts and actions.

But Western culture has made progress. No longer are we interested in having only men fix telephones and only women be telephone operators; today, we encourage women and men to be everything they might be, without regard to gender. Astronauts are both men and women. If Neil Armstrong, referred to in chapter 6, had made his famous "One small step for a man" speech today, he would have been likely to say, "One small step for an individual." Despite some lingering sexism, today boys *and* girls in primary school grades are more likely to be encouraged to solve problems creatively, to approach science and math problems with excitement, and to be caring, warm human beings.

---

tion years, we guess about the likelihood of a Democratic or a Republican victory. On the basis of our past experience, we estimate the probability of staying on a study schedule, an exercise regime, or a diet. We can judge that a particular event increases or decreases the probability of another event. When several factors are involved, their compounding and mitigating effects alter the probability. For example, the probability that there will be rain when there are thunderclouds, high winds, and low barometric pressure is much higher than the probability of rain when there are only a few thunderclouds.

Subjects asked to make probability judgments about the real world, particularly about fairly rare events, are more likely to fail than are subjects given laboratory problems (Swets, 1992). The further the prediction is in the future, the more ambiguity exists for the predictor; and people are likely to be affected by past behavior and make mistakes about the future (Payne, Bettman, & Johnson, 1992). People make mistakes and errors in judgment and may act irrationally. They may ignore key pieces of data and thus make bad (or irrational) decisions not based on probability. Sometimes, people's world views color their probability decision making. If a moral system, religious belief, or political view is pointed in one direction (for example, Christianity versus Buddhism or capitalism versus communism), a person's strategies and decision esti-

FOCUS

▶ What are the advantages of using syllogisms in research? pp. 248–249

▶ What is the fundamental difference between a compensatory model and one based on elimination by aspects? p. 249

▶ What evidence exists to support the idea that people are often not good at estimating the probability of events in the world?   pp. 249–252

mates will be influenced. The Diversity box on page 250 examines how language (semantics) can influence thought. Finally, people are not machines or computers; their creativity, past experiences, and humanness affect results, sometimes in unpredictable ways. However, cognitive psychologists suggest ways for people to become the most efficient learners and thinkers they can be, and they have found that people can be taught to better weigh costs and benefits and be less influenced by their past frames of reference (Larrick, Morgan, & Nisbett, 1990; Payne, Bettman, & Johnson, 1992).

Problem Solving

How do you study for your psychology exam when you have an English paper due tomorrow? How can you arrange your minuscule closet so all of your clothes and other belongings will fit? Your car gets a flat tire; what should you do? These are problems to be solved. In important ways, they represent some of the highest levels of cognitive functioning.

Human beings are wonderful at **problem solving;** we excel at confronting a situation that requires insight or some unknown elements to be determined to deal with it. Because we can form concepts and we can group things together in logical ways, we are able to organize our thoughts and attack a problem to be solved. Psychologists believe there are four stages in problem solving (see Figure 7.4):

▶ Realizing that a problem exists.

▶ Assessing its complexity.

▶ Devising ways of solving the problem (which might include formulating a number of strategies that will lead to an insight and then actually implementing the problem-solving strategy).

▶ Assessing whether the problem-solving approach has been successful.

Huge differences exist in people's problem-solving abilities; but psychologists, with their understanding of the processes of thought and of problem solving, can help people become more effective problem solvers. Recall from chapters 1 and 3 that Gestalt psychologists analyzed the world in terms of perceptual frameworks and argued that the mind organizes the elements of experience to form something unique. As we saw in chapter 5, Wolfgang Köhler (1927), a Gestalt researcher, showed that chimps could solve problems by developing insights into methods of retrieving food that was beyond their reach. They discovered they could pile up boxes to reach food or attach poles together to make a long stick with which to grab the food. Once the insight occurred, no further instruction, investigation, or training was necessary. Insight is not essential to problem solving; but hints, cues, and prior experience all give the process of developing insight and finding essential elements an advantage in problem solving (Kaplan & Simon, 1990).

Although our problem-solving abilities are usually quite good, we may create our own limitations to problem solving. Among them are functional fixedness and psychological set, which are discussed next. Researchers study these hindrances to gain a better understanding of the processes of problem solving.

Problem solving: The behavior of individuals when confronted with a situation or task that requires some insight or some unknown elements to be ascertained to deal with it.

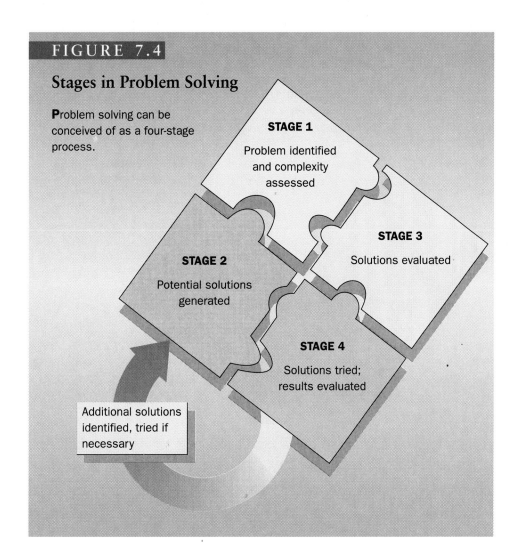

FIGURE 7.4

Stages in Problem Solving

Problem solving can be conceived of as a four-stage process.

STAGE 1

Problem identified and complexity assessed

STAGE 3

Solutions evaluated

STAGE 2

Potential solutions generated

STAGE 4

Solutions tried; results evaluated

Additional solutions identified, tried if necessary

Functional Fixedness: Cognition with Constraints

When my daughter Sarah was 4 years old, she observed me taking her raincoat out of the closet before our trip to the zoo. Sarah insisted that it was not raining outside and that raincoats are for rain. I explained that the coat could also be used as a windbreaker or a light spring jacket. Reluctantly, she put on the coat. In this exchange, Sarah exhibited a basic characteristic of most people: functional fixedness. **Functional fixedness** is the inability to see that an object can have a function other than its stated or usual one. When people are functionally fixed, they have limited their choices and conceptual framework. In many ways, this constitutes a breakdown in problem solving.

Studies of functional fixedness show that often the name given to a tool limits its function. In a typical study, a subject is presented with a task and provided tools that can be used in various ways. One laboratory problem used to show functional fixedness is the two-string problem (see Figure 7.5 on page 254). In this task, the subject is put in a room in which there are two strings hanging from the ceiling and some objects lying on a table. The task is to tie the two strings together, but it is impossible to reach one string while holding the other. The only solution is to tie a

Functional fixedness: The inability to see that an object can have a function other than the one normally associated with it.

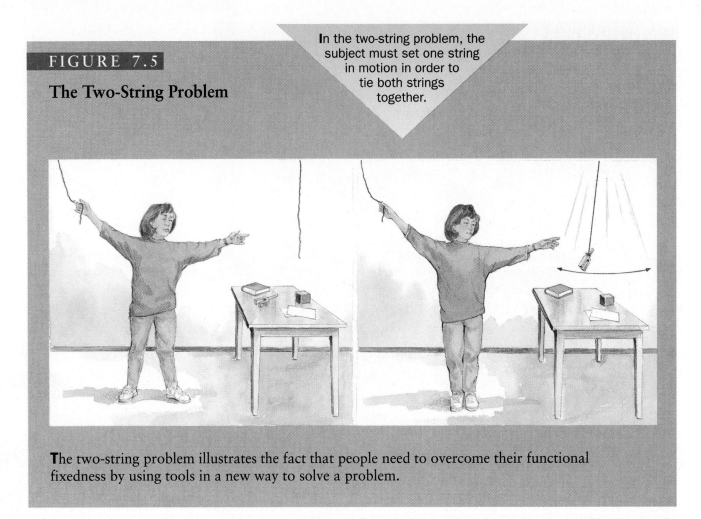

FIGURE 7.5

The Two-String Problem

In the two-string problem, the subject must set one string in motion in order to tie both strings together.

The two-string problem illustrates the fact that people need to overcome their functional fixedness by using tools in a new way to solve a problem.

weight (such as a magnet or a pair of pliers) to one string, set it swinging back and forth, take hold of the second string, and wait until the first string swings within reach. This task is difficult because people's previous experiences with an object (such as the pliers) may prevent them from considering it as a potential tool in new problem-solving situations.

Psychological Set

Psychologists have found that most individuals are flexible in their approaches to solving problems. In other words, they do not use preconceived, or "set," solutions. However, thinking about objects, people, and situations in new ways becomes especially important when we realize that people sometimes develop a rigid strategy, or approach, to certain types of problems. Avoiding a rigid approach allows a painter to work in charcoal, pastels, latex, and oils all at once. A flexible scientist will rely on existing technology, technology that needs to be developed, and even technology beyond the realm of modern science. President John F. Kennedy was able to conceive of an innovative solution to a complex problem, such as engendering a better relationship with developing countries: the Peace Corps. All of these solutions require limber thought processes.

Creative thinking requires that people break out of their *psychological set*—their limited ways of thinking about possibilities. Having a psychological set is the opposite of being creative. According to the principle underlying this problem-solving limitation, prior experience predisposes a person to make a particular

FIGURE 7.6

The Nine-Dot Problem

Try to connect all nine dots with no more than four lines running through them, and do it without lifting your pen from the paper.

Because people tend to group things in familiar ways, it is hard for them to overcome their psychological set to connect the nine dots as instructed.

response. Most of the time, this predisposition, or readiness, is useful and adaptive; for the most part, what worked in the past will work in the future. Sometimes, however, the biasing effect of a set is not productive. It limits innovation and prevents a person from solving new and complex problems (Holland, 1975). In an increasingly complex and changing world, such limitations are problematic. (The Applications box on page 256 offers suggestions for avoiding limitations and barriers to effective critical thinking.)

Here's a problem that is difficult because of a psychological set. In Figure 7.6, draw no more than four lines that will run through all nine dots—without lifting your pen from the paper. The answer is provided in Figure 7.7 on page 257.

Creative Problem Solving

The owners of a high-rise professional building were deluged with complaints that the building's elevators were too slow. The owners called in a consultant, who researched the problem and discovered that tenants often had to wait several minutes for an elevator. Putting in new, faster elevators would cost tens of thousands of dollars, more than the owners could afford. Eventually, the consultant devised a creative solution that ended the complaints but cost only a few hundred dollars: He installed wall mirrors at each elevator stop so people could look at themselves while waiting.

Creativity is the process of developing original, novel, and appropriate responses to a problem. An *original response* is a response not copied from or imitative of another response; that is, the respondent originated the idea. In this discussion, it means a response that is not usually given. A *novel response* is a response that is new or that has no precedent. Unless an original and novel solution is also appropriate, however, psychologists do not call it creative. An *appropriate response* is a response that is deemed reasonable in terms of the situation. Building your home out of soap bubbles may be an original and novel idea, but it is clearly not appropriate. A key issue in creativity is how people can become more creative in their thinking (Greeno, 1989).

You don't have to be an Einstein or a Picasso to be creative, as the building consultant demonstrated. To make sure that a creative solution is appropriate, effective problem solvers form a hypothesis and then test it to evaluate potential solutions. Creativity is simply a different way of thinking.

Creative problem solving has been effective in breaking down some of the barriers individuals with handicaps face in their daily lives.

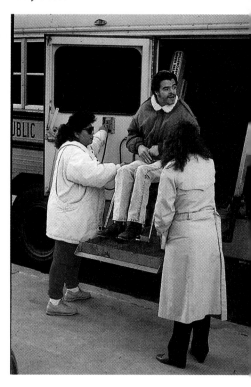

Creativity: A process of thought and problem solving, generally considered to include originality, novelty, and appropriateness.

APPLICATIONS

Be a Critical Thinker

Every day, people have to make judgments, classify ideas, follow logic, and solve complex problems. We say that they are involved in reasoning. Yet reasoning abilities vary from person to person, and some people are better at forming concepts, making decisions, or solving problems without giving the issue at hand systematic critical thought. As we saw in chapter 1, being a critical thinker means that, among other things, you have to:

► Avoid biases.
► Be evaluative.
► Avoid oversimplifications.
► Determine the relevance of facts.
► Question facts.
► Consider all arguments.

There are several other key ideas to make you especially good at critical thinking.

Don't focus on availability. Things that come to mind quickly are not necessarily the best solutions to problems. Don't necessarily choose the first answer.

Don't generalize too quickly. That most elements in a grouping follow a pattern does not mean *all* elements in the grouping will follow the pattern. For example, the fact that you have seen dozens of red roses does not mean all roses are red.

Don't stick with an easy decision. People often stick with solu-tions that work even though better solutions exist. Look at all the alter-natives.

Don't stick with a decision that fits preexisting ideas. People often accept too quickly ideas that con-form to their previously held views. This is a serious mistake for re-searchers who want to be open to new ideas.

Don't test only some of the available ideas or premises. If re-searchers do not evaluate all of the available ideas, premises, alterna-tives, or conclusions, they are likely to miss the correct, or most logical, answer.

Don't be emotional. Sometimes people become emotionally tied to a specific idea, premise, or conviction. When this happens, the likelihood that they can critically evaluate the evidence drops sharply. Critical thinkers are cool and evaluative, not headstrong and emotional.

Don't be constrained by old ideas. Committees formed to evalu-ate problems and recommend solu-tions are often composed of people with different viewpoints. After the committee members define the prob-lem, they may write down all possi-ble solutions, order them, and evalu-ate the possibilities. In doing so, they are using an effective problem-solving tool called brainstorming.

Brainstorming is a problem-solv-ing technique whereby people con-sider all possible solutions without making any initial judgments about the worth of those solutions. It can be used to illuminate alternative so-lutions to problems as diverse as how a city can dispose of its waste and how a topic for a group project can be selected. The rationale behind brainstorming is that people will pro-duce more high-quality ideas if they do not have to evaluate the sugges-tions immediately. Brainstorming at-tempts to release the potential of the participants, to free them from po-tential functional fixedness, to in-crease the diversity of ideas, and to promote creativity.

Brainstorming can be an effective problem solving process for groups in diverse settings.

Brainstorming: A technique for problem solving that involves considering all possi-ble solutions without making prior evaluative judgments.

Creativity as a Three-Stage Process. Morris Stein (1974) defined creativity as a process involving three stages: hypothesis formation, hypothesis testing, and com-munication of results. In hypothesis formation, a person tries to formulate a new response to a problem, which is not an easy task. A person must confront the situ-ation and think of it in nonstereotyped ways, exploring paths not previously explored.

Next, the hypothesis must be tested against reality. At this stage, it is crucial to apply the criterion of appropriateness. If the result is original, novel, and appropriate, the person can move toward the third stage—the communication of results. A creative idea or expression is worthless if it is not shared with other people.

When people sort through alternatives to try to solve a problem, they attempt to focus their thinking, discarding inappropriate solutions until a single appropriate option is left. To do so, they *converge* on an answer (or use convergent thinking skills). **Convergent thinking** is narrowing down choices and alternatives to arrive at a suitable answer. **Divergent thinking,** in contrast, is widening the range of possibilities and expanding the options for solutions; this lessens the likelihood of functional fixedness or psychological set.

Guilford (1967) defined creative thinking as divergent thinking. According to other psychologists, any solution to a problem that can be worked out only with time and practice is not a creative solution. To foster creativity, people need to rethink their whole approach to a task (Greeno, 1989). Successful entrepreneurs know this to be the case (McClelland, 1987); and those who develop new technologies, products, and services are often well rewarded for their creativity. Business schools are paying closer attention to developing creativity in marketing courses, and researchers are examining the roles of creativity and insight in solving problems (Kaplan & Simon, 1990).

Brain Structure and Creativity. Are some people born creative? It is not clear whether the brain is organized in some special way in highly creative individuals. Researchers have conducted electroencephalographic studies to see if there are any observable differences in the brain waves of gifted and talented people. So far, problems in clearly defining the subject population (see Young & Ellis, 1981) and the appropriate testing tasks affect the validity of the findings. Moreover, individual differences in the brain-wave patterns of normal subjects are sufficiently great that a difference in the brain-wave pattern of an especially creative or talented individual would not necessarily be significant. Also, no firm evidence exists that creative individuals are either more or less intelligent than other people. The data relating IQ scores and creativity are inconclusive. However, new research programs for enhancing creativity in adults are showing promising results (Goff, 1992). The Applications box on page 258 presents strategies for improving your problem-solving abilities.

Problem Solving and Computers

Because human beings invented computers, it is not surprising that computers handle information in much the same manner as the human brain, though the brain has far more options and strategies for information processing than a computer does. By simulating specific models of the human brain, computers help psychologists understand human thought processes. Specifically, computers help shape theoretical development (as in hypotheses about information processing and about perception), assist researchers in investigating how people solve problems, and enable psychologists to test models of certain aspects of behavior, such as memory.

Researchers who program computers to work like a human brain are designing *computer simulations.* When computer programs implement some types of human activities, they are said to involve *artificial intelligence (AI),* particularly if the programs are designed to optimize the efficiency of the activities. The researchers' task is formidable, because, as we saw in chapter 2, the brain is complex, with billions of interconnections. In chapters 3 and 6, we saw how researchers break down many perception and memory problems into small steps, using the information-processing approach.

Information Processing. The information-processing approach to perception, memory, and problem solving is a direct outgrowth of computer simulations. Flowcharts showing how information from sensory memory reaches short- and long-term

Convergent thinking: The process by which possible options are selectively narrowed until they converge (come together) into one answer.

Divergent thinking: The production of new information from known information or the generation of logical possibilities.

FIGURE 7.7

The Nine-Dot Solution

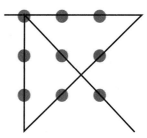

Here is a creative solution to the nine-dot problem found in Figure 7.6. Notice that you have to think beyond your normal psychological set and not see the nine dots as a square.

APPLICATIONS

Improve Your Problem-Solving Abilities

Each of us solves problems regularly; it thus makes sense that we should try to become the best problem solvers possible. Problem solving is deliberate and time-consuming and affects day-to-day decisions. Ashcraft (1989) has suggested the following ways to improve problem-solving abilities.

Increase Your Knowledge. A person with limited knowledge about a topic is far less able to solve problems than is a well-informed problem solver. Learn about bicycles if you are going to buy one. Study computer programming if you are going to program a computer.

Automate Some Tasks. Become an expert at some simple tasks involved in solving your problem. Because you have a limited attention span (see chapter 3), you should free your mental resources to solve more complex aspects of a problem by automatically solving smaller ones. In chess, have a couple of opening moves prepared; in studying, make an outline first. These tasks will then be routine and automatic.

Follow a Plan. Set a plan of action. If your problem is remembering material for an exam, use the SQ3R plus approach described in the "To the Student" section at the beginning of this book. Identify the problem,

explore alternative approaches, look at the effects, and think critically (see chapter 1, p. 32).

Effective problem solvers often map out their choices before making a decision.

Draw Inferences and Develop Subgoals. Try to draw inferences about the known facts and the possible ways to solve the problem. Then break down large problems into smaller, more manageable tasks. In planning a Thanksgiving dinner, think first about the appetizers, then about the main course, and last about the desserts.

Work Backwards. Trace a solution in reverse order, working back toward the fact that you know. In

writing a computer program, first decide what the output should look like, and then decide on the steps needed to produce that output.

Search for Contradictions and Relations. Are there possibilities that can be ruled out right away because they violate basic rules, guidelines, or assumptions? Actively consider things you already know to help you eliminate inconsistencies. This means using your existing framework of knowledge to help you solve new problems.

Reformulate the Problem and Represent it Physically. Go back to the beginning of the problem and try to restate it; rethink it in different terms. For example, if you have been thinking in terms of building with wood, think about other materials to achieve a fresh look. Draw, build, or in some way represent the problem physically—make it tangible and concrete instead of abstract and ethereal. Don't use just your brain to solve a problem. Some of the most creative solutions have been sketched out on napkins by problem solvers attempting to represent the problem in some new way.

Practice. To be good at problem solving, practice doing it. Practice makes perfect—or at least makes you better. For example, the more often you solve algebra word problems that focus on two unknowns, the better you will be at solving them.

memory rely implicitly on a computer analogy. Those who study memory extend the computer analogy further by referring to storage areas as "buffers" and information-processing mechanisms as "central processors."

In addition, computers have been programmed to understand and produce human language. These programs store in their memory information about the rules for generating English sentences and even speech. For example, in programs written for blind people, information can be typed at a keyboard, and the computer vocalizes what has been typed. The information-processing approach is widely used, although it has come under attack as reducing everything to its smallest element (Bruner, 1990).

Computer Programs. The most widely investigated aspect of computer simulation and artificial intelligence is problem solving. As we saw at the beginning of this chapter, chess was one of the first problems attacked by computers. Computers have been taught to play other games, such as checkers and backgammon, and to solve simple number completion tasks. They also solve complicated problems involving large amounts of memory. The most sophisticated programs include aspects of human memory systems.

Problem-solving programs use two basic approaches: algorithms and heuristics. **Algorithms** involve reaching a solution to a problem by using a set of rules to implement a particular procedure's steps over and over again until the problem is solved. Many mathematics problems (for example, finding a square root) make use of algorithms. Algorithms are precise and are usually implemented exhaustively until the solution is reached. For example, in a chess game, a particular chess algorithm might involve having the computer use a procedure to examine every permutation and combination of possible plays before choosing the one move that has the highest probability of success.

Algorithms are also used in a wide variety of real-life problems, from increasing the output of a recipe (say by doubling each ingredient) to writing a computer program (even a relatively simple program would need a number of algorithms). To implement an algorithm, you follow the rules regarding which task to implement at which point in the procedure. For example, an algorithm for doubling a recipe might be: "Find the list of ingredients. For each ingredient, find the measured amount of the ingredient, multiply that amount by 2, and use the product as the new amount for the ingredient. Repeat this procedure until there are no more ingredients listed in the recipe." It's tedious, monotonous, and uninspired, but it works.

However, because algorithms are a set of rules and procedures that *must* be followed, the time and effort might make them impractical for some uses. Human problem solvers, such as chess master George Koltanowski, learn things and use rules-of-thumb so they do not have to follow a rigid set of rules to solve a problem. These rules-of-thumb are integral to heuristic strategies.

Heuristics are sets of strategies that act as flexible guidelines—not strict rules and procedures—for discovery-oriented problem solving. Heuristic procedures reflect the processes used by the human brain; they involve making rough estimates, guesses, and subjective evaluations that might be called hunches or intuition. To contrast heuristics with algorithms, we can return to the chess example. When deciding on a move, a person using an algorithm strategy would repeatedly consider *every* possible move in terms of its probability for success, then choose the one with the highest likelihood of success. A person using a heuristic strategy would consider only the moves believed most likely to be successful. These moves would not be given statistical probabilities of outcomes; instead, the heuristic strategist would ask: Which move has usually enhanced my strategic position in the game?

A number of heuristic approaches exist; most of them center on the goal that the problem's solution should achieve. For example, in **subgoal analysis,** a problem is taken apart or broken down into several smaller steps, each of which has a subgoal. In **means-ends analysis,** the current situation or position is compared with the desired end (the goal) in order to determine the most efficient means for getting from one (the current position) to the other (the goal). The objective is to reduce the number of steps needed to reach the goal. A **backward search** involves working backward from the goal or endpoint to the current position, both to analyze the problem and to reduce the steps needed to get from the goal to the current position.

Human beings often use all three of these heuristic approaches, but they may be limited, by a psychological set, to using only one approach or problem-solving set. Human beings are also hampered by their limited attention span and limited ability to work on a number of tasks at one time. In contrast, computers can have hundreds

Algorithms: [AL-go-rith-ums] Simple, specific, exhaustive procedures that provide a solution to a problem after a step-by-step analysis.

Heuristics: [hyoo-RISS-ticks] Sets of selective strategies that act as guidelines for discovery-oriented problem solving but are not strict rules.

Subgoal analysis: A heuristic procedure in which a task is broken down into smaller, more manageable parts.

Means-end analysis: A heuristic procedure in which efforts are made to move the problem solver closer to a solution by finding intervening steps (subgoals) and making changes that will bring about the solution as efficiently as possible.

Backward search: A heuristic procedure in which a problem solver starts at the end of a problem and systematically works in reverse steps to discover the subparts necessary to achieve a solution.

TABLE 7.1

Algorithms and Heuristics Are Two Different but Equally Viable Approaches to Problem Solving

Approach	Procedure	Advantages	Disadvantages	Example
Algorithm	Exhaustive, systematic consideration of all possible solutions; a set of rules	Solution is guaranteed	Can be very inefficient, effortful, time-consuming	Computer chess programs are typically based on a set of predefined rules and moves
Heuristics	Strategies; rules-of-thumb that have worked in the past	Efficient; saves effort and time	Solution not guaranteed	Person attempting to repair a car uses past experience to rule out a whole range of potential problems

or even thousands of processors operating at once. Today's supercomputers are made up of many powerful computers that operate simultaneously (in parallel) to solve problems.

Although computers can be programmed to process information the way human beings do, they lack human ingenuity and spontaneity. In addition, computers do not have a referential context in which to judge situations. When you say to a grocer, "Halibut?" and the grocer responds, "Wednesday, after 4 o'clock, downtown only," you understand that halibut will be available on Wednesday, after 4 o'clock, when the shipment has arrived at the downtown branch of the grocery chain. Human beings understand the context of fresh fish being shipped in only occasionally, to some stores, at certain times during the week. They understand the context of branch stores, shipments, fresh fish, and selective shipments. Computers do not have such contexts. Further, they cannot evaluate their own ideas and improve their own problem-solving abilities by developing heuristics.

Table 7.1 summarizes the major advantages and disadvantages of algorithms and heuristics.

Neural Networks

The comparison of our brain to a computer is a compelling one. Interesting new research has been focusing on the brain's ability to represent information in a number of locations simultaneously. Take a moment and imagine a computer. You may conjure up an image of an IBM, a Macintosh, a laptop, or a mainframe terminal. You might also start thinking about programming code, computer screens, and even Nintendo. Your images of a specific computer or representations of what the computer can do are each stored and coded at different places in the brain. No one suggests that you have a computer corner where all information about computers is stored. Since various pieces of information are stored in different portions of the brain, their electrical energy must be combined at some point, in some way, for you to use the word *computer*, understand it, and visualize it. When information is represented neuronally, it is represented in different portions of the brain.

The brain has specific processing areas. However, these areas themselves are located throughout the brain and need a "convergence" zone, or center, to mediate and organize the information, according to researchers University of Iowa researchers Damasio and Damasio (1992). Thus, physically distant clusters of neuronal activity are taken together in convergence zones to evoke words, develop sentences, and fully process ideas and images about the subject at hand—for example, computers. That convergence zones are located away from specific pieces of information helps explain why some stroke victims and patients with various lesions can tell you some things about computers but not everything they once knew. For example, a stroke victim may be able to look at a picture and tell you that it has a keyboard and a screen but be unable to say that it is a picture of a computer. From Damasio and Damasio's view, a key convergence zone has been corrupted. The idea of convergence zones has led to the development of models of where and how the brain operates to represent the world, develop concepts, and solve problems.

In recent years, mathematicians, physiologists, and psychologists have joined forces to develop specific models of how neural structures learn to represent complicated information (e.g., Hinton, 1992). Their work often comes in the study of *parallel distributed processing (PDP)*, which suggests that many operations take place simultaneously and at many locations within the brain (an idea introduced in chapter 6).

The brain in some ways acts as a computer, processing events and information. Unlike most computers used in offices today, the brain can process many operations simultaneously. Most computers can perform only one operation at a time—admittedly very quickly but still only one at a time. PDP is appealing to theoreticians because in the brain thousands of signals arrive simultaneously. PDP models assert that we can process many events and store them simultaneously. PDP models are models not only of memory but also of perception and learning.

To study parallel distributed processing, researchers have devised neural networks. These networks are typically composed of interconnected "units" that serve as model neurons. Each artificial unit, or neuron, receives signals of varying and modifiable weight to represent signals that would be received by a real neuronal dendrite. Activity generated by the unit is transmitted as a single outgoing signal to other neural units. Both input and output to units can be varied electronically, as can interconnections among units. Layers of units can be connected to other layers, and the output of one layer may be the input to another.

A neural network can be physically built, but today researchers prefer to use computers to create complex, fast, efficient neural networks that simulate specific activities. For example, neural networks can be taught to recognize handwritten numbers and other simple patterns. In the teaching, a network can be shown a stimulus, say, the letter *A*. If the network (the computer program) responds that the stimulus was an *H,* the signal strength of some of the synaptic junctions can be altered to make the network respond appropriately. In addition, a network can learn to recognize a range of forms that look like the letter *A*. We say in this case that the network has learned a *prototype*. The prototypes may constitute the network's basis of form and letter perception.

An interesting element of networks is what happens when one portion of a network is partially destroyed: The network does not crash, but it makes some mistakes, much as our brain would. When portions of the brain are ablated, or injured, in an accident, the person is still able to complete some tasks. (Remember the split-brain patients who could name an object by means of one hemisphere but who could point to the object only by means of the other hemisphere—see p. 62.)

FOCUS

▶ What is the rationale behind brainstorming?   p. 256

▶ On the basis of research findings, identify and describe three ways to improve your problem-solving abilities. p. 258

▶ What are the fundamental differences between heuristics and algorithms?   pp. 259–260

Language

The doorbell rings. You open the door and see someone wearing sunglasses, a T-shirt, and pink and green neon swim trunks. The person says: "Tell your roommate to get her stick. It's 6-foot and glassy." Some people might interpret this to mean they'd better arm themselves with a club because a shiny 6-foot monster is running loose. However, a surfer would grab a surfboard (stick) and head out to the beach, where 6-foot-high waves are breaking on a beautiful, windless day (making the ocean's surface "glassy"). Although the words sound the same to surfer and non-surfer, the interpretation made by each is radically different because surfers use special expressions when talking about their sport.

This difference in interpretation highlights the amazing structure of language and our ability to process it effortlessly despite its complexity. Some researchers have wondered: If two people who speak the same language use different expressions to describe conditions, does this mean they think about the world in different ways? Does language determine thought, or do all people think alike, regardless of their language?

Thought and Language

In the 1950s researchers discovered that Eskimo language had many more nouns to describe snow than English does; anthropologist and linguist Benjamin Whorf reasoned that verbal and language abilities must affect thought directly. In Whorf's view, the structure of the language that people speak directly determines their thoughts and perception (Whorf, 1956).

To investigate Whorf's claim, cognitive psychologist Eleanor Heider Rosch studied the language structure and color-naming properties of two cultures with different languages (Heider, 1971, 1972; Heider & Olivier, 1972; Rosch, 1973). Every language has ways of classifying colors, although no language includes more than 11 basic colors (Berlin & Kay, 1969). Rosch's subjects were English-speaking Americans and native speakers of Dani, the language of a primitive Stone Age tribe (the Dani) in Indonesian New Guinea. In Dani, there are only two basic color names: *mola* for bright colors and *mili* for dark colors. In English, there are many ways of classifying color, usually based on hues (red, blue, yellow, green, turquoise, pink, and brown are examples). If language determines thought, as Whorf claimed, then the English speakers and the Dani would show two different ways of thinking about color.

Rosch showed both groups of subjects single-color chips for 5 seconds each. After 30 seconds, she asked the subjects to pick the same color from a group of 40 color chips. Whorf's hypothesis predicted that since the Dani have only two basic color-naming words, they would confuse colors within a group. Two different hues from the *mola* category of color would be considered the same basic color, *mola*. Neither the Dani nor the English-speaking subjects, however, confused colors within categories. The Dani's two-color language structure did not limit the ability of the subjects to discriminate, remember, or think about colors.

Rosch's studies showed that language does not determine thought. Although various languages have developed specific grammars and thought processes, they have probably done so in response to specific environments, events, and cultures, as shown in the Diversity box on page 250. It might be adaptive to discriminate among many kinds of snow, but language does not determine thoughts.

Language and thought play a role in many forms of unspoken communication. This Japanese father and son are playing a hand game, the structure of which may have been verbally explained at one time, but which is now understood and unspoken.

Rather, thoughts about snow help shape language and the words in it. Thus, strong statements about language determining thought are wrong, but there is some truth to Whorf's original ideas. As Hunt and Agnoli (1991, p. 377) assert, "The language people speak is a guide to the language in which they think."

In the same manner, even though human beings are sensitive to odors, they have an impoverished language structure to describe them. Research shows that although odors are easily detected, descriptions are difficult. They are often based on personal experiences and sometimes are coded in terms of a personal biographical event (for example, grandad's pipe tobacco, mother's perfume, Aunt Maria's upstairs attic) (Richardson & Zucco, 1989). Linguistic processes play a limited role in the processing of smell; and like the description of snow, our language of odors is determined by other factors. Nonetheless, linguistic processes are far from simple and have been carefully researched and studied, as the following sections show.

Linguistics

Throughout the ages and in every culture, human beings have rendered their thoughts into language and have employed words to order their thoughts. Tens of thousands of years ago, our cave-dwelling ancestors put their thoughts into words to organize hunting parties. Several millennia later, Egyptian scribes used hieroglyphics (writing in pictorial characters) to represent the spoken word. Still later, Socrates was sentenced to drink hemlock for preaching corrupting ideas to the youth of ancient Greece. Today, world leaders employ oratory to rouse their constituencies to moral behavior and social progress, professors verbally instruct students in the various fields of human knowledge, and people from all walks of life use language to exchange ideas with others or to mentally solve problems. Without this ability, human civilization could never exist. In many ways, language and thinking define humanity.

We learn language as children. Children are astonishingly adept at understanding and utilizing the basic rules of language. A 3-year-old, noticing that many nouns can be turned into verbs by the addition of a suffix, may say, "It sunned today," meaning it was a sunny day. The miracle of language acquisition in children has long puzzled linguists and psycholinguists.

Linguistics is the study of language, including speech sounds, meaning, and grammar. **Psycholinguistics** is the study of how language is acquired, perceived, understood, and produced. Among other things, psycholinguists seek to discover how children learn the complicated rules necessary to speak correctly. Psychological studies since the early 1970s show that children first acquire the simple aspects of language, then learn progressively more complex elements and capabilities.

Studies have also revealed *linguistic structures*—the rules and regularities that exist in and make it possible to learn a language. This section examines the study of three major areas of psycholinguistic study: *phonology,* the study of the sounds of language; *semantics,* the study of the meanings of words and sentences; and *syntax,* the study of the relationships among words and how they combine to form sentences.

Phonology

The gurgling, spitting, and burping noises infants first make are caused by air passing through the vocal apparatus. At about 6 weeks, infants begin to make speech-like cooing sounds. During their first 12 months, their vocalizations become more varied and frequent. Eventually, infants can combine sounds into pronounceable units.

Phonemes. The basic units of sound that compose the words in a language are called **phonemes.** In English, phonemes are the sounds of single letters, such as *b, p,*

Linguistics: [ling-WIST-icks] The study of language, including speech sounds, meaning, and grammar.

Psycholinguistics: The study of how language is acquired, perceived, understood, and produced.

Phonemes: [FOE-neems] The basic units of sound that compose the words in a language.

Morphemes: [MORE-feems] The basic units of meaning in a language.

Semantics: The study of the meaning of language components.

f, and *v,* and of combinations of letters, such as *t* and *h* in *th*ese. All the sounds in the English language are expressed in 45 phonemes; of those, just 9 make up nearly half of all words.

Morphemes. At about 1 year of age, children make the first sounds that psychologists classify as real speech. Initially, they utter only one word. But soon they are saying as many as four or five words. Words consist of **morphemes,** the basic units of meaning in a language. A morpheme consists of one or more phonemes combined into a meaningful unit. The morpheme *do,* for example, consists of two phonemes, the sounds of the letters *d* and *o.* Other words can be formed by adding prefixes and suffixes to morphemes. Adding *un* or *er* to the morpheme *do,* for example, gives *undo* or *doer. Morphology* is the study of these meaningful sound units.

No matter what language people speak, one of their first meaningful utterances is the morpheme *ma.* It is coincidental that *ma* is a word in English. Other frequently heard words of English-speaking people are *bye-bye, mama,* and *bebe.* In any language, the first words often refer to a specific object or person, especially food, toys, and animals. In the second year, a child's vocabulary increases to about 50 words and in the third year to as many as 1,000 words. (Figure 7.8 shows vocabulary increases through age 7.)

Semantics

At first, infants do not fully understand what their parents' utterances mean. But as more words take on meaning, they develop semantic capability. **Semantics** is the analysis of the meaning of language, but especially of its individual words, the relationships among words, and the placement of words in a context that generates thought.

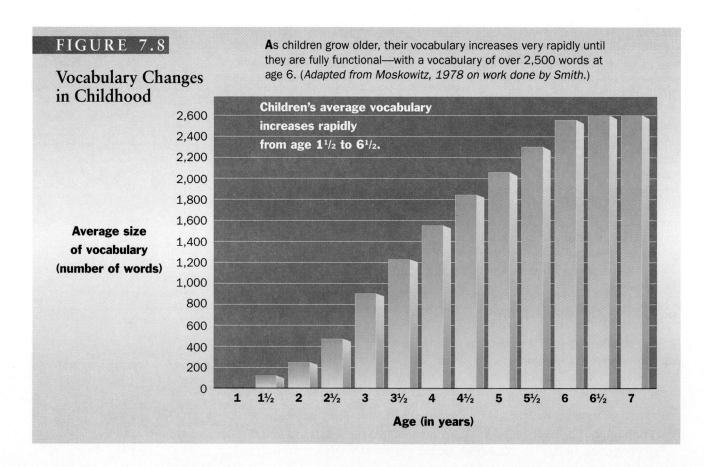

FIGURE 7.8

Vocabulary Changes in Childhood

As children grow older, their vocabulary increases very rapidly until they are fully functional—with a vocabulary of over 2,500 words at age 6. (*Adapted from Moskowitz, 1978 on work done by Smith.*)

Children's average vocabulary increases rapidly from age 1½ to 6½.

Average size of vocabulary (number of words)

Age (in years)

Consider how a 4-year-old child might misconstrue what her father says to her mother: "I've had a terrible day. First, the morning traffic made me a nervous wreck. Then, I got into an argument with my boss, who became so furious he almost fired me." The child might think her dad got into a car accident and was nearly set on fire. In trying to understand what is being said, a child is faced with understanding not only the meanings of single words but also their relationships to other words. As everyone who has attempted to learn a new language knows, the meaning of a sentence is not the same as the definitions of the individual words added together. Although children acquire about 5 to 10 words a day from about the 15th month onward until they begin school, the words they acquire mean different things, depending on their context. For example, a Chinese exchange student studying English at a California college needed a light for his cigarette and followed these directions printed on a red box: PULL FOR FIRE.

Syntax

Once children can use words that have distinct meanings, they begin to combine those words into short sentences, such as "Mama look" or "Bye-bye, mama." That is, they develop a syntactic capability. **Syntax** is the study of how words and groups of words combine to form phrases, clauses, and sentences. Syntactic capability enables children to convey more meaning. For example, children acquire a powerful new way of making their demands known when they learn to combine the words *I want* or *give me* with appropriate nouns Suddenly, they can ask for cookies, toys, or mommy, without any of them being within pointing range. The rewards that such linguistic behavior brings children are powerful incentives for them to learn more language. Children do not really need external rewards to want to learn language, though. (This concept will be examined later in the chapter in a comparison of chimpanzees and human beings.) Children begin to use sentences at different ages; but once they begin, they tend to develop at similar rates (R. Brown, 1970). Moreover, the average length of sentences increases at a fairly regular rate as children grow older.

Early studies of children's short sentences suggested that descriptions of the positions and types of words used could characterize early speech, but later analyses showed these descriptions to be inadequate. Later investigations suggested that young children possess an innate grammar and that they use grammatical relationships in much the same ways that adults do (McNeill, 1970). **Grammar** is the linguistic description of how a language functions, especially in terms of the rules and patterns used for generating appropriate and comprehensible sentences. Table 7.2 on page 266 presents some of the linguistic milestones in a child's life.

Transformational Grammar

In 1957, linguist Noam Chomsky described a radical approach to grammar that changed many psychologists' views of language development. Chomsky claimed that each person is born with the ability to transform a particular kernel of meaning into an infinite number of meaningful sentences. In Chomsky's grammar, the meaningful message of a sentence is stored differently from the words used to compose it (Chomsky, 1986, 1990). Psychologists are especially interested in transformational grammar because it helps explain unique features of human language.

Surface and Deep Structures. The fundamental idea of Chomsky's **transformational grammar** is that each sentence has both a surface structure and a deep structure. The **surface structure** is the organization of a sentence that is closest to its written or spoken form. It shows the words and phrases that can be analyzed

Syntax: [SIN-tacks] The study of how groups of words are related and how they are arranged in phrases and sentences.

Grammar: The linguistic description of how a language functions, especially the rules and patterns used for generating appropriate and comprehensible sentences.

Transformational grammar: An approach to the study of language that assumes that each surface structure of a sentence has a deep structure associated with it.

Surface structure: The organization of a sentence that is closest to its written or spoken form.

TABLE 7.2

Linguistic Milestones of Children

AGE	LANGUAGE ACTIVITY
12 weeks	Smiles when talked to; makes cooing sounds spontaneously
16 weeks	Turns head in response to human voices
20 weeks	Makes vowel and consonant sounds while cooing
6 months	Changes from cooing to babbling
12 months	Imitates sounds; understands some words
18 months	Uses from 3 to 50 words; understands basic speech
24 months	Uses more than 50 words; uses two-word phrases
30 months	Uses new words daily; has good comprehension of speech; vocabulary of up to 1000 words
36 months	Has vocabulary of over 1000 words; makes grammatical mistakes, but their number decreases significantly with each passing week

Does this sign really mean that the children are slow? Common usage can change the meaning of words and word groupings.

Deep structure: The organization of a sentence that is closest to its underlying meaning.

through the diagramming procedures often taught in junior high school. The **deep structure** is the underlying pattern of the words that helps convey meaning. Thus, the sentences *Alex gave Mary a dog* and *Alex gave a dog to Mary* have different surface structures but the same deep structure. (See Figure 7.9 for an example of how transformational rules work.)

To understand transformational grammar more clearly, consider this sentence: Visiting relatives can be a pain. Although the sentence is simple, it has two distinct meanings. It can mean that relatives who visit can be annoying guests or that going to visit relatives is an annoying chore. Transformational

FIGURE 7.9

Chomsky's Concepts of Surface Structure and Deep Structure

Two different surface structures lead to the same meaning through a series of transformational rules.

Two Different Surface Structures →   Alex gave Mary a dog.   Mary was given a dog by Alex.

TRANSFORMATIONAL RULES

Deep Structure →   Mary now has a dog; Alex gave it to her.

grammar accounts for these two meanings by showing that, for the same surface structure, there are two possible deep structures. To a great extent, the meaning of a word or a sentence is far more important than its surface form or structure. There is no doubt that the structure of a sentence conveys meaning, but semantic (meaning) factors help convey the abstract significance of a word or sentence.

Abstraction in Language. Imagine that a friend phones you to tell you about a severe-storm warning he just heard over the radio. Most likely, he won't recite the radio announcement verbatim but instead will relay in his own words estimates of the storm's arrival time, wind velocities, and probable amount of precipitation. That is, your friend will tell you what he remembers best from the announcement—its concepts, not its exact wording. This suggests that our memory of verbal exchanges is not literal-minded and passive but rather an active compilation of concepts.

Researchers more than 50 years ago made the same argument. In 1932, English psychologist F. C. Bartlett published results from studies that made history and are consistent with recent studies. Bartlett had his subjects read a short story packed with plot information. After a few minutes, the subjects had to recall the story. They retold the story to another subject, who retold it to another, and so forth. Bartlett examined the retelling of the story from person to person to see what happened to the details as time passed. Bartlett found that the stories grew shorter, less detailed, and more informal; some events were altered, and others were made up to fit the altered story line. He argued that his subjects built a *schema* (an organized structure in memory) of the events of the story, and the schema was what they remembered (see chapter 6, p. 228). Bartlett thus asserted that his subjects had abstracted the key elements for memory organization and recall.

FOCUS

▶ What evidence did researchers use to determine whether the structure of spoken language determines people's thoughts and perception?   pp. 262–263

▶ Identify the fundamental difference between surface and deep structure.   pp. 265–267

▶ Identify Bartlett's evidence for the existence of a schema. p. 267

Language Acquisition

Research shows that language and thought are sensitive to both genetic inheritance (nature) and experience (nurture). As in other areas of human behavior, the debate continues about the relative contribution of each factor. If language is based on biology, two things should be true: (1) Many aspects of language ability should be evident early in life. (2) All children, regardless of their culture or language, should develop grammar (an understanding of language patterns) in a similar way. If environmental factors account for language acquisition, the role of learning should be preeminent.

Consider what happens when people take their first course in Spanish, French, or Latin. They recognize that they will learn to communicate in a new language which includes a new grammar, new written forms, and new pronunciation. They may buy study aids: books, dictionaries, and tapes. They may read about the country of the new tongue, talk to someone who speaks the language, and rely on foreign language teachers. In general, they prepare to acquire the new language. But when you learned your very first language, how were you prepared to learn it? Were you prepared at all? In trying to resolve the nature-nurture debate over language acquisition, researchers investigate the development of language through observational studies of infants and children, case histories of sensory-deprived infants, studies of reading-disabled or brain-damaged individuals, and experiments with chimpanzees.

Learning Theories

Learning theories emphasize the role of environmental influences, or nurture, in language acquisition. The basic idea is that language is a natural unfolding of traditional learning.

One learning theory, the *conditioning approach,* highlights the importance of language experiences during the formative years. According to this theory, both other-person reinforcement (in the form of parental approval) and self-reinforcement (in the form of speech) increase the probability that children will use words and sentences. As the sole explanation of language, the conditioning approach has one serious weakness: parental inattention to reinforcing language structure. Slobin (1975, p. 290) says, "A mother is too engaged in interacting with a child to pay attention to the linguistic form of his utterances." Despite this inattention, however, children eventually learn to form sentences.

Another learning theory claims that children acquire language through *imitation*—that is, by copying adult speech. Through imitation, children learn to use the proper forms of language. An example of learning by imitation is picking up regional terminology, such as, "Y'all come back now."

Studies have examined the ability of adults and children to use new words grammatically. Brown and Berko (1960) presented adults and children with a sentence containing both real words and nonsense words—for example, "Let's wug some fish"—then asked them to use the nonsense word correctly in another sentence. Both adults and children responded with sentences such as "The fish were wugged yesterday"—using *wug* as a verb, as in the original sentence. Brown and Berko also found that scores on this type of test improved regularly with age. They concluded that formal changes in word associations and skill in placing words in their proper grammatical context are part of a child's developing ability to use English syntax. Children respond to the rules. They develop the ability to use abstract rules in addition to their growing vocabulary.

Learning approaches have several weaknesses, however. They do not explain how children (who learn grammar in a short period of time) are able to generate an infinite number of new sentences, given the small sample of sentences they have heard. Additionally, learning approaches do not consider biological or maturational readiness. If readiness were not to some extent biologically determined, parents could teach their children to speak, read, and write soon after birth. Thus, psychologists speak of acquiring the first language, not learning it.

Biological Theories

Psychologist George Miller (1965) asserts that human beings have an innate, unique capacity to acquire and develop language. Although he does not exclude experience as a factor in shaping children's language, Miller claims that it is human nature itself that allows children to pay attention to language in their environment and ultimately to use it.

Nonetheless, even the strongest proponents of the nature (biological) argument do not contend that a specific language is inborn. Rather, they agree that a predisposition toward language exists and that a blueprint for language is "preprinted." As a child matures, this blueprint provides the framework through which the child learns a language and its rules (e.g., Kuhl et al., 1992). Three major sources of evidence support the biological side of the nature versus nurture debate: (1) studies of brain structure, lateralization, and convergence zones; (2) studies of learning readiness; and (3) language acquisition in children and chimpanzees.

Brain Structure, Lateralization, and Convergence Zones. As early as the 1800s, researchers knew that the brain of a human being is specialized for different functions. At that time, researchers began mapping the brain and discovering that if certain areas were damaged (usually through accidents), the injured person would suffer from severe disorders in language abilities. Later work, some of it by Norman Geschwind (1972), led to the idea of **lateralization**—the localization of a particular brain function primarily in one hemisphere. As chapter 2 showed, considerable evidence suggests that the left and right hemispheres of the brain (normally connected by the corpus callosum) handle distinctly different functions.

> **Lateralization:** The localization of a particular brain function primarily in one hemisphere.

Some researchers argue that studies show the brain has unique processing abilities in each hemisphere. For example, important language functions are predominantly, but not exclusively, left hemisphere functions (Corina, Vaid, & Bellugi, 1992). However, the available data do not make an airtight case; each hemisphere seems to play a dominant role in some functions and to interact with the other hemisphere in the performance of others.

Damasio and Damasio (1992) assert that the brain has specific language-processing areas, some of which are lateralized. However, these language areas are located throughout the brain and need a "convergence" zone or center to mediate and organize the information. Thus, physically distant clusters of neuronal activity are taken together in convergence zones to evoke words, develop sentences, and fully process language.

Learning Readiness. Researcher Erik Lenneberg (1921–1975) claimed that human beings are born with a grammatical capacity and a readiness to produce language (Lenneberg, 1967). He theorized that language simply develops as people interact with their environment. One important aspect of this theory is that a child's capacity to learn language depends on the maturation of specific neurological structures. For example, the structural maturation that has occurred at about 18 to 24 months permits children to acquire grammar so they can interact linguistically with others. On the other hand, lack of maturity in certain structures limits infants' ability to speak in the first months of life. Lenneberg's view derives in part from observations that most children learn the rules of grammar at a very early age.

Lenneberg believed that the brain continues to develop from birth until about age 13, with optimal development at age 2. During this period, children develop grammar and learn the rules of language. After age 13, there is little room for improvement or change in their neurological structure. Lenneberg supported his argument with the observation that brain-damaged children can relearn some speech and language, whereas brain-damaged adolescents or adults who lose language and speech are unable to completely regain the lost ability. Lenneberg's view is persuasive, but some of his original claims have been seriously criticized—particularly his idea of the role of a critical time period in language development (e.g., Kinsbourne, 1975).

Some researchers claim that not only human beings but also other organisms—for example, chimpanzees—are born with a grammatical capacity and a readiness for language.

Language Studies with Chimpanzees

Do animals communicate with one another through language? If they do, is that language the same as, similar to, or totally different from the language of human beings? Most important, what can human beings learn from animals about the inborn aspects of language?

The biological approach to language suggests that human beings are "prewired"—born with a capacity for language. Experience is the key that unlocks this existing capacity and makes it available for expression. The arguments for and against the biological approach to language acquisition use studies showing that chimpanzees naturally develop some language abilities. Researchers can control and shape the environment in which chimps learn language, something they cannot do in studies involving human subjects.

Chimpanzees are generally considered among the most intelligent animals; in addition, they resemble human beings more closely than any other animal. Playful and curious, chimps share many common physical and mental abilities with human beings. For these reasons, they have been the species of choice when psychologists have studied language in animals.

However, all attempts to teach animals to talk have failed. Until recently, this failure had led most psycholinguists to conclude that only human beings have the capacity to acquire language. Two decades ago, however, some major research projects showed that even though chimpanzees lack the necessary vocal apparatus to speak, they can learn to use different methods of communication (Rumbaugh & Savage-Rumbaugh, 1978). Studies of chimpanzees have taken place both in the field in near natural environments and in laboratory settings using computer technology. With results from sharply different environments, clear conclusions are emerging.

Washoe. From age 1, the chimpanzee Washoe was raised like a human child in the home of Allen and Beatrice Gardner (1969). During the day, Washoe was in the house or in the large fenced yard. At night, she slept in a trailer. The Gardners and their research assistants did not speak to Washoe. Instead, they used Ameslan (American Sign Language, the sign language used by the deaf) to communicate with her. Rather than being taught to speak words, Washoe was taught to make signs that stood for words as well as for such simple commands and concepts as *more, come, give me, flower, tickle,* and *open.*

Within 7 months, Washoe learned 4 signs; after 12 months, she had learned 12 signs. At 22 months, she had a vocabulary of 34 signs; by age 4, she knew 85 signs; and by the end of her 5th year, Washoe had accumulated 160 signs (J. D. Fleming, 1974). Washoe learned a large number of signs that refer to specific objects or events. She was able to generalize these signs and to combine them in a meaningful order to make sentences. There is no proof, however, that she used a systematic grammar (with rules to transform and generate novel sentences).

Sarah. The chimp Sarah was raised in a cage, with more limited contact with human beings than Washoe had. Psychologist David Premack (1971) used magnetized plastic symbols and instrumental training methods to teach Sarah words and sentences (see Figure 7.10). Initially, Premack placed several plastic symbols on a board in front of Sarah and placed a banana slightly out of reach. Each time Sarah chose the appropriate symbol, he would give her the banana as a reward. Eventually, through shaping, Sarah came to associate a specific symbol with a banana and learned to place the token on the board when she wanted a banana.

Gradually, Sarah developed a small but impressive vocabulary. She learned to make compound sentences, to answer simple questions, and to substitute words in a sentence construction—for example, "Place banana dish," "Place apple dish," and "Place orange dish." There is no evidence, however, that she could generate a new sentence, such as, "Is the apple in the dish?" or "Where are the apples?"

Lana. The chimp Lana learned to interact with a computer at the Yerkes Primate Research Center at Emory University. Researchers Rumbaugh, Gill, and Von Glaserfeld (1973) gave Lana 6 months of computer-controlled language training.

FIGURE 7.10

Symbols Used by Sarah in Premack's Study

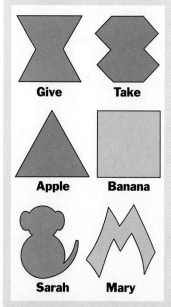

Give   Take

Apple   Banana

Sarah   Mary

Sarah learned to construct sentences using pieces of plastic that varied in color, size, and shape.

Lana learned to press a series of keys with imprinted geometric symbols. Each symbol represented a word in an artificial language called Yerkish. The computer varied the location of each Yerkish word and the color and brightness of the keys. Through instrumental conditioning, Lana was able to demonstrate some of the rudiments of language acquisition. However, like Washoe and Sarah, Lana did not show that she could manipulate grammatical relations in meaningful and regular ways.

So far, most studies of chimps show that their language is similar to that of young children: It is concrete, specific, and limited. However, chimps do not show the ability to generate an infinite number of grammatically correct sentences, an ability that human beings acquire with age.

Nim. A Columbia University psychologist, H. S. Terrace (1979, 1980), claims that even the limited results with chimps are greatly overvalued. He suggests that chimps do not have language abilities and that the data reported so far with chimps show only that they were mimicking their teachers' signs.

Terrace reports significant differences between chimp language and the language of young children. In raising his chimp, Nim Chimpsky (named after the famous linguist Noam Chomsky), Terrace found that Nim's utterances did not increase in length, as young children's do. Nim acquired many words, but she did not use them in longer and longer sentences as time passed. In addition, only 12 percent of Nim's utterances were spontaneous; the remaining 88 percent were responses to her teacher. Terrace points out that a significantly greater percentage of children's utterances are spontaneous. Terrace also found no evidence of grammatical competence either in his own data or in that of other researchers.

Kanzi. Recent work with a little-known species of ape, the pygmy chimpanzee, shows that chimps can acquire symbols without training. According to well-known language researcher Sue Savage-Rumbaugh, these chimps comprehend symbols before they produce them, and they also comprehend human speech. According to Savage-Rumbaugh (1987), they have the ability to construct a rudimentary grammar.

Kanzi, a pygmy chimp, uses a keyboard to talk to his human trainers. His keyboard has 256 symbols, and he has mastered more than 150. Recordings of interactions with Kanzi have shown that he comprehends both individual words and sentences and responds appropriately. He learned his language by being enmeshed in a language environment, not through training procedures. His unique contribution is that he understands human speech and syntax and has learned to do so without training. He learned language steadily and rapidly, and Savage-Rumbaugh believes this sets him apart from all other apes who have learned language and have shown that learning through the production of language (Greenfield & Savage-Rumbaugh, 1990).

Researchers have gained valuable knowledge about the nature of language by studying chimps and other animals. Researcher Sue Savage-Rumbaugh taught her chimp, Kanzi, to communicate using a special keyboard. (Photo courtesy of CNN.)

Chimp Language? Terrace's work challenged the findings of previous investigators and made them think about language in new ways. Other researchers at the Yerkes Primate Center have presented additional challenges to primate language acquisition (Savage-Rumbaugh et al., 1983). They claim not only that chimp lan-

FOCUS

▶ The two learning approaches to language acquisition—conditioning and imitation—operate differently with respect to one key underlying principle. Identify the principle (think back to chapter 5).   p. 268

▶ What is the crucial assumption of biological approaches to language acquisition?   pp. 268–269

▶ Terrace claimed an important difference between chimp language and the language of human children. What is that difference?   p. 271

guage is different from that of human beings but also that the purpose of chimp language is different.

Unlike young children, who spontaneously learn to name and to point at objects (often called *referential naming*), chimps do not spontaneously develop such communication skills. For Savage-Rumbaugh and her colleagues, such skills are crucial components of human language. Terrace (1985) agrees that the ability to name is a basic part of human consciousness. He argues that, as part of our socialization, we learn to refer to our various inner states: our feelings, thoughts, and emotions.

Chimps can be taught some naming skills, but the procedure is long and tedious. Children, on the other hand, develop these skills easily and spontaneously at a young age. Accordingly, researchers such as R. J. Sanders (1985) assert that chimps do not interpret the symbols they use in the same way children do. These researchers question the comparability of human and chimp language.

Although few psychologists are completely convinced about the role of language in chimp communication, their criticisms do not diminish the chimps' language abilities or their accomplishments in other areas, such as mathematics (Rumbaugh, Savage-Rumbaugh, & Hegel, 1987; Boysen & Berntson, 1989). They also do not rule out language and speech processing in some chimps (Savage-Rumbaugh, 1987). Chimp language remains an emerging part of psychology; the answers are far from complete, but the quest is exciting.

Concluding Note

Our language does not determine our thoughts, but clearly our thoughts influence our language and the way we approach the world. Human beings are unique in that we get to form concepts, make decisions, and solve problems. In doing so, we not only learn but remember and plan for the future. Our ability to operate in our complex world is shaped by our society, especially by our parents and teachers. However, parents and teachers today are facing special tasks. Professional educators are focusing on critical thinking skills (see pages 32 and 256). They are encouraging logical decision making, creativity, and effective problem-solving strategies. In addition, they are being challenged to be gender-neutral in their language, to encourage women in the sciences, and to foster analytical thought.

In the classroom, these challenges are opportunities, but the opportunities have not been made equal for all students. Traditionally, math teachers have been more likely to call on males and college professors have been more likely to reward males for alternative points of view. In general, both male and female teachers make more disapproving comments to their female students than to their male students. Students also have stereotyped ideas and try to take advantage of female professors more than male professors—for example, by asking for time extensions and special favors. Thus, while the task for teachers is to foster critical thinking, they must first evaluate sexism in their classroom, so that creativity and good decision making become a possibility for *all* of the students in the class.

Summary & Review

Cognitive Psychology: An Overview

What is cognitive psychology?

Cognitive psychology is the study of the overlapping fields of learning, memory, perception, and thought. Cognitive psychology focuses on encoding, storage, retrieval, analysis, recall, reconstruction, elaboration, and memory. Cognitive psychologists study thinking; they assume that mental processes exist, are systematic and can be studied scientifically. Cognitive psychologists believe that we are active participants in analyzing our world.   pp. 244–245

KEY TERMS: *cognitive psychology,* p. 244; *reasoning,* p. 244.

Concept Formation

What is concept formation?

In concept formation, we classify and organize objects by grouping them with or isolating them from others on the basis of a common feature. In concept-learning studies, stimuli vary along dimensions, or features, which set them apart from others. Within each dimension are different values or attributes.   pp. 245–247

What is the selection method?

Concept-learning studies using the reception method present a subject with a series of instances. The task is to classify the instances as positive or negative. Studies using the selection method present all the possible instances at once. The subject chooses one instance at a time, asking if it is positive or negative.   p. 247

KEY TERMS: *concepts,* p. 245; *positive instance,* p. 246; *negative instance,* p. 246; *mediation theory,* p. 247; *conservative focusing,* p. 247.

Reasoning and Decision Making

What are reasoning and decision making?

Reasoning is the process by which we generate and evaluate situations and reach conclusions. The procedure we use to reach a valid conclusion is called *logic. Decision making* is the assessment of alternatives; we make decisions that sometimes involve the probability of a certain event's occurrence and the expected value.   p. 248

How are syllogisms used in psychological research?

A *syllogism* is a sequence of statements or premises (assumed to be true), followed by a conclusion; the task is to decide (deduce) if the conclusion is valid. Psychologists analyze the decision-making process by asking participants to trace their thought processes into a series of steps—often by saying them out loud. pp. 248–249

What are two important decision-making approaches?

A decision-making approach in which some factors take on more importance than others is called a *compensatory model.* In the *elimination by aspects* approach, people rule out alternatives that do not meet minimum criteria; this approach is generally a fast and efficient way to make decisions.   pp. 249–251

KEY TERMS: *logic,* p. 248; *decision making,* p. 248.

Problem Solving

What is problem solving?

Problem solving consists of realizing that a problem exists, assessing its complexity, devising solutions, implementing those solutions, and assessing results. Problem solving implies confronting a situation that requires an insight to deal with it. p. 252

What are functional fixedness and brainstorming?

Functional fixedness is the inability to see that an object can have a function other than its stated or usual one. Functional fixedness has proven detrimental in problem solving. To help eliminate functional fixedness some people use the technique of brainstorming. *Brainstorming* is a problem-solving technique whereby people consider all possible solutions without making any initial judgments about the worth of those solutions.   pp. 253–255

What is creative thought?

Creative responses are original, novel, and appropriate. According to Guilford, creative thinking is divergent thinking. *Divergent thinking* is the production of new information from known information, or the generation of logical possibilities. By contrast, *convergent thinking* is the process by which possible options are selectively narrowed until they converge onto one answer. pp. 255–257

continued

Summary & Review

What are algorithms and heuristics?

Algorithms are procedures that provide a solution by routinely following a set of rules and implementing a set of specific procedures in accordance with the rules. *Heuristics* are sets of strategies that act as guidelines, not strict rules, for problem solving.   pp. 259–260

What are the assumptions of PDP models?

The study of *parallel distributed processing* suggests that many operations take place simultaneously and at many locations within the brain. Neural networks have been devised to simulate brain activity.   p. 261

KEY TERMS: *problem solving*, p. 252; *functional fixedness*, p. 253; *creativity*, p. 255; *convergent thinking*, p. 257; *divergent thinking*, p. 257; *algorithms*, p. 259; *heuristics*, p. 259; *subgoal analysis*, p. 259; *means-end analysis*, p. 259; *backward search*, p. 259.

Language

What was Whorf's assumption about language structure?

Whorf assumed that language structure determined thought. However, research shows that language structure alone is unlikely to account for the way people think.   pp. 262–263

What are psycholinguistics and the key parts of grammar?

Psycholinguistics is the study of how people acquire, perceive, comprehend, and produce language. *Grammar* is the linguistic description of a language. It consists of the rules and patterns for generating correct, comprehensible sentences in the language. *Phonemes* are the basic units of sounds in a language. *Morphemes* are the basic units of meaning. *Semantics* is the study of the meaning of language components. *Syntax* is how groups of words are related and how words are arranged into phrases and sentences.   pp. 263–265

What is transformational grammar?

Transformational grammar, developed by Chomsky, is an approach to studying the structure of a language. It assumes that each sentence has both a *surface structure* and a *deep structure*. In general, researchers conclude that the meaning of a sentence (deep structure) and the level of its analysis are more important than the specific words or word structure.   pp. 265–267

KEY TERMS: *linguistics*, p. 263; *psycholinguistics*, p. 263; *phonemes*, p. 263; *morphemes*, p. 264; *semantics*, p. 264; *syntax*, p. 265; *grammar*, p. 265; *transformational grammar*, p. 265; *surface structure*, p. 265; *deep structure*, p. 266.

Language Acquisition

How do children acquire language?

Learning plays an important part in language acquisition. However, people have the ability to generate an infinite number of correctly formed sentences in their language. Because this ability cannot be acquired solely through imitation or instruction, it suggests the existence of an innate grammar, or language ability.   p. 267–269

What do psychologists conclude about chimp language?

Few psychologists are completely convinced about the ways in which chimps use language, but their criticisms do not diminish the chimps' language abilities or accomplishment in other areas such as mathematics. Language and speech processing in some chimps is not ruled out, but a healthy skepticism still exists among most psychologists.   pp. 269–272

KEY TERM: *lateralization*, p. 269.

CONNECTIONS

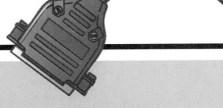

If you are interested in...

Child Development

Each class I teach usually includes at least one pair of twins. Their experiences as twins are often similar. Identical (monozygotic) twins not only look alike but share a remarkable number of interests, abilities, and traits. They tend to enjoy the same sports, have the same talents, and be similar in personality; they may both be outgoing or shy or enjoy being pranksters. Some twins talk at length about their similarities. Beth and Melissa, for example, described their highly similar choices in dates, their shared preference for spicy foods, and their insecurity in group settings. Another pair of twins, Gene and Mark, related their similar career goals (both wanted to be engineers) and recognized that they often had similar dreams, although not necessarily on the same night.

When twins recount their similarities, other students in my class are always intrigued and often ask a number of questions. In discussing the similarities, students quickly acknowledge that one reason the twins are so much alike is, of course, genetics. They also note that the twins are raised by the same parents at the same time in history, attend the same school, and so on. My

277

students are expressing the same view as many psychologists. However, the role of genetics in personal traits may be stronger than we once believed.

To assess the roles played by genetics and environment, researchers have studied identical twins who have been reared apart; and they have found extraordinary similarities between them (Lykken, McGue, Tellengen, & Bouchard, 1992). Lykken and his colleagues found one identical twin who was an accomplished storyteller with a collection of amusing anecdotes. Later, his twin brother was asked if he knew any funny stories. "Why, sure," he responded; and leaning back with a practiced air, he continued, "I'll tell you a story." Other twins shared interests in dogs, smoked the same cigarettes, and were both politically conservative. One pair of twins shared a phobia for water at the beach; both would enter the water backward, and then only up to their knees. In the Lykken study, there were two fire fighters, two gunsmiths, and two people who obsessively counted things; all the pairs were identical twins.

Lykken and his colleagues (1992) argue that genetics plays an especially important role in our development. They assert that traits such as musical ability, leadership, and mathematical reasoning are determined in large part by genetics. But many psychologists—and parents—believe that while genetics may play a crucial role in a person's life, the environment in which a child is raised has an equal, if not even more important, impact. Many parents think they can enhance their children's genetic endowment and optimize the likelihood of their living well-educated, well-reasoned, satisfying lives.

However, parents sometimes push their children too fast and too far. According to David Elkind (1987), a well-known psychologist and professor of child development, pushing children can have adverse consequences. Elkind asserts that parents sometimes take a "superkid" approach to child rearing. They hurry their children, expecting them to think, feel, and act much older than they are. Elkind's ideas about hurried children are based on his recognition of individual differences among children and their abilities. Some children develop slowly; others develop rapidly. Some are cognitively advanced; others are average or slow.

In this chapter, we will focus on normal development in children and see how people's inborn characteristics interact with their environments to produce individuals who are unique in both experience and heredity. The next chapter will examine adolescence, adulthood, and aging—showing that development is a continual process.

Approaches to Child Development

Psychologists study development to find out how people change throughout their lives and to learn what causes those changes. They are especially interested in discovering whether the developing infant's abilities, interests, and personality are determined by *nature* (at or before birth) or by *nurture* (their experiences after they are born). The nature versus nurture issue has been raised before in chapter 2. Separating biological from environmental causes of behavior is complicated, and the answer to any specific question about human behavior often involves the interaction of both nature and nurture.

In their study of development, psychologists adopt various research methods and viewpoints to unravel the causes of behavior. Two widely used methods are the cross-sectional method and the longitudinal method. In the *cross-sectional research method*, many subjects of different ages are compared to determine if they differ on

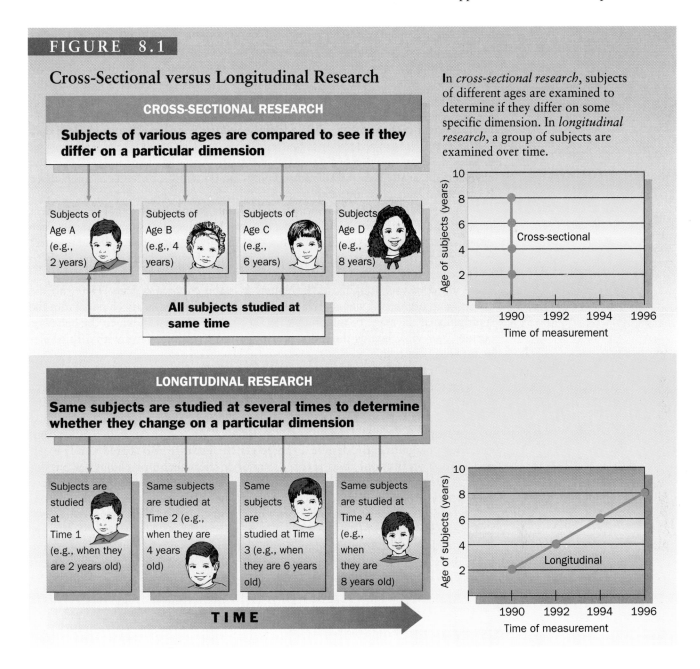

FIGURE 8.1

Cross-Sectional versus Longitudinal Research

CROSS-SECTIONAL RESEARCH

Subjects of various ages are compared to see if they differ on a particular dimension

Subjects of Age A (e.g., 2 years)

Subjects of Age B (e.g., 4 years)

Subjects of Age C (e.g., 6 years)

Subjects of Age D (e.g., 8 years)

All subjects studied at same time

In *cross-sectional research*, subjects of different ages are examined to determine if they differ on some specific dimension. In *longitudinal research*, a group of subjects are examined over time.

Cross-sectional

Age of subjects (years)

1990 1992 1994 1996

Time of measurement

LONGITUDINAL RESEARCH

Same subjects are studied at several times to determine whether they change on a particular dimension

Subjects are studied at Time 1 (e.g., when they are 2 years old)

Same subjects are studied at Time 2 (e.g., when they are 4 years old)

Same subjects are studied at Time 3 (e.g., when they are 6 years old)

Same subjects are studied at Time 4 (e.g., when they are 8 years old)

TIME

Longitudinal

Age of subjects (years)

1990 1992 1994 1996

Time of measurement

some important dimension. In the *longitudinal research method,* a group of people is compared at different ages to determine whether changes have occurred over a long period of time. See Figure 8.1 for a comparison of the cross-sectional and longitudinal research methods.

Each method has advantages and disadvantages. For example, the cross-sectional method suffers from the fact that the subjects' backgrounds (parents, family income, nutrition) differ and the subjects may have learned various things in different ways. Further, the subjects' behavior, performance in a specific task, or ability might reflect a predisposition, a liking of the task, or some other variable unrelated to changes that come from development or aging. With this method, individual differences are impossible to assess. The longitudinal method also has problems. For one thing, it requires repeated access to the same subjects; but some subjects may move, withdraw from the study, or even die. Also, after repeated testing on the same task (even though the tests are months or years apart), subjects may do better because of practice. Moreover, longitudinal research sometimes takes years to complete; and during that time, important changes may occur in the environment and in the social world of the subjects. Finally, the research is time-consuming and expensive.

Regardless of the method used, most psychologists have a point of view—a theoretical orientation. Some theorists adopt the *reductionistic* (mechanistic) *view;* they believe that if we can reduce an organism's behavior to its essential elements, we can explain the behavior. According to this view, organisms wait for influences in the environment to affect them: All human beings are born alike; differences come about because of different experiences.

The *organismic view,* in contrast, asserts that people go through development stages that are qualitatively different and cannot be reduced to simple elements. The organism actively affects its world rather than simply waiting for the world to affect it. Development occurs in a series of stages in which key characteristics are likely to emerge.

A third way of looking at development is the *contextual view.* Here, all the events in an organism's life are related. The contextualist looks at behavior from the standpoint of the stage of the organism's life and the context in which the behavior occurs. This view blends the reductionistic and organismic views with a third element: social context.

Each of these views must look at the general behavior of people in order to generate laws of human development, sometimes called *nomothetic laws.* In addition, they must provide *idiographic patterns*—patterns that are unique to individuals. Researchers must be sensitive to the idea that the environments for each individual are not shared by others, even by family members. Family members often differ from one another significantly, despite a shared genetic heritage and shared family experiences. In a presidential address to a group of developmental psychologists, Sandra Scarr (1992, p. 14) argues that the individuality of behavior is so different because each person has unique experiences, so that "the ways they evoke behavior from others, actively select or ignore opportunities, and construct their own experience" determine their individuality.

We will now begin looking at events that influenced us even before we were born. These events are heavily influenced by biology as well as by the environment in which we live.

The First Nine Months

Conception occurs when an ovum and a sperm join in the Fallopian tube to form a **zygote**—a fertilized egg. During the next 5 to 7 days, the zygote descends through the Fallopian tube and implants itself in the blood-lined wall of the uterus. From that time until the 49th day after conception, the organism is called an **embryo.** Then, from the 8th week until birth, the organism is called a **fetus.** On the average, maturation and development take 266 days, or 9 months. For descriptive purposes, this period is divided into three trimesters (3-month periods). Table 8.1 describes the prenatal (before birth) and postnatal (after birth) periods of development.

Prenatal Development

The First Trimester. Within minutes after the zygote is formed, basic characteristics are established. They include the color of the hair, skin, and eyes; the sex (gender); the likelihood that the person will be tall or short, fat or lean; and per-

Zygote: A fertilized egg.

Embryo: [EM-bree-o] The human organism from the 5th through the 49th day after conception.

Fetus: The human organism from the 49th day after conception until birth.

haps basic intellectual abilities and personality traits. Within 10 hours, the zygote divides into four cells. During the 1st week, about a dozen cells descend from the Fallopian tube to the uterus, where they begin the process of *differentiation* (organs and other parts of the body begin to form). Some cells form the *umbilical cord*—a group of blood vessels and tissues that connect the zygote to the placenta. The **placenta** is a mass of tissue in the uterus that acts as the life-support system for the fetus by supplying it with oxygen,

TABLE 8.1 *Life Stages and Approximate Ages in Development*

Life Stage	Approximate Age
Prenatal period	
Zygote	Conception to day 5 or 6
Embryo	Day 5 to day 49
Fetus	Week 8 to birth
Postnatal period	
Infancy	Birth to age 2
Toddlerhood	Age 2 to 3
Early childhood	Age 3 to 6
Middle childhood	Age 6 to 13
Adolescence	Age 13 to 20
Young adulthood	Age 20 to 40
Middle adulthood	Age 40 to 65
Late adulthood	Age 65 on

Conception occurs when an ovum and sperm join to form a fertilized egg.

food, and antibodies from the mother and by eliminating wastes by way of the mother. By the end of the 1st week, the developing organism is an embryo made up of as many as 150 cells attached to the wall of the uterus.

During the 1st month, the embryo begins to take shape. Although only a half inch long, its arms and legs begin to form and it acquires the rudiments of eyes, ears, mouth, and brain. By the 25th day, a primitive version of the heart is beating.

During the 2nd month, the embryo begins to resemble a human being. Each day, it grows about a millimeter, and new parts begin to take shape. The nose begins to form about the 33rd day, and the first true bone cells appear on about the 47th day.

In the 3rd month, growth continues, features become more defined, and sex characteristics begin to appear. The digestive, breathing, and musculature systems become stronger. At the end of the 3rd month, the fetus is about 3 inches long and weighs 1 ounce. It can kick its legs, turn its feet, and swallow, although the mother cannot yet feel its movement.

The Second Trimester. During the second 3-month period, the fetus consumes a good deal of food, oxygen, and water through the placenta; and its weight and strength increase. In the 4th or 5th month, it can be up to 10 inches long, its muscles are significantly stronger, and its heartbeat can be heard with a stethoscope. Late in the 4th month or in the 5th month, the mother may begin to feel the movement of the fetus.

In the 5th and 6th months, the fetus grows about 2 inches per month. At the end of the second trimester (about 28 weeks), it is about 14 inches long. Its respiratory system is mature enough to enable it to live outside the uterus, increasing the chances of survival if it is born prematurely.

The Third Trimester. In the last trimester, the fetus gains weight rapidly—usually a pound in the 7th month, 2 pounds in the 8th, and a pound a week in the 9th. Its respiratory system and internal organs continue to develop, and its muscles mature significantly. The mother can feel strong kicking and movement.

Table 8.2 on page 282 summarizes the major physical developments during the prenatal period.

Placenta: [pluh-SENT-uh] A group of blood vessels and membranes in the uterus connected to the fetus by the umbilical cord and serving as the mechanism for the exchange of nutrients and waste products.

TABLE 8.2

Major Developments during the Prenatal Period

AGE	SIZE	CHARACTERISTICS
1 week	150 cells	Ovum attaches to uterine lining.
2 weeks	Several thousand cells	Placental circulation established.
3 weeks	1/10 inch	Heart and blood vessels begin to develop. Basics of brain and central nervous system form.
4 weeks	1/4 inch	Kidneys and digestive tract begin to form. Rudiments of ears, nose, and eyes are present.

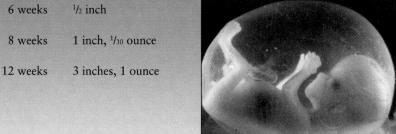

AGE	SIZE	CHARACTERISTICS
6 weeks	1/2 inch	Arms and legs develop. Jaws form around mouth.
8 weeks	1 inch, 1/30 ounce	Bones begin to develop in limbs. Sex organs begin to form.
12 weeks	3 inches, 1 ounce	Gender can be distinguished. Kidneys are functioning, and liver is manufacturing red blood cells. Fetal movements can be detected by a physician.

AGE	SIZE	CHARACTERISTICS
16 weeks	6½ inches, 4 ounces	Heartbeat can be detected by a physician. Bones begin to calcify.
20 weeks	10 inches, 8 ounces	Mother feels fetal movements.
24 weeks	12 inches, 1½ pounds	Vernix (white waxy substance) protects the body. Eyes open, eyebrows and eyelashes form, skin is wrinkled and red, respiratory system is not mature enough to support life.

AGE	SIZE	CHARACTERISTICS
28 weeks	15 inches, 2½ pounds	Fetus is fully developed but needs to gain in size, strength, and maturity of systems.
32 weeks	17 inches, 4 pounds	A layer of fat forms beneath the skin to regulate body temperature.
36 weeks	19 inches, 6 pounds	Fetus settles into position for birth.
38 weeks	21 inches, 8 pounds	Fetus arrives at full term—266 days from conception.

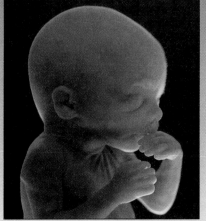

Harmful Environmental Influences on the Fetus

People have long assumed that the behavior of a pregnant woman affects her unborn child's development. Medieval European doctors advised pregnant women that uplifting thoughts would help the baby develop into a good, happy person, while fright, despondency, and negative emotions might disrupt the pregnancy and possibly influence the infant to become sad or mean-spirited. Today, some pregnant women wear fetal belts that play soothing music to the unborn child, who can listen and thereby gain a benevolent perspective of the outside world.

While a fetus may not be affected by the mother's condition to the extent suggested by medieval doctors, it is known that, from conception until birth, the environment and life-support systems provided by the mother influence the fetus. Environmental factors such as diet, infection, radiation, and drugs affect both the mother and the fetus.

Substances that can produce developmental malformations (birth defects) in a fetus are known as **teratogens.** These defects are the leading cause of death of infants in their first year of life. If the mother drinks alcoholic beverages in early and middle pregnancy, the baby is more likely to be born prematurely, to have a lower birth weight, and to suffer from mental retardation or hyperactivity (Streissguth, Barr, & Martin, 1983). One study showed that drinking more than 3 ounces of 100 proof liquor per day during pregnancy was significantly related to a small decrease in a 4-year-old's intelligence test scores (Streissguth et al., 1989).

Studies show that any drug can affect fetal development. High doses of aspirin, for example, may cause fetal bleeding, although this evidence is controversial (Werler, Mitchell, & Shapiro, 1989). Cigarette smoking constricts the oxygen supply to the fetus. Babies born to mothers who smoke tend to be smaller and may be at increased risk for cleft palate, mental retardation, and hyperactivity (Hunt, 1983). Cocaine, marijuana, and tranquilizers can all be teratogenic, producing major irreversible malformations and neurological disorders (Lester & Dreher, 1989; Kopp & Kaler, 1989). Unfortunately, in the last few years, hundreds of thousands of infants have been born each year addicted to cocaine or related drugs. The influence of drugs is especially important during the embryonic stage of development, when the mother may not realize she is pregnant.

Animal studies also support the idea that prenatal stress has negative consequences in offspring (Pfister & Muir, 1992). Even a human mother's mood during pregnancy or shortly thereafter may have an effect. One study (Dawson et al., 1991) indicated that children of depressed mothers showed unusual brain-wave activity. This study is just a first step in the examination of such relationships, and its results are likely to generate debate and further research.

The Birth Process

Approximately 9 months after conception, the mother goes into **labor**—the process in which the uterus contracts to open the cervix so the fetus can descend through the birth canal to the outside world. The process is divided into three stages: early labor, active labor, and transition. Although each woman's labor is different, most women experience characteristic sensations during the three stages.

To allow the fetus to descend through the birth canal, the cervix has to open (dilate) to about 10 centimeters (4 inches). In *early labor,* the cervix dilates to about 3 centimeters. Labor pains from contractions of the uterine muscles occur at regular intervals, from 5 to 30 minutes apart, and last approximately 30 seconds each. In *active labor,* the cervix dilates to 7 centimeters. Contractions are about 3 to 5 minutes apart and more intense. During this stage, the woman usually goes to a hospital or birthing center if she is not giving birth at home. During *transition,* the mother is likely to experience major discomfort or pain. The cervix dilates to the full 10 centimeters, and contractions are much stronger and last longer.

The baby is now ready to be born. When people speak about the birth of a baby, they are usually referring to the slow descent through the birth canal. For anywhere from 5 minutes to 2 hours, the mother will bear down with her abdominal muscles, pushing the baby from the uterus through the birth canal. Until delivery, the fetus is

Teratogens: [ter-AT-oh-jen] Substances that can produce developmental malformations in a fetus.

Labor: The process in which the uterus contracts to open the cervix so the fetus can descend through the birth canal to the outside world.

attached to its mother by the umbilical cord. Within a few minutes after delivery, the placenta at the end of the cord detaches from the wall of the uterus and is also delivered.

Natural Childbirth. Throughout most of human history, women delivered babies without the aid of doctors, nurses, or medication. Only during the past 70 years have women in developed countries given birth in hospitals, where professionals can respond quickly to complications. In these settings, few babies or mothers die in childbirth.

Since the 1970s, a movement has developed to keep medical intervention to a minimum during childbirth. A number of techniques help reduce the pain and discomfort of childbirth without drugs. The best-known technique is the *Lamaze method,* which has five basic components: (1) information about anatomy and physiology to reduce fear of the unknown; (2) respiratory techniques to maintain a steady oxygen supply during labor; (3) conditioned relaxation and training to respond to a uterine contraction by relaxing other muscles in the body; (4) a process of cognitive (thought) restructuring, which enables the mother to distract herself from the activities of the labor room; and (5) social support provided by a labor coach (usually the spouse), who attends the Lamaze classes with the mother and helps her through the labor.

The psychological benefits of Lamaze and other natural childbirth methods have not been adequately studied. However, most couples who have attended Lamaze classes are thankful for the preparation and feel more confident about the impending birth.

FOCUS

▶ What are the fundamental differences between the organismic view and the contextual view of development? p. 280

▶ What is the evidence that the embryonic stage is crucial for fetal development? pp. 280–281

Newborns, Infancy, and Early Childhood

Newborns are not nearly as helpless as many people believe. At birth, they can hear, see, smell, and respond to the environment in adaptive ways; in other words, they have good sensory systems. They also are directly affected by experience. To help them develop in optimal ways, psychologists try to find out how experience affects their perception. In doing so, psychologists need to discover how infants think, what they perceive, and how they react to the world. Researchers have therefore devised ingenious ways of "asking" newborns questions about their perceptual world. Some of these questions are: What are a child's inborn abilities and reflexes? When do inborn abilities become evident? How are inborn abilities affected by the environment?

The Newborn's Reflexes and Perceptual World

Babinski reflex: A reflex in which an infant projects its toes outward and up when the soles of its feet are touched.

Touch the palm of a newborn baby and you'll probably find one of your fingers held in the surprisingly firm grip of a tiny fist. The baby is exhibiting a reflexive reaction. Babies are born with innate *primary reflexes*—unlearned responses to stimuli. Some help ensure the baby's survival, and most disappear over the course of the 1st year of life. One primary reflex exhibited by infants is the **Babinski reflex**—a projection of the toes outward and up in response to a touch to the sole of the foot. Another is the **Moro reflex**—an outstretching of the arms and legs and crying in response to a loud noise or change in the environment. Infants also exhibit the **rooting reflex**—the turning of their head toward a mild stimulus (such as a breast or hand) that touches their lips or cheek. They show the **sucking reflex** in response to objects that touch their lips and the **grasping reflex** in response to an object touching the palms of their hands—infants vigorously grasp objects touching their fingers. Physicians use the presence or absence of primary reflexes at birth to assess neurological damage and to evaluate an infant's rate of development. The first illustration on page 292a summarizes the primary reflexes and their duration.

At first, an infant's abilities and reflexes are biologically determined through genetic transmission. Gradually, learned responses, such as reaching for desired objects or grasping a cup, replace reflex reactions. New experiences in the environment become more important in determining behavior. These complex interactions between nature and nurture follow a developmental time course that continues throughout life (see the illustrations on page 292a).

Fantz's Viewing Box. An avalanche of research on infant perception shows that newborns have surprisingly well-developed perceptual systems. Some of the early work was done by Robert Fantz (1961), who designed a viewing box in which he placed infants; he then had a hidden observer or camera record their responses to stimuli (see Figure 8.2). The exciting part of Fantz's work was not so much that he asked interesting questions but that he was able to get "answers" from the

Moro reflex: A reflex in which an infant stretches out its arms and legs and cries when there is a loud noise or abrupt change in the environment.

Rooting reflex: A reflex in which an infant turns its head toward a mild stimulus applied to its lips or cheeks.

Sucking reflex: A reflex in which an infant makes sucking motions when presented with a stimulus to the lips, such as a nipple.

Grasping reflex: A reflex in which an infant grasps vigorously any object touching its palm or fingers or placed in its hand.

FIGURE 8.2

Results of Fantz's Study

Using a viewing box to observe newborns' eye movements, Fantz (1961) recorded the total time infants spent looking at various patterns. He found that they looked at faces or patterned material much more often than they looked at homogeneous fields.

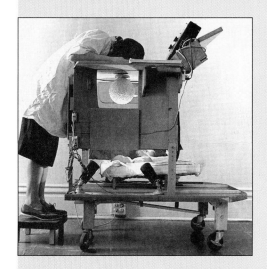

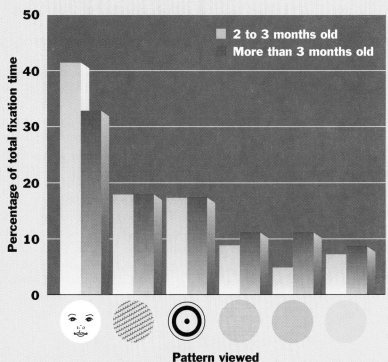

infants. By showing infants various pictures of faces and patterns and recording their eye movements, he discovered the infants' visual preferences. He recorded how long and how often the infants looked at each picture and calculated the total time they spent viewing each type of picture. Because they spent more time looking at pictures of faces than at pictures of random squiggles, Fantz concluded that they could see different patterns and that they preferred faces.

Infants prefer complex visual fields over simple ones, curved patterns over straight or angular ones, and human faces over random patterns or faces with mixed-up features (Haaf, Smith, & Smitley, 1983; Walton & Bower, 1993). Even in the first few months of life, babies can discriminate among facial features (Nelson, 1987) and prefer attractive faces to less attractive ones (Langlois et al., 1991). Newborns look at pictures of their parents more than at pictures of strangers and at eyes more than at other features (Mauer & Salapatek, 1976). We also know that babies respond to caregivers by imitating their facial gestures some of the time (Kaitz, Meschulach-Sarfaty, & Auerbach, 1988), although research in this area is controversial and the findings are not always consistent (Nelson & Ludemann, 1989).

Using a procedure similar to Fantz's, Walker-Andrews (1986) observed 5- and 7-month-old infants who saw films of people with angry or happy facial expressions making angry or happy sounds. (The lower third of the people's faces was covered so the infants could not match the sounds to the lips.) The researcher showed that 7-month-old infants could tell when the sound and facial expression did not match, but 5-month-olds could not. Walker-Andrews's research supports the idea of a timetable by which infants develop the ability to discriminate among facial expressions.

The Visual Cliff. One of the best-known developmental research studies was done by Walk and Gibson in 1961. They devised the *visual cliff method* to determine the extent of infants' depth perception. In this method, the researcher places an infant on a glass surface, half of which is covered with a checkerboard pattern. The same pattern is placed several feet below the transparent half of the glass surface. Infants can crawl easily from the patterned area onto the transparent area. Infants who lack depth perception should be willing to crawl onto the transparent side as often as onto the patterned side. Conversely, infants who have depth perception should refuse to crawl onto the transparent side, even when encouraged to do so by their mothers. Walk and Gibson found that infants who can crawl will avoid the transparent surface, thus proving that they have depth perception.

Sorce and his colleagues (1985) used the visual cliff method to study infants' responses to parents' facial expressions. They placed each 12-month-old baby on the "shallow" side of the visual cliff and put an attractive toy on the "deep" side, where the

When placed on the visual cliff, most babies over 6 months of age will not crawl to the "deep" side; this reticence indicates that they have developed depth perception.

mother was standing. At first, each mother smiled to encourage her baby to crawl toward the toy. When a baby could see the change in depth, the mother either looked fearful or angry or continued to smile. The researchers found that a baby who was uncertain about what to do at the visual cliff used the mother's facial expression to help the baby decide. If the mother looked fearful or angry, few babies crossed; if the mother smiled, most of the babies crossed. Sorce and his colleagues concluded that the mother's facial expression is a key source of information for infants. Babies are responsive to facial expression, and even to attractiveness (Langlois, Roggman, & Rieser-Danner, 1990).

In sum, newborns enter the world with the ability to experience, respond to, and learn from the environment. In general, therefore, we say that the sensory systems of newborns are well formed but still developing; their development is subject to experience, which ultimately alters brain connections permanently (M. Leon, 1992). Babies' development occurs in a certain order and on a rough timetable of developmental events during infancy and early childhood. These events are the topics considered next.

Physical and Emotional Changes in Infancy and Childhood

An infant who weighs 7.5 pounds at birth may weigh as much as 20 or 25 pounds by 12 months. At 18 months, the infant is usually walking and beginning to talk. For psychologists, infancy ends when the child begins to represent the world abstractly through language. Thus, *infancy* is the period from birth to 18 months; and *childhood* is the period from 18 months to about age 13—when *adolescence* begins.

In the 1970s and 1980s, it was widely held that bonding occurs. **Bonding** is a special process of emotional attachment suggested to occur between parents and babies immediately after birth. It is neither a reflex nor a learned behavior, though some psychologists claim it is inborn. Marshall Klaus and John Kennell (1983) believe that a mother is in a state of heightened sensitivity to her child immediately after delivery, and she begins to form unique, specific attachments to her child. Klaus argues that babies should have as much physical and emotional contact as possible with their mothers and fathers; keeping parents and infants together shortly after birth should be the rule, not the exception (Kennell, Voos, & Klaus, 1979). Research has not especially supported claims for bonding (Eyer, 1992). Eyer asserts that there is no evidence to support its existence and that it is a fictional concept; Eyer has offered a scathing critique of the bonding literature. The issue of the existence of bonding is not yet resolved, but many parents have welcomed the increased contact with their newborns that is reputed to facilitate bonding.

In the first weeks and months of life, the parent-infant attachment deepens as some of the infant's reflexes disappear and new behaviors appear. At about 4 to 8 weeks, infants may sleep for 4 to 6 hours during the night, uninterrupted by the need to eat (to the great relief of their weary parents). When awake, they smile at the mother, stare intently at mobiles and other moving objects, listen attentively to human voices, and reach out to touch objects. At 4 months, they have greater control over head movements and posture, they can sit with support, and they play with toys for longer periods.

At about 7 months, infants begin to crawl, giving them more freedom to seek out favorite toys and people and avoid threatening situations. The ability to crawl is accompanied by important changes in behavior. Infants now show strong preferences for the mother or other caregiver. During the period from 8 to 15 months, attachment to the mother may become so strong that her departure from the room

Bonding: A special process of emotional attachment suggested to occur between parents and babies in the minutes and hours immediately after birth.

Separation anxiety: In children from 8 to 15 months, the fear response displayed when the mother or caregiver is absent.

causes a fear response, especially to strangers; this response is known as **separation anxiety.** Some researchers have found that infants who show strong attachment at this age tend to be more curious and self-directed later in life (Ainsworth, 1979).

At the end of the 1st and the beginning of the 2nd year of life, children can walk, climb, and manipulate their environment—skills that often lead to the appearance of safety gates that block stairways, fasteners that lock cabinets, medicine bottles with childproof caps, and other safety features in the home. There is significant variability in the age at which a child begins to walk or climb. Some babies mature early; others are slow to develop these abilities. The age at which these specific behaviors occur seems unrelated to any other major developmental abilities. Figure 8.3 shows the major achievements in motor development for the first 15 months.

Attachment. Mothers of newborns form a close attachment to their babies. The mothers recognize their infants by smell, touch, and sound (Kaitz et al., 1992); and the infants similarly recognize the mothers (M. Leon, 1992). Some psychologists consider the establishment of a close and warm parent-child relationship one of the major accomplishments of the 1st year of life. A secure baby has a mother who is affectionate and especially responsive (Isabella, Belsky, & von Eye, 1989). This relationship makes later cognitive and emotional development easier (Sroufe & Waters, 1977). Not all researchers agree, but experimental studies show that the quality and nature of the mutual closeness formed between the newborn and the mother can make a difference in later life (P. Schwartz, 1983). Children who have not formed warm, close attachments early in life lack a sense of security and become anxious and overly dependent (Bowlby, 1977). As 6-year-olds, they are perceived as more aggressive and less competent than their more secure counterparts (D. A. Cohn, 1990). Those who have close attachments require less discipline and are less easily distracted (Bus & Van Ijzendoorn, 1988; Lewis & Feiring, 1989).

Can adoptive parents form the same type of secure, close attachment to the child as biological parents? Even without the initial post-delivery bonding that Klaus and Kennell describe (p. 287), adoptive parents form supportive, healthy family relationships. A caretaking atmosphere that is warm, consistent, and governed by the infant's needs is the key. Both adoptive and biological parents can provide such an atmosphere, and both adoptive and biological children can form strong attachments to their parents (Singer et al., 1985).

Once established, early attachment is fairly permanent. Brief separations from parents, as in child-care centers, do not adversely affect it. Influential psychologist Mary Ainsworth (1979) asserts that these parental attachments affect the child's later friendships, relations with relatives, and enduring adult relationships.

Verbal and Emotional Exchanges: Cross-Cultural Data

The extent to which infants focus on their caregivers increases significantly as they mature. Dialogues in the form of gestures, smiles, and vocalizations become more common. Mothers and fathers initiate these interactions as often as the infants do. This early play is good for babies as long as the babies are not overstimulated and annoyed by too much excitement (Singer & Singer, 1990).

Verbal exchanges help establish ties, teach language, inform infants about the world, and socialize infants. These exchanges seem to occur between all infants and parents—they are universal. In a cross-cultural study, parents in four countries—Argentina, France, Japan, and the United States—all used similar speech categories and spoke to older infants less than younger ones (Bornstein et al., 1992). There were some differences, too, of course. For example, Japanese mothers were willing to speak more ungrammatically to their infants, using nonsense words, songs, and

FIGURE 8.3

Infants' Development of Motor Abilities

Of the 1,036 normal Denver babies tested in the Denver Development Screening Test, 50 percent had mastered these motor skills at the ages indicated.

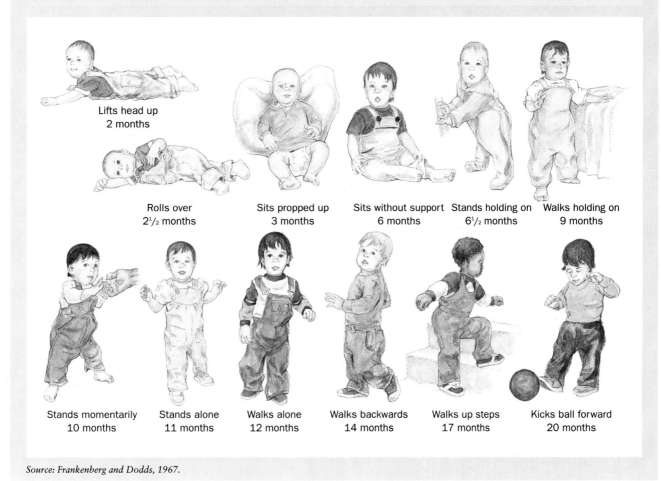

Lifts head up
2 months

Rolls over
2½ months

Sits propped up
3 months

Sits without support
6 months

Stands holding on
6½ months

Walks holding on
9 months

Stands momentarily
10 months

Stands alone
11 months

Walks alone
12 months

Walks backwards
14 months

Walks up steps
17 months

Kicks ball forward
20 months

Source: Frankenberg and Dodds, 1967.

rhythms more than mothers from the other countries did. However, the similarities among cultures outweigh the differences. The researchers concluded, "[The] universal aspects of infancy... appear... to exert control over the content of maternal speech" (p. 601).

Interactions between parents and babies are especially important in development. In an experiment in which mothers remained still and expressionless, their infants appeared sad and turned away from them (Cohn & Tronick, 1983). The implication is that the mere presence of a parent is not enough; the parent must interact both physically and vocally with the infant (Sorce & Emde, 1981) and must pay attention to the infant (Jones & Raag, 1989).

There are some cultural differences in responsiveness to infants. In a study of mother-infant interactions with participants from Kenya, Mexico, and the United States, researchers found that a mother's culture and schooling affect her responsiveness. In comparing women from Mexico and the United States, the researchers found that women who had more schooling—and therefore more institutionalized communication—were more verbally responsive than were women with less schooling (Richman, Miller, & LeVine, 1992). Emotional responsiveness also varied with culture. Women from Kenya were more likely to be soothing and protective to young infants; women from the United States were more verbally active and played a great deal. The cultural differences that appeared were evident at 4 months, and were even more pronounced at 9 months. How such verbal and emotional responsiveness on the part of mothers affects later development is a matter of speculation and a promising area for future research.

Several other important variables influence the type and amount of interaction between parents and infants. One is the baby's physical attractiveness, or cuteness (Hildebrandt, 1983). People judge especially beautiful babies as more competent, more likable, and healthier than average or unattractive babies (Stephan & Langlois, 1984). They are more likely to play with, speak to, tweak, jiggle, or smile at attractive children. This is not surprising; psychologists know that people are biased by the attractiveness of others, whether children or adults (Ritter & Langlois, 1988).

The baby's own behavior is also important. Clarke-Stewart (1973) found that the more often the child looked, smiled, or vocalized to his mother, the more affectionate and attached to the child she became, and further, the more responsive she was to her child's distress. Tronick and Cohn (1989) concur. They have found that infants and mothers both change their behavior in reaction to each other, and they argue that neither the baby nor the mother is a passive recipient of the other's emotions. Both are active participants in forming the attachment. The illustrations on page 292a present the approximate time at which various emotions generally emerge in infants.

Personality, Shyness, and Temperament

During the earliest months of life, some infants smile or reach out to a new face and readily accept being held or cuddled. Others are more inhibited. Still others exhibit extreme reticence, even distress, in the presence of strangers. As adults, the xenophobic infants (those who fear strangers) are likely to be inhibited, meek, and wavering (Caspi, Elder, & Bem, 1988).

Some psychologists believe each of us is born with a specific temperament: easygoing, willful, outgoing, or shy, to name a few. Newborns, infants, and children, like the adults they will eventually grow to be, are all different from one another. Generalizations from one child to all children are impossible, and even generalizations from a sample of children must be made with caution. So many variables can affect a child's growth and development that researchers painstakingly try to separate all the important ones. With this caution in mind, let us look at a study of temperament.

To examine shyness and temperament in infancy, Daniels and Plomin (1985) conducted a study with adopted infants, who were tested for shyness at 1 and 2 years of age. The researchers gathered information about both the adoptive and the biological parents of the infants and also collected data about children living with their biological parents. They found that in both biological and adoptive homes, parental ratings of an infant's shyness were associated with the mother's self-reports of her own shyness. These findings led them to conclude that the infant's environment plays an important role in the development of shyness.

Many researchers contend that some specific personality traits, including shyness, are long-lasting and may be biologically based. For example, Jerome Kagan and his colleagues found that 2- and 3-year-olds who were extremely cautious and shy tended to remain that way for 4 more years. They also found physiological evidence (an increase in autonomic nervous system activity, for example) that these children may be more responsive to change and unfamiliarity (Kagan & Snidman,

1991a). Daniels and Plomin (1985) found an important relationship between the shyness of the biological mother and the shyness of the adopted infant at 2 years of age. These findings suggest that genetic factors also play a role in shyness. Studies of identical twins on a range of emotional dimensions, especially temperament, also show support for a strong genetic component (Emde et al., 1992). However, shyness and other temperaments can be changed; human behavior is the product of deliberative thought processes as well as biological forces. Parents recognize that they affect a child's temperament and personality; they assume that their child-rearing practices will have important influences on development.

FOCUS

▶ Identify Robert Fantz's working hypothesis in his experiments about the perceptual abilities of infants.   p. 285

▶ What evidence is there for the existence of attachment? pp. 287–288

▶ Cite evidence to suggest that some traits, such as shyness, are inborn. p. 290

Intellectual Development

Why do some automobiles have childproof locks and windows? Why do parents use gates to guard stairs and gadgets to keep kitchen cabinets closed? Why are young children's toys made so that small parts cannot come off? The answer: Children are inquisitive and much more intelligent than many people give them credit for being.

The physical and social development of infants is visible and dramatic; the parents of infants will tell you that their babies seem to grow and change every day. The changes that occur in young children are less visible but no less dramatic. Children are continually developing intellectually; the changes they experience center on their ability to cope with an ever-expanding world. Older children can determine the difference between external and internal causes of behavior more easily than younger children. Much of this difference is intellectually based (Miller & Aloise, 1989).

The noted Swiss psychologist Jean Piaget (1892–1980) believed that the fundamental development of all intellectual abilities takes place during the first 2 years of life; many psychologists and educators agree. Piaget devised procedures for examining the intellectual development of young children. He described one such procedure as follows (Piaget, 1963, p. 283):

> Initially we relied exclusively on interviews and asked the children only verbal questions. . . . We now try to start with some action that the child must perform. We introduce him into an experimental setting, presenting him with objects and— after the problem has been stated—the child must do something, he must experiment. Having observed his actions and the manipulation of objects we can then pose the verbal questions that constitute the interview.

Piaget's theory focuses on *how* people think (thought processes) instead of on *what* they think (content), making it applicable to people in all societies and cultures. However, perhaps Piaget's greatest strength is his description of how a person's inherited capacities interact with the environment to produce an intellectually functioning child and adult. Although psychologists were initially skeptical of Piaget's ideas, and some criticisms persist, many researchers have shown that his assumptions are generally correct and can be applied cross-culturally. There are also dissenters (notably Russian psychologist Lev Vygotsky), who stress society's role in establishing thought processes (Rogoff & Morelli, 1989).

According to Piaget, both children and adults use two processes to deal with new ideas: assimilation and accommodation. **Assimilation** is the process by which a

Jean Piaget (1892–1980) devised procedures for examining the intellectual development of young children. His work continues to be extraordinarily influential in the field of child development.

Assimilation: According to Jean Piaget, the process by which new concepts and experiences are incorporated into existing mental frameworks so as to be used in a meaningful way.

Accommodation: According to Jean Piaget, the process by which new concepts and experiences modify existing cognitive structures and behaviors.

Sensorimotor stage: The first of Piaget's four stages of intellectual development (covering roughly the first 2 years of life), during which the child begins to interact with the environment and the rudiments of intelligence are established.

person absorbs new ideas and experiences, incorporates them into existing cognitive structures (thought processes) and behaviors, and uses them later in similar situations. **Accommodation** is the process of modifying previously developed cognitive structures and behaviors to adapt them to a new concept.

A child who learns to grasp a spoon demonstrates assimilation by later grasping similar objects, such as forks, crayons, and sticks. This assimilated behavior then serves as a foundation for accommodation. The child can learn the new, more complex behavior of grasping a sphere (such as a ball) by modifying the earlier response and widening the grasp. People accommodate new information every day by learning new words and then assimilating them by using the words themselves—only to be confronted with more new information. The two processes alternate in a never-ending cycle of intellectual and behavioral growth.

Assimilation and accommodation occur throughout four stages of development that Piaget described. The illustrations on page 292b show activities typical of each stage of an infant's first 12 months.

Piaget's Four Stages

Four *stages* of intellectual development are central to Piaget's theory. Piaget believed that just as standing must precede walking, some stages of intellectual development must precede others. For example, if a parent presents an idea that is too advanced, the child will not understand the new concept and no real learning will take place. A 4-year old who asks how babies are made will probably not understand the mother's biologically accurate explanation and will not learn or remember it. If the same child asks the question a few years later, the explanation will be more meaningful and more likely to be remembered. Piaget's stages are associated with approximate ages, and his theory brings the biological component of behavior into sharp focus. Although he acknowledged the role of environmental influences, Piaget clearly had a strong biological bias, especially in referring to stages of development. The four developmental stages are the sensorimotor stage, the preoperational stage, the concrete operations stage, and the formal operations stage.

The Sensorimotor Stage. Piaget considered the **sensorimotor stage,** which extends from birth to about age 2, to be the most important because the foundation for all intellectual development is established during this period. Consider the enormous changes that take place during the first 2 years of life. At birth, an infant is a totally dependent, reflexlike organism. Within a few weeks, infants learn some simple habits. They smile at the mother or other caretaker; they seek the stimulation offered by a colorful musical mobile hanging overhead; they reach out and anticipate events in the environment, such as the mother's breast or a bottle. At 2 to 3 months, infants develop a rudimentary memory for past events and are able to predict future visual events (Haith & McCarty, 1990). According to Piaget, the acquisition of memory is a crucial foundation for further intellectual development.

By the age of 6 to 8 months, infants seek new and more interesting kinds of stimulation. They can sit up and crawl. No longer willing just to watch what goes on around them, they begin to manipulate their environment, attempting what Piaget called "making interesting sights last." Karen Wynn (1992) suggests that, even at this age, infants have some key numerical reasoning abilities that lay the foundation for further arithmetic reasoning development. At about 8 months, infants begin to develop a sense of their own intentions, and they attempt to overcome obstacles to reach goals. They can now crawl to the other side of a room to where the cat is lying or follow the mother into the next room.

From about 9 months on, children develop *object permanence*—the ability to realize that objects continue to exist even when they are out of sight. Prior to the

For the next few years, the child will be unable to see situations from the point of view of another person. Intellectual immaturity makes a young child continue to pester Mom even after she says she has a headache and wants to be left alone (Elkind, 1981a). Children cannot usually put themselves in the mother's (or anyone else's) position.

The Preoperational Stage. At the end of Piaget's sensorimotor stage, children are just beginning to understand the difference between their ideas, feelings, and interests and those of others. This process of **decentration** continues for several years (M. E. Ford, 1979). Simultaneously, children may also become manipulative, difficult to deal with, and belligerent. Parents often describe this stage as the terrible 2s; it is characterized by the appearance of the ever-popular "No!" The child's behavior vacillates between charming and awful. This vacillation and annoying new habits, such as being difficult to dress and bathe, are signs of normal development and mark the beginning of the stage of preoperational thought.

In the **preoperational stage,** which lasts from about age 2 to age 6 or 7, children begin to represent the world symbolically. As preschoolers, they play with objects in new ways and try, through let's-pretend games, to represent reality. Nonetheless, they remain somewhat egocentric, continue to think concretely, and cannot deal with abstract thoughts that are not easily represented. They make few attempts to make their speech more intelligible or to justify their reasoning, and they may develop behavior problems such as inattentiveness, belligerence, and temper tantrums. During this stage, adults begin to teach children how to interact with others (Flavell, 1963), but major social and intellectual changes will not become fully apparent until the next stage of development.

The Concrete Operations Stage. According to Piaget, the preoperational stage is followed by the concrete operations stage. The **concrete operations stage** is Piaget's third stage of intellectual development, lasting from approximately age 6 or 7 to age 11 or 12, during which a child develops the ability to understand constant factors in the environment, rules, and higher-order symbolism such as arithmetic and geography. Children in this stage attend school, have friends, can take care of themselves, and may take on household responsibilities. They can look at a situation from more than one viewpoint and evaluate different aspects of it. The child has gained sufficient mental maturity to be able to distinguish between appearances and reality, and to think ahead one or two moves in checkers or other games. During this stage, children discover constancy in the world; they learn rules and understand the reasons for them. For example, a child learns to wear a raincoat on a cloudy morning, anticipating rain later in the day.

The hallmark of this stage is **conservation**—the ability to recognize that objects may be transformed, visually or physically, yet still have the same amount of weight, substance, or volume. This concept has been the subject of considerable research. In a typical conservation task, a child is shown three beakers. Two beakers are short, squat, and half full of water; a third is tall, thin, and empty (see Figure 8.5). The experimenter pours the water from one short, squat beaker into the tall, narrow one and asks the child, "Which beaker has more water?" A child who does not understand the principles of conservation will claim that the taller beaker contains more water. A child who is able to conserve volume will recognize that the same amount of water is in both the tall and the short beaker. A child who has mastered one type of conservation (for example, volume) often cannot immediately transfer that knowledge to other conservation tasks (for example, those involving weight).

A child who masters the concept of conservation realizes that specific facts are true because they follow logically, not simply because they are observed. Abundant research supports this claim. An example is the work of distinguished psychologist John H. Flavell (1988). Flavell and his colleagues have been studying a pheno-

Decentration: The process, beginning at about age 2, of changing from a totally self-oriented point of view to one that recognizes other people's feelings, ideas, and viewpoints.

Preoperational stage: Piaget's second stage of intellectual development (lasting from about age 2 to age 6 or 7), during which initial symbolic thought is developed.

Concrete operations stage: Piaget's third stage of intellectual development (lasting from approximately age 6 or 7 to age 11 or 12), during which the child develops the ability to understand constant factors in the environment, rules, and higher-order symbolism.

Conservation: The ability to recognize that something that changed in some way (such as the "shape" of liquid in a container) still has the same weight, substance, or volume.

Newborns' Reflexes

REFLEX	INITIATED BY	RESPONSE	DURATION
Eye blink	Flashing a light in the infant's eyes	Closing of both eyes	Lifelong
Babinski	Gently stroking the side of the infant's foot	Flexing of the big toe; fanning out of the other toes	Usually disappears near the end of the first year
Withdrawal	Pricking the sole of the infant's foot	Flexing of the leg	Present during the first 10 days; present but less intense later
Plantar	Pressing a finger against the ball of the infant's foot	Curling all the toes under	Disappears between 8 and 12 months
Moro	Making a sudden loud sound	Extending the arms and legs and then bringing the arms toward each other in a convulsive manner	Begins to decline in 3rd month; gone by 5th month
Rooting	Stroking the infant's cheek lightly with a finger or a nipple	Turning the head toward the finger, opening the mouth, and trying to suck	Disappears at approximately 3 to 4 months
Sucking	Inserting a finger into the infant's mouth	Sucking rhythmically	Often less intense and less regular during the first 3 to 4 days of life but continues for several months

Newborns' Emotional Responses

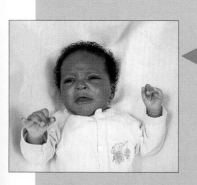

EMOTIONS	APPROXIMATE AGE OF EMERGENCE
Interest	Birth
Neonatal smile	Birth
Distress	Birth
Disgust	Birth
Social smile	4–6 weeks
Anger	3–4 months
Surprise	3–4 months
Sadness	3–4 months
Fear	5–7 months
Shame	6–8 months
Guilt	2nd year

Infants' Perceptual and Cognitive Milestones

1st WEEK

- **C**an see patterns, light, and dark
- **B**ecome sensitive to the location of sounds
- **C**an distinguish volume and pitch
- **P**refer high voices
- **W**ill grasp object if they touch it accidentally
- **S**top sucking to look at a person momentarily

1st MONTH

- **B**ecome excited at the sight of a person or toy
- **L**ook at objects only if in their line of vision
- **P**refer patterns to any color, brightness, or size
- **C**an coordinate eyes sideways, up, and down
- **C**an follow a toy from the side to the center of the body

2nd MONTH

- **P**refer people to objects
- **S**tare at human faces, become quiet at the sound of a human voice
- **A**re startled at sounds and make a facial response
- **R**each out voluntarily instead of grasping reflexively
- **C**an perceive depth
- **C**an coordinate eye movements
- **C**an discriminate among voices, people, tastes, and objects

3rd MONTH

- **F**ollow moving objects
- **G**lance from one object to another
- **C**an distinguish near objects from distant objects
- **S**earch with eyes for source of sounds
- **B**ecome aware of self through exploration
- **S**how signs of memory

4 to 7 MONTHS

- **S**ee the world in color and with near-adult vision
- **C**an pull dangling objects toward them
- **F**ollow dangling or moving objects
- **T**urn to follow sound and vanishing objects
- **V**isually search out fast-moving or fallen objects
- **B**egin to anticipate a whole object by seeing only part of it
- **D**eliberately imitate sounds and movements
- **R**emember a segment representing an entire situation
- **C**an recall a short series of actions
- **C**an look briefly for a toy that disappears

8 to 12 MONTHS

- **P**ut small objects into and pull them out of containers
- **S**earch behind a screen for an object if they see it hidden
- **C**an hold and manipulate one object while looking at a second
- **R**ecognize dimensions of objects

(Source: After Clarke-Stewart, Friedman, and Koch, 1985, p. 191)

292b

development of object permanence, when a mother leaves the room and the child can no longer see her, she no longer exists. After object permanence develops, the baby realizes that she is just out of view. Although the exact age at which object permanence becomes evident has not yet been established, Renée Baillargeon (1991) has shown the existence of object permanence for some tasks in 4-month-olds—earlier than Piaget believed possible. Various aspects of object permanence evolve gradually throughout the sensorimotor stage (see Figure 8.4).

In the second half of the sensorimotor stage (from about 12 to 24 months), children begin to walk, talk, and use simple forms of logic. Object permanence is more fully developed; the child can now follow a ball that rolls away and can search for the mother after she has left the room. Children also begin to use language to represent the world, an ability that takes them beyond the concrete world of visual imagery. By age 2, a child can talk about Grandma, Daddy, doggy, cookies, Big Bird, going bye-bye, and other objects and events. No longer an uncoordinated, reflex-oriented organism, the child has become a thinking, walking, talking human being.

Throughout the sensorimotor stage, few demands are made on the child. **Egocentrism,** or *self-centeredness*, shapes all behavior; it is the inability to perceive a situation or event except in relation to oneself. Children are unable to understand that the world does not exist solely to satisfy their interests and needs. They respond to questions such as Why does it snow? with answers such as "So I can play in it."

> **Egocentrism:** [ee-go-SENT-rism] The inability to perceive a situation or event except in relation to oneself. Also known as *self-centeredness*.

FIGURE 8.4

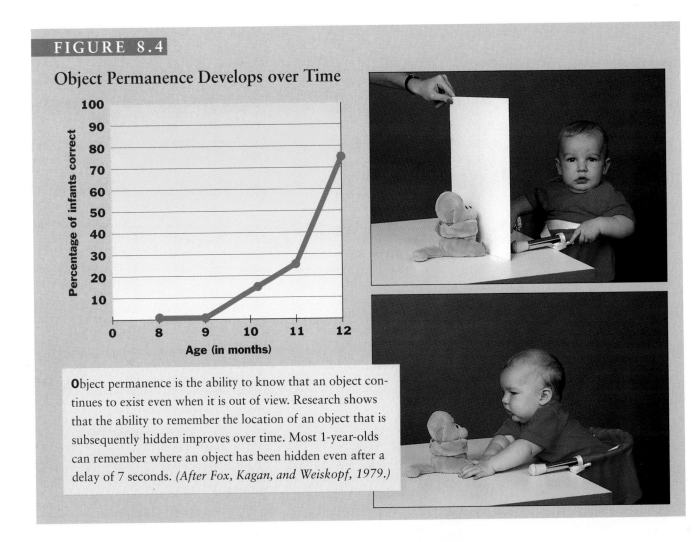

Object Permanence Develops over Time

Object permanence is the ability to know that an object continues to exist even when it is out of view. Research shows that the ability to remember the location of an object that is subsequently hidden improves over time. Most 1-year-olds can remember where an object has been hidden even after a delay of 7 seconds. *(After Fox, Kagan, and Weiskopf, 1979.)*

Lift page to see illustrations on pages 292a & b.

FIGURE 8.5

Development of Conservation

Conservation is the ability to recognize that an object that has been transformed is still the same object, regardless of any changes it has undergone.

1 A child examines two beakers (B and C) and sees that they are the same.

2 A researcher pours the contents of one beaker (C) into a taller and slimmer beaker (A).

3 The child is asked to indicate which beaker has "more" in it. Children who have not yet developed the ability to conserve will choose the tall beaker and often declare, "It has more in it; it's bigger."

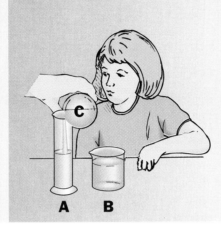

menon closely associated with conservation: the ability of children to distinguish between appearance and reality. They assert that, by the age of 6, children possess some knowledge about the difference between appearance and reality and can sense what a task is all about.

Piaget further held that children's understanding of space and their construction of alternative perspectives is limited until this stage has been mastered. Recent evidence, however, suggests that Piaget may have underestimated the perspective abilities of children. Researchers now find that even 5-year-olds can solve certain perspective problems previously thought to be solely in the domain of 9- to 10-year-olds (Newcombe & Huttenlocher, 1992). Even 3-year-olds have abilities to represent and remember the past that Piaget suggested were impossible (Gopnik, 1993).

Intellectual and perceptual cognitive abilities continue to develop as children mature and, slowly and in different ways, begin to grasp new and ever-more-difficult concepts (Flavell, Green, & Flavell, 1989). For example, at around age 7, children come to realize the connectedness of their thoughts and they become especially conscious of their inner mental life (Flavell, Green, & Flavell, 1993).

The Formal Operations Stage. The **formal operations stage** is Piaget's fourth and final stage of intellectual development (beginning at about age 12), during which the individual can think hypothetically, can consider all future possibilities, and is capable of deductive logic. Unlike children in the concrete operations stage, whose thought is still tied to immediate situations, adolescents can engage in abstract thought. They do this by forming hypotheses that allow them to think of different ways to represent situations, organizing them into all possible relationships and outcomes. The intellectual world of adolescents is full of informal theories of logic and ideas about themselves and life (Flavell, 1963).

By age 12, the egocentrism of the sensorimotor and preoperational stages has for the most part disappeared, but a new egocentrism has developed. According to

Formal operations stage: Piaget's fourth and final stage of intellectual development (beginning at about age 12), during which the individual can think hypothetically, can consider all future possibilities, and is capable of deductive logic.

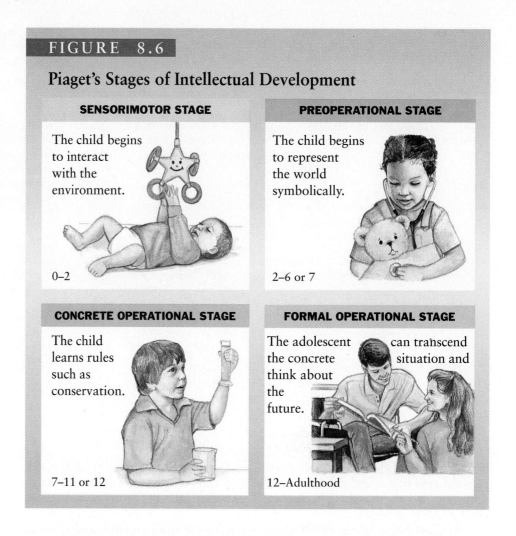

FIGURE 8.6

Piaget's Stages of Intellectual Development

SENSORIMOTOR STAGE

The child begins to interact with the environment.

0–2

PREOPERATIONAL STAGE

The child begins to represent the world symbolically.

2–6 or 7

CONCRETE OPERATIONAL STAGE

The child learns rules such as conservation.

7–11 or 12

FORMAL OPERATIONAL STAGE

The adolescent can transcend the concrete situation and think about the future.

12–Adulthood

Inhelder and Piaget (1958, pp. 345–346): "The adolescent goes through a phase in which he attributes an unlimited power to his own thoughts so that the dream of a glorious future or of transforming the world through ideas (even if this idealism takes a materialistic form) seems to be not only fantasy, but also an effective action which in itself modifies the empirical world." The egocentrism and naive hopes of adolescents eventually decrease as they face and deal with the challenges of life.

Piaget's stages of intellectual development are illustrated in Figure 8.6. A summary of some important points in Piaget's theory is presented in Table 8.3.

Implications and Criticisms of Piaget's Theory. Parents, educators, and psychologists can enhance children's intellectual development by understanding how cognitive abilities develop. For example, Piaget recognized that parental love and parent-child interaction are always important to a child's development, but he asserted that they are *essential* in the first 2 years of life. He also stressed the importance of providing a great deal of physical and intellectual stimuli, especially stimuli that move and change color, shape, and form. Research confirms that children and animals given sensory stimulation from birth through the early months develop more quickly both intellectually and socially than those who are not given such stimulation. Parents and educators who agree with Piaget have devoted their efforts to ensuring that the first years of life are ones in which stimulation is great, curiosity is encouraged, and exploration is maximized. From Piaget's point of view, they are optimizing children's potential.

> **TABLE 8.3 *Important Points in Piaget's Theory of Intellectual Development***
>
> 1. Cognitive development is a process in which each stage builds on the previous one.
> 2. The egocentrism of infants and children is reduced over a period of several years through the process of decentration.
> 3. The exact age at which each stage of development appears differs from one child to another, but all children in all societies go through the same stages.
> 4. To psychologists, the actual content of children's thoughts is less important than the nature of their thinking. By discovering how children think, psychologists can find ways to facilitate learning.

While acknowledging that it is possible to accelerate children's development, Piaget stressed that children should not be pushed too fast. Parents serve their children best by providing intellectual stimulation that is appropriate to their current developmental level. Noted psychologist David Elkind (1981b), in his book *The Hurried Child,* supports this view; he argues that overacceleration ultimately has deleterious effects. Yale psychologist Edward Zigler (1987, p. 257) concurs: "We are driving our children too hard and thereby depriving them of their most precious commodity—their childhood. . . . Children are growing up too fast today, and prematurely placing four-year-olds and five-year-olds into full-day preschool education programs will only compound the problem." In Zigler's view, developmentally appropriate care programs that focus on social interaction and recreation should be the focus for preschoolers. He asserts that the real business of a preschooler is socialization, not education.

Although Piaget's ideas have had an enormous influence on the ways psychologists think about children's development, some researchers have problems with his approach. For example, Fischer and Silvern (1985) remind psychologists that there is a great deal of variation in maturation and that a strict view of Piaget's stage approach reduces the role of the environment. Other researchers claim that Piaget's specific questions and tasks focus people's thinking about children on the wrong abilities and issues. Many studies of young children measure development by giving the same task to children of various ages. Children who cannot do the task are thought to be cognitively deficient.

Psychologist Rochel Gelman argues that researchers tend to underestimate younger children's abilities. Studies by Gelman and others show that to understand cognitive development fully, psychologists should ask children of different ages different questions. For example, Shatz and Gelman (1973) found that 2-year-olds change the length of their sentences on the basis of whom they are talking to, using shorter sentences when speaking to younger children. The researchers point to the cognitive maturity of a child who has decentered enough to make such a shift in point of view. Like Gelman, many researchers claim that Piaget may have overestimated the extent of egocentrism in young children. Baillargeon asserts that Piaget underestimated the abilities of infants. She holds that abilities that Piaget saw at 18 months are now found at 6 months of age (Miller & Baillargeon, 1990).

We know that cognitive maturity is impressive in 2-year-olds. Can such maturity, along with social maturity, be enhanced? Can the competency of young children be given a push, a leg up, a head start? In the 1960s, the federal government thought it could. As the Applications box on page 298 shows, the psychologists who advised the government were correct.

Did Project Head Start Work?

Project Head Start was initiated in the 1960s in an effort to break the poverty cycle by raising the social and educational competency of disadvantaged preschool children. Head Start has received federal support for more than 2 decades and is often referred to as a milestone in psychology. The multimillion-dollar project showed what can be done to provide remedial education, equal education, and effective use of child development techniques. Did it really work?

Project Head Start takes preschool-age children and provides them an enriched preschool environment for a year or two. Disadvantaged children are placed in a school with a low teacher-student ratio, and are provided nutritional and medical services. Parent involvement is central; parents work on school boards and in the classroom, and also receive related social services such as family counseling.

During the past several years there have been many reports documenting the success of Head Start. Preschool children score sharply higher at the end of their Head Start year than they did at the beginning (Haskins, 1989). However, Lee, Schnur, and Brooks-Gunn (1988) have questioned whether Head Start actually put disadvantaged children on an equal footing with others.

The investigators reanalyzed the data from Head Start, focusing on intellectual differences. They compared gains made by three groups of economically disadvantaged children: (1) students in Head Start, (2) students who attended no preschool program, and (3) students who attended another preschool program. More than 78 percent of the 900 participants in the study were members of minority groups. The aim was to determine whether the Head Start students made gains and, if so, whether those gains were equal to or better than those made by other students from low-income families.

The analysis showed clearly that children enrolled in Head Start programs made important gains and had an advantage over children who did not attend preschool and over children who attended another preschool program. However, although they made significant gains in cognitive abilities, Head Start children still did not do as well as children from upper socioeconomic status homes.

Research clearly shows that Project Head Start works well.

Why? One reason is that Head Start children tended to be especially disadvantaged, even compared with other disadvantaged groups. The researchers suggest that 1 year of Head Start may not be enough to close the gap. They argue that their data should be seen as a mandate for enhancing the program, suggesting that a second year would be likely to magnify and solidify the Head Start advantage.

Today, Head Start enrolls about 600,000 children a year, most of them from the neediest families—mostly African American and from the lower socioeconomic classes. Socioeconomic class is a critical determinant in school success (Duyme, 1988). As children from other racial minorities and from single-parent homes enter the program, different kinds of gains may be seen. Moreover, many of the benefits of Head Start may not be evident till later in life.

Many psychologists consider it imperative that programs such as Head Start and follow-up programs be expanded and funded at higher levels so they can reach out to a wider community. For example, the federal government's school breakfast program, which provides nutritious meals for low-income children, also produces increases in academic performance (Meyers et al., 1989). As Zigler (1987, p. 258) has written, "We simply cannot inoculate children in one year against the ravages of a life of deprivation." Clearly, it is essential that economically disadvantaged children be given an equal educational start in life—not just for a year but throughout their childhood (Woodhead, 1988).

Language Development

One of the most important aspects of children's development is the acquisition of language, as we saw in chapter 7. Young children have ways of communicating their desires and needs nonverbally—through facial expressions, hand motions, and other behaviors—but effective communication begins with the acquisition of language.

In the first few months of life, babies cry and coo. By 6 months, the sounds they make, called babbling, may become differentiated. Often, 6- to 8-month-old babies repeat the same sounds for hours or days at a time. By the end of a year, they have learned a few simple words, perhaps including *mama* and *dada*. From this naming stage, they go on to develop simple two- and three-word utterances. These utterances are often characterized as telegraphic because the infants use few words, as if they are trying to be economical.

Through their telegraphic two-word sentences, young children can convey an amazingly large number of thoughts. Sentences such as "No peas," "More ice cream," and "Change diaper" are quite explicit and make a child's needs and desires known.

However, even more important than the utterances themselves is the way they evolve into more complex statements as the children learn grammar (the rules and patterns for generating sentences in a language). Children learn grammar at an early age. Although 5- and 6-year-olds have not yet been taught all the grammar of their language, their speech includes the essentially correct use of nouns, verbs, and adjectives. The ability to use language produces dramatic changes in their lives, allowing them to interact on a more mature level with other people and to represent the world in increasingly complex ways.

FOCUS

▶ From Piaget's view, why are the first 2 years the most important time for intellectual development?   p. 290

▶ What was a key criticism of Piaget's research method? p. 296

▶ What evidence did researchers use to show that Head Start is a worthwhile program?   p. 298

Moral Reasoning

The physical and intellectual development of childhood is paralleled by growth in the capacity for moral reasoning. From childhood on, people develop **morality**—a system of learned attitudes about social practices, institutions, and individual behavior that allows people to evaluate situations and behavior as being right or wrong, good or bad. Morality lets people evaluate situations and act according to their beliefs.

Attitudes about morals develop and change throughout life. At an early age, children learn from their parents the behaviors, attitudes, and values considered appropriate and correct in their culture. Morality is aided by teachers and bolstered by church and community leaders as well as by family and friends. As children mature, they acquire attitudes that accommodate an increasingly complex view of the world and of reality. Your views of morality when you were a 10-year-old probably differ from your views today. The United States Supreme Court has restricted adolescents' rights to make important life decisions, in part because the Court believes adolescents lack moral maturity (Gardner, Scherer, & Tester, 1989). However, do they? Is the reasoning and judgment of a child, a preteen, or an adolescent like that of an adult?

Piaget and Morality

Piaget examined children's ability to analyze questions of morality and found the results to be consistent with his ideas about intellectual development. Young children's ideas about morality are rigid and rule-bound; children expect justice to follow from a particular act. When playing a game, a young child will not allow the

Morality: A system of learned attitudes about social practices, institutions, and individual behavior used to evaluate situations and behavior as being right or wrong, good or bad.

rules to be modified. Older children, on the other hand, recognize that rules are established by social convention and may need to be altered, depending on the situation. They have developed a sense of *moral relativity*, which allows them to recognize that situational factors affect the way things are perceived and that people may or may not receive their just reward or punishment (Piaget, 1932).

According to Piaget, as children mature, they move from inflexibility toward relativity in their moral judgments; they develop new cognitive structures and assimilate and accommodate new ideas. When young children are questioned about lying, for example, they respond that it is always and under any circumstances bad—a person should never lie. Sometime between the ages of 5 and 12, however, children recognize that lying may be permissible in some special circumstances.

Kohlberg: Heinz's Dilemma

Piaget's theory of moral development was based on descriptions of how children respond to specific kinds of questions and at what age they switch and use other forms of answers. The research of Harvard psychologist Lawrence Kohlberg (1927–1987) grew out of Piaget's work. Kohlberg believed that moral development in general proceeds through three levels, each of which is divided into two stages. The central concept in Kohlberg's theory is that of justice. In his studies of moral reasoning, Kohlberg presented different types of stories to people of various ages and asked them what the stories meant to them and how they felt about them (Kohlberg, 1969). In one story, Heinz, a poor man, stole a drug for his wife, who would have died without it:

> In Europe a woman was near death from a special kind of cancer. There was one drug that doctors thought might save her. It was a form of radium that a druggist in the same town recently discovered. The drug was expensive to make, but the druggist was charging ten times what the drug cost him to make. He paid $200 for the radium and charged $2,000 for a small dose of the drug. The sick woman's husband, Heinz, went to everyone he knew to borrow the money, but he could only get together $1,000, which is half of what it cost. He told the druggist that his wife was dying, and asked him to sell it cheaper or let him pay later. But the druggist said, "No, I discovered the drug, and I'm going to make money from it." So Heinz got desperate and broke into the man's store to steal the drug for his wife. (p. 379)

Kohlberg asked his subjects about the morality and justice of Heinz's action: Would a good husband steal for his wife? Was it actually wrong? Why? Adults' interpretations of Heinz's plight differed from those of adolescents and 5-year-olds. Children had difficulty seeing that Heinz's circumstances might influence the way his action could be judged (Kohlberg, 1976). Kohlberg found that people's judgments of the behavior of others vary with their level of moral development.

Three Levels of Morality. Presented with the story of Heinz, children at level 1 morality either condemn Heinz's behavior (explaining that he should be punished because he stole) or justify it (explaining that Heinz was good because he tried to save his wife's life). People at level 2 morality say that Heinz broke the law by stealing and should go to jail. Only people who have reached level 3 can see that although Heinz was justified in his action, the ethical dilemma is complex (see Figure 8.7).

Young children at level 1, *preconventional morality,* base their decisions about right and wrong on the likelihood of avoiding punishment and obtaining rewards. A child in this stage would say it is "bad" to pull the cat's tail, "because Mom will spank me." School-age children, who are at level 2, adopt *conventional morality;* they conform in order to avoid the disapproval of other people. At this stage, a 10-year-old might choose not to try cigarettes because his parents and friends disap-

Lawrence Kohlberg

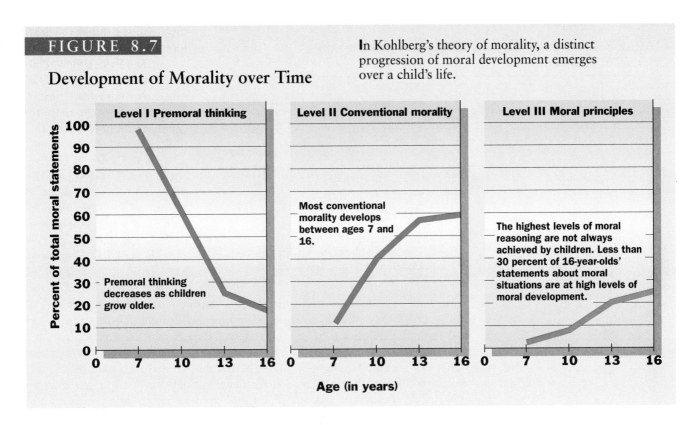

FIGURE 8.7

Development of Morality over Time

In Kohlberg's theory of morality, a distinct progression of moral development emerges over a child's life.

Level I Premoral thinking

Percent of total moral statements

Premoral thinking decreases as children grow older.

Level II Conventional morality

Most conventional morality develops between ages 7 and 16.

Level III Moral principles

The highest levels of moral reasoning are not always achieved by children. Less than 30 percent of 16-year-olds' statements about moral situations are at high levels of moral development.

Age (in years)

prove of smoking. Level 2 judgments are also governed by a process that considers the implications of a person's behavior. Why did he do it? What will be the consequences for him and for others?

Level 3, or *postconventional morality*, is concerned with contracts, moral conscience, and laws. In level 3 morality, people make judgments on the basis of their perception of the needs of society, with the goal of maintaining community welfare and the legal order. In advanced stages of level 3, people make judgments on the basis of their personal moral beliefs and values rather than those of society. Conscientious objection to legally sanctioned behaviors would be associated with this stage. For example, a person may be opposed to capital punishment, even though it is legal in some states. Most adults reach at least the first parts of level 3. Table 8.4 on page 302 compares Piaget's and Kohlberg's theories on moral development.

Extending Initial Ideas. Piaget set the stage for 2 decades of research by Kohlberg, whose work was monumental in scope. Like other great thinkers, Kohlberg laid down a theory that he knew would be tested, evaluated, and revised—a firm foundation for the next generation of research.

Piaget and Kohlberg studied moral reasoning, not moral behavior. Both theorists focused on how people make decisions, not on the behavior that might result from those decisions. However, their theories differ. Piaget thought of the stages of moral development as discrete, whereas Kohlberg viewed them as overlapping. Kohlberg also went further than Piaget in systematizing the development of morality. He elaborated on ideas about how children's interactions with parents and friends may influence their conceptions of morality. For example, when children realize that working within or around the rules affects other family members, their view of the rules changes. Thus, an older girl will spare her mother embarrassment and respond favorably when asked her opinion about her mother's carefully chosen new dress; a younger child will refuse to break the rules about lying and will tell her

TABLE 8.4 *A Comparison of Piaget and Kohlberg on Moral Development*

Piaget	Kohlberg
Sensorimotor and preoperational (birth–6 or 7 years)	Level 1—*Preconventional morality* Stage 1: Obedience and punishment orientation Stage 2: Naively egoistic orientation
Concrete operations (7–11 or 12 years)	Level 2—*Conventional morality* Stage 3: Good-child orientation Stage 4: Authority-and-social-order-maintaining orientation
Formal operations (12 years and beyond)	Level 3—*Postconventional morality* Stage 5: Contractual-legalistic orientation Stage 6: Conscience or principle orientation

mother if she thinks the dress looks ugly (Blasi, 1980).

In Kohlberg's view, children may use earlier levels of moral reasoning from time to time, even though they are capable of higher levels; this finding has been substantiated by the work of DeVries and Walker (1986). They asked university students to fill out an attitude questionnaire and write an essay on capital punishment. The results showed that the subjects had achieved high levels of moral reasoning but often did not reason at those levels in supporting their positions on capital punishment. In fact, 24 percent of the subjects used a level of moral reasoning that was a full stage lower than that which they were capable of using. Researchers are expanding on the original Kohlberg research, using different contexts—for example, a classroom where perceptions of fairness are being evaluated across the age span (Thorkildsen, 1989).

Kohlberg's theory has not gone unchallenged. Some have suggested that his views are culturally bound and that he did not examine issues with which normal adults have to deal. For example, Yussen (1977) has shown that older children and teenagers consider other moral issues in their lives more important than the Heinz dilemma. This criticism does not make Kohlberg's work any less important; however, it does raise some significant questions.

Gender Differences: Gilligan's Work

A major addition to the study of morality has been the work of Carol Gilligan (1982), who found that people look at more than justice when they analyze moral conflicts. She discovered that people are also concerned with caring, with relationships, and with connections with other people.

Carol Gilligan

Though Kohlberg and his colleagues had not generally reported any gender differences, Gilligan did. *Gender differences* are, of course, differences between males and females in behavior or mental processes. She examined differences between girls and boys in their inclinations toward caring and justice. She found that girls are more concerned with care, relationships, and connections with other people. As younger children, girls gravitate toward a morality of caring, while boys gravitate toward a morality of justice. Gilligan asserts that the difference between boys and girls is established by gender and by the child's relationship with the mother. Because of the gender difference between boys and their mothers, boys see that they are essentially different from other people, whereas girls develop a belief in their similarity (connectedness) with others. As older children, Gilligan asserts that the transition to adolescence turns out to be a crucial time during which girls may develop their own voice—a voice too often muted and suppressed (Brown & Gilligan, 1992). Gilligan shows that boys respond to the Heinz dilemma by indicating that sometimes people must act on their own to do the right thing. Girls, by contrast, are more likely to look for ways to talk out differences or to seek some compromise. Like Kohlberg, Gilligan argues that the development of caring follows a time course, with initial caring only toward oneself, later caring toward others as well, and ultimately (in some people) a more mature stage of caring for truth.

Gilligan's work has been influential in psychologists' evaluations of morality. Yet her approach fosters a continuation of gender stereotyping—women as caring, men as logical. Moreover, her work has been limited to white, middle-class children; it needs a broader, more multicultural perspective.

Cross-Cultural Gender Differences. Does women's inclination toward caring show itself in other cultures? Three researchers from Brigham Young University examined questionnaire responses of women in Korea, China, Thailand, and the United States (Stimpson, Jensen, & Neff, 1992). Their results show that Gilligan's work holds up in the three non-Western cultures, and they suggest that differences in caring between men and women may initially have a biological origin.

Caring and Justice Are Not Incompatible. Caring and justice are not incompatible values; indeed, they go together. That boys and girls develop them differently need not be seen as negative. Recognizing the differences between boys and girls allows us to expand the horizons of each to the full limit of their human potential (Damon, 1988).

The study of morality, justice, and caring has gone beyond Kohlberg's original view. For example, Kitwood (1990) argues that only after people have developed a sense of themselves can they fully care about others; he thus combines personality theory (discussed in chapter 12) with studies of morality. Moral reasoning and behavior, and especially promoting morality, have to be studied within the context of the total person.

Promoting Morality in Children

Although parents are the main source of children's moral values, Kohlberg suggested that other people can also help promote the development of morality and conscience (Windmiller, 1980). Kohlberg recommended that teachers as well as parents talk to children about moral issues related to situations such as war, death, education, and even cheating on taxes. These discussions are especially worthwhile when adults understand the stages of moral development (Damon, 1980).

Role taking—the ability to adopt perspectives different from one's own—is another way to foster morality. According to Kohlberg, children who have opportunities in classrooms, churches, and at home to consider moral dilemmas from another person's point of view are more likely to develop a mature sense of morality (Kohlberg, 1971). Through such consideration, people learn not only what society's values are but also how to think independently. Moreover, they achieve higher levels of moral reasoning, thereby gaining greater flexibility and independence in both judgment and behavior. For example, when older children and teenagers form a self-image and adopt gender-based characteristics, they often rely on the opinions and standards of others. However, a study of 13-, 17-, and 21-year-olds showed that both males and females at higher levels of moral reasoning tended to be less rigid than those at lower levels about incorporating some characteristics associated with the other gender into their own self-image (Leahy & Eiter, 1980). They could escape gender stereotyping and decide for themselves which characteristics would enhance their self-image.

FOCUS

▶ Distinguish the key differences among the preconventional, conventional, and postconventional levels of morality. pp. 300–301

▶ What is a potential research problem with the stories that Kohlberg used to discern moral development?   p. 301

▶ What was Gilligan's main criticism of Kohlberg's work? p. 302

Social Development

As society changes, so do ideas and practices related to children's social development. In a 1959 study of masculinity and father-son relationships, Paul Mussen and Luther Distler concluded that a father's importance and involvement in his son's life are crucial in determining the child's gender-based interests. A generation ago, when Mussen and Distler conducted their research, parents tended to encourage "masculine" traits such as athletic prowess in their sons and "feminine" traits such as shyness in their daughters. They accepted and promoted a gender-based social environment. Today, many parents deemphasize gender-based interests in their children, seeking to reduce or eliminate society's tendency to stereotype people, their interests, and their occupations on the basis of gender. The Diversity box examines the issue of gender stereotyping in greater depth.

Early Social Development

Social development begins at birth with the development of an attachment between parents and their newborn. The nature of a child's beginning and early interactions with parents is a crucial part of personality development. Infants have a great need to be hugged and cuddled, nurtured, and made to feel good. However, as psychoanalyst Bruno Bettelheim said, "Love is not enough." Eventually, parents must teach their children to interact with others and to become independent.

The First Months. In the first year of life, social interaction is limited because infants are largely egocentric. They seldom distinguish their needs and desires from those of others. In about the second half of the 1st year, children exhibit strong attachments to parents and other caregivers and fear of strangers. At 18 to 24 months, they have matured sufficiently to have specific desires and needs; however, they lack the language skills to make those needs known. A child cannot tell her father, for example, that she wants the green bib, not the blue one, although she can indicate her displeasure, often quite loudly (Ames et al., 1979). As early as 9 months, infants show they like to play games by indicating their unhappiness when an adult stops playing with them (Ross & Lollis, 1987). They play by themselves; but as they grow older, especially beyond 2 years of age, they engage in more social play with other children (Howes, Unger, & Seidner, 1989).

By the end of their second year, children have begun to understand that they are separate from their parents. They learn to differentiate themselves from others, to manipulate the world, and to interact with other people. As they enter the preoperational stage, egocentrism gives way to increased social interaction. At age 2, children generally play alone or alongside other children, but with little interaction. They prefer to play with an adult rather than with another 2-year-old (Jennings, Curry, & Connors, 1986). They are now better at controlling their emotional responses than they were at 18 months. Gradually they begin to socialize with their peers.

Sharing. The noted pediatrician Benjamin Spock once said that the only two things children will share willingly are communicable diseases and their mother's age. Actually, from age 2 until they begin school, children vacillate between quiet conformity and happy sharing, on the one hand, and making stubborn negative demands and exhibiting egocentric behavior, on the other. Because sharing is a socially desirable behavior, children must learn to share when they enter child-care centers, nursery school, or kindergarten.

Infants need to be held, cuddled, and nurtured.

Boys and Girls Behave Differently—Sometimes

Socialization starts at the moment of birth, when parents may begin treating their children differently on the basis of gender. Psychologists are especially aware of *gender stereotyping*—patterns of behavior expected of people according to their gender. Young boys are given footballs; young girls are given Barbie dolls. Boys wear blue, girls pink. Is this a problem?

You may believe that most gender-stereotyped behavior comes from parents—that boys and girls are treated differently in their formative years and for this reason develop differently. The reality is that most of the differences in the way boys and girls are raised are small (Lytton & Romney, 1991). In Western cultures, some of the differences are the following: (1) Boys receive physical punishment more often than girls. (2) Fathers tend to differentiate between sons and daughters more than do mothers. (3) The extent to which parents treat boys and girls differently tends to decrease as the children grow older.

However, the gender differences that do exist in the way parents raise their children tend to result from many factors. For example, boys tend to be assigned chores that take them away from people (such as yard work and feeding pets), whereas girls tend to be assigned in-house activities. As a consequence, some researchers assert, girls interact more with people and may therefore become more nur-

turing. In the same manner, boys may excel at manipulating objects and tools, while girls have fewer opportunities for inventive play. Not only are reinforced behaviors important, but (as we know from social learning theory) children learn gender-based ideas merely by watching the behavior of adults of their own gender. Moreover, there may be biological influences; that is, children may have preexisting preferences for gender-based behaviors.

We know that 18-month-old boys and girls show greater involvement with toys conventionally associated with their own gender—even if parents have not promoted play with same-gender stereotyped toys (Caldera, Huston, & O'Brien, 1989). This suggests a biological influence (Berenbaum & Hines, 1992). Further, starting at age 3 and continuing for several years, children prefer same-gender playmates. According to Eleanor Maccoby and Carol Jacklin (1987), this characteristic is reliable, cuts across a variety of situations, and is difficult to change. Gender segregation does not happen solely because children have been given "boy" toys or "girl" toys; nor does it result solely from inborn temperamental differences that lead to rough-and-tumble play for boys and more sedate play for girls. Children know they are members of one gender or the other. This knowledge binds

members of each gender together and differentiates them from members of the other one. Children with widely different personalities are drawn together solely on the basis of their shared gender. Maccoby (1990) asserts that gender differences are minimal when children are observed individually but become more evident in social situations.

It is apparent that nurturing and biological influences on children are both important factors in determining gender differences. However, gen-

der differences in behavior are small and are obvious only in certain situations (Oliver & Hyde, 1993), such as on the playground. As parents consider the implications of research on gender differences, they must use critical thinking skills. They should foster, among other things, children's achievement, moral values, and sense of self-esteem. None of these values is gender-based; both boys and girls can and should be taught to play, learn, reason, and solve problems. All children should be taught basic human values, and these too are not gender-specific.

Very young children do not understand the concept of sharing—particularly the idea that if you share with another child, the other child is more likely to share with you. In a laboratory study of sharing, researchers observed groups of two children separated by a gate. Initially, one child was given toys and the other wasn't; then the situation was reversed. The researchers found that none of the children shared spontaneously; however, 65 percent shared a toy when asked to do so by the mother.

Moreover, a child who was deprived of a toy after having shared one often approached the child who now had the toy. One child even said: "I gave you a toy. Why don't you give me one?" Children do not initiate sharing at a young age; but once they share, they seem to exhibit knowledge about reciprocal arrangements (Levitt et al., 1985).

Entry into kindergarten helps lead to a breakdown of egocentrism; however, many factors can either promote or retard this aspect of development. One variable is the type of toys children play with. Quilitch and Risley (1973) provided young children with two kinds of toys—those generally played with by one child at a time (isolate toys) and those designed for use by two or more children at the same time (social toys). All the children played with both kinds of toys, but some were first given social toys and others were first given isolate toys. After the initial play period, more of the children who had been given social toys first chose to play with other children. The researchers concluded that the kinds of toys given to children altered the degree of egocentrism exhibited in their play.

Single Parenting

Before this century, fathers were more likely than mothers to head one-parent families. Mothers rarely had the financial means to support children after divorce. High maternal mortality rates at birth also tended to make men the heads of single-parent households.

Today, more children than ever are being raised in single-parent homes. In the decade between 1970 and 1980 the number of single parents raising children increased by at least 28 percent. Only 4 percent of American households fit the traditional description of a working father, a mother who stays at home, and two or more school-age children. This means that 15 million children in the United States live with only one parent. According to the Bureau of the Census, 24 percent of children under the age of 6 live with just one parent (Bureau of the Census, 1989).

For the millions of divorced, widowed, or never-married parents who are rearing children alone, many of the traditional supports (such as the assistance of grandparents) are unavailable. Single parents tend to work longer hours than married parents, and their own parents and other relatives seldom live in the same community. Still, evidence exists that the effects of single parenthood are indirect and that single parents in some cases can do just as well as, if not better than, they did when they were married (if they were married) (M. N. Wilson, 1989).

Researchers are just beginning to ask about the role of absent parents on children's emotional development and maladjustment (Phares, 1992). They are now examining the effects of single parenting. Only recently have they realized the extent to which school-age children are being raised by single parents and the extent to which younger children are being cared for in child-care centers (Amato & Keith, 1991).

Child Care

According to the Bureau of the Census (1990), 58 percent of mothers with children under the age of 6 are working or looking for work outside the home; the figure increases to 74 percent for women whose children are between 6 and 13. By 1995, it is expected that 34 million children will have working mothers (Hofferth & Phillips, 1987). For families in which both parents have jobs, as well as for single-parent families, child care can be a necessity. Child-care centers provide care for about 23 percent of preschool children who have working mothers.

Child-care situations are becoming increasingly diverse as parents seek alternative arrangements for their children. While their mothers work, most preschool children are cared for in their own or other people's homes, often by babysitters, relatives, friends, fathers, former spouses, or grandparents (Presser, 1989; Bureau of the Census, 1987). Many Americans believe that when children are reared by people other than their parents, their development is less than optimal (Kagan, Kearsley, & Zelazo, 1980). In the past decade, this issue has been the subject of intensive research.

It isn't easy to determine the effects of child care because of a number of variables. These variables include the child's age at entry into a child-care program, the child's family background, the security of the child's attachment to parents, and the stability of the child-care arrangements (Belsky, 1990). All these factors can affect a child's response to the child-care experience (Howes & Stewart, 1987; Clarke-Stewart, 1989). Psychologists are especially interested in the relationship of child care and attachment because they believe that a child's emotional security depends on a strong, loving bond with a parent or primary caretaker (Kagan, Kearsley, & Zelazo, 1980). Contrary to popular belief, studies of attachment behaviors find that nonparental care does not reduce a child's emotional attachment to the mother (Etaugh, 1980). Moreover, there is no firm evidence that temporary separations, such as those caused by child care for preschool children, create later psychological trauma (Lamb et al., 1988).

Considerable evidence suggests that a stimulating, varied environment is necessary for optimal intellectual development and that high-quality child-care centers provide a sufficiently stimulating environment. High-quality child care means an experienced and highly qualified staff, a low staff-to-child ratio, and low staff turnover (Farber & Egeland, 1982). Belsky and Steinberg (1978) found no differences in intellectual functioning between middle-class children enrolled in high-quality child-care centers and children reared at home. In fact, high-quality child-care centers may increase children's positive social interactions with peers (Schindler, Moely, & Frank, 1987), may make the children appear happier (Vandell, Henderson, & Wilson, 1988), and may help prevent the declines in intellectual functioning that sometimes occur in children from low-income families who are not exposed to varied environments (e.g., Burchinal, Lee, & Ramey, 1989).

However, recent research has questioned the conventional wisdom of child care. The new research suggests that child-care centers may have negative effects on social development for children who spend more than 20 hours per week there. Jay Belsky of Pennsylvania State University asserts that extensive nonmaternal care in the 1st year of life is associated with insecurity in infants. Infants who received more than 20 hours of child care per week displayed more avoidance of their mothers when they were reunited than did infants who spent only a couple of hours in child care (Belsky & Rovine, 1988). In related work with noninfant children, Clarke-Stewart (1989) argues that studies indicate that children who spend extensive periods of time in child-care settings show increased disobedience, aggressiveness, bossiness, and brattiness—and that these children want their own way but do not know how to comfortably achieve it. Interestingly, this effect may be associated with the academic training of child-care workers, which emphasizes children's independence and assertiveness. Clarke-Stewart suggests that this problem may be considered the "dark side" of children's social training: "In good or poor day-care programs, it seems children do not follow social rules or resolve social conflicts without resorting to aggression unless special efforts are made by their caregivers" (p. 271).

A child's home environment and socialization can, of course, moderate some of these negative consequences. The sharing activities not normally done with children can produce positive effects (Moorehouse, 1991). First-class child-care centers do not necessarily produce negative effects. However, a short-staffed center, lengthy periods spent in child care, children who are difficult temperamentally, and parents who are not especially attentive to a child's needs may have deleterious effects.

Fathers and Their Children

The American family is undergoing dramatic changes. During the past 2 decades, women have entered the work force in unprecedented numbers and, in so doing, have changed the shape, structure, and fabric of family life. Women are spending less time with their young children. Are fathers taking up the slack? Do fathers spend enough time with their children? Is it "quality" time?

Assertions Lead to Hypotheses.

Today's fathers are more interested in their newborns and may be involved in their upbringing from the first moments of the child's life, as evidenced by the fact that many more fathers are now present in the delivery room during their children's birth. They are also affectionate and responsive care-givers (Parke & O'Leary, 1976). Two words often used in describing fathers' interactions with children are *quality* and *quantity*. Fathers sometimes assert that they spend limited time with their children but that this time is quality time. Grossman, Pollack, and Golding (1988) looked at the quality and quantity of interactions between fathers and their first-born 5-year-old children to determine whether this is true.

Methods.

The researchers studied 23 families participating in a Boston University pregnancy and parenthood project. They met with the parents during early pregnancy and within 2 weeks of the child's 5th birthday. On the first occasion, they measured a number of psychological, marital, and sociocultural variables. For example, they examined both the husband's and the wife's adapta-tion to life as an adult—their levels of anxiety, autonomy, marital adjustment, and age. At the 5-year follow-up, they measured both the quantity and the quality of time fathers spent with their children. To measure quantity, the researchers had the fathers estimate the average amount of time they spent with their children on weekdays and weekends, with respect to both playtime and care-taking. To measure quality, the researchers had the subjects perform a task that involved both parents and the child in their home. The researchers recorded the quality of the interactions during play in terms of warmth (was the parent critical or reinforcing?), attention, and responsiveness.

Results.

Quality and quantity of time were not directly related but were affected by numerous vari-

---

Today, researchers generally assert that good quality child care "is neither a benefit nor a detriment to the development of children from stable low-risk families" (Scarr & Eisenberg, 1993, p. 638). Yet, Belsky's and some of Clarke-Stewart's arguments contradict the findings of previous research. As a result, most psychologists are maintaining an open mind regarding child care and its effects. As Scarr, Phillips, and McCartney (1990) assert, we must consider the facts about child care—the evidence—not just the fantasies and the hopes of parents and psychologists. The research is far from complete.

Maternal employment is a reality in the 1990s. Thus, the issue for many parents is not whether infants should be in child care but rather how to make the best of the child-care experience (Clarke-Stewart, 1989). Parents considering child care either as an option or as a necessity should first establish specific care goals both for themselves and for their child. Sensitive and responsive care for children has to be the first priority (Belsky, 1990). If those goals can be met through child care, the parents should find the highest-quality child care affordable within a reasonable distance of home and work. Finally, they must also provide a supportive home environment.

The Research Process box explores the changing relationships of fathers and their children.

Latchkey Children

Millions of children come home from school to empty houses or apartments, where they take care of themselves until their parents return from work. They are known

ables. Some fathers spent enormous amounts of time with their children, others very little. Some spent quality time; others did not. Men who had been well adjusted during the wife's pregnancy spent relatively more time with their 5-year-olds. Men who enjoyed and were involved in their work spent less time with their children. Interestingly, women played a key role in the amount of time fathers spent with their children. Self-sufficient and autonomous women tended to have husbands who spent less time with their children and had happier, better-adjusted children (MacEwen & Barling, 1991.) These women tended to be willing and able to "do it all." (Of course, women who do it all may create situations that allow husbands to spend less time with their children.) On the quality issue, men who were happy, well adjusted, and satisfied at work were supportive of their children and spent quality time with them. The same was true of men who valued their own independence.

Conclusions. A striking conclusion of the Grossman, Pollack, and Golding study is that the amount of time men spend with their children is directly affected by their wives. Men married to autonomous, self-sufficient, competent women spend less time with their children. The quality of their time seems to be affected more by their own feelings of self-worth and adjustment.

The quality and quantity of time men spend with their children cannot be analyzed in simple terms because it is affected by personal psychological variables as well as by marital factors and even the gender of th'e child (Ross & Taylor, 1989). For example, men are more likely to engage in affectionate touch with younger sons than older ones, and daughters receive less attention from fathers than do sons (Harris & Morgan, 1991; Salt, 1991). In general, fathers are seen as less affectionate than are mothers (Berndt et al., 1993). There are still many unanswered questions: Do some types of men marry autonomous women because they want little to do with their children? Why is it that the wife's autonomy keeps men from spending time with their children? Do children seek out the more autonomous parent? The research continues.

as self-care, or latchkey, children. Most parents who leave their children in self-care arrangements establish rules for them to follow and maintain telephone contact with them in order to supervise them even while the parents are not present in the home. Do these latchkey arrangements work? Are there behavioral consequences for children left to care for themselves?

Rodman and his colleagues compared self-care children with adult-supervised children. A self-care child is a child between the ages of 6 and 13 who spends time alone or with a younger sibling on a periodic basis (Rodman, Pratto, & Nelson, 1988). The researchers found children who were alike with respect to age, gender, grade in school, family composition, and mother's and father's occupation and matched them to form comparable groups of self-care and adult-supervised children. When fourth- and seventh-graders in both groups were compared on measures of psychological and social functioning, there were no important differences between the groups. The researchers (Rodman, Pratto, & Nelson, 1985, p. 417) concluded, "The growing public and professional concern about the negative effects of self-care arrangements is premature and may not be warranted."

Considerable caution must be used in interpreting data on latchkey children because of the immense variability in the situations in which such children are studied (Vandell & Ramanan, 1991). Further, not all researchers find similar results or focus on similar problems. For example, self-care has been implicated in substance abuse in eighth-grade children (Richardson et al., 1989). But among former latchkey children, college students do not seem to differ on personality or academic variables (Messer, Wuensch, & Diamond, 1989). We also know that after-school programs aimed at latchkey children at risk for substance abuse are effective (Ross et al.,

1992). One of the most frequent problems reported among self-care children is loneliness and boredom; yet we do not know the long-term impact of these feelings (Guerney, 1991).

For now, the overall developmental effects of self-care and child care seem to be minimal. However, although research shows there are not necessarily problems with latchkey children, the idea that there are *no* problems is premature. Other family variables must be considered when researchers look at the impact of a variable such as after-school care (Vandell & Ramanan, 1991). Researchers who study such topics as single parenting, child care, and self-care must focus on the multiplicity of personality and academic differences between children raised in these environments and children raised in non-child-care or non-self-care homes.

FOCUS

▶ What is the research evidence on why gender segregation occurs among boys and girls?   p. 305

▶ Identify two key variables that affect the quality of child care.   pp. 306–307

Concluding Note

In any bookstore, you'll find shelves lined with how-to books on child rearing written by physicians, parents, psychologists, and others. The variety of ideas and experts shows that ideas about child rearing are complicated and constantly changing. Today, many researchers and applied psychologists stress that parenting must be considered in the social context of the family. For example, a mother's behavior toward her child is influenced by her life circumstances, health, education, and ethnicity (Feiring et al., 1987) and even by the extent to which she thinks she is a parent who controls her child's behavior (Donovan & Leavitt, 1989).

Although hundreds of applied psychology articles have explored such issues as the effects of breast-feeding, feeding schedules, and spoiling, the reality is that these topics are less important than the emotional climate in which child rearing takes place. A mother can provide warmth, love, closeness, and nutrients for her infant whether she chooses breast-feeding or bottle feeding. The choice is less important than making feeding a pleasurable, relaxed experience for both the parent and the child.

Research into child-rearing practices is difficult because of the wide array of individual variables that affect development. But certain key ideas have resulted from research: Babies follow a developmental progression, there is much variability among children on developmental issues, and babies are egocentric and unable to delay their gratification. In addition, research shows that children's genetic endowment, home environment, child-care situation, and intellectual development all affect how parents interact with their children. Bringing up children is no simple matter.

Summary & Review

Approaches to Child Development

Distinguish between cross-sectional and longitudinal research methods.

In the *cross-sectional method*, many subjects of different ages are compared to determine if they differ on some important dimension. In the *longitudinal method*, a single group of people is compared at different ages, usually over a long period of time, to determine whether changes have occurred.   pp. 278–280

Identify three major theories of child development.

The reductionistic view states that if we can reduce an organism's behavior to its essential elements, we can explain the behavior; the organismic view asserts that people go through qualitatively different developmental stages that cannot be reduced to simple elements. In the contextual view, all the events in an organism's life are seen as interrelated.   p. 280

The First Nine Months

Trace embryonic development.

From the 5th through the 49th day after conception, an unborn human being is called an *embryo;* from then until birth, it is called a *fetus*. During the 1st month, the embryo begins to take shape. During the 2nd month, the embryo begins to resemble a human being. In the 3rd month, growth continues, features become more defined, and sex characteristics begin to appear.   pp. 280–281

What is a teratogen?

A *teratogen* is a substance that can produce developmental malformations in a fetus; common teratogens include alcohol and cocaine. In the first months of life an embryo is especially sensitive to teratogens.   p. 283

KEY TERMS: *zygote*, p. 280; *embryo*, p. 280; *fetus*, p. 280; *placenta*, p. 281; *teratogens*, p. 283; *labor*, p. 283.

Newborns, Infancy, and Early Childhood

With what reflexes are newborns born, and how well do they perceive the world?

Infants are born with a set of primary reflexes; among them are the *Babinski reflex*, the *Moro reflex*, the *rooting reflex*, and the *sucking reflex*. Newborns have surprisingly well-developed perceptual systems. Research shows that they prefer complex visual fields, curved patterns, and human faces.   pp. 284–286

When does infancy end and childhood begin and end?

Infancy is the period from birth to 18 months, and *childhood* is the period from 18 months to about age 13, when adolescence begins.   p. 287

What are bonding and separation anxiety?

Bonding is a special process of emotional attachment between parent and child in the minutes and hours immediately after birth; bonding is a controversial idea that is widely accepted, but has little research support. As infants grow, the extent to which they focus on their caregivers increases significantly. Infants may develop *separation anxiety*, a fear response in children from 8 to 15 months, displayed when a parent is absent.   pp. 287–288

KEY TERMS: *Babinski reflex*, p. 284; *Moro reflex*, p. 285; *rooting reflex*, p. 285; *sucking reflex*, p. 285; *grasping reflex*, p. 285; *bonding*, p. 287; *separation anxiety*, p. 288.

Intellectual Development

What are Piaget's concepts of assimilation and accommodation?

Piaget identified two processes that enable the individual to gain new knowledge: assimilation and accommodation. *Assimilation* is the process of absorbing, incorporating, and utilizing new information in a meaningful way. *Accommodation* is the process of modifying one's existing thought processes and framework of knowledge.   pp. 291–292

Identify Piaget's four stages of intellectual development.

Piaget believed that intellectual development occurs in four stages, each of which must be completed before the next stage begins. In the *sensorimotor stage*, covering roughly the first two years of life, the child begins to interact with the environment, and the rudiments of intelligence are established. The *preoperational stage* lasts from about age 2 to age 7, when initial symbolic thought is developed. The *concrete operations stage* lasts from approximately ages 7 to 12, when the child develops the ability to understand constant factors in the environment, rules, and higher-order symbolism. The *formal operations stage* begins at about age 12,

continued

Summary & Review

when the individual can think hypothetically, consider all future possibilities, and is capable of deductive logic.   pp. 292–295

What is egocentrism?

Egocentrism is the inability to perceive a situation or event except in relation to oneself and is a characteristic of the sensorimotor stage. At birth, infants are totally egocentric. At the end of the sensorimotor period, they begin the process of decentration, gradually moving away from self-centeredness.   pp. 293–294

KEY TERMS: *assimilation*, p. 292; *accommodation*, p. 292; *sensorimotor stage*, p. 292; *egocentrism*, p. 293; *decentration*, p. 294; *preoperational stage*, p. 294; *concrete operations stage*, p. 294; *conservation*, p. 294; *formal operations stage*, p. 295.

Moral Reasoning

What is morality and how has it been studied?

Morality is a system of learned attitudes about social practices, institutions, and individual behavior used to evaluate situations and behavior as being right or wrong, good or bad. Piaget and Kohlberg studied moral reasoning, focusing on how people make moral judgments about hypothetical situations. Their theories differ in that Piaget thought of the stages of moral development as discrete, whereas Kohlberg viewed them as overlapping. Kohlberg proposed that children's interactions with parents and friends may influence their conceptions of morality.   pp. 299–301

What was Carol Gilligan's basic finding?

Whereas Kohlberg showed that young children base their decisions about right or wrong on the likelihood of avoiding punishment and obtaining rewards, Gilligan found that children were also concerned with caring, relationships, and connections with other people. Most important, Gilligan found important differences between boys and girls. As younger children, girls gravitate toward a morality of caring, while boys gravitate to a morality of justice, a difference established by virtue of the child's gender and the child's relationship with the mother.   pp. 302–303

KEY TERM: *morality*, p. 299.

Social Development

What is gender stereotyping?

Gender stereotyping is expectations for specific behavior patterns according to a person's gender. While parents do reinforce children selectively based on their gender, especially at young ages, gender differences in behavior are small and apparent only in certain situations, such as on the playground and in groups. p. 305

What is a latchkey child?

When children take care of themselves until their parents arrive home from work, they are known as self-care, or latchkey, children. One of the most frequent problems reported among self-care children is loneliness and boredom, but researchers do not know the long-term impact of these feelings. The overall developmental effects of self-care and child care seem to be minimal, but the idea that there are "no problems" is still premature.   pp. 308–309

What are the effects of day care?

Studies of attachment behaviors find that nonparental care does not reduce a child's emotional attachment to parents. Moreover, there is no firm evidence that temporary separations, such as those caused by child care for preschool children, create later psychological trauma. Still, studies show that children who spend *extensive* periods of time in child-care settings show increased disobedience and aggressiveness. Most psychologists agree that some time in child care may help the socialization process and they maintain an open mind regarding the long-term effects of child care.   pp. 306–310

CONNECTIONS

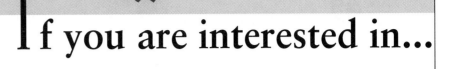

I f you are interested in...

The role of early childhood experiences in development, see ...

CHAPTER 2, pp. 60–64

The way the brain of a newborn is modifiable and continues to develop until age 13.

CHAPTER 7, pp. 264–265

How language development proceeds very rapidly once it begins at about 18 months of age.

CHAPTER 17, pp. 621–623

How viewing violence and sexual situations on television proves to have longlasting effects on children.

Gender differences in development, see ...

CHAPTER 9, p. 322

How psychologists have found that cognitive differences in development are, in most cases, overexaggerated.

CHAPTER 17, pp. 622–625 ▲

The aggressive behaviors males and females exhibit and their different modes of expression.

Social development in childhood, see ...

CHAPTER 10, pp. 364–366

The way children develop specific motives, for example, to achieve, succeed, or be successful.

CHAPTER 12, pp. 429–431

Freud's view that the first six years of a child's life is crucial for later personality development.

CHAPTER 16, pp. 515–516

How a child's early interactions with parents, peers, church, and school shape his or her attitudes.

9

Adolescence
and
Adulthood

In the past year, my daughter Jesse has matured physically into a woman; yet I have to admit I sometimes still treat her like a child. She is eager to finish her high school years, but she occasionally worries about leaving friends and family to start college. She constantly asks herself what sort of career she should have. Although I know she finds her life exciting, she is looking forward to becoming an adult and leaving behind the uncertainty of adolescence.

At 75, Jesse's grandmother finds life more rewarding now than ever before. Her youngest child left home to start his own family years ago, and since then she has devoted most of her spare time to painting. She and her husband have opened a gallery in which they sell her artwork. But she is struggling with the physical challenges of old age, including arthritis, which threatens to end her painting career.

Jesse and her grandmother are both facing new challenges. Every age—infancy, childhood, adolescence, early adulthood, and late adulthood—brings its own joys and difficulties. Psychologists see aging as a process of continued growth that is influenced by a person's biological inheritance, life experiences, frame of mind, and a certain amount of chance. For example, moving from one state to another changes people's lives; a divorce is unsettling; a death in the family can be devastating; winning the lottery can jolt a person from poverty to luxury and from anonymity to fame. So, in addition to normal, predictable maturational and developmental changes, a once-in-a-lifetime happening can permanently alter physical, social, and personality development. This chapter discusses some of the developmental changes that occur during adolescence and adulthood and traces the psychological processes that underlie these stages of development.

Adolescence

In our culture, the transition from childhood to adulthood brings dramatic intellectual, social, emotional, and physical changes. Generally, this transition occurs between the ages of 12 and 20, a period known as *adolescence,* when children bridge the gap to adulthood. **Adolescence** is the period extending from the onset of puberty to early adulthood. **Puberty** is the period during which the reproductive system matures; it begins with an increase in sex hormone production, occurring at and signaling the end of childhood. Although adolescents are in many ways like adults—they are nearly mature physically and mentally, and their moral development is fairly advanced—their emotional development may be far from complete.

Adolescence is often referred to as a time of storm and stress—of raging hormones—and for some adolescents this is indeed the case. It is the popular stereotype that adolescents are in a state of conflict resulting in part from the lack of congruity in their physical, intellectual, social, and emotional development. Consider alcohol abuse. Most adolescents know, intellectually, that drinking is illegal, harmful, and potentially deadly when combined with driving. Yet most are not mature enough to stand up to peer pressure by making a conscious decision not to drink.

Storm and stress is not the whole of adolescence, though. Many adolescents go through this period of multiple changes without significant psychological difficulty. Although hormones are rushing and changing adolescents' reactions, nonbiological factors seem to be especially important in moderating the role of hormones in adolescents' moods (Buchanan, Eccles, & Becker, 1992; Eccles et al., 1993). According to A. C. Petersen (1988), adolescence may be a challenging life period, just as adulthood is, but only 11 percent of adolescents have serious difficulties and only 32 percent have even sporadic difficulties. Also, 57 percent of adolescents have basically positive, healthy development during these years.

The current consensus among psychologists is that adolescence is not ordinarily a time of great psychological turmoil (Powers, Hauser, & Kilner, 1989) and that adolescents have no more psychological disturbances than the rest of the population (Hauser & Bowlds, 1990). This does not mean that adolescence is conflict-free and that parent-child relationships do not change during this period (Larson & Ham, 1993); what it does mean is that adolescence does not have to be a stressful time (Galambos, 1992; Paikoff & Brooks-Gunn, 1991).

Adolescence in a Cultural Context

Adolescence has not always been seen as a problem period; nor is it considered so in all societies today. Some experts link the "invention" of the adolescent life stage

Adolescence: [add-oh-LESS-since] The period extending from the onset of puberty to early adulthood.

Puberty: [PEW-burr-tee] The period during which the reproductive system matures; it begins with an increase in sex hormone production and occurs at (and signals) the end of childhood.

with certain social and historical events. In the middle of the 19th century, waifs in large cities roamed the streets as pickpockets, prostitutes, and purse snatchers; and many used drugs, including opium. By 1860, the number of young people living by their wits on the streets of New York City had reached 30,000. Their plight led to a reform movement that put many of them in school and helped stretch the age of dependence from 14 to 18.

Today, it is common for an American teenager to feel "no one understands me," but it's difficult to imagine a teenage tribeswoman growing up in the jungles of New Guinea expressing the same sentiment. Thus, the problems of adolescence must be considered in a cultural context. Even when adolescents grow up in the same country, they experience life's joys and disappointments in different ways. Some come from disadvantaged economic groups, perhaps from a Chicago ghetto or a Native American reservation. Some grow up in luxury, perhaps in a wealthy suburb of Los Angeles. Others are exposed to racial prejudice, alcohol and other drug abuse, non-supportive families, or other stressful situations that lead them to feel a lack of control over their own lives.

Research shows that youths from differing backgrounds have sharply different rates of drug use. For example, among high school seniors, African-American and Hispanic-American rates for cocaine use are similar to those of whites. On Native American reservations, however, youths have high rates of cocaine use. Special populations and subgroups can thus be seen as having differing values, needs, and behavior patterns (Oetting & Beauvais, 1990).

Unfortunately, most of the research on adolescence has been conducted on white, middle-class American teenagers. But researchers now understand that the life experiences of whites, Navajos, Hispanic Americans, African Americans, Asian Americans, and other groups are not all alike. Each year, more studies compare the experiences of different groups and sensitize both professionals and the public to cultural differences among groups as well as to the diversity that exists within cultural groups. Not all Asian Americans are mathematically inclined; nor do all African Americans live in poverty. The reality is that, in many domains, there is more within-group diversity than between-group diversity; researchers are recognizing the similarities between groups as well as the differences.

The experiences of adolescents, such as this girl growing up on a reservation, are not all alike.

Physical Development

The words *adolescence* and *puberty* are often used interchangeably, but in fact they mean different things. As noted earlier, *puberty* is the period during which the reproductive system matures; it begins with an increase in sex hormone production and occurs at (and signals) the end of childhood. *Adolescence* is the period extending from the onset of puberty to early adulthood. Psychologists observe this distinction when studying adolescence. (See Figure 9.1 on page 318.)

The age when puberty begins varies widely; some girls begin to mature physically as early as age 8, some boys at 9 or 10 (Marshall & Tanner, 1969). The average age of puberty is 13, plus or minus a year or two (on average, girls enter puberty a year or two before boys). Just before the onset of puberty, boys and girls experience significant growth spurts, gaining as much as 5 inches in a single year.

By the end of the 1st or 2nd year of the growth spurt, changes have occurred in body proportions, fat distribution, bones and muscles, and physical strength and agility. In addition, the hormonal system has begun producing secondary sex characteristics. **Secondary sex characteristics** are the physical features of a person's gender identity that are not directly involved with reproduction but that help distinguish men from women. (Primary sex characteristics are those associated principally with the genitalia and gonads.) Boys experience an increase in body mass as well as the growth of pubic, underarm, and facial hair. Girls experience an increase in the size

Secondary sex characteristics: The physical features of a person's gender identity that are not directly involved with reproduction but that help distinguish men from women.

FIGURE 9.1

The In-Between World of the Adolescent

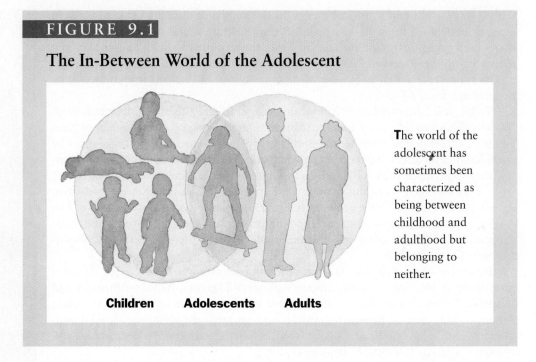

The world of the adolescent has sometimes been characterized as being between childhood and adulthood but belonging to neither.

Children   Adolescents   Adults

of the breasts, a widening of the hips, and the growth of underarm and pubic hair. Puberty ends with the maturation of the reproductive organs, at which time boys produce sperm and girls produce ova and begin to menstruate. These physical changes generally take several years to complete.

Puberty has received a good deal of research attention. For example, researchers have found that as boys pass through puberty, they feel more positive about their bodies, whereas girls are more likely to have negative feelings. Researchers assert that puberty itself does not create psychological maladjustment. Becoming an adolescent means emerging as an adult, socially and sexually. New forces affect the self-image of adolescents; and although these forces create new stressors, most adolescents perceive their new status as desirable.

In junior high school, the most popular boys complete puberty at an early age. Boys who mature early often enjoy several advantages, including increased confidence, superior athletic prowess, greater sexual appeal, and higher expectations from teachers and parents. Early-maturing girls, on the other hand, seem to be at a disadvantage because their female peers often treat them as outsiders. Thus, maturation has implications for social development.

Social Development

An adolescent's personality is affected both by the timing of puberty (a biological factor) and by how people react to that timing (an environmental factor). Parents and teachers can help both early- and late-maturing adolescents with feelings about body image. For example, research shows that involvement with athletics can be a buffer against the negative feelings that arise during this period. Increased time spent in sports is associated with increased satisfaction and higher self-ratings of strength and attractiveness for both girls and boys. Physical activity is associated with achievement, weight reduction, muscle tone, and stress reduction, all of which foster a positive self-image (Kirshnit, Richards, & Ham, 1988).

The environmental factors that influence adolescents' social development and self-image affect later adult behavior as well. The two most important groups of people who influence the social behavior of adolescents are parents and peers. There is no question that adolescents are responsive to parental influence and put up serious resistance to parental authority only in making life-altering decisions (Scherer & Reppucci, 1988). The Diversity box on page 320 examines the influence of parents on academic achievement. Studies disagree about the influence of peers versus parents, but most indicate that adolescents' attitudes fall somewhere between those of their parents and those of their peers (Paikoff & Brooks-Gunn, 1991).

The influence of peer groups is formidable. *Peer groups* are people who identify with and compare themselves to one another. They often consist of people of the same age, gender, and race, although adolescents may change their peer group memberships and may belong to more than one group. As adolescents spend more time away from parents and home, they experience increasing pressure to conform to the values of their peer groups, especially same-sex peer groups (Bukowski et al., 1993).

Peer groups have an enormous influence on adolescents.

Peer groups are a source of information about society, educational aspirations, and group activities. Peers sometimes praise, sometimes cajole, and constantly pressure one another to conform to behavioral standards, including standards for dress, social interaction, and forms of rebellion, such as shoplifting or drug taking (Farrell & Danish, 1993). Most important, they influence the adolescent's developing self-concept.

Gender Development and Gender Differences

We saw in chapter 8 that **gender differences** are differences between males and females in behavior or mental processes. Research on the biological factors that affect gender differences has been extensive and has shown few important differences between the genders. Although adolescent girls often reach milestones earlier than boys, the difference between the genders usually disappears by late adolescence (L. Cohn, 1991). Experience and learning—the way a person is raised and taught—have a far more profound impact on behaviors.

Gender Identity. As noted earlier, a key feature of adolescence is that it is a period of transition and change. Adolescents must develop their own *identity*, a sense of themselves as independent, mature individuals. One important aspect of identity is **gender identity**—a person's sense of being male or female. Children develop gender identity by age 3. By age 4 or 5, children realize their identity is permanent. By age 8, they know that changing their hair, clothing, or behavior does not alter their gender. Consider, for example, the experience that adolescents have when their bodies change in appearance very rapidly, sometimes in unpredictable ways. During the transition to adulthood, adolescents often try out various types of behaviors, including those relating to male-female relationships and dating. Some adolescents become extreme in their orientation toward maleness or femaleness. Boys, especially in groups, may become aggressive and boisterous; girls may act submissively, be overly concerned with their looks, and focus on bonding with other girls. This exaggeration of traditional male or female behaviors is often short-lived.

Many psychologists believe that once gender identity is firmly established, children and adolescents attempt to bring their behavior and thoughts within generally accepted gender-specific roles. **Gender schema theory** asserts that children and adolescents use gender as an organizing theme to classify and understand their perceptions about the world (S. L. Bem, 1985; Maccoby, 1988). Young children use gender

Gender differences: Differences between males and females in behavior or mental processes.

Gender identity: A person's sense of being male or female.

Gender schema theory: The theory that children and adolescents use gender as an organizing theme to classify and understand their perceptions about the world.

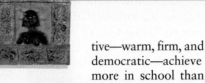

DIVERSITY

Ethic Differences in Achievement

Which group does best in school: Hispanic Americans, Asian Americans, or African Americans? There is a widely held belief that students of Asian American descent do better, thanks to inherited differences and to achievement-oriented socialization and other cultural values. A research team set out to determine how a person's ethnic background affects academic achievement.

Steinberg, Dornbusch, and Brown (1992) administered a 30-page questionnaire to over 15,000 students at nine high schools that varied geographically, ethnically, and socioeconomically. The questionnaire gathered information about the students' adjustment, schooling, behavior problems, and potential maladjustment. The researchers focused on peer relationships, family relationships, and such family variables as ethnicity, socioeconomic status, immigration history, and patterns of language use.

The researchers found that adolescents whose parents are authorita- tive—warm, firm, and democratic—achieve more in school than do their peers. Peer interactions also turn out to be important; strong peer support for academics can make up for a lack of authoritative parenting. Conversely, peer disdain of academics weakens a strong parental voice.

What about ethnic differences? Regardless of ethnic group, youngsters from authoritative homes fared better in social functioning than did their counterparts from nonauthoritative homes. In school performance, there was a slight difference among ethnic groups: White teenagers were more likely to benefit from authoritative parenting than were African Americans and Asian Americans.

Why would authoritativeness benefit African Americans and Asian Americans in social development more than in academic performance? The social versus academic difference may come from world views (basic attitudes toward life) that are sharply different. The researchers found that while all of the students believed a good ed- ucation would pay off, Asian Americans in particular feared the conse- quences of a poor education. By contrast, African American and Hispanic American students were more likely to believe that a positive life could still follow after a poor education. Not surprisingly, youngsters who are taught and believe that they can suc- ceed without doing well in school will devote far less energy to academic pur- suits than will students who are more fearful of negative consequences.

A child's world view, taught by parents and reinforced by peers, shapes future success. Ethnic minori- ties may vary little in many ways; but when it comes to school, some dis- tinctly different world views may al- ter motivation, performance, and later success in the job market. Stein- berg, Dornbusch, and Brown (1992) have been careful in their conclu- sions; they realize that their study is of a small sample and that many dif- ferent factors interact to affect per- formance. Still, they assert that their research provides a foundation for future research—an agenda for fur- ther questions.

---

as a social category. In doing so, they decide on appropriate and inappropriate gen- der behaviors by processing a wide array of social information. In fact, children's and adolescents' self-esteem and feelings of worth often are tied to their gender- based perceptions about themselves, many of which are determined by identification with the same-gender parent (Heilbrun, Wydra, & Friedberg, 1989). For example, they may relate their self-worth to how much their behavior matches that of adult males or females or how well they fulfill society's view of gender roles. (See Figure 9.2 for a description of gender schema theory.)

Gender Roles. **Gender roles,** or *sex roles,* are the full range of behaviors gen- erally associated with one's gender; these roles help people establish who they are. However, in the course of establishing a sexual identity, people sometimes adopt **gender role stereotyping**—typical beliefs about gender-based behaviors that are strongly expected, regulated, and reinforced by society. Men, for example, may learn to hide their emotions, because society frowns on men who cry in public and rein- forces men who appear strong and stoic when faced with sorrow or stress. Gender- based ideas about professions are especially likely to become stereotyped. Even

Gender roles: The full range of behaviors generally associ- ated with one's gender; they help people establish who they are. Also known as *sex roles.*

Gender role stereotyping: Typical beliefs of society con- cerning the patterns of behav- ior expected, regulated, and reinforced based on gender.

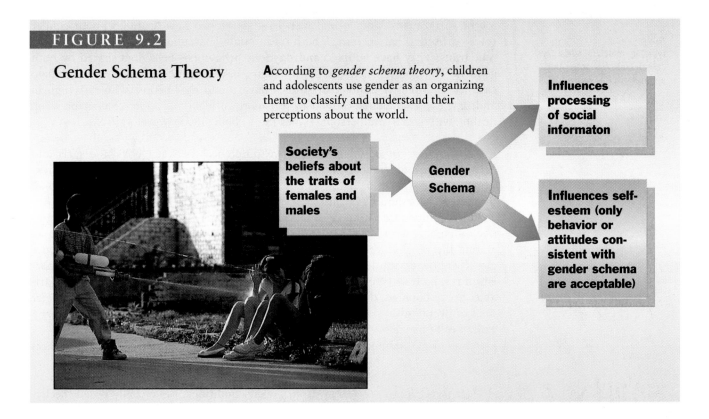

FIGURE 9.2

Gender Schema Theory

According to *gender schema theory*, children and adolescents use gender as an organizing theme to classify and understand their perceptions about the world.

Society's beliefs about the traits of females and males → Gender Schema →

Influences processing of social informaton

Influences self-esteem (only behavior or attitudes consistent with gender schema are acceptable)

today, how many little girls aspire to be doctors, fire fighters—or President of the United States? Gender role stereotypes are difficult to change; from the early 1970s to the early 1980s, for example, the percentage of men in nursing, teaching, and social work remained low, even though many people became more accepting of men in these professions.

In the workplace, gender role stereotypes still exist and heavily influence wages and promotions (Hoffman & Hurst, 1990). On average, women earn about two-thirds of each dollar that a man earns. Although almost 50 percent of law school students are women, only about 10 percent of partners in large law firms are women (Repa, 1988). Women are taking positions of major responsibility in corporate America, but only 2 percent of senior executives are female.

As we saw in chapter 8, parents are the first and most important sources of gender-based stereotyping; they influence the child from birth. Peers and schools are also especially important sources of gender information. In addition, the media, especially television, have a profound impact on people's perceptions about gender. When we view television programs and commercials, we see that they often portray men and women in strongly gender-stereotyped roles. From classic television, we see the well-defined traditional gender roles of June and Ward Cleaver in "Leave It to Beaver." Ward would never do the laundry, for example. Today's television programs are more likely to cast women in roles outside the house; but beer commercials still show men chasing scantily clad women on the beach, and toy commercials often focus on girls playing house.

Androgyny. Asserting a gender identity in adolescence has always been part of the transition to adulthood. Today, this task is more complicated, especially for women. In earlier decades, women were expected to pursue marriage and home-making, which were considered full-time careers. Today, women's plans often include a career outside the home, which may be interrupted for child rearing. In

Androgynous: Having some typically male and some typically female characteristics apparent in one individual.

recent years, many women and men have developed new attitudes about gender roles—attitudes that encourage both traditionally masculine and traditionally feminine traits. They have adopted **androgynous** behaviors—behaviors shared by both genders. Thus, both men and women fix cars, have careers, do housework, and help care for children. A number of studies have found that people who rate high in androgynous characteristics tend to feel more fulfilled and more competent when dealing with social and personal issues (S. L. Bem, 1975; Worell, 1978).

Differences in Abilities. Cognitive differences between boys and girls and between male and female adolescents are minimal; in fact, they are generally nonexistent. As you will see in chapter 11, gender differences in verbal ability are so small that researchers should not say they exist (Hyde & Linn, 1988); differences in mathematical abilities are also very small (Hyde, Fennema, & Lamon, 1990). The cognitive differences found today exist only in certain special populations—for example, among the very brightest mathematics students, where boys continue to outscore girls (Benbow & Stanley, 1983). This does not mean that no differences are apparent in certain tests (such as the SAT). What it does mean is that when cultural variables are discounted, the remaining differences are small and unimportant and refer only to overall group differences, not individual accomplishments. There are many examples of females who outperform, outanalyze, and outwrite males.

Biological differences between men and women certainly exist, but researchers are still trying to determine whether basic intellectual differences exist and, if so, under what conditions. Biologically based mechanisms may account for some gender-based behaviors, but learning is far more potent in establishing and maintaining gender role stereotypes and gender-specific attitudes (see chapter 5, p. 196). Our society continues to reinforce gender-based activities (Pomerleau et al., 1990). This shapes the behavior of children and adolescents into gender roles. But as our society's views change, so will gender-based activities.

FOCUS

▶ Why are gender differences so sharply delineated in the study of adolescence?   p. 319

▶ What evidence exists to show that gender-based behaviors are strongly expected, regulated, and reinforced by society?   pp. 319–322

▶ What can we conclude about gender differences between men and women?   pp. 319–322

Erik Erikson and the Search for Identity

Society does not make it easy for adolescents to form an image of who they are and what they want in life. After years of being allowed to behave like children, suddenly adolescents are expected to behave like adults. Trying to achieve the freedom and responsibilities of adulthood, such as taking responsibility for contraception while giving up the security of childhood, can create stress.

Erikson's Theory. Perhaps no one is more closely associated with the challenges of adolescence than Erik H. Erikson (1902–1990), who studied with Freud in Austria. With sharp insight, a linguistic flair, and a logical, coherent approach to studying human behavior, Erikson is a key figure in the history of psychology. Erikson developed a theory of *psychosocial* outcomes of development; each of his stages leads to the development of a unique personality, and the stages help define how a person develops a role as a member of society. A series of basic psychological conflicts determine the course of development. His theory is noted for its integration of a person's disposition and environment with historical forces in the shaping of the person's life.

Erikson saw that environment-person relationships were interactive; he asserted that people have to accept responsibility for their lives and their place in history. Nowhere is this idea more evident than in adolescence. According to Erikson, the growth and turmoil of adolescence creates an "identity crisis"; the major task for adolescents is to resolve that crisis successfully by forming an identity. People's *identity* is who they are, where they perceive themselves to be going, and what their place is in the world. The failure to form an identity leaves the adolescent confused about adult roles and unable to cope with the demands of adulthood, including the development of mature relationships with members of the opposite sex (Erikson, 1963, 1968).

Erikson believed people form self-images from their perceptions of themselves as well as from other people's perceptions of them (expressed through behavior). Membership in political, religious, or ideological groups, for example, helps adolescents discover what they believe in and what satisfies their needs. Erikson maintained that psychosocial development continues throughout life.

Erikson's theory describes a continuum of stages (including dilemmas and crises) through which all individuals must pass. Each stage can have either a positive or a negative outcome. New dilemmas emerge as a person grows older and faces new responsibilities, tasks, and social relationships. A person may experience a dilemma as an opportunity and face it positively or view the dilemma as a catastrophe and fail to cope with it effectively. For example, an adolescent may be pressured to engage in drug use or shoplifting; whether the teen succumbs to peer pressure or emerges as a victor able to withstand it affects the teen's self-image. To emerge as a fully mature, stable adult, a person has to pass through each stage successfully. Table 9.1 on page 324 lists the psychosocial stages in Erikson's theory and the important events associated with them. We will now take a closer look at each stage.

Erikson's Eight Stages of Development.   Stages 1 through 4 of Erikson's theory cover birth through age 12. Stage 1 (birth to 12–18 months) involves the development of *basic trust versus basic mistrust.* During their first months, infants make distinctions about the world and decide whether it is a comfortable, loving place in which they can feel basic trust. At this stage, they develop beliefs about the essential truthfulness of people. If their needs are adequately met, they learn that the world is a predictable and safe place. Infants whose needs are not met learn to distrust the world.

During stage 2 (18 months to 3 years), the toddler must resolve the crisis of *autonomy versus shame and doubt.* Success in toilet training and other tasks involving control leads to a sense of autonomy and more mature behavior. Difficulties dealing with control during this stage result in fears and a sense of shame and doubt.

Stage 3 (ages 3 to 6) is that of *initiative versus guilt,* when children develop the ability to use their own initiative. During this stage, they either gain a sense of independence and good feelings about themselves or develop a sense of guilt, lack of acceptance, and negative feelings about themselves. If children learn to dress themselves, clean their rooms, and develop friendships with other children, they can feel a sense of mastery; alternatively, they can be dependent or regretful.

Stage 4 (6 to 12 years) covers *industry versus inferiority.* Children either develop feelings of competence and confidence in their abilities or experience inferiority, failure, and feelings of incompetence.

Erikson's stage 5, *identity versus role confusion,* marks the end of childhood and the beginning of adolescence. At this time, adolescents must decide who they are and what they want to do in life. Otherwise, they will become confused and rebellious.

TABLE 9.1 Erikson's Eight Stages of Psychosocial Development

Stages	Approximate Age	Important Event	Description
1. Basic trust versus basic mistrust	Birth to 12–18 months	Feeding	The infant must form a first loving, trusting relationship with the caregiver, or develop a sense of mistrust.
2. Autonomy versus shame/doubt	18 months to 3 years	Toilet training	The child's energies are directed toward the development of physical skills, including walking, grasping, controlling the sphincter. The child learns control but may develop shame and doubt if not handled well.
3. Initiative versus guilt	3 to 6 years	Independence	The child continues to become more assertive and to take more initiative but may be too forceful, which can lead to guilt feelings.
4. Industry versus inferiority	6 to 12 years	School	The child must deal with demands to learn new skills or risk a sense of inferiority, failure, and incompetence.
5. Identity versus role confusion	Adolescence	Peer relationships	The teenager must achieve a sense of identity in occupation, gender roles, politics, and religion.
6. Intimacy versus isolation	Young adulthood	Love relationships	The young adult must develop intimate relationships or suffer feelings of isolation.
7. Generativity versus stagnation	Middle adulthood	Parenting	Each adult must find some way to satisfy and support the next generation.
8. Ego integrity versus despair	Late adulthood	Reflection on and acceptance of one's life	The culmination is a sense of acceptance of oneself as one is and a sense of fulfillment.

The special problems of adolescence—which sometimes include rebellion, suicide, and drug problems—must be dealt with at this stage.

Stage 6 (young adulthood) involves *intimacy versus isolation*. Young adults begin to select other people with whom they can form intimate relationships. They learn to relate on a warm, social basis with members of the opposite sex. The alternative is to become isolated.

In stage 7 (middle adulthood), *generativity versus stagnation*, people hope to convey information, love, and warmth to others, particularly their children. As adults, they hope to influence their family and the world; otherwise, they will stagnate, feeling that life is unexciting.

In stage 8 (late adulthood), *ego integrity versus despair*, people decide whether their existence is meaningful, happy, and cohesive or wasteful and unproductive. Many individuals never fully complete stage 8, and some do so with regrets and a feeling that time is too short. Those who do master and complete this stage feel fulfilled, with a sense that they understand, at least partly, what life is about.

A key point of Erikson's theory is that people must go through each stage, resolving the crises of that stage as best they can. Of course, people grow older whether or not they are ready for the next stage. A person may still have unresolved conflicts, opportunities, and dilemmas from previous stages. This can cause anxiety and discomfort and make resolution of advanced stages more difficult. Because adolescence is such a crucial stage for the formation of a firm identity, the environment surrounding an adolescent becomes especially important. In the United States today, that environment is often a home with only one parent or a home with one parent and a step-parent—the topic we consider in the Applications box on page 326.

Sexual Behavior during Adolescence

In human beings, learned attitudes have a greater influence than biological factors in determining sexual behavior; and people first learn about such behavior at home. Children are affected by their parents' attitudes and behavior—whether, for instance, they hug and kiss openly, seem embarrassed by their bodies, or talk freely about sexual matters.

The influence of parents in sexual matters was shown in a study that examined how parents' discipline and control influence teenagers' sexual attitudes and behavior. Miller and colleagues (1986) surveyed more than 2,000 teenagers and their parents about parental discipline and teenage sexual behavior. The results showed that sexual permissiveness and intercourse were more frequent among adolescents who viewed their parents as not having rules or not being strict. Sexual behaviors, especially intercourse, were less frequent among teenagers who reported that their parents were strict. In addition, close relationships with parents and feelings of support have been associated with later age at first intercourse (Brooks-Gunn & Furstenberg, 1989).

Relaxed Attitudes. American adolescents view sexual intimacy as an important and normal part of growing up; and premarital heterosexual activity has become increasingly common among adolescents, especially 13- to 17-year-olds. Three-fifths (60 percent) of white male teenagers have intercourse by age 18, and the same percentage of white female adolescents do so by just a year later, age 19. For African Americans, 60 percent of males have intercourse by age 16, and 60 percent of females do so by age 18. There are great individual differences in the age at first intercourse and in the subsequent frequency of intercourse. It is not uncommon for first intercourse to occur at age 14 or 15 and then for the teenager not to have relations again for a year or two (Furstenberg, Brooks-Gunn, & Chase-Lansdale, 1989). Dreyer (1982) suggests several reasons for the early expression of sexual behavior:

▶ Adolescents are reaching sexual maturity at younger ages than in previous decades.

▶ Knowledge and use of contraception are becoming more widespread, thus eliminating the fear of pregnancy.

▶ Adults' sexual attitudes and behaviors are changing.

▶ Adolescents consider sexual behavior normal in an intimate relationship.

More relaxed attitudes about adolescent sexual behavior have brought about increased awareness of contraception and of the problems of teenage pregnancy. Nevertheless, 1 in 10 teenage girls became pregnant in the early 1990s (Alan Guttmacher Institute, 1991). More than 1 million teenage girls become pregnant

Life in One-Parent Families

Of the approximately 62 million family households in the United States, about 1 out of every 4 is a single-parent household; and most of these single parents are women. This family situation can be particularly problematic for some adolescents, although as the number of one-parent families has increased, some of the problems seem to have lessened.

A father's absence may be due to death, desertion, separation, or divorce, among other things. Well-known researcher Mavis Hetherington points out that almost half the children born in the last decade will experience the divorce of their parents (Hetherington, Stanley-Hagan, & Anderson, 1989). Most of these children

will also experience the remarriage of their parents. The responses of children to these rapidly changing situations are diverse. Some children of divorced parents seem less able to cope than those who have lost a parent through death. They often have to deal with parental conflict, the divorce process itself, continuing poor adjustment of parents, and disagreements between their parents (Forehand et al., 1990). They may blame themselves; and as a result, their self-esteem, which is just beginning to strengthen, suffers. Children of divorce often refuse to accept its permanency (Wallerstein & Blakeslee, 1989). This is especially true of emerging adolescents, who tend to be more affected by divorce than are very young children or older adolescents (Amato, 1993; Amato & Keith, 1991).

The negative effects of an absent father are different for boys and girls. Boys seem to have a harder time, perhaps because they do not have as many opportunities to interact with adult men; and they may end up learning masculine behaviors, often highly stereotyped ones, from peers (Wallerstein & Blakeslee, 1989). Girls can also have a hard time when their father is absent. They see boys having more freedom and status, while they must struggle for independence. Also, girls from one-parent homes report less positive attitudes toward the father and more sexual experimentation than do girls from two-parent homes. Gender differences are not always apparent, and sometimes they disappear by late adolescence. Wallerstein and Blakeslee argue that although girls may not appear to be affected as much

---

each year in the United States, and nearly 500,000 give birth. The consequences of childbearing for teen mothers are great. A young woman's chances for future education and employment become more limited, and many young women are forced to rely on public assistance. Most studies indicate that women who bear children early will not achieve economic equality with women who postpone parenthood until they are adults (Furstenberg, Brooks-Gunn, & Chase-Lansdale, 1989).

A variety of trends are erasing the differences between the sexual behavior of men and women; they include improved transportation and communication, the women's movement, and more equal opportunities in education (Sprecher, McKinney, & Orbuch, 1987). Today, almost 40 percent of 20-year-old women have had at least one pregnancy as a teenager (that is about 1 million teenagers), and 15 percent have had an abortion. In fact, current studies show that, despite the fear of AIDS, teenagers and college students still engage in regular sexual activity. Further, adolescents in the United States are substantially more likely to experience a pregnancy than their counterparts in other Western countries (Miller & Moore, 1990).

Contraception. Teenagers are still largely uninformed or ill informed about reproductive physiology and contraception. Too many underestimate the likelihood of pregnancy and have negative attitudes toward contraception, although they have trouble explaining why. Low levels of self-esteem, and feelings of powerlessness and alienation, are also associated with the personalities of those who fail to use contraceptives. School-based, comprehensive health-care programs that emphasize the complete picture of sexuality (attitudes, contraception, motivation, behavior) reduce the risks of pregnancy in teenagers (Ford Foundation, 1989).

About one out of every four U.S. households is headed by a single parent, most often the mother.

as boys, in later adolescence they show the negative effects.

One of the problems in researching children and divorce is that large representative samples are seldom used, so the negative outcomes of divorce may tend to be overemphasized (Barber & Eccles, 1992). Another problem is that preexisting behavior problems are rarely considered when the effects of divorce are evaluated (Cherlin et al., 1991). Some children and adolescents exhibit remarkable resiliency when faced with a divorce. In fact, Hetherington asserts that, in the long run, some may actually be strengthened by having to cope with family transitions (Hetherington, Stanley-Hagan, & Anderson, 1989).

In addition, today women and their children, who were once at extreme economic disadvantage after a divorce, are faring better financially, achieving more education, and obtaining better job opportunities. Another reason one-parent families are doing better is that parents are increasingly sharing custody and working toward the best interests of their children. In addition, most people remarry after a divorce; thus, the time a child or an adolescent spends in a single-parent household can be brief. As Hetherington and her colleagues maintain, "Divorce and remarriage can remove children from stressful and acrimonious family relationships and many children eventually emerge as competent or even enhanced individuals" (Hetherington, Stanley-Hagan, & Anderson, 1989, p. 310). Barber and Eccles (1992) agree that although two parents can generally do a better job than one, it does not follow that all children are better off if their parents stay together.

Not surprisingly, younger adolescents in less committed, less stable relationships are less likely to use contraceptives (Milan & Kilmann, 1987) or to make sure unwanted pregnancies do not take place (Gerrard, 1987). The data show that older, more mature adolescents are more likely to use contraception (Brooks-Gunn & Furstenberg, 1989), but fewer than 50 percent of all college students use condoms (DeBuono et al., 1990).

FOCUS

▶ In each of Erikson's eight stages, people face dilemmas. What are the overall consequences of a poor outcome at any one stage? pp. 323–325

▶ What impact can a father's absence have on children? pp. 326–327

Adulthood

Adults in the 1990s have vastly different life experiences than did adults of the 1950s, whose lives followed predictable and prescribed timetables. People married when they were in their late teens or early 20s and had children soon after. Wives stayed at home to raise the children, while husbands went to work to support the family. Today's adults are marrying later, some not at all; and parenting is often postponed or rejected. While some women choose to stay at home to raise the children, many are concentrating on careers, working side by side with their male coworkers.

Many grown children are returning home after college, and divorce has broken up numerous families. The 1950s stereotype of a well-ordered, simple family structure has changed sharply, and in a relatively short period of time.

The American adult life experience of the 1990s is also different from that of other cultures. Americans share some commonalities with people from other Western cultures, but their experience is vastly different from that in Third World countries. These differences have been studied little. Until the 1970s, developmental psychologists concentrated largely on white middle-class children, especially those in infancy and early childhood.

Psychologists are now focusing on development throughout the life span, recognizing that new challenges are faced in every stage of a person's life. They study adult development by looking at the factors that contribute to stability or frustration, to a sense of accomplishment or feelings of despair, and to physical factors that may affect functioning. Researchers today are also examining the differences between men and women, with emphasis on the unique experiences of women in U.S. culture. Minorities are being studied, and theories now are recognizing and focusing on cultural diversity. Psychologists are also recognizing that a person's career, not just the person's family or life stage, is a defining characteristic of adulthood. Adults spend an enormous amount of time and energy on their careers, which have been examined relatively little by psychologists. Building Table 9.1 summarizes the major changes in functioning in young adulthood.

Physical Development

Although physical development in adulthood is slower, less dramatic, and sometimes less visible than in childhood and adolescence, it does occur. Barbara Newman (1982) traced various types of physical changes that occur in adulthood. We will examine some of her findings here.

Fitness Changes. Fitness involves both a psychological and a physical sense of well-being. Physically, human beings are at their peak of agility, speed, and strength between ages 18 and 30. From 30 to 40, there is some loss of agility and speed. And between 40 and 60, much greater losses occur. In general, strength, muscle tone, and overall fitness deteriorate from age 30 on. People become more susceptible to disease. Respiratory, circulatory, and blood pressure problems are more apparent; lung capacity and physical strength are significantly reduced.

BUILDING TABLE 9.1

Major Changes in Important Domains of Adult Functioning

AGE	PHYSICAL CHANGE	COGNITIVE CHANGE	WORK ROLES	PERSONALITY DEVELOPMENT	MAJOR TASKS
Young Adulthood 18-25	Peak functioning in most physical skills; optimum time for childbearing	Cognitive skills high on most measures	Choose career, which may involve several job changes; low work satisfaction is common	Conformist; task of intimacy	Separate from family; form partnership; begin family; find job; create individual life pattern

Sexual Changes. In adulthood, sexual changes occur in adults of both sexes. For example, women often experience an increase in sexual desire, but men achieve erections less rapidly. In the childbearing years, women's and men's sexual desires are sometimes moderated by the stresses of raising a family and juggling a work schedule. For women, midlife changes in hormones lead to the cessation of ovulation and menstruation at about 50 years, a process known as *menopause.* At about the same age, men's testosterone levels decrease, their ejaculations are weaker and briefer, and their desire for sexual intercourse decreases from adolescent levels.

Sensory Changes. In early adulthood, most sensory abilities remain fairly stable, and many women and men increase their involvement in fitness and better nutrition. As the years pass, however, adults must contend with inevitable sensory losses. Reaction time slows, visual acuity decreases, the risks of glaucoma and retinal detachment increase, and hearing loss occurs. By 65 years, most people can no longer hear very-high-frequency sounds, and some are unable to hear ordinary speech. Ronald Reagan, for example, suffered from a serious hearing loss during his presidency, despite being in generally good health otherwise.

Social Development: Midlife Crises

It is popular to believe that people pass through predictable life crises. In the movies, a midlife crisis is seen as a time when people reevaluate their choices, change their life, reorient, become depressed in the process, buy a fast sports car, and perhaps throw over their spouse for another. The idea that people between 35 and 50 will have a life crisis is widely accepted and considered inevitable.

But are crises unavoidable? Does everyone go through a midlife crisis? We know that people go through transitions. At certain junctures, new decisions must be made and people must reassess who they are, where they are going, and how they want to get there. A distinction should be drawn between a transition and a crisis, however. A *transition* suggests that a person has reached a time in life when old ways of coping no longer work, old tasks have been accomplished, and new methods of living are forthcoming. A person in transition must face new dilemmas, challenges, and responsibilities, which often require reassessment, reappraisal, and the development of new skills. A *crisis*, by contrast, occurs when old ways of coping become ineffective and a person is helpless—not knowing what to do and needing new, radically different coping strategies. Crises are often perceived as painful turning points and catastrophes in a person's life.

Not everyone experiences the infamous midlife crisis, but most people pass through a midlife transition; and some pass through two, three, or even more transitions. Often, a transition occurs at the beginning of adulthood, when people must give up adolescent freedom and accept adult responsibilities. At around age 30, another transition may occur; during this transition, careers and relationships begun in a person's 20s are reevaluated and sometimes rejected. In the transitions of early and middle adulthood, people reorient their career and family choices—the midlife "crisis" at about age 40. Sometimes, parents experience another transition, called the *empty nest syndrome,* when their children leave home—although it is less likely to occur in people who are engaged in paid employment outside the home (Adelmann et al., 1989). Transitions also occur at retirement, not only for the retiree but for the spouse.

Consider my friend Sarah, a single 44-year-old, who has operated her own greeting card distributing company for 20 years. Although the company earns her a comfortable living, it has yet to produce enough profit to enable Sarah to establish a retirement fund; and she worries about how she'll make ends meet in another 20 years. Moreover, Sarah would like to try another career, perhaps in interior decorating. Although she finds the idea of a career change exciting, she questions whether she has the skill and energy to start over. Sarah may be experiencing a midlife "crisis" that may help her become a happier, wiser, and more secure adult.

People who experience midlife transitions normally show no evidence of increased maladjustment or increased rates of suicide or alcoholism. In fact, suicide rates are at their lowest during midlife transitions. For some people, however, midlife changes can be difficult. These midlife changes must be examined for each individual, rather than across all individuals. Like adolescents, some adults face the transitions in their lives, while others merely go through them, not perceiving them as difficult or painful. Their attitudes depend on their unique personalities and ways of coping with the world. The term *midlife crisis* may be a misnomer. As Levinson (1980) suggests, it should more properly be called a midlife transition—a transition that may be more difficult for some individuals than others.

Personality Development

A basic tenet of most personality theories is that, regardless of day-to-day variations, an individual's personality remains stable over time. That is, despite the frequently observed deviations from people's normal patterns or stages of development, the way people cope with life tends to remain fairly consistent throughout the lifetime. But research shows that personality may be sensitive to the unique experiences of the individual, especially during the adult years. According to Haan, Millsap, and Hartka (1986), children's and adolescents' personalities tend to remain stable, while those of adults change over time. The researchers collected data from a longitudinal sample of subjects, who were asked to describe themselves on variables such as self-confidence, assertiveness, dependability, and warmth. The researchers found important shifts in many variables once the subjects reached adulthood. Adults are likely to be more assertive and self-confident than when they were younger, for example. Further, major life events—for example, a child's tragic death, a highly stressful job situation, or a divorce—can alter a person's overall outlook on life.

The data from this study are not easily generalized because the researchers did not take into account changing societal values and expectations. Nevertheless, the data suggest that the adult years are filled with great personal challenges and opportunities and therefore are the years in which people need to be innovative, flexible, and adaptive. Positive changes during adulthood—the development of a sense of generativity, the fulfillment of yearnings for love and respect—usually depend on some degree of success at earlier life stages. Adults who continue to operate with youthful ideals and false assumptions are less likely to experience personality growth in later life.

Women have undergone special scrutiny since the early 1970s. Researchers now recognize that the male-dominated psychology profession of the 1950s generated a host of personality theories that failed to highlight women's unique personality and development issues adequately. Personality researchers now acknowledge that the life experiences of contemporary women are unique. Women face challenges in the work force and the home that were not conceived of 3 decades ago. Managing careers, creating homes, and developing a sense of personal satisfaction have given rise to the "supermom" phenomenon of women trying to have it all—home, family, career, personal satisfaction. Serious research into supermom and the psychological life of women is just beginning to emerge. Aspects of personality development are discussed further in chapter 12.

Building Table 9.2 presents a summary of changes in important domains of adult functioning for both men and women.

BUILDING TABLE 9.2

Major Changes in Important Domains of Adult Functioning

AGE	PHYSICAL CHANGE	COGNITIVE CHANGE	WORK ROLES	PERSONALITY DEVELOPMENT	MAJOR TASKS
Young Adulthood 18-25	Peak functioning in most physical skills; optimum time for childbearing	Cognitive skills high on most measures	Choose career, which may involve several job changes; low work satisfaction is common	Conformist; task of intimacy	Separate from family; form partnership; begin family; find job; create individual life pattern
Early Adulthood 25-40	Still good physical functioning in most areas: health habits during this time establish later risks	Peak period of cognitive skill on most measures	Rising work satisfaction; major emphasis on career or work success; most career progress steps made	Task of generativity	Rear family; establish personal work pattern and strive for success
Middle Adulthood 40-65	Beginning signs of physical decline in some areas— strength, elasticity of tissues, height, cardiovascular function	Some signs of loss of cognitive skill on timed, unexercised skills	Plateau on career steps, but higher work satisfaction	Increase in self-confidence, openness; lower use of immature defenses	Launch family; redefine life goals; redefine self outside of family and work roles; care for aging parents

Adult Stage Theories

Some people—perhaps the more poetic among us—think of life as a journey that each person takes along a road from birth to death. The concept of a journey through life is similar to Erik Erikson's stage theory, in which people move through a series of stages, resolving a different dilemma in each stage. An important aspect of Erikson's theory is that people progress in a specific direction from the beginning of life to the end.

One noted theorist, Daniel Levinson (mentioned previously in relation to transitions versus crises), has devised a different stage theory of adult development. He agrees that people go through stages and that they have similar experiences at certain points in their lives. He also agrees that studying those shared experiences allows psychologists to help people manage their lives. However, unlike Erikson, Levinson does not see life as a journey toward some specific goal or objective, nor as a blueprint that everyone must follow. Rather, a theory of development should lay out the stages (or eras) during which individuals work out various developmental tasks. In his words (Levinson, 1980, p. 289): "We change in different ways, according to different timetables. Yet, I believe that everyone lives through the same developmental periods in adulthood . . . though people go through them in their own ways."

Levinson (1978) suggests that, as people grow older, they adapt to the demands and tasks of life. He describes four basic eras in the adult life cycle, each with distinctive qualities and different life problems, tasks, and situations. Each also brings with it different *life structures*—unique patterns of behavior and ways of interacting with the world. However, because no two people have the same life situation, no two people adapt in exactly the same way. Each person develops a life structure to deal with each era. A young man in his early 30s, for example, may become involved in religious work and learn how groups function to achieve common goals; those skills may be less necessary during his 40s, when he concentrates more on his sales career.

In each era, people develop stable life structures that get them through the period successfully. They then enter a new era, in which they encounter new life conditions, challenges, and dilemmas. Because the old life structures no longer work, they must go through a period of transition, during which they adjust to their new situation. Sometimes, the transition is difficult, characterized by anxiety and even depression. Thus, according to this theory, we can think of a person's life as alternating between stable periods and transitional periods. The four eras outlined by Levinson are:

▶ Ages 11–17—adolescence.

▶ Ages 18–45—early adulthood.

▶ Ages 46–65—middle adulthood.

▶ Ages 66 on—late adulthood.

During *adolescence,* young people enter the adult world but are still immature and vulnerable. During *early adulthood,* they make their first major life choices regarding family, occupation, and style of living. Throughout this period, adults move toward greater independence and senior positions in the community. They raise their children, strive to advance their careers, and launch their offspring into the adult world. Early adulthood is an era of striving for gaining and accepting responsibility. By the end of this era, at about age 45, people no longer have to care for their children, but they may assume the responsibility of caring for their parents.

The much discussed midlife crisis occurs at the end of early adulthood. During this era, people realize that their lives are half over—that if they are to change their lives, they must do so now. Of those who are dissatisfied with the life they have made, some resign themselves to their original course; others decide to change, grow, and strive to achieve new goals. (This era is equivalent to Erikson's stage of generativity versus stagnation.)

Middle adulthood spans the years from 46 to 65. Adults who have gone through a midlife crisis now live with the decisions they made during early adulthood. Career and family are usually well established. People experience either a sense of satisfaction, self-worth, and accomplishment or a sense that much of their life has been wasted. It is often during this period that people reach their peak in creativity and achievement (Simonton, 1988). In the middle of this era, some people go through a crisis similar to that of early adulthood. Sometimes, it is a continuation of the earlier crisis; at other times, it is a new one.

The years after age 50 are ones of mellowing. People approaching their 60s begin to prepare for late adulthood, making whatever major career and family decisions are necessary before retirement. People in their early 60s generally learn to assess their lives not in terms of money or of day-to-day successes but according to whether life has

In middle adulthood, careers are usually well established and people reach their peak in creativity and achievement.

been meaningful, happy, and cohesive. At this time, people stop blaming others for their problems. They are less concerned about disputes with other people. They try to optimize their life because they know that at least two-thirds of it has passed and they wish to make the most of their remaining years. Depending on how well they come to accept themselves, the next decade may be one of great fulfillment or great despair.

Levinson's fourth and final era, *late adulthood*, covers the years from age 66 on. During retirement, many people relax and enjoy the fruits of their labors. Children, grandchildren, and even great-grandchildren can become the focus of an older person's life.

Gender Differences in Adult Stages

Levinson developed his theory by studying 40 men in detail over several years. His subjects were interviewed weekly for several months and were then interviewed again after 2 years. Spouses were interviewed, and extensive biographical data were collected. Levinson's theory has achieved wide acclaim, but it has also been challenged. A major shortcoming is that it is based on information gathered from a small sample of middle-class men. It does not consider socioeconomic class or gender differences.

Women do not necessarily follow the same life stages or changes as men. As children, women are taught different values, goals, and approaches toward life; and these are often reflected later in their choice of vocations, hobbies, and intellectual pursuits (Kalichman, 1989). Women have traditionally sought different career opportunities, although this is changing. In the field of law, for example, women now compose nearly half of all law school students. However, female attorneys often choose careers that do not follow the traditional male associate-partnership ladder.

The developmental course of women, and especially of women's transitions, is similar to that of men; but women tend to experience transitions and life events at later ages and in more irregular sequences than those reported by Levinson. In a major study of women's transitions, Mercer, Nichols, and Doyle (1989) found a developmental progression for women. They considered especially the role of motherhood and how it influences the life courses of women. The researchers broke the developmental progression into five eras at which there are important transitions:

▶ Ages 16–25—launch into adulthood.
▶ Ages 26–30—leveling.
▶ Ages 36–40—liberation.
▶ Ages 61–65—regeneration/redirection.
▶ Ages 66 on—creativity/destructiveness.

In the *launch into adulthood era*, women break away from families to go to school, marry, or work. In the *leveling era*, many women readjust their life course; this is often a time for marriage, separation, or divorce. In the *liberation era*, women focus their aspirations and grow personally. In the *regeneration/redirection era*, women, like men, adjust to their lifetime choices and prepare for retirement and a more leisurely lifestyle. In the last stage of life, the *creativity/destructiveness era*, women are challenged to adapt to health changes and the loss of spouses and friends; this time is also characterized by a surge of creativity or sometimes depression. With its five-stage approach, this women's developmental life stage theory is similar to Levinson's, but it has its own unique flavor and recognizes differences in the life courses of men and women.

Today, many universities, recognizing that there are special issues relating to women, have departments of women's studies. Women still face discrimination in the work force, and society continues to vacillate in its expectations for women and for child care. Women still have the primary burden of family responsibilities, especially child care; in the aftermath of a divorce, the woman usually gets physical custody of the children. Women must often juggle multiple roles; these roles place on them enormous burdens, which alter their moods and their ability to function at their peak (K. J. Williams et al., 1991). The assumption of child care after divorce has sharp economic consequences that alter the lifestyle, mental health, and course of life stages for women (McBride, 1990). Clearly, these are obvious differences in the life stages of men and women, whether upper-, middle-, or lower-class.

A comprehensive picture of adult development must also include minorities and their special life experiences. For example, the life cycle, family responsibilities, and beliefs of a Navajo woman, a recent immigrant from Cuba, or a poor farmer are all different. As cultural differences in development are systematically studied, global theories such as Levinson's will be adjusted to explain adult development more completely.

FOCUS

▶ What is the difference between a transition and a crisis in an adult's life? p. 329

▶ Levinson's four eras describe important characteristics of adult development. How did he infer such eras? p. 331

▶ Mercer, Nichols, and Doyle found a different developmental progression for women. What distinguishes their approach from Levinson's? p. 333

Aging

As people grow older, they age experientially as well as physically; that is, they gather experiences and expand their worlds. Nevertheless, in Western society, growing older is not always easy, especially because of the negative stereotypes associated with the aging process. Today, however, people are healthier than ever before, are approaching later years with vigor, and look forward to second and sometimes third careers.

Although most older adults face aging from a mature and experienced vantage point and look forward to a fruitful retirement, they also face challenges. Sometimes, failing health (their own or a spouse's) complicates life; sometimes society's negative attitudes complicate it. In general, being over age 65 brings with it new developmental tasks—retirement, health issues, and maintenance of a long-term standard of living.

An Aging Population

How older people view themselves depends, in part, on how society treats them. Many Asian cultures greatly respect the elderly for their wisdom and maturity; in such societies, gray hair is a mark of distinction, not embarrassment. In contrast, the United States is a youth-oriented society where people spend a fortune on everything from hair dyes to facelifts to make themselves look younger. However, because the average age of Americans is climbing, how we perceive the elderly and how they perceive themselves may be changing.

In the first 5 years of the 1990s, approximately 12 percent of the U.S. population—more than 30 million Americans—will be 65 or older. According to the Bureau of the Census (1992), the proportion of elderly people is expected to increase to between 20 and 25 percent by 2030, and the number of Americans past 65 will exceed 60 million (see Figure 9.3). At present, the average life expectancy at birth

Modern Japan's increasingly fast-paced and high-pressure society is causing many of its senior citizens to view themselves as a burden to the younger generation. Suicide is on the increase and some, like this woman, pray to die. (Photo courtesy of CNN.)

FIGURE 9.3

A Nation Growing Older

In the year 2030, the U.S. population will be distributed fairly evenly among 10-year age groups ranging from birth through age 69.

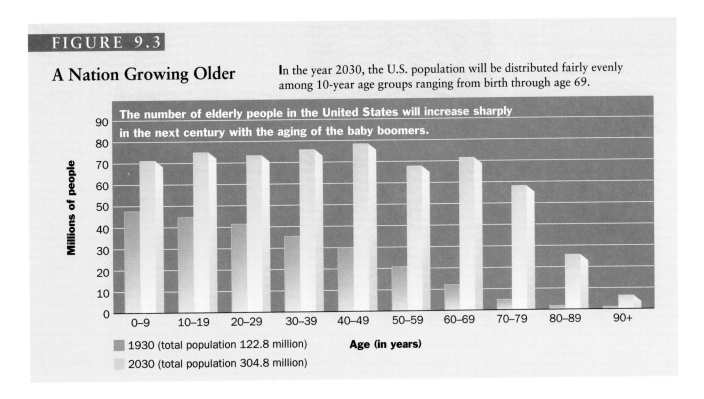

The number of elderly people in the United States will increase sharply in the next century with the aging of the baby boomers.

■ 1930 (total population 122.8 million)
□ 2030 (total population 304.8 million)

Age (in years)

in the United States is about 74.7 years. Life expectancy is different for men and women, however. Women live about 4 years longer than men, on the average; and at birth their life expectancy is 7 years greater (at age 65, the difference is about 3 years).

For many people, the years after age 60 are filled with excitement. Financially, two-thirds of American workers are covered by pension plans provided by their employers. Socially, most maintain close friendships and family ties. Some, however, experience financial problems, and others experience loneliness and isolation because many of their friends and relatives have died or they have lost touch with their families. In the United States, there are now as many people over the age of 60 as there are under the age of 7. Yet funding for programs involving the health and psychological well-being of older people is relatively limited.

Myths, Realities, and Stereotypes

There is a widely held myth that older people are less intelligent than younger people, less able to care for themselves, inflexible, and sickly. The reality is that many elderly people are as competent and capable as they were in their earlier adulthood. They work, play golf, compete in races, socialize, and stay politically aware and active. Healthy elderly people maintain a good sex life (Bretschneider & McCoy, 1988); and if they were not depressed earlier in life, they are unlikely to be depressed now. Building Table 9.3 on page 337 summarizes important changes in adult functioning from young adulthood to late, late adulthood.

Stereotypes about the elderly have given rise to **ageism**—prejudice against the elderly and the discrimination that follows from it. Ageism is prevalent in the job market, in which older people are not given the same opportunities as their younger coworkers, and in housing and health care. It is exceptionally prevalent in the media—on television and in newspapers, cartoons, and magazines—and in everyday language (Schaie, 1993).

Ageism: Prejudice against the elderly and the discrimination that follows from it.

As the elderly population of America continues to grow, many of the myths about aging are being dispelled. As these women prove, growing old does not automatically relegate people to their rocking chairs.

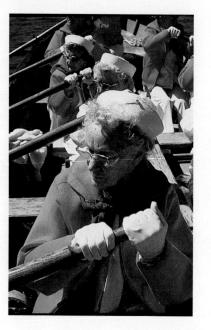

Schmidt and Boland (1986) examined everyday language to learn how people perceive older adults. They found interesting differences. For example, *elder statesman* implies that a person is experienced, intelligent, or perhaps conservative. However, *old statesman* might suggest that a person is past his prime, tired, or useless. The term *old people* may allude to positive elements in older adults— for example, the perfect grandparent—or to negative qualities such as grouchiness or mental deficiencies. What does *old* mean?

Older people who are perceived to represent negative stereotypes are more likely to suffer discrimination than those who appear to represent more positive stereotypes. This means that an older person who appears healthy, bright, and alert is more likely to be treated with the same respect shown to younger people. By contrast, an older adult who appears less capable may not be given the same respect or treatment. In chapter 17, we'll see that first impressions have a potent effect on people's behavior. This seems to be particularly true for older people. An older person's physical appearance may invoke ageism, whereas a younger person's appearance seems less likely to have such an immediate effect. In any case, ageism can be reduced if people recognize the diversity that exists among aging populations (Kimmel, 1988).

Theories of Aging

The quest for eternal youth has inspired extravagant attempts to slow, stop, or reverse the aging process. Ponce de Leon organized an expedition to the New World in 1512 to find the fabled fountain of youth. Alchemists in the Middle Ages tried in vain to concoct an elixir of life. And in the past hundred years, quacks have attempted to reclaim youthful vigor with everything from strong laxative therapy (to clean the colon) to injections of cells from lamb fetuses. In recent years, scientists seem to have dramatically increased the life span of some laboratory animals by feeding them calorie-restricted diets. However, so far the maximum life span attained by human beings has been between 100 and 120 years.

Despite the centuries-long search for the secret of eternal youth, psychologists and physicians have been examining the behavioral and physiological changes that accompany aging only since the early 1970s. Three basic types of theories have been developed to explain why people age. These theories are based on heredity, external factors, and physiology. Although each emphasizes a different cause for aging, it is most likely that aging results from a combination of all three.

Heredity. Genes determine much of a person's physical makeup; thus, it is probable that heredity, to some extent, determines how long a person will live. Much supporting evidence exists for this component. For example, we know that long-lived parents tend to have long-lived offspring. However, researchers still do not know *how* heredity exerts its influence over the aging process.

External Factors. Kimmel (1980) suggests that external factors affect how long a person will live. For example, people who live on farms live longer than those in cities; normal-weight people live longer than overweight people; and people who

BUILDING TABLE 9.3

Major Changes in Important Domains of Adult Functioning

AGE	PHYSICAL CHANGE	COGNITIVE CHANGE	WORK ROLES	PERSONALITY DEVELOPMENT	MAJOR TASKS
Young Adulthood 18-25	Peak functioning in most physical skills; optimum time for childbearing	Cognitive skills high on most measures	Choose career, which may involve several job changes; low work satisfaction is common	Conformist; task of intimacy	Separate from family; form partnership; begin family; find job; create individual life pattern
Early Adulthood 25-40	Still good physical functioning in most areas: health habits during this time establish later risks	Peak period of cognitive skill on most measures	Rising work satisfaction; major emphasis on career or work success; most career progress steps made	Task of generativity	Rear family; establish personal work pattern and strive for success
Middle Adulthood 40-65	Beginning signs of physical decline in some areas—strength, elasticity of tissues, height, cardiovascular function	Some signs of loss of cognitive skill on timed, unexercised skills	Plateau on career steps, but higher work satisfaction	Increase in self-confidence, openness; lower use of immature defenses	Launch family; redefine life goals; redefine self outside of family and work roles; care for aging parents
Late Adulthood 65-75	Significant physical decline on most measures	Small declines for virtually all adults on some skills	Retirement	Perhaps integrated level; perhaps more inferiority; or perhaps self-actualized; task of ego integrity	Cope with retirement; cope with declining health; redefine life goals and sense of self
Late, Late Adulthood 75+	Marked physical decline on virtually any measure, including speed, strength, work capacity, elasticity, system functioning	Often significant loss in many areas, including memory	Work roles now unimportant	Perhaps integrated or self-actualized, at least for some people	Come to terms with death

do not smoke cigarettes, who are not constantly tense, and who do not expose themselves to disease or radiation live longer than others. Because data on external factors are often obtained from correlational studies, cause-and-effect statements cannot be based on them; but it is reasonable to assume that external factors such as disease, smoking, and obesity affect a person's life span.

Physiology. Several theories use physiological and genetic explanations to account for aging. Because a person's physiological processes depend on both hereditary and environmental factors, these theories rely on both concepts. The *wear-and-tear theory* of aging claims that the human organism simply wears out from overuse, much like the parts of a machine (Rowland, 1977). Although a commonsense notion, this view does not have much experimental support.

A related theory, the *homeostatic theory,* suggests that the body's ability to adjust to varying situations decreases with age. For example, as the ability to maintain a constant body temperature decreases, cellular and tissue damage occur and aging results. Similarly, when the body can no longer control the use of sugar through the output of insulin, signs of aging appear (Eisdorfer & Wilkie, 1977). On the other hand, aging may be the *cause* of deviations from homeostasis, rather than the result.

Whatever the causes of aging, people go through a number of predictable changes as they age. These are often called biobehavioral changes, and we will consider them next.

Biobehavioral Changes

Elderly people must contend with significant biological changes. These changes include alterations in calcium metabolism, which make the bones more brittle; increased susceptibility to diseases of the joints, such as arthritis; decreased elasticity in the skin, creating folds and wrinkles. Some biological changes interact with behavioral ones. For example, people who live alone may not eat properly and may suffer vitamin deficiencies as a result. The changes that come about from the interaction of biology and behavior are termed *biobehavioral changes.* Figure 9.4 shows some symptoms seen in elderly patients as a result of aging.

Brain Disorders. You might assume that aging is inevitably accompanied by *senility,* a term once used to describe cognitive changes that occur in older people. Today, these cognitive deficits are known to be caused by brain disorders that

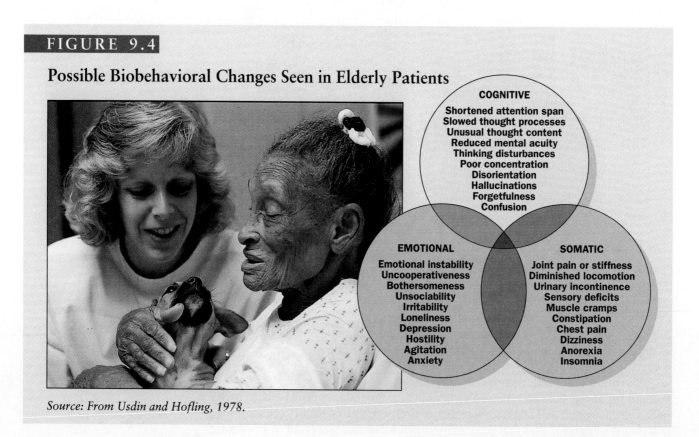

FIGURE 9.4

Possible Biobehavioral Changes Seen in Elderly Patients

COGNITIVE
Shortened attention span
Slowed thought processes
Unusual thought content
Reduced mental acuity
Thinking disturbances
Poor concentration
Disorientation
Hallucinations
Forgetfulness
Confusion

EMOTIONAL
Emotional instability
Uncooperativeness
Bothersomeness
Unsociability
Irritability
Loneliness
Depression
Hostility
Agitation
Anxiety

SOMATIC
Joint pain or stiffness
Diminished locomotion
Urinary incontinence
Sensory deficits
Muscle cramps
Constipation
Chest pain
Dizziness
Anorexia
Insomnia

Source: From Usdin and Hofling, 1978.

occur only in *some* older people. Brain disorders are sometimes termed *dementias*. **Dementias** are impairments in mental functioning and global cognitive abilities of longstanding duration in otherwise alert individuals, causing a loss of memory and related symptoms. The leading cause in the United States is Alzheimer's disease. Only 0.4 percent of people aged 60 to 65 suffer from dementias. The percentage increases to 3.6 for people aged 75 to 79 and to 23.8 for individuals aged 85 to 93 (Selkoe, 1992).

More than 70 conditions cause dementias. Among them is AIDS; patients have a failing immune system, which can cause brain infections, which in turn can lead to dementia. Some conditions that cause dementia can be treated, and that treatment often halts (but does not reverse) the dementia. Memory loss can occur for recent events (short-term memory) as well as for past events. Additional symptoms of dementias include loss of language skills, reduced capacity for abstract thinking, personality changes, and loss of a sense of time and place. Severe and disabling dementias affect about 1.5 million Americans. With the increasing number of elderly citizens, these statistics are on the rise.

Reversible dementias, which are caused by malnutrition, alcoholism, or toxins (poisons), usually affect younger people. *Irreversible dementias* are of two types—multiple infarcts and Alzheimer's disease (which we'll examine in the Research Process box on p. 340). *Multiple infarct dementia* is usually caused by two or more small strokes (ruptures of small blood vessels in the brain); it results in a slow degeneration of the brain.

Sensory Abilities. Older people are likely to experience decreased sensory abilities. Their vision, hearing, taste, and smell require a higher level of stimulation to respond the way younger people's senses do. Older people, for example, usually are unable to make fine visual discriminations without the aid of glasses, have limited capacity for dark adaptation, and often have some degree of hearing loss, especially in the high-frequency ranges.

Changes in the Nervous System. One change that can be seen easily in older individuals is a slowing of their reaction time in specific situations. Although the sensory systems themselves may not be impaired, older people respond less quickly to events. In an emergency, for example, an elderly driver may be unable to stop a car as quickly as a younger driver could. Many explanations for this decreased response time have been suggested, but none has been proven conclusively. Other changes include alterations in brain-wave activity and in autonomic nervous system activity. Some researchers have suggested that older individuals appear to be underaroused. However, studies of autonomic nervous system responsiveness in old and young adults show little support for this once-popular idea (Powell, Milligan, & Furchtgott, 1980).

Overall Health. People's overall health deteriorates as they age. For men, the probability of dying doubles in each decade after midlife. Blood pressure rises, cardiac output decreases, and the likelihood of stroke increases. One impact of this deterioration is that cardiovascular disease influences intellectual functioning by decreasing blood flow to the brain (Hertzog, Schaie, & Gribbin, 1978).

Some individuals experience *terminal drop*—a rapid decline in intellectual functioning in the year before death. Some researchers attribute this change to cardiovascular disease, claiming that the decreased blood flow (and resulting decrease in oxygen) to the brain causes declining mental ability and, ultimately, failing health. However, although there is evidence for the terminal drop, no satisfactory method exists for predicting death on the basis of poor performance on intelligence or neuropsychological tests (Botwinick, 1984).

Dementias: Impairments in mental functioning and global cognitive abilities of long-standing duration in otherwise alert individuals, causing memory loss and related symptoms.

THE RESEARCH PROCESS

Alzheimer's Disease

Alzheimer's disease is a chronic and progressive disorder of the brain that is a major cause of degenerative dementia. It could well be the most widespread neurological disorder of all time (Bloom, Lazerson, & Hofstadter, 1985). As the population grows older, the number of cases of Alzheimer's disease increases. Currently, there are about 1.5 to 2 million diagnosed Alzheimer's patients in the United States; in addition, there is a large number of undiagnosed cases. A recent estimate suggests that the numbers may be even greater than once thought: 1 in 10 people over 65 may have the disease, and almost half of those over 85 may have it (Evans et al., 1989). Because Alzheimer's is a degenerative disease, its progression cannot be stopped; it is irreversible and ultimately ends in death. To date, there is no fully effective method of prevention, treatment, or cure.

What causes this disease? What is its psychological impact on our population? How does it affect families?

What Causes Alzheimer's Disease? A definitive diagnosis of Alzheimer's disease can be made only by an examination of brain tissue after death; tangled neurons is the typical finding. Brain scans usually confirm that explanation: The patient's neurons seem to be twisted and gnarled and coated with *plaque* (fibrous tissue that impedes neural transmission). Levels of neurotransmitter substances are usually low.

Correlational research shows that Alzheimer's disease tends to run in families, which suggests a genetic basis or at least a predisposition to the disorder. Some researchers posit a depletion of enzymes; others suggest an accumulation of toxins; still others focus on neurotransmitters and metabolic patterns. Blood supply problems, immune system factors, head

injuries, and viruses have also been implicated in the disease. Proteins that accumulate in the brain of Alzheimer's patients are now being found elsewhere in the body, which makes the proteins easier to extract and study. Rabizadeh et al., (1993) found a protein that seems to kill cells involved in memory unless another specific protein (called a nerve growth factor, or NGF) is bound to that protein. There has been speculation that memory loss might be averted or stopped by treating cells with NGF or other drugs that mimic the action of NGF.

No one yet knows the causes of Alzheimer's disease or has developed an effective treatment. Researchers are beginning to think that there are many types of Alzheimer's disease, some of which may be hereditary (Bondareff et al., 1993; Martin et al., 1990) and some of which may have been generated by early life events, such as head injuries (Roberts, 1988).

Alzheimer's disease: [ALTZ-hy-merz] A chronic and progressive disorder of the brain that is a major cause of degenerative dementia; it may be a group of related disorders tied together loosely under one name.

Intellectual Changes

Perhaps the most distressing change that occurs with aging is a decline in intellectual ability. Many researchers who once believed that general intellectual functioning remains stable throughout life now acknowledge that certain aspects of intelligence may deteriorate with age. However, it is difficult to know exactly what and how much change occurs.

Many researchers have studied changes in intellectual functioning. A major problem, however, is defining it. Aged people are likely to do poorly on standardized intelligence tests, not because their intelligence is low but because the tests require the manipulation of objects during a timed interval—and older people have a slower reaction time or decreased manual dexterity (often because of arthritis). To overcome these disadvantages, researchers have devised different methodologies for studying intelligence in older people.

Although most research indicates that cognitive and intellectual abilities decrease with advancing age, many of the changes are of little importance for day-to-day functioning. For example, overall vocabulary decreases only slightly (Shneidman, 1989). Moreover, some of the changes observed in laboratory tasks (for example, reaction-time tasks) are either small or reversible (Baltes, Reese, & Lipsitt, 1980). In addition, many older people do not do well on intelligence tests because they are not as motivated as younger people to do well. Finally, extreme variability in both the types and causes of intellectual deficits suggests that changes in health

Psychological Effects. The impact of Alzheimer's disease on the patient is enormous; the disease severely damages the quality of life. Patients are not necessarily stripped of their vigor or strength, but they slowly become confused and helpless. Initially, they may forget to do small things. Later, they may forget appointments, anniversaries, and the like. The forgetfulness is often overlooked at first. Jokes and other coping strategies cover up for memory losses and lapses. The memory losses are not always apparent; some days are better than others. Ultimately, however, the disorder grows worse. Eventually, Alzheimer's patients have trouble finding their way home and remembering their own name and the names of their spouse and children. Sometimes fact retrieval is more impaired than is general accumulated knowledge (Bäckman & Lapinska, 1993). Their personality also changes. They may become abrupt, abusive, and hostile to family members. Within months, or sometimes years, they lose their speech and language functions. Eventually, they lose all control of memory and even of simple bodily functions.

Implications for Families. In addition to studying the effects of Alzheimer's disease on patients, researchers are also studying the impact on patients' families. Caring for the patient imposes great physical, emotional, and financial hardships (Aronson, Levin, & Lipkowitz, 1984). Because families cannot care for relatives with Alzheimer's indefinitely, hospitalization, or at least day care, is often necessary. The patient's loved ones "walk a tightrope between meeting the patient's needs and preserving their own well-being" (Heckler, 1985, p. 1241). Alzheimer's disease changes family life in irreversible ways; most patients are placed in nursing homes after extensive and exhausting care at home. Brody, Lawton, and Liebowitz (1984, p. 1331) assert, "In the overwhelming majority of cases, nursing home placement occurs only after responsible family caregivers have endured prolonged, unrelenting caring (often for years) and no longer have the capacity to continue their caregiving efforts." It is estimated that, by 1995, the cost of nursing home care for Alzheimer's patients may be as high as $41 billion per year.

and family situation may produce the severe biological and psychological consequences that in turn affect intellectual functioning. See Table 9.2 on page 342 for a summary of age changes in intellectual skills through adulthood.

Whatever the causes, deficits in intellectual functioning that occur with age and that influence behavior are seldom devastating. Up to the ages of 60 to 65, there is little decline in learning or memory; motivation, interest, and lack of recent educational experience are probably more important in learning complex knowledge than is age. At later ages, evidence exists for some modest decreases in abilities, particularly in such functions as short-term (working) memory (Craik, Morris, & Gick, 1990).

Despite evidence that old age takes a toll, there exist many remarkable examples of intellectual achievement by people 70 years old or older. Golda Meir, for example, became prime minister of Israel at age 70. Benjamin Franklin invented bifocal eyeglasses at 74 and helped to frame the Constitution of the United States at 81. Arthur Rubinstein, the Polish-born American concert pianist, gave one of his greatest recitals (at New York's Carnegie Hall) at age 89.

Dying: The End of the Life Span

Everyone recognizes that death is inevitable; but in the 20th century, few people actually witness death (Aiken, 1985). Before this century, most people died in bed at home, where other people were likely to be with them. Today, nearly 80 percent

TABLE 9.2   *Summary of Age Changes in Intellectual Skills*

Age 20–40	Age 40–65	Age 65 and Older
Peak intellectual ability between about 20 and 35	Maintenance of skill on measures of verbal intelligence; some decline of skill on measures of performance intelligence; decline usually not functionally significant till age 60 or older	Some loss of verbal intelligence; most noticeable in adults with poorer health, lower levels of activity, and less education
Optimal performance on memory tasks	Little change in performance on memory tasks, except perhaps some slowing later in this period	Slowing of retrieval processes and other memory processes; less skillful use of coding strategies for new memories
Peak performance on laboratory tests of problem solving	Peak performance on real-life problem-solving tasks and many verbal abilities	Decline in problem-solving performance on both laboratory and real-life tests

of people die in hospitals and nursing homes. About 8 million Americans experience the death of an immediate family member each year. We are all affected by death, but most people avoid discussing it.

Thanatology—the study of psychological and medical aspects of death and dying—has become an interdisciplinary specialty. Researchers and theorists in several areas—including theology, law, history, psychology, sociology, and medicine—have come together to better understand death and dying. For psychologists, dealing with the process of dying is especially complicated because people do not like to talk or think about death. Nevertheless, considerable progress has been made toward understanding the psychology of dying.

Kübler-Ross's Stage Theory. Elisabeth Kübler-Ross has become famous for her studies of the way people respond psychologically to their impending death (see, e.g., Kübler-Ross, 1969, 1975). She believes that people in Western society fear death because it is unfamiliar, often hidden away in hospitals. She suggests that a way to reduce this fear is to involve members of a dying person's family more closely in what is, in fact, a very natural process. She contends that it is better for people to die at home than in an unfamiliar hospital room.

Kübler-Ross was one of the first researchers to use a stage theory to discuss people's fear of their own death and that of loved ones. People who learn they are terminally ill, in Kübler-Ross's view, typically go through five stages: *denial,* which serves as a buffer against the shocking news; *anger* directed against family, friends, or medical staff; *bargaining,* in which people try to gain more time by "making a deal" with God, themselves, or their doctors; *depression,* often caused by the pain of their illness and guilt over inconveniencing their family; and finally, *acceptance,* in which people stop fighting and accept death.

Criticisms of Kübler-Ross's Theory. Kübler-Ross's theory has been subject to considerable criticism. Not all researchers find the same sequence of events in the dying process (Stephenson, 1985). They argue that the sequence outlined by Kübler-Ross does not work for all people and that the stages are not necessarily experienced in the order she suggests. However, Kübler-Ross contends that her theory was meant to be an overall outline, not a strict set of stages or steps.

Kübler-Ross has also been criticized for her research techniques. Her interviews have not been very systematic; she offers few statistics, and some of her ideas rely

Thanatology: The study of the psychological and medical aspects of death and dying.

APPLICATIONS

Hospice Care

Hospices are special facilities established to provide efficient and humane care to terminally ill patients and their families. They address emotional, social, and spiritual needs in addition to physical ones, and they combine humane treatment with sensitivity to the financial costs of patient care (Butterfield-Picard & Magno, 1982; Smyser, 1982). Hospice care takes psychological principles used in therapy and puts them to work in the day-to-day care of the terminally ill. A hospice often focuses

on the psychological needs of the patient, while acknowledging that death is inevitable and imminent.

Hospice care is not appropriate for every dying person. It requires specific kinds of commitment from the patient and family members. Therefore, before admitting a patient, hospices evaluate both the patient and the family. Hospices operate under a different set of guidelines from hospitals and nursing homes that care for the terminally ill (Butterfield-Picard & Magno, 1982):

▶ Control of decisions concerning the patient's care rests with the patient and the family.

▶ Many aspects of traditional care, such as life-support procedures, are discontinued when the patient no longer desires them.

▶ Pain is kept to a minimum so the patient can experience life as fully as possible until death.

▶ A team of professionals provide care around the clock.

▶ Surroundings are homelike rather than clinical.

▶ When possible, family members and the hospice team are the caregivers.

▶ Family members receive counseling before and after the patient dies.

There are more than 440 hospices in the United States today, with at least 360 more under construction. Yet relatively few terminally ill patients receive hospice care. For those who do, family members, friends, and practitioners have to answer ethical and practical questions about care and costs, life-support systems, and medications. To help them, researchers and applied psychologists are exploring such issues as exactly when death occurs, how the dying should be treated, and how families can cope better with the dying process. They are examining issues such as how to help the families cope with grief over their loss and guilt about their feeling of relief.

more on intuition than on facts established through scientific methods. Specifically, her data-gathering techniques have been highly subjective. Schaie and Willis (1986) have suggested that Kübler-Ross's ideas should not be considered a theory but "an insightful discussion of some of the attitudes that are often displayed by people who are dying" (p. 483). Although Kübler-Ross's ideas about death and dying may not actually be true in every case, many practitioners find them useful in guiding new medical staff through the difficult task of helping the dying, especially those who are facing premature death because of illnesses such as cancer.

Whether or not one accepts Kübler-Ross's stages as typical, it is clear that, as in all areas of life, people approach death with different attitudes and behaviors. In general, people fear death, although they are more fearful of death in middle age than at any other time in the life cycle. Religious people fear death less than others, older women fear it less than older men, and financially stable people have less negative attitudes toward death than do poor people. Moreover, most psychologists believe that the ways in which people have dealt with previous stresses in their lives largely predict how they will deal with death.

FOCUS

► In what ways do biobehavioral changes that occur as a result of aging affect the lives of older adults?   p. 338

► What is the evidence that intelligence test scores among aging subjects decrease because of non-intelligence-related factors?   p. 340

► What are the implications for mental health professionals of the large number of people affected by Alzheimer's disease?   pp. 340–341

In addition to imposing emotional stress on the terminally ill patient, impending death also causes stress for the patient's family. Kübler-Ross has drawn attention to the additional stress on family members created by interactions with doctors, especially in traditional impersonal hospital settings. Like many other physicians and psychologists, she believes that a more homelike setting can help patients and their families deal better with death. One answer to the problem of death in institutional settings is the hospice, discussed in the Applications box on page 343.

Concluding Note

The study of adolescence and adulthood, like the study of childhood, focuses on change. Today, people in general and psychologists in particular are especially aware of the effects of change on the day-to-day lives of adolescents and adults. Adolescents go through physical, emotional, and intellectual changes that sometimes turn their world upside-down. Hormones change, first loves appear, and life goals are established. Moral development matures, and new values are established. It can be a trying time.

Teenagers are not alone in facing change; adulthood also brings with it continuous change. This chapter highlighted the possibilities of midlife transitions and described how career, family, and physical changes affect adults. Change is again the key to understanding. Change is usually for the better, and it is toward maturity and fulfillment. Nevertheless, there are times in an adult's life when change is difficult. For example, no single event has such wrenching effects as divorce. Adults must cope with new lifestyles, settings, and economic situations. Eventually, the two new family units that evolve will function adequately, although their functioning will often be very different from what it was before. From a psychologist's point of view, the changes that occur in the life cycle are not only observable but in many ways predictable. It is the task of the developmental psychologist to study life-cycle changes, incorporate them into comprehensive theories, and make predictions so as to allow individuals to better manage their lives.

As research unfolds over the next decade, we are likely to see a greater focus on the effects of change and transitions, such as divorce, on individuals, families, and family structures. Blended families, remarriages, and living alone bring new challenges. Each change has to be studied by researchers who can ask the appropriate developmental questions to build stronger, sounder developmental theories.

Summary & Review

Adolescence

Distinguish between puberty and adolescence.

Puberty is the period during which the reproductive system matures; it occurs at, and signals, the end of childhood. There is considerable variation among individuals as to its onset. *Adolescence* is the period extending from the onset of puberty to early adulthood.   p. 316

What is the origin of the adolescent identity crisis?

Changing intellectual abilities, body proportions, and sexual urges (together with parental expectations for more adult behavior) create the classic adolescent identity crisis of Western culture. However, the problems of adolescence must be considered in a cultural context because most of the research on adolescence has been conducted with white, middle-class American teenagers—and this is clearly not representative of all teenagers. pp. 316–318

What are gender identity and gender schema theory?

Gender identity is a person's sense of being male or female. Parents are the first and most important forces shaping gender identity; they influence a child from birth. Peers and schools are especially important sources of information as well. *Gender schema theory* asserts that children and adolescents use gender as an organizing theme to classify and understand their perceptions about the world. pp. 319–320

What is androgyny?

Androgyny is the condition in which some typically male and some typically female characteristics are apparent in one individual.   pp. 321–322

Briefly describe Erikson's psychosocial theory of development.

Erikson describes psychosocial development throughout life as a continuum of stages during which people resolve various psychosexual issues. His stage theory suggests that at each stage a successful or unsuccessful resolution of a dilemma determines personality and social interactions. His approach emphasizes the gradual development of complex feelings, beliefs, and experiences, usually through successful completion of one stage at a time.   pp. 322–325

How have adolescent sexual behavior and attitudes changed in the last twenty years?

Adolescents view sexual intimacy as a normal part of growing up, and premarital heterosexual activity has become common among adolescents, especially 13- to 17-year-olds. More relaxed attitudes about adolescent sexual behavior have brought about increased awareness among adolescents about contraception and teenage pregnancy. Yet teen pregnancy is on the rise; thus, increased awareness does not imply that the problem is being solved.   pp. 325–326

KEY TERMS: *puberty,* p. 316; *adolescence,* p. 316; *secondary sex characteristics,* p. 317; *gender differences,* p. 319; *gender identity,* p. 319; *gender schema theory,* p. 319; *gender roles,* p. 320; *gender role stereotyping,* p. 320; *androgynous,* p. 322.

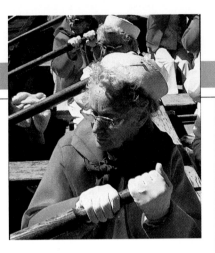

Adulthood

What are the key physical changes that occur in adulthood?

Physical development continues throughout adulthood as overall fitness decreases, especially after age 40; sexual changes, including the effects of decreasing levels of sex hormones; and, sensory changes, including increased reaction time after the age of 65.   pp. 327–329

Do people have midlife crises?

Nearly everyone has transitions in life, but not everyone experiences them as crises. A *transition* suggests that a person has reached a time in life when old ways of coping no longer work. A *crisis* occurs when old ways of coping become ineffective and a person feels helpless, not knowing what to do.   pp. 329–330

Briefly describe two adult stage theories of development—one for men, and one for women.

Daniel Levinson's stage theory of adulthood asserts that everyone lives through the same developmental periods in adulthood, though people go through them in their own ways. His theory of adult development (which was generated from data on males)

continued

Summary & Review

describes four basic eras, each with distinctive qualities and different life problems, tasks, and situations: adolescence, early adulthood, middle adulthood, and late adulthood. Women do not necessarily follow the same life stages as men. Women tend to experience transitions and life events at later ages and in more irregular sequences than those reported by Levinson; consequently, Mercer, Nichols, and Doyle suggested a developmental progression for women broken into five eras: launch into adulthood, leveling, liberation, regeneration/redirection, and creativity/destructiveness. pp. 331–334

Aging

Who are the aged?

In general, being over age 65 classifies a person as being aged. In the first five years of the 1990s approximately 12 percent of the U.S. population—more than 30 million Americans—will be 65 or older.   pp. 334–335

What is ageism?

Ageism is discrimination on the basis of age, often resulting in the denial of rights and services to the elderly.   p. 335

Describe the biobehavioral changes in the elderly.

Changes that occur from the interaction of biology and behavior are called *biobehavioral changes.* In the elderly they fall into the categories of brain disorders (especially dementias), loss of sensory abilities (especially visual), changes in the nervous system (especially in reaction time), and decreases in overall health. pp. 338–339

What are dementias?

Brain disorders, sometimes called *dementias,* involve losses of cognitive or mental functioning. Reversible dementias, caused by malnutrition, alcoholism, or toxins (poisons), usually affect younger people. Irreversible dementias are of two types, multiple infarcts and *Alzheimer's disease.*   pp. 339–341

What are the effects of Alzheimer's disease?

Currently, there are about 1.5 to 2 million diagnosed Alzheimer's patients in the United States. Alzheimer's is a degenerative disease whose progression cannot be stopped; it is irreversible and ultimately ends in death. Individuals who suffer from Alzheimer's disease slowly lose their memory. Within months, or sometimes years, they lose their speech and language functions. Eventually, they lose all bodily and mental control.   p. 341

What are the essential elements of Kübler-Ross's theory of dying?

Elisabeth Kübler-Ross has described dying as a process involving five stages: denial, anger, bargaining, depression, and finally, acceptance. Although controversial and not widely accepted by the scientific community, Kübler-Ross's ideas have generated much interest.   pp. 342–344

What is a hospice?

A hospice is a special facility established to provide efficient and humane care to terminally ill patients and their families. Hospice care is not appropriate for every dying person. It requires specific kinds of commitment from the patient and family members.   p. 343

KEY TERMS: *ageism,* p. 335; *dementias,* p. 339; *Alzheimer's disease,* p. 340; *thanatology,* p. 342.

CONNECTIONS

If you are interested in...

Sexual behavior and the process of development, see ...

CHAPTER 15, pp. 515–516

How many psychological disorders exhibit themselves in the sexual domain of a person's life.

CHAPTER 12, pp. 427–428

Freud's argument that a person's life energy is sexual in nature.

CHAPTER 17, pp. 633–634

People are attracted to those who share their attitudes and who like them.

◀

Midlife transitions and how people respond to stressful situations, see ...

CHAPTER 10, p. 369

How a person's emotional life is to a great extent determined by how he or she appraises a situation.

CHAPTER 13, pp. 488–489

The way people's health can be affected by their reactions to life-cycle events, as well as to stressors in the environment.

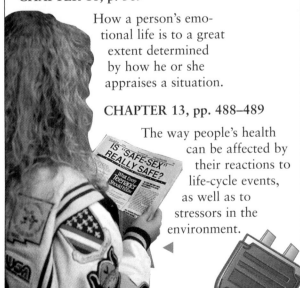

◀

Stereotypes about certain types of people, including adolescents and the elderly, see ...

CHAPTER 5, pp. 174–177

The way operant conditioning, used by parents to reinforce certain ideas in their children, leads to long-lasting ideas and evaluations.

CHAPTER 16, pp. 577–579

Changing stereotyped ideas, which is possible only when a person views an argument as very powerful and delivered in an expert way by an important communicator.

CHAPTER 17, pp. 625–628

How stereotypes, usually based on wrong information from a limited or nonexistent sample of behavior, lead to prejudice.

▶

10

Motivation and Emotion

Jim Abbott set his goals high—and achieved them. Abbott was the star pitcher on his high school baseball team, led the U.S. Olympic baseball team to a gold medal, and can throw a fastball at 93 miles per hour. If these statistics are not enough to separate Jim Abbott from other athletes, the fact that he has only one hand ensures his distinction.

As a youngster, Abbott, whose right arm is 10 inches shorter than his left, was never treated as disabled; instead, he was encouraged to try harder. He was motivated by his parents to work hard, and he developed a can-do attitude about life. He practiced, practiced, practiced—as do all superb athletes—and he is now pitching full-time with an incredible degree of success for the New York Yankees.

Why do some people strive to achieve success while others are content to enjoy life at a more relaxed pace? Why will one person spend a free afternoon watching soap operas and munching potato chips while another will use the time for a 5-mile run and a quick study session before dinner? Why do some people crave the excitement of competition while others seem to shy away from it? The most important question is: What drives people to take some action?

Defining Motivation

The study of motivation is as old as the study of psychology. Researchers have always sought to know what impels people to take various actions—from simple actions such as eating to complex actions such as learning a foreign language. Many theories of motivation have been developed to explain the causes of people's behaviors, but no single theory can explain all behavior. In fact, most psychologists believe that inborn motivation and learning cause people to behave in different ways. To understand these interacting forces, we must first define *motivation*.

Motivation is any condition, usually internal, that appears by inference to initiate, activate, or maintain an organism's goal-directed behavior. Let's examine the four basic parts of motivation: (1) internal condition; (2) inference; (3) initiation, activation, or maintenance; and (4) goal-directed behavior.

Motivation reflects an *internal condition*. The condition may develop from physiological needs and drives or from complex desires, such as the desire to help others, to obtain approval, or to earn a high income. Motivation is an *inferred concept* that links a person's internal conditions to external behavior. It cannot be observed directly, but we can infer its presence by its behavioral effects. Motivation *initiates, activates, or maintains behavior*. Because Jim Abbott was motivated to become a good ball player, he initiated a regimen of practice, which he may maintain throughout the competitive season. Motivation generates *goal-directed behavior*. Goals vary widely across individuals and situations. Some goals are concrete and immediate—for example, to get up and eat food, to remove a painful stimulus, or to win a diving match. Other goals are more abstract and long term; the behavior of someone who studies hard, for example, may be to maximize learning, obtain good grades, and get a good job.

Motivation theories fall into three broad categories: drive theory, theories about learned motives, and cognitive and humanistic theories. We will examine each of these theories in turn and then look at how motivation affects emotions.

Motivation: Any condition, although usually an internal one, that appears by inference to initiate, activate, or maintain an organism's goal-directed behavior.

Drive theory: An explanation of behavior emphasizing internal factors that energize organisms to seek, attain, reestablish, balance, or maintain some goal that helps with survival.

Drive: An internal aroused condition that directs an organism to satisfy physiological needs.

Need: A physiological condition arising from an imbalance and usually accompanied by arousal.

Biologically Based Motives: Drive Theory

Some of the most influential and best-researched motivation theories are forms of drive theory. **Drive theory** is an explanation of behavior that assumes that an organism is motivated to act because of a need to attain, reestablish, balance, or maintain some goal that helps with the survival of the organism or the species. Stimuli such as hunger and pain create, energize, and initiate behavior. An organism deprived of food for 24 hours will spend most of its time looking for food; it will be driven to seek food.

A **drive** is an internal aroused condition that directs an organism to satisfy physiological needs. Drive theory focuses on **need**—a state of physiological imbalance usually accompanied by arousal. Physiological needs are said to be mechanistic,

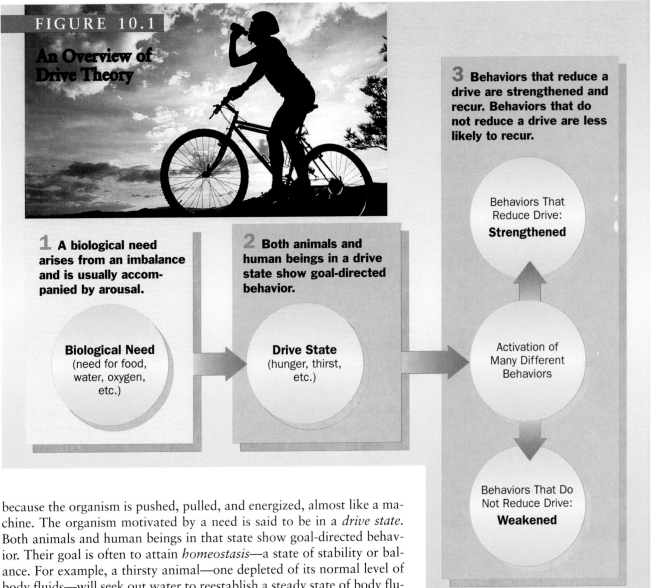

FIGURE 10.1

An Overview of Drive Theory

1 A biological need arises from an imbalance and is usually accompanied by arousal.

Biological Need
(need for food, water, oxygen, etc.)

2 Both animals and human beings in a drive state show goal-directed behavior.

Drive State
(hunger, thirst, etc.)

3 Behaviors that reduce a drive are strengthened and recur. Behaviors that do not reduce a drive are less likely to recur.

Behaviors That Reduce Drive: **Strengthened**

Activation of Many Different Behaviors

Behaviors That Do Not Reduce Drive: **Weakened**

because the organism is pushed, pulled, and energized, almost like a machine. The organism motivated by a need is said to be in a *drive state*. Both animals and human beings in that state show goal-directed behavior. Their goal is often to attain *homeostasis*—a state of stability or balance. For example, a thirsty animal—one depleted of its normal level of body fluids—will seek out water to reestablish a steady state of body fluids. The processes by which organisms seek to reestablish homeostasis are a key idea in drive theory. Behaviors that reduce a biological need (and reestablish homeostasis) are strengthened and are therefore likely to recur. Behaviors that do not reduce a biological need are less likely to recur. (See Figure 10.1 for an overview of drive theory.)

In examining motivation from a drive reduction point of view, psychologists seek to understand such simple behaviors as eating and drinking. As Abraham Maslow (1962, 1969) suggested, a person's physiological need for food and water must be satisfied before any other needs. Hunger and thirst are motivated by both physiological and psychological factors.

Physiological Determinants of Hunger

When you are hungry, you may feel stomach pain or become weak or dizzy—all sensations that cause you to seek food. What causes these sensations? Physiological explanations of hunger focus on the glucostatic approach, its relation to specific centers of the brain, and hormones.

The *glucostatic approach* to explaining hunger argues that the principal physiological cause of hunger is a low blood sugar level, which accompanies food deprivation and creates a chemical imbalance. In the body, sugar is quickly broken down into glucose, which is crucial to cellular activity. When the blood sugar level is low, the body sends warning signals to the brain; the brain immediately responds by generating hunger pain in the stomach. Hunger depends directly on blood sugar levels and other metabolites that trigger the central nervous system circuitry controlling eating. Experiments with animals whose nerves between stomach and brain were severed show that the animals continued to eat at appropriate times—when their blood sugar levels were low. These experiments provide evidence for the glucostatic approach.

The amount of food people eat does not necessarily affect the feeling of hunger—at least not right away. A hungry adult who eats steadily for 5 minutes may still feel hungry on stopping. But 30 minutes later, after the food has been converted into sugar, the person may no longer feel hungry. The type of food eaten determines how soon the feeling of hunger disappears. A candy bar loaded with easily converted sugar will take away hunger pain faster than will foods high in protein. High-protein foods such as meat, cheese, and milk take more time to digest and to convert into glucose.

Much of our understanding of hunger and eating behavior comes from studies of the brain, particularly of the hypothalamus, a region of the forebrain (see chapter 2, p. 58). Researchers now know that two areas of the hypothalamus are partly responsible for eating behavior: the ventromedial hypothalamus and the lateral hypothalamus.

The *ventromedial hypothalamus* (stop-eating center) is activated to stop an organism from eating when the blood sugar level is high, or when this part of the hypothalamus is electrically stimulated. The *lateral hypothalamus* (start-eating center) is activated to drive the organism to start eating when the blood sugar level is low, or when this part of the hypothalamus is stimulated.

The ventromedial hypothalamus may influence eating by stimulating the hormonal and metabolic systems (Powley, 1977). As we saw in chapter 2, insulin is a hormone secreted by the pancreas; it is released into the bloodstream when sugar (glucose) is present to allow the blood sugar to be metabolized into the body's cells. Eating food that quickly increases blood sugar levels also triggers the pancreas to release insulin quickly. The body then quickly metabolizes the blood sugar and once again lowers the blood sugar level. Thus, a person generally finds that after an initial feeling of relief from hunger, hunger will rapidly recur; the blood sugar level is now low again, often even lower than before eating. The rapid increase in insulin (often too much insulin) allows the rapid metabolization of the sugar. Thus, eating a sugar-laden candy bar relieves hunger initially but may cause an even greater level of hunger within a half hour or so.

As Figure 10.2 points out, researchers have used lesioning techniques to destroy the ventromedial and lateral areas of the hypothalamus in rats. This destruction caused the opposite effects of stimulation. As researchers have become more sophisticated, they have learned that few behaviors, including eating, are controlled by one single area of the brain. Usually, several areas work together, with one area mainly in control. For eating, that area of control is the hypothalamus.

What happens when the motivation to eat, the hormonal system, or perhaps genetics leads a person to overeat and eventually to become obese?

Hunger and Obesity

In an address to the American Psychological Association, Yale University psychologist Judith Rodin (1981, p. 361) summarized the plight of fat people:

FIGURE 10.2

The Impact of the Hypothalamus on Eating Behavior

The stimulation or destruction of a rat's hypothalamus alters the rat's eating behavior; in addition, the location of the hypothalamic stimulation—ventromedial or lateral—affects the results.

SECTION OF HYPOTHALAMUS	DESTRUCTION (ABLATION)	STIMULATION
Lateral	Animal stops eating	Animal eats continuously
Ventromedial	Animal eats continuously	Animal stops eating

First, heavy people are forced to wear the consequences of their affliction on their body and have probably built up a whole armamentarium of defenses to deal with that circumstance. No other physical characteristic except skin color is so stigmatized in our society. Second is the delightful but problematic fact that food is a positive and reinforcing stimulus for most of us. . . . Third, and probably most unfair of all, obesity is unusual because being fat is one of the factors that may keep one fat. . . . [T]he perverse fact is that it often does take fewer calories to keep people fat than it did to get them fat in the first place. This occurs because obesity itself changes the fat cells and body chemistry and alters levels of energy expenditure.

How do we explain obesity? Two types of explanations are genetic and psychological.

Genetic Explanations of Obesity. Some researchers insist that problems of obesity are genetically based. Grilo and Pogue-Geile (1991) analyzed the results of a series of genetic studies and concluded that inherited traits are the principal determinants of obesity. Other researchers concur, offering a number of explanations.

For example, Richard Nisbett (1972), a psychologist at the University of Michigan, proposed an explanation based on *fat cells*. He asserted that people are born with different numbers of fat cells and that the number of fat cells a person is born with determines the person's eating behavior and propensity toward obesity. Body fat is stored in fat cells, so people born with many fat cells are more likely to be obese than are those born with few fat cells. Although the number of fat cells a person has is genetically determined, the size of each cell is affected both by genetics and by nutritional experience early in life.

Dieting, in this explanation, decreases only the *size*, not the *number*, of fat cells. Moreover, the body wants to maintain the size of fat cells at a constant level, so people who have shrunk the normal size of their fat cells by dieting will experience a constant state of food deprivation. In addition, each significant weight gain may add new fat cells. Thus, permanent weight loss becomes extremely difficult. This accounts for the finding that about two-thirds of the people who lose weight will gain it back within a year.

The Pima Indians of Arizona have unusually low metabolisms, resulting in an inherited tendency toward being overweight.

Closely associated with the fat cell explanation of eating and obesity is the view that each person has a *set point*—a level of body weight that is maintained by the body. The central idea of the set point explanation is that the body seeks to maintain and will always reestablish a homeostatic weight. The set point is determined by many factors, including genetics, early nutrition, current environment, and learned habits. Further, some studies suggest that people can inherit both a tendency to overeat and a slow metabolism. For example, the Pima Indians of Arizona are prone to obesity; 80 to 90 percent of the tribe's young adults are dangerously overweight. According to Ravussin et al. (1988), who spent 4 years researching their habits, the Pimas have unusually low metabolisms. During any 24-hour period, the typical Pima (who is as active as other people) burns about 80 calories less than is considered normal for the person's body size.

People don't have the luxury of choosing their genetic heritage, but that does not condemn those who inherit a predisposition toward obesity to become fat. Keesey and Powley (1986) agree that the body's natural predisposition is to maintain homeostasis and that therefore the individual's attempts to lose weight through intake regulation (such as dieting) are prone to failure. However, they argue that weight control is achievable by increased energy expenditure through exercise.

Psychological Explanations of Obesity. Our physiological makeup isn't the only important factor in our eating behavior. Our experiences also teach us how to interact with food. The social environment is rampant with food-oriented messages that have little to do with nutritional needs. People use lunch to discuss business and attend dinner parties to celebrate special occasions. Advertisements proclaim that merriment can be found at a restaurant or a supermarket. Parents coax good behavior from their children by promising them desserts or fat-laden snacks. Thus, eating acquires a significance that far exceeds its role in satisfying physiological needs: It serves as a rationale for social interaction, a means to reward good behavior, and a way to fend off unhappy thoughts.

Consider my own attempts to maintain my weight after losing 75 pounds through diet and exercise. Suddenly, I noticed food even more than before. Every time I saw food advertised on billboards or television, I wanted to eat. All the social events I attended seemed to feature a delectable spread of appetizers, which I was tempted to sample in order to be "sociable." And whenever I became anxious, my first impulse was to seek the comfort of food. However, by separating eating behaviors linked to hunger from those that were learned responses to emotions, I controlled my eating behavior and avoided gaining weight even 2 years after my major weight loss.

Researchers continue to explore the causes of overeating. Their efforts have led to some interesting findings, especially when dieters are compared to nondieters. This topic is examined in the Research Process box on page 356.

Eating Disorders

Eating disorders: Psychological disorders characterized by gross disturbances in eating behavior and in the way individuals respond to food.

Anorexia nervosa: [an-uh-REX-see-uh ner-VOH-suh] An eating disorder characterized by an intense fear of becoming obese, dramatic weight loss, concern about weight, disturbances in body image, and an obstinate and willful refusal to eat.

Eating, one of the great joys in life, is also the focus of two important psychological disorders that are now widely recognized. **Eating disorders** are psychological disorders characterized by gross disturbances in eating behavior and in the way individuals respond to food. Two important eating disorders are anorexia nervosa and bulimia nervosa.

Anorexia Nervosa. **Anorexia nervosa,** a starvation disease that affects as many as 40 out of every 10,000 young women in the United States, is an eating disorder characterized by an obstinate and willful refusal to eat. Individuals with the disorder, usually adolescent girls from middle-class families, have a distorted body image. They perceive themselves as fat if they lack muscle tone or deviate from their idealized body image. They intensely fear being fat and relentlessly pursue thinness. The anorexic's refusal to eat eventually brings about emaciation and malnutrition (which may bring about a further loss of muscle tone and distortion of body image). Victims may sustain permanent damage to their heart muscle tissue, sometimes dying as a result.

Many therapists believe that anorexia nervosa has strictly psychological origins. They cite poor mother-daughter relationships, overprotective parents, other negative family interactions, and escapes from self-awareness as the main causes (Heatherton & Baumeister, 1991; Pike & Rodin, 1991). Others are exploring possible physiological origins of the disease, including the many changes taking place at puberty that might influence its emergence (Attie & Brooks-Gunn, 1989). Some psychologists believe that people with eating disorders may lack a hormone that is thought to induce a feeling of fullness after a meal.

Anorexia nervosa victims require a structured setting and are often hospitalized to help them regain weight. To ensure that the setting is reinforcing, hospital staff members are always present at meals, and individual and family therapy is provided. Clients are encouraged to eat and are rewarded for consuming specified quantities of food. Generally, psychotherapy is also necessary to help these people maintain a healthy self-image and body weight. Even with treatment, however, as many as 50 percent suffer relapses within a year.

Society contributes to eating disorders by imposing unrealistic definitions of the perfect female body. In the 1950s, Jayne Mansfield's hourglass figure was the ideal. Today's models are many pounds lighter.

Bulimia Nervosa. **Bulimia nervosa** is an eating disorder characterized by binge eating followed by purging. It tends to occur in normal-weight women with no history of anorexia nervosa (e.g., Garfinkel, Moldofsy, & Garner, 1980). The binging (recognized by the person to be abnormal) is accompanied by a fear of not being able to stop eating. Individuals who engage in binge eating become fearful of gaining weight; they become preoccupied with how others see them (Striegel-Moore, Silberstein, & Rodin, 1993). Therefore, they often purge themselves of unwanted calories, mostly through vomiting, laxatives, and diuretics. Other methods include compulsive exercising and weight reduction drugs. Bulimics become depressed (Hinz & Williamson, 1987), and the medical complications are serious. They include cardiovascular and gastrointestinal problems, menstrual irregularities, blood and hormone dysfunctions, muscular and skeletal problems, and sharp swings in mood and personality (Kaplan & Woodside, 1987).

The ratio of female to male bulimics is 10 to 1. Researchers theorize that women more readily than men believe that fat is bad and thin is beautiful. Women of higher socioeconomic classes are at greater risk of becoming bulimic, as are professionals whose weight is directly related to achievement, such as dancers, athletes, and models. Disharmonious family life and maladjusted parents appear to increase the likelihood of bulimia (Striegel-Moore, Silberstein, & Rodin, 1986). Bulimics also have lower self-esteem than people who eat normally, and they may have experienced some kind of clinical depression in the past.

Bulimia nervosa: [boo-LEE-me-uh ner-VOH-suh] An eating disorder characterized by repeated episodes of binge eating (and a fear of not being able to stop eating) followed by purging.

THE RESEARCH PROCESS

What Causes Overeating?

There are laws of nature that cannot be broken. Unfortunately, one law is that calories not expended will be stored as fat; and a continued imbalance between high food intake and low calorie expenditure will result in obesity. What causes people to eat more food than they need? Answers to this question have evolved slowly through research spanning 3 decades.

Initial Studies. Stanley Schachter and colleagues (Schachter, Goldman, & Gordon, 1968) investigated the eating patterns of obese people.

The researchers disguised the true purpose of the experiments because people often alter their behavior when told they are being watched. In one experiment, some subjects were given roast beef sandwiches to eat and others were not. The subjects were then seated in front of bowls of crackers and were presented with rating scales. They were told to eat as many of the crackers as necessary to judge whether each bowl contained crackers that were salty, cheesy, or garlicky. The researchers' actual goal was to observe how many crackers the subjects ate in making their judgments.

Initial Results. As shown in Figure 10.3, the normal-weight subjects ate far fewer crackers than they would have if they had not eaten the roast beef sandwiches. In contrast, the obese subjects ate even more than they would have if they had not eaten the sandwiches. Schachter and his colleagues concluded that the eating behavior of the obese subjects was determined principally by external factors.

Focus on External Cues. In another study, Schachter (1971) asked both obese and normal-weight subjects to sit at a desk and complete a personality test. The subjects were invited to munch from a bag of almonds while they worked on the test. Schachter set up two situations. In one, the almonds were shelled; in the other, they were unshelled. Schachter's question was whether one group would eat more than the other of each kind of nut.

About half of the normal-weight subjects ate nuts, whether or not the nuts were shelled. In contrast, 19 of 20 obese subjects ate the shelled nuts, but only 1 of 20 ate the unshelled ones. Schachter concluded that obese people tend to eat more than people of normal weight when food is readily available and less when the food is difficult to get.

Schachter also showed that obese adults will eat more from a bowl

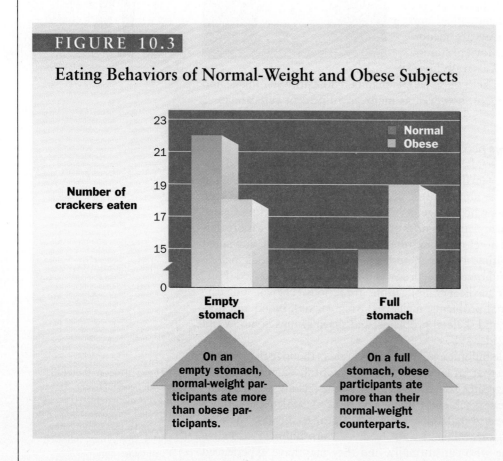

FIGURE 10.3

Eating Behaviors of Normal-Weight and Obese Subjects

Number of crackers eaten

Empty stomach

Full stomach

On an empty stomach, normal-weight participants ate more than obese participants.

On a full stomach, obese participants ate more than their normal-weight counterparts.

of nuts that is brightly illuminated than from a dimly illuminated bowl. Adults of normal weight are unaffected by the degree of illumination. This evidence led Schachter to infer that the sight of food motivates overweight people to eat. He contended that the availability of food, its prominence, and other external cues tell obese individuals when to eat (too much, too fast, and too often). In contrast, normal-weight individuals eat more in response to internal physiological mechanisms, such as hunger. In the end, under similar conditions, obese subjects eat more than normal-weight subjects, and the effect is more pronounced when there are external cues to trigger eating.

Contradictions. Schachter's work set off wide-ranging research into the psychological variables that cause overeating. His work focused on external cues, but other researchers argue that obese people are not necessarily more responsive to external cues than are normal-weight people. Stunkard and others suggest that differences between the eating habits of obese and normal-weight individuals are small and inconsistent (Rodin, 1981; Stunkard et al., 1980). They contend instead that the physiological responses of obese individuals may be triggered more quickly than those of normal-weight people.

According to physicians Hirsch and Leibel (1988), people who have lost weight often must take in fewer calories to maintain their weight than do those who have never been obese. This means that formerly obese people have a more difficult time keeping their weight down. Other researchers agree, asserting that a cycle of dieting and regaining weight makes permanent weight loss difficult (Heatherton, Polivy, & Herman, 1991; Klesges, Isbell, & Klesges, 1992). In addition, researchers Grilo and Pogue-Geile (1991) argue that genetics may play a stronger role than the environment in weight maintenance. Others believe that disorders of the autonomic nervous system may be keeping obese people fat (see Peterson, Seligman, & Vaillant, 1988).

The newest research and assertions are forcing a critical evaluation of all previously collected data. They imply that physiological mechanisms may play a much larger role than psychological ones in eating behavior. Today, there is no simple answer to the nature versus nurture question of obesity, but the research continues. Some of the latest research even suggests a relationship between socioeconomic status and obesity. Sobal and Stunkard (1989) report that in developed countries, such as the United States, obesity is more common among women of lower socioeconomic status than among women of higher socioeconomic status. Research into the causes is just beginning.

Attempts to treat obesity must incorporate a "reasonable weight" based on aesthetic and health standards for the wide range of individuals with obesity problems (Brownell & Wadden, 1992). Such plans must also incorporate the biological and environmental factors that affect each person (see Table 10.1).

TABLE 10.1 *Influences on Eating*

Biological factors	Environmental factors
Number and size of fat cells	Sight of food
Set point	Aromas of food
Hormones (especially insulin)	Acquired food preferences
Metabolism	Eating habits
Hypothalamus	Mood fluctuations
Stimulation from a full stomach	Visual stimuli (including clocks on the wall)
Raised or lowered glucose levels in bloodstream and cells	Acquired taste aversions (remember the Garcia effect in chapter 5)

According to Johnson and Larson (1982), some women may eat as a means of lightening their mood, regulating tension, and escaping from self-awareness (Heatherton & Baumeister, 1991). However, after binging, they feel guilty. To lessen their guilt and the potential consequence of gaining weight, they purge themselves. Researchers believe the purges reduce post-binge guilt feelings. Bulimics may become so involved in food-related behaviors that they will avoid contact with other people.

Efforts are under way to reduce the likelihood that adolescents will develop the disorder, as is research into its potential biological causes. Researchers suggest that prevention programs be established at home, in high schools and colleges, and in the community (Fairburn et al., 1991; Shisslak et al., 1987).

FOCUS

▶ With what evidence would a biologically based theorist respond to Schachter's studies?   pp. 353, 356

▶ What evidence is there that the relationship between eating and obesity can be explained by external cues? pp. 356–357

▶ Human beings do not always respond to food in the same manner. What variables might have affected Schachter's subjects to cause them to behave differently in his studies?   p. 357

Thirst

A human embryo is made up of more than 80 percent water, a newborn child is about 75 percent water, and a normal adult is about 60 to 70 percent water. It is thus understandable that the human body is highly sensitive to water losses. Although you can live for weeks without food, you can live only a few days without replenishing your supply of fluid. Thirst is therefore a strong drive.

A delicate balance (homeostasis) of fluid intake is necessary for proper physiological functioning; any imbalance results in a drive to restore the balance. When a person experiences fluid deprivation and the resulting cellular dehydration, homeostatic mechanisms come into play. The person is put into a drive state in which the mouth and throat become dry, cueing the person to drink. Thirst is not a *result* of dryness in the mouth or throat, and simply placing water in the mouth will not reduce thirst.

Approximately two-thirds of the body's fluid is contained within the cells. The regulation of fluid within the cells is controlled primarily by the hypothalamus; the regulation of fluid between the cells and in blood plasma is controlled primarily by the pituitary gland and the kidneys.

When the body does not have an adequate supply of fluid, cells in the hypothalamus and the pituitary respond. Consider fluid loss between cells: Recall from chapter 2 (p. 66) that the pituitary initiates the release of an antidiuretic hormone that acts on the kidneys to increase fluid absorption and to decrease the amount of urine produced by the body. Thus, when the pituitary is stimulated in this way, a person urinates less frequently. If a person consumes a great deal of sodium (found in table salt, soy sauce, and many junk foods), the body responds by requiring more fluids.

Thirst is a body response that triggers fluid consumption; it is not the cause of fluid consumption. Cells in the hypothalamus and pituitary initiate fluid consumption and respond to cellular changes and ratios of chemicals to fluids in the body. We are motivated to drink because of internal processes. Of course, we can drink too much or too little; and we develop many learned preferences. For example, we may prefer to quench our thirst with Coke or Pepsi, coffee or tea, or plain water. The roles of learning and preferences become especially important in more complex behaviors, such as sex.

Sexual Motivation and Behavior

The sexual drive in human beings is to a great extent under psychological control. In contrast, the sexual behavior of lower organisms is controlled largely by their physiological and hormonal systems.

Sex Hormones. When hormones are released, they exert profound effects on behavior. If the hormone-generating testes of male rats are removed, the animals show a marked decrease in sexual activity. Similarly, most female animals are sexually responsive only when hormones are released into the bloodstream (when they are "in heat"). Human beings, on the other hand, can choose whether or not to respond sexually to encounters at any given time. In fact, in human beings, the removal of hormone-generating organs may not affect sexual behavior at all (depending on the person's age at removal). In rats, early social experience is not necessary for adult sexual functioning. But if dogs, cats, and monkeys are isolated from sexual experiences early in life, they later show a lack of sexual responsiveness. The human sexual response cycle is even more complex.

Sexual Response Cycle. When human beings become sexually aroused, they go through a series of four phases (stages). The phases, which together are known as the *sexual response cycle,* are the excitement phase, the plateau phase, the orgasm phase, and the resolution phase.

The **excitement phase** is the first phase of the cycle, during which there are initial increases in heart rate, blood pressure, and respiration. A key characteristic of this phase is **vasoconstriction**—a constriction of the blood vessels, particularly in the genital area. In women, breasts swell and vaginal lubrication increases; in men, the penis becomes erect. The excitement phase is anticipatory and may last from a few minutes to a few hours. It may be initiated by physical contact, fantasy, or activity in any of the senses.

The **plateau phase** is the second phase of the sexual response cycle, during which the sexual partners are preparing for orgasm. Autonomic nervous system activity, such as the heart rate, increases. In women, the vagina becomes engorged and fully extended; in men, the penis becomes fully erect and turns a darker color.

The **orgasm phase** is the third phase of the sexual response cycle, during which autonomic nervous system activity reaches its peak and muscle contractions occur throughout the body, especially in the genital area, in spasms. An *orgasm* is the peak of sexual activity. In men, muscles throughout the reproductive system contract to help expel semen; in women, muscles surrounding the outer vagina contract. Although men experience only one orgasm during each sexual response cycle, women are capable of multiple orgasms. An orgasm is an all-or-none activity lasting only a few seconds; once a threshold for orgasm is reached, the orgasm occurs.

The **resolution phase** is the fourth phase of the sexual response cycle, during which the body naturally returns after orgasm to its resting, or normal, state. This return takes from 1 to several minutes, varying considerably from person to person. During this phase, men are usually unable to achieve an erection for some period of time, called the *refractory period.*

Like many other physiological events, the sexual response cycle is subject to considerable variation. Some people go through a lengthy plateau phase; others may have a longer resolution phase.

People who are unable to experience pleasure from sexual activity and who consider sexual behavior too difficult, painful, or aversive may suffer from a sexual dysfunction.

Excitement phase: The first phase of the sexual response cycle, during which there are initial increases in heart rate, blood pressure, and respiration.

Vasoconstriction: In the sexual response cycle, a constriction of the blood vessels, particularly in the genital area.

Plateau phase: The second phase of the sexual response cycle, during which the sexual partners are preparing for orgasm. Autonomic nervous system activity increases and there is further vasoconstriction.

Orgasm phase: The third phase of the sexual response cycle, during which autonomic nervous system activity reaches its peak, and muscle contractions occur throughout the body, but especially in the genital area, in spasms.

Resolution phase: The fourth phase of the sexual response cycle, during which the body naturally returns after orgasm to its resting, or normal, state.

Sexual Dysfunction. **Sexual dysfunction** is the inability to obtain satisfaction from sexual behavior, often accompanied by the inability to experience orgasm. It sometimes is caused by too much alcohol or other drugs or by fatigue or some physical ailment. It may also result from early experience in which faulty sexual behaviors or attitudes were learned. Most people experience some type of sexual problem at one time or another, but generally these problems are temporary.

Sexual problems have been carefully researched. Starting with the work of Masters and Johnson (1966, 1970), psychologists and physicians have been attempting to help people with sexual dysfunction. The Masters and Johnson approach has a strong commitment toward treating pairs of people. Thus, when a man or woman comes for treatment, a typical procedure is to treat not only the client but also the partner.

Two types of sexual dysfunction in men are erectile dysfunction and premature ejaculation. Sexual dysfunction in women is termed orgasmic dysfunction. **Erectile dysfunction** is the inability of a man to attain or maintain an erection of sufficient strength to allow him to engage in sexual intercourse. It may be caused by anatomical defects, damage to the central nervous system, or the excessive use of alcohol or other drugs. More often, however, erectile dysfunction is caused by emotional problems.

There are two kinds of erectile dysfunction: primary and secondary. **Primary erectile dysfunction** is the inability of a man *ever* to have attained an erection of sufficient strength to have allowed him to engage in sexual intercourse. Masters and Johnson have argued that fear and unusual sensitivity or anxiety regarding sexual incidents that may have happened early in a man's life generally contribute to primary erectile dysfunction.

The second type of erectile dysfunction occurs more frequently. With this type of dysfunction, a man may have had successful sexual intercourse in the past but is now incapable of consistently engaging in sexual intercourse. Specifically, **secondary erectile dysfunction** is the inability of a man to achieve an erection in 25 percent or more of his sexual attempts. One of the key symptoms and major blocks to curing men with secondary erectile dysfunction is that once a man has had a problem in achieving or maintaining an erection, he maintains such a distinct memory of the incident that it may inhibit him in future attempts.

Premature ejaculation is the inability of a man to delay ejaculation long enough to satisfy his sexual partner in at least half of his sexual encounters. Instead, ejaculation occurs at, just before, or just following insertion of the penis into the vagina. Premature ejaculation is usually caused by emotional and psychological factors. With the cooperation of his partner, however, a man can learn to delay his orgasm until he wants it to happen. Fear and anxiety caused by previous failures often deprive the man of his "staying power," just as fear can cause secondary erectile dysfunction.

Women suffer from two types of orgasmic dysfunction: primary and secondary dysfunction. **Primary orgasmic dysfunction** is the inability of a woman *ever* to achieve an orgasm through any method of sexual stimulation. Some causes of primary orgasmic dysfunction are physical, but more often they are psychological. They may result from extreme religious orthodoxy, unfavorable communication about sexual activities, or some childhood trauma.

Secondary orgasmic dysfunction, or *situational orgasmic dysfunction,* is the inability of a woman who has achieved orgasm by one technique or another in the past to achieve it in a given situation. Often, this dysfunction occurs when a woman is unable to achieve orgasm because she finds her mate sexually unattractive, undesirable, or in some other way unacceptable. In addition, many women find that orgasm brings about feelings of guilt, shame, and fear. Like her male counterpart, a woman may have experienced traumatic sexually related events that now inhibit her sexual feelings.

Sexual dysfunction: The inability to obtain satisfaction from sexual behavior, often accompanied by the inability to experience orgasm.

Erectile dysfunction: In men, the inability to attain or maintain an erection of sufficient strength to allow sexual intercourse.

Primary erectile dysfunction: The inability of a man *ever* to have attained an erection of sufficient strength for sexual intercourse.

Secondary erectile dysfunction: The inability of a man to achieve an erection in 25 percent or more of his sexual attempts.

Premature ejaculation: The inability of a man to delay ejaculation long enough to satisfy his sexual partner in at least half of his sexual encounters.

Primary orgasmic dysfunction: The inability of a woman *ever* to achieve orgasm through any means of sexual stimulation.

Secondary orgasmic dysfunction: A woman's inability to achieve orgasm in a given situation, even though she has achieved orgasm in the past by one technique or another. Also known as *situational orgasmic dysfunction.*

Treatment of orgasmic dysfunction involves several steps. According to Masters and Johnson, the key is understanding the client's sexual value system and the reasons for her inability or unwillingness to achieve orgasm. Masters and Johnson argue that the sexual partners and the therapist should take part in a round table discussion where the woman reveals her own ideas about sex and about what attracts and repels her. Using the woman's value system, the therapist can teach her to respond to sexual stimulation. The couple are directed not to have intercourse at first. They are taught through a series of sessions to seek and sustain pleasure so that, in successive days, they obtain an increasing amount of erotic pleasure. Orgasm is not the focus, but ultimately it is achieved in an unhurried situation in which neither partner is under pressure to perform.

Sensory Stimulation and Arousal Theory

A characteristic of all motivational systems is that they involve arousal. Arousal is generally thought of in terms of activation of the central nervous system, the autonomic nervous system, and the muscles and glands. Some motivational theorists suggest that organisms seek to maintain optimal levels of arousal by actively varying their exposure to arousing stimuli.

Unlike hunger and thirst, the lack of sensory experience does not result in a physiological imbalance; yet both human beings and animals seek sensory stimulation. When deprived of a normal amount of visual, auditory, or tactile stimulation, some adults become irritable and consider their situation or environment intolerable. Kittens like to explore their environment; young monkeys will investigate mechanical devices and play with puzzles; and people seem motivated or impelled to seek sensory stimulation. (However, in some situations people seek to avoid stimulation—for example, when they are sick or in need of rest.)

Neither a lack of sensory stimulation nor drive reduction theory explains many basic behaviors. *Arousal theory* attempts to bridge the gap by explaining the link between our behavior and our state of arousal. Think of some activity that you practice often and in which you occasionally either compete or perform publicly. For example, you may be a diver, an actor, or a member of a debating team. Chances are, you performed most poorly when you were not interested in practicing or when you were exceedingly nervous about your performance, such as during a competition. Conversely, you probably did your best when you were eager to practice or when you were moderately excited by the competition. This phenomenon explains why some baseball players perform exceptionally well at the beginning of the season, when pressure is only moderately high, and then commit numerous errors when pressure increases—for instance, in the final games of the World Series.

The link between performance and arousal was first scientifically explored in 1908 by R. M. Yerkes and J. D. Dodson. They described a relationship involving arousal and performance, called the *Yerkes-Dodson law.* Contemporary researchers have extended that relationship by suggesting that when a person's level of arousal and anxiety is either too high or too low, performance will be poor, especially on complex tasks (e.g., Brehm & Self, 1989). Thus, people who do not

People are motivated to seek sensory stimulation. Some people (this bungee jumper, for example) seek higher and higher levels of arousal by engaging in potentially dangerous activities.

FOCUS

▶ What is the evidence that we are motivated to drink because of a lack of fluid in the cells of the body? p. 358

▶ What evidence exists to suggest that thought plays an especially important role in human sexual behavior? pp. 359–361

care about what they are doing have little anxiety but also have little arousal and therefore usually perform poorly in both work and play. If arousal increases to the point of high anxiety, performance suffers.

Researcher Donald Hebb (1904–1985) suggested that behavior varies from disorganized to effective, depending on a person's level of arousal. He argued that human functioning is most efficient when people are at an optimal level of arousal (Hebb, 1955). People seek, and are most efficient at, specific arousal levels (K. J. Anderson, 1990). The inverted U-shaped curve in Figure 10.4 shows the relationship between level of arousal and level of performance.

Fundamental to all motivation theories is the notion that it is not the stimulus itself but the organism's internal response to it that determines how the organism behaves. Hebb's idea shifted researchers' focus from stimuli, drives, and needs to the idea that arousal energizes behavior but does not direct it. The development of optimal-arousal theories helped psychologists explain the variation in people's responses to situations in terms of a state of internal arousal rather than solely in terms of responses to stimuli. This shift in emphasis marked a subtle but important transi-

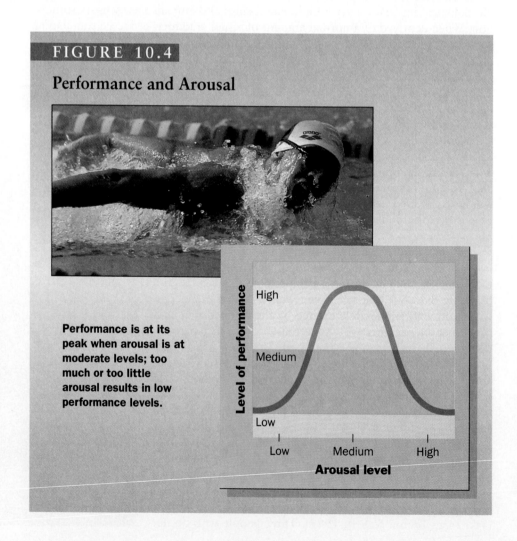

FIGURE 10.4

Performance and Arousal

Performance is at its peak when arousal is at moderate levels; too much or too little arousal results in low performance levels.

BUILDING TABLE 10.1

Drive Theory of Motivation

THEORY	THEORIST	PRINCIPALLY EXPLAINS	KEY IDEA	VIEW OF BEHAVIOR
Drive	a. Nisbett b. Schachter c. Hebb	a. Obesity b. Hunger and obesity c. Optimal arousal	a. Number of fat cells determines obesity. b. External cues energize eating behavior. c. Performance depends on level of arousal.	a. Mechanistic—obesity is biologically determined. b. Partially mechanistic but recognizes the role of learning. c. Mostly mechanistic—the efficiency of behavior is determined by the level of physiological arousal.

tion from a strictly mechanistic drive reduction theory toward learning and more cognitive theories. In the latter theories, a person's expectations, past experiences, and thought processes play an important role in motivation. (See Building Table 10.1 for a comparison of the various explanations for drive theory.)

Learned Motives

In tracing the history of motivation theory, we find distinct shifts from one concept to another. For example, many early researchers focused on internal conditions—needs—that impel organisms to action. However, contemporary researchers recognize and embrace the idea that some motives are biological, others are learned through conditioning, and still others result from human beings thinking about and evaluating their needs and their behaviors. The idea that human beings evaluate their situation is most aptly expressed in expectancy theories, which connect thought and motivation.

Expectancy theories are explanations of behavior that focus on our expectation of success in reaching a goal and our need for achievement as energizing factors. A key element of these theories is that our thoughts guide our behaviors. The social motives and needs we develop are not initiated because of some physiological imbalance. Rather, we learn through our interactions in the environment to have needs for mastery, affiliation, and competition. These needs lead to expectations about the future and about how various efforts will lead to various outcomes.

Motives and Social Needs

To understand some important concepts related to expectancy theories, we can consider Jim Abbott's desire to be a professional baseball player. The desire, hard work, and long hours of practice meant that Abbott had to deprive himself of other pleasures. But winning, being a pro, and being among the best obviously added to his self-esteem.

A **motive** is a specific condition, usually internal and usually involving some form of arousal, that directs an organism's behavior toward a goal. Unlike a drive, which always has a physiological origin, a motive does not necessarily need to have

Expectancy theories: Explanations of behavior that focus on the expectation of success and the need for achievement as energizing factors for human beings.

Motive: A specific internal condition, usually involving some sort of arousal, that directs an organism's behavior toward a goal

a physiological explanation. Thus, although Abbott was motivated to be among the best, there was no urgent physiological need for him to do so.

A **social need** is an aroused condition that directs people toward establishing feelings about themselves and others and toward establishing and maintaining relationships. Abbott's social needs, for example, probably have included winning approval from family, friends, and other ball players. The needs for achievement, affiliation, and good feelings about oneself are affected by many factors, including socioeconomic status and race (Littig & Williams, 1978) and experiences from birth onward. Our need to feel good about ourselves often leads to specific behaviors through which we strive to be evaluated positively (Geen, 1991). This topic will be explored in more detail when we consider social psychology in chapters 16 and 17.

Social Need for Achievement

Personality psychologists such as Henry Murray assert that key events and situations in people's environment determine behavior. Murray called these environmental situations that have direct implications for a person "press" (Murray, 1938). The environment might *press* an individual to excel at sports, be a loving caretaker to a grandparent, or achieve great wealth. The *press* of poverty might produce a social need for financial security; it might therefore cause a person to work hard, train, and become educated to achieve wealth. The most notable theories for measuring the results of press are expectancy theories that focus specifically on the **need for achievement**—a social need that directs people to strive constantly for excellence and success. According to achievement theories, people engage in behaviors that satisfy their desires for success, mastery, and fulfillment. Tasks not oriented toward these goals are not motivating and are either not undertaken or are performed without energy and commitment.

One of the leaders in early studies of achievement motivation was David C. McClelland (b. 1917), whose early research focused on the idea that people have strong social motives for achievement (McClelland, 1958). McClelland showed that achievement motivation is learned in a person's home environment during childhood. Adults with a high need for achievement had parents who stressed excellence and who provided physical affection and emotional rewards for high achievement. These adults also generally walked early, talked early, and had a high need for achievement even in elementary school (e.g., Teevan & McGhee, 1972). A high need for achievement is most pronounced in firstborn children, perhaps because parents typically have more time to give them direction and praise. Achievement motives are often measured through scores derived from coding the thought content of imaginative stories.

Early studies of people's need for achievement used the *Thematic Apperception Test (TAT)*. In this test, subjects are shown scenes with no captions and vague themes, which are thus open to interpretation. The subjects are instructed not to think in terms of right or wrong answers but to answer four basic questions for each scene:

▶ What is happening?

▶ What has led up to this situation?

▶ What is being thought?

▶ What will happen next?

Using a complex scoring system, researchers analyze subjects' descriptions of each scene. They have found that subjects with a high need for achievement tell stories that stress success, getting ahead, and competition (Spangler, 1992).

Social need: An aroused condition that directs people toward establishing feelings about themselves and others and toward establishing or maintaining relationships.

Need for achievement: A social need that directs people to strive constantly for excellence and success.

High versus Low Need for Achievement. In tests such as the TAT, a researcher can quickly discern which subjects have a high need for achievement and which have a low need. Lowell (1952), for example, found that when he asked subjects to rearrange scrambled letters (such as *wtse*) to construct a meaningful word (such as *west*), subjects with a low need for achievement improved only slightly over successive testing periods. In contrast, subjects who scored high in the need for achievement showed greater ongoing improvement over several periods of testing (see Figure 10.5). The researchers concluded that, when presented with a complex task, subjects with a high need for achievement find new and better ways of performing the task as they practice it, whereas subjects with a low need for achievement try no new methods. People with a high need for achievement constantly strive toward excellence and better performance; they have developed a belief in their self-efficacy and in the importance of effort in determining performance (Carr, Borkowski, & Maxwell, 1991; McClelland, 1961).

Risk and Achievement. The need for achievement seems closely related to the amount of risk people are willing to take. Some researchers claim that children exposed to praise are likely to be more achievement-oriented and thus willing to take on higher levels of risk. To test this idea, Canavan-Gumpert (1977) presented first- and sixth-grade girls in a New York suburban school with math problems, then praised them for correct answers and criticized them for incorrect answers. After a practice task in which they were praised or criticized, the girls chose problems to do at one of eight levels of difficulty.

The praised subjects had more optimistic expectations, higher standards, and greater confidence about their future performance. They chose problems at the highest level of difficulty, accepting the risk of failure. The criticized subjects were dissatisfied with their performance and chose problems at the lowest difficulty level. The most important finding of the Canavan-Gumpert study is that praise and criticism directly affect children's risk-taking behavior and, ultimately, their need for achievement. (The Applications box on page 366 discusses how working in groups can affect motivation and achievement in learning.)

The goals people set and the amount of risk they are willing to take are also affected by the kind of needs that motivate them, their experiences, and even their moods (Hom & Arbuckle, 1988). The expression *self-fulfilling prophecy* suggests that those who expect to succeed will do so and those

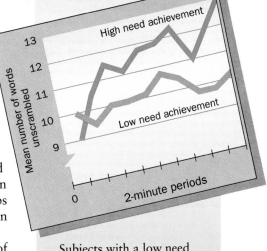

FIGURE 10.5

Performance on a Scrambled-Letter Task

Performance on a scrambled-letter task over 2 successive minutes is shown. Task achievement is affected by a person's overall approach to achievement-related tasks. (Based on data from Lowell, 1952.)

Subjects with a low need for achievement improved overall but subjects with a high need for achievement improved even more.

Cooperative Learning

Most American teachers attempt to motivate students by having them compete against one another. However, research from the University of Minnesota, Johns Hopkins University, and the University of California shows that cooperative interactions among students—not just between students and teachers or students and books—play a significant role in real learning. Teachers who overlook student-to-student teaching may be failing their own courses (Kohn, 1992).

Studies show that forming teams of students in which no one gets credit until everyone understands the material is far more effective than competitive or individualized learn-ing. Whether the students are pre-schoolers or college-age, in English or physics class, they have more fun, enjoy the subject matter more, and learn more when they work together. What's the secret? Learning stems more from providing explanations than from receiving them. In a cooperative group, everyone has an incentive to help everyone else. The result is that high-, medium-, and low-ability students all benefit from a sharing of skills.

Our society associates excellence with being Number 1. However, the data show that competition—some students succeeding and others failing—actually impedes learning. David Johnson, a social psychologist and education professor at the University of Minnesota, noted the ef-fectiveness of team learning by asserting that there is almost nothing that American education has seen that compares with its level of empirical support (Argyle, 1991; Kohn, 1986). Achievement and attitude of students are improved through cooperative learning (Hwong et al., 1993).

Cooperative education isn't as simple as grouping students around a table and telling them to work together. It means carefully establish-

who don't expect to succeed won't. Expectations for success and failure can influence the outcome of an effort if those expectations help shape the person's behavior (Elliott & Dweck, 1988). A teacher who expects a student to fail, for example, may treat the student in ways that increase the likelihood of the student's failure; things tend to turn out just the way the teacher expected (or prophesied) they would. Expectancy thus becomes a key component in explaining behavior, especially in subjects with a high need for achievement. For example, a person pushed toward success by parents, drama instructors, or sports coaches may develop a high need for achievement; after positive experiences, such an individual will typically set challenging but attainable performance goals (Dweck & Leggett, 1988).

Importance of Achievement Motivation. For most adults in our culture, social motivation, with its emphasis on achievement, focuses on a sense of satisfaction and well-being throughout life. It would thus follow that people whose high need for achievement is met might be happier than others. Studies show that older individuals with high aspirations are more satisfied with life than those with low aspirations.

Erik Erikson's psychosocial developmental theory, which we explored in chapter 9, sees middle adulthood as a period of generativity, or productivity. Late adulthood, from Erikson's view, is a time of integration, when achievement is not a focus. Although the nature of achievement motivation changes during development, these changes are difficult to ascertain because individuals' needs for achievement alter as their culture changes. Both culture and development significantly affect achievement motivation.

Achievement motivation seems to be highly valued and related to people's sense of well-being. It is affected by many variables, including age, gender, education, career and culture. But as a concept, it still needs much more study.

ing a positive interdependence that makes each student dependent on and accountable to the rest of the group. The students start to think of themselves as a team. Knowing that they will sink or swim together, they start swimming.

There are several ways to put this theory into practice. One approach, called the *jigsaw method,* was invented by Elliot Aronson, a social psychologist at the University of California, Santa Cruz. He divided a study project into parts and gave one piece to each student in a group. Then he told the students that everyone would be responsible for all the material. Students had to learn from each other, and they did. In addition, Aronson found other results. Self-esteem went up as each student saw

that others were depending on him or her. Also, each one realized that being a good student didn't depend on besting others. Moreover, students in the groups grew to like one another more, including those of different races and levels of ability.

According to Alfie Kohn (1992), competition gets in the way of real learning by making students anxious. It also makes them doubt their own abilities and become nasty toward losers, envious of winners, more prejudiced toward those from other ethnic groups, and suspicious of just about everyone. In a book on competition, Kohn documented the case against competitive learning and asserted that we should move toward cooperative ventures to stimulate motivation and success.

Cooperation works in a variety of settings. For example, cooperative ventures are better than competitive ones when workers and managers are involved (Tjosvold & Chia, 1989). But such ventures depend on the makeup of each group, including such variables as gender (Garza & Borchert, 1990) and culture (Domino, 1992).

Psychologists and educators continue to fine-tune the techniques of cooperative learning. In fact, some of them formed an organization, the International Association for the Study of Cooperation in Education (IASCE). The group conducts research and tries to spread the message that cooperation works better than competition in the classroom.

Personality and Motivation

Expectancy theories show that if people hold beliefs or expectations for success, they will behave, operate, or cooperate in specific ways. However, people's beliefs and expectations are determined partly by how people perceive the causes of success or failure. If a person believes a task is impossible, for example, then the cause of the ultimate failure will have little to do with expectations for success. Similarly, if a person believes that a task is so simple that anyone can do it properly, then success at the task will provide little reward or satisfaction.

Human beings not only have expectancies about their success and failure but also hold causal beliefs. They may believe that some tasks are especially easy, that they are especially lucky persons, or that they are destined to be successful. Such dispositions toward tasks affect behavior directly. (We will examine these dispositions in more detail in chapter 16.)

Personality also affects motivation, and, conversely, motivation is one determiner of personality. For example, a shy person, although motivated to succeed, may be inhibited and reticent about taking chances in front of people. Some aspects of personality may even have health consequences. Friedman and Rosenman (1974) proposed classifying people according to two distinct personality styles or behavior patterns that can be used to predict the likelihood of suffering a heart attack. They designated people who had a great sense of urgency about all things and were impatient, aggressive, easily roused to anger, and extremely achievement-oriented as Type A individuals (who are at greater risk for heart attacks). They designated all other people as Type B. Although their primary goal was to help Type A people become Type B people (Kahn et al., 1982), their research also provided information on what motivates people.

BUILDING TABLE 10.2

Drive and Expectancy Theories of Motivation

THEORY	THEORIST	PRINCIPALLY EXPLAINS	KEY IDEA	VIEW OF BEHAVIOR
Drive	a. Nisbett	a. Obesity	a. Number of fat cells determines obesity.	a. Mechanistic—obesity is biologically determined.
	b. Schachter	b. Hunger and obesity	b. External cues energize eating behavior.	b. Partially mechanistic but recognizes the role of learning.
	c. Hebb	c. Optimal arousal	c. Performance depends on level of arousal.	c. Mostly mechanistic—the efficiency of behavior is determined by the level of physiological arousal.
Expectancy	a. McClelland	a. Achievement motivation	a. Humans learn the need to achieve.	a. Partly cognitive, partly mechanistic—achievement is a learned behavior.
	b. Friedman and Rosenman	b. Type A and Type B behavior	b. Time urgency (Type A behavior) leads to competitiveness—and to heart disease.	b. Partly cognitive, partly mechanistic—Type A behavior is initiated early in life.

Using behavior patterns such as Type A and Type B, psychologists can infer a great deal about individuals' motivations and how people will respond to various situations. Type A people, for example, possess an intense desire to control their environment, and they become irritated and distressed when others slow down their rapid pace (Suarez & Williams, 1989; Suls & Wan, 1989b). Furthermore, they find it difficult to develop new motives and new behaviors to help themselves slow down and relax. Type B people do not seem to be motivated by the same desires for mastery and success. When they desire greatness or achievement, they are willing to pursue these objectives at a far more deliberate pace.

As we will see in chapter 13, the Type A–Type B classification system has become popular, but it lacks rigorous scientific support. It does frame specific and important questions for motivation researchers, however. Among these questions are: Who is likely to be motivated? Can motivation predict behavior?

Building Table 10.2 summarizes both drive and expectancy theories of motivation.

Cognitive and Humanistic Theory

One of Jim Abbott's goals has been to constantly improve his pitching. Pitching well obviously provides him with a sense of accomplishment. The reasons for his goals and pride are viewed differently by cognitive and humanistic theorists, whose views we will now consider.

Cognitive Theory

In the study of motivation, **cognitive theory** is an explanation of behavior that asserts that people are actively and regularly involved in determining their goals and their means of achieving them. Like expectancy theories, cognitive theory focuses on thought as an initiator and determinant of behavior. However, more than expectancy theories, cognitive theory emphasizes the role of active decision making in all areas of life. For example, you are actively involved in deciding how much time you will spend studying for an exam, how hard you will work to become an accomplished pianist, or how strictly you will follow a new diet or exercise program.

> **Cognitive theory:** An explanation of behavior that emphasizes the role of thought and individual choices regarding life goals and the means of achieving them.

As early as 1949, Donald Hebb anticipated how cognitive theory would influence psychology to move away from mechanistic views of motivation and behavior:

> As far as one can see at present, it is unsatisfactory to equate motivation with biological need. Theory built on this base has a definiteness that is very attractive; but it may have been obtained at too great a cost. (Hebb, 1949, p. 179)

Hebb recognized that mechanistic drive- or need-reduction theories were incomplete and that other factors, such as arousal and attention, are important determinants of motivation. As a result of Hebb's brilliant theorizing, contemporary researchers emphasize the role of active decision making and the human capacity for abstract thought. These cognitive theorists assume that individuals set their goals and decide how to achieve them.

Cognitive Controls. It may seem like common sense that if you are aware of—and think about—your behavior, motivation, and emotions and you attempt to alter your thoughts, you can control your behavior. Cognitive psychologists maintain that if human beings are aware of their thought patterns, they can control their reasoning and ultimately their overt behavior. We will see in chapter 15 that this idea is used extensively by therapists to help people with various maladjustments. In explaining motivation, cognitive psychologists show that arousal (which Hebb and other researchers equated with drive) is under voluntary cognitive control.

In a classic study, Lazarus and Alfert (1964) monitored the arousal levels of three groups of subjects under conditions capable of inducing great stress. The subjects watched a film showing the primitive ritual of subincision, in which an adolescent's penis is deeply cut. The film included five such operations.

The first group saw the film without any commentary. The second group listened during the film to a commentary denying that pain and harm were associated with the operation; this group was termed the *denial commentary group*. The third group listened to the same commentary before the film; this group was termed the *denial orientation group*. The levels of arousal of the subjects were measured by their electrodermal response (EDR)—a measure of the electrical response of the skin and usually correlated with arousal (see Figure 10.6 on page 370).

With the start of the film, the EDR increased in all groups. However, the levels of arousal varied among the groups. The group that heard no commentary had the highest overall level of arousal. The denial commentary group (commentary during the film) had a lower arousal increase than the no-commentary group. And the denial orientation group (commentary before the film) had the lowest level of increased arousal. Lazarus and Alfert believed the subjects in the denial orientation group were able to build up their psychological defenses against the potentially stressful content of the film. In other words, they had some degree of cognitive control to insulate themselves against their physiological and emotional reactions.

Through instruction and self-help techniques, people can alter their behavior by changing their thoughts and thus their expectancies (e.g., Norris, 1989). That our

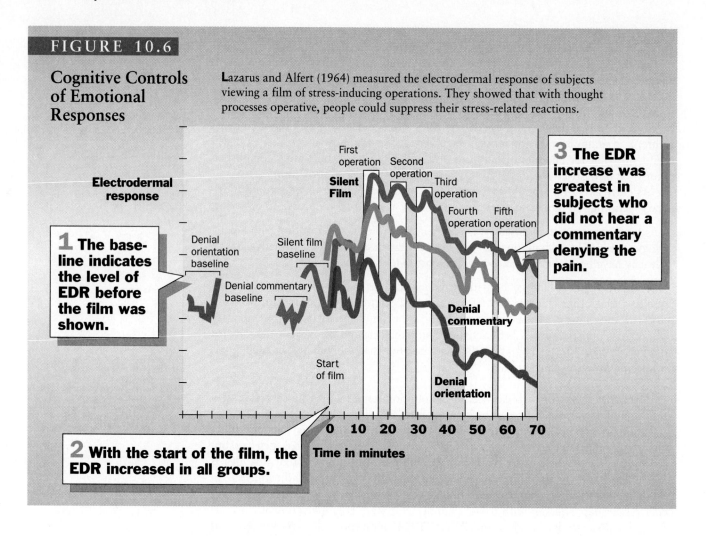

FIGURE 10.6

Cognitive Controls of Emotional Responses

Lazarus and Alfert (1964) measured the electrodermal response of subjects viewing a film of stress-inducing operations. They showed that with thought processes operative, people could suppress their stress-related reactions.

Electrodermal response

1 The baseline indicates the level of EDR before the film was shown.

Denial orientation baseline

Denial commentary baseline

Silent film baseline

Silent Film

First operation

Second operation

Third operation

Fourth operation

Fifth operation

3 The EDR increase was greatest in subjects who did not hear a commentary denying the pain.

Denial commentary

Start of film

Denial orientation

0 10 20 30 40 50 60 70

2 With the start of the film, the EDR increased in all groups.

Time in minutes

---

thoughts can alter our behavior also becomes evident when we think about our intrinsic and extrinsic motivation.

Intrinsic and Extrinsic Motivation. For fun, people engage in a wide variety of behaviors that bring no external tangible rewards. Infants play with mobiles, children build erector set cities and then tear them down, and adults do crossword and jigsaw puzzles. Psychologists call behaviors engaged in for no apparent reward except the pleasure and satisfaction of the activity itself **intrinsically motivated behaviors.** Edward Deci (1975) suggests that people engage in such behaviors for two reasons: to achieve stimulation and to achieve a sense of accomplishment, competence, and mastery over the environment.

In studies focusing on intrinsic motivation, Deci compared two groups of college-age subjects engaged in puzzle solving. One group received no external rewards, and the other group did receive rewards. Deci found that subjects who were initially given rewards generally spent less time solving puzzles when rewards were no longer given. Those who were never rewarded, on the other hand, spent the same amount of time solving puzzles on all trials (Deci, 1971, 1972). Similar studies of younger children yielded comparable results (Lepper, Greene, & Nisbett, 1973) and also showed that if rewards are expected before the activity is performed, the effect of not giving them is even greater (Ryan, Mims, & Koestner, 1983). Building Table 10.3 adds Deci's cognitive theory to our summary of motivation theories.

Intrinsically motivated behaviors: [in-TRINZ-ick-lee] Behaviors that a person engages in in order to feel more competent, satisfied, and self-determined.

BUILDING TABLE 10.3

Drive, Expectancy, and Cognitive Theories of Motivation

THEORY	THEORIST	PRINCIPALLY EXPLAINS	KEY IDEA	VIEW OF BEHAVIOR
Drive	a. Nisbett b. Schachter c. Hebb	a. Obesity b. Hunger and obesity c. Optimal arousal	a. Number of fat cells determines obesity. b. External cues energize eating behavior. c. Performance depends on level of arousal.	a. Mechanistic—obesity is biologically determined. b. Partially mechanistic but recognizes the role of learning. c. Mostly mechanistic— the efficiency of behavior is determined by the level of physiological arousal.
Expectancy	a. McClelland b. Friedman and Rosenman	a. Achievement motivation b. Type A and Type B behavior	a. Humans learn the need to achieve. b. Time urgency (Type A behavior) leads to competitiveness—and to heart disease.	a. Partly cognitive, partly mechanistic—achievement is a learned behavior. b. Partly cognitive, partly mechanistic—Type A behavior is initiated early in life.
Cognitive	Deci	Intrinsic motivation	Intrinsic motivation is self-rewarding because it makes people feel competent.	Cognitive—motivation is inborn, but extrinsic rewards often decrease it.

Other research (e.g., McGraw & Fiala, 1982) shows that offering rewards for engaging in an already attractive task results in a lower level of involvement and often permanent disengagement. Lepper and Greene (1978) refer to this phenomenon as the *hidden cost of reward*. When people think about the causes of their actions, such thought will lead to changes in their behavior. (The hidden cost of reward was examined in more detail in chapter 5, p. 188.)

Extrinsic rewards are rewards that come from the external environment. Praise, a high grade, or money for a particular behavior are extrinsic rewards. Such rewards can strengthen existing behaviors, provide people with information about their performance, and increase feelings of self-worth and competence. As already noted, however, extrinsic rewards can decrease intrinsic motivation (Pittman & Heller, 1987). Verbal extrinsic rewards (such as praise) are less likely to interfere with intrinsic motivation than are tangible rewards (such as money) (Anderson, Manoogian, & Reznick, 1976).

Psychologists continue to explore the effects of extrinsic rewards for intrinsically motivated behaviors. Baumeister and Tice (1985) showed that people with high self-esteem aspire to excel and seek opportunities to do so when they are rewarded for intrinsically motivated behaviors. But people with low self-esteem aspire to be only adequate or satisfactory when given rewards for intrinsically motivated behavior. It is not surprising, then, that intrinsic motivation is, at least in part, related to a person's past experiences and current level of self-esteem. Other variables, such as the

Extrinsic rewards: [ecks-TRINZ-ick] Rewards that come from the external environment.

type of task undertaken and the type of reward received, can influence the level of intrinsic motivation. The combination of intrinsic motivation, external rewards, self-esteem, and perhaps new and competing needs affect day-to-day behavior. (We will consider in chapter 13 what happens when goals and needs conflict and how animals and human beings behave in situations that have both positive and negative aspects.)

Humanistic Theory

Jim Abbott's physiological readiness, his expectations, and his learned behavior all work together to determine his success in baseball. One of the appealing aspects of humanistic theory is that it recognizes the interplay of behavioral theories and incorporates some of the best elements of the drive, expectancy, and cognitive approaches for explaining behavior.

Humanistic theory is an explanation of behavior that emphasizes the entirety of life rather than the individual components of behavior. It focuses on human dignity, individual choice, and self-worth. Humanistic psychologists believe that individuals' behavior must be viewed within the framework of the individual's environment and values.

As we saw in chapter 1, one of the founders and leaders of the humanistic approach was Abraham Maslow (1908–1970), who assumed that people are essentially good—that they possess an innate inclination to develop their potential and to seek beauty, truth, and harmony. Like other humanistic theorists, Maslow believed that people are born open and trusting and can experience the world in healthy ways. In his words, people are naturally motivated toward **self-actualization**—the process by which individuals strive to fulfill themselves.

Maslow described the characteristics he found in self-actualized people. Although few self-actualized people have all of these traits, all such people strive (and are directed) toward acquiring them, he believed. Self-actualized people, according to Maslow:

Are realistically oriented.	Accept themselves.
Are unconventional.	Are problem-centered.
Have a need for privacy.	Are independent.
Have a fresh appreciation of people.	Have spiritual experiences.
Identify with people.	Have intimate relationships.
Are democratic.	Do not confuse means with ends.
Have a good sense of humor.	Are creative and nonconformist.
Appreciate the environment.	Are spontaneous.

Humanistic theory: An explanation of behavior that emphasizes the role of human qualities such as dignity, individual choice, and self-worth.

Self-actualization: The process of realizing one's uniquely human potential for good; the process of achieving everything that one is capable of achieving.

Maslow's influential theory conceived of people's motives as forming a pyramid-shaped structure, with fundamental physiological needs at the base and the needs for love, achievement, understanding, and self-actualization near the top (see Figure 10.7). According to Maslow, as lower-level needs are satisfied, people strive for the next higher level; the pyramid culminates in self-actualization. Maslow claimed that once someone's basic physiological needs are met, the person is in a better position to satisfy emotional needs. He did not claim that a person's basic physiological needs have to be satisfied completely before the person can achieve a higher level of fulfillment. However, unless basic physiological needs are met, people are unlikely to grow and develop physically or to acquire social and aesthetic motives that might direct behavior. Only if people's needs for food, shelter, and physical safety are met

FIGURE 10.7

Maslow's Hierarchy of Needs

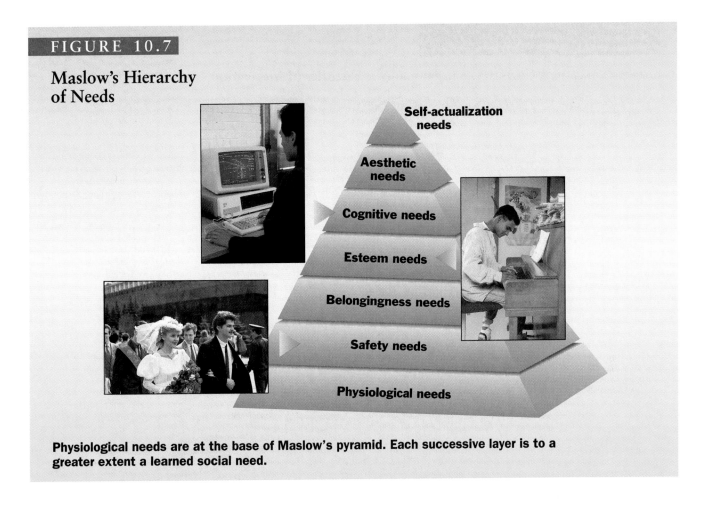

Self-actualization needs

Aesthetic needs

Cognitive needs

Esteem needs

Belongingness needs

Safety needs

Physiological needs

Physiological needs are at the base of Maslow's pyramid. Each successive layer is to a greater extent a learned social need.

can they attend to developing a sense of self-respect or a sense of beauty. (See Building Table 10.4 on page 374 for a summary of Maslow's humanistic theory compared with other motivation theories.)

Although Maslow's theory provides an interesting way to organize aspects of motivation and behavior and their relative importance, its global nature makes experimental verification difficult. Moreover, his levels of motivation seem closely tied to middle-class American cultural experience, so the theory may not be valid for all cultures or socioeconomic strata. Maslow's theory, like many other motivation theories, does not explain how other components of our lives interact with behavior. For example, how do we maintain a need for privacy and independence and fulfill our need to be with other people? Humanistic theory does not deal with how people develop the need to seek beauty, truth, and harmony. In addition, it never directly addresses how our motivation to self-actualize affects our emotional experiences—the subject discussed next.

FOCUS

▶ What do researchers mean when they use the term *cooperative interdependence*? p. 366

▶ What evidence exists to show that intrinsic motivation is lessened when rewards are offered for a behavior? p. 370

▶ Why are humanistic theories difficult to test experimentally? p. 372

BUILDING TABLE 10.4

Drive, Expectancy, Cognitive, and Humanistic Theories of Motivation

THEORY	THEORIST	PRINCIPALLY EXPLAINS	KEY IDEA	VIEW OF BEHAVIOR
Drive	a. Obesity b. Hunger and obesity c. Optimal arousal	a. Nisbett b. Schachter c. Hebb	a. Number of fat cells determines obesity. b. External cues energize eating behavior. c. Performance depends on level of arousal.	a. Mechanistic—obesity is biologically determined. b. Partially mechanistic but recognizes the role of learning. c. Mostly mechanistic— the efficiency of behavior is determined by the level of physiological arousal.
Expectancy	a. McClelland b. Friedman and Rosenman	a. Achievement motivation b. Type A and Type B behavior	a. Humans learn the need to achieve. b. Time urgency (Type A behavior) leads to competitiveness—and to heart disease.	a. Partly cognitive, partly mechanistic—achievement is a learned behavior. b. Partly cognitive, partly mechanistic—Type A behavior is initiated early in life.
Cognitive	Deci	Intrinsic motivation	Intrinsic motivation is self-rewarding because it makes people feel competent.	Cognitive—motivation is inborn, but extrinsic rewards often decrease it.
Humanistic	Maslow	Learned needs for fulfillment and feelings of self-actualization.	Self-actualization	Cognitive—humans seek to self-actualize after they have fulfilled basic needs for food and security.

Emotion

Anger can cause you to hurl an object across a room or lash out at a friend. Happiness can make you smile all day, donate your change to the Salvation Army, and stop to help a motorist with a flat tire. Fear can electrify you, making your legs pump faster as you sprint down a dark, shadowy alley. Although emotions, including love, joy, and fear, can direct people's behavior, these states and categories remain fuzzy (Rosch, 1978). Even psychologists have difficulty agreeing on their definitions.

What Is Emotion?

The word *emotion* is an umbrella term referring to a wide range of subjective states, such as love, fear, hate, and disgust. We all have emotions, talk about them, and agree on what represents them, but this agreement is not scientific. The psychological investigation of emotion has led to a more precise definition. An **emotion** is a subjective response (feeling), usually accompanied by a physiological change, that is interpreted by the individual, then readies the individual for some action that is associated with a change in behavior. People cry when they are sad, find increased energy when they are excited, and breathe faster, sweat, feel nauseated, and salivate less (causing a dry mouth) when they are afraid (see Kleinginna & Kleinginna, 1981). Some physiological changes precede an emotional response. For example, just before an automobile crashes, the people in it show physiological arousal, muscle tension, and avoidance responses—that is, they brace themselves in anticipation. Other changes are evident only after an emotion-causing event. It is only after the auto accident that people shake with fear, disbelief, or rage.

People often respond to physiological changes by altering their behavior. When they are afraid, they may scream. When they are angry, they may seek revenge or retribution. When they are in love, they may act tenderly toward others. In some situations, people think about acting out such behaviors but may not express them in directly observable ways. Emotional expressions sometimes seem contradictory; think about Juliet's claim that "parting is such sweet sorrow." Although emotions may seem to be written all over people's faces, appearances can be deceiving and difficult to interpret.

Psychologists focus on different aspects of emotional behavior. The earliest researchers cataloged and described basic emotions (Bridges, 1932; Wundt, 1896). Others tried to discover the physiological bases of emotion (Bard, 1934). Still others focused on how people perceive bodily movements and on how they convey emotions to others through nonverbal mechanisms such as gestures or eye contact (Tagiuti, 1968). More recent studies have investigated people's ability to control their emotional responses (Meichenbaum, 1977). Table 10.2 provides a series of laws through which theoreticians have attempted to codify the regularity of emotional behavior (Frijda, 1988).

> **Emotion:** A subjective response, usually accompanied by a physiological change, that is interpreted by the individual, then readies the individual for some action that is associated with a change in behavior.

TABLE 10.2   *The Laws of Emotion*

1. Emotions are elicited by specific events.
2. Emotions are specific responses that are subjective in nature.
3. Emotions arise in response to goals or motives important to the individual.
4. Emotions are responses to events appraised as real, and the extent of an emotion is determined by the extent of the realness of the event.
5. Emotions are elicited by people's expectations for change in conditions.
6. Pleasure disappears with continuous satisfaction; pain may persist for longer periods.
7. Emotional events retain their power to evoke emotion indefinitely.
8. One emotion leads to another.
9. When possible, people view a situation in the lightest emotional way.

Source: Frijda, 1988.

FIGURE 10.8

Alternative Conceptions of Our Emotional Range: Plutchik's Circle

Robert Plutchik (1980) suggests that our emotions can be mixed (just as colors are) to yield new varieties of emotional experience.

Many psychologists acknowledge that emotion consists of three elements: feelings, physiological responses, and behaviors. People experience the same kinds of emotions, but the intensity and quality vary. One person's sense of joy is different from another's. Thus, emotions have a private, personal, and unique component. This subjective element is called *feelings*. Subjective feelings are difficult to measure, so most researchers focus on the other two aspects of emotion—physiological responses and behaviors. This focus shifts research from the internal process to action or readiness for action.

Today, researchers are studying the following observable and measurable aspects of emotions: whether one hemisphere of the brain dominates emotion (R. J. Davidson, 1992; Fox, 1991); the biochemical components of emotions, including blood glucose levels and hormone changes (Baum, Grunberg, & Singer, 1992); physiological responses such as heart rate and blood pressure; and behavioral responses such as smiling and crying.

Robert Plutchik (1980) suggests that our emotions can be mixed (just as colors are) to yield new varieties of emotional experience. He has devised a conceptual circle to characterize emotional responses (see Figure 10.8). Primary emotions (shown in the center of the circle) are mixed with neighboring emotions to yield more complex emotions (shown on the outside of the circle). Such models are interesting ways to think about the range of our emotional responses; however, there is little data to support them.

Richard Lazarus (1991) concludes that there are four *types* of emotions: (1) emotions resulting from harm, loss, or threats; (2) emotions resulting from benefits; (3) borderline emotions, such as hope and compassion; and (4) more complex emotions, such as grief, disappointment, bewilderment, and curiosity. Turner and Ortony (1992) assert that we should think in terms of basic components of emotions rather than basic emotions. Lewis and Saarni (1985) suggest that the following five basic *elements* of emotions must be considered:

1. *Emotional elicitors*—the events that trigger emotions. (They include painful as well as pleasant experiences.)

2. *Emotional receptors (brain mechanisms)*—central nervous system mechanisms responsible for processing emotional reactions. (They are discussed later in this chapter.)

3. *Emotional states*—changes in neural, biochemical, and general physiological activity that occur when an organism is activated emotionally.

4. *Emotional expressions*—observable and measurable changes in an organism that convey information to others about emotional states.

5. *Emotional experience*—a subjective state determined by cognitive and social factors. (This is the individual's interpretation and evaluation of an emotional reaction.)

Not all researchers consider all elements of a definition of emotion in their studies. One may focus on emotional expression; another may focus on emotional experiences. Physiological psychologists sometimes trace pathways and confine their research to brain mechanisms such as the hypothalamus. Researchers such as Izard

DIVERSITY

Cultural Differences in Emotional Terms

If you live in the United States and speak English, your emotional life is categorized differently than if you come from Japan or Indonesia. Some words that describe emotions in the English language, and therefore reflect the North American experience, have no real equivalent in other languages. Are there emotions that exist in English that do not exist in German, Chinese, or Japanese? If such differences exist, what do they tell us about emotion?

According to James A. Russell (1991), who has conducted extensive research into cross-cultural comparisons of emotional terms, enormous differences exist. For example, languages differ in the number of words they provide to categorize emotions. There are 2,000 words to describe emotions in English, but only 1,500 in Dutch, 750 in Taiwanese Chinese, and 230 in Malay.

More important than the number of specific terms, however, are the categories of emotion. Some English words have no real equivalent in other languages. Russell points out that English distinguishes among *terror, horror, dread, apprehension,* and *timidity* as types of fear. However, in Gidjingali, an Australian aboriginal

language, one word, *gurakadj,* suffices. What English treats as different emotions—for example, *anger* and *sadness*—other languages treat as one emotion. The English distinction between *shame* and *embarrassment* is not made by the people of Japan. In China, there exists no term for *anxiety*; in Sri Lanka, there exists no term for *guilt*. In addition, some languages have words without an equivalent in English.

The categorization of words to describe emotion is important because it shows researchers that the emotional experience across all cultures may not be the same. Cultural differences in emotion are probably due to differences in the way each culture approaches, appraises, and

responds to various life events (Mesquita & Frijda, 1992). For example, the definition of *shameful events* among the Awlad 'Ali, a tribe of Egyptian Bedouins, is highly specific: Shameful events are those that injure one's honor; therefore, how a person codes an event is a central element in their language (Mesquita & Frijda, 1992). In addition, just because a language does not have a particular word does not mean that the concept does not exist; it might, for example, be expressed in a phrase rather than in a single word.

From psychologists' point of view, the use of language to describe emotion is important because any discussion of emotion that names emotions uses specific words in a specific language. To describe a theory of emotion that is truly universal to all people, in all cultures, in all languages, a theory must be cross-culturally valid—not bound by specific lexical (word) entries in a dictionary. This is an enormous challenge. Most psychologists believe that all human beings experience the same emotions (Mauro, Sato, & Tucker, 1992), but psychologists have to use terminology that is consistent across cultures. Without such consistency, cross-cultural differences will be hard to separate from cross-cultural similarities.

(1993) assert that emotion is a multistage process with neural systems at the beginning and cognitive systems at the end. Before going on to the biologically based theories of emotion, read the Diversity box, which examines cultural differences in the use of emotional terms.

Physiological Theories of Emotion

The wide range of emotions that human beings express is in large part controlled by a series of neurons located in an area deep within the brain, the limbic system. The *limbic system* is composed of cells in the hypothalamus, the amygdala, and other cortical and subcortical areas. Studies of these crucial areas began in the 1920s, when Bard (1934) found that the removal of portions of the cortex of cats produced sharp emotional reactions to simple stimuli such as a touch or a puff of air. The cats would hiss, claw, bite, arch their backs, and growl—and their reactions did not seem directed at any specific person or target. Bard referred to this behavior as sham rage. Later researchers stimulated portions of the brain with electrical current and found that the visual system was also important in emotions. They deduced that the cortex was integrating visual information and hypothalamic information to produce emotional behavior. In general, two major physiological (biological) approaches to the study of emotion developed: the James-Lange theory and the Cannon-Bard theory. Both are concerned with the physiology of emotions and with whether physiological change or emotional feelings occur first.

The James-Lange Theory. According to a theory proposed by both William James (1842–1910) and Carl Lange (1834–1900) (we give them joint credit since the two approaches were so similar), people experience physiological changes and then interpret them as emotional states (see Figure 10.9). People do not cry because they feel sad; they feel sad because they cry. People do not perspire because they are afraid; they feel afraid after they perspire. In other words, the James-Lange theory says that people do not experience an emotion until after their bodies become aroused and begin to respond with physiological changes; that is, feedback from the body produces feelings or emotions (James, 1884; Lange, 1922). For this approach, *feeling* is the essence of emotion. Thus, James (1890, p. 1006) wrote, "Every one

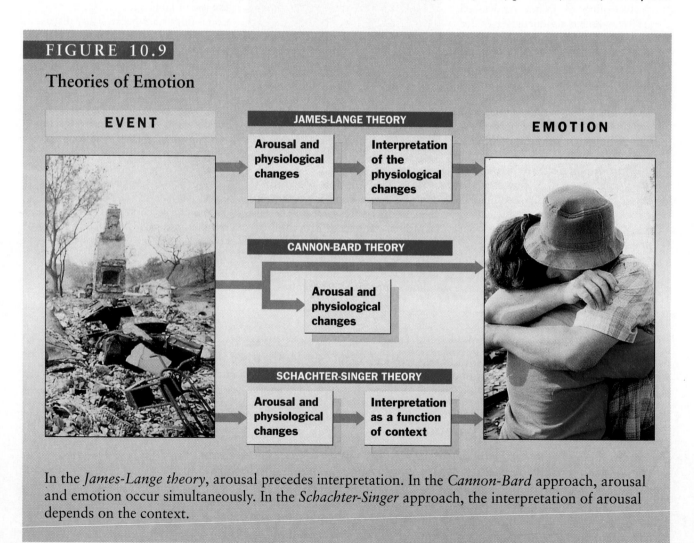

FIGURE 10.9

Theories of Emotion

EVENT

JAMES-LANGE THEORY

Arousal and physiological changes → Interpretation of the physiological changes

EMOTION

CANNON-BARD THEORY

Arousal and physiological changes

SCHACHTER-SINGER THEORY

Arousal and physiological changes → Interpretation as a function of context

In the *James-Lange theory*, arousal precedes interpretation. In the *Cannon-Bard* approach, arousal and emotion occur simultaneously. In the *Schachter-Singer* approach, the interpretation of arousal depends on the context.

of the bodily changes whatsoever it be is felt, acutely or obscurely, the moment it occurs."

A modern physiological approach suggests that facial movements, by their action, create emotions. In some ways, this approach is similar to the James-Lange theory. For example, when specific facial movements create a change in blood flow to and temperature of the brain, pleasant feelings occur. According to Zajonc, Murphy, and Inglehart (1989), a facial movement such as a smile or an eye movement may release the appropriate emotion-linked neurotransmitters. Some neurotransmitters may bring about pleasant emotions and others may bring about unpleasant ones. Zajonc and his colleagues argue that facial movements alone are capable of inducing emotions. This theory is still relatively new and has not yet been tested extensively by other researchers.

The Cannon-Bard Theory. Physiologists, notably Walter Cannon (1871–1945), were critical of the James-Lange theory. Cannon and P. Bard, a colleague, argued that the physiological changes in many emotional states were identical. They reasoned as follows: If increases in blood pressure and heart rate accompany feelings of both anger and joy, how can people determine their emotional state simply from their physiological state?

Cannon argued that when a person is emotional, two areas of the brain—the thalamus and the cerebral cortex—are stimulated simultaneously (he did not realize the full nature of the limbic system). Stimulation of the cortex produces the emotional component of the experience; stimulation of the thalamus produces physiological changes in the sympathetic nervous system. According to Cannon (1927), emotional feelings *accompany* physiological changes (see Figure 10.9); they do not produce such changes. A problem with the Cannon-Bard approach is that physiological changes in the brain do not happen exactly simultaneously. Further, people report that they often have an experience and then have physiological and emotional reactions to it. Neither the James-Lange nor the Cannon-Bard approach considered the idea that people's interpretations of or thoughts about a situation might alter their physiological reactions and emotional responses. An interesting and controversial use of the physiological changes involved in emotion, lie detector tests, is examined in the Applications box on page 380.

Cognitive Theories of Emotion

Cognitive theories of emotion, focusing on interpretation as well as physiology to explain emotions, developed in response to the older physiological approaches. They follow logically in the history of psychology because thought processes have become extremely influential in the past 3 decades. Cognitive theorists argue that appraisal is a sufficient cause for emotion (R. S. Lazarus, 1991).

The Schachter-Singer Approach. The Schachter-Singer view of emotion is a cognitive approach that, focusing on emotional activation, incorporates elements of both the James-Lange and the Cannon-Bard theories. Stanley Schachter and Jerome Singer observed that people do indeed interpret their emotions, but not solely from bodily changes. They argued that people interpret physical sensations within a specific context (see Figure 10.9). Observers cannot interpret what a person's crying means unless they know the situation in which that behavior occurs. If a man cries at a funeral, we suspect he is sad; if he cries at his daughter's wedding, we suspect he is joyful.

To prove their contention, Schachter and Singer (1962) injected volunteer subjects with epinephrine (adrenaline), a powerful stimulant that increases physiological signs of arousal such as heart rate, excitement, energy, and even sensations of

APPLICATIONS

Lie Detectors

Many physiological changes are due to an increase in activity in the sympathetic branch of the autonomic nervous system. When the sympathetic branch is activated, a whole range of activities take place almost simultaneously. Fear, for example, may slow or halt digestion, increase blood pressure and heart rate, deepen breathing, dilate pupils, decrease salivation (causing a dry mouth), and tense muscles. Researchers recognize that the autonomic nervous system provides direct, observable, measurable responses that can be quantified in a systematic manner. This realization led to the development of what is commonly called the lie detector.

The polygraph test (recordings of many physiological responses) is perhaps the most widely recognized recorder of emotion. When people refer to a lie detector test, they are referring to a polygraph test. A polygraph device records changes in the activity of the sympathetic branch of a subject's autonomic nervous system. Most autonomic nervous system activity is involuntary, and lying is usually associated with an increase in autonomic activity. A trained polygraph operator compares a person's autonomic responses to a series of relatively neutral questions to the person's responses to questions about the issue being explored. During noncontroversial questions (such as a request for the person's name or address), autonomic activity remains at what is considered the baseline level. During critical questions (such as whether the person used a knife as a holdup weapon), however, a person with something to hide usually shows a dramatic increase in autonomic nervous system activity.

A lie detector test can be useful in indicating whether a person is lying. Not all people, however, show distinct or marked autonomic nervous system changes when emotionally aroused (Bashore & Rapp, 1993). Habitual liars, for example, show little or no change in autonomic activity when they lie; they seem to be able to lie without becoming emotionally aroused. Equally important is the finding that some people who tell the truth may register changes in autonomic nervous system activity because of anxiety. This means that a truthful individual who takes a lie detector test might be called a liar when the individual is in fact telling the truth.

In a study of lie detectors, researchers examined innocent and guilty individuals accused of theft (Kleinmuntz & 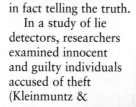 Szucko, 1984). Although guilty people were often declared guilty by the lie detector and innocent people often were declared innocent, 37 percent of innocent people were declared guilty! In summary, studies show that lie detectors are subject to significant errors in both directions (Szucko & Kleinmuntz, 1981; Kleinmuntz & Szucko, 1984; Patrick & Iacono, 1989).

Today, most states do not accept the lie detector as valid evidence in court, especially in criminal cases. A federal law now restricts businesses from using the polygraph to test prospective employees. The American Psychological Association has also expressed strong reservations about the use of polygraph tests, asserting that they may cause psychological damage to innocent persons. The association's concerns stem in part from the knowledge that some people can control their emotions and do not respond automatically to external stimuli, whereas other people are less able to control their emotions and may overreact to external stimuli.

butterflies in the stomach. The subjects were not aware of the usual results of the injection. To see if they could affect how subjects interpreted their aroused state, Schachter and Singer manipulated the settings in which the subjects experienced their arousal. The researchers hired undergraduates and paid them to act either happy and relaxed or sad, depressed, and angry. The hired subjects—called stooges—pretended that they, too, were volunteers in the drug study. However, they were given injections of salt water, not epinephrine. Their emotional behavior was strictly an act. The "happy" stooges shot wads of paper into a wastebasket and flew paper airplanes around the room. The "angry" ones complained about the questionnaire they had to fill out and voiced their dissatisfaction with the experiment.

All the experimental subjects showed increased physiological arousal. Those with the happy stooges reported that the drug made them feel good; those with the angry ones reported feeling anger. Schachter and Singer reasoned that when people have no immediate explanation for their physiological arousal, especially when arousal levels are low, they will label their feelings in terms of the thoughts available to them.

The cognitive view receives support from anecdotal data as well as experiments. When people first smoke marijuana or take other psychoactive drugs, for example, they tend to approach the experience with definite expectations. If told the drug will produce feelings of hunger, new users will report feeling hunger; if told the drug is a downer, new users often interpret their bodily sensations as depressive. In Schachter and Singer's view, people experience internal arousal, become aware of the arousal, seek an explanation for it, identify an external cue, and then label the arousal. This labeling determines the emotion that is felt.

Other Cognitive Theories of Emotion. Valins (1966) and Reisenzein (1983) challenged Schachter and Singer's view. Valins showed that thoughts alone are sufficient to produce emotional behavior. He showed male subjects slides of nude women and, at the same time, played a soundtrack of previously recorded heartbeats. The subjects were told that the heartbeats were their own but to ignore them. The heartbeats were speeded up or slowed down as the slides were shown. This meant that the subjects were being cued by the heartbeats as to their supposed arousal level, even though their arousal level may not actually have changed. A control group saw the same slides, heard the same sounds, but was told that the sounds were meaningless and to ignore them.

When the two groups were asked to judge the attractiveness of the nude women, the experimental group rated them more positively than did the control group. Valins concluded that actual physiological arousal is not a prerequisite for labeling of emotion; cognitive processes alone will suffice (see Harris & Katkin, 1975). Reisenzein (1983) argues that Schachter and Singer's theory overestimates the role of arousal and that arousal at best merely intensifies an emotional experience.

Shaver's Multicultural Prototypes. Phillip Shaver and his colleagues have sought to identify the basic emotions that all people experience and the ways in which they are experienced. Shaver showed that there are six emotions that almost all people will describe when asked to identify emotions: love, joy, anger, sadness, fear, and surprise (Shaver et al., 1987). Of course, these six basic categories can overlap, and many other emotional states can be grouped under them.

Schwartz and Shaver (1987) contend that people's emotional knowledge is organized around these six emotional categories and that people exhibit characteristic behaviors with each emotion. They also assert that these emotions appear cross-culturally and that researchers have to understand this overall structure before they can define an overall theory of emotion. Each culture may put its own value on an emotion and have different traits that trigger it. For example, love is an extremely powerful emotion in the United States; but in Sumatra, one of the chief islands of Indonesia, nostalgia is the most powerful emotion (Heider, 1991).

Shaver asserts that people understand and interpret emotional events by comparing the events to basic emotional concepts. For example, when a mother sees her child fall and start to cry, she rushes toward the child. An observer sees this event and assumes the mother is frightened and concerned. This assumption is based on general knowledge about fear and love. Schwartz and Shaver (1987) claim that people make use of implicit learned knowledge to understand and manage social interactions. Only by understanding this structure of emotion can we begin to place cognitive interpretations within a reasonable framework.

Shaver does not deny the role of cognition. On the contrary, he argues that cognitive interpretations are critical. But before we can understand the cognitions, he believes, we have to understand the overall structure and concept of emotion. To some extent, he argues, we have jumped too far into our analysis of emotion, and we need to step back and review the basics. Paul Ekman (1993) concurs and asserts that some aspects of emotion may be culture specific and others may be universal. He also believes that we have just begun asking the proper questions.

Frijda: Appraisal and Readiness. Another view of emotion sees appraisal as important but also considers the idea that people ready themselves for action. Nico Frijda asserts that each emotional experience is not only a cognitive appraisal of a situation but also a set of action tendencies or behaviors that are being prepared as the cognitive appraisal takes place.

For Frijda, when a situation is potentially threatening, a person prepares to flee or attack and autonomic nervous system arousal is invoked (Frijda, Kuipers, & ter Schure, 1989). Frijda supports Shaver's contention that emotions can be arranged around several distinct categories. But he does not suggest that arousal is necessary, nor does he necessarily invoke the limbic system. He supports his ideas by a research study showing that subjects' specific action tendencies are closely associated with specific cognitive appraisals. Thus, Frijda has introduced responses along with appraisals. This approach looks again at how emotions develop—an area of research that has often followed different avenues.

Development of Emotional Responses

Harlow found that young monkeys raised in isolation would not thrive as well those those raised with a cloth-covered wire surrogate mother.

People's ability to express emotion develops from birth through adulthood. Some aspects seem to be learned, others inborn. Naturalistic observations of human infants indicate that they follow a relatively fixed pattern of emotional development. They are born with a startle (Moro) reflexive response; they smile, coo, and gurgle at about 6 weeks; they develop a fear of strangers at 6 to 9 months. Attachment behaviors encouraged in the early weeks and months of life are also nurtured during adolescence and adulthood, when people form close loving bonds with others.

Emotional expressions appear in all cultures; fear, joy, surprise, sadness, anger, and disgust are common expressions. These expressions are also found in deaf and blind people and in people without limbs, who have limited touch experiences (Izard & Saxton, 1988). Most researchers therefore consider those emotional expressions innate even though they unfold slowly over the first year of life and are reinforced by caregivers.

Emotional Development in Rhesus Monkeys. To find out how people develop emotional responses, Harry Harlow (1905–1981), a psychologist at the University of Wisconsin, focused on the development of emotion in rhesus monkeys (we examined some of Harlow's work in chapter 1). Harlow's initial studies were on the nature of early interactions among monkeys. He found that monkeys raised from birth in isolated bare-wire cages away from their mothers did not survive, even though they were well fed. Other monkeys, raised in the same conditions but with scraps of terry cloth in their cages, survived.

Terry cloth is hardly a critical variable in the growth and development of monkeys, yet its introduction into a wire cage made the difference between life and death for rhesus monkeys. Harlow inferred that the terry cloth provided some measure of security. That conclusion led him to attempt to discover whether infant monkeys had an inborn desire for love or warmth that might be satisfied by soft, warm objects such as terry cloth.

In a classic experiment, Harlow placed infant monkeys in cages along with two wire-covered shapes resembling adult monkeys. One figure was covered with terry cloth; the other was left bare. Both could be fitted with bottles to provide milk. In some cases, the wire mother surrogate had the bottle of milk; in other cases, the terry cloth mother surrogate had the bottle.

Harlow found that the infant monkeys clung to the terry cloth mother surrogates whether or not they provided milk. He concluded that the wire mother surrogate, even with a bottle of milk, could not provide the comfort that a terry cloth–covered mother surrogate could provide (Harlow & Zimmerman, 1958).

Another result of Harlow's experiment was that neither group of monkeys grew up to be totally normal. Harlow's monkeys were more aggressive and fearful than normally raised monkeys. They were also unable to engage in normal sexual relations. And some of the infants raised with wire mother surrogates exhibited self-destructive behaviors (Harlow, 1962).

Harlow next suggested that the emotions of fear, curiosity, and aggression are inborn and that the brain mechanisms underlying them develop over time and in a specific sequence. To test this idea, he isolated monkeys of various ages for different periods of time. As Harlow expected, certain behaviors, such as attachment and nurturing, were more affected by early isolation; and other behaviors were more affected by later isolation. When monkeys were deprived of social contacts with other monkeys from the ages of 18 to 24 months, for example, their later social behaviors relating to mating were essentially normal. Harlow concluded that nature and nurture must interact at specific times (when the relevant brain mechanisms are ready to mature) for normal emotional and social development.

Emotional Development in Human Beings. Although it is a broad leap from Harlow's monkeys to human infants, it is reasonable to assume that infants, like monkeys, have an inborn need for social stimulation. Klaus and Kennell (1983) suggest that there is a period in which emotional relationships are formed between caregiver and child. They contend that infants deprived of periods of social stimulation will not develop as well emotionally as do infants who go through a period of close social attachment. They add that the presence or absence of bonding may exert an extraordinary influence later in life (M. H. Bornstein, 1989). (We examined the controversial issue of bonding and attachment in chapter 8.) It is easy to see parent-infant attachment on the faces of new parents and newborn children.

Behavioral Expression of Emotions

Since 1898, psychologists have recognized that facial expressions provide reliable clues to people's feelings. This *behavioral expression of emotions* is easily observed and interpreted by others. Most important, facial expressions are generally an accurate index of a person's emotional states. Recent research suggests that there are asymmetries in facial expressions in both infants and adults, and that adults can easily discern those differences. Best and Queen (1989) found that the left side of the face (controlled by the right side of the brain in most people) may be more expressive than the right side of the face, especially in adults (Rothbart, Taylor, & Tucker, 1989). They argue that the right side of the face may be more readily under control by the left side of the brain, and so people are able to inhibit right-face expression more easily than left-face expression. Nevertheless, though facial expressions (either side) are good indicators of emotion, they are only indicators; real emotions can be masked by a happy face or a turned-down mouth. For a demonstration that emotions are both easy and difficult to read, see Figure 10.10 on page 384.

People also display emotion through gestures, body language, and voice tone and volume (Izard & Saxton, 1988). Examples include a lowered head, shaking fists, and laughter, as well as clenched teeth, limpness, and loss of energy. The autonomic

FIGURE 10.10

Recognizing and Naming Emotions

Look carefully at the following six photographs. Which of the following six emotions is portrayed in each?

A. Happiness   B. Sadness   C. Fear   D. Anger   E. Surprise   F. Disgust

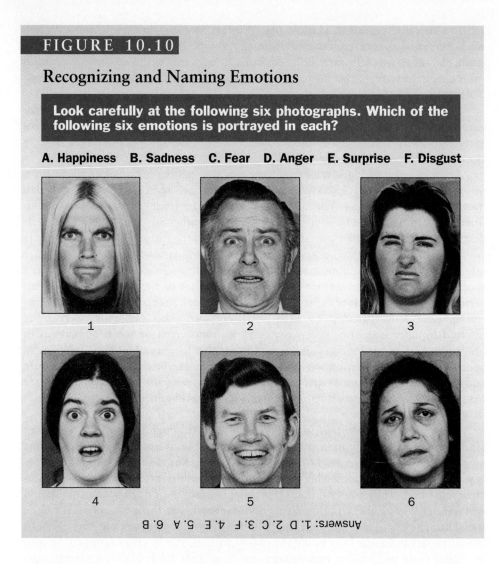

Answers: 1. D 2. C 3. F 4. E 5. A 6. B

nervous system responds differently to differences among emotions (Levenson, 1992). Researchers have studied the smiling responses of infants, children, and adults by examining when and under what conditions smiling is evoked and then lost (Carlson, Gantz, & Masters, 1983). Researchers have also studied smiling cross-culturally (Levenson et al., 1992; Sogon & Masutani, 1989) and have found commonalities in what brings about emotional responses such as smiling, although not all researchers find the same results (Ekman, 1992). Some researchers have focused on the variables that bring laughter and smiles to people's lives.

Researchers observe animals and human beings in situations that might induce stress and emotional responses. For example, psychologists have studied the emotional expressions of store clerks and their responses to customers. In one study (Rafaeli, 1989), a range of variables was considered: the clerk's gender, the wearing of a smock with a name tag, the presence of other clerks, and the customer's gender. Although the results were complicated, the emotional expressions of clerks were affected by nearly all the variables. Female clerks displayed positive emotions more often than male clerks, male customers received positive emotional responses more often than female customers, and clerks especially aware of their role (wearing smocks) were more expressive than other clerks. The expression of emotion was thus affected by context and by subtle variables that are still being investigated.

Controlling Emotions

Another aspect of cognitive theory is the self-regulation view of emotional expression, which emphasizes that people are not passive—that they do not respond automatically to environmental or internal stimuli. This view asserts that people manage or determine their emotional states in purposeful ways by constantly evaluating their environment and their feelings. Through this appraisal, individuals can alter their level of arousal.

Arousal. Arousal is an essential component in emotion, and researchers show that people can use cognitive means to control their arousal level and therefore their emotions. For psychologists studying the behavior of disturbed individuals, the interaction of arousal, emotion, and thought has become increasingly important. Even in normal individuals, too high a level of arousal can produce extreme emotional responses and lead to disorganized, less effective behavior (see Figure 10.11). Many maladjusted individuals, such as those suffering from the manic stages of bipolar disorders, have so high a level of arousal that they cannot organize their thinking or behavior (see chapter 14, p. 517). Even young infants show some forms of emotional restraint and control, and an infant's control of emotion continues to develop, especially at the end of the first year (Kopp, 1989).

Responses to Emotions. Some studies show that people can control their body's biochemistry. In the study by Lazarus and Alfert (1964) discussed earlier, for example, subjects were able to manipulate their electrodermal response when told in advance about a subincision ritual shown in a film. Thus, emotion and its expression reflect a person's motivations and basic biochemistry (Carver & Scheier, 1990). People also control their emotions because of strong cultural expectations.

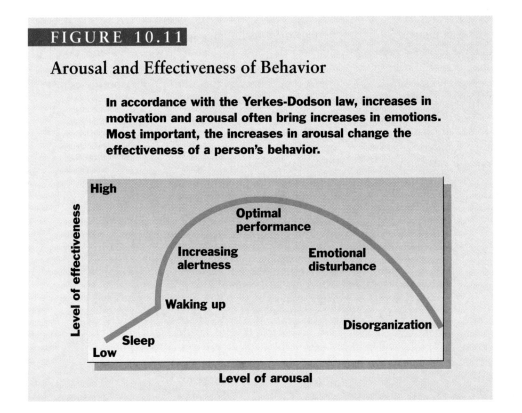

FIGURE 10.11

Arousal and Effectiveness of Behavior

In accordance with the Yerkes-Dodson law, increases in motivation and arousal often bring increases in emotions. Most important, the increases in arousal change the effectiveness of a person's behavior.

In the United States, for example, children and women have greater permission to cry and express emotion than men do. But in Latin America, men are expected to be emotional. Expectations and cognitive appraisals of situations seem to be key elements in physiological and subsequent behavioral expressions of emotion (C. A. Smith, 1989). Expectations that are biased in one direction or another can lead to some unusual consequences; for example, if a person suffers from hypochondriasis (see chapter 14, p. 511), any ache, pain, or quickness of breath might lead the person to dire feelings about health.

FOCUS

▶ Identify the fundamental ideas that distinguish the James-Lange, Cannon-Bard, and Schachter-Singer theories of emotion. p. 378

▶ What is the evidence to suggest that lie detectors are unscientific? pp. 380–382

▶ What are the implications of Harlow's studies with infant monkeys? p. 382

Concluding Note

We study motivation to learn the causes of behavior. Drives determine some of our behaviors. We eat and drink at least in part in response to physiological imbalances in our body. But our eating and drinking behavior is determined to a great extent by external forces and by our thoughts. We often eat not because of physiological need but because of external events—clocks on the wall, billboards, and offers of food. Our physiological needs are thus tempered by our learned needs. Psychologists have learned that if people hold beliefs or expectations, they will behave, operate, or cooperate in specific ways. Our expectations and learned motives even affect our health. We know that when people have extraordinarily high expectations for success, their expectations can put them at risk for serious health problems. Some applied psychologists have focused on ways in which simple day-to-day behaviors can facilitate good health and improve our emotional lives.

Psychologists are seeking to improve people's health and well-being by helping them modulate their emotional life. Our emotions are determined in part physiologically and in part by our experiences. We can learn to modulate our emotional response to events in our world. Psychologists are teaching stress management techniques to Type A individuals (see chapters 13 and 15), and they are helping people manage their motivations and acquire realistic ideas about their goals so they do not develop maladjustments (chapter 15). Health science professionals are focusing on preventive measures to enhance the sense of well-being and purpose and to help people manage their motivational and emotional lives in productive, worthwhile ways.

Summary & Review

Defining Motivation

What is motivation?

Motivation is an internal condition that appears by inference to initiate, activate, or maintain an organism's goal-directed behavior. Motivation is inferred from behavior and caused by needs, drives, or desires. A need is a state of physiological imbalance that is usually accompanied by arousal. p. 350

KEY TERM: *motivation,* p. 350.

Biologically Based Motives: Drive Theory

What is a mechanistic theory of behavior?

A mechanistic explanation of behavior views the organism as pushed, pulled, and energized almost like a machine. Expectancy theories incorporate aspects of both mechanistic and cognitive theories. They try to predict a limited range of behavior and emphasize that individuals can choose among various forms of behavior. An individual's expectation of success and achievement is thought to help determine how and when to respond.   pp. 350–351

What causes hunger?

The glucostatic approach to hunger argues that the principal physiological cause of hunger is a low blood sugar level, which accompanies food deprivation. Genetics and disorders of the autonomic nervous system may also play a role. Physiological makeup isn't the only important factor in eating behavior; our experiences also teach us how to interact with food. There is no clear, convincing, simple answer to the questions of nature versus nurture in obesity.   pp. 351–354

What are anorexia nervosa and bulimia nervosa?

Anorexia nervosa, a starvation disease, is an *eating disorder* characterized by obstinate and willful refusal to eat. *Bulimia nervosa* involves binge eating accompanied by fear of not being able to stop eating. Bulimics often purge themselves of unwanted calories through vomiting, laxatives, and diuretics.   pp. 354–355

What causes thirst?

Although humans can live for weeks without food, we can live only a few days without replenishing our supply of fluid. Any imbalance in fluid is reflected in a drive to restore the balance. A delicate balance of fluid intake—*homeostasis*—is necessary for proper functioning. When people experience fluid deprivation and the resulting cellular dehydration, homeostatic mechanisms come into play. A person is put into a drive state and his or her mouth and throat becomes dry. This cues a person to drink. It is important to note that thirst is not a *result* of dryness in the throat or mouth.   p. 358

Define and describe sexual dysfunctions.

Sexual dysfunction is the inability to obtain satisfaction from sexual behavior, often accompanied by the inability to experience orgasm. *Erectile dysfunction* is the inability of a man to attain or maintain an erection of sufficient strength to allow him to engage in sexual intercourse. A woman unable to achieve orgasm is said to suffer from an *orgasmic dysfunction.*   pp. 360–361

How is behavior affected by arousal?

According to optimal arousal theories, individuals seek an optimal level of stimulation. The *Yerkes-Dodson*

law basically asserts that behavior varies from disorganized to effective to optimal, depending on the person's level of arousal. Contemporary researchers have extended the idea by suggesting that when a person's level of arousal and anxiety is too high *or* too low, performance will be poor, especially on complex tasks. An inverted U-shaped curve describes the relationship between arousal and effectiveness of behavior. pp. 361–362

KEY TERMS: *drive theory,* p. 350; *drive,* p. 350; *need,* p. 350; *eating disorders,* p. 354; *anorexia nervosa,* p. 354; *bulimia nervosa,* p. 355; *excitement phase,* p. 359; *vasoconstriction,* p. 359; *plateau phase,* p. 359; *orgasm phase,* p. 359; *resolution phase,* p. 359; *sexual dysfunction,* p. 360; *erectile dysfunction,* p. 360; *primary erectile dysfunction,* p. 360; *secondary erectile dysfunction,* p. 360; *premature ejaculation,* p. 360; *primary orgasmic dysfunction,* p. 360; *secondary orgasmic dysfunction,* p. 360.

continued

Summary & Review

Learned Motives

What is expectancy theory?

Expectancy theory focuses on people's expectations of success and need for achievement; the theory suggests that people's thoughts guide and direct their behavior.   p. 363

What is a motive and what affects people's motives?

A *motive* is a specific internal condition directing an organism's behavior toward a goal. People's motives and their motivated behavior is affected by (1) physiology, (2) emotional state (including arousal), (3) ability, and (4) thought processes. High motivation without ability will not yield high performance, nor will high ability without motivation.   pp. 363–364

Distinguish between a social motive and a social need.

A social motive is a condition that directs people toward establishing or maintaining relationships with others. A social need is an internal aroused condition involving feelings about self and others and toward establishing and maintaining relationships. pp. 363–364

What is need for achievement?

Need for achievement is a social need that directs a person to strive constantly for excellence and success. According to expectancy theory, people engage in behaviors that satisfy their desires for success, mastery, and fulfillment. Tasks not oriented toward these goals are not motivating and either are not undertaken or are done without energy and commitment. Need for achievement can be measured by tests such as the TAT. pp. 363–364

KEY TERMS: *expectancy theories,* p. 363; *motive,* p. 363; *social need,* p. 364; *need for achievement,* p. 364.

Cognitive and Humanistic Theory

What is cognitive theory?

Cognitive theory emphasizes the role of active decision making in all areas of life. It is an explanation of behavior that emphasizes the role of thoughts and individual choices regarding life goals and the means of achieving them. Cognitive theory moves away from mechanistic descriptions of behavior and focuses on the role of human choice and expression.   pp. 368–370

What is intrinsic motivation and behavior?

Intrinsically motivated behaviors are behaviors that a person performs in order to feel competent and self-determining. *Extrinsic rewards* are rewards that comes from the external environment and decrease the recurrence of intrinsically motivated behavior.   pp. 370–372

What is humanistic theory?

Humanistic theory is an explanation of behavior that emphasizes the role of human qualities such as dignity, individual choice, and self-concept. Maslow's humanistic theory assumes that people are basically good and that they strive for *self-actualization,* the process of fulfilling one's potential for good to the greatest degree possible.   pp. 372–374

KEY TERMS: *cognitive theory,* p. 369; *intrinsically motivated behaviors,* p. 370; *extrinsic rewards,* p. 371; *humanistic theory,* p. 372; *self-actualization,* p. 372.

Emotion

What is emotion?

An *emotion* is a subjective response (feeling), usually accompanied by a physiological change, that is interpreted by the individual, readies the individual toward some action, and is associated with a change in behavior. Emotions are aroused internal states; they may occur in response to either internal or external stimuli. pp. 375–377

Describe the three main theories of emotion.

The James-Lange theory of emotion states that people experience physiological changes and interpret those changes as emotions. The Cannon-Bard theory states that when people experience emotions, two areas of the brain are stimulated simultaneously, one creating an emotional response and the other creating physiological change. According to the Schachter-Singer approach, people interpret physiological changes within specific contexts and infer emotions from these cues.   pp. 377–381

Do lie detectors work?

Many physiological changes are due to an increase in activity in the sympathetic branch of the autonomic nervous system. A polygraph device records these changes. However, not all people show marked autonomic nervous system changes when emotionally aroused. Thus, lie detector tests are subject to significant errors. p. 380

What are the basic emotional expressions?

Shaver showed that there are six emotions that most people display regardless of their culture: love, joy, anger, sadness, fear, and surprise. These six categories can overlap, and many other emotional states can be grouped under them.   pp. 383–384

KEY TERM: *emotion,* p. 375.

CONNECTIONS

If you are interested in...

The role of motivation in learning, memory, and intelligence, see ...

CHAPTER 5, p. 176

How an organism in a need state (for example, hungry), learns more quickly, and better.

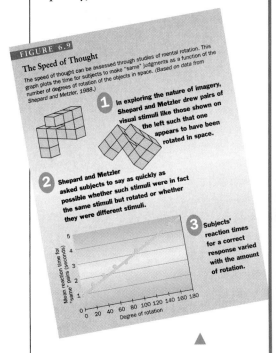

FIGURE 6.9

The Speed of Thought

The speed of thought can be assessed through studies of mental rotation. This graph plots the time for subjects to make "same" judgments as a function of the number of degrees of rotation of the objects in space. (Based on data from Shepard and Metzler, 1988.)

1. In exploring the nature of imagery, Shepard and Metzler drew pairs of visual stimuli like those shown on the left such that one appears to have been rotated in space.

2. Shepard and Metzler asked subjects to say as quickly as possible whether such stimuli were in fact the same stimuli but rotated or whether they were different stimuli.

3. Subjects' reaction times for a correct response varied with the amount of rotation.

CHAPTER 6, pp. 224–225

Ways to improve your memory.

CHAPTER 11, pp. 408–411

The relationship between innate intelligence and motivation to succeed on a test.

How thoughts influence motives and behavior, see ...

CHAPTER 5, pp. 190–191

How cognitive learning takes place without specific observable motives or reinforcement.

CHAPTER 12, pp. 448–454

How personality theorists are introducing thought into the equation of how a person develops and maintains a personality.

CHAPTER 15, pp. 553–556

The way treatment approaches to various disorders consider the role of motivation and a person's appraisal of situations in determining behavior.

The emotional responses people make to various situations, see ...

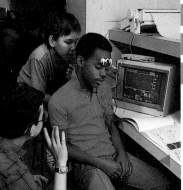

CHAPTER 4, pp. 137–141

How a person can learn to manipulate his or her body's response and subsequent emotions through techniques such as hypnosis and biofeedback.

CHAPTER 13, pp. 471–479, 486–489

How people's health can be affected by their overall emotional responses when faced with stressful situations.

CHAPTER 13, pp. 474–477

The interaction between physiological disorders and emotional responses.

11

Intelligence

onsider the experience of a former student of mine, Maria Helton, when she was in high school. Maria Helton waited anxiously as her high school adviser examined her school records. The adviser told Maria that her intelligence test score was well above average and high enough for the accelerated physics class. Students in that class were required to have an intelligence test score of 125 or more, a recommendation from the school psychologist, and permission from the instructor. The adviser noted that Maria excelled in creative pursuits and that she was keenly interested in science and had always received As in science courses. The adviser sought the approval of the physics teacher, and Maria was thrilled when the teacher granted her request. Through diligent studying, Maria managed to score consistently in the top third of the class on the course exams. Beyond this, her best talents were revealed when the physics class was divided into groups and assigned projects for the school science fair. Maria was chosen to lead her group, and she thought of an especially creative experiment that won her group first place.

Estimating intellectual capabilities is a complex task, but there is more to intelligence than test scores. Intelligence tests do not measure several mental characteristics that are important to success, such as motivation, creativity, and leadership skills. That is, they do not measure all of a person's special, unique capabilities.

Intelligence is difficult to measure because it is hard to define. People demonstrate effective and intelligent behavior in many ways, but not necessarily in all areas. Some people, for example, can write a complicated computer program but not a short story. Moreover, intelligence must be defined in terms of the situations in which people find themselves. Intelligent behavior for a dancer is very different from intelligent behavior for a scientist, and both types of behavior are different from intelligent behavior for a child with a learning disability.

No single test—such as a test of verbal ability, English literature, or math—is a clear measure of intelligence. Psychologists therefore use a variety of tests as well as other data—among them interviews, teacher evaluations, and writing and drawing samples—to evaluate an individual's current standing, to make predictions about future performance or behavior, and to offer suggestions for remedial work or therapy. In spite of their drawbacks, tests do have strong predictive value; for example, intelligence tests can generally predict academic achievement, and achievement tests can generally predict whether someone will profit from further training in a specific area.

In this chapter, we will measure individual differences in intelligence by way of theories, tests, and controversies. We also will examine two special populations with respect to intelligence: the gifted and the mentally retarded. We begin with the question: What is intelligence?

What Is Intelligence?

Why do two students who study the same material for the same amount of time get different scores on an examination? Why do some people succeed in medical school and others have difficulty finishing high school? One factor might be that one person is more intelligent than the other, and high intelligence enhances a person's chances of succeeding academically.

Intelligence is one of the most widely used yet highly debated concepts in science and everyday life. In 1921, a group of psychologists attempted to answer the question, What is intelligence? They could not come to an agreement. Sternberg and Detterman (1986), 65 years later, posed the same question to 25 respected researchers, but the researchers still could not reach agreement on this question.

Defining Intelligence

For some psychologists, intelligence is all mental abilities; for others, it is the basic general factor (*g factor*) necessary for all mental activity; for still others, it is a group of specific abilities (A. R. Jensen, 1987). J. F. Fagan III (1992) asserts that intelligence is not a trait or a faculty of the mind but instead is processing by the brain. Quinn McNemar (1964) contended, "All intelligent people know what intelligence is—it is the thing that the other guy lacks!" Nearly all psychologists agree that intelligence is a concept, not a thing (Howard, 1993). Most of the various definitions of intelligence all share certain key concepts:

▶ Intelligence is defined in terms of observable, objective behavior.

▶ Intelligence takes in both an individual's capacity to learn and the person's acquired knowledge.

▶ One sign of intelligence is the ability to adapt to the environment.

Perhaps the most widely accepted definition of intelligence is that of the well-known test constructor David Wechsler (1958, p. 7): "**Intelligence** is the aggregate or global capacity of the individual to act purposefully, to think rationally, and to deal effectively with the environment." In Wechsler's definition, intelligence is expressed behaviorally. It is the way people act and their ability to learn new things and to use previously learned knowledge. Most important, intelligence deals with people's ability to adapt to the environment. Wechsler's definition of intelligence has had far-reaching effects on how test developers devise intelligence tests and investigate the nature of intelligence.

Theories of Intelligence

Human beings show intelligent behavior in a variety of ways, and sometimes they choose not to act intelligently. We cannot say that all people are intelligent all of the time; nor can we specify the exact conditions under which people will exhibit their intelligence. This realization of individual differences in behavior has been a problem for psychology from its beginnings. E. B. Titchener, an early psychologist, studied the speed of subjects' mental processes and paid little or no attention to variations (differences) among the subjects. John Watson, known as the father of behaviorism, denied the relevance of individual differences for behaviorism.

Intelligence is evident in the ability of Lapp herders to adapt to their harsh environment.

However, researchers who examine intelligence focus on individual differences. In the early 1900s, a large body of data describing the characteristics thought to be involved in intelligence emerged. The data included information on age, race, gender, socioeconomic status, and environmental factors. From these data, researchers developed theories about the nature of intelligence and ways in which to test it. Today, the most influential approaches to the study of intelligence are Piaget's and Wechsler's theories, factor theories, Jensen's two-level theory, and the relatively new theory proposed by Sternberg.

Piaget's Theory. According to Jean Piaget, intelligence is a reflection of a person's adaptation to the environment, and intellectual development consists of changes in the way the individual accomplishes that adaptation. Every child goes through invariant (in terms of sequence) stages in intellectual development, with different levels of cognitive processes determining the types of intellectual tasks the child can accomplish. (We examined this developmental process in chapter 8.) Three-year-olds cannot learn calculus because they are not ready to perform the mental operations needed to grasp the necessary concepts. Piaget's theory of intellectual development focuses on the interaction of biological readiness and learning. In Piaget's view, neither predominates in the development of intelligence; they work together.

Intelligence: According to Wechsler, "the aggregate or global capacity of the individual to act purposefully, to think rationally, and to deal effectively with the environment."

Factor analysis: A statistical procedure designed to discover the mutually independent elements (factors) in any set of data.

Factor theory approach to intelligence: Theories of intelligence based on factor analysis, including those of Spearman and Thurstone.

Wechsler's Theory. David Wechsler viewed intelligence from the perspective of a test examiner. As one of the developers of a widely used and widely respected intelligence test (which we will examine later), Wechsler knew that tests were made up of many subparts, each measuring a different aspect of a person's functioning and resourcefulness. He therefore examined closely the components of intelligence and argued that intelligence tests involving spatial relations and verbal comprehension reveal little about someone's overall capacity to deal with the world. In Wechsler's view, psychologists need to remember that intelligence is more than simply mathematical or problem-solving ability; it is the broad ability to deal with the world.

Factor Theories. Factor theories of intelligence use a correlation technique known as *factor analysis* to discover what makes up intelligence. **Factor analysis** is a statistical procedure designed to discover the mutually independent elements (factors) in any set of data. Results of tests of verbal comprehension, spelling, and reading speed, for example, usually correlate highly, suggesting that some underlying attribute of verbal abilities determines a person's score on those three tests.

Early in this century, Charles E. Spearman (1863–1945) used factor analysis to show that intelligence consists of two parts: a general factor affecting all tasks and several specific factors necessary to perform specific tasks. According to Spearman, some amounts of both the general and the specific factors were necessary for the successful performance of any task. This basic approach to intelligence is known as the *two-factor theory of intelligence.*

Louis L. Thurstone (1887–1955) further developed Spearman's work by postulating a general factor analogous to Spearman's, as well as seven other factors, each representing a unique mental ability. His theory is known as the **factor theory approach to intelligence.** In it, he developed a computational scheme for sorting out the seven factors that he considered to be the abilities of human beings: verbal comprehension, word fluency, number facility, spatial visualization, associative memory, perceptual speed, and reasoning.

Thurstone's factor theory approach led to and culminated in J. P. Guilford's multifactor approach to intelligence testing. Guilford was one of the last students to work with Titchener, and his work focuses on individual mental abilities. He is concerned with developing a testable scheme of intelligence. Guilford gave large numbers of tests to diverse populations and found a whole range of factors that seemed appropriate in describing intelligence. He looked for a rational scheme of grouping them together and he eventually found it; he called it the *structure of intellect model.* According to Guilford (1967), human intellectual abilities and activities can be described in terms of three major dimensions: the mental operations performed, the content of those operations, and the resulting product of the operations (see Figure 11.1). Guilford's three-dimensional model produces 150 factors, 98 of which have been demonstrated experimentally, according to Guilford. These varieties of intelligence are often, but not always, independent of one another.

Guilford (1985) contends that more than a few scores are necessary for a correct assessment of an individual's intellectual abilities. He also asserts that intelligence should be defined as "a systematic collection of abilities or functions for processing information of different kinds in different forms" (p. 231). Research supports Guilford's theory and suggests that optimally weighted composite scores may best predict achievement, school learning, and work performance (Guilford, 1985). The multifactor approach is not universally accepted, however. Some researchers continue to assert that there is a general factor of intelligence and that it cannot be separated into distinct parts accounting for specific processes; rather, it accounts for success in both academic and work pursuits (Kranzler & Jensen, 1991; Ree & Earles, 1992).

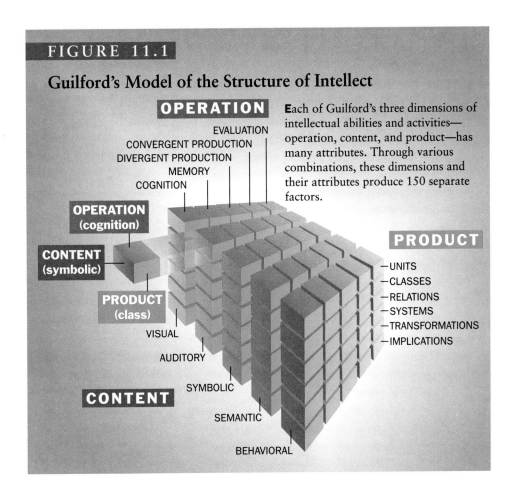

FIGURE 11.1

Guilford's Model of the Structure of Intellect

OPERATION

EVALUATION
CONVERGENT PRODUCTION
DIVERGENT PRODUCTION
MEMORY
COGNITION

OPERATION
(cognition)

CONTENT
(symbolic)

PRODUCT
(class)

VISUAL
AUDITORY
SYMBOLIC
SEMANTIC
BEHAVIORAL

CONTENT

PRODUCT

—UNITS
—CLASSES
—RELATIONS
—SYSTEMS
—TRANSFORMATIONS
—IMPLICATIONS

Each of Guilford's three dimensions of intellectual abilities and activities—operation, content, and product—has many attributes. Through various combinations, these dimensions and their attributes produce 150 separate factors.

Jensen's Two-Level Theory. Arthur Jensen approaches intelligence testing not from the viewpoint of a test constructor but from the viewpoint of a theoretician. A. R. Jensen (1969, 1970) suggests that intellectual functioning consists of associative abilities and cognitive abilities. *Associative abilities* enable us to connect stimuli and events; they require little reasoning or transformation. Questions testing associative abilities include the following: asking someone to repeat from memory a seven-digit number sequence or to name the first president of the United States. *Cognitive abilities,* on the other hand, deal with reasoning and problem solving. Solving word problems and defining new words or concepts are examples of cognitive ability tasks.

Jensen's idea is not new; even the founders of the testing movement suggested that different kinds of intellectual functioning are involved in intelligence. What is new is Jensen's claim that associative and cognitive abilities are inherited, adding more information to the nature versus nurture controversy about intelligence (discussed later in this chapter).

Sternberg's View. Robert J. Sternberg takes an information-processing view of intelligence. His view is triarchic, dividing intelligence into three dimensions: componential, experiential, and contextual. Other researchers have proposed that there are multiple types of intelligence. Gardner and Hatch (1989) present seven (see Table 11.1 on page 396). Like Gardner and Hatch, Sternberg believes in multiple types of intelligence, but he focuses on *how* people use their intellectual capacities. His aim

TABLE 11.1 *Gardner and Hatch's Seven Types of Intelligence*

Type of Intelligence	End State	Core Components
Logical-mathematical	Scientist Mathematician	Sensitivity to and capacity to discern logical or numerical patterns; ability to handle long chains of reasoning.
Linguistic	Poet Journalist	Sensitivity to the sounds, rhythms, and meanings of words; sensitivity to the the different functions of language.
Musical	Composer Violinist	Ability to produce and appreciate rhythm, pitch, and timbre; appreciation of the forms of musical expressiveness.
Spatial	Navigator Sculptor	Capacity to perceive the visual-spatial world accurately and to perform transformations on initial perceptions.
Bodily-kinesthetic	Dancer Athlete	Ability to control bodily movements and to handle objects skillfully.
Interpersonal	Therapist Salesperson	Capacity to discern and respond appropriately to the moods, temperaments, motivations, and desires of other people.
Intrapersonal	Person with detailed, accurate self-knowledge	Access to one's own feelings and the ability to discriminate among them and draw on them to guide behavior; knowledge of one's own strengths, weaknesses, desires, and intelligence.

Source: H. Gardner & T. Hatch, Multiple intelligences go to school: Educational implications of the theory of multiple intelligences, *Educational Researcher, 18* (8) (1989), 6.

is to relate a person's intelligence to the person's internal and external world. Sternberg's ideas, which are relatively new in the domain of intelligence theories, are presented next.

A New Theory of Intelligence

A psychologist in search of a field for important research with far-ranging practical implications could confidently choose intelligence and intelligence testing. Robert J. Sternberg of Yale University did—and his life has never been the same. Fully aware that traditional theories of intelligence are purported to be the building blocks of today's intelligence tests, Sternberg has criticized most of the widely used tests.

Sternberg (1986a) finds intelligence tests too narrow and contends that they don't adequately account for intelligence in the everyday world. He argues that researchers have focused for too long on how to measure intelligence, rather than on the more important questions: What is intelligence? How does it change? What can individuals do to enhance it? Sternberg reasons that some tests measure individual mental abilities while others measure the way the individual operates in the environment. He asserts that a solid theory of intelligence must account for both individual mental abilities and the ability of people to use their capabilities in the environment. Sternberg focuses not on how much intelligence people have but on how they use it.

New Ideas. Sternberg (1985, 1986a) has described the new "triarchic" theory of intelligence in his book *Beyond IQ*. The theory's three dimensions can be viewed

FIGURE 11.2

Sternberg's Triarchic Theory of Intelligence

CONTEXTUAL INTELLIGENCE

Ability to adapt to a changing environment and to shape one's world to optimize opportunities. Contextual intelligence deals with an individual's ability to prepare for problem solving in specific situations. For example, this Lapp herder in northern Scandinavia stuffs his boots with dried grasses for warmth.

EXPERIENTIAL INTELLIGENCE

Ability to formulate new ideas and combine unrelated facts. A test of experiential intelligence assesses a person's ability to deal with novel tasks in an automatic manner. Examples include learning to remember all the words containing the letter *t* in a particular paragraph and diagnosing a problem with an automobile engine.

COMPONENTIAL INTELLIGENCE

Ability to think abstractly, process information, and determine what needs to be done. Tasks that can be used to measure the elements of componential intelligence are analogies, vocabulary, and syllogisms.

as three subparts, or subtheories, each covering a different aspect of intelligence: contextual, experiential, and componential (see Figure 11.2).

The *contextual subtheory* deals with an individual's ability to use intelligence to prepare for problem solving in specific situations. This part of the triarchic theory focuses on how people shape their environments so their competencies can be best utilized. For example, an individual might organize problems in a meaningful way, perhaps by grouping similar items together. The contextual subtheory does not refer to any mental operations needed to carry out problem solving.

The *experiential subtheory* deals with the individual and the person's external world. According to this theory, a test measures intelligence if it assesses a person's ability to master the handling of novel tasks in an automatic manner. An example of such a task is learning to remember all the words containing the letter *T* in a particular paragraph. Initially, finding and remembering such words is tedious, but with much practice the task becomes automatic.

The *componential subtheory* is the glue that holds the other two subtheories together. It describes the mental mechanisms that underlie what are commonly considered intelligent behaviors. A component is a basic method of information processing. It includes a person's ability to determine the tasks that need to be done, to determine the order in which the subtasks should be undertaken, to analyze their subparts, to decide which information should be processed, and to monitor performance. Tasks that can be used to measure the elements of the componential subtheory are analogies, vocabulary, and syllogisms.

To be intelligent, a behavior has to involve all three subtheories of intelligence. For example, Sternberg suggests that eating is a behavior that is adaptive but does not show novelty or the use of nontrivial abilities. Similarly, turning on a light switch is adaptive and automatic but does not demonstrate the other components of intelligence. Few behaviors involve all three components, so Sternberg asserts that various tasks measure intelligence to a different extent.

Future Tests. Good predictors of a person's academic achievement must look at the person's knowledge of the world, in addition to the person's verbal comprehension and mathematical reasoning. Too often, children do poorly in school and society despite their obvious intellectual skills. They often do not know how to allocate their time and work effectively with other people. These skills need to be taught, because some students do not develop them on their own. As Ceci (1991) asserts, schools foster the learning of specific skills, not necessarily general problem-solving abilities. In addition, schools often foster specific ways of thinking about problems, but researchers and tests need to value alternative modes of thought and creativity. Sternberg and Gardner have teamed up on a research project to develop a curriculum to help students develop "practical intelligence."

Does Sternberg support the continued use of intelligence tests? Yes, if the tests are used prudently. Sternberg argues that existing tests do not do justice to the theories from which they evolved and that new tests examining all aspects of intelligent behavior need to be established. Existing tests measure some people's intelligence some of the time; however, they are often misleading. From Sternberg's viewpoint, new batteries of tests are needed to analyze fully the three basic subcomponents of intelligent behavior.

FOCUS

▶ Identify the key aspects of a good definition of *intelligence.* p. 392

▶ Wechsler and Sternberg criticize intelligence tests on what fundamental grounds? pp. 394–397

▶ Describe Sternberg's triarchic theory of intelligence. pp. 396–398

Principles of Test Development

Like Maria Helton, who was profiled at the beginning of this chapter, you probably have taken one or more intelligence tests during your school years. The results of these tests—often rendered in precise numbers—may have determined your educational curriculum from elementary school onward. Psychologists are among the first to admit that intelligence tests have shortcomings, and researchers continue to revise these tests to correct their inadequacies.

Intelligence tests have had a long and interesting history. In the late 19th and early 20th centuries, Alfred Binet (1857–1911), a Frenchman, became interested in psychology and began to study the relationship of physiology and behavior. He later employed Theodore Simon (1873–1961), a physician; their friendship and collaboration became famous.

Binet and Simon are known as the founders of the psychological testing movement. Interestingly, the first intelligence tests weren't developed for the general population. In 1904, Binet was commissioned to identify procedures for educating children in Paris who suffered from mental retardation. Binet was chosen for the task because he had been lobbying for action to help the schools. (Only recently had schools been made public, and disadvantaged children were doing poorly and dropping out.) In 1905, Binet and Simon set a goal to separate normal children from children with mental retardation. As Stagner (1988) suggests, this may have been the first government-sponsored psychological research. Binet and Simon were concerned only with measuring general intelligence in children, not with why some children were retarded in intellectual development or what their future might be.

Binet coined the phrase *mental age,* meaning the age level at which a child is functioning cognitively. He and Simon developed everyday tasks, such as counting, naming, and using objects, to determine mental age. The scale they developed is often considered the first useful and practical test of intelligence. Ninety years later, psychologists are still following some of their recommendations about how tests should be constructed and administered. In fact, one of the most influential intelligence tests in use today—the Stanford-Binet test—is a direct result of Binet and Simon's early tests.

Developing a Test

Imagine that you are a 7-year-old child taking an intelligence test. You come to the following question: Which one of the following tells you the temperature? Below the question are pictures of the sun, a radio, a thermometer, and a pair of mittens. Is the thermometer the only correct answer? Suppose there are no thermometers in your home, but you often hear the temperature given on radio weather reports. Or imagine that you "test" the temperature each morning by standing outside to feel the sun's strength, or that you know it's cold outside when your parents tell you to wear mittens. According to your experiences, any one of the answers to the question might be an appropriately intelligent response.

What Does a Test Measure? The ambiguity and cultural biases of this hypothetical test question illustrate the complexity of intelligence test development. In general, we say that a *test* is a standardized device for examining a person's responses to specific stimuli, usually questions or problems. Because there are many potential pitfalls in creating a test, psychologists follow an elaborate set of guidelines and procedures to make certain that their questions are properly constructed.

First, a psychologist must decide what the test is to measure. For example, will it measure musical ability or knowledge of geography, mathematics, or psychology? Second, the psychologist needs to construct and evaluate items for the test that will give examiners a reasonable expectation that success on the test will mean something. Third, the test must be standardized.

Standardization. **Standardization** is the process of developing a uniform procedure for administering and scoring a test and for establishing norms. **Norms** are the scores and corresponding percentile ranks of a large and representative sample of subjects from the population for which the test was designed. The **representative sample** is a sample of individuals who match the population with whom they are to be compared, with regard to key variables such as socioeconomic status and age (this idea is also discussed in Module A). Thus, a test designed for all college freshmen

Standardization: The process of developing a uniform procedure for administering and scoring a test, and for establishing norms.

Norms: The scores and corresponding percentile ranks of a large and representative sample of subjects from the population for which the test was designed.

Representative sample: A sample of individuals who match the population with whom they are to be compared, with regard to key variables such as socioeconomic status and age.

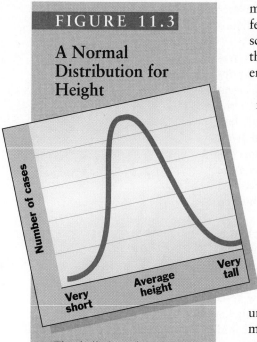

FIGURE 11.3

A Normal Distribution for Height

This bell-shaped curve shows the normal distribution of height in the general population. As with normal distributions of weight and even intelligence, very few people are represented at the extremes.

Normal curve: A bell-shaped graphic representation of data arranged so that a certain percentage of the population falls under each part of the curve.

Raw score: An examinee's score on a test which has not been transformed or converted in any way.

Standard score: A score that expresses an individual's position relative to the mean, based on the standard deviation.

Percentile score: A score indicating what percentage of the test population would obtain a lower score.

might be given to 2,000 freshmen, including an equal number of males and females 16 to 20 years old who were graduated from large and small high schools and from different areas of the country. Standardization ensures that there is a basis for comparing future test results with those of a standard reference group.

After a test is designed and administered to a representative sample, the results are examined to establish a norm score for different segments of the test population. Knowing how people in the representative sample have done allows psychologists and educators to interpret future test results properly. In other words, the scores of those in the sample serve as a reference point for comparing individual scores.

Normal Curve. Test developers generally plot the scores of the representative sample on a graph that shows how frequently each score occurs. On most tests, some people score very well, some score very poorly, and most score in the middle. When test scores are distributed that way, psychologists say the data are normally distributed or fall on a normal curve. A **normal curve** is a bell-shaped graphic representation of data arranged so that a certain percentage of the population falls under each part of the curve. As Figure 11.3 shows, most people are in the middle range, with a few at each extreme. Tests are often devised so that comparisons can be made of individual scores against a normal distribution. (Module A discusses the normal distribution in detail on pages 653–655.)

Scores. The simplest score on a test is the **raw score**—the number of correct answers not converted or transformed in any way. However, the raw score is seldom a true indicator of a person's ability. On many tests, particularly intelligence tests, raw scores need to be adjusted to take into account a person's age, gender, and grade level. Such scores are commonly expressed in terms of a **standard score**—a score that expresses an individual's position relative to that of others and based on the mean and how scores are distributed around it. If, for example, a 100-item intelligence test is administered to students in the 3rd and 11th grades, we would expect those in the 11th grade to answer more items correctly than those in the 3rd grade. To adjust for the differences, after the test each student's score is compared to the score typically achieved by other students at the same grade level. Thus, if 11th-graders typically answer 70 questions correctly, an 11th-grader who answers 90 questions correctly will have done better than most other students at that grade level. Similarly, if 3rd-graders usually answer 25 questions correctly, then a 3rd-grader who answers 15 questions correctly will have done worse than most other students at that grade level.

A standard score is generally a **percentile score**—a score indicating what percentage of the test population would obtain a lower score. If, for example, someone's percentile score is 84, then 84 percent of the people taking the test obtained a lower score than that person did.

Intelligence Quotients. Perhaps the oldest and most widely recognized test is the intelligence test. In the early 1900s, intelligence was measured by a simple formula. An intelligence quotient (IQ) was calculated by dividing a person's mental abilities, or mental age, by the person's chronological age and multiplying the result by 100. Mental ages of children were calculated from the number of correct answers on a series of test items; the higher the number, the higher the mental age. (See Figure 11.4 for examples.)

A problem with the traditional formula of mental age divided by chronological age times 100 is that, at each age, the intelligence test shows different variability.

FIGURE 11.4

How to Calculate an Intelligence Quotient

To calculate an IQ using the traditional formula, a person's mental age is divided by his or her chronological age, and the result is multiplied by 100. Three people's IQs are calculated here.

	RALPH	LUCINDA	SHEALY
Mental Age (MA)	6 years	15 years	15 years
Chronological Age (CA)	6 years	18 years	12 years
MA ÷ CA	6 ÷ 6 = 1	15 ÷ 18 = 0.83	15 ÷ 12 = 1.25
MA ÷ CA × 100	1 × 100 = 100	0.83 × 100 = 83	1.25 × 100 = 125
IQ	100	83	125

Young children are far more variable in their answers than are older children or adults; it is as if their intelligence were less stable, less repeatable, and more subject to change. This variability makes predictions and comparisons difficult. To simplify measures of IQ, psychologists and testers began using **deviation IQ**—a standard IQ test score for which the mean and standard deviation remain constant at all ages. (The standard deviation is a measure of variability or dispersion of scores—see pages 649–651 in Module A.) Thus, a child of 9 and an adolescent of 16, each with an IQ of 116, have the same position relative to others who have taken the same IQ test. Both are above the 84th percentile; that is, both scored better than 84 percent of all others their age who took the same IQ test.

Of all the achievements by psychologists in making tests useful, perhaps the most important is to ensure that tests are both reliable and valid. If a student obtains different scores on two versions (or forms) of the same test, which score is correct? Furthermore, does the test measure what it is supposed to measure and *only* that? We will now consider reliability and validity.

Reliability

Reliability refers to the consistency of test scores. **Reliability** is the ability of a test to yield the same score for the same individual through repeated testings. (The consistency of test scores assumes that the person is in the same emotional and physiological state at each time of administration of the test.) If a test's results are not consistent from one testing session to another, or for two comparable groups of people, meaningful comparisons are impossible.

There are several ways to determine whether a test is reliable. The simplest, termed *test-retest,* is to administer the same test to the same person on two or more

Deviation IQ: A standard IQ test score that has the same mean and standard deviation at all ages.

Reliability: The ability of a test to yield the same score for the same individual through repeated testings.

Validity: The ability of a test to measure only what it is supposed to measure.

occasions. If, for example, the person achieves a score of 87 one day and 110 another, the test is probably not reliable (see Figure 11.5). Of course, the person might have remembered some of the test items from one occasion to the next. To avoid that problem, testers use the *alternative-form method,* which involves giving two different versions of the same test. If the two versions test the same characteristic, differing only in the test items used, both should yield the same result. Another way to test reliability is to use the *split-half method,* which involves dividing a test into two parts; on a reliable test, the scores from each half yield similar, if not identical, results.

Even the most reliable test will not yield identical results each time it is taken; however, a good test will have a relatively small standard error of measurement. The *standard error of measurement* is the number of points by which a score varies because of imperfect reliability. Consider an IQ test that has a standard error of measurement of 3, for example. If someone scores 115 on that test, a practitioner can state with a high degree of confidence that the individual's real score is between 112 and 118—3 points above or below the obtained score.

Validity

If your psychology exam includes questions such as What is the square root of 647? and Who wrote *The Grapes of Wrath*? it is not a valid measure of your knowledge of psychology. That is, it is not measuring what it is supposed to measure. To be useful, a test must have not only reliability but also **validity**—the ability to measure only what it is supposed to measure and to predict only what it is supposed to predict.

Types of Validity. Content validity is a test's ability to measure the knowledge or behavior it is intended to measure. A test designed to measure musical aptitude should not include items that assess mechanical aptitude or personality characteristics. Similarly, an intelligence test should measure only intelligence, not musical training, cultural experiences, or socioeconomic status.

In addition to content validity, a test should have *predictive validity*—the ability to predict a person's future achievements with at least some degree of accuracy.

FIGURE 11.5

Test-Retest Reliability

In *test-retest reliability*, when people are given the same or a similar test on repeated occasions, their scores remain similar.

		HIGH-RELIABILITY TEST		LOW-RELIABILTY TEST	
		First Testing	Second Testing	First Testing	Second Testing
	 **Ralph**	92	90	92	74
	 **Lucinda**	87	89	87	96
	 **Shealy**	78	77	78	51

TABLE 11.2   *Types of Validity Used to Assess Tests*

Validity	Aspect Measured
Content validity	The extent to which a test reflects a sample of the actual behavior to be measured
Predictive validity	The extent to which a test can predict a person's behavior in some other setting
Face validity	The extent to which a test "looks" appropriate just from a reading of the items
Construct validity	The extent to which a test actually measures a particular trait (such as intelligence, anxiety, or musical ability)

However, critics of intelligence tests like to point out that test scores are not always accurate predictors of people's performance. Tests cannot take into account a high level of motivation or creative abilities. Nevertheless, many colleges rely on the Scholastic Aptitude Test (SAT) scores of high school students to predict their ability to do college-level work and thus use these scores to evaluate who should be accepted for admission. Two additional types of validity are *face validity,* the extent to which a test looks appropriate, and *construct validity,* the extent to which a test actually measures a particular trait. Table 11.2 shows four types of validity: content, predictive, face, and construct validity.

A Critique of Test Validity. There are five basic criticisms of—and defenses for—the validity of tests and testing. The first is that there is no way to measure intelligence because no clear, agreed-upon *definition of intelligence* exists. The defense against this argument is that, although different IQ tests seem to measure different abilities, the major tests have face validity. Face validity is the appropriateness of test items "on their face"—that is, their appropriateness to experts. Intelligence tests have face validity; they generally contain items requiring problem solving and rational thinking, which in white middle-class society are appropriate tests of intelligence.

The second criticism is that, because IQ test items usually consist of *learned information,* they reflect the quality of a child's schooling rather than the child's actual intelligence. The response to this challenge is that most vocabulary items on IQ tests are learned in the general environment, not in school; moreover, the ability to learn vocabulary terms and facts seems to depend on the ability to reason verbally.

The third criticism is that *school settings* may adversely affect IQ and other test scores, not only because tests are often administered inexpertly but also because of the halo effect (e.g., Crowl & MacGinitie, 1974). The **halo effect** is the tendency to allow one particular or outstanding characteristic about an individual to influence the evaluation of other characteristics. A test administrator can develop a positive or negative feeling about a person, a class, or a group of students that might influence the administration of tests or the interpretation of test scores (Nathan & Tippins, 1990). People who defend testing against this charge acknowledge that incorrectly administered tests are likely to result in inaccurate test scores, but they claim that this effect is less powerful than opponents think it is.

The two other criticisms of testing are less directly related to the issue of validity. One is that some people are *testwise.* These individuals make better use of their time than others do, guess the tester's intentions, and find clues in the test. Practice in taking tests improves these people's performance. The usual responses are that the

Halo effect: The tendency to let one of an individual's characteristics influence the evaluation of other characteristics.

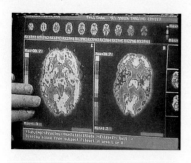

PET scans reveal that brains that work the hardest on intelligence tests (left) score lowest, while brains that work less (right) score highest. (Photo courtesy of CNN.)

items on IQ tests are unfamiliar even to experienced test takers and that the effects of previous practice are seldom or never evident on IQ tests.

The final criticism is that individuals' scores often depend on their *motivation to succeed* rather than on actual intelligence. Members of minority groups often do not have the same motivation to succeed as do members of the majority. Defenders of IQ tests agree that the motivation of examinees and their attitude toward tests are important; however, they deny that the IQ tests themselves influence motivation.

Critics of IQ tests are concerned with the interpretation of scores. They note that test scores without interpretation can foster narrow conceptions about students' ability in both students and teachers. One result is the neglect of talents and abilities unmeasured by such tests. This neglect may lead to an inappropriate career or a wrong placement in school.

Test Interpretation

Tests are generally made up of different subtests or subscales, each yielding a score. There may also be one general score for the entire test. All these scores require knowledgeable interpretation; that is, test scores must be given in a context that is meaningful to the person who receives the information, perhaps a parent or a teacher. Without such a context, the scores are little more than numbers.

Many intelligence tests provide a single IQ score. These tests, however, contain far more information than that single score. Consider one of the most popular IQ tests for children, the Wechsler Intelligence Scale for Children–Revised (WISC–R). In addition to an overall IQ score, the WISC–R test yields scores for verbal IQ, performance IQ (measuring visual-spatial ability, numerical ability, and other nonverbal abilities), and various other subtests.

Although single and multiple scores are useful in evaluating an individual accurately, global or overall IQ scores should be de-emphasized and test examiners should look instead at the components of the IQ score. The interpretation of test scores is the key to understanding IQs; without such interpretation, a single IQ score can be biased, inaccurate, or misleading.

FOCUS

▶ What is the fundamental assumption that underlies a representative sample?   p. 399

▶ Why is the normal curve an essential part of understanding the process of standardization?   pp. 399–400

▶ Why is validity such an essential part of the test process?   p. 402

▶ Which of the basic criticisms of and defenses for the validity of tests and testing have empirical research support?   p. 403

Three Important Intelligence Tests

What is the best intelligence test? What does it measure? Can you study for an intelligence test to get a higher score? As in other areas in science, theory leads to application; many intelligence theorists applied their theoretical knowledge to the development of IQ tests. The three tests we will examine here are all based on the theories of their developers; they are the Stanford-Binet Intelligence Scale, the Wechsler scales, and the Kaufman Assessment Battery for Children.

Stanford-Binet Intelligence Scale

Most people associate the beginning of intelligence testing with Alfred Binet and Theodore Simon. As noted earlier, in 1905 Binet collaborated with Simon to develop the Binet-Simon Scale. The original test was actually 30 short tests arranged in order of difficulty and consisting of such tasks as distinguishing food from nonfood and pointing to objects and naming them.

The Binet-Simon Scale was heavily biased toward verbal questions and was not well standardized. From 1912 to 1916, Lewis M. Terman revised the scale and developed an intelligence test now known as the Stanford-Binet Intelligence Scale. (*Stanford* refers to Stanford University, where the test was further developed.) A child's mental age (intellectual ability) is divided by the child's chronological age and multiplied by 100 to yield an intelligence quotient (IQ).

Decades of psychologists have used the original and revised versions of the Stanford-Binet scale. This test has traditionally been a good predictor of academic performance, and many of its simplest subtests correlate highly with one another. A new version of the Stanford-Binet Intelligence Scale, published in 1986, contains items that minimize gender and racial characteristics. It is composed of four major subscales and one overall IQ score, and it tests individuals aged 2 through 23.

The test administration time varies with the examinee's age, because the number of subtests given is determined by age. All examinees are first given a vocabulary test; and along with their age, this test determines the level at which all other tests begin. There are 15 possible subtests, varying greatly in content. Some require verbal reasoning, others quantitative reasoning, and still others abstract visual reasoning. In addition, there are tests of short-term memory. Each of the subtests consists of a series of levels, with two items at each level. The test begins with test items for each subscale at the entry level and continues until a higher level on each subscale is established (until a prescribed number of items are failed). (See Figure 11.6 on page 406 for a description of the new Stanford-Binet Intelligence Scale.)

Raw scores, determined by the number of items passed, are converted to a standard score for each age group. The new Stanford-Binet is a potent test; one great strength is that it can be used over a wide range of ages and abilities. Nonetheless, like all tests, it has limitations; one of its limitations is that examinees are not given the same battery of tests across age levels. This makes the comparison of individuals difficult (Sattler, 1992). However, the new Stanford-Binet scale correlates well with the old one, as well as with the WISC–R and the Kaufman Assessment Battery for Children (both of which are examined next).

Wechsler Scales

David Wechsler (1896–1981), a Rumanian immigrant who earned a PhD in psychology from Columbia University, was influenced by Charles Spearman and Karl Pearson, two English statisticians with whom he studied. In 1932, Wechsler was appointed chief psychologist at Bellevue Hospital in New York City; there, he began making history. In the 1930s, Wechsler recognized that the Stanford-Binet Intelligence Scale was inadequate for testing the IQ of adults. He also maintained that some of the Stanford-Binet items lacked validity. In 1939, Wechsler developed the Wechsler-Bellevue Intelligence Scale to test the IQ of adults. In 1955, the Wechsler Adult Intelligence Scale (WAIS) was published; it eliminated some technical difficulties of the Wechsler-Bellevue scale. The 1981 revision of the test is the WAIS–R.

Wechsler also developed the Wechsler Intelligence Scale for Children (WISC), which covers children aged 6 through 16. It was revised in 1974, becoming the WISC–R; the 1991 revision is the WISC–III. Table 11.3 on page 407 shows some typical subtests included in this scale. In 1967, the Wechsler Preschool and Primary Scale of Intelligence (WPPSI) was developed for children aged 4 through 6-1/2; it was revised in 1989 as the WPPSI–R.

The Wechsler scales group test items by content. For example, all the information questions are presented together, and all the arithmetic problems are presented

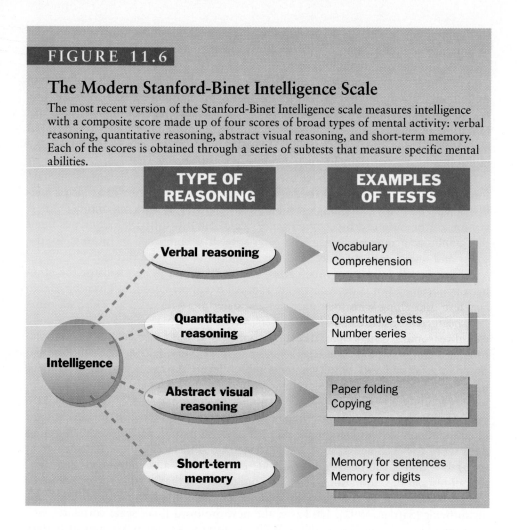

FIGURE 11.6

The Modern Stanford-Binet Intelligence Scale

The most recent version of the Stanford-Binet Intelligence scale measures intelligence with a composite score made up of four scores of broad types of mental activity: verbal reasoning, quantitative reasoning, abstract visual reasoning, and short-term memory. Each of the scores is obtained through a series of subtests that measure specific mental abilities.

TYPE OF REASONING	EXAMPLES OF TESTS
Verbal reasoning	Vocabulary Comprehension
Quantitative reasoning	Quantitative tests Number series
Abstract visual reasoning	Paper folding Copying
Short-term memory	Memory for sentences Memory for digits

Intelligence

together. The score on each subtest is calculated and converted to a standard (or scaled) score, adjusted for the subject's age. The scaled scores allow for a comparison of scores across age levels. Thus an 8-year-old's scaled score of 7 is comparable to an 11-year-old's scaled score of 7.

The Wechsler scales have been well researched; thousands of studies have been conducted to assess their reliability and validity. They are valid cross-culturally (Insua, 1983), for special education students (Covin & Sattler, 1985), for learning disabled students (Clarizio & Veres, 1984), and for populations of maladjusted individuals (Eppinger et al., 1987).

Kaufman Assessment Battery for Children

Many intelligence tests have been criticized for being biased; some of their questions are geared toward the white middle-class male experience. Psychologists Alan and Nadeen Kaufman contend that their Kaufman Assessment Battery for Children (K-ABC) uses tasks that tap the experience of all people, regardless of background. A memory task in the K-ABC, for example, might have a subject look at a picture of a face and a few moments later pick it out from among pictures of other faces.

The K-ABC was designed especially for assessment, intervention, and remediation of school problems. School psychologists, who are the primary users of the K-

TABLE 11.3

Typical Subtests on the WISC–R

VERBAL TEST		PERFORMANCE TEST	
Subtest	Type of Task	Subtest	Type of Task
Information	Given a question, recall a general fact that has been acquired in both formal and informal school settings.	Picture completion	Given an incomplete picture, point out the part that is missing.
Similarities	Given two ideas, use another concept in describing how both are alike.	Picture arrangement	Given a series of pictures that tell a story, put them in the right sequence.
Arithmetic	Given a word problem, solve it without pencil and paper.	Block design	Given a picture of a block design, use real blocks to reproduce it.
Digit span	Given an orally presented string of digits, recall them.	Object assembly	Given a jigsaw-type puzzle, put the pieces together to form a complete object.
Vocabulary	Given a vocabulary word, define it.	Coding	Given a key that matches numbers to geometric shapes, fill in a blank form with the shapes that go with the numbers.
Comprehension	Given a question requiring practical judgment and common sense, answer it.		

ABC, act as evaluators and consultants to families and schools, helping them to set and achieve appropriate educational goals.

The K-ABC consists of four global scales. Three measure mental processing abilities (sequential processing, simultaneous processing, and a composite of the two); the fourth assesses achievement. The Kaufmans believe that the sequential- and simultaneous-processing scales measure abilities synonymous with intelligence— that is, the ability to process information and the ability to solve problems (Kaufman, 1983). A sequential task requires the manipulation of stimuli in sequential order. For example, a child, might be asked to repeat a series of digits in the order in which the examiner presented them. A simultaneous-processing task involves organizing and integrating many stimuli at the same time. Here, a child might be asked to recall the placement of objects on a page that was presented only briefly.

The K-ABC assesses how well and in what way an individual solves problems on each task, minimizing the role of language and of acquired facts and skills. A separate part of the test, the achievement scale, involves demonstrating such skills as reading comprehension, letter and word identification, and computation. These tasks resemble those typically found on other IQ tests; they are heavily influenced by language experience and verbal ability.

Although early research on the K-ABC shows it to be a promising IQ test (German, 1983; Zins & Barnett, 1983), it is not without its critics. A. R. Jensen (1984) and Sternberg (1984) have been especially critical of the assumptions on which the

FOCUS

▶ What is the chief difference between the Kaufman Assessment Battery for Children (K-ABC) and the Stanford-Binet and Wechsler scales?   pp. 404–407

K-ABC is founded, particularly the ideas about sequential-processing abilities. Kaufman (1984) argues that his test is valid and reliable and that it is evolving. He wants it to be an alternative to the WISC–III and the Stanford-Binet scales. Many practitioners consider it child-oriented and easy to administer. Final evaluations of the K-ABC are still probably a decade away.

Testing Controversy

In 1986, a federal court in California upheld a 1979 ruling barring the administration of IQ tests to African-American students in the state. According to the judge who made the original ruling, the tests are culturally biased and therefore discriminate against African Americans for "special education" purposes; the result is a disproportionate number of African Americans being assigned to classes for the mentally retarded. The California court case illustrates the political, cultural, and scientific issues involved in the debate over what intelligence tests actually measure. Minority groups have joined psychologists and educators in challenging the usefulness of testing in general and of intelligence testing in particular.

The complexity of the issues related to testing has caused researchers to attempt to address several key issues: Are there cultural biases in tests? To what extent are tests free from educational influences? How do genetics and child-rearing practices affect IQ scores? Does family size and composition affect IQ scores? Finally, are there ethnic, gender, or age differences in IQ scores; and if there are, what do they mean? All of these issues are addressed in this section.

Cultural Biases?

A major argument against IQ testing is that the tests are culturally biased and thus are used to discriminate against individuals who do not come from the test makers' environments, which are usually white, male, middle-class, and suburban. A test item or subscale is considered culturally biased when, with all other factors held constant, its content is more difficult for members of one group than for those of other groups. To understand how a test can be culturally biased, imagine that the child of an impoverished migrant worker is given the temperature problem posed earlier. If the child is unfamiliar with thermometers and radios, the child might choose the sun as the best answer. On the basis of experiments that have shown some tests to be culturally or racially biased, some educators and parents have urged a ban on tests in all public schools, especially IQ tests. They argue that some groups of individuals who are not exposed to the same education and experiences as the middle-class group for whom the tests were designed are bound to perform less well.

Clearly, those who interpret IQ tests must be particularly sensitive to any potential biases. Nonetheless, although researchers find differences among the IQ scores of various racial and cultural groups, they find no consistent and conclusive evidence of bias in the tests themselves. Differences between siblings are usually as great as differences between racial groups; there is as great a variability between individuals as between groups. That IQ tests systematically discriminate in terms of race is not true. Biases can exist, but they do not exist in such tests as the WISC–R; and well-respected psychologists support this view (Sattler, 1992; Vernon, 1979). A key to any bias that exists on an IQ test is how the results are used (a point to be examined shortly). When cultural differences occur, they can be eliminated by better test construction, but this still does not explain the meaning of those differences (Helms, 1992).

Culture and Testing: Conclusions

IQ tests cannot predict or explain all types of intellectual behavior. They are derived from a small sample of a restricted range of cognitive activities. Intelligence can be demonstrated in many ways; an IQ test tells little about someone's ability to be flexible in new situations and to function in mature and responsible ways. Intelligence tests reflect many aspects of people's environments—how much individuals are encouraged to express themselves verbally, how much time they spend reading, and the extent to which parents have urged them to engage in academic pursuits (e.g., Barrett & Depinet, 1991).

In the past 2 decades, the public, educators, and psychologists have scrutinized the weaknesses of IQ tests and have attempted to eliminate bias in testing by creating better tests and establishing better norms for comparison. The tests have attempted to control the influences of different cultures (Helms 1992). However, even the courts acknowledge the complexity of the issues involved in tests and testing (Elliott 1987). In isolation, IQ scores mean little. Information about an individual's home environment, personality, socioeconomic status, and special abilities is crucial to understanding intellectual functioning.

The same argument must be made about the SAT, which is widely criticized as being a poor predictor of success in college. However, some researchers claim that, in combination with high school grades, it is a good predictor of success in college for students from different cultural groups and income levels (R. M. Kaplan, 1982). Interestingly, despite its good predictive ability, the SAT has undergone a major revision. The new version has fewer culturally biased items and a greater emphasis on reading comprehension. This is an important change, since performance on reading comprehension tests can sometimes be above chance levels, even when examinees do not read passages (Katz et al., 1990). The Diversity box on page 410 further examines cultural differences in testing.

Critics of standardized testing have been vocal and persuasive, and their arguments cannot be discounted. Research into test construction, test validation, and the causes of differences among individuals' scores continues. Overall, experts believe that these tests, despite their flaws, adequately measure the most important elements of intelligence (Snyderman & Rothman, 1987). The components of tests, including their subscales and specific questions, not only help researchers evaluate their validity but also help distinguish the elements most affected by nature from those most affected by nurture. Table 11.4 on page 411 summarizes some misconceptions about intelligence tests and testing.

Nature or Nurture?

Psychologists have long recognized that both the genetic heritage established even before birth (nature) and people's life experiences (nurture) play an important role in intelligence. Researchers have often used child-rearing studies to help unravel the key variables. In a classic environmental study, a researcher administered IQ tests to children reared in different communities in the Blue Ridge Mountains, an isolated area 100 miles west of Washington, DC (Sherman & Key, 1932). Most of the adults in each community were illiterate, and communication with the outside world was limited. The investigators concluded that lack of language training and school experience accounted for the children's poor scores on standardized tests, particularly on

DIVERSITY

Cultural Differences Are Small and Narrowing

Cultural differences, particularly between African Americans and whites, in IQ scores, SAT scores, and other measures of achievement or ability are narrowing. This may be due to a generation of desegregation, more equal opportunities under the law, federal intervention programs for the culturally disadvantaged, socioeconomic factors that affect home environments, or other factors (L. V. Jones, 1984). Jones suggests that the more minorities enroll in mathematics courses in high school, the better they will do on achievement tests. Consistent with this reasoning is a cross-cultural study comparing Mexican Americans with caucasian Americans; it showed that with acculturation to U.S. society, the Mexican-American IQ score differences disappeared (Gonzales & Roll, 1985). Further, differences within groups are often greater than differences between groups, a fact that minimizes the importance of between-group differences (Zuckerman, 1990).

The relative importance of three factors in creating differences between groups has yet to be established. The first is the possibility of a genetic component. The second is that racial and ethnic minorities are disproportionately represented among those who live in culturally impoverished areas. The third is that IQ tests may contain a built-in bias against members of racial and ethnic minorities. Perhaps more important than any of these three factors, however, is the recognition that the differences among individuals of a particular racial or ethnic group are greater than the differences among the various groups.

People from different cultures and backgrounds differ—there is no doubt about that. A cross-cultural study of 320 Israeli children whose parents had emigrated from Europe, Iraq, North Africa, or Yemen showed that the four groups tended to exhibit four different patterns of cognitive abilities (Burg & Belmont, 1990). Differing patterns of cognitive ability are not surprising; cultures vary considerably in their worldview and in their conception of time, space, people, and what is important. Thus, historical and cultural background have a significant effect on people's patterns of mental ability. When Flynn (1987) showed that IQ scores are changing around the world, he concluded that schooling, educational emphasis, and family values in specific cultures were affecting test scores—not that people in certain cultures were getting smarter. Schooling clearly fosters the cognitive processes that contribute to high IQ scores (Ceci, 1991).

One conclusion is becoming strikingly clear: *Rather than measuring innate intellectual capacity, IQ tests measure the degree to which people adapt to the culture in which they live.* In many cultures, to be intelligent is to be socially adept. In Western society, the more schooling you have, the higher your IQ score is likely to be (Ceci, 1991). Moreover, the extent to which a person's IQ score is changeable is far more important than the amount of intelligence the person may have inherited. All individuals have special capabilities (both intellectual and other), and how those capabilities are regarded depends on the social environment. Being a genius in Africa may mean being a fine hunter or a good storyteller; in the United States, it may mean being an astute and aggressive sales manager. In the United States, however, the concept of giftedness is too often attached to high academic achievement alone. This limited conception of intelligence is one reason educators in some settings are placing less emphasis on IQ scores.

Researchers today assert that the typical intelligence test is too limited because it does not take into account the many forms of intelligent behavior that occur outside the testing room (Frederiksen, 1986; Sternberg & Wagner, 1993). Frederiksen suggests that real-life problem situations might be used to supplement the usual psychological tests. This view is consistent with Sternberg's (1986a) idea that intelligence must be evaluated on many levels, including the environment in which a person lives and works. If this type of evaluation were to take place, IQ scores could become better at predicting both academic and occupational success (Barrett & Depinet, 1991). Yet, for all the limitations of IQ scores, research continues to show that they are still the best overall predictor of job performance (Ree & Earles, 1992 and 1993).

---

tests involving calculations and problem solving. Moreover, because the IQ scores of the children were highest in communities with the best social development and lowest in communities with the poorest social development, the researchers concluded that the children's IQs developed only as their environment demanded development. Angoff (1988) has asserted that children from impoverished homes can

TABLE 11.4

Some Misconceptions about Intelligence Tests and Testing

MISCONCEPTION	REALITY
Intelligence tests measure innate intelligence.	IQ scores measure some of an individual's interactions with the environment; they never measure only innate intelligence.
IQs never change.	People's IQs change throughout life, but especially from birth through age 6. Even after this age, significant changes can occur.
Intelligence tests provide perfectly reliable scores.	Test scores are only estimates. Every test score should be reported as a statement of probability, such as: There is a 90 percent chance that the child's IQ falls between X and Y.
Intelligence tests measure all we need to know about a person's intelligence.	Most intelligence tests do not measure the entire spectrum of abilities related to intellectual behavior. Some stress verbal and nonverbal intelligence but do not adequately measure other areas, such as mechanical skills, creativity, and social intelligence.
A battery of tests can tell us everything we need to know in making judgments about a person's competence.	No battery of tests can give a complete picture of any person. A battery can only illuminate various areas of functioning.

Source: Adapted from Sattler, 1988.

Intelligence Tests

CANNOT PREDICT

Musical Ability

CAN PREDICT

Academic Ability

achieve more on IQ tests, the SAT, and other standardized tests if "cognitive training begins early in life and continues for an extended period . . . and is carried out in a continuously supportive and motivating atmosphere" (p. 719).

However, it is important to remember that tests can be constructed with a bias toward urban or rural children. Myra Shimberg (1929) standardized two tests on urban and rural schoolchildren in New York State. Each test contained 25 questions. The examples in Table 11.5 on page 412 show clearly that they test for different kinds of information. Shimberg found that rural children scored significantly lower than urban children on Test A but higher than urban children on Test B. The difference between the scores of the two groups was in part a function of the tests themselves, not of any real difference in the children's intellectual capacities. Test A was biased toward urban children, Test B toward rural children.

TABLE 11.5   *Tests Can Be Constructed to Have a Bias*

Test A	Test B
1. What are the colors in the American flag?	1. Of what is butter made?
2. Who is the president of the United States?	2. Name a vegetable that grows above ground.
3. What is the largest river in the United States?	3. Why does seasoned wood burn more easily than green wood?
4. How can banks afford to pay interest on the money you deposit?	4. About how often do we have a full moon?
5. What is the freezing point of water?	5. Who was president of the U.S. during the World War?
6. What is a referendum in government?	6. How can you locate the pole star?

Few would debate the idea that the environment has a potent effect on intellectual tasks. But to unravel the fixed genetic component from the environmental impact has required some sophisticated research and statistical techniques. Such unraveling has often taken place in studies of adopted children, who are raised apart from their biological parents because of poverty, death, or unwanted pregnancies. Intelligence test scores and other measures of cognitive ability are examined so as to compare the adopted person's score with that of biological parents, adoptive parents, biological siblings, and adoptive siblings. The goal is to see whether scores later in life more greatly resemble those of biological relatives or adoptive relatives.

One type of adoptive study compares the intellectual abilities of adopted children with the abilities of their adoptive parents (Horn, 1983). Many of these studies use identical twins who were separated at birth; because the twins share the same genetic heritage, any differences in IQ scores *must* be the result of environmental influences. A French adoption study showed a 14-point increase in IQ scores in children whose biological parents were unskilled workers but whose adoptive parents were in a higher socioeconomic class (Schiff et al., 1982). This study demonstrated that the environment has a strong effect on intellectual abilities. Other data from adoptive homes, however, strongly suggest that the biological mother's IQ score has a more important effect than the adoptive home environment on a child's IQ score (Bouchard et al., 1990; McGue & Bouchard, 1989).

There are volumes of data from child-rearing studies attempting to demonstrate the genetic and environmental components of intelligence. In general, research shows that, to a great extent, genetics and environment contribute equally to IQ scores, especially in certain parts of an IQ test (Pedersen, Plomin, Nesselroade, & McClearn, 1992.)

The nature versus nurture controversy is by no means resolved. Each year, new data emerge to lend support to one side or the other in establishing intellectual abilities. However, to frame nature and nurture as a debate with a winner and loser is a mistake; the two work together. There is a myth that if a behavior or characteristic is genetic, it cannot be changed. However, genes do not fix behavior; instead they establish a range of possible reactions. Environments determine whether the full range of the genetic potential will be expressed.

Figure 11.7 summarizes the correlations between IQ scores and child-rearing environments for both related and unrelated children in different studies. If genetics were the sole determinant of IQ scores, the correlation for identical twins should be 1.0 whether they are reared together or apart. Also, the correlation should not decrease when any two siblings (twins or not) are brought up apart from each other. However, identical twins raised together and apart do not have identical IQ scores—although their scores are similar (Bouchard et al., 1990). Bouchard and colleagues conclude that about half of the similarities between identical twins can be accounted for by genetics—not the 70 to 80 percent that some researchers claim. This finding lends strong support to the idea that the environment must play an equally important role in determining IQ scores (e.g., F. W. Johnson, 1991). Interestingly, most of

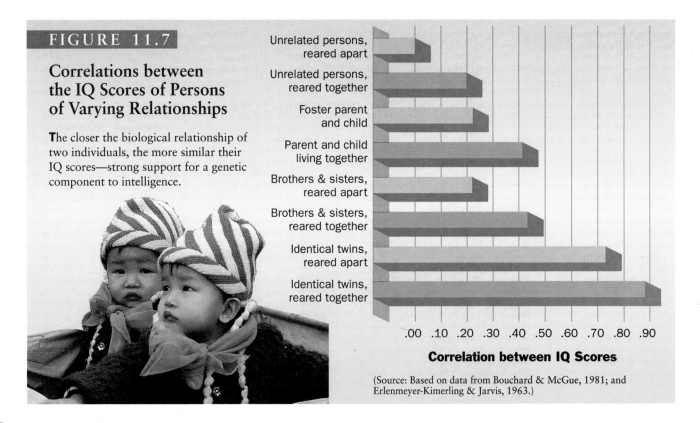

FIGURE 11.7

Correlations between the IQ Scores of Persons of Varying Relationships

The closer the biological relationship of two individuals, the more similar their IQ scores—strong support for a genetic component to intelligence.

Correlation between IQ Scores

.00 .10 .20 .30 .40 .50 .60 .70 .80 .90

(Source: Based on data from Bouchard & McGue, 1981; and Erlenmeyer-Kimerling & Jarvis, 1963.)

the data about IQ scores and the role of genetics come from studies of identical twins and their performance early in life; only recently have data been emerging from studies of older identical twins who have lived full lives and had a wide range of experiences (Pedersen et al., 1992).

Family Structure

An inspiring English teacher, a stimulating television series, or a neighbor with a chemistry set may be enough to create differences among the IQ scores of siblings (McCall, 1983). Although siblings are often very similar to one another on a number of dimensions, they are also very different from one another (Dunn & Plomin, 1990). Few doubt that genetic influences are important; the real issue is how important the nonshared environment is (Plomin & Neiderhiser, 1991). Although siblings share a genetic heritage, they experience the same or a similar environment differently (Dunn, 1992). Since a number of variables create differences among brothers and sisters, it is easy to see why it is very difficult to estimate the effects of such variables among racial or ethnic groups.

Belmont and Marolla (1973) found that children from large families score lower on intelligence tests than do those from smaller families. They suggest that the third and fourth children have a less optimal intellectual environment than does the first or second child. In a later study, Zajonc and Markus (1975) theorized that, within a family, the intellectual growth of every member depends on the other members. Moreover, they suggested that the overall level of intellectual performance is likely to decrease for each new member of a family. Consider what happens when two adults have a child. The intellectual climate at home becomes that of two mature adults and one child. Imagine that each adult is assigned 30 units and the child is assigned 0 units. The average level of intellectual ability in the home drops from 30 to 20. With a second child, the intellectual average decreases again to 15.5. (See Table 11.6 on page 414 for the calculations.)

TABLE 11.6

The Zajonc-Markus Model of Intellectual Climate in the Home

Year of Birth of Child	Number of Children	VALUE OF INTELLECTUAL CLIMATE	
		Formula	Average Number of Units
1976	1	$\dfrac{\text{Mother (30) + Father (30) + Baby (0)}}{\text{Number in family (3)}}$	= 20.0
1978	2	$\dfrac{\text{Mother (30) + Father (30) + First Child (2)* + Baby (0)}}{\text{Number in family (4)}}$	= 15.5
1980	3	66 ÷ 5	13.2
1982	4	72 ÷ 6	12.0
1984	5	80 ÷ 7	11.4
1986	6	90 ÷ 8	11.3
1988	7	102 ÷ 9	11.3
1990	8	116 ÷ 10	11.6
1992	9	132 ÷ 11	12.0
1994	10	150 ÷ 12	12.5

*This example assumes that for each 2 years of life, a child is credited with 2 units toward the intellectual climate in the home.

Because family size has decreased in the past 2 decades and the spacing between children has increased, Zajonc and Markus predicted that the declining trend in SAT scores that began in the late 1960s would be reversed. In fact, SAT scores did decrease from 1973 to 1979 and then rose from 1980 to 1985. Zajonc (1986) claimed his model predicted the turnaround. His predictions have been confirmed in other cultures as well (Wilson, Mundy-Castle, & Panditji, 1990). However, other researchers assert that the model makes wrong predictions and is based on wrong assumptions (Flynn, 1988; Rodgers, 1988).

Keep in mind that the family size model is a statistical one; Zajonc acknowledges that it will not hold true for all individuals and all families. Even when it does apply, the effects are small; and many researchers discount its importance (e.g., Sattler, 1992). Furthermore, the researchers point out that other important factors, such as increased spacing between the birth of children, can minimize the negative effects. Large families also may contribute to the growth of individual members in areas other than intelligence by nurturing social competence, moral responsibility, and ego strength.

Gender Differences

Remember Maria? She excelled at science, and her adviser suggested that she take an accelerated physics class. Was Maria's success in science genetically based? As a girl, was she more analytical? Are girls better than boys at some tasks and boys better than girls at others, or are they equal?

Many psychologists believe there are gender differences in verbal ability, with girls exceeding boys in most verbal tasks in the early school years. However, at least some of the differences have been due to the cultural expectations of parents and teachers. For example, parents and teachers have long encouraged boys to engage in spatial, mechanical tasks. Two interesting events have occurred in the past 2 decades, though. First, parents have been encouraging both girls and boys to acquire math, verbal, and spatial skills; that is, there has been less gender role stereotyping recently. Second, the observed cognitive differences between boys and girls have been diminishing each year. Referring to girls catching up to boys in mathematical abilities, Rosenthal and Ruben (1982, p. 711) stated, "We can say that whatever the reason, in these studies females appear to be gaining in cognitive skill relative to males faster than the gene can travel!"

It turns out that the old consensus about gender differences is at least exaggerated and at most simply wrong. Hyde and Linn (1988) examined 165 research studies on gender differences in verbal ability; these studies had tested a total of 1,418,899 subjects. Although Hyde and Linn found a gender difference in favor of females, it was so small that they claim it is not worth mentioning. They further argue that more refined tests and theories of intelligence are needed to examine any gender differences that might exist. The differences found today exist only in certain special populations. For example, among the very brightest mathematics students, boys continue to outscore girls (Kimball, 1989). But these too may have a basis in cultural expectations (Jacklin, 1989). In general, it is fair to say that differences between the test scores of males and females are disappearing and that this change has been occurring in a number of cultures (A. Feingold, 1988b; Lummis & Stevenson, 1990).

An outcome of Hyde and Linn's findings is the realization that since verbal ability tests provide gender-unbiased measures of cognitive ability, they should be used to select students for academic programs. Selection procedures for academic programs are especially important when special students, such as the gifted, are being considered. If you had to design a series of selection procedures for a high school, a college, or a program for gifted students, what procedures would you choose?

Stability of Intelligence Test Scores

Nearly every American has taken an intelligence test at some time. Was the test you took in the second grade a good predictor of your academic ability when you were a sophomore in high school, or should you have been retested? Does an IQ score remain stable over a long period of time?

Early examinations of IQ score stability showed that the IQ scores of infants did not correlate well with their IQ scores when they were school aged (Bayley, 1949). Researchers quickly realized that it is not possible to measure the same capabilities in infants that can be measured in older children and adults. Further, correlations of the IQ scores of school-age children and adults show that such scores can change, sometimes substantially; yet some research indicates that certain predictions from infant to school-age IQ can be made (DiLalla et al., 1990). In general, psychologists have shown that intelligence and achievement test scores at first increase with age, then level off in adulthood.

What about the IQ scores of adults? Do IQ scores remain stable throughout adulthood? The results of a 40-year IQ study showed that, in general, the intellectual functioning of men increased a bit around age 40 and gradually declined to earlier levels when the men were in their 50s (Schwartzman et al., 1987). Despite the passage of 40 years, cognitive performance remained relatively stable. IQ scores and aging are a complicated issue because some aspects of the scores decrease with age

Recent research has uncovered subtle biases in our public schools that favor boys over girls, especially in math and science. (Photo courtesy of CNN.)

FOCUS

▶ With respect to intelligence testing, what is the fundamental issue in the nature versus nurture controversy? p. 409

▶ What is the evidence to show that cultural variables affect test scores and the gender differences that sometimes appear with them?   p. 410

▶ If IQ tests do not examine innate ability, what do the tests measure?   p. 411

▶ What conclusion about nature versus nurture can be drawn when correlations between IQ scores and child-rearing environments for both related and unrelated children are examined?   pp. 411–412

and others do not. For example, performance-based portions of IQ tests tend to show a decrease with age, but verbal-based portions do not. In addition, not everyone shows age-related IQ declines; people who continue their education throughout their lives show relatively small decreases.

Ample evidence now exists to confirm that IQ scores remain relatively stable once subjects reach adulthood. However, the scores of infants and children are so prone to change that they are not reliable predictors of later IQ scores. Of course, a child who achieves a high score on an IQ test at age 9 is likely to do well at age 18—perhaps better. The data show enough fluctuation, though, especially at younger ages, to make predictions uncertain.

Giftedness and Mental Retardation

American society is oriented toward looking for, testing, and educating special or exceptional children. As early as the first weeks of the first grade, most students take some kind of reading readiness test; by the end of the fourth grade, they are usually classified and labeled as to their projected future development, again largely on the basis of tests. The term *exceptional* refers to people who are gifted as well as to those who suffer from learning disabilities, physical impairments, and mental retardation.

Children often display their intellectual development in their use of language. For example, a child who learns to read at age 3 or who can do multiplication at age 4 is obviously bright, whereas a child who has not learned to differentiate colors or simple shapes on entering first grade is obviously showing slower intellectual development than other children.

Giftedness

Gifted individuals represent one end of the continuum of intelligence and talent. However, exceptional ability is not limited to cognitive skills. Most 6-year-olds enrolled in a ballet class will probably show average ability; dance teachers report that only an occasional child has a natural ability for dance. In the same way, many children and adults learn to play the piano, but few excel. Over a wide range of behaviors, some people excel in a particular area but are only average in other areas.

The phenomenon of gifted children has been recognized and discussed for centuries. Some gifted children, like Mozart, display their genius musically. Others display it in science; many great scientists made their most important theoretical discoveries very early in their careers. Although there is no universally accepted definition of *giftedness* (just as there is no universally agreed-upon definition of *intelligence*), one was given in section 902 of the federal government's Gifted and Talented Children's Act of 1978:

> The term *gifted and talented* means children, and whenever applicable, youth who are identified at the preschool, elementary, or secondary level as possessing demonstrated or potential abilities that give evidence of high performance responsibility

in areas such as intellectual, creative, specific academic or leadership ability, or in the performing or visual arts and who by reason thereof require services or activities not ordinarily provided by the school.

Thus, gifted children may have superior cognitive, leadership, or performing arts abilities. Moreover, they require special schooling that goes beyond the ordinary classroom. Without it, these children may not realize their potential.

Even though the federal government acknowledges the need for special education for gifted individuals, states and communities bear the major financial burden (about 92 percent) of their education. Some states—including California, Pennsylvania, and Illinois—spend more per year than the federal government on educating gifted and talented students. Nearly every state has a special program for the gifted; however, some school systems have none and others allocate special instruction only in brief periods or to small groups. Some systems provide special schools for children with superior cognitive abilities, performing talents, or science aptitude. Most do not offer gifted programs for all grades (Reis, 1989). However, the special needs of gifted students (and of those suffering from mental retardation—considered next) should not be addressed only 1 day a week or only in grades 1 through 6.

Mental Retardation Defined

Mental retardation covers a wide range of behaviors, from slow learning to severe mental and physical impairment. Many people with mental retardation are able to cope well with their environment. Most learn to walk and to feed and dress themselves; many learn to read and are able to work. In 1992, the American Association on Mental Retardation adopted a new formal definition of mental retardation:

> **Mental retardation** refers to substantial limitations in present functioning. It is characterized by significantly subaverage intellectual functioning, existing concurrently with related limitations in two or more of the following applicable adaptive skill areas: communication, self-care, home living, social skills, community use, self-direction, health and safety, functional academics, leisure, and work. Mental retardation manifests before age 18.

The definition requires that practitioners consider (1) cultural and linguistic diversity, (2) how adaptive skills interact with a person's community setting, (3) that specific skills often exist with limitations, and (4) that life functioning will generally improve with age.

There are a variety of causes for mental retardation—from deprived environments (especially for those with mild retardation) to genetic abnormalities, infectious diseases, and physical trauma (including drugs taken by pregnant women). There are two broad ways to classify retardation. The first focuses on biological versus environmental causes; the second, more prevalent approach focuses on levels of retardation as reflected in behavior.

Levels of Retardation

A diagnosis of mental retardation involves three criteria: a lower-than-normal (below 70) IQ score as measured on a standardized test such as the WISC–R or the WAIS–R, difficulty adapting to the environment, and the presence of such problems before age 18. There are four basic levels of mental retardation, each corresponding to a different range of scores on a standardized IQ test (see Figure 11.8 on page 418): mild, moderate, severe, and profound.

Mild Retardation. People with mild mental retardation (Wechsler IQs of 55–69) account for approximately 90 percent of the people classified as mentally

Mental retardation: Below-average intellectual functioning, as measured on an IQ test, accompanied by substantial limitations in present functioning that originated during childhood.

FIGURE 11.8

Mental Retardation as Measured on the Stanford-Binet and Wechsler Scales

Classification	Stanford-Binet IQ Score	Wechsler IQ Score	Percentage of the Mentally Retarded	Educational Level Possible
Mild	52–68	55–69	90	Sixth grade
Moderate	36–51	40–54	6	Second to fourth grade
Severe	20–35	25–39	3	Limited speech
Profound	Below 20	Below 25	1	Unresponsive to training

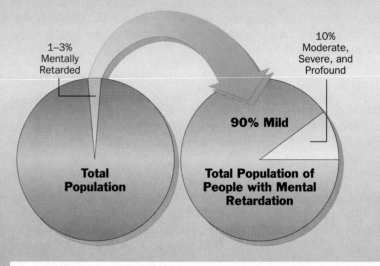

retarded. Through special programs, they are able to acquire academic and occupational skills but generally need extra supervision of their work (e.g., Allington, 1981). As adults, people with mild mental retardation function intellectually at the level of 10-year-olds. Thus, with some help from family and friends, most people with mild mental retardation can cope successfully with their environment. The Applications box examines the employment of people with mental retardation.

Moderate Retardation. People with moderate mental retardation (Wechsler IQs of 40–54) account for approximately 6 percent of those classified as mentally retarded. Most live in institutions or as dependents of their families. Those who are not institutionalized need special classes; some can hold simple jobs, although few are employed. People with moderate mental retardation are able to speak, write, and interact with friends; but their motor coordination, posture, and social skills are clumsy. Their intellectual level is equivalent to that of 5- to 6-year-olds.

Severe Retardation. Only about 3 percent of the people with mental retardation are severely retarded (Wechsler IQs of 25–39). People with severe mental retardation show great motor, speech, and intellectual impairment and are almost totally dependent on others to take care of their basic needs. Severe retardation often results from birth disorders or traumatic injury to the brain.

Profound Retardation. Only 1 percent of the people with mental retardation are classified as profoundly retarded (IQs below 25). These people are unable to

Employing Workers with Mental Retardation

Companies are realizing that if people with mild mental retardation are placed in the right job, are properly trained, and are effectively motivated, they can be counted on to be good workers. As a result, many companies now hire workers with mental retardation who were once thought unemployable.

Drawbacks do exist in hiring such workers. One is that training them often requires extra patience. A more detailed and carefully defined training program is usually necessary; behavioral techniques such as those described in chapter 5 are used extensively. Even a relatively simple task may be broken down into 30 or 40 individual steps. Workers with mental retardation sometimes need help to keep them focused on their job; such help might include prompts from supervisors or a checklist to follow. Mentally retarded individuals may work more slowly than others in the same position. They may also require some training in social skills—for example, in being friendly toward and smiling at coworkers. Also, workers who have lower IQs may be less adept at personal grooming and may not read, write, tell time, or handle money well.

Nonetheless, there also are great successes. Those workers who have been brought through training programs do exceptionally well. Workers with mental retardation are likely to stay with jobs others tire of. They may be more dependable, motivated,

and industrious than other workers. After they are trained, they have few problems adjusting to the routine of a 9-to-5 job. Owners of fast food restaurants who hire workers with mental retardation (such as McDonald's) report that these workers are rarely late for work or sick. The employers consider these workers reliable and dependable. Marriott Corporation employs more than 1,000 workers who have been diagnosed as mentally retarded. People diagnosed as mentally retarded are working, earning a wage, and handling their lives impressively. They do far better in their lives outside of their jobs than they ever did before—because of the law and mainstreaming discussed on page 420.

The federal government has taken an extensive role in the education and support of individuals with mental retardation. It provides Supplemental Social Security Income payments to unemployed workers with mental retardation. It also provides tax benefits to employers of the mentally or physically handicapped. Advocates for individuals with mental retardation are concerned because the costs of such support programs are rising very quickly. This makes work training programs even more valuable. Various states are providing funds formerly reserved only for institutions to businesses and colleges for the purpose of training workers with mental retardation. Such programs are money savers for local governments; workers who earn money pay taxes and do not require support payments. The task for government is substantial; and the challenge, in terms of numbers and cost, is formidable.

master even simple tasks and require total supervision and constant care. Their motor and intellectual development is minimal, and many are physically underdeveloped. Physical deformities and other congenital defects (such as deafness, blindness, and seizures) often accompany profound mental retardation.

The Law and Education

Until recently, thousands of children were given a substandard education after doing poorly on an intelligence test. Labeled as slow learners or perhaps even as mentally retarded, these children received neither special education nor special attention. However, in 1975, the U.S. Congress passed Public Law 94–142 (PL 94–142), the Education for All Handicapped Children Act. Originally intended to improve school programs for physically handicapped children, its passage ensures individualized testing and educationally relevant programs for all children.

The law holds that all school-age children must be provided an appropriate, free public education. After testing, children with special needs are not to be grouped separately unless they have severe handicaps. Tests for identification and placement

Mainstreaming: The administrative practice of placing exceptional children in regular classroom settings with the support of special education services.

must be unbiased. Further, educational programs for these children must be arranged to make them as close to normal as possible, with the unique needs of each child considered. An individualized educational program or plan (IEP) must be arranged by the school in consultation with the parents. The law also mandates that schools must follow specific procedures: offering an explanation of rights, evaluation procedures, regular reevaluation, and reasons for any changes in a student's status.

PL 94–142 has significantly increased the amount of testing in public school systems, leading to more classification and labeling. Many see this as a disadvantage. However, the implementation of the law has also guaranteed thousands of children with special needs an appropriate education. This is costly for local school districts; but when students need a special education, they can rely on the courts to make sure that the school system provides it.

FOCUS

▶ A diagnosis of mental retardation involves a lower-than-normal IQ score. What does this imply about IQ tests as a predictor of behavior? pp. 417–420

▶ What are the implications of the Education for All Handicapped Children Act ? p. 419

Since the passage of PL 94–142, there has been a shift toward **mainstreaming**—integrating all children with special needs into regular classroom settings as appropriate, with the support of special education services. Technically, the law requires students to be placed in the least restrictive or unusual environment feasible. Its purpose is to make life as normal as possible for these children by requiring that they and their teachers and classmates cope with their current skill level and expand it as much as possible. In mainstreaming, children are assigned to a regular class for at least half of their school day. For the rest of the day, they are often in special education classrooms or in vocational training situations. Although research studies have produced conflicting data on the effectiveness of mainstreaming, psychologists and educators generally support it (Zigler & Hodapp, 1991).

Real progress has been made with mainstreaming, but some problems remain. Most mainstreamed children, for example, get mainstreamed not into the academic side of school but into the social side (athletics, lunch). A more troubling event is that fewer children are being diagnosed as mentally retarded. This is being done to avoid stigmatization, but a consequence is the failure to provide special services to children who require them (Zigler & Hodapp, 1991).

Concluding Note

The history of the study of intelligence shows a shift from early attempts to separate normal individuals from those with mental retardation, to later attempts to carefully measure intellectual functioning through tests, to the most recent attempt to measure brain functioning and develop curricula to teach practical intelligence. Underlying much of the research and theory have been attempts to discern what creates intelligent behavior: nature or nurture. However, researchers are beginning to realize that the important thing is not nature versus nurture but how the two combine to create individuals who cope with the world effectively. To state the nature-nurture issue as a debate is a mistake. Nature sets the framework for our intellectual life, and nurture shapes our day-to-day interactions and how we use our inherited potential.

If researchers are to understand how and under what conditions people exhibit intelligent behavior, they have to ask what are the fundamental components of intelligence. They have to look not only at specific skills such as mathematical ability but also at practical skills such as time management. Intelligent people have specific and general skills. Wechsler was correct in his assessment of what intelligence is: People who are intelligent act purposefully, think rationally, and deal effectively with the environment.

Summary & Review

What Is Intelligence?

Define intelligence.

Intelligence must be defined in terms of observable, objective behavior; it must take in both an individual's capacity to learn and the person's acquired knowledge; and it must indicate an ability to adapt to the environment. A widely accepted definition of intelligence is Wechsler's: The aggregate or global capacity of the individual to act purposefully, to think rationally, and to deal effectively with the environment.   pp. 392–393

What is a factor analysis approach to intelligence?

A *factor analysis approach* to intelligence uses correlational techniques to determine which tasks are involved in intellectual ability. In factor analysis, many tasks are given to a subject, scores are derived for each task, and correlations are computed. The assumption is that tasks with high correlations test similar aspects of intellectual functioning. An example of the factor analysis approach is Guilford's approach. According to Guilford, human intellectual abilities and activities can be described in terms of three major dimensions: the mental operations performed, the content of those operations, and the resulting product of the operations. pp. 394–395

Compare Piaget's and Sternberg's approaches to intelligence.

According to Jean Piaget, intelligence is a reflection of a person's adaptation to the environment, and intellectual development consists of changes in the way the individual accomplishes that adaptation. Robert Sternberg takes an information processing view of intelligence. He divides intelligence into three dimensions: componential, experiential, and contex-

tual. Sternberg, like Piaget, focuses on adaptation.   pp. 393–398

KEY TERMS: *intelligence,* p. 393; *factor analysis,* p. 394; *factor-theory approach to intelligence,* p. 395.

Principles of Test Development

How were the first intelligence tests developed?

In 1905, Binet and Simon set a goal to distinguish normal children from children with mental retardation. Binet coined the phrase mental age, meaning the age level at which a child is functioning cognitively. He and Simon developed everyday tasks, such as counting, naming, and using objects, to determine mental age. The scale they developed can be considered the first useful and practical test of intelligence.   pp. 398–399

What is standardization?

Standardization is the process of developing a uniform procedure for administering and scoring a test. This includes developing *norms*—the scores and corresponding percentile ranks of a large and *representative sample* of subjects from the population for which the test was designed. pp. 399–400

What is reliability and validity?

A test is considered reliable if it yields the same score on repeated testings. There are several types of *reliability.* All tests have some degree of unreliability. The standard error of measurement is the number of points by which a score varies because of the imperfect reliability of a test. A test's *validity* tells a test developer whether a test measures what it is presumed to measure; without validity, proper inferences from test results cannot be made.   pp. 401–403

Critique the validity of tests and testing.

There are five basic criticisms of—and defenses for—the validity of tests and testing. The first focuses on the definition of intelligence. The second focuses on learned information. The third is that school settings may adversely affect IQ scores. The remaining criticisms of testing focus on the fact that some people are testwise and on people's motivation to succeed.   pp. 403–404

What do IQ tests actually measure?

Most intelligence tests do not measure the full spectrum of abilities related to intellectual behavior. Some test verbal and nonverbal intelligence but do not adequately measure areas such as mechanical skills, creativity, and social intelligence. IQ test scores do not measure innate ability, and overall IQ test scores must be deemphasized.   pp. 404–408

KEY TERMS: *standardization,* p. 399; *norms,* p. 399; *representative sample,* p. 399; *normal curve,* p. 400; *raw score,* p. 400; *standard score,* p. 400; *percentile score,* p. 400; *deviation IQ,* p. 401; *reliability,* p. 401; *validity,* p. 402; *halo effect,* p. 403.

Three Important Intelligence Tests

Describe three widely used IQ tests.

The Stanford-Binet Intelligence Scale consists of four major subscales and one overall IQ test score. It has been a good predictor of academic perfor-

continued

Summary & Review

mance, and many of its tests correlate highly with one another; its newer items minimize gender and racial characteristics. The Wechsler Scales group test items by content. The score on each subtest is calculated and converted to a standard (or scaled) score, adjusted for the subject's age. The test yields a verbal, performance, and overall IQ score. The K-ABC consists of four global scales. Three measure mental processing abilities—sequential processing, simultaneous processing, and a composite of the two; the fourth assesses achievement.   pp. 404–407

Testing Controversy

Is there a cultural bias in IQ tests?

Although researchers find differences among the IQ test scores of various racial and cultural groups, they find little or no consistent and conclusive evidence of bias in the tests themselves. The evidence of many studies conducted with a variety of intelligence tests and ethnic minority groups indicates that intelligence tests are not culturally biased. IQ test scores alone mean little and must be interpreted in the context of a person's life (including schooling). We must recognize that intelligence can be demonstrated in many ways. pp. 408–409

Characterize the nature versus nurture issue regarding intelligence.

Proponents of the genetic (nature) view generally assert that intelligence

tests portray intelligence accurately. Proponents of the environmental (nurture) view believe that today's intelligence tests are inadequate, that they do not measure a person's adaptation to a constantly changing environment. Many researchers claim that current theorizing will never resolve the issue of nature versus nurture because factors such as family structure, family size, and other environmental variables are important and impossible to measure accurately. Genetics does not fix a person's intelligence; it sets a framework for environment to shape it.   pp. 409–413

Are there cultural and gender differences in intelligence?

Cultural differences exist and express themselves in IQ test scores; for this reason many psychologists assert that we must (1) de-emphasize an overall test score, (2) focus on interpretation of tests, (3) remember that IQ test scores do not measure innate ability, and (4) focus on intellectual functioning in the context of real-life situations. The old consensus about gender differences between men and women is at least exaggerated, and at most simply wrong; gender differences in verbal ability are so small that researchers should not say that they exist.   pp. 410, 414–415

Giftedness and Mental Retardation

What is giftedness?

Giftedness is having superior cognitive, leadership, or performing arts

abilities. Gifted children represent one end of a continuum of intelligence abilities. Such individuals need special schooling to meet their special needs.   pp. 416–417

What is mental retardation?

Mental retardation is below-average intellectual functioning together with substantial limitations in adaptive behavior, originating before age 18. Retardation can affect communication, self-care, home living, social skills, community use, self-direction, health and safety, leisure activities, and work. There are four basic levels of mental retardation, each corresponding to a specific range of scores on a standardized intelligence test. The behaviors associated with mental retardation vary from slow learning to an inability to care for oneself because of impaired physical, motor, and intellectual development. pp. 417–419

What is mainstreaming and what is its goal?

Mainstreaming is the integration of all children with special needs into regular classroom settings wherever appropriate and with the support of special services. The purpose of mainstreaming is to help normalize the life experiences of children with special needs; unfortunately this is most often done in social settings rather than academic ones.   p. 420

KEY TERMS: *mental retardation,* p. 417; *mainstreaming,* p. 420.

CONNECTIONS

If you are interested in...

12

Personality and Its Assessment

Around the 11th week of each semester, I ask the students in my introductory psychology class to describe my personality. We have been together for 3 hours every week. I have talked a great deal about psychology and the relationship of psychology to other disciplines, including economics, politics, and education. My students think they know my views well. Thus, when I ask them to describe my personality, they are fairly sure they can describe me well. But can they? Although we have spent more than 30 hours together in class, do my students have an accurate perception of what I am like at home, with my children, with my friends, or at a party? I always ask: At a party, would I be a shy and quiet type, or would I be the type who would wear a lampshade on his head and be very outgoing?

My students characterize me fairly well. I'm not a lampshade type of person, but I'm not shy either. The students talk about my sense of humor and my relationship with my wife and daughters—people whom I often use as examples. Yet they quickly realize that they have seen me in only limited circumstances, always doing much the same thing. Although we have spent many hours together—far more time than one spends on a first or second date—it is hard to judge how I would act with my mother or how I felt about the Vietnam War. At this juncture, I usually point out the complexity of personality, of making judgments about what people are like, and of trying to characterize people from a very small sample of the range of behaviors in which they engage. The reality is that no other phenomenon is as resistant to easy definition and assessment as the human character.

Most people describe the way they respond to the world by using catchwords: They say they are shy, sensitive, outgoing, concerned, or aggressive. They also use these words to describe their personality. Psychologists, on the other hand, describe personality in a systematic and scientific way. For psychologists, **personality** is a set of relatively enduring behavioral characteristics (including thoughts) and internal predispositions that describe how a person reacts to the environment. However, psychologists also recognize that an individual's behavior is not consistent all the time or in every situation.

What gives people consistency in their behavioral characteristics? To answer this question, some personality theorists focus on day-to-day behaviors that characterize people; others focus on the inner conflicts that shape personality. Some see a human being as an individual who reacts to the environment. Others emphasize the internal, even genetic, influences that impel a person to action. Personality theorists must consider social psychological concepts such as attitudes, motivational concepts such as expectancies, and even biological theories such as those suggesting predispositions toward such personality characteristics as shyness.

The earliest personality theorists (for example, Freud) tended to think of personality as something stable within the individual. Later theorists began to recognize that personality depends on a host of environmental situations. Contemporary theorists, especially the behavioral and cognitive ones, often focus more on environmental determinants of personality than on internal predispositions.

Personality theories are a set of interrelated ideas and facts put forward to coherently explain and predict behavior and mental processes. Being able to predict and explain behavior enables psychologists to help people anticipate situations and express their feelings in manageable and reasonable ways. Personality theories focus on a few key questions:

▶ Does nature or nurture play a greater role in day-to-day behavior?

▶ Do unconscious processes direct behavior?

▶ Are human behavior patterns fixed, or are people free to chose their own destinies?

▶ Does our behavior depend on our situation?

▶ What makes people consistent in their behavior?

Personality: A set of relatively enduring behavioral characteristics and internal predispositions that describe how a person reacts to the environment.

No personality theory considers all these issues; nor does every theory explain all of personality. Thus, each theory we will consider is incomplete, but each is important because it addresses some key element of personality. We will begin by examining psychoanalytic theory—an approach to personality that focuses on the unconscious and how thoughts and ideas contained therein direct day-to-day behavior. This approach is the well-known and widely disputed theory of Sigmund Freud.

Psychoanalytic Theory

Sigmund Freud (1856–1939) was an Austrian physician whose influence on psychology became so great that some of his basic ideas and concepts are often taken for granted. Such Freudian terms as *ego, oral fixation, death wish,* and *Freudian slip* and such Freudian concepts as *unconscious motivation* and *Oedipus complex* are part of everyday language. However, when Freud introduced his ideas, he was seen as strange, heretical, and simply off base. Psychologists of the time (including Wundt, Titchener, and Köhler) thought that the proper subject matter of psychology was the study of the mind and how it works. Studying the unconscious and suggesting that children have sexual experiences were, to say the least, out of the mainstream.

Sigmund Freud

Freud used hypnosis to treat people with physical and emotional problems. Most of his patients were from the middle and upper classes of Austrian society. Many were socialites who, because they lived in a repressive society, had limited opportunities for the release of anxiety and tension. Freud noticed that many of them needed to discuss their problems and often felt better after having done so. From his studies of hypnosis and his work with these patients, he began to conceptualize a theory of behavior; many of his early conclusions focused on the role of sexual frustrations in producing physical symptoms. Over time, Freud developed an elaborate theory of personality and an accompanying approach to therapy. His approach to personality came to be called *psychoanalytic theory,* his method of therapy *psychoanalysis.*

Three Key Concepts

Many psychological theories have a key concept around which they grow. Freud's theory has three such concepts: psychic determinism, unconscious motivation, and conflict. **Psychic determinism** is a psychoanalytic assumption that all feelings, thoughts, actions, gestures, and speech have a purpose and are determined by some action or event that happened to an individual in the past. Adults, for example, do not have accidental slips of the tongue; nor do they frown or change mood by accident. Instead, past events affect all of today's actions. Moreover, most of a person's thoughts and behavior are determined by **unconscious motivation**—a psychoanalytic assumption that behavior is determined by desires, goals, and internal states of which an individual is unaware because they are buried deep within the unconscious. By definition, people are unaware of the contents of the unconscious and even of its very existence. These two ideas—that behavior is caused by previous events and that people are no longer aware of these events—guided much of Freud's theory.

Freud also theorized that people are constantly in *conflict.* They are energized and act the way they do because of two basic instinctual drives—*life,* which prominently features sex and sexual energy, and *death,* which features aggression. These instincts are buried deep within the unconscious and are not always socially acceptable. Freud wrote little about aggression until late in his life; he focused mainly on sexual instincts, which he termed the **libido**—the instinctual (and usually sexual) life force that, working on the pleasure principle and seeking immediate gratification, energizes the id (discussed in more detail shortly). In his later writings, Freud referred to the *libido* as "life energy." His critics assert that he was inordinately preoccupied with sexual matters.

When people exhibit socially unacceptable behaviors or have feelings they consider socially unacceptable, especially sexual feelings, they often experience self-

Psychic determinism: [SIE-kick] A psychoanalytic assumption that everything a person feels, thinks, and does has a purpose and that all behaviors are caused by past events.

Unconscious motivation: A psychoanalytic assumption that behavior is determined by desires, goals, and internal states, buried deep within the unconscious, of which an individual is unaware.

Libido: [lih-BEE-doe] In Freud's theory, the instinctual (and usually sexual) life force that, working on the pleasure principle and seeking immediate gratification, energizes the id.

punishment, guilt, and anxiety—conflict. Freud's theory thus describes a conflict between a person's instinctual (often unconscious) need for gratification and the demands of society for socialization. In other words, it paints a picture of human beings caught in a conflict between basic sexual and aggressive desires and society's demands. A person might wish to strike an offensive drunk, but social rules do not allow that behavior. For Freud, a person's basic desire is to maximize instinctual gratification while minimizing punishment and guilt.

Structure of Consciousness and the Mind

In his theory, Freud considered the sources and consequences of conflict and how people deal with it. For Freud, a person's source of energy to deal with conflict is biologically determined and lies in the structure of consciousness.

Structure of Consciousness. According to Freud, consciousness consists of three levels of awareness. The first level, the **conscious,** consists of the thoughts, feelings, and actions of which people are aware. The second level, the **preconscious,** consists of mental activities that people can become aware of if they closely attend to them. The third level, the **unconscious,** consists of the mental activities beyond people's normal awareness. They become aware of these activities only through specific therapeutic techniques, such as dream analysis.

Suppose a woman decides to become a psychotherapist for a *conscious* reason. She tells her family and friends that she wants to help people. Later, during an introspective moment, she realizes that her *preconscious* motivation for becoming a psychotherapist stems from a desire to resolve her own unhappiness. Finally, through psychoanalysis, she discovers that she hungers for love and intimacy, which her parents denied her. *Unconsciously,* she hopes that her future patients will satisfy that hunger by making her feel needed. Freud's theory focuses on people's unconscious level of awareness and how it influences their behavior.

Id, Ego, and Superego. According to Freud's theory, the primary structural elements of the mind and personality are three mental forces (not physical structures of the brain) that reside, fully or partially, in the unconscious—the id, the ego, and the superego. Each force accounts for a different aspect of functioning.

The **id** is the source of a person's instinctual energy, which, according to Freud, is either sexual or aggressive. The id works through the *pleasure principle;* that is, it tries to maximize immediate gratification through the satisfaction of raw impulses. Deep within the unconscious, the demanding, irrational, and selfish id seeks pleasure. It does not care about morals, society, or other people.

While the id seeks to maximize pleasure and obtain immediate gratification, the **ego** (which grows out of the id) is the part of the personality that seeks to satisfy the individual's instinctual needs in accordance with reality; that is, it works by the *reality principle.* The ego acts as a manager, adjusting cognitive and perceptual processes to balance the person's functioning, to control the id, and to stay in touch with reality. For example, the id of a boy who wakes up shivering demands to be warmed. The ego may recognize that the boy could steal a blanket from his older brother, who is sleeping in the next bed. Working on the reality principle, the boy realizes that he can gratify his id by stealing the blanket.

The **superego** in Freud's theory is the moral aspect of mental functioning, comprising the ego ideal and the conscience and taught by parents and society. The

Conscious: Freud's first level of awareness, consisting of the thoughts, feelings, and actions of which people are aware.

Preconscious: Freud's second level of awareness, consisting of the mental activities of which people gain awareness by attending to them.

Unconscious: Freud's third level of awareness, consisting of the mental activities beyond people's normal awareness.

Id: In Freud's theory, the source of instinctual energy, which works mainly on the pleasure principle.

Ego: In Freud's theory, the part of personality that seeks to satisfy the id and superego in accordance with reality.

Superego: [super-EE-go] In Freud's theory, the moral aspect of mental functioning, comprising the ego ideal (what a person would ideally like to be) and the conscience, and taught by parents and society.

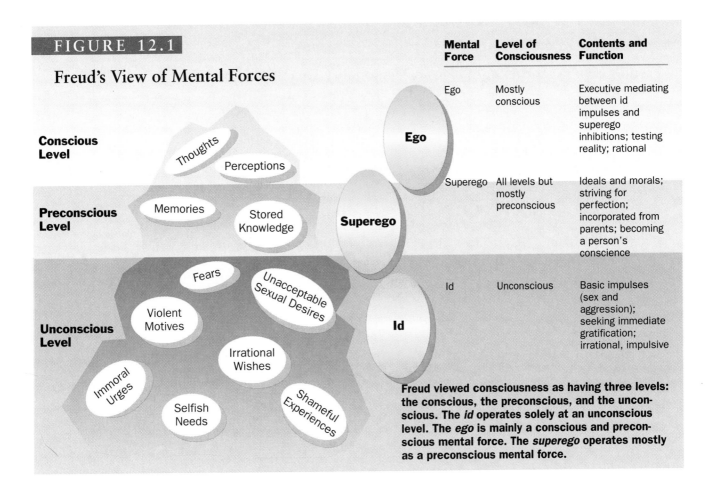

FIGURE 12.1

Freud's View of Mental Forces

Conscious Level — Thoughts, Perceptions

Preconscious Level — Memories, Stored Knowledge

Unconscious Level — Fears, Unacceptable Sexual Desires, Violent Motives, Irrational Wishes, Immoral Urges, Selfish Needs, Shameful Experiences

Ego

Superego

Id

Mental Force	Level of Consciousness	Contents and Function
Ego	Mostly conscious	Executive mediating between id impulses and superego inhibitions; testing reality; rational
Superego	All levels but mostly preconscious	Ideals and morals; striving for perfection; incorporated from parents; becoming a person's conscience
Id	Unconscious	Basic impulses (sex and aggression); seeking immediate gratification; irrational, impulsive

Freud viewed consciousness as having three levels: the conscious, the preconscious, and the unconscious. The *id* operates solely at an unconscious level. The *ego* is mainly a conscious and preconscious mental force. The *superego* operates mostly as a preconscious mental force.

superego tells the id and the ego whether gratification in a particular instance is ethical. It attempts to control the id by internalizing parental authority (whether rational or irrational) through the process of socialization and by punishing transgressions with feelings of guilt and anxiety. The superego may tell the boy that stealing a blanket from his older brother, who may then become cold, is immoral and that his brother might punish him for stealing the blanket. By asking his parents for another blanket, the boy can satisfy his id without feeling guilty, fearful, or anxious. The ego and superego attempt to modulate the id and direct it toward appropriate ways of behaving (See Figure 12.1 for a description of Freud's levels of consciousness and mental forces.)

Development of Personality

Freud strongly believed that if people looked at their past they could gain insight into their current behavior. This belief led him to create an elaborate critical psychosexual stage theory of personality development. Freud believed that the core aspects of personality are established early, remain stable throughout life, and are changed only with great difficulty. He argued that all people pass through five critical stages of personality development: oral, anal, phallic, latency, and genital (see Figure 12.2 on page 430). At each of the key stages, Freud asserted that people have conflicts and issues associated with *erogenous zones*—areas of the body that, when stimulated, give rise to erotic or sexual sensations.

Test Bank questions 12.61–12.77 relate to material on these pages.

430   *Chapter 12* Personality and Its Assessment

FIGURE 12.2

Freud's Five Psychosexual Stages of Personality Development

STAGE	ORAL Birth to 2 years	ANAL 2 to 3 years	PHALLIC 3 to 7 years	LATENCY 7 to Puberty	GENITAL Puberty On
Erogenous Zone	Mouth	Anus	Genitals	None	Genitals
Conflicts/ Experiences	Infant achieves gratification through oral activities such as feeding, thumb sucking, and cooing.	The child learns to respond to some parental demands (such as for bladder and bowel control).	The child learns to realize the differences between males and females and becomes aware of sexuality.	The child continues developing but sexual urges are relatively quiet.	The growing adolescent shakes off old dependencies and learns to deal maturely with the opposite sex.
Adult Traits Associated with Problems at Stage	Optimism, gullibility, passivity, hostility.	Excessive cleanliness, orderliness, messiness, rebelliousness.	Flirtatiousness, vanity, promiscuity, chastity.	—	—

Oral Stage. The **oral stage** is based on the fact that the instincts of infants (from birth to about age 2) are focused on the mouth—the primary pleasure-seeking center. Infants receive oral gratification through feeding, thumb sucking, and cooing; their basic feelings about the world are established during the early months of life. Relying heavily on symbolism, Freud contended that adults who consider the world a bitter place (referring to the mouth and taste senses) probably had difficulty during the oral stage of development and may have traits associated with passivity and hostility. Their problems would tend to focus on nurturing, warmth, and love.

Anal Stage. The **anal stage** is Freud's second stage of personality development, from age 2 to about 3, during which children learn to control the immediate gratification they obtain through defecation and to become responsive to the demands of society. At about age 2 or 3, children learn to respond to some parents' and society's demands.

Oral stage: Freud's first stage of personality development, from birth to about age 2, during which infants obtain gratification primarily through the mouth.

Anal stage: Freud's second stage of personality development, from about age 2 to about age 3, during which children learn to control the immediate gratification they obtain through defecation and to become responsive to the demands of society.

In Freud's first stage of personality development, infants focus on oral gratification.

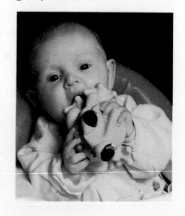

One parental demand is that children control their bodily functions of urination and defecation. Most 2- and 3-year-olds experience pleasure in moving their bowels, and the anal area is the focus of their pleasurable feelings. This stage therefore establishes the basis for conflict between the id and the ego—between the desire for infantile pleasure and the demand for adult, controlled behavior. Freud claimed that, during the anal stage, children develop certain lasting personality characteristics related to control, such as neatness and extreme orderliness, that reflect their toilet-training. Thus, adults who had difficulty in the anal stage would tend to have problems that focus on orderliness and also might be compulsive in many behaviors.

Phallic Stage. The **phallic stage** is Freud's third stage of personality development, from about age 4 to 7, during which children obtain gratification primarily from the genitals. During this stage, children pass through the Oedipus (or Electra) complex. At about age 4 or 5, children become aware of their sexuality. Freud claimed that, during this stage, numerous feelings are repressed so deeply that children (and later adults) are unaware of many of their sexual urges. Nonetheless, gender role development begins during this period.

The **Oedipus complex** occurs during the phallic stage, and includes feelings of rivalry with the parent of the same sex and love of the parent of the opposite sex, ultimately resolved through identification with the parent of the same sex. The Oedipus complex for males thus refers to a boy's love for his mother, hostility toward his father, and consequent fear of castration and punishment by the father. In resolving the Oedipus complex, the boy eventually accepts his father's close relationship with his mother. Rather than feel excluded by it, he chooses to gratify his need for his mother's attention by identifying with his father. In this way, a young boy begins to identify with and model his behavior after that of his father.

For females, Freud argued that the Oedipus complex, sometimes termed the *Electra complex,* follows a slightly different course. Freud held that when a young girl realizes that she has no penis, she develops what Freud called *penis envy.* He suggested that she can symbolically acquire a penis by attaching her love to her father. A young girl may then ask her father to marry her so they can raise a family together. When she realizes that this is unlikely, she may identify with her mother and copy her mother's behavior as a means of obtaining (or sharing in) her father's affection. Like the young boy, the young girl identifies with the parent of the same sex in the hope of obtaining affection from the parent of the opposite sex. For both boys and girls, the critical component in resolving the Oedipus complex is the development of identification with the parent of the same sex. Adult traits that are associated with problems at this stage usually involve sexuality and may be seen in vanity, promiscuity, or excessive worry about chastity.

The existence of an Oedipus complex is controversial and widely debated, especially because many people find it sexist and degrading to women. There is no doubt about Freud's views of women; he saw them as weaker and less rational than men and believed they should be subservient to men. Today, most researchers believe that Freud's notion of penis envy was imaginative but unconvincing, overdrawn, and lacking credibility (Stagner, 1988).

Latency Stage. Freud's fourth stage of development, the **latency stage,** lasts from about age 7 until puberty. During this period, children develop physically, but sexual urges are inactive (latent). Sexual urges, fears, and frustrations are repressed; and much of children's energy is channeled into social or achievement-related activities. Some modern psychoanalysts (considered in the next section) believe that this stage has disappeared from American society because of the fast-paced maturation of children into adolescence. They assert that children move from the phallic stage directly to the genital stage.

Phallic stage: [FAL-ick] Freud's third stage of personality development, from about age 4 to about age 7, during which children obtain gratification primarily from the genitals.

Oedipus complex: [ED-i-pus] Occurring during the phallic stage, feelings of rivalry with the parent of the same sex and love of the parent of the opposite sex, ultimately resolved through identification with the parent of the same sex; *Electra complex* is this process specifically in girls.

Latency stage: [LAY-ten-see] Freud's fourth stage of personality development, from about age 7 until puberty, during which sexual urges are inactive.

Genital stage: [JEN-it-ul] Freud's last stage of personality development, from the onset of puberty through adulthood, during which the sexual conflicts of childhood resurface at puberty and are often resolved during adolescence.

Fixation: An excessive attachment to some person or object that was appropriate only at an earlier stage of development.

Defense mechanism: A largely unconscious way of reducing anxiety by distorting perceptions of reality.

Repression: A defense mechanism by which people block anxiety-provoking feelings from conscious awareness and push them into the unconscious.

Projection: A defense mechanism by which people attribute their own undesirable traits to other people or objects.

Genital Stage. When people reach the last stage of development, the **genital stage,** the sexuality, fears, and repressed feelings of earlier stages are once again exhibited. Many of an adolescent's repressed feelings of sexuality toward the parents resurface. During the genital stage, the adolescent shakes off dependence on parents and learns to deal with members of the opposite sex in socially and sexually mature ways. Members of the opposite sex, who may have been ignored during the latency stage, are now seen as attractive and desirable. Many unresolved conflicts and repressed urges affect behavior during this stage. Ideally, if people passed through previous stages of development without major incident, they will develop conventional relations with members of the opposite sex. If not, they may continue to have unresolved conflicts within their unconscious.

Unresolved Conflicts

As children proceed from one developmental stage to the next, they adjust their views of the world. However, if they do not successfully pass through a stage, they acquire a fixation and an unrelenting use of defense mechanisms.

Fixations. A **fixation** is an excessive attachment to some person or object that was appropriate only at an earlier stage of development. A person who becomes fixated is said to be arrested at a particular stage of development. Fixation at one developmental stage does not prevent all further development; but unless people master each stage successfully, they cannot fully master the later stages. For example, a child who does not successfully pass through the phallic stage probably has not resolved the Oedipus complex and may feel hostility toward the parent of the same sex. The child may suffer the consequences of this unresolved conflict throughout life.

According to Freud, good personality adjustment generally involves a balance among competing forces. The child, and later the adult, is neither too self-centered nor too moralistic. Restrictive, punitive, and overbearing parents or parents who are indifferent, smothering, or overindulgent produce emotionally disturbed children who have a difficult time coping with life because of the resulting fixations. Fixations or partial fixations usually occur because of frustration or overindulgence that hinders the expression of sexual or aggressive energy at a particular psychological stage.

What happens when a person becomes fixated? According to Freud, the person develops defense mechanisms and sometimes maladjustment.

Defense Mechanisms. A **defense mechanism** is a largely unconscious way of reducing anxiety by distorting perceptions of reality. Everyone defends against anxiety from time to time. Defense mechanisms allow the ego to deal with the uncomfortable feelings that anxiety produces. In fact, people are typically unaware that they are using defense mechanisms. Nonetheless, people who use them to such an extent that reality is sharply distorted can become maladjusted.

Freud described many kinds of defense mechanisms but identified repression as the most important. In **repression,** anxiety-provoking thoughts and feelings are totally relegated to the unconscious. When people repress a feeling or desire, they become unaware of it. Thus, a young girl who has been taught that assertiveness is inappropriate in women may repress her own assertiveness.

In addition to repression, Freud observed five other key defense mechanisms:

▶ **Projection**—the mechanism by which people attribute their own undesirable traits to others. A woman who unconsciously recognizes her own aggressive tendencies may see other people as acting in an excessively aggressive way. A man who is anxious about his own anger may see others as being overly hostile.

▶ **Denial**—the mechanism by which people refuse to accept reality and the true source of their anxiety. Someone with strong sexual urges may deny interest in sex rather than deal with those urges.

▶ **Reaction formation**—the mechanism by which people defend against anxiety by adopting behaviors opposite to their true feelings. A classic example of reaction formation is the behavior of someone with strong sexual urges who becomes extremely chaste.

▶ **Sublimation**—the mechanism by which socially unacceptable impulses are redirected into acceptable ones. Thus, a man who has sexual desire for someone he knows is off limits (perhaps a cousin) may channel that desire into painting nudes.

▶ **Rationalization**—the mechanism by which people reinterpret undesirable feelings or behavior to make them appear acceptable. For example, a thief may rationalize that her victims acquired their wealth through illegal or immoral means or that she needs the money more than they do.

The work of a prison artist may represent sublimation, in which unacceptable impulses are rechanneled into socially acceptable behaviors.

When defense mechanisms cause reality to become distorted and maladaptive, a person must be concerned about using them. Over-reliance on defense mechanisms leads to maladjustment.

Freud Today

When Freud's psychosexual theory of development was first proposed around 1900, it received considerable unfavorable attention. It was considered absurd that young children had sexual feelings toward their parents. Freud's theory, however, has to be considered in a cultural context. Austrian society, with its rigid standards of behavior, and Freud's wealthy patients biased him in directions that few theorists would adopt today.

Yet, as we watch young children and the way in which they identify with their parents, we can see that there are elements of truth to this conception of how personality development proceeds. Little girls do tend to idolize their fathers, and little boys often become strongly attached to their mothers. However, Freud was not nearly as interested in normal development as he was in the pathologies, or disorders, that appeared as a result of imperfect development. In many ways, Freud's theory paved the way for other developmental stage theorists, such as Piaget, Erikson, and Levinson, who made more specific predictions about specific behaviors (see Figure 12.3 on page 434).

Freud's theories have been sharply criticized for a number of reasons. Some psychologists object to Freud's basic conception of human nature, his emphasis on sexual urges, and his idea that human behavior is biologically determined. Others reject his predictions about psychosexual stages and fixations. Still others assert that his theory does not account for changing situations and the contexts in which people find themselves. Many people find Freud's ideas about women patently offensive. At

Denial: A defense mechanism by which people refuse to accept the true source of their anxiety.

Reaction formation: A defense mechanism by which people behave in a manner opposite to their true but anxiety-provoking feelings.

Sublimation: [sub-li-MAY-shun] A defense mechanism by which people redirect socially unacceptable impulses into acceptable ones.

Rationalization: A defense mechanism by which people reinterpret undesirable feelings or behaviors in terms that make them appear acceptable.

FIGURE 12.3

A Comparison of Four Prominent Stage Theories

The stage theories of Freud, Piaget, Erikson, and Levinson all suggest that individuals must master each stage before they can pass successfully through the next.

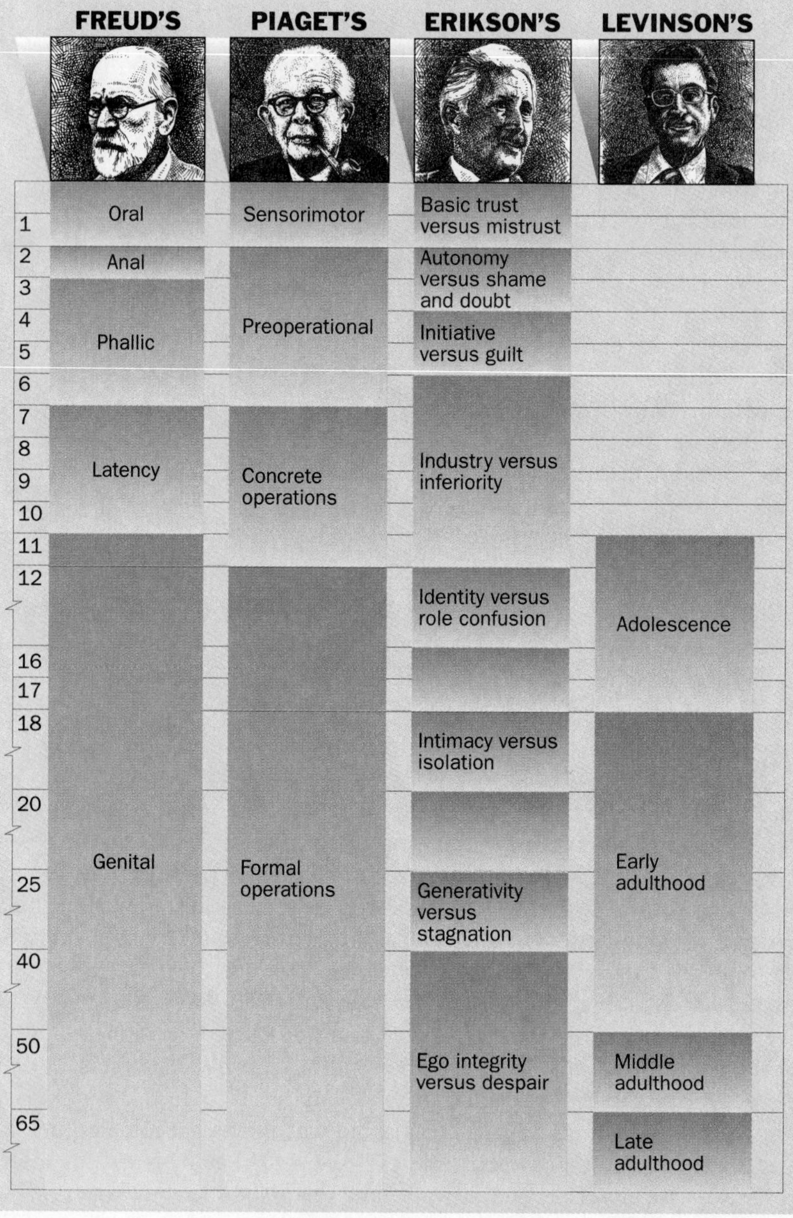

	FREUD'S	PIAGET'S	ERIKSON'S	LEVINSON'S
1	Oral	Sensorimotor	Basic trust versus mistrust	
2	Anal		Autonomy versus shame and doubt	
3				
4	Phallic	Preoperational	Initiative versus guilt	
5				
6				
7				
8	Latency	Concrete operations	Industry versus inferiority	
9				
10				
11				
12			Identity versus role confusion	Adolescence
16				
17				
18		Formal operations	Intimacy versus isolation	Early adulthood
20				
25	Genital		Generativity versus stagnation	
40				
50			Ego integrity versus despair	Middle adulthood
65				Late adulthood

a minimum, his ideas are controversial; and many psychologists do not regard them as valid. Almost all agree that his theory makes specific predictions about an individual's behavior almost impossible. Regardless of whether Freud's theory is right or wrong, his influence on psychology and on Western culture exceeds that of any other personality theorist, present or past. His theory weaves together his clinical experiences with patients, his speculations about human nature, and his own extraordinary personality.

Cultural Determinants of Personality

When I first mentioned Freud, I noted that his practice was with Austrian society matrons. This seems simple enough, but consider the implications. Freud developed a theory from dealing with a particular group of patients. Their day-to-day behavior, personalities, and problems were shaped by the culture in which they lived. *Culture,* as we have seen, refers to the norms, ideals, values, rules, patterns of communication, and beliefs adopted by a group of people. Different nations have different cultures. Within a culture, there may be different social classes, but all of the people have the same basic sets of norms.

We see cultural diversity as we travel from one country to another—for example, in Europe. Traveling from England, to Spain, through France, and then to Germany and onward to Turkey, one sees distinctly different value systems, lifestyles, and personalities. Modes of dress and attitudes about work, family, and religion all differ. The implication is significant because our culture shapes how we raise our children, what values we teach, and what family life is like.

Cultural values shape personality. Therefore, personality theories must be considered in a cultural context. Western society values competitiveness, autonomy, and self-reliance; in addition, Western conceptions of personality focus on the individual. By contrast, non-Western cultures value interdependence and cooperation; they also focus more on groups in constructing conceptions of personality. For developing adolescents, one culture may stress conformity to rules, strict adherence to religious values, and obedience to parental authority. By contrast, another culture may stress independence, free thought, experimentation, and resistance to parental authority. Within Western culture, there are significant variations based on heritage. People from a white Anglo-Saxon Protestant background bring to the culture a sharply different heritage than do people of African-American descent.

The many cultural variables make the study of culture and personality a complicated task. Adjustments and refinements for variations must be made to take account of ethnicity, gender, age, class, and culture. Accordingly, every personality theory, concept, and approach must be considered and evaluated from a multicultural perspective. We know that a person from Japan is likely to view embarrassment and saving face differently from a person from the United States. We will come back to this multicultural theme later in this chapter, when we examine the theory of Walter Mischel. He asserts that the context in which behavior occurs must be a focus of personality psychologists.

FOCUS

▶ What are the fundamental assumptions about human behavior and the mind on which Freud's theory is based? p. 427

▶ Why did Freud believe the unconscious to be so important in his theory of personality?   p. 428

▶ What is the fundamental assumption of all of Freud's defense mechanisms?   p. 432

Neo-Freudians—Dissent and Revision

There is no question that Freud has had an enormous impact on psychological thought. But his theory has been attacked by modern theorists, including some of his students, who have found what they consider serious omissions, errors, and biases in Freudian theory. Many have developed new ideas loosely based on Freud's original conception but usually attributing greater influence to cultural and interpersonal factors; they have become known as **neo-Freudians.**

Some neo-Freudians have argued that people are not driven solely by sexual instincts (Alfred Adler, for instance). Others have argued that the ego has more of a

Neo-Freudians: Personality theorists who have proposed variations on the basic ideas of Freud, usually attributing a greater influence to cultural and interpersonal factors than did Freud.

role than Freud thought in controlling behavior (Erich Fromm, for instance). Still others have focused on the central role of anxiety in shaping personality and maladjustment (Karen Horney, for instance). Many theories have attributed a greater influence to cultural and interpersonal factors (Harry Stack Sullivan, for example). A number of the theories have been more optimistic and future-oriented (Carl Jung's, for instance). While traditional psychoanalysts begin by focusing on unconscious material in the id and only later try to increase the patient's ego control, many neo-Freudians focus on helping people to develop stronger control of their ego and to feel better about their "selves." Carl Jung is one of the best known of the neo-Freudians, and we will explore his influential theory next.

Carl Jung's Analytical Psychology

Carl Gustav Jung

Carl Gustav Jung (1875–1961) was a psychiatrist who became a close friend and follower of Freud. However, Jung, a brilliant thinker, ultimately broke with Freud over several key issues. Compared to Freud, Jung placed relatively little emphasis on sex. He focused instead on people's desire to blend their basic drives (including sex) with real-world demands. Thus, Jung saw people's behavior as less rigidly fixed and determined than Freud. He also emphasized the search for meaning in life. When Jung declared his disagreements with Freud, in 1917, he and Freud severed their relationship; Freud was intolerant of followers who deviated too much from his position.

Jung chose to differentiate his approach from Freud's by terming it an *analytic approach* rather than a *psychoanalytic approach*. Like Freud, Jung emphasized unconscious processes as determinants of behavior; and he believed that each person houses past events in the unconscious. Jung's version of the unconscious was slightly different, however. Unlike Freud, Jung held that the unconscious anticipates the future and redirects a person when the person is leaning too much in one psychological direction.

In addition, Jung developed a new concept central to his ideas—that of the collective unconscious. The **collective unconscious** is a storehouse (collection) of primitive ideas and images in the unconscious that are inherited from our ancestors. These inherited ideas and images, which are termed **archetypes,** are emotionally charged, rich in meaning and symbolism, and contained within a person's collective unconscious. The archetypes of our collective unconscious emerge in art, in religion, and especially in dreams.

One especially important archetype is the *mandala,* a mystical symbol, generally circular in form, that in Jung's view represents the striving for unity within a person's self. Jung pointed out that many religions have mandalalike symbols; indeed, Hinduism and Buddhism use such symbols as aids to meditation. Another archetype is the concept of mother; each person is born with a predisposition to react to certain types of people or institutions as mother figures. Such figures are considered warm, accepting, and nurturing; some examples are the Virgin Mary, one's alma mater, and the Earth. There are archetypes for wise older men and wizards. Jung found rich symbolism in dreams and used archetypes such as the mandala and mothers to help people understand their own mental processes and behavior.

Jung's ideas are widely read but not widely accepted by mainstream psychologists. Although his impact on psychoanalysis is important, Jung himself never achieved prominence in leading psychological thought because his ideas, even more than Freud's, cannot be verified. Some theorists even view them as mere poetic speculation.

Another psychologist who broke with Freud—but who made a more lasting impact on psychological thought—was Alfred Adler, whom we will consider next.

Collective unconscious: In Jung's theory, a storehouse (collection) of primitive ideas and images in the unconscious that are inherited from our ancestors.

Archetypes: [AR-ki-types] In Jung's theory, emotionally charged ideas and images that have rich meaning and symbolism and are contained within the collective unconscious.

Alfred Adler's Fulfillment Approach

Alfred Adler (1870–1937) was heavily influenced by Freud, and some psychologists consider his theory simply an extension of Freud's. Adler was a Viennese physician who had an unhappy childhood. He recalled being compared to his older brother, who seemed to be better liked because of his physical prowess and attractiveness. Perhaps his unhappy childhood and feelings of inferiority led Adler to believe that people strive to become the best they can be. When Adler broke with Freudian traditions, he focused much more on human values and social interactions.

Adler differed with Freud on two key points. First, Adler viewed human beings as striving to overcome obstacles in order to fulfill themselves rather than for pleasure. Second, Adler viewed the social nature of human beings as much more important than did Freud. Adler met with Freud weekly; but in 1911, Freud denounced him because of sharp, irreconcilable differences in their views of personality.

Alfred Adler

Structure of Personality. According to Adler, people are motivated, or energized, by natural feelings of inferiority, which lead them to strive for completion, superiority, and ultimately perfection. Thus, feelings of inferiority are not always detrimental. A sense of inferiority can compel people to strive for superiority and thereby express their core tendencies, both as individuals and as members of society.

Adler recognized that people seek to express their need for superiority in different areas of life. Some seek to be superior artists; others seek to be superior social advocates, parents, teachers, or corporate executives. Thus, each person develops a unique lifestyle, one in which attitudes and behaviors express a specific life goal or an ideal approach to achieving superiority. Adler eventually sought to develop an "individual" psychology, arguing that people have to be analyzed as unique human beings.

Adler stressed fulfillment through striving toward specific goals. Some life goals, which Adler called *fictional finalism,* are unrealistic and unlikely to be achieved by most people. Examples are winning the Nobel Prize for literature, becoming a billionaire, or earning worldwide fame (Adler, 1969). However, it is these fictional goals, which are often unconscious, that motivate people and set up unique patterns of striving.

Development of Personality. Adler believed children's social interactions are particularly important in determining eventual personality characteristics. (Later, Carl Rogers would come to the same conclusion.) Adler and his followers relied heavily on the idea that early relationships with siblings, parents, and other family members determine the lifestyle an individual eventually chooses. It therefore follows that birth order is important. A firstborn child, for example, is likely to have a different relationship with people and is likely to thus develop a lifestyle different from that of a thirdborn child. Firstborns are pushed by parents toward success,

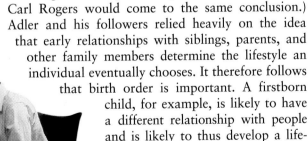

Adler believed that people are driven by the desire to overcome obstacles in their lives.

leadership, and independence and thus tend to have a high need for achievement. Their early experiences make it likely that they will choose a career reflecting that need for achievement, such as that of a corporate president or U.S. senator. Third-born children, on the other hand, are usually more relaxed about achievement. A young child who feels competitive with an older sibling, however, may develop a strong need for achievement that will drive the child toward success.

Foundations for Other Theories. To a great extent, psychologists see Adler as stressing an interpersonal route to fulfillment. His ideas about inferiority feelings and lifestyle have made their way into other popular theories of psychology. In addition, his ideas serve as the foundation of many child-care development centers.

Adler's theory, developed 20 years before the humanistic theories, laid the foundation for these theories. Adler emphasized an innate social need, motivated by feelings of inferiority, to strive toward perfection and superiority. Humanistic theories (considered next) stressed internal forces that motivate people to strive for self-actualization.

Humanistic Approaches

Unlike Freudians and neo-Freudians, who want to understand relationships between children and parents, humanistic theorists are more interested in people's conceptions of themselves and what they would like to become. In general, *humanistic theories* assume that people are motivated by internal forces to achieve personal goals. Humanistic psychology focuses not on disturbed individuals but on healthy people coping with human motives such as self-esteem.

Humanistic theories, which emphasize fulfillment, were developed partly in response to Freud's theory, which stresses the conflict of inner forces. Whereas Freud saw people in conflict warding off evil thoughts and desires with defenses, humanists see people as basically decent and worthwhile (although some of their specific behaviors might not be). Moreover, humanistic fulfillment theories enable theoreticians and practitioners to make predictions about specific behaviors.

Sometimes humanistic theories are also called *phenomenological approaches* because they focus on the individual's unique experiences with and ways of interpreting the world (phenomena). These approaches are more likely to examine immediate experiences than past ones and are more likely to deal with an individual's perception of the world than with a therapist's perception of the individual. Finally, they focus on self-determination; people carve their own destinies, from their own vantage points, and in their own ways. The humanistic approaches are represented by two well-known psychologists, Abraham Maslow and Carl Rogers, whose theories are examined next.

Abraham Maslow

Abraham Maslow

No single individual is more closely associated with humanistic phenomenological psychology than Abraham Maslow (1908–1970). In chapter 10, we examined Maslow's theory of motivation, which states that human needs are arranged in a pyramidal hierarchy in terms of importance and potency. Lower needs—food and water, for example—are powerful and drive people toward fulfilling them. At the middle of the pyramid of needs are safety, then belongingness, then self-esteem. At the top of the pyramid is self-actualization. The higher the need on the hierarchy, the more distinctly human the need.

As a humanist, Maslow believed that human beings are born healthy and undamaged, and he had a strong bias toward studying well-adjusted people. He spoke about personality in terms of human uniqueness and the human need for self-actualization—the process of growth and the realization of human potential. He focused not on what was missing from personality or life but on what one might achieve in realizing one's full potential. The process of realizing potential and of growing is the process of becoming self-actualized.

Critics of Maslow find his notions too fuzzy (as they do Freud's). His approach to psychology is viewed as romantic and never fully developed, and his theory is virtually untestable. A more complete and scientific humanistic approach was presented by Carl Rogers.

Carl Rogers and Self Theory

Carl Rogers (1902–1987) began to formulate his personality theory during the first years of his practice as a clinician in Rochester, New York. He listened to thousands of patients and was among the first psychologists to record and transcribe his interactions with them. What Rogers's patients said about their experiences, their thoughts, and themselves led him to make three basic assumptions about behavior:

▶ Behavior is goal-directed and worthwhile.

▶ People are innately good, so they will almost always choose adaptive, enhancing, and self-actualizing behaviors.

▶ How people see their world determines how they will behave.

Carl Rogers

Key Concepts. Rogers believed that personal experiences provide an individual with a unique and subjective internal frame of reference and world view. He believed that **fulfillment**—an inborn tendency directing people toward actualizing their inherited nature and thus attaining their potential—is the motivating force of personality development. Thus, people strive naturally to express their capabilities, potential, and talents to the fullest extent.

Rogers's personality approach is *unidirectional* because it always moves in the direction of fulfillment. This does not mean that a person's personality undergoes uninterrupted growth. During some periods, no growth is evident. However, for Rogers, a person's core tendency is to actualize, maintain, and enhance life. Rogers liked the analogy of a seed, which if watered grows into a strong, healthy plant—a representative sample of other members of its species.

Structure of Personality. Rogers's theory of personality is structured around the concept of self. What he means by **self** are the perceptions individuals have of themselves and of their relationships to other people and to various aspects of life. The self is how people see their own behavior and internal characteristics. As mentioned before, Rogers's theory assumes that individuals are constantly engaged in the process of fulfilling their potential—of actualizing their true selves.

Rogers suggested that each person has a concept not only of self but also of an ideal self. The **ideal self** is the self a person would ideally like to be (such as a competent professional, a devoted mate, or a loving parent). According to Rogerian theory, each person's happiness lies within that person's conception of self. A person is generally happy when agreement exists between the real (Rogers used the term *phenomenal*) self and the ideal self. Great discrepancies between the real and the ideal selves create unhappiness, dissatisfaction, and, in extreme cases, major maladjustment.

Rogers's focus on the self led him to his basic principle—that people tend to maximize their self-concept through **self-actualization.** In this process, the self

Fulfillment: In Rogers's personality theory, an inborn tendency directing people toward actualizing their inherited nature and thus attaining their potential.

Self: In Rogers's theory of personality, the perceptions individuals have of themselves and of their relationships to other people and to various aspects of life.

Ideal self: The self that a person would ideally like to be.

Self-actualization: The process of growth and the realization of human potential.

grows, expands, and becomes social. People are self-actualized when they have expanded their self-concepts and developed their potential to approximate their ideal selves. When people's self-concepts are not what they would like them to be, anxiety develops. Like Freud, Rogers saw anxiety as useful because it motivates people to try to actualize their best selves, to become all they are capable of being.

Development of Personality. Unlike Freud, Rogers suggested that development occurs continuously, not in stages. He contended that personality development involves learning self-assessment techniques to master the process of self-actualization—which takes a lifetime.

Rogers was particularly aware that children develop basic feelings about themselves early in life. This awareness led him to understand the role of social influences in the development of self-concepts. The self-assessments of children who are told that they are beautiful, intelligent, and clever are radically different from those of children who are told that they are bad, dirty, shameful, and a general nuisance. Rogers did not claim that negative feelings toward children's behavior should not be expressed. Instead, he suggested that children must grow up in an atmosphere in which they can experience life fully. This involves their recognizing both the good and the bad sides of their behavior.

Self-Concepts. People with rigid self-concepts guard themselves against potentially threatening feelings and experiences. Rogers suggested that these people become unhappy when they are unable to fit new types of behavior into their existing self-concepts. They then distort their perceptions of their behavior in order to make the perceptions compatible with the self-concepts. A person whose self-concept includes high moral principles, rigid religious observances, and strict self-control, for example, probably becomes anxious when he feels envy. Such a feeling is inconsistent with his self-concept. To avoid anxiety, he denies or distorts what he is truly experiencing. He may deny that he feels envy, or he may insist that he is entitled to the object he covets.

A changing world may threaten a person's self-concept. The person may then screen out difficult ideas or thoughts, creating a narrow view, a limited conception of the world, and a restriction on personal growth. But individuals can reduce or eliminate their fear by broadening their frame of reference and by considering alternative behaviors. People with healthy self-concepts can allow new experiences into their lives and can accept or reject them. Such people move in a positive direction. With each new experience, their self-concepts become stronger and more defined, and the goal of self-actualization is brought closer.

Individual Development. Rogers's concept of personality shows an abiding concern for *individual development*. Rogers stressed that each person must evaluate her or his own situation from a personal (internal) frame of reference, not from the external framework of others.

Freud's and Rogers's theories of personality make fundamentally different assumptions about human nature and about how personality is expressed. Freud saw biologically driven human beings in conflict; Rogers saw human beings as inherently good and trying to be everything they could be. Where Freud was strongly deterministic, humanists are strongly oriented toward free will. Humanists believe people can rise above their biologically inherited traits and can use decision-making processes to guide behavior. The treatment procedures that developed from the theories of Freud and Rogers—psychoanalysis and client-centered therapy (the latter discussed in chapter 15)—are fundamentally different. (See Building Table 12.1 for a summary of the psychoanalytic and humanistic approaches.)

Next, we examine an approach to personality that focuses on traits and on the specific behavioral responses that individuals make throughout their lives.

BUILDING TABLE 12.1

Psychoanalytic and Humanistic Approaches to Personality

APPROACH	MAJOR PROPONENT	CORE OF PERSONALITY	STRUCTURE OF PERSONALITY	DEVELOPMENT	CAUSE OF PROBLEMS
Psychoanalytic	Sigmund Freud	Maximizes gratification while minimizing punishment or guilt; instinctual urges direct behavior	Id, ego, superego	Five stages: oral, anal, phallic, latency, genital	Imbalances between the id, ego, and superego resulting in fixations
Humanistic	Carl Rogers	Actualizes, maintains, and enhances the experiences of life through the process of self-actualization	Self	Process of cumulative self-actualization	Wide discrepancy between self and concept of ideal self

Trait and Type Theories

Both ancient philosophers and medieval physicians believed that the proportion of body fluids (called humors) determined a person's temperament and personality. Cheerful, healthy people, for example, were said to have a *sanguine* (cheerful, hopeful, and self-confident) personality because blood was their primary humor; those who had a preponderance of yellow bile were considered hot-tempered.

Like their medieval counterparts, some early psychologists based their personality theories on the behaviors people openly exhibit, such as shyness, impulsiveness, and aggressiveness. Research shows that many of these easily observed characteristics do predict other behaviors. For example, extremely shy people are more likely than others to be anxious and lonely and to have low self-esteem (DePaulo et al., 1989); and adolescents with behavior problems often have low self-esteem (Harper & Marshall, 1991). Theories based on these observations—personality trait and type theories—make intuitive sense and thus have been very popular.

Trait theorists study specific traits. A **trait** is any readily identifiable stable behavior that characterizes the way in which an individual differs from other individuals. Someone might characterize Bill Clinton as being energetic and forward-looking and George Bush as having been tough and especially patriotic. Such characterizations present specific ideas about these people's behaviors, or traits. Traits can be evaluated on a continuum, so a person can be extremely shy, very shy, shy, or mildly shy. For some personality theorists, traits are the elements that personality is made of.

Type theorists group together traits common to specific personalities. **Types,** therefore, are broad collections of traits loosely tied together and interrelated. Although the distinction between traits and types sometimes blurs, according to Gordon Allport (1937, p. 295): "A man can be said to *have* a trait; but he cannot be said to *have* a type. Rather he *fits* a type."

Trait: Any readily identifiable stable behavior that characterizes the way in which an individual differs from other individuals.

Types: Broad collections of traits loosely tied together and interrelated.

We will now examine the trait and type theories of Gordon Allport, Raymond Cattell, and Hans Eysenck. We will end with an examination of a newer model of traits: the Big Five.

Allport's Trait and Cattell's Factor Theory

Gordon Allport

The distinguished psychologist Gordon Allport (1897–1967) was a leading trait theorist who suggested that each individual has a unique set of personality traits. According to Allport (1937), if a person's traits are known, it is possible to predict how the person will respond to various environmental stimuli. Allport quickly discovered that there are thousands of traits to characterize people's behavior but that some are more dominant than others.

Allport decided that people's behavior could be categorized into three kinds of traits: cardinal, central, and secondary. *Cardinal traits* are ideas and behaviors that determine the direction of a person's life. A clergyman's cardinal trait may be devotion to God; a civil rights leader's, the desire to rectify social and political injustices. Allport noted that many people have no cardinal traits.

The more common *central traits* are reasonably easy to identify; they are the behaviors that characterize a person's daily interactions (the basic units of personality). Allport believed that central traits—including control, apprehension, tension, self-assuredness, forthrightness, and practicality—adequately describe many personalities. For example, boxing legend Muhammad Ali could be characterized as forthright and self-assured; Woody Allen's typical film persona could be described as tense and apprehensive.

Secondary traits are specific behaviors that occur in response to specific situations. For example, a person may have a secondary trait of a prejudice toward minorities, a keen interest in psychology lectures, or a love of spectator sports. Being less characteristic of an individual's behavior than central traits, secondary traits are more easily modified and are not necessarily shown on a daily basis.

Allport asserted that central traits—for example, being forthright and self-assured, as is Governor Ann Richards of Texas—are the basic units of personality.

Everyone has different combinations of traits, which is why Allport claimed that each person is unique. To identify a person's traits, Allport recommended an in-depth study of that individual. If Allport's theory is true, knowing a person's traits would allow a psychologist to predict how that person would respond to the environment—that is, what the person's behavior would be. This has not yet come about.

Psychologists such as Allport and Raymond B. Cattell (b. 1905) have argued that it is possible to tell a great deal about a person just by knowing a few of the person's traits. Cattell (1965) used the technique of factor analysis—a statistical procedure in which groups of variables (factors) are analyzed to detect which are related—to show that groups of traits tend to cluster together. Thus, people who describe themselves as warm and accepting also tend to rate themselves as high on nurturance and tenderness and low on aggression, suspiciousness, and apprehensiveness. Researchers also see patterns within professions; for example, artists may see themselves as creative, sensitive, and open, while accountants may describe themselves as careful, serious, conservative, and thorough-minded. Cattell termed the obvious, day-to-day cluster of traits *surface traits* and the higher-order cluster of traits *source traits.*

Eysenck's Type Theory

Whereas Allport and Cattell focused on the trait level, Hans Eysenck (b. 1916) focused on higher levels of trait organization, or what he called *types.* Eysenck (1970) argued that all personality traits can be reduced to three basic dimensions: emotional stability, introversion or extroversion, and psychoticism.

Hans Eysenck

Emotional stability is the extent to which people have control over their feelings. People can be spontaneous, genuine, and warm; or they can be controlled, calm, flat, unresponsive, and stilted. *Introversion or extroversion* refers to the extent to which people are withdrawn or open. Introverts are socially withdrawn and shy; extroverts are socially outgoing and open and like to meet new people. Eysenck's third dimension, *psychoticism,* is sometimes called tough- or tender-mindedness. At one extreme, people are troublesome, opposed to authority, sensation-seeking, insensitive, and risk taking; at the other end, they are warm, gregarious, and tender. Each type incorporates elements at a lower level (traits), and each trait incorporates lower-order qualities (habits).

Eysenck argued that personality has a biological basis but emphasized that learning and experience also shape an individual's behavior. For example, he said that introverts and extroverts possess different levels of arousal in the cortex of the brain. Accordingly, persons of each type seek the amount of stimulation necessary to achieve their preferred level of arousal. For example, a person who prefers a low level of arousal, in which stimulation is less intense, may become a security guard or a librarian; a person who prefers a high level of arousal, which is reflected in outward behavior, may become a race-car driver or a politician. The idea of a biological component to some of these traits is hotly debated (Heath & Martin, 1990). Most psychologists assert that some traits may be genetically passed on—at least to some extent (e.g., Tellegen et al., 1988)—but that environmental influences are so strong that most of a person's personality is shaped by day-to-day interactions.

The Big Five

Because of trait theory's popular appeal and commonsense approach, researchers today still find it attractive. However, rather than speak of hundreds of traits or a few types, many theorists agree that there are five broad trait categories that describe individuals. The categories have become known as the *Big Five* (McCrae & Costa, 1987):

▶ *Extroversion-introversion*—the extent to which people are social or unsocial, talkative or quiet, affectionate or reserved.

▶ *Agreeableness-antagonism*—the extent to which people are good-natured or irritable, courteous or rude, flexible or stubborn, lenient or critical.

▶ *Conscientiousness-undirectedness*—the extent to which people are reliable or undependable, careful or careless, punctual or late, well organized or disorganized.

▶ *Neuroticism-stability*—the extent to which people are worried or calm, nervous or at ease, insecure or secure.

▶ *Openness to experience*—the extent to which people are open to experience or closed, original or conventional, independent or conforming, creative or uncreative, daring or timid.

Although dozens of traits describe people, researchers think of the Big Five as types of "supertraits," the important dispositions that characterize personality (McCrae & Costa, 1990). Research has been supportive (Goldberg, 1990, 1993). However, we must remember this is only a model used to help us understand personality; it is not necessarily a final or complete description of personality (Wiggins & Trapnell, 1992).

Criticisms of Trait and Type Theories

Trait and type theories are appealing because they characterize people along important dimensions, providing simple explanations for how individuals behave. However, psychologists have criticized these theories on five basic fronts.

First, they say trait theories are not actually personality theories. That is, they do not make predictions about behaviors and explain why the behaviors occur. Some psychologists claim that trait theories are merely lists of behaviors arranged into a hierarchy. Second, most trait theories do not tell which personality characteristics last a lifetime and which are transient. Events that do not happen every day can alter traits and types. Third, since an individual's behavior depends on the situation or context, traits cannot predict behavior. Some researchers contend that the failure of trait theories to account for situational differences is a crucial weakness. Fourth, trait theories do not account for changing cultural elements. If you test the same persons at 10-year intervals, the person's traits are likely to be different. But society will also be different, as will people's values and ideas. Trait and type theories do not account for these changing cultural norms. Finally, trait and type theories do not

BUILDING TABLE 12.2

Psychoanalytic, Humanistic, and Trait Approaches to Personality

APPROACH	MAJOR PROPONENT	CORE OF PERSONALITY	STRUCTURE OF PERSONALITY	DEVELOPMENT	CAUSE OF PROBLEMS
Psychoanalytic	Sigmund Freud	Maximizes gratification while minimizing punishment or guilt; instinctual urges direct behavior	Id, ego, superego	Five stages: oral, anal, phallic, latency, genital	Imbalances between the id, ego, and superego resulting in fixations
Humanistic	Carl Rogers	Actualizes, maintains, and enhances the experiences of life through the process of self-actualization	Self	Process of cumulative self-actualization	Wide discrepancy between self and concept of ideal self
Trait and Type	Gordon Allport	A series of interrelated hierarchically arranged traits that characterize the day-to-day behaviors of the individual	Traits	Process of learning new traits	Having learned faulty or inappropriate traits

explain why people develop traits. Nor do they explain why traits change.

Although trait and type theories continue to evolve, psychologists want theories that explain (a) the development of personality, (b) how personality theory can predict maladjustment, and especially (c) why a person's behavior can be dramatically different in different situations.

Building Table 12.2 on the facing page presents a summary of the approaches discussed so far. Theories that attempt to describe, explain, and predict behavior with more precision tend to be behavioral ones, the next major group of theories that we will examine.

FOCUS

▶ The neo-Freudians reacted to what fundamental assumptions of Freud?   pp. 435–436

▶ Alfred Adler's view of personality development was radically different from that of Freud. What implications did this difference have for Adler's theory of personality development?   p. 437

▶ What is a fundamental criticism of trait and type theories?   p. 444

Behavioral Approaches

Inner drives, psychic urges, and the need for self-actualization are hard-to-define concepts referring to internal characteristics. The behaviorists assert that these concepts are not the proper subject matter of personality study. Behavioral theorists are practical. They believe that people often need to change aspects of their lives quickly and efficiently and that many people do not have the time, money, or energy for lengthy therapy or personality analysis.

Consider the behavioral self-treatment Redford Williams proposes for Type A people—those hard-driving, ambitious, highly competitive people who, according to cardiologists, are at high risk of heart attacks (R. L. Williams, 1989). Williams says that hostility and cynical mistrust are the lethal elements of Type A individuals, and he outlines steps they can take to reduce hostility and develop a more trusting attitude and a healthier heart. One step is cynicism monitoring—recording angry feelings in a "hostility" journal. Another is thought stopping—mentally yelling "Stop!" whenever hostile thoughts start forming.

If behaviorists are correct in saying that personality is equivalent to the sum of a series of responses, then Williams's self-treatment program should help Type A individuals change their health-endangering personalities.

Key Behavioral Concepts

Behavioral personality theorists assert that personality develops as people learn from their environments. The key word is *learn*. According to behaviorists, personality characteristics are not long-lasting; instead they are subject to change. Thus, for behaviorists such as Skinner personality is the sum of a person's learned tendencies. Behaviorists look at personality very differently from any of the theorists described so far. They generally do not look inward; they look only at overt behavior. Behavioral approaches are often viewed as a reaction to the conceptual vagaries of traditional personality theories.

Precisely Defined Elements. Behavioral theories tend to center on precisely defined elements, such as the relationship between stimuli and responses, the strength of stimuli, and the strength, duration, and timing of reinforcers. All these can be tested in a laboratory or clinical setting. By focusing on stimuli and responses, behaviorists avoid conceptualizing human nature and concentrate instead on predicting behavior in specific circumstances. As a result, their assertions are more easily tested. Behaviorists see the development of personality simply as a change in response characteristics—a person learns new behaviors in response to new environments and stimuli.

Responses to Stimuli. For most behaviorists, the structural unit of personality is the response to stimuli. Any behavior, regardless of the situation, is seen as a response to stimuli or a response awaiting reinforcement (or punishment). When an identifiable stimulus leads to an identifiable response, researchers predict that every time that stimulus occurs, so will the response. This stimulus-response relationship helps explain the constancy of personality. If, for example, a teenager complains about his financial predicament and his father responds by talking about sports, the teenager may stomp out of the room. If this scene is repeated often, it becomes predictable: The stimulus of avoidance (sports talk) leads to the response of withdrawal.

Behavior Patterns. Using a behavioral analysis, psychologists can discover how people develop behavior patterns (such as eating their vegetables or being hostile) and why behavior is in constant flux. The behavioral approach suggests that learning is the process that shapes personality and that learning takes place through experience. Because new experiences happen all the time, a person is constantly learning about the world and changing response patterns accordingly. Just as there are several learning principles involving the use of stimuli, responses, and reinforcement (for a review, see chapter 5), there are several behavioral personality theories. These theories are based on classical conditioning, operant conditioning, and observational learning.

Classical Conditioning

Most people are fearful or anxious at some time. Some are fearful more often than not. How do people become fearful? What causes constant apprehension and anxiety?

Many behavioral psychologists maintain that people develop fear, anxiety, and a timid personality through classical conditioning, in which a neutral stimulus is paired with another stimulus that elicits some response. Eventually, the neutral stimulus can elicit the response on its own. For example, many people fear rats. Because rats are often encountered in dark cellars, a person may learn to fear dark cellars; that is, dark cellars become a feared stimulus. Later, the person may develop a generalized fear of dark places. If the first time the person sees a train, it's in a darkened station that looks like a cellar, the person may learn to fear trains. Classical conditioning thus allows researchers to explain the predictability of a person's day-to-day responses to specific stimuli. It describes the relationship between one stimulus and a person's expectation of another, as well as the predictable response the person makes (Rescorla, 1988).

Operant Conditioning

In operant conditioning, spontaneous behavior is followed with a consequence, such as reinforcement or punishment. According to behaviorists, personality can be explained as spontaneous behavior that is reinforced. For example, when a person is affectionate and that behavior is reinforced, the person is likely to continue to be affectionate.

Behavioral psychologists often use the operant learning principles of reward and punishment to help children control themselves and shape their own personalities. Consider a problem of school discipline. A 10-year-old child in a Florida public school frequently used obscenities (Lahey, McNees, & McNees, 1973). In an hour's time, the child would utter as many as 150 obscene words and phrases. Each time the child uttered an obscene word, the behavioral psychologists would take him out of the classroom for a minimum of 5 minutes and place him in a well-lit, empty room. They told him he would be placed in the time-out room every time he made an obscene statement. In a few days, the number of obscenities decreased dramatically, from 2 a minute to fewer than 5 an hour. Using time-out, the researchers were able to modify an element of personality.

The time-out procedure is often used in learning situations in both classrooms and laboratories. As with any reinforcement or punishment procedure, the subject learns that the procedure is contingent on behavior. In the example, the time-out was punishment. The child found it rewarding to be in the classroom and punishing to be in the time-out room. Thus, to remain in the classroom and avoid being put in the time-out room, he learned not to utter obscenities.

Observational Learning

Observational learning theories assume that people learn new behaviors simply by watching the behaviors of others. The theory contends that an observer will imitate the specific behaviors of a model and thus develop a set of personality characteristics. Personality is thus seen as developing through the process of observation and imitation.

Observational learning theories stress the importance of the relationship between the observer and the model in eliciting imitative behavior. When children view the behavior of a parent or other important figure, their imitative behavior is significantly more extensive than when they observe the actions of someone less important to them. A son is more likely to adopt his father's hurried behavior than his neighbor's relaxed attitude.

People can learn abnormal, as well as acceptable, behavior and personality characteristics through imitation. In fact, the most notable behavior that people observe and then imitate may be violence on television. As we will see in chapter 17, children who observe a violent television program are more willing to hurt others after watching the program. If children observe people who are reinforced for violent, aggressive behavior, they are more likely to imitate that behavior than more socially desirable behaviors.

Observational learning theories assume that learning a new response can occur without reinforcement. However, although personality develops as a function of imitating the behavior of other people, later reinforcement acts to maintain such learned behavior. Most people, for example, have observed aggressive, hostile behavior in others but still choose different ways to express emotions. Together, the imitative aspects of observational learning theories and the reinforcement properties of conditioned learning can account for most behaviors. For example, a daughter may become logical and forthright by watching her lawyer mother prepare arguments for court cases and seeing her win.

Researchers who focus on observational learning recognize that people choose to show some behaviors and to omit others. Accordingly, some researchers focus on observational learning in combination with another element—thought (cognition). The cognitive approaches to personality, which we will examine next, focus on the interaction of thoughts and behavior.

Research shows that television leads children to believe that violence is acceptable and sometimes even admirable.

Cognitive Approaches

In some important ways, cognitive approaches to personality appeared as a reaction to strict behavioral models, adding a new dimension. The cognitive emphasis is on the interaction of a person's thoughts and behavior. It considers the uniqueness of human beings, especially of their thought processes; and it assumes that human beings are decision makers, planners, and evaluators of behavior. (Strict behavioral approaches did not consider thought processes.)

Cognitive views have been influenced by the humanistic idea that people are essentially good and strive to be better. George Kelly (1955) was one of the first psychologists to assert that people make rational choices in trying to predict and manage events in the world. Many contemporary researchers claim that people can change their behavior, their conceptions of themselves, and their personalities in a short time if they are willing to change their thoughts.

Key Cognitive Concepts

From a cognitive point of view, the mere association of stimuli and responses is not enough for conditioning and learning to occur in human beings; thought processes also have to be involved. According to cognitive theory, we exhibit learned behavior that is based on our situation and personal needs at a particular time. If thought and behavior are closely intertwined, then when something affects our thoughts, it should also affect our behavior. The man who mentally yells "Stop!" whenever his thoughts become hostile should be successful in quelling his violent behaviors.

One of the key concepts of the cognitive approach to personality is the idea that people develop self-schemata. As we saw in chapter 6 (p. 228), a *schema* is a conceptual framework by which people make sense of the world. Self-schemata (*schemata* is the plural of *schema*) are a series of ideas and self-knowledge that organize how people think about themselves. They are global and help us define ourselves. A man may have a self-schema that involves exercise, his wife, his schoolwork, his family, and religious feelings. Cognitive researchers assert that people's self-schemata help shape their day-to-day behavior. They may affect people's adjustment, maladjustment, and ability to regulate their own behavior.

Over the years, a number of smaller theories (*microtheories*) have developed, dealing with how people perceive themselves and their relationship with the world. We will consider three of these theories next: locus of control (developed by Julian Rotter), self-efficacy (Albert Bandura), and cognitive social learning (Albert Mischel). Each takes a different view and helps us understand different aspects of personality.

Locus of Control

Many classic theories that attempt to explain all aspects of personality and behavior have been criticized because they are difficult to study scientifically. The ego in Freud's theory, for example, is not a physiological structure or state that can be manipulated or studied. Similarly, the concepts of self and of maximizing potential in Rogers's theory are difficult to measure and assess. As a reaction to imprecise grand theories, psychologists have developed smaller, better-researched theories. These microtheories, some of which follow a cognitive approach, account for specific behaviors in specific situations. Because of their smaller scope, they are easier to test.

One widely studied cognitive-behavioral theory is locus of control, introduced in the 1950s and 1960s, and systematically developed by Julian Rotter and Herbert

TABLE 12.1   *Statements Reflecting Internal versus External Locus of Control*

Internal Locus of Control		External Locus of Control
People's misfortunes result from the mistakes they make.	*versus*	Many of the unhappy things in people's lives are partly due to bad luck.
With enough effort, we can wipe out political corruption.	*versus*	It is difficult to have much control over the things politicians do in office.
There is a direct connection between how hard I study and the grade I get.	*versus*	Sometimes I can't understand how teachers arrive at the grades they give.
What happens to me is my own doing.	*versus*	Sometimes I feel that I don't have enough control over the direction my life is taking.

Lefcourt. *Locus of control* involves the extent to which individuals believe that a reinforcement or an outcome is contingent on their own behavior or personal characteristics versus the extent to which they believe that a reinforcement or outcome is a function of luck, chance, or fate or is simply unpredictable (Lefcourt, 1992; Rotter, 1990). Rotter focused on whether people place their locus of control inside themselves (internal) or in their environments (external). Locus of control influences how people view the world and how they identify the causes of success or failure in their lives. In an important way, it reflects people's personalities—their views of the world and their reactions to it. To examine locus of control, Rotter developed a test consisting of a series of statements about oneself and other people. Try responding to the statements in Table 12.1 to determine whether your locus of control is internal or external.

People with an internal locus of control (determined by their choice of statements) feel a need to control their environment. They are more likely to engage in preventive health measures and dieting than are external people. College students characterized as internal are more likely than others to profit from psychotherapy and to show high academic achievement (Lefcourt & Davidson-Katz, 1991). In contrast, people with an external locus of control believe they have little control over their lives. A college student characterized as external may attribute a poor grade to a lousy teacher, feeling there was nothing he or she could have done to get a good grade. In contrast, individuals who develop an internal locus of control feel they can master any course they take because they believe that, through hard work, they can do well in any subject.

People develop expectations based on their beliefs about the sources of reinforcement in their environments. These expectations lead to specific behaviors described as personality. Reinforcement of these behaviors in turn strengthens expectancy and leads to increased belief in internal or external control.

Locus of control integrates personality theory, expectancy theories, and reinforcement theory (see Figure 12.4 on page 450). It describes several specific behaviors but is not comprehensive enough to explain all, or even most, of an individual's behavior. For example, people often develop disproportionately negative thoughts about themselves and acquire a poor sense of self-esteem. Sometimes, this is shown in the behavior we call shyness, which is discussed in the Applications box on page 451. Bandura's theory, which we will examine next, specifically addresses people's convictions (thoughts) about their own effectiveness.

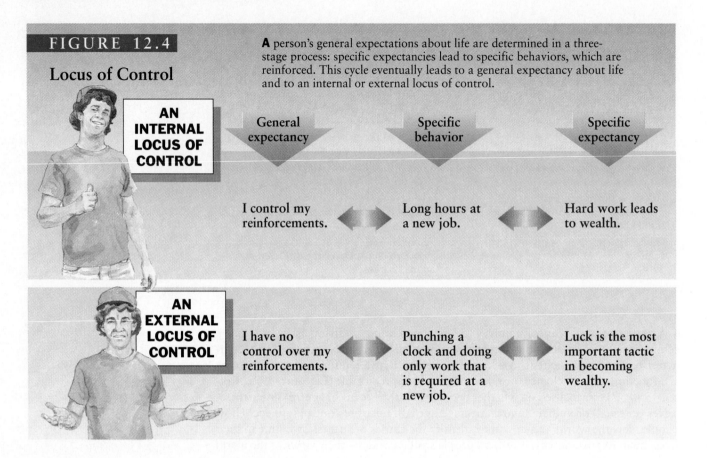

FIGURE 12.4

Locus of Control

A person's general expectations about life are determined in a three-stage process: specific expectancies lead to specific behaviors, which are reinforced. This cycle eventually leads to a general expectancy about life and to an internal or external locus of control.

AN INTERNAL LOCUS OF CONTROL

General expectancy → Specific behavior → Specific expectancy

I control my reinforcements. ⟷ Long hours at a new job. ⟷ Hard work leads to wealth.

AN EXTERNAL LOCUS OF CONTROL

I have no control over my reinforcements. ⟷ Punching a clock and doing only work that is required at a new job. ⟷ Luck is the most important tactic in becoming wealthy.

Self-Efficacy

One of the most influential cognitive theories of personality was developed by Albert Bandura (b. 1925), a former president of the American Psychological Association. His conception of personality began with observational learning theory and the idea that human beings observe, think about, and imitate other's behavior (Bandura, 1977a). Bandura played a major role in reintroducing thought processes into learning and personality theory.

Bandura argued that people's expectations of mastery and achievement and their convictions about their own effectiveness determine the types of behavior they will engage in and the amount of risk they will undertake (Bandura, 1977a, 1977b). He used the term **self-efficacy** to describe a person's belief about whether he or she can successfully engage in and execute a specific behavior. Judgments about self-efficacy determine how much effort people will expend and how long they will persist in the face of obstacles (Bandura, 1986). A strong sense of self-efficacy allows people to feel free to select, influence, and even construct the circumstances of their own lives.

Also, people's feeling that they can control a situation increases their perceived self-efficacy in managing it (Bandura & Wood, 1989). Thus, people who have a high level of self-efficacy are more likely than others to attribute success to variables within themselves rather than to chance factors and are more likely to pursue their tasks (Bandura, 1988; McAuley, Duncan, & McElroy, 1989). Because people can think about their motivation, and even their own thoughts, they can effect changes in themselves and persevere during tough times (Bandura, 1989; Haaga & Stewart, 1992).

Bad luck or nonreinforcing experiences can damage a developing sense of self-efficacy. Observation of positive, prosocial models during the formative years, on the other hand, can help people to develop a strong sense of self-efficacy that will

Self-efficacy: A person's belief about whether he or she can successfully engage in and execute a specific behavior.

APPLICATIONS

Overcoming Shyness

About 40 percent of adults report being shy; and for at least 2 million adults, **shyness** is a serious behavior problem that inhibits personal, social, and professional growth. Shy people show extreme anxiety in social situations; they are extremely reticent and often overly concerned with how others view them. They fear acting foolishly; as a consequence, they may develop clammy hands, dry mouth, excessive perspiration, trembling, nausea, blushing, and a need to go to the bathroom frequently. Shyness makes people avoid social situations and makes them speak softly, when they speak at all. Shy people avoid approaching other people (Asendorpf, 1989). Most shy people report that they have always been shy, and half of all shy people feel that they are shyer than other people in similar situations (Carducci & Stein, 1988).

Personality researchers contend that certain personality traits, including shyness, are long-lasting. Jerome Kagan found that 2- and 3-year-olds who were extremely cautious and shy tended to remain that way for years (Kagan, 1989). Daniels and Plomin (1985) also found an important relationship between biological mothers' shyness and adopted infants' shyness

at 2 years of age. This finding suggests that genetic factors play an important role in shyness (Lykken et al., 1992).

Although Kagan suggests that extreme shyness may have a biological basis, we also know that shyness emerges because people develop distorted self-concepts—negative views about their competencies and a lack of self-esteem. Such individuals view themselves in a poor light and see themselves as having very few social graces. These thoughts, combined with such actions as withdrawal and nervousness, set a person up for so-

cial failure. When negative events occur, the person then says, "See, I was right." A person's thoughts about her or his shyness, bodily reactions, and social behaviors thus perpetuate the shyness.

Treatment programs exist to help people overcome extreme shyness (Carducci & Stein, 1988). If you are shy, here are some things you can do:

▶ Rehearse what you want to say before speaking.

▶ Build your self-esteem by focusing on your good points.

▶ Accept who you are, and think about your distinctive, positive traits.

▶ Practice smiling and making eye contact.

▶ Observe the behavior of others whom you admire, and copy it.

▶ Think about how others feel; remember that about 40 percent of all people feel the way you do.

▶ Engage in relaxation training, which might include self-hypnosis, yoga, or even biofeedback.

▶ Read self-help books on putting your best foot forward.

▶ Think positively; a positive attitude about yourself and other people can go a long way toward helping to overcome shyness.

encourage and reinforce them in directing their own lives. Bandura's theory allows individual flexibility in behavior. People are not locked into specific responses to specific stimuli, as some strict behaviorists might assert. According to Bandura, people choose the behaviors they will imitate, and they are free to adapt their behavior to any situation. Self-efficacy both determines and flows from feelings of self-worth. Accordingly, people's sense of self-efficacy determines how they might present themselves to other people. For example, a person whom others view as successful may not share that view, and a person who has achieved little of note to society may consider himself a capable and worthy person.

Bandura's theory is optimistic. It is a long way from Freud's deterministic theory, which argues that conflicting biologically based forces determine human behavior. It is also a long way from a strict behavioral theory, which suggests that environmental contingencies shape behavior. Bandura believes that human beings have choices, that they direct the course of their lives. He also believes that society, parents, experiences, and even luck help shape those lives.

Shyness: Extreme anxiety in individuals who are socially reticent and often overly concerned with how they appear to others, often leading to avoidance of social situations.

Women's Personality Changes from College to Midlife

Does personality change over time, or does it stay the same from adolescence through old age? Are personality changes the same for men and women?

Trait theorists assume that personality remains much the same over the life span. Shy people remain shy; high school pranksters become retirement home pranksters. Stage theorists such as Erik Erikson and Daniel Levinson (chapter 9), on the other hand, contend that people change during their life span. These psychologists believe in an adult life cycle.

But are there gender differences in the course of personality development? Many researchers think there are, particularly before and during adolescence (L. D. Cohn, 1991).

Questions Are Formulated. Unfortunately, most personality and adult life-cycle studies have been conducted with men—who represent less than half the population. Do women's personalities change in a similar way? Do the personalities of career-oriented women change and those of family-oriented women stay the same? Helson and Moane (1987), of the University of California at Berkeley, studied the personalities of a group of women, starting when the women were of college age and continuing to when they were at midlife. The primary objective was to discover whether personality changes are obvious across different life paths and whether those changes support theories of adult development and personality. A second objective was to compare the life cycles of men and women, since previous long-term studies had failed to address that vital issue. The researchers asked whether life cycles in adulthood need to be rethought. Do women have midlife transitions, as men do?

Method. Helson and Moane began their work in 1958 at Mills College, a private women's college located in Oakland, California. They gathered information from the same 81 women at ages 21, 27, and 43. In using this longitudinal method, they studied a single group of people at different times to determine whether changes had occurred over time. (For a review of this method, see chapter 8, p. 278.) The researchers used several measures of personality, including the California Personality Inventory (CPI). The CPI, which is commonly used to study people from mid-adolescence to old age, is a test of normal personality. Designed to assess effectiveness in interpersonal functioning, it examines confidence, independence, responsibility, socialization, self-control, tolerance, and flexibility, among other dimensions.

Correlational Results. The results, reported as correlations among the different measures of personality, showed interesting stabilities and changes. For example, when the women were between the ages of 21 and 27, they took control of their lives, acknowledged differences in the way the world ought to be and the way it was, and scored higher on tolerance, social maturity, and femininity than they did later in life. At

Gender and Self-Efficacy. Men and women develop differently, both physiologically and socially; and this difference affects their self-efficacy. As children, boys are more likely than girls to play in large groups where opportunities for discussion are minimized; girls, by contrast, are more likely than boys to play in small groups in which interpersonal awareness is more likely to be heightened. In addition, boys more than girls may be encouraged to become involved in competitive, achievement-related activities (L. D. Cohn, 1991). Research that has manipulated a participant's view of performance on various tasks shows that a person's sense of self-efficacy is related to the person's fulfillment of culturally mandated, gender-appropriate norms (Josephs, Markus, & Tafarodi, 1992). Men more than women focus on independence and distinctiveness; women more than men focus on interdependence and good relations. From these different focuses, both men and women derive a sense of self-efficacy.

Mischel's Cognitive Social Learning

Walter Mischel

Like Bandura, Walter Mischel (b. 1930) claims that thought is crucial in determining human behavior; but Mischel also believes that both past experiences and current reinforcement are important. What's more, Mischel is an *interactionist*—he focuses on the interaction of people and their environment (Mischel, 1983). Mischel and other cognitive theorists (e.g., Cantor & Kihlstrom, 1982) argue that people

ages 27 to 43, they scored higher in the areas of dominance, independence, and confidence, but lower in flexibility and femininity. The changes from 27 to 43 were greater than the changes from 21 to 27. As the women grew older, they became more organized, committed, and work-oriented, but less open to change.

The results of this study are consistent with adult life-cycle theories of development that have focused on men. From ages 21 to 43, there were increases in self-discipline and commitment to duties; this typically occurs with men. The women became more confident, independent, and work-oriented. Until age 27, the changes were small, but after age 27, the women became less feminine, focusing less on gender-specific tasks such as child care and more on gaining independence and confidence and on developing a career.

Conclusions. Helson and Moane (1987) maintain that women's personalities change in consistent and predictable ways between the ages of 21 (young adulthood) and 43 (mid-

dle age). They believe, for example, that a career requires a woman to develop skills, confidence, and insight into others—things that were not necessary at earlier life stages. From Helson and Moane's view, personality is not static but is a constantly evolving set of skills and abilities acquired to cope with the demands and dilemmas that face maturing individuals. This view is consistent with that of some stage theorists who have focused on men, but it presents problems for trait theorists, who assert that personality is stable during the life span.

Remaining Issues. Helson and Moane conducted their studies during a time of rapid change in women's roles in society, from 1960 through 1985. Were the changes that occurred then similar to the changes that are taking place now or to the changes that will occur in the next 20 years? Is the United States likely to experience a decade similar to the one that saw the Vietnam War, the women's liberation movement, and Watergate? Today, women aged 21 to

27 may not show the same patterns. Research is now addressing various possibilities. For example, Helson and Picano (1990) have shown that traditional women who later in life join the labor force juggle their various roles with success.

The 1960–1985 research did not specifically address certain lifestyle variations; many women, for example, opt for careers first and children later. Socioeconomic status and societal changes determine so many lifestyle, educational, and work issues that they too need to be examined. Further, new research must consider results in a historical context, taking into account changing political, social, and moral values. Last, it will take a longitudinal study of college women of the 1980s traced over 20 years to determine whether Helson and Moane's findings are still valid for today's generation. Women may achieve somewhat different milestones, at somewhat different times than do men, particularly during the adolescent years; but far more research is needed to make that determination (L. D. Cohn, 1991).

respond flexibly to various situations. They change their responses on the basis of their past experiences and their current assessment of the present situation. This process of adjustment is called *self-regulation*. People make subtle adjustments in their tone of voice and overt behavior (their personality), depending on the context in which they find themselves. Those who tend to be warm, caring, and attentive, for example, can become hostile and aggressive in certain situations.

People's personalities, and particularly their responses to a stimulus, are determined by the following (Mischel, 1979): *competencies* (what they know and can do), *encoding strategies* (the way they process, attend to, and select information), *expectancies* (their anticipation of outcomes), *personal values* (the importance they attach to various situations), and *self-regulatory systems* (the systems of rules people have established for themselves to guide their behavior).

Mischel has had a great impact on psychological thought because he has forced researchers to consider the idea that traits alone cannot predict behavior, that the context of the situation must be considered. The context means not only the immediate situation but also the culture in which a person lives and was raised as well as other situational variables, such as the gender and age of the person whose behavior is being predicted.

The Research Process box discusses how two researchers studied the constancy of personality by examining the behavioral characteristics of a group of women over a period of 20 years.

Cognitive Theories Evolve

From the view of personality theorists such as Rotter, Bandura, and Mischel, human uniqueness can best be explained by the idea that reinforcement, past experiences, current feelings, future expectation, and subjective values all influence people's responses to their environments. Human beings have characteristic ways of responding, but those ways (their personalities) change, depending on specific circumstances.

Cognitive theories of personality are well researched but not yet complete; they do not, for example, clearly explain the development of personality from childhood to adulthood. They are also not well integrated. Bandura, for example, has shifted his focus from observational learning to self-regulation to self-efficacy without tying together the threads of those research areas. What this incompleteness and lack of coherence signify is that personality research and theory are still in their infancy, with further research and new ideas needed to tie up loose ends and generate more sophisticated, complete theories.

Personality theories are diverse, and their explanations and accounts of specific behaviors vary sharply; each one views the development of personality and maladjustment from a different vantage point. See Building Table 12.3 for an overall summary of the theories presented in this chapter.

When a practitioner, regardless of orientation, meets a client, there are several ways the client can be evaluated. These techniques are the focus of psychological assessment, the topic we will consider next.

FOCUS

► Identify three key behavioral concepts used to explain personality development.   pp. 445–446

► For a cognitive psychologist, what explains the constancy of personality?   p. 448

► Why is Mischel called an interactionist?   pp. 452–453

Psychological Assessment

Assessment is the process of evaluating individual differences among human beings by using tests, interviews, observations, and recordings of physiological processes. Psychologists who conduct assessments are constantly seeking ways to evaluate personality in order to explain behavior, to diagnose and classify maladjusted people, and to develop treatment plans when necessary. Many individuals and institutions give tests—school systems often give IQ tests, for example—but these are not assessments. Assessments are done by psychologists who have a relationship with a client, and the type of examination used is determined by the client's needs (Matarazzo, 1990).

Often, more than one assessment procedure is needed to provide all the necessary information, and many psychologists administer a group, or *battery*, of tests. The goal of the examiner is to use a variety of available tests so that, when the information taken together is added up, an intelligent conclusion can be drawn. As Kaufman (1990, p. 29) asserts, "Psychologists need to be shrewd detectives to uncover test interpretations that are truly 'individual' . . . and will ultimately help the person referred for evaluation."

A psychologist may assess personality with the Minnesota Multiphasic Personality Inventory–2nd edition (MMPI–2) (discussed later in this section), intelligence with the WAIS–R (described in chapter 11), and a specific skill (such as coordination) with some other specific test. More confidence can be placed in the data from several tests than in the data from a single test; further, with several measures, cur

Assessment: The process of evaluating individual differences among human beings by using tests and direct observation of behavior.

BUILDING TABLE 12.3

Psychoanalytic, Humanistic, Trait and Type, Behavioral, and Cognitive Approaches to Personality

APPROACH	MAJOR PROPONENT	CORE OF PERSONALITY	STRUCTURE OF PERSONALITY	DEVELOPMENT	CAUSE OF PROBLEMS
Psychoanalytic	Sigmund Freud	Maximizes gratification while minimizing punishment or guilt; instinctual urges direct behavior	Id, ego, superego	Five stages: oral, anal, phallic, latency, genital	Imbalances between the id, ego, and superego resulting in fixations
Humanistic	Carl Rogers	Actualizes, maintains, and enhances the experiences of life through the process of self-actualization	Self	Process of cumulative self-actualization	Wide discrepancy between self and concept of ideal self
Trait and Type	Gordon Allport		Traits	Process of learning new traits	Having learned faulty or inappropriate traits
Behavioral	B. F. Skinner	Reduction of social and biological needs that energize behavior through the emission of learned responses	Responses	Process of learning new responses	Having learned faulty or inappropriate behaviors
Cognitive	Several, including Rotter, Bandura, and Mischel	Learned responses depend on a changing environment, and the person responds after thinking about the context of the environment	Changing responses	Process of thinking about new responses	Inappropriate thoughts or faulty reasoning

rent levels of functioning are better characterized. Hundreds of psychological tests exist. According to Barrios (1988), there are over 100 tests just for measuring the various elements of anxiety. The purpose of the testing determines the type of tests administered.

Intelligence Tests

Often, the first test given in a psychological assessment is an *intelligence test*. (Chapter 11 is devoted extensively to an examination of intelligence and intelligence tests.) These tests provide specific information about a person's level of intellectual functioning and therefore can be good predictors of academic achievement—an important part of personality development. They may give an overall IQ score, separate verbal IQ and performance IQ scores (e.g., in the Wechsler Intelligence Scale for Children–III), or all three types of scores. In addition, verbal IQ tests (scales) can have subscales that examine specific components of verbal intelligence and are thus helpful in assessing the reasons for, say, a student's low grades. However, intelligence tests are limited because they provide only a general indication of a person's behavior pattern.

Objective Personality Tests

Next to intelligence tests, the most widely given tests are *objective personality tests*. These tests, sometimes termed *personality inventories,* generally consist of true-false or check-the-best-answer questions. The aims of objective personality tests vary. Raymond Cattell developed a test called the 16PF (16PF refers to 16 personality factors) to screen job applicants and to examine individuals who fall within a normal range of personality functioning. The California Personality Inventory (CPI) is used primarily to identify and assess normal aspects of personality. Using a large sample of normal subjects as a reference group, it examines personality traits such as sociability, self-control, and responsibility.

One of the most widely used and well-researched personality tests is the Minnesota Multiphasic Personality Inventory–2nd edition (the MMPI–2). The original MMPI was widely used; and the new MMPI–2, published in 1989, is considered a major revision. The MMPI–2 consists of 567 true-false statements that focus on attitudes, feelings, motor disturbances, and bodily complaints. A series of subscales examine different aspects of functioning and measure the truthfulness of the subjects' responses; these subscales, called the clinical and validity scales, are shown in Table 12.2. In 1992, a special version of the MMPI was developed for adolescents, called the MMPI–A. Items have been written for this test that cover adolescent issues such as eating disorders, substance abuse, and family and school problems. Typical statements on the MMPI–2 are as follows:

I tire easily.

I become very anxious before examinations.

I worry about sex matters.

I become bored easily.

The MMPI–2 can be administered individually or to a group. The test takes 90 minutes to complete and can be scored in less than a half hour. It provides a profile that lets psychologists assess an individual's current level of functioning and characteristic way of dealing with the world, and it provides a description of some specific personality characteristics. The MMPI–2 also enables psychologists to make reasonable predictions about a person's ability to function in specific situations, such as working in a mental hospital or as a security guard.

Generally, the MMPI–2 is used as a screening device for maladjustment. Its norms are based on the profiles of thousands of normal people and a smaller group of psychiatric patients. Each scale tells how most normal individuals score. In general, a score significantly above normal may be considered evidence of maladjustment.

Nearly 5,000 published studies have examined the validity and reliability of the original MMPI. For the most part, these studies have supported the MMPI as a valid and useful predictive tool. The MMPI–2 has a better representative sample (one that reflects the overall population), a much larger sample (2,600 people) of subjects for standardization (the subjects are also more representative of the population than were the initial group of subjects). The MMPI–2 includes questions that focus on eating disorders and drug abuse. Older questions that had a gender bias have been revised. Studies are now evaluating the MMPI–2. Because many of the traditional

TABLE 12.2   *The Clinical and Validity Scales of the MMPI–2*

Scale Name	Interpretation
Clinical Scales	
1. Hypochondriasis (Hs)	High scorers reflect an exaggerated concern about their physical health.
2. Depression (D)	High scorers are usually depressed, despondent, and distressed.
3. Hysteria (Hy)	High scorers complain often about physical symptoms, with no apparent organic cause.
4. Psychopathic deviate (Pd)	High scorers show a disregard for social and moral standards.
5. Masculinity/femininity (Mf)	Extreme scorers show "traditional" masculine or feminine attitudes and values.
6. Paranoia (Pa)	High scorers demonstrate extreme suspiciousness and feelings of persecution.
7. Psychasthenia (Pt)	High scorers tend to be highly anxious, rigid, tense, and worrying.
8. Schizophrenia (Sc)	High scorers tend to be socially withdrawn and to engage in bizarre and unusual thinking.
9. Hypomania (Ma)	High scorers are highly emotionally excitable, energetic, and impulsive.
10. Social introversion (S)	High scorers tend to be modest, self-effacing, and shy.
Validity Scales	
1. Cannot say (?)	High scorers are evasive in filling out the questionnaire.
2. Lie (L)	High scorers attempt to present themselves in a very favorable light and possibly tell lies to do so.
3. Infrequency (F)	High scorers are presenting themselves in a particularly bad way and may well be "faking bad."
4. Defensiveness (K)	High scorers may be very defensive in filling out the questionnaire.

features of the test remain unchanged, the refinements and modifications should only improve the test's predictive validity (Butcher et al., 1990). Still, the MMPI–2 is by no means a perfect instrument for valid predictions about future behavior and it should be considered only one test in a battery of tests (Helmes & Reddon, 1993).

Projective Tests

The fundamental idea underlying the use of projective tests is that a person's unconscious motives direct daily thoughts and behavior. **Projective tests** are a variety of devices or instruments used to assess personality in which an examinee is shown a standard set of ambiguous stimuli and asked to respond in an unrestricted manner. The examinees are assumed to project unconscious feelings, drives, and motives onto the ambiguous stimuli. Clinicians assess the deeper levels of their personality structure and uncover motives of which the examinees may not be aware. Projective tests are used when it is important to determine whether the examinee is trying to hide something from the psychologist. They tend to be less reliable than objective personality tests, but they help complete a picture of psychological functioning.

Projective tests: Personality-assessing devices or instruments by which examinees are shown a standard set of ambiguous stimuli and asked to respond in an unrestricted manner.

FIGURE 12.5

Example of a Rorschach Inkblot Test

In a Rorschach inkblot test, the psychologist asks the subject to describe what he or she sees in an inkblot such as this one. From the subject's descriptions, the psychologist makes inferences about the subject's drives, motivations, and unconscious conflicts.

Rorschach Inkblot Test. One widely used projective test is the *Rorschach Inkblot Test* (see Figure 12.5). Ten inkblots are shown to a subject, one at a time. Five are black and white, two have some red ink, and three have various pastel colors. They are symmetrical, with a specific shape or form.

Subjects tell the clinician what they see in the design, and a detailed report of the response is made for later interpretation. Aiken (1988, p. 390) reports a typical response to a Rorschach inkblot:

> My first impression was a big bug, a fly maybe. I see in the background two facelike figures pointing toward each other as if they're talking. It also has a resemblance to a skeleton—the pelvis area. I see a cute little bat right in the middle. The upper half looks like a mouse.

After the inkblots have been shown, the examiner asks specific questions, such as: "Describe the facelike figures." or "What were the figures talking about?" Although norms are available for responses, skilled interpretation and good clinical judgment are necessary for placing a subject's responses in a meaningful context. Long-term predictions can be formulated only with great caution (Exner, Thomas, & Mason, 1985).

Thematic Apperception Test. The *Thematic Apperception Test* (TAT) is much more structured than the Rorschach. (It was discussed in chapter 10 as one way to assess a person's need for achievement.) It consists of black-and-white pictures, each depicting one or more people in an ambiguous situation; and subjects are asked to tell a story describing the situation. Specifically, they are asked what led up to the situation, what will happen in the future, and what the people are thinking and feeling. The TAT is particularly useful as part of a battery of tests to examine a person's characteristic way of dealing with others and of interacting with the world.

To some extent, projective tests have a bad reputation among nonpsychologists. Most argue that the interpretation of pictures is too subjective and prone to error. Practicing clinicians, even when they use projective tests, are likely to rely heavily on behavioral assessment approaches, discussed next.

Behavioral Assessment

Traditionally, *behavioral assessment* focused on overt behaviors that could be examined directly. Today, practitioners and researchers examine cognitive activity as well. Their aim is to gather information both to diagnose maladjustment and to prescribe treatment. Four popular and widely used behavioral assessment techniques are behavioral assessment interviews, naturalistic observation, self-monitoring, and neuropsychological assessment.

Behavioral Assessment Interviews. Any psychological assessment is likely to begin with an interview. Interviews are personal, giving the client (and the client's family) an opportunity to express feelings, facts, and experiences that might not be expressed through other assessment procedures. Interviews yield important information about the client's family situation, occupational stresses, and other events that affect the behavior being examined. They also allow psychologists to evaluate the client's motivations as well as to inform the client about the assessment process.

Behavioral assessment interviews tend to be systematic and structured, focusing on overt and current behaviors and paying attention to the situations in which these behaviors occur. The interviewer will ask the examinee about the events that led up to a specific response, how the examinee felt while making the response, and whether the same response might occur in other situations. Through this type of interview, the clinician has the opportunity to select the problems to be dealt with in therapy and to set treatment goals. Many clinicians consider their first interview with a client a key component in the assessment process.

Interviews reveal only what the interviewee wishes to disclose, however, and are subject to bias on the part of the interviewer. Nonetheless, together with other behavioral measures, interviews are a good starting point.

Naturalistic Observation. In behavioral assessment, *naturalistic observation* involves two or more observers entering a client's natural environment and recording the occurrence of specified behaviors at predetermined intervals. In a personality assessment, for example, psychologists might observe how often a child in a classroom uses obscene words or how often a hospitalized patient refers to her depressed state. The purpose of naturalistic observation as a behavioral assessment technique is to observe people without interference. The strength of the approach is in providing information that might otherwise be unavailable or difficult to piece together. For example, observation can help psychologists realize the sequence of actions that may lead up to an outburst of depressed feelings or to antisocial behaviors.

Naturalistic observation is not without its problems, however. How does a researcher record behavior in a home setting without being observed? Do naturalistic samples of behavior represent interactions in other settings? Does the observer have any biases, make inaccurate judgments, or collect inadequate data? Although naturalistic observation is not perfect, it is a powerful technique.

Self-Monitoring. **Self-monitoring** is an assessment procedure in which a person systematically counts and records the frequency and duration of specific behaviors in himself or herself. One person might record the number and duration of specific personality traits or of such symptoms as migraine headaches, backaches, or feelings of panic. Another person might self-monitor eating or sleeping patterns, sexual behavior, or smoking.

Self-monitoring is inexpensive, easy to do, and applicable to a variety of problems. It reveals information that might otherwise be inaccessible and enables practitioners to probe the events that preceded the monitored activity to see whether some readily identifiable pattern exists. In addition, self-monitoring helps clients become more aware of their own behaviors and the situations in which they occur.

Neuropsychological Assessment. The newest branch of assessment is *neuropsychological assessment.* (*Neurologists* are physicians who study the physiology of the brain and its disorders; *neuropsychologists* are psychologists who study the brain and its disorders as they relate to behavior.) Though neuropsychology is a traditional area in experimental psychology, its techniques are now employed by practitioners. Practitioners now routinely watch for signs of neuropsychological disorders.

Often personality changes and some forms of maladjustment result from a brain disorder or a malfunction in the nervous system (see Table 12.3 on page 460 for examples). The signs may become evident through the use of traditional assessment

Self-monitoring: An assessment procedure in which a person systematically counts and records the frequency and duration of specific behaviors in him- or herself.

TABLE 12.3

Some Brain-Behavior Characteristics for Selected Sites in the Brain

SITE	CHARACTERISTIC
Parietal lobes	These lobes contain reception areas for the sense of touch and for the sense of body position. Damage to this area may result in deficits in the sense of touch; disorganization; and distorted self-perception.
Frontal lobes	These lobes are integrally involved in ordering information and sorting out stimuli. Damage to this area may affect concentration and attention, abstract thinking ability, concept formation ability, foresight, problem-solving ability, speech, and gross and fine motor ability.
Temporal lobes	These lobes contain auditory reception areas as well as certain areas for the processing of visual information. Damage to this area may affect sound discrimination, recognition, and comprehension; music appreciation; voice recognition; and auditory or visual memory storage.
Occipital lobes	These lobes contain visual reception areas. Damage to this area could result in blindness in all or part of the visual field or deficits in object recognition, visual scanning, visual integration of symbols into wholes, and recall of visual imagery.

Source: Adapted from Cohen et al., 1988.

devices such as histories (a history of headaches, for example), intelligence tests (showing slow reaction times), or observation of the client during a session (the occurrence of head motions or muscle spasms). Thus, if a child who frequently and inappropriately makes obscene gestures or remarks accompanies them with facial tics, the practitioner may suspect the existence of the neurological disorder known as Tourette syndrome, in which such behaviors are often evident. Psychologists who see evidence of neuropsychological deficits often refer the afflicted clients to neuropsychologists or neurologists for further evaluation.

FOCUS

▶ What evidence is there that the MMPI–2 is a good test of potential maladjustment?   p. 456

▶ Identify the techniques used in behavioral assessment. pp. 458–460

Concluding Note

Personality theories are so diverse that students often have trouble trying to decide which ones make the most sense. The truth is that they all make a certain amount of sense. Each theory is coherent, predicts behavior (some of the time), and is based on some fundamental assumptions about human nature and behavior. The differences among the theories are especially instructive. Freud was biologically oriented and spoke of dark forces within an individual that propelled the individual forward. Maslow, by contrast, spoke of inner drives toward self-fulfillment. Cognitive-behaviorists such as Mischel are much more people-environment oriented.

Each of the personality theories must take into account the wide diversity of human behavior. Cultural diversity is so strong, ethnic differences are so varied, and gender differences are so pronounced that a comprehensive theory of personality cannot be as global as was Freud's or as specific as is Rotter's. A youth from a Native American reservation in Arizona brings to his emerging personality sharply different experiences from those of a youth from the San Fernando valley of California or the son of a migrant farm worker from the rural South. Even if people are from the same geographic area, they have sharply different family expectations, gender-based roles, and religious experiences.

Personality theories tend to neglect age and experience. How does our personality change as we mature? We know that people change, but we need to know what triggers such change. Our theories about and studies of personality have come a long way; however, we still have a long way to go. The journey is very exciting for those of us who study personality and try to incorporate into our theories the diversity of the human experience.

Summary & Review

Psychoanalytic Theory

Identify three key concepts of psychoanalytic theory.

Psychic determinism suggests that all thoughts, feelings, actions, gestures, and speech are determined by some action or event that happened to an individual in the past. *Unconscious motivation* suggests that behavior is determined by desires, goals, and internal states of which an individual is generally unaware. Freud also theorized that people are constantly in *conflict* because of two basic instinctual drives buried deep within the unconscious—life, which prominently features sex and sexual energy, and death, which features aggression. pp. 427–428

According to Freud, what is the structure of personality?

Freud's structure of *personality* includes awareness that exists at three levels: *conscious, preconscious,* and *unconscious.* The primary structural elements of the mind and personality—the id, the ego, and the superego—are three forces that reside, fully or partially, in the unconscious. The *id,* which works through the pleasure principle, is the source of human instinctual energy. The *ego* tries to satisfy the instinctual needs in accordance with reality. The *superego* is the moral branch or aspect of mental functioning.   pp. 428–429

Describe Freud's view of the development of personality.

Freud described the development of personality in terms of five consecutive stages: oral, anal, phallic, latency, and genital. The *oral stage* is based on the fact that newborns' instincts are focused on their mouths—their primary pleasure-seeking center. In the *anal stage* children learn to control the immediate gratification obtained through defecation and become responsive to the demands of society. In the *phallic stage* children

continued

Summary & Review

obtain gratification primarily from the genitals. During this stage, children pass through the *Oedipus* (or Electra) *complex*. In the *latency stage*, sexual urges are inactive. The *genital stage* is Freud's last stage of personality development, during which the sexual conflicts of childhood resurface at puberty and are resolved in adolescence. pp. 429–432

What are defense mechanisms?

Defense mechanisms, such as *projection*, *denial*, *reaction formation*, *sublimation*, and *rationalization*, are ways in which people reduce anxiety by distorting their perceptions of reality. Defense mechanisms allow the ego to deal with anxiety. For Freud, the most important defense mechanism is *repression*—in which people block anxiety-provoking feeling from conscious awareness and push them into the unconscious. pp. 432–433

Who are the neo-Freudians?

A *neo-Freudian* (such as Jung or Adler) is a person who modified or varied some of the basic ideas of Freud; they usually attributed a greater influence to cultural and interpersonal factors than did Freud. The neo-Freudians argued that Freud stressed sex too much and left out many key issues. Other neo-Freudians asserted that the ego has more of a role than Freud thought in controlling behavior and shaping personality. pp. 435–436

Briefly describe the approaches of Jung and Adler.

Jung emphasized unconscious processes as determinants of behavior and believed that each person houses past events in the unconscious. The *collective unconscious* is a collection of emotionally charged ideas and images that have rich meaning and symbolism. In Alfred Adler's theory, people strive for superiority or perfection. This tendency is often prompted

by feelings of inferiority. According to Adler, individuals develop a lifestyle that allows them to express their goals in the context of human society. pp. 436–438

KEY TERMS: *personality*, p. 426; *psychic determinism*, p. 427; *unconscious motivation*, p. 427; *libido*, p. 427; *conscious*, p. 428; *preconscious*, p. 428; *unconscious*, p. 428; *id*, p. 428; *ego*, p. 428; *superego*, p. 428; *oral stage*, p. 430; *anal stage*, p. 430; *phallic stage*, p. 431; *Oedipus complex*, p. 431; *latency stage*, p. 431; *genital stage*, p. 432; *fixation*, p. 432; *defense mechanism*, p. 432; *repression*, p. 432; *projection*, p. 432; *denial*, p. 433; *reaction formation*, p. 433; *sublimation*, p. 433; *rationalization*, p. 433; *neo-Freudians*, p. 435; *collective unconscious*, p. 436; *archetypes*, p. 436.

Humanistic Approaches

What is self-actualization?

Self-actualization is the process of realizing our innate human potential to become the best we can be. The process of realizing potential, and of growing, is the process of becoming self-actualized. pp. 438–439

Describe Rogers's theory of personality.

The humanistic approach of Rogers states that *fulfillment* is the motivating force of personality development and is structured around the concept of *self*. The *ideal self* is the self a person would ideally like to be. Persons with rigid self-concepts guard themselves against threatening feelings; they become unhappy when they are unable to fit new types of behavior into their current self-concepts. pp. 439–440

KEY TERMS: *fulfillment*, p. 439; *self*, p. 439; *ideal self*, p. 439; *self-actualization*, p. 439

Trait and Type Theories

Distinguish between a trait and a type.

Traits are any readily identifiable stable behaviors that characterize the way in which an individual differs from other people; *types* are broad collections of traits loosely tied together and interrelated. A person can be said to have a trait; the person cannot be said to have a type; rather, the person fits a type. p. 441

Describe the ideas of Allport, Cattell, and Eysenck.

Allport argued that if you know a person's traits, it is possible to predict how he or she will respond to stimuli. *Cardinal traits* are ideas and behaviors that determine the direction of a person's life. *Central traits* are the behaviors that characterize a person's daily interactions. *Secondary traits* are specific behaviors that occur in response to specific situations. Cattell used the technique of *factor analysis* to show that groups of traits tend to cluster together. Cattell termed the obvious, day-to-day cluster of traits surface *traits* and the higher-order cluster of traits *source traits*. Eysenck focused on higher levels of trait organization, *types*. Eysenck argued that all personality traits can be reduced to three basic dimensions: emotional stability, introversion or extroversion, and psychoticism. pp. 442–443

What is meant by the term "the big five"?

Although dozens of traits exist, researchers think of "the big five" as "supertraits," the important dispositions that characterize personality. These are: Extroversion-introversion—the extent to which people are social or calm; agreeableness-antagonism—the extent to which people are good natured or irritable; conscientiousness-undirectedness—the extent to which people are reliable or undependable; neuroticism-stability—the extent to which people are nervous or at ease; and openness to experience—the extent to which people are independent or conforming.   p. 443

KEY TERMS: *trait*, p. 441; *types*, p. 441.

Behavioral Approaches

What are the key ideas of behavioral approaches to personality?

Behavioral theories of personality center on precisely defined elements, such as the relationship between stimuli and responses, the strength of stimuli, and the strength, duration, and timing of reinforcers. For behaviorists, the structural unit of personality is the response. All behaviors are seen as responses to stimuli or as responses waiting for reinforcement. Behavioral psychologists try to use the learning principles to help clients control their behavior and shape their personalities.   pp. 445–446

How do learning theorists account for behavior?

Behavioral psychologists who focus on classical conditioning maintain that people develop personalities that focus on anxiety and fear through processes in which a neutral stimulus is paired with another stimulus that elicits some response. According to behaviorists who focus on operant conditioning, personality can be explained as spontaneous behavior that is reinforced. The social learning theorist sees personality as developing through the process of observation and imitation and that learning can occur independent of reinforcement.   pp. 446–447

Cognitive Approaches

What are the key ideas of the cognitive approach to personality?

The cognitive approach emphasizes the interaction of a person's thoughts and behavior. This approach considers the uniqueness of human beings and assumes that human beings are decision makers, planners, and evaluators of behavior. Cognitive views assert that individuals make rational choices in trying to predict and manage events in the world. One of the key concepts of the cognitive approach is the idea that people develop self-schemata—a series of ideas and self-knowledge that organize how a person thinks about himself or herself.   p. 448

What is locus of control?

Locus of control is the extent to which individuals believe that a reinforcement or an outcome is contingent on their own behavior or personal characteristics as opposed to luck, chance, fate, or is simply unpredictable. People classified as internal feel in control of their environment and future; people with an external locus of control believe that they have little control over their lives.   pp. 448–449

What is self-efficacy?

Self-efficacy is a person's belief about whether he or she can successfully engage in and execute a specific task or behavior. Judgments about self-efficacy determine how much effort people will expend and how long they will persist in the face of obstacles. A strong sense of self-efficacy allows people to feel free to select, influence, and even construct the circumstances of their lives.   pp. 450–452

How do Mischel and other cognitive theorists view the effect of situations on personality?

The cognitive theories of Bandura, Mischel, and Rotter have reintroduced thought into the equation of personality and situational variables. They have focused on how people interpret the situations in which they find themselves and then alter their behavior. Mischel argues that people change their responses based on their past experiences and their current assessment of the situation to suit the present situation. This process of adjustment is called self-regulation. pp. 452–454

KEY TERMS: *self-efficacy*, p. 450; *shyness*, p. 451.

Psychological Assessment

What is assessment?

Assessment is the process of evaluating individual differences among human beings using techniques such as tests, interviews, observations, and recordings of physiological processes. Many psychologists administer a group or battery of tests. The goal is to use the variety of tests available so that when the information taken together is added up, intelligent, informed conclusions can be drawn.   pp. 454–456

Briefly describe the MMPI–2.

The MMPI–2 consists of 567 true-false statements that focus on attitudes, feelings, motor disturbances, and bodily complaints. A series of subscales examines different aspects of functioning and measures the truthfulness of the subject's responses; these are called the clinical and validity scales. The MMPI–2 is used as a screening device for maladjustment. It provides a profile that allows

continued

Summary & Review

psychologists to assess an individual's current level of functioning and characteristic way of dealing with the world and to make reasonable predictions about the person's ability to function in specific situations. pp. 456–457

Describe projective tests.

Projective tests such as the TAT use ambiguous stimuli and ask examinees to respond in an unrestricted manner. Examinees are thought to reflect or project unconscious feelings, drives, and motives onto the ambiguous stimuli. pp. 457–458

What are four widely used methods of behavioral assessment?

Four popular and widely used behavioral assessment techniques are behavioral assessment interviews, naturalistic observation, self-monitoring, and neuropsychological assessment. Behavioral assessment interviews tend to be systematic and structured, focusing on overt and current behaviors and paying attention to the situations in which these behaviors occur. Naturalistic observation involves observing a client in the natural environment and recording the occurrence of specified behaviors at predetermined intervals. *Self-monitoring* is an assessment procedure in which a person systematically records the frequency and duration of specific behaviors in himself or herself. Neuropsychological assessment is the study of the brain and its disorders as they relate to behavior. pp. 458–460

KEY TERMS: *assessment*, p. 454; *projective tests*, p. 457; *self-monitoring*, p. 459.

CONNECTIONS

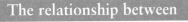

If you are interested in...

13

Stress and Health Psychology

A good friend's life changed drastically 2 years ago. Tricia was in therapy to help her sort out some career and marital problems when one day she started to remember some awful events that had taken place many years before. As a young adolescent, Tricia had been sexually abused by her father. Over a period of several months in therapy, she slowly and painfully began to recall the details of her ordeal. After her memories surfaced, she began waking up in the middle of the night, drenched in a cold sweat. Her dreams were terrifying re-creations of the horrors she had experienced. She became depressed, unable to concentrate at work, and increasingly withdrawn from her family. As a consequence of her depression, she lost weight, had great difficulty sleeping, developed a series of physical complaints, and lost interest in her usual activities. This once vibrant, active woman was taken over by her memories. Her stress level was unbearable.

As a student, you face a variety of stressors: studying for several final exams in a single week, juggling your studies with a part-time job to help with your tight finances, getting along with your roommate in small living quarters. Stress, ranging from the minor hassle of being caught in a traffic jam to the major trauma of fighting in a war, is a reality for all of us. We can deal with stress in either positive or negative ways; unfortunately, many people don't cope effectively with stress. Some suffer from stress-related health problems, such as high blood pressure and insomnia. Others try to escape from stress by turning to alcohol and other drugs.

In this chapter, we will examine the nature of stress, learn how to cope with stress, and see the relationship of health and stress. We will also look into how motivation, learning, and personality work together to influence our ability to cope with stress in day-to-day life.

Stress

Eating antacid tablets like candy, launching into tirades at coworkers or friends, banging their fists on a table, and consuming cocktails each night are a way of life for many people who succumb to the stress of their jobs, families, or financial burdens. One person may have a high-pressure job that affects her social life and causes daily migraines. A coworker might manage the same amount of stress in more positive ways, without suffering negative health consequences. Herein lies an important difference: Stress is evaluated and handled in different ways, depending on the person.

What Is Stress?

A **stressor** is an environmental stimulus that affects an organism in physically or psychologically injurious ways, usually producing anxiety, tension, and physiological arousal. **Anxiety** is a generalized feeling of fear and apprehension that might be related to a particular event or object and is often accompanied by increased physiological arousal. Physiological arousal is often the first change that appears when a person experiences a stressor. Arousal refers to changes in the autonomic nervous system, including increased heart rate, breathing, and blood pressure; sweating palms; and dilation of the pupils.

Whenever something negatively affects someone, physically or psychologically, the person may experience the effect as stress. **Stress** is a nonspecific, often global, response by an organism to real or imagined demands made on it; it is an emotional response. The key is that not all people view a stimulus or a situation in the same way; *a person must appraise a situation as stressful for it to be stressful.* This broad definition recognizes that everyone experiences stress at some time; however, stress is an interpreted state, a response on the part of a person. Richard Lazarus (1993), a leader in the study of emotion and stress, asserts that people *actively negotiate* between the demand of the environment (stressors) and personal beliefs and behaviors. This active negotiation is what cognitive researchers refer to as appraisal. Sometimes, the arousal that stressors bring about initiates positive actions; sometimes its effects are detrimental.

What determines whether a particular event will be stressful? The answer lies in the extent to which people are familiar with the event, how much they had anticipated the event, and how much they can control the event and themselves.

The first day of a new course brings excitement and some apprehension about an instructor's expectations and whether the time commitments for the course will

Stressor: An environmental stimulus that affects an organism in physically or psychologically injurious ways, usually producing anxiety, tension, and physiological arousal.

Anxiety: A generalized feeling of fear and apprehension that might be related to a particular event or object and is often accompanied by increased physiological arousal.

Stress: A nonspecific, often global, response by an organism to real or imagined demands made on it (a person must appraise a situation as stressful for it to be stressful).

be burdensome; the second or third time a class meets is usually much less worrisome. When people can predict events, they feel that they are more in control and can have some impact on the future. This is a two-step process: First, you decide whether a situation is threatening; then you decide whether you can cope with it.

Types and Sources of Stress

During rehearsal for a choral concert, 41 grade-schoolers developed nausea, shortness of breath, and abdominal pains. At the choir performance that evening, 29 of the children collapsed on stage. At another school, 34 sixth-grade students became dizzy and fainted during their graduation program. In both cases, the children were diagnosed as suffering from stress-related disorders. Feeling stress and trapped in situations that didn't allow them to escape from it, the children responded with symptoms of physical illness. Three broad types of events cause stress: frustration, conflict, and pressure.

Frustration. When people are hindered from meeting their goals, they often feel frustrated. **Frustration** is the emotional state or condition that results when a goal—work, family, or personal—is thwarted or blocked. When people believe they cannot achieve a goal (often because of situations beyond their control), they may experience frustration. When you are unable to obtain a summer job because of a lack of experience, it can cause feelings of frustration. When a grandparent becomes ill, you may feel helpless; and this can causes frustration. When there is an environmental threat over which you have no control, frustration is often the result (Hallman & Wandersman, 1992).

Some frustrations are externally caused. Examples are your lack of experience for a specific job or your grandparent's illness. Other frustrations are caused by specific people; your boss may be unfair in his appraisal of you, or your roommate may be too stingy to chip in for new furniture. You can sometimes alleviate the frustration of dealing with other people by taking some action; this action, however, may place you in conflict, another type of stress.

Conflict. When people must make difficult decisions, we say that they are in a state of **conflict**—the emotional state or condition in which people have to make difficult decisions about two or more competing motives, behaviors, or impulses. Consider the difficult decisions of American draftees who did not want to fight in the Vietnam War but did not want to flee to Canada or face imprisonment. What happens if a person's goals and needs conflict—if a student must choose between two equally difficult academic courses, both of which will advance the student's career plans, but in different directions?

One of the first psychologists to describe and quantify such conflict situations was Neal Miller (1944, 1959). Miller developed hypotheses about how animals and human beings behave in situations that have both positive and negative aspects. In general, he described three types of situations that involve competing demands: approach-approach conflicts, avoidance-avoidance conflicts, and approach-avoidance conflicts.

Approach-approach conflict is the conflict that results when a person must choose between two equally attractive alternatives or goals (for example, two wonderful jobs). This conflict generates discomfort and a stress response; however, people can usually tolerate it because either alternative is pleasant. **Avoidance-avoidance conflict** is the conflict that results from having to choose between two equally distasteful alternatives or goals (for example, mowing the lawn or painting the garage). **Approach-avoidance conflict** is the conflict that results from having to choose an alternative or goal that has both attractive and repellent aspects. Studying for an

Frustration: The emotional state or condition that results when a goal—work, family, or personal—is thwarted or blocked.

Conflict: The emotional state or condition in which a person has to make difficult decisions about two or more competing motives, behaviors, or impulses.

Approach-approach conflict: The conflict that results from having to choose between two equally attractive alternatives or goals.

Avoidance-avoidance conflict: The conflict that results from having to choose between two equally distasteful alternatives or goals.

Approach-avoidance conflict: The conflict that results from having to choose an alternative or goal that has both attractive and repellent aspects.

FIGURE 13.1

Three Types of Conflict

In approach-approach conflict, people have to choose between equally appealing situations. In avoidance-avoidance conflict, people have to choose between two equally distasteful situations. In approach-avoidance conflict, people have to choose an alternative that is both appealing and distasteful.

APPROACH–APPROACH CONFLICT

Movies (+) ← → Theatre (+)

France (+) ← → England (+)

AVOIDANCE–AVOIDANCE CONFLICT

Studying (−) ← → Cleaning (−)

Unemployment (−) ← → Degrading job (−)

APPROACH–AVOIDANCE CONFLICT

Studying (−)

Good grades (+)

Delicious meal (+)

High calories (−)

exam, which can lead to good grades but is boring and difficult, is an approach-avoidance situation.

As Figure 13.1 shows, any of the three types of conflict situations will lead to stress. Miller developed principles to predict behavior in conflict situations, particularly in approach-avoidance situations:

1. The closer a subject is to a goal, the stronger the tendency is to approach the goal.

2. When two incompatible responses are available, the stronger one will be expressed.

3. The strength of the tendency to approach or avoid is correlated with the strength of the motivating drive. (Thus, a child who is both hungry and thirsty will seek food if he is more hungry than thirsty.)

We regularly face conflict situations that may cause us to become anxious and upset. Moreover, if conflicts affect our day-to-day behavior, we may exhibit symptoms of maladjustment.

Pressure: Work, Time, and Life Events. Arousal and stress may occur when people feel **pressure**—the emotional state or condition resulting from the real or imagined expectations of others for certain behaviors or results. Although individual situations differ, pressure is common to almost everyone. Most of the time, it is associated with work, a lack of time, and life events.

Work that is either too overstimulating or understimulating can cause stress. Work-related stress also can come from fear of retirement, from being passed over for promotion, and from organizational changes. In addition, the physical work setting may be too noisy or crowded or too isolated. Work-related pressure from deadlines, competition, and professional relationships (to name just a few possibilities) can cause a variety of physical problems. People suffering from work stress may experience migraines, sleeplessness, hunger for sweets, overeating, and ulcers and other intestinal distress. Stress at work often leads to illness, resulting in lost efficiency and absenteeism (Levi, 1990).

Individuals with high-stress jobs, particularly when the stress is constant, show the effects convincingly. Air traffic controllers and surgeons, for example, are responsible for the lives of other people every day and must be alert and organized at all times. If they work too many hours without relief, they may even make a fatal mistake. Others with high-stress jobs include inner-city high school teachers, customer service agents, waiters and waitresses, and emergency workers.

Lack of time is another common source of stress. Everyone faces deadlines: Students must complete tests before class ends, auto workers must keep pace with the assembly line, and tax returns must be filed by April 15. People have only a limited number of hours each day in which to accomplish tasks; therefore, most people carefully allocate their time to reduce time pressure. They may establish routines, make lists, set schedules, leave optional meetings early, and set aside leisure time in which to rid themselves of stressful feelings. If they do not handle time pressures successfully, they may begin to feel overloaded and stressed.

A third common source of stress is life events, which may be both positive and stressful at the same time. Consider marriage. Marriage unites people as partners, companions, lovers, and friends. Nonetheless, adjusting to married life means becoming familiar with new experiences, responding to unanticipated events, and having less control over many aspects of day-to-day experiences—all of which can be stressful. Also, at times, interpersonal discord arises. One partner may not be fulfilling marital or role obligations or may be causing the spouse to feel left out; both possibilities may bring about stress and even health problems (Burman & Margolin, 1992). We will examine stressful life events in more detail on pages 474–478.

Responses to Stress

People react to stress in a wide variety of ways. Some experience modest increases in physiological arousal, while others may exhibit significant physical symptoms. In extreme cases, people become so aroused, anxious, and disorganized that their behavior becomes maladaptive or maladjusted. The basic idea underlying the work of many researchers is that stress activates a potential predisposition toward maladjustment (Monroe & Simons, 1991).

Emotion, Physiology, and Behavior. Psychologists who study stress typically divide the stress reaction into emotional, physiological, and behavioral components. *Emotionally,* people's reactions often depend on their frustration, their work-related pressures, and their day-to-day conflicts. When frustrated, people become angry or annoyed; when pressured, they become aroused and anxious; when placed in situations of conflict, they may vacillate or become irritable and hostile.

Physiologically, the stress response is characterized by arousal. When psychologists refer to arousal, they usually mean changes in the autonomic nervous system,

Pressure: The emotional state or condition resulting from others' real or imagined expectations for success or for specific behaviors or results; the feelings that result from coercion.

FIGURE 13.2

Effects of Arousal on Task Performance

When arousal is low, task performance is poor or non-existent. Performance is usually best at moderate levels of arousal. High levels of arousal on complex tasks usually impair performance.

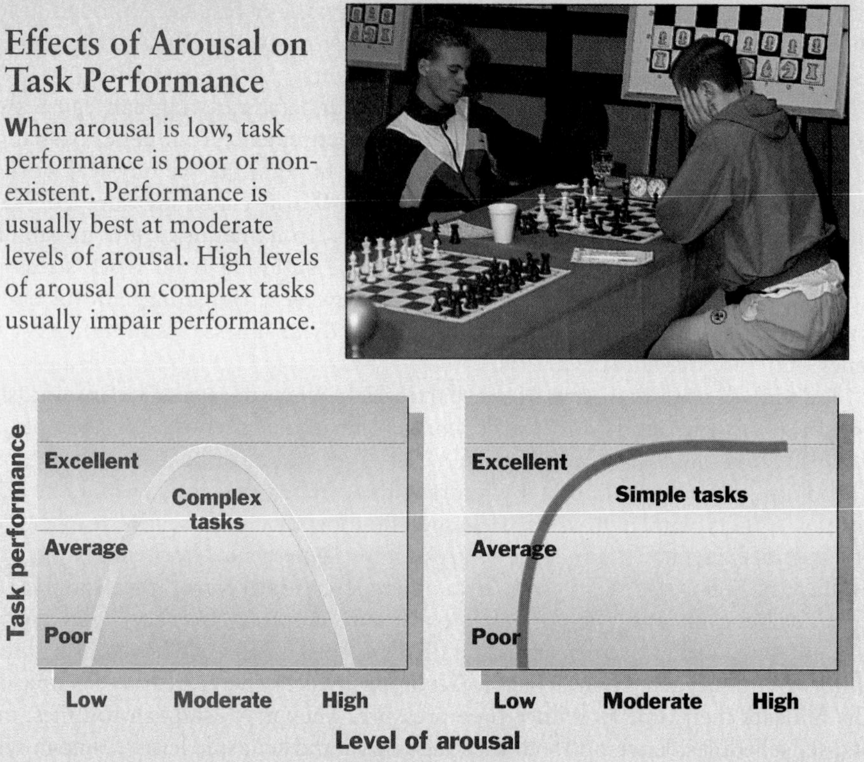

ncluding increased heart rate, breathing, and blood pressure; sweating palms; and dilation of the pupils. Arousal is often the first change that occurs when a person feels stressed.

Behaviorally, stress and its arousal response are related. As we saw in chapter 10, psychologist Donald Hebb (1972) has argued that effective behavior depends on a person's state of arousal. When people are moderately aroused, they behave with optimal effectiveness; when they are underaroused, they lack the stimulation to behave effectively. Overarousal tends to produce disorganized behavior in which people become ineffective, particularly if the tasks they undertake are complex. (Figure 13.2 shows the effects of arousal on task performance.)

A moderate amount of stress is necessary and desirable. Stress and the accompanying arousal are what keep us active and involved. They impel students to study, drive athletes to excel during competition, and help businesspeople to strive toward greater heights. In short, stress and arousal can help people achieve their potential. See Figure 13.3 for an overview of the responses to stressors that occur after an appraisal.

Burnout. A stress reaction especially common to people with high standards is **burnout**—a state of emotional and physical exhaustion, lowered productivity, and feelings of isolation, often caused by work-related pressures (Kalimo & Mejman, 1987). People who face high-stress conditions on a daily basis often feel debilitated, hopeless, and emotionally drained, and may eventually stop trying. Although burnout is most often caused by work-related problems and stress, family, financial, and social pressures can create the same feelings. Burnout victims develop negative self-concepts because they are unable to maintain the high standards they have set for themselves. They often cease to be concerned about others and have physical as well as social problems.

Burnout: A state of emotional and physical exhaustion, lowered productivity, and feelings of isolation, often caused by work-related pressures.

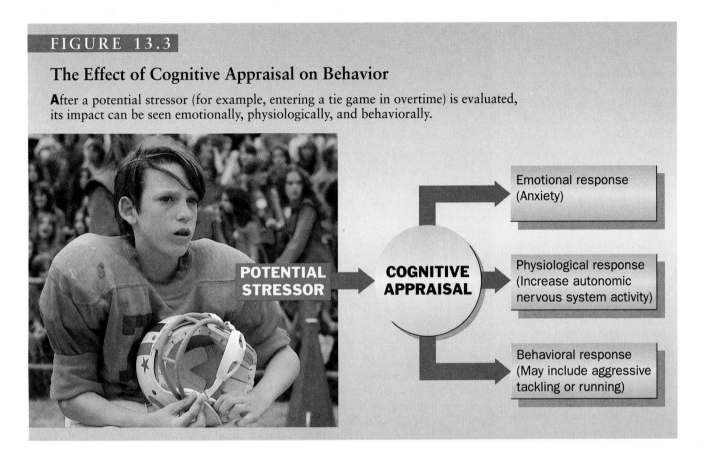

FIGURE 13.3

The Effect of Cognitive Appraisal on Behavior

After a potential stressor (for example, entering a tie game in overtime) is evaluated, its impact can be seen emotionally, physiologically, and behaviorally.

POTENTIAL STRESSOR → COGNITIVE APPRAISAL →

Emotional response (Anxiety)

Physiological response (Increase autonomic nervous system activity)

Behavioral response (May include aggressive tackling or running)

Health Consequences. A recent research study found that stress contributes to a person's susceptibility to catching the common cold (Cohen, Tyrrell, & Smith, 1993). Mothers and self-help books have long told people to reduce their levels of stress to keep from getting sick, and research now supports their advice.

Stress does not directly cause disease. However, it contributes to many diseases, including the six major causes of death in the United States: heart disease, cancer, lung ailments, accidental injuries, cirrhosis of the liver, and suicide. In general, stress affects the immune system, making people more vulnerable to disease (Cohen, Tyrrell, & Smith, 1991; Cohen & Williamson, 1991). It may lead to headaches, backaches, decreased productivity, and family arguments. At a minimum, stress-related illnesses are causing an increase in medical costs for both individuals and employers. Extreme stress has been implicated in sudden heart attacks (Kamarck & Jennings, 1991).

Stress afflicts children as well as adults. Children are usually unable to change or control the circumstances in which they find themselves (Band & Weisz, 1988). They may experience stress in school, stress caused by an abusive parent, stress from their parents divorce, or stress from peer pressure. Like adults, they often show their stress response in physical symptoms. Also like adults, children have to appraise a situation as stressful for it to be stressful; and some children are more vulnerable than others.

Ethnic Differences in Responses to Stress. In March 1989, the oil tanker *Exxon Valdez* ran aground on the rocks of Prince William Sound in Alaska and created an ecologically disastrous oil spill. It also had profound effects on the people living in the region, who experienced a marked increase in physical and psychological disorders. A research team sought to explore whether stress reactions to the disaster varied with the ethnicity of the residents (Palinkas et al., 1992). The team

When the Exxon Valdez *ran aground in March of 1989, it caused both ecological and psychological damage for native Alaskans, many of whom make their living in the fishing industry.*

examined Native Alaskans and white Euro-Americans in 13 communities in Alaska that were affected by the oil spill. The Native Alaskans live a distinctly different lifestyle and work in different types of jobs compared to the Euro-Americans. The Euro-Americans are more likely resemble the population of the other 49 U.S. states.

Although both groups reported more psychological problems than usual, the Native Alaskans reported more participation in clean-up activities than did the Euro-Americans. The Native Alaskans were also more affected in their business dealings (fishing, for example), and the clean-up activities dominated their work, social, and cultural lives. Consequently, they saw the *Valdez* accident as having a far greater social and psychological impact, and they experienced far more stress than did the Euro-Americans. As we have seen before, people have a cultural framework that shapes their point of view; that framework also determines which events they will see as stressful.

Studying Stress: Focus on Physiology

Psychologists want to know how today's increasingly complex lifestyles affect the physical and psychological well-being of individuals. For example, does intense competition make businesspeople more susceptible to heart attacks? How can psychologists help people cope with life stresses, such as having a baby? How can therapists help veterans who are traumatized by war? These questions have helped researchers develop theories of stress. One of the best-known theories is Hans Selye's general adaptation syndrome, which we will look at next.

Selye's General Adaptation Syndrome. In the 1930s, Hans Selye (1907–1982) began a systematic study of stressors and stress. He investigated the physiological changes in people who were experiencing various amounts of stress. Selye conceptualized people's responses to stress in terms of a *general adaptation syndrome* (1956, 1976). (A *syndrome* is a set of responses; in the case of stress, it is a set of behaviorally defined physical symptoms.) Selye's work initiated thousands of studies on stress and stress reactions, and Selye himself published more than 1,600 articles on the topic.

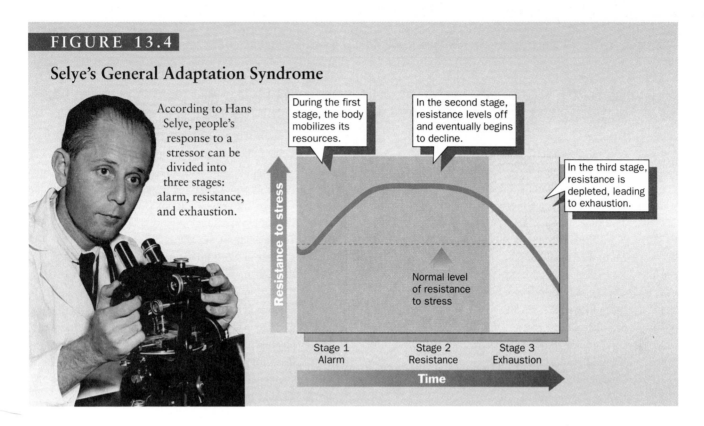

FIGURE 13.4

Selye's General Adaptation Syndrome

According to Hans Selye, people's response to a stressor can be divided into three stages: alarm, resistance, and exhaustion.

During the first stage, the body mobilizes its resources.

In the second stage, resistance levels off and eventually begins to decline.

In the third stage, resistance is depleted, leading to exhaustion.

Resistance to stress

Normal level of resistance to stress

Stage 1 Alarm   Stage 2 Resistance   Stage 3 Exhaustion

Time

According to Selye, people's response to a stressor occurs in three stages: (1) an initial short-term stage of alarm, (2) a longer period of resistance, and (3) a final stage of exhaustion (see Figure 13.4). During the *alarm stage*, people experience increased physiological arousal. They become excited, anxious, or frightened. Bodily resources are mobilized. Metabolism speeds up dramatically, and blood is diverted from the skin to the brain, resulting in a pale appearance. (The response is much like the fight-or-flight syndrome, in which the sympathetic nervous system is activated; see chapter 2.) People also may experience loss of appetite, sleeplessness, headaches, ulcers, or hormone imbalances; their normal level of resistance to stress decreases.

Because people cannot stay highly aroused for very long, the initial alarm response usually leads to *resistance*. During this stage, physiological and behavioral responses become more moderate and sustained. People in the resistance stage often are irritable, impatient, and angry; and they may experience chronic fatigue. This stage can persist for a few hours, several days, or even years, although eventually resistance begins to decline. Couples who suffer traumatic divorces sometimes exhibit anger and emotional fatigue years after the conflict has been resolved in court.

The final stage is *exhaustion*. Stress saps psychological energy; resistance is depleted. If people don't relieve their stress, they can become too exhausted to adapt. At that point, they again become extremely alarmed, and they finally give up. Maladjustment, withdrawal, or, in extreme cases, death may follow. Of course, not everyone shows the same behaviors.

Holmes-Rahe Scale. Among the many researchers Selye inspired to study stressors and refine his theory are Holmes and Rahe. Their basic assumption is that stressful life events to which people must adapt, especially in combination, will damage health (Holmes & Rahe, 1967; Rahe, 1989). *Stressful life events* are prominent events in a person's day-to-day circumstances that necessitate change.

TABLE 13.1 *A Portion of the Holmes-Rahe Social Readjustment Rating Scale*

Rank	Life Event	Value	Rank	Life Event	Value
1	Death of spouse	100	23	Son or daughter leaving home	29
2	Divorce	73	24	Trouble with in-laws	29
3	Marital separation	65	25	Outstanding personal achievement	28
4	Jail term	63	26	Wife begins or stops work	26
5	Death of close family member	63	27	Begin or end school	26
6	Personal injury or illness	53	28	Change in living conditions	20
7	Marriage	50	29	Revision of personal habits	24
8	Fired at work	47	30	Trouble with boss	23
9	Marital reconciliation	45	31	Change in work hours or conditions	20
10	Retirement	45	32	Change in residence	20
11	Change in health of family member	44	33	Change in schools	20
12	Pregnancy	40	34	Change in recreation	19
13	Sex difficulties	39	35	Change in church activities	19
14	Gain of new family member	39	36	Change in social activities	18
15	Business readjustment	39	37	Loan for lesser purchase (under $10,000)	17
16	Change in financial state	38	38	Change in sleeping habits	16
17	Death of close friend	37	39	Change in number of family get-togethers	15
18	Change to different line of work	36	40	Change in eating habits	15
19	Change in number of arguments with spouse	35	41	Vacation	13
20	Mortgage or loan for major purchase	31	42	Christmas	12
21	Foreclosure of mortgage or loan	30	43	Minor violations of the law	11
22	Change in responsibilities at work	29			

To test their assumption, the researchers devised the Social Readjustment Rating Scale—a scale on which individuals circle significant life events that they've recently experienced (see Table 13.1 for part of this scale). Each event is rated for its influence on a person. The death of a spouse, divorce, and illness are rated as high stressors; changes in eating habits, vacations, and holidays are rated lower. A person's total score is an index of stress and the likelihood of illness in the next 2 years. According to Holmes and Rahe, a person who scores above 300 points will be likely to suffer a stress-induced physical illness.

Although widely used, the Holmes-Rahe scale has been sharply criticized on a number of dimensions. First, for many people who score high on the scale, a direct relationship between health and life events has not been found (Krantz, Grunberg, & Baum, 1985). People have support systems, friends, and activities that influence how, when, and under what conditions stress will affect them. Some psychologists therefore question the validity of the scale in predicting illness (Theorell et al., 1986).

Another criticism stems from the fact that the scale was based on a study of young male navy personnel, whose characteristics do not necessarily match those of the general population, especially older people and women (Dohrenwend & Shrout, 1985). In addition, the scale includes only major life events. The stressors faced by most people are seldom crises; they are the day-to-day hassles and irritations that add up over the years (Kanner et al., 1981). Table 13.2 presents the 10 most frequently cited hassles.

The results of a study of the effect of both major life events and daily hassles on the reported health of elderly subjects showed that hassles are more closely related to psychological and physical ill health than are major life events (Chamberlain & Zika, 1990). Another study found that flu, headaches, sore throats, and backaches also were significantly related to daily hassles and stress (DeLongis, Folkman, & Lazarus, 1988). It is not surprising that people with an external locus of control (see chapter 12, p. 448), little social support (to be discussed in a following section), and high levels of stress see life as much more difficult than do others (Jorgensen & Johnson, 1990). The Diversity box on page 478 examines the influence of culture in perceiving and handling stressors.

Heart Disease and Stress

Heart disease and high blood pressure account for more than half the deaths each year in the United States. Among African Americans, high blood pressure is the number 1 health problem (N. B. Anderson, 1989). Physicians and psychologists view this silent killer as a disorder of lifestyle and quality of life (R. M. Kaplan, 1988). Three components of day-to-day life that are particularly important in heart disease are: work-site stress, Type A behavior, and physiological reactivity. Intense research into each of these biobehavioral factors has altered heart patient treatment.

Work-Site Stress. The likelihood that you will have a heart attack increases significantly if you are an air traffic controller or a surgeon. This occurs because these kinds of work are loaded with potential stressors. Other jobs may demand too little or too much of a worker. Stress is also affected by *autonomy*—the extent to which a person controls the speed, flow, and level of work. A position with high demands and low control increases stress. A factory worker, for example, usually has little control over the work and may therefore experience stress. Work-site stress increases the prevalence of heart attacks (Levi, 1990).

Men are more likely than women to develop heart disease. However, in the last decade, the work and home situations of men and women have become much more parallel. When their situations are similar, men and women seem to have similar rates of heart disease (Hamilton & Fagot, 1988).

Type A Behavior. In the late 1950s, physicians Friedman and Rosenman identified a pattern of behavior that they believe contributes to heart disease: Type A behavior (Friedman & Rosenman, 1974). **Type A behavior** occurs in individuals who are competitive, impatient, hostile, and always striving to do more in less time. (**Type B behavior** occurs in people who are calmer, more patient, and less hurried.) Do you see yourself as a Type A person or a Type B person? Do you know anyone who is Type A?

Early studies of Type A behavior showed a positive association with heart disease; that is, Type A individuals were more likely than Type B individuals to have

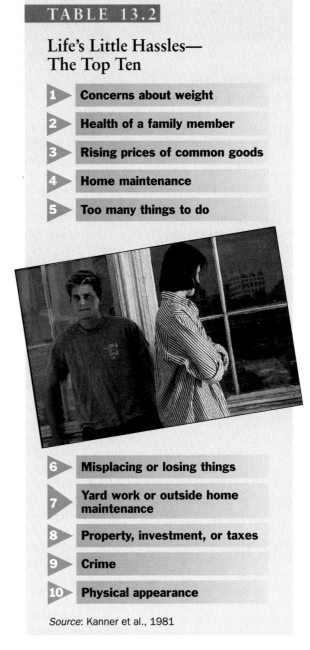

TABLE 13.2

Life's Little Hassles— The Top Ten

1 ▸ **Concerns about weight**
2 ▸ **Health of a family member**
3 ▸ **Rising prices of common goods**
4 ▸ **Home maintenance**
5 ▸ **Too many things to do**

6 ▸ **Misplacing or losing things**
7 ▸ **Yard work or outside home maintenance**
8 ▸ **Property, investment, or taxes**
9 ▸ **Crime**
10 ▸ **Physical appearance**

Source: Kanner et al., 1981

Type A behavior: Behavior characterized by competitiveness, impatience, hostility, and always striving to do more in less time.

Type B behavior: Behavior characterized by more calmness, more patience, and less hurrying than that of Type A individuals.

DIVERSITY

Stress and Hispanic Culture

Researchers have long known that stress drains people's psychological resources. They also recognize that stress is often a result of specific life events such as loss of a job, daily hassles, and long-term strains such as poor economic conditions. A relatively unexplored research area has been cultural differences in coping with such stresses and strains. For example, are Hispanic Americans more vulnerable than non-Hispanic whites? This question was investigated by three California researchers, Jacqueline Golding, Marilyn Potts, and Carol Aneshensel.

Question and Method. Golding, Potts, and Aneshensel (1991) questioned whether Hispanic Americans are more at risk for stress and strain than are non-Hispanic whites. They examined the data from a large epidemiological study by the National Institute of Mental Health, which estimated the prevalence of mental disorders in the general population.

Over 2,300 persons responded to interviews that asked a set of questions about psychiatric disorders, use of health services, and demographic characteristics. The study was conducted in Los Angeles County, California and included 1244 respondents who were Hispanic (538 of whom were born in the United States and 706 of whom were born in Mexico and immigrated to the United States). In addition, there were 1,149 non-Hispanic white respondents.

Measures. Respondents indicated whether they had experienced stress from life events in the past six months. These events included such items as undesirable family or relationship events, such as divorce; undesirable work- or money-related events, such as being fired or bad financial situations; legal events, such as arrests; crime victimization, such as being burglarized; housing changes, such as moving; medical or psychological problems, such as a physical illness or drug problems; and deaths in the family. In addition to the questions about psychological stress, the researchers sought to know if ongoing and persistent economic strain was evident among respondents. They explored whether respondents had difficulty affording clothes, food, and medical care or paying bills.

heart attacks. However, more recent research suggests that no such relationship exists (Matthews, 1988). Some elements of Type A behavior seem related to heart disease (Byrne & Reinhart, 1989), but not the overall Type A behavior pattern. For example, hostility and anger have been related to heart disease (Krantz et al., 1988), as have suspiciousness and mistrust (Weidner et al., 1989). People who are extremely anxious, depressed, angry, and unhappy have a higher rate of heart disease than do normally adjusted people (T. Q. Miller et al., 1991). In sum, Type A behavior patterns exist; however, a direct relationship to heart disease is minimal or nonexistent (Friedman & Booth-Kewley, 1988; Matthews, 1988).

Physiological Reactivity. A possible third factor relating stress to heart disease is how our bodies react to stress. This is called *reactivity,* or *physiological reactivity.* A situation interpreted as stressful may cause our bodies to react physiologically, triggering processes that lead to heart disease. Research shows that Type A behavior patterns are associated with increased physiological reactivity (Contrada, 1989), long-lasting emotional distress (Suls & Wan, 1989a, 1989b), and feelings of anger and hostility (Suarez & Williams, 1989). It is still not clear whether people predisposed to heart disease show reactivity or whether reactivity predisposes them to heart disease. Further, people who are physically fit react better physiologically to stressful situations than those who are not fit.

Although work-site stress, Type A behavior, and physiological reactivity may be individually linked to heart disease, research suggests that they are interactive, that is, they affect one another (Krantz et al., 1988). From a psychologist's viewpoint, this is an important implication requiring further investigation. First, much more research is needed to sort out the factors. Second, although behavioral factors contribute to heart disease, we need to learn how important they are. Third, and most

Results. To make appropriate comparisons, the researchers had to ensure that equivalent subjects were studied. They did not want to compare more wealthy Hispanic American participants with poor participants, for example; accordingly, a variety of statistical and sampling techniques were used to ensure comparable groups of subjects—this is a strength of the research study. Golding, Potts, and Aneshensel (1991) found that life events were fairly similar among Hispanic and white participants. However, the ongoing stress caused by economic strains were greater for Hispanic than for white participants, especially if the Hispanics were immigrants, rather than born in the United States.

Many similarities were found among the Hispanic Americans and whites; the uneducated were more likely to be burglarized, to suffer from unemployment, and to have marital problems, regardless of their culture. The only important differences were related to economic strain. Hispanic participants, especially those who were immigrants, reported more economic and household strain than did non-Hispanic whites. Being poor, female, and coming from a large household was associated with greater strains.

Conclusions. There are few differences in the life events of Hispanic and non-Hispanic whites in terms of stressful life events. The stressors of divorce, unemployment, and moving occurred equally frequently when comparable groups were analyzed. But the economic strains and the day-to-day hassles of being economically disadvantaged and unable to afford life's necessities seemed to affect the Hispanic participants more than whites, especially Hispanic immigrants. The researchers point out that adverse life events and economic strains are difficult to separate because they invariably occur together.

Research into ethnicity and behavior often shows striking differences because the world view and life experiences of different groups is unique. But as the research of Golding, Potts, and Aneshensel (1991) shows, stress levels in comparable groups of Hispanic Americans and non-Hispanic whites are similar. All of us, regardless of our culture, are adversely and similarly affected by the difficult times in our lives.

important, psychologists need to find interventions that will lessen the stressful conditions and decrease the likelihood of heart disease.

Posttraumatic Stress Disorder

In 1989, a group of army veterans returned with several therapists to Vietnam, where they had waged war more than 2 decades earlier. This time, however, their mission was not to fight an enemy but to heal their own psychological wounds. One veteran reported that he had been haunted for years by nightmares of his combat experiences. This severe stress-related disorder is termed **posttraumatic stress disorder**—a category of mental disorders that becomes evident after a person has undergone the stress of some type of disaster.

Origins and Symptoms. Victims of rape, natural disasters (tornadoes, earthquakes, hurricanes, floods), and disasters caused by human beings (wars, train wrecks, toxic chemical spills) often suffer from posttraumatic stress disorder. Many survivors of the 1989 San Francisco earthquake still fear the double-decker freeways of California, which took several lives when they collapsed in the quake. Posttraumatic stress disorder is also still evident long after the 1980 volcanic eruption of Mt. St. Helens (Shore, Vollmer, & Tatum, 1989). The 1993 bombing at the World Trade Center is now affecting hundreds of people who were trapped and many others who witnessed the event. Victims of the recent flooding along the Missouri and Mississippi rivers are also likely to suffer from posttraumatic stress syndrome for years to come.

Common symptoms of posttraumatic stress disorder are vivid, intrusive recollections or reexperiences of the traumatic event and occasional lapses of normal consciousness (Wood et al., 1992). People may develop anxiety, depression, or

Posttraumatic stress disorder: A category of mental disorders that becomes evident after a person has undergone the stress of some type of disaster; common symptoms include vivid, intrusive recollections or reexperiences of the traumatic event and occasional lapses of normal consciousness.

exceptionally aggressive behavior; and they may avoid situations that resemble the traumatizing events. Such behaviors may eventually interfere with daily functioning, family interactions, and health. Research on posttraumatic stress disorder is growing, with an increasing number of studies focusing on such natural disasters as earthquakes, tornadoes, and floods (Wood et al., 1992). Many more studies have focused on Vietnam veterans (e.g., Pitman et al., 1990).

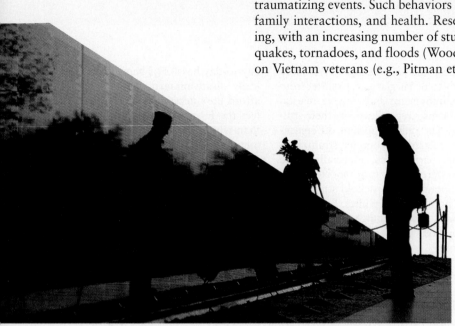

The Vietnam war created unique psychological problems, and its veterans are particularly vulnerable to posttraumatic stress disorders.

The Vietnam Veteran. Vietnam veterans are particularly vulnerable to posttraumatic stress disorder. Although most of them do not suffer from the disorder, thousands of them do. Decades later, they still endure feelings of alienation, sleeping problems, the reliving of painful experiences, and concentration difficulties.

Many did not experience symptoms until months or even years after their return home. Those who suffer from the disorder seem more likely than others to have other stressful events in their lives and other adjustment problems, which in turn make the disorder worse—a vicious cycle (McFall, Mackay, & Donovan, 1991).

The Vietnam War created unique psychological problems. Survival—not heroism—was the primary concern of many military personnel. Some turned to drugs such as alcohol to alleviate fear. Moreover, the combatants, most of whom were drafted, knew that many people in the United States vehemently opposed the conflict. Finally, many of the soldiers were whisked home without ceremony or a chance to reacclimate gradually (Hobfoll et al., 1991).

For a number of complicated psychological, political, and social reasons, mental health practitioners have not always been as responsive as they might have been to individuals suffering from posttraumatic stress disorder. Too often, clients have been held responsible for how they react to stress. Now that psychologists recognize the disorder, special help in the form of workshops and therapy is becoming available, and drug therapies are being assessed (Lerer et al., 1987).

Suicide: The Ultimate Escape

Fortunately, most people who think about suicide do not actually commit the act; however, life's stressors can take a heavy toll. When people become depressed, the likelihood that they will commit suicide increases. Each day, about 80 people in the United States commit suicide; that's almost 30,000 people each year. These individuals are often lonely, guilt-ridden, and depressed. They believe things cannot and will not get better, and that suicide is their best option.

A distinction must be drawn between attempters and completers. *Attempters* try to commit suicide but are unsuccessful. They tend to be young, more often women, impulsive, and more likely to make nonfatal attempts, such as wrist slashing. *Completers* succeed in taking their lives. They tend to be male and older, and they use highly lethal techniques of self-destruction, such as handguns.

Who commits suicide? More than three times as many men as women actually succeed in ending their lives, although four times as many women attempt to do so. Among adolescents, suicide is the second leading cause of death (after accidents); 1 out of every 1,000 adolescents attempts suicide each year, and nearly 5,000 young people between the ages of 15 and 24 are successful (B. P. Allen, 1987; Garland & Zigler, 1993). The elderly, the divorced, and former patients with psychological disorders have a higher likelihood than others of attempting and committing suicide. In fact, the elderly make up 23 percent of those who commit suicide. Alcoholics have a high rate of suicide, as do Native Americans (Murphy et al., 1992; T. J. Young, 1991). People who have been suffering from major depression are more likely to attempt suicide while they are recovering, when their energy level is higher. At the depths of depression, a person is usually too weak, divided, and lacking in energy to commit suicide. Although only 15 percent of depressed people are suicidal, most suicide-prone individuals are depressed.

Are there warning signs of suicide? Research shows that predicting suicide is difficult (R. B. Goldstein et al., 1991). However, there are several indicators: changes in personal appearance, a dramatic drop in quality of schoolwork, changes in drug abuse patterns, decreased appetite, the giving away of prized possessions, and, most important, a depressed attitude. Nearly everyone who is suicidal exhibits depression; such individuals show changes in sleeping patterns, a diminished ability to concentrate, fatigue, and feelings of worthlessness. In addition, 86 percent of those who are successful have attempted suicide before. Clearly, suicide attempters may become suicide completers if no one intervenes.

Causes. The causes of suicide are as complex as the people who commit suicide and may lie both within the individual (psychological) and outside the individual in society (societal). For some individuals who take their own lives, societal pressures serve as a catalyst. For others, the catalysts may be ill parents, substance abuse that impairs judgment, or traumatic events. For still others, a long-standing series of psychological disorders may predispose them to suicide. Table 13.3 presents some of the many myths about suicide and counters them with facts.

Psychologists cite a broad array of factors that may influence a suicide attempt. *Biological psychologists* assert that certain neurotransmitters have been linked to

---

TABLE 13.3   *Myths and Facts about Suicide*

Myth	Fact
1. Suicide happens without warning.	1. Suicidal individuals give many clues; 80 percent have to some degree discussed with others their intent to commit suicide.
2. Once people become suicidal, they remain so.	2. Suicidal persons remain so for limited periods; thus the value of restraint.
3. Suicide occurs almost exclusively among affluent or very poor individuals.	3. Suicide tends to occur proportionately in all economic levels of society.
4. Virtually all suicidal individuals are mentally ill.	4. This is not so, although most are depressed to some degree.
5. Suicidal tendencies are inherited or run in families.	5. There is no evidence for a direct genetic factor.
6. Suicide does not occur in primitive cultures.	6. Suicide occurs in almost all societies and cultures.
7. Ritual suicide is common in Japan.	7. Ritual suicide is rare in modern Japan; the most common method is barbiturate overdose.
8. Writers and artists have the highest suicide rates because they are "a bit crazy to begin with."	8. Physicians and police officers have the highest suicide rates; they have access to the most lethal means, and their work involves a high level of frustration.
9. Once a person starts to come out of a depression, the risk of suicide dissipates.	9. The risk of suicide is highest in the initial phase of an upswing from the depth of depression.
10. People who attempt suicide fully intend to die.	10. People who attempt suicide have a diversity of motives.

Source: Meyer and Salmon, 1988.

Most people who attempt suicide show prior signs of depression.

disorders that predispose an individual to suicide (Roy et al., 1991). *Behavioral psychologists* suggest that past experiences with suicide (by observing the effects of suicides on friends and relatives of a person who committed suicide) reinforce people's attempts to commit suicide. Other people who have taken their lives may also serve as models for the behavior, but this is not always the case (Davidson et al., 1989; Gibson & Range 1991; Kessler et al., 1989).

Psychodynamically oriented psychologists suggest that the suicidal person is turning hostility and anger inward. Freud might argue that the act of suicide is the ultimate release of the aggressive instinct. *Cognitive psychologists* assert that suicide is the failure of a person's problem-solving abilities in response to stress or, alternatively, that a person's cognitive assessment is that the future is hopeless. *Humanistic psychologists* see suicide as a waste of a human being's potential, and they attempt to help suicidal and depressed patients focus on the meaning in their lives so that they might fulfill rather than destroy themselves. Many theorists, regardless of orientation, focus on a person's attempt to escape from aversive self-awareness (Baumeister, 1990).

Adolescent suicide has received a great deal of attention. Adolescents who attempt suicide often see a wide discrepancy between their high personal ambitions and meager results. The causes of adolescent suicide are still not fully understood, but the increasing pressures and stress encountered by adolescents today certainly contribute to the rising number of suicides. Adolescents face an extremely competitive work force, alternating pressures to conform and to be an individual, and a social situation teeming with violence, crime, and drugs. Often, angry and frustrated adolescents exhibit other self-destructive behaviors, such as drug use, in addition to feeling hopelessness and low self-esteem (Kashani, Reid, & Rosenberg, 1989; Stivers, 1988).

Prevention. Most individuals who attempt suicide want to live. However, their stress and their sense of helplessness about the future tell them that death is the only way out. This is even more true of adults than of adolescents (D. A. Cole, 1989). Some are helped by crisis intervention and by counselors they can talk to on suicide hot lines.

When a person makes a suicide threat, take it seriously. Most people who commit suicide leave clues to their intentions ahead of time. Statements such as "I don't want to go on" or "I'm a burden to everyone, so maybe I should end it all" should be taken as warning signs. When people begin to give things away or to write letters with ominous tones to relatives and friends, these too are signs. If you know someone you think may be contemplating suicide, here are some steps you can take (Curran, 1987):

▶ Talk to the person. Don't be afraid to talk with your friend or relative about suicide; it will not influence him or her to commit suicide.

▶ Talk about stressors with a person who is at risk. The more the suicidal individual talks, the better.

▶ Help a person who is contemplating suicide to seek out a psychologist, counselor, or parent. A person thinking of suicide needs counseling.

▶ Tell your friend's spouse, parent, guardian, or counselor. Unless you are certain that these people know, you should tell someone responsible for your friend's welfare.

▶ Do not keep a contemplated suicide a secret. Resist your friend's attempt to keep you quiet about such confidences. Despite a friend's wish for secrecy, be responsible and tell the friend's relatives or guardian.

Coping

Most people need a way to cope with anxiety and with the physical ailments produced by stress. Some people seek medical and psychological help; others turn to alcohol and other drugs. From your own experience, do you know some coping techniques that are more effective than others?

What Is Coping?

In general, *coping* means dealing with a situation. However, for a psychologist, **coping** is the process by which a person takes some action to manage environmental and internal demands that cause or might cause stress and that will tax the individual's inner resources. This definition of coping involves five important components. First, the coping is constantly changing and being evaluated and is therefore a process or strategy. Second, coping involves managing situations, not necessarily bringing them under complete control. Third, coping is effortful; it does not happen automatically. Fourth, coping aims to manage behavioral as well as cognitive events. Finally, coping is a learned process.

Many types of coping strategies exist; a person may use a few or many of them. Coping begins at the biological level. People's bodies respond to stress with specific reactions, including changes in hormone levels, autonomic nervous system activity, and the amount of neurotransmitters in the brain. Effective coping strategies occur at the psychological level when people learn new ways of dealing with their vulnerabilities.

Vulnerability, Coping Skills, and Social Support

A crucial factor that determines how well people cope with their problems is **vulnerability**—the extent to which people are easily impaired by an event and thus respond maladaptively to the external or internal demands being placed on them. A person who is vulnerable is said to be not very resilient. Vulnerability depends on **coping skills**—the techniques people use to deal with stress and changing situations. People who have effective coping skills to guide them are prepared to deal with stress-related situations and are thus less vulnerable (Wiebe, 1991). People with poor coping skills may be extremely vulnerable and incapable of dealing with stress. In some cases, they may even develop a sense of *learned helplessness;* they may have found that rewards and punishments are not contingent on their behavior, so they learn not to try to cope, thereby remaining helpless. Faced with poor coping skills and a loss of control, some people stop responding. (We will examine learned helplessness further in chapters 14 and 16.)

A person's vulnerability is also affected by the level of social support available to them. **Social support** includes comfort, recognition, approval, and encouragement from other people, including friends, family, members of organizations, and

Coping: The process by which a person takes some action to manage environmental and internal demands that cause or might cause stress and that will tax the individual's inner resources.

Vulnerability: The extent to which people are easily impaired by an event and thus respond maladaptively to the external or internal demands being placed on them.

Coping skills: The techniques people use to deal with stress and changing situations.

Social support: The availability of comfort, recognition, approval, and encouragement from other people, including friends, family, members of organizations, and coworkers.

coworkers. When people feel supported by others' emotional concern and displays of caring, such as phone calls or notes, they can cope better with extraordinary pressure. The support is especially valuable when it is offered by someone who is important to the vulnerable person (Dakof & Taylor, 1990; Kessler et al., 1992). In addition to (and sometimes in place of) friends and family, group therapy (examined in chapter 15) can be especially effective in alleviating anxiety. In group therapy, other people in similar situations can offer emotional concern and support. Even animals can provide social support (J. M. Siegel, 1990).

According to psychologist Richard S. Lazarus (1982), people faced with constant stress use either defense- or task-oriented coping strategies. We will consider them next.

Defense-Oriented and Task-Oriented Coping Strategies

Defense-oriented coping strategies do not reduce stress; however, they help people protect themselves from its effects. These strategies ease stress, thereby enabling people to tolerate and deal with disturbances. As we saw in chapter 12, people may use defense mechanisms to distort reality in order to defend themselves against life's pressures. One such mechanism is *rationalization,* in which people reinterpret reality to make it more palatable. If your boyfriend (or girlfriend) dumps you, you might cope by telling your friends that you "never really liked him (or her) anyway." Similarly, a person who is turned down for a job may rationalize that he didn't want to work for the company after all. Another defense mechanism is *reaction formation.* A woman who raves about her new job but who is feeling a lot of stress and fear at work has developed a reaction formation. She is expressing a feeling that is the opposite of her true one.

Stress management is becoming increasingly important to highly stressed individuals. Counselors commonly treat stress first by identifying the source and then by helping the client modify behavior to cope with it. Through therapy, a person troubled by stressful situations can learn to cope by untangling personal feelings, understanding the sources of the stress, and then modifying behavior to alleviate it. Students about to enter college, for example, often show signs of stress. They're worried about academic pressures, social life, and overall adjustment. At some schools, incoming college students can receive counseling to learn how to deal with their stress. Similarly, stress management seminars, in which psychologists help business executives deal with stress in the corporate world, are becoming increasingly popular. The aim of both the counseling and the seminars is the same: to modify people's response to stress by replacing maladaptive responses with more useful ones.

Most psychologists, and especially behavioral psychologists, recommend *task-oriented coping strategies* for managing stress. The strategies usually involve several tasks, or steps (see Figure 13.5), essentially: (1) identifying the source of stress, (2) choosing an appropriate course of action for stress reduction, (3) implementing the plan, and (4) evaluating its success. Each of these steps (which are not always undertaken in order) is affected by a person's biases, attitudes, value systems, and previous environmental stressors.

Identifying the Source. Since stress-producing situations exist in many areas, identifying the source of stress is often difficult. A woman may be experiencing problems with her workload, her finances, her social life, and her roommate. She must decide what is causing her the most stress and whether her problems with her social life, for example, are in some way tied to her work situation. Older people seem to have as much difficulty as younger people in identifying and controlling the sources of stress (Lazarus & DeLongis, 1983).

FIGURE 13.5

Developing a Stress Reduction Program

1 Identifying the stressor: What is distressing me?

2 What am I willing to do about it?

3 How am I handling it now?

4 What am I going to do about it?

5 How have I put my plan into action?

6 What results can I see?

▶ Biases
▶ Background
▶ Assumptions
▶ Environment
▶ Value system
▶ Inferences
▶ Attitudes

Choosing the Action. Once the source of stress is found, people need to choose among several coping strategies. For example, they can withdraw from a competitive, stress-inducing situation by quitting work, leaving a spouse, or declaring bankruptcy. More often, they turn to other people or other methods of coping.

Because stress is usually accompanied by arousal and excitement, people may cope by using *relaxation techniques.* These techniques include biofeedback, hypnosis, and meditation, all of which help people to refocus their energies. Exercise such as aerobics, jogging, and racquetball is another effective way to relax and relieve stress (Imm, 1990).

Many people manage stress and anxiety with *cognitive coping strategies;* that is, they prepare themselves for pressure through gradual exposure to increasingly higher stress levels (Janis, 1985). Chapter 10 discussed a study in which subjects viewing a film with painful scenes were able to control their emotional responses (Lazarus & Alfert, 1964). This study suggests that people can learn to manage their stress, to some extent, by using their thought processes. A major goal of current research on stress is to prepare people to react in constructive ways to early warning signs of stress.

Research shows that people can help themselves cope with stress by talking to themselves (Turk, 1978). The self-talk procedure, which is used widely, is effective in helping people confront stressors and cope with pain and the feeling of being overwhelmed (Turk, Meichenbaum, & Genest, 1983). By talking to themselves, people gain control over their emotions, arousal, and stress reactions; this technique is especially useful before noxious or painful medical procedures such as chemotherapy or root canal work (Ludwick-Rosenthal & Neufeld, 1988).

APPLICATIONS

Coping, Health, and a Positive Attitude

Applied psychologists claim that simply maintaining a positive attitude can have beneficial effects on coping with stress and reducing its physical symptoms. People who believe they have control over their lives, health, and well-being are more relaxed than those who do not (Rodin, 1986). An upbeat mood, a positive sense of personal control, and even a self-serving bias can facilitate such worthwhile behaviors as helping others and evaluating people favorably. Some researchers suggest that people who have positive attitudes may even live longer.

Sometimes, reframing or rethinking a situation is a rationalization to make it less anxiety-producing, as we saw in chapter 12. One study, however, showed that people engaged in such small self-deceptions may be healthier than people who focus on their anxiety. In an unpublished study of people from 1946 through 1988, Peterson, Seligman, and Vaillant (reported in DeAngelis, 1988) found that those who made excuses for negative events in 1946 had better health in 1988.

Such results indicate that people who emphasize the downside of life's events may develop learned helplessness. They may then choose inaction because they believe themselves to be powerless in controlling events. Taking a positive approach and believing in your own abilities help you ward off stress and avoid the fear and arousal that come from feelings of despair and low self-esteem (Bandura et al., 1988). Seligman (1988) argues that optimism helps people achieve goals and cope more effectively; for example, optimistic salespeople substantially outsell their pessimistic colleagues. Maintaining an optimistic attitude is likely to help people engage in self-protective behaviors that will foster change for the better (Ewart, 1991; Scheier & Carver, 1993).

Conservation of Resources. People can develop a positive attitude by conserving resources. Hobfoll (1989) suggests that people strive to retain, protect, and build resources; the potential or actual loss of these valued resources is threatening. A person's home, marriage, or status as a community leader are all resources. In Hobfoll's view, when these resources are under attack, people try to defend themselves against the attack. They attempt to ward off the attack or replace the lost resources by, say, seeking a new marriage or leadership position or by gaining some new competence or financial strength. Treatment might mean shifting a person's focus of attention and reinterpreting the threat, helping them to see how they might replace lost resources (for example, by finding a new job), and reevaluating the threat.

Positive Attitudes and Psychoneuroimmunology. One effect of a positive approach is that it may harness the body's own defense mechanisms. **Psychoneuroimmunology (PNI)** is the study of how psychological processes and the nervous system affect and in turn are affected by the body's natural defense system—the immune system. Recent studies of PNI show that the immune system (which fights disease) responds to a person's moods, stress, and basic attitudes about life. According to PNI researchers, the brain provides information to the immune system about how and when to respond. The two systems seem to be linked, each producing substances that alter the other's functions. The brain sends signals to the immune system that trigger its disease-fighting ability. The immune system sends signals to the brain that alter its functioning (Glaser & Kiecolt-Glaser, 1988). Thus, the immune system of a person with a pos-

Psychoneuroimmunology (PNI): [sie-ko-NEW-ro-IM-you-NOLL-oh-gee] The study of how psychological processes and the nervous system affect and in turn are affected by the body's natural defense system, the immune system.

Stress inoculation: [in-OK-you-LAY-shun] The procedure of giving people realistic warnings, recommendations, and reassurances to help them prepare for and cope with impending dangers or losses.

Implementing the Plan. Helping people prepare for stressful situations by providing them with new ideas is called stress inoculation. **Stress inoculation** is the procedure of giving people realistic warnings, recommendations, and reassurances to help them prepare for and cope with impending dangers or losses. Sometimes it involves a single technique, such as breathing deeply and regularly. At other times it is more elaborate, involving graded exposure to various levels of threats or detailed information about a forthcoming procedure (Janis, 1985). Janis likens stress inoculation to an antibiotic given to ward off disease. It helps people to defend themselves and to cope with an event when it occurs. Essentially, it does the following:

▶ Increases the predictability of stressful events.

▶ Fosters coping skills.

▶ Generates self-talking.

▶ Encourages confidence about successful outcomes.

▶ Builds a commitment to personal action and responsibility for an adaptive course of action.

Evaluating the Success of the Plan. A well-designed coping plan includes evaluation of the plan's success. Have the techniques been effective? Is there still more to do? Are new or further actions needed? All of these questions need to be answered to complete the task-oriented coping strategy.

Health Psychology

At least half of all the premature deaths in the United States are the result of unhealthy lifestyles. In the past, most people died from causes beyond their control—influenza, tuberculosis, and pneumonia, for example. Today, the leading causes of death—heart disease, cancer, stroke, and accidents—can be largely controlled by environmental and behavioral variables. Psychologists believe there is a direct relationship between people's health and their behavior. **Health psychology** is the psychological subfield concerned with the use of psychological ideas and principles in health enhancement, illness prevention, diagnosis and treatment of disease, and rehabilitation processes. It is an action-oriented discipline and assumes that people's ideas and behaviors contribute to the onset and prevention of illness. A closely related field, *behavioral medicine,* integrates behavioral science with biomedical knowledge and techniques; it is narrower in focus than health psychology (Agras, 1992).

Traditionally, physicians have looked at health as the absence of disease. A person who was not infected with a virus, bacterial infection, cold, and so on was considered healthy. Now, however, physicians and psychologists acknowledge that health refers not just to the absence of disease but to the total welfare of a person in terms of social, physical, and mental well-being. The concentration on social, physical, and mental well-being now places health and psychology in the same corner (Seeman, 1989). Health and wellness are now seen as conditions people can actively pursue by eating well, exercising regularly, and managing stress effectively (Cowen, 1991). Unlike medicine, which focuses on specific diseases, health psychology looks at the broad principles of thought and behavior that clarify fundamental psychosocial mechanisms and enhance all areas of a person's life.

Variables That Affect Health and Illness

Health and illness are affected by complex interrelationships among many events. Accordingly, health researchers have explored five variables that correlate strongly with health and illness: personality, cognitions, social environment, gender, and sociocultural variables (Rodin & Salovey, 1989).

Personality. Do certain personality variables predispose people to illness? Or does illness predispose people to a specific personality? Some evidence suggests that angry, hostile people are more prone to illness than are optimists. However, which comes first? Perhaps the lack of illness causes optimism, or at least positive lifestyles. The role of personality variables in illness and health is still unclear, and much more research is needed (as we saw when we examined the role of Type A behavior in heart disease, p. 477). One important personality variable is the extent to which people believe they control their lives, health, and illness. When people sense that they can control their own their health, they are more likely to engage in health-conscious behaviors, such as eating complex carbohydrates, decreasing their consumption of saturated fat, and exercising more (Taylor, 1990).

Health psychology: Psychological subfield concerned with the use of psychological ideas and principles in health enhancement, illness prevention, diagnosis and treatment of disease, and rehabilitation processes.

Health, Wellness, and Lifestyle

Students are interested in staying fit; more than 9 out of 10 work exercise into their schedules.

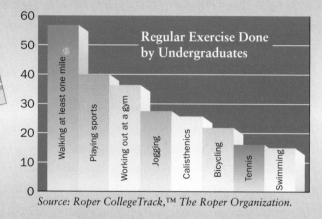

Regular Exercise Done by Undergraduates

- Walking at least one mile
- Playing sports
- Working out at a gym
- Jogging
- Calisthenics
- Bicycling
- Tennis
- Swimming

Source: Roper CollegeTrack,™ The Roper Organization.

Extent of knowledge about issues related to AIDS

Percent answering that they know a great deal about . . .	Under-graduate students
The way AIDS is transmitted	59
Groups in society that practice behaviors that put them at risk for AIDS	47
Blood test for the virus which causes AIDS	25
The way AIDS is treated medically	17

Source: Roper CollegeTrack,™ The Roper Organization.

After being diagnosed as having the virus that causes AIDS, Magic Johnson became a forceful advocate for AIDS education.

How adults are believed to have become infected. Worldwide estimates are for those infected with H.I.V.; U.S. figures are for reported AIDS cases.

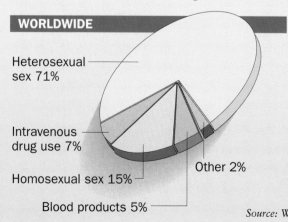

WORLDWIDE

- Heterosexual sex 71%
- Intravenous drug use 7%
- Homosexual sex 15%
- Blood products 5%
- Other 2%

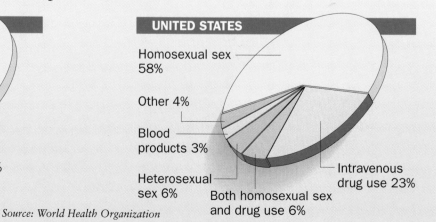

UNITED STATES

- Homosexual sex 58%
- Other 4%
- Blood products 3%
- Heterosexual sex 6%
- Both homosexual sex and drug use 6%
- Intravenous drug use 23%

Source: World Health Organization

The leading cause of premature death in the United States is an unhealthy lifestyle, including poor diet, lack of exercise, alcohol and drug abuse, smoking, and unsafe sex.

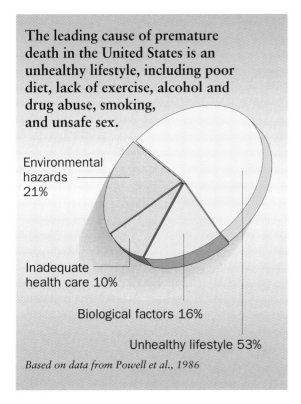

Environmental hazards 21%

Inadequate health care 10%

Biological factors 16%

Unhealthy lifestyle 53%

Based on data from Powell et al., 1986

Nearly half (45%) of undergraduates watch the amount and kind of foods they eat.

Asked about their current eating habits, students report the following:

I follow a planned diet, but not under a doctor's supervision	3%
I tend to watch the amount and kinds of food I eat	42%
I eat pretty much whatever I want	54%

Source: Roper CollegeTrack,™ The Roper Organization.

Students' top five concerns on campus

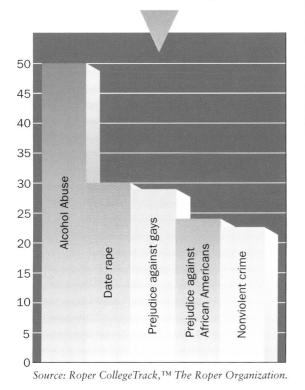

Alcohol Abuse

Date rape

Prejudice against gays

Prejudice against African Americans

Nonviolent crime

Source: Roper CollegeTrack,™ The Roper Organization.

If you smoke, your risk of developing the following diseases and disorders increases substantially.

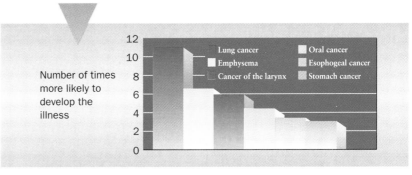

Number of times more likely to develop the illness

Lung cancer
Emphysema
Cancer of the larynx
Oral cancer
Esophogeal cancer
Stomach cancer

itive, upbeat attitude responds better and faster than does that of a person who is depressed and lethargic (Ader & Cohen, 1993; O'Leary, 1990). Consider people who have recently lost loved ones to death; they consistently show higher rates of illness. Today, many AIDS patients are provided with counseling to bolster their immune systems by improving their attitudes; this may help them live longer.

Some psychologists find it difficult to accept the fact that the immune system responds to mental attitudes. Researchers, however, are now beginning to realize the power that positive thinking may have on a number of bodily processes (Herbert & Cohen, 1993; O'Leary, 1990). Of course, even though positive attitudes and thoughts can be beneficial, they can go only so far in helping to alleviate illness (DeAngelis, 1988) and only with some people (Manuck et al., 1991). Sometimes, having a positive attitude and practicing hypnosis, meditation, and the other traditional stress-reduction techniques fail to reduce stress. Sometimes the failure occurs because of half-hearted attempts; at other times, the problem is a lack of expertise. More often, though, people just lack coping skills or even the knowledge that such skills exist.

Wearing rose-colored glasses from time to time can be beneficial; however, continuous self-deception can lead to maladjustment, lies, and a badly distorted view of reality.

Effective Coping Strategies. Taking responsibility for preventive behaviors can be an important step toward better physical and mental health (Ewart, 1991). There are a number of steps you can take to cope, manage stress, and stay healthy:

▶ **Increase exercise.** People cope better when they improve their physical fitness, usually through exercise. In addition, increased exercise will lower blood pressure and reduce the risk of heart disease.

▶ **Eat well.** People feel better and cope better when they eat well and have a balanced diet. This also means not being overweight.

▶ **Sleep well.** People react better to life when they have had a good night's sleep; reaction time improves, as does judgment.

▶ **Learn to relax.** In our fast-paced society, few people take the time to relax and let uncomfortable ideas and feelings leave them. Learn meditation, yoga, or deep breathing. Schedule some time each day for yourself.

▶ **Be flexible.** Our lives are unpredictable; accept that fact, and day-to-day surprises will be easier to handle.

▶ **Keep stress at school or the office.** Work-related pressures should be kept in the work environment. Bringing stress home will only make it worse. People are more likely to be involved in substance abuse and domestic violence when they bring stress home with them.

▶ **Communicate.** Share your ideas, feelings, and thoughts with the significant people in your life. This will decrease misunderstanding, mistrust, and stress.

▶ **Seek support.** Social support from family, friends, and self-help groups helps you appraise situations differently. Remember, you have to appraise a situation as stressful for it to be stressful. Social support helps you keep stressful situations in perspective.

▶ Gives people realistic warnings, recommendations, and reassurances to help them prepare for and cope with impending dangers or losses.

To cope well both at home and at work, people should be task-oriented, self-monitoring, realistic, open to supportive relationships, and patient (Sarason & Sarason, 1987). They also need to eat sensibly, get enough sleep, stand up to the boss from time to time, find a hobby, take refuge in family, and sometimes, when things get too extreme, quit. Most important, people have to believe in themselves and their ability to cope well with stressors (Bandura et al., 1988). The Applications box above examines the importance of a positive attitude in coping with stress.

FOCUS

▶ Why is appraisal such a key component of stress? p. 468

▶ What is the link between stress and ill health? pp. 471–474

▶ What is the evidence that the immune system is implicated in the relationship of attitudes and health? p. 486

Lift page to see illustrations on pages 486a & b.

Cognitions. People's thoughts and beliefs about themselves, other people, and situations affect health-related behaviors. For example, people with an internal locus of control (examined in chapter 12) are more likely to take charge of their illnesses and attempt to get better than are people with an external locus of control (who believe that there is nothing that they can do to affect their health). People who have assumed control over their health are also more likely to follow healthy lifestyles.

Social Environment. Family, close friends, and work can be sources of social support—a key element in maintaining health and recovering from illness. Greater self-esteem, positive feelings about the future, and a sense of control are characteristic of people with strong social support. Adults in stable long-term relationships such as marriage are less likely to be ill than are people devoid of strong social support networks; in addition, the children of stable marriages are likely to be healthier (Gottman & Katz, 1989). Support from coworkers and supervisors in the work environment may also facilitate health (Repetti, Matthews, & Waldron, 1989). Individuals with support are more likely to engage in preventive dental health, proper eating habits, and the use of safety practices, such as seat belts.

Gender. Some health concerns apply only to women (menopause, for example), and others disproportionately affect women (for example, eating disorders). Therefore, the health concerns of women differ from those of men. Seventy percent of all psychoactive medications prescribed are for women, and two-thirds of all surgical procedures are performed on women (Ogur, 1986; Travis, 1988). While women have always enjoyed an advantage in longevity, the gap in the life span between men and women has been decreasing. Women's changing lifestyles and work are highly correlated with increased medical problems and a decreased life span. Further, as Rodin and Ickovics (1990) assert, the redefinition of gender roles and the changing social support structure for women affect health, medical treatment, and psychological functioning.

Sociocultural Variables. Gender, age, ethnic group, and socioeconomic class all are important variables that affect health. Although we know that women tend to visit physicians more often than men, in some cultures the quality of their treatment is not equal to that given men. With advancing age, people are more likely to become ill or depressed (although there is much individual variation) (Dura, Stukenberg, & Kiecolt-Glaser, 1990). Often, illness among the elderly is affected by other variables, such as loneliness, loss of a spouse, and isolation from family. Ethnicity also seems to be an important sociocultural variable. Some ethnic minorities and people from lower socioeconomic groups may lack knowledge, funds, or access to preventive care. In addition, older, less educated, and less affluent individuals are far less likely to engage in exercise, which helps to prevent illness.

Disease prevention is the focus of many health psychologists. In recent years, preventing the spread of AIDS, considered in the Applications box on page 490, has been of great concern.

The Psychology of Being Sick

When a person is sick with an illness that impairs day-to-day functioning, the effects can be devastating. The impact on the individual can be profound both psychologically and economically. Illness seriously affects both the sick person and family members. Health psychologists are concerned not only with the links between stress and health, but also with how people cope with illness when it occurs.

Seeking Health Care. When do people seek health care? What are the variables that prompt a person to become well and healthy? Most people avoid medical

AIDS (Acquired Immune Deficiency Syndrome)

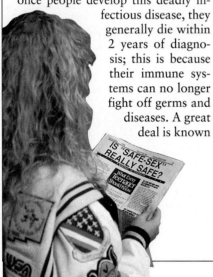

A major concern of health psychologists is AIDS (acquired immune deficiency syndrome). People who contract the human immunodeficiency virus (HIV—the virus that causes AIDS) can harbor it for many years without developing AIDS. However, once people develop this deadly infectious disease, they generally die within 2 years of diagnosis; this is because their immune systems can no longer fight off germs and diseases. A great deal is known about AIDS, but at present there are no preventive vaccines or cures and few treatments to slow its destructive course. Moreover, some people, fearing contamination, shun AIDS patients. Because most people with AIDS acquire the disease through sexual contact or intravenous drug use, some see it as a moral stigma. For all these reasons, AIDS is accompanied by devastating psychological consequences.

One in 250 persons in the United States is infected with HIV. HIV infection/AIDS is the third leading cause of death among people 25–44. Reports from the Centers for Disease Control show that by 1994 more than 200,000 deaths from AIDS will have occurred in the United States, and an estimated 1.5 million U.S. inhabitants will be infected with HIV. Worldwide, 13 to 14 million persons are infected. Most people who have AIDS are between 20 and 49 years of age; and although, at present, some states have a greater percentage of cases than others (especially New York and California), most experts believe that this unevenness will disappear in time.

Few other diseases are accompanied by so many losses. AIDS patients face the loss of physical strength, mental acuity, ability to work and care for their families, self-sufficiency, social roles, income and savings, housing, the emotional support of friends and loved ones, and ultimately life itself. Some schools have prohibited any children who have AIDS, or even who have family members with AIDS, from attending classes. People with AIDS have been fired, coworkers have quit their jobs to avoid them, and judges have held legal hearings on closed-circuit television to avoid contact with people who have AIDS. For many people with AIDS, self-esteem fades rapidly as they blame themselves for having contracted the disease. This self-blame leads to depression, anxiety, self-anger, and a negative outlook on life. Fam-

care and advice except when it becomes absolutely necessary. Usually, when people have a visible symptom (rashes, cuts, swellings, fever) and the symptom appears threatening, painful, and persistent, they seek professional help. They are more likely to seek such help when they are sure the problem is physical rather than psychological and when they think medical attention will provide a cure. If they think medical attention will be a waste of time, or if they dread a diagnosis, they often delay seeking help.

There are gender differences in people's willingness to seek medical attention. Women seek medical help more than men do, have more medical visits, and take more prescription medication (Rosenstock & Kirscht, 1979). Yet men have a shorter life span than do women and have higher rates of ulcers, heart disease, and stroke. Men may be less willing to seek medical attention because they perceive illness as a weakness in character. Because some women are not in the work force, they may have more time to think about their symptoms or to get away for a medical visit. In addition, women have nonpathological problems (problems not caused by disease), such as childbirth and menopause, that require medical attention.

The Sick Role. When people do what they think will help them get well, we say they are adopting a *sick role*. For most people, this means taking specific steps to get well, relieving themselves of normal responsibilities, and realizing that they are not at fault for their illness. (Of course, a person can adopt behaviors associated with illness when in fact there is no illness or pathology.)

ilies and friends become similarly affected as they cope with a dying loved one and face their own inability to understand the disease.

Psychologists pay particular attention to high-risk behaviors in AIDS prevention. Such behaviors directly expose people to the blood or semen of others who are likely to have been exposed to the virus—in other words, to others who are likely to have engaged in high-risk behaviors. Often, individuals who have engaged in high-risk behaviors are sexually promiscuous men and women, homosexual or bisexual men, or present or past intravenous drug abusers. Heterosexuals who have had sexual contact with carriers of AIDS are also at risk. In the United States, about 6 percent of known cases of AIDS occur from heterosexual sex; worldwide, heterosexual sex accounts for 71 percent of the reported AIDS cases. Ethnic minorities, particularly African Americans (29 percent) and Hispanic Americans (16 percent), make

up a disproportionately large share of AIDS patients in the United States according to the Centers for Disease Control.

Health professionals agree that the way to control the spread of AIDS is to educate people to decrease the behaviors that put them at risk. People will not get AIDS if they make informed, conscientious decisions about their personal behaviors. Individuals who are not in long-term monogamous relationships must use condoms, and intravenous drug users must avoid sharing needles.

Health psychologists can play a major role in setting up AIDS prevention programs, especially for hard-hit high-risk groups. Adolescents are especially at risk because they, more than adults, are likely to engage in unprotected sexual activity. AIDS education aimed at this group and others is critically important because education is effective in changing behavior (Fisher & Fisher, 1992). Although AIDS education and preven-

tion campaigns have resulted in profound behavior changes among gay men, not enough is being done to educate other high-risk groups or the general population, and people are still engaging in casual sex with strangers (R. D. Clark III, 1990). Interestingly, women who have had a previous sexually transmitted disease are more likely than men to alter their high-risk behaviors, though men seem to alter their behaviors when they experience cognitive changes, such as fear of the disease (Cochran & Mays, 1989; Kalichman, Hunter, & Kelly, 1992).

Research shows that when people believe they have control over their health, such as by eliminating risk-related behaviors, they maintain a sense of optimism that offers health benefits (S. E. Taylor et al., 1992). Thus, thoughts and ideas play an important role both in disease prevention and in how people respond to becoming sick.

Unfortunately, many people blame the ailing person for being sick, even though the illness may be unrelated to any preventive measures a person might have taken. Sick people usually are relieved of normal responsibilities, such as working or taking care of the family. When they are in the hospital, they give over to physicians and nurses the responsibility for their care, and they give up family and work responsibilities. Although our society fosters an approach that says we should be cheerful when we are sick, it is normal for sick people to be slightly depressed or even angry, especially when hospitalized (R. S. Lazarus, 1984). Because sickness is generally seen as a temporary state, we expect people to get well and to work toward that end—taking medication, sleeping, and, especially, complying with medical advice.

Compliance with Medical Advice. Getting people to adhere to a health regimen has long been a focus of health psychologists. We know, for example, that cigarette smoking is one of the largest health problems today, causing about a half million deaths annually in the United States alone. Yet people continue to smoke. People will comply with specific recommendations for a specific disease, such as: "Take three tablets a day for 10 days." However, they are less likely to adhere to general recommendations for diet, exercise, and overall health conditions, such as quitting smoking or relaxing more. The impact of many general recommendations of physicians can be great. For example, a 10-percent weight reduction through diet and exercise in men aged 35 to 55 would produce an estimated 20 percent reduction in heart attacks (American Heart Association, 1984). However, people are more receptive to medical treatment when it is specific, simple, and easy to do and has minimal side effects.

Compliance with medical advice depends on the severity of the problem. People seeking a cure or relief of specific symptoms are more likely to be cooperative than are people merely seeking wellness or prevention. When exercise is the prescribed treatment, most people drop out of a program within 6 months. Even when the impact of not taking a medication is serious, people are not especially compliant; this is especially true for lengthy or difficult treatments, such as four-times-daily insulin injections (Hanson et al., 1989). If an illness causes pain or discomfort, people are more likely to comply with a regimen of treatment to alleviate the discomfort.

Compliance with a health-care regimen is increased when the regimen is tailored to the person's lifestyle and habits. Even written agreements between practitioners and clients can be helpful. Health psychologists have found clients more likely to adhere to treatments when a physician's influence and the family support systems are substantial. Social support from family and friends turns out to be especially valuable in getting even very sick people to comply with guidelines for treatment (DiMatteo & DiNicola, 1982). Teaching resourcefulness and stress management, and explaining the implications of their medical regimen, are all key variables (Aikens et al., 1992). In the next section, we will examine how health psychologists try to help people adapt and cope with their situations.

Health Psychology and Adaptive Behavior

Health psychologists focus on adaptive behaviors that will improve people's day-to-day lives. They encourage preventive programs at work (Antonovsky, 1987) and educate people about ways to manage stress and about other positive approaches toward health (Beech, 1987) that will enhance and prolong life. They frequently conduct stress management workshops to help managers and workers cope with increasing pressures and workloads, and they are involved in helping people quit smoking, control their alcohol intake, follow exercise programs, and practice good nutrition.

Today, health psychologists attempt to change people's behavior before it gets out of hand. Health psychology is an action-oriented discipline; and as we move through the 1990s, with many men and women seeking more healthful lifestyles, psychologists are playing an instrumental role in their quest. Sometimes, they focus on preventive behaviors—using condoms to prevent the spread of AIDS, exercising regularly, and so on. At other times, they help people deal with existing problems such as obesity, diabetes, and high stress levels. See the illustrations on pages 486a & 486b for more information on these topics. We will now examine three ways of dealing with health problems: behavioral interventions, pain management, and stress management.

Behavioral Interventions. To manage existing health disorders and help prevent disease, behavioral interventions are necessary and important. Health psychologists know that many lifestyle behavior problems can be modified; they include obesity, smoking, hypertension, and alcohol and other drug abuse.

Consider drug abuse. The principal places where people are introduced to drugs are schools, in both city and suburban settings. As a result, in the mid-1980s—under the direction of the Secretary of Education—a national plan was laid out for achieving drug-free schools. To a great extent, the plan is an effort to help students cope without drugs; it is action-oriented and incorporates the efforts of educating students, involving the family and community in dealing with drug use and abuse, and especially prevention.

Pain Management. Severe and disabling pain is symptomatic of some illnesses. It can take three forms: (1) *chronic pain,* which is long-lasting and ever-present; (2) *periodic pain,* which comes and goes; (3) and *progressive pain,* which is ever-present and increasing in severity as the illness progresses. Many people suffer from chronic pain, such as headache pain, lower back pain, and arthritis pain. Some types of chronic pain can be treated with drugs, surgery, or other medical interventions; but other types, such as pain caused by cancer, sometimes call for nontraditional psychological techniques.

Two nontraditional techniques for pain management are hypnosis and biofeedback (examined in chapter 4). Other techniques include behavior modification and cognitive therapy (see chapters 5 and 15). Behavior modification uses learning principles to teach people new effective behaviors and to help them unlearn old maladaptive behaviors. People undergoing this type of therapy learn to relax after a twinge of pain rather than focusing on the pain and thus making it worse. (Chapter 15 looks into how cognitive therapy uses behavior modification techniques to help people acquire new thoughts, beliefs, and values that can help in pain management.)

Stress Management. Because stress exists in all our lives—whether from school exams, parent or peer pressures, natural disasters, illness, death, divorce, inflation, or financial difficulties—many health psychologists focus on stress and its management. With the help of health psychologists, employers are sponsoring programs for managing stress in the workplace (Glasgow & Terborg, 1988). The programs usually involve education, exercise, nutrition, and counseling. The results are fewer workdays lost to illness and lower health-care costs.

Stress management also results in fewer lost lives (Gebhardt & Crump, 1990). When patients who were hospitalized for heart attacks were treated for stress symptoms after their release from the hospital, they had fewer subsequent heart attacks than did a control group who did not receive specific stress treatments (Frasure-Smith & Prince, 1989).

The task of managing stress in people's daily lives is becoming greater each day, as new and potent forces impinge on people's health (Ilgen, 1990). In the 1990s, people are concerned not only about managing day-to-day illness and stress but also about potential threats from the environment.

FOCUS

▶ What impact does the vast number of AIDS patients have on society? p. 490

▶ What are the implications of the finding that men seem more affected than women by cognitive (thought) changes, such as fear of AIDS? p. 490

▶ Under what conditions do people comply with medical advice? p. 491

Concluding Note

Helping people stay healthy and helping to keep stress at manageable levels are two goals to which psychologists have dedicated a great deal of research. The word *people,* however, is somewhat misleading in this context. Earlier, I pointed out that glib generalizations about ethnicity and age are difficult or impossible to make in our multicultural society. It is equally important to remember that men and women are different biologically and that their experiences in society also differ.

When psychologists refer to people's health and people's responses to stress, the people they are talking about are often male. Nevertheless, we know that women's responses to drugs, high blood pressure, and medical advice, and their risk of alcoholism, depression, and death, are often different from men's. Psychological research has assumed a model of nor-

malcy that is often based on the experience of the average white, middle-class, college-educated man. There are indeed great numbers of such individuals in our society; however, women represent half the population, and they often respond differently. Moreover, as students of psychology, you have to remember that the role of women in the work force and society is continuing to change.

Similarly, the roles of minorities are also changing. Our theories of stress and health, of coping and failure, and of normalcy and maladjustment are relative to the time they are studied and are determined by the population we study. Researchers are becoming more sensitive to the health of women and minorities, and this is benefiting both science and, ultimately, the human condition.

Summary & Review

Stress

What is stress, and what causes it?

Stress is a set of nonspecific global responses by an organism to real and imagined environmental demands. It is a normal part of living and depends on a person's appraisal of a situation. Stress is caused by *stressors*—environmental stimuli that affect an organism in either physically or psychologically injurious ways.   pp. 468–469

Describe approach-approach and avoidance-avoidance conflicts.

Approach-approach conflicts arise when a person must choose between two equally pleasant alternatives, such as two wonderful jobs. *Avoidance-avoidance conflicts* occur when a choice involves two equally distasteful alternatives, such as mowing the lawn or painting the garage.   pp. 469–470

Describe the emotional, physiological, and behavioral reactions to stress.

Emotionally, people's reactions often depend on their *frustration*, their work-related pressures, and their day-to-day *conflicts*. Physiologically, the stress response is characterized by arousal. Behaviorally, stress and its arousal response are related. When people are moderately aroused, they behave with optimal effectiveness; when they are underaroused, they lack the stimulation to behave effectively.   pp. 471–473

What are the stages of Selye's general adaptation syndrome?

Selye characterized stress responses as a general adaptation syndrome with three stages: alarm, resistance, and exhaustion. During the *alarm stage*, people experience increased physiological arousal and mobilize bodily resources. During *resistance*, physiological and behavioral responses be-

come more moderate and sustained. During *exhaustion*, if people don't relieve their stress, they can become too exhausted to adapt; at that point, they once again become extremely alarmed, and they finally give up.   pp. 474–475

Characterize Type A behavior.

Type A behavior occurs in individuals who are competitive, impatient, hostile, and always striving to do more in less time. Some elements of Type A behavior seem related to heart disease, but not the overall Type A behavior pattern.   p. 477

What are the consequences of being exposed to stress?

People exposed to high levels of stress for long periods of time may develop stress-related disorders, including physical illness. *Posttraumatic stress disorder* is a disorder that becomes evident after a person has undergone the stress of some type of disaster.   pp. 478–480

Who attempts suicide?

Most people who think about suicide do not actually commit the act. Attempters try to commit suicide but are unsuccessful; completers succeed in taking their lives. More than three times as many men as women actually succeed in ending their lives, although four times as many women attempt to do so; 1 out of every 1,000 adolescents attempts suicide each year.   pp. 480–481

KEY TERMS: *stressor*, p. 468; *anxiety*, p. 468; *stress*, p. 468; *frustration*, p. 469; *conflict*, p. 469; *approach-approach conflict*, p. 469; *avoidance-avoidance conflict*, p. 469; *approach-avoidance conflict*, p. 469; *pressure*, p. 471; *burnout*, p. 472; *Type A behavior*, p. 477; *Type B behavior*, p. 477; *posttraumatic stress disorder*, p. 479.

Coping

What is coping?

Coping is the process by which a person takes some action to manage environmental and internal demands that cause or might cause stress and that will tax the individual's inner resources. Coping skills are the techniques people use to deal with stress and changing situations.   p. 483

Distinguish between defense-oriented and task-oriented coping strategies.

Defense-oriented coping strategies do not reduce stress but instead help people protect themselves from its effects. Most psychologists recommend task-oriented coping strategies; these strategies usually involve several tasks, or steps, essentially: (1) identifying the source of stress, (2) choosing an appropriate course of action for stress reduction, (3) implementing the plan, and (4) evaluating its success.   pp. 484–488

What are the effects of stress inoculation?

Stress inoculation increases the predictability of stressful events, fosters coping skills, generates self-talking, encourages confidence about successful outcomes, builds a commitment to personal action and responsibility to an adaptive course of action, and gives people realistic warnings, recommendations, and reassurances to help them prepare for and cope with impending dangers or losses.   pp. 486–487

continued

Summary & Review

What is psychoneuro-immunology?

Psychoneuroimmunology is the study of how psychological processes and the nervous system affect the body's immune system and how, in turn, the immune system influences psychological processes.   pp. 486–487

KEY TERMS: *coping,* p. 483; *vulnerability,* p. 483; *coping skills,* p. 483; *social support,* p. 483; *stress inoculation,* p. 486; *psychoneuroimmunology,* p. 486.

Health Psychology

What is health psychology?

Health psychology is the study of ideas and principles from many fields that enhance health, prevent illness, diagnose and treat disease, and rehabilitate people. Health psychology is an action-oriented discipline that focuses on preventive health measures as well as intervention in existing conditions.   pp. 488–489

How can health psychologists help combat AIDS problems?

Health psychologists can highlight the distinction between high-risk and low-risk behavior in AIDS prevention. They can be involved in educating youth, the uneducated, and other high-risk populations; and they can counsel AIDS patients and their families.   pp. 490–491

What is a sick role, and how do perceptions of health risk shape behavior?

When people do what they think will help them get well, we say they are adopting a sick role. Research shows that people are more receptive to medical treatments when the treatments are specific, simple, and easy and have minimal side effects. Perceptions of health risks and consequences are an important factor in determining attitudes and behaviors toward new technologies and toward risky behaviors and diseases such as AIDS.   pp. 490–492

KEY TERM: *health psychology,* p. 488.

CONNECTIONS

I f you are interested in...

How people cope with everyday problems, see ...

CHAPTER 4, pp. 137–141

Various coping techniques (such as biofeedback and self-hypnosis) that can be practiced at home to effectively manage stressors.

CHAPTER 10, pp. 385–386

How people can learn to control their emotional responses to situations through self-instruction.

CHAPTER 14, pp. 518–520

How seriously depressed people often feel there is no hope and that they cannot cope any longer.

CHAPTER 15, pp. 553–556
Cognitive therapy, which focuses on changing people's distorted ideas of reality and helps them to develop positive self-esteem.

The role of stress in everyday life, see ...

CHAPTER 10, pp. 361–363

The relationship between arousal and stress.

CHAPTER 14, pp. 505–508

How certain psychological disorders have a strong component of anxiety.

CHAPTER 17, pp. 620–623

How frustration can lead to stress and, ultimately, ▶ aggression.

Psychology's role in health and well-being, see ...

CHAPTER 5, pp. 169–170

How the immune system can be conditioned to respond to environmental stimulation.

CHAPTER 9, pp. 338–341

The inevitable physical deterioration that occurs with aging.

CHAPTER 14, pp. 510–512, 518–520

Various disorders that affect both physical and mental health.

◀

14

Psychological Disorders

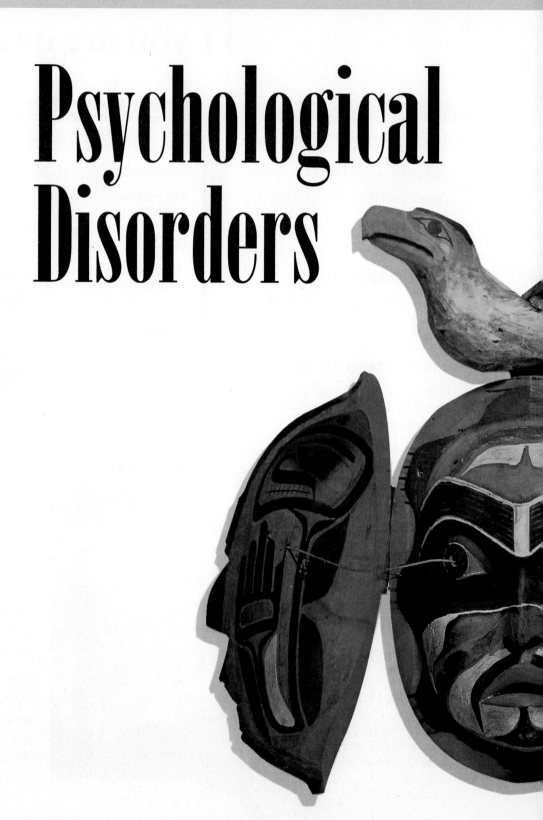

Under a 1987 directive issued by Mayor Edward Koch to help New York City's mentally ill homeless, Joyce Brown was forcibly committed to Bellevue Hospital. The 40-year-old former secretary had lived on a Manhattan sidewalk for a year, feeding herself on $7 a day and huddling over a hot-air vent in winter to stay warm. She was dirty and incoherent, cursed at passersby, defecated in her clothes, and tore up and burned dollar bills given to her. Brown, however, didn't want to be "helped." "Some people are street people," she said. "That's the life they choose to lead."

Brown took her battle to court, and the judge found her to be educated, intelligent, and fiercely independent. In explaining her odd behavior, Brown said that after she had eaten enough for the day, she burned any excess money because carrying cash at night was dangerous. She attributed her filthy condition to the inaccessibility of public toilets. Neither suicidal nor malnourished, Brown seemingly posed little threat to herself or others. Three psychiatrists hired by Brown's attorneys testified that the woman was odd but not crazy. Four psychiatrists for the city said she was maladjusted. The judge ruled in Brown's favor, noting that street life may be aesthetically offensive but that the mentally ill are as entitled as everyone else to freedom.

Joyce Brown's case raises two important questions about mental illness: How different must a person's behavior be to qualify as abnormal? And what should public policy be regarding mental illness and crime?

Is Brown's behavior any stranger than that of an old man who leaves a multi-million dollar fortune to his cats? Is it any more eccentric than taking a mid-winter bath in an ice-covered lake (as do members of the Polar Bear club) or undergoing extensive cosmetic surgery to obtain a perfect face and body?

What Is Abnormal Behavior?

Is Joyce Brown merely odd, or is she abnormal? To some extent, it depends on where you live, because every society has its own definition of abnormal behavior. In Russia, for example, people were once regularly placed in mental institutions for political dissent (Faraone, 1982). Generally, however, the behavior of people classified as abnormal is more than odd. Recent data suggest that, in any single month, about 15 percent of adults in the U.S. population meet the criteria for having a mental disorder; that is, they exhibit symptoms of abnormality (Reiger et al., 1988).

A Definition

Abnormal behavior is behavior characterized as:

1. atypical,
2. socially unacceptable,
3. distressing,
4. maladaptive, or
5. the result of distorted cognitions.

Let us consider these five distinguishing characteristics.

First, abnormal behavior is *atypical*. Many behaviors are unusual; however, abnormal behaviors tend to be so unusual as to be statistically rare. For example, you would not consider ear piercing among teenage boys to be abnormal because the practice is fairly common in our society today. However, washing one's hands every few minutes during the day until they are raw is abnormal. Of course, not all atypical behavior is necessarily abnormal. The Olympic feats of runner Carl Lewis are statistically uncommon but not abnormal.

Second, in addition to being atypical, abnormal behavior is also often *socially unacceptable*. Society is fickle. Ideas about what is normal and abnormal vary according to cultural values, which are in a constant state of flux. What is normal in one culture may be labeled abnormal in another. Similarly, behavior that was considered abnormal 20 years ago, such as a woman calling a man for a date, may be considered normal today. For behavior to be judged abnormal, it is usually unacceptable to society.

Third, a person's abnormal behavior often causes *distress* to the person or to those around the person. While feelings of anxiety are normal in many situations, prolonged anxiety (distress) may indicate abnormal behavior. You may feel anxious while you are preparing to speak in front of a large group; but constant, unrelent-

Abnormal behavior: Behavior characterized as atypical, socially unacceptable, distressing, maladaptive, or the result of distorted cognitions.

ing anxiety, the avoidance of any situation that might require public speaking, and fear of people in general suggests abnormal behavior.

Fourth, abnormal behavior is usually *maladaptive,* or self-defeating to the person exhibiting it. Maladaptive behavior, such as drug abuse, is harmful and nonproductive. It often leads to more misery and prevents people from making positive changes in their lives.

Last, abnormal behavior is often the result of *distorted cognitions* (thoughts). For example, a young man with distorted cognitions may falsely believe that people are out to get him. A woman suffering from major depression may believe that she is worthless, stupid, and unlovable.

In recent years, psychologists have begun to describe behavior in terms of *maladjustment* rather than *abnormality.* The distinction is important because it implies that maladaptive behavior can, with treatment, become adaptive and productive. The term *maladjustment* also emphasizes specific behaviors rather than labeling the entire person.

To summarize, abnormal behavior is characterized as atypical, socially unacceptable, distressing, maladaptive, or the result of distorted cognitions. There are, of course, exceptions to this definition. For example, we do not hesitate to label drug abuse as abnormal, but that behavior is not as atypical as it once was. Nevertheless, this definition provides psychologists with a solid framework from which to explore abnormal behavior and its treatment.

Is dressing like Spiderman and climbing the wall of a skyscraper abnormal behavior?

Perspectives on Abnormality

Before prescribing treatment, mental health practitioners want to know why a person is maladjusted, because the cause of a disorder can sometimes help define a treatment plan. Therefore, they often turn to theories and models that attempt to explain the causes of abnormality. A **model** is an analogy, a perspective, or an approach that helps scientists discover relationships among data; it uses a structure from one field to help describe data in another. Psychologists use models to make predictions about behavior. These models form the basis of **abnormal psychology,** the field of psychology concerned with the assessment, treatment, and prevention of maladaptive behavior. Several models help explain abnormal behavior: medical-biological, psychodynamic, humanistic, behavioral, cognitive, sociocultural, legal, and interactionist.

Medical-Biological Model. Thousands of years ago, our ancestors believed that abnormal behavior was caused by demons that invaded people's bodies. The "cure" often involved *trephination*—drilling a hole into the skull to allow the evil force to escape. Even as recently as a few hundred years ago, people with psychological disorders were caged and treated like animals. Early reformists, such as Philippe Pinel, advocated the medical model and proposed that abnormal behavior could be treated and cured. When scientists showed that syphilis could cause mental disorders, the medical model gained even greater acceptance and led to more humane treatment and improved conditions for patients.

Model: A perspective or approach derived from data in one field, used to help describe data in another field.

Abnormal psychology: The field of psychology concerned with the assessment, treatment, and prevention of maladaptive behavior.

*Philippe Pinel (1745–1826)
released the patients at a Paris
Hospital from their shackles,
introducing more humane
treatment of people suffering
from mental disorders.*

The *medical-biological model* of abnormal behavior focuses on the biological and physiological conditions that initiate abnormal behaviors. This model adequately deals with a range of mental ailments, such as those caused by mercury poisoning or viral attacks on brain cells. It focuses on genetic abnormalities, problems in the central nervous system, and hormonal changes. It also helps explain and treat individuals with substance abuse problems and with schizophrenia, two disorders that may have a strong biological component. Proponents of the medical-biological model might explain Joyce Brown's behavior (introduced at the beginning of the chapter) as a result of a chemical or hormonal imbalance that altered her judgment.

Many of the terms and concepts used in psychology and psychiatry are borrowed from medicine; they include *treatment, case, symptom, syndrome,* and *mental illness.* The medical model assumes that abnormal behavior, like other illnesses, can be diagnosed, treated, and often cured. This approach has not gone unchallenged, however. Its critics say that it does not take advantage of modern psychological insights, such as those of learning theory. A major—but not surprising—disadvantage of the medical model is that it emphasizes hospitalization and drug treatment rather than solving psychological problems by psychological means. Use of the medical model also has fostered the notion that abnormal behavior can be infectious, much like a disease.

Psychodynamic Model. The *psychodynamic model* of abnormal behavior is loosely rooted in Freud's theory of personality (discussed in chapter 12). It assumes that psychological disorders result from anxiety produced by unresolved conflicts and forces of which a person may be unaware. It asserts that maladjustment occurs when a person relies on too many defense mechanisms or when defense mechanisms fail. Joyce Brown's behavior might be explained as anger turned inward against the self. Although Brown is bright and capable, her behavior might be seen as a reaction to her fear of competing caused by low-self esteem that was initiated in childhood. Treatment usually involves helping a patient become aware of motivations, conflicts, and desires so the person can have a healthier lifestyle. We will explore psychodynamic approaches in more detail in chapter 15.

Humanistic Model. Like the psychodynamic model, the *humanistic model* of abnormal behavior assumes that inner psychic forces are important in establishing and maintaining a normal lifestyle. However, unlike psychodynamic theorists, humanists believe that people have a good deal of cognitive control over their lives. The humanistic model focuses on individual uniqueness and decision making. It contends that people become maladjusted when their expectations far exceed their achievements. In Joyce Brown's case, a humanist might focus on her dignity, self-respect, and quest for independence. Treatment usually involves helping maladjusted people discover and accept their true selves, formulate more realistic self-concepts and expectations, and become more like their ideal selves.

Behavioral Model. The *behavioral model* of abnormal behavior states that such behavior is caused by faulty or ineffective learning and conditioning patterns. Two fundamental assumptions of behavioral (learning) theorists are that disordered behavior can be reshaped and that more appropriate, worthwhile behaviors can be substituted through traditional learning techniques (see chapter 5).

Behavioral theorists assume that events in a person's environment reinforce or punish various behaviors selectively and, in doing so, shape personality and may create maladjustment. They thus contend that an abusive husband may have learned to assert his dominance over women through physical abuse because as a child he was rewarded for typically masculine behaviors (such as fighting) and punished for typically feminine behaviors (such as nurturance). Proponents of the behavioral model might explain Joyce Brown's behavior by noting that she did not find significant reinforcers in the work world and she felt she could take care of herself and manage better on a day-to-day basis on the streets.

Cognitive Model. The *cognitive model* of abnormal behavior asserts that human beings engage in both prosocial and maladjusted behaviors because of ideas and thoughts. As thinking organisms, individuals decide how to behave; abnormal behavior is based on false assumptions or unrealistic situations.

Practitioners from the cognitive perspective treat people with psychological disorders by helping them develop new thought processes that instill new values. Joyce Brown might be assumed to have developed wrong ideas about the world; these ideas might be irrational and might have led her to maladaptive behaviors. A practitioner might assert that a client (such as Brown) can replace maladjusted behaviors with worthwhile ones. Using the cognitive model, a practitioner might treat Joyce Brown by helping her to formulate more rational self-concepts and to adopt more effective coping strategies.

Sociocultural Model. According to the *sociocultural model* of abnormal behavior, people develop abnormalities within a context—the context of the family, the community, and society. Researchers, especially cross-cultural researchers, have shown that people's personality development and their disorders reflect their culture, the stressors in their society, and the types of disorders prevalent in their society. Relying heavily on the learning and cognitive frameworks, the sociocultural model focuses on cultural variables as key determinants of maladjustment.

As researchers examine the frequency and types of disorders that occur in different societies, they also note some sharp differences within each society. Within a specific society, disorders vary as a function of the decade being examined and the age and gender of the clients. In China, for example, depression is relatively uncommon, but stress reactions in the form of physical ailments are common. Understanding cross-cultural perspectives on abnormality helps us frame our questions and interpret our data. Thus, a sociocultural approach is often illuminating.

Legal Model. The *legal model* of abnormal behavior defines such behavior differently. Think about John W. Hinckley, Jr., the man who attempted to assassinate President Ronald Reagan. A jury declared him "not guilty by reason of insanity," and he was acquitted of murder charges. During the public outcry that followed, states sought to prohibit the insanity plea. At least half the states changed their insanity plea, 12 adopted the new plea "guilty but mentally ill," and 3 chose to eliminate the insanity plea altogether.

The term *insane* is a legal term, not a psychological one. Insanity refers to a condition that excuses people from responsibility and protects them from punishment. From the legal point of view, a person cannot be held responsible for a crime if, at the time of the crime, the person lacked the capacity to recognize right from wrong or to obey the law.

Think back to the example of Joyce Brown. Do any of the legal criteria describe her? The answer is no. Although useful for judicial purposes, the legal definition of abnormal behavior is too focused to be useful in treating clients; also, it is a misconception that it is widely used in court as a defense.

Interactionist Model. Each of the models described—medical-biological, psychodynamic, humanistic, behavioral, cognitive, sociocultural, and legal—explains maladjustment from a different perspective. No single model can explain every kind of abnormal behavior; however, each has value. For some disorders (such as phobias), learning theory explains the cause and prescribes an effective course of treatment. For other disorders (such as schizophrenia), medical-biological theory explains a significant part of the problem. Consequently, many psychologists use an *interactionist model* of abnormal behavior, one drawing on all these perspectives (sometimes termed an eclectic model). For example, a therapist could treat a depressed patient by arranging for antidepressant drugs (medical-biological approach); helping the patient develop new, optimistic thought processes (cognitive approach); and teaching the patient adaptive behaviors to eliminate depression-inducing stress (behavioral approach).

As you examine each of the psychological disorders presented in this chapter, think about why you favor one of the explanations of maladjustment over another. Do you have a cognitive bent, or do you favor a more psychodynamic approach? Perhaps you are more behavioral in your beliefs. Regardless of a practitioner's predispositions, it is important that the symptoms be carefully evaluated so proper diagnoses can be made. Next, we will consider a system that has been developed to help practitioners make diagnoses. The system is presented in the work known as the *Diagnostic and Statistical Manual of Mental Disorders.*

Diagnosing Maladjustment: The DSM-IV

Three psychiatrists hired by Joyce Brown's attorneys testified that she was odd but not crazy. Four psychiatrists hired by the city said she was insane. This controversy underscores the fact that diagnosing maladjusted behavior is a complicated process.

Diagnostic and Statistical Manual of Mental Disorders. The American Psychiatric Association has devised a system for diagnosing maladjusted behavior—the *Diagnostic and Statistical Manual of Mental Disorders (DSM).* Its goals are (1) to improve the reliability of diagnoses by categorizing disorders according to observable behaviors and (2) to make sure that the diagnoses are consistent with research evidence and practical experience (Widiger et al., 1991). The system designates 16 major categories of maladjustment and more than 200 subcategories. (Table 14.1 lists some of the major classifications.) The *DSM* also cites the **prevalence** of each disorder—the percentage of the population displaying a disorder during any specified period. For most psychological disorders, we also know the lifetime prevalence—the statistical likelihood that a person will develop the disorder during his or her lifetime.

You might think that a diagnostic manual would be straightforward, like an encyclopedia of mental disorders. However, the *DSM* has met with some resistance and controversy. Some psychologists applaud its recognition of social and environmental influences on behavior. Others argue that it is too precise and complicated. Some assert that despite its rigor, it is still not precise enough. Others worry about a bias against women. Still others believe the *DSM* should go beyond diagnosis and include problem-oriented and problem-solving information rather than just symptoms. Many psychologists are unhappy with the use of psychiatric

Prevalence: The percentage of a population displaying a disorder during any specified period.

terms that perpetuate a medical rather than a behavioral model. The current edition is the *DSM-IV*, published in 1994. The manual is constantly being revised to reflect the latest scientific knowledge and thus is an evolving system of classification.

Diversity and Diagnoses. The *DSM-IV* is by no means the final word in diagnosing maladjustment, and its reliability is not completely known; it continues to evolve. It especially needs to become more sensitive to issues of diversity. Not all ethnic groups exhibit symptoms of every disorder; nor do members of one ethnic group have an equal likelihood of exhibiting specific symptoms.

Research shows that the likelihood of a specific diagnosis is indeed related to ethnicity. For example, Asian Americans and African Americans receive more diagnoses of the disorder schizophrenia than do whites; Hispanic Americans receive fewer diagnoses of schizophrenia than do whites (Flaskerud & Hu, 1992). Similarly, Koreans are more likely to report being depressed than are individuals from Taiwan, the Philippines, or the United States (Crittenden et al., 1992). Culture and its effects on clinical diagnosis and treatment plans is under-researched and an important area of concern for practicing psychologists. According to the American Psychological Association (1993), practitioners must

▶ Recognize cultural diversity;

▶ Understand the role of culture and ethnicity in development;

▶ Help clients understand their own sociological identification; and

▶ Understand the influence of culture, race, gender, and sexual orientation on behavior.

In the remainder of this chapter, we will explore some of the most important disorders in *DSM-IV* and their consequences. We will begin with anxiety disorders.

TABLE 14.1 *Major Classifications of the* Diagnostic and Statistical Manual of Mental Disorders, *Fourth Edition*

Disorders First Diagnosed in Infancy, Childhood, and Adolescence

Delirium, Dementia, and other Cognitive Disorders

Substance Related Disorders

Schizophrenia and other Psychotic Disorders

Mood Disorders

Anxiety Disorders

Somatoform Disorders

Factitious Disorders

Dissociative Disorders

Sexual Disorders and Gender Identity Disorders

Eating Disorders

Sleep Disorders

Impulse Control Disorders

Adjustment Disorders

Personality Disorders

Note: Each classification is further broken down into subtypes (with some minor modifications).

FOCUS

▶ What are the advantages and disadvantages of the medical-biological model of abnormal behavior?   p. 502

▶ Identify the distinguishing characteristics of the psychodynamic, humanistic, and cognitive models of abnormal behavior.   pp. 502–503

▶ What does it mean for a psychologist to be interactionist?   p. 504

▶ What are the goals of the *DSM*, and what are its potential advantages and disadvantages?   pp. 504–505

Anxiety, Somatoform, and Dissociative Disorders

Psychologists know that almost everyone experiences anxiety. Most people feel anxious in specific situations, such as before taking an examination, competing in a swim meet, or delivering a speech. Although anxiety can be a positive, motivating force, its effects can also be debilitating; left untreated, it may eventually impair a person's health and lead to hospitalization. Anxiety disorders are so common in the general population that they warrant special consideration. Research into them, however, is not extensive; and there is a real paucity of research on special populations—for example, African Americans (Neal & Turner, 1991).

Defining Anxiety

Karen Horney

Karen Horney (pronounced HORN-eye), a neo-Freudian renowned for her work on anxiety, described it as the central factor in both normal and abnormal behavior (Horney, 1937). **Anxiety** is customarily considered a generalized feeling of fear and apprehension that might be related to a particular event or object, often accompanied by increased physiological arousal. Horney considered it a motivating force, an intrapsychic urge, and a signal of distress. Horney argued that anxiety underlies many forms of maladjustment. She believed that maladjustment occurs when too many defenses against anxiety pervade an individual's personality.

Freud, in contrast, saw anxiety as the result of constant conflict among the id, ego, and superego; and he called nearly all forms of behavior associated with anxiety *neurotic*. Freud's term *neurosis* has made its way into everyday language, to the point where nonpsychologists tend to describe any behavioral quirk as neurotic. Today, psychologists believe that, as a general catchall term, *neurosis* is neither appropriate nor efficient. Precise and consistent diagnosis of maladjustment is essential to appropriate treatment; however, anxiety (and what Freud called neurotic behaviors) refers to a wide range of symptoms, including fear, apprehension, inattention, palpitation, respiratory distress, and dizziness.

Psychologists recognize anxiety as a key symptom of maladjustment—not necessarily the cause of maladjustment. Apprehension, fear, and its accompanying autonomic nervous system arousal are caused by thoughts, environmental stimuli, or perhaps some long-standing and as yet unresolved conflict. This is clearly the case with generalized anxiety disorders, considered next.

Generalized Anxiety Disorders

Every disorder represents a different pattern of behavior and maladjustment, and *DSM-IV* classifies disorders under a variety of diagnostic categories. Those in which anxiety is the prominent feature are designated generalized anxiety disorders. **Generalized anxiety disorders** are anxiety disorders characterized by persistent anxiety occurring more days than not for at least six months, sometimes with problems in motor tension, autonomic hyperactivity, apprehension, and concentration. People with a generalized anxiety disorder feel anxious almost constantly. They often report sleep disturbances, excessive sweating, muscle tension, headaches, and insomnia. They are tense and irritable, unable to concentrate, have difficulty making decisions, and may hyperventilate (Rapee, 1986).

For this diagnosis, *DSM-IV* states that a person must show persistent anxiety for at least six months. When such chronic anxiety has no obvious source, it is called free-floating anxiety. **Free-floating anxiety** is persistent anxiety not clearly related to any specific object or situation, accompanied by a sense of impending doom. On the other hand, the source of such extreme anxiety may be, and often is, a specific stressor in the environment, such as being in a prisoner-of-war camp.

People with a generalized anxiety disorder show impairment in three areas of functioning. One area is *motor tension,* whereby the person is unable to relax and exhibits jumpiness, restlessness, and tension. The second area is *autonomic hyperactivity,* whereby the person sweats, has a dry mouth, has a high resting pulse rate, urinates frequently, and may complain of a lump in the throat. The third area is *vigilance,* whereby the person has difficulty concentrating and is irritable and impatient. Unlike people who feel anxious almost constantly, those who suffer from phobic disorders, considered next, have far more focused anxiety and fear.

Anxiety: A generalized feeling of fear and apprehension that might be related to a particular event or object, often accompanied by increased physiological arousal.

Generalized anxiety disorders: Anxiety disorders characterized by persistent anxiety for at least 6 months, occurring more days than not sometimes with problems in motor tension, autonomic hyperactivity, apprehension, and concentration.

Free-floating anxiety: Persistent anxiety not clearly related to any specific object or situation, accompanied by a sense of impending doom.

Phobic Disorders

Do you know someone who is petrified at the thought of an airplane ride, who avoids crowds at all cost, or who shudders at the sight of a harmless garden snake? That person may suffer from a **phobic disorder**—an anxiety disorder involving the excessive, unreasonable, and irrational fear of, and consequent attempt to avoid, specific objects or situations. People with phobic disorders exhibit avoidance and escape behaviors, show increased heart rate and irregular breathing patterns, and report thoughts of disaster and severe embarrassment. Many psychologists agree that, once established, phobias are maintained by the relief a person derives from escaping or avoiding the feared situation.

One key to diagnosing a phobic disorder is that the fear must be excessive and disproportionate to the situation. Most people who fear heights would not avoid visiting a friend who lived on the top floor of a tall building; however, a person with a phobia of heights would. Fear alone does not distinguish a phobia; both fear and avoidance must be evident.

Mild phobic disorders occur in about 7.5 percent of the population. They are, in fact, relatively common in well-adjusted people. Severe, disabling phobias occur in less than 0.05 percent of the population and typically appear in patients with other disorders (Seif & Atkins, 1979). Phobias occur most frequently between the ages of 30 and 60 and about equally in men and women (Marks, 1977). There are an infinite number of objects and situations toward which people become fearful. Because of their diversity and number, *DSM-IV* classifies three basic kinds of phobias: agoraphobia, social phobia, and specific phobia; we consider them next.

Agoraphobia. **Agoraphobia** is a marked fear and avoidance of being alone or isolated in open and public places from which escape might be difficult or embarrassing. It is accompanied by avoidance behaviors that may eventually interfere with normal activities. It can become so debilitating that it prevents the individual from going into any open space, traveling in airplanes, or being in crowds. People with severe cases may decide to never leave their home. Agoraphobia is often brought on by stress, particularly interpersonal stress. It is far more common in women than in men and is often accompanied by other disorders.

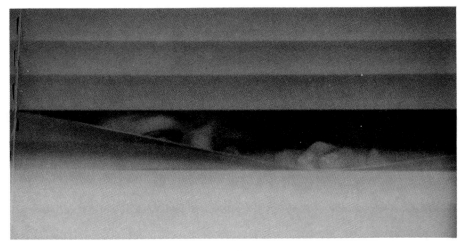

People suffering from extreme cases of agoraphobia are afraid to leave the safety of their own homes.

The disorder brings about hyperventilation, extreme tension, and even cognitive disorganization (Zitrin, 1981). Agoraphobics feel weak and dizzy when they have an attack and often suffer from severe panic attacks. *Panic attacks* are characterized as acute anxiety accompanied by sharp increases in autonomic nervous system arousal that is not triggered by a specific event; persons experiencing such attacks often avoid the situations that are associated with them (McNally, 1990). Agoraphobics often are seriously depressed (Breier, Charney, & Heninger, 1984).

Agoraphobia is complicated, incapacitating, and extraordinarily difficult to treat (Mathews, Gelder, & Johnston, 1981). According to Freud and other psy-

Phobic disorder: An anxiety disorder characterized by excessive, irrational, and unreasonable fear and subsequent attempted avoidance of specific objects or situations, acknowledged by the person as unreasonable.

Agoraphobia: [AG-or-uh-FOE-bee-uh] An anxiety disorder characterized by fear and avoidance of being alone or in public places from which escape might be difficult or embarrassing.

TABLE 14.2   *Some Common Specific Phobias*

Name	Object or Situation Feared
Acrophobia	High places
Ailurophobia	Cats
Algophobia	Pain
Anthropophobia	Men
Aquaphobia	Water
Astraphobia	Storms, thunder, and lightning
Claustrophobia	Closed places
Cynophobia	Dogs
Hematophobia	Blood
Mysophobia	Contamination
Nyctophobia	Darkness
Pathophobia	Disease
Pyrophobia	Fire
Thanatophobia	Death
Xenophobia	Strangers
Zoophobia	Animals

choanalysts, traumatic childhood experiences may cause people to avoid particular objects, events, and situations that produce anxiety. Freudians speculate that agoraphobics may have feared abandonment by a cold or nonnurturing mother and that the fear has generalized to a fear of abandonment or helplessness. Most researchers today find Freudian explanations of phobic behavior unconvincing. As an alternative, modern learning theory suggests that agoraphobia may develop because people avoid situations they have found painful or embarrassing. Failed coping strategies and low self-esteem have been implicated (Williams, Kinney, & Falbo, 1989). Despite much research, no simple cause for the disorder has been found.

Social Phobia. A **social phobia** is an anxiety disorder characterized by fear of, and desire to avoid, situations in which the person might be exposed to scrutiny by others and might behave in an embarrassing or humiliating way. A person with a social phobia avoids eating in public or speaking before other people. The person also avoids evaluation by refusing to deal with people or situations in which it might occur.

Specific Phobia. A **specific phobia** is an anxiety disorder characterized by irrational and persistent fear of a specific object or situation along with a compelling desire to avoid it. Most people are familiar with specific phobias. Among them are *claustrophobia* (fear of closed spaces), *hematophobia* (fear of the sight of blood), and *acrophobia* (fear of heights). Table 14.2 lists some common specific phobias. Many develop in childhood, adolescence, or early adulthood. Most people who fear heights, doctors, or flying can calm themselves and deal with their fear; those who cannot (true phobics) often seek the help of a psychotherapist when the phobia interferes with their health or with day-to-day functioning. Behavior therapy is typically effective. The Diversity box examines the prevalence of specific phobias and other anxiety disorders among African Americans.

Obsessive-Compulsive Disorders

Being orderly and organized is an asset for most people in today's fast-paced, complex society. However, when orderliness becomes the primary concern, a person may be suffering from an obsessive-compulsive disorder. An **obsessive-compulsive disorder** is an anxiety disorder characterized by persistent and uncontrollable thoughts and irrational beliefs that cause performance of compulsive rituals that are intrusive and inappropriate and interfere with daily life. Obsessive-compulsive disorders are characterized by the presence of unwanted thoughts, urges, and actions that focus on maintaining order and control. About 2 percent of the population suffer from obsessive-compulsive disorders; of these, about 20 percent have only obsessions or compulsions, and about 80 percent have both.

People with obsessive-compulsive disorders com-

Social phobia: [FOE-bee-uh] An anxiety disorder characterized by fear of, and desire to avoid, situations in which the person might be exposed to scrutiny by others and might behave in an embarrassing or humiliating way.

Specific phobia: An anxiety disorder characterized by irrational and persistent fear of an object or situation, along with a compelling desire to avoid it.

Obsessive-compulsive disorders: [ob-SESS-iv kom-PULS-iv] Anxiety disorders characterized by persistent and uncontrollable thoughts and irrational beliefs that cause the performance of intrusive and inappropriate compulsive rituals that interfere with daily life.

DIVERSITY

Anxiety Disorders among African Americans

Here are two important facts: (1) Anxiety disorders are one of the most common problems presented to clinical psychologists. (2) By the year 2000, one-third of the U.S. population will be composed of ethnic minorities. Nonetheless, little attention has been given to anxiety disorders among ethnic minorities such as African Americans.

Recently, however, two researchers from the University of Pittsburgh, Angela Neal and Samuel Turner (1991), conducted a study of anxiety disorders among African Americans. They found a higher rate of anxiety disorders among African Americans than among white Americans.

Neal and Turner (1991) found that African Americans had a higher prevalence of specific phobia than any other ethnic group; the same was true for agoraphobia. The percentage of African Americans who are diag-nosed as agoraphobic is 50 percent higher than for whites. Further, the percentage of African-American Vietnam veterans who suffer from posttraumatic stress disorder is also higher than for whites. For specific and social phobia, African Americans are nearly twice as likely as whites to report recent phobias (Brown, Eaton, & Sussman, 1990). As with the other disorders, childhood anxiety disorders are less likely among white adolescents than among African-American adolescents (Kashani & Orvaschel, 1988).

Researchers are not sure why these differences exist, and certain research problems make finding out difficult. Among these problems are the following five: (1) Within the African-American community, research does not have an honorable reputation because of abuses that occurred in the past. As a consequence, few individuals wish to participate in research studies. (2) At times of emotional distress, African Americans are more likely to seek help from an emergency room physician or a minister than from a mental health professional. Again, the lack of participants makes research difficult. (3) Researchers have unwittingly neglected anxiety disorders in African Americans. (4) The number of African Americans who are themselves engaged in clinical research is exceptionally small. (5) It is also not clear how African Americans view anxiety, anxiety disorders, and coping with anxiety.

Today community psychologists are often the researchers who are asking the questions. They know the appropriate questions to ask. However, as Neal and Turner (1991) assert, they often lack the personnel and the resources to fully implement their ideas.

The apparent high frequency of anxiety disorders among African Americans and complicating social factors that may lead to these disorders are part of the multicultural research problems that psychologists are only now beginning to recognize.

---

bat anxiety by carrying out ritual behaviors that reduce tension; they feel that they have to *do* something. For example, a man obsessed with avoiding germs may wash his hands a hundred times a day and may wear white gloves to avoid touching contaminated objects. If he does not perform these compulsive acts, he may develop severe anxiety. A woman obsessed with punctuality may become extremely anxious if dinner guests arrive 5 minutes late. A person may compulsively write notes about every detail of every task before permitting herself or himself to take any action. Here is an account of obsessive-compulsive behavior:

> I used to write notes to remind myself to do a particular job, so in my mind there was a real risk that one of these notes might go out of the window or door. . . . My fear was that if one of these papers blew away, this would cause a fatality to the person carrying out my design project. . . . I found it difficult to walk along the street, as every time I saw paper I wondered if it was some of mine. I had to pick it all up, unless it was brown chocolate paper, or lined paper, which I didn't use. And before I got on my bike, I checked that nothing was sticking out of my pockets and got my wife to recheck. . . . I would have to sit in a certain seat on the bus so that, when I walked downstairs, I could look back up and check that no papers were on the seat. I couldn't smoke a cigarette without taking it to bits and checking there was no document between the paper and tobacco. I couldn't even have

People with obssessive-compulsive disorders carry out ritual behaviors that reduce tension and anxiety.

sex because I thought a piece of paper might get intertwined into the mattress. (Melville, 1977, pp. 66–67)

Freud and other psychodynamic theorists believed that obsessive-compulsive disorders come largely from difficulties during the anal stage of development, when orderliness and cleanliness are often stressed. Learning theorists argue that bringing order to a person's environment reduces uncertainty and risk and thus is reinforcing. Because reinforced behaviors tend to recur, these behaviors become exaggerated during times of stress. Biologically oriented theorists believe that such factors as chronic elevated levels of arousal are implicated (Turner, Beidel, & Nathan, 1985), and some researchers suggest a genetic link for anxiety disorders (Last et al., 1991).

Practitioners report that true obsessive-compulsive disorders are relatively rare. Treatment often includes drugs (such as Anafrinil, Prozac, or Zoloft) combined with relaxation exercises. Such treatment helps change ideas about stress and the consequences of anxiety (e.g. Christensen et al., 1987). Family support and family psychotherapy are also helpful; families are taught that they should neither encourage the behaviors nor participate in the person's rituals. Today, self-help groups and greater awareness of the disorders are leading to successful treatment.

Somatoform and dissociative disorders, discussed next, are harder to understand and treat.

Somatoform Disorders

If you were a television writer for a soap opera, you might have on your desk a copy of *DSM-IV*, with the page turned to somatoform and dissociative disorders. These disorders are relatively rare and are studied less than other disorders; however, they make for fascinating reading and study. They are naturals for interesting television storylines.

Somatoform disorders are disorders that involve real physical symptoms that are not under voluntary control and for which no apparent physical cause exists. Evidence suggests that the causes are psychological. Three types of somatoform disorders are somatization disorders, conversion disorders, and hypochondriasis.

Somatization Disorders. **Somatization disorders** are somatoform disorders characterized by recurrent and multiple complaints of several years' duration for which medical attention has been ineffective. Those with the disorder, however, tend to seek medical attention at least once a year. The disorder typically begins before age 30. It is diagnosed in only about 1 percent of females and is even rarer in males.

Patients feel sickly for a good part of their lives and may report muscle weakness, double vision, memory loss, and hallucinations. Other commonly reported symptoms include gastrointestinal problems such as vomiting and diarrhea; painful menstrual periods with excessive bleeding; sexual indifference; and pains in the back, chest, and genitals. Patients are often beset by anxiety and depression.

Individuals with somatization disorders often have a host of emotional problems that cause their medical complaints. However, some of the medical conditions are not psychologically caused, and physicians must be especially careful to treat medically those conditions that need treatment and not to dismiss all the patient's problems as psychological.

Conversion Disorders. **Conversion disorders** are somatoform disorders characterized by the loss or alteration of physical functioning for no apparent physiological reason. People suffering from conversion disorders often lose the use of their arms, hands, or legs or their vision or other sensory modality. They may develop a combination of ailments. For example, a patient may become not only blind but also deaf, mute, or totally paralyzed.

Somatoform disorders: [so-MAT-oh-form] Disorders characterized by real physical symptoms not under voluntary control and for which no evident physical cause exists.

Somatization disorders: Somatoform disorders characterized by recurrent and multiple complaints of several years' duration for which medical attention has been ineffective.

Conversion disorders: Somatoform disorders characterized by the loss or alteration of physical functioning for no apparent physiological reason.

Although the patient may be unaware of the relationship, conversion disorders are generally considered a way to escape from or avoid upsetting situations. Also, the attention and support patients sometimes receive because of the symptoms may cause them to maintain the disorder. Conversion disorders are often associated with a history of psychosomatic illness. Men and women are equally likely to develop conversion disorders, which, like somatization disorders, are rare.

Hypochondriasis. When a person spends a lot of time going to physicians with all types of bodily complaints for which the physicians can find no cause, psychologists suspect hypochondriasis. **Hypochondriasis** is a somatoform disorder characterized by an inordinate preoccupation with health and illness, coupled with excessive anxiety about disease. Hypochondriacs believe, erroneously, that they have grave afflictions. They become preoccupied with minor aches and pains and often miss work and create alarm among family members. Every ache, every minor symptom, is examined, interpreted, and feared.

Psychodynamic views of hypochondriasis focus on how the symptoms of the illness keep the person from dealing with some other painful source of stress. Behavioral psychologists focus on how the illness can be reinforcing: People are given extra attention and care, and the illness diverts attention from tasks at which the individual may not be succeeding. By focusing on illness, a person may avoid marital problems, financial affairs, and educational goals. Of course, to the hypochondriac, the fears and anxiety are real. Only through psychotherapy can the true causes of the overattention to symptoms be addressed.

Dissociative Disorders

Dissociative disorders are disorders characterized by a sudden but temporary alteration in consciousness, identity, sensory/motor behavior, or memory. These disorders are quite noticeable and sharply delineated, although relatively rare. They include psychogenic amnesia and multiple personality.

Dissociative Amnesia. Psychogenic amnesia, one of several dissociative disorders, used to be grouped with other disorders. Today, however, psychologists recognize it as a separate disorder. **Dissociative amnesia** is a dissociative disorder characterized by the sudden and extensive inability to recall important personal information, usually of a traumatic or stressful nature. The memory loss is too extensive to be explained by ordinary forgetfulness. Often, the amnesia is brought on by a traumatic incident involving the threat of physical injury or death. The condition, which is relatively rare, occurs most often during wars or natural disasters.

Dissociative Identity Disorder: Multiple Personality. Another form of dissociative disorder, often associated with psychogenic amnesia but presenting a dramatically different kind of behavior, is **dissociative identity disorder,** more commonly known as multiple personality. Multiple personality is a dissociative disorder characterized by the existence within an individual of two or more distinct personalities, each of which is dominant at particular times and directs the individual's behavior at those times. Each personality has a unique style and different memories and behavioral patterns. For example, one personality may be adaptive and efficient at coping with life, while an-

Hypochondriasis: [hy-po-kon-DRY-a-sis] A somatoform disorder characterized by an inordinate preoccupation with health and illness, coupled with excessive anxiety about disease.

Dissociative disorders: Disorders characterized by a sudden but temporary alteration in consciousness, identity, sensory/motor behavior, or memory.

Dissociative amnesia: A dissociative disorder characterized by the sudden and extensive inability to recall important personal information, usually of a traumatic or stressful nature.

Dissociative identity disorder: Often called *multiple personality,* a dissociative disorder characterized by the existence within an individual of two or more distinct personalities, each of which is dominant at particular times and directs the individual's behavior at those times.

other may exhibit maladaptive behavior. Some people's alternate personalities are of the opposite sex. Each personality is usually unaware of any other one, although in some cases they eavesdrop on each other (Schacter et al., 1989). The different personalities (when active) acknowledge that time has passed but cannot account for it. The switch from one personality to another is usually brought on by stress.

Despite the impression left by popular movies and books, such as *The Three Faces of Eve* and *Sybil,* multiple personality as a diagnosed disorder is extremely rare, with only a few hundred actual well-documented cases in history. Many people confuse multiple personality with schizophrenia, a much more common disorder (which we'll examine later in this chapter).

Psychologists have little data on the causes of multiple personality and debate about how best to classify it (see Greaves, 1980). There is even controversy as to whether multiple personality actually exists. Some psychologists think people invent multiple personalities to avoid taking responsibility for their own behavior, especially when they have committed criminal acts. Others think some therapists subtly encourage patients to show symptoms of this disorder so the therapists can achieve recognition. Multiple personality is a well-known disorder nonetheless; it is vivid and interesting, and much more research is needed before comprehensive theories and effective treatments will become available.

FOCUS

▶ Why is free-floating anxiety a central concept to anxiety disorders?   p. 506

▶ Identify the central elements of an obsessive-compulsive disorder.   p. 508

▶ What evidence suggests that a person is displaying the symptoms of dissociative identity disorder (multiple personality)?   p. 511

▶ What are the implications of multiple personality for traditional theories of personality?   pp. 511–512

Personality and Sexual Disorders

People who exhibit inflexible and long-standing maladaptive ways of dealing with the environment that typically cause stress or social or occupational difficulties may have one of the **personality disorders.** Often, these disorders begin in childhood or adolescence and persist throughout adulthood. People with personality disorders are easy to spot but difficult to treat.

Types of Personality Disorders

People with personality disorders are divided into three broad types: those whose behavior appears (1) odd or eccentric, (2) fearful or anxious, or (3) dramatic, emotional, and erratic. We will now consider five specific personality disorders: paranoid, dependent, histrionic, narcissistic, and antisocial.

Personality disorders: Disorders characterized by inflexible and long-standing maladaptive ways of dealing with the environment, which typically cause stress and social or occupational problems.

Paranoid Personality Disorder. People who have unwarranted feelings of persecution and who mistrust almost everyone are said to be suffering from *paranoid personality disorder.* They are hypersensitive to criticism and have a restricted range of emotional responses. They have strong fears of being exploited and losing control and independence. Sometimes they appear cold, humorless, and even scheming. As you might expect, people with paranoid personality disorder are suspicious and seldom able to form close, intimate relationships with others.

Dependent Personality Disorder. Fearful or anxious behaviors are characteristic of people with a *dependent personality disorder.* Such people are submissive and clinging; they let others make all the important decisions in their lives. They try to appear pleasant and agreeable at all times. They act meek, humble, and affectionate in order to keep their protectors. Battered wives often suffer from the dependent personality disorder. Overprotective, authoritative parenting seems to be a major initiating cause of dependency (R. F. Bornstein, 1992).

Histrionic Personality Disorder. A *histrionic personality disorder* is characterized by dramatic, emotional, and erratic behaviors. People with this disorder seek attention by exaggerating situations in their lives. They have stormy personal relationships, are excessively emotional, and demand constant reassurance and praise.

Narcissistic Personality Disorder. Closely related to histrionic personality disorder is *narcissistic personality disorder.* People with this disorder have an extremely exaggerated sense of self-importance, expect special favors, and need constant admiration and attention. They show a lack of caring for others, and they react to criticism with rage, shame, or humiliation.

Antisocial Personality Disorder. Perhaps the most widely recognized personality disorder is the antisocial personality disorder. An **antisocial personality disorder** is characterized by egocentricity, by behavior that is irresponsible and that violates the rights of other people—lying, theft, delinquency and other violations of social rules; and by a lack of guilt feelings, an inability to understand other people, and a lack of fear of punishment. Individuals with this disorder may be superficially charming, but their behavior is destructive and often reckless. A person so diagnosed must be at least 18 years old and usually displays a blatant disregard for others.

A person who frequently changes jobs, does not take proper care of his or her children, is arrested often, fails to pay bills, and lies constantly displays behaviors typical of antisocial personality disorder. Such people are relatively unsocialized adults; they are unwilling to conform to and live by society's rules, and their behavior often brings them into conflict with society. Antisocial people consistently blame others for their behavior. They seldom feel guilt or learn from experience or punishment. The disorder occurs six times more often in men than in women. Extreme forms of this disorder are displayed by cold-blooded killers, such as Charles Manson and Ted Bundy, although most people with the disorder reveal their sociopathy through less deadly and sensational means. As much as 3 percent of the population may be diagnosed with antisocial personality disorder.

Adopted children who were separated at birth from antisocial parents are likely to show antisocial behavior later in life (Cadoret, 1978). This suggests a genetic (nature) contribution to the disorder. Another fact that suggests a genetic cause is that the nervous systems of people diagnosed as having antisocial personality disorder may be different from those of normal people. When normal people do something wrong, their autonomic nervous system reacts with symptoms of anxiety, such as fear, heart palpitations, and sweating. Evidence suggests that *decreased* autonomic arousal is characteristic in people with antisocial personality disorders (Waid, 1976). These people do not function at sufficiently high levels of autonomic nervous system arousal, do not experience the physiological symptoms of anxiety, and thus do not learn to associate those symptoms with antisocial behavior.

On the environmental (nurture) side, some psychologists believe that poor child-rearing practices and unstable family situations have rendered individuals with an antisocial personality disorder unable to learn fear, guilt, and punishment avoidance. Such people seem to have learned maladaptive functioning from their family situations and consequently to have developed inappropriate behaviors. If the environ-

Antisocial personality disorder: A personality disorder characterized by egocentricity, by behavior that is irresponsible and that violates the rights of other people—lying, theft, delinquency, and other violations of societal rules—and by a lack of guilt feelings, an inability to understand other people, and a lack of fear of punishment.

mental viewpoint is correct, antisocial personality disorder may be a learned behavior.

The symptoms of antisocial personality disorder often are seen first in a person's interactions with family members. Family relationships become strained, and some people suffering with the disorder may become involved in domestic violence—including child abuse, which we will examine next.

Child Abuse

Child abuse is not classified as a personality disorder, but many child abusers suffer from personality disorders. **Child abuse** is the physical, emotional, or sexual mistreatment of children. It has been implicated in children's development of antisocial personality disorder. In one year, of the families reported for abuse or neglect in New York City, 50 percent had at least one child who was later taken to court for conduct disorders or for being ungovernable (Alfaro, 1981). The impact on an abused child's self-esteem is profound (Trickett & Putnam, 1993), although victimized children can recover well with treatment (Kendall-Tackett, Williams, & Finkelhor, 1993).

Child abuse is clearly an important psychological and social problem. Between 350,000 and 2 million children in the United States are the victims of abuse each year (Helfer, 1987); 1,200 children die each year from child abuse and neglect. Research shows that, of all the reported cases of child abuse, 30 to 40 percent are substantiated by professionals such as social workers (Eckenrode et al., 1988). Moreover, not all cases are reported; even some treated cases go unreported by therapists, although the therapists are bound by law to report them (Kalichman & Craig, 1991).

The Child Abuser. Who are the child abusers? Only about 5 percent of child abusers exhibit symptoms of very disturbed behavior. Most abusive parents seem quite normal by traditional social standards and sometimes have a prominent place in the community.

A distinction must be made between those who physically abuse children and those who sexually abuse them. Physically abusive parents often have unusually high expectations for their children and distorted perceptions of the children's behavior. They are generally less satisfied with their children than are nonabusive parents, and they perceive child rearing as more difficult than do nonabusive parents (Trickett & Susman, 1988). Abusive parents are not necessarily more discipline-oriented, power-oriented, or authoritarian with their children, but they tend to rely on ineffective child management techniques, including aversive control, blaming, scapegoating, threats, verbal degradations, and physical punishment (Emery, 1989a, b). Parents who were abused as children are far more likely than others to be abusers themselves, especially if they do not have a stable, emotionally satisfying, supportive relationship with a mate (Egeland, Jacobvitz, & Sroufe, 1988).

Prevention. Most psychologists and social workers consider child abuse an interactive process involving parental incompetence, environmental stress, and poor child management techniques. Therefore, both psychologists and social workers focus on changing family systems and patterns of interaction (Emery, 1989a, b). Parents can be taught different coping skills, impulse control, effective child management techniques, and constructive ways to interact with their children. When these techniques are applied in an early intervention program for parents at risk of child abuse, they produce encouraging results. Children of potentially abusive parents who have undergone such therapy have fewer and less intense behavior problems

Child abuse: Physical, emotional, or sexual mistreatment of children.

(Wolfe et al., 1988). Yet evaluations of such programs are equivocal. Reppucci and Haugaard (1989), for example, conclude, "We cannot be sure whether prevention programs are working, nor can we be sure that they are doing more good than harm" (p. 1274). These researchers argue that extensive investigation of the full range of preventive efforts is urgent. It is impossible not to concur.

The Applications box on page 516 explains another behavior that, while it is not a *DSM-IV* classification, is an urgent problem for individuals and society—rape.

Sexual Disorders

Few behaviors arouse more anxiety, fear, and superstition than those involving human sexuality. However, many sexual problems (for example, orgasmic dysfunction) are often temporary symptoms of some other type of problem that is not sexual in nature (for example, anxiety or poor communication between partners). We considered some of the sexual dysfunctions in chapter 10 when we examined sexual motivation (p. 359). Sexual *disorders* range from disorders of desire, arousal, and orgasm to disorders that focus on pain to disorders induced by substance abuse. We will focus on sexual *deviations* in the next few paragraphs.

Sexual deviations, or *paraphilias* are sexual practices directed toward objects rather than people, sexual encounters involving real or simulated suffering or humiliation, or sexual activities with nonconsenting partners. The *DSM* classifies only a few true sexual deviations; some researchers, however, maintain that there are many more (Money, 1984). A diagnosis of sexual deviation is made when the causes are psychological rather than physical and when these behaviors are the primary source of sexual stimulation or gratification for the individual.

Following are some unconventional sexual activities that characterize sexual disorders. A person who has such urges, acts on those urges, or is markedly distressed by these urges can be characterized as having the disorder. *Fetishism,* which is more common in men than in women, involves sexual arousal and gratification brought about by nonliving objects rather than by people. For example, a man may have a fetish about a woman's shoes and may receive sexual gratification from them instead of from her.

In *transvestic fetishism,* also known as transvestism or *cross-dressing,* a man receives gratification (often but not always sexual) by dressing in the clothing of a woman. (The number of women diagnosed with this disorder is very small.) Interference with cross-dressing produces frustration. Transvestites consider themselves members of their own sex, and most are heterosexual.

A person who achieves sexual satisfaction by watching other people in different states of undress or sexual activity is practicing *voyeurism.* Most voyeurs, or "peeping Toms," are men. Some researchers suggest that because voyeurs generally do not want to be seen, they are excited by the risk of discovery involved in watching other people.

Another unconventional sexual activity is *exhibitionism,* in which adult men expose their genitals to unsuspecting observers, who are almost always female. Exhibitionists find the startled reactions of their victims sexually arousing.

Some people derive sexual satisfaction through sexual contact with children, a disorder known as *pedophilia.* Most pedophiles are well acquainted with the child; sometimes they are even close relatives. Many are married and seemingly well adjusted, both sexually and socially. Pedophiles may suffer from loneliness or schizophrenia. Fifty percent were themselves sexually abused as children (Ames & Houston, 1990).

Two other types of deviations are *sexual sadism* and *sexual masochism.* A sadist achieves sexual gratification by inflicting pain on a sexual partner. A masochist

Sexual deviations: Sexual practices directed toward objects rather than people, sexual encounters involving real or simulated suffering or humiliation, or sexual activities with a nonconsenting partner. Also known as *paraphilias.*

Rape

Rape is not a *DSM-IV* classification; it is a crime that often is committed by an individual with an antisocial personality disorder. **Rape** is the forcible sexual assault of an unwilling partner, usually a woman. Today, the definition of *rape* is growing broader, to include any forcible sexual assault without freely given permission.

Most rapes are planned, often in a meticulous manner; they are generally not impulsive acts prompted by a spur-of-the-moment sexual or aggressive feeling. Rape should be considered a violent crime rather than a sexual crime. Labeling rape a sexual assault obscures the violent, brutal nature of the crime and often places the woman on the defensive in the courtroom, even though she was the victim. Research shows that people often blame the victim, particularly if she knew the rapist (Kanekar et al., 1991).

More than 90,000 rapes are reported each year, according to the FBI; however, many experts assert that this is only one-fourth of the actual number. For example, one research study found that 27 percent of college women had experienced situations in which rape was attempted, and 7.5 percent of college men reported initiating acts that meet the definition of rape (Koss, Gidycz, & Wisniewski, 1987). Although these results are not generalizable to the entire population, rape and attempted rape seem to be far more common than was previously believed; and many rape victims know their assailants. Today, on college campuses, rape or attempted rape by an acquaintance—sometimes known as *date rape*—is receiving increased attention by law enforcement officials.

The Rapist. Because rape is such a violent crime, it has come under the critical eye of researchers seeking to understand the characteristics and motivations of the rapist. Several facts about rapists are coming into focus. They tend to be young, often between 15 and 25 (Sadock, 1980). Many are poor, culturally disadvantaged, and uneducated. Many have willing sex-

achieves sexual gratification from experiencing pain inflicted by someone else. Sadists and masochists are often sexual partners; the sadist provides the pain for the masochist, and both achieve sexual satisfaction. The pain involved can be physical or emotional.

Most psychologists agree that sexual disorders are learned behaviors. According to Freudians, problems during the Oedipal period create sexual problems later in life. Most behavioral practitioners agree in part with Freud, saying that sexual deviants are people whose normal gender role stereotyping went haywire early in their lives. They argue that a difficult adolescence and a poor emerging self-concept are learning factors that may predispose someone to sexual disorders. Individuals who had a difficult time with their parents and peers, for example, may display some of those problems through sexual disorders when they are adults. Often, anger, hostility, shame, and doubt are present in people who suffer from sexual disorders.

FOCUS

► Identify the distinguishing characteristics of a person diagnosed as having an antisocial personality disorder. p. 513

► Identify one preventative program that could be instituted to help decrease child abuse. p. 514

► What is implied by the term *date rape*? p. 516

Rape: Forcible sexual assault of an unwilling partner, usually a woman.

Unfortunately, the causes and treatment of sexual disorders have not been studied much. Thus, psychologists know less than they would like to know about biological and environmental contributions. Most practitioners focus on behavioral treatments and on teaching people new, more adaptive ways of expressing feelings, fears, and sexual urges. These techniques can be effective and do not require hospitalization or drug therapy, unlike treatment for some of the more debilitating disorders considered in the remainder of this chapter.

ual partners, and half are married, although their high level of aggressiveness probably precludes a happy and stable marriage or other relationship.

Rapists may have some history of sexual dysfunctions; however, this finding is not consistent across all studies. They often have committed another sex-related offense, although this finding also is not consistent across all studies (Furby, Weinrott, & Blackshaw, 1989). Rapists tend to be more responsive to violence than are other men (Quinsey, Chaplin, & Upfold, 1984) and less able to understand cues and messages from women who say no. Levels of maladjustment of rapists vary from slight to extreme when measured on psychological tests (Kalichman et al.,

1989). Men who assault and rape women often view their attacks not as rape but as "mere" assault (Bourque, 1989). Various classifications of

rapists have emerged—from rapists who rape on a whim, to angry rapists, to violent, sadistic, angry rapists. No firm classification system is yet in place.

Most research studies show that between 15 and 25 percent of male college students engage in some level of sexual aggression, usually toward women (Malamuth & Sockloskie, 1991). Most rapists think the likelihood of being punished is small, and this is considered one of the contributory factors in rape (L. Ellis, 1991). A comprehensive theory of rape is going to have to account for both its aggressive and its sexual nature (Barbaree & Marshall, 1991).

Mood Disorders

All of us experience depression at one time or another. Ending a long-term intimate relationship, feeling overwhelmed during final exams, mourning the death of a close friend, and experiencing serious financial problems are all sources of depression. When people become so depressed or sad that a change occurs in their outlook and overt behavior, they may be suffering from clinical depression. Depression is considered a type of mood disorder. Mood disorders, which include *bipolar disorder* and *major depressive disorder,* are often caused or at least initiated by a specific event, although for many individuals the symptoms occur gradually.

Bipolar Disorders

Gustav Mahler, a 19th-century Austrian composer-conductor, apparently suffered from a bipolar disorder. At age 19, he wrote to a friend:

> Much has happened within me since my last letter; I cannot describe it. Only this: I have become a different person. I don't know whether this new person is better; he certainly is not happier. The fires of a supreme zest for living and the most gnawing desire for death alternate in my heart, sometimes in the course of a single hour.

Bipolar disorders, which originally were known as *manic-depressive disorders,* get their name from the fact that patients' behavior vacillates between two extremes: mania and depression. The *manic phase* is characterized by rapid speech, inflated self-esteem, impulsiveness, and decreased need for sleep. Patients in the manic phase are easily distracted, get angry when things do not go their way, and seem to have

Bipolar disorders: Mood disorders characterized by vacillation between two extremes: mania and depression. Originally known as *manic-depressive disorders.*

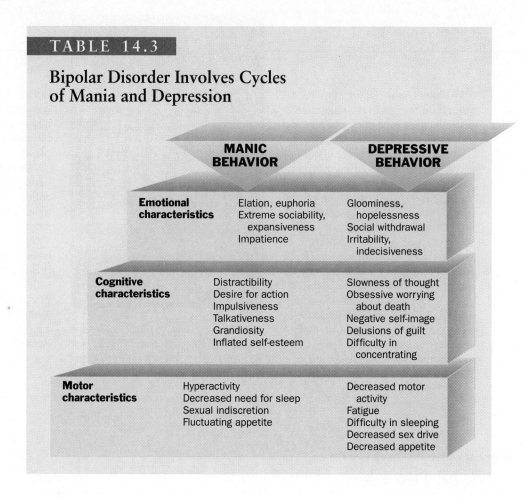

TABLE 14.3

Bipolar Disorder Involves Cycles of Mania and Depression

	MANIC BEHAVIOR	DEPRESSIVE BEHAVIOR
Emotional characteristics	Elation, euphoria Extreme sociability, expansiveness Impatience	Gloominess, hopelessness Social withdrawal Irritability, indecisiveness
Cognitive characteristics	Distractibility Desire for action Impulsiveness Talkativeness Grandiosity Inflated self-esteem	Slowness of thought Obsessive worrying about death Negative self-image Delusions of guilt Difficulty in concentrating
Motor characteristics	Hyperactivity Decreased need for sleep Sexual indiscretion Fluctuating appetite	Decreased motor activity Fatigue Difficulty in sleeping Decreased sex drive Decreased appetite

boundless energy. A person in the *depressed phase,* which often follows the manic phase, is moody and sad, with feelings of hopelessness.

Almost 2 million Americans suffer from bipolar disorders, which typically begin in late adolescence and continue throughout life. Patients can be relatively normal for a few days, weeks, or months between episodes of excitement and depression, or they can rapidly vacillate between excitement and depression. The key component of bipolar disorders is the shift from excited states to depressive states of sadness and hopelessness. Although Mahler's bipolar disorder started much earlier, people who suffer from bipolar disorders are often in their late 20s before they begin to overtly manifest the symptoms. The disorder seems to have a biological basis (Leber, Beckham, & Danker-Brown, 1985), and patients respond fairly well to drug treatment, especially to Lithium (which will be discussed in the next chapter). Table 14.3 lists the signs and symptoms of mania and depression in bipolar disorders.

Major Depressive Disorder

Bonnie Strickland, former president of the American Psychological Association, said during the 1988 APA meetings, "Depression has been called the common cold of psychological disturbances, . . . which underscores its prevalence, but trivializes its impact." Strickland noted that, at any one time, about 14 million people are suffering from this disabling disorder.

Depressive disorders are a general category of mood disorders in which people show extreme and persistent sadness, despair, and loss of interest in life's usual activ-

Depressive disorders: A general category of mood disorders in which people show extreme and persistent sadness, despair, and loss of interest in life's usual activities.

ities on a day-to-day basis. The main difference between depressive disorders and bipolar disorders is that people with depressive disorders show no vacillation between excitement and depression; they tend to be depressed constantly. One type of depressive disorder is major depressive disorder; it is eight times more common than bipolar disorders.

Major depressive disorder is characterized by loss of interest in almost all of life's usual activities, as evidenced by a sad, hopeless, or discouraged mood; sleep disturbance; loss of appetite; loss of energy; and feelings of unworthiness and guilt. Someone experiencing it is not merely experiencing fleeting anxiety with sadness but is displaying a relatively extreme reaction to a specific event, such as the loss of a loved one, a job, or a home or some failure in life. Sufferers show at least some impairment of social and occupational functioning, although their behavior is not necessarily bizarre.

Symptoms. The symptoms of major depressive disorder include poor appetite, insomnia, weight loss, loss of energy, feelings of worthlessness and intense guilt, inability to concentrate, and sometimes thoughts of death and suicide (Benca et al., 1992; Buchwald & Rudick-Davis, 1993; Irwin, Smith, & Gillin, 1992). Depressed patients have a gloomy outlook on life, an extremely distorted view of current problems, and a tendency to blame themselves. They often withdraw from social and physical contact with others. Every task seems to require a great effort, thought is slow and unfocused, and problem-solving abilities are impaired (Danion et al., 1991; Hartlage et al., 1993; Marx, Williams, & Claridge, 1992).

Depressed people may also have **delusions**—false beliefs that are inconsistent with reality and held in spite of contradictory evidence that often induce feelings of guilt, shame, and persecution. Seriously disturbed patients show even greater disruptions in thought and motor processes and a total lack of spontaneity and motivation. Such patients typically report that they have no hope for themselves or the world; nothing seems to interest them. Some feel responsible for serious world problems such as economic depression, disease, or hunger. They report strange diseases and may insist that their body is disintegrating or that their brain is being eaten from the inside out. Most people who exhibit symptoms of major depression can describe their reasons for feeling sad and dejected; however, they may be unable to explain why their response is so deep and so prolonged.

Psychologists say that people suffering from major depression are poor at reality testing. *Reality testing* is a person's ability to accurately judge the demands of the environment and to deal with those demands. People with poor reality testing are unable to cope with the demands of life in rational ways because their reasoning ability is grossly impaired.

Onset and Duration. A major depressive episode can occur at any age, although it usually first occurs before age 40. Symptoms are rapidly apparent and last for a few days, weeks, or months. Because so many different circumstances can bring about a depressive reaction, the extent of depression varies dramatically from individual to individual. Episodes may occur once or many times. Sometimes, depressive episodes are separated by years of normal functioning followed by two or three brief incidents of depression a few weeks apart. Stressful life events are sometimes predictors of depression (Monroe, Simons, & Thase, 1991). Major depressive disorder is not exclusively an adult disorder; many researchers find evidence of it in children and young adolescents (Larson et al., 1990). When children show depression, they often have other symptoms, especially anxiety and loneliness. Treatment plans must be flexible and account for the wide array of family situations in which children find themselves—divorce or foster homes or an environment of alcoholism or child abuse, for example.

Major depressive disorder: A depressive disorder characterized by loss of interest in almost all of life's usual activities, as evidenced by a sad, hopeless, or discouraged mood on a day-to-day basis; sleep disturbance; loss of appetite; loss of energy; and feelings of unworthiness and guilt.

Delusions: False beliefs, inconsistent with reality, held in spite of evidence to the contrary.

A recent study of 43,000 people in 9 different countries shows that depression is increasing across all cultures—the result of changing social, economic, and demographic factors. (Photo courtesy of CNN.)

Prevalence. According to the National Institutes of Mental Health, major depressive disorders strike about 14 to 15 million Americans each year. Women are twice as likely as men to be diagnosed as depressed and are more likely to express feelings of depression openly (Allgood-Merten, Lewinsohn, & Hops, 1990). In the United States, about 19 to 23 percent of women and 8 to 11 percent of men have experienced a major depressive episode at some time. About 6 percent of women and 3 percent of men have experienced episodes sufficiently severe to require hospitalization. It is unclear why women experience more depression than men; research on gender differences in both causes and treatment is limited (Strickland, 1992).

According to a number of studies, Americans born around 1960 suffer up to 10 times the incidence of major depression as did their grandparents or great-grandparents (Lewinsohn et al., 1993). This may be due to changes in diagnosis, in reporting frequency, or perhaps in the stressors in our society; the answer is not yet clear. In addition, people in developing cultures are far less likely to develop the passivity, feelings of hopelessness, diminished self-esteem, and suicidal tendencies that typify Westerners afflicted by major depressive disorder. Martin Seligman (1988) suggests that the increased incidence of depression in the United States stems from too much emphasis on the individual, coupled with a loss of faith in such supportive institutions as family, country, and religion.

Clinical Evaluation. How does a practitioner know if a person is suffering from major depressive disorder? A complete clinical evaluation comprises three parts: a physical examination, a psychiatric history, and a mental status examination. The *physical examination* is given to rule out thyroid disorders, viral infection, and anemia—all of which cause a slowing down of behavior. A neurological check of coordination, reflexes, and balance is part of this exam, to rule out brain disorders. The *psychiatric history* attempts to trace the course of the potential illness, genetic or family factors, and past treatments. Finally, the *mental status examination* scrutinizes thought, speaking processes, and memory; it may include interviews, tests for psychiatric symptoms (among them the MMPI–2), and projective tests such as the TAT (see chapter 12 for details).

Causes of Major Depressive Disorder

Most psychologists believe major depressive disorder is caused by a combination of biological, learning, and cognitive factors. Biological theories suggest that chemical and genetic processes can account for depression. Learning theories suggest that people develop faulty behaviors. Cognitive theories suggest that irrational ideas guide behavior. Learned helplessness theories suggest that people may choose not to respond and give up. We will examine each theory in more detail next.

Biological Theories. Are people born with a predisposition to depression? Depression may be genetically based, according to Tsuang and Faraone (1990). Weissman and colleagues (1987) found that children of depressed patients are more likely than other children to be depressed. Further, twin studies assert that genetic factors play a substantial role in depression (Kendler et al., 1992, 1993).

A different approach is the *norepinephrine hypothesis,* which states that an insufficient amount of norepinephrine (a neurotransmitter in the brain, which we examined in chapter 2) may cause depression. Research has shown that if the level of norepinephrine at the receptor site in the brain is increased, depression is alleviated. Because aversive stimuli decrease norepinephrine levels, however, being in a stressful situation could bring about depression.

Recent research suggests that, although the norepinephrine hypothesis is not false, the biological underpinnings of depression are more complex. That is, depression may be caused by many substances in the brain (in addition to norepinephrine) that are not functioning properly or because of genetics, or both (Faraone, Kremen, & Tsuang, 1990). New evidence even suggests a relationship between allergies and depression; this research suggests that allergic reactions in a small group of depressed patients may accentuate brain chemical imbalances (P. S. Marshall, 1993).

Other evidence for a biological explanation of depression is that antidepressant drugs seem to help certain types of depressed patients. In one study, every depressed patient was given one of three treatments: psychotherapy alone, an antidepressant drug alone, or a combination of psychotherapy and drug therapy. Psychotherapy and drug therapy proved equally effective in reducing depressive symptoms. However, the combination of psychotherapy and drug therapy helped the most (DiMascio et al., 1979).

Learning and Cognitive Theories.   Learning and cognitive theorists argue that people learn depressive behaviors and thoughts. People with poor social skills who never learn to express prosocial behaviors and who are punished for the behaviors they do exhibit experience the world as aversive and depressing. In support of this idea is the finding that children of depressed patients, having been exposed to depressive behaviors so much, are more likely then other children to be depressed (Downey & Coyne, 1990). In addition, Peter Lewinsohn (1974) believes that people who have few positive reinforcements in their lives (often the old, the sickly, and the poor) become depressed. Other people find them unpleasant and avoid them, thus creating a nonreinforcing environment (Lewinsohn & Talkington, 1979). Lewinsohn stresses that depressed people often lack the social skills needed to obtain reinforcement, such as asking a neighbor or friend for help with a problem. See Figure 14.1 for details of Lewinsohn's view.

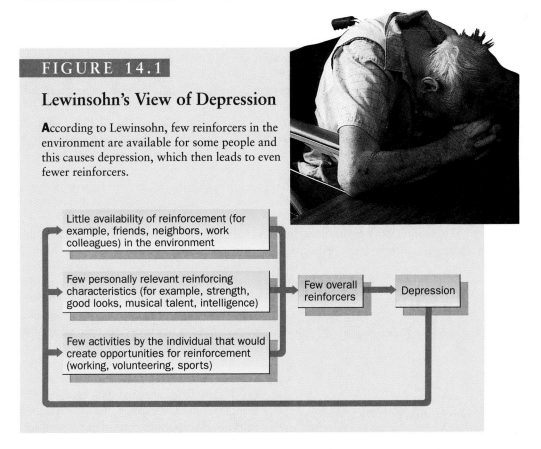

FIGURE 14.1

Lewinsohn's View of Depression

According to Lewinsohn, few reinforcers in the environment are available for some people and this causes depression, which then leads to even fewer reinforcers.

Little availability of reinforcement (for example, friends, neighbors, work colleagues) in the environment

Few personally relevant reinforcing characteristics (for example, strength, good looks, musical talent, intelligence)

Few activities by the individual that would create opportunities for reinforcement (working, volunteering, sports)

Few overall reinforcers → Depression

Learned helplessness: The behavior of giving up or not responding, exhibited by people or animals exposed to negative consequences or punishment over which they have no control.

Psychiatrist Aaron Beck proposed another influential learning theory. Beck (1967) suggested that depressed people already have negative views of themselves, the environment, and the future; and these views cause them to magnify their errors. They compare themselves to other people, usually unfairly; and when they come up short, they see the difference as disastrous. They see the human condition as universally wretched, become angry (Riley, Treiber, & Woods, 1989), and view the world as a place that defeats positive behavior. Their poor self-concept along with negative expectations about the world produce negative future expectations that lead to depression. All of this is magnified in adolescents, who are going through many bodily changes, and may heighten their risk of depression (Allgood-Merton, Lewinsohn, & Hops, 1990).

Beck (1967, 1972, 1976) theorized that depression does not cause negative feelings but that negative feelings and expectation cause depression. Research supports Beck's theory. Depressed people are harsher on themselves than nondepressed people are, and they have particularly low levels of self-expectations and self-esteem (Drennen, 1991). They make judgments based on insufficient data, they overgeneralize, and they exaggerate the negative outcomes in their lives. According to Beck, being depressed causes poor judgments and thus affects people's cognitions. Research support for this claim, however, is not strong (Haaga, Dyck, & Ernst, 1991).

Beck's theory is influential among psychologists for two reasons. First, it is consistent with the notion that depression stems from a lack of appropriate positive reinforcements in people's environments. Second, it acknowledges both cognitive and environmental variables such as family interactions.

Learned Helplessness. What would you do if you failed every exam you took, regardless of your efforts? What happens when a person's hopes and dreams are constantly thwarted, regardless of the person's behavior? The result may be **learned helplessness** (which we will consider in more detail in chapter 16)—the behavior of giving up or not responding, exhibited by people or animals who have learned that rewards and punishments are not contingent on behavior.

Seligman (1976) has suggested that people's beliefs about the causes of their failures determine whether they will become depressed. When they attribute their failures to unalterable conditions within themselves ("my own weakness, which is unlikely to change"), they acquire low self-esteem (Raps et al., 1982). That is, when people come to believe that eventual outcomes are unrelated to anything under their control, they develop learned helplessness. For example, a man who comes to believe that his effort to meet new people by being outgoing and friendly never works may stop trying. Eventually, he will choose not to respond to the environment because he has learned that his behavior makes no difference (Peterson & Seligman, 1984).

Seligman (1988) argues that the environment, not genetics, is the cause of depression and helplessness, especially when people believe they are responsible for long-standing failures in many areas of their lives. This idea is fully developed in a model presented by Abramson, Metalsky, and Alloy (1989), who assert that when learned helplessness is operative, people adopt the view that they cannot change highly aversive life events.

The idea that learned helplessness is a key factor in depression has received research support, although the way learned helplessness operates is not yet fully understood (DeVellis & Blalock, 1992; Metalsky

FOCUS

▶ Identify the key characteristics of a bipolar disorder. p. 517

▶ What are the essential characteristics of major depressive disorder? pp. 518–519

▶ Describe how learned helplessness can lead to depression. p. 522

& Joiner, 1992). The effects of helplessness and depression are poignant and painful. They influence the day-to-day life of the individual, the person's work environment, and the person's family—especially parenting (Downey & Coyne, 1990). The inability to function on a day-to-day basis becomes especially apparent in the study of an even more disabling disorder, schizophrenia, which we'll examine next.

Schizophrenia

Schizophrenia is considered the most devastating, complex, and frustrating of all mental disorders; people with this disorder lose touch with reality and are often unable to function in a world that makes no sense to them. A person with schizophrenia is said to have a schizophrenic disorder, because schizophrenia really represents a range of disorders. **Schizophrenia** is a group of disorders characterized by a lack of reality testing and by deterioration of social and intellectual functioning, beginning before age 45 and lasting at least 6 months. People diagnosed as having a schizophrenic disorder often show serious personality disintegration with significant changes in thought, mood, perception, and behavior. They may be considered **psychotic**—suffering from a gross impairment in reality testing that is wide ranging and interferes with their ability to meet the ordinary demands of life.

Schizophrenia begins slowly, with more symptoms developing as time passes. It affects 1 of every 100 people in the United States and accounts for almost 25 percent of all mental hospital admissions each year (Sartorius, 1982). The diagnosis occurs more frequently among lower socioeconomic groups (Dohrenwend et al., 1992) and nonwhites and more frequently among younger people (Lindsey & Paul, 1989). As Figure 14.2 shows, African Americans are more likely than whites to be diagnosed as schizophrenic.

Schizophrenia: [SKIT-soh-FREN-ia] A group of disorders characterized by a lack of reality testing and by deterioration of social and intellectual functioning and beginning before age 45 and lasting at least 6 months. Schizophrenics often show serious personality disintegration with significant changes in thought, mood, perception, and behavior.

Psychotic: [sie-KOT-ick] Suffering from a gross impairment in reality testing that interferes with the ability to meet the ordinary demands of life.

FIGURE 14.2

Cultural Factors in the Diagnosis of Schizophrenia and Mood Disorders

African Americans are more likely than whites to be diagnosed as schizophrenic. By contrast, whites and Hispanic Americans are more likely than African Americans to suffer from mood disorders. (Source: Based on data from Snowden & Cheung, 1990.)

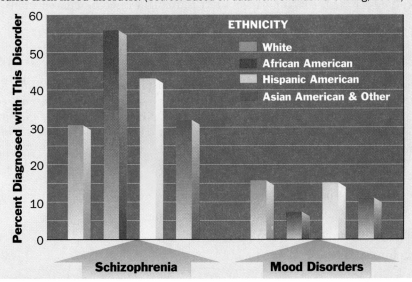

Hallucinations: [ha-LOOSE-in-AY-shuns] Compelling perceptual (visual, tactile, olfactory, or auditory) experiences without a real physical stimulus.

Affect: A person's emotional responses.

Essential Characteristics of Schizophrenia

People with schizophrenia display sudden changes in thought, perception, emotion, and overall behavior. Those changes are often accompanied by distortions of reality and an inability to respond appropriately in thought, perception, or emotion.

Thought Disorders. One of the first signs of schizophrenia is difficulty maintaining logical thought and coherent conversation. People with schizophrenia show disordered thinking and impaired memory (Sengel & Lovallo, 1983). They may also suffer from *delusions.* Many have delusions of persecution and believe that the world is a hostile place. These delusions are often accompanied by delusions of grandeur, in which the patient erroneously believes that he or she is a particularly important person. This importance becomes the reason for the persecution. Sometimes the patients take on the role of an important character in history—for example, General Norman Schwarzkopf, Jesus Christ, or the Queen of England—and delude themselves that people are conspiring to harm them.

Perceptual Disorders. Another sign of schizophrenia is the presence of **hallucinations**—compelling perceptual (visual, tactile, olfactory, or auditory) experiences without a real physical stimulus. Auditory hallucinations are the most common. The patient reports hearing voices originating outside his or her head. The voices may comment on the patient's behavior or direct the patient to behave in certain ways (Bentall, 1990). For example, convicted murderer David Berkowitz (known to the media as Son of Sam) claimed that his neighbor's dog told him to kill. Hallucinations have a biological basis and are caused by abnormal brain responses (Asaad & Shapiro, 1986).

Emotional Disorders. One of the most striking characteristics of schizophrenia is the display of inappropriate **affect**—emotional responses. A patient with schizophrenia may become depressed and cry when her favorite food falls on the floor, yet laugh hysterically at the death of a close friend or relative. Some patients display no emotion (either appropriate or inappropriate) and seem incapable of experiencing a normal range of feeling. Their emotional range is constricted, or *flat.* They show blank, expressionless faces, even when presented with a deliberately provocative remark or situation. Other patients exhibit *ambivalent* affect. They go through a wide range of emotional behaviors in a brief period, seeming happy one moment and dejected the next. An ambivalent affect is usually caused by internal conflicts.

Types of Schizophrenia

The term *schizophrenia* is a catchall for patients displaying many symptoms; however, there are actually five types of schizophrenia—disorganized, paranoid, catatonic, residual, and undifferentiated—each with different symptoms, diagnostic criteria, and causes (see Table 14.4). A diagnosis of schizophrenia, regardless of the type, requires the presence of the following features:

▶ Lack of reality testing;

▶ Involvement of more than one area of psychological functioning;

▶ Deterioration in social and intellectual functioning;

▶ Onset of illness generally before age 45;

▶ Duration of illness at least 6 months.

Disorganized Type. The **disorganized type** of schizophrenia is characterized by severely disturbed thought processes, frequent incoherence, delusions, and inappropriate affect. Patients may exhibit bizarre emotions, with periods of giggling, crying, or irritability for no apparent reason. Their behavior can be silly, inappropriate, or even obscene. They show a severe disintegration of normal personality, a loss of reality testing, and often poor personal hygiene. Their chances for recovery are poor.

Paranoid Type. The paranoid type of schizophrenia is one of the most difficult to identify and study because outward behavior often seems appropriate to the situation. **Paranoid type** of schizophrenia is characterized by hallucinations and delusions of persecution or grandeur (or both), and sometimes irrational jealousy. Paranoid schizophrenics may actively seek out other people and not show extreme withdrawal from social interaction. Their degree of disturbance varies over time. (The paranoid type of schizophrenia is different from the paranoid personality disorder, which is discussed on p. 512 and which has less likelihood of being biologically caused.)

Paranoid schizophrenics may be alert, intelligent, and responsive. However, their delusions and hallucinations impair their ability to deal with reality and their behavior is often unpredictable and sometimes hostile. They may see bizarre images and are likely to have auditory hallucinations. They may think they are being chased by ghosts or by intruders from another planet. They have extreme delusions of persecution and, occasionally, of grandeur. They may believe certain events in the world have a particular significance to them. If, for example, the President of the United States makes a speech deploring crime, a paranoid schizophrenic patient may believe that the President is referring specifically to the patient's crimes. Patients with the paranoid type of schizophrenia have a better chance of recovery than do patients with other types of schizophrenia.

Disorganized type: A major type of schizophrenia, characterized by frequent incoherence, absence of systematized delusions, and blunted, inappropriate, or silly affect.

Paranoid type: [PAIR-uh-noid] A major type of schizophrenia, characterized by delusions and hallucinations of persecution or grandeur (or both), and sometimes irrational jealousy.

TABLE 14.4

Types and Symptoms of Schizophrenia

TYPE	SYMPTOMS
Disorganized	Frequent incoherence, absence of systematized delusions, and blunted, inappropriate, or silly affect
Paranoid	Delusions and hallucinations of persecution or grandeur (or both) and sometimes irrational jealousy
Catatonic	Stupor in which there is a negative attitude and marked decrease in reactivity to the environment or an excited phase in which there is agitated motor activity not influenced by external stimuli and which may appear or disappear suddenly
Residual	History of at least one previous episode of schizophrenia with prominent psychotic symptoms but at present a clinical picture without any prominent psychotic symptoms and continuing evidence of the illness, such as inappropriate affect, illogical thinking, social withdrawal, or eccentric behavior
Undifferentiated	Prominent delusions, hallucinations, incoherence, or grossly disorganized behavior, without meeting the criteria for any of the other types or meeting the criteria for more than one type

Catatonic type: [CAT-uh-TONN-ick] A major type of schizophrenia, characterized by displays of excited or violent motor activity or by stupor (in which the individual is mute, negative, and basically unresponsive).

Residual type: A schizophrenic disorder characterized by inappropriate affect, illogical thinking, or eccentric behavior but with the patient generally in touch with reality.

Undifferentiated type: A schizophrenic disorder characterized by a mixture of symptoms and which does not allow for clear diagnoses to meet criteria of other diagnostic categories.

Catatonic Type. **Catatonic type** of schizophrenia is characterized by displays of excited or violent motor activity or by stupor in which the individual is mute, negative, and basically unresponsive. There are actually two subtypes of the catatonic type of schizophrenia—excited and withdrawn—both of which involve extreme overt behavior. *Excited* catatonic patients show excessive activity. They may talk and shout continuously and engage in seemingly uninhibited, agitated, and aggressive motor activity. These episodes usually appear and disappear suddenly. *Withdrawn* catatonic patients tend to appear stuporous—mute, negative, and basically unresponsive. Although they occasionally exhibit some signs of the excited type, they usually show a high degree of muscular rigidity. They are not immobile but have a decreased level of speaking, moving, and responding, although they are usually aware of events around them. Withdrawn catatonic patients may use immobility and unresponsiveness to maintain control over their environment; their behavior relieves them of the responsibility of responding to external stimuli.

Residual and Undifferentiated Type. People who show symptoms attributable to schizophrenia but who remain in touch with reality are said to have the **residual type** of schizophrenia. Such patients show inappropriate affect, illogical thinking, or eccentric behavior. They have a history of at least one previous schizophrenic episode.

Sometimes, it is difficult to determine which category a patient most appropriately fits into (Gift et al., 1980). Some patients exhibit all the essential features of schizophrenia—prominent delusions, hallucinations, incoherence, and grossly disorganized behavior—but do not fit neatly into the categories of disorganized, catatonic, paranoid, or residual. Individuals with these characteristics are said to have the **undifferentiated type** of schizophrenia.

Causes of Schizophrenia

What causes people to lose their grasp on reality with such devastating results? Are people born with schizophrenia, or do they develop it as a result of painful childhood experiences? Researchers of schizophrenia take markedly different positions about its origins. Biologically oriented psychologists focus on chemicals in the brain and a person's genetic heritage; their basic argument is that schizophrenia is a brain disease (Heinrichs, 1993; D. L. Johnson, 1989). Learning theorists argue that a person's environment and early experiences cause schizophrenia. The arguments for each approach are compelling, and there are data to support them.

Biological Causes. Evidence exists to suggest the presence of some kind of biological determinant of, or predisposition to, schizophrenia. People born with that predisposition have a greater probability of developing schizophrenia than do other people. It is now generally accepted that schizophrenia runs in families (Gottesman, 1991); the children and siblings of schizophrenic patients are more likely to exhibit maladjustment and schizophrenic symptoms than are other people (Walker & Emory, 1983). Researchers have been looking for a gene that might carry specific traits associated with schizophrenia, although such efforts have had only limited success (Markow, 1992).

About 1 percent of the U.S. population is schizophrenic; however, when one parent has schizophrenia, the probability that an offspring also will develop it increases to between 3 and 14 percent. If both parents have schizophrenia, their children have about a 35 percent probability of developing it (D. Rosenthal, 1970). (Figure 14.3 shows the likelihood of the relatives of schizophrenics developing the disorder.)

Researchers are aware that the family environment of children of schizophrenics is typically unusual, and they acknowledge that the genetic evidence is only suggestive and that environment is likely to play a role in the development of the disorder. If schizophrenia were totally genetic, then the likelihood that identical (monozygotic) twins, who have identical genes, would show the disorder would be 100 percent. (This likelihood of shared traits is referred to as the **concordance rate**.) Studies of schizophrenia in identical twins show concordance rates from 0 to 86 percent (Dalby, Morgan, & Lee, 1986; Gottesman & Shields, 1982), suggesting that other factors are involved. In one important study, analysis of brain structures showed subtle but important brain abnormalities in a schizophrenic individual whose identical twin did not show the abnormality. Such studies assert that nongenetic factors must exert an important influence on schizophrenia and also be critical in its development (Gottesman, 1991; Suddath et al., 1990).

Nevertheless, most researchers agree that genetics is a fundamental cause of the disorder. The concordance rate for schizophrenia in identical twins is almost five times that in fraternal twins. Moreover, identical twins reared apart from their natural parents and from each other show a higher concordance rate than do fraternal twins or control subjects (Stone, 1980).

Other support for a biological basis for schizophrenia comes from researchers who discovered that chemicals in the bloodstream may contribute to the development of schizophrenia. Several studies note the importance of the neurotransmitter *dopamine* in schizophrenia. Dopamine pathways are considered one of the main sites of biochemical disturbance in the brain (M. B. Bowers, Jr., 1982). A class of drugs, the *phenothiazines*, appears to block receptor sites in the dopamine pathways. When patients with schizophrenia are given phenothiazines, many of their disturbed thought processes and hallucinations disappear. Conversely, drugs that stimulate the dopamine system (such as amphetamines) aggravate existing schizophrenic disorders. See Figure 14.4 on page 528 for an overview of the dopamine hypothesis.

Certain portions of the brains of schizophrenic patients exhibit abnormalities, although it is not yet clear whether schizophrenia causes the abnormalities or the abnormalities cause schizophrenia. For example, the *brain ventricles* (hollow areas normally filled with fluid) are enlarged in some schizophrenic patients (Raz & Raz, 1990; Suddath et al., 1990). Furthermore, some structures, notably the frontal lobes, show reduced blood flow and functioning (Buchsbaum, 1990; Resnick, 1992).

In sum, researchers now assert that biological and genetic factors predict a specific risk for schizophrenia. While many stress factors (which are the focus of environmental researchers) may contribute to schizophrenia or other disorders, a strong genetic component seems to be essential.

Environmental Factors. Some psychologists believe that in addition to genetics, environmental interactions determine the development of schizophrenia. Freudian psychologists, for example, suggest that early childhood relationships determine whether a person will become fixated at the oral stage and develop a disorder such as schizophrenia. Such a person has not developed an ego and will make

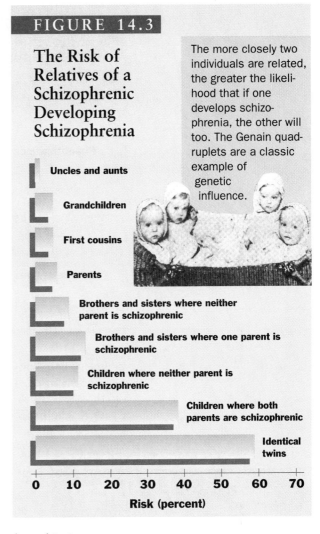

FIGURE 14.3

The Risk of Relatives of a Schizophrenic Developing Schizophrenia

The more closely two individuals are related, the greater the likelihood that if one develops schizophrenia, the other will too. The Genain quadruplets are a classic example of genetic influence.

- Uncles and aunts
- Grandchildren
- First cousins
- Parents
- Brothers and sisters where neither parent is schizophrenic
- Brothers and sisters where one parent is schizophrenic
- Children where neither parent is schizophrenic
- Children where both parents are schizophrenic
- Identical twins

0   10   20   30   40   50   60   70
Risk (percent)

Concordance rate: The percentage of occasions when two groups or individuals show the same trait.

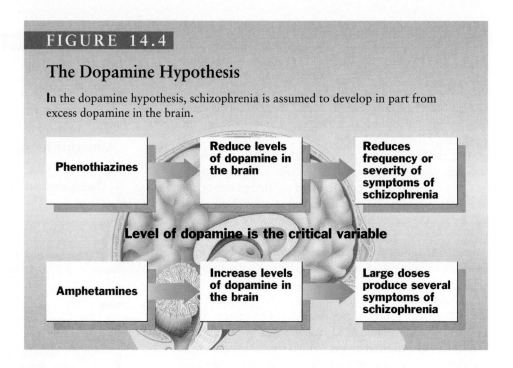

FIGURE 14.4

The Dopamine Hypothesis

In the dopamine hypothesis, schizophrenia is assumed to develop in part from excess dopamine in the brain.

| Phenothiazines | → | Reduce levels of dopamine in the brain | → | Reduces frequency or severity of symptoms of schizophrenia |

Level of dopamine is the critical variable

| Amphetamines | → | Increase levels of dopamine in the brain | → | Large doses produce several symptoms of schizophrenia |

judgments based on the id's pleasure principle. Lacking the ego, which uses the reality principle in making judgments, the individual will seek immediate gratification and thus be unable to deal effectively with reality. Freudian psychologists assert that a person who has successfully passed through the oral stage and has developed a strong ego is unlikely to suffer from schizophrenia; however, there is a lack of rigorous scientific evidence to support this assertion.

Behavioral explanations of schizophrenia are based on traditional learning principles (explored in chapter 5). The behavioral approach argues that faulty reinforcement and extinction procedures, as well as social learning processes, can account for schizophrenia. Imagine a child brought up in a family where the parents constantly argue, where the father is an alcoholic, and where neither parent shows much affection for the other or for anyone else. Such a child, receiving no reinforcement for interest in events, people, and objects in the outside world, may become withdrawn and begin to exhibit schizophrenic behavior. Lidz (1973) argues that children who grow up in such homes adopt the family's faulty view of the world and of relationships and thus are likely to expect reinforcement for abnormal behaviors. Growing up in such an emotionally fragmented environment may predispose individuals to emotional disorder and eventual schizophrenia (Walker et al., 1983). In addition, if the parents themselves are schizophrenic and they mistreat the child, this increases the likelihood of problems such as schizophrenia in the child's future (Walker, Downey, & Bergman, 1989).

Even in families in which marital conflict is absent, parents sometimes confuse their children. Some parents, for example, place their children in a situation that offers two different and inconsistent messages, a **double bind.** Initially proposed by Bateson (Bateson et al., 1956), double bind situations usually occur between individuals with a strong emotional attachment, such as that of a child and parents (Mishler & Waxler, 1968). In play, parents may hold up a toy and say, "No, you may not have this," while smiling and giving other nonverbal assurances that the child may have the toy. Generally, the child understands that the parent is teasing. However, not all children understand this and not all situations are so clearly cued.

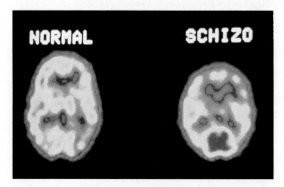

This PET scan shows decreased neural activity in the brain of a person diagnosed with schizophrenia as compared to that of a normal person.

Double bind: A situation in which an individual is given two different and inconsistent messages.

Games of this kind, if played consistently, may shape an environment of confusion conducive to the development of schizophrenia.

Learning theory suggests that schizophrenics are likely to develop and maintain the disorder because of faulty reinforcement patterns. A person who receives a great deal of attention for behaviors that other people see as bizarre is likely to continue those behaviors. People who fail to develop effective social skills are more at risk (Mueser et al., 1990). Other reinforcement theories suggest that bizarre behavior and thoughts are themselves reinforcing because they allow the person to escape from both acute anxiety and an overactive autonomic nervous system.

FOCUS

▶ Identify the essential characteristics of the five major types of schizophrenia. p. 525

▶ How are concordance rates used to discern the causes of schizophrenia? p. 527

▶ Why would researchers place special emphasis on longitudinal research rather than cross-sectional research in the study of schizophrenia (see p. 278 for a review of longitudinal versus cross-sectional research)? p. 530

Nature or Nurture? Many variables determine whether an individual will develop schizophrenia. Some people, because of family environment, genetic history, or brain chemistry, are more vulnerable than others (see Figure 14.5). **Vulnerability** is a person's diminished ability to deal with demanding life events. The more vulnerable the individual is, the less necessary are environmental stress or other disorders (such as anxiety) to the initiation of a schizophrenic episode. The Research Process box on page 530 examines the vulnerability-stress hypothesis.

To summarize, although the exact causes of schizophrenia are still unknown, research suggests the following:

▶ A connection exists between genetics and schizophrenia, although genetics alone cannot account for its development.

▶ Specific types of chemical substances in the brain are associated with schizophrenia.

▶ Environmental factors (such as the presence of marital conflict and double binds) contribute to the development of schizophrenia. Among these factors, early childhood relationships may be especially important.

▶ The most likely cause of schizophrenia is a biological predisposition in the individual, which is aggravated by a climate of emotional immaturity, lack of communication, and emotional instability.

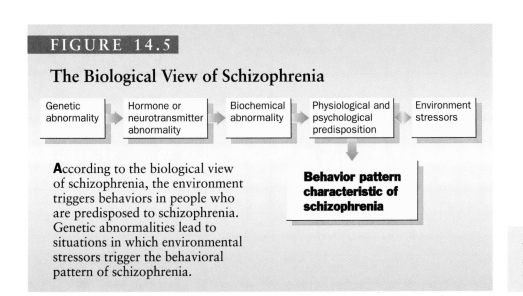

FIGURE 14.5

The Biological View of Schizophrenia

Genetic abnormality → Hormone or neurotransmitter abnormality → Biochemical abnormality → Physiological and psychological predisposition → Environment stressors

↓

Behavior pattern characteristic of schizophrenia

According to the biological view of schizophrenia, the environment triggers behaviors in people who are predisposed to schizophrenia. Genetic abnormalities lead to situations in which environmental stressors trigger the behavioral pattern of schizophrenia.

Vulnerability: A person's diminished ability to deal with demanding life events.

THE RESEARCH PROCESS

High-Risk Children and Schizophrenia

Can schizophrenia be prevented? Do some people have a vulnerability to schizophrenia that is triggered by stressful situations? According to the vulnerability-stress hypothesis, a person's susceptibility to schizophrenia depends on genetic factors, birth factors, and stress during infancy, childhood, and adolescence. This approach assumes that when stressors appear, schizophrenia and its symptoms may appear; the more stressors, the more likely that schizophrenia will surface. Some people can tolerate a great deal of stress; others can tolerate very little before schizophrenia materializes.

Psychologists have conducted longitudinal studies of schizophrenia by following children of schizophrenic mothers and fathers from birth to adulthood. These studies, known as *high-risk studies* because the subjects are at higher risk than the general population, have produced landmark results. The high-risk approach is effective because of the following:

▶ Subjects can be studied before the disorder develops.

▶ The data are relatively unbiased because it is not known whether the child will become schizophrenic.

▶ Data can be gathered from the individuals and their families (not from doctors or hospital records) and are therefore not influenced by patients likelihood of seeking particular medical assistance.

Many high-risk studies under way throughout the world, including some that started in the 1960s, are now assessing the likelihood of schizophrenia in mature adults. The Copenhagen High-Risk Project is one such study. Since 1962, Mednick, Parnas, and Schulsinger (1987) have followed a sample of 207 children who were at high risk for schizophrenia, as well as 104 control children. This study focused on mothers and their children. The mothers of the high-risk children were schizophrenic; the mothers who were control subjects were not schizophrenic. The schizophrenic and control mothers were matched for age, social class, education, and urban-rural differences. Psychological tests were given at periodic intervals. The results showed that if a child's mother was schizophrenic, the child was at least eight times more likely than usual to develop schizophrenia. If the birth experience was traumatic, there was increased likelihood of schizophrenia. The results also showed that poor maternal supervision was related to the development of schizophrenia.

Other high-risk projects report similar results. The University of Rochester Child and Family Study, which began in 1972, shows that parental maladjustment leads to children who will need psychological care (Wynne, Cole, & Perkins, 1987). The Stony Brook High-Risk Project reports that considerable family discord, poor parenting skills, and marital conflict are related to psychological problems in children. The relationship is magnified when there is a schizophrenic parent (Weintraub, 1987).

There is no doubt that children of schizophrenic parents are at greater risk for developing schizophrenia. However, researchers are most interested in the high-risk children who never develop the disorder. What makes them different? Researchers believe that family relationships are an important dimension. If children of schizophrenic parents are in a household filled with discord, fighting, alcoholism, and poor discipline, they are much more likely to develop the disorder. Burman and colleagues (1987, p. 364) conclude, "Stressful environments will tend to produce schizophrenia in genetically predisposed individuals."

The vulnerability-stress hypothesis might prove to be the most accurate predictor of schizophrenia. It appears that in some people who are more vulnerable than others, stressors may spark the psychiatric disorder (or relapse), as will such events as alcohol abuse. The longitudinal research continues.

Concluding Note

When people are vulnerable, they are more easily affected by stressors in their environment and more likely to develop some type of maladjustment. However, people who lack strong coping skills do not necessarily develop abnormal behavior.

Two individuals who are faced with the same stressors in their lives—death, loss of work, or abuse—may respond very differently. One may develop a serious and long-lasting clinical depression; the other may be energized and develop a plan to solve the problem. Thus stress is interpreted differently by different people; and the extent of maladjustment, if any, is determined by learned coping skills. Often the cop-

Concluding Note *cont.*

ing skills mean relying on social support, on therapy, and even on taking positive steps such as exercise, a new sleep regimen, or a new diet.

There is no doubt that a significant number of people in our country are maladjusted, in need of therapy, and suffering daily. Some whole groups of people seem more vulnerable; we saw earlier that ethnic minorities seem at a particular disadvantage. The tasks for psychologists are to recognize people's needs, to help people prevent maladjustment, to help people through their adjustment problems, and to empower people to live more worthwhile, fulfilling lives. Recognizing individual needs and individual differences is difficult, especially when determining even group needs is hard. This task is the focus of the next chapter—psychotherapy.

Summary & Review

What Is Abnormal Behavior?

What are the characteristics of abnormal behavior?

Abnormal behavior is atypical, socially unacceptable, distressing, maladaptive, or the result of distorted cognitions.   pp. 500–501

Explain the major perspectives on abnormality.

The *medical-biological model* focuses on biological/physiological conditions that initiate abnormal behaviors. The *psychodynamic model* focuses on unresolved conflicts and forces of which a person may be unaware. The *humanistic model* focuses on individual uniqueness and decision making. The *behavioral model* states that abnormal behavior is caused by faulty or ineffective learning. The *cognitive model* looks at ideas and thoughts. The *sociocultural model* examines abnormalities within the context of family, community, and society. The *legal model* defines abnormal behavior in terms of guilt, innocence, and sanity. The *interactionist model* draws on all these perspectives.   pp. 501–504

What is the DSM-IV?

The *DSM-IV* is the diagnostic manual by which mental health practitioners diagnose and classify mental disorders. It describes behavior in terms of its characteristics and its *prevalence.*   pp. 504–505

KEY TERMS: *abnormal behavior,* p. 500; *model,* p. 501; *abnormal psychology,* p. 501; *prevalence,* p. 504.

Anxiety, Somatoform, and Dissociative Disorders

Describe the central characteristics of anxiety.

Anxiety is a generalized feeling of fear and apprehension, often accompanied by increased physiological arousal, that may or may not be related to a specific event or object.   p. 506

What are the chief characteristics of a generalized anxiety disorder and a phobic disorder?

A *generalized anxiety disorder* is characterized by persistent anxiety of at least a month's duration. A *phobic disorder* is characterized by irrational fear and avoidance of certain objects or situations.   pp. 506–507

What are the chief symptoms of obsessive-compulsive disorders?

Individuals with *obsessive-compulsive disorders* have persistent and uncontrollable thoughts and irrational be-

liefs, which cause them to perform compulsive rituals that interfere with normal daily functioning. The focus of these behaviors is often on maintaining order and control.   pp. 508–509

What are the chief characteristics of somatization disorders, conversion disorders, and dissociative disorders?

Somatization disorders are somatoform disorders characterized by recurrent and multiple complaints of several years' duration for which medical attention has not been effective. *Conversion disorders* are somatoform disorders characterized by the loss or alteration of physical functioning for no apparent physiological reason. People lose the use of their arms, hands, or legs, or their vision or another sensory modality. They may develop a combination of ailments. *Dissociative disorders* are disorders characterized by a sudden but temporary alteration in consciousness, identity, sensory/motor

continued

Summary & Review

behavior or memory. These disorders, though quite noticeable, are relatively rare. pp. 510–512

KEY TERMS: *anxiety,* p. 506; *generalized anxiety disorders,* p. 506; *free-floating anxiety,* p. 506; *phobic disorder,* p. 507; *agoraphobia,* p. 507; *social phobia,* p. 508; *specific phobia,* p. 508; *obsessive-compulsive disorders,* p. 508; *somatoform disorders,* p. 510; *somatization disorders,* p. 510; *conversion disorders,* p. 510; *hypochondriasis,* p. 511; *dissociative disorders,* p. 511; *dissociative amnesia,* p. 511; *dissociative identity disorder,* p. 511.

Personality and Sexual Disorders

What are the chief characteristics of the paranoid, dependent, histrionic, narcissistic, and antisocial personality disorders?

People who have unwarranted feelings of persecution and who mistrust almost everyone are said to be suffering from *paranoid personality disorder.* Fearful or anxious behaviors are characteristic of people with a *dependent personality disorder.* Dramatic, emotional, and erratic behaviors are characteristic of the *histrionic personality disorder.* The *narcissistic personality disorder* is characterized by an extremely exaggerated sense of self-importance, an expectation of special favors, and a constant need for attention. The *antisocial personality disorder* is characterized by behavior that is irresponsible and violates the rights of others; persons with antisocial personality disorder have no fear of punishment and are egocentric. pp. 512–514

Characterize the essential components of sexual deviations.

Sexual deviations are sexual practices directed toward objects rather than people or involving real or sim-

ulated suffering, humiliation, or non-consenting partners. p. 515

KEY TERMS: *personality disorders,* p. 512; *antisocial personality disorder,* p. 513; *child abuse,* p. 514; *sexual deviations,* p. 515; *rape,* p. 516.

Mood Disorders

Where does the term bipolar disorders *come from?*

The name *bipolar disorders* is derived from the fact that patients' behavior vacillates between two extremes: mania and depression. pp. 517–518

What are the essential characteristics of major depressive disorder?

Patients diagnosed with *major depressive disorder* have a gloomy outlook on life, especially slow thought processes, loss of appetite, an exaggerated view of current problems, loss of energy, and a tendency to blame themselves. pp. 518–519

Identify two major hypotheses for the causes of depression.

The norepinephrine hypothesis suggests that an insufficient amount of norepinephrine in the brain causes depression. Learning theories stress that reinforcement patterns and social interactions determine the course and nature of depression. pp. 520–522

KEY TERMS: *bipolar disorders,* p. 517; *depressive disorders,* p. 518; *major depressive disorder,* p. 519; *delusions,* p. 519; *learned helplessness,* p. 522.

Schizophrenia

What are the essential components of schizophrenia?

Schizophrenia is a group of disorders characterized by a lack of reality testing and by deterioration of social and intellectual functioning. Individuals often show serious personality disintegration, with significant changes in

thought, mood, perception, and behavior. p. 524

Identify the five major types of schizophrenia.

The *disorganized type* of schizophrenia is characterized by severely disturbed thought processes, hallucinations, delusions, and frequently incoherence. *Paranoid type* schizophrenia is among the most difficult to identify and study because outward behavior often seems appropriate to the situation. Patients may not show extreme withdrawal from social interaction. There are two subtypes of *catatonic type* schizophrenia—excited and withdrawn. People who show symptoms attributable to schizophrenia but who remain in touch with reality are characterized as *residual type.* Some patients exhibit all the essential features of schizophrenia but do not fall prominently into the other categories—these individuals are classified as *undifferentiated type.* pp. 524–526

What is a concordance rate?

The *concordance rate* is the percentage of occasions when two groups or individuals show the same trait. Concordance rates often are examined between siblings, especially twins. p. 527

What is the claim of psychologists who support a biological explanation of schizophrenia?

Biological studies suggest that the cause of schizophrenia must be to some extent genetic, as is shown by higher concordance rates for identical twins than for fraternal twins. pp. 526–527

KEY TERMS: *psychotic,* p. 523; *schizophrenia,* p. 523; *hallucinations,* p. 524; *affect,* p. 524; *disorganized type,* p. 525; *paranoid type,* p. 525; *catatonic type,* p. 526; *residual type,* p. 526; *undifferentiated type,* p. 526; *concordance rate,* p. 527; *double bind,* p. 528; *vulnerability,* p. 529.

CONNECTIONS

If you are interested in...

The biological bases of psychological disorders, see ...

CHAPTER 2, pp. 43–44, 65–69

Hormonal and genetic influences on behavior.

CHAPTER 10, pp. 352–358

How overeating, or even eating the wrong foods, can affect behavior. ▶

CHAPTER 15, pp. 565–567

The use of drugs to treat various forms of maladjustment.

The role of anxiety in normal behavior and in maladjustment, see ...

CHAPTER 10, pp. 361–362

How behavior is affected when a person is feeling anxious and aroused. ▼

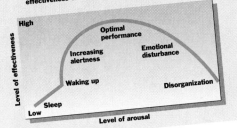

FIGURE 10.11
Arousal and Effectiveness of Behavior

In accordance with the Yerkes-Dodson law, increases in motivation and arousal often bring increases in emotions. Most important, the increases in arousal change the effectiveness of a person's behavior.

High

Optimal performance

Increasing alertness

Emotional disturbance

Waking up

Disorganization

Level of effectiveness

Sleep

Low

Level of arousal

CHAPTER 13, pp. 471–479

How a person's health can deteriorate due to continually high levels of anxiety, stress, and autonomic nervous system arousal.

The role of learning in the development of various forms of maladjustment, see ...

CHAPTER 5, pp. 174–180

How children's behavior, both good and bad, is learned through conditioning procedures. ▼

CHAPTER 12, pp. 450–452

How self-esteem, often learned in the formative years of childhood, affects the ability to cope with the simple as well as the complex demands of life.

CHAPTER 16, pp. 575–576, 591–594

How attitudes and self-perceptions develop through a process of repeated experiences.

15

Approaches
to
Treatment

C
hapter 13 introduced a friend of mine, Tricia, who suffered from stress and depression after remembering the long-forgotten sexual abuse by her father that she had endured as a young adolescent. Tricia became angry and despondent, and her mood affected all areas of her life. A software consultant and sales manager, she became overly concerned about her monthly sales totals and began inviting coworkers to join her at a local bar after work to relieve tension. Often, Tricia telephoned her husband to say she was going to be home late. Over time, there were many harsh words between them. Tricia soon began to come into work late and sometimes skipped work altogether.

Angry and anxious, losing sleep, losing weight, and verging on alcoholism, Tricia finally made an appointment with a counselor at a hospital's psychological services center. She ultimately was involved in months of counseling on several issues, including her self-esteem, her distorted ideas about work demands, and her marital relationship; and for a short time, she also received some drug therapy.

People often find it difficult to cope with problems related to stress, maladjustment, peer pressure, and abuse in families. For some, these problems become overwhelming, creating a need for professional help. Approaches to these issues are the major topics of this chapter.

Therapy Comes in Many Forms

Many types of treatment are available for people who are having difficulty coping with their problems. When a person seeks help from a physician, mental health counseling center, or drug treatment center, an initial working diagnosis is necessary. Does the person have medical problems? Should the person be hospitalized? Is the person dangerous? If talking therapy is in order, what type of practitioner is best suited for the person? There are two broad types of therapy: biologically based therapy and psychotherapy.

Biologically Based Therapy and Psychotherapy

Biologically based therapy has traditionally been called *somatic therapy*; it refers to treatments for the body, including therapy that affects hormone levels and the brain. For example, severely depressed individuals may need antidepressants; those diagnosed as having schizophrenia may need antipsychotic drugs; those with less severe disorders may be advised to change their diet and exercise more. We will examine some of these biological therapies later in this chapter; for now, we will explore the broad array of psychological therapies that are available for people suffering from maladjustment.

Psychotherapy is the treatment of emotional or behavioral problems through psychological techniques. It is a change-oriented process whose goal is to help people cope better with their problems and to achieve more emotionally satisfying lifestyles. It accomplishes its goal by teaching people how to relieve stress, improve interpersonal communication, understand previous events in their lives, and modify their faulty ideas about the world. Psychotherapy helps people improve their self-image and adapt to new and challenging situations.

Types of Psychotherapy

There are about 200 different forms of psychotherapy. Some focus on individuals, some on groups of individuals (group therapy), and others on families (family therapy). Some psychologists even deal with whole communities; these *community psychologists* focus on helping individuals, groups, and communities develop a more action-oriented approach to individual and social adjustment.

A therapist's training will usually determine the type of treatment approach taken. Rather than using just one type of psychotherapy, many therapists take an *eclectic* approach—that is, they combine a number of different techniques in their treatment. Here is an overview of the psychotherapeutic approaches in use today; each will be defined and examined in greater detail later in the chapter.

Some practitioners use *psychodynamically based approaches*, which loosely or closely follow Freud's basic ideas. Their aim is to help patients understand the motivations underlying their behavior. They assume that maladjustment and abnormal behavior occur when people do not understand themselves adequately. *Humanistic*

Psychotherapy: [SIE-ko-THAIR-uh-pee] The treatment of emotional or behavioral problems through psychological techniques.

therapists assume that people are essentially good—that they have an innate disposition to develop their potential and to seek beauty, truth, and goodness. This type of therapy tries to help people realize their full potential and find meaning in life. In contrast, *behavior therapy* is based on the assumption that most behaviors, whether normal or abnormal, are learned. Behavior therapists encourage their clients to learn new adaptive behaviors. Growing out of behavior therapy and cognitive psychology (see chapters 1 and 7) is *cognitive therapy,* which focuses on changing a client's thoughts and perceptions. See Figure 15.1 for a graphic representation of the primary orientations of clinical psychologists—those psychologists who focus on maladjustment.

Which Therapy, Which Therapist?

The appropriate type of therapy and its effectiveness vary with the type of disorder being treated and the goal of the client. For example, individual psychodynamic therapy has a good success rate for people with anxiety and maladjustment disorders, but it is less successful for those with schizophrenia. Long-term group therapy is more effective than short-term individual therapy for people with personality disorders. Behavior therapy is usually the most effective approach with children regardless of the disorder (Casey & Berman, 1985).

Tricia could therefore receive effective treatment from a variety of therapists. One therapist might focus on discovering the root causes of her maladjustment. Another might concentrate on eliminating her symptoms: depression, drinking, and poor work performance. Research to discover the best treatment method is often conducted for specific disorders, such as depression (Robinson, Berman, & Neimeyer, 1990). Results from such studies usually limit their conclusions to a specific method with a specific problem. Besides the therapeutic approaches, some characteristics of the therapists themselves affect the treatment; among these characteristics are gender, ethnicity, personality, level of experience, and degree of empathy.

Although there are differences among the various psychotherapies and therapists, there are also some commonalities. In all the therapies, clients usually expect a positive outcome, which helps them strive for change. In addition, they receive attention, which helps them maintain a positive attitude. More-

FIGURE 15.1

Orientation of Clinical Psychologists

The primary orientation of clinical psychologists who belong to the American Psychological Association has remained fairly stable over the last decade.

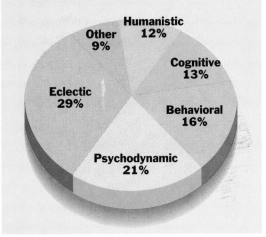

Humanistic 12%
Cognitive 13%
Behavioral 16%
Psychodynamic 21%
Eclectic 29%
Other 9%

over, no matter what type of therapy is involved, certain characteristics must be present in both therapist and client for therapeutic changes to occur. For example, good therapists communicate interest, understanding, respect, tact, maturity, and ability to help. They respect the clients' ability to cope with their troubles (C. T. Fischer, 1991). They use suggestion, encouragement, interpretation, examples, and perhaps rewards to help clients change or rethink their situations. But clients must be willing to make some changes in their lifestyles and ideas. A knowledgeable, accepting, and objective therapist can facilitate behavior changes, but the clients are the ones who make the changes (Lafferty, Beutler, & Crago, 1989). Figure 15.2 on page 538 presents an overview of the outcomes of psychotherapy plus efforts to change.

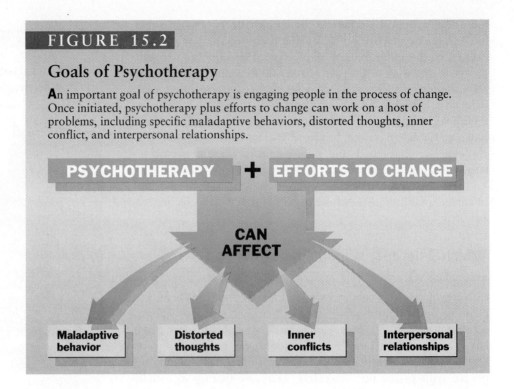

FIGURE 15.2

Goals of Psychotherapy

An important goal of psychotherapy is engaging people in the process of change. Once initiated, psychotherapy plus efforts to change can work on a host of problems, including specific maladaptive behaviors, distorted thoughts, inner conflict, and interpersonal relationships.

PSYCHOTHERAPY **+** EFFORTS TO CHANGE

CAN AFFECT

| Maladaptive behavior | Distorted thoughts | Inner conflicts | Interpersonal relationships |

Variables such as the client's social class, age, education, therapeutic expectations, and level of anxiety are also important. For example, therapists need to understand the unique life stresses experienced by women. Similarly, they must address the special obstacles facing clients of various ethnic and other minority groups (Sue, 1988). In general, the therapist and client must form an alliance to work together purposefully (Luborsky, Barber, & Crits-Cristoph, 1990); such alliances are helped if the therapist and client share some values (Kelly & Strupp, 1992). Table 15.1 presents an overview of the major practitioners of psychotherapy including their earned degrees and their activities. The table includes a number of practitioners who do not have as much training in psychotherapy as do psychologists, for example, nurses and social workers.

Challenges to Psychotherapy

Is therapy really necessary? Some researchers note that many clients could achieve relief from their symptoms without psychotherapy. Others assert that psychotherapy is more art than science. Still others believe psychotherapy provides only temporary relief of symptoms.

Placebo Effect. A **placebo effect** is a nonspecific therapeutic change that occurs as a result of a person's expectations of change rather than as a result of any specific treatment. Physicians report that sometimes people experience relief from their symptoms when they are given sugar pills and told that the pills are medicine. In much the same way, patients in psychotherapy may show relief from their symptoms simply because they have entered therapy and now expect change. For some people, just the attention of a therapist and the chance to express their feelings can be therapeutic. One research study showed that clients who paid for therapy had a better therapeutic outcome than clients who did not pay (Yoken & Berman, 1984).

The placebo effect in psychotherapy is likely to be temporary. Any long-lasting therapeutic effects will generally come about from the client's and therapist's efforts

Placebo effect: [pluh-SEE-bo] A nonspecific therapeutic change that occurs as a result of a person's expectations of change rather than as a direct result of any specific treatment.

TABLE 15.1   *Psychotherapy Practitioners and Their Activities*

Type of Practitioner	Degree	Years beyond Undergraduate Degree	Activities
Clinical or counseling psychologist	PhD *(Doctor of Philosophy)* or PsyD *(Doctor of Psychology)*	5–8	Diagnosis, testing, and treatment using a wide array of techniques, including insight and behavior therapy
Psychiatrist	MD *(Doctor of Medicine)*	8	Biomedical therapy, diagnosis, and treatment, often of a psychoanalytic nature
Social worker	MSW *(Master of Social Work)*	2	Family therapy, behavior therapy, often in community-based settings such as hospitals
Psychiatric nurse	BSN or MA *(Bachelor of Science in Nursing or Master of Arts)*	0–2	Inpatient psychiatric care, supportive therapy of various types
Counselor	MA *(Master of Arts, often in counseling)*	2	Supportive therapy, family therapy, vocational readjustment, alcoholism and drug abuse counseling

(P. Horvath, 1988). Research studies that compare traditional psychotherapies with placebo treatments show that the traditional therapies are more effective (Clum & Bowers, 1990).

Psychotherapy Research. In 1952, an important paper by Hans Eysenck challenged the effectiveness of psychotherapy, claiming that it produces no greater change in maladjusted individuals than do naturally occurring life experiences. Thousands of studies attempting to investigate the effectiveness of therapy followed.

These studies showed what clients and therapists have known for decades: that Eysenck was wrong. Analyses of large amounts of data using sophisticated statistical techniques found psychotherapy effective (Smith, Glass, & Miller, 1980). Although many psychologists challenge the data, techniques, and conclusions of these analyses, most are still convinced that psychotherapy is effective with a wide array of clients (e.g., Kazdin, 1991; Matt, 1989).

Is one type of therapy more effective than another? Many researchers contend that most psychotherapies are equally effective; that is, regardless of the approach a therapist uses, the results are often the same. Many more psychotherapy research strategies are under development; they will lead to a clearer picture of which approaches are best for certain disorders and for particular types of clients (Beutler, 1991). Table 15.2 presents some generally recognized signs of good progress in therapy.

TABLE 15.2   *Signs of Good Progress in Therapy*

Signs of Good Progress in Therapy

► The client is providing personally revealing and significant material.
► The client is exploring the meaning of feelings and occurrences.
► The client is exploring material avoided earlier in therapy.
► The client is expressing significant insight into personal behavior.
► The client's method of communicating is active, alive, and energetic.
► There is a valued client-therapist working relationship.
► The client feels free to express strong feelings toward the therapist—either positive or negative.
► The client is expressing strong feelings outside of therapy.
► The client moves toward a different set of personality characteristics.
► The client is showing improved functioning outside of therapy.
► The client indicates a general state of well-being, good feelings, and positive attitudes.

Source: Mahrer & Nadler, 1986.

FOCUS

➤ What is the essential difference between biologically based therapy and psychotherapy? p. 536

➤ Identify some things that you think might happen as a result of treatment. What would you expect to gain, lose, or change during therapy? p. 537

Next, we'll explore psychodynamic therapy, which focuses on helping clients discover their unconscious motivations. It has a point of view that differentiates it from other therapies that we will consider later in the chapter.

Psychodynamic Therapy

Psychoanalysis is a lengthy insight therapy developed by Freud that aims at uncovering conflicts and unconscious impulses through special techniques, including free association, dream analysis, and transference. It is used by therapists who are specifically trained in its theory and practice. There are about 3,000 practicing psychoanalysts in the United States, and many other psychologists use a therapy loosely connected to or rooted in Freudian theory. These psychologists refer to their therapies as **psychodynamically based therapies**—therapies that use the theory, approach, or techniques derived from Freud, but that sometimes reject some of the elements of Freud's theory.

Sigmund Freud believed that the exchange of words in psychoanalysis causes therapeutic change. According to Freud (1920/1966, p. 21):

> The patient talks, tells of his past experiences and present impressions, complains, and expresses his wishes and his emotions. The physician listens, attempts to direct the patient's thought-processes, reminds him, forces his attention in certain directions, gives him explanations and observes the reactions of understanding or denial thus evoked.

Freud's therapy is an **insight therapy**—a therapy that attempts to discover relationships between unconscious motivations and current abnormal behavior. It has two basic assumptions: (1) that becoming aware of one's motivations helps a person change and become more adaptable; and (2) that the causes of maladjustment are unresolved conflicts, which the person was unaware of and therefore unable to deal with. The goal of insight therapy is to treat the causes of abnormal behavior rather than the behaviors themselves. In general, insight therapists try to help people see life from a different perspective so they can choose more adaptive lifestyles.

Because psychoanalysis is based on the development of a unique relationship between the therapist and the patient, compatibility is especially critical. The patient and the therapist usually decide within the first few sessions whether they feel comfortable working with each other.

Goals of Psychoanalysis

Many individuals who seek psychotherapy are unhappy with their behavior but are unable to change it. As we saw in the discussion of Freud's theory of personality (chapter 12), Freud believed that conflicts among a person's unconscious thoughts and processes produce maladjusted behavior. The general goal of psychoanalysis is to help patients understand the unconscious motivations that direct their behavior. Only when they become aware of those motivations can they begin to choose behaviors that lead to more fulfilling lives. In psychoanalysis, patients are encouraged to

Psychoanalysis: [SIE-ko-uh-NAL-uh-sis] A lengthy therapy developed by Freud that aims at uncovering conflicts and unconscious impulses through special techniques, including free association, dream analysis, and transference.

Psychodynamically based therapies: [SIE-ko-die-NAM-ick-lee] Therapies based loosely on Freud's theory of psychoanalysis, using a part of the approach but rejecting some elements of Freud's theory.

Insight therapy: A therapy that attempts to discover relationships between unconscious motivations and current abnormal behavior in order to change that behavior.

express healthy impulses, strengthen day-to-day functioning based on reality, and perceive the world as a positive rather than a punishing place.

To illustrate the psychoanalytical approach, suppose that Tricia seeks the help of a psychologist who uses a psychodynamically based therapy. The psychologist might attempt to discover the source of Tricia's problems by asking her to describe how she relates to her parents—in Tricia's case, especially to her father. She realizes that she has sought her father's approval all her life.

Through therapy, Tricia realizes she is torn between her desire to please her father, her anger toward her father, and her dislike of sales. In fact, she thinks she might prefer being a photographer. She also discovers that she has been incapable of expressing anger appropriately toward her father. Frustrated and hostile, she has lost interest in work and begun using alcohol to numb the pain of her past memories and her diminishing self-esteem.

Freud's study in London contained the couch that has become the symbol of psychoanalysis.

Techniques of Psychoanalysis

In general, psychoanalytic techniques are geared toward the exploration of early experiences. In traditional psychoanalysis, the patient lies on a couch and the therapist sits in a chair out of the patient's view. Freud believed this arrangement would allow the patient to be more relaxed and feel less threatened than the person would be in viewing the therapist. Today, however, many followers of Freud prefer to use face-to-face interactions with patients.

Two major techniques used in psychoanalysis are free association and dream analysis. In **free association,** the patient is asked to report whatever comes to mind, regardless of order, how trivial it might seem, or how disagreeable it might feel. A therapist might say, "I can help you best if you say whatever thoughts and feelings come to your mind, even if they seem irrelevant, immaterial, foolish, embarrassing, upsetting, or even if they're about me, even very personally, just as they come, without censoring or editing" (Lewin, 1970, p. 67). The purpose of free association is to help patients learn to recognize connections and patterns among their thoughts and to allow the unconscious to express itself freely.

In **dream analysis,** patients are asked to describe their dreams in detail; a patient's dreams are interpreted and used to gain insight into unconscious motivations. Sometimes lifelike, sometimes chaotic, sometimes incoherent, dreams may at times replay a person's life history and at other times venture into the person's current problems. Freud believed dreams represent some element of the unconscious seeking expression. Psychodynamically oriented therapists see much symbolism in dreams; they assert that the content of a dream hides its true meaning. Many therapists use patients' dreams to gain insight into patients' current problems. The goal of dream analysis is to disclose patients' unconscious desires and motivations by discovering the meaning of their dreams.

Both free association and dream analysis involve the therapist's interpretation. **Interpretation,** in Freud's theory, is the technique of providing a context, meaning, or cause of a specific idea, feeling, or set of behaviors; it is the process of tying a set

Free association: A psychoanalytic technique in which a person reports to the therapist his or her thoughts and feelings as they occur, regardless of how trivial, illogical, or objectionable their content may appear.

Dream analysis: A psychoanalytic technique in which a patient's dreams are interpreted and used to gain insight into the individual's unconscious motivations.

Interpretation: In Freud's theory, the technique of providing a context, meaning, or cause of a specific idea, feeling, or set of behaviors; the process of tying a set of behaviors to its unconscious determinant.

of behaviors to its unconscious determinant. With this technique, the therapist tries to find common threads in a patient's behavior and thoughts. Patients' use of *defense mechanisms* (ways of reducing anxiety by distorting reality, examined in chapter 12) is often a sign of an area that may need to be explored. For example, if a patient becomes jittery every time he speaks about women, the psychotherapist may speculate that the patient's nervousness results from early difficulties with women, perhaps with his mother. The therapist may then encourage the patient to explore his attitudes and feelings about women in general and about his mother in particular.

Two processes are central to psychoanalysis: resistance and transference. **Resistance** is an unwillingness to cooperate by which a patient signals a reluctance to provide the therapist with information or to help the therapist understand or interpret a situation, sometimes to the point of belligerence. For example, a patient disturbed by her counselor's unsettling interpretations might become angry and start resisting treatment by missing appointments or failing to pay for therapy. Analysts usually interpret resistance as meaning either that the patient wishes to avoid discussing a particular subject or that an especially difficult stage in psychotherapy has been reached. To minimize resistance, analysts try to accept patients' behavior. When a therapist does not judge but merely listens, a patient is more likely to describe feelings thoroughly (Butler & Strupp, 1991).

Transference is a psychoanalytic procedure in which a therapist becomes the object of a patient's emotional attitudes about an important person in the patient's life, such as a parent. For example, if Tricia's therapist is a man, she may become hostile toward him. A psychoanalyst would say that she is acting as if the therapist were her father; that is, she is acting out with the therapist attitudes and emotional reactions from an earlier relationship (Butler & Strupp, 1991). Most importantly, because the psychotherapist will respond differently from the way Tricia's father might have, Tricia can experience the conflict differently, which will lead her to a better understanding of the issue. By permitting transference, the therapist gives patients a new opportunity to understand their feelings and can guide them in the exploration of repressed or difficult material. The examination of thoughts or feelings that were previously considered unacceptable (and therefore were often repressed) helps patients understand and identify the underlying conflicts that direct their behavior.

Psychotherapy, with its slowly gained insights into the unconscious, is a gradual and continual process. Through their insights, patients learn new ways of coping with instinctual urges and develop more mature means of dealing with anxiety and guilt. The entire process of interpretation, resistance to interpretation, and transference is sometimes referred to as **working through.**

Ego Analysts

Freud's theory has not been universally accepted; even his followers have disagreed with him. One group of psychoanalysts, referred to as ego analysts, or ego psychologists, have modified some of Freud's basic ideas. **Ego analysts** are psychoanalytic practitioners who assume that the ego has greater control over behavior than Freud suggested and who are more concerned with reality testing and control over the environment than with unconscious motivations and processes. Like Freud, they assume that psychoanalysis is the appropriate method for treating patients with emotional problems. Unlike Freud, however, they assume that people have voluntary control over whether, when, and in what ways their biological urges will be expressed.

A major disagreement has to do with the role of the id and the ego. (Recall from chapter 12, p. 428, that the id is based on the pleasure principle and the ego is based on the reality principle and tries to control the id's impulsive behavior.) Whereas traditional psychoanalysts begin by focusing on unconscious material in the id and only later try to increase the patient's ego control, ego analysts aim at helping clients

Resistance: In psychoanalysis, an unwillingness to cooperate by which a patient signals a reluctance to provide the therapist with information or to help the therapist understand or interpret a situation.

Transference: A psychoanalytic procedure in which a therapist becomes the object of a patient's emotional attitudes about an important person in the patient's life, such as a parent.

Working through: The gradual, often repeated, slow process in therapy of interpretation, resistance to interpretation, and transference.

Ego analysts: Psychoanalytic practitioners who assume that the ego has greater control over behavior than Freud suggested and who are more concerned with reality testing and control over the environment than with unconscious motivations and processes. Also known as *ego psychologists.*

develop stronger control of their egos. From an ego analyst's point of view, a weak ego may cause maladjustment through its failure to understand and control the id. Thus, by learning to master and develop their egos—including moral reasoning and judgment—people gain greater control over their lives.

Criticisms of Psychoanalysis

Some critics of psychoanalysis contend that the approach is unscientific, imprecise, and subjective; they assert that its concepts (such as id, ego, and superego) are not linked to real things or to day-to-day behavior. Other critics object to Freud's biologically oriented approach, which suggests that human beings are bundles of energy caught in conflict and driven toward some hedonistic goal. These critics ask: Where is the free will in human behavior? Also, elements of Freud's theory are sexist and untestable. Freud conceived of men and women in prescribed roles; most practitioners today find this idea objectionable.

Quite aside from these criticisms, the effectiveness of psychoanalysis is open to question. Research shows that psychoanalysis is more effective for some people than for others. It is more effective, for example, for people with anxiety disorders than for those diagnosed as schizophrenic. In addition, younger patients improve more than older ones. In general, studies show that psychoanalysis can be as effective as other therapies, but it is no more so (Garfield & Bergin, 1986).

Psychoanalysis also has a number of disadvantages. The problems addressed in psychoanalysis are difficult, and a patient must be highly motivated and articulate to grasp the complicated and subtle relationships explored. Also, because traditional psychoanalysis involves the patient meeting with the therapist for an hour at a time, 5 days a week, for approximately 5 years, a typical psychoanalysis might cost $100,000. Many people who seek therapy cannot afford the money or the time for this type of therapy.

Building Table 15.1 presents a summary of the key components of the psychoanalytic view of therapy. Humanistic therapies, which we will examine next, are neither as time-consuming nor as comprehensive in their goals as psychoanalysis.

FOCUS

▶ Explain what is meant by resistance and transference. p. 542

▶ What basic criticism of Freudian psychoanalysis do ego analysts offer?   p. 542

▶ Identify the disadvantages of psychoanalysis.   p. 543

BUILDING TABLE 15.1

Key Issues in Psychoanalytic Therapy

THERAPY	NATURE OF PSYCHO-PATHOLOGY	GOAL OF THERAPY	ROLE OF THERAPIST	ROLE OF UNCONSCIOUS MATERIAL	ROLE OF INSIGHT	TECHNIQUES
Psychoanalytic	Maladjustment reflects inadequate conflict resolution and fixation in early development.	Attainment of maturity, strengthened ego functions, reduced control by unconscious/repressed impulses.	An *investigator*, uncovering conflicts and resistances.	Primary in classical psychoanalysis, less emphasis in ego analysis.	Comes not solely from intellectual understanding but also from emotional experiences.	Analyst takes an active role in interpreting the dreams and free associations of patients.

Client-centered therapy: An insight therapy, developed by Carl Rogers, that seeks to help people evaluate the world and themselves from their own perspective by providing a nondirective environment and unconditional positive regard for the client. Also known as *person-centered therapy*.

Nondirective therapy: A form of therapy in which the client determines the direction of therapy while the therapist remains permissive, almost passive, and accepts totally the client's feelings and behavior.

Humanistic Therapies

Humanistic therapies, unlike psychoanalytic therapies, emphasize the uniqueness of the human experience and the idea that human beings have free will to determine their destinies. Humanistic psychologists assert that human beings are conscious, creative, and born with an innate desire to fulfill themselves. To some extent, humanistic approaches are an outgrowth of psychodynamically based insight therapies: They help people understand the causes of their behavior, both normal and maladjusted. Client-centered therapy and Gestalt therapy are two types of humanistic therapies.

Client-Centered Therapy

Client-centered therapy is an insight therapy that seeks to help people evaluate the world and themselves from their own perspective by providing a nondirective environment and unconditional positive regard for the client. Client-centered therapy, or person-centered therapy, was developed by Carl Rogers (1902–1987). Rogers was a quiet, caring man who turned the psychoanalytic world upside-down when he introduced his approach. He focused on the person, listening intently to his clients and encouraging them to define their own "cures." Rogers saw people as basically good, competent, social beings who move forward and grow. He believed that, throughout life, we move toward our ideal selves, maturing into fulfilled individuals through the process of self-actualization.

Rogerian therapists hold that problem behaviors occur when the environment prevents a person from developing innate potential. If children are given love and reinforcement only for their achievements, for example, then as adults they may see themselves and others only in terms of achievement. Rogerian treatment involves helping people evaluate the world from their own perspective and develop improved self-regard. A Rogerian therapist might treat my friend Tricia by encouraging her to explore her past goals, current desires, and expectations for the future, and then asking whether she can achieve what she wants through sales, photography, or some other option. Table 15.3 presents the basic assumptions underlying Rogers's approach to treatment.

Carl Rogers

Techniques of Client-Centered Therapy. Because its goal is to help clients discover and actualize their as-yet-undiscovered selves, client-centered therapy is nondirective. **Nondirective therapy** is a form of therapy in which the client determines the direction of therapy while the therapist remains permissive, almost passive, and accepts totally the client's feelings and behavior. In nondirective therapy the therapist does not dominate the client, but instead encourages the client's search for growth.

The use of the word *client* rather than *patient* is a key aspect of Rogers's approach to therapy (*patient* connotes a medical model). In psychoanalysis, therapists *direct* the patients' "cure" and help the patients understand their behavior; in client-centered therapy, therapists *guide* the clients and help them to realize what the clients feel is right for them. The clients direct the conversation, and the therapists help

---

TABLE 15.3 *Carl Rogers's Assumptions about Human Beings*

1. People are innately good and are effective in dealing with their environments.
2. Behavior is purposeful and goal-directed.
3. Healthy people are aware of all their behavior; they choose their behavior patterns.
4. A client's behavior can be understood only from the client's point of view. Even if a client has misconstrued events in the world, the therapist must understand how the client sees those events.
5. Effective therapy occurs only when a client modifies his or her behavior, not when the therapist manipulates it.

them organize their thoughts and ideas simply by asking the right questions and by responding with words such as "Oh," and reflecting back the clients' feelings. Even a small movement, such as a nod or gesture, can help clients stay on the right track. Clients learn to evaluate the world from their own vantage point, with little interpretation by the therapist.

A basic tenet of client-centered therapy is that the therapist must be a warm, accepting person who projects positive feelings toward clients. To counteract clients' negative experiences with people who were unaccepting, and who thus taught them that they are bad or unlikable, client-centered therapists accept clients as they are, with good and bad points; they respect them for their worth as individuals and show them positive regard and respect. *Empathic understanding,* whereby therapists communicate acceptance and recognition of clients' emotions and encourage clients to discuss whatever feelings they have, is an important part of the therapeutic relationship.

Client-centered therapy can be viewed as a consciousness-raising process that helps people expand their awareness. Initially, clients tend to express attitudes and ideas they have adopted from other people. Thus, Tricia might say, "I should get top sales figures," implying "because my father counts on my success." As therapy progresses and she experiences the empathic understanding of the therapist, she will begin to use her own ideas when evaluating herself (Rogers, 1951). As a result, she will talk about herself in more positive ways and try to please herself rather than others. She may say, "I should make top sales figures only if they mean something to me," reflecting a more positive, more accepting attitude about herself. As she feels better about herself, she will eventually suggest to the therapist that she knows how to deal with the world and may be ready to leave therapy.

Criticisms of Client-Centered Therapy. Client-centered therapy is widely acclaimed for its focus on the therapeutic relationship. No other therapy makes clients feel so warm, accepted, and safe. These are important characteristics of any therapy, but critics argue that they may not be enough to bring about long-lasting change.

Critics of client-centered therapy assert that lengthy discussions about past problems do not necessarily help people with their present difficulties and that an environment of unconditional positive regard may not be enough to bring about behavior changes. They believe that this therapy may be making therapeutic promises that cannot be fulfilled and that it focuses on concepts that are hard to define, such as self-actualization.

Gestalt Therapy

With the aim of creating an awareness of a person's whole self, Gestalt therapy differs significantly from psychoanalysis. **Gestalt therapy** is an insight therapy that emphasizes the importance of a person's being aware of current feelings and situations. It assumes that human beings are responsible for themselves and their lives and that they need to focus not on the past but on the present. As such, Gestalt therapy is concerned with current feelings and behaviors and their representation in a meaningful, coherent whole.

Frederick S. ("Fritz") Perls (1893–1970), a physician and psychoanalyst trained in Europe, was the founder and principal proponent of Gestalt therapy. He was a dynamic, charismatic therapist, and many psychologists followed him and his ideas closely. Perls assumed that the best way to help clients come to terms with anxiety and other unpleasant feelings was to focus on their current understanding and awareness of the world, not on past situations and experiences.

Frederick S. Perls

Gestalt therapy: [Gesh-TALT] An insight therapy that emphasizes the importance of a person's being aware of current feelings and situations.

Goals of Gestalt Therapy. The goals of Gestalt therapy are to help clients be in touch with current feelings, to help them resolve old conflicts, and to enable them to resolve future conflicts. The therapy aims at expanding clients' awareness of their current attitudes and feelings so they can respond more fully and appropriately to current situations. Gestalt therapy does not attempt to "cure" people; rather, it helps them become complete and enables them to continue to adapt in the future. Gestalt psychologists help people deal with feelings of what Perls termed *incomplete Gestalts*—that is, unfinished business or unresolved conflicts, such as previously unrecognized feelings of anger toward a spouse or envy of a brother or sister.

From Perls's point of view, the client needs to expand conscious awareness by reconnecting fragments of past and current experience. Perls argued that people develop false lives and are not in touch with their real selves. Only when they become aware of the here and now can they become sensitive to the tension and repression that made their previous behavior maladaptive. Also, once they become aware of their current feelings and accept themselves, clients can understand earlier behaviors and plan appropriate future behaviors. From a Gestalt viewpoint, healthy people are in touch with their feelings and reality. Thus, a major goal of therapy is to get people in touch with their feelings so they can construct an accurate picture of their psychological world.

Guided by a Gestalt-oriented therapist, Tricia might explore her current relationship with her parents. She might realize that her anger and poor sales reflect low self-esteem and hostile feelings toward her father. After constructing an accurate picture of her psychological world, she could adopt new behaviors that would help her explore other careers while she continued her sales work.

Techniques of Gestalt Therapy. Gestalt therapy examines current feelings and behaviors of which a client may be unaware. Usually, the therapist asks the client to concentrate on current feelings about a difficult past experience. For example, a Gestalt therapist may ask a client to relive a situation and discuss it as if it were happening in the present. The underlying assumption is that feelings expressed in the present can be understood and dealt with more easily than can feelings remembered from the past.

Many Gestalt techniques are designed to help clients become more alert to significant sensations in themselves and to their surroundings. One such technique is to have clients change the way they talk; a client who thinks she has trouble expressing aggression might be asked to talk aggressively to each member of a group. Another technique is to ask clients to behave in a manner opposite to the way they feel; a man who feels hostile or aggressive toward his boss, for example, might be asked to behave as if their relationship were warm and affectionate. For these reasons, Gestalt therapy is considered an experiential therapy.

Hypnosis (described in chapter 4), while not exactly a psychodynamic or a humanistic technique, is used by many practitioners as an adjunct to their therapies. Gestalt therapists use it from time to time to help bring clients to a more complete awareness of their surroundings. Evidence suggests that a subject's susceptibility to hypnosis can affect the outcome of some therapeutic interventions, although Spanos, Lush, and Gwynn (1989) assert that other techniques work just as well. Therapists may use hypnosis to help clients relax, remember past events, reduce their anxiety, quit smoking, raise their consciousness, or even lose weight (Cochrane, 1987).

FOCUS

▶ Why is Carl Rogers's therapy considered client-centered? p. 544

▶ What is the fundamental aim of Gestalt therapy? p. 545

▶ Briefly describe the major differences between psychoanalysis, client-centered therapy, and Gestalt therapy. pp. 540, 544, 545

BUILDING TABLE 15.2

Key Issues in Psychoanalytic and Humanistic Therapy

THERAPY	NATURE OF PSYCHO-PATHOLOGY	GOAL OF THERAPY	ROLE OF THERAPIST	ROLE OF UNCONSCIOUS MATERIAL	ROLE OF INSIGHT	TECHNIQUES
Psychoanalytic	Maladjustment reflects inadequate conflict resolution and fixation in early development.	Attainment of maturity, strengthened ego functions, reduced control by unconscious/repressed impulses.	An *investigator*, uncovering conflicts and resistances.	Primary in classical psychoanalysis, less emphasis in ego analysis.	Comes not solely from intellectual understanding but also from emotional experiences.	Analyst takes an active role in interpreting the dreams and free associations of patients.
Humanistic	Pathology reflects an incongruity between the real self and the potential, desired self. Over-dependence on others for gratification and self-esteem.	Foster self-determination; release human potential; expand awareness.	An *empathic person* in true encounter with patient, sharing experience.	Emphasis is primarily on conscious experience.	Used by many, but there is more emphasis on *how* and *what* questions than on *why* questions.	Patient is asked to see the world from a different perspective and is encouraged to focus on current situations rather than past ones.

Criticisms of Gestalt Therapy. Gestalt therapy encourages clients to get in touch with their feelings. This approach is seen as both a strength and a weakness. Some critics believe Perls was too focused on individuals' happiness and growth, that he encouraged the attainment of these goals at the expense of other goals. Gestalt therapy is also criticized for focusing too much on feelings and not enough on thought and decision making. Some psychologists think Gestalt therapy might work well for healthy people who want to grow but that it might not be as successful with severely maladjusted people who cannot make it through the day.

Building Table 15.2 presents a summary of the key components of the psychoanalytic and humanistic views of therapy.

Behavior Therapy

Sometimes, people have certain problems that may not warrant an in-depth discussion of early childhood experiences, an exploration of unconscious motivations, a lengthy discussion about current feelings, or a resolution of inner conflicts. Examples of such problems are fear of heights, anxiety about public speaking, marital conflicts, and sexual dysfunction. In these cases, behavior therapy may be more appropriate than psychodynamically based or humanistic therapies.

Goals of Behavior Therapy

Behavior therapy is a therapy based on the application of learning principles to human behavior. Synonymous with *behavior modification,* it focuses on changing overt behaviors rather than on understanding subjective feelings, unconscious processes, or motivations. It uses learning principles to help people replace maladaptive behaviors with new, better ones. Behavior therapists assume that people's

Behavior therapy: A therapy, based on the application of learning principles to human behavior, that focuses on changing overt behaviors rather than on understanding subjective feelings, unconscious processes, or motivations. Also known as *behavior modification.*

behavior is influenced by changes in their environment, in the way they respond to that environment, and in the way they interact with other people. Unlike psychodynamically based therapies, behavior therapy does not aim to discover the origins of a behavior; it works only to alter it. For a person with a nervous twitch, for example, the goal would be to eliminate the twitch. Thus, behavior therapists treat people by having them first unlearn old, faulty behaviors and then learn new, more effective ones.

Behavior therapists do not always focus on the problems that caused the client to seek therapy. If they see that the client's problem is caused by some other situation, they may focus on changing that situation. A client may seek therapy because of a faltering marriage. However, the therapist may discover that the marriage is suffering because of the client's excessive arguments with his wife, each of which is followed by a period of heavy drinking. The therapist may then discover that both the arguments and the drinking are brought on by stress at work, aggravated by the client's unrealistic expectations regarding his performance (Goldfried & Davison, 1976). In this situation, the therapist might focus on helping the client to develop standards that will ease the original cause of the problem—the tension felt at work—and that will be consistent with the client's capabilities, past performance, and realistic future performance.

Unlike psychodynamic and humanistic therapies, behavior therapy does not encourage clients to interpret past events to find their meaning. Although a behavior therapist may uncover a chain of events leading to a specific behavior, that discovery will not generally prompt a close examination of the client's early experiences.

When people enter behavior therapy, many aspects of their behavior may change, not just those specifically being treated. Thus, a person being treated for extreme shyness might find not only that the shyness decreases but also that she can engage more easily in discussions about emotional topics and can perform better on the job. Behaviorists argue that once a person's behavior has changed, it may be easier for the person to manage attitudes, fears, and conflicts.

Behavior Therapy versus Psychodynamic and Humanistic Therapies

Behaviorists are dissatisfied with psychodynamic and humanistic therapies for three basic reasons: (1) psychodynamic and humanistic therapies use concepts that are almost impossible to define and measure (such as the id, the ego, and self-actualization); (2) some studies show that patients who do not receive psychodynamic and humanistic therapies improve anyway; and (3) once a person has been labeled as abnormal, the label itself may lead to maladaptive behavior. (Although this is true with any type of therapy, psychodynamic therapy tends to use labels more than behavior therapy does.) Behavior therapists assume that people display maladaptive behavior not because they are abnormal but because they are having trouble adjusting to their life situations; if they are taught new ways of coping, the maladjustment will disappear. A great strength of behavior therapy is that it provides a coherent conceptual framework.

However, behavior therapy is not without its critics. Most insight therapists, especially those who are psychodynamically based, believe that if only *overt* behavior is treated, as is often done in behavior therapy, symptom substitution may occur. **Symptom substitution** is the appearance of one symptom to replace another that has been eliminated by treatment. Thus, insight therapists argue that if a therapist eliminates a nervous twitch without examining its underlying causes, the client will express the disorder by developing some other symptom, such as a speech impediment. Behavior therapists, on the other hand, contend that symptom substitution

Symptom substitution: The appearance of one symptom to replace another that has been eliminated by treatment.

does not occur if the treatment makes proper use of behavioral principles. Research shows that behavior therapy is at least as effective as insight therapy and in some cases is more effective (Jacobson, 1991; McGlynn, 1990; Snyder, Wills, & Grady-Fletcher, 1991).

Techniques of Behavior Therapy

Behavior therapy uses an array of techniques to help people change their behavior. Among them are operant conditioning, counterconditioning, and modeling, often in combination. In addition to using several behavioral techniques, the therapist may use some insight techniques. A good therapist will use whatever combination of techniques will help a client most efficiently and effectively. The more complicated the disorder being treated, the more likely it is that a practitioner will use a mix of therapeutic approaches—a *multimodal approach* (e.g., Blanchard et al., 1990).

Behavior therapy usually involves three general procedures: (1) identifying the problem behavior and its frequency; (2) treating the client, perhaps by reeducation, communication training, or some type of counterconditioning; and (3) assessing whether there is a lasting behavior change. If the client exhibits the new behavior for several weeks or months, the therapist concludes that treatment was effective. Let's now explore the three major behavior therapy techniques: operant conditioning, counterconditioning, and modeling.

Operant Conditioning

Operant conditioning procedures are used with different people in different settings to achieve a wide range of desirable behaviors, including increased reading speed, improved classroom behavior, and the maintenance of personal hygiene. As we saw in chapter 5, operant conditioning to establish new behaviors often depends on a *reinforcer*—any event that increases the probability that a particular response will recur. Tricia could employ operant conditioning to help herself adopt more positive responses toward her father. For example, she could ask her husband to praise her every time she responds to her father in an appropriate manner.

One of the most effective uses of operant conditioning is with children who are antisocial, slow learners, or in some way maladjusted. Operant conditioning is also effective with patients in mental hospitals. Ayllon and Haughton (1964), for example, instructed staff members to reinforce hospitalized patients for psychotic verbalizations during one period and for neutral verbalizations during another. As expected, the frequency of psychotic verbalizations increased when they were reinforced and decreased when they were not reinforced (see Figure 15.3 on page 550).

Token Economies. One way of rewarding adaptive behavior is with a **token economy**—an operant conditioning environment in which patients who engage in appropriate behavior receive tokens that they can exchange for desirable items or activities. Some examples are candy, new clothes, games, or time with important people in their lives. The more tokens people earn, the more items or activities they can obtain.

Token economies are used to modify behavior in social settings, usually with groups of people. They aim to strengthen behaviors that are compatible with social norms. For example, a patient in a mental hospital might receive tokens for cleaning tables, helping in the hospital laundry, and maintaining certain standards of personal hygiene and appearance. The number of tokens earned is determined by the level of difficulty of the behavior or task and how long the person performs it. Thus, patients might receive 3 tokens for brushing their teeth but 40 tokens for engaging in helping behaviors.

Token economy: An operant conditioning environment in which patients who engage in appropriate behavior receive tokens that they can exchange for desirable items or activities.

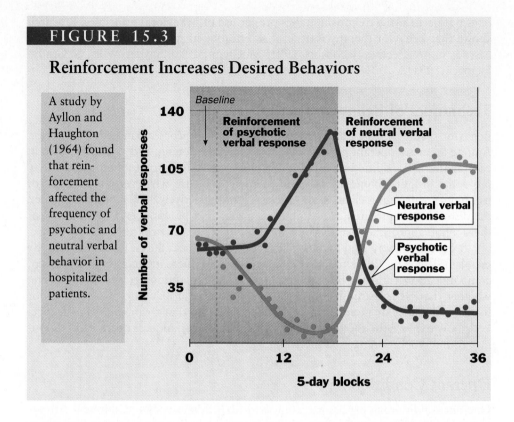

FIGURE 15.3

Reinforcement Increases Desired Behaviors

A study by Ayllon and Haughton (1964) found that reinforcement affected the frequency of psychotic and neutral verbal behavior in hospitalized patients.

Ayllon and Azrin (1965) monitored the performance of a group of hospitalized patients who were involved in doing simple work tasks for 45 days. They found that when tokens (reinforcement) were contingent on performance, the patients produced about four times as much work per day as when tokens were not delivered. (See Figure 15.4, in which some of their results are presented.) Such techniques become especially effective when combined with other behavioral techniques (Miller, Cosgrove, & Doke, 1990). We will examine two of these techniques next—first extinction and punishment and then time-out procedures.

Extinction and Punishment. As we saw in chapter 5, extinction and punishment are conditioning techniques that can decrease the frequency of an undesired behavior. If reinforcers are withheld, extinction of a behavior will occur. Suppose a 6-year-old refuses to go to bed at the designated time. When she is taken to her bedroom, she cries and screams violently. If the parents give in and allow her to stay up, they are reinforcing the crying behavior: The child cries; the parents give in. A therapist might suggest that the parents stop reinforcing the crying behavior by insisting that the child go to bed and stay there. Chances are that the child will cry loudly and violently for two or three nights, but the behavior will eventually be extinguished (C. D. Williams, 1959).

Another way to decrease the frequency of an undesired behavior is to punish it. Punishment often involves the presentation of an aversive stimulus. In the laboratory, researchers might provide slight electric shocks to get adult subjects to stop performing a specific behavior. Usually, punishment for undesired behaviors is combined with positive reinforcement for desired behaviors.

Time-Out. As we saw in chapter 5, the **time-out**—the physical removal of a person from sources of reinforcement to decrease the occurrence of undesired behaviors—is an effective operant conditioning procedure. Suppose a child regularly

Time-out: A punishment procedure in which a person is physically removed from a desired or reinforcing situation to decrease the likelihood that an undesired behavior will recur.

FIGURE 15.4

Token Economies Change Performance Effectively

Ayllon and Azrin (1965) found that tokens increased the number of hours worked by patients.

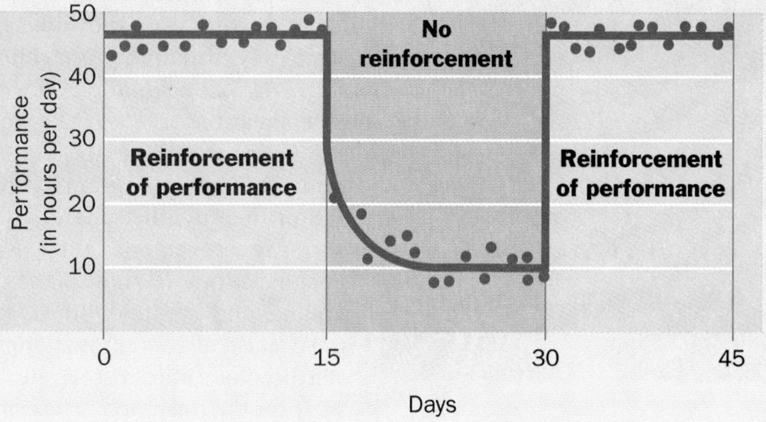

Token economics have also proven effective in some school settings.

throws temper tantrums each time he wants a piece of candy, an ice-cream cone, or his little brother's toys; and suppose that, out of frustration and embarrassment, his parents often give in. In the time-out procedure, whenever the child misbehaved, he would be placed in a restricted area away from the rest of the family, without toys, television, or other people. He would be kept in the restricted area (such as a chair or a time-out room) for a short period, such as 5 or 10 minutes; if he left, more time would be added. Not only would the child not be getting what he wanted, he would also be removed from any potential source of reinforcement. Time-out is principally used with children and young adolescents and is especially effective when it is combined with positive reinforcers for appropriate behavior and is administered by a child-care specialist (Crespi, 1988).

Counterconditioning

A second major approach to behavior therapy is **counterconditioning**—a process of reconditioning in which a person is taught a new, more adaptive response to a familiar stimulus. For example, anxiety is one of the first responses people show when they are maladjusted, fearful, or lacking in self-esteem. If a therapist can inhibit anxiety by conditioning a person to respond with something other than fear—that is, by *counterconditioning* the person—a real breakthrough in therapy will be achieved.

Joseph Wolpe (b. 1915) was one of the initial proponents of counterconditioning. His work in classical conditioning, especially in situations in which animals show conditioned anxiety responses, led him to attempt to inhibit or decrease anxiety as a response in human beings. His therapeutic goal was to replace anxiety with some other response, such as relaxation, amusement, or pleasure.

Behavior therapy using counterconditioning begins with a specific stimulus (S_1) which elicits a specific response (R_1). After the person undergoes counterconditioning, the same stimulus (S_1) should elicit a new response (R_2) (Wolpe, 1958). There are two basic approaches to counterconditioning: systematic desensitization and aversive counterconditioning.

Counterconditioning: A process of reconditioning in which a person is taught a new, more adaptive response to a familiar stimulus.

Using systematic desensitization, this therapist is gradually acclimating his client to a previously frightening situation—flying.

Systematic Desensitization. **Systematic desensitization** is a three-stage counterconditioning procedure in which people are taught to relax when presented with stimuli that formerly elicited anxiety. First, the subject learns how to relax; then the subject describes the specific situations that arouse anxiety; and finally the subject, while deeply relaxed, imagines increasingly vivid scenes of the situations that elicit anxiety. In this way, the subject is gradually, step by step, exposed to the source of anxiety, usually by imagining a series of progressively more fearful or anxiety-provoking situations. Eventually, the subject actually approaches the real-life situation.

Flying in an airplane, for example, is a stimulus situation (S_1) that can bring about an inappropriate fear response (R_1). With systematic desensitization therapy, the idea of flying (S_1) can eventually elicit a response of curiosity or even relaxation (R_2). The therapist might first ask the client to imagine sitting in an airplane on the ground, then to imagine the airplane taxiing, and eventually to imagine flying though the billowing clouds. As the client realizes that imagining the scene will not result in harm, the person becomes able to tolerate more stressful imagery and may eventually perform the imagined behavior—in this case, flying in an airplane.

Systematic desensitization is most successful for people who have problems such as impulse control or who exhibit forms of anxiety, such as phobias. It is not especially effective for people who exhibit serious psychotic symptoms; nor is it the best treatment for situations involving interpersonal conflict.

Aversive Counterconditioning. Before therapy, clients often do not avoid a stimulus that prompts inappropriate behavior. This is where another form of counterconditioning can be used, aversive counterconditioning. **Aversive counterconditioning** is a counterconditioning technique that pairs an aversive or noxious stimulus with a stimulus that elicits undesired behavior so that the subject will adopt a new, desirable behavior in response to the original stimulus. As with systematic desensiti-

zation, the objective is to teach a new response to the original stimulus. A behavior therapist might use aversive counterconditioning to teach a client a new response to alcohol. The first step might be to teach the person to associate alcohol (the original stimulus) with the sensation of nausea (a noxious stimulus). If verbal instruction is not enough, the therapist might administer a drug that causes nausea whenever alcohol is consumed. The goal is to make the drinking of alcohol unpleasant. Eventually, the treatment will make the client experience nausea just at the thought of consuming alcohol, thus causing the client to avoid alcohol (the new, desired response) (W. S. Davidson, 1974).

Systematic desensitization: A counterconditioning procedure in which a person first learns deep relaxation and then imagines a series of progressively fearful situations; with each successive experience, the person learns relaxation rather than fear as a new response to a formerly fearful stimulus.

Aversive counterconditioning: A counterconditioning technique that pairs an aversive or noxious stimulus with a stimulus that elicits undesirable behavior so the subject will adopt a new, desirable behavior in response to the original stimulus.

Cigarette smoking can be reduced or eliminated through aversive counterconditioning.

Modeling

Both children and adults learn behaviors by watching and imitating other people—in other words, by observing models. Children learn table manners, toilet behavior, and appropriate responses to animals by observing and imitating their parents and other models. Similarly, the music you listen to, the clothing styles you wear, and the social or political causes you support are determined, in part, by the people around you.

According to Albert Bandura (1977a), modeling is most effective in three areas: (1) learning new behavior; (2) helping to eliminate fears, especially phobias; and (3) expressing already existing behavior. By watching the behavior of others, people learn to exhibit more adaptive and appropriate behavior. Bandura, Blanchard, and Ritter (1969), for example, asked people with a snake phobia to watch other people handling snakes. Afterward, the subjects' fear of snakes was reduced.

Many specific phobias, such as fear of snakes, can be extinguished through modeling.

One problem with modeling is that people may observe and imitate the behavior of inappropriate models. We will see in chapter 17 that people imitate violent behaviors that they have observed on television and in movies. Further, many adolescents become involved in alcohol and other drug abuse because they imitate their peers. Such imitation often occurs because of faulty thinking about situations, people, or lifelong goals. When people have developed a faulty set of expectations that guide their behavior, cognitive therapy may be in order.

Building Table 15.3 on page 554 presents a summary of the key components of the psychoanalytic, humanistic, and behavioral views of therapy.

FOCUS

▶ Identify two fundamental reasons that behaviorists are dissatisfied with psychodynamic and humanistic therapies. p. 548

▶ As a behavior therapy technique, operant conditioning is especially effective with what disorders? p. 549

▶ Why would modeling be especially effective in treating phobias? p. 553

Cognitive Therapy

Cognitive psychologists have had a profound impact in many areas of psychology, especially in therapy. In the past, most behavior therapists were concerned only with overt behavior, but today many incorporate thought processes into their treatments. Researchers now suggest that thought processes may hold the key to managing many forms of maladjustment.

Therapists who use *cognitive restructuring* (cognitive therapy) are interested in modifying the faulty thought patterns of disturbed people (Mahoney, 1977). This type of therapy is effective for people who have attached overly narrow or otherwise inappropriate labels to certain situations; for example, they may believe that sex is dirty or that assertiveness is unwomanly. Whenever they are presented with a situation that involves sex or assertiveness, they respond in a way that is determined by their thoughts about the situation rather than by facts of the situation.

Cognitive therapy offers three basic propositions:

▶ Cognitive activity affects behavior.

BUILDING TABLE 15.3

Key Issues in Psychoanalytic, Humanistic, and Behavior Therapy

THERAPY	NATURE OF PSYCHO-PATHOLOGY	GOAL OF THERAPY	ROLE OF THERAPIST	ROLE OF UNCONSCIOUS MATERIAL	ROLE OF INSIGHT	TECHNIQUES
Psychoanalytic	Maladjustment reflects inadequate conflict resolution and fixation in early development.	Attainment of maturity, strengthened ego functions, reduced control by unconscious/repressed impulses.	An *investigator*, uncovering conflicts and resistances.	Primary in classical psycho-analysis, less emphasis in ego analysis.	Comes not solely from intellectual understanding but also from emotional experiences.	Analyst takes an active role in interpreting the dreams and free associations of patients.
Humanistic	Pathology reflects an incongruity between the real self and the potential, desired self. Over-dependence on others for gratification and self-esteem.	Foster self-determination; release human potential; expand aware-ness.	An *empathic person* in true encounter with patient, sharing experi-ence.	Emphasis is primarily on con-scious experience.	Used by many, but there is more emphasis on *how* and *what* questions than on *why* questions.	Patient is asked to see the world from a different perspective and is encouraged to focus on current situations rather than past ones.
Behavior	Symptomatic be-havior stems from faulty learning or learning of mala-daptive behaviors. The symptom is the problem; there is no "underlying disease."	Relieving symp-tomatic behavior by suppressing or replacing maladaptive behaviors.	A *helper* helping subject unlearn old behaviors and learn new ones.	No concern with unconscious processes.	Irrelevant and unnecessary.	Subjects learn new responses; used to establish new behaviors and eliminate faulty or un-desirable ones.

▶ Cognitive activity can be monitored.

▶ Behavior changes can be effected through cognitive changes.

Like other forms of behavior therapy, cognitive therapy focuses on current behavior and current thoughts. It is not especially concerned with uncovering forgotten child-hood experiences, although it can be used to alter thoughts about those experiences. It has been used effectively to treat depression, bulimia, weight loss, anger, and ado-lescent behavior problems (e.g., Butler et al., 1991; Hollon, Shelton, & Davis, 1993; Kendall, 1993). Cognitive therapy has gone through three decades of development and its future looks promising (Mahoney, 1993).

Rational-Emotive Therapy

Rational-emotive therapy: A cognitive behavior therapy that emphasizes the impor-tance of logical, rational thought processes.

The best-known cognitive therapy is **rational-emotive therapy**—behavior therapy that emphasizes the importance of logical, rational thought processes. This therapy was developed by researcher Albert Ellis (b. 1913) more than 30 years ago. Most behavior therapists assume that abnormal behavior is caused by faulty and irrational *behavior* patterns. Ellis and his colleagues, however, assume that it is caused by

TABLE 15.4 *Albert Ellis Outlined Ten Irrational Assumptions*

1. It is a necessity for an adult to be loved and approved by almost everyone for virtually everything.
2. A person must be thoroughly competent, adequate, and successful in all respects.
3. Certain people are bad, wicked, or villainous and should be punished for their sins.
4. It is catastrophic when things are not going the way one would like.
5. Human unhappiness is externally caused. People have little or no ability to control their sorrows or to rid themselves of negative feelings.
6. It is right to be terribly preoccupied with and upset about something that may be dangerous or fearsome.
7. It is easier to avoid facing many of life's difficulties and responsibilities than it is to undertake more rewarding forms of self-discipline.
8. The past is all-important. Because something once strongly affected someone's life, it should continue to do so indefinitely.
9. People and things should be different from the way they are. It is catastrophic if perfect solutions to the grim realities of life are not immediately found.
10. Maximal human happiness can be achieved by inertia and inaction or by passively and without commitment "enjoying oneself."

Source: Ellis & Harper, 1961.

faulty and irrational *thinking* patterns (Ellis, 1970; Ellis & Harper, 1961). They believe that if faulty thought processes can be replaced with rational ones, maladjustment and abnormal behavior will disappear.

According to Ellis, psychological disturbance is a result of events in a person's life that give rise to irrational beliefs leading to negative emotions and behaviors. Moreover, these beliefs are a breeding ground for further irrational ideas (Dryden & Ellis, 1988). Ellis (1988) argues that people make formal demands on themselves and on other people, and they rigidly hold onto them no matter how unrealistic and illogical they are.

Albert Ellis

Thus, a major goal of rational-emotive therapy is to help people examine the past events that produced the irrational beliefs. Ellis, for example, tries to focus on a client's basic philosophy of life and how it is inevitably self-defeating. He thus tries to uncover the client's thought patterns and help the client recognize that the underlying beliefs are faulty. Table 15.4 lists 10 irrational assumptions that, according to Ellis, cause emotional problems and maladaptive behaviors. They are based on people's needs to be liked, to be competent, to be loved, and to feel secure. When people place irrational or exaggerated value on these needs, the needs become maladaptive and lead to emotional disturbance, anxiety, and abnormal behavior. If rational-emotive therapy is successful, the client adopts different behaviors based on new, more rational thought processes. Research supports the effectiveness of the approach (Haaga & Davison, 1993) and Ellis (1993) asserts that rational-emotive therapy has broad applications in both therapy and classroom settings.

Beck's Approach

Another cognitive therapy that focuses on irrational ideas is that of Aaron Beck (1963). As we saw in chapter 14, Beck's theory assumes that depression is caused by people's distorted cognitive views of reality, which lead to negative views about the

Group therapy: The treatment of emotional and behavioral problems, or any psychotherapeutic process, in which several people meet as a group with a therapist.

Aaron Beck

world, themselves, and the future, and often to gross overgeneralizations. For example, people who think they have no future—that all of their options are blocked—and who undervalue their intelligence are likely to be depressed. Such individuals form appraisals of situations that are distorted and based on insufficient (and sometimes wrong) data. The goal of therapy, therefore, is to help them to develop realistic appraisals of the situations they encounter and to solve problems (Beck, 1993). The therapist acts as a trainer and coinvestigator, providing data to be examined and guidance for understanding how cognitions influence behavior (Beck & Weishaar, 1989).

According to Beck, a successful client passes through four stages as he corrects his faulty views and moves toward improved mental health:

> First, he has to become aware of what he is thinking. Second, he needs to recognize what thoughts are awry. Then he has to substitute accurate for inaccurate judgments. Finally, he needs feedback to inform him whether his changes are correct. (Beck, 1976, p. 217)

Meichenbaum's Approach

Some researchers, among them Donald Meichenbaum, believe that what people *say* to themselves determines what they will do. Therefore, a goal of therapy is to change the things people say to themselves. According to Meichenbaum, the therapist has to change clients' appraisal of stressful events and use of self-instructions, thus normalizing clients' reactions (Meichenbaum, 1993).

A strength of Meichenbaum's theory is that self-instruction can be used in many settings for many different problems (Dobson & Block, 1988). It can help people who are shy or impulsive, people with speech impediments, and even those who are schizophrenic (Meichenbaum, 1974; Meichenbaum & Cameron, 1973). Rather than attempting to change their irrational beliefs, clients learn a repertoire of activities they can use to make their behavior more adaptive. For example, they may learn to conduct a private monologue in which they work through adaptive ways of thinking and coping with situations. They can then discuss with a therapist the quality and usefulness of these self-instructional statements. They may learn to organize their responses to specific situations in an orderly, more easily exercised set of steps.

Cognitive therapy in its many forms has been used with adults, children, and specialized groups such as women and the elderly (Davis & Padesky, 1989; DiGiuseppe, 1989; Glantz, 1989). It can be applied to such problems as anxiety disorders, marital relations, chronic pain, and (as we saw in Beck's work) depression. Cognitive therapy continues to make enormous strides and to influence an increasing number of theorists and practitioners who conduct both long-term therapy and brief therapy. The latter is considered in the Applications box on page 558.

Building Table 15.4 provides a summary of the key components of the psychoanalytic, humanistic, behavioral, and cognitive views of therapy. Next, we will look into group therapy, which focuses on treating groups of people rather than individuals.

Group Therapy

When several people meet as a group to receive psychological help, the treatment is referred to as **group therapy.** This technique was introduced in the early 1900s and has become increasingly popular since World War II. One reason for its popularity is that the demand for therapists exceeds the number available. Individually, a ther-

BUILDING TABLE 15.4

Key Issues in Psychoanalytic, Humanistic, Behavior, and Cognitive Therapy

THERAPY	NATURE OF PSYCHO-PATHOLOGY	GOAL OF THERAPY	ROLE OF THERAPIST	ROLE OF UNCONSCIOUS MATERIAL	ROLE OF INSIGHT	TECHNIQUES
Psychoanalytic	Maladjustment reflects inadequate conflict resolution and fixation in early development.	Attainment of maturity, strengthened ego functions, reduced control by unconscious/repressed impulses.	An *investigator*, uncovering conflicts and resistances.	Primary in classical psycho-analysis, less emphasis in ego analysis.	Comes not solely from intellectual understanding but also from emotional experiences.	Analyst takes an active role in interpreting the dreams and free associations of patients.
Humanistic	Pathology reflects an incongruity between the real self and the potential, desired self. Over-dependence on others for gratification and self-esteem.	Foster self-determination; release human potential; expand awareness.	An *empathic person* in true encounter with patient, sharing experience.	Emphasis is primarily on conscious experience.	Used by many, but there is more emphasis on *how* and *what* questions than on *why* questions.	Patient is asked to see the world from a different perspective and is encouraged to focus on current situations rather than past ones.
Behavior	Symptomatic behavior stems from faulty learning or learning of maladaptive behaviors. The symptom is the problem; there is no "underlying disease."	Relieving symptomatic behavior by suppressing or replacing maladaptive behaviors.	A *helper* helping subject unlearn old behaviors and learn new ones.	No concern with unconscious processes.	Irrelevant and unnecessary.	Subjects learn new responses; used to establish new behaviors and eliminate faulty or undesirable ones.
Cognitive	Maladjustment occurs because of faulty, irrational thought patterns.	To change the way subjects think about themselves and the world.	A trainer and co-investigator helping the client learn new, rational ways to think about the world.	Little or no concern with unconscious processes.	Irrelevant, but may be used if some insight does occur.	Subjects learn to think situations through logically and to reconsider many of their irrational assumptions.

apist can generally see up to 40 clients a week for 1 hour each. But in a group, the same therapist might see 8 to 10 clients in just 1 hour. Another reason for the popularity is that the therapist's fee is shared among the members of the group, making group therapy less expensive than individual therapy.

Group therapy can also be more effective than individual therapy in the treatment of interpersonal conflicts, since groups provide frequent and varied opportunity for mutual reinforcement and support (Rose, 1991). The social pressures that operate in a group can help shape the members' behavior; in addition, group members provide useful models of behavior for one another. Successful self-help organizations such as Weight Watchers, Gamblers Anonymous, and Alcoholics Anonymous practice a form of group therapy. Such self-help groups grow in popularity each year; currently, about 6 million American adults are members of such groups.

Brief Therapy

There is a new model for psychotherapy in town—and it is often a cognitive therapy. The new model rejects many of the traditional ideas of the various therapies we've discussed so far in this chapter. Its proponents reject the idea that one therapeutic approach can help all people with any behavioral or emotional problem. They also reject the belief that a person's unconscious or life history must be understood fully before the client can end therapy. Finally, they disavow the idea that the therapist and client have to resolve past or future psychological problems in one group of psychotherapy sessions.

In an award-winning address to the American Psychological Association, Nicholas Cummings (1986) described the new model. Termed **brief intermittent therapy,** or *brief therapy,* it is a therapeutic approach that is based on a blend of psychotherapeutic orientations and skills and focuses on identifying the client's current problem and treating it with the most effective treatment as quickly as possible. A basic goal of brief therapy is to give clients what they need; the therapy therefore focuses on treating clients' problems efficiently and getting clients back on their own as quickly as possible. One of its objectives is to save clients time and money. There are no limits on the number of sessions, and clients remain in therapy as long as they find it necessary. They can also return if they need help in the future. The key distinction of this changing approach to therapy is that more and more therapists are thinking in terms of *planned* short-term treatments (Wells & Phelps, 1990).

The therapist makes sure that treatment begins in the first session of brief therapy. He or she strives to perform an *operational diagnosis* that answers the question: Why is the client here today instead of last week or last month, last year, or next year? The answer indicates to the therapist the specific problem for which the client is seeking help. Also in the first session, "every client makes a therapeutic contract with every therapist" (N. A. Cummings, 1986, p. 430; Goulding, 1990). The goals of therapy are established and agreed on by the client and the therapist; and the therapy is precise, active, and directive, with no unnecessary extra steps (Clarkin & Hull, 1991; Lazarus & Fay, 1990).

Because it is relatively new, there is not a great deal of published research on the effectiveness of brief therapy; but what has been published is encouraging (e.g., Zeig & Gilligan, 1990). Research has been limited to relatively few clients with a narrow range of problems. Nonetheless, researchers have found brief therapy to be effective when treatment goals and procedures are tailored to the client's needs and the time available (Brom, Kleber, & Defares, 1989). It can be especially effective when combined with thought restructuring (Ellis, 1990) and is effective for relapse prevention for alcoholics (Sandahl & Ronnberg, 1990). Brief therapy is not a cure-all. Like all therapies, its aim is to help relieve clients' suffering (L. Segal, 1991); and it will be effective with some clients some of the time and with some problems (Clarkin & Hull, 1991). More research on brief therapy is being conducted now, and its future will depend on the results of that research.

Brief intermittent therapy: A therapeutic approach that focuses on identifying the client's current problem and solving it with the most effective treatment as quickly as possible. Also known as *brief therapy.*

Techniques and Formats

The techniques used by a therapy group are determined largely by the nature of the group and the orientation of its therapist. The group may follow a psychoanalytic, client-centered, Gestalt, behavioral, or other approach. No two groups are alike, and no two groups deal with individual members in the same way.

In traditional group therapy, from 6 to 12 clients meet on a regular basis (usually once a week) with a therapist in a clinic or hospital or in the therapist's office. Generally, the therapist selects members on the basis of what they can gain from and offer to the group. The goal is to construct a group whose members are compatible (but not necessarily the same) in terms of age, needs, and problems. The duration of group therapy varies, usually longer than 6 months, but there are a growing number of short-term groups (under 12 weeks) (Rose, 1991).

The format of traditional group therapy varies, but generally each member describes her or his problems to the other members, who in turn relate their experiences with similar problems and how they coped with them. This gives individuals a chance to express their fears and anxieties to people who are warm and accepting; each member eventually realizes that every person has emotional problems. Group members also have opportunities to role play (try out) new behaviors in a safe but evaluative environment. In a mental health center, for example, a therapist might help members relive past traumas and cope with their continuing fears. Finally, in group therapy, members can exert pressure on an individual to behave in more appropriate ways. Sometimes, the therapist is directive in helping the group cope with a specific problem. At other times, the therapist allows the group to work through its problems independently.

Nontraditional Group Therapy

Two nontraditional techniques sometimes used in group therapy are psychodrama and encounter groups. **Psychodrama** is a group therapy procedure in which members act out their situations, feelings, and roles. It stems from the work of J. L. Moreno, a Viennese psychiatrist who used this technique in the 1920s and 1930s. Those who participate can practice expressing their feelings and responding to the feelings of others. Even those who do not participate can see how others respond to different emotions and situations. Psychodrama can help open the floodgates of emotion and can be used to help refine social skills and define problem areas that need to be worked on further (Naar, 1990).

Encounter groups are groups of people who meet together to learn more about their feelings, behavior, and interactions. They are designed to offer people experiences that will help them self-actualize and develop better interpersonal relationships. (Self-actualization, which we examined in chapters 10 and 12, is the process by which people move toward fulfilling their potentials.) Encounter groups also enable their members to work on resolving their own problems and perceiving—and ultimately minimizing—the effects of their problems on others. Each encounter group is unique. Some are like regular therapy groups. In others, the therapist participates minimally, if at all. Some researchers believe that encounter groups made up of specific types of people—such as female athletes, drug addicts, alcoholics, homosexuals, anorexics, or singles—have an advantage in therapy.

Family Therapy

A special form of group therapy is family therapy. **Family therapy** is therapy in which two or more people who are committed to each other's well-being are treated at once in an effort to change the ways in which they interact. A *family* is defined as any group of people who are committed to one another's well-being, preferably for life (Bronfenbrenner, 1989). Widely used by a large number of practitioners, especially social workers, family therapy aims to change the ways in which family members interact. From a family therapist's point of view, the real patient in family therapy is the family's structure and organization (Jacobson & Bussob, 1983). While parents may identify one member of their family—perhaps a delinquent child—as the problem, family therapists believe that that person, in many cases, may simply be a scapegoat. The so-

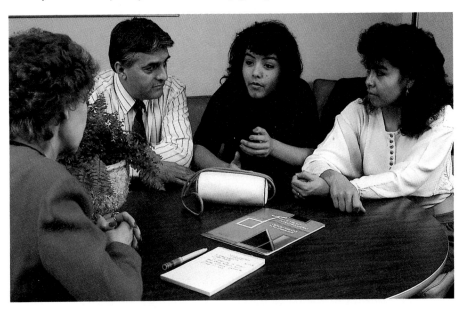

Family therapy focuses on the family system as a whole, rather than on the specific problems of any one family member.

> **Psychodrama:** [SIE-ko-drama] A group therapy procedure in which members act out their situations, feelings, and roles.
>
> **Encounter groups:** Groups of people who meet together to learn more about their feelings, behavior, and interactions.
>
> **Family therapy:** Therapy in which two or more people who are committed to one another's well-being are treated at once, in an effort to change the ways in which they interact.

called problem member diverts the family's attention from problems that are difficult to confront. Sometimes, family therapy is termed *relationship therapy*, because this is often the focus of the intervention (Becvar & Becvar, 1988).

Family therapists attempt to change *family systems*. This means that treatment takes place within an ongoing, active social system such as a marriage or family (Fruzzetti & Jacobson, 1991). Therapists assume that there are multiple sources of psychological influence: Individuals within a family affect family processes, and family processes affect individuals; the family is an interactive system (Bednar, Burlingame, & Masters, 1988). The family systems approach has become especially popular in universities that have social work colleges, in departments of psychology, and even in colleges of medicine, where patients are often seen in a family setting.

A useful technique in family therapy is to *restructure* the family's interactions. If a son is responding too submissively to his domineering mother, for example, the therapist may suggest that the son be assigned household chores only by his father.

Many psychologists, social workers, and psychiatrists use family therapy to help individuals and families change. However, not all families profit equally from such interventions. Family therapy is difficult, for example, with families that are disorganized or in which not all members participate.

Some researchers believe the family systems approach is as effective as individual therapy—and in some situations more effective (Bednar, Burlingame, & Masters, 1988). A clinician who is presented with a person who has some type of adjustment problem must also consider the impact of this problem on other people. This is one of the main focuses of the study of codependence, which we will consider in the Applications box. In the next section, we will examine how disorders, both mild and severe, affect a person's life as well as coworkers, family members, and, ultimately, the community.

FOCUS

▶ According to Ellis, what are the consequences of developing irrational beliefs? pp. 554–555

▶ Compare and contrast rational-emotive therapy with Beck's approach to therapy. pp. 554–556

▶ Identify the advantages group therapy has over individual therapy. pp. 556–559

Community Psychology

The therapies we've confronted so far in this chapter are based on the assumption that people need help to adapt to society in healthy and productive ways. However, some psychologists try to help people in a broader way. Community psychology has emerged in response to a widespread desire for a more action-oriented approach to individual and social adjustment. **Community psychology** is a branch of psychology that seeks to reach out to society to provide services, such as community mental health centers, and especially to effect social change through empowerment, planning, prevention, early intervention, research, and evaluation.

In the 1960s, many psychologists recognized that individual therapy was at best imprecise and at worst inefficient for treating large numbers of maladjusted people. Researchers and practitioners, as well as politicians, sought a more efficient and effective approach. President John F. Kennedy's 1963 message to Congress called for "a bold new approach" to the treatment of mental illness and was followed by legislation and funding for community mental health centers.

The general aims of community psychology are to strengthen existing social support networks and to stimulate the formation of new networks to meet new challenges (Gonzales et al., 1983). A key element is community involvement leading to

Community psychology: The branch of psychology that seeks to reach out to society to provide services such as community mental health centers and especially to effect social change through empowerment of individuals, planning, prevention, early intervention, research, and evaluation.

APPLICATIONS

Codependence

Recently, practitioners have focused on how families often become enmeshed in a patient's problems—for example, depression, alcoholism, drug abuse, child abuse, or anxiety disorders. Such involvement with the life of the patient often becomes devastating for the family. This problem is termed *codependence*. Codependence is not a disorder in the *DSM-IV*. In fact, the families of people with such disorders as substance abuse have often gone relatively unnoticed. Although practitioners often treat whole families, not just the person suffering from maladjustment, they view codependence as an additional type of adjustment problem—not for the patient but for the patient's family and friends.

In codependence, families often cling to a person with serious problems in a dependent way. The codependents—the family members or friends—are often plagued by intense feelings of shame, fear, anger, or pain; but they cannot express those feel-

ings because of an intense desire to please and care for the person suffering from the disorder or addiction. Codependent children may believe their job is to take care of their maladjusted parents. Codependent adults may strive to help their maladjusted families or friends with their problems. They often think that if they were perfect, they could help the maladjusted individual. In some cases, people actually *need* the patient to stay disordered; for example, families sometimes unwittingly want a patient to remain dependent on them so they can stay in a controlling position. Practitioners often see patients who are facing alcoholism or cocaine addiction and friends or family members who are codependent.

Here are some warning signs that people may be codependent:

▶ They always choose to be with the wrong people—alcoholics or verbally or physically abusive people, for example.

▶ They assume responsibility for others with whom they have relationships.

▶ They avoid confronting their feelings about their current relationships.

▶ They are anxious a great deal of the time, especially about their friend or relative with problems.

▶ They close out all of their own feelings because they are focused on other people's feelings.

Pia Mellody and colleagues (Mellody, Miller, & Miller, 1989) assert that people who suffer from codependence lack the necessary skills to lead mature, satisfying, adult lives. Codependents have difficulty experiencing positive self-esteem, setting psychological boundaries between themselves and others, and defining and meeting their own day-to-day needs. They become wrapped up in another person and in doing so suffer themselves and retard the growth of the other person. The problem of codependence is just being realized and evaluated. Mellody suggests a family-oriented therapeutic approach for treating codependence, and future research will evaluate this idea.

---

social change. A church or synagogue group, for example, could mobilize its senior citizens for a foster grandparent program.

Another key element of community psychology is **empowerment**—helping people to enhance existing skills and develop new skills, knowledge, and motivation so they can gain control over their own lives (Rappaport, 1987). Community psychology focuses on prevention, early intervention, planning, research, and evaluation. Community psychologists work in schools, churches, planning commissions, and prisons. They plan and set up programs for bringing psychological skills and knowledge into the community.

A special focus of community psychology is *primary prevention*—lowering the rate of new cases of a disorder or counteracting harmful circumstances that might lead to maladjustment. Primary prevention usually works on groups rather than on individuals. It may focus on an entire community, on mild-risk groups (such as children from families of low socioeconomic status), or on high-risk groups (such as children of schizophrenic parents).

Psychology as a Community Activity

In response to growing public awareness of mental health problems, a special kind of service agency—*the neighborhood clinic*—has been developed. Such clinics help

Empowerment: Facilitating the development of skills, knowledge, and motivation in individuals so they can act for themselves and gain control over their own lives.

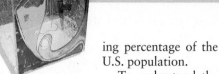

DIVERSITY

Asian Americans and Mental Health

Asian Americans are as difficult to characterize as a group as are African Americans or Protestants. That is, there are considerable differences within each group, including diversity in language, education, traditions, and socioeconomic levels. However, the Asian-American experience is typical of other ethnic experience, in that it brings a unique perspective to the study of psychology. By recognizing the cultural values—the diversity—of Asian Americans, this perspective raises psychologists' sensitivity and understanding of this rich cultural heritage. This is necessary because Asian Americans are a rapidly increasing percentage of the U.S. population.

To understand the mental health of Asian Americans, Tsai and Uemura (1988) assert, one must understand three core cultural values that shape the responses of Asian Americans to stress and to the world: family, harmony, and stoicism.

In traditional Asian culture, the *family* is the primary source of emotional support. The most important family relationship is not the global husband-wife-children relationship but the parent-child relationship. A person is defined by roles in the family, which include parent roles, grandparent roles, and child roles. A deferential and respectful relationship among family members to their elders is maintained, with an emphasis on the prescribed roles; these family roles and responsibilities provide support.

Harmony means keeping shame minimized and dignity intact. This is a key goal if an Asian American is to have a good relationship with family and self. Preserving dignity, or "face," maintains a person and the person's family and community. If everyone preserves such dignity, interpersonal harmony is optimized.

Asian Americans also rely on personal strength and a sense of *stoicism;* the open expression of emotion is discouraged. Restraint and emotional maturity mean suffering silently and suppressing emotions.

These three values—family, harmony, and stoicism—tend to keep

Community outreach programs seek to empower people to solve problems and improve life for all members of a community.

communities cope with problems created by mental illness, unemployment, and lack of education. Some clinics provide free, confidential treatment for such problems as drug addiction, alcoholism, and emotional and psychological disorders. They offer a variety of services, including partial hospitalization programs for people who require hospitalization during the day and outpatient care for people who live at home while receiving therapy. They also offer consultation, education programs, and lectures and literature on such topics as therapy, family planning, and drug rehabilitation.

Crisis intervention centers help people deal with short-term, stressful situations that require immediate therapeutic attention. Often, the crisis is a specific event; for example, a person may be contemplating suicide, or a woman may have been raped. The focus of crisis intervention is on the immediate circumstances, not on past experiences. Some studies show that crisis intervention therapy can be especially effective (Sawicki, 1988), but one problem in evaluating such therapy is that a variety of techniques are used, making controlled comparisons difficult (Slaikeu, 1990).

An important aim of community psychology is to serve all members of the community, including people who might not otherwise be able to afford the services of a psychotherapist or counselor. Community psychologists are change-oriented. Because they believe that some social conditions and organizational procedures result in maladjusted individuals, they often advocate changes in community institutions and organizations. For example, they seek to improve the court system, develop programs to prevent drug use in schools, help energy conservation groups

fore seeking outside help; they tend, as a group, to seek such help only in extreme crises. They are far more likely to ask for help from family, thus avoiding shame, maintaining harmony, and saving face by being stoic.

For example, Japanese Americans suffered many emotional problems during World War II, when they were incarcerated at the Manzanar relocation center in California. (Asian Americans were ordered by the U.S. government to be held in camps isolated from the rest of the population during the war.) Those who were confined at the Manzanar camp and at other, similar camps suffered with great dignity and stoicism; however, to this day, survivors of the camps still bear emotional burdens.

A challenge for community psychologists is to reach out to the Asian-American community by making psychological services available in a way that minimizes shame, improves family unity, and respects cultural differences. The therapeutic alliance that is established in the delivery of mental health services to Asian Americans must respect the Asian family, its life cycle, its traditions, and the types of problems presented to practitioners (McGoldrick et al., 1991). This often means that utilizing family bonds—perhaps through family therapy—is an effective technique, as is using traditional and familiar Asian-American philosophical traditions. We are not all one people with exactly the same needs.

Asian Americans from utilizing mental health services provided in the community (Tsai & Uemura, 1988). Asian Americans may subject themselves to enormous levels of stress be-

educate the public, consult with industry about reducing stress on the job, help churches develop volunteer programs to aid the homeless, and help hospitals set up preventive-medicine programs. The Diversity box explores the need for community psychology to take into account the importance of cultural values and beliefs when devising ways to help various communities.

Biologically Based Therapies

When an individual is referred to a practitioner for help, the usual approach involves some form of psychological treatment. This generally means a talking therapy that may be based on psychodynamic, humanistic, behavioral, or cognitive theories. However, for some patients, talking therapy is not enough. Some may be too depressed; others may be exhibiting symptoms of bipolar disorders (manic depression); still others may need hospitalization because they are suicidal.

This is where biologically based therapies enter the picture. These therapies may include medication, hospitalization, and the involvement of physicians. They are generally used in combination with traditional forms of psychotherapy—a multimodal approach. Biologically based therapies fall into three broad classes: psychosurgery (rarely used), electroconvulsive shock therapy (occasionally used), and drug therapies (often used).

Electroconvulsive shock therapy (ECT): [eel-ECK-tro-con-VUL-siv] A treatment for severe mental illness in which a brief application of electricity to the head is used to produce a generalized seizure. Also known as *shock treatment*.

Psychosurgery and Electroconvulsive Shock Therapy

Psychosurgery is brain surgery; it was used in the past to alleviate symptoms of mental disorders. A particular type of psychosurgery was commonly performed in the 1940s and 1950s: *prefrontal lobotomies*. They involved severing parts of the brain's frontal lobes from the rest of the brain. The frontal lobes were thought to control emotions; their removal destroyed connections within the brain, making patients docile. Patients lost the symptoms of their mental disorders, but they also became overly calm and completely unemotional. Some became unable to control their impulses, and an estimated 1 to 4 percent died from the operation.

Today, despite advances in technology and in the precision of the operation, psychosurgery is rarely used, for three basic reasons. First, drug therapy has proven more effective than surgical procedures. Second, the long-term effects of psychosurgery are questionable. Third, and most important, the procedure is irreversible and therefore morally objectionable to most practitioners and to patients and their families. Its earlier widespread use is considered by many to have been a serious mistake.

Electroconvulsive shock therapy (ECT), or *shock treatment*, once widely employed for depressed individuals, is a treatment for severe mental illness in which a brief application of electricity to the head is used to produce a generalized seizure (convulsion). The duration of the shock is less than a second, and patients are treated in 3 to 12 sessions over several weeks. In the 1940s and 1950s, ECT was routinely given to severely disturbed patients in mental hospitals. Unfortunately, it was often used on patients who did not need it (mostly women) and by overzealous physicians who wished to control unruly patients. Today, ECT is not a common treatment. According to the National Institutes of Health, fewer than 2.5 percent of all psychiatric hospital patients are treated with ECT.

Is ECT at all effective? Could drug therapy or traditional psychotherapy be used in its place? ECT is effective in the *short-term* management of severely depressed individuals and is sometimes used when a patient is at risk of suicide (Abrams, Swartz, & Vedak, 1991). However, its effects are only temporary if it is not followed by drug therapy and psychotherapy (Parker et al., 1992). Generally speaking, ECT should be used as a last resort, when other forms of treatment have been ineffective. ECT is not appropriate for treating schizophrenia or for managing unruly behaviors associated with other disorders.

The medical risk of death during the administration of ECT is low (Coffey et al., 1991). However, there is a potential for mem-

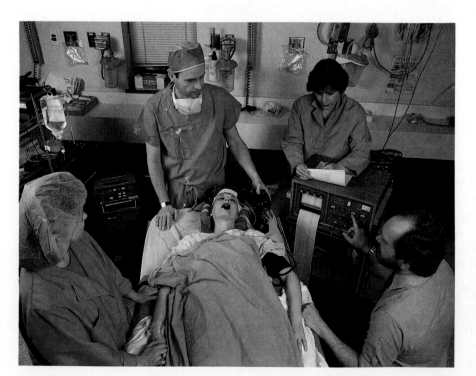

In electroconvulsive shock therapy, a mild electric current passes through the brain for less than a second, causing a brief seizure.

ory loss and for a decreased ability to learn and retain new information that may endure for several weeks. In addition, ECT may frighten patients and can leave them with feelings of shame and of being stigmatized.

If practitioners determine that ECT is warranted, the law requires (and medical ethics demands) that the patient has the right to accept or reject the treatment. Much more research is needed to determine the full effects of ECT and the groups for whom the treatment might be beneficial, if any (Pearlman, 1991).

Drug Therapy

Drug therapy attempts to manage psychological problems through the use of drugs. When physicians (often psychiatrists) administer drugs, people may experience relief from symptoms of anxiety, mania, depression, and schizophrenia. Drugs for the relief of mental problems are sometimes termed *psychotropic drugs;* they are usually grouped into four classes: antianxiety drugs, antidepressant drugs, antimania drugs, and antipsychotic drugs. See Table 15.5 for a list of some common drugs used to treat psychological disorders.

Antianxiety Drugs. Calming and anxiety reducing, antianxiety drugs, or tranquilizers, are mood-altering substances. Widely used in the United States (and probably overprescribed), these drugs (technically *anxiolytics*) reduce stressful feelings, calm patients, and lower excitability. Miltown, Tranxene, and Valium are trade names of the most widely prescribed drugs. When taken occasionally to help a person through a stressful situation, such drugs are useful. They also help manage anxiety in a person who is extremely anxious, particularly when the person is also receiving some form of psychotherapy. However, long-term use of antianxiety drugs

---

TABLE 15.5   *Common Drugs Used to Treat Psychological Disorders*

Effect Group	Chemical Group	Generic Name	Trade Name
Antianxiety (anxiolytic)	Propanediol	Meprobamate	Equanil Miltown
	Benzodiazepine	Clorazepate dipotassium Alprazolam Diazepam	Tranxene Xanax Valium
Antidepressant (thymoleptic)	Tricyclic	Amoxapine Nortriptyline Amitriptyline Imipramine Maprotiline	Asendin Aventyl Elavil Tofranil Ludiomil
	Monoamine oxidase inhibitor (MAO)	Phenelzine Tranylcypromine	Nardil Parnate
	Atypical antidepressant	Fluoxetine	Prozac
Antimania (thymoleptic)	Lithium carbonate	Lithium	Eskalith
Antipsychotic (neuroleptic)	Phenothiazine	Chlorpromazine Trifluoperazine Thioridazine	Thorazine Stelazine Mellaril
	Butyrophenone	Haloperidol	Haldol

without some adjunct therapy is usually ill-advised. Today, physicians are wary of patients seeking antianxiety drugs for management of daily stressors; they worry about substance abuse and an overreliance on drugs to get through the day.

Antidepressant Drugs. As their name suggests, antidepressants (technically *thymoleptics*) are sometimes considered mood elevators. They work by altering the level of neurotransmitters in the brain. The extremely depressed people who take antidepressants become more optimistic and less sad and often redevelop a sense of purpose in their lives. These medications allow many people to function outside a hospital setting. The drugs can take as long as 4 weeks to reach their full effectiveness, and daily use is necessary to maintain their benefit.

Antidepressants come from two major categories of drugs: tricylics and monoamine oxidase (MAO) inhibitors. Both types of drugs are potent. The tricylics are prescribed much more often than the MAO inhibitors because they pose less danger of medical complications. (Patients on MAO inhibitors have to adhere to special diets and some other restrictions to prevent adverse physical reactions to the drugs.) To help a patient suffering from a severe bout of depression, a physician might prescribe a commonly used tricyclic such as imipramine (Tofranil) or amitriptyline (Elavil), which works with fewer serious side effects and alleviates symptoms in the majority of people with depressive problems.

Research on the effects of antidepressant drugs is controversial. Some researchers assert their profound effects, and others report only modest help from the drugs (Greenberg et al., 1992). Research using double-blind and carefully controlled conditions continues. The impact of new research will be intense because the number of individuals with depressive disorders is substantial.

Antimania Drugs. Lithium carbonate, the only effective antimania drug (technically also a *thymoleptic*), has come into wide use for patients with bipolar (manic-depressive) disorders because it relieves the manic elements. Psychiatrists find that when a daily maintenance dose is taken, lithium is especially helpful in warding off future episodes of mania. The dosage of any drug is important, but in the case of lithium it is especially important. Too much produces noxious side effects; too little has no effect. No drug will cure depressive individuals of all their symptoms and solve all their problems; however, lithium allows patients to cope better, to control their symptoms, and to seek other therapies that allow them to manage their lifestyles in the most productive way possible.

Antipsychotic Drugs. Antipsychotic drugs (technically *neuroleptics*) are used mainly for people who suffer from the disabling disorder of schizophrenia. These drugs reduce hostility and aggression in violent patients and make their disorders more manageable. They also reduce delusions and allow some patients to manage life outside a hospital setting.

Most of the antipsychotic drugs prescribed are phenothiazines, the most common of which is chlorpromazine (Thorazine). They seem to work by altering the level and uptake of brain neurotransmitters—but this is uncertain (Goldenberg, 1990). As with antidepressants, dosages of antipsychotic drugs are crucial. Further, if patients are maintained on antipsychotic drugs for too long, other problems can emerge. One such problem is

FOCUS

► Why did community psychology emerge and what do community psychologists mean by *empowerment?* p. 561

► What are the ethical implications of psychosurgery and of electroconvulsive shock therapy (ECT)?   p. 564

► What are the major classes of drugs, and what evidence exists to show their effectiveness in which situations? pp. 565–566

APPLICATIONS

Talking Therapy, Drug Therapy, and Depression

Depression is the most common disorder seen by the medical, psychiatric, and psychological communities. Nearly 20 percent of the population will experience a depressive episode at one time or another. Women are twice as likely as men to be diagnosed as depressed; the aged are more likely than others to be depressed, as are widows and people with lower incomes (Coryell, Endicott, & Keller, 1992; Umberson, Wortman, & Kessler, 1992).

Treatment for depression has traditionally involved insight-oriented therapy, drug therapy, or a combination of the two. Insight therapy has been used to help patients gain an understanding of the causes of their feelings of sadness. Drug therapy has proven especially effective in altering brain activity in ways that alleviate depressive symptoms. Prozac and Norpramin are two popular and effective drugs. A commonly held belief of practitioners and theoreticians is that the most effective treatment is

drugs in combination with psychotherapy.

New research is challenging this traditionally held idea, however. In the last decade, psychologists have found that (1) psychotherapy is especially effective for depression; (2) the benefits of psychotherapy for depression are long-lasting; and (3) most important, combinations of psychotherapy and drug therapy are *not* necessarily more effective than either of the treatments alone. In an important review of the research literature on the treatment of depression, Robinson, Berman, and Neimeyer (1990), of Memphis State University, show that drug therapy alone and traditional psychotherapy alone are equally effective. Their finding startled some members of the psychological community because they challenged the long-held idea that combination treatments are the most effective. The three researchers acknowledge that drug therapy plus psychotherapy may be the most effective treatment for some other disorders. However, for the types of drugs they examined and with patients suffering from clinical depression, the result was clear: The combination treatment provided no additional benefit over drug therapy alone or psychotherapy alone.

The work of these researchers raises the question: How many widows, other women, and people from lower socioeconomic status are being given drugs when they don't need them? The answer is unclear; but with each passing month, new research on various types of depression and on the role of psychotherapy and drug therapy continues to emerge (Hollon, Shelton, & Loosen, 1991). For example, Wexler and Cicchetti (1992) assert that psychotherapy alone has the advantage. They add, however, that initial treatment with psychotherapy alone might perhaps be followed by combination treatment. We are likely to see other studies showing which types of depressive disorders can best benefit from drug therapy, which from traditional insight therapy, which from cognitive therapy, and which from combinations of drug therapy and traditional talking therapies.

tardive dyskinesia—a central nervous system disorder characterized by involuntary, spasmodic movements of the upper body, especially the face and fingers, and includes leg jiggling and tongue protrusions, facial ticks, and involuntary movements of the mouth and shoulders.

Drug therapy can be an effective method for treating a variety of disorders, but it is often sought out only after traditional forms of psychotherapy have been tried. It is sometimes used in combination with traditional talking therapy, as is shown in the Applications box.

Concluding Note

No matter what type of therapy is involved, certain key characteristics must be present in both therapist and client for therapeutic change to occur. A therapist who is knowledgeable, accepting, and objective can facilitate a client's behavior change, but it is always the client who makes the change.

In our fast-paced society, people seem to want quick fixes. Every 4 years, politicians promise a quick fix to the economy, a new plan to eliminate poverty, or a simple solution to racial tension. In the same manner, people often want to take drugs to alleviate emotional problems.

Drug therapy is an important form of treatment, especially for anxiety, depression, and schizophrenia. It is the most widely used biologically based therapy, and it is effective when used correctly and carefully.

But several key issues must be stressed. Dosages are especially important and must be monitored; too much or too little of certain drugs is dangerous. Long-term continued usage of many drugs is ill-advised. Further, no drug will permanently cure the maladjustments of people who are not coping well. Last, physicians and psychiatrists must be sensitive to the issues of overmedication and long-term dependence on drugs.

People with emotional problems usually need to reevaluate their situations, explore the causes of their behavior, and modify existing ideas and behaviors. For disorders such as schizophrenia, drugs are necessary; but for the day-to-day stresses of modern life, drug therapy must be used with extreme caution.

Summary & Review

Therapy Comes in Many Forms

What is psychotherapy?

Psychotherapy is the treatment of emotional or behavioral problems through psychological techniques.   p. 536

What is a placebo effect?

A *placebo effect* is a nonspecific therapeutic change that occurs as a result of a person's expectations of change rather than as a direct result of a certain treatment.   p. 538

KEY TERMS: *psychotherapy,* p. 536; *placebo effect,* p. 538.

Psychodynamic Therapy

Distinguish between insight and behavior therapies.

Insight therapies, including *psychodynamically based therapies,* assume that maladjustment and abnormal behavior are caused by people's failure to understand their own motivations and needs. Insight therapists believe that once patients understand the motivations that produce maladjusted behavior, the behavior can be changed. Behavior therapists apply learning principles to produce specific changes in behavior. They concentrate on changing people's overt behaviors rather than on understanding their unconscious motivations.   p. 540

According to psychoanalysis, what causes maladjustment and what are some processes involved in treatment?

According to classical Freudian psychoanalysis, conflicts among a person's unconscious thoughts and processes produce maladjusted behavior. Treatment often involves the process of *interpretation, resistance* to interpretation, and *transference;* collectively, these processes are referred to as *working through.*   pp. 541–542

KEY TERMS: *psychoanalysis,* p. 540; *psychodynamically based therapies,* p. 540; *insight therapy,* p. 540; *free association,* p. 541; *dream analysis,* p. 541; *interpretation,* p. 541; *resistance,* p. 542; *transference,* p. 542; *working through,* p. 542; *ego analysts,* p. 542.

Humanistic Therapies

What are the goals and major treatment techniques of client-centered therapy?

Client-centered therapy aims to help clients realize their potential by learning to evaluate the world and themselves from their own point of view. The approach is *nondirective* and includes a therapist who conveys unconditional positive regard while letting the client set the agenda for therapy. pp. 544–545

What are the goals of Gestalt therapy?

Gestalt therapy encourages individuals to get in touch with their current feelings and become aware of their current situations. Gestalt techniques are designed to help clients become more alert to their significant feelings and to their surroundings. pp. 545–546

KEY TERMS: *client-centered therapy,* p. 544; *nondirective therapy,* p. 544; *Gestalt therapy,* p. 545.

Behavior Therapy

What is behavior therapy?

Behavior therapy is a therapy based on the application of learning principles to human behavior. It is synonymous with *behavior modification* and focuses on changing overt behaviors rather than on understanding subjective feelings, unconscious processes, or motivations. It focuses on replacing old behaviors with new, more adaptive ones.   pp. 547–548

What is systematic desensitization?

Systematic desensitization is a typically three-stage counterconditioning procedure in which a person is taught to relax while imagining increasingly fearful situations.   p. 552

In what areas is modeling especially effective?

According to social learning theory, modeling as a technique is especially effective in three areas: (1) learning new behavior; (2) helping to eliminate fears, especially phobias; and (3) expressing already existing behavior.   p. 553

KEY TERMS: *behavior therapy,* p. 547; *symptom substitution,* p. 548; *token economy,* p. 549; *time-out,* p. 550; *counterconditioning,* p. 551; *systematic desensitization,* p. 552; *aversive counterconditioning,* p. 552.

Cognitive Therapy

What are the three basic propositions of cognitive therapy?

The three basic propositions are (1) cognitive activity affects behavior, (2) cognitive activity can be monitored, and (3) behavior changes can be effected through cognitive changes. pp. 553–554

Describe the key characteristics of rational-emotive therapy.

Rational-emotive therapy emphasizes the role of logical, rational thought processes in behavior. It assumes that

continued

Summary & Review

faulty, irrational thinking patterns are the cause of abnormal behavior. pp. 554–555

KEY TERMS: *rational-emotive therapy,* p. 554; *brief intermittent therapy,* p. 558.

Group Therapy

What is group therapy, and how are its techniques determined?

Group therapy is therapy used to treat several people simultaneously for emotional and behavioral problems. The techniques used by a therapy group are determined by the nature of the group and the orientation of its therapist. pp. 556–557

What do family therapists attempt to achieve in therapy?

Family therapists attempt to change family systems. Treatment takes place within an ongoing, active social system such as a marriage or family, be-cause individuals affect family processes and family processes affect individuals. pp. 559–560

KEY TERMS: *group therapy,* p. 556; *psychodrama,* p. 559; *encounter group,* p. 559; *family therapy,* p. 559.

Community Psychology

What are the goals of community psychologists?

Community psychologists seek to provide psychological services to people who might not otherwise seek them. The general aims of community psychologists are (1) to empower people, (2) to strengthen existing social support networks, and (3) to stimulate the formation of new networks to meet new challenges. pp. 560–561

KEY TERMS: *community psychology,* p. 560; *empowerment,* p. 561.

Biologically Based Therapies

What are the major types of biologically based therapies?

The major types of biologically based therapies are psychosurgery, electroconvulsive shock therapy, and drug therapy. Psychosurgery (brain surgery) is a generally outmoded method of treatment used to alleviate symptoms of mental disorders. *Electroconvulsive shock therapy* (ECT) is a treatment for severe mental illness in which a brief application of electricity to the head is used to produce a generalized seizure. Drugs for the relief of mental problems are usually grouped into four classes: anti-anxiety drugs, antidepressant drugs, antipsychotic drugs, and antimania drugs. pp. 563–566

KEY TERM: *electroconvulsive shock therapy,* p. 564.

CONNECTIONS

If you are interested in...

Freud's theory of psychoanalysis as a therapeutic approach, see ...

CHAPTER 12, pp. 427–433

Freud's theory of personality, which later developed into a full-blown treatment approach.

▼

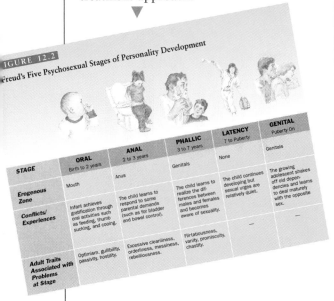

IGURE 12.2
Freud's Five Psychosexual Stages of Personality Development

STAGE	ORAL Birth to 2 years	ANAL 2 to 3 years	PHALLIC 3 to 7 years	LATENCY 7 to Puberty	GENITAL Puberty On
Erogenous Zone	Mouth	Anus	Genitals	None	Genitals
Conflicts/ Experiences	Infant achieves gratification through oral activities such as feeding, thumb sucking, and cooing.	The child learns to respond to some parental demands (such as for bladder and bowel control).	The child learns to realize the differences between males and females and becomes aware of sexuality.	The child continues developing but sexual urges are relatively quiet.	The growing adolescent shakes off old dependencies and learns to deal maturely with the opposite sex.
Adult Traits Associated with Problems at Stage	Optimism, gullibility, passivity, hostility.	Excessive cleanliness, orderliness, messiness, rebelliousness.	Flirtatiousness, vanity, promiscuity, chastity.	—	—

CHAPTER 12, pp. 432–433

How defense mechanisms are often overused by individuals in need of therapy.

The behavioral approach to therapy, see ...

CHAPTER 1, pp. 10–11

How early behaviorists focused only on overt, observable behavior.

CHAPTER 5, pp. 159–189, 193–195

Classical conditioning, operant conditioning, and modeling, which can help explain long-standing behaviors—some of which may become maladaptive. ▶

CHAPTER 14, p. 521

How disorders such as depression often have a cognitive basis, which requires a change in thought processes and overt behavior.

Biological approaches to therapy, see ...

CHAPTER 2, pp. 49–50, 65–69

How certain chemicals in the blood and brain that affect behavior can be used as part of a multi-modal treatment approach.

CHAPTER 13, pp. 471–479 ▶

How stress can lead to a number of health-related issues that can be alleviated in part through psychotherapy and in part through drug treatments.

CHAPTER 14, p. 520

Depression's biological basis and how it can sometimes be alleviated through drug therapy.

16

The Social World

In 1978, a team of 40 eminent scientists assembled in Turin, Italy, to study a yellowed, 14-foot strip of linen bearing the ghostly imprint of a bearded man wearing a crown of thorns. Purported to be Christ's burial cloth, the Shroud of Turin has been worshipped by multitudes since its earliest known exhibition in 1354. After 6 days of extensive testing—including X-ray fluorescence, surface sampling, photographic computer analysis, and image enhancement—the scientists announced that the cloth's imprint was not paint or pigment and may have resulted from a brief flash of radiation emanating from a body. In a news service interview, the team's leader said, "Every one of the scientists I have talked to believes the cloth is authentic." Convinced that the shroud was genuine, one Jewish member of the scientific team converted to Christianity.

In the fall of 1988, the Vatican permitted small swatches of the shroud to be submitted to a new carbon-14 dating technique (earlier carbon-14 procedures would have destroyed too much of the cloth). All three laboratories that analyzed the linen concluded it was woven between 12 and 13 centuries after Christ's death. One expert declared the shroud to be the work of a brilliant medieval hoaxer. However, the new scientific proof didn't shake the faith of those who ardently believed the shroud legend. Some believers questioned the accuracy of carbon-14 dating; others said that the image—regardless of its age—was created by a miracle.

The Shroud of Turin case exemplifies how human beings acquire, maintain, and change their attitudes. Preliminary "proof" of the shroud's authenticity convinced one well-educated man to change his long-standing religious beliefs. Yet even stronger scientific evidence debunking the shroud proved unpersuasive to others. Why would people hold such strong and different attitudes about a piece of cloth?

Social psychology is the study of how individuals influence and are influenced by the thoughts, feelings, and behaviors of other individuals. Although it may not always be apparent, your behavior is directly affected by the social world in which you live. Look at what you are wearing right now. Look at what other people are wearing. Are the similarities only a matter of chance? On a grander scale, in the 1992 presidential election, George Bush came to be seen as out of touch with middle America, particularly on such issues as the economy, health care, family leave, and women's concerns. How was this image created? How did it come to be adopted by a majority of voters?

In this chapter, we will look at some of the traditional concepts in social psychology: attitudes, social cognition, and social influence. These concepts help us form an understanding of behavior when more than one person is involved—that is, of our social world. Our focus will be on how individual behavior is affected by other people. We will begin with attitudes.

Attitudes

In 1989, the film *Roger and Me* tried to shape public opinion (attitudes) toward General Motors, its leadership, corporate America, and the plight of U.S. workers in general. Its message, "The American dream is dead," had a profound impact not only on morale at General Motors but on public debates about the path of American industry (Bateman, Sakano, & Fujita, 1992).

Attitudes are lasting patterns of feelings, beliefs, and behavior tendencies toward other people, ideas, or objects which are based in our experiences and shape our future behavior; they are usually evaluative and serve certain functions (Eagly & Chaiken, 1993). They determine whether we will respond to a given situation positively or negatively, with enthusiasm or reluctance. Our attitudes are shaped by how other people perceive us and by how we think other people see us. Social psychologists are concerned with how the behavior and attitudes of others influence an individual's behavior. For example, the scientist who underwent the religious conversion while studying the Shroud of Turin was undoubtedly influenced by the beliefs of his fellow investigators. Moreover, his attitude toward the shroud was shaped by professional training that made the existing scientific proof very convincing.

Dimensions and Functions of Attitudes

Attitudes reflect experiences, beliefs, and behaviors from our past and they involve feelings, often evaluative, that are long-lasting. However, they represent more than just feelings; they serve a function. They help guide new behaviors and help people interpret the world efficiently.

Attitudes are generally considered to have three dimensions each of which serves a function; the dimensions are cognitive, emotional, and behavioral. The *cognitive*

Social psychology: The study of how individuals influence and are influenced by the thoughts, feelings, and behaviors of other individuals.

Attitudes: Lasting patterns of feelings, beliefs, and behavior tendencies toward other people, ideas, or objects which are based in our experiences, shape our future behavior, are evaluative in nature, and serve certain functions.

dimension of attitudes consists of thoughts and beliefs, such as the belief that science or religious faith can reveal truths. The *emotional dimension* involves evaluative feelings such as like or dislike. For example, some people may like the idea that the Shroud of Turin is authentic because it makes them feel more spiritual. The *behavioral dimension* is how people show their evaluative beliefs and feelings (Eagly, 1992), such as by publicly announcing the shroud's authenticity or undergoing a religious conversion.

When people form attitudes about a group of people, a series of events, or a political philosophy, those attitudes serve a function by helping them categorize, process, and remember the people, events, and philosophy (Hymes, 1986). When people have strongly held attitudes and adopt a specific belief, they are said to have a *conviction*. Once people acquire a conviction, they think about it, become involved with it, and may become emotional over it (which makes convictions long-lasting and resistant to change). This is especially true of religious and political convictions (Abelson, 1988). For example, despite strong scientific evidence to the contrary, many people still believe that the Shroud of Turin was Christ's burial cloth. Further, once people have adopted a conviction, they use it to guide a wide range of behaviors and to process new information about events in the world.

Individuals do not always publicly display their attitudes, especially when their attitudes are not yet firmly established or when their attitudes and behaviors are inconsistent. For example, despite widespread support of a nuclear arms freeze, few people give their time, energy, or money to organizations that support this cause (Gilbert, 1988). What variables determine when attitudes are displayed or changed? Why are some attitudes hard to modify and others relatively easy? Most important, how are attitudes formed?

Forming Attitudes

Attitudes are formed through learning that begins early in life. Thus, psychologists rely on learning theories to explain how children form attitudes. Three learning theory concepts that help explain attitude formation are classical conditioning, operant conditioning, and observational learning (see chapter 5 for a detailed explanation of these concepts).

Classical Conditioning. The pairing of people, events, and ideologies with attitudes often goes unnoticed because it is so effortless. However, such pairings can shape children's views and emotional responses to the world, thereby forming the basis of their attitudes as both children and adults. (See Figure 16.1 on page 576 for an application of this process.) For example, suppose a child overhears a parent make a negative comment about a neighbor. Classical conditioning pairs the formerly neutral stimulus (neighbor) with an unconditioned stimulus (negative comment). Because negative comments naturally elicit negative feelings as a response, we treat the resulting negative feelings as an unconditioned response. If the child overhears such remarks repeatedly, the neighbor eventually evokes a negative response (now a conditioned response) in the child.

Operant Conditioning. A key principle of operant conditioning is that reinforced behaviors are likely to recur; this principle helps explain how attitudes are maintained over time. In socializing their children, parents express and reinforce ideas and behaviors consistent with their own "correct" view of the world. Such expression and reinforcement help children adopt the parents' "correct" attitudes.

Observational Learning. According to the concept of observational learning, people establish attitudes by watching the behavior of someone they consider significant and then imitating that behavior. The new attitudes people learn eventually

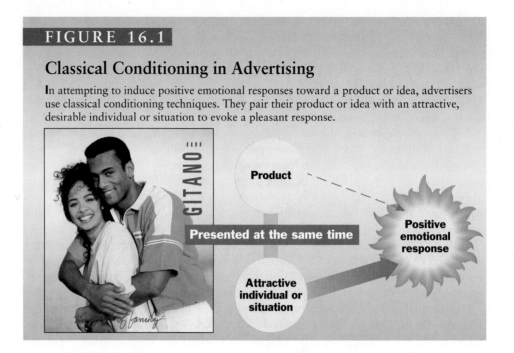

FIGURE 16.1

Classical Conditioning in Advertising

In attempting to induce positive emotional responses toward a product or idea, advertisers use classical conditioning techniques. They pair their product or idea with an attractive, desirable individual or situation to evoke a pleasant response.

become their own. Suppose that a young girl sees her father react angrily to a television news story that contradicts the family's religious faith. The next time the child hears a similar argument, she will likely mimic her father's attitude.

Predicting Behavior from Attitudes

Social psychologists can assess people's attitudes, but whether those attitudes predict behavior depends on a number of variables. Among these variables are attitude strength, vested interest, specificity of attitudes, and accessibility of attitudes.

Attitude Strength. Attitudes are better predictors of behavior when they are strongly held and there are few competing outside influences, such as conflicting advertising appeals and advice from friends. A Catholic man who believes strongly in religious miracles will more readily accept the Shroud of Turin's authenticity if he hears only arguments supporting that attitude.

Vested Interest. Attitudes people consider personally important (in which they have a vested interest) are more likely to be shown in behavior and to stay intact, regardless of how situations change over time (Krosnick, 1988). Behavior is also more likely to follow from attitudes if the attitudes are established by personal experience. People who have experienced job hiring discrimination firsthand are more likely to base their own hiring practices on applicants' actual qualifications than are people who were never unfairly denied employment (Fazio & Zanna, 1981).

Specificity of Attitudes. Attitudes are more likely to foretell behavior when they are specific and the situation requiring a decision closely matches the situation to which the attitude applies. For example, general attitudes about a healthy environment have less impact on an individual's behavior than do specific attitudes about littering or recycling (Ajzen & Fishbein, 1977). Global attitudes do not predict specific behaviors very well. For example, a person may have a broad attitude about politics; but only a specific attitude about health care, welfare reform, or government waste will predict voting behavior toward a specific candidate.

Accessibility of Attitudes. Attitudes predict behavior best when they are accessible and easily remembered (Fazio, 1989, 1990). When people know their attitudes about a political candidate's various positions, they can easily decide how favorably they rate the candidate. When their views about a person are not easily remembered, making such judgments is more time-consuming and less reliable.

Changing Attitudes

Just as people learn attitudes, they can unlearn them and learn new ones. New attitudes may impel a person to try a particular brand of soap, vote Democratic, or undergo a religious conversion.

A common avenue by which people's attitudes change is the mass media, particularly television. The goal of television commercials is to either change or reinforce people's behavior. Commercials exhort viewers to drink Pepsi, not Coke; to drive a Volvo instead of a Saab; to say no to drugs; or to vote for a Democrat instead of a Republican. Their appeal may be cognitive (one product tastes better than the other) or emotional (owning this product will make you feel proud). Whatever their appeal, commercials aim to influence people's convictions and overt behavior. Research shows that television advertising is the most influential medium of attitude change in the Western world; this is no surprise given the fact that, in the average American household, the television is on for more than 4 hours every day (Huston, Watkins, & Kunkel, 1989).

To change an attitude, a person must be motivated and receptive. Moreover, the person who wishes to effect the change—the communicator—must be persuasive. Social psychologists have identified four components of attitude change: the communicator, the communication, the medium, and the audience.

The Communicator. To be persuasive, a communicator—the person trying to influence the attitude change—must project integrity, credibility, and trustworthiness. If people don't trust, respect, or like the communicator, they are unlikely to change their attitudes. An unknown conservationist is less likely to convince an audience of the importance of preserving wildlife than is a well-known scientist such as Carl Sagan.

Researchers find that the perceived power, prestige, celebrity, prominence, and degree of attractiveness of the communicator are extremely important (Chaiken & Eagly, 1983). For example, the Surgeon General has a greater ability to change your views about cigarette smoking in the workplace than does a local school board member. Yet a speaker who is regarded as knowledgeable and important but who speaks inexpertly or uses too technical a vocabulary is not likely to effect attitude change (Lee & Ofshe, 1981).

Information received from friends is considered more influential than information from the communications media. Costanzo and colleagues (1986, p. 528) suggest, "Media sources are effective in creating awareness of a new technology, but interpersonal sources exert a far greater influence on the decision to adopt a new technology." Leonard-Barton (1981) showed that the best predictor of whether a customer will purchase solar energy equipment is the number of the person's acquaintances who currently own such devices. Similarly, a teenager is more likely to follow a close friend's advice on the use of condoms than that of an unknown public health official (Jaccard et al., 1990).

Well-trained communicators can be especially effective. In a research study promoting energy conservation (Gonzales, Aronson, & Costanzo, 1988), energy auditors were specially trained to change attitudes and help people effectively conserve home energy. The auditors learned to communicate vividly, personalize their recommendations, get their clients involved, and induce a sense of economic loss through inaction on the part of the homeowners. Their training had dramatic results. Clients were more likely to become involved in energy conservation measures when the home auditor had the special training. They were also more likely to be involved if they thought about their new knowledge and set out to tell others about it (Boninger et al., 1990).

The Communication. A clear, convincing, and logical argument is the most effective tool for changing attitudes—especially attitudes with emotional content, such as those concerning capital punishment, abortion, or school desegregation (Millar & Millar, 1990). Attitude change is more likely when the targeted attitude is not too different from an existing one; it is also more likely when the audience is not highly involved with a particular point of view (Johnson & Eagly, 1989). Research shows that people who expect to receive the content of a new idea are likely to exhibit attitude change (Boninger et al., 1990). Thus, political candidates can influence voters to vote for them when their ideas are consistent with those of the voters. Changing the ideas of politically involved citizens is more difficult than altering those of noninvolved citizens (Johnson & Eagly, 1989; Ottati, Fishbein, & Middlestadt, 1988).

Communicating fear is effective in motivating attitude change, especially when health issues are concerned and the communicator does not overdo the fear appeal (Robberson & Rogers, 1988). For example, think of some of the antismoking ads you've seen on television. What techniques do they use to induce fear? Fear works; we know that college students who come to fear AIDS are more likely to use condoms (Boyd & Wandersman, 1991) and that fear of cancer can be motivating in some situations (Wandersman & Hallman, 1993). Fear approaches work well in changing people's attitudes about their health, but positive approaches stressing enhanced self-esteem also work well—and sometimes better—especially when combined with the positive influence of peers (Robberson & Rogers, 1988).

Researchers have found that if people hear a persuasive message often enough, they begin to believe it, regardless of its validity. Repeated exposure to certain situations can also change attitudes (R. F. Bornstein, 1989). For example, after seeing numerous commercials that show one battery brand outperforming the competition, a television viewer may change his attitude toward the product from neutral to positive. Similarly, a name that is heard more often is more likely to be liked than is one heard infrequently; this is called the *mere exposure effect* (Jacoby et al., 1989).

The Medium. The way in which communication is presented—its medium—influences people's receptiveness to change. For example, face-to-face communication has more impact than communication through television or in writing. Thus, although candidates for public office rely heavily on TV, radio, and printed ads, they also try to meet people face-to-face. Bill Clinton's bus tours through the country during the 1992 presidential campaign proved to be an especially effective way to get his message across to people. Even the location of the delivery of the message is important; messages delivered from a church pulpit have more impact than those delivered in a bowling alley.

The Audience. From time to time, people actually want to have their attitudes changed, and they seek out alternative views. At other times, they fold their arms across their chest and announce, "It's going to take an act of Congress to change my mind" (Johnson & Eagly, 1989). This is in part age-related. People are most susceptible to attitude changes in their early adult years; susceptibility to change drops off in later years (Krosnick & Alwin, 1989). People of high intelligence are less likely to have their opinions changed, and those of high self-esteem tend to be similarly unyielding (Rhodes & Wood, 1992).

Changing attitudes, and ultimately behavior, can be difficult if people have well-established habits (which often come with advancing age) or are highly motivated in the opposite direction. Consider attitudes toward seat belts. Although people believe in the effectiveness of seat belts and hold positive attitudes about using them, few people use them all the time. Mittal (1988) showed that getting people to use seat belts takes more than developing positive attitudes; it also takes instilling a use habit. Mittal argues that the more often people use seat belts, the more likely they will be to use them in the future. Thus, education and devices to promote remembering (such as warning buzzers) can be helpful (Geller, Patterson, & Talbot, 1982).

Finally, people in a good mood are more likely than others to pay attention to a message and have their attitudes changed (Bless, Mackie, & Schwarz, 1992). The idea that the message and emotional factors are separate elements that have separate effects is highlighted in the elaboration likelihood model, which we'll examine in the next section.

> **Elaboration likelihood model:**
> A theory of attitude change suggesting that there are two routes to persuasion: central, which focuses on thoughtful, elaborative considerations; and peripheral, which focuses on less careful, more emotional, and even superficial considerations.

Cognitive Approaches to Attitude Change

Decades of research have identified the components of attitude change. But for all of our knowledge about when and how persuasion takes place, only recently have researchers begun to focus on what happens to the individuals whose attitudes are being changed. What are their thought processes, and what other events affect attitude change?

Elaboration Likelihood Model. Researchers have long known that mood affects attitude change. People in a good mood are more receptive to change; however, motivation and ability to think about relevant arguments are also important. Richard Petty and John Cacioppo (1981, 1985) have presented an **elaboration likelihood model**—a theory of attitude change suggesting that there are two routes to persuasion: central and peripheral. (See Figure 16.2 for an overview of their model.)

The *central route* emphasizes conscious and direct information concerning a given issue. It relies on how effective, authoritative, and logical a communication is. Confronted with scientific evidence that the Shroud of Turin is only 6 centuries old, many people would conclude through the central route that the relic is not Christ's burial cloth. That is, unless they were highly motivated to believe otherwise, they

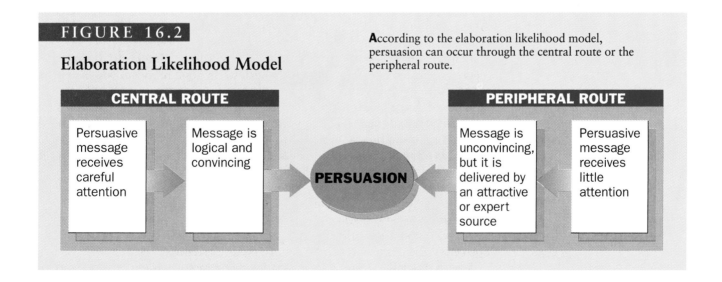

FIGURE 16.2

Elaboration Likelihood Model

According to the elaboration likelihood model, persuasion can occur through the central route or the peripheral route.

CENTRAL ROUTE

Persuasive message receives careful attention → Message is logical and convincing → **PERSUASION**

PERIPHERAL ROUTE

PERSUASION ← Message is unconvincing, but it is delivered by an attractive or expert source ← Persuasive message receives little attention

would conclude that the scientific arguments against the shroud's authenticity are too strong to refute.

The *peripheral route* emphasizes less careful, more emotional, and even superficial considerations. This route has an indirect but very powerful effect, especially when there are no convincing or powerful arguments that can force the use of the central route—for example, in political messages (DeBono, 1992; Petty et al., 1993). Whether a person accepts a message depends on how the person perceives its pleasantness, its delivery, its similarity to well-established personal attitudes, and the communicator. The peripheral route may convince someone that the Shroud of Turin is not genuine; but in this case, the attitude change stems largely from emotional rather than logical arguments and therefore may not be long-lasting (Petty et al., 1993). For example, the person may doubt the shroud's authenticity only because a respected religious leader has expressed such doubt. Whether or not a person changes an attitude depends in large part on what functions the attitude serves.

Attitude Functions. When people hold a strong conviction, they can use their attitude to help them organize the world. Cognitive researchers assert that attitudes serve a function. They can help individuals to categorize events as good or bad and to process information. Attitudes also permit people to hold a group of values or beliefs; thus, they are ways by which people express their identity. Still another function of attitudes is to help people maintain their self-esteem by preferring their own attitudes or beliefs to those held by other people.

Whether a person is willing to change attitudes depends on the functions of the attitude and how and when a persuasive message is delivered. The passage of time can increase the impact of some messages, a phenomenon we will consider next.

Delayed Attitude Change: The Sleeper Effect

Are you influenced to buy shampoo A instead of shampoo B after watching a television commercial? Do you choose tire X instead of tire Z after reading ads in your daily newspaper? Can you think of one particular ad campaign that has had a long-term effect on your attitude and behavior? Persuasive messages can change a person's attitudes, but the effectiveness usually decreases as time passes. However, in the 1940s, psychologists discovered that, in some cases, the passage of time can *increase* the impact of some messages because of the sleeper effect. According to the *sleeper effect,* the impact of a message delivered by a highly credible source decreases as time passes, but the impact of a message delivered by a source of low credibility can actually increase over time.

Consider, for example, the 1992 Bush versus Clinton presidential campaign. Suppose you held the view that President Bush was a good president who had done important things for the country. During the campaign, you saw supermarket tabloids espousing him as the greatest president of all time. Because you held such supermarket tabloids in disdain, you discounted the message. As time passed, however, you forgot who proclaimed Bush to be a national hero and you were moved to believe it, even more than before. The source of the message was forgotten, but the message was not. This is the sleeper effect.

For the sleeper effect to occur, the message must have a high impact, the low-credibility source must be discounted, and the relationship between the message and its deliverer must be dissociated over time (Gruder et al., 1978). Because of these limiting conditions, the effect is hard to substantiate (Greenwald et al., 1986). Nonetheless, there is new research confirming its existence.

When a discounting cue (a cue indicating that a message is not credible, such as a counterargument or an undermining of source credibility) is presented *after* a message (instead of before, as is usually the case), reliable sleeper effects can be discerned more easily, according to Ohio State University researchers A. R. Pratkanis and colleagues (1988). They showed that sleeper effects are obtainable and more easily explainable through what they termed a differential decay interpretation. The *differential decay interpretation* suggests that the sleeper effect is obtained when the message and the discounting cue have opposite, but nearly equal, immediate impacts that are not well-integrated into memory. For the sleeper effect to occur, the discounting cue (say, the earlier-mentioned message from a low-class tabloid) must be received after or simultaneously with the message. But the impact of the cue *decays* (lessens) faster than the message does (you continue to remember the idea that Bush was the greatest president of all time). With the faster decay rate of the negative influence of the discounting cue, sleeper effects can be obtained. Although someday another interpretation may more powerfully describe and explain the sleeper effect, the current one is fairly convincing and based on well-done cognitive research.

That people's thoughts determine their actions is seen especially clearly when people are placed in situations where there are inconsistencies in beliefs or behavior, the topic we will consider next.

Searching for Cognitive Consistency

Although basic ideas about life and morals are established early, attitudes continually develop and change. Some people seek change, trying to keep pace with friends or relatives; others resist change. Most people try to maintain consistency among their various attitudes and between their attitudes and behavior. Consistency leads to orderly living and enables people to make decisions about future behavior without having to filter out numerous alternatives (Cialdini, 1993).

Cognitive Dissonance. Imagine the dilemma faced by the Jewish scientist who converted to Christianity on the basis of preliminary proof of the Shroud of Turin's authenticity. As a scientist, he must have found the physical evidence of the shroud compelling; as a Jew, he must have been bewildered by the apparent proof of Christ's divinity. How could he reconcile these opposite attitudes? Moreover, what further confusion did he suffer when he later learned that the cloth was not really Christ's shroud?

Whenever our attitudes conflict with one another or with our behavior, we feel uncomfortable. For example, if a student believes he should be saving part of his income toward tuition but spends every dime of it, his attitudes and behavior conflict. He may feel uncomfortable or even upset. Leon Festinger (1919–1989) termed this feeling as **cognitive dissonance**—the state of discomfort that results when a discrepancy exists among two or more of a person's beliefs or between a person's beliefs and overt behavior.

On the basis of the concept that people seek to reduce dissonance, Festinger (1957) proposed a cognitive dissonance theory. According to the theory, when people experience conflict among their attitudes or between their attitudes and their behavior, they are motivated to change either their attitudes or their behavior. (See Figure 16.3 on page 582.) For example, suppose you are a strong proponent of animal rights. You support the American Society for the Prevention of Cruelty to Animals (ASPCA) and Greenpeace, refrain from eating meat, and are repulsed by fur coats. Then you win a raffle and are awarded a stylish black leather coat. Wearing the coat goes against your beliefs; but it feels good, you know it looks great on you, and all your friends admire it. According to cognitive dissonance theory, you are experiencing conflict between your attitudes (animal rights) and your behavior (wearing the coat). To relieve the conflict, you either stop wearing the coat or modify your beliefs. (Some psychologists consider cognitive dissonance theory a type of motivation theory because people become energized to do something.)

Cognitive dissonance: [COG-nuh-tiv DIS-uh-nins] A state in which individuals feel uncomfortable because they hold two or more thoughts, attitudes, or behaviors that are inconsistent with one another.

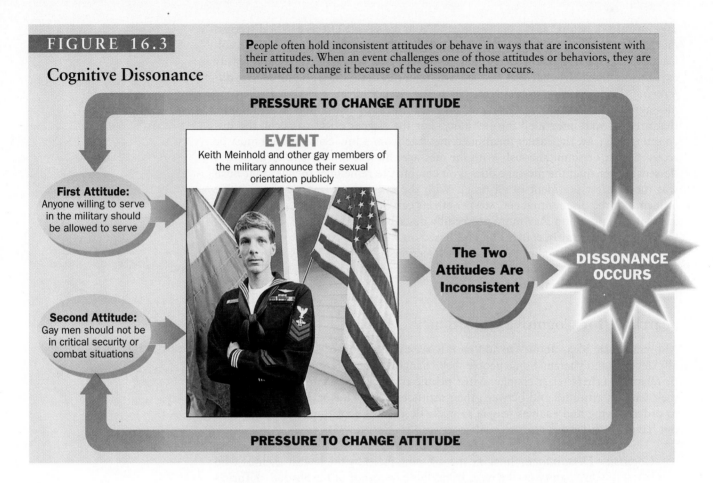

FIGURE 16.3

Cognitive Dissonance

People often hold inconsistent attitudes or behave in ways that are inconsistent with their attitudes. When an event challenges one of those attitudes or behaviors, they are motivated to change it because of the dissonance that occurs.

PRESSURE TO CHANGE ATTITUDE

EVENT
Keith Meinhold and other gay members of the military announce their sexual orientation publicly

First Attitude:
Anyone willing to serve in the military should be allowed to serve

Second Attitude:
Gay men should not be in critical security or combat situations

The Two Attitudes Are Inconsistent

DISSONANCE OCCURS

PRESSURE TO CHANGE ATTITUDE

Research supports Festinger's claim that, for an attitude or behavior to change, negative consequences (dissonance) have to be associated with the maintenance of existing attitudes or behaviors. But other studies find that people often engage in activities that help reduce their cognitive discomfort without changing an inconsistent set of beliefs (Steele, 1975). A smoker, for example, might take up jogging to improve his cardiovascular health but still not change his dissonant smoking habit.

An Alternative to Cognitive Dissonance Theory. Although cognitive dissonance theory has wide popularity, not all psychologists subscribe to it. Social psychologist Daryl Bem (1972) claims that people do not change their attitudes because of internal states such as dissonance. He has proposed instead **self-perception theory**—an approach to attitude formation in which people are assumed to not understand the causes of their own attitudes and behavior—to infer their attitudes and emotional states and the causes of their behavior from the situations in which they find themselves. According to Bem, people can perceive their behavior only after the fact and in the context in which it occurred; that is, they can interpret their behavior only in a situational context. His approach suggests that people simply look at their behavior and say, "If I behaved in this way, I must have had this (consistent) attitude." See Figure 16.4 for a comparison of the traditional view of attitude formation with Bem's view.

Bem's research is supported to some extent by the work of Stanley Schachter (which we reviewed in chapter 11). Schachter showed that subjects infer aspects of their emotional states from both their physical states and the situations in which they find themselves. A subject who is physically aroused and surrounded by happy people reports feeling happy. A subject who is physically aroused and in a tense situation reports feeling angry.

Self-perception theory: An approach to attitude formation in which people are assumed to infer their attitudes on the basis of observations of their own behavior.

Bem's self-perception model is a distinct theoretical alternative to Festinger's cognitive dissonance theory. But research supports both theories. For example, Tybout and Scott (1983) investigated what happened to attitudes when information about the taste of a product was provided or withheld. They discovered that when information was available, internal states (such as beliefs and predispositions) were the keys to attitude formation and change, much as Festinger suggests. However, when information was unavailable, subjects used a process of self-perception (such as that described by Bem) to determine their attitudes.

People may infer not only their own attitudes but also the thoughts and attitudes of other people. This is the substance of balance theory, which we will examine next.

Balance Theory. According to **balance theory,** we prefer satisfying and harmonious relationships between our beliefs and the beliefs of others whom we like. For instance, if Don likes both Paula and heavy metal music, he will be in a state of cognitive balance if he thinks Paula also likes heavy metal music. However, he will be in a state of imbalance if he thinks Paula does not like heavy metal music (see Figure 16.5).

Like cognitive dissonance theory, balance theory can be considered a motivation theory. The unpleasant tension that results from disagreement motivates people to change. Also, like cognitive dissonance theory, balance theory assumes that people are decision makers whose thoughts ultimately determine their behavior.

According to balance theory, people who wish to maintain stable, balanced relationships must agree with each other in order to avoid unpleasant situations. In fact, research studies on balance theory have shown that friendships are based, in part, on the extent of the perceived agreement between two friends regarding which of their other acquaintances are acceptable. Suppose, for example, Sue likes both Mary and Jeff but thinks that Mary does not like Jeff. Sue experiences an unpleasant state of tension. She can either change her belief about Mary's attitude toward Jeff, or decide that she herself does not like Jeff. In either case, the imbalance will no longer exist.

Reactance Theory. Have you ever been ordered (perhaps by a parent) to do something that caused you to want to do the exact opposite? According to social psychologist Jack Brehm (1966), whenever people feel their freedom of choice is

FIGURE 16.4

Two Views of Attitudes

Does behavior follow from attitudes (the traditional view), or do attitudes follow from behavior (Bem's view)?

TRADITIONAL VIEW

Attitudes → Behavior

Attitudes shape behaviors; behaviors follow from attitudes

BEM'S VIEW

Behavior → Attitudes

Situations are interpreted and then attitudes are formed

Balance theory: An attitude theory stating that people prefer to hold consistent beliefs and try to avoid incompatible beliefs.

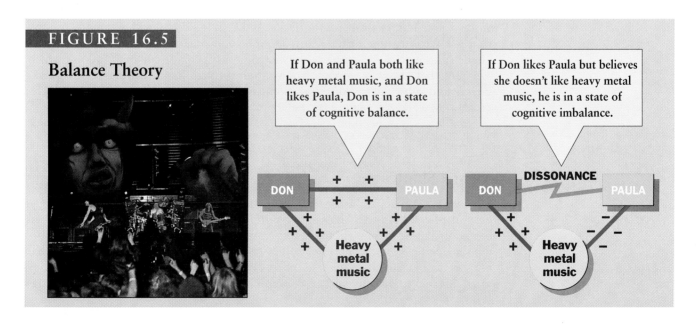

FIGURE 16.5

Balance Theory

If Don and Paula both like heavy metal music, and Don likes Paula, Don is in a state of cognitive balance.

If Don likes Paula but believes she doesn't like heavy metal music, he is in a state of cognitive imbalance.

DON + + PAULA
+ +
+ + +
+ + + +
+ **Heavy metal music**

DON **DISSONANCE** PAULA
+ + –
+ + –
+ + + –
+ **Heavy metal music** –

being unjustly restricted, they are motivated to reestablish that freedom. Brehm terms this form of negative influence *reactance*. In reactance, what is inconsistent is the image of ourselves as free to choose and the realization that someone is trying to force us to choose a particular alternative.

Reactance theory is derived from the notion of forbidden fruit. When people are forbidden to do something, that activity often becomes more attractive. Choosing the forbidden fruit may provide an individual with a sense of autonomy. An adolescent who is told he cannot be friends with members of a minority group might seek out members of that group more often. When coercion is used, resistance follows.

FOCUS

► Under what conditions are attitudes most likely to predict future behaviors?   pp. 576–577

► What is the evidence that a good communicator can effectively change attitudes?   p. 578

► How does the sleeper effect work?   pp. 580–581

► How does cognitive dissonance theory explain attitude change?   pp. 581–582

According to reactance theory, the extent of reactance is usually directly related to the extent of the restrictions on behavior. If the person does not consider the behavior very important and if the restriction is slight, little reactance develops. The wording or delivery of the restriction also affects the extent of reactance. A person who is told she *must* respond in a certain way is more likely to react negatively than if she merely receives a suggestion or is given a relatively free choice in responding.

Social Cognition

After meeting someone for the first time, you might say, "I really like him!" or "I can't explain why, but she irritates me." Often, first impressions are based on nothing more than the other person's appearance, body language, and speech patterns. Yet these impressions can have lasting effects. How do we form attitudes about others?

Social cognition is the thought process of making sense of events, other people, ourselves, and the world in general through analyzing and interpreting them. It focuses on social information in memory and how it affects judgments, choices, evaluations, and, ultimately, behavior (Fiske, 1992). It is a useful and pragmatic process in which we often use mental shortcuts to help us organize the world. The process often begins with our attempts to understand other people's communications, which can be verbal (through words) or nonverbal (through looks, gestures, body movements, and other means of expression), and to form impressions of them. The process by which people use the behavior and appearance of others to infer their internal states and intentions is known as **impression formation;** usually, but not always, the impressions are accurate.

Social cognition: The thought process of making sense of events, people, ourselves, and the world in general through analyzing and interpreting them.

Impression formation: The process by which people use the behavior and appearance of others to infer their internal states and intentions.

Mental Shortcuts

We saw earlier that people use their attitudes to help them make decisions and organize their lives. Many decisions about morality are neatly categorized in good or bad behaviors. Using mental shortcuts to help process information decreases the information overload that people might otherwise experience in their complex lives. People seek to be "cognitive misers," processing information superficially unless they are motivated to do otherwise. As Susan Fiske (1992, p. 879) asserts, "Social cognition operates in the service of practical consequences." To help themselves make decisions, people develop pragmatic rules of thumb.

One rule of thumb is *representativeness;* individuals or events that appear to be representative of other members of a group are quickly classified as such, despite a complete lack of evidence. Another rule of thumb is *availability;* the easier it is to bring to mind instances of one category, type, or idea, the more likely it is that that category, type, or idea will be used to describe an event. Still another rule of thumb is the *false consensus effect;* people tend to believe that others believe the same thing they do. The last rule of thumb is *framing;* the way people present information to us helps determine whether we are likely to categorize it in an acceptable, easy manner.

When people's behavior fits neatly into our conceptions of the world, we can use little effort to make judgments about it. One of the most powerful ways people can send signals that can be easily interpreted by others is through nonverbal communication.

Nonverbal communication: Information provided by cues or actions that involve movements of the body, especially the face, and sometimes the vocal cords.

Nonverbal Communication

Impression formation often begins with nonverbal communication. **Nonverbal communication** is provided by cues or actions that involve movements of the body, especially the face, and sometimes the vocal cords. When a person irritates you, it may be a gesture, a grimace, or an averting of the eyes that generates your bad feelings. Nonverbal communication is difficult to suppress and is easily accessible to observers (DePaulo, 1992). Based on small samples of people's behavior, adults make good use of nonverbal information in judging others (Ambady & Rosenthal, 1993). (The four major sources of nonverbal communication are facial expressions, body language, physical contact, and eye contact.

Facial Expressions and Body Language. Many of the conclusions we draw from other people's communications are based on their facial expressions. Most people can distinguish six basic emotions in the facial expressions of other people: love, joy, anger, sadness, fear, and surprise (Shaver et al., 1987). A simple gesture such as smiling gives people a powerful cue about a person's truthfulness. Research shows that when people smile, both the smile and the muscular activity around the eyes help determine if the truth is being told or if the person is smiling to mask another emotion (Ekman, Friesen, & O'Sullivan, 1988). The Research Process box on page 586 examines this research in more detail.

Facial expressions and body language are universal means of communication.

THE RESEARCH PROCESS

Hiding the Truth

Can you deceive others by smiling when you're telling a lie? Not very well, according to researchers Ekman, Friesen, and O'Sullivan (1988). More than 20 years ago, two of these researchers noted that facial features and gestures provide complex information to an observer, especially when a person tries to be deceitful. They observed that subtle facial cues accompany various types of smiling and that people cannot mask true emotions with a grin. They tested their idea experimentally by having subjects view people telling about pleasant experiences and then view people lying about experiences, trying to make unpleasant ones seem pleasant.

Method. Ekman and his colleagues identified several types of smiles: happy smiles, false smiles, smiles of a listener, and masking smiles. They asserted that facial muscles around the eyes and nose signal the real meaning of a smile. The research team videotaped (with a concealed camera) subjects who first truthfully described a film that was mildly enjoyable. Then the subjects watched an unpleasant film about skin burns and amputations and were asked to conceal negative feelings when describing the film. Could the participants convince another person that they had watched a pleasant film?

Results. Close-ups of the subjects' faces were scored with respect to which facial muscles moved. Facial muscle movements such as pulling the brows together, wrinkling the nose, and raising the brows were categorized, and the results showed that smiles of true enjoyment involved eye muscle activity more often than did feigned smiles of enjoyment. When subjects tried to conceal negative emotions with a happy but false smile, there were specific changes in the muscles.

Of course, not everyone is good at interpreting facial gestures. For example, some children find it difficult to decode nonverbal cues, and this leaves them with poor social skills. According to Nowicki and Duke (1989), 5- to 10-year-old children sometimes have difficulty interpreting emotional states through facial expressions, posture, and gestures. Their misjudgments may cause them anxiety and confusion that carry over to the classroom and make learning difficult.

Facial expressions are especially potent in televised communication. Mullen and colleagues (1986) wished to find out if newscasters exhibited biased facial expressions. The researchers asked college students to rate videotaped segments of newscasters referring to presidential candidates; there was no sound from the television monitors. The subjects rated the newscasters' facial expressions on a scale from extremely negative to extremely positive. The results showed that, in the 1984 presidential election, Peter Jennings had a bias in favor of one candidate. Tom Brokaw and Dan Rather showed no bias; they remained scrupulously neutral. Although fascinating, the effects of the newscaster experiment were not large. Also, it is not clear from the study whether viewers' political views influenced their decision to watch Jennings, Brokaw, or Rather in the first place. However, by using a scientific method, the researchers showed the existence of a bias. The results suggest that some small portion of voting behavior may be affected by nonverbal gestures, not only of the candidate but also of television newscasters.

People also convey information about their moods and attitudes through body positions and gestures—**body language.** Such movements as crossing the arms, lowering the head, and standing rigidly can all communicate negative attitudes.

Body language may differ by age and gender. The energetic and forceful way younger people walk makes them appear sexier, more carefree, and happier than older people (Montepare & Zebrowitz-McArthur, 1988). Additionally, research shows that women are often better than men at communicating and interpreting nonverbal messages, especially facial expressions. Women are more likely to send nonverbal facial messages but are also more cautious in interpreting nonverbal messages sent to them by men (Rosenthal & DePaulo, 1979).

Body language: The communication of information through body positions and gestures.

The results support the researchers' contention that genuinely happy smiles differ from other smiles in the amount of time it takes for the smile to appear and how long it remains on the face before fading.

Conclusions. This study shows that smiles are not a single category of behavior but are multifaceted. A person can exhibit different social signals through a smile. From a social psychologist's view, this is important because it shows that people are tuned in to fine elements of behavior. For example, a person can say that he likes or dislikes your smile. Moreover, another person's smile can affect your own behavior. Your boss may be smiling, but a mere lift of an eyebrow or a couple of millimeters of space between the eyebrows can have

a dramatic impact on your thoughts or overt behavior.

Research shows that deceptive salespersons can be detected through nonverbal cues (DePaulo & DePaulo, 1989). Cross-cultural research also shows that people are adept at judging deception (Bond et al., 1992). However, this issue is not yet fully resolved. Researcher Bella DePaulo (1992) asserts that people can use nonverbal messages to lie or deceive only sometimes. Some people have developed the skill more than others and use it to present their "best selves," but it works best when people are just editing or slightly altering their true selves or attitudes.

Physical Contact. Argyle (1972) found that individuals convey information nonverbally through such physical contact as touching, hitting, striking, embracing, and kissing; they also convey information through proximity—the physical distance maintained during interaction with other people. We see this in professional ball players, who use a variety of physical gestures, including high-fives, after scoring in a game. Other ways of giving nonverbal messages include orientation and posture—the angle at which a person sits or stands, such as leaning forward or backward. The more cues available, the greater the information conveyed (Schwarz, Foa, & Foa, 1983). We will consider some of these cues in more detail in the next chapter. Interestingly, when two people are talking, body movements, hand movements, and other nonverbal gestures decrease when a third person is present, even if that person is passive (Guerin, 1989).

Eye Contact. Researchers are well aware of another source of nonverbal communication: The eyes convey a surprising amount of information about feelings. A person who is looking at you may gaze briefly or may stare. You may glance or stare back. Psychologists term this process *making eye contact.* You would probably gaze tenderly at someone you found attractive but avoid eye contact with someone you did not trust or like or did not know well (Teske, 1988). When people are looked at, they accept it as a sign of being liked. Frequent eye contact between a man and a woman may indicate that they are sexually attracted to each other.

We tend to judge people by the eye contact they make with us. Generally, people prefer modest amounts of eye contact rather than constant or no eye contact. Job applicants, for example, are rated more favorably when they make moderate amounts of eye contact, and speakers who make more rather than less eye contact are preferred. Therapists report that a lack of eye contact in therapy suggests a lack of involvement. However, this is true only in Western cultures; some non-Western cultures consider direct eye contact a sign of disrespect. Witnesses in a court trial are perceived as more credible when they make eye contact with the attorney. People make inferences (attributions) about others' internal dispositions from the degree of eye contact.

Attribution: The process by which someone infers other people's motives and intentions from observing their behavior and deciding whether the causes of the behavior are *dispositional* (internal) or *situational* (external).

Attribution

If it's noon and you see people eating hamburgers and french fries, you can be fairly certain that they are eating because they are hungry. Similarly, if you see a man at a bus stop reading the Muslim holy book, the Koran, you might infer that he is a devout Muslim. In getting to know other people, we often infer the causes of their behavior. When we do, we are making attributions.

Attribution is the process by which someone infers other people's motives and intentions from observing their behavior and deciding whether the causes of the behavior are *dispositional* (internal) or *situational* (external). Through attribution, people decide how they will react toward others; they attempt to evaluate and to make sense of their social world.

At first, attribution seems like a fairly straightforward process based on common sense. However, it must take into account internal as well as external causes of behavior. Someone making an *internal attribution* thinks the behavior comes from within the person, from the individual's personality or abilities. Someone making an *external attribution* believes the person's behavior is caused by outside events, such as the weather or luck. In other words, if internal causes seem to predominate, a person's behavior will be attributed to personality or abilities; if external causes seem to predominate, the behavior will be attributed to the situation.

People can be mistaken when they infer the causes of another person's behavior. Suppose that the man toting the Koran is actually a Catholic taking a world religion class that uses the book as a text. In that case, the original attribution (that he is a Muslim) would be wrong. To learn about attribution and how it can be more precise, researchers have tried to conceptualize its processes.

Harold Kelley's (1972, 1973) popular theory of attribution contains three criteria to help determine whether the causes of a behavior are internal or external: *consensus, consistency,* and *distinctiveness* (see Figure 16.6). According to Kelley, to infer that someone's behavior is caused by internal characteristics, you must believe the following:

▶ That few other people in the same situation would act in the same way (low consensus).

▶ That the person has acted in the same way in similar situations in the past (high consistency).

▶ That the person acts in the same way in different situations (low distinctiveness).

To infer that a person's behavior is caused by external factors, you must believe the following:

▶ That most people would act that way in that sort of situation (high consensus).

▶ That the person has acted that way in similar situations in the past (high consistency).

▶ That the person acts differently in other situations (high distinctiveness).

To see how Kelley's theory works, suppose that someone in a restaurant acts rudely to a certain waiter but other people in the same restaurant are not rude to the waiter (low consensus). Also suppose that the person has acted rudely toward this waiter on other occasions (high consistency). Finally, assume that the person acts rudely to all waiters (low distinctiveness). In such a case, people would no doubt attribute the rudeness to the individual's personality; that person is simply rude.

Now suppose (1) that many other customers act rudely toward the waiter (high consensus), (2) that our target person has acted rudely toward this waiter in the past (high consistency), but (3) that our target person does not act rudely toward any other waiters (high distinctiveness). People would then be more likely to attribute the rudeness to situational factors, such as the waiter's incompetence.

FIGURE 16.6

Attributional Thinking

Assigning an internal attribution to a person is usually the result of low consensus, high consistency, and low distinctiveness. When a person shows high consensus, consistency, and distinctiveness, people tend to attribute the causes of behavior to external reasons. These are the fundamental guidelines of Kelley's attibutional model.

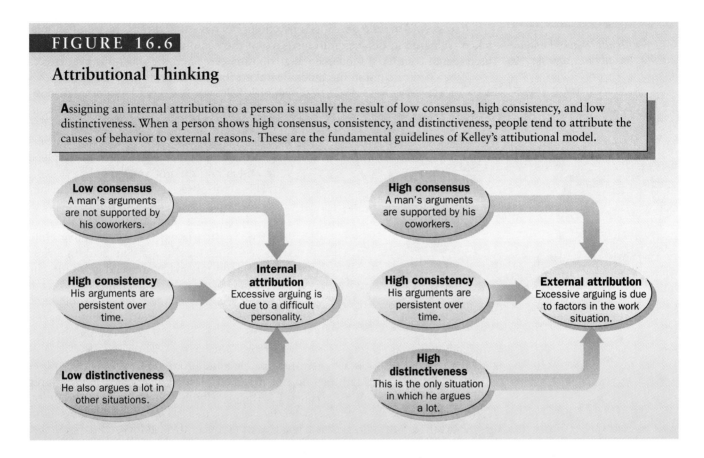

Why People Make Attributions. Why do we make attributions? What motivates us to want to know the causes of other people's behavior? A traditional idea is that we engage in the process of attribution to maintain a sense of control over our environment. It helps us feel competent and masterful because we think that knowledge about the causes of behavior will help us control and predict similar events in the future. Burger and Hemans (1988) showed that subjects who have an intense desire to control events around them are more likely than others to make attributions.

People also make attributions to help maintain a sense of balance, thereby resolving inconsistencies between old and new information about themselves (Snyder & Higgins, 1988). Often, a person who makes an excuse about some personal behavior that has had negative outcomes has shifted the cause of the behavior to a less central element of personality or to situational factors. This behavior results in enhanced image building and a sense of control.

People make attributions to quickly make sense of their world. If a person's behavior fits in with a pattern you have seen before, why analyze it in depth? People are quick to make causal attributions if the behavior being observed is not unusual.

Attribution theory is a rapidly emerging specialty in social psychology, but theorists do not agree about the nature of attributions. For example, Hilton (1990) asserts that the traditional view of the individual as a rational being trying to sort out relevant facts does not consider such factors as who is doing the explaining, to whom, or why an explanation is needed. He therefore proposes an extension of the traditional causal explanation that accounts for the form of attributions, particularly when they are presented in conversation. His new model has an interpersonal focus; it is yet to be fully evaluated by other researchers.

It's difficult to avoid making attributions about other people. What was your initial reaction to these truck drivers?

Errors in Attribution. Social psychologists have found that we are often mistaken or biased in our attributions. Two of the common types of errors that have been identified are the fundamental attribution error and the actor-observer effect.

When people commit the **fundamental attribution error,** they assume that other people's behavior is caused by internal dispositions and they underestimate situational influences. A man may have lost his temper after being overcharged for an item; a woman may have become hostile because the waiter spilled soup on her and did not apologize.

The **actor-observer effect** is the tendency for people to attribute the behavior of others to dispositional causes but to attribute their own behavior to situational causes. A young child who gets hurt may say, "You made me hurt myself." However, when a friend gets hurt, the same child may say, "You're clumsy." If you fail an exam, you may blame it on your roommate, whose radio kept you from concentrating on your studies. However, when someone else fails an exam, you may wonder about the person's intelligence.

Errors in attribution are often judgments made in a limited context, with limited knowledge; and often they do not help people cope any better—they simply assign blame (Funder, 1987; Tennen & Affleck, 1990). Some errors in attribution come from the fact that people generally perceive themselves as having more positive traits than others do and as being more flexible in their ability to adapt (Sande, Goethals, & Radloff, 1988); this tendency is evident cross-culturally (Liebrand, Messick, & Wolters, 1986). Can you think of any useful functions that errors in attribution might serve?

A Just World? According to Melvin Lerner (1970), many people believe that an appropriate relationship exists between what they do and what happens to them. In other words, they believe that the world is just—that people get what they deserve. A negative consequence of the just-world belief is that victims of crime, poverty, and other misfortunes are often treated as if they brought these things on themselves (Connors & Heaven, 1989). People may blame female rape victims for wearing seductive clothing or too much makeup, for acting too friendly toward men, or for going out alone after dark (see McCaul et al., 1990). The realization that bad things can happen to good people threatens our belief that the world is just and makes us feel vulnerable. Our ability to see that someone else has been treated unfairly can upset our belief in a just world and perhaps motivate us to rectify the situation or compensate someone who was unfairly punished—in an effort to reestablish justice.

Fundamental attribution error: The tendency to attribute other people's behavior to dispositional (internal) causes rather than situational (external) causes.

Actor-observer effect: The tendency for people to attribute the behavior of others to dispositional causes but to attribute their own behavior to situational causes.

Learned Helplessness. People want to have control over their lives so they can determine their own destinies. They want to be able to attribute the causes of their behavior to rational events in the world. Most people believe they can control their environment to a reasonable extent. But what happens to people in a situation in which they feel they have little control? How do they react when negative things happen to them?

Assume that you are a subject in an experiment in which you have to solve puzzles. The puzzles appear to be relatively simple; yet no matter what you do, you cannot solve them. You probably become frustrated. Research shows that both people and animals, when put in situations in which they have no control over the negative things happening to them, often stop responding. Martin Seligman (1975) and his colleagues showed, for example, that dogs first exposed to a series of inescapable shocks and then given a chance to escape further punishment fail to learn the escape response. Seligman termed this behavior learned helplessness. **Learned helplessness** is the behavior of giving up or not responding, exhibited by subjects exposed to negative consequences or punishment over which they have no control. According to Seligman, the major cause of learned helplessness is an organism's belief that its response will not affect what happens to it in the future. The result of this belief is anxiety, depression, and, eventually, nonresponsiveness. We saw in chapter 14 (p. 522) that learned helplessness is a major cause of depression.

The opposite of learned helplessness is *learned optimism*—a sense that the world has positive outcomes from which people can see happy things in their lives (Seligman, 1991). Seligman asserts that *learning* is the key to a sense of doom or optimism.

Feeling overwhelmed and without resources, some people give up on changing the negative aspects of their lives.

Many researchers believe that Seligman's views are not comprehensive enough to explain learned helplessness. Thus, other researchers have proposed attribution models of learned helplessness that take into account such variables as a person's locus of control, gender, and previous expectations. Research on learned helplessness must be expanded to approximate real-life situations more closely than laboratory situations with animals can (Mikulincer & Nizan, 1988).

Attribution has an important influence on people's judgments about their own behavior and other people's. Did John Smith rob the store because he is a violent man? Did he need the money to support his heroin addiction or to pay for his sick child's operation? Did his father beat him when he was a child? Did his mother abandon him? Is he discouraged over his inability to find a decent job? Is he taking medication that has altered his behavior? We constantly seek the reasons for people's behavior to help us make judgments about them. You probably reflect on the causes of your own behavior at times; that behavior is often shaped by your self-perceptions.

Self-Perceptions

Self-perception is people's attitudes toward and beliefs about themselves, largely formed during childhood and adolescence and often a reflection of other people's perceived attitudes. How would you describe yourself? Self-perceptions are greatly affected by other people's perceived attitudes. Thus, when social psychologists study self-perceptions, they examine how other people and social situations affect how people see themselves and how that perception influences everyday behavior.

Established early in life and reevaluated frequently, self-perceptions develop over time and from experience. At first, children use answers to such questions as, "Mommy, am I pretty?" and "Mommy, do you like me?" to help form their self-perceptions. Adolescents then reassess their early self-perceptions, which enables them to establish a firm identity consistent with both previous attitudes and new values. The successful completion of adolescence (which Erikson calls the *identity crisis*) results in a person's ability to adapt to new situations while retaining a firm understanding of self and personal values.

Learned helplessness: The behavior of giving up or not responding, exhibited by subjects exposed to negative consequences or punishment over which they have no control.

Self-perceptions: People's attitudes toward and beliefs about themselves, largely formed during childhood and adolescence and often a reflection of other people's perceived attitudes.

Role: A set of behaviors expected from a certain category of individuals; a person's roles may change depending on the group within which the person finds himself or herself.

Self-serving bias: People's tendency to evaluate their own behavior as worthwhile, regardless of the situation.

Over the years, people develop a sense of themselves by combining aspects of their family, occupational, recreational, and gender roles. A **role** is a set of behaviors expected from a specific group of individuals. Our culture, for example, has certain expectations for men, women, various ethnic groups, leaders, and those in various social positions. For example, we expect integrity, leadership, and strict compliance with the law from an Attorney General. In 1993, President Clinton nominated Zoë Baird, a leading Connecticut lawyer, for the post. When it was revealed that Baird had hired illegal aliens to care for her children, the public was outraged. Most people believed she had to be held to at least the same standards as everyone else. Baird withdrew.

Roles for individuals are sometimes established on the basis of prominent physical cues, such as height; people expect tall men and women to play basketball and do not expect shorter people to enjoy or play the game. In some ways, people are lazy about paying attention to other aspects of a person's behavior (Fiske, 1989). Other roles are defined by the individual, but these too often follow from cultural expectations. Research shows these roles to be related to the fact that men often have more status than women and men are more often engaged in the distinctive behaviors, such as political leadership, of national groups (Eagly & Kite, 1987). The Diversity box further examines the influence of culture in self-perception.

People also develop self-perceptions by comparing themselves to others and seeing how they measure up. Thus, athletes compare themselves to better athletes as well as to less competent ones, and high school juniors compare their academic and social skills both to those of other juniors and to those of sophomores and seniors. Individuals also receive feedback from other people that helps them evaluate themselves. Research, however, shows that the extent to which people accept feedback varies with their level of self-esteem; people with higher levels of self-esteem are more willing to accept feedback. Further, when people are in a good mood, they are more willing to accept feedback (Esses, 1988). Last, although people are good at estimating how most other people generally perceive them, they are not as good at sensing how they are viewed by individuals (Kenny & DePaulo, 1993).

Self-Serving Biases. Social psychologists have found that most people are not realistic in evaluating themselves, their capabilities, or their behavior. The **self-serving bias** is people's tendency to evaluate their own behavior as worthwhile, regardless of the situation. Most people consider themselves more charitable, more giving, more intelligent, more considerate, more sensitive, more likely to succeed, and more of a leader than they consider most other people.

Psychologists have focused on two possible explanations for the development and role of self-serving biases. First, a self-serving bias meets people's *need for self-esteem* and need to feel good about themselves in comparison to other people. It can be seen as an adaptive response that helps people deal with their limitations and gives them the courage to venture into areas they normally might not explore. The extent to which people use a self-serving bias varies by culture; for example, Americans use it more than some Europeans (Nurmi, 1991). The other explanation involves *self-presentation:* Self-serving biases allow people to present themselves to other people in a positive light (Weary et al., 1982). This allows people to believe they are presenting themselves well to others in their social world.

Errors in attribution, which we considered earlier, contribute to self-serving biases. People tend to take credit for their successes and blame others for their failures; that is, people assume that good things happen to them because they deserve them and that bad things happen to other people because they deserve them. When something bad happens to you, you may blame it on bad luck or circumstances; when something bad happens to others, you may blame it on their careless or reckless behavior. This combination of attribution errors and a self-serving bias

DIVERSITY

Self-Perceptions of African-American Women

Psychologists know that men and women perceive themselves differently. So do teenagers and people over age 65, people from the north and from the south, and African Americans and white Americans.

Victoria Binion (1990) undertook a study of self-perception in a sample of African-American and white women. Among other things, she was interested in the relationship between culture and gender role attitudes and perceptions. Binion interviewed over 175 women in a low-income community near downtown Detroit. Her questionnaire asked the participants about their gender identity, gender role attitudes, and self-perceptions. The participants either agreed or disagreed (on a scale of 1 to 5) with statements such as: "The only way for women to survive is to have men protect them"; and "Women can handle a lot more hurt than men can." The women were young (about 26 years of age) and were all high school graduates. In terms of age, education, and marital status, the African-American and white women in the study were quite similar.

The results of the study showed that African-American women characterized themselves as either androgynous (37 percent), masculine (24 percent), feminine (18 percent), or undifferentiated (none of the above) (22 percent). Women who saw themselves as masculine showed traits such as independence and courage. Women who saw themselves as feminine tended to view themselves as weak and needing help. Androgynous women showed traits and agreed with statements that were both masculine and feminine.

There is a strong cultural component in determining self-perception and gender identity. Binion showed that African-American women were more than twice as likely as white women to characterize themselves as androgynous (having many characteristics of both genders), and they were less likely than white women to characterize themselves as feminine. Further, African-American women reported that they were less liberal than white women about the female role in the family. Moreover, they expressed less cultural freedom and less liberal gender role attitudes than white women. Although African-American women tended to report more traditional gender role attitudes (women as weaker and dependent), many identified themselves as being androgynous.

The relationship among culture, gender identity, and self-perceptions is complex. For example, women who are college graduates have more liberal views about the female role regardless of their culture. A woman's relationship with her parents is affected by her self-report of masculinity or femininity; for example, women who were brought up with a father in the home tended to have more liberal views about the woman's role in the family.

There exists enormous diversity among individual women, individual families, and cultural values within any community. A person's self-perception is affected by parenting, education, and ethnicity. When social psychologists develop theories of self-perception, ethnicity is a variable they are going to have to take into account. We are a diverse people, and the data show that culture affects how people perceive themselves.

helps some people maintain self-esteem and appear competent. Such an attitude, however, may inhibit people from having realistic goals, thus setting them up for disappointment.

Neither view of self-serving biases—self-esteem or self-presentation—has received substantial research support. Research has shown that, although self-serving biases exist, they are not present in all people at all times. People find other ways to cope. Individuals who suffer from depression and loneliness, for example, often have low levels of self-esteem but do not seem to develop a self-serving bias. Instead, they may develop and exhibit maladjusted or abnormal behavior, as we saw in chapter 14.

Locus of Control.   People may use self-serving biases and attribution errors to develop a sense of control that enables them to maintain self-esteem and a belief in their own ability to succeed and be happy. Therefore, although people misrepresent reality through biases and errors, they think they gain control over their lives and over their ability to get what they need. Psychologist Julian Rotter (1966) described such misrepresentations in terms of developing an internal locus of control. A person's *locus of control* (which we examined briefly in chapter 12) influences how the person views the world and identifies the causes of success or failure in life.

Rotter found that people have either an external or an internal locus of control, and this affects them in many situations. In therapy, for example, individuals with an external locus of control often place the blame for their problems on other people. In daily situations, people with an external locus of control may attribute bad scores on examinations to poor instruction. Those with an internal locus of control, on the other hand, believe they can master any subject. On the negative side, people with an internal locus of control may also accept blame and intense guilt feelings for various failures in their lives. In general, though, people with an internal locus of control can use that disposition to evaluate situations and be responsive and creative (Strickland, 1989).

Perceiving Others

We perceive others in relation to our own self-perceptions. An assertive person, for example, may view other assertive people as expressing normal, appropriate behavior. A quiet, shy, passive person, on the other hand, may view assertive people as loud or even aggressive.

A person's frame of reference usually starts with himself or herself. Then the person compares an individual to other people or an absolute standard and makes an overall evaluation. Both children and adults have conceptions of an ideal man or woman; these are determined by gender and culture (Gibbons et al., 1988).

Physical Appearance. Many factors determine how we perceive others. Among them are work habits, athletic abilities, and success as a parent or mate. According to a substantial body of literature, one of the most important factors is physical appearance. Appearance sharply affects people's attitudes toward others and ultimately influences how people perceive themselves (T. Horvath, 1981).

In general, attractive people are judged to have more positive traits and characteristics than unattractive people, especially when appearance is the first information provided (Benassi, 1982). For example, teachers believe that attractive children will get higher grades and will misbehave less than will unattractive children. Attractive children are also predicted to have more successful careers (Dion, Berscheid, & Walster, 1972; Lerner & Lerner, 1977). The same process occurs with adults: Attractive people are granted more freedom and are perceived as being more fair and competent than unattractive people (Cherulnik, Turns, & Wilderman, 1990). For example, attractive college professors are seen as better teachers and are less likely to be blamed if a student receives a failing grade in a course (Romano & Bordieri, 1989).

It is unfortunate that people's self-concepts and their status in other people's eyes may be determined largely by superficial characteristics such as physical attractiveness, which can set them up for a lifelong pattern of reinforcement or punishment. Physically unattractive and different people tend to be isolated, to be ignored by members of both sexes, and to have negative traits attributed to them. Employers are less likely to hire them, regardless of their qualifications (Forsythe, 1990). In addition, people who perceive themselves as being physically unattractive are more likely to have anxiety problems in dealing with members of the opposite sex.

How important is attractiveness when it comes to dating? Do people always select the most attractive person for a date? Research shows that people prefer attractive dates, and some studies show that people seek out those of their own level of attractiveness. But other variables also seem to play an important role; educational level, intelligence, socioeconomic status, and similarity of previous experiences all weigh heavily in the choice of whom to date and eventually marry (Feingold, 1988a). Although physical attractiveness is initially important in selecting dates and mates, it is just one variable among many.

FOCUS

► Can people mask a lie through facial expressions such as a smile?   pp. 585–586

► Describe the fundamental difference between *dispositional* and *situational* interpretations of the causes of behavior. p. 588

► Identify the assumptions of the fundamental attribution error.   p. 590

► What is learned helplessness?   pp. 590–591

Social Influence

Social influence is the way in which one or more people alter the attitudes or behavior of others. For example, parents try to instill specific values in their children. An adolescent may notice the hair style or mannerism of an attractive peer and decide to adopt it. Professors urge students to shed preconceived ideas. The behavior or appearance of a celebrity may be emulated by adoring fans. Religious leaders exhort their followers to live in certain ways. People exert a powerful influence on others, and psychologists have attempted to understand how this influence operates. Studies of social influence have focused on two topics: conformity and obedience.

Conformity

People conform to the behaviors and attitudes of their peer or family groups. A successful young executive might wear conservative dark suits and drive a BMW in order to fit in with office colleagues. Similarly, the desire to conform can induce people to do things they might not do otherwise. An infamous example is the My Lai massacre, in which American soldiers slaughtered Vietnamese civilians during the Vietnam War. While several factors account for the soldiers' behavior (including combat stress, hostility toward the Vietnamese, and obedience to authority), the soldiers also yielded to extreme group pressure. The few soldiers who refused to kill the civilians hid that fact from their comrades. One soldier even shot himself in the foot to avoid becoming part of the slaughter.

Conformity occurs when a person changes attitudes or behaviors to be consistent with other people or with social norms; people try to fit in. The behaviors they might adopt include positive, prosocial behaviors such as wearing seat belts, volunteering time and money for a charity, or buying only products that are safe for the environment. Sometimes, however, people conform to counterproductive, antisocial behaviors, such as drug use, fraternity hazing, or mob action.

Conformity in Groups. Groups strongly influence conformity. Solomon Asch (1955) found that people in a group adopt its standard, which may be as restricted as an individual refraining from speaking during a public address or as pervasive as a whole nation discriminating against a particular ethnic group. Studies also show that individuals conform to group norms even when they are not pressured to do so. Consider what happens when an instructor asks a class of 250 students to answer a relatively simple question, but no one volunteers. When asked, most students will

Social influence: The way in which one or more people alter the attitudes or behavior of others.

report that they did not raise their hand because no one else did. Unpressured conformity also is illustrated by the fact that people generally dress appropriately for specific occasions such as weddings, black-tie parties, and funerals. Asch (1955, p. 6) stated:

> The tendency to conformity in our society [is] so strong that reasonably intelligent and well-meaning young people willing to call white black is a matter of concern. It raises questions about our ways of education and about the values that guide our conduct.

Asch's Conformity Experiment. Suppose you have agreed to participate in an experiment of line discriminations. You are seated at the end of a table next to four other students. The experimenter holds up a card and asks each of you to pick which of two lines is longer, A or B. You quickly discover that the task is simple. The experimenter proceeds to hold up successive pairs of lines, with each participant correctly identifying the longest. Suddenly, after several rounds, you notice that the first person has chosen line A instead of line B, though B is obviously longer. You are surprised when the second person also chooses line A, then the third, then the fourth. Your turn is next. You are sure that line B is longer. What do you do?

In 1951, Asch performed a similar experiment to explore conformity. Seven to nine subjects were brought into a room and told that they would be participating in an experiment involving visual judgment. The subjects were to judge which of three lines matched a standard (see Figure 16.7). However, only one group member was unaware of the purpose of the study; we call such a participant a naive subject; the others were collaborators of the researcher, and they deliberately gave false answers to try to influence the naive subject. Asch found that the naive subject would generally go along with the group, even though the majority answer was obviously

FIGURE 16.7

Asch's Classic Study of Conformity

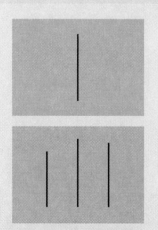

Subjects were shown the cards at the left and asked to choose the line in the picture on the bottom that was the same length as the line in the picture on the top. The confederates deliberately chose incorrect answers to see if the unsuspecting subject (#6) would go along with the majority.

wrong and even though the group exerted no explicit or directly observable pressure on the subject.

Although only some of the naive subjects conformed in Asch's experiments, enough did so that psychologists researched the phenomenon further. They found that the number of people in the group is a critical variable. When 1 or 2 individuals collaborate with the researcher, the tendency to conform is considerably less than when 10 do. Another important variable is the number of dissenting votes. If even 1 of 15 people disagrees with the other collaborating subjects, the naive subject is more likely to choose the correct line.

Variables in Conformity. How do groups influence individual behavior? One conformity variable is the *amount of information* provided when a decision is to be made. When people are uncertain of how to behave in ambiguous situations, they seek the opinions of others. For example, people who are unsure of how they should vote in an election will often ask trusted friends for advice. We tend to accept the advice of those whom we like and who are like us.

Another important variable that determines the degree of conformity is the *relative competence* of the group. People are more likely to conform to the decision of a group if they perceive its members as being more competent than they themselves are. This pressure becomes stronger as group size increases. A student in a large class, for example, may not answer even a simple question if he assumes that his classmates are more competent than he is.

Position within a group also affects individual behavior. A person who confidently believes that a group holds her in high esteem will respond independently. If she feels insecure about her status, even though it is high, she may respond as the group does because she fears losing her status.

The extent to which *behavior is public* also determines people's responses. Individuals are more willing to make decisions that are inconsistent with those of their group when the behavior is private. In a democracy, for example, voting is done privately so as to minimize group pressure on how individuals vote.

Theories of Conformity. Why do people tend to conform? Several theories have attempted to explain this phenomenon. The *social conformity approach* states that people conform to avoid the stigma of being wrong, deviant, out of line, or different from others. According to this view, people want to do the right thing and define as right whatever is generally accepted (Festinger, 1954). For example, in high school, a boy might be considered socially correct if he joins the football team but not if he enrolls in a modern dance class. Neighbors would likely approve if a homeowner built a picket fence that looked like their fences but would consider the homeowner deviant if she enclosed her property with a 10-foot concrete wall.

Another explanation for the presence or absence of conformity in a group relies on *attribution*. When a person can identify causes for other people's behavior in a group, and strongly disagrees with those causes, conformity disappears (Ross, Bierbrauer, & Hoffman, 1976). Suppose you hear several people arguing vehemently for the construction of a toxic waste incinerator near your town because it will boost the local economy. At first you agree, but later you discover that all the incinerator proponents own land at the proposed building site and stand to make money by selling the land to the incinerator company. After attributing the incinerator proponents' attitude to a desire for personal profit, you may no longer agree.

The issue of *independence* also helps explain conformity (or the lack of it). Although people in a group would like to be independent, independence is risky. People would have to face the consequences of their independence, such as serious disapproval, peer pressure to conform, being seen as deviant, and becoming less powerful.

Conformity is the course most people choose, but some prefer a greater degree of independence and are willing to risk social disapproval for it.

Last, conformity is *expedient* and conserves mental energy. Cialdini (1993) argues that too many events, circumstances, and changing variables exist for people to be able to analyze all the relevant data. People therefore need shortcuts to help them make decisions. It is efficient and easy for people to go along with others whom they trust and respect, especially if key elements of a situation fit in with their views.

All four variables—social conformity, attribution, risks of independence, and expediency—interact to produce the conformity effect. As psychologists try to sort out the variables and examine different theories, they approach an understanding of how groups influence individual behavior. But not everyone conforms to group pressures all the time—especially when other people disagree with the group.

Dissenting Opinions. Both everyday experience and research show that *dissenting opinions* help counteract group influence and conformity. Even one or two people in a large group can seriously influence decision making. Moreover, when group decision making occurs, a consistent minority (think of South African leader Nelson Mandela) can exert substantial influence, even when the minority is devoid of power, status, or competence (Mungy, 1982).

The Indian leader Mahatma Gandhi provides one of the most remarkable examples of a dissenter counteracting group influence. At age 24, after being subjected to humiliating racial discrimination in South Africa, where he lived, Gandhi began drafting petitions on behalf of the South African Indian community. A decade later, a South African minister was negotiating with the formerly powerless Gandhi on the issue of Indian rights. Later, Gandhi was instrumental in wresting India's independence from the powerful British. In 1946, Gandhi fasted to stop the fighting between Muslims and Hindus during the transfer of British power to India and Pakistan. The *London Times* reported that his lone fast did what several troop divisions could not have done to restore peace. Can you think of any other famous dissenters through history? How did their refusal to conform to group pressure affect their lives? How did their dissension influence society?

Obedience and Milgram's Study

According to psychologists, **obedience** is the process by which a person complies with the orders of another person or group of people. The studies on obedience by Stanley Milgram (1933–1984) are classic. Today, Milgram's results and interpretations still generate debate.

Milgram's work focused on the extent to which an individual will obey a significant person. His studies, which showed that ordinary people were remarkably

Obedience: The process by which a person complies with the orders of another person or group of people.

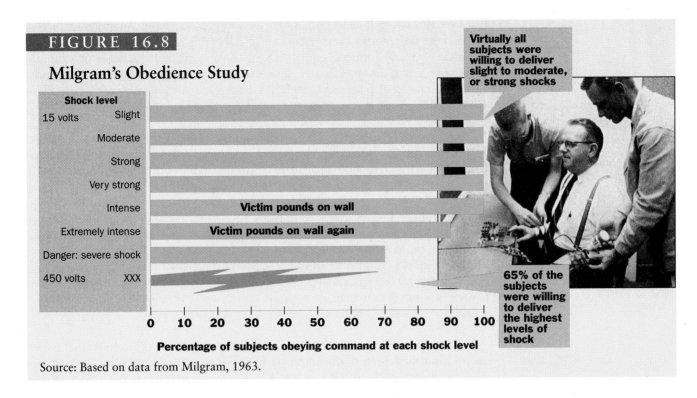

FIGURE 16.8

Milgram's Obedience Study

Virtually all subjects were willing to deliver slight to moderate, or strong shocks

65% of the subjects were willing to deliver the highest levels of shock

Shock level

15 volts   Slight
Moderate
Strong
Very strong
Intense   Victim pounds on wall
Extremely intense   Victim pounds on wall again
Danger: severe shock
450 volts   XXX

0 10 20 30 40 50 60 70 80 90 100

Percentage of subjects obeying command at each shock level

Source: Based on data from Milgram, 1963.

willing to comply with the wishes of others, especially if they saw the others as important, reveals a great deal about the social world, about social influence in general, and about obedience in particular. They also reveal something about people's self-perceptions, values, and early interactions in life.

Imagine that you are one of the participants in Milgrams 1963 study. You and another person are brought into a laboratory and are told that you will be participating in an experiment on paired-associate learning. You and the other person draw lots to determine who will be the teacher and who will be the learner. In actuality, the drawing is rigged so that you will be the teacher and the other person, who is actually collaborating with the experimenter, will be the learner.

The learner-collaborator is taken to an adjoining room, where you cannot see him. You are shown a shock-generating box containing 30 switches, with labels that range from *low shock* to *danger—severe shock*. You are told to shock the learner by hitting one of the switches every time he makes an error.

As the test continues, the experimenter and an assistant, both wearing white lab coats, encourage you to increase the shock voltage one level each time the learner makes a mistake. As the shock level rises, the learner-collaborator screams as if he is suffering increasing pain. When the intensity reaches the point of severe shock, the learner stops responding vocally to the paired-associate stimulus and pounds on the walls of the booth. The experimenter tells you to treat the learner's lack of response as an error and to continue increasing the levels of shock. What would you do?

This was the basic scenario of the Milgram study. As Figure 16.8 shows, 65 percent of the subjects in the study continued to shock the learner as directed until shocks at all levels were delivered. (You may have guessed by now that the learner-collaborators were not actually receiving shocks; they were only pretending to be in pain.)

However, not all of Milgram's subjects were obedient. Moreover, the presence of other subjects who refused to participate reduced the probability of obedience to as little as 10 percent (Milgram, 1965; Powers & Geen, 1972). These data suggest that behavior is sensitive to both authority and peer behavior. An individual's ability to resist coercion in the presence of an ally who also resists indicates the importance of social influences on behavior. A person's personality—for example, submissive versus domineering—is also likely to affect the willingness to conform, although individual personality variables have been studied relatively little (Blass, 1991).

Background Authority. Did conducting the study at the prestigious Yale University influence the subjects? Milgram (1965) suggested that his experiment might have involved a particular type of experimental bias—*background authority.* To investigate the issue, Milgram conducted a second study in an office building in Bridgeport, Connecticut. Subjects were contacted by mail and had no knowledge that Milgram or his associates were from Yale. In this second study, 48 percent of the office subjects, as compared with the 65 percent at Yale, delivered the maximum level of shock. Milgram therefore concluded that the perceived function of an institution can induce compliance in subjects. Moreover, an institution's qualitative position within a category (such as a prestigious as opposed to an unknown university) may be less important than the type of institution it is (for example, a university rather than an office building).

Explaining Milgram's Results. Why did so many subjects in Milgram's experiments obey the wishes of the authority figure? One reason is that the subjects were volunteers. Volunteers often bring undetected biases to an experimental situation, and one such bias is their willingness to go along with authority. Another reason is that the experimental situation can itself bias the outcome. Perhaps the subjects were willing to administer the shocks only because they knew they were participating in an experiment or because they were instructed to do so by the experimenter, and they might not act the same way without being told to do so or when outside the experimental context.

Obedience to authority figures can also be explained by learning theories. Children learn that authority figures, such as teachers and parents, know more than they do and that taking their advice generally proves beneficial. As adults they maintain those beliefs, with the authority figures being employers, judges, government leaders, and so on. Cialdini (1993) also notes that obedience has practical advantages, such as helping people make decisions quickly: "It is easy to allow ourselves the convenience of automatic obedience. . . . We don't have to think, therefore we don't" (p. 178).

We not only obey those in authority, we also take directives from people who merely look authoritative. People who take on the trappings of power (expensive clothes, uniforms, prestigious cars, fancy offices) are often treated as authority figures. We are more likely to heed security guards who dress in uniforms that look like police garb than those who wear clothing of a less official appearance. As we saw in Milgram's conformity studies, people rely on symbols to make quick decisions, although the decisions are sometimes irrational.

Researchers repeated Milgram's methods, and the results of one study suggest that obedience to authority is not specific to Western culture (Shanab & Yahya, 1978). Students at the University of Jordan participated in a similar study. As in the original Milgram study, about 65 percent were willing to give high levels of shock to other students. Milgram's findings are cross-cultural and apply to men and women, old and young; they show that the social world and our interactions within it are strongly affected by other people. Powerful people in positions of authority can change the course of events and potentially influence history (consider Hitler, Khaddafi, or the Pope). Milgram's studies challenge social psychologists to learn why people obey and why people in lower positions in a hierarchy (for example, in government, a school, or an industry) will not challenge authority. They also encour-

APPLICATIONS

Techniques to Induce Compliance

How can we influence others? How can others influence us? What techniques facilitate compliance, or at least attitude change? Managers, salespeople, parents, and politicians all apply the principles of social psychology. They influence people regularly by using social psychological techniques such as foot-in-the-door, door-in-the-face, ask-and-you-shall-be-given, low-balling, modeling, and incentives.

Foot-in-the-Door Technique. To get someone to change an attitude or grant a favor, begin by asking for a small attitude change or a small favor. In other words, get your foot in the door. Ask to borrow a quarter today, a dollar next week, and money for your tuition within a month.

The essence of the *foot-in-the-door technique* is that a person who grants a small request is likely to comply with a larger request later. It works, however, only if the person first grants the small favor; and it works best if there is some time between the first, small request and the later, large one. If the person says no to the first favor, the person may find it even easier to say no to subsequent ones. Although the foot-in-the-door technique is relatively easy to find in American society, cross-cultural studies show that it is not as easily found in all countries (Kilbourne, 1989).

Door-in-the-Face Technique. To use the *door-in-the-face technique,* first ask for something outrageous; then later ask for something much smaller and more reasonable. Ask a friend to lend you $100; after being turned down, ask to borrow $5. Your friend may be relieved to grant the smaller favor.

The principle of the door-in-the-face technique is that a person is more likely to grant a small request after turning down a larger one. It appears to work because people do not want to be seen as turning someone down twice, and it works best if there is little time in between requests. To look good and maintain a positive self-image, people agree to the lesser of two requests.

Ask-and-You-Shall-Be-Given Technique. When people ask for money for a good cause, whether the request is large or small, they usually will get a positive response. Ask someone who has given before, and the request is even more likely to be granted (Doob & McLaughlin, 1989). Fundraisers for universities, churches, and museums know that asking usually will get a positive response.

Low-Balling Technique. Low-balling is a compliance technique by which a person is influenced to make a decision or commitment because of the low stakes associated with it. Once the decision is made, the stakes might increase; but the person will likely stick with the original decision. For example, if a man agrees to buy a car for $9,000, he may still buy it even if the saleswoman increases the price to $10,000. Low-balling works because people tend to stick to their commitments, even if the stakes are raised. Changing one's mind may suggest a lack of good judgment, cause stress, and make the person feel as if he or she were violating an (often imaginary) obligation.

Modeling Technique. Showing someone good behavior, such as conserving energy or saying no to drugs, increases the likelihood that the person will behave similarly. The person being observed is a model for the desired behavior. *Modeling,* which we examined in chapter 5, is a powerful technique through which people learn and adopt new behaviors and attitudes by witnessing others engaged in those behaviors and expressing those attitudes. When well-known athletes publicly declare their attitudes about the scourge of drugs, they act as models for youngsters who aspire to careers such as theirs.

Incentives Technique. Nothing succeeds better in eliciting a particular behavior than a desired incentive. Offering a 16-year-old unlimited use of the family car for setting the dinner table every day usually results in a neatly set dinner table. Offering a large monetary bonus to a sales agent for higher-than-usual year-end sales performance usually boosts sales efforts.

We can influence others and induce attitude change by using techniques that researchers have studied in the laboratory. Researchers have shown that the way a request is framed, the approach that a person takes, or the incentives that are offered can be critical in determining whether people will comply.

age us to ask how other people influence us to comply with their wishes (see the Applications box for some possible techniques to induce compliance).

A Matter of Ethics—Implications of Milgram's Work. In any study of social influence, researchers worry about ethical issues; they never want to induce compliance unwillingly in research participants. Milgram's experimental methods raise several ethical issue. The primary issue is deception and potential harm to the subjects

Debriefing: A procedure to inform subjects about the true nature of an experiment after its completion.

who participated. Obtaining unbiased responses in psychological research often requires deceiving naive subjects. After the experiment, the subjects are debriefed. **Debriefing** is a procedure to inform subjects about the true nature of the experiment after its completion, including hypotheses, methods, and expected or potential results. It preserves the validity of the responses and takes account of ethical considerations. Of course, debriefing must be done clearly and with sensitivity, especially in studies which could reflect on a participant's self-esteem.

Milgram's subjects were fully debriefed and shown that they had not actually harmed the other person. Nevertheless, critics argue, the subjects realized that they were capable of inflicting severe pain on other people. Milgram therefore had a psychiatrist interview a sample of his obedient subjects a year after the study. No evidence was found of psychological trauma or injury. Moreover, one study reported that subjects viewed participation in the obedience experiment as a positive experience. They did not regret having participated, nor did they report any short-term negative psychological effects (Ring, Wallston, & Corey, 1970).

FOCUS

▶ Identify the principal finding in studies of obedience. pp. 598–599

▶ What evidence exists to show that modeling is a way of inducing compliance?   p. 601

▶ Identify the ethical issues in Milgram's study.   pp. 601–602

Concluding Note

Human behavior is profoundly affected by subtle yet strong social influences. The Asch studies showed that people conform in their judgments and behavior, even when not directly asked to do so. Milgram's obedience studies showed that people are willing to comply with the desires of a scientific researcher, even when it is psychologically difficult to do so. Social psychologists recognize that our behavior is shaped by early experiences, by others in our lives, and by daily influences such as advertising. We are not programmed machines; we examine other people's nonverbal messages, we read between their smiles, and we resist (or give in to) attempts to change our attitudes or to cause us to comply with others' wishes. Our day-to-day behavior is affected by the situation and the context in which it occurs. No person is an island, unaffected by other people's attitudes and behavior.

In this chapter, we have examined the components and characteristics that make up the social world of individuals. We have seen that other people affect attitudes, help shape our individual self-perceptions, and exert powerful influences on individual behavior. However, this is only half the story. In the next chapter, we will explore the interactions that occur among individuals and focus on the variables that can influence those interactions. We will see in studies of environment, groups, and aggression that many other factors operate to influence individual behavior.

Summary & Review

Attitudes

What is social psychology?

Social psychology is the study of how individuals influence and are influenced by the thoughts, feelings, and behaviors of other individuals. p. 574

What are the essential characteristics of attitudes?

Attitudes are lasting patterns of feelings, beliefs, and behavior tendencies toward other people, ideas, or objects which are based in our experiences and shape our future behavior. Our attitudes are usually evaluative in nature and have cognitive, emotional, and behavioral dimensions, each of which serves a function. pp. 574–575

What are the key components of attitude change?

Social psychologists have identified four components of attitude change: the communicator, the communication, the medium, and the audience. pp. 577–579

The elaboration likelihood model focuses on what two routes of attitude change?

The *elaboration likelihood model* proposed by Petty and Cacioppo asserts that there are two routes to persuasion: central and peripheral. The central route emphasizes rational decision making; the peripheral route, which is more indirect and superficial, emphasizes emotional and motivational influences. pp. 579–580

What is cognitive dissonance?

Cognitive dissonance is the discomfort that results when an individual maintains two or more beliefs, attitudes, or behaviors that are inconsistent with one another. p. 581

KEY TERMS: *social psychology,* p. 574; *attitude,* p. 574; *elaboration likelihood model,* p. 574; *cognitive dissonance,* p. 581; *self-perception theory,* p. 582; *balance theory,* p. 583.

Social Cognition

What is social cognition?

Social cognition is the thought process of making sense of events, people, ourselves, and the world in general through analyzing and interpreting them. Often, people use mental shorts in making sense of the world to save time; they develop rules of thumb. pp. 584–585

What is nonverbal communication, and how is it used in social cognition?

Nonverbal communication is information provided by cues or actions that involve movements of the body, especially the face, and sometimes the vocal cords. These sources of information help people make judgments about other people and about events in the world.   pp. 585–587

What is attribution, and how is it used?

Attribution is the process by which someone infers other people's motives and intentions from observing their behavior and deciding whether the causes of the behavior are *dispositional* (internal) or *situational* (external). Attribution helps people make sense of the world, organize their thoughts quickly, and maintain a sense of control over the environment. It helps people feel competent and masterful and maintain a sense of balance because it helps them predict similar events in the future.   pp. 588–589

Describe the most common attribution errors.

Two of the most common errors are the fundamental attribution error and the actor-observer effect. The *fundamental attribution error* is the tendency to attribute other people's behavior to dispositional causes rather than situational causes. The *actor-observer effect* is the tendency for people to attribute the behavior of others to dispositional causes but to attribute their own behavior to situational causes.   p. 590

What is learned helplessness?

Learned helplessness is the behavior of giving up or not responding, exhibited by subjects exposed to negative consequences or punishment over which they feel they have no control. pp. 590–591

How do people develop self-perceptions?

Early social interactions with parents, peers, and institutions strongly affect *self-perception* and social behavior. Behavior may be influenced not only by personal thoughts but also by environmental factors such as television, direct reinforcement, or group pressures. People's self-perceptions are determined in part by how they interact with and view others. p. 591

What is locus of control?

People's locus of control may be either external or internal. Individuals who place the causes of what happens to them in the outside world are said to have an external locus of control. Those who believe they control what happens to them have an internal locus of control.   pp. 593–594

KEY TERMS: *social cognition,* p. 584; *impression formation,*

continued

Summary & Review

p. 584; *nonverbal communication,* p. 585; *body language,* p. 586; *attribution,* p. 588; *fundamental attribution error,* p. 590; *actor-observer effect,* p. 590; *learned helplessness,* p. 591; *self-perceptions,* p. 591; *role,* p. 592; *self-serving bias,* p. 592.

Social Influence

Explain social influence and conformity.

Social influence is the way in which one or more people alter the attitudes or behavior of others. Social influence is easily seen in studies of conformity. *Conformity* occurs when a person changes attitudes or behaviors to be consistent with other people or with social norms.   p. 595

What is obedience, and what did Milgram's studies of obedience demonstrate?

Obedience is the process by which a person complies with the orders of another person or group of people. Milgram's studies demonstrated that an individual's ability to resist coer-

cion is limited (65 percent of subjects in one study delivered what they thought were the highest possible levels of shock to other participants), although the presence of an ally who refuses to participate reduces obedience and indicates the importance of social influences on behavior. pp. 598–600

KEY TERMS: *social influence,* p. 595; *obedience,* p. 598; *debriefing,* p. 602.

CONNECTIONS

I f you are interested in...

The way people form self-concepts, see ...

CHAPTER 8, pp. 304–308

How early interactions with parents, friends, and relatives help shape a child's developing self-concept.

CHAPTER 12, pp. 439–440

How humanists such as Carl Rogers focused their theories around the idea of an emerging and satisfying self-concept.

CHAPTER 15, pp. 553–554

How cognitive psychologists claim that a person's self-concept can be bolstered through cognitive (thought) reshaping.

Gender differences and social behavior, see ...

CHAPTER 8, p. 305

How gender segregation often begins in childhood years during play.

CHAPTER 9, pp. 333–334

Why and when men and women follow different life courses, especially when it comes to midlife transitions.

CHAPTER 14, pp. 505, 507, 520

The finding that some psychological disorders are more prevalent in women than in men.

The formation of attitudes, see ...

CHAPTER 5, pp. 193–195

How social (observational) learning theory claims that people learn attitudes by observing the behavior and attitudes of others.

CHAPTER 8, p. 305

The way children's and adolescents' developing attitudes, which are often based on sex role stereotypes, have their roots in childhood learning.

17

Social Interactions

Two years ago, there was a toxic waste spill, which flowed into a stream that flowed into a small lake in my neighborhood. Children occasionally swim in this lake, and fish are regularly caught there. The reaction of the neighborhood was swift; people became alarmed about their health and welfare. Signs went up warning people to stay away, and property owners worried about the value of their homes.

My neighbors feared cancer and monetary losses from the disintegration of their community. The phone lines buzzed, the press was brought in, and the local environmental control agency was mobilized. In the end, the spill turned out to be very localized, the levels of toxins were low, and no one was hurt. There were some small legal claims against the chemical company that had spilled the waste. However, from a social psychologist's view, the mobilization of the residents in my neighborhood was classic. In a neighborhood group, people became empowered; discussions ensued, and people were energized. Individuals who had never met one another started sharing ideas, and people who had never given much thought to hazardous waste became knowledgeable and outspoken on the subject.

Human behavior is affected by powerful social interactions, which are affected by a wide range of variables. Environmental psychologists study how physical settings such as people's homes and neighborhoods affect behavior. They are interested in such issues as the effects of crowding, how personal space can be changed to meet changing needs, and neighborhood reactions to toxic waste spills. These psychologists examine not only whole neighborhoods but also smaller groups. They study some of the darker sides of human behavior, such as aggression and prejudice, and more prosocial behaviors, such as helping, friendship, attraction, and love. These topics are the focus of this chapter.

Environmental Psychology

Imagine that it is a cool spring day and you are relaxing on a park bench, when the baby of the man seated next to you begins to cry. Now imagine that it is 90 degrees on a very crowded, stuffy airplane and you have spent the last 15 minutes getting your assigned seat, when, suddenly, the baby of the woman standing next to you starts bawling. The infant in the park was unhappy and needed attention; the baby on the airplane is a screaming brat. Clearly, environmental conditions influence our reactions. **Environmental psychology** is the study of how physical settings affect human behavior and how people change their environment, often to make it more comfortable and acceptable.

Studying the Environment

Environmental psychologists study the physical and social aspects of the environment, how the individual behaves in it, and how it might be changed. The studies are often conducted in institutional settings, such as schools, hospitals, and churches. For example, consider the design of a nursing station in a hospital. The station is the center of activity on each floor, and in traditional hospital floor plans it is usually placed between two long corridors. An alternative is to place it at the hub of a wheel-like arrangement of rooms (a radial design). Most of the patient rooms would then be closer to the nursing station, and nurses could reach them faster and more efficiently. When Trites and his coworkers (1970) investigated worker satisfaction with different hospital designs, they found a distinct preference for the radial design. That result led to the redesigning of many hospital floors (Proshansky & O'Hanlon, 1977).

Environmental Variables

The environment includes not only the shape of a building, the layout of a hospital floor or a dormitory, or the arrangement of buildings in a housing project or shopping mall. It also includes such variables as furniture and fixtures, climate, noise level, and the number of people per square foot. Environmental psychologists study the relationships among the many variables. Whether a room is perceived as crowded, for example, is determined not only by the number of people in it but also by the room's size and shape, furniture layout, ceiling height, number of windows, wall colors, lighting—as well as the time of day. Researchers who look at global environmental systems such as cities, communities, and neighborhoods must consider all these variables and more. Two of the easiest environmental variables to control for people's well-being are temperature and noise.

Environmental psychology: The study of how physical settings affect human behavior and how human behavior affects the environment.

FIGURE 17.1

Heat and Aggression

A study of violence in Houston, Texas, showed that over a 2-year period, as the temperature increased, so did the rate of murders and rapes. (*Based on data from Anderson & Anderson, 1984.*)

Temperature. Very hot or very cold climates can cause behavioral effects ranging from annoyance to an inability to function. New England industrial workers, for example, would never survive the winter without proper shelter, heating, and warm clothes; and southern industrial workers would be less productive without air conditioning during the summer.

Environmental variables that impair work performance are considered stressors. As we saw in chapter 13, a **stressor** is a stimulus that affects an organism in physically or psychologically injurious ways and usually elicits feelings such as anxiety, tension, and physiological arousal. Temperature can be a stressor that affects many areas, including academic performance, driving an automobile, and being attracted toward others. In general, performance is optimal at moderate temperatures and becomes progressively worse at high or low temperatures.

When the temperature rises and people become uncomfortable, they are more likely to make risky decisions, be less accurate, behave erratically, and be less controlled (Kudoh et al., 1991). Research shows that as temperature rises, aggression increases. Hotter regions of the world show more aggression; and hotter years, months, and days have all been associated with more aggressive behaviors, such as murder, riots, and wife beatings (C. A. Anderson, 1989). (See, for example, Figure 17.1.) Laboratory research on temperature can never be identical to situations in a normal office or home; therefore, ongoing field-based work is likely to provide better evidence about the exact nature of a relationship between heat and aggression (Anderson & DeNeve, 1992; Bell, 1992).

Noise. Another environmental variable that can affect behavior is *noise*—unwanted sound. Noise is a stressor that can stimulate people to uncommonly high levels of arousal and poor performance.

Stressor: A stimulus that affects an organism in physically or psychologically injurious ways and elicits feelings such as anxiety, tension, and physiological arousal.

Some noises are almost always present. Among them are the buzzing of fluorescent lights, the humming of refrigerators, the banging of doors as they open or close, the chirping of birds, the engine sounds of moving cars, and the chattering of people as they talk. Although some of these sounds may be unwanted, they are usually not too disruptive; nor are they stressors. They rarely raise levels of arousal or interfere with daily activities.

However, an unpredictable and intermittent noise of moderate intensity, such as a train whistle, can impair performance on tasks that involve sustained attention or memory. And if noise raises physiological arousal to very high levels, it may impair performance in general and even cause hearing damage (see chapter 3). Thus, noise acts as a stressor when it interferes with communication, raises physiological arousal, or is so loud it causes pain. More commonly, noise simply interferes with our ability to concentrate.

Crowding

Another environmental variable is the number of people. In some situations that involve many people, you may feel closed in and crowded. In other situations, the excitement of a crowd may make you feel exhilarated. It is not the size of a space or the number of people that causes you to feel crowded; rather, **crowding** is the perception that your space is too limited. Thus, crowding is a psychological state. One person might feel crowded and uncomfortable in a mall filled with Christmas shoppers; someone else might think that throngs promote a holiday ambiance.

Crowding is affected by both social and spatial density. *Social density* is the number of people in a given space; *spatial density* is the size of a space with a fixed number of people in it. (See Figure 17.2 for a graphic view of social versus spatial density.) For example, in an empty theater, a person might feel lonely; but in a full, or even half-full, theater, the person might feel crowded. Similarly, the first few people who arrive at a party often feel awkward and ill at ease; yet, within an hour, with perhaps only 20 people there, they may feel closed in. Researchers must be careful to separate the variables of social and spatial density (Baum, 1987).

Crowding in Dorms. A study on the effects of crowding in dormitories was done in 1973 by Valins and Baum. The dormitories were of two designs: (1) corridors with long hallways, 2 people per room, 34 people per floor, and a shared bathroom and lounge; or (2) suites, with 4 or 6 students sharing a bathroom and lounge, and several suites per floor. The actual space per student was about the same in both types of dormitories. Corridor residents reported too many people on their floor and too many unwanted interactions; 67 percent of corridor residents found their living space crowded, compared with 25 percent of suite residents. Valins and Baum (1973) concluded that corridor designs promoted "excessive social interaction and that such interaction is associated with the experience of crowding" (p. 249).

If some dormitories produce feelings of crowding, as Valins and Baum suggested, these feelings should be evident in people's behavior. In a now classic study, Bickman and colleagues (1973) compared the helping behavior shown by students living in housing of different densities. They used a measure called the *lost-letter technique,* in which unmailed letters were purposely dropped in dormitory corridors. They reasoned that someone finding the letter would assume that a person in the dormitory had lost it.

The dependent variable was the number of "lost" letters that were subsequently mailed. The independent variable was the density of housing. The experiment involved high-density dormitories (high-rise, 22-story towers, each housing more than 500 students), medium-density dorms (4- to 7-story buildings, each housing about 165 students), and low-density dorms (2- to 4-story buildings, with about 58

Crowding: The perception that one's space is too restricted.

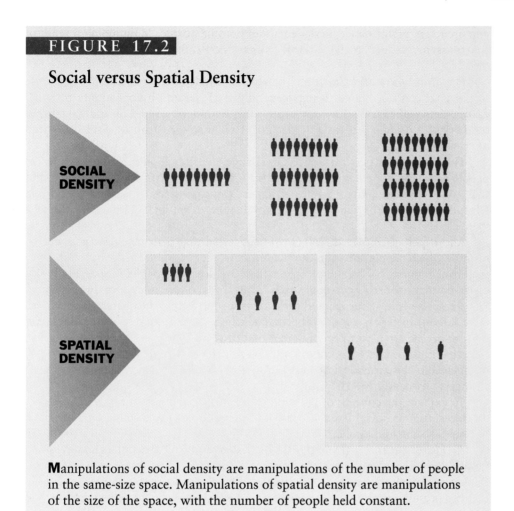

FIGURE 17.2

Social versus Spatial Density

Manipulations of social density are manipulations of the number of people in the same-size space. Manipulations of spatial density are manipulations of the size of the space, with the number of people held constant.

students each). Letters were dropped unobtrusively in areas near stairwells and elevators, with no more than one letter per corridor. The letters were addressed, sealed, and stamped but had no return address.

The results showed that helping behavior was 63 percent in high-density dorms, 87 percent in medium-density dorms, and 100 percent in low-density dorms. When questionnaires were distributed to the students in the dorms, the answers generally reflected attitudes related to the kind of housing in which the students lived. For example, students in high-density dorms reported feeling less trust, cooperativeness, and responsibility than did students in the lower-density dorms. The researchers concluded that students living in the higher-density dormitories behaved in a less socially responsible manner toward other dormitory residents. Baum believes that in situations of high density, people feel stressed, out of control, and crowded. All of this contributes to potential problems in situations of high density—for example, in prisons (Fleming, Baum, & Weiss, 1987).

Controlling the Environment

Although many of the effects of crowding are not consistent across all situations or populations, certain effects seem to be universal. In high-density situations, people feel stressed and sometimes overaroused. They may feel alone or anonymous, and they may withdraw from the situation. They may become apathetic, exhibit impaired task performance, and sometimes become hostile. Maintaining a sense of control seems to be a crucial variable (Ruback & Pandey, 1991).

Personal Space and Culture. To help assert individuality and maintain a sense of personal control, human beings generally try to establish appropriate personal spaces. **Personal space** is the area or invisible boundary around an individual that the person considers private. Encroachment on that space causes displeasure and often withdrawal.

The size of your personal space can change, depending on the situation and the people near you. For example, you may walk arm in arm with a family member but will avoid physical contact with a stranger. You may stand close to a friend and whisper in his ear but will keep a certain distance from an elevator operator or a store clerk.

Anthropologist Edward Hall (1966) suggested that personal space is a mechanism by which people communicate with others. He proposed that people adhere to established norms of personal space that are learned in childhood. Hall also observed that the use of personal space varies from culture to culture. In the United States, especially in suburban and rural areas, people are used to generous space and large homes. In Japan, on the other hand, where there is little space available per person, people are used to small homes that provide little private space. In general, Western cultures insist on a fair amount of space for people, reserving proximity for intimacy and close friends; but Arab cultures allow much smaller distances between strangers (Rustemli, 1991).

To explain the concept of personal space, Hall classified four *spatial zones,* or distances, used in social interactions with other people. The distances are intimate, personal, social, and public.

An *intimate distance* (from 0 to 18 inches) is reserved for people who have great familiarity with one another. It is acceptable for comforting someone who is hurt, for lovers, for physicians, and for athletes. The closeness enables a person to hold another person, examine the other's hair and eyes, and hear the other's breath.

An acceptable distance for close friends and everyday interactions is *personal distance* (1.5 to 4 feet). It is the distance used for most social interactions. At 1.5 to 2 feet, someone might tell a secret to a close friend. At 2 feet, people can walk together while conversing. At 2 to 4 feet, they maintain good contact with a coworker without seeming too personal or impersonal.

Social distance (4 to 12 feet) is used for business and for interactions with strangers. At 4 to 6 feet, people are close enough to communicate their ideas effectively but far enough away to remain separated. Personal space in the social zone may be controlled by physical barriers, such as a desk to separate a clerk, receptionist, or boss from the people with whom the person interacts.

Public distance (12 to 25 feet) minimizes personal contact. It is the distance at which politicians speak at lunch clubs, teachers instruct classes of students, and actors and musicians perform. Public distance is sufficiently great to eliminate personal communication between individuals and their audiences.

Of course, determining personal space is a tricky endeavor, and researchers are trying to sort out distance estimations (Zakay, Hayduk, & Tsai, 1992). Figure 17.3 presents generally accepted estimates of the space people use when seated and when standing.

Privacy. Irwin Altman (1975) has suggested that the key to understanding why people feel crowded and need personal space is privacy. **Privacy** is the result of the process of controlling boundaries between people so that access is limited. Everyone needs privacy. According to Altman, privacy allows people to develop and nurture a sense of self. Without it, people feel they have no control over who and what can

Personal space: The area around an individual that is considered private and around which the person feels an invisible boundary.

Privacy: The result of the process of limiting the access of other people by controlling the boundaries between those people and oneself.

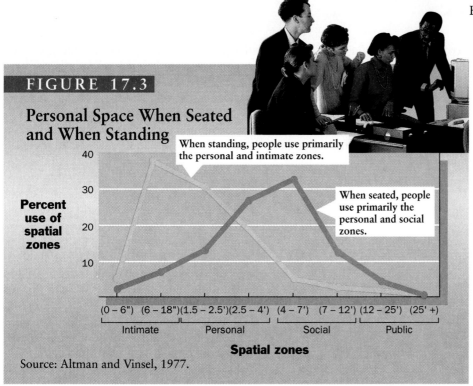

FIGURE 17.3

Personal Space When Seated and When Standing

When standing, people use primarily the personal and intimate zones.

When seated, people use primarily the personal and social zones.

Percent use of spatial zones

(0 – 6")	(6 – 18")	(1.5 – 2.5')	(2.5 – 4')	(4 – 7')	(7 – 12')	(12 – 25')	(25' +)
Intimate		Personal		Social		Public	

Spatial zones

Source: Altman and Vinsel, 1977.

intrude on them. This sense of helplessness can lead to low self-esteem and poor social adaptations. Understanding people's need for privacy is central to understanding the behavior of human beings in their environment.

One way in which people maintain a sense of privacy is to change their immediate environment. When a teenager goes into a room and closes the door, she closes herself off from other people; she limits their access to her. The teenager has set up a boundary—a closed door—behind which she can do what she wants when she wants to. Similarly, two people may enter a room and close the door, thereby controlling other people's access to them.

Maintaining a sense of privacy is closely related to territoriality, another important aspect of many people's lives. **Territorial behavior** is behavior involved in establishing, maintaining, personalizing, and defending a delineated space. It helps regulate the exclusive use of a specific area by a person or a group of people by marking a space as a private area where intruders are not welcome. Homeowners put up fences and signs that say "No Trespassing," teenagers lock their bedroom doors, street gangs defend their turf, and nations wage war in defense of national boundaries. Like personal-space behaviors, territorial behaviors are privacy-regulating mechanisms.

Preserving the Environment

An emerging area of environmental research is in controlling people's behavior in the environment, such as preventing them from littering. Research studies by Scott Geller at Virginia Polytechnic Institute found that littering can be significantly reduced if instructions for proper disposal of objects are provided; and the more specific the instructions, the less littering (Geller, 1975; Geller, Witmer, & Tuso, 1977).

Another area of research is finding out what variables make people want to preserve the environment. Consider energy conservation, including driving smaller, more fuel-efficient cars and investing in solar panels for the home. Research on these issues has shown that tax laws that reward energy savings, signs about energy conservation, and new equipment for saving energy help people adopt more energy-

Territorial behavior: Behavior involved in establishing, maintaining, personalizing, and defending a delineated space.

saving behaviors. As with littering, when people are given specific energy-saving instructions and prompts, they are more likely to comply (Geller, Winett, & Evertt, 1982).

Some tremendous worldwide problems must be solved. Geller (1989) suggests that marketing principles be combined with behavioral analysis to solve such problems as preserving the rain forests and managing wastes. First, socially beneficial ideas and behaviors must be advanced; this helps move people to intend to do such things as wear seat belts (Stasson & Fishbein, 1990). Products or ideas can be promoted by making them affordable, accessible, easy to use, and desirable (Burn, 1991). Psychologists must then analyze the wants, needs, and perceptions of the people being targeted. After these steps have been taken, the results should be evaluated to see whether the strategy has been effective. Geller claims that behavioral interventions combined with social marketing and policy strategies can provide an integrative program for environmental preservation. He also hopes for a collaboration of social action research and scholarship to preserve the quality of our environment (Geller, 1992).

Many of the social problems that need to be solved, whether environmental, social, economic or political, are often done with other people and in the context of groups. For example, the President alone does not make and implement policy; he does it with the Congress and the judiciary. Individuals working together in groups are our next topic.

FOCUS

▶ How do environmental stressors affect our behavior? p. 609

▶ Describe the hypothesis and results of the lost-letter experiment in the dormitory. pp. 610–611

▶ What is the effect of the four spatial zones that define personal space? p. 612

Behavior in Groups

"Membership has its privileges," according to American Express. By appealing to people's desire to be part of a group, the charge card company employs psychological principles to sell its product and engender loyalty. To make the American Express group as attractive as possible, the company runs magazine ads featuring famous athletes, actors, politicians, and businesspeople who are cardholders. Who wouldn't want to identify with such an elite group?

Membership does confer certain advantages, which is why people belong to all kinds of groups. There are formal groups, such as the American Association of University Students, and informal ones, such as peer groups. A **group** can be either a large number of people working toward a common purpose or a small number of people (even two) who are loosely related and have some common goals or interests. By joining a group, people indicate that they agree with or have a serious interest in its purpose. If a major function of the American Cancer Society is to raise money for cancer research, a person's membership indicates an interest in finding a cure for cancer.

Group: A number of individuals who are loosely or cohesively related and who share some common characteristics and goals.

Social facilitation: A change in performance that occurs when people believe they are in the presence of other people.

Social Facilitation

Individual behavior is affected not only by membership in a group but also by the mere presence of a group. For example, **social facilitation** is a change in performance that occurs when people believe they are in the presence of other people. For example, one person practicing a sport with a degree of success may do even better when

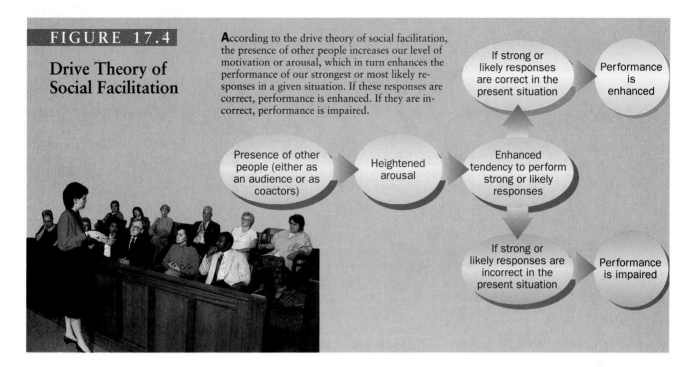

FIGURE 17.4

Drive Theory of Social Facilitation

According to the drive theory of social facilitation, the presence of other people increases our level of motivation or arousal, which in turn enhances the performance of our strongest or most likely responses in a given situation. If these responses are correct, performance is enhanced. If they are incorrect, performance is impaired.

Presence of other people (either as an audience or as coactors) → Heightened arousal → Enhanced tendency to perform strong or likely responses

If strong or likely responses are correct in the present situation → Performance is enhanced

If strong or likely responses are incorrect in the present situation → Performance is impaired

other people are watching. Another person, however, may do worse when other people are around.

How the presence of others changes our behavior, and whether it changes the behavior for better or worse, is illustrated in Figure 17.4. This figure is based on Robert Zajonc's (1965) drive theory of social facilitation. According to Zajonc, the presence of others produces heightened arousal, which leads to a greater likelihood of performing a particular response (Jackson & Latané, 1981; Zajonc, 1965). But just what is the nature of the heightened arousal? This is a source of some debate.

One theory of social facilitation suggests that fear of evaluation—not the mere presence of people—brings about changes in performance (see Innes & Young, 1975). If an auto mechanic knows that a customer is watching him repair an engine, he will likely increase his work speed to convince the observer of his efficiency and professionalism.

However, Bond and Titus (1983) suggest that the effects of social facilitation are often overestimated and the effects of believing oneself to be observed are often underestimated. They caution that a model of social facilitation must take into account the actual and believed presence of observers, as well as the perceived importance of the evaluation by the perceived observers. Thus, being evaluated by a friend or relative has a different effect from being evaluated by a stranger (Buck et al., 1992).

Social Loafing

A decrease in an individual's effort and productivity as a result of working in a group is known as **social loafing.** Suppose you and your friends are asked to help someone move a grand piano; in order to move the piano, you join forces with your friends and accomplish the task. Did you expend as much effort as a member of the group as you would have expended if you had had to move the piano by yourself? Research says that people exert more effort alone than when other people help—social loafing. In an experiment in which individuals were instructed to clap their hands and cheer, they clapped and cheered less loudly when they were part of a group (Latané, Williams, & Harkins, 1979).

Social loafing: The decrease in productivity that occurs when an individual works in a group instead of alone.

Social loafing may occur when an individual's performance within a group cannot be evaluated.

Most psychologists claim that social loafing occurs when individual performance within a group cannot be evaluated; that is, poor performance may go undetected, and exceptional performance may go unrecognized. Consequently, people feel less pressure to work hard or efficiently. One study showed that as group size increased, individual members believed their own efforts were more dispensable—the group could function without their help. "Let George do it!" became the prevailing attitude (Kerr & Bruun, 1983).

Social loafing is minimized when the task is attractive and rewarding and the group is committed to high task performance (Zaccaro, 1984). It is also less apparent when a group is small, when the members know one another well, and when a group leader calls on individuals by name or lets it be known that individual performance may be evaluated (Williams, Harkins, & Latané, 1981). Some researchers have noted decreased social loafing when people have the opportunity to assess their own performance relative to other people's, even though no one else evaluated them (Szymanski & Harkins, 1987). Social loafing is also minimized when people are asked to weigh their performance against an objective standard, even though they are not evaluated by anyone else (Harkins & Szymanski, 1988). Further, social loafing is minimized when coworkers perform poorly on meaningful tasks (Williams & Karau, 1991). Thus, as with so many other social phenomena, a wide array of variables can alter the extent of social loafing.

Group Polarization

In groups, people may be willing to adopt behaviors slightly more extreme than their individual behavior tendencies. They may be willing to make decisions that are risky or even daring. A person who by herself is unwilling to invest money in a venture may change her mind on hearing that other members of her group are investing. Some early research on group decision making focused on the willingness of individuals to accept more risky alternatives when other members of the group did so; this research described such individuals as making a *risky shift* in their decisions.

In a group, individuals initially perceive themselves as being more extreme than the other members of the group. They believe they are more fair, more right-minded, more liberal, and so on. When they discover that their positions are not very different from those of others in the group, they shift, or become *polarized,* to show that they are even more right-minded, more fair, or more liberal. They also may become more assertive in expressing their views. Shifts or exaggerations that take place among group members after group discussions are referred to as **group polarization;** in individuals, we refer to the shift as a *choice shift* (Zuber, Crott, & Werner, 1992). See Figure 17.5 for a diagram of how group polarization occurs.

A *persuasive arguments* explanation of the phenomenon asserts that people tend to become more extreme after hearing views similar to their own. A person who is mildly liberal on an issue becomes even more liberal, more polarized. As more argu-

Group polarization: The exaggeration of individuals' preexisting attitudes as a result of group discussion.

ments favoring the person's view are presented in the group discussion, the individual's view is likely to become more extreme. The explanation therefore suggests that people in a group often become more wedded to their initial views instead of becoming more moderate. If other people in the group hold similar views, that may polarize them even more.

The effects of group polarization are particularly evident among juries. After group discussion, jury members are likely to decide on their initial views and argue for them more strongly. Thus, individual jury members with an initially mild view toward a defendant will have an even milder view after group discussions; their initial view becomes a verdict.

Another explanation for group polarization is **diffusion of responsibility**—the feeling of individual members of a group that they cannot be held responsible for the group's actions. If a church youth group makes a decision to invest money, for example, no single individual is responsible. Diffusion of responsibility allows the teenagers to make far more extreme investment decisions as a group than they would individually.

Social comparison may also play a role in group polarization. People compare their view with others whom they respect and who may hold more extreme views than theirs. Feeling as right-minded as their colleagues, they become at least as liberal or fair as their peer group—they polarize their views. After a group becomes polarized, many people in the group may share the same opinion. When such an event occurs (as it often does with government officials), people sometimes fall into a trap called *groupthink*.

Groupthink

Studies of decision making in government have often focused on the concept of **groupthink**—the tendency of people in a group to seek concurrence with one another when reaching a decision, usually prematurely. Groupthink occurs when group members reinforce commonly held beliefs in the interest of getting along, rather than effectively evaluating alternative solutions to the problem. The group does not allow its members to disagree or to take dissenting opinions and evaluate options realistically (Janis, 1983). It discredits or ignores information not held in common. See Figure 17.6 on page 618 for a summary of the factors leading to groupthink.

Studies of history and government offer several examples of groupthink resulting in defective decision making: consider the Bay of Pigs invasion. In the Bay of Pigs incident, President Kennedy decided to go ahead with a CIA plan, devised by anti-Castro exiles, to invade Cuba. When the President asked for counsel from his advisers—an impressive group with wide political experience—no one voted against the plan, and the mission was carried out. The Bay of Pigs invasion turned out to be a major political fiasco and nearly resulted in war between the United States and the Soviet Union. Janis (1982) and McCauley (1989) cite this episode as an example of groupthink.

Social psychologist Ivan Steiner (1982) suggests that groupthink occurs when members' overriding concern is to maintain group cohesiveness and harmony. Maintaining cohesiveness helps individuals believe that the group cannot make mistakes.

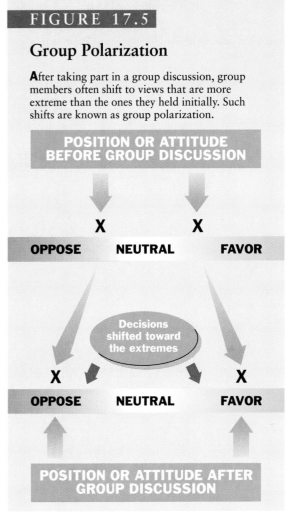

FIGURE 17.5

Group Polarization

After taking part in a group discussion, group members often shift to views that are more extreme than the ones they held initially. Such shifts are known as group polarization.

POSITION OR ATTITUDE BEFORE GROUP DISCUSSION

X   X

OPPOSE   NEUTRAL   FAVOR

Decisions shifted toward the extremes

X   X

OPPOSE   NEUTRAL   FAVOR

POSITION OR ATTITUDE AFTER GROUP DISCUSSION

Diffusion of responsibility: The feeling of individual members of a group that they cannot be held responsible for the group's actions.

Groupthink: The phenomenon of people in a group reinforcing one another and seeking concurrence and group cohesiveness, rather than effectively evaluating choices and reasoning.

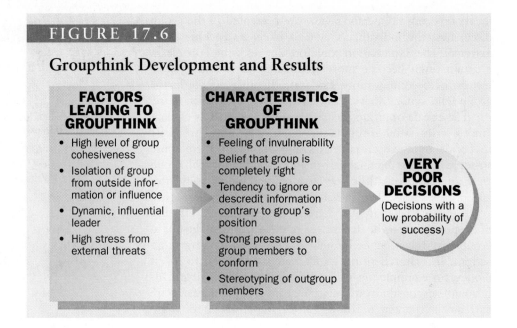

In addition, strong leaders often insulate a group from information or from other people to keep the group thinking in one direction (McCauley, 1989).

Although groupthink is not inevitable, it is common enough that social psychologists consider it an important issue in group influence on decision making. They look at it in terms of group behavior, social influence, and a self-serving and self-reinforcing mechanism. Students of political science and history can use the concept of groupthink in training new leaders in decision making. Group leaders can help deter groupthink by fostering open inquiry into issues, by creating subgroups to look at specific parts of a decision, and by planning for additional meetings before a final decision is made.

Despite its intuitive appeal, research support for groupthink is minimal. Aldag and Fuller (1993) assert that despite its lack of empirical support, groupthink continues to be viewed as a defective process that we should guard against. They argue that groupthink can happen, but that research into leaders and committees needs to focus on other variables. For example, among other things, small group research needs to examine the group structure, the decisions that have to be made, the degree of stress associated with the decisions, perceptions of invulnerability, how groups will make the actual decision, and the political consequences of the decision for its members and leaders. Aldag and Fuller's assertion that groupthink is not as potent as once believed will be evaluated in the next decade by social psychologists; this evaluation may alter the way leaders run groups and the way social psychologists think about group behavior.

Unrestrained Group Behavior

When placed in a group, normally thoughtful people have been known to take part in irrational behaviors. In the early 1970s, for example, streaking became popular on college campuses. A naked person darted out from behind a bush, ran across campus or through a crowded lobby, and disappeared. Soon, streaking groups with hundreds of students began to form. The behavior was not considered a matter of individual responsibility but was instead a group decision.

A key component of unrestrained behavior such as streaking or mob violence is *anonymity.* Anonymity produces a lack of self-awareness and self-perception that leads to decreased concern with social evaluation. When people have fewer concerns about being evaluated, they are more willing to engage in inappropriate or irrational behaviors. Without accurate self-perception, people exhibit behaviors they would normally avoid.

The view that no single individual can be held responsible for the behavior of a group focuses on **deindividuation**—the process by which individuals lose their sense of self-awareness and distinctive personalities in the context of a group (Diener et al., 1980). Deindividuation (and its accompanying arousal) can lead to shifts in people's perceptions of how their behavior will be viewed—and thus to less controlled or less careful decisions about their behavior (see Prentice-Dunn & Rogers, 1984). With deindividuation, people alter their thoughts about decisions.

Groups such as the military, prisons, and cults use deindividuation to encourage their members to conform. In boot camp, military recruits are made to feel that they are there to serve the group, not their conscience. In prisons, inmates are made to wear uniforms and cut their hair short and are assigned numbers. With their unique personality stripped away, they are no longer treated as individuals and are made to behave as members of one large prison group. A cult persuades members to go along with group beliefs and acquire a sense of obligation to the group by asking individual members to perform increasingly taxing services on the group's behalf.

We have looked at the characteristics and dynamics of individuals within group settings. Let us now examine one particular aspect of social behavior that may occur within or between groups: aggression.

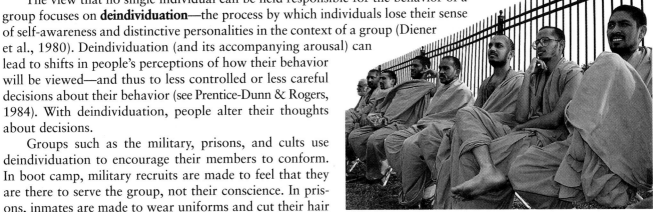

Some groups use deindividuation to encourage their members to conform.

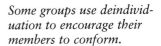

FOCUS

▶ Explain the principle of social loafing.   pp. 615–616

▶ Describe the phenomenon of group polarization and give an example from your own experience.   pp. 616–617

▶ Identify the social variables that are important in explaining unrestrained group behavior.   pp. 618–619

Aggression

We killed, killed, killed. The Malays would stop and go through people's pockets and take their watches and money. We did not think of watches or money. We thought only of killing. . . . [W]e were drunk with blood.

A Semai soldier told that tale to American anthropologist Robert K. Dentan (1968), who lived with the man's tribe for more than a year. What is most remarkable about the story is that the Semais are among the most gentle people on earth. Not a single murder has been recorded among this central Malayan tribe, adults never physically attack one another, children are taught to be nonviolent, and the tribe has no police force. The Semai even regret having to kill their chickens for food. Yet, despite their pacifist heritage, Semai tribesmen were recruited and trained by the British to fight Communist guerrillas in the early 1950s. When their comrades fell in battle, the Semai avenged themselves on the enemy with terrible ferocity. One veteran even reported drinking the blood of a man he killed. Upon their return home, however, the Semai soldiers returned to their pacifist ways.

In contrast to the Semai, the Yanomamo Indians of Brazil and Venezuela are among the most violent people on earth. Their murder rate is three times that of the

Deindividuation: The process by which individuals in a group lose their sense of self-awareness and concern with evaluation.

city of Detroit, and an estimated 44 percent of the men aged 25 or older have participated in at least one killing. But other South American Indian tribes are as peaceful as the Yanomamo are violent. If people can be either loving or violent, what compels them to act one way or the other?

When people feel unable to control situations that affect their lives, they may become frustrated, angry, and aggressive. Social psychologists define **aggression** as any behavior designed to harm another person or thing. An aggressive person may attempt to harm others physically through force; verbally through gossip, rumors, or irritating comments; or emotionally by withholding love. On a larger scale, whole countries attempt to harm others by acts of war. Three major theories attempt to explain aggressive behavior; they involve instincts, acquired drives, and social learning.

Instincts

Some psychologists believe that many aspects of behavior, including aggression, are inborn (see DiLalla & Gottesman, 1991); but most psychologists and the American Psychological Association (1990) do not agree. Those who believe that people are genetically predisposed toward aggression are termed *nativists*. One nativist, Freud, suggested that people have a destructive desire to release aggression against themselves, a death instinct he called *thanatos*. However, Freud never fully developed the concept of a death instinct, and today it is not widely accepted.

Another nativist, ethologist and Nobel laureate Konrad Lorenz (1903–1989), investigated aggressive behavior through naturalistic observation. He noted that although animals of the same species fight with one another, they often use signals that tell them to stop fighting, well before death would occur. Recent research argues that both animals and human beings can be aggressive; whether that aggression is inhibited or expressed depends on previous experiences and the organism's current social context, such as whether the organism is being provoked or whether it has been raised in a hostile environment (Lore & Schultz, 1993).

According to Lorenz (1964), aggression is instinctive and spontaneous; the aggressive instinct serves to maximize the use of food, space, and resources. Lorenz stressed the social implications of people's aggressive instincts, focusing on their adaptive values.

Acquired Drives

Another explanation for aggressive behavior is that the frustration of goal-directed behavior leads to aggression—the **frustration-aggression hypothesis,** initially proposed by Dollard and colleagues (1939). This theory relies on everyday experience demonstrating that people involved in goal-oriented tasks often become aggressive or angry when frustrated. For example, ordinarily, you may be unlikely to become upset if another car pulls out into traffic in front of you. However, if you are in a hurry to get to work, you might honk angrily at the other driver. On a larger scale, the violence between Catholics and Protestants in Northern Ireland is fueled in part by intense competition for decent jobs in a depressed economy.

Berkowitz (1964) examined the evidence for the frustration-aggression hypothesis and proposed a modified view of it. He suggested that frustration creates a *readiness* for aggressive acts rather than creating actual aggression. He showed that, even when frustration is present, certain events or situations must exist before aggression occurs—for example, a weapon lying on a table. In a later reformulation, Berkowitz (1989) suggested that frustrations generate aggressive inclinations to the extent that they arouse negative feelings in the person affected (Berkowitz, 1990). Berkowitz's conception accounts for the times people don't become aggressive when frustrated.

Aggression: Any behavior designed to harm another person or thing.

Frustration-aggression hypothesis: The view that frustration of goal-directed behavior leads to aggression.

Many psychologists find the frustration-aggression hypothesis too simple, but it is still beneficial—in part because it has led to other research that helps describe behavior, for example, social learning theory.

Social Learning

Danny is engrossed in watching André the Giant in a professional wrestling match on a Saturday afternoon. Almost without realizing it, he lurches over and tackles his sister, Lori, whose screams prompt their mother to burst into the room and turn off the TV.

From a psychologist's viewpoint, Danny's mother did the right thing. When children are in situations for which they have not established their own standard responses, they copy the behavior of others. Thus, they imitate characters they see in movies or on television. According to Bandura, aggressive behavior can be both established and eliminated through *observational learning,* as we saw in chapter 5. Bandura argues that children are not born with aggressive instincts but learn aggression (or nonaggression) by seeing other people, including parents, teachers, and peers, exhibiting such behavior. A child will learn to be aggressive by imitating another child using a toy gun or by watching parents or teachers act aggressively. On the other hand, a child will learn to be nonaggressive if he or she sees parents acting nonaggressively or someone being punished for aggressive behavior. Semai children learned gentleness from their parents; then, as soldiers, they were taught to kill by the British.

Many researchers point out that conclusions about the effects of social learning and violence on children cannot accurately be made from experimental settings. We define *violence* as aggression in which a person seeks to inflict injury through physical force. Laboratories are not people's homes, and they have other distracting elements that make them unlike real-life situations. Despite such problems, the results of studies suggest that after being exposed to aggressive situations, children imitate them in subsequent play. However, contrary to a widely held belief, not all children

After watching an adult model take aggressive action against an inflatable doll, children imitated the aggressive behavior.

who grow up in homes in which they are exposed to violence become violent adults (Widom, 1989). It is true that many, if not most, people who are child abusers were abused themselves; but being abused does not make a person an abuser (remember, correlations do not mean causation). A wide array of positive events in a child's life may mitigate many early negative experiences.

In a classic study, Bandura, Ross, and Ross (1963) found that children who viewed aggression either live, on films, or in TV cartoons were nearly twice as aggressive in subsequent play as those who did not view aggression. Much research supports this finding (Wood, Wong, & Chachere, 1991). Worchel, Hardy, and Hurley (1976), for example, had adult subjects view films with either violent or nonviolent content and then interact with a series of research assistants. One research assistant was directed to assume a bumbling and inadequate manner by purposely making mistakes. After the subjects had viewed and interacted with the assistants, they were asked to rate them to help determine which of the assistants would be rehired. The subjects who had viewed the violent films rated the bumbling assistant lower than did those who had viewed the nonviolent films; they also were the only ones to recommend not rehiring. Their judgments were more aggressive.

Considerable evidence exists to suggest that exposure to media violence increases a person's tendency to be aggressive. In one experiment, men were angered by a female accomplice. They then watched either a violent film with scenes of torture or another film containing no violence. When the men were given an opportunity to shock the accomplice (by means of fake electrical shocks), those exposed to the violent film showed higher levels of aggression (as measured by willingness to shock the accomplice) than did those who saw the nonviolent film (Donnerstein et al., 1987). Again, exposure to films can affect subsequent behavior and especially people's thoughts about violence. Beginning in 1993, the U.S. Congress began a series of debates and threatened legislation unless the television networks became more sensitive to the impact of media violence. Their arguments were based on data such as those examined in the Applications box.

Cognitive Psychology and Aggression

Ideas are highly perishable; they become rapidly outdated and are replaced by newer, more modern ones. This has been especially true in the study of aggression. Early research was based on learning theory explanations popular in the 1950s and 1960s. Later, with the increasing influence of Skinner's behaviorism, researchers focused on operant interpretations of aggression. They studied the implications of punishing children for aggressive behavior and rewarding them for nonaggressive behavior. A shift toward social learning theory occurred in the 1970s, and the effects of television viewing were a prime focus. In the 1980s, cognitive explanations of aggression became prevalent, and researchers began to speak in terms of thought, interpretations, and expectations.

Leonard Eron (1987) conducted a longitudinal study of aggression over 22 years. He tracked the entire third-grade population (870 students) of Columbia County, a semirural area in New York State. Eron's early work, in the 1960s, examined psychological conditions that might cause aggression, especially parental attitudes toward children. He found that children rated as aggressive when they were 8 were still rated as aggressive when they were 19—and were three times more likely to have been in trouble with the law as were those rated as nonaggressive (Lefkowitz et al., 1977).

In the late 1970s, Eron and other aggression researchers looked at the same data in a new light. The full blossoming of the cognitive influence on theory and on data collection led them to probe the influences in children's lives that cause them to *interpret* the world in a way that makes them aggressive. They looked at the data with a cognitive frame of reference: An aggressive child responds to the world with combativeness because the child has internalized aggressive ideas. Eron (1987, p. 441) argued, "It was what the subjects were saying to themselves about what they wanted . . . what might be an effective or appropriate response . . . that helped determine how aggressive they are today."

Eron's work is typical of much social psychological research. He shifted his explanations from simple motivational drive reduction ideas (described in chapter 10) to social learning ideas, and finally to a cognitive-behavioral analysis of aggression.

Gender Differences in Aggression

Many people believe that men are naturally more aggressive than women. They refer to aggressive contact sports such as football and boxing, the aggressive role of men in business, the overwhelming number of violent crimes committed by men, and the

APPLICATIONS

Television and Violence

Most children spend more hours watching television than they spend in any other activity except sleep, and they are often indiscriminate viewers (Huston et al., 1992; Kubey & Csikszentmihalyi, 1990). Because children watch so much television, it serves as a major source of imitative behavior and may alter their overall aggressive thoughts and their views of life (Bushman & Geen, 1990; Cairns, 1990). The fact that television portrays so much aggressive behavior concerns parents and educators, as well as social psychologists. Half of all prime-time television characters are involved in violent activity of some kind; about one-tenth kill or are killed. Moreover, about 20 percent of television males are engaged in law enforcement, whereas fewer than 1 percent are in law enforcement in the real world (Gerbner & Gross, 1976).

In general, research supports the contention that viewers who frequently watch violent television programs are more likely to be aggressive than are viewers who see less television violence (Wood, Wong, & Chachere, 1991). Further, one study found that children exposed to large doses of television violence are less likely to help a real-life victim of violence; and another found that viewers of violence were less sympathetic to victims than were non-

viewers (Huston et al., 1992). Viewers of violence also are more fearful of becoming victims of violent acts. One study found that the viewing of violence at age 8 predicted aggressive behavior at age 19 (Eron & Huesmann, 1980). Children who play violent video games also seem to act more aggressively at later ages (Schutte et al., 1988), and even infants can become fearful by watching television (Meltzoff, 1988).

How does watching violence on television affect viewers? Baron and Byrne (1991) describe four primary effects of viewing television violence:

▶ It weakens the inhibitions of viewers.

▶ It may suggest new ideas and techniques to the uninitiated.

▶ It may prime or stimulate existing aggressive ideas.

▶ It may reduce a person's overall emotional sensitivity to violence.

Television can also have positive effects on children. Children exposed to such shows as *Sesame Street* and *Mister Rogers' Neighborhood,* which focus on topics such as sharing and caring, were more likely to engage in prosocial behavior with other children than were children in a control group who did not watch those shows (Coates, Pusser, & Goodman, 1976).

Generally, researchers have concentrated on the outcomes of watching television. Recently, however, why children watch so much television has been explored. Although environmental reasons are important (parents and brothers and sisters watch a lot), so are genetic reasons. Children of adoptive parents watched a great deal of television if their biological parents did! This is a surprising finding and is currently undergoing more extensive research (Plomin et al., 1990)

Research on the effects of television has had important social implications. Children under the age of 5 believe what they see on television to be the truth; thus, the content of television shows influences children in profound ways. Further, researchers are concerned about the widespread availability of cable television, which offers programs that portray violence more frequently and explicitly than network television does. Such shows can act as a cue for children who might already be aggressive (Josephson, 1987). Social psychologists interested in public policy are suggesting requirements for at least a certain amount of educational programming for children on every station and for controls to protect children from advertising that exploits their special vulnerability (Huston et al., 1992; Huston, Watkins, & Kunkel, 1989).

---

traditional view that men are more likely than women to be ruthless and unsympathetic. It is also generally accepted that more masculine people are more aggressive (Kogut, Langley, & O'Neal, 1992). But are men really more aggressive than women?

To learn more about gender differences in aggression, two psychologists at Purdue University, Alice Eagly and Valerie Steffen (1986), searched the psychological literature over a 15-year period for studies of adults exposed to standardized situations designed to induce aggressive behavior. They found 63 experiments that compared gender differences in aggressive behaviors. Most of the studies were conducted in laboratories, although some were conducted in field settings. The laboratory experiments were often teacher-learner situations, where a teacher had to deliver shocks to a learner (similar to the Milgram studies described in chapter 16). The

The Domestic Assault of Women

Will today's children create a gentler society? Will they deal with marital conflict through reason and caring? Or will the adults of tomorrow be even more violent than today's adults? Don Dutton, a professor of psychology at the University of British Columbia, is asking these questions to determine the causes of domestic violence, spousal abuse, and the inability of battered women to leave abusive relationships. Dutton is a social psychologist whose research into aggression and its causes led him to write *The Domestic Assault of Women* (1988), in which he encapsulates current knowledge about why many married women are violently abused by their husbands.

Prevalence. As many as 2 million women a year may be beaten by their husbands, and nearly 30 percent of all married couples report at least one violent episode. Sexual abuse and assault have been experienced by 38 to 67 percent of adult women before age 18 (Koss, 1990). Many women, long before marriage, have thus experienced assault in various forms. High levels of conflict, low socioeconomic status, and exposure to violence as a child are correlated with domestic violence (Sugarman & Hotaling, 1989). Further, younger adults (under age 30) are more likely to engage in domestic violence than are older adults (O'Leary et al., 1989); and such behaviors (pushing, shoving, slapping) are fairly stable—a person who is aggressive early in a relationship stays that way. While domestic violence against men exists, the vast majority of cases involve men abusing women.

Causes. Is there some event, action, or predisposition that makes a man abuse his wife? Early explanations of domestic violence focused on *mental disorders,* and many research studies show that men who assault women suffer from personality disorders such as those we examined in chapter 14.

Other explanations of domestic violence focus on *biological predispositions* (which will be explained further on p. 629). Sociobiological theory, for example, explains aggressive behaviors as attempts to maximize the likelihood that the aggressors and their offspring will survive. Sociobiologists argue that human beings have a genetic predisposition toward aggression. For example, a man's anger about his wife's infidelity, her intention to end a marriage, or her decisions about offspring can lead to domestic violence.

Differing from these psychiatric and biological theorists, many sociologists and psychologists believe that assaults on women by their husbands are generated by the *social rules* supporting male dominance. Although society is changing, a traditional wife is submissive and willing to be dom-

---

field experiments typically involved the experimenter cutting in line in front of a naive subject, causing mild frustration that could turn into anger and aggression.

Using a painstaking statistical procedure, Eagly and Steffen confirmed what people already expected—men are more physically aggressive than women. But they also found that both men and women use psychological aggression such as verbal abuse and angry gestures. They offer an interesting interpretation of the findings. They suggest that the differences in aggression that appear between men and women are directly related to the perceived consequences of the aggression. Women in our culture have been raised with values that make them feel especially guilty if they induce physical pain; men have not been raised with those values, at least not to the same extent. However, gender roles in our society are changing; the number of women in the work force clearly attests to that fact. Therefore, it is likely that the gender differences in willingness to induce pain—and act aggressively—will diminish in the next decade.

The environment in which people work, study, and live has such a sharp impact on their lives that social psychologists have investigated how it affects social behavior in particular. What they have found is that people's environment, including the places where they live and work, influences their aggressiveness, their thoughts, and their actions. Thus, Southerners are more likely to endorse

FOCUS

▶ What did Bandura's studies of aggression and imitation show? pp. 621–622

▶ Identify the central element of the social learning approach to aggression. pp. 621–622

inated by her husband (see Stets & Pirog-Good, 1989). According to this view, men are merely living up to cultural expectations.

None of these explanations is substantiated by all the data, and Dutton proposes a *nested ecological approach*. This approach views people as growing and developing within a social context and suggests that a valid explanation of domestic violence must examine at least four factors:

▶ The cultural values of the individuals. (Are men and women equal?)

▶ Their social situation. (Are they employed?)

▶ Their family unit. (Do they communicate as a couple?)

▶ Their level of individual development. (Do they express feelings well? Do they excuse violence? Have they witnessed family violence?)

In a comprehensive theory of assault, a potentially assaultive male must be evaluated in each of the four areas suggested. Thus, Dutton (1988, p. 25) argues:

Wife assault would be viewed as likely when a male has strong

needs to dominate women . . . and exaggerated anxiety about intimate relationships, . . . has had violent role models . . . and has poorly developed conflict-resolution skills,

. . . is currently experiencing job stress, . . . is isolated from support systems , . . . is experiencing relationship stress . . . and power struggles, . . . and exists in a culture where maleness is defined by the ability to respond to conflict aggressively.

While some see violence against women as the misuse of power by men (L. Walker, 1989), the nested ecological approach considers a complex mix of variables as determinants of assaultive behavior. Unlike most wife assault models, which focus on one level of analysis (communication, personal values, or perhaps job stress), the nested ecological approach suggests multiple levels, with the importance of each level differing in each assault case. Although it is tempting to rely on simple models of domestic assault, the reality is that human beings are complex, and the causes of assault must be understood in a larger context.

violence as a response to threats to their property or integrity than are Northerners. Such responses are rooted in long-standing frustration as well as in child-rearing. Our culture, and even our region, has a strong impact on how we interact with others (Nisbett, 1993). This becomes especially apparent in the study of violence and aggression toward women, which we examine in the Applications box. It also becomes apparent through the study of prejudice. Researchers have found a close relationship between prejudice and aggression. We will explore the causes of prejudice next.

Prejudice

There has been a long and heated debate about American productivity, especially in comparison to Japanese productivity. In 1992, Senator Ernest Hollings from South Carolina joked to factory workers about dropping the atomic bomb on Japan in World War II: "Made in America by lazy and illiterate Americans and tested in Japan." His remark followed that of a top politician in Japan who called American workers lazy. The salvo of remarks and apologies that followed made the nightly news and highlighted the fact that people have deeply entrenched ideas that may not be based in fact.

What happens when you do not share ideas, values, or activities with another person or another group of people? What happens when you do not know another group of people well, or at all? Why do some people form negative evaluations of certain groups, such as African Americans, Asians, Jews, or homosexuals? What is prejudice, and how can it be prevented?

What Is Prejudice?

Prejudice is a negative evaluation of an entire group of people that is typically based on unfavorable (and often wrong) ideas about the group. It is generally based on a small sample of experience, or even on no experience, with an individual from the group being evaluated. People sometimes develop prejudices because of stereotypes about others they do not know well. **Stereotypes** are fixed, overly simple (and often wrong) ideas, usually about traits, attitudes, and behaviors attributed to groups of people. Often, stereotypes are negative. People hold stereotyped ideas about Native Americans, Catholics, women, and mountain folk; the stereotypes can lead to prejudice. Stereotypes usually have a historical basis; for example, the idea that all African Americans are natural musicians or athletes probably stems from the fact that historically African Americans were barred from avenues of upward mobility except through the entertainment and sports industries.

Prejudice is an attitude. As we saw in chapter 16, an attitude is composed of a belief (all *X*s are stupid), an emotional element (I hate those *X*s), and often a behavior (I intend to keep those *X*s out of my neighborhood). When prejudice is translated into behavior, it is called **discrimination**—behavior targeted at individuals or groups, with the aim of holding them apart and treating them differently. One widely held type of discrimination is *sexism*—prejudice based on gender; sexism involves accepting the strong and widely held beliefs of rigid gender role stereotyping. We examined gender role stereotyping in chapter 9, where we saw that gender differences tend to be small, when they exist at all. Overt discrimination based on gender is illegal; but it still exists, and many women's expectations for themselves are still based on their gender. Of course, not all people are sexist, but sexism remains a societal problem.

Sometimes people are prejudiced but do not show that attitude in behavior— that is, they do not discriminate (see, for example, Table 17.1). Merton (1949) referred to such individuals as *cautious bigots* (true bigots are prejudiced and discriminate). Also, sometimes people show *reverse discrimination*, bending over backward to treat an individual more positively than they should, solely to counter their own preexisting biases or stereotypes (Chidester, 1986). Thus, someone prejudiced toward African Americans may treat an African-American person oversolicitously and may evaluate the person favorably on the basis of standards different from those used for others. This too is discrimination.

A related concept is *tokenism,* in which prejudiced people engage in positive but trivial actions toward members of a group they dislike. A man may make a token gesture toward the women on his staff, or a manager may hire a token Hispanic American. By engaging in tokenism, a person often attempts to put off more important actions, such as changing overall hiring practices. The trivial behavior justifies, in this person's mind, the idea that the person has done something for the disliked group. Tokenism has negative consequences for the self-esteem of the person it is applied to, and it perpetuates discrimination.

What Causes Prejudice?

The causes of prejudice cannot be tied to a single theory or explanation. Like so many other psychological phenomena, prejudice has multiple causes and can be examined within an individual, between individuals, within a group, or within society (Duckitt, 1992). We will consider four theories to explain prejudice: social learning theory, motivational theory, cognitive theory, and personality theory.

Prejudice: A negative evaluation of an entire group of people that is typically based on unfavorable (and often wrong) ideas about the group.

Stereotypes: Fixed, overly simple (and often wrong) ideas, usually about traits, attitudes, and behaviors attributed to groups of people.

Discrimination: Behavior targeted at individuals or groups, with the aim of holding them apart and treating them differently.

TABLE 17.1

Prejudice and Discrimination

Prejudice and discrimination interact in such a way that one can be evident without the other.

	PREJUDICE	
DISCRIMINATION	**PRESENT**	**ABSENT**
PRESENT	An employer believes that nonwhites cannot do quality work and does not promote them, regardless of their performance.	An employer believes that all people can do quality work but does not promote minorities because of long-held company policies.
ABSENT	An employer believes that nonwhites cannot do quality work, but promotes them on the basis of their performance rather than following preconceived ideas.	An employer believes that all people can do quality work and promotes people on the basis of their performance on the job.

Social Learning Theory. According to social learning theory, children learn to be prejudiced; they watch parents, other relatives, and neighbors engaged in acts of discrimination, which often include stereotyped judgments and racial slurs; and then they incorporate those ideas into their own behavioral repertoire. After children have observed such behaviors, they are then reinforced (operant conditioning techniques) for exhibiting similar behaviors. Thus, through imitation and reinforcement, a prejudiced view is transmitted from parents to children, from one generation to the next.

Motivational Theory. We saw in chapter 10 that people are motivated to succeed, to get ahead, and to provide for basic as well as high-level emotional needs. If people are raised to compete against others for scarce resources, the competition can elicit negative views against competitors. Motivational theory thus asserts that individuals learn to dislike specific individuals (competitors) and then generalize that dislike to whole classes of similar individuals (races, religions, or colors). This helps make those groups of people (often seen as competitors) into scapegoats—such as the Jews in Nazi Germany, Japanese Americans during World War II, and blacks in South Africa today. Research with children, adolescents, and adults shows that people who are initially seen as friends or as neutral others are sometimes treated badly when turned into competitors. Competition for jobs among immigrants can also create prejudice, particularly in times of economic hardship.

Children learn prejudice, in part, from the attitudes and actions of their parents and others.

Cognitive Theory. Cognitive theorists assert that people think about individuals and the groups they come from as a way of organizing the world. Recall from chapter 16 Cialdini's (1993) argument: There are so many events, circumstances, and changing variables in our lives that people cannot easily analyze all the relevant data. People thus devise mental shortcuts to help them make decisions. One of those shortcuts is to stereotype individuals and the groups they belong to—for example, all Hispanics, all homeless people, all men, all attorneys. By devising such shortcuts in thinking, people develop ideas about who is in an *in-group*—that is, who is a member of a group to which they belong or want to belong. People tend to see themselves and other members of an in-group in a favorable light.

As we saw in chapter 16, when judging other people, individuals make fundamental attribution errors. They assume that other people's behavior is caused by internal dispositions—which might not be true—and that other people are all alike (Judd & Park, 1988). They underestimate situational influences and overestimate dispositional influences on other people's behavior, and then they use those behaviors as evidence for their attitudes (prejudices). Thus, hostilities between Arabs and Israelis in the Middle East, Catholics and Protestants in Ireland, and blacks and whites in South Africa are perpetuated.

Personality Theory. Some psychologists assert that people develop prejudices because they have a prejudice-prone personality. Some personality tests examine the extent to which people are likely to be prejudiced. For example, one type of personality that appears to be prevalent is the *authoritarian personality*. Authoritarian people were fearful and anxious as children and may have been raised by cold, love-withholding parents who regularly used physical punishment. To gain control and mastery as adults, such individuals become aggressive and controlling over others. They see the world in absolutes—good versus bad, black versus white. They also tend to blame others for their problems and become prejudiced toward those people (Adorno et al., 1950). The relationship between personality and prejudice has its roots in psychoanalytic theory, but it is not widely accepted by many theorists who study prejudice today. However, the idea that some people have personality traits that lead them toward prejudice has guided some personality theory research.

How to Reduce and Eliminate Prejudice

To reduce and eliminate prejudice, we can teach rational thinking, judge people by their behavior, and promote equality. For example, once people have worked on a community project with a member of a different culture, lived with a person of another race, or prayed with members of a different church, their views of them as individuals change (Wilder & Thompson, 1980).

As a society, we can pass laws that mandate equal treatment for all people; for example, we can legally eliminate discrimination in the workplace and housing market. We can also elect officials on the basis of their competence, throw them out on the basis of their incompetence, and make gender-neutral judgments of performance. Margaret Thatcher, former Prime Minister of Great Britain, was widely judged by her performance, not by her gender.

As students of psychology, we can become especially sensitive to thinking about *individuals* rather than about groups. Through examining individuals, we can be sensitive to the wide diversity of human behavior. Although it is tempting to derive broad generalizations about behavior when making attributions about the causes of behavior, we must focus on individuals. When we focus on individuals, we see that human beings are engaged in and are affected by a whole array of behaviors—some of them destructive and harmful and others prosocial, worthwhile, and helpful.

Prosocial Behavior

Are country people more helpful than city people? It turns out that they are (Steblay, 1987); but what factors are at work, and under what conditions are people helpful? For example, if you are walking down the street with a bag of groceries and you drop them, what is the likelihood that someone will help you pick them up? Will a bystander who observes a serious accident or crime help the victim? Psychologists who ask these questions want to find out when, and under what conditions, someone will help a stranger. They are examining the likelihood of **prosocial behavior**—an act that benefits someone else or society but that generally offers no obvious benefit to the person performing it and that might even involve some personal risk or sacrifice.

Altruism: Helping without Rewards

Why does Peter Beneson, the founder of Amnesty International, devote so much time and effort to helping "prisoners of conscience" around the world? What compels Mother Teresa to wander Calcutta's streets and attend to the wounds and diseases of people no one else will touch? Why did people risk their lives to help Jews avoid the Nazi death camps during World War II?

Altruistic acts are behaviors that benefit other people and for which there is no discernible extrinsic reward, recognition, or appreciation. A person who helps someone in need when there is no obvious reward is generally referred to as altruistic (Quigley, Gaes, & Tedeschi, 1989). However, does an altruistic person truly expect no reward for good acts? Isn't the feeling of well-being after performing an altruistic act a type of reward? Does the altruist expect a reward in an afterlife?

Behavioral Explanations. Behavioral psychologists have a difficult time explaining altruism, because altruistic acts are performed without overt or even anticipated reinforcement. Many behaviorists contend that it is an element of personality that directs people to seek social approval by helping; for example, self-monitoring individuals tailor their behavior to help other people (White & Gerstein, 1987). People with a high need for achievement are also more likely than others to be helpful (Puffer, 1987). Some people may develop altruistic behaviors because the consequences of their actions are self-reinforcing (Batson et al., 1991). Research also shows that when we have a relationship with a person, we are more likely to be caring and helpful (Batson, 1990). Intrinsically rewarding activities tend to become powerful behavior initiators. Thus, such activities become established as regular activities; and people are later impelled to help others, such as the homeless, disadvantaged senior citizens, and orphans.

Sociobiology. Consider the following scenario. An infant crawls into a busy street. A truck is just about to run the infant over when the mother darts in front of the speeding vehicle and carries her child to safety. Most people would say that love impelled the mother to risk her life to save the child. Sociobiologists would argue that the mother committed her heroic deed so her genes would be passed on to another generation.

Prosocial behavior: An act that benefits someone else or society but that generally offers no obvious benefit to the person performing it and that might even involve some personal risk or sacrifice.

Altruistic acts: [ahl-true-ISS-tick] Behaviors that benefit other people and for which there is no discernible extrinsic reward, recognition, or appreciation.

Was the mother's brave action altruistic or merely in accordance with her biological drives? The idea that we are genetically predisposed toward certain behaviors was described by Harvard University zoologist Edward Wilson in his 1975 book, *Sociobiology: A New Synthesis.* Wilson argued that biological, genetic factors underlie all behavior. But he went one step further. He asserted, in his theory of **sociobiology,** that even day-to-day behaviors are determined by the process of natural selection—that social behaviors that contribute to the survival of a species are passed on through the genes from one generation to the next and account for the mechanisms that have evolved to produce behaviors like altruism (Crawford & Anderson, 1989). For the sociobiologist, genetics, not learning, is the key to daily behavior.

At the heart of the sociobiology theory is the issue of altruism. Sociobiologists account for altruism by saying that when a person lays down his or her life for another, that person is passing on the likelihood that the other person's genes will be transmitted to another generation. They point out that people are much more likely to be altruistic toward relatives than toward strangers; that is, people are instinctively driven to help pass on their family's gene pool to another generation.

Sociobiological theory is hotly debated by psychologists because it places genetics in a position of primary importance and minimizes the role of learning. Most psychologists feel strongly that learning plays a key role in the day-to-day activities of human beings. We *learn* to love, to become angry, to help or hurt others, and to develop relationships with those around us. But although sociobiology is too fixed and rigid for most psychologists, it does raise our consciousness about the role of biology and genetics in social behavior. Behavioral theories and sociobiology are two ways of explaining why people help others. People don't always help, however. One important area of research is explaining why help is sometimes withheld.

Bystander Apathy: Failing to Help

The study of helping behavior has taken some interesting twists and turns. For example, psychologists have found that in large cities, where potentially lethal emergencies (accidents, thefts, stabbings, rapes, and murders) occur frequently, people often exhibit bystander apathy—they watch, but seldom help. **Bystander apathy** is the unwillingness of witnesses to an event to help, an effect that increases with the number of observers. Such was the case in a well-known incident in New York City in 1964. Kitty Genovese was walking home when a man approached her with a knife. A chase ensued, during which she screamed for help. He stabbed her, and she screamed some more. When lights came on in nearby buildings, the attacker fled. But when he saw that no one was coming to his victim's aid, he returned and stabbed her again. The murder lasted more than 30 minutes and was heard by dozens of neighbors; yet no one came to the victim's aid. This is a classic case of bystander apathy.

Bibb Latané and John Darley (1970) investigated bystander apathy in a long series of studies. They found that in situations requiring uncomfortable responses, people must choose between helping or standing by apathetically. They must decide whether to introduce themselves into a situation, especially when there are other bystanders.

Latané and Darley reasoned that when people are aware of other bystanders in an emergency situation, they might be less likely to help because they experience *diffusion of responsibility* (the feeling that they cannot be held responsible). To test their hypothesis, the researchers brought college students to a laboratory and told them they were going to be involved in a study of people who were interested in discussing college life. They explained that, in the interest of preserving people's anonymity, a group discussion would be held over an intercom system rather than face-to-face; they noted that each person in the group would talk in turn. In fact,

Sociobiology: The theory that even day-to-day behaviors are determined by the process of natural selection—that social behaviors that contribute to the survival of a species are passed on through the genes from one generation to the next and account for the mechanisms that have evolved to produce behaviors such as altruism.

Bystander apathy: The unwillingness of witnesses to an event to help; an effect that increases when there are more observers.

there was only one true subject in each experimental session. All the other conversations were prerecorded with assistants who worked for the researchers.

The independent variable in this study was the number of people the naive subject thought were in the discussion group. The dependent variable was whether and how fast the naive subject reported as an emergency an apparent serious nervous seizure of one of the assistants.

The future "seizure victim" spoke first; he talked about his difficulties getting adjusted to New York City and mentioned that he was prone to seizures, particularly when studying hard. Next, the naive subject spoke. Then came the prerecorded discussions of assistants. Then the "seizure victim" talked again. After a few relatively calm remarks, his speech became increasingly loud and incoherent; he stuttered and indicated that he needed help because he was having "a-a-a real problem-er-right now and I-er-if somebody could help me out it would-it would-er-er sh-sure be good." At this point, the experimenter began timing the speed of the naive subject's response.

The naive subjects were led to believe that their discussion group contained either two, three, or six people. In the two-person group, they believed they were the only bystander; in the three-person group, they thought there was one other bystander. When the subjects thought they were the only bystander, 85 percent of them responded before the end of the seizure. If there was one other bystander, 62 percent of the subjects responded by the end of the seizure. When subjects thought there were four other bystanders, only 31 percent responded by the end of the seizure. (See Figure 17.7 for some typical results of bystander apathy studies.) Thus,

FIGURE 17.7

The Bystander Apathy Effect

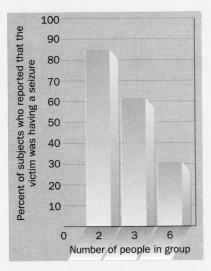

In bystander apathy studies, as the number of people in the group increased, the willingness of naive subjects to inform the experimenter that the victim had suffered a seizure decreased. (*Source: Latané and Darley, 1970.*)

Observing someone in need and failing to come to their aid is a common phenomenon. Studies show that the greater the number of observers, the less the chances are that an individual will choose to help.

cast in the role of bystanders to an emergency, the naive subjects were less likely to respond if they thought other people were present who might help. In general, Latané (1981) found that speed of assistance decreases as the number of bystanders believed to be present increases (see Shotland & Heinold, 1985).

Did the subjects not help because they were cold and callous? Apparently not. They seemed to be very concerned about the seizure victim. Why did they not respond? Latané and Darley suggest that they were worried about the guilt and shame they would feel if they did not help, but they also feared making fools of themselves if they did help.

In general, research has shown that bystanders will help under some conditions. For one thing, people's self-concepts and previous experiences affect their willingness to intercede. Bystanders who see themselves as being especially competent in emergencies (such as doctors and nurses) are likely to help a victim regardless of the number of people present (Pantin & Carver, 1982). If the person who needs help has a relationship with the person who can offer help, help is more likely to be given (Batson, 1990). Also, personality characteristics of the individual involved in a bystander situation are important. Men respond more often than women (Salminen & Glad, 1992); but Tice and Baumeister (1985) found that subjects with a high degree of masculinity were less likely to respond. They contended that highly masculine subjects might be especially fearful of embarrassment. In our society, the personality characteristics of men, in general, emphasize strength and aggression rather than sensitivity.

FOCUS

▶ Name specific actions people can take to eliminate prejudice.   pp. 628–629

▶ What is the key psychological explanation for bystander apathy?   pp. 630–632

Relationships and Attraction

What is it about your friends that attracts you and makes you want to maintain a relationship with them? We saw in chapter 10 that people develop relationships to fulfill their needs for warmth, understanding, and emotional security. Social psychologists study **interpersonal attraction**—the tendency of one person to evaluate another person (or a symbol or image of another person) in a positive way. Psychologists know that people are attracted to those who live or work near them, whom they consider good-looking, who share their attitudes, and with whom they spend time.

Proximity

Interpersonal attraction: The tendency of one person to evaluate another person (or a symbol or image of another person) in a positive way.

People are more likely to develop a relationship with a neighbor than with someone who lives several blocks or miles away. Three decades of research show that the closer people are to someone geographically—whether it is where they work or where they live—the more attracted they will be to that person. A simple explanation is that they are likely to see that person often, and repeated exposure leads to familiarity, which leads to attraction. Another reason is that attraction is facilitated by the anticipation of a relationship with someone one encounters frequently. In addition, if people are members of a group, such as a computer club, a volunteer organization, or an aerobics class, they perceive themselves as sharing the same feelings, attitudes, and values as others in the group. That perception leads to attraction.

Physical Characteristics

Research shows that people ascribe more power, status, competence, and personal regard to individuals they find physically attractive than to those they don't; we saw this in chapter 16 when we looked into who could best change people's attitudes (Dion, Pak, & Dion, 1990; Feingold, 1992a&b). Volumes of research show that people are attracted romantically, at least at first, to those whom they find attractive (Cunningham, Barbee, & Pike, 1990). But research also shows that physical attraction in romantic relationships is only one important element among many others (Eagly et al., 1991; Feingold, 1988a). In the workplace and other venues, a woman's physical appearance is very important—more so than a man's appearance. This gender difference is not surprising; it is a holdover from years of discrimination against women and a society that has valued women more for beauty than for other qualities (L. Jackson, 1992).

In a typical physical attractiveness experiment, subjects are given two identical job résumés, each with a different picture attached to it. Results show that people will evaluate the résumé of the person they find physically attractive more highly than that of the other person, even though their qualifications are the same (e.g., Frieze, Olson, & Russell, 1991). Attractive people are preferred in the workplace, as dates, and as friends; they are thought to be less menacing (Eagly et al., 1991). In one research study, for example, subjects were given information about a hypothetical sex offender, including a facial photograph and a conviction record (Esses & Webster, 1988). The subjects judged physically unattractive sex offenders as less likely to restrain their behavior in the future than better-looking but equally dangerous sex offenders.

The culture in which we live helps define our views of physical attractiveness.

We know that, for broadcast media stars, physical attractiveness is important. Paula Zahn, Katie Couric, Jane Pauley, and Connie Chung are all exceptional journalists. However, it is difficult not to notice that they are all attractive. Good looks are not confined to female anchors; Arthur Kent, Tom Brokaw, and Ed Bradley are also attractive. As Jackson (1992) asserts, physical attractiveness can get people into places and provide avenues for success that otherwise are not available. If physical attraction is only one characteristic of attraction, what are others?

Liking Those Who Like Us and Share Our Attitudes

Learning theorists contend that we are attracted to and form relationships with those who give us positive reinforcement and that we dislike those who punish us. The basic idea is simple: We like people who like us. Moreover, if we like someone, we tend to assume (sometimes incorrectly) that the other person likes us in return and that we share similar qualities. This is especially true for people who need social approval—for example, when their self-esteem is low (Jacobs, Berscheid, & Walster, 1971).

Another attribute that affects the development of relationships is real or perceived similarity in attitudes and opinions. If you perceive someone's attitudes as similar to your own, there is an increased probability that you will like that person. Having similar values, interests, and background is a good predictor of a friendship (e.g., L. Miller, 1990). Similarly, voters who agree with the views of a particular candidate tend to rate the person as more honest, friendly, and persuasive than the politicians with whom they disagree.

Researchers have also found that, if you already like someone, you will perceive that person's attitudes as being similar to your own. For example, voters who like a particular candidate, perhaps because the candidate is warm-hearted or physically attractive, will tend to minimize their attitudinal differences. The slogan "I Like Ike" helped elect Eisenhower, and some political analysts have suggested that Bill Clinton defeated George Bush in the 1992 presidential election because voters perceived him as being a more caring person.

That we like those who like us is explained by cognitive consistency theory, which suggests that sharing similar attitudes reduces cognitive dissonance (a phenomenon we examined in chapter 16). To avoid dissonance, we feel attracted to those we believe share similar attitudes; shared attitudes in turn lead to attraction and liking. Learning theories also suggest that we like people with similar attitudes because similar attitudes are reinforcing to us. As long as we think the other person's attitudes are genuine, such liking will continue.

Friendships and the Role of Equity

Friendship is a special two-way relationship between people. A key component of this close relationship is the extent to which people are connected with each other's lives. According to one influential group of researchers, if two people's behaviors, emotions, and thoughts are related, then the people are dependent on one another—and we can say a relationship exists (Kelley et al., 1983). Closeness is reported by many researchers as the key variable that defines a friendship, although *close* must be defined operationally so all researchers mean the same thing when they use the word (Berscheid, Snyder, & Omoto, 1989).

Variables in Friendships. Ideally, friends participate as equals, enjoy each other's company, have mutual trust, provide mutual assistance, accept each other as they are, respect each other's judgment, feel free to be themselves, understand each other in fundamental ways, and are intimate and share confidences (Davis & Todd, 1984). Reciprocity and commitment between people who see themselves as equals are essentials of friendship (Hartup, 1989). Compared with casual friends, close friends interact more frequently across a greater range of settings, are more exclusive, and offer each other more benefits (Hays, 1989).

As we saw in chapter 9, friendships among children tend to be of the same gender; cross-gender friendships are rare. With youngsters, friendships lead to cooperation rather than competition, at least more than with nonfriends (Hartup, 1989). Furthermore, when children have friends in the classroom, they do better in school (Ladd, 1990). Adolescent friendships sometimes provide a place for sharing and intimacy, although they can also be filled with conflict over social or political issues, drugs, gangs, and sexual behavior (Berndt, 1992). Among adults, friendships between two women differ from those between two men; and both differ from friendships between a man and a woman. Women talk more about family, personal matters, and doubts and fears than do men; men talk more about sports and work than do women. Cultural expectations for specific gender-based behaviors often determine such interactions.

Equity. Equity plays an important role in relationships. *Equity theory* states that people attempt to maintain stable, consistent interpersonal relationships in which the ratio of each member's contribution is equal to that of the other members. This ensures that all members are treated fairly. People in close relationships usually have a sense of balance in the relationships and believe they will stay together for a long time (Clark & Reis, 1988).

According to equity theory, one way in which people maintain a balanced relationship is to make restitution when it is demanded. Apologies help restore a sense of autonomy and fairness to the injured individual. Similarly, people who do favors expect favors in return, often using the principle of equity unconsciously in day-to-day life. When a politician running for reelection responds to her constituents' desires by having a playground built, she expects their votes on election day. Research shows that when a person senses inequity in a situation, this affects her or his feeling about the other person—especially when the other person is being treated better (Griffeth, Vecchio, & Logan, 1989).

Intimate Relationships and Love

Intimacy. People involved in a close relationship may also be intimate with one another. *Intimacy* generally refers to the willingness of a person to be self-disclosing and to express important feelings and information to another person; in response, the other person usually acknowledges the first person's feelings, making the individual feel valued and cared for (Reis & Shaver, 1988). Self-disclosure and emotional openness are key elements in intimate relationships; they come through direct reports, nonverbal messages, and even touching. Self-disclosure tends to be reciprocal; people who disclose themselves to others are usually recipients of intimate information.

Unfortunately, there is little research on intimate relationships outside of marriage. Communication, affection, consideration, and self-disclosure between friends have been studied relatively little. However, we know that important individual and gender differences exist in friendships. For example, men are more self-disclosing with a woman than they are with another man, and in general men are less likely to be self-disclosing and intimate than are women (Dindia & Allen, 1992). Psychologists know much more about intimate relationships between pairs of people, especially men and women, where sex, love, and marriage become involved (Miller, 1990).

People in intimate relationships often express feelings in unique ways—they give flowers, take moonlight walks, write lengthy letters, and have romantic dinners. Love, emotional commitment, and sex may be part of an intimate relationship. According to psychologists, love has psychological, emotional, and social factors. Consider this array of definitions:

▶ Mature love is possible only if a person achieves a secure sense of self-identity. When people are in love, they become one and yet remain two individuals (Fromm, 1956).

▶ Love "is a condition in which the happiness of the other person is essential to your own" (Heinlen, 1961).

▶ Love is "a passionate spiritual, emotional, sexual attachment between a man and a woman that reflects a high regard for the value of each other's person" (Branden, 1980).

▶ The ultimate in romantic love is a state called limerance; this is a head-over-heels involvement and preoccupation with thoughts of the loved one (Tennov, 1981).

▶ Love is characterized by exclusiveness, fascination, and sexual desire (Davis & Todd, 1982).

Elements in a Love Relationship. Researchers have identified some common elements in love relationships. *Love* usually involves the idealization of another person; people see their loved ones in a positive light. It also involves caring for another person and being fascinated with that person. Love includes trust, respect, liking, honesty, companionship, and sexual attraction. A key element is commitment; however, researchers disagree as to whether love and commitment can be separated, because one usually follows from, or is part of, the other (Fehr, 1988; Fehr & Russell, 1991).

Many classifications of love have been suggested, and all have some overlapping components. One influential classification is Sternberg's (1986b) view, which sees love as having three components: intimacy, commitment, and passion. *Intimacy* is a sense of emotional closeness. *Commitment* is the extent to which a relationship is permanent and long-lasting. *Passion* is arousal, some of it sexual, some intellectual, and some motivational. Another view of love (Hendrick and Hendrick, 1986) includes six distinct varieties: passionate, game-playing, friendship, logical, possessive, and selfless (see Table 17.2).

TABLE 17.2

Varieties of Love

Hendrick and Hendrick's (1986) description of love includes six distinct varieties.

Varieties of Love	Sample Items Measuring Each Variety
Passionate love	My lover and I were attracted to each other immediately after we first met.
	My lover and I became emotionally involved rather quickly.
Game-playing love	I have sometimes had to keep two of my lovers from finding out about each other.
	I can get over love affairs pretty easily and quickly.
Friendship love	The best kind of love grows out of a long friendship.
	Love is really a deep friendship, not a mysterious, mystical emotion.
Logical love	It is best to love someone with a similar background.
	An important factor in choosing a partner is whether or not he (she) will be a good parent.
Possessive love	When my lover doesn't pay attention to me, I feel sick all over.
	I cannot relax if I suspect that my lover is with someone else.
Selfless love	I would rather suffer myself than let my lover suffer.
	Whatever I own is my lover's to use as he (she) chooses.

What happens when love disappears? People in a close emotional relationship who break up, whether married or not, experience emotional distress. Sadness, anger, loss, and despair are among the emotions experienced by people who have broken a close relationship. However, research shows that the extent of those feelings is determined by an individual's level of security. If you lose a close friend, lover, or spouse, your reaction will be determined not only by the loss of your relationship but also by your own basic feelings of security, attachment, and anxiety (Simpson, 1990).

Love is a state, but it is also an act and a series of behaviors. Thus, although a person may be in love, most psychologists think of love in terms of the behaviors that demonstrate it, including remaining faithful sexually and showing caring behaviors (D. Buss, 1988). Can you think of other specific behaviors that may demonstrate love? While love may be thought of solely in emotional terms, we also wish to know whether love has a biological basis—an element we'll consider next.

The Origins of Love. According to David McClelland (1986), two sources exist for understanding love: analytical self-reports governed by the left side of the brain and emotional reports governed by the right side of the brain (an idea we examined in chapters 2 and 4). In McClelland's view, the right brain can tell us about the emotional experiences that are not consciously processed. McClelland argues that these emotional processes influence physiological processes and behaviors that are not directly under conscious control. In some ways, McClelland writes, there are two psychologies of love: an analytic left-brain understanding and an emotional right-brain understanding. McClelland's view, particularly his physiologically based explanation of love, has yet to achieve wide acceptance.

Love is a complicated emotion that defies easy characterizations. Every culture expresses love differently, and even within a culture there are enormous variations in its expression (see the Diversity box for more on this topic). Yet love is a basic human emotion that is nurtured from birth to death and is easily seen in every culture. As psychologists discern the key elements of friendships, they will be more likely to tackle the even more complicated topic of love and how it should be nurtured.

FOCUS

▶ Describe the factors involved in developing close relationships. pp. 632–634

▶ Provide a psychological explanation of why, if you perceive someone's attitudes as similar to your own, you will probably like that person. pp. 633–634

▶ Identify some key elements in developing a love relationship. p. 636

DIVERSITY

Friends and Lovers— A Cross-Cultural Comparison

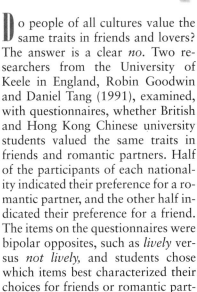

Do people of all cultures value the same traits in friends and lovers? The answer is a clear *no*. Two researchers from the University of Keele in England, Robin Goodwin and Daniel Tang (1991), examined, with questionnaires, whether British and Hong Kong Chinese university students valued the same traits in friends and romantic partners. Half of the participants of each nationality indicated their preference for a romantic partner, and the other half indicated their preference for a friend. The items on the questionnaires were bipolar opposites, such as *lively* versus *not lively*, and students chose which items best characterized their choices for friends or romantic partners.

Results showed that, overall, romantic partners were expected to be more honest and caring than friends were expected to be. In addition, the British students stressed the importance of sensitivity and humor in both romantic partners and friends, but the Chinese students stressed money-mindedness and creativity.

This was a simple study using straightforward questions and methodology; however, it illustrates the complexity of human interactions and the role that our culture plays in determining our choices. Goodwin and Tang (1991) showed that we choose different people for friends and lovers; and most important from a cross-cultural perspective, our choices depend on our culture.

Other results support these conclusions. When Susan Sprecher and her colleagues (1992) compared the cultural similarities in love attitudes and experiences among Japanese, Americans, and Russians, they found some sharp differences. For example, the Japanese were less romantic than the other groups, the Americans were more likely to associate love with marriage than were the other groups, and the Russians were the most ex-

citable and had the most trouble staying calm when in love. Similar findings have been shown in other cross-cultural studies of mate preferences (Buss et al., 1990). Other studies often show gender differences in addition to cultural differences. For example, men value attractiveness more than women; and women accord more weight than men to socioeconomic status, ambitiousness, and character. These gender differences vary little with culture (Feingold, 1990, 1992a).

As these studies show, there are cultural differences in the way love is felt and expressed, especially when it comes to the importance of factors leading up to the love experience. Yet similarities abound. In the arena of love, culture seems to have a somewhat less predictable impact than we might expect (Sprecher et al., 1992). In addition, cross-cultural studies often are of college students; as researchers study a wider sample of participants, our knowledge of relationships and love will grow more comprehensive.

Concluding Note

Our social interactions are shaped by a wide array of events in our lives. How we behave in groups and whether we succumb to pressure, develop prejudices, or act aggressively is shaped by our day-to-day experiences. Among these experiences is television, which helps shape our behavior, our attitudes, group processes, and the way we view our environment.

In 1986, the American Psychological Association created a task force to evaluate the effects of television. Three major principles that guided the work of the task force were the following: (1) All television viewing is educational; that is, every time a person watches television, the person learns something, for better or for worse. (2) Gradually and cumulatively, television influences our view of the world. (3) The effect of television depends not only on the content of a program but also on the individual who is watching it—including the person's family and personality and the milieu in which television is viewed (Huston et al., 1992).

Like so many other social psychological phenomena, television viewing is not a simple cause-and-effect situation; its results depend on an array of variables—cultural, social, ethnic, and age-related. Psychologists are concerned about television viewing by youngsters, particularly when programs involve sex, violence, and negative cultural views. The situation cannot be fixed with a pull of the plug or an appointed censor, however. Psychological studies need to continue to study the impact of television on prejudice, aggression, and prosocial behavior if any changes in viewing are to be made in the future.

As researchers study the impact of our social interactions and our social world on day-to-day behavior, they learn that even some of our simplest behaviors are exceedingly complex. Thus, viewing television, helping a bystander in distress, and developing a friendship turn out to be complex social phenomena with intricate variables affecting how people behave. This is what makes the study of social behavior so exciting.

Summary & Review

Environmental Psychology

What do environmental psychologists study?

Environmental psychologists study how physical settings and social aspects of the environment affect human behavior and how people change their environments to meet their psychological needs.   p. 608

Define crowding, and explain the difference between social density and spatial density.

Crowding is the perception that one's space is too limited. *Social density* is the number of people in a given space. *Spatial density* is the size of a space with a fixed number of people in it. p. 610

What is personal space?

Personal space is the immediate area around an individual at any given time. Four spatial zones, or distances, used in social interactions are intimate, personal, social, and public. p. 612

KEY TERMS: *environmental psychology,* p. 608; *stressor,* p. 609; *crowding,* p. 610; *personal space,* p. 612; *privacy,* p. 612; *territorial behavior,* p. 613.

Behavior in Groups

What are social facilitation and social loafing?

Social facilitation is a change in performance that occurs when people believe they are in the presence of other people. The change can be either positive or negative. *Social loafing* is a decrease in an individual's effort and productivity as a result of working in a group.   pp. 614–616

Identify three processes that may occur within a group when the group is involved in decision making.

Group polarization is the exaggeration of preexisting attitudes as a result of group discussion. *Groupthink* is the tendency of people in a group to seek concurrence with one another. *Deindividuation* is the process by which individuals in a group lose their sense of self-awareness, self-perception, and concern with evaluation.   pp. 616–619

KEY TERMS: *group,* p. 614; *social facilitation,* p. 614; *social loafing,* p. 615; *group polarization,* p. 616; *diffusion of responsibility,* p. 617; *groupthink,* p. 617; *deindividuation,* p. 619.

Aggression

What are the major theories to explain aggression?

Aggression can be viewed as an instinct, an acquired drive, or a learned social behavior. Many psychologists assert that observational learning theory accounts for a great deal of aggression: People learn aggression (or nonaggression) by seeing other people exhibiting such behaviors. pp. 619–620

What is the basic finding about violence on television?

In general, research shows that viewers who frequently watch violent television programs are more likely to be aggressive after watching television than are viewers who see less television violence.   pp. 621–623

KEY TERMS: *aggression,* p. 620; *frustration-aggression hypothesis,* p. 620.

Prejudice

Define prejudice, and identify the theories that explain it.

Prejudice is a negative evaluation of an entire group of people that is typically based on unfavorable (and often wrong) ideas about the group. Prejudice has multiple causes and can be accounted for, at least to some extent, by social learning theory, motivational theory, cognitive theory, and personality theory.   pp. 625–626

KEY TERMS: *prejudice,* p. 626; *stereotypes,* p. 626; *discrimination,* p. 626.

Prosocial Behavior

Distinguish between prosocial behavior and bystander apathy.

Prosocial behavior is an act that benefits someone else or society but that generally offers no obvious benefit to the person performing it. In contrast, *bystander apathy* is the unwillingness of witnesses to an event to help, especially when there are a number of observers.   pp. 629–630

KEY TERMS: *prosocial behavior,* p. 629; *altruistic acts,* p. 629; *sociobiology,* p. 630; *bystander apathy,* p. 630.

continued

Summary & Review

Relationships and Attraction

Define interpersonal attraction, and indicate key findings in studies of interpersonal attraction.

Interpersonal attraction is the tendency of one person to evaluate another person (or a symbol or image of another person) in a positive way. The process of attraction involves the characteristics of both the people involved and the situation. Research shows that people ascribe more power, status, competence, and personal regard to people they find attractive than to those they don't. pp. 632–634

What are some key elements in a friendship?

Reciprocity, closeness, and commitment between individuals who see themselves as equals are essentials of friendship; equity also plays an important role. Equity theory holds that people attempt to maintain stable, consistent relationships in which the ratio of each member's contribution is equal.   pp. 634–635

Define love, and describe some of its key components.

Love usually involves the idealization of another person. People see their loved ones in a positive light, care for them, and are fascinated with them; love also involves trust and commitment. According to Sternberg, love has three components: intimacy (a sense of emotional closeness), commitment (the extent to which a relationship is permanent), and passion (arousal, some of it sexual, some intellectual, and some motivational). pp. 635–636

KEY TERM: *interpersonal attraction*, p. 632.

CONNECTIONS

If you are interested in...

The influence of the environment on our perceptions of the world, see ...

CHAPTER 3, pp. 94–100

How our perceptions of the world depend on past experiences in the environment as well as current stimulation.

CHAPTER 13, pp. 471–477

The way stressors in the environment such as worksite pressures can eventually lead to health problems.

CHAPTER 16, pp. 588–591

How people make decisions about the causes of other people's behavior, especially if the causes are due to environmental situations.

How people behave in groups, see ...

CHAPTER 9, pp. 318–319

Adolescents and peer pressure.

CHAPTER 15, pp. 556–557

Why individuals sometimes improve more in group therapy than they do in individual therapy.

Prejudice, see ...

CHAPTER 5, p. 162

How people develop classically conditioned, discriminatory responses to formerly neutral stimuli.

CHAPTER 9, pp. 318–319

How adolescents conform, and how this may affect their attitudes about other people, especially peers.

CHAPTER 16, pp. 574–577

How attitudes are formed and how they shape future behaviors.

Module A

Scientific and Statistical Methods

U ntil recently, Shirley could not hold a job because she suffered from debilitating schizophrenic symptoms, including disordered thinking and bizarre auditory hallucinations. Now, however, Shirley works 40 productive hours a week at a floral shop, and she rarely experiences the mental aberrations that once made her life a living hell. Shirley's improvement is due in part to phenothiazine, a drug that helps control the brain's use of the neurotransmitter dopamine, and in part to a caring psychotherapist. But credit must also be given to researchers who discovered that children of schizophrenic parents have a statistically greater risk for developing schizophrenia. By helping uncover the disorder's biological connection, they spurred the search for drugs such as phenothiazine.

Scientific progress is in many ways directly linked to our ability to measure and quantify data. In the physical sciences, the need to precisely measure time, weight, and distance has given rise to terms describing mind-boggling minuteness, including femtosecond (one-quadrillionth of a second), nanogram (one-billionth of a gram), and angstrom (one ten-billionth of a meter). Examining behavioral phenomena in numerical terms enables scientists to be exact, consistent, and objective.

Statistics is the branch of mathematics that deals with collecting, classifying, and analyzing data. To rule out coincidence and discover the true causes of behavior, psychologists control the variables in experiments, then use statistics to describe, summarize, and present results.

Conducting Experiments

The following account of a therapy experiment will help illustrate how proper methodology and statistics help scientists interpret results: A psychologist was interested in proving whether a new therapeutic approach he had been using was effective with couples who were experiencing marital conflict. His approach focused on relaxation. For 3 years, he had been teaching couples relaxation techniques to help them cope better with their problems, and he had found it effective—the couples were better able to communicate after they had gone through relaxation exercises. But now he wanted to show, by experiment, whether relaxation training *caused* the marital improvement.

Hypotheses

The psychologist hypothesized that relaxation training can be crucial to communication in marriage. A **hypothesis** is a tentative statement about a causal relationship between two variables or situations to be evaluated in an experiment. Recall from chapter 1 that an **experiment** is a procedure in which a researcher systematically manipulates certain variables in order to describe objectively the relationship between the variables of concern and the resulting behavior. Well-designed experiments permit inferences about cause and effect.

The psychologist advertised in the newspaper for couples experiencing marital problems. He told the couples who answered the ad that they would be participating in a study of "therapy for marriage difficulties." He explained that all of the couples would receive effective therapy, although not all at the same time or in the same order, and that some would have to be on a waiting list for a few months.

Variables

The psychologist wanted to know if his therapeutic technique (relaxation training) would be effective; thus, the independent variable in his study would be the delivery of therapy. Recall from chapter 1 that the **independent variable** is the variable in an experiment that is directly and purposefully manipulated by the experimenter to determine what effect the differences in it will have on the variables under study. The **dependent variable** is the behavior measured by an experimenter in order to assess whether changes in the independent variable affect the behavior under study. The

Statistics: The branch of mathematics that deals with collecting, classifying, and analyzing data.

Hypothesis: A tentative statement about a causal relationship between two variables or situations to be evaluated in an experiment.

Experiment: A procedure in which a researcher systematically manipulates certain variables in order to describe objectively the relationship between the variables of concern and the resulting behavior.

Independent variable: The variable in an experiment that is directly and purposefully manipulated by the experimenter to determine what effect the differences in it will have on the variables under study.

Dependent variable: The behavior measured by an experimenter in order to assess whether changes in the independent variable affect the behavior under study.

dependent variable in this study would be scores in three areas: the couples' levels of anxiety and marital satisfaction and the frequency of sexual contact.

To later know whether his treatment would be effective, the psychologist asked each of the couples in his study to answer a battery of questions measuring their level of anxiety, their level of marital satisfaction, and the frequency of their sexual contact. With these answers, he could later assess whether his subjects had changed over the course of treatment.

The psychologist divided 75 couples into three groups. He put every third couple into a control group and told them they would have to wait several months for therapy to begin. (The **control group**—the group that does not receive the treatment under investigation—provides a standard for comparison, as we saw in chapter 1.) The couples in the other two groups would be compared to those in the control group to see if relaxation training produced any measurable effect in their marriages. These second and third groups were **experimental groups;** they received training in relaxation over a 6-month period. One of the experimental groups received relaxation training alone, and the other received relaxation training along with communication exercises.

Every week for 20 weeks, the couples in the two experimental groups were treated. At the end of the study, the researcher again examined the 75 couples' level of anxiety, level of marital satisfaction, and frequency of sexual contact. He expected those who received the experimental treatments to do better than the control group. (At the end of the 20 weeks, the control group was then given the treatment that involved both relaxation and communication.)

The researcher found, as expected, that the control group had changed very little (or not at all) over the course of the experiment; but the experimental groups showed major changes. The couples who had received relaxation treatment—especially when it was combined with communication training—were less anxious, happier in their marriages, and had more frequent sexual contact. The researcher concluded that the independent variable (the relaxation training) caused a change in the subjects' lives. This experiment is a simple one, and there are things the researcher might do to make it better; but it has the elements of a good experiment.

Carefully Conducted Experiments

What makes a good experiment? As we saw in chapter 1, to be generalizable to a population, a good experiment must have a sufficient number of carefully selected subjects in each group. Experiments have one or more experimental groups and a control group.

Inferences. If researchers are to make valid inferences from the collected data, it is important that the subjects represent the larger population. With human beings, this may mean that the subjects should have the same socioeconomic status, perhaps come from the same community, or be nearly the same age; the goal is to provide a balanced group, or sample, with regard to important characteristics. Thus, as chapter 1 showed, a **sample** is a group of subjects or participants who are generally representative of the population about which an inference is being made. Any differences among the groups must be due only to the experimental manipulation. If other variables in the relaxation training study were properly controlled (i.e., held constant), the researchers could conclude that any difference in the couples' marital relationship at the end of the experiment was a result of therapy. If the sample was not carefully balanced, then it would be difficult or impossible to conclude that therapy alone made the difference.

Subject Selection. Proper selection is a key element of good research. Sometimes subjects are selected randomly; for example, researchers may administer a

Control group: In an experiment, the group of subjects that does not receive the treatment under investigation.

Experimental group: In an experiment, the group of subjects that receives the treatment under investigation.

Sample: A group of subjects or participants who are generally representative of the population about which an inference is being made.

newly developed achievement test to randomly chosen members of the general population in order to derive an average test score. At other times, subjects are chosen with respect to a specific variable, such as gender or age. In any case, experimental subjects must be representative of the population to which they will be compared, and the researchers must make enough observations to ensure that the behaviors observed are representative and characteristic.

Carefully Defined Variables. The description of the independent and dependent variables is especially important. The independent variable has to be spelled out accurately, and how it is administered or delivered to subjects has to be painstakingly specified. If, for example, the variable is a particular drug dosage, the dosage must be specified carefully. If an experiment states that rats will receive 10 milligrams of a drug for each kilogram of body weight, then each rat, regardless of its weight, would receive the proper amount of the drug.

Similarly, the dependent variable has to be carefully defined: How is it to be measured, with what instruments, how frequently, and by whom? Some dependent variables, such as running speed, are easily specified; others, such as arousal, anxiety, and depression, are more difficult to define precisely. In most cases, researchers offer an **operational definition** of the variable—a concrete description of how the variable being studied will be measured. In the relaxation therapy example, marital adjustment could be operationally defined as scores on an adjustment scale or anxiety scale or as self-reports monitored on a weekly basis. If the behavior being measured is anxiety, it can be defined operationally as a change in the electrodermal response (a measure of nervous system arousal).

After researchers have specified the variables and chosen the subjects, they conduct the experiment, hoping it will yield interpretable, meaningful results. But extraneous, or irrelevant, variables can affect the results, making interpretation difficult. *Extraneous variables* are factors that affect the results of an experiment but that are not of interest to the experimenter. A lightning storm that occurs during an experiment in which anxiety is being measured through electrodermal response is an extraneous variable. It would be difficult or impossible for the researchers to ascertain which parts of the increased electrodermal response were due to manipulations of the independent variable and which parts were due to anxiety associated with lightning storms. When extraneous variables occur during an experiment (or just before it), they may *confound results*—make data difficult to interpret.

FOCUS

▶ Distinguish between the independent and the dependent variable. pp. 643–644

▶ Why is proper subject selection so important, especially in studies examining small groups of individuals who are not widely represented in the whole population—for example, Alzheimer's patients, the physically disabled, or Native Americans? pp. 644–645

▶ How can extraneous variables render an experiment uninterpretable? p. 645

Descriptive Statistics

Researchers use statistics to evaluate and organize data. Specifically, they use **descriptive statistics**—a general set of procedures to summarize, condense, and describe samples of data. Descriptive statistics makes it possible for researchers to interpret the results of their experiments. Similarly, your professors use descriptive statistics to interpret exam results. For example, a statistical description of a 100-point midterm exam may show that 10 percent of a class scored more than 60 points, 70 percent scored between 40 and 60 points, and 20 percent scored fewer

Operational definition: A definition based on a set of concrete steps used to define a variable.

Descriptive statistics: A general set of procedures used to summarize, condense, and describe samples of data.

Frequency distribution: A chart or array, usually arranged from the highest to the lowest score, showing the number of instances of each obtained score.

Frequency polygons: Graphs of frequency distributions that show the number of instances of obtained scores, usually with the data points connected by straight lines.

than 40 points. On the basis of this statistical description, the professor might conclude that the test was exceptionally difficult and might arrange the grades so that anyone who earned 61 points or more received an A. But before inferences can be drawn or grades can be arranged, the data from a research study must be organized in a meaningful way.

Organizing Data

When psychologists do research, they often produce large amounts of data that must be assessed. Suppose a social psychologist asks parents to monitor the number of hours their children watch television. The parents might report between 0 and 20 hours of television watching a week. Here is a list of the actual number of hours of television watched by 100 children in a particular week:

11	18	5	9	6	20	2	5
9	7	15	3	6	11	9	14
6	1	10	3	4	4	10	4
8	8	9	10	13	12	9	8
16	1	15	9	4	3	7	10
10	5	6	12	8	2	13	8
14	12	6	9	8	12	5	17
10	7	3	14	13	7	9	2
10	17	11	13	16	7	5	4
15	11	9	11	16	8	15	17
14	7	10	10	12	8	10	11
11	1	12	7	6	0	5	13
19	18	9	8				

The first step in making these numbers meaningful is to organize them in such a way that we can see the number of times each one occurs; this type of organization is known as a **frequency distribution.** As the frequency distribution in Table A.1 shows, the number 9 occurs more frequently than any other, indicating that more children watched 9 hours of TV a week than any other number of hours.

Researchers often construct graphs from the data in frequency distributions. Such graphs, called **frequency polygons,** show the possible results or scores (for example, the number of hours children watched TV) on the horizontal axis, or *abscissa,* and the frequency of each score (for example, the number of children who watched TV for those hours) on the vertical axis, or *ordinate.* Figure A.1 is a frequency polygon of the data from the frequency distribution in Table A.1. Straight lines connect the data points.

FIGURE A.1

A frequency polygon showing the number of hours of TV watched by 100 children.

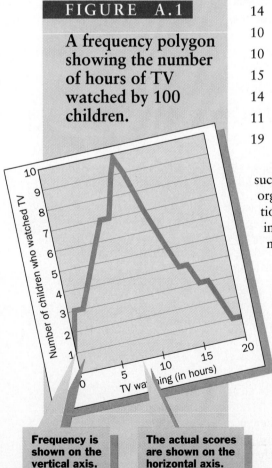

Frequency is shown on the vertical axis.

The actual scores are shown on the horizontal axis.

Measures of Central Tendency

People who use the term *average* to describe a variety of commonalities or tendencies. A woman asks a clerk to help her find a sweater for her average-sized husband. The owner of a new sedan boasts that his car averages 40 miles to a gallon of gasoline. A doctor tells her patient that his serum cholesterol level is average because it falls halfway between low and high measurements. In each of these cases, the person is using *average* to depict a type of norm. A descriptive statistic that tells us which

TABLE A.1

A Frequency Distribution for the Number of Hours of TV Watched in a Week by 100 Children

Number of Hours of TV Watching	Number of Individuals Watching	Total Number of Individuals Watching
0		1
1		3
2		3
3		4
4		5
5		6
6		7
7		7
8		9
9		10
10		9
11		7
12		6
13		5
14		4
15		4
16		3
17		3
18		2
19		1
20		1

Few individuals score very high or low—most score in the middle range.

result or score best represents an entire set of scores is a **measure of central tendency.** It is used to summarize and condense data. Also, because almost every group has members who score higher or lower than the group, researchers often use a measure of central tendency to describe the group *as a whole*.

Consider the statement: Men are taller than women. Because we know that some women are taller than some men, we assume that the statement means: *On the average,* men are taller than women. In other words, if we compare the heights of all the men and all the women in the world, we will find that, *on the average,* men are taller.

Mean. How could we investigate the truth of the statement that men are taller than women? One way would be to measure the height of thousands of men and women, taking a careful sample from each country, race, and age group. We could then calculate the average heights of the men and women in the sample and plot the results on a graph.

Table A.2 on page 648 lists height data from a small sample of men and women; these data are plotted in Figure A.2 on page 648. For each group, the heights of the subjects were measured, added together, and divided by the number of subjects in the group. The resulting number is the **mean,** or *arithmetic average* (in this case, in terms of height for the men and women in the group). The mean is the most frequently used measure of central tendency.

Mode. Another statistic used to describe the central tendency of a set of data is the mode. The **mode** is the most frequently observed data point. Figure A.3 on page 649 plots the frequency of different heights for all the heights in Table A.2. It shows that only one person is 58 inches tall, three people are 79 inches, and more people are 70 inches tall than any other height. The mode of that group therefore is 70 inches.

Measure of central tendency: An index of the average, or typical, value of a distribution of scores.

Mean: A measure of central tendency calculated by dividing the sum of the scores by the number of scores. Also known as the *arithmetic average.*

Mode: A measure of central tendency, the most frequently observed data point.

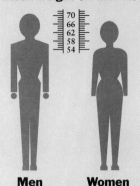

FIGURE A.2

Mean Heights for Men and Women

Mean height (in inches)

Men   Women

These mean heights for men and women reflect an average computed for the people in each group.

Median: A measure of central tendency, the point at which 50 percent of all observations occur above and 50 percent below.

Median. The **median** is the 50 percent point: Half the observations fall above it and the other half fall below it. Figure A.4 arranges the heights for men and women in Table A.2 from lowest to highest. It shows that half the heights fall above 68 and half fall below 68. The median of the data set, therefore, is 68. You have probably read news reports about median income in the United States being on the rise. For example, a typical news report might be, "According to the U.S. Census Bureau, the median income in the United States rose to $36,000 this year." What this means is that half of the U.S. families earn more than this amount and half earn less.

Table A.3 on page 650 presents a set of data from an experiment on memory. The scores are the number of correctly recalled items. There are three groups of subjects: a control group, which received no special treatment; Experimental Group 1, which received task-motivating instructions (such as think hard, focus your attention); and Experimental Group 2, which was hypnotized and told under hypnosis that its members would have better recall. The results of the study show that the task-motivated group did slightly worse than the control group; its mean was 10.3, compared with the control group mean of 10.6. But the hypnosis group did better, recalling 15.4 words on average, compared with the control group's recall of 10.6 words—a difference of 4.8 words. Hypnosis therefore seemed to have a positive effect on memory—or did it?

The medians for the control group and the task-motivated group were equal: 10.5 words. The difference between the control group and the hypnosis group was

TABLE A.2

Calculation of Mean Height for Men and Women, in Inches

Men	Height in Inches	Women	Height in Inches
Davis	62	Leona	58
Baird	62	Golde	59
Jason	64	Marcy	61
Ross	67	Mickey	64
David	68	Sharon	64
Cary	68	Rozzy	66
Mark	69	Bonnie	66
Evan	70	Diane	66
Michael	70	Cheryl	66
Davey	70	Carol	67
Steven	70	Iris	67
Morry	70	Nancy	67
Alan	70	Theresa	67
Bernie	70	Sylvia	67
Lester	70	Jay	68
Al	70	Linda	68
Arnold	73	Elizabeth	71
Andrew	79	Jesse	75
Corey	79	Gabrielle	76
Stephen	79	Sarah	77
Total height	**1400**	**Total height**	**1340**

Mean: $\dfrac{\Sigma S}{N} = \dfrac{1400}{20} = 70$ in.   Mean: $\dfrac{\Sigma S}{N} = \dfrac{1340}{20} = 67$ in.

Note: ΣS means add up each score; N means number of scores.

FIGURE A.3

The Mode for Men's and Women's Heights

```
58  I
59  I
60
61  I
62  II
63
64  II
65
66  IIIII
67  IIIIII
68  IIII
69
70  IIIIIIII  Mode
              (the most frequently
              observed height)
71  I
72
73  I
74  I
75  I
76  I
77  I
78
79  III
```

4 words. The median difference (4 words) is smaller than the mean difference (4.8 words), because the median discounts very high and very low scores. For example, if you average a 0 in with five other test scores (where the average score is about 70), it will drop your *average* substantially; averaging in a 60 would not have as big an impact. But with medians, an extreme score (be it a 0 or a 60) would count the same. With a small sample such as this one, where a single score can have a big impact, the median is often a better measure of central tendency.

The mean, mode, and median are descriptive statistics that are measures of central tendency. They each tell researchers something about the average (or typical) subject. Sometimes, they are the same number; but more often, enough variability exists (one very tall person or two very short ones, for example) that each central tendency measure yields a slightly different result. If you had to guess the height of a woman you had never met, a good guess would be the mean, or the average, height for women. If you were a buyer for a clothing store and had to pick one dress size or one shoe size to order, you might be more likely to pick the modal size—the size that will occur more often than any other.

Measures of Variability

A measure of central tendency is a single number that describes a hypothetical "average" subject. In real life, however, people do not always reflect the central tendency. Consequently, knowing how an average subject might score is more useful when we know how the scores in the group are distributed relative to one another. If you know that the mean of a group of numbers is 150, you do not know how widely dispersed are the scores that are averaged to calculate that mean.

A statistic that describes the extent to which scores differ from one another in a distribution is called a measure of variability. **Variability** is a measure of the extent to which scores differ from one another and especially the extent to which they differ from the mean. If all the subjects obtain the same score, no variability exists; this, however, is unlikely to occur. It is more usual that, in any group of subjects being tested or measured in some way, personal and situational characteristics will cause some to score high and some to score low. If researchers know the extent of the variation, they can estimate the extent to which subjects differ from the mean, or "average," subject.

Range. One measure of variability, the **range,** shows the spread of scores in a distribution; it is calculated by subtracting the lowest score from the highest score. If the lowest score on a test was 20 points and the highest was 85, the range was 65 points. Whether the mean was 45, 65, or 74 points, the range remained 65. There was always a 65-point spread from the lowest score to the highest.

Variability: A measure of the extent to which scores differ from one another and especially the extent to which they differ from the mean.

Range: A measure of variability that describes the spread of scores in a distribution, calculated by subtracting the lowest score from the highest score.

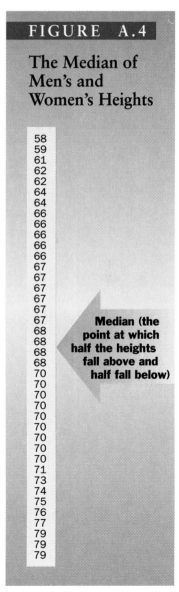

FIGURE A.4

The Median of Men's and Women's Heights

```
58
59
61
62
62
64
64
66
66
66
66
67
67
67
67
67
67
68
68
68
68
70
70
70
70
70
70
70
71
73
74
75
76
77
79
79
79
```

Median (the point at which half the heights fall above and half fall below)

TABLE A.3

Calculations of the Mean and the Median for Three Groups of Subjects (with 10 Subjects in Each Group)

Subject	Control Group	Experimental Group 1 (Task-Motivated)	Experimental Group 2 (Hypnosis)
1	10	11	16
2	12	13	14
3	14	14	16
4	10	12	12
5	11	12	10
6	9	8	9
7	5	10	15
8	12	5	12
9	16	10	18
10	7	8	32
Total	106	103	154
Mean	10.6	10.3	15.4
Median	10.5	10.5	14.5

Control Group (scores are reordered lowest to highest)

$$\text{Mean} = \frac{5 + 7 + 9 + 10 + 10 + 11 + 12 + 12 + 14 + 16}{10} \quad \frac{106}{10} = 10.6$$

$$\text{Median} = 5 \quad 7 \quad 9 \quad 10 \quad \boxed{10 \quad 11} \quad 12 \quad 12 \quad 14 \quad 16$$
$$\downarrow$$
$$10.5$$

The point at which half the scores fall above and half the scores fall below is 10.5; that is, 10.5 is the median.

Experimental Group 1 (scores are reordered lowest to highest)

$$\text{Mean} = \frac{5 + 8 + 8 + 10 + 10 + 11 + 12 + 12 + 13 + 14}{10} \quad \frac{103}{10} = 10.3$$

$$\text{Median} = 5 \quad 8 \quad 8 \quad 10 \quad \boxed{10 \quad 11} \quad 12 \quad 12 \quad 13 \quad 14$$
$$\downarrow$$
$$10.5$$

The point at which half the scores fall above and half the scores fall below is 10.5; that is, 10.5 is the median.

Experimental Group 2 (scores are reordered lowest to highest)

$$\text{Mean} = \frac{9 + 10 + 12 + 12 + 14 + 15 + 16 + 16 + 18 + 32}{10} \quad \frac{154}{10} = 15.4$$

$$\text{Median} = 9 \quad 10 \quad 12 \quad 12 \quad \boxed{14 \quad 15} \quad 16 \quad 16 \quad 18 \quad 32$$
$$\downarrow$$
$$14.5$$

The point at which half the scores fall above and half the scores fall below is 14.5; that is, 14.5 is the median.

The range is a relatively crude measure of the extent to which subjects vary within a group. In a group of 100 students, for example, nearly all may have scored within 10 points of the mean score of 80. But if the lowest score was 20 and the highest was 85, the range would be 65. More precise measures of the spread of scores within a group are available, however. They indicate how scores are distributed as well as the extent of their spread.

Standard Deviation. Consider a reaction-time study that measures how fast subjects press a button when a light is flashed. The following list gives the number of milliseconds it took each of 30 randomly chosen 10th-graders to press the button when the light was flashed; clearly, the reaction times vary.

450	490	500
610	520	470
480	492	585
462	600	490
740	700	595
500	493	495
498	455	510
470	480	540
710	722	575
490	495	570

A person who was told only that the mean reaction time was 540 milliseconds would assume that 540 is the best estimate of how long it takes a 10th-grade student to respond to the light. But these data are variable—not everyone took 540 milliseconds; some took more time and some took less. Psychologists say that the data were variable, or that variability existed.

To find out how much variability exists among data, and to quantify it in a meaningful manner, we need to know the standard deviation. A **standard deviation** is a descriptive statistic that measures the variability of data from the mean of the sample; it is calculated by figuring the extent to which each score differs from the mean.

The calculations for a standard deviation are shown in Table A.4 on page 652. The general procedure involves subtracting the mean from each score and then squaring that difference. Next, the squared differences are added up and divided by the number of scores minus 1. (In a small sample, to get a better estimate of the population's standard deviation, you typically divide by one less than the number of scores.) Last, you take the square root of the answer. You have now calculated a standard deviation.

Table A.5 on page 652 shows the reaction times for two groups of subjects responding to a light. The mean is the same for both groups; but Group 1 shows a large degree of variability, while Group 2 shows little variability. The standard deviation (the estimate of variability) for Group 1 subjects will be substantially higher than that for Group 2 subjects because the scores differ from the mean much more in the first group than in the second.

A standard deviation gives information about all the members of a group, not just an average member. Knowing the standard deviation—that is, the variability associated with each mean—enables a researcher to make more accurate predictions. Since the standard deviation for subjects in Group 2 of Table A.5 is small, a researcher can more confidently predict that a subject will respond to light in about 555 milliseconds (the mean response time). However, the researcher cannot

Standard deviation: A descriptive statistic that measures the variability of data from the mean of the sample.

TABLE A.4

Computation of the Standard Deviation for a Small Distribution of Scores

Score	Score – Mean	(Score – Mean)²
10	10 – 6 = 4	16
10	10 – 6 = 4	16
10	10 – 6 = 4	16
5	5 – 6 = –1	1
4	4 – 6 = –2	4
4	4 – 6 = –2	4
4	4 – 6 = –2	4
1	1 – 6 = –5	25
48		86

$$\sqrt[2]{\frac{\Sigma(X - \overline{X})^2}{N - 1}}$$

Σ means sum up.

X = score.

N refers to the number of scores.

Sum of scores = 48.

Mean = sum of scores ÷ 8 = 6.

Sum of squared difference from mean = 86.

Average of squared differences from mean (dividing by the number of scores –1)
= 86 ÷ 7 = 12.3.

Square root of average squared difference from the mean = 3.5.

Standard deviation = 3.5.

TABLE A.5

Reaction times in milliseconds, mean reaction times, and standard deviations for two groups of subjects responding to a light.

Group 1		Group 2
380		530
400	Group 1 shows a wider range	535
410	of scores and thus great vari-	540
420	ability. Group 2, by contrast,	545
470	shows a narrow range of	550
480	scores and little variability.	560
500		565
720		570
840		575
930		580
Mean = 555		**Mean = 555**
Standard deviation = 197		**Standard deviation = 17**

confidently make the same prediction for subjects in Group 1, since that group's standard deviation is high.

Confidence in predictions turns out to be a key issue for statisticians; they want to be as sure as possible that the mean of a group actually represents the mean of the larger population that group (sample) represents. This concern is important because researchers want to infer that a difference between a control group and an experimental group is due to the experimenter's statistical manipulations, extraneous variables, or one or two deviant scores. It turns out that many of the manipulations and controls that researchers devise are necessary if they wish to make sound inferences, the topic we will consider next.

Inferential Statistics and the Normal Curve

Researchers use inferential statistics in making decisions about data. **Inferential statistics** are procedures used to reach conclusions (generalizations) about larger populations from a small sample of data with a minimal degree of error. There are usually two issues to be explored: First, does the mean of a sample (a small group of subjects) actually reflect the mean of the larger population? Second, is a difference found between two means (for example, between the means for a control group and an experimental group) a real and important difference, or is it a result of chance? Psychologists hope to find a **significant difference**—a difference in performance between two groups that can be repeated experimentally using similar groups of subjects and that is not a result of chance variations. Generally, psychologists assume that a difference is statistically significant if the likelihood of its occurring by chance is less than 5 out of 100 times. But many researchers assume a significant difference only if the likelihood of its occurring by chance is fewer than 1 out of 100 times.

It is sometimes difficult to decide whether a difference is significant. Let us go back to Table A.3, where calculations were performed for a set of data. The data represent scores from a memory study in which the participants had to learn lists of unrelated words. There were three groups of subjects: One was given task-motivating instructions such as thinking hard (Experimental Group 1), a second was hypnotized (Experimental Group 2), and a third was given no special instructions (the control group). The dependent variable was the average number of words correctly recalled by each subject. The results showed that the task-motivated group recalled no more words, on the average, than the control group (in fact, 0.3 words less). The hypnosis group recalled 4.8 more words, on the average, than the control group.

Since the hypnosis group did better than the control group, can we conclude that hypnosis is a beneficial memory aid? Did the hypnosis group do *significantly* better than the control group? Was a 4.8-word difference significant? It is easy to see that if the difference between the recall of the two groups had been 10 words, and if the variability within the groups had been very small, the difference would be considered significant. A 1- or 2-word difference would not be considered significant if the variability within the groups was large. In the present case, a 4.8-word difference was not significant; the scores were highly variable, and only a small sample of subjects was used. When scores are variable (widely dispersed), both statistical tests and researchers are unlikely to view a small difference between two groups as significant or important. (See Figure A.5 on page 654 for an illustration of this point.)

Even if statistically significant differences are obtained, most researchers require that an experiment be repeated and that the results be the same. Repeating an experiment to verify a result is called *replicating* the experiment. If the results of a repli-

Inferential statistics: Procedures used to reach conclusions (generalizations) about larger populations from a small sample of data with a minimal degree of error.

Significant difference: A statistically determined likelihood that a behavior has not occurred because of chance alone.

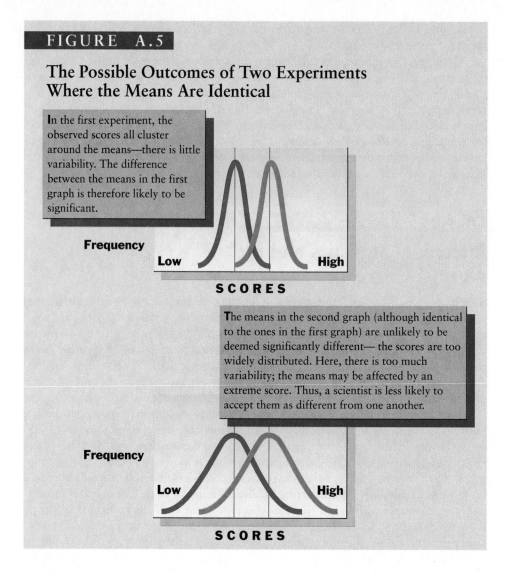

FIGURE A.5

The Possible Outcomes of Two Experiments Where the Means Are Identical

In the first experiment, the observed scores all cluster around the means—there is little variability. The difference between the means in the first graph is therefore likely to be significant.

Frequency

Low   High

S C O R E S

The means in the second graph (although identical to the ones in the first graph) are unlikely to be deemed significantly different— the scores are too widely distributed. Here, there is too much variability; the means may be affected by an extreme score. Thus, a scientist is less likely to accept them as different from one another.

Frequency

Low   High

S C O R E S

cated experiment are the same, a researcher will generally say that the observed difference between the two groups is important.

The Normal Curve

When a large number of scores are involved, a frequency polygon often takes the form of a bell-shaped curve called a **normal curve,** or *normal distribution.* Normal distributions usually have a few scores at each end and progressively many more scores toward the center. Height, for example, is approximately normally distributed: More people are of average height than are very tall or very short (see Figure A.6). Weight, shoe sizes, intelligence, and scores on psychology exams also tend to be normally distributed.

Characteristics of a Normal Curve

A normal curve has certain characteristics. The mean, mode, and median are assumed to be the same; and the distribution of scores around that central point is symmetrical. Also, most individuals have a score that occurs within six standard deviations—three above the mean and three below it (see Figure A.7).

To explain this phenomenon, Figure A.8 shows a normal curve for test scores. The mean is 50, and the standard deviation is 10. Note how each increment of 10

Normal curve: A bell-shaped curve, drawn as a frequency polygon, that depicts the approximately expected distribution of scores when a sample is drawn from a large population. Also known as *normal distribution.*

FIGURE A.6

A Normal Curve for Height

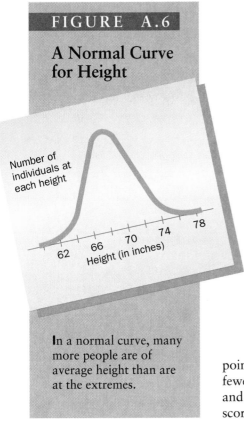

In a normal curve, many more people are of average height than are at the extremes.

FIGURE A.7

Percentages of Population in a Normal Curve

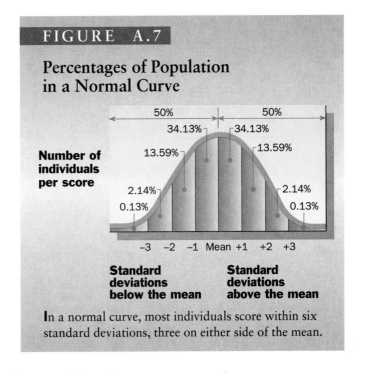

In a normal curve, most individuals score within six standard deviations, three on either side of the mean.

points above or below the mean accounts for fewer and fewer individuals. Scores between 50 and 60 account for 34.13 percent of those tested; scores between 60 to 70 account for 13.59 percent; and scores above 70 account for under 2.5 percent. The sum of these percentages (34.13 + 13.59 + 2.14 + 0.13) represents 50 percent of the scores.

When you know the mean and standard deviation of a set of data, you can estimate where an individual in the sample population stands relative to others. In Figure A.9, Dennis, for example, is 74 inches tall. His height is one standard deviation

FIGURE A.8

A Normal Curve, with a Standard Deviation of 10 Points

FIGURE A.9

A Normal Curve with a Mean of 70 and a Standard Deviation of 4 Points

Dennis, who is 74 inches tall, is taller than 84 percent of the sample population; Rob, who is 66 inches tall, is taller than only 16 percent of the population.

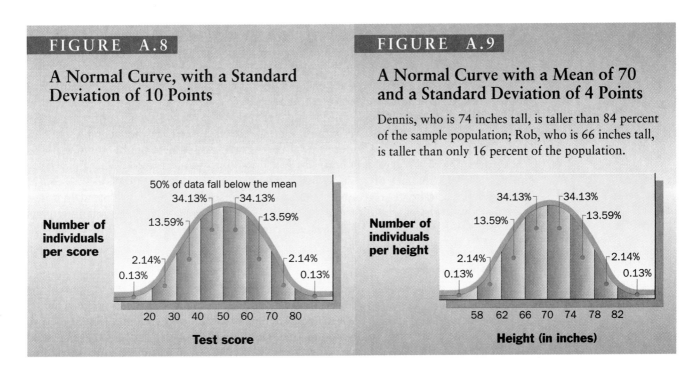

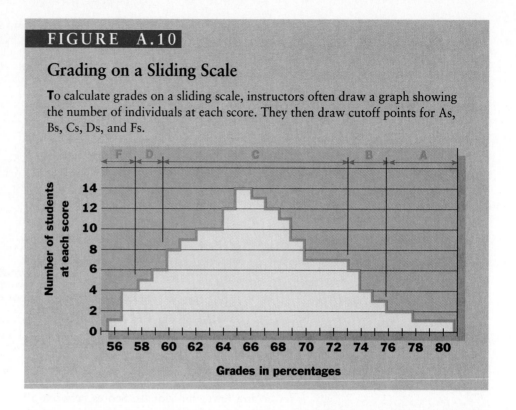

FIGURE A.10

Grading on a Sliding Scale

To calculate grades on a sliding scale, instructors often draw a graph showing the number of individuals at each score. They then draw cutoff points for As, Bs, Cs, Ds, and Fs.

above the mean, which means that he is taller than 84 percent of the population (0.13 + 2.14 + 13.59 + 34.13 + 34.13 = 84.12 percent). Rob, who is 66 inches tall, is taller than only 16 percent of the population. His height is one standard deviation below the mean.

Normal Curves: A Practical Example

Your grade on an examination is often determined by how other members of the class do on the exam. This is what instructors mean when they say that a grade is on a "sliding scale" or "curve." If the average student in a class answers only 50 percent of the questions correctly, a student who answers 70 percent correctly has done a good job. But if the average student scores 85 percent, then someone who scores only 70 percent has not done so well.

Before they assign grades on a sliding scale, testing services and instructors generally plot the test results on a graph in order to calculate a mean. They then inspect the scores and "slide the scale" to an appropriate level. Figure A.10 shows the scores on a trigonometry test. Since the average score is 65 percent, students who score 65 percent will receive a C, those who do better will receive an A or a B, and those who do worse will receive a D or an F.

For a number of reasons, it is sometimes impractical or impossible to collect experimental data for control groups or experimental groups or to do research that involves manipulations of an experimental variable. In these cases, correlations (considered next) may be calculated; they can tell a scientist a great deal.

Correlation

Sometimes researchers wish to compare data that were gathered in different surveys and questionnaires. To do so, they perform a *correlation study*. A correlation implies that an increase in the value of one variable will be accompanied by an increase or decrease in the value of a second variable. The degree and direction of relationship between two variables is expressed by a numerical value called the **correlation coefficient.** Correlation coefficients range from –1, through 0, to +1. Any correlation coefficient greater or less than 0, regardless of its sign, indicates that the variables are related. When two variables are perfectly correlated, they are said to have a correlation coefficient of 1. A perfect correlation occurs when knowing the value of one variable allows one to predict *precisely* the value of the second, but this is a rare occurrence in psychological research.

Most variables are not perfectly correlated. Consider height and weight, for example. Although tall people generally weigh more than short people, some tall people weigh less than some short people. Figure A.11 illustrates the fact that knowing a person's height does not enable one to predict the person's weight exactly. The two variables have a correlation coefficient of only 0.65.

Another example of imperfectly correlated variables is found in the incidence of children of schizophrenic parents. If a parent is schizophrenic, the likelihood that the child will be schizophrenic increases sharply. Thus, there is a correlation between parents and children with respect to schizophrenia. Because this correlation is not perfect—that is, not every child born to a schizophrenic parent will develop the disorder—psychologists believe that genetics is only one of several contributing factors in the development of the disorder.

When one variable shows an increase in value and a second also shows an increase, the two variables are positively related, and the relationship is known as a *positive correlation.* Height and weight show a positive correlation: Generally, as height increases, so does weight. On the other hand, if one variable decreases as the other increases, the variables are negatively correlated, and the relationship is known as a *negative correlation.* Figure A.12 offers a hypothetical example. The relationship between the number of hours of therapy and the extent of anxiety in the figure shows a negative correlation. As the number of hours of therapy increases, anxiety decreases. These variables have a negative correlation coefficient of about –0.6 or –0.7.

Another example of a negative condition is that between time and memory. A person might be able to recall an entire list of 10 words immediately after reading it; the next day, the person may remember only 5 of the words, and a week later only 1 word. Thus, as time increases, memory decreases. Similarly, people who live close to an airport report that aircraft noise is painfully loud; those who live farther away report less noise. The loudness of the aircraft noise is negatively correlated with the distance from the airport: As distance increases, loudness decreases.

A correlation coefficient of +0.7 is no stronger than one of –0.7. That is, the *direction,* not the strength, of a relationship is changed by the plus or minus sign. The strength is determined by the number: The larger the number, the greater the strength of the correlation. A correlation coefficient of –0.8 is greater than one of +0.7; a correlation coefficient of +0.6 is greater than one of –0.5.

Some variables show absolutely no correlation; this is expressed by a correlation coefficient of 0. Figure A.13 plots data for IQ and height. The figure shows

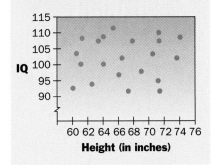

FIGURE A.11

The Correlation of Height and Weight

When two variables are related, knowing the value of one helps a person predict the value of the other.

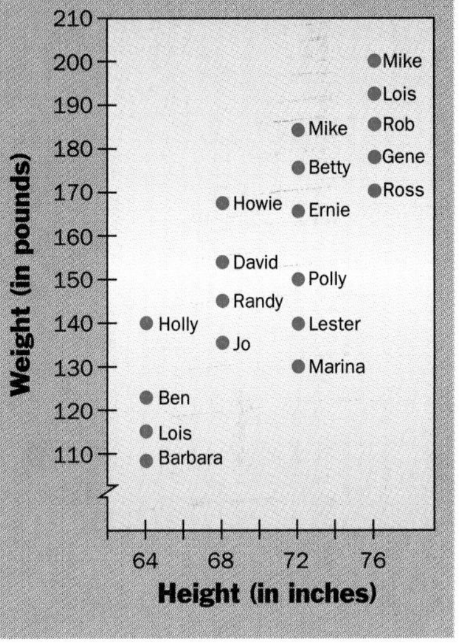

FIGURE A.13

A Correlation Coefficient of 0 (zero) Shows That There Is No Relationship

Correlation coefficient: A number that expresses the degree and direction of a relationship between two variables, ranging from –1 (a perfect negative correlation) to +1 (a perfect positive correlation).

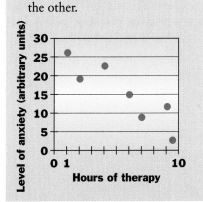

FIGURE A.12

A Negative Correlation

In a negative correlation, an increase in one variable is associated with a decrease in the other.

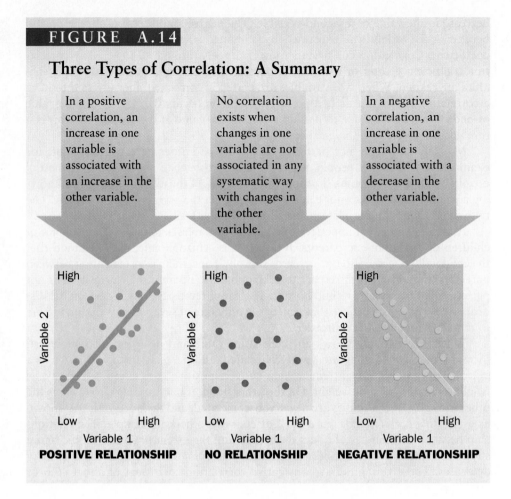

FIGURE A.14

Three Types of Correlation: A Summary

In a positive correlation, an increase in one variable is associated with an increase in the other variable.

No correlation exists when changes in one variable are not associated in any systematic way with changes in the other variable.

In a negative correlation, an increase in one variable is associated with a decrease in the other variable.

POSITIVE RELATIONSHIP

NO RELATIONSHIP

NEGATIVE RELATIONSHIP

no correlation between IQ and height, so the two variables have a correlation coefficient of 0. (See Figure A.14 for a summary of correlations.)

As we saw in chapter 1, correlation studies make no statements about cause and effect. They simply show that if there is an increase in one variable, there will probably be an increase or decrease in another variable. It is only through experimental studies that researchers can make cause-and-effect statements. Many of the studies reported in this text are correlational, but far more are experimental. Whenever possible, researchers wish to draw causal inferences.

FOCUS

▶ When one is considering small samples of human participants, particularly those of a racial or ethnic group, what is the best measure of central tendency, and why? pp. 646–649

▶ Distinguish the key differences among the mean, mode, and median. pp. 647–648

▶ Describe the underlying characteristics of a normal curve. pp. 654–656

Summary & Review

Conducting Experiments

What is a hypothesis?

A *hypothesis* is a tentative statement about a causal relationship between two variables or situations to be evaluated in an experiment. p. 643

What are three key components of a good experiment?

A good *experiment* must have one or more *experimental groups*, a *control group*, carefully defined variables, and a sufficient number of carefully selected subjects in each group. The experiment must include a good *sample*—a group of subjects or participants who are generally representative of the population about which an inference is to be made. pp. 643–645

What are the roles in an experiment of the independent and dependent variables?

The independent and dependent variables in an experiment must be carefully specified. The *independent variable* is directly and purposefully manipulated by the experimenter to see what effect differences in it will have on the variables under study. The *dependent variable* is the behavior measured by the experimenter to assess whether changes in the independent variable affect the behavior under study. If a variable cannot be defined precisely, it must be defined operationally, in the form of a concrete description of how it will be measured. p. 645

KEY TERMS: *statistics*, p. 643; *hypothesis*, p. 643; *experiment*, p. 643; *independent variable*, p. 643; *dependent variable*, p. 643; *control group*, p. 644; *experimental group*, p. 644; *sample*, p. 644; *operational definition*, p. 645.

Descriptive Statistics

What is descriptive statistics, and what is a frequency distribution?

Descriptive statistics is a general set of procedures to summarize, condense, and describe samples of data. A *frequency distribution* is a way of organizing data to show the number of times each item of data occurs; the graphic version of a frequency distribution is a *frequency polygon*. pp. 645–646

What are measures of central tendency?

Measures of central tendency are descriptive statistics that indicate which single score best represents an entire set of scores. The most frequently used measure of central tendency is the *mean*, or arithmetic average. Also used are the *mode*, or most frequently observed data point; and the *median*, the 50 percent point. pp. 646–647

What is a measure of variability?

A measure of *variability* is a statistic that describes the extent to which scores differ from one another in a distribution. One such measure, the *range*, shows the spread of scores in a distribution. Another, the *standard deviation*, shows the extent to which all members of a group will vary from the mean. pp. 649–651

KEY TERMS: *descriptive statistics*, p.645; *frequency distribution*, p. 646; *frequency polygons*, p. 646; *measure of central tendency*, p.647; *mean*, p. 647; *mode*, p. 647; *median*, p. 648; *variability*, p. 649; *range*, p. 649; *standard deviation*, p. 651.

Inferential Statistics and the Normal Curve

What is the role of inferential statistics?

Inferential statistics enable the researcher to determine whether two or more groups differ from one another and whether the difference is a result of chance. When a difference is significant, it can be repeated experimentally using similar groups of subjects. Repeating an experiment to verify a result is called replicating the experiment. p. 653

What are the key characteristics of a normal curve?

The mean, mode, and median of a normal curve are generally assumed to be the same, and the distribution of scores around that central point is symmetrical. pp. 654–656

KEY TERMS: *inferential statistics*, p. 653; *significant difference*, p. 653; *normal distribution*, p. 654.

Correlation

What are the essential characteristics of a correlation coefficient?

The correlation coefficient expresses the degree of relationship between two variables. When two variables are perfectly correlated, they are said to have a correlation of 1. The direction, not the strength, of a correlation relationship is changed by a plus or minus sign in front of the number. The strength is determined by the number: the larger the number, the greater the strength of the correlation. pp. 656–658

continued

Summary & Review

Compare correlational studies and experiments with regard to cause and effect.

Correlation studies make no statements about cause and effect. They simply show that if there is an increase in one variable, there will probably be an increase or decrease in another variable. Only through experimental studies can researchers make cause-and-effect statements. pp. 657–658

KEY TERM: *correlation coefficient,* p. 657.

Module B

Industrial/Organizational Psychology

Many business experts thought that Sharp Corporation of Japan made a big mistake when it built an electronics factory in Memphis. In 1966, RCA had built a TV plant in that city; but wildcat strikes, product sabotage, and abysmal quality forced RCA to shut the factory down. The Japanese plant proved successful, however. What made the difference? A possible explanation is that the Japanese bosses treated their American employees like family, while demanding the highest levels of quality control. In return, the employees were motivated and found their work fulfilling.

Industrial/organizational (I/O) psychology: The study of how individual behavior is affected by the work environment, coworkers, and organizational practices.

As productivity has become increasingly important to American industry, industrial/organizational psychology has grown in importance. **Industrial/organizational (I/O) psychology** is the study of how individual behavior is affected by the work environment, coworkers, and organizational practices. It is used in government, hospitals, universities, and public service agencies, in addition to large and small for profit organizations. In all these environments, how well individuals perform their duties and relate to one another is a key concern.

I/O psychology can be divided into three broad areas: personnel psychology, organizational psychology, and human factors. *Personnel psychology* focuses on the relationship of people and their jobs, training, promotions, benefits, discrimination, and performance evaluation, and on determining who has the skills and abilities to perform various jobs. Such functions take place both before people begin to work for an organization and as an ongoing process within the organization. *Organizational psychology* is concerned with organizations—their issues and structure and especially how people adapt, in both large and small settings. Last, the subfield of *human factors,* or human engineering, is the study of how environments can be designed to optimize performance by dealing with workers' limitations and meeting workers' personal needs.

Personnel Psychology

Personnel psychologists are involved in a broad array of activities, including helping employers choose among prospective job candidates, helping determine compensation packages, and arranging termination programs when business must cut back. Among the most important tasks is to help businesses select among well-trained qualified candidates for specific positions. Today, finding the right people for jobs occurs within the context of an organization's *strategic planning.* This planning includes forecasting the organization's future needs, establishing specific objectives, and implementing programs to ensure that appropriate people will be available when needed (Jackson & Schuler, 1990).

Job Analyses

As a first step in the strategic planning process, companies often prepare *job analyses*—careful descriptions of the various tasks and activities of employees, along with the knowledge, skills, and abilities necessary for the employees to do their jobs. This means specifying performance criteria—behaviors—that are required of employees. It also means enumerating the specifications for successful employment (for example, a computer programmer might need good eyesight, a college education, and top-notch computing skills).

Employers need to ensure that jobs are appropriate and have the correct scope. A job should not be too big or encompass too many tasks; nor should it be too limiting and so focused that it becomes boring and repetitive. Ideally, jobs should allow employees some level of responsibility for and control over how they do their tasks. Balancing the scope and complexity of jobs and helping employers create jobs that will be motivating are two of the key tasks of an I/O psychologist.

Employers want to hire people who will enjoy their work, suit the company's needs, and be productive. I/O psychologists use specific selection procedures, including tests, to produce the best match between employers and employees. The selection procedures for jobs with large firms are often complicated and time-consuming.

Selection Procedures

Selection procedures have one basic goal—predicting the success of job candidates so as to determine which candidates to make offers to and which to reject. Employers and researchers use applications, interviews, work samples, and tests to make comparisons between people. Subtle factors can be at work in selection procedures, and interviewers have to pay particular attention to these factors to make sure that such things as their own moods or an applicant's clothes do not influence their evaluation of an applicant's capabilities (Forsythe, 1990).

Standardized cognitive tests, such as those for general ability and specific knowledge, are good predictors of both academic success and job performance (Schmidt, Ones, & Hunter, 1992). However, an important question for I/O psychologists is whether tests, which are widely used in industry, are the best predictors of job performance. This question has become especially important because of a large number of lawsuits filed by those who think the tests discriminate against them (Guion & Gibson, 1988).

Standardized tests are not limited to intellectual abilities. Depending on the job, there may be tests of spatial abilities, perceptual accuracy, motor abilities, personality, and personal interests. Each test is used to help the employer determine if a job candidate's abilities match a job's requirements. Tests of personality and interests, though, are difficult to correlate with job performance; for example, outgoing individuals may be good salespeople, but quiet, introspective individuals can be just as successful.

Training

When a company hires a new employee, a period of training nearly always follows. *Training* is the process by which employees are systematically taught skills to improve their job performance. A new employee may need to learn specific skills, such as how to use a computer program or how to sell in a new industry. Most corporations offer systematic training, which typically involves teaching employees about the organization and its goals. Training individuals about specific tasks can be simple or complex. For example, a new sales manager must learn not only about the range of products she will sell but also about the territory she will manage, the employees she will supervise, and the specific needs of her customers.

Even seasoned employees need training and retraining. In large organizations, training is an ongoing process, as new products are introduced and new technologies are discovered. I/O psychologists typically break training into a multistep set of learning objectives. This method of training often provides specific knowledge and skills and helps employees identify their strengths and weaknesses in regard to new tasks. It also helps employees identify obstacles to overcome and opportunities to grow and advance.

Training may be the simple process of reviewing a new product or procedure. It may also be an elaborate process that involves the employee in active participation on the job—perhaps programming a robot or pitching a product to clients. Training may include repetitive practice, particularly with highly technical equipment. It often involves moving from a teaching classroom or sales meeting to the field, store, or actual workplace. Last, training usually involves feedback, so employees can learn if the new skills or knowledge have been successfully acquired.

Performance Appraisal

Have you ever been evaluated by an employer? Bosses are sometimes good at appraising work; but they may forget your best efforts and remember your mistakes,

Performance appraisal: The process by which a supervisor periodically evaluates the performance of a subordinate.

or they may not accurately convey how they feel about your performance. What makes a boss good at evaluating employees?

Performance appraisal is the process by which a supervisor periodically evaluates the performance of a subordinate. Supervisors have always made such appraisals; and in the past 70 years, researchers have tried to find ways for them to do it systematically. Performance appraisals are especially important because they are often used in making determinations about salaries, layoffs, firings, transfers, and promotions (Cleveland, Murphy, & Williams, 1989).

The problem with performance appraisal is that it is often done inaccurately by people with few skills in evaluation and with few diagnostic aids. Supervisors generally report that they dislike conducting appraisals. They don't like to review their subordinates, and many acknowledge that they do not have strong evaluative skills. Further, some managers have inappropriate biases (Swim et al., 1989).

Despite similarities in work performance, men and women approach being evaluated differently. Research shows that men are likely to deny the information given in evaluations; women, by contrast, are likely to approach evaluations as opportunities to gain information about their abilities (T. A. Roberts, 1991). Roberts asserts that women may take evaluations very seriously in the short term in order to reach long-term goals.

Many companies require periodic evaluations, but reluctant managers do them as infrequently as possible, and sometimes in a cursory manner. They often evaluate everybody about the same—average, or perhaps very good, which may leave employees feeling unappreciated. Ways to improve the process typically involve more active thinking on the part of supervisors. We see this in the Research Process box.

FOCUS

▶ What are the goals of selection procedures and training efforts in the workplace? p. 663

▶ In the DeNisi, Robbins, and Cafferty study, what was the hypothesis that the researchers generated? p. 665

Organizational Psychology

I/O psychologists help people work together in organizations, work at satisfying the emotional and social needs of employees, and help organizations motivate management and workers. One obvious motivator is economics; people need money to live. Nonetheless, a successful employer-employee relationship relies on factors in addition to economic motivation.

Job Performance

We know that job performance is affected by *intrinsically motivated behavior*—behavior engaged in strictly because it brings pleasure. (We examined intrinsic and extrinsic motivation in chapters 5 and 10.) Recall that when intrinsically motivated behaviors are constantly reinforced with direct external rewards (such as money), productivity often drops. Money is often not that important to job performance. A well-paid plumber may find her work tedious and unfulfilling, while a lower-paid clerical worker who has a job that he sees as important and challenging will perform well and increase his responsibilities.

Often, with the help of I/O psychologists, employers try to find ways to motivate employees to be more productive (and hence to provide the companies with more profits). One theory, proposed by Victor Vroom (1964), suggests that job per-

THE RESEARCH PROCESS

Performance Appraisal and Cognition

"I distinctly remember you goofing off last Thursday. On Friday, I saw you behaving rudely to a customer. Don't do it again!" the boss shouted at an intimidated clerk. The frightened clerk shook his head and walked away muttering. He had been out sick on Thursday; furthermore, his boss didn't know the nature of his interaction with the customer, who had yelled at him and insulted him and done everything but slap him. He felt that his performance appraisal was inaccurate, to say the least.

Managers have to observe employees, evaluate their performance, remember it after intervening activities have taken place, and then recall specific behaviors accurately. Cognitive processes are crucial in making accurate performance appraisals (DeNisi & Williams, 1988). One important cognitive process in appraisals is memory. Do supervisors remember their appraisals of workers? Does a worker's most recent work bias a performance appraisal?

Hypotheses. Although an employee's work may be consistently good, a bad period of performance just before an appraisal can bias an observer toward a poor decision. Steiner and Rain (1989) argue that there are recency effects in performance appraisals, just as there are in memory studies (as we saw in chapter 6). Are there other memory effects as well in performance appraisal? Are there techniques that can be used to ensure more accurate appraisals, such as taking notes?

Method. DeNisi, Robbins, and Cafferty (1989) asked subjects to watch videotapes of carpenters who were sawing, sanding, and staining and then to evaluate their performance. The subjects were provided with a guide to correct performance, and some received a set of diary cards with tabs on them. The tabbed cards included either the names of the carpenters or the task names, or they were blank. The subjects who were not given cards were asked to remember the workers' performance without help. The researchers wanted to know if using diaries would help people to make better performance evaluations.

Results and Conclusion. The results showed that the diaries produced better recall and more accurate ratings. Keeping a diary provided a way to organize information and made the subjects less dependent on memory. This would obviously help eliminate the recency efforts found by Steiner and Rain. Performance appraisals are a cognitive task affected by traditional cognitive variables, such as intervening activity, memory loss, and recency effects. The research shows that keeping a diary can minimize the negative effects and improve appraisals. Diary recording is not a complete solution to improving performance evaluations; a wide range of factors influence evaluations, including who was evaluated just before you and how you were rated in your last evaluation, among other things (Maurer, Palmer & Ashe, 1993). Still, the use of diaries has a generally positive impact on the process of performance evaluations.

Implications. Employers need to be sensitive to how and when they do performance appraisals. Psychologists seek to help employers be fair, professional, and accurate. In addition, because laws have been passed to protect employees from discrimination, employers have been forced to be more responsive to employees by doing regular appraisals. In the process, larger companies with better-trained staffs are helping workers by specifying tasks to be mastered during the next appraisal period. I/O psychologists have also worked to develop better rating forms, to train managers to evaluate performance more effectively, and especially to help managers conduct unbiased appraisals.

---

formance is determined by both motivation and ability. Vroom's is an expectancy theory (we examined expectancy theories in chapter 10); it states that motivation is determined by what people expect to get from performing a task—a rewarding experience or a frustrating one. According to Vroom, a person must first have the ability to perform the task; without that, the experience will be frustrating and hence nonmotivating. However, a person's conscientiousness and general overall abilities are very important; specific abilities to do a task seem less crucial in determining job performance (Schmidt & Hunter, 1992).

Lawler and Porter (1967) modified and expanded Vroom's theory. They contended that performance is determined by motivation, ability, and *role perceptions*—the ways people think about themselves and their jobs (see Figure B.1 on page 666).

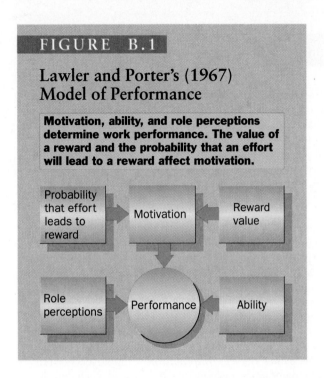

FIGURE B.1

Lawler and Porter's (1967) Model of Performance

Motivation, ability, and role perceptions determine work performance. The value of a reward and the probability that an effort will lead to a reward affect motivation.

They believed workers must fully understand the nature of their positions and all that is required of them. Too often, people fail not because of lack of motivation or ability but because they do not know what is expected of them or how to achieve a sense of control or power in the organization (Ragins & Sundstrom, 1989).

Today, researchers claim that the motivation to work can be explained by integrating theories that focus on goals, experiences, and thoughts (Locke & Latham, 1990a). Locke and Latham (1990b) assert that, if a high challenge is accompanied by high expectations for success, then high performance is likely; however, employees must also be committed to the goals of the company and be sensitive to feedback. Success is also based on effort, persistence, and specific task strategies. When people are given incentives, when they think their contributions are important, and when the effort required of them is not excessive, productivity will be high (Shepperd, 1993). When performance is high, job satisfaction is likely; this in turn facilitates commitment to the organization and its goals.

Job Satisfaction

Job satisfaction is different from job motivation. Motivation (the internal conditions that direct a person to act) is always shown in behavior; job satisfaction (a person's attitude about the work and workplace) may not be shown in behavior. A tired, bored, and overworked electrician may feel discouraged and angry—and may even hate her job—but she can still be motivated to work. Her motivation may stem from the high pay she receives, from her obligation to complete a job, or from some other source. Both her motivation and her job performance are high—as is seen in her work. Thus, although her job satisfaction is low, it does not affect her performance.

Job satisfaction must be viewed in the context of the work setting and workers' standards (Locke & Latham, 1990b). Workers' motivations and values have to be consistent with the available opportunities and resources if potential advancement and satisfaction are to be facilitated (Katzell & Thompson, 1990). The level of satisfaction depends on the extent to which people see a discrepancy between their expectations for satisfaction and actual satisfaction. That discrepancy is based on various aspects of a job. People can be pleased or dissatisfied about hours, pay, client contact, and promotion opportunities, for example (Algera, 1990). People have standards for comparison that determine the extent to which they feel they are doing well or poorly. One of those standards is fairness; when people believe decisions, evaluations, and resource allocations are made fairly, their job satisfaction tends to be high. This finding is true for both men and women in a number of settings (Witt & Nye, 1992). Table B.1 presents some key factors related to job satisfaction.

Motivation Management

Both employers and psychologists know that people are motivated by different variables. Monetary rewards are important, for example; but so is the likelihood of success. I/O psychologists study not only rewards and success but also workers' effects on management and management's concerns about itself. Psychologists recognize the complexity of motivation management and have developed three basic approaches to it: paternalistic, behavioral, and participatory.

TABLE B.1   *Some Key Factors Related to Job Satisfaction*

▶ The work is interesting.
▶ There is adequate recognition.
▶ The work contributes to self-esteem.
▶ There are opportunities for advancement.
▶ The pay is perceived as being adequate and equitable.
▶ There is job security.
▶ There are good relationships with supervisory personnel.
▶ There are opportunities for enjoyable social interactions.
▶ There is a positive attitude toward the work environment.
▶ The work is perceived to be challenging.
▶ There are opportunities to apply one's own judgment.
▶ There is some degree of autonomy.
▶ Opportunities exist to influence company policy and procedures.
▶ There is adequate information and equipment.

The fundamental idea of the *paternalistic approach* to motivation is that a company takes care of its employees' needs and desires in a fatherly manner. This approach was common in the mining companies of Appalachia, which provided housing, schools, recreation, and churches for employees. It is contrary to many psychologists' views on behavior. Instrumental conditioning studies show that, for a behavior (such as work) to be established and maintained, reinforcement must be contingent on performance. In a paternalistic system, all employees—productive as well as nonproductive—are given reinforcement if they fulfill their role as workers. Reinforcement without the need for performance does not encourage people to work hard.

Behavioral approaches to motivation assume that people will work only if they receive tangible rewards for specific task performance. Examples include paying a factory worker by the piece and a typist by the page. In such a system, hardworking employees obtain more rewards—commissions, salary increases, bonuses, and so on—because they produce more; but little attention is paid to the emotional needs of workers.

The *participatory approach* to motivation is based on the belief that individuals who have a say in the decisions that affect their lives are more motivated to work. Participation, it is argued, provides a setting in which managers and employees can exchange information to solve problems (Tjosvold, 1987). Supporters of this approach believe that a sense of competence and self-determination is likely to increase individuals' levels of motivation (Deci, 1975). *Quality circles,* in which workers at all levels assemble to discuss ways to promote excellence, is one technique employers use to involve workers in the management process (Matsui & Onglatco, 1990).

Many variables affect the success of participatory programs: the work setting, the individuals involved, the kinds of decisions to be made, and the hiring policies, for example. When participatory approaches to work are undertaken there are positive effects on workers' values, thoughts, and motivation. This leads to less conflict among workers, increased productivity, and better overall performance on the job (see Figure B.2 on page 668). When workers feel comfortable and involved with

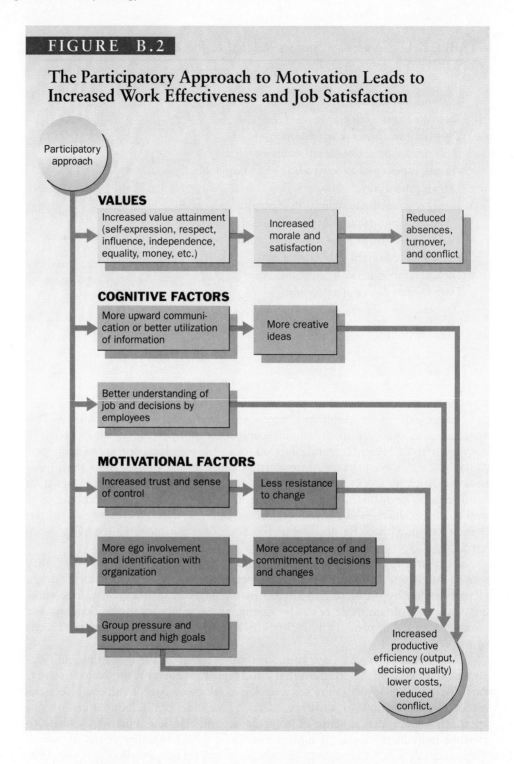

FIGURE B.2

The Participatory Approach to Motivation Leads to Increased Work Effectiveness and Job Satisfaction

their work and their organization, they are more likely to be spontaneous, to help coworkers, to protect the organization, and so on. Many of these behaviors depend on feeling positive about the work environment and having a good attitude at work (George & Brief, 1992).

If you were setting up your own company, which approach would you use to motivate your workers? Would you be the paternalistic boss, would you set objectives to be met, or would you let workers participate in decision making?

Leadership

In every organization, some individuals emerge as *leaders*—people who influence other people's behavior toward the attainment of some agreed-upon goals. In some organizations, leaders emerge spontaneously; in others, they are formally chosen by a governing body. Leaders are expected to help further the purposes of their organization. Thus, one of their primary roles is to motivate employees to be involved in and work hard at their tasks. They also are responsible for setting goals and making policy decisions.

The study of leadership has gone through three major phases, each with a characteristic focus: traits, behaviors, and situations. The right combination of these elements ultimately describes an effective leader.

The specific personality traits of individual leaders were studied intensively until the early 1950s. This research tried to isolate the characteristics that make individuals good or poor leaders (for example, are good leaders assertive, directive, or authoritarian?), but the approach was doomed to failure. Leaders cannot be universally characterized by traits such as assertiveness or passivity. Many leaders are assertive, but many others are not. In fact, individual differences among leaders are extreme. One reason the early studies were unable to find a common denominator was that each leader and each organization has different goals. An individual's personality traits will tell psychologists something about leadership, but the differences among leaders tend to be greater than the similarities

After the early 1950s, the focus of research moved from leaders' personalities to their behaviors. The second group of studies tried to find characteristic ways in which leaders interact with other members of their organizations. Some of the pioneering work on leadership was done at the University of Michigan's Institute for Social Research. The Michigan studies (as they are often called) found that leaders tend to be either employee- or task-oriented. Whether a leader is employee- or task-oriented is determined by how the leader chooses to influence behavior. An employee-oriented leader acts to maintain and enhance individual employees' feelings of self-worth or self-esteem. Such leaders try to make employees and coworkers feel valued and important. A task-oriented leader focuses on getting the job done efficiently and quickly, with as little effort as possible.

There tend to be gender-related styles in leadership, with women being more employee-oriented and men more task-oriented (Eagly & Johnson, 1990). Recent studies show that the gender of the leader and of the followers has other important effects. For example, female leaders or managers tend to be evaluated as positively as their male counterparts. However, when they behave in stereotypically male ways, they are devalued—especially if the evaluators are men (Eagly, Makhijani, & Klonsky, 1992).

Further research has confirmed that individual differences among leaders are great and that a leader's behavior is determined by personal traits, by overall orientation (employee or task), and sometimes by the group of people being led. Some groups of individuals have characteristics that demand an employee orientation. For example, an underpaid, overworked, but dedicated social worker may have a great need for self-esteem, feel that his work is worthwhile, but also know that he is underpaid. A supervisor must motivate this person not with authoritarian task-oriented directions but with concern for his need for self-worth. Everyone has a need for self-esteem. Highly paid executives, however, may be more easily motivated by a task-oriented approach, because they recognize that their high salary reflects their productivity. Job performance, job satisfaction, and the way a worker is treated are closely related. In motivating workers, leaders must consider their own personal traits, the various possible behaviors they might use to influence others, and the conditions in which they and their coworkers work.

In the 1970s, research shifted from investigating leader behavior to investigating the situations in which behaviors were performed. Some situations lend themselves to leadership, and even to specific forms of leadership; others need little leadership or direction. Thus, a warm, friendly, employee-oriented leader (or supervisor) is generally very useful for a group of service workers. However, if the organization encounters financial trouble and its workers must be laid off, with the supervisor having no control over who is let go, the climate of uncertainty may counteract the usefulness of that leader's approach. The organization may then have to find a task-oriented leader who can keep the organization functioning.

A complex interplay of factors determines the most effective style of leadership in different situations, even within one organization. Effective leaders may simply be better at perceiving the goals and needs of their organization. Two major theories that try to account for leadership effectiveness are the Fiedler contingency model and Vroom's leadership model.

The Fiedler Contingency Model. Fred Fiedler (1964, 1974) has developed a contingency model of leadership that acknowledges that traits, behaviors, and situations can vary among individuals and over time and that leadership is contingent on all other factors. Fiedler's model assumes that there are a number of possible situations in which leaders may find themselves: Relations between leaders and followers can be good or bad, tasks for the organization can be structured or unstructured, and the leader's power can be weak or strong. A leader is in a favorable position if he or she has good relations with followers, has a task that is structured, and is in a position of power. In contrast, a leader is in an unfavorable position if he or she has poor relations with followers, is dealing with an unstructured task, and lacks power. Fiedler has developed scales for rating leadership ability and effectiveness and has correlated them with the various possible situations. His results show that relationship-oriented leaders have the best overall functioning; and leaders who are task-oriented have very effective organizations, but only in extremely favorable circumstances.

The key element of Fiedler's theory is that people can change their behavior according to the situation in which they find themselves. This model allows people to adopt the most effective leadership role possible for a particular situation. Fiedler made a great inferential leap in assuming that a combination of situations affects behavior. Ultimately, his approach may not explain leadership, but it provides a solid theory with practical implications.

Vroom's Leadership Model. Unlike Fiedler, Vroom believes there are a variety of ways of making decisions in organizations. A leader can make an authoritarian decision and simply announce it; she can present a problem, listen to advice, and then make a decision; or she can allow other people to make the decision. When a manager makes a decision and announces it, subordinates and coworkers have little freedom of choice; this style of leadership is called boss-centered (Vroom, 1974; Vroom & Yetton, 1973). As a leader's use of authority increases, the freedom of others in the group decreases. According to Vroom's view, each time a decision is to be made, managers or leaders can ask themselves a series of questions about the best possible approach to solving a problem that will help them determine the best leadership approach for the situation.

The strength of Vroom's model is that it recognizes that leaders have options—that they can choose how to behave on the basis of their own previous experiences and knowledge and on the basis of situations or conditions. Vroom's model has received some research support, but its practical implications in the workplace have not been evaluated systematically. Like Fiedler's model, it emphasizes the important role of situational variables in determining which leadership approach is most appropriate to a situation.

Psychologists' knowledge of how people influence and manage others has grown dramatically. Effective leadership depends not only on personal traits and specific techniques or behaviors but also on the situation. Workers may exaggerate the leadership characteristics of a boss if their environment is productive and they are happy (Shamir, 1992). Thus, leadership, workers' perceptions of leadership, and motivation are interrelated.

A good leader must assess worker motivation and levels of satisfaction. Sensitivity to motivation, satisfaction, and performance can help a leader set solid personnel selection policies. Good selection procedures help establish a favorable working situation, and a favorable situation makes for better leadership possibilities. Better leadership, in turn, may make workers more productive and more satisfied.

Human Factors

The study of human factors focuses on the relationship of human beings to machines and their environment. A human factors psychologist might focus on health-care products, cooking utensils, educational products, or the interaction of machines and the environment in which they are placed. Most human factors research focuses on the work environment, especially the areas of efficiency and safety.

Efficiency

In the work environment, researchers have examined the abilities of workers to operate machines effectively. Much of this research centers on **ergonomics**—the study of the fit between people, their anatomy or physiology, and the demands of a particular task or piece of equipment, and the environment in which the task occurs. In the early part of this century, working with machinery meant reading dials, turning wheels, and lifting equipment. Human factors researchers focused on creating machine-human interfaces that required as little energy as possible and created few errors on the part of the machine operator. This might mean developing display screens that are visible and meaningful to all who might view them.

Today, working with machinery often means operating a computer, monitoring computer-controlled devices, programming equipment, and working in teams with other highly skilled employees. To a great extent, *controlling* equipment, rather than operating it, has become a focus of human factors research. If equipment is to be properly controlled, dials, computer screens, and display devices have to be designed well enough that errors are minimized. For example, a pilot must be able to read a computer screen accurately to land a plane safely; a nuclear power plant operator must be able to read the temperature of nuclear devices. The design of computer display screens has dominated research in human factors (Howell, 1993).

Nonetheless, computer screens and displays are only one part of the study of human factors. Today, jobs are more complex, and more likely to require cognitive rather than physical skills. Workers are increasingly task interdependent, hence there has been an increased emphasis on social factors in the workplace. Today, researchers are studying groups of pilots and navigators in the cockpit, in addition to instrumentation displays. A growing area is the study of robotics. In industries such as auto manufacturing, robots have been programmed to do many tasks that human beings once did. They must be designed effectively to duplicate the abilities of human beings. Much of the work of robotics engineers is to make sure that robots are both effective and safe.

Even the tools of carpenters, technicians, and tailors can be designed using the principles of human factors. For example, what is the best weight for a hammer?

Ergonomics: The study of the fit between people, their anatomy or physiology, and the demands of a particular task or piece of equipment, and the environment in which the task occurs.

How tall should a drill press be? Can the design of sewing machines, computers, and robotic controls take into account the size of an operator's hand? Each of these human factors considerations can improve accuracy, productivity, and safety.

Safety

Human factors research can provide a work environment that is not only efficient but also safe. Many industrial accidents occur despite attempts to protect workers' safety. Human factors research can help reduce accidents by designing safe equipment. Psychologists can also help design work schedules that optimize the safe use of equipment—especially potentially dangerous equipment. They can help choose people who can work the equipment with the fewest accidents; some people have greater manual dexterity than others, and some are more attentive than others. Last, psychologists can help promote safety through programs that improve people's attitudes about safety and therefore promote safer work behavior. Only when workers believe that safety is valued and personally helpful are they likely to make safety-promoting changes. A company may comply with government safety regulations; but unless its workers cooperate in safety efforts, major work-site accidents can occur. Nuclear power plants are an obvious case in point. Safety regulations must be followed; if they are not, the lives of thousands of people are put at risk.

FOCUS

► Identify and characterize three approaches to motivation management. pp. 666–668

► Identify the key characteristics of good leaders. pp. 669–671

► What are the implications of the fact that jobs increasingly require more cognitive rather than physical skills? pp. 671–672

Summary & Review

Personnel Psychology

What is industrial/ organizational (I/O) psychology?

Industrial/organizational psychology is the study of how individual behavior is affected by the work environment, coworkers, and organizational practices. It can be divided into three broad areas: personnel psychology, organizational psychology, and human factors. p. 662

What is performance appraisal?

Performance appraisal is the process by which a supervisor periodically evaluates the performance of a subordinate. pp. 663–664

KEY TERMS: *industrial/organizational psychology,* p. 662; *performance appraisal,* p. 664.

Organizational Psychology

What does Vroom's expectancy theory say about job performance?

Vroom's expectancy theory asserts that performance is determined by motivation and ability. pp. 664–666

What is a leader, and who makes the best leader?

A *leader* is a person who influences other people's behavior toward the attainment of some agreed-upon goals.

Leaders can be employee-oriented or task-oriented; the context of the situation or organization is a key determinant of which type of leader will be more effective. pp. 669–671

Human Factors

What is ergonomics?

Ergonomics is the study of the fit between people, their anatomy or physiology, and the demands of a particular task or piece of equipment, and the environment in which the task occurs. pp. 671–672

KEY TERM: *ergonomics,* p. 671.

REFERENCES

Aarons, L. (1976). Sleep assisted instruction. *Psychological Bulletin, 83,* 1–40.

Abed, F. (1991). Cultural influences on visual scanning patterns. *Journal of Cross-Cultural Psychology, 22,* 525–534.

Abelson, R. P. (1988). Conviction. *American Psychologist, 43,* 267–276.

Abrams, R., Swartz, C. M., & Vedak, C. (1991). Antidepressant effects of high-dose right unilateral electroconvulsive therapy. *Archives of General Psychiatry, 48,* 746–748.

Abramson, L. Y., Metalsky, G. I., & Alloy, L. B. (1989). Hopelessness depression: A theory-based subtype of depression. *Psychological Review, 96,* 358–372.

Adelmann, P. K., Antonucci, T. C., Crohan, S. E., & Colemen, L. M. (1989). Empty nest, cohort, and employment in the well-being of midlife women. *Sex Roles, 20,* 173–180.

Ader, R., & Cohen, N. (1993). Psychoneuroimmunology: Conditioning and stress. *Annual Review of Psychology, 44,* 53–85.

Ader, R., Cohen, N., & Bovbjerg, D. (1982). Conditioned suppression of humoral immunity in the rat. *Journal of Comparative and Physiological Psychology, 96,* 517–521.

Adler, A. (1969). *The science of living.* Garden City, NY: Anchor Books. (Original work published 1929.)

Adorno, T., Frenkel-Brunswick, E., Levinson, D., & Sanford, R. (1950). *The authoritarian personality.* New York: Harper & Row.

Agnew, H. W., Jr., & Webb, W. B. (1973). The influence of time course variable on REM sleep. *Bulletin of the Psychonomic Society, 2,* 131–133.

Agras, W. S. (1992). Some structural changes that might facilitate the development of behavioral medicine. *Journal of Consulting and Clinical Psychology, 4,* 499–509.

Aiken, L. R. (1985). *Dying, death, and bereavement.* Boston: Allyn and Bacon.

Aiken, L. R. (1988). *Psychological testing and assessment* (6th ed). Boston: Allyn and Bacon.

Aikens, J. E., Wallander, J. L., Bell, D. S. H., & Cole, J. A. (1992). Daily stress variability, learned resourcefulness, regimen adherence, and metabolic control in type I diabetes mellitus: Evaluation of a path model. *Journal of Consulting and Clinical Psychology, 60,* 113–118.

Ainsworth, M. D. S. (1979). Infant-mother attachment. *American Psychologist, 34,* 932–937.

Ajzen, I., & Fishbein, M. (1977). Attitude-behavior relations: A theoretical analysis and review of empirical research. *Psychological Bulletin, 84,* 888–918.

Akshoomoff, N. A., & Courchesne, E. (1992). A new role for the cerebellum in cognitive operations. *Behavioral Neuroscience, 106,* 731–738.

Alan Guttmacher Institute (1991). *Facts in brief.* New York: Author.

Aldag, R. J., & Fuller, S. R. (1993). Beyond fiasco: A reappraisal of the groupthink phenomenon and a new model of group decision processes. *Psychological Bulletin, 113,* 533–552.

Alfaro, J. D. (1981). Report on the relationship between child abuse and neglect and later socially deviant behavior. In R. J. Hunner & Y. E. Walker (Eds.), *Exploring the relationship between child abuse and delinquency* (pp. 175–219). Montclair, NJ: Allanheld, Osmun.

Algera, J. A. (1990). The job characteristics model of work motivation revisited. In U. Kleinbeck, H. Quast, H. Thierry, & H. Hacker (Eds.), *Work motivation.* Hillsdale, NJ: Erlbaum.

Alkon, D. L. (1989, July). Memory storage and neural systems. *Scientific American,* pp. 42–50.

Allen, B. P. (1987). Youth suicide. *Adolescence, 22,* 271–290.

Allen, G. L. (1981). A developmental perspective on the effects of "subdividing" macrospatial experience. *Journal of Experimental Psychology: Human Learning and Memory, 7,* 120–132.

Allen, G. L. (1987). Cognitive influences on the acquisition of route knowledge in children and adults. In P. Ellen & C. Thinus-Blanc (Eds.), *Cognitive processes and spatial orientation in animal and man: Vol. 2. Neurophysiology and developmental aspects.* Boston: Martinus Nijhoff.

Allen, K. E., Turner, K. D., & Everett, P. M. (1970). A behavior modification classroom for Head Start children with problem behaviors. *Exceptional Children, 37,* 119–127.

Allgood-Merten, B., Lewinsohn, P. M., & Hops, H. (1990). Sex differences and adolescent depression. *Journal of Abnormal Psychology, 99,* 55–63.

Allington, R. L. (1981). Sensitivity to orthographic structure in educable mentally retarded children. *Contemporary Educational Psychology, 6,* 135–139.

Allport, G. W. (1937). *Personality: A psychological interpretation.* New York: Holt.

Altman, I. (1975). *The environment and social behavior.* Monterey, CA: Brooks/Cole.

Altman, I., & Vinsel, A. M. (1977). Personal space: An analysis of E. T. Hall's proxemics framework. In I. Altman, A. Rapoport, & J. F. Wohlwill (Eds.), *Human behavior and environment: Vol. 2. Advances in theory and research.* New York: Plenum Press.

Amato, P. R. (1993). Children's adjustment to divorce: Theories, hypotheses, and empirical support. *Journal of Marriage and the Family, 55,* 23–38.

Amato, P. R., & Keith, B. (1991). Parental divorce and the well-being of children: A meta-analysis. *Psychological Bulletin, 110,* 26–46.

Ambady, N., & Rosenthal, R. (1993). Half a minute: Predicting teacher evaluations from thin slices of nonverbal behavior and physical attractiveness. *Journal of Personality and Social Psychology, 64,* 431–441.

American Association on Mental Retardation (1992). *Mental retardation.* Washington, DC: Author.

American Heart Association (1984). *Exercise and your heart.* Dallas, TX: Author.

American Psychiatric Association (1987). *Diagnostic and statistical manual of mental disorders* (3rd ed. rev.) (DSM-III-R). Washington, DC: Author.

American Psychological Association (1990). The Seville statement on violence. *American Psychologist, 45,* 1167–1168.

American Psychological Association (1992a). *Demographic characteristics of APA members by membership status, 1991.* Washington, DC: Office of Demographic, Employment, and Educational Research, APA Education Directorate.

American Psychological Association (1992b, December). Ethical principles of psychologists and code of conduct. *American Psychologist.*

American Psychological Association (1993). Guidelines for providers of psychological services to ethnic, linguistic, and culturally diverse populations. *American Psychologist, 48,* 45–48.

Ames, L. D., Gillespie, C., Haines, J., & Ilg, F. L. (1979). *The Gesell Institute's child from one to six.* New York: Harper & Row.

Ames, M. A., & Houston, D. A. (1990). Legal, social, and biological definitions of pedophilia. *Archives of Sexual Behavior, 19,* 333–342.

Anderson, C. A. (1989). Temperature and aggression: Ubiquitous effects of heat on occurrence of human violence. *Psychological Bulletin, 106,* 74–96.

Anderson, C. A., & Anderson, D. C. (1984). Ambient temperature and violent crime: Tests of the linear and curvilinear hypotheses. *Journal of Personality and Social Psychology, 46,* 91–97.

Anderson, C. A., & DeNeve, K. M. (1992). Temperature, aggression, and the negative affect escape model. *Psychological Bulletin, 111,* 347–351.

Anderson, K. J. (1990). Arousal and the inverted-U hypothesis: A critique of Neiss's "reconceptualizing arousal." *Psychological Bulletin, 107,* 96–100.

Anderson, N. B. (1989). Racial differences in stress-induced cardiovascular reactivity and hypertension: Current status and substantive issues. *Psychological Bulletin, 105,* 89–105.

Anderson, R., Manoogian, S., & Reznick, J. (1976). Undermining and enhancing of intrinsic motivation in pre-school children. *Journal of Personality and Social Psychology, 34,* 915–922.

Andrews, J. D. W. (1989). Integrating visions of reality: Interpersonal diagnosis and the existential vision. *American Psychologist, 44,* 803–817.

Angoff, W. H. (1988). The nature-nurture debate, aptitudes, and group differences. *American Psychologist, 43,* 713–720.

Antonovsky, A. (1987). Health promoting factors at work: The sense of coherence. In R. Kalimo, M. A. El-Batawi, & C. L. Cooper (Eds.), *Psychological factors at work and their relation to health.* Geneva: World Health Organization.

Aoki, C., & Siekevitz, P. (1988, December). Plasticity in brain development. *Scientific American,* pp. 56–64.

Appel, J. B., & Peterson, N. J. (1965). What's wrong with punishment? *Journal of Criminal Law, Criminology, and Police Science, 156,* 450–453.

Argyle, M. (1972). Nonverbal communication in human social interaction. In R. Hinte (Ed.), *Nonverbal communication.* New York: Cambridge University Press.

Argyle, M. (1991). *Cooperation.* New York: Routledge.

Aronson, M. K., Levin, G., & Lipkowitz, R. (1984). A community based family/patient group program for Alzheimer's disease. *Gerontologist, 24,* 339–342.

Asaad, G., & Shapiro, B. (1986). Hallucinations: Theoretical and clinical overview. *American Journal of Psychiatry, 143,* 1088–1097.

Asch, S. E. (1951). Effects of group pressure upon the modification and distortion of judgments. In J. Guetzkow (Ed.), *Groups, leadership, and men.* Pittsburgh: Carnegie Press.

Asch, S. E. (1955, November). Opinions and social pressure. *Scientific American,* pp. 31–35.

Asendorpf, J. B. (1989). Shyness as a final common pathway for two different kinds of inhibition. *Journal of Personality and Social Psychology, 57,* 481–492.

Ashcraft, M. H. (1989). *Human memory and cognition,* Glenview, IL: Scott, Foresman.

Attie, I., & Brooks-Gunn, J. (1989). Development of eating problems in adolescent girls: A longitudinal study. *Developmental Psychology, 25,* 70–79.

Ayllon, T., & Azrin, N. H. (1965). The measurement and reinforcement behavior of psychotics. *Journal of the Experimental Analysis of Behavior, 8,* 357–383.

Ayllon, T., & Haughton, E. (1964). Modification of symptomatic verbal behavior of mental patients. *Behavior Research and Therapy, 2,* 87–97.

Azrin, N. H., & Holtz, W. C. (1966). Punishment. In W. K. Honig (Ed.), *Operant behavior: Areas of research and application.* New York: Appleton-Century-Crofts.

Backman, L., & Lipinska, B. (1993). Monitoring of general knowledge: Evidence for preservation in early Alzheimer's disease. *Neuropsychologia, 31,* 335–345.

Baddeley, A. D., & Hitch, G. (1974). Working memory. In G. Bower (Ed.), *Recent advances in learning and motivating* (Vol. 8). New York: Academic Press.

Baddeley, A. D., & Longman, D. J. A. (1966). The influence of length and frequency of training session on rate of learning to type. In A. D. Baddeley (Ed.), *The psychology of memory.* New York: Basic Books.

Bahrick, H. P., & Hall, L. K. (1991). Lifetime maintenance of high school mathematics content. *Journal of Experimental Psychology: General, 120,* 20–33.

Baillargeon, R. (1991). Reasoning about the height and location of a hidden object in 4.5- and 6.5-month-old infants. *Cognition, 38,* 2–17.

Baird, J. C., Wagner, M., & Fuld, K. (1990). A simple but powerful theory of the moon illusion. *Journal of Experimental Psychology: Human Perception and Performance, 16,* 675–677.

Bak, M., Girvin, J. P., Hambrecht, F. T., Kufta, C. V., Loeb, G. E., & Schmidt, E. M. (1990). Visual sensations produced by intracortical microstimulation of the human occipital cortex. *Medical and Biological Engineering and Computing, 28,* 257–259.

Balay, J., & Shevrin, H. (1988). The subliminal psychodynamic activation method. *American Psychologist, 3,* 161–174.

Baldwin, E. (1993). The case for animal research in psychology. *Journal of Social Issues, 49,* 121–131.

Baltes, P. B., Reese, H. W., & Lipsitt, L. P. (1980). Life-span developmental psychology. *Annual Review of Psychology, 31,* 65–110.

Banaji, M. R. & Crowder, R. G. (1989). The bankruptcy of everyday memory. *American Psychologist, 44,* 1185–1193.

Band, E. B., & Weisz, J. R. (1988). How to feel better when it feels bad: Children's perspectives on coping with everyday stress. *Developmental Psychology, 24,* 247–253.

Bandura, A. (1969). *Principles of behavior modification.* New York: Holt, Rinehart & Winston.

Bandura, A. (1977a). Self-efficacy: Toward a unifying theory of behavioral change. *Psychological Review, 84,* 191–215.

Bandura, A. (1977b). *Social learning theory.* Englewood Cliffs, NJ: Prentice-Hall.

Bandura, A. (1982). Self-efficacy: Mechanism in human agency. *American Psychologist, 37,* 122–147.

Bandura, A. (1986). *Social foundations of thought and action: A social cognitive theory.* Englewood Cliffs, NJ: Prentice-Hall.

Bandura, A. (1988). Self-regulation of motivation and action through goal systems. In V. Hamilton, G. H. Bower, & N. H. Frijda (Eds.), *Cognitive perspectives on emotion and motivation* (pp. 37–61). Dordrecht, Netherlands: Kluwer Academic Publishers.

Bandura, A. (1989). Human agency in social cognitive theory. *American Psychologist, 44,* 1175–1184.

Bandura, A., Blanchard, E. B., & Ritter, B. (1969). Relative efficacy of desensitization and modeling approaches for inducing behavioral, affective, and attitudinal changes. *Journal of Personality and Social Psychology, 13,* 173–199.

Bandura, A., Cioffi, D., Taylor, B., & Brouillard, M. E. (1988). Perceived self-efficacy in coping with cognitive stressors and opioid activation. *Journal of Personality and Social Psychology, 55,* 479–488.

Bandura, A., & Menlove, F. L. (1968). Factors determining vicarious extinction of avoidance through symbolic modeling. *Journal of Personality and Social Psychology, 8,* 99–108.

Bandura, A., Ross, D., & Ross, S. A. (1963). Imitation of film-mediated aggressive models. *Journal of Abnormal and Social Psychology, 66,* 3–11.

Bandura, A., & Walters, R. (1963). *Social learning and personality development.* New York: Holt, Rinehart & Winston.

Bandura, A., & Wood, R. (1989). Effect of perceived controllability and performance standards on self-regulation of complex decision making. *Journal of Personality and Social Psychology, 56,* 805–814.

Barbaree, H. E., & Marshall, W. L. (1991). The role of male sexual arousal in rape: Six models. *Journal of Consulting and Clinical Psychology, 59,* 621–630.

Barber, B. L., & Eccles, J. S. (1992). Long-term influence of divorce and single parenting on adolescent family- and work-related values, behaviors, and aspirations. *Psychological Bulletin, 111,* 108–126.

Barber, T. X., Spanos, N. P., & Chaves, J. F. (1974). *Hypnosis, imagination, and human potentialities.* New York: Pergamon Press.

Bard, P. (1934). Emotion: 1. The neuro-humoral basis of emotional reactions. In C. Murchison (Ed.), *Handbook of general experimental psychology.* Worcester, MA: Clark University Press.

Bardon, J. I. (1983). Psychology applied to education: A specialty in search of an identity. *American Psychologist, 38,* 185–196.

Baron, R. A., & Byrne, D. (1991). *Social psychology* (6th ed.). Boston: Allyn and Bacon.

Barrett, G. V., & Depinet, R. L. (1991). A reconsideration of testing for competence rather than for intelligence. *American Psychologist, 46,* 1012–1024.

Barrios, B. A. (1988). On the changing nature of behavioral assessment. In A. S. Bellack & M. Hersen (Eds.), *Behavioral assessment.* New York: Pergamon Press.

Bartlett, F. C. (1932). *Remembering: A study in experimental and social psychology.* New York: Macmillan.

Bashore, T. R., & Rapp, R. E. (1993). Are there alternatives to traditional polygraph procedures? *Psychological Bulletin, 113,* 3–22.

Bateman, T. S., Sakano, T., & Fujita, M. (1992). Roger, me, and my attitude: Film propaganda and cynicism toward corporate leadership. *Journal of Applied Psychology, 77,* 768–771.

Bateson, G., Jackson, D. D., Haley, J., Weakland, J. (1956). Toward a theory of schizophrenia. *Behavioral Science, 1,* 214–264.

Batson, C. D. (1990). How social an animal? *American Psychologist, 45,* 336–346.

Batson, C. D., Batson, J. G., Slingsby, J. K., Harrell, K. L., Peekna, H. M., & Todd, R. M. (1991). Empathic joy and the empathy-altruism hypothesis. *Journal of Personality and Social Psychology, 61,* 413–426.

Baum, A. (1987). Crowding. In D. Stokols & I. Altman (Eds.), *Handbook of environmental psychology.* New York: Wiley.

Baum, A., Grunberg, N. E., & Singer, J. E. (1992). Biochemical measurements in the study of emotion. *Psychological Science, 3,* 56–62.

Baumeister, R. F. (1990). Suicide as escape from self. *Psychological Review, 97,* 90–113.

Baumeister, R. F., & Tice, D. M. (1985). Self-esteem and responses to success and failure: Subsequent performance and intrinsic motivation. *Journal of Personality, 53,* 450–467.

Bayley, N. (1949). Consistency and variability in the growth of intelligence from birth to eighteen years. *Journal of Genetic Psychology, 25,* 165–196.

Beck, A. T. (1963). Thinking and depression: 1. Idiosyncratic content in cognitive distortions. *Archives of General Psychiatry, 9,* 324–333.

Beck, A. T. (1967). *Depression: Clinical, experimental, and the theoretical aspects.* New York: Hober.

Beck, A. T. (1972). *Depression: Causes and treatment.* Philadelphia: University of Pennsylvania Press.

Beck, A. T. (1976). *Cognitive therapy and emotional disorders.* New York: International Universities Press.

Beck, A. T. (1991). Cognitive therapy. *American Psychologist, 46,* 368–375.

Beck, A. T., & Weishaar, M. (1989). Cognitive therapy. In A. Freeman, K. M. Simon, L. E. Beutler, & H. Arkowitz (Eds.), *Comprehensive handbook of cognitive therapy.* New York: Plenum Press.

Beck, J. (1966). Effects of orientation and of shape similarity on perceptual grouping. *Perception and Psychophysics, 1,* 311–312.

Becvar, D. S., & Becvar, R. J. (1988). *Family therapy: A systemic integration.* Boston, MA: Allyn and Bacon.

Bednar, R. L., Burlingame, G. M., & Masters, K. S. (1988). Systems of family treatment: Substance or semantics? *Annual Review of Psychology, 39,* 401–434.

Bee, H. L. (1987). *The journey of adulthood.* New York: Macmillan.

Beech, H. R. (1987). The use of behavioural therapy in somatic stress reactions. In R. Kalimo, M. A. El-Batawi, & C. L. Cooper (Eds.), *Psychological factors at work and their relation to health.* Geneva: World Health Organization.

Begg, I. M., Needham, D. R., & Bookbinder, M. (1993). Do backward messages unconsciously affect listeners? No. *Canadian Journal of Experimental Psychology, 47,* 1–14.

Bekerian, D. A., & Bowers, J. M. (1983). Eyewitness testimony: Were we misled? *Journal of Experimental Psychology: Learning, Memory, and Cognition, 9,* 139–145.

Bekhtereva, N. P., Gilerovich, E. G., Gurchin, F. A., Lukin, V. A., et al. (1990). The first results of the use of embryonal nervous tissue transplantation for the treatment of parkinsonism. *Zhurnal Nevropatologii-i-Psikhiatrii-imeni—S. S. Korsakova, 90,* 10–13.

Belenky, M. F., Clinchy, B. M., Goldberger, N. R., & Tarule, J. M. (1986). *Women's ways of knowing.* New York: Basic Books, Inc.

Bell, B. E., & Loftus, E. F. (1989). Trivial persuasion in the courtroom: The power of (a few) minor details. *Journal of Personality and Social Psychology, 56,* 669–679.

Bell, P. A. (1992). In defense of the negative affect escape model of heat and aggression. *Psychological Bulletin, 111,* 342–346.

Belmont, L., & Marolla, F. A. (1973). Birth order, family size, and intelligence. *Science, 182,* 1096–1101.

Belsky, J. (1990). Parental and nonparental child care and children's socioemotional development: A decade in review. *Journal of Marriage and the Family, 52,* 885–903.

Belsky, J., & Rovine, M. J. (1988). Nonmaternal care in the first year of life and the security of infant-parent attachment. *Child Development, 59,* 157–167.

Belsky, J., & Steinberg, L. D. (1978). The effects of day care: A critical review. *Child Development, 49,* 929–949.

Bem, D. J. (1972). Self-perception theory. In L. Berkowitz (Ed.), *Advances in experimental social psychology.* New York: Academic Press.

Bem, S. L. (1975). Sex-role adaptability: One consequence of psychological androgyny. *Journal of Personality and Social Psychology, 31,* 634–643.

Bem, S. L. (1985). Androgyny and gender schema theory: A conceptual and empirical integration. In T. B. Sonderegger (Ed.), *Nebraska symposium on motivation.* Lincoln: University of Nebraska Press.

Bem, S. L. (1993). *The lenses of gender.* New Haven: Yale University Press.

Benassi, M. A. (1982). Effects of order of presentation, primacy, and attractiveness on attributions of ability. *Journal of Personality and Social Psychology, 43,* 48–58.

Benbow, C. P., & Stanley, J. C. (1983). Sex differences in mathematical reasoning ability: More facts. *Science, 222,* 1029–1031.

Benca, R. M., Obermeyer, W. H., Thisted, R. A., & Gillin, C. (1992). Sleep and psychiatric disorders. *Archives of General Psychiatry, 49,* 651–655.

Benjamin, L. T., Jr., Durkin, M., Link, M., Vestal, M., & Acord, J. (1992). Wundt's American doctoral students. *American Psychologist, 47,* 123–131.

Benson, K., & Feinberg, I. (1977). The beneficial effect of sleep in a Jenkins and Dallenbach paradigm. *Psychophysiology, 14,* 375–384.

Bentall, R. P. (1990). The illusion of reality: A review and integration of psychological research on hallucinations. *Psychological Bulletin, 107,* 82–95.

Berenbaum, S. A., & Hines, M. (1992). Early androgens are related to childhood sex-typed toy preferences. *Psychological Science, 3,* 203–206.

Berkowitz, L. (1964). *The effects of observing violence.* San Francisco: Freeman.

Berkowitz, L. (1989). Frustration-aggression hypothesis: Examination and reformulation. *Psychological Bulletin, 106,* 59–73.

Berkowitz, L. (1990). On the formation and regulation of anger and aggression. *American Psychologist, 45,* 494–503.

Berlin, B., & Kay, P. (1969). *Basic color terms: Their universality and evolution.* Berkeley: University of California Press.

Bernal, G., & Berger, S. M. (1976). Vicarious eyelid conditioning. *Journal of Personality and Social Psychology, 34,* 62–68.

Berndt, T. J. (1992). Friendship and friends' influence in adolescence. *Psychological Science, 1,* 156–159.

Berndt, T. J., Cheung, P. C., Lau, S., Hau, K. T., & Lew, W. J. F. (1993). Perceptions of parenting in mainland China, Taiwan, and Hong Kong: Sex differences and societal differences. *Developmental Psychology, 29,* 156–164.

Bernstein, D., & Ebbesen, E. (1978). Reinforcement and substitution in humans: A multiple-response analysis. *Journal of the Experimental Analysis of Behavior, 30,* 243–253.

Bernstein, I. L. (1988, September 9). *What does learning have to do with weight loss and cancer?* Paper presented at a science and public policy seminar sponsored by the Federation of Behavioral, Psychological, and Cognitive Sciences, Washington, DC.

Berscheid, E., Snyder, M., & Omoto, A. M. (1989). The relationship closeness inventory: Assessing the closeness of interpersonal relationships. *Journal of Personality and Social Psychology, 57,* 792–807.

Best, C. T., & Queen, H. F. (1989). Baby, it's in your smile: Right hemiface bias in infant emotional expressions. *Developmental Psychology, 25,* 264–276.

Betancourt, H. & Lopez, S. R. (1993). The study of culture, ethnicity, and race in American psychology. *American Psychologist, 48,* 629–637.

Beutler, L. E. (1991). Have all won and must all have prizes? Revisiting Luborsky et al.'s verdict. *Journal of Consulting and Clinical Psychology, 59,* 226–232.

Bexton, W. H., Heron, W., & Scott, T. H. (1954). Effects of decreased variation in the sensory environment. *Canadian Journal of Psychology, 8,* 70–76.

Bickman, L., Teger, A., Gabriele, T., McLaughlin, C., Berger, M., & Sunaday, E. (1973). Dormitory density and helping behavior. *Environment and Behavior, 5,* 465–466.

Bierman, D., & Winter, O. (1989). Learning during sleep: An indirect test of the erasure-theory of dreaming. *Perceptual and Motor Skills, 69,* 139–144.

Binet, A., & Simon, T. (1905). Méthodes nouvelles pour le diagnostic de niveau intellectuel des anororaux. *L'Année Psychologique, 11,* 191–244.

Binet, A., & Simon, T. (1916). *The development of intelligence in children.* (E. S. Kite, Trans.). Baltimore: Williams & Wilkins. (Original work published 1905)

Binion, V. J. (1990). Psychological androgyny: A black female perspective. *Sex Roles, 22,* 487–507.

Bishop, J. E. (1986, February 14). Technology: Researchers track pain's path, develop new kind of reliever. *Wall Street Journal,* p. 23.

Blakemore, C., & Cooper, G. F. (1970). Development of the brain depends on the visual environment. *Nature, 228,* 477–478.

Blanchard, E. B., Appelbaum, K. A., Radnitz, C. L., Michultka, D., Morrill, B., Kirsch, C., Hillhouse, J., Evans, D. D., Guarnieri, P., Attanasio, V., Andrasik, F., Jaccard, J., & Dentinger, M. P. (1990). Placebo-controlled evaluation of abbreviated progressive muscle relaxation and of relaxation combined with cognitive therapy in the treatment of tension headache. *Journal of Consulting and Clinical Psychology, 58,* 210–215.

Blasi, A. (1980). Bridging moral cognition and moral action: A critical review of the literature. *Psychological Bulletin, 88,* 1–45.

Blass, T. (1991). Understanding behavior in the Milgram obedience experiment: The role of personality, situations, and their interactions. *Journal of Personality and Social Psychology, 60,* 398–413.

Bless, H., Mackie, D. M., & Schwarz, N. (1992). Mood effects on attitude judgments: Independent effects of mood before and after message elaboration. *Journal of Personality and Social Psychology, 63,* 585–595.

Bloom, F. E. (1981, October). Neuropeptides. *Scientific American,* pp. 148–168.

Bloom, F. E., Lazerson, A., & Hofstadter, L. (1985). *Brain, mind, and behavior.* New York: Freeman.

Bohannon, J. N., III (1988). Flashbulb memories for the space shuttle disaster: A tale of two theories. *Cognition, 29,* 179–196.

Bond, C. F., Jr., Omar, A., Pitre, U., Lashley, B. R., Skaggs, L. M., & Kirk, C. T. (1992). Fishy-looking liars: Deception judgment from expectancy violation. *Journal of Personality and Social Psychology, 63,* 969–977.

Bond, C. F., Jr., & Titus, L. J. (1983). Social facilitation: A meta-analysis of 241 studies. *Psychological Bulletin, 94,* 265–292.

Bondareff, W., Mountjoy, C. Q., Wischik, C. M., Hauser, D. L., LaBree, L. D., & Roth, M. (1993). Evidence of subtypes of Alzheimer's disease and implications for etiology. *Archives in General Psychiatry, 50,* 350–354.

Boninger, D. S., Brock, T. C., Cook, T. D., Gruder, C. L., & Romer, D. (1990). Discovery of reliable attitude change persistence resulting from a transmitter tuning set. *Psychological Science, 1,* 268–271.

Bonnet, M. H. (1980). Sleep, performance, and mood after the energy-expenditure equivalent of 40 hours of sleep deprivation. *Psychophysiology, 17,* 56–63.

Borg, E., & Counter, S. A. (1989, August). The middle-ear muscles. *Scientific American,* pp. 74–80.

Bornstein, M. H. (1989). Sensitive periods in development: Structural characteristics and causal interpretations. *Psychological Bulletin, 105,* 179–197.

Bornstein, M. H., Tal, J., Rahn, C., Galperin, C. Z., Pecheux, M. G., Lamour, M., Toda, S., Azuma, H., Ogino, M., & Tamis-Lemonda, C. S. (1992). Functional analysis of the contents of maternal speech to infants of 5 and 13 months in four cultures: Argentina, France, Japan, and the United States. *Developmental Psychology, 28,* 593–603.

Bornstein, R. F. (1989). Exposure and affect: Overview and meta-analysis of research, 1968–1987. *Psychological Bulletin, 106,* 265–289.

Bornstein, R. F. (1992). The dependent personality: Developmental, social, and clinical perspectives. *Psychological Bulletin, 112,* 3–23.

Borrie, R. A. (1991). The use of restricted environmental stimulation therapy in treating addictive behaviors. *International Journal of the Addictions, 25,* 995–1015.

Botwinick, J. (1984). *Aging and behavior: A comprehensive integration of research findings* (3rd ed.). New York: Springer-Verlag.

Bouchard, T. J., Jr., Lykken, D. T., McGue, M., Segal, N. L., & Tellegen, A. (1990). Sources of human psychological differences: The Minnesota study of twins reared apart. *Science, 250,* 223–228.

Bouchard, T. J., Jr., & McGue, M. (1981). Familial studies of intelligence: A review. *Science, 212,* 1055–1058.

Bourque, L. B. (1989). *Defining rape.* Durham, NC: Duke University Press.

Bovbjerg, D. H., Redd, W. H., Jacobsen, P. B., Manne, S. L., Taylor, K. L., Surbone, A., Crown, J. P., Norton, L., Gilewski, T. A., Hudis, C. F., Reichman, B. S., Kaufman, R. J., Currie, V. E., & Hakes, T. B. (1992). An experimental analysis of classically conditioned nausea during cancer chemotheraphy. *Psychosomatic Medicine, 54,* 623–637.

Bower, G. H. (1981). Mood and memory. *American Psychologist, 36,* 126–148.

Bower, T. G. R. (1966, December). The visual world of infants. *Scientific American,* pp. 80–92.

Bowers, K. S. (1979). Time distortion and hypnotic ability: Underestimating the duration of hypnosis. *Journal of Abnormal Psychology, 88,* 435–439.

Bowers, M. B., Jr. (1982). Biochemical processes in schizophrenia: An update. *Schizophrenia Bulletin, 6,* 393–403.

Bowlby, J. (1977). The making and breaking of affectional bonds: Etiology and psychopathology in the light of attachment theory. *British Journal of Psychiatry, 130,* 201–210.

Boyd, B., & Wandersman, A. (1991). Predicting undergraduate condom use with the Fishbein and Ajzen and the Triandis attitude-behavior models: Implications for public health interventions. *Journal of Applied Social Psychology, 21,* 1810–1830.

Boynton, R. M. (1988). Color vision. *Annual Review of Psychology, 39,* 67–101.

Boysen, S. T., & Berntson, G. G. (1989). Numerical competence in a chimpanzee (Pan troglodytes). *Journal of Comparative Psychology, 103,* 23–31.

Boysen, S. T., & Berntson, G. G. (1990). The development of numerical skills in chimpanzee (Pan troglodytes). In S. T. Parker and K. R. Gibson (Eds.), *"Language" and intelligence in monkeys and apes.* New York: Cambridge University Press.

Bradley, B. P. (1990). Behavioural addictions: Common features and treatment implications. *British Journal of Addiction, 85,* 1417–1419.

Branden, N. (1980). *The psychology of romantic love.* Los Angeles: Tarcher.

Brazelton, T. B., & Cramer, B. G. (1990). *The earliest relationship.* Reading, MA: Addison-Wesley.

Brehm, J. W. (1966). *A theory of psychological reactance.* New York: Academic Press.

Brehm, J. W., & Self, E. A. (1989). The intensity of motivation. *Annual Review of Psychology, 40,* 109–131.

Breier, A., Charney, D., & Heninger, G. R. (1984). Major depression in patients with agoraphobia and panic disorder. *Archives of General Psychiatry, 41,* 1129–1135.

Bretschneider, J. G., & McCoy, N. L. (1988). Sexual interest and behavior in healthy 80- to 102-year-olds. *Archives of Sexual Behavior, 17,* 109–129.

Bridges, K. M. B. (1932). Emotional development in early infancy. *Child Development, 3,* 324–341.

Brody, E. M., Lawton, M. P., and Liebowitz, B. (1984). Senile dementia: Public policy and adequate institutional care. *American Journal of Public Health, 74,* 1381–1383.

Brom, D., Kleber, R. J., & Defares, P. B. (1989). Brief psychotherapy for posttraumatic stress disorders. *Journal of Consulting and Clinical Psychology, 57,* 607–612.

Bronfenbrenner, U. (1989, September 7). *Who cares for children?* Invited address, UNESCO, Paris.

Brooks-Gunn, J., & Furstenberg, F. F., Jr. (1989). Adolescent sexual behavior. *American Psychologist, 44,* 249–257.

Broughton, R. J. (1991). Field studies of sleep/wake patterns and performance: A laboratory experience. *Canadian Journal of Psychology, 45,* 240–253.

Brown, A. S. (1989). *How to increase your memory power.* Glenview, IL: Scott, Foresman.

Brown, D. R., Eaton, W. W., & Sussman, L. (1990). Race differences in prevalence of phobic disorders. *Journal of Nervous and Mental Disease 178*(7), 434–441.

Brown, L. M., & Gilligan, C. (1992). *Meeting at the crossroads.* Cambridge, MA: Havard University Press.

Brown, R. (1970). The first sentences of child and chimpanzee. In R. Brown (Ed.), *Psycholinguistics: Selected papers.* New York: Free Press.

Brown, R., & Berko, J. (1960). Word association and the acquisition of grammar. *Child Development, 31,* 1–14.

Brown, R., & Kulik, J. (1977). Flashbulb memories. *Cognition, 5,* 73–99.

Brownell, K. D., & Wadden, T. A. (1992). Etiology and treatment of obesity: Understanding a serious, prevalent, and refractory disorder. *Journal of Consulting and Clinical Psychology, 60,* 505–517.

Bruner, J. (1990). *Acts of meaning.* Cambridge, MA: Harvard University Press.

Bryant, R. A., & McConkey, K. M. (1989). Hypnotic blindness: A behavioral and experiential analysis. *Journal of Abnormal Psychology, 98,* 71–77.

Buchanan, C. M., Eccles, J. S., & Becker, J. B. (1992). Are adolescents the victims of raging hormones? Evidence for activational effects of hormones on moods and behavior at adolescence. *Psychological Bulletin, 111,* 62–107.

Buchsbaum, M. S. (1990). The frontal lobes, basal ganglia, and temporal lobes as sites for schizophrenia. *Schizophrenia Bulletin, 16,* 379–382.

Buchwald, A. M., & Rudick-Davis, D. (1993). The symptoms of major depression. *Journal of Abnormal Psychology, 102,* 197–205.

Buck, R., Losow, J. I., Murphy, M. M., & Costanzo, P. (1992). Social facilitation and inhibition of emotional expression and communication. *Journal of Personality and Social Psychology, 6,* 962–968.

Bukowski, W. M., Gauze, C., Hoza, B., & Newcomb, A. F. (1993). Differences and consistency between same-sex and other-sex peer relationships during early adolescence. *Developmental Psychology, 29,* 255–263.

Burchinal, M., Lee, M., & Ramey, C. (1989). Type of day-care and preschool intellectual development in disadvantaged children. *Child Development, 60,* 128–137.

Bureau of the Census (1987, May). *Statistical Brief* (Survey of Income and Program Participation, SB-2-87). Washington, DC: U.S. Government Printing Office.

Bureau of the Census (1989). *Single parents and their children* (Statistical Brief, SB-3-89). Washington, DC: U.S. Government Printing Office.

Bureau of the Census (1990, June). *Time off for babies: Maternity leave arrangements.* Washington, DC: U.S. Government Printing Office.

Bureau of the Census (1992). *Statistical abstract of the United States* (112th ed.). Washington, DC: U.S. Government Printing Office.

Burg, B., & Belmont, I. (1990). Mental abilities of children from different cultural backgrounds in Israel. *Journal of Cross-Cultural Psychology, 21,* 90–108.

Burger, J. M., & Hemans, L. T. (1988). Desire for control and the use of attribution processes. *Journal of Personality, 56,* 531–546.

Burman, B., & Margolin, G. (1992). Analysis of the association between marital relationships and health problems: An interactional perspective. *Psychological Bulletin, 112,* 39–63.

Burman, B., Mednick, S. A., Machon, R. A., Parnas, J., & Schulsinger, F. (1987). Children at high risk for schizophrenia: Parent and offspring perceptions of family relationships. *Journal of Abnormal Psychology, 96,* 364–366.

Burn, S. M. (1991). Social psychology and the stimulation of recycling behaviors: The block leader approach. *Journal of Applied Social Psychology, 21,* 611–629.

Burr, D. C., Morrone, M. C., & Spinelli, D. (1989). Evidence for edge and bar detectors in human vision. *Vision Research, 29,* 419–431.

Bus, A. G., & Van Ijzendoorn, M. H. (1988). Mother-child interactions, attachment, and emergent literacy: A cross-sectional study. *Child Development, 59,* 1262–1272.

Bushman, B. J., & Geen, R. G. (1990). Role of cognitive-emotional mediators and individual differences in the effects of media violence on aggression. *Journal of Personality and Social Psychology, 58,* 156–163.

Buss, A. H. (1989). Personality as traits. *American Psychologist, 44,* 1378–1388.

Buss, A. H., et al. (1990). International preferences in selecting mates. *Journal of Cross-Cultural Psychology, 21,* 5–47.

Buss, D. M. (1988). Love acts: The evolutionary biology of love. In R. J. Sternberg & M. L. Barnes (Eds.), *The psychology of love.* New Haven, CT: Yale University Press.

Butcher, J. N., Graham, J. R., Dahlstrom, W. G., & Bowman, E. (1990). The MMPI-2 with college students. *Journal of Personality Assessment, 54,* 1–15.

Butler, G., Fennell, M., Robson, P., & Gelder, M. (1991). Comparison of behavior therapy and cognitive behavior therapy in the treatment of generalized anxiety disorder. *Journal of Consulting and Clinical Psychology, 59,* 167–175.

Butler, R., & Nisan, M. (1986). Effects of no feedback, task-related comments, and grades on intrinsic motivation and performance. *Journal of Educational Psychology, 78,* 210–216.

Butler, S. F., & Strupp, H. H. (1991). Psychodynamic psychotherapy. In M. Hersen, A. E. Kazdin, & A. S. Bellack (Eds.), *The clinical psychology handbook* (2nd ed.). New York: Pergamon Press.

Butterfield-Picard, H., & Magno, J. B. (1982). Hospice the adjective, not the noun: The future of a national priority. *American Psychologist, 37,* 1254–1259.

Byrne, D. G., & Reinhart, M. I. (1989). Occupation, Type A behavior, and self-reported angina pectoris. *Journal of Psychosomatic Research, 33,* 609–619.

Cadoret, R. J. (1978). Psychopathology in adopted-away offspring of biologic parents with antisocial behavior. *Archives of General Psychiatry, 35,* 176–184.

Cairns, E. (1990). Impact of television news exposure on children's perceptions of violence in northern Ireland. *Journal of Social Psychology, 130,* 447–452.

Caldera, Y. M., Huston, A. C., & O'Brien, M. (1989). Social interactions and play patterns of parents and toddlers with feminine, masculine, and neutral toys. *Child Development, 109,* 70–76.

Canavan-Gumpert, D. (1977). Generating reward and cost orientations through praise and criticism. *Journal of Personality and Social Psychology, 35,* 501–513.

Cannon, W. B. (1927). The James-Lange theory of emotion: A critical examination and an alternative theory. *American Journal of Psychology, 39,* 106–124.

Cantor, N., & Kihlstrom, J. F. (1982). Cognitive and social processes in personality. In G. T. Wilson & C. M. Franks (Eds.), *Contemporary behavior therapy.* New York: Guilford.

Carducci, B. J., & Stein, N. D. (1988, April). *The personal and situational pervasiveness of shyness in college students: A nine-year comparison.* Paper presented at the meeting of the Southeastern Psychological Association, New Orleans.

Carlson, C. R., Gantz, F. P., & Masters, J. C. (1983). Adults' emotional states and recognition of emotion in young children. *Motivation and Emotion, 7,* 81–102.

Carlson, R. A., Sullivan, M. A., & Schneider, W. (1989). Practice and working memory effects in building procedural skill. *Journal of Experimental Psychology: Learning, Memory, and Cognition, 15,* 517–526.

Carr, M., Borkowski, J. G., & Maxwell, S. E. (1991). Motivational components of underachievement. *Developmental Psychology, 27,* 108–118.

Carver, C. S., & Scheier, M. F. (1990). Origins and functions of positive and negative affect: A control-process view. *Psychological Review, 97,* 19–35.

Casey, R. J., & Berman, J. S. (1985). The outcome of psychotherapy with children. *Psychological Bulletin, 98,* 388–400.

Caspi, A., Elder, G. H., & Bem, D. J. (1988). Moving away from the world: Life-course patterns of shy children. *Developmental Psychology, 24,* 824–831.

Cattell, R. B. (1965). *The scientific analysis of personality.* Baltimore: Penguin.

Cavanagh, P., & Leclerc, Y. G. (1989). Shape from shadows. *Journal of Experimental Psychology: Human Perception and Performance, 15,* 3–27.

Ceci, S. J. (1991). How much does schooling influence general intelligence and its cognitive components? A reassessment of the evidence. *Developmental Psychology, 27,* 703–722.

Ceci, S. J., & Bronfenbrenner, U. (1991). On the demise of everyday memory. *American Psychologist, 46*, 27–31.

Ceci, S. J., & Bruck, M. (1993). Suggestibility of the child witness: A historical review and synthesis. *Psychological Bulletin, 113*, 403–439.

Cermak, L. S. (1975). *Improving your memory*. New York: Norton.

Chaiken, S., & Eagly, A. H. (1983). Communication modality as a determinant of persuasion: The role of communicator salience. *Journal of Personality and Social Psychology, 45*, 241–256.

Chaiken, S., & Stangor, C. (1987). Attitudes and attitude change. *Annual review of psychology, 28*, 575–630.

Chamberlain, K., & Zika, S. (1990). The minor events approach to stress: Support for the use of daily hassles. *British Journal of Psychology, 81*, 469–481.

Chamizo, V. D., & Mackintosh, N. J. (1989). Latent learning and latent inhibition in maze discriminations. *Quarterly Journal of Experimental Psychology, 41B*, 21–31.

Chang, F. I. F., Isaacs, K. R., & Greenough, W. T. (1991). Synapse formation occurs in association with the induction of long-term potentiation in two-year-old rat hippocampus in vitro. *Neurobiology of Aging, 12*, 517–522.

Chassin, L., Pillow, D. R., Curran, P. J., Molina, B. S. G., & Barrera, M., Jr. (1993). Relation of parental alcoholism to early adolescent substance use: A test of three mediating mechanisms. *Journal of Abnormal Psychology, 102*, 3–19.

Cherlin, A. J., Furstenberg, F. F., Jr., Chase-Lansdale, L., Kiernan, K. E., Robins, P. K., Morrison, D. R., & Teitler, J. O. (1991). Longitudinal studies of effects of divorce on children in Great Britain and the United States. *Science, 252*, 1386–1389.

Cherry, E. C. (1953). Some experiments on the recognition of speech with one and with two ears. *Journal of the Acoustical Society of America, 25*, 975–979.

Cherulnik, P. D., Turns, L. C., & Wilderman, S. K. (1990). Physical appearance and leadership: Exploring the role of appearance-based attribution in leader emergence. *Journal of Applied Social Psychology, 20*, 1530–1539.

Chidester, T. R. (1986). Problems in the study of interracial interaction: Pseudo-interracial dyad paradigm. *Journal of Personality and Social Psychology, 50*, 74–79.

Chomsky, N. (1957). *Syntactic structures*. The Hague, Netherlands: Mouton.

Chomsky, N. (1972). *Language and mind* (rev. ed.). New York: Harcourt Brace Jovanovich.

Chomsky, N. (1975). *Reflections on language*. New York: Pantheon.

Chomsky, N. (1986). *Knowledge of language: Its nature, origin, and use*. New York: Praeger.

Chomsky, N. (1990). On the nature, use and acquisition of language. In W. G. Lycan (Ed.), *Mind and cognition* (pp. 627–646). Oxford: Blackwell.

Christensen, H., Hadzi-Pavlovic, D., Andrews, G., & Mattick, R. (1987). Behavior therapy and tricyclic medication in the treatment of obsessive-compulsive disorder: A quantitative review. *Journal of Consulting and Clinical Psychology, 55*, 701–771.

Cialdini, R. B. (1988). *Influence* (2nd ed.). Glenview, IL: Scott, Foresman.

Cialdini, R. B. (1993). *Influence* (3rd ed.). New York: HarperCollins.

Clarizio, H., & Veres, V. (1984). A short-form version of the WISC-R for the learning disabled. *Psychology in the Schools, 21*, 154–157.

Clark, M. S., & Reis, H. T. (1988). Interpersonal processes in close relationships. *Annual Review of Psychology, 39*, 609–672.

Clark, R. D., III (1990). The impact of AIDS on gender differences in willingness to engage in casual sex. *Journal of Applied Social Psychology, 20*, 771–782.

Clarke-Stewart, A. (1973). Interactions between mothers and their young children: Characteristics and consequences. *Monographs of the Society of Research in Child Development, 38*.

Clarke-Stewart, A., Friedman, S., & Koch, J. B. (1985). *Child development: A topical approach*. New York: Wiley.

Clarke-Stewart, A. (1989). Infant day care: Maligned or malignant? *American Psychologist, 44*, 266–273.

Clarkin, J. F., & Hull, J. W. (1991). The brief psychotherapies. In M. Hersen, A. E. Kazdin, & A. S. Bellack (Eds.), *The clinical psychology handbook* (2nd ed.). New York: Pergamon Press.

Cleveland, J. N., Murphy, K. R., & Williams, R. E. (1989). Multiple uses of performance appraisal: Prevalence and correlates. *Journal of Applied Psychology, 74*, 130–135.

Clum, G. A., & Bowers, T. G. (1990). Behavior therapy better than placebo treatments: Fact or artifact? *Psychological Bulletin, 107*, 110–113.

Coates, B., Pusser, H. E., & Goodman, I. (1976). The influence of "Sesame Street" and "Mister Rogers' Neighborhood" on children's social behavior in the preschool. *Child Development, 47*, 138–144.

Cochran, S. D., & Mays, V. M. (1989). Women and AIDS-related concerns. *American Psychologist, 44*, 529–535.

Cochrane, G. J. (1987). Hypnotherapy in weight-loss treatment: Case illustrations. *American Journal of Clinical Hypnosis, 30*, 20–27.

Coffey, C. W., Weiner, R. D., Djang, W. T., Figiel, G. S., Soady, S. A. R., Patterson, L. J., Holt, P. D., Spritzer, C. E., & Wilinson, W. E. (1991). Brain anatomic effects of electroconvulsive therapy. *Archives of General Psychiatry, 48*, 1013–1021.

Cohen, R. J., Montague, P., Nathanson, L. S., & Swerdlik, M. E. (1988). *Psychological testing*. Mountain View, CA: Mayfield.

Cohen, S., Tyrrell, D. A. J., & Smith, A. P. (1991). Psychological stress and susceptibility to the common cold. *New England Journal of Medicine, 325*, 606–612.

Cohen, S., Tyrrell, D. A., & Smith, A. P. (1993). Negative life events, perceived stress, negative affect, and susceptibility to the common cold. *Journal of Personality and Social Psychology, 64*, 131–140.

Cohen, S., & Williamson, G. M. (1991). Stress and infectious disease in humans. *Psychological Bulletin, 109*, 5–24.

Cohn, D. A. (1990). Child-mother attachment of six-year-olds and social competence at school. *Child Development, 61*, 152–162.

Cohn, J. F., & Tronick, E. Z. (1983). Three-month-old infants' reaction to simulated maternal depression. *Child Development, 54*, 185–193.

Cohn, L. (1991). Sex differences in the course of personality development: A meta-analysis. *Psychological Bulletin, 109*, 252–266.

Cole, D. A. (1989). Psychopathology of adolescent suicide: Hopelessness, coping beliefs, and depression. *Journal of Abnormal Psychology, 98*, 248–255.

Comer, J. P. (1988, November). Educating poor minority children. *Scientific American*, pp. 42–51.

Connors, J., & Heaven, P. C. L. (1989). Belief in a just world and attitudes toward AIDS sufferers. *Journal of Social Psychology, 130*, 559–560.

Contrada, R. J. (1989). Type A behavior, personality hardiness, and cardiovascular responses to stress. *Journal of Personality and Social Psychology, 57*, 895–903.

Conway, M. A. (1991). In defense of everyday memory. *American Psychologist, 46*, 19–26.

Coppola, D. M., & O'Connell, R. J. (1988). Behavioral responses of peripubertal female mice towards puberty-accelerating and puberty-delaying chemical signals. *Chemical Senses, 13*, 407–424.

Coren, S., & Aks, D. J. (1990). Moon illusion in pictures: A multimechanism approach. *Journal of Experimental Psychology: Human Perception and Performance, 16*, 365–380.

Coren, S., & Halpern, D. F. (1991). Left-handedness: A marker for decreased survival fitness. *Psychological Bulletin, 109*, 90–106.

Corina, D. P., Vaid, J., & Bellugi, U. (1992). The linguistic basis of left hemisphere specialization. *Science, 255*, 1258–1260.

Coryell, W., Endicott, J., & Keller, M. (1992). Major depression in a nonclinical sample. *Archives of General Psychiatry, 49*, 117–125.

Costanzo, M., Archer, D., Aronson, E., & Pettigrew, T. (1986). Energy conservation behavior: The difficult path from information to action. *American Psychologist, 41*, 521–528.

Covin, T. M., & Sattler, J. M. (1985). A longitudinal study of the Stanford-Binet and WISC-R with special education students. *Psychology in the Schools, 22*, 274–276.

Cowan, N. (1988). Evolving conceptions of memory storage, selective attention, and their mutual constraints within the human information-processing system. *Psychological Bulletin, 104*, 163–191.

Cowen, E. L. (1991). In pursuit of wellness. *American Psychologist, 46*, 404–408.

Craik, F. I. M., & Lockhart, R. S. (1972). Levels of processing: A framework for memory research. *Journal of Verbal Learning and Verbal Behavior, 11*, 671–784.

Craik, F. I. M., Morris, R. G., & Gick, M. L. (1990). Adult age differences in working memory. In G. Vallar and T. Shallice (Eds.), *Neuropsychological impairments of short-term memory* (pp. 247–267). New York: Cambridge University Press.

Craik, F. I. M., & Tulving, E. (1975). Depth of processing and the retention of words in episodic memory. *Journal of Experimental Psychology: General, 104*, 268–294.

Crawford, C. B., & Anderson, J. L. (1989). Sociobiology. *American Psychologist, 44*, 1449–1459.

Crawford, M., & MacLeod, M. (1990). Gender in the college classroom: An assessment of the "chilly climate" for women. *Sex Roles, 23*, 101–122.

Crespi, T. D. (1988). Effectiveness of time-out: A comparison of psychiatric, correctional, and day-treatment programs. *Adolescence, 23*, 805–811.

Crick, F., & Koch, C. (1992, September). The problem of consciousness. *Scientific American*, pp. 153–159.

Crittenden, K. S., Fugita, S. S., Bae, H., Lamug, C. B., & Lin, C. (1992). A cross-cultural study of self-report depressive symptoms among college students. *Journal of Cross-Cultural Psychology, 23*, 163–178.

Crowl, R. K., & MacGinitie, W. H. (1974). The influence of students' speech characteristics on teachers' evaluations of oral answers. *Journal of Educational Psychology, 66*, 304–308.

Cummings, N. A. (1986). The dismantling of our health system: Strategies for the survival of psychological practice. *American Psychologist, 41*, 426–431.

Cunningham, M. R., Barbee, A. P., & Pike, C. L. (1990). What do women want? Facialmetric assessment of multiple motives in the perception of male facial physical attractiveness. *Journal of Personality and Social Psychology, 59*, 61–72.

Curran, D. K. (1987). *Adolescent suicidal behavior.* Washington, DC: Hemisphere.

Cutler, W. B., Preti, G., Krieger, A., Huggins, G. R., Garcia, C. R., & Lawley, H. J. (1986). Human axillary secretions influence women's menstrual cycles: The role of donor extract from men. *Hormones and Behavior, 20,* 463–473.

Czeisler, C. A., Johnson, M. P., Duffy, J. F., Brown, E. N., Ronda, J. M., & Kronauer, R. E. (1990). Exposure to bright light and darkness to treat physiologic maladaptation to night work. *New England Journal of Medicine, 322,* 1253–1259.

Dakof, G. A., & Taylor, S. E. (1990). Victims' perceptions of social support: What is helpful from whom? *Journal of Personality and Social Psychology, 58,* 80–89.

Dalby, J. T., Morgan, D., & Lee, M. L. (1986). Single case study. Schizophrenia and mania in identical twin brothers. *Journal of Nervous and Mental Disease, 174,* 304–308.

Damasio, A. R., & Damasio, H. (1992, September). Brain and language. *Scientific American,* pp. 89–95.

Damon, W. (1980). Structural-development theory and the study of moral development. In M. Windmiller, N. Lambert, & E. Turiel (Eds.), *Moral development and socialization.* Boston: Allyn and Bacon.

Damon, W. (1988). *The moral child.* New York: Free Press.

Daniels, D., & Plomin, R. (1985). Origins of individual differences in infant shyness. *Developmental Psychology, 21,* 118–121.

Danion, J. M., Willard-Schroeder, D., Zimmermann, M. A., Grange, D., Schlienger, J. L., & Singer, L. (1991). Explicit memory and repetition priming in depression. *Archives of General Psychiatry, 48,* 707–711.

Darley, J. M., & Latané, B. (1968). Bystander intervention in emergencies: Diffusion of responsibility. *Journal of Personality and Social Psychology, 8,* 377–383.

Davidson, L. E., Rosenberg, M. L., Mercy, J. A., Franklin, J., & Simmons, J. T. (1989). An epidemiologic study of risk factors in two teenage suicide clusters. *Journal of the American Medical Association, 262,* 2687–2692.

Davidson, R. J. (1992). Emotion and affective style: Hemispheric substrates. *Psychological Science, 3,* 39–43.

Davidson, W. S. (1974). Studies of aversive conditioning for alcoholics: A critical review of theory and research methodology. *Psychological Bulletin, 81,* 571–581.

Davis, D., & Padesky, C. (1989). Enhancing cognitive therapy with women. In A. Freeman, K. M. Simon, L. E. Beutler, & H. Arkowitz (Eds.), *Comprehensive handbook of cognitive therapy.* New York: Plenum Press.

Davis, K. E., & Todd, M. J. (1982). Friendship and love relationships. In K. E. Davis & M. J. Todd (Eds.), *Advances in descriptive psychology* (Vol. 2). Greenwich, CT: JAI Press.

Davis, K. E., & Todd, M. J. (1984). Prototypes, paradigm cases, and relationship assessment: The case of friendship. In S. Duck & D. Perlman (Eds.), *Sage series in personal relationships* (Vol. 1). Beverly Hills, CA: Sage Publications.

Dawson, G., Grofer, L., Panagiotides, H., Hill, D., & Spieker, S. (1991). Frontal lobe activity and affective behavior of infants of mothers with depressive symptoms. Manuscript submitted for publication.

Day, R. H., & McKenzie, B. E. (1977). Constancies in the perceptual world of the infant. In W. Epstein (Ed.), *Stability and constancy in visual perception.* New York: Wiley.

DeAngelis, T. (1988). In praise of rose-colored specs. *APA Monitor, 19*(1), 11.

DeBono, K. G. (1992). Pleasant scents and persuasion: An information processing approach. *Journal of Applied Social Psychology, 22,* 910–919.

DeBuono, B. A., Zinner, S. H., Daamen, M., & McCormack, W. M. (1990). Sexual behavior of college women in 1975, 1986, and 1989. *New England Journal of Medicine, 322,* 821–825.

Deci, E. L. (1971). Effect of externally mediated rewards on intrinsic motivation. *Journal of Personality and Social Psychology, 18,* 105–115.

Deci, E. L. (1972). Effects of contingent and non-contingent rewards and controls on intrinsic motivation. *Organizational Behavior and Human Performance, 8,* 217–229.

Deci, E. L. (1975). *Intrinsic motivation.* New York: Plenum Press.

Deffenbacher, J. L. (1988, August). *Cognitive-behavioral approaches to anger reduction: Some treatment considerations.* Paper presented at the 96th Annual Convention of the American Psychological Association, Atlanta.

Delmonte, M. M. (1983). Mantras and mediation: A literature review. *Perceptual and Motor Skills, 57,* 64–66.

DeLongis, A., Folkman, S., & Lazarus, R. S. (1988). The impact of daily stress on health and mood: Psychological and social resources as mediators. *Journal of Personality and Social Psychology, 54,* 486–495.

Dement, W. C., Greenberg, S., & Klein, R. (1966). The effect of partial REM sleep deprivation and delayed recovery. *Journal of Psychiatric Research, 4,* 141–152.

Dement, W. C., & Kleitman, N. (1957). The relation of eye movements during sleep to dream activity: An objective method for the study of dreaming. *Journal of Experimental Psychology, 53,* 339–346.

Dement, W. C., & Wolpert, E. A. (1958). The relation of eye movements, body motility, and external stimuli to dream content. *Journal of Experimental Psychology, 55,* 543–553.

DeNisi, A. S., Robbins, T., & Cafferty, T. P. (1989). Organization of information used for performance appraisals: Role of diary-keeping. *Journal of Applied Psychology, 74,* 124–129.

DeNisi, A. S., & Williams, K. J. (1988). Cognitive approaches to performance appraisal. *Personnel and Human Resources Management, 6,* 109–155.

Dennett, D. C. (1991). *Consciousness explained.* Boston: Little, Brown.

Dentan, R. K. (1968). *The Semai: A nonviolent people of Malaya.* New York: Holt, Rinehart & Winston.

DePaulo, B. M. (1992). Nonverbal behavior and self-presentation. *Psychological Bulletin, 111,* 203–243.

DePaulo, B. M., Dull, W. R., Greenberg, J. M., & Swaim, G. W. (1989). Are shy people reluctant to ask for help? *Journal of Personality and Social Psychology, 56,* 834–844.

DePaulo, P. J., & DePaulo, B. M. (1989). Can deception by salespersons and customers be detected through nonverbal behavioral cues? *Journal of Applied Social Psychology, 19,* 1552–1577.

Deregowski, J. B. (1980). Perception. In H. C. Triandis & J. J. Berry (Eds.), *Handbook of cross-cultural psychology: Vol. 3. Basic processes.* Boston: Allyn and Bacon.

Dershowitz, A. M. (1986). *Reversal of fortune inside the Von Bulow case.* New York: Random House.

DeValois, R. L., & Jacobs, G. H. (1968). Primate color vision. *Science, 162,* 533–540.

DeValois, R. L., Thorell, L. G., & Albrecht, D. G. (1985). Periodicity of striate-cortex-cell receptive fields. *Journal of the Optical Society of America (A), 2,* 1115–1123.

DeVellis, B. M., & Blalock, S. J. (1992). Illness attributions and hopelessness depression: The role of hopelessness expectancy. *Journal of Abnormal Psychology, 101,* 257–264.

DeVries, B., & Walker, L. J. (1986). Moral reasoning and attitudes toward capital punishment. *Developmental Psychology, 22,* 509–513.

Dewsbury, D. A. (1991). Animal learning (and behavior?). *Bulletin of the Psychonomic Society, 29,* 57–58.

Deyo, R. A., Straube, K. T., & Disterhoft, J. F. (1989). Nimodipine facilitates associative learning in aging rabbits. *Science, 243,* 809–811.

Diener, E. (1983). Subjective well-being. *Psychological Bulletin, 95,* 542–575.

Diener, E., Lusk, R., DeFour, D., & Flax, R. (1980). Deindividuation: Effects of group size, density, number of observers, and group member similarity on self-consciousness and disinhibited behavior. *Journal of Personality and Social Psychology, 39,* 449–459.

Dietvorst, T. F. (1978). Biofeedback assisted relaxation training with patients recovering from myocardial infarction. *Dissertation Abstracts International, 38*(7-B), 3389.

DiGiuseppe, R. (1989). Cognitive therapy with children. In A. Freeman, K. M. Simon, L. E. Beutler, & H. Arkowitz (Eds.), *Comprehensive handbook of cognitive therapy.* New York: Plenum Press.

DiLalla, L. F., & Gottesman, I. I. (1991). Biological and genetic contributors to violence—Widom's untold tale. *Psychological Bulletin, 109,* 125–129.

DiLalla, L. F., Thompson, L. A., Plomin, R., Phillips, K., Fagan, J. F., III, Haith, M. M., Cyphers, L. H., & Fulker, D. W. (1990). Infant predictors of preschool and adult IQ: A study of infant twins and their parents. *Development Psychology, 26,* 759–769.

DiMascio, A., Weissman, M. M., Prusoff, B. A., Neu, C., Zwilling, M., & Klerman, G. L. (1979). Differential symptom reduction by drugs and psychotherapy in acute depression. *Archives of General Psychiatry, 36,* 1450–1456.

DiMatteo, M. R., & DiNicola, D. D. (1982). *Achieving patient compliance: The psychology of the medical practitioner's role.* New York: Pergamon Press.

Dindia, K., & Allen, M. (1992). Sex differences in self-disclosure: A meta-analysis. *Psychological Bulletin, 112,* 106–124.

DiNicola, D. D., & DiMatteo, M. R. (1984). Practitioners, patients, and compliance with medical regimens: A social psychological perspective. In A. Baum, S. E. Taylor, & J. E. Singer (Eds.), *Handbook of psychology and health: Vol. 4. Social psychological aspects of health.* Hillsdale, NJ: Erlbaum.

Dion, K. K., Berscheid, E., & Walster, E. (1972). What is beautiful is good. *Journal of Personality and Social Psychology, 24,* 285–290.

Dion, K. K., Pak, A. W., & Dion, K. L. (1990). Stereotyping physical attractiveness. *Journal of Cross-Cultural Psychology, 21,* 158–179.

Dobson, K. S., & Block, L. (1988). Historical and philosophical bases of the cognitive-behavioral therapies. In K. S. Dobson (Ed.), *Handbook of cognitive-behavioral therapies.* New York: Guilford.

Doerfler, L. A. (1988, August, 14). *Well-being at work: Profits, programs, and prevention.* Symposium abstract presented at the Center for Health and Fitness, Division of Preventative and Behavioral Medicine, University of Massachusetts Medical School.

Dohrenwend, B. P., Levav, I., Shrout, P. E., Schwartz, S., Naveh, G., Link, B. G., Skodol, A. E., & Stueve, A. (1992). Socioeconomic status and psychiatric disorders: The causation-selection issue. *Science, 255,* 946–952.

Dohrenwend, B. P., & Shrout, P. E. (1985). "Hassles" in the conceptualization and measurement of life stress variables. *American Psychologist, 40,* 780–785.

Dollard, J., Doob, L. W., Miller, N. E., Mowrer, O. H., & Sears, R. R. (1939). *Frustration and aggression.* New Haven, CT: Yale University Press.

Domino, G. (1986). Sleep habits in the elderly: A study of three Hispanic cultures. *Journal of Cross-Cultural Psychology, 17*, 109–120.

Domino, G. (1992). Cooperation and competition in Chinese and American children. *Journal of Cross-Cultural Psychology, 23*, 456–467.

Donnerstein, M., Donnerstein, E., Berkowitz, L., & Linz, D. (1987). Research on pornography. In E. Donnerstein, D. Linz, & S. Penrod (Eds.), *The question of pornography: Research findings and policy implications.* New York: Free Press.

Donovan, W. L., & Leavitt, L. A. (1989). Maternal self-efficacy and infant attachment: Integrating physiology, perceptions, and behavior. *Child Development, 60*, 460–472.

Doob, A. N., & McLaughlin, D. S. (1989). Ask and you shall be given: Request size and donations to a good cause. *Journal of Applied Social Psychology, 19*, 1049–1056.

Dowling, J. E., & Boycott, B. B. (1966). *Proceedings of the Royal Society (London)* (Series), *166*, 80–111.

Downey, G., & Coyne, J. C. (1990). Children of depressed parents: An integrative review. *Psychological Bulletin, 108*, 50–76.

Drennen, W. T. (1991). Negative schemas and depression in normal college student volunteers. *Psychological Reports, 68*, 521–522.

Drennen, W. T., & Holden, E. W. (1984). Trait/set interactions in EMG biofeedback. *Psychological Reports, 54*, 843–849.

Dreyer, P. H. (1982). Sexuality during adolescence. In B. B. Wolman (Ed.), *Handbook of developmental psychology.* Englewood Cliffs, NJ: Prentice-Hall.

Dryden, W., & Ellis, A. (1988). Rational-emotive therapy. In K. S. Dobson (Ed.), *Handbook of cognitive-behavioral therapies.* New York: Guilford.

Duckitt, J. (1992). Psychology and prejudice. *American Psychologist, 47*, 1182–1193.

Dunant, Y., & Israel, M. (1985, April). The release of acetylcholine. *Scientific American*, pp. 58–83.

Duncan, J. (1980). The locus of interference in the perception of simultaneous stimuli. *Psychological Review, 87*, 272–300.

Dunn, J. (1992). Siblings and development. *Current Directions in Psychological Science, 1*, 6–9.

Dunn, J., & Plomin, R. (1990). *Separate lives.* New York: Basic Books.

Dura, J. R., Stukenberg, K. W., & Kiecolt-Glaser, J. K. (1990). Chronic stress and depressive disorders in older adults. *Journal of Abnormal Psychology, 99*, 284–290.

Dutton, D. G. (1988). *The domestic assault of women.* Boston: Allyn and Bacon.

Duyme, M. (1988). School success and social class: An adoption study. *Developmental Psychology, 24*, 203–209.

Dweck, C. S. (1986). Motivational processes affecting learning: Special Issue. Psychological science and education. *American Psychologist, 41*, 1040–1048.

Dweck, C. S., & Leggett, E. L. (1988). A socio-cognitive approach to motivation and personality. *Psychological Review, 95*, 256–273.

Eagly, A. H. (1992). Uneven progress: Social psychology and the study of attitudes. *Journal of Personality and Social Psychology, 63*, 693–710.

Eagly, A. H., Ashmore, R. D., Makhijani, M. G., & Longo, L. C. (1991). What is beautiful is good, but...: A meta-analytic review of research on the physical attractiveness stereotype. *Psychological Bulletin, 110*, 109–128.

Eagly, A. H., & Chaiken, S. (1993). *The psychology of attitudes.* Fort Worth, TX: Harcourt Brace Jovanovich.

Eagly, A. H., & Johnson, B. T. (1990). Gender and leadership style: A meta-analysis. *Psychological Bulletin, 108*, 233–256.

Eagly, A. H., & Kite, M. E. (1987). Are stereotypes of nationalities applied to both women and men? *Journal of Personality and Social Psychology, 53*, 451–462.

Eagly, A. H., Makhijani, M. G., & Klonsky, B. G. (1992). Gender and the evaluation of leaders: A meta-analysis. *Psychological Bulletin, 111*, 3–22.

Eagly, A. H., & Steffen, V. J. (1986). Gender and aggressive behavior: A meta-analytic review of the social psychological literature. *Psychological Bulletin, 100*, 309–330.

Eccles, J. S., Medgley, C., Wigfield, A., Buchanan, C. M., Reuman, D., Flanagan, C., & MacIver, D. (1993). Development during adolescence. *American Psychologist, 48*, 90–101.

Eckenrode, J., Powers, J., Doris, J., Munsch, J., & Bolger, N. (1988). Substantiation of child abuse and neglect reports. *Journal of Consulting and Clinical Psychology, 56*, 9–16.

Egeland, B., Jacobvitz, D., & Sroufe, L. A. (1988). Breaking the cycle of abuse. *Child Development, 59*, 1080–1088.

Eich, E., & Metcalfe, J. (1989). Mood dependent memory for internal versus external events. *Journal of Experimental Psychology: Learning, Memory, and Cognition, 15*, 443–455.

Eisdorfer, C. (1983). Conceptual models of aging. *American Psychologist, 2*, 197–202.

Eisdorfer, C., Wilkie, F. (1977). Stress, disease, aging, and behavior. In J. E. Birren & K. W. Schaie (Eds.). *Handbook of the psychology of aging.* New York: Van Nostrand Reinhold.

Ekman, P. (1992). Facial expressions of emotion: New findings, new questions. *Psychological Science, 3*, 34–38.

Ekman, P. (1993). Facial expression and emotion. *American Psychologist, 48*, 384–392.

Ekman, P., Friesen, W. V., & O'Sullivan, M. (1988). Smiles when lying. *Journal of Personality and Social Psychology, 54*, 414–420.

Elkind, D. (1981a). Giant in the nursery—Jean Piaget. In E. M. Hetherington & R. D. Parke (Eds.), *Contemporary readings in child psychology* (2nd ed.). New York: McGraw-Hill.

Elkind, D. (1981b). *The hurried child.* Reading, MA: Addison-Wesley.

Elkind, D. (1987). *Miseducation.* New York: Knopf.

Elliott, E. S., & Dweck, C. S. (1988). Goals: An approach to motivation and achievement. *Journal of Personality and Social Psychology, 54*, 5–12.

Elliott, R. (1987). Litigating intelligence IQ tests, special education, and social science in the courtroom. Dover, MS: Auburn House.

Ellis, A. (1970). *The essence of rational psychotherapy: A comprehensive approach to treatment.* New York: Institute for Rational Living.

Ellis, A. (1988, August). *The philosophical basis of rational-emotive therapy (RET).* Paper presented at the 96th Annual Convention of the American Psychological Association, Atlanta.

Ellis, A. (1990). How can psychological treatment aim to be briefer and better? The rational-emotive approach to brief therapy. In J. K. Zeig & S. G. Gilligan (Eds.), *Brief therapy myths, methods, and metaphors*, New York: Brunner/Mazel.

Ellis, A. (1993). Reflections on rational-emotive therapy. *Journal of Consulting and Clinical Psychology, 61*, 199–201.

Ellis, A., & Harper, R. A. (1961). *A guide to rational living.* North Hollywood, CA: Wilshire Book.

Ellis, L. (1991). A synthesized (biosocial) theory of rape. *Journal of Consulting and Clinical Psychology, 59*, 631–642.

Ellis, R. J., & Oscar-Berman, M. (1989). Alcoholism, aging, and functional cerebral asymmetries. *Psychological Bulletin, 106*, 128–147.

Emde, R. N., Plomin, R., Robinson, J., Corley, R., DeFries, J., Fulker, D. W., Reznick, J. S., Campos, J., Kagan, J., & Zahn-Waxler, C. (1992). Temperament, emotion, and cognition at fourteen months: The MacArthur longitudinal twin study. *Child Development, 63*, 1437–1455.

Emery, R. E. (1989a). Family violence. *American Psychologist, 44*, 321–328.

Emery, R. E. (1989b, September 15). *Family violence: Has science met its match?* Edited transcript of a science and public policy seminar presented by the Federation of Behavioral, Psychological, and Cognitive Sciences in the Rayburn House Office Building, Washington, DC.

Eppinger, M. G., Craig, P. L., Adams, R. L., & Parsons, O. A. (1987). The WAIS-R index for estimating premorbid intelligence: Cross-validation and clinical utility. *Journal of Consulting and Clinical Psychology, 55*, 86–90.

Epstein, R. (1991). Skinner, creativity, and the problem of spontaneous behavior. *Psychological Science, 2*, 362–370.

Epstein, S., & O'Brien, E. J. (1985). The person-situation debate in historical and current perspective. *Psychological Bulletin, 98*, 513–537.

Erdelyi, M. H. (1992). Psychodynamics and the unconscious. *American Psychologist, 47*, 784–787.

Ericsson, K. A., Chase, W. G., & Faloon, S. (1980). Acquisition of a memory skill. *Science, 208*, 1181–1182.

Erikson, E. H. (1963). *Childhood and society* (2nd ed.). New York: Norton.

Erikson, E. H. (1968). *Identity: Youth and crisis.* New York: Norton.

Erlenmeyer-Kimling, L., & Jarvik, L. F. (1963). Genetics and intelligence: A review. *Science, 142*, 1477–1479.

Eron, L. D. (1987). The development of aggressive behavior from the perspective of a developing behaviorism. *American Psychologist, 42*, 435–442.

Eron, L. D., & Huesmann, L. R. (1980). Adolescent aggression and television. *Annals of the New York Academy of Sciences, 347*, 319–331.

Esses, V. M. (1988, August). *Mood moderates the effect of feedback on self-image.* Paper presented at the 96th Annual Convention of the American Psychological Association, Atlanta.

Esses, V. M., & Webster, C. D. (1988). Physical attractiveness, dangerousness, and the Canadian criminal code. *Journal of Applied Social Psychology, 18*, 1017–1031.

Etaugh, C. (1980). Effects of nonmaternal care on children. *American Psychologist, 35*, 309–319.

Evans, D. A., Funkenstein, H. H., Albert, M. S., Scherr, P. A., Cook, N. R., Chown, M. J., Hebert, L. E., Hennekens, C. H., & Taylor, J. O. (1989). Prevalence of Alzheimer's disease in a community population of older persons. *Journal of the American Medical Association, 262*, 2551–2556.

Ewart, C. K. (1991). Social action theory for a public health psychology. *American Psychologist, 46*, 931–946.

Exner, J. E., Jr., Thomas, E. A., & Mason, B. (1985). Children's Rorschachs: Description and prediction. *Journal of Personality Assessment, 49*, 13–14.

Eyer, D. E. (1992). *Mother-infant bonding: A scientific fiction.* New Haven, CT: Yale University Press.

Eysenck, H. J. (1952). The effects of psychotherapy: An evaluation. *Journal of Consulting and Clinical Psychology, 16*, 319–324.

Eysenck, H. J. (1970). *The structure of human personality* (3rd ed.). London: Methuen.

Fabrega, H., Mezzich, J., & Ulrich, R. F. (1988). Black-white differences in psychopathology in an urban psychiatric population. *Comprehensive Psychiatry, 29*, 285–297.

Fagan, J. F., III (1992). Intelligence: A theoretical viewpoint. *Current Directions in Psychological Science, 1,* 82–86.

Fagan, T. K. (1986). School psychology's dilemma. *American Psychologist, 41,* 851–861.

Fagan, T. K. (1992). Compulsory schooling, child study, clinical psychology, and special education. *American Psychologist, 47,* 236–243.

Fairburn, C. G., Jones, R., Peveler, R. C., Carr, S. J., Solomon, R. A., O'Connor, M. E., Burton, J., & Hope, R. A. (1991). Three psychological treatments of bulimia nervosa. *Archives of General Psychiatry, 48,* 463–469.

Fajardo, D. M. (1985). Author race, essay quality, and reverse discrimination. *Journal of Applied Social Psychology, 15,* 255–268.

Fantz, R. L. (1961, May). The origin of form perception. *Scientific American,* pp. 66–72.

Faraone, S. V. (1982). Psychiatry and political repression in the Soviet Union. *American Psychologist, 37,* 1105–1112.

Faraone, S. V., Dion, K. K., Berscheid, E., & Walster, E. (1972). What is beautiful is good. *Journal of Personality and Social Psychology, 24,* 285–290.

Faraone, S. V., Kremen, W. S., & Tsuang, M. T. (1990). Genetic transmission of major affective disorders: Quantitative models and linkage analyses. *Psychological Bulletin, 108,* 109–127.

Faraone, S. V., & Tsuang, M. T. (1985). Quantitative models of the genetic transmission of schizophrenia. *Psychological Bulletin, 98,* 41–66.

Farber, E. A., & Egeland, B. (1982). Developmental consequences of out-of-home care for infants in low-income population. In E. F. Zigler & E. W. Gordon (Eds.), *Day care: Scientific and social policy issues.* Boston: Auburn House.

Farrell, A. D., & Danish, S. J. (1993). Peer drug associations and emotional restraint: Causes or consequences of adolescents' drug use? *Journal of Consulting and Clinical Psychology, 61,* 327–334.

Fazio, R. H. (1989). On the power and functionality of attitudes: The role of attitude accessibility. In A. R. Pratkanis, S. J. Breckler, & A. G. Greenwald (Eds.), *Attitude structure and function.* Hillsdale, NJ: Erlbaum.

Fazio, R. H. (1990). Multiple processes by which attitudes guide behavior: The MODE model as an integrative framework. In M. P. Zanna (Ed.), *Advances in experimental social psychology* (Vol. 23, pp. 75–109). San Diego: Academic Press.

Fazio, R. H., & Zanna, M. P. (1981). Direct experience and attitude-behavior consistency. In L. Berkowitz (Ed.), *Advances in experimental social psychology* (Vol. 14). New York: Academic Press.

Feeney, D. M. (1987). Human rights and animal welfare. *American Psychologist, 42,* 593–599.

Fehr, B. (1988). Prototype analysis of the concepts of love and commitment. *Journal of Personality and Social Psychology, 55,* 557–579.

Fehr, B., & Russell, J. A. (1991). The concept of love viewed from a prototype perspective. *Journal of Personality and Social Psychology, 60,* 425–438.

Feingold, A. (1988a). Cognitive gender differences are disappearing. *American Psychologist, 43,* 95–103.

Feingold, A. (1988b). Matching for attractiveness in romantic partners and same-sex friends: A meta-analysis and theoretical critique. *Psychological Bulletin, 104,* 226–235.

Feingold, A. (1990). Gender differences in effects of physical attractiveness on romantic attraction: A comparison across five research paradigms. *Journal of Personality and Social Psychology, 59,* 981–993.

Feingold, A. (1992a). Gender differences in mate selection preferences: A test of the parental investment model. *Psychological Bulletin, 112,* 125–139.

Feingold, A. (1992b). Good-looking people are not what we think. *Psychological Bulletin, 111,* 304–341.

Feiring, C., Fox, N. A., Jaskir, J., & Lewis, M. (1987). The relation between social support, infant risk status, and mother-infant interaction. *Developmental Psychology, 3,* 400–405.

Fenwick, P., Donaldson, S., Gillies, L., Bushman, J., Fenton, G., Perry, I., Tilsley, C., & Serafinowicz, H. (1977). Metabolic and EEG changes during transcendental meditation. *Biological Psychology, 5,* 101–118.

Fernandez, E., & Turk, D. C. (1992). Sensory and affective components of pain: Separation and synthesis. *Psychological Bulletin, 112,* 205–217.

Festinger, L. (1954). A theory of social comparison processes. *Human Relations, 7,* 117–140.

Festinger, L. (1957). *A theory of cognitive dissonance.* Evanston, IL: Row, Petersen.

Fiedler, F. E. (1964). A contingency model of leadership effectiveness. In L. Berkowitz (Ed.), *Advances in experimental social psychology* (Vol. 1). New York: Academic Press.

Fiedler, F. E. (1974). Personality, motivational systems, and behavior of high and low LPC persons. *Human Relations, 25,* 391–412.

Fine, A. (1986, August). Transplantation in the central nervous system. *Scientific American,* pp. 52–67.

Finke, R. A., Pinker, S., & Farah, M. J. (1989). Reinterpreting visual patterns in mental imagery. *Cognitive Science, 13,* 51–78.

Finn, P. R., & Pihl, R. O. (1987). Men at high risk for alcoholism: The effect of alcohol on cardiovascular response to unavoidable shock. *Journal of Abnormal Psychology, 96,* 230–236.

Fischer, C. T. (1991). Phenomenological-existential psychotherapy. In M. Hersen, A. E. Kazdin, & A. S. Bellack (Eds.), *The clinical psychology handbook* (2nd ed.). New York: Pergamon Press.

Fischer, J., & Gochros, H. L. (1975). *Planned behavior change: Behavior modification in social work.* New York: Free Press.

Fischer, K. W., & Silvern, L. (1985). Stages and individual differences in cognitive development. *Annual Review of Psychology, 36,* 613–648.

Fisher, J. D., & Fisher, W. A. (1992). Changing AIDS-risk behavior. *Psychological Bulletin, 111,* 455–474.

Fiske, S. T. (1989, August 13). *Interdependence and stereotyping: From the laboratory to the Supreme Court (and back).* Paper presented at the American Psychological Association Convention, New Orleans.

Fiske, S. T. (1992). Thinking is for doing: Portraits of social cognition from daguerreotype to laserphoto. *Journal of Personality and Social Psychology, 63,* 877–889.

Fitzgerald, L. F., & Osipow, S. H. (1986). An occupational analysis of counseling psychology. *American Psychologist, 41,* 535–544.

Flaskerud, J. H., & Hu, L. T. (1992). Relationship of ethnicity to psychiatric diagnosis. *Journal of Nervous and Mental Disease, 180,* 296–303.

Flavell, J. H. (1963). *The developmental psychology of Jean Piaget.* New York: Van Nostrand Reinhold.

Flavell, J. H. (1986). The development of children's knowledge about the appearance-reality distinction. *American Psychologist, 41,* 418–425.

Flavell, J. H., Green, F. L., & Flavell, E. R. (1989). Young children's ability to differentiate appearance-reality and level 2 perspectives in the tactile modality. *Child Development, 60,* 201–213.

Flavell, J. H., Green, F. L., & Flavell, E. R. (1993). Children's understanding of the stream of consciousness. *Child Development, 64,* 387–398.

Fleming, I., Baum, A., & Weiss, L. (1987). Social density and perceived control as mediators of crowding stress in high-density residential neighborhoods. *Journal of Personality and Social Psychology, 52,* 899–906.

Fleming, J. D. (1974, July). Field report: The state of the apes. *Psychology Today,* pp. 31–46.

Flor, H., & Turk, D. C. (1989). Psychophysiology of chronic pain: Do chronic pain patients exhibit symptom-specific psychophysiological responses? *Psychological Bulletin, 105,* 215–259.

Flynn, J. R. (1987). Massive gains in 14 nations: What IQ tests really measure. *Psychological Bulletin, 101,* 171–191.

Flynn, J. R. (1988). The decline and rise of scholastic aptitude scores. *American Psychologist, 43*(6), 479–480.

Ford, M. E. (1979). The construct validity of egocentrism. *Psychological Bulletin, 86,* 1169–1188.

Ford Foundation (1989). *The common good, social walfare, and the American future.* New York: Author.

Forehand, R., Thomas, A. M., Wierson, M., Brody, G., & Fauber, R. (1990). Role of maternal functioning and parenting skills in adolescent functioning following parental divorce. *Journal of Abnormal Psychology, 99,* 278–283.

Forsythe, S. M. (1990). Effect of applicant's clothing on interviewer's decision to hire. *Journal of Applied Social Psychology, 20,* 1579–1595.

Foster, R. G. (1993). Photoreceptors and circadian systems. *Current Directions in Psychological Science, 2,* 34–39.

Fox, N. A. (1991). If it's not left, it's right. *American Psychologist, 46,* 863–872.

Fox, N. A., Kagan, J., & Weiskopf, S. (1979). The growth of memory during infancy. *Genetic Psychology Monographs, 99,* 91–130.

Frable, D. E. (1989). Sex typing and gender ideology: Two facets of the individual's gender psychology that go together. *Journal of Personality and Social Psychology, 56,* 95–108.

Framo, J. L. (1991). The integration of marital therapy with sessions with family of origin. In A. S. Gurman & D. P. Kniskern (Eds.), *Handbook of family therapy* (Vol. 1). New York: Brunner/Mazel.

Frankenberg, W. K., & Dobbs, J. B. (1967). The Denver Developmental Screening Tests. *Journal of Pediatrics, 71,* 191–192.

Frasure-Smith, N., & Prince, R. (1989). Long-term follow-up of the ischemic heart disease life stress monitoring program. *Psychosomatic Medicine, 51,* 485–513.

Frederiksen, N. (1986). Toward a broader conception of human intelligence. *American Psychologist, 41,* 445–452.

Freud, S. (1933). *New introductory lectures on psycho-analysis.* New York: Norton.

Freud, S. (1953). The interpretation of dreams. In J. Strachey (Ed. and Trans.), *The standard edition of the complete psychological works of Sigmund Freud* (Vols. 4, 5). London: Hogarth Press. (Original work published 1900)

Freud, S. (1966). *A general introduction to psychoanalysis* (J. Riviere, Trans.). New York: Washington Square Press. (Original work published 1920.)

Frezza, M., di Padova, C., Pozzato, G., Terpin, M., Baraona, E., & Lieber, C. S. (1990). High blood alcohol levels in women. *New England Journal of Medicine, 322,* 95–99.

Friedman, H. S., & Booth-Kewley, S. (1988). Validity of the Type A construct: A reprise. *Psychological Bulletin, 104,* 381–384.

Friedman, M., & Rosenman, R. H. (1974). *Type A behavior and your heart.* Greenwich, CT: Fawcett.

Friedman, W. J. (1993). Memory for the time of past events. *Psychological Bulletin, 113,* 1, 44–66.

Frieze, I. H., Olson, J. E., & Russell, J. (1991). Attractiveness and income for men and women in management. *Journal of Applied Social Psychology, 21,* 1039–1057.

Frijda, N. H. (1988). The laws of emotion. *American Psychologist, 43,* 349–358.

Frijda, N. H., Kuipers, P., & ter Schure, E. (1989). Relations among emotion, appraisal, and emotional action readiness. *Journal of Personality and Social Psychology, 57,* 212–228.

Fromm, E. (1956). *The art of loving.* New York: Harper & Row.

Fruzzetti, A. E., & Jacobson, N. S. (1991). Marital and family therapy. In M. Hersen, A. E. Kazdin, & A. S. Bellack (Eds.), *The clinical psychology handbook* (2nd ed.). New York: Pergamon Press.

Funder, D. C. (1987). Errors and mistakes: Evaluating the accuracy of social judgment. *Psychological Bulletin, 101,* 75–90.

Furby, L., Weinrott, M. R., & Blackshaw, L. (1989). Sex offender recidivism: A review. *Psychological Bulletin, 105,* 3–30.

Furstenberg, F. F., Jr., Brooks-Gunn, J., & Chase-Lansdale, L. (1989). Teenaged pregnancy and childbearing. *American Psychologist, 44,* 313–320.

Furumoto, L., & Scarborough, E. (1986). Placing women in the history of psychology: The first American women psychologists. *American Psychologist, 41,* 35–42.

Galambos, N. L. (1992). Parent-adolescent relations. *Current Directions, 1,* 146–149.

Galin, D. (1974). Implications for psychiatry of left and right cerebral specialization: A neurophysiological context for unconscious processes. *Archives of General Psychiatry, 31,* 572–583.

Gallup, G. G., Jr., & Suarez, S. D. (1985). Alternatives to the use of animals in psychological research. *American Psychologist, 40,* 1104–1111.

Galotti, K. M. (1989). Approaches to studying formal and everyday reasoning. *Psychological Bulletin, 105,* 331–351.

Garcia, J., Gustavson, C. R., Kelly, D. J., & Sweeney, M. (1976). Prey–lithium aversions: 1. Coyotes and wolves. *Behavioral Biology, 16,* 61–72.

Garcia, J., & Koelling, R. A. (1971). The use of ionizing rays as a mammalian olfactory stimulus. In H. Autrum, R. Jung, W. R. Loewenstein, D. M. MacKay, & H. L. Teuber (Eds.), *Handbook of sensory physiology: Vol. 4. Chemical senses* (Pt. 1). New York: Springer-Verlag.

Gardner, H., & Hatch, T. (1989). Multiple intelligences go to school: Educational implications of the theory of multiple intelligences. *Educational Research, 18*(8), 6.

Gardner, R. A., & Gardner, B. T. (1969). Teaching sign language to a chimp. *Science, 165,* 664–672.

Gardner, W., Scherer, D., & Tester, M. (1989). Asserting scientific authority: Cognitive development and adolescent legal rights. *American Psychologist, 6,* 895–902.

Garfield, S. L., & Bergin, A. E. (1986). *Handbook of psychotherapy and behavior change* (3rd ed.). New York: Wiley.

Garfinkel, P. E., Moldofsy, H., & Garner, D. M. (1980). The heterogeneity of anorexia nervosa: Bulimia as a distinct subgroup. *Archives of General Psychiatry, 37,* 1036–1040.

Garland, A. F., & Zigler, E. (1993). Adolescent suicide prevention. *American Psychologist, 48,* 169–182.

Garza, R. T., & Borchert, J. E. (1990). Maintaining social identity in a mixed-gender setting: Minority/majority status and cooperative/competitive feedback. *Sex Roles, 22,* 679–691.

Gazzaniga, M. S. (1983). Right hemisphere language following brain bisection: A 20-year perspective. *American Psychologist, 38,* 525–537.

Gazzaniga, M. S. (1989). Organization of the human brain. *Science, 245,* 947–952.

Gebhardt, D. L., & Crump, C. E. (1990). Employee fitness and wellness programs in the workplace. *American Psychologist, 45,* 262–272.

Geen, R. G. (1991). Social motivation. *Annual Review of Psychology, 42,* 377–399.

Geldard, F. (1972). *The human senses.* New York: Wiley.

Geller, E. S. (1975). Increasing desired waste disposals with instructions. *Man-Environment Systems, 5,* 125–128.

Geller, E. S. (1989). Applied behavior analysis and social marketing: An integration for environmental preservation. *Journal of Social Issues, 45,* 17–36.

Geller, E. S. (1992). It takes more than information to save energy. *American Psychologist, 47*(6) 814–816.

Geller, E. S., Patterson, L., & Talbot, E. (1982). A behavioral analysis of incentive prompts for motivating safety belt use. *Journal of Applied Behavior Analysis, 15,* 403–415.

Geller, E. S., Winett, R. A., & Evertt, P. B. (1982). *Preserving the environment: New strategies for behavior change.* New York: Pergamon Press.

Geller, E. S., Witmer, J. F., & Tuso, M. E. (1977). Environmental intervention for litter control. *Journal of Applied Psychology, 62,* 344–351.

George, J. M., & Brief, A. P. (1992). Feeling good—doing good: A conceptual analysis of the mood at work-organizational spontaneity relationship. *Psychological Bulletin, 112,* 310–329.

Gerbner, G., & Gross, L. (1976, September). The scary world of TV's heavy viewer. *Psychology Today,* pp. 41–45.

German, D. (1983). Analysis of word-finding disorders on the Kaufman Assessment Battery for Children (K-ABC). *Journal of Psychoeducational Assessment, 1,* 121–134.

Gerrard, C. K., Reznikoff, N., & Riklan, N. (1982). Level of aspiration, life satisfaction, and locus of control in older adults. *Experimental Aging Research, 8,* 119–121.

Gerrard, M. (1987). Sex, sex guilt, and contraceptive use revisited: The 1980s. *Journal of Personality and Social Psychology, 52,* 975–980.

Geschwind, N. (1972, April). Language and the brain. *Scientific American,* pp. 76–83.

Gevins, A. S. (1989). Signs of model making by the human brain. In E. Basar & T. H. Bullock (Eds.), *Brain dynamics* (Vol. 2). Berlin and Heidelberg: Springer-Verlag.

Gevins, A. S., & Illes, J. (1990). Neurocognitive networks of the human brain. In R. A. Zappulla (Ed.), *Windows on the brain: Neuropsychology's technological frontiers.* San Francisco: EEG Systems Laboratory.

Gibbons, J. L., Stiles, D. A., Schnellmann, J. de-la-Garza, & Hidalgo, I. M. (1988, August). *Guatemalan adolescents view the ideal person as hard-working.* Paper presented at the 96th Annual Convention of the American Psychological Association, Atlanta.

Gibson, E. J. (1988). Exploratory behavior in the development of perceiving, acting, and the acquiring of knowledge. *Annual Review of Psychology, 39,* 1–41.

Gibson, J. A. P., & Range, L. M. (1991). Are written reports of suicide and seeking help contagious? High schoolers' perceptions. *Journal of Applied Social Psychology, 21,* 1517–1523.

Gift, T. E., Strauss, J. S., Ritzler, B. A., Kokes, R. F., & Harder, D. W. (1980). How diagnostic concepts of schizophrenia differ. *Journal of Nervous and Mental Disease, 168,* 3–8.

Gilbert, R. K. (1988). The dynamics of inaction. *American Psychologist, 43,* 755–764.

Gilligan, C. (1982). *In a different voice: Psychological theory and women's development.* Cambridge, MA: Harvard University Press.

Glantz, M. D. (1989). Cognitive therapy with the elderly. In A. Freeman, K. M. Simon, L. E. Beutler, & H. Arkowitz (Eds.), *Comprehensive handbook of cognitive therapy.* New York: Plenum Press.

Glaser, R., & Kiecolt-Glaser, J. (1988). Stress-associated immune suppression and acquired immune deficiency syndrome (AIDS). In T. P. Bridge, A. F. Mirsky, & F. K. Goodwin (Eds.), *Psychological, neuropsychiatric, and substance abuse aspects of AIDS.* New York: Raven Press.

Glasgow, R. E., & Terborg, J. R. (1988). Occupational health promotion programs to reduce cardiovascular risk. *Journal of Consulting and Clinical Psychology, 56,* 365–373.

Gloor, P., Olivier, A., Quesney, L. F., Andermann, F., & Horowitz, S. (1982). The role of the limbic system in experiential phenomena of temporal lobe epilepsy. *Annals of Neurology, 12,* 129–144.

Goff, K. (1992). Enhancing creativity in older adults. *Journal of Creative Behavior, 26,* 40–49.

Goldberg, L. R. (1990). An alternative "description of personality": The Big Five factor structure. *Journal of Personality and Social Psychology, 59,* 1216–1229.

Goldberg, L. R. (1993). The structure of phenotypic personality traits. *American Psychologist, 48,* 26–34.

Goldenberg, M. M. (1990). *Pharmacology for the psychotherapist.* Muncie, IN: Accelerated Development, Inc.

Goldfried, M. R., & Davison, G. C. (1976). *Clinical behavior therapy.* New York: Holt, Rinehart & Winston.

Golding, J. M., Potts, M. K., & Aneshensel, C. S. (1991). Stress exposure among Mexican Americans and non-hispanic whites. *Journal of Community Psychology, 19,* 37–59.

Goldman, M. S., Brown, S. A., Christiansen, B. A., & Smith, G. T. (1991). Alcoholism and memory: Broadening the scope of alcohol-expectancy research. *Psychological Bulletin, 110,* 137–146.

Goldstein, R. B., Black, D. W., Nasrallah, A. M., & Winokur, G. (1991). The prediction of suicide. *Archives of General Psychiatry, 48,* 418–423.

Goleman, D. (1985). *Vital lies, simple truths.* New York: Simon & Schuster.

Gonzales, L. R., Hays, R. B., Bond, M. A., & Kelly, J. G. (1983). Community mental health. In M. Hersen, A. E. Kazdin, & A. S. Bellack (Eds.), *The clinical psychology handbook.* New York: Pergamon Press.

Gonzales, M. H., Aronson, E., & Costanzo, M. (1988). Using social cognition and persuasion to promote energy conservation: A quasi-experiment. *Journal of Applied Social Psychology, 18,* 1049–1066.

Gonzales, R. R., & Roll, S. (1985). Relationship between acculturation, cognitive style, and intelligence. *Journal of Cross-Cultural Psychology, 16,* 190–205.

Goodwin, R., & Tang, D. (1991). Preferences for friends and close relationship partners: A cross-cultural comparison. *Journal of Social Psychology, 131,* 579–581.

Gopnik, A. (1993). How we know our minds: The illusion of first-person knowledge of intentionality. *Behavioral and Brain Sciences, 16,* 1–14.

Gottesman, I. I. (1991). *Schizophrenia genesis.* New York: Freeman.

Gottesman, I. I., & Shields, J. (1982). *Schizophrenia: The epigenetic puzzle.* Cambridge, England: Cambridge University Press.

Gottman, J. M., & Katz, L. F. (1989). Effects of marital discord on young children's peer interaction and health. *Developmental Psychology, 25,* 373–381.

Goulding, M. M. (1990). Getting the important work done fast: Contract plus redecision. In J. K. Zeig & S. G. Gilligan (Eds.), *Brief therapy myths, methods, and metaphors.* New York: Brunner/Mazel.

Greaves, G. B. (1980). Multiple personality: 165 years after Mary Reynolds. *Journal of Nervous and Mental Disease, 168,* 577–596.

Green, R. J., & Stanton, M. E. (1989). Differential ontogeny of working memory and reference memory in the rat. *Behavioral Neuroscience, 103,* 98–105.

Greenberg, R. P., Bornstein, R. F., Greenberg, M. D., Fisher, S. & Seymour, F. (1992). A meta-analysis of antidepressant outcome under "blinder" conditions. *Journal of Consulting and Clinical Psychology, 60,* 664–669.

Greenfield, P. M., & Savage-Rumbaugh, E. S. (1990). Grammatical combination in Pan paniscus: Processes of learning and invention in the evolution and development of language. In S. T. Parker and K. R. Gibson (Eds.), *"Language" and intelligence in monkeys and apes.* New York: Cambridge University Press.

Greeno, J. G. (1989). A perspective on thinking. *American Psychologist, 44,* 134–141.

Greenwald, A. G. (1992). New look 3. *American Psychologist, 47,* 766–779.

Greenwald, A. G., Pratkanis, A. R., Leippe, M. R., & Baumgardner, M. H. (1986). Under what conditions does theory obstruct research progress? *Psychological Review, 93,* 216–229.

Griffeth, R. W., Vecchio, R. P., & Logan, J. W., Jr. (1989). Equity theory and interpersonal attraction. *Journal of Applied Psychology, 74,* 394–401.

Grilo, C. M., & Pogue-Geile, M. F. (1991). The nature of environmental influences on weight and obesity: A behavior–genetic analysis. *Psychological Bulletin, 110,* 520–537.

Grossman, F. K., Pollack, W. S., & Golding, E. (1988). Fathers and children: Predicting the quality and quantity of fathering. *Developmental Psychology, 1,* 91–92.

Gruder, C. L., Cook, T. D., Hennigan, K. M., Flay, B. R., Alessis, C., & Halamaj, J. (1978). Empirical tests of the absolute sleeper effect predicted from the discounting cue hypothesis. *Journal of Personality and Social Psychology, 42,* 412–425.

Guerin, B. (1989). Social inhibition of behavior. *Journal of Social Psychology, 129,* 225–233.

Guerney, L. F. (1991). A survey of self-supports and social supports of self-care children. *Elementary School Guidance and Counseling, 25,* 243–254.

Guilford, J. P. (1967). *The nature of human intelligence.* New York: McGraw-Hill.

Guilford, J. P. (1985). The structure of intellect model. In B. B. Wolman (Ed.), *Handbook of intelligence: Theories, measurements, and applications.* New York: Wiley.

Guion, R. M., & Gibson, W. M. (1988). Personnel selection and placement. *Annual Review of Psychology, 39,* 349–375.

Gulevich, G., Dement, W., & Johnson, L. (1966). Psychiatric and EEG observations on a case of prolonged (264 hours) wakefulness. *Archives of General Psychiatry, 15,* 29–35.

Haaf, R. A., Smith, P. H., & Smitley, S. (1983). Infant response to facelike patterns under fixed-trial and infant-control procedures. *Child Development, 54,* 172–177.

Haaga, D. A. F., & Davison, G. C. (1993). An appraisal of rational-emotive therapy. *Journal of Consulting and Clinical Psychology, 61,* 215–220.

Haaga, D. A. F., Dyck, M. J., & Ernst, D. (1991). Empirical status of cognitive theory of depression. *Psychological Bulletin, 110,* 215–236.

Haaga, D. A. F., & Stewart, B. L. (1992). Self-efficacy for recovery from a lapse after smoking cessation. *Journal of Consulting and Clinical Psychology, 60,* 24–28.

Haan, N., Millsap, R., & Hartka, E. (1986). As time goes by: Change and stability in personality over fifty years. *Psychology and Aging, 1,* 220–232.

Haber, R. N. (1969, April). Eidetic images. *Scientific American,* pp. 36–44.

Haber, R. N. (1979). Twenty years of haunting eidetic imagery: Where's the ghost? *Behavioral and Brain Sciences, 2,* 583–629.

Haith, M. M., & McCarty, M. E. (1990). Stability of visual expectations at 3.0 months of age. *Developmental Psychology, 26,* 68–74.

Hale, R., Nevels, R. M., Lott, C., & Titus, T. (1990). Cultural insensitivity to sexist language toward men. *Journal of Social Psychology, 130,* 697–698.

Halgren, E., Walter, R. D., Cherlow, A. G., & Crandall, P. H. (1978). Mental phenomena evoked by electrial stimulation of the human hippocampal formation and amygdala. *Brain, 101,* 83–117.

Hall, E. T. (1966). *The hidden dimension.* Garden City, NY: Doubleday.

Hall, J. F. (1982). *An invitation to learning and memory.* Boston: Allyn and Bacon.

Hall, S. M., Havassy, B. E., & Wasserman, D. A. (1991). Effects of commitment to abstinence, positive moods, stress, and coping on relapse to cocaine use. *Journal of Consulting and Clinical Psychology, 59,* 526–532.

Hallahan, D. P., & Kauffman, J. M. (1991). *Exceptional children.* Englewood Cliffs, NJ: Prentice-Hall.

Hallman, W. K., & Wandersman, A. H. (1992). Attribution of responsibility and individual and collective coping with environmental threats. *Journal of Social Issues, 48,* 101–118.

Halpern, D. F. (1986). *Sex differences in cognitive abilities.* Hillsdale, NJ: Erlbaum.

Hamilton, S., & Fagot, B. I. (1988). Chronic stress and coping styles: A comparison of male and female undergraduates. *Journal of Personality and Social Psychology, 5,* 819–823.

Hanson, C. L., Cigrang, J. A., Harris, M. A., Carle, D. L., Relyea, G., & Burghen, G. A. (1989). Coping styles in youths with insulin-dependent diabetes mellitus. *Journal of Consulting and Clinical Psychology, 57,* 644–651.

Harkins, S. G., & Szymanski, K. (1988). Social loafing and self-evaluation with an objective standard. *Journal of Experimental Social Psychology, 24,* 354–365.

Harlow, H. F. (1962). The heterosexual affectional system in monkeys. *American Psychologist, 17,* 1–9.

Harlow, H. F., & Zimmerman, R. R. (1958). The development of affectional responses in infant monkeys. *Proceedings of the American Philosophic Society, 102,* 501–509.

Harmon, T. M., Hynan, M. T., & Tyre, T. E. (1990). Improved obstetric outcomes using hypnotic analgesia and skill mastery combined with childbirth education. *Journal of Consulting and Clinical Psychology, 58,* 525–530.

Harper, J. F., & Marshall, E. (1991). Adolescents' problems and their relationship to self-esteem. *Adolescence, 26,* 799–803.

Harris, C. M., Hainline, L., Abramov, I., Lemerise, E., & Camenzuli, C. (1988). The distribution of fixation durations in infants and naive adults. *Vision Research, 28,* 419–432.

Harris, K. M., & Morgan, S. P. (1991). Fathers, sons, and daughters: Differential paternal involvement in parenting. *Journal of Marriage and the Family, 53,* 531–544.

Harris, V. A., & Katkin, E. S. (1975). Primary and secondary emotional behaviour: An analysis of the role of autonomic feedback on affect, arousal, and attribution. *Psychological Bulletin, 82,* 904–916.

Harrison, J. R., & Barabasz, A. F. (1991). Effects of restricted environmental stimulation therapy on the behavior of children with autism. *Child Study Journal, 21,* 153–166.

Hartlage, S., Alloy, L. B. Vazquez, C., & Dykman, B. (1993). Automatic and effortful processing in depression. *Psychological Bulletin, 113,* 247–278.

Hartup, W. W. (1989). Social relationships and their developmental significance. *American Psychologist, 44,* 120–126.

Haskins, R. (1989). Beyond metaphor: The efficacy of early childhood education. *American Psychologist, 44,* 274–282.

Hauser, S. T., & Bowlds, M. K. (1990). Stress, coping, and adaptation. In S. S. Feldman & G. R. Elliott (Eds.), *At the threshold.* Cambridge, MA: Harvard University Press.

Hawkins, J. D., Catalano, R. F., & Miller, J. Y. (1992). Risk and protective factors for alcohol and other drug problems in adolescence and early adulthood: Implications for substance abuse prevention. *Psychological Bulletin, 112,* 64–105.

Hays, R. B., (1989). The day-to-day functioning of close versus casual friendships. *Journal of Social and Personal Relationships, 6,* 21–37.

Heath, A. C., & Martin, N. G. (1990). Psychoticism as a dimension of personality: A multivariate genetic test of Eysenck and Eysenck's psychoticism construct. *Journal of Personality and Social Psychology, 58,* 111–121.

Heatherton, T. F., & Baumeister, R. F. (1991). Binge eating as escape from self-awareness. *Psychological Bulletin, 100,* 86–108.

Heatherton, T. F., Polivy, J., & Herman, C. P. (1991). Restraint, weight loss, and variability of body weight. *Journal of Abnormal Psychology, 100,* 78–83.

Hebb, D. O. (1949). *Organization of behavior.* New York: Wiley.

Hebb, D. O. (1955). Drives and the C.N.S. (conceptual nervous system). *Psychological Review, 62,* 243–254.

Hebb, D. O. (1972). *Textbook of psychology* (3rd ed.). Philadelphia: Saunders.

Heckler, M. M. (1985). Psychology in the public forum: The fight against Alzheimer's disease. *American Psychologist, 40,* 1240–1244.

Heider, E. R. (1971). "Focal" color areas and the development of color names. *Developmental Psychology, 4,* 447–455.

Heider, E. R. (1972). Universals in color naming and memory. *Journal of Experimental Psychology, 93,* 10–21.

Heider, E. R., & Olivier, D. C. (1972). The structure of the color space in naming and memory for two languages. *Cognitive Psychology, 3,* 337–354.

Heider, K. G. (1991). *Landscapes of emotion: Lexical maps and scenarios of emotion terms in Indonesia.* Cambridge, England: Cambridge University Press.

Heilbrun, A. B., Jr., Wydra, D., & Friedberg, L. (1989). Parent identification and gender schema development. *Journal of Genetic Psychology, 150,* 293–299.

Heinlein, R. (1961). *Stranger in a strange land.* New York: Putnam.

Heinrichs, R. W. (1993). Schizophrenia and the brain. *American Psychologist, 48,* 221–233.

Held, R., & Hein, A. (1963). Movement produced stimulation in the development of visually guided behavior. *Journal of Comparative and Physiological Psychology, 56,* 872–876.

Helfer, R. E. (1987). The developmental basis of child abuse and neglect: An epidemiological approach. In R. E. Helfer & R. S. Kempe (Eds.), *The Battered Child* (4th ed.). Chicago: University of Chicago Press.

Hellige, J. B. (1993). Unity of thought and action: Varieties of interaction between the left and right cerebral hemispheres. *Current Directions in Psychological Science, 2,* 21–25.

Helmes, E., & Reddon, J. R. (1993). A perspective on developments in assessing psychopathology: A critical review of the MMPI and MMPI-2. *Psychological Bulletin, 113,* 453–471.

Helms, J. E. (1992). Why is there no study of cultural equivalence in standardized cognitive ability testing? *American Psychologist, 47,* 1083–1101.

Helson, R., & Moane, G. (1987). Personality change in women from college to midlife. *Journal of Personality and Social Psychology, 53,* 176–186.

Helson, R., & Picano, J. (1990). Is the traditional role bad for women? *Journal of Personality and Social Psychology, 59,* 311–320.

Hendrick, C., & Hendrick, S. S. (1986). A theory and method of love. *Journal of Personality and Social Psychology, 50,* 392–402.

Hendrick, C., & Hendrick, S. S. (1989). Research on love: Does it measure up? *Journal of Personality and Social Psychology, 56,* 784–794.

Herbert, T. B., & Cohen, S. (1993). Depression and immunity: A meta-analytic review. *Psychological Bulletin, 113,* 472–486.

Hertzog, C., Schaie, K. W., & Gribbin, K. (1978). Cardiovascular disease and changes in intellectual functioning from middle to old age. *Journal of Gerontology, 33,* 872–883.

Hetherington, E. M., Stanley-Hagan, M., & Anderson, E. R. (1989). Marital transitions: A child's perspective. *American Psychologist, 44,* 303–312.

Hildebrandt, K. A. (1983). Effect of facial expression variations on ratings of infant's physical attractiveness. *Developmental Psychology, 29,* 414–417.

Hilgard, E. R. (1965). *Hypnotic susceptibility.* New York: Harcourt, Brace & World.

Hilgard, E. R., & Morgan, A. H. (1975). Heart rate and blood pressure in the study of laboratory pain in man under normal conditions and as influenced by hypnosis. *Acta Neurobiologiae Experimentalis, 35,* 501–513.

Hilton, D. J. (1990). Conversational processes and causal explanation. *Psychological Bulletin, 107,* 65–81.

Hines, T. (1991). The myth of right hemisphere creativity. *Journal of Creative Behavior, 25,* 223–227.

Hinton, G. E. (1992, September). How neural networks learn from experience. *Scientific American,* pp. 145–151.

Hinz, L. D., & Williamson, D. A. (1987). Bulimia and depression: A review of the affective variant hypothesis. *Psychological Bulletin, 102,* 150–158.

Hirsch, H. V. B., & Spinelli, D. N. (1971). Modification of the distribution of receptive field orientation in cats by selective exposure during development. *Experimental Brain Research, 13,* 509–527.

Hirsch, J., & Leibel, R. L. (1988). New light on obesity. *New England Journal of Medicine, 318,* 509–510.

Hobfoll, S. E. (1989). Conservation of resources: A new attempt at conceptualizing stress. *American Psychologist, 44,* 513–524.

Hobfoll, S. E., Spielberg, C. D., Breznitz, S., Figley, C., Folkman, S., Lepper-Green, B., Meichenbaum, D., Milgram, N. A., Sandler, I., Sarason, I., & van der Kolk, B. (1991). War-related stress. *American Psychologist, 46,* 848–855.

Hobson, J. A. (1989). *Sleep.* New York: Freeman.

Hobson, J. A., & McCarley, R. W. (1977). The brain as a dream state generator: An activation-synthesis of the dream process. *American Journal of Psychiatry, 134,* 1335–1348.

Hochberg, J. E. (1974). Organization and the Gestalt tradition. In E. C. Carterette & M. P. Friedman (Eds.), *Handbook of perception.* New York: Academic Press.

Hochberg, J. E. (1979). Sensation and perception. In E. Hearst (Ed.), *The first century of experimental psychology.* New York: Wiley.

Hofferth, S. L., & Phillips, D. A. (1987). Child care in the United States, 1970 to 1995. *Journal of Marriage and the Family, 49,* 559–571.

Hoffman, C., & Hurst, N. (1990). Gender stereotypes: Perception or rationalization? *Journal of Personality and Social Psychology, 58,* 197–208.

Holder, M. D., Yirmiya, R., Garcia, J., & Raizer, J. (1989). Conditioned taste aversions are not readily disrupted by external excitation. *Behavioral Neuroscience, 103,* 605–611.

Holland, M. K. (1975). *Using psychology: Principles of behavior and your life.* Boston: Little, Brown.

Hollon, S. D., Shelton, R. C., & Davis, D. D. (1993). Cognitive therapy for depression: Conceptual issues and clinical efficacy. *Journal of Consulting and Clinical Psychology, 61,* 270–275.

Hollon, S. D., Shelton, R. C., & Loosen, P. T. (1991). Cognitive therapy and pharmacotherapy for depression. *Journal of Consulting and Clinical Psychology, 59,* 88–99.

Holloway, F. A. (1977). State-dependent retrieval based on time of day. In B. Ho, D. Chute, & D. Richards (Eds.), *Drug discrimination and state-dependent learning.* New York: Academic Press.

Holmes, D. S. (1984). Mediation and somatic arousal reduction. *American Psychologist, 39,* 1–10,

Holmes, T. H., & Rahe, R. H. (1967). The social readjustment rating scale. *Journal of Psychosomatic Research, 11,* 213–218.

Hom, H. L., Jr., & Arbuckle, B. (1988). Mood induction effects upon goal setting and performance in young children. *Motivation and Emotion, 12,* 113–122.

Horn, J. M. (1983). The Texas adoption project: Adopted children and their intellectual resemblance to biological and adoptive parents. *Child Development, 54,* 268–275.

Horne, J. (1988). *Why we sleep.* New York: Oxford University Press.

Horney, K. (1937). *The neurotic personality of our time.* New York: Norton.

Hornstein, G. A. (1992). The return of the repressed. *American Psychologist, 47,* 254–263.

Horvath, P. (1988). Placebos and common factors in two decades of psychotherapy research. *Psychological Bulletin, 204,* 214–225.

Horvath, T. (1981). Physical attractiveness: The influence of selected torso parameters. *Archives of Sexual Behavior, 10,* 21–24.

Howard, K. I., Kopta, S. M., Krause, M. S., & Orlinsky, D. E. (1986). The dose-effect relationships in psychotherapy. *American Psychologist, 41,* 159–164.

Howard, R. W. (1993). On what intelligence is. *British Journal of Psychology, 84,* 27–37.

Howarth, E. (1986). What does Eysenck's psychotism scale really measure? *British Journal of Psychology, 77,* 223–227.

Howe, M. J. A., & Smith, J. (1988). Calendar calculating in "idiots savants": How do they do it? *British Journal of Psychology, 79,* 371–386.

Howell, W. C. (1993). Engineering psychology in a changing world. *Annual Review of Psychology, 44,* 231–263.

Howes, C., & Stewart, P. (1987). Child's play with adults, toys, and peers: An examination of family and child-care influences. *Developmental Psychology, 23,* 423–430.

Howes, C., Unger, O., & Seidner, L. B. (1989). Social pretend play in toddlers: Parallels with social play and with solitary pretend. *Child Development, 60,* 77–84.

Hoyt, I. P., Nadon, R., Register, P. A., Chorny, J., Fleeson, W., Grigorian, E. M., & Otto, L. (1989). Daydreaming, absorption, and hypnotizability. *International Journal of Clinical and Experimental Hypnosis, 37,* 332–342.

Hubel, D. H., & Wiesel, T. N. (1962). Receptive fields, binocular interaction, and functional architecture in the cat's visual cortex. *Journal of Physiology, 160,* 106–164.

Hudspeth, A. J. (1983, January). The hair cells of the inner ear. *Scientific American,* pp. 54–73.

Hunt, E. B. (1983). On the nature of intelligence. *Science, 219,* 141–146.

Hunt, E. B., & Agnoli, F. (1991). The Whorfian hypothesis: A cognitive psychology perspective. *Psychological Review, 98,* 377–389.

Hurvich, L., & Jameson, D. (1974). Opponent processes as a model of neural organization. *American Psychologist, 30,* 88–102.

Huston, A. C., Donnerstein, E., Fairchild, H., Feshback, N. D., Katz, P. A., Murray, J. P., Rubinstein, E. A., Wilcox, B. L., & Zuckerman, D. (1992). *Big world, small screen.* Lincoln: University of Nebraska Press.

Huston, A. C., Watkins, B. A., & Kunkel, D. (1989). Public policy and children's television. *American Psychologist, 44,* 424–433.

Hwong, N. C., Caswell, A., Johnson, D. W., & Johnson, R. T. (1993). Effects of cooperative and individualistic learning on prospective elementary teachers' music achievement and attitudes. *The Journal of Social Psychology, 133*(1), 53–64.

Hyde, J. S., Fennema, E., & Lamon, S. J. (1990). Gender differences in mathematics performance: A meta-analysis. *Psychological Bulletin, 107,* 139–155.

Hyde, J. S., & Linn, M. C. (1988). Gender differences in verbal ability: A meta-analysis. *Psychological Bulletin, 104,* 53–69.

Hymes, R. W. (1986). Political attitudes as social categories: A new look at selective memory. *Journal of Personality and Social Psychology, 51,* 233–241.

Ilgen, D. R. (1990). Health issues at work: Opportunities for industrial/organizational psychology. *American Psychologist, 45,* 273–283.

Imm, P. S. (1990). Perceived benefits of participants in an employees' aerobic fitness program. *Perceptual and Motor Skills, 71,* 753–754.

Ingbar, D. H., & Gee, J. B. L. (1985). Pathophysiology and treatment of sleep apnea. *Annual Review of Medicine, 36,* 369–395.

Inhelder, B., & Piaget, J. (1958). *The growth of logical thinking from childhood to adolescence.* New York: Basic Books.

Inhoff, A. W., Morris, R., & Calabrese, J. (1986). Eye movements in skilled transcription typing. *Bulletin of the Psychonomic Society, 2,* 113–114.

Innes, J. M., & Young, R. F. (1975). The effect of presence of an audience, evaluation apprehension, and objective self-awareness on learning. *Journal of Experimental Social Psychology, 11,* 35–42.

Insua, A. M. (1983). WAIS-R factor structures in two cultures. *Journal of Cross-Cultural Psychology, 14,* 427–438.

Intraub, H. (1980). Presentation rate and the representation of briefly glimpsed pictures in memory. *Journal of Experimental Psychology: Human Learning and Memory, 6,* 1–12.

Intraub, H., & Nicklos, S. (1985). Levels of processing and picture memory: The physical superiority effect. *Journal of Experimental Psychology: Learning, Memory, and Cognition, 11,* 284–298.

Irwin, D. E., Brown, J. S., & Sun, J. S. (1988). Visual masking and visual integration across saccadic eye movements. *Journal of Experimental Psychology: General, 117,* 276–287.

Irwin, M., Smith, T. L., & Gillin, J. C. (1992). Electroencephalographic sleep and natural killer acitivity in depressed patients and control subjects. *Psychosomatic Medicine, 54,* 10–21.

Isabella, R. A., Belsky, J., & von Eye, A. (1989). Origins of infant-mother attachment: An examination of interactional synchrony during the infant's first year. *Developmental Psychology, 25,* 12–21.

Izard, C. E. (1993). Four systems for emotion activation: Cognitive and noncognitive processes. *Psychological Review, 100,* 68–90.

Izard, C. E., & Saxton, P. M. (1988). Emotions. In R. C. Atkinson, R. J. Herrnstein, G. Lindzey, & R. D. Luce, (Eds.), *Stevens handbook of experimental psychology: Vol. 1. Perception and motivation.* New York: Wiley.

Jaccard, J., Helbig, D. W., Wan, C. K., Gutman, M. A., & Kritz-Silverstein, D. C. (1990). Individual differences in attitude-behavior consistency: The prediction of contraceptive behavior. *Journal of Applied Social Psychology, 20,* 575–617.

Jacklin, C. N. (1989). Female and male: Issues of gender. *American Psychologist, 44,* 127–133.

Jackson, J. M., & Latané, B. (1981). All alone in front of all those people: Stage fright as a function of number and type of co-performers and audience. *Journal of Personality and Social Psychology, 40,* 73–85.

Jackson, L. A. (1992). *Physical appearance and gender.* Albany: State University of New York Press.

Jackson, S. E., & Schuler, R. S. (1990). Human resource planning: Challenges for industrial/organizational psychologists. *American Psychologist, 45,* 223–239.

Jacobs, L., Berscheid, E., & Walster, E. (1971). Self-esteem and attraction. *Journal of Personality and Social Psychology, 17,* 84–91.

Jacobson, N. S. (1991). Behavioral versus insight-oriented marital therapy: Labels can be misleading. *Journal of Consulting and Clinical Psychology, 59,* 142–145.

Jacobson, N. S., & Bussob, N. (1983). Marital and family therapy. In M. Herson, A. E. Kazdin, and A. S. Bellack (Eds.), *The clinical psychology handbook.* New York: Pergamon Press.

Jacoby, L. L., Kelley, C., Brown, J., & Jasechko, J. (1989). Becoming famous overnight: Limits on the ability to avoid unconscious influences of the past. *Journal of Personality and Social Psychology, 56,* 326–338.

James, W. (1884). What is an emotion? *Mind, 9,* 188–205.

James, W. (1890). *Principles of psychology.* New York: Dover.

Janis, I. L. (1982). *Groupthink* (2nd ed.). Boston: Houghton Mifflin.

Janis, I. L. (1983). The role of social support in adherence to stressful decisions. *American Psychologist, 38,* 142–160.

Janis, I. L. (1985). Stress inoculation in health care: Theory and research. In A. Monat & R. S. Lazarus (Eds.), *Stress and coping* (2nd ed.). New York: Columbia University Press.

Jaynes, J. (1976). *The origin of consciousness in the breakdown of the bicameral mind.* Boston: Houghton Mifflin.

Jenkins, H. M., & Harrison, R. H. (1960). Effect of discrimination training on auditory generalization. *Journal of Experimental Psychology, 59,* 244–253.

Jenkins, J. G., & Dallenbach, K. M. (1924). Oblivescence during sleep and waking. *American Journal of Psychology, 35,* 605–612.

Jennings, K. D., Curry, N. E., & Connors, R. (1986). Toddlers' social behaviors in dyads and groups. *Journal of Genetic Psychology, 147,* 515–528.

Jensen, A. R. (1969). How much can we boost IQ and scholastic achievement? *Harvard Educational Review, 39,* 1–123.

Jensen, A. R. (1970). Can we and should we study race differences? In J. Hellmuth (Ed.), *Disadvantaged child* (Vol. 3). New York: Brunner/Mazel.

Jensen, A. R. (1984). The black-white difference on the K-ABC: Implications for future tests. *Journal of Special Education, 18,* 377–408.

Jensen, A. R. (1987). Psychometric g as a focus on concerted research effort. *Intelligence, 11,* 193–198.

John, E. R., Chesler, P., Bartlett, F., & Victor, I. (1968). Observational learning in cats. *Science, 159,* 1489–1491.

Johnson, B. T., & Eagly, A. H. (1989). Effects of involvement on persuasion: A meta-analysis. *Psychological Bulletin, 106,* 290–314.

Johnson, C., & Larson, R. (1982). Bulimia: An analysis of moods and behavior. *Psychosomatic Medicine, 44,* 341–351.

Johnson, D. L. (1989). Schizophrenia as a brain disease. *American Psychologist, 44,* 553–555.

Johnson, F. W. (1991). Biological factors and psychometric intelligence: A review. *Genetic, Social, and General Psychology Monographs, 117,* 315–357.

Johnson, L. C., Slye, E. S., and Dement, W. (1965). Electroencephalographic and autonomic activity during and after prolonged sleep deprivation. *Psychosomatic Medicine, 27,* 415–423.

Jones, L. V. (1984). White-black achievement differences: The narrowing gap. *American Psychologist, 39,* 1207–1213.

Jones, S. S., & Raag, T. (1989). Smile production in older infants: The importance of a social recipient for the facial signal. *Child Development, 60,* 811–818.

Jorgensen, R. S., & Johnson, J. H. (1990). Contributors to the appraisal of major life changes: Gender, perceived controllability, sensation seeking, strain, and social support. *Journal of Applied Social Psychology, 20,* 1123–1138.

Josephs, R. A., Markus, H. R., & Tafarodi, R. W. (1992). Gender and self-esteem. *Journal of Personality and Social Psychology, 63,* 391–402.

Josephson, W. L. (1987). Television violence and children's aggression: Testing the priming, social script, and disinhibition predictions. *Journal of Personality and Social Psychology, 53,* 882–890.

Judd, C. M., & Park, B. (1988). Out-group homogeneity: Judgments of variability at the individual and group levels. *Journal of Personality and Social Psychology, 54,* 778–788.

Jussim, L. (1989). Teacher expectations: Self-fulfilling prophecies, perceptual biases, and accuracy. *Journal of Personality and Social Psychology, 57,* 469–480.

Kagan, J. (1988). The meanings of personality predicates. *American Psychologist, 43,* 614–620.

Kagan, J. (1989). Temperamental contributions to social behavior. *American Psychologist, 44,* 668–674.

Kagan, J., Kearsley, R. B., & Zelazo, P. R. (1980). *Infancy: Its place in human development.* Cambridge, MA: Harvard University Press.

Kagan, J., & Snidman, N. (1991a). Infant predictors of inhibited and uninhibited profiles. *Psychological Science, 2,* 40–44.

Kagan, J., & Snidman, N. (1991b). Temperamental factors in human development. *American Psychologist, 46,* 856–862.

Kahn, J. P., Kornfield, D. S., Blood, D. K., Lynn, R. B., Heller, S. S., & Frank, K. A. (1982). Type A behavior and the thallium stress test. *Psychosomatic Medicine, 44,* 431–436.

Kaitz, M., Lapidot, P., Bronner, R., & Eidelman, A. I. (1992). Parturient women can recognize their infants by touch. *Developmental Psychology, 28,* 35–39.

Kaitz, M., Meschulach-Sarfaty, O., & Auerbach, J. (1988). A reexamination of newborns' ability to imitate facial expressions. *Developmental Psychology, 1,* 3–7.

Kales, A., Tan, T. L., Kollar, E. J., Naithoh, P., Preson, T. A., & Malmstrom, E. J. (1970). Sleep patterns following 205 hours of sleep deprivation. *Psychosomatic Medicine, 32,* 189–200.

Kalichman, S. C. (1989). Sex roles and sex differences in adult spatial performance. *Journal of Genetic Psychology, 150,* 93–100.

Kalichman, S. C., & Craig, M. E. (1991). Professional psychologists' decisions to report suspected child abuse: Clinician and situation influences. *Professional Psychology: Research and Practice, 22,* 84–89.

Kalichman, S. C., Hunter, T. L., & Kelly, J. A. (1992). Perceptions of AIDS susceptibility among minority and nonminority women at risk for HIV infection. *Journal of Consulting and Clinical Psychology, 60,* 725–732.

Kalichman, S. C., Szymanowski, D., McKee, G., Taylor, J., & Craig, M. E. (1989). Cluster analytical derived MMPI profile subgroups of incarcerated adult rapists. *Journal of Clinical Psychology, 45,* 149–155.

Kalil, R. E. (1989, December). Synapse formation in the developing brain. *Scientific American,* pp. 76–85.

Kalimo, R., & Mejman, T. (1987). Psychological and behavioural responses to stress at work. In R. Kalimo, M. A. El-Batawi, & C. L. Cooper (Eds.), *Psychosocial factors at work and their relation to health.* Geneva: World Health Organization.

Kamarck, T., & Jennings, J. R. (1991). Biobehavioral factors in sudden cardiac death. *Psychological Bulletin, 109,* 42–75.

Kanekar, S., Shaherwalla, A., Franco, B., Kunju, T., & Pinto, A. J. (1991). The acquaintance predicament of a rape victim. *Journal of Applied Social Psychology, 21,* 1524–1544.

Kanner, A. D., Coyne, J. C., Schaefer, C., & Lazarus, R. S. (1981). Comparison of two modes of stress measurement: Daily hassles and uplifts versus major life events. *Journal of Behavioral Medicine, 4,* 1–39.

Kaplan, A. S., & Woodside, D. B. (1987). Biological aspects of anorexia nervosa and bulimia nervosa. *Journal of Consulting and Clinical Psychology, 55,* 645–653.

Kaplan, C. A., & Simon, H. A. (1990). In search of insight. *Cognitive Psychology, 22,* 374–419.

Kaplan, R. M. (1982). Nader's raid on the testing industry: Is it in the best interest of the consumer? *American Psychologist, 37,* 15–23.

Kaplan, R. M. (1988). Health-related quality of life in cardiovascular disease. *Journal of Consulting and Clinical Psychology, 56,* 382–392.

Kashani, J. H., & Orvaschel, H. (1988). Anxiety disorders in mid-adolescence: A community sample. *American Journal of Psychiatry, 145,* 960–964.

Kashani, J. H., Reid, J. C., & Rosenberg, T. K. (1989). Levels of hopelessness in children and adolescents: A developmental perspective. *Journal of Consulting and Clinical Psychology, 57,* 496–499.

Katsuki, Y. (1961). Neutral mechanisms of auditory sensation in cats. In W. A. Rosenblith (Ed.), *Sensory communication.* Cambridge, MA: MIT Press.

Katz, S., Lautenschlager, G. J., Blackburn, A. B., & Harris, F. H. (1990). Answering reading comprehension items without passages on the SAT. *Psychological Science, 1,* 122–127.

Katzell, R. A., & Thompson, D. E. (1990). Work motivation. *American Psychologist, 45,* 144–153.

Kaufman, A. S. (1983). Some questions and answers about the Kaufman Assessment Battery for Children (K-ABC). *Journal of Psychoeducational Assessment, 1*, 205–218.

Kaufman, A. S. (1984). K-ABC and controversy. *Journal of Special Education, 18*, 409–444.

Kaufman, A. S. (1990). *Assessing adolescent and adult intelligence.* Boston: Allyn and Bacon.

Kazdin, A. E. (1991). Effectiveness of psychotherapy with children and adolescents. *Journal of Consulting and Clinical Psychology, 59*, 785–798.

Kazdin, A. E. (1991). Treatment research: The investigation and evaluation of psychotherapy. In M. Hersen, A. E. Kazdin, & A. S. Bellack (Eds.), *The clinical psychology handbook* (2nd ed.). New York: Pergamon Press.

Keesey, R. E., & Powley, T. L. (1986). The regulation of body weight. *Annual Review of Psychology*, 109–135.

Kelley, H. H. (1972). Attribution in social interaction. In E. E. Jones et al. (Eds.), *Attribution: Perceiving the causes of behavior.* Morristown, NJ: General Learning Press.

Kelley, H. H. (1973). Process of causal attribution. *American Psychologist, 28*, 107–128.

Kelley, H. H., Berscheid, E., Christensen, A., Harvey, J. H., Huston, T. L., et al. (1983). *Close relationships.* New York: Freeman.

Kelly, G. (1955). *The psychology of personal constructs.* New York: Norton.

Kelly, T. A., & Strupp, H. H. (1992). Patient and therapist values in psychotherapy: Perceived changes, assimilation, similarity, and outcome. *Journal of Consulting and Clinical Psychology, 60*, 34–40.

Kendall, P. C. (1993). Cognitive-behavioral therapies with youth: Guiding theory, current status, and emerging developments. *Journal of Consulting and Clinical Psychology, 61*, 235–247.

Kendall-Tackett, K. A., Williams, L. M., & Finkelhor, D. (1993). Impact of sexual abuse on children: A review and synthesis of recent empirical studies. *Psychological Bulletin, 113*, 164–180.

Kendler, K. S. (1980). The nosologic validity of paranoia (simple delusional disorder): A review. *Archives of General Psychiatry, 37*, 699–706.

Kendler, K. S., Neale, M. C., Kessler, R. C., Heath, A. C., & Eaves, L. J. (1992). A population-based twin study of major depression in women. *Archives of General Psychiatry, 49*, 257–266.

Kendler, K. S., Neale, M. C., MacLean, C. J., Heath, A. C., Eaves, L. J., & Kessler, R. C. (1993). Smoking and major depression. *Archives of General Psychiatry, 50*, 36–43.

Kennell, J. H., Voos, D. K., & Klaus, M. H. (1979). Parent-infant bonding. In J. D. Osofsky (Ed.), *Handbook of infant development.* New York: Wiley.

Kenny, D. A., & DePaulo, B. M. (1993). Do people know how others view them? An empirical and theoretical account. *Psychological Bulletin, 114*, 145–161.

Kerr, N., & Bruun, S. E. (1983). Dispensability of member effort and group motivation losses: Free-rider effects. *Journal of Personality and Social Psychology, 44*, 78–94.

Kessler, R. C., Downey, G., Stipp, H., & Milavsky, J. R. (1989). Network television news stories about suicide and short-term changes in total U.S. suicides. *Journal of Nervous and Mental Disease, 177*, 551–555.

Kessler, R. C., Kendler, K. S., Heath, A. C., Neale, M. C., & Eaves, L. J. (1992). Social support, depressed mood, and adjustment to stress: A genetic epidemiologic investigation. *Journal of Personality and Social Psychology, 62*, 257–272.

Kihlstrom, J. F., Barnhardt, T. M., & Tataryn, D. J. (1992). The psychological unconscious. *American Psychologist, 47*, 788–791.

Kilbourne, B. K. (1989). A cross-cultural investigation of the foot-in-the-door compliance induction procedure. *Journal of Cross-Cultural Psychology, 20*, 3–38.

Kim, J. J., & Fanselow, M. S. (1992). Modality-specific retrograde amnesia of fear. *Science, 256*, 675–677.

Kimball, M. M. (1989). A new perspective on women's math achievement. *Psychological Bulletin, 105*, 198–214.

Kimmel, D. C. (1980). Adulthood and aging: An interdisciplinary view (2nd ed.). New York: Wiley.

Kimmel, D. C. (1988). Ageism, psychology, and public policy. *American Psychologist, 43*, 175–178.

Kimura, D. (1988). Sex differences in the brain. Paper presented at the Society for Neuroscience meeting in Toronto, Canada.

Kimura, D. (1992, September). Sex differences in the brain. *Scientific American*, pp. 119–125.

Kingsbury, S. J. (1987). Cognitive differences between clinical psychologists and psychiatrists. *American Psychologist, 42*, 152–156.

Kinsbourne, M. (1975). The ontogeny of cerebral dominance. In D. Aaronson & R. W. Rieber (Eds.), *Developmental Psycholinguistics and Communication Disorders: Annals of the New York Academy of Science, 263*, 244–250.

Kirshnit, C. E., Richards, M. H., & Ham, M. (1988, August). *Athletic participation and body-image during early adolescence.* Paper presented at the 96th Annual Convention of the American Psychological Association, Atlanta.

Kitwood, T. (1990). *Concern for others.* New York: Routledge.

Klatzky, R. L. (1991). Let's be friends. *American Psychologist, 46*, 43–45.

Klaus, M. H., & Kennell, J. H. (1983). In Antonia W. Hamilton (Ed.), *Bonding: The beginnings of parent-infant attachment* (rev. ed.). New York: New American Library.

Kleinginna, P. R., Jr., & Kleinginna, A. M. (1981). A categorized list of definitions with suggestions for a consensual definition. *Motivation and Emotion, 5*, 345–380.

Kleinmuntz, B., & Szucko, J. J. (1984). Lie detection in ancient and modern times: A call for contemporary scientific study. *American Psychologist, 39*, 766–776.

Klesges, R. C., Isbell, T. R., & Klesges, L. M. (1992). Relationship between dietary restraint, energy intake, physical activity, and body weight: A prospective analysis. *Journal of Abnormal Psychology, 101*, 668–674.

Kluver, H. (1936). An analysis of the effects of the removal of the occipital lobes in monkeys. *Journal of Psychology, 2*, 49–61.

Koenig, O., Reiss, L. P., & Kosslyn, S. M. (1990). The development of spatial relation representation: Evidence from studies of cerebral lateralization. *Journal of Experimental Child Psychology, 50*, 119–130.

Kogut, D., Langley, T., & O'Neal, E. C. (1992). Gender role masculinity and angry aggression in women. *Sex Roles, 26*, 355–365.

Kohlberg, L. (1969). The cognitive-developmental approach to socialization. In D. A. Goslin (Ed.), *Handbook of socialization theory and research.* Chicago: Rand McNally.

Kohlberg, L. (1971). From is to ought: How to commit the naturalistic fallacy and get away with it in the study of moral development. In T. Mischel (Ed.), *Cognitive development and epistemology.* New York: Academic Press.

Kohlberg, L. (1976). Moral stages and moralization: The cognitive-developmental approach. In T. Lickona (Ed.), *Moral development and behavior.* New York: Holt, Rinehart & Winston.

Kohler, W. (1973). *The mentality of apes* (2nd ed.). New York: Liveright. (Original work published 1927)

Kohn, A. (1986). *No contest: The case against competition.* Boston: Houghton Mifflin.

Kohn, A. (1992). *No contest.* Boston: Houghton Mifflin.

Kohout, J., & Pion, G. (1990). Participation of ethnic minorities in psychology: Where do we stand? In G. Stricker, E. Davis-Russell, E. Bourg, E. Duran, W. R. Hammond, J. McHolland, K. Polite, & B. E. Vaughn (Eds.), *Toward ethnic diversification in psychology education and training.* Hyattsville, MD: American Psychological Association.

Kohout, J., Wicherski, M., & Cooney, B. (1992). *Characteristics of graduate departments of psychology: 1989–1990.* Washington, DC: Office of Demographic, Employment, and Educational Research, American Psychological Association.

Kolb, B. (1989). Brain development, plasticity, and behavior. *American Psychologist, 44*, 1203–1212.

Konish, M. (1993). Listening with two ears. *Scientific American, 4*, 66–73.

Koocher, G. P. (1991). Questionable methods in alcoholism research. *Journal of Consulting and Clinical Psychology, 59*, 246–248.

Kopp, C. B. (1989). Regulation of distress and negative emotions: A developmental view. *Developmental Psychology, 25*, 343–354.

Kopp, C. B., & Kaler, S. R. (1989). Risk in infancy: Origins and implications. *American Psychologist, 44*, 224–230.

Koss, M. P. (1990). The women's mental health research agenda. *American Psychologist, 45*, 374–380.

Koss, M. P., Gidycz, C. A., & Wisniewski, N. (1987). The scope of rape: Incidence and prevalence of sexual aggression and victimization in a national sample of higher education students. *Journal of Consulting and Clinical Psychology, 55*, 162–170.

Kosslyn, S. M. (1975). Information representation in visual images. *Cognitive Psychology, 7*, 341–370.

Kosslyn, S. M. (1978). Measuring the visual angle of the mind's eye. *Cognitive Psychology, 7*, 341–370.

Kosslyn, S. M. (1987). Seeing and imagining in the cerebral hemispheres: A computational approach. *Psychological Review, 94*, 148–175.

Koulack, D. (1991). *To catch a dream.* Albany: State University of New York Press.

Krantz, D. S., Contrada, R. J., Hill, D. R., & Friedler, E. (1988). Environmental stress and biobehavioral antecedents of coronary heart disease. *Journal of Consulting and Clinical Psychology, 56*, 333–341.

Krantz, D. S., Grunberg, N. E., & Baum, A. (1985). Health psychology. *Annual Review of Psychology, 36*, 349–383.

Kranzler, J. H., & Jensen, A. R. (1991). The nature of psychometric g: Unitary process or a number of independent processes? *Intelligence, 15*, 397–422.

Krosnick, J. A. (1988). Attitude importance and attitude change. *Journal of Experimental Social Psychology, 24*, 240—255.

Krosnick, J. A., & Alwin, D. F. (1989). Aging and susceptibility to attitude change. *Journal of Personality and Social Psychology, 57*, 416–425.

Krosnick, J. A., Betz, A. L., Jussim, L. J., & Lynn, A. R. (1992). Subliminal condition of attitudes. *Society for Personality and Social Psychology, 18*, 152–162.

Kubey, R., & Csikszentmihalyi, M. (1990). *Television and the quality of life.* Hillsdale, NJ: Erlbaum.

Kübler-Ross, E. (1969). *On death and dying.* New York: Macmillan.

Kübler-Ross, E. (1975). *Death: The final stage of growth*. Englewood Cliffs, NJ: Prentice-Hall.

Kudoh, N., Tajima, H., Hatayama, T., Maruyama, K., Shoji, Y., Hayashi, T., & Nakanishi, M. (1991). Effects of room environment on human cognitive activities. *Tohoku Psychologica Folia, 50*, 45–54.

Kuhl, P. K., Williams, K. A., Lacerda, F., Stevens, K. N., & Lindblom, B. (1992). Linguisitic experience alters phonetic perception in infants by 6 months of age. *Science, 255*, 606–255.

Ladd, G. W. (1990). Having friends, keeping friends, making friends, and being liked by peers in the classroom: Predictors of children's early school adjustment? *Child Development, 61*, 1081–1100.

Lader, M. (1975). The nature of clinical anxiety in modern society. In C. D. Spielberger & I. G. Sarason (Eds.), *Stress and anxiety* (Vol. 1). Washington, DC: Hemisphere Publishing.

Laessle, R. G., Tuschl, R. J., Waadt, S., & Pirke, K. M. (1989). The specific psychopathology of bulimia nervosa: A comparison with restrained and unrestrained (normal) eaters. *Journal of Consulting and Clinical Psychology, 57*, 772–775.

LaFerla, J. J., Anderson, D. L., & Schalch, D. S. (1978). Psychoendocrine response to sexual arousal in human males. *Psychosomatic Medicine, 40*, 166–0172.

Lafferty, P., Beutler, L. E., & Crago, M. (1989). Differences between more and less effective psychotherapists: A study of select therapist variables. *Journal of Consulting and Clinical Psychology, 57*, 76–80.

Lahey, B. B., McNees, M. P., & McNees, M. C. (1973). Control of an obscene "verbal tic" through timeout in an elementary school classroom. *Journal of Applied Behavior Analysis, 6*, 101–104.

Lamb, M. E., Hwang, C., Bookstein, F. L., Broberg, A., Hult, G., & Frodi, M. (1988). Determinants of social competence in Swedish preschoolers. *Developmental Psychology, 1*, 58–70.

Landers, S. (1988, November 30). Survey verifies teen risk-taking. *APA Monitor*.

Landrine, H., Klonoff, E. A., & Brown-Collins, A. (1992). Cultural diversity and methodology in feminist psychology. *Psychology of Women Quarterly, 16*, 145–163.

Lange, C. G. (1922). *The emotion* (English translation). Baltimore: Williams & Wilkins. (Original work published 1885)

Langlois, J. H., Ritter, J. M., Roggman, L. A., & Vaughn, L. S. (1991). Facial diversity and infant preferences for attractive faces. *Developmental Psychology, 27*, 79–84.

Langlois, J. H., Roggman, L. A., & Rieser-Danner, L. A. (1990). Infants' differential social responses to attractive and unattractive faces. *Developmental Psychology, 26*, 153–159.

Langman, B., & Cockburn, A. (1975). Sirhan's gun. *Harper's, 250*, 16–27.

Larrick, R. P., Morgan, J. N., & Nisbett, R. E. (1990). Teaching the use of cost-benefit reasoning in everyday life. *Psychological Science, 1*, 362–370.

Larson, R., & Ham, M. (1993). Stress and "storm and stress" in early adolescence: The relationship of negative events with dysphoric affect. *Developmental Psychology, 29*, 130–140.

Larson, R. W., Raffaelli, M., Richards, M. H., Ham, M., & Jewell, L. (1990). Ecology of depression in late childhood and early adolescence: A profile of daily states and activities. *Journal of Abnormal Psychology, 99*, 92–102.

Last, C. G., Hersen, M., Kazdin, A., Orvaschel, H., & Perrin, S. (1991). Anxiety disorders in children and their families. *Archives of General Psychiatry, 48*, 928–931.

Latané, B. (1981). The psychology of social impact. *American Psychologist, 36*, 343–356.

Latané, B., & Darley, J. M. (1970). *The unresponsive bystander: Why doesn't he help?* New York: Meredith.

Latané, B., Williams, K., & Harkins, S. (1979). Many hands make light work: The causes and consequences of social loafing. *Journal of Personality and Social Psychology, 37*, 822–832.

Lavach, J. R. (1991). Cerebral hemisphericity, college major and occupational choices. *Journal of Creative Behavior, 25*, 218–222.

Lawler, E. E., & Porter, L. W. (1967). Antecedent attitudes of effective managerial performance. *Organizational Behavior and Human Performance, 2*, 122–142.

Lazarus, A. A., & Fay, A. (1990). Brief psychotherapy: Tautology or oxymoron? In J. K. Zeig & S. G. Gilligan (Eds.), *Brief therapy myths, methods, and metaphors*. New York: Brunner/Mazel.

Lazarus, R. S. (1974). Cognitive and coping processes in emotion. In B. Weiner (Ed.), *Cognitive views of human motivation*. New York: Academic Press.

Lazarus, R. S. (1982). The psychology of stress and coping, with particular reference to Israel. In C. D. Spielberger, I. G. Sarason, & N. A. Milgram (Eds.), *Stress and anxiety* (Vol. 8). Washington, DC: Hemisphere Publishing.

Lazarus, R. S. (1984). The trivialization of distress. In B. L. Hammonds & C. J. Scheirer (Eds.), *Psychology and health: The master lecture series*. Washington, DC: American Psychological Association.

Lazarus, R. S. (1991a). Cognition and motivation in emotion. *American Psychologist, 46*, 352–367.

Lazarus, R. S. (1991b). The cognitive-motivational-relational theory. In R. S. Lazarus (Ed.), *Emotion and adaptation*. New York: Oxford University Press.

Lazarus, R. S. (1991c). *Emotion and adaptation*. New York: Oxford University Press.

Lazarus, R. S. (1991d). Progress on a cognitive-motivational-relational theory of emotion. *American Psychologist, 46*, 819–834.

Lazarus, R. S. (1993). From psychological stress to the emotions: A history of changing outlooks. *Annual Review of Psychology, 44*, 1–21.

Lazarus, R. S., & Alfert, E. (1964). Short-circuiting of threat by experimentally altering cognitive appraisal. *Journal of Abnormal and Social Psychology, 69*, 195–205.

Lazarus, R. S., & DeLongis, A. (1983). Psychological stress and coping in aging. *American Psychologist, 38*, 245–254.

Lazarus, R. S., DeLongis, A., Folkman, S., & Gruen, R. (1985). Stress and adaptational outcomes. *American Psychologist, 40*, 770–779.

Leahey, T. H. (1992). The mythical revolutions of American psychology. *American Psychologist, 47*, 308–318.

Leahy, R. L., & Eiter, M. (1980). Moral judgment and the development of real and ideal androgynous self-image during adolescence and young adulthood. *Developmental Psychology, 16*, 362–370.

Leber, W. R. Beckham, E. E., & Danker-Brown, P. (1985). Diagnostic criteria for depression. In E. E. Beckham & W. R. Leber (Eds.), *Handbook of depression: Treatment, assessment, and research*. Homewood, IL: Dorsey Press.

Lee, M. T., & Ofshe, R. (1981). The impact of behavioral style and status characteristics on social influence: A test of two competing theories. *Social Psychology Quarterly, 44*, 73–82.

Lefcourt, H. M. (1992). Durability and impact of the locus of control construct. *Psychological Bulletin, 112*, 411–414.

Lefcourt, H. M., & Davidson-Katz, K. (1991). Locus of control and health. In C. R. Snyder & D. R. Forsyth (Eds.), *Handbook of social and clinical psychology* (pp. 246–266). New York: Pergamon Press.

Lefkowitz, M. M., Eron, L. D., Walder, L. O., & Huesmann, L. R. (1977). *Growing up to be violent*. New York: Pergamon Press.

Lefley, H. P. (1989). Family burden and family stigma in major mental illness. *American Psychologist, 44*, 556–560.

Leibowitz, H. W. (1971). Sensory, learned, and cognitive mechanisms of size perception. *Annals of the New York Academy of Sciences, 1988*, 47–62.

Leiner, H. C., Leiner, A. L., & Dow, R. S. (1986). Does the cerebellum contribute to mental skills? *Behavioral Neuroscience, 100*, 443–454.

Lenneberg, E. H. (1967). *Biological foundations of language*. New York: Wiley.

Leon, M. (1992). The neurobiology of filial learning. *Annual Review of Psychology, 43*, 377–399.

Leonard-Barton, D. (1981). The diffusion of active residential solar energy equipment in California. In A. Shama (Ed.), *Marketing solar energy innovations* (pp. 243–257). New York: Praeger.

Lepper, M. R., & Greene, D. (1978). Overjustification research and beyond: Toward a means-end analysis of intrinsic motivation. In M. R. Lepper & D. Greene (Eds.), *The hidden cost of reward*. Hillsdale, NJ: Erlbaum.

Lepper, M. R., Greene, D., & Nisbett, R. E. (1973). Undermining children's intrinsic interest with extrinsic reward: A test of the overjustification hypothesis. *Journal of Personality and Social Psychology, 28*, 129–137.

Lerer, B., Bleich, A., Kotler, M., Garb, R., Hertzberg, M., & Levin, B. (1987). Posttraumatic stress disorder in Israeli combat veterans. *Archives of General Psychiatry, 44*, 976–977.

Lerner, M. J. (1970). The desire for justice and reactions to victims. In J. Macaulay & L. Berkowitz (Eds.), *Altruism and helping behavior: Social psychological studies of some antecedents and consequences*. New York: Academic Press.

Lerner, R. M., & Lerner, J. V. (1977). Effects of age, sex, and physical attractiveness on child-peer relations, academic performance, and elementary school adjustment. *Developmental Psychology, 13*, 585–590.

Lester, B. M., & Dreher, M. (1989). Effects of marijuana use during pregnancy on newborn cry. *Child Development, 60*, 765–771.

Levenson, R. W. (1992). Autonomic nervous system differences among emotions. *Psychological Science, 3*, 23–27.

Levenson, R. W., Ekman, P., Heider, K., & Firesen, W. V. (1992). Emotion and autonomic nervous system activity in the Minangkabau of West Sumatra. *Journal of Personality and Social Psychology, 62*, 972–988.

LeVere, T. E., Brugler, T., Sandin, M., & Gray-Silva, S. (1989). Recovery of function after brain damage: Facilitation by the calcium entry blocker nimodipine. *Behavioral Neuroscience, 103*, 561–565.

Levi, L. (1990). Occupational stress. *American Psychologist, 46*, 1142–1145.

Levin, D. J. (1990). *Alcoholism*. New York: Hemisphere Publishing.

Levine, M. (1975). *Hypothesis testing: A cognitive theory of learning*. Hillsdale, NJ: Erlbaum.

Levinson, D. J. (1978). *The seasons of a man's life*. New York: Knopf.

Levinson, D. J. (1980). Toward a conception of the adult life course. In N. J. Smelser & E. H. Erikson (Eds.), *Themes of work and love in adulthood*. Cambridge, MA: Harvard University Press.

Levitt, M. J., Weber, R. A., Clark, M. C., & McDonnell, P. (1985). Reciprocity of exchange in toddler sharing behavior. *Developmental Psychology, 21*, 122–123.

Lewin, K. K. (1970). *Brief psychotherapy*. St. Louis: Warren H. Green.

Lewinsohn, P. M. (1974). Classical and theoretical aspects of depression. In I. S. Calhoun, H. E. Adams, & K. M. Mitchell (Eds.), *Innovative treatment methods in psychopathology.* New York: Wiley Interscience.

Lewinsohn, P. M., Rohde, P., Seeley, J. R., & Fischer, S. A. (1993). Age-cohort changes in the lifetime occurrence of depression and other mental disorders. *Journal of Abnormal Psychology, 102,* 110–120.

Lewinsohn, P. M., & Talkington, J. (1979). Studies on the measurement of unpleasant events and relations with depression. *Applied Psychological Measurement, 3,* 83–101.

Lewis, M., & Feiring, C. (1989). Infant, mother, and mother-infant interaction behavior and subsequent attachment. *Child Development, 60,* 831–837.

Lewis, M., & Saarni, C. (1985). Culture and emotions. In M. Lewis and C. Saarni (Eds.), *The socialization of emotions.* New York: Plenum Press.

Lidz, T. (1973). *The origin and treatment of schizophrenic disorders.* New York: Basic Books.

Liebrand, W. B. G., Messick, D. M., & Wolters, F. J. M. (1986). Why we are fairer than others: A cross-cultural replication and extension. *Journal of Experimental Social Psychology, 22,* 590–604.

Lilly, J. C. (1956). Mental effects of reduction of ordinary levels of physical stimuli in intact, healthy persons. *Psychiatric Research Reports, 5,* 1–28.

Linberg, M. A., Beggs, A. L., Chezik, D. D., & Ray, D. (1982). Flavor-toxicosis associations: Tests of three hypotheses of long delay learning. *Physiology and Behavior, 29,* 439–442.

Lindsay, D. S. (1993). Eyewitness suggestibility. *Current Directions in Psychological Science, 2,* 86–89.

Lindsey, K. P., & Paul, G. L. (1989). Involuntary commitments to public mental institutions: Issues involving the overrepresentation of blacks and assessment of relevant functioning. *Psychological Bulletin, 106,* 171–183.

Lindvall, O. (1991). Prospects of transplantation in human neurodegenerative diseases. *Trends in Neurosciences, 14,* 376–384.

Lindvall, O., Brundin, P., Widner, H., Rehncrona, S., Gustavi, B., Frackowiak, R., Leenders, K. L., Sawle, G., Rothwell, J. C., Marsden, C. D., & Bjorklund, A. (1990). Grafts of fetal dopamine neurons survive and improve motor function in Parkinson's disease. *Science, 247,* 374–577.

Linn, M. C., & Petersen, A. C. (1985). Emergence and characterization of sex differences in spatial ability: A meta-analysis. *Child Development, 56,* 1479–1498.

Linney, J. A., & Seidman, E. (1989). The future of schooling. *American Psychologist, 44,* 336–340.

Littig, L. W., & Williams, C. E. (1978). Need for affiliation, self-esteem, and social distance of black Americans. *Motivation and Emotion, 2,* 369–374.

Locke, E. A., & Latham, G. P. (1990a). Work motivation: The high performance cycle. In U. Kleinbeck, H. Quast, H. Thierry, & H. Hacker (Eds.), *Work Motivation.* Hillsdale, NJ: Erlbaum.

Locke, E. A., & Latham, G. P. (1990b). Work motivation and satisfaction: Light at the end of the tunnel. *Psychological Science, 1,* 240–246.

Lockhart, R. S., & Craik, F. I. M. (1990). Levels of processing: A retrospective commentary on a framework for memory research. *Canadian Journal of Psychology, 44,* 87–112.

Loehlin, J. C., Willerman, L., & Horn, J. M. (1987). Personality resemblance in adoptive families: A 10-year follow-up. *Journal of Personality and Social Psychology, 53,* 961–969.

Loftus, E. F. (1979). The malleability of human memory. *American Scientist, 67,* 310–320.

Loftus, E. F. (1991). *Witness for the defense.* New York: St. Martin's Press.

Loftus, E. F. (1993). The reality of repressed memories. *American Psychologist, 48,* 518–537.

Loftus, E. F., & Hoffman, H. G. (1989). Misinformation and memory: The creation of new memories. *Journal of Experimental Psychology: General, 118,* 100–104.

Lore, R. K., & Schultz, L. A. (1993). Control of human aggression. *American Psychologist, 48,* 16–25.

Lorenz, K. (1964). Ritualized fighting. In J. D. Carthy & F. J. Ebling (Eds.), *The natural history of aggression.* New York: Academic Press.

Lowell, E. L. (1952). The effect of need for achievement on learning and speed of performance. *Journal of Psychology, 33,* 31–40.

Luborsky, L., Barber, J. P., & Crits-Christoph, P. (1990). Theory-based research for understanding the process of dynamic psychotherapy. *Journal of Consulting and Clinical Psychology, 58,* 281–287.

Ludwick-Rosenthal, R., & Neufeld, W. J. (1988). Stress management during noxious medical procedures: An evaluative review of outcome studies. *Psychological Bulletin, 3,* 326–342.

Luger, G. F., Bower, T. G. R., & Wishart, J. G. (1983). A model of the development of the early infant object concept. *Perception, 12,* 21–34.

Lummis, M., & Stevenson, H. W. (1990). Gender differences in beliefs and achievement: A cross-cultural study. *Developmental Psychology, 26,* 252–263.

Lundin, R. W. (1961). *Personality: An experimental approach.* New York: Macmillan.

Lykken, D. T., McGue, M., Tellegen, A., & Bouchard, T. J., Jr. (1992). Emergenesis. *American Psychologist, 47,* 1565–1577.

Lynch, G., & Baudry, M. (1984). The biochemistry of memory: A new and specific hypothesis. *Science, 224,* 1057–1063.

Lytton, H., & Romney, D. M. (1991). Parents' differential socialization of boys and girls: A meta-analysis. *Psychological Bulletin, 109,* 267–296.

Maccoby, E. E. (1988). Gender as a social category. *Developmental Psychology, 24,* 755–765.

Maccoby, E. E. (1990). Gender and relationships. *American Psychologist, 45,* 513–520.

Maccoby, E. E., & Jacklin, C. N. (1987). Gender segregation in childhood. *Advances in Child Development and Behavior, 20,* 239–287.

MacEwen, K. E., & Barling, J. (1991). Effects of maternal employment experiences on children's behavior via mood, cognitive difficulties, and parenting behavior. *Journal of Marriage and the Family, 53,* 635–644.

MacLeod, C. M. (1991). Half a century of research on the Stroop effect: An integrative review. *Psychological Bulletin, 109,* 163–203.

MacNichol, E. F. (1964, December). Three-pigment color vision. *Scientific American,* pp. 48–56.

Madrazo, I., Drucken-Colin, R., Diaz, V., Martinez-Mata, J., Toress, C., & Becerril, J. J. (1987). Open microsurgical autograft of adrenal medulla to the right caudate nucleus in two patients with intractable Parkinson's disease. *New England Journal of Medicine, 316,* 831–834.

Magolda, M. B. (1990). Gender differences in epistemological development. *Journal of College Student Development, 31,* 555–561.

Mahoney, M. J. (1977). Reflections on the cognitive-learning trend in psychotherapy. *American Psychologist, 32,* 5–13.

Mahoney, M. J. (1993). Introduction to special section: Theoretical developments in the cognitive psychotherapies. *Journal of Consulting and Clinical Psychology, 61,* 187–193.

Mahrer, A. R., & Nadler, W. P. (1986). Good moments in psychotherapy: A preliminary review, a list, and some promising research avenues. *Journal of Consulting and Clinical Psychology, 54,* 10–15.

Maier, N. R. F., & Klee, J. B. (1941). Studies of abnormal behavior in the rat: 17. Guidance versus trial and error and their relation to convulsive tendencies. *Journal of Experimental Psychology, 29,* 380–389.

Malamuth, N. M., & Sockloskie, R. J. (1991). Characteristics of aggressors against women: Testing a model using a national sample of college students. *Journal of Consulting and Clinical Psychology, 59,* 670–681.

Mamelak, M. (1991). A model for narcolepsy. *Canadian Journal of Psychology, 45,* 194–220.

Manuck, S. B., Cohen, S., Rabin, B. S., Muldoon, M. F., & Bachen, E. A. (1991). Individual differences in cellular immune response to stress. *Psychological Science, 2,* 111–115.

Margraf, J., Ehlers, A., Roth, W. T., Clark, D. B., Sheikh, J., Agras, W. S., & Taylor, C. B. (1991). How "blind" are double-blind studies? *Journal of Consulting and Clinical Psychology, 59,* 184–187.

Markow, T. M. (1992). Genetics and developmental stability: An integrative conjecture on aetiology and neurobiology of schizophrenia. *Psychological Medicine, 22,* 295–305.

Marks, I. M. (1977). Clinical phenomena in search of laboratory models. In J. D. Maser & M. E. P. Seligman (Eds.), *Psychopathology: Experimental models.* San Francisco: Freeman.

Marks, W. B., Dobell, W. H., & MacNichol, J. R. (1964). The visual pigments of single primate cones. *Science, 142,* 1181–1183.

Marlatt, G.A, Baer, J. S., Donovan, D. M., & Kivlahan, D. R. (1988). Addictive behaviors: Etiology and treatment. *Annual Review of Psychology, 39,* 223–252.

Marquis, D. P. (1931). Can conditioned responses be established in the newborn infant? *Journal of Genetic Psychology, 39,* 479–492.

Marschark, M., Yuille, J. C., Richman, C. L., & Hunt, R. R. (1987). The role of imagery in memory: On shared and distinctive information. *Psychological Bulletin, 102,* 28–41.

Marshall, P. S. (1989). Attention deficit disorder and allergy: A neurochemical model of the relation between the illnesses. *Psychological Bulletin, 106,* 434–446.

Marshall, P. S. (1993). Allergy and depression: A neurochemical threshold model of the relation between the illnesses. *Psychological Bulletin, 113,* 23–43.

Marshall, W. A., & Tanner, J. M. (1969). Variations in the pattern of pubertal changes in girls. *Archives of Disease in Childhood, 44,* 291–303.

Martin, G. M., Schellenberg, G. D., Wijsman, E. M., & Bird, T. D. (1990). Dominant susceptibility genes. *Science, 347,* 124.

Martin, R., & Haroldson, S. (1977). Effect of vicarious punishment on stuttering frequency. *Journal of Speech and Hearing Research, 20,* 21–26.

Marx, E. M., Williams, J. M. G., & Claridge, G. C. (1992). Depression and social problem solving. *Journal of Abnormal Psychology, 101,* 78–86.

Maslow, A. H. (1962). *Toward a psychology of being.* New York: Van Nostrand.

Maslow, A. H. (1969). Toward a humanistic biology. *American Psychologist, 24,* 734–735.

Massaro, D. W., & Cowan, N. (1993). Information processing models: Microscopes of the mind. *Annual Review of Psychology, 44,* 383–425.

Masson, J. M. (1990). *Final analysis.* Reading, MA: Addison-Wesley.

Masters, A. (1990). Sexism and psychohistory: Our failure to confront feminist scholarship. *Journal of Psychohistory, 17,* 383–385.

Masters, W. H., & Johnson, V. E. (1966). *Human sexual response.* Boston: Little, Brown.

Masters, W. H., & Johnson, V. E. (1970). *Human sexual inadequacies.* Boston: Little, Brown.

Matarazzo, J. D. (1990). Psychological assessment versus psychological testing. *American Psychologist, 45,* 999–1017.

Mathews, A. M., Gelder, M. G., & Johnston, D. W. (1981). *Agoraphobia: Nature and treatment.* London: Guilford.

Matsui, T., & Onglatco, M. L. U. (1990). Relationships between employee quality circle involvement and need fulfillment in work as moderated by work type: A compensatory or a spillover model? In U. Kleinbeck, H. Quast, H. Thierry, & H. Hacker (Eds.), *Work motivation.* Hillsdale, NJ: Erlbaum.

Matsuoka, K., Onizawa, T., Hatakeyama, T., & Yamaguchi, H. (1987). Incidence of young adult eidetikers, and two kinds of eidetic imagery. *Tohoku Psychologica Folia, 46,* 62–74.

Matt, G. E. (1989). Decision rules for selecting effect sizes in meta-analysis: A review and reanalysis of psychotherapy outcome studies. *Psychological Bulletin, 105,* 106–115.

Matthews, K. A. (1988). Coronary heart disease and Type A behaviors: Update on and alternative to the Booth-Kewley and Friedman (1987) quantitative review. *Psychological Bulletin, 104,* 373–380.

Matthies, H. (1989). Neurobiological aspects of learning and memory. *Annual Review of Psychology, 40,* 381–404.

Mauer, D., & Salapatek, P. (1976). Development changes in the scanning of faces by young infants. *Child Development, 47,* 523–527.

Maurer, T. J., Palmer, J. K., & Ashe, D. K. (1993). Diaries, checklists, evaluations, and contrast effects in measurement of behavior. *Journal of Applied Psychology, 78,* 226–231.

Mauro, R., Sato, K., & Tucker, J. (1992). The role of appraisal in human emotions: A cross-cultural study. *Journal of Personality and Social Psychology, 62,* 301–317.

May, J., & Kline, P. (1987). Measuring the effects upon cognitive abilities of sleep loss during continuous operations. *British Psychological Society, 78,* 443–455.

McAuley, E., Duncan, T. E., & McElroy, M. (1989). Self-efficacy cognitions and causal attributions for children's motor performance: An exploratory investigation. *Journal of Genetic Psychology, 150,* 65–73.

McBride, A. B. (1990). Mental health effects of women's multiple roles. *American Psychologist, 45,* 381–384.

McCall, R. B. (1983). Environmental effects on intelligence: The forgotten realm of discontinuous nonshared within-family factors. *Child Development, 54,* 408–415.

McCarty, D., Argeriou, M., Huebner, R. B., & Lubran, B. (1991). Alcoholism, drug abuse, and the homeless. *American Psychologist, 46,* 1139–1148.

McCaul, K. D., Veltum, L. G., Boyechko, V., & Crawford, J. J. (1990). Understanding attributions of victim blame for rape: Sex, violence, and foreseeability. *Journal of Applied Social Psychology, 20,* 1–26.

McCauley, C. (1989). The nature of social influence in groupthink: Compliance and internalization. *Journal of Personality and Social Psychology, 57,* 250–260.

McClearn, G. E., Plomin, R., Gora-Maslak, G., & Crabbe, J. C. (1991). The gene chase in behavioral science. *Psychological Science, 2,* 222–229.

McClelland, D. C. (1958). Methods of measuring human motivation. In J. W. Atkinson (Ed.), *Motives in fantasy, action, and society.* Princeton, NJ: Van Nostrand.

McClelland, D. C. (1961). *The achieving society.* Princeton, NJ: Van Nostrand.

McClelland, D. C. (1986). Some reflections on the two psychologies of love. *Journal of Personality, 54,* 334–353.

McClelland, D. C. (1987). Characteristics of successful entrepreneurs. *Journal of Creative Behavior, 21,* 219–233.

McClintock, M. K. (1971). Menstrual synchrony and suppression. *Nature, 229,* 244–245.

McCloskey, M., Wible, C. G., & Cohen, N. J. (1988). Is there a special flashbulb-memory mechanism? *Journal of Experimental Psychology: General, 117,* 171–181.

McConkey, K. M., & Kinoshita, S. (1988). The influence of hypnosis on memory after one day and one week. *Journal of Abnormal Psychology, 97,* 48–53.

McConkie, G. W., Kerr, P. W., Reddix, M. D., & Zola, D. (1988). Eye movement control during reading: 1. The location of initial eye fixations on words. *Vision Research, 28,* 1107–1118.

McCrae, R. R., & Costa, P. T., Jr. (1987). Validation of the Five-Factor Model of Personality across instruments and observers. *Journal of Personality and Social Psychology, 52,* 81–90.

McCrae, R. R., & Costa, P. T., Jr. (1990). *Personality in adulthood.* New York: Guilford.

McDonaugh, G. R. (1992). *An examination of racial stereotypes: The differential effects of gender and social class on their content.* Dissertation research, Purdue University, West Lafayette, IN.

McFall, M. E., Mackay, P. W., & Donovan, D. M. (1991). Combat-related PTSD and psychosocial adjustment problems among substance abusing veterans. *Journal of Nervous and Mental Disease, 179,* 33–38.

McGaugh, J. L. (1990). Significance and remembrance: The role of neuromodulatory systems. *Psychological Science, 1,* 15–25.

McGinty, D., & Szymusiak, R. (1988). Neuronal unit activity patterns in behaving animals: Brainstem and limbic system. *Annual Review of Psychology, 39,* 135–168.

McGlynn, S. M. (1990). Behavioral approaches to neuropsychological rehabilitation. *Psychological Bulletin, 108,* 420–441.

McGoldrick, M., Preto, N. G., Hines, P. M., & Lee, E. (1991). Ethnicity and family therapy. In A. S. Gurman & D. P. Kniskern (Eds.), *Handbook of family therapy* (Vol. 2). New York: Brunner/Mazel.

McGrath, M. J., & Cohen, D. B. (1978). REM sleep facilitation of adaptive waking behavior: A review of the literature. *Psychological Bulletin, 85,* 24–57.

McGraw, K. O., & Fiala, J. (1982). Undermining the Zeigarnik effect: Another hidden cost of reward. *Journal of Personality, 50,* 58–66.

McGue, M., & Bouchard, T. J., Jr. (1989). Genetic and environmental determinants of information processing and special mental abilities: A twin analysis. In R. J. Sternberg (Ed.), *Advances in the psychology of human intelligence.* Hillsdale, NJ: Erlbaum.

McGue, M., Pickens, R. W., & Svikis, D. S. (1992). Sex and age effects on the inheritance of alcohol problems: A twin study. *Journal of Abnormal Psychology, 101,* 3–17.

McKeachie, W. J. (1988). Teaching thinking. *Update: National Center for Research to Improve Postsecondary Teaching and Learning, 2,* 1.

McKeachie, W. J., Pintrich, P. R., & Lin, Y. (1985). Learning to learn. In G. d'Ydewalle (Ed.), *Cognition, information processing, and motivation.* New York: Elsevier–North Holland.

McKenzie, B. E., Tootell, H. E., & Day, R. H. (1980). Development of visual size constancy during the 1st year of human infancy. *Developmental Psychology, 16,* 163–174.

McManus, I. C., & Bryden, M. P. (1991). Geschwind's theory of cerebral lateralization: Developing a formal, causal model. *Psychological Bulletin, 110,* 235–237.

McMinn, M. R., Lindsay, S. F., Hannum, L. E., & Troyer, P. K. (1990). Does sexist language reflect personal characteristics? *Sex Roles, 23,* 389–396.

McMinn, M. R., Troyer, P. K., Hannum, L. E., & Foster, J. D. (1991). Teaching nonsexist language to college students. *Journal of Experimental Education, 59,* 153–161.

McNally, R. J. (1990). Psychological approaches to panic disorder: A review. *Psychological Bulletin, 108,* 403–419.

McNeill, D. (1970). Explaining linguistic universals. In J. Morton (Ed.), *Biological and social factors in psycholinguistics.* London: Logos Press.

McNemar, Q. (1964). Lost: Our intelligence. Why? *American Psychologist, 19,* 871–882.

McReynolds, P. (1987). Lightner Witmer: Little-known founder of clinical psychology. *American Psychologist, 42,* 849–858.

Medin, D. L. (1989). Concepts and conceptual structure. *American Psychologist, 44,* 1469–1481.

Mednick, S. A., Parnas, J., & Schulsinger, F. (1987). The Copenhagen high-risk project, 1962–1986. *Schizophrenia Bulletin, 13,* 485–495.

Meichenbaum, D. (1974). *Cognitive behavior modification.* Morristown, NJ: General Learning Press.

Meichenbaum, D. (1977). *Cognitive behavior modification.* New York: Plenum Press.

Meichenbaum, D. (1993). Changing conceptions of cognitive behavior modification: Retrospect and prospect. *Journal of Consulting and Clinical Psychology, 61,* 202–204.

Meichenbaum, D., & Cameron, R. (1973). Training schizophrenics to talk to themselves: A means of developing attentional controls. *Behavior Therapy, 4,* 515–534.

Mellody, P., Miller, A. W., & Miller, J. K. (1989). *Facing codependence.* New York: Harper & Row.

Meltzoff, A. N. (1988). Imitation of televised models by infants. *Child Development, 59,* 1221–1229.

Melville, J. (1977). *Phobias and compulsions.* New York: Penguin.

Melzack, R. (1990, February). The tragedy of needless pain. *Scientific American,* pp. 27–33.

Melzack, R., & Wall, P. D. (1970). Psychophysiology of pain. *International Anesthesiology Clinics, 8,* 3–34.

Mercer, R. T., Nichols, E. G., & Doyle, G. C. (1989). *Transitions in a woman's life* (Vol. 12). New York: Springer Publishing.

Merikle, P. M., & Reingold, E. M. (1990). Recognition and lexical decision without detection: Unconscious perception? *Journal of Experimental Psychology: Human Perception and Performance, 16,* 574–583.

Merton, R. K. (1949). Merton's typology of prejudice and discrimination. In R. M. MacIver (Ed.), *Discrimination and national welfare.* New York: Harper & Row.

Mesquita, B., & Frijda, N. H. (1992). Cultural variations in emotions: A review. *Psychological Bulletin, 112,* 179–204.

Messer, S. C., Wuensch, K. L., & Diamond, J. M. (1989). Former latchkey children: Personality and academic correlates. *Journal of Genetic Psychology, 150,* 301–309.

Metalsky, G. I., & Joiner, T. E., Jr. (1992). Vulnerability to depressive symptomatology: A prospective test of the diathesis-stress and causal mediation components of the hopelessness theory of depression. *Journal of Personality and Social Psychology, 63,* 667–675.

Meyer, R. G., & Salmon, P. (1988). *Abnormal psychology* (2nd ed.). Boston: Allyn and Bacon.

Meyers, A. F., Sampson, A. E., Wetzman, M., Rogers, B. L., & Kayne, H. (1989). School breakfast program and school performance. *American Journal of Diseases of Children, 143,* 1234–1239.

Meyers-Levy, J., & Maheswaran, D. (1991). Exploring differences in males' and females' processing strategies. *Journal of Consumer Research, 18,* 63–70.

Middaugh, S. J. (1990). On clinical efficacy: Why biofeedback does—and does not—work. *Biofeedback and Self-Regulation, 15,*(3), 191–208.

Mikhailova, N. G., Zukhar, A. V., Loseva, E. V., & Ermakova, I. V. (1991). Influence of transplantation of embryonal brain tissue (early periods) on reactions of avoidance of artificial and zoosocial stimuli in rats. *Neuroscience and Behavioral Physiology, 21,* 34–37.

Mikulincer, M., & Nizan, B. (1988). Causal attribution, cognitive interference, and the generalization of learned helplessness. *Journal of Personality and Social Psychology, 55,* 470–478.

Milan, R. J., & Kilmann, P. R. (1987). Interpersonal factors in premarital contraception. *Journal of Sex Research, 23,* 289–321.

Milgram, S. (1963). Behavioral study of obedience. *Journal of Abnormal and Social Psychology, 67,* 371–378.

Milgram, S. (1965). Liberating effects of group pressure. *Journal of Personality and Social Psychology, 1,* 127–134.

Millar, M. G., & Millar, K. U. (1990). Attitude change as a function of attitude type and argument type. *Journal of Personality and Social Psychology, 39,* 217–228.

Miller, B. C., McCoy, J. K., Olson, T. D., & Wallace, C. M. (1986). Parental discipline and control attempts in relation to adolescent sexual attitudes and behavior. *Journal of Marriage and the Family, 48,* 503–512.

Miller, B. C., & Moore, K. A. (1990). Adolescent sexual behavior, pregnancy, and parenting: Research through the 1980s. *Journal of Marriage and the Family, 52,* 1025–1044.

Miller, G. A. (1956). The magic number seven, plus or minus two: Some limits on our capacity for processing information. *Psychological Review, 63,* 81–97.

Miller, G. A. (1965). Some preliminaries to psycholinguistics. *American Psychologist, 20,* 15–20.

Miller, K. F., & Baillargeon, R. (1990). Length and distance: Do preschoolers think that occlusion brings things together? *Developmental Psychology, 26,* 103–114.

Miller, L. C. (1990). Intimacy and liking: Mutual influence and the role of unique relationships. *Journal of Personality and Social Psychology, 59,* 50–60.

Miller, N. E. (1944). Experimental studies of conflict. In J. M. Hunt (Ed.), *Personality and behavioral disorders* (Vol. 1). New York: Ronald Press.

Miller, N. E. (1959). Liberalization of basic S-R concepts: Extensions to conflict behavior, motivation, and social learning. In S. Koch (Ed.), *Psychology: A study of a science* (Vol. 2). New York: McGraw-Hill.

Miller, N. E. (1969). Learning of visceral and glandular responses. *Science, 163,* 434–445.

Miller, N. E. (1985). The value of behavioral research on animals. *American Psychologist, 40,* 423–440.

Miller, P. H., & Aloise, P. A. (1989). Young children's understanding of the psychological causes of behavior: A review. *Child Development, 60,* 257–285.

Miller, R. P., Cosgrove, J. M., & Doke, L. (1990). Motivating adolescents to reduce their fines in a token economy. *Adolescence, 25,* 97–104.

Miller, T. Q., Turner, C. W., Tindale, R. S., Posavac, E. J., & Dugoni, B. L. (1991). Reasons for the trend toward null findings in research on type A behavior. *Psychological Bulletin, 110,* 469–485.

Milner, B. (1966). Amnesia following operation on the temporal lobes. In C. W. M. Whitty & O. L. Zangwill (Eds.), *Amnesia.* London: Butterworth.

Milner, B., Corkin, S., & Teuber, H. L. (1968). Further analysis of hippocampal amnesic syndrome: 14-year follow-up study of H.M. *Neuropsychologia, 6,* 215–234.

Milner, P. M. (1989). A cell assembly theory of hippocampal amnesia. *Neuropsychologia, 27,* 23–30.

Milner, P. M. (1991). Brain stimulation reward: A review. *Canadian Journal of Psychology, 45,* 1–36.

Mischel, W. (1973). Toward a cognitive social learning reconceptualization of personality. *Psychological Review, 80,* 252–283.

Mischel, W. (1979). On the interface of cognition and personality: Beyond the person-situation debate. *American Psychologist, 34,* 740–754.

Mischel, W. (1983). Alternatives in the pursuit of the predictability and consistency of persons: Stable data that yield unstable interpretations. *Journal of Personality, 51,* 578–604.

Mischel, W., & Grusec, J. E. (1966). Determinants of the rehearsal and transmission of neutral and averse behaviors. *Journal of Personality and Social Psychology, 3,* 197–205.

Mishler, E. G., & Waxler, N. E. (1968). Family interaction processes and schizophrenia: A review of current theories. In E. G. Mishler & N. E. Waxler (Eds.), *Family processes and schizophrenia.* New York: Science House.

Mittal, B. (1988). Achieving higher seat belt usage: The role of habit in bridging the attitude-behavior gap. *Journal of Applied Social Psychology, 18,* 993–1016.

Money, J. (1984). Paraphilias: Phenomenology and classification. *American Journal of Psychotherapy, 38,* 164–168.

Monroe, S. M., & Simons, A. D. (1991). Diathesis-stress theories in the context of life stress research: Implications for the depressive disorders. *Psychological Bulletin, 110,* 406–425.

Monroe, S. M., Simons, A. D., & Thase, M. E. (1991). Onset of depression and time to treatment entry: Roles of life stress. *Journal of Consulting and Clinical Psychology, 59,* 566–573.

Montepare, J. M., & Zebrowitz-McArthur, L. (1988). Impressions of people created by age-related qualities of their gaits. *Journal of Personality and Social Psychology, 55,* 547–556.

Montgomery–St. Laurent, T., Fullenkamp, A. M., & Fischer, R. B. (1988). A role for the hamster's flank gland in heterosexual communication. *Physiology and Behavior, 44,* 759–762.

Moorehouse, M. J. (1991). Linking maternal employment patterns to mother-child activities and children's school competence. *Developmental Psychology, 27,* 295–303.

Morgan, W. P. (1992). Hypnosis and sport psychology. In J. Rhue, S. J. Lynn, & I. Kirsch (Eds.), *Handbook of clinical hypnosis.* Washington, DC: American Psychological Association.

Morrison, D. M. (1985). Adolescent contraceptive behavior: A review. *Psychological Bulletin, 98,* 538–568.

Moskowitz, B. A. (1978, November). The acquisition of language. *Scientific American,* pp. 92–108.

Mueser, K. T., Bellack, A. S., Morrison, R. L., & Wade, J. H. (1990). Gender, social competence, and symptomatology in schizophrenia: A longitudinal analysis. *Journal of Abnormal Psychology, 99,* 138–147.

Mullen, B., Tice, D. M., Baumeister, R. F., Dawson, K. E., Riordan, C. A., Radloff, C. E., Goethals, G. R., Kennedy, J. G., & Rosenfeld, P. (1986). Newscasters' facial expressions and voting behavior of viewers: Can a smile elect a president? *Journal of Personality and Social Psychology, 51,* 291–295.

Mungy, G. (1982). The power of minorities. In H. Tajfel (Ed.), *European monographs in social psychology* (Vol. 31). London: Academic Press.

Murphy, G. E., Wetzel, R. D., Robins, E., & McEvoy, L. (1992). Multiple risk factors predict suicide in alcoholism. *Archives of General Psychiatry, 49,* 459–463.

Murray, H. A. (1938). *Explorations in personality.* New York: Oxford University Press.

Mussen, P. H., & Distler, L. (1959). Masculinity, identification, and father-son relationships. *Journal of Abnormal and Social Psychology, 59,* 350–356.

Muuss, R. E. (1989). Carol Gilligan's theory of sex differences in the development of moral reasoning during adolescence. *Adolescence, 23,* 229–243.

Naar, R. (1990). Psychodrama in short-term psychotherapy. In R. A. Wells & V. J. Giannetti (Eds.), *Handbook of the brief psychotherapies.* New York: Plenum Press.

Nace, E. P. (1987). *The treatment of alcoholism.* New York: Brunner/Mazel.

Nash, M. (1987). What, if anything, is regressed about hypnotic age regression? A review of the empirical literature. *Psychological Bulletin, 102,* 42–52.

Nathan, B. R., & Tippins, N. (1990). The consequences of halo "error" in performance ratings: A field study of the moderating effect of halo on test validation results. *Journal of Applied Psychology, 75,* 290–296.

Nathan, P. E. (1988). The addictive personality is the behavior of the addict. *Journal of Consulting and Clinical Psychology, 56,* 183–188.

Nathan, P. E., & Skinstad, A. H. (1987). Outcomes of treatment for alcohol problems: Current methods, problems, and results. *Journal of Consulting and Clinical Psychology, 55,* 332–340.

Nathans, J. (1989, February). The genes for color vision. *Scientific American,* pp. 42–49.

Navon, D. (1990). How critical is the accuracy of an eyewitness's memory? Another look at the issue of lineup diagnosticity. *Journal of Applied Psychology, 75,* 506–510.

Neal, A. M., & Turner, S. M. (1991). Anxiety disorders research with African Americans: Current status. *Psychological Bulletin, 109,* 400–410.

Nelson, C. A. (1987). The recognition of facial expressions in the first two years of life: Mechanisms of development. *Child Development, 58,* 889–909.

Nelson, C. A., & Ludemann, P. M. (1989). Past, current, and future trends in infant face perception research. *Canadian Journal of Psychology, 43,* 183–198.

Nelson, K. (1993). The psychological and social origins of autobiographical memory. *Psychological Science, 4,* 7–14.

Nemeroff, C. B., Knight, D. L., Kirshnan, R. R., Slotkin, T. A., Bissette, G., Melville, M. L., & Blazer, D. G. (1988). Marked reduction in the number of platelet-tritiated imipramine binding sites in geriatric depression. *Archives of General Psychiatry, 45,* 919–923.

Newcomb, M. D., & Bentler, P. M. (1988). Impact of adolescent drug use and social support on problems of young adults: A longitudinal study. *Journal of Abnormal Psychology, 97,* 64–75.

Newcomb, M. D., & Bentler, P. M. (1989). Substance use and abuse among children and teenagers. *American Psychologist, 44,* 242–248.

Newcombe, N., & Huttenlocher, J. (1992). Children's early ability to solve perspective-taking problems. *Developmental Psychology, 28,* 635–643.

Newman, B. M. (1982). Mid-life development. In B. B. Wolman (Ed.), *Handbook of developmental psychology.* Englewood Cliffs, NJ: Prentice-Hall.

Nilsson, K. M. (1990). The effect of subject expectations of "hypnosis" upon vividness of visual imagery. *International Journal of Clinical and Experimental Hypnosis, 38,* 17–24.

Nisbett, R. E. (1972). Hunger, obesity, and the ventromedial hypothalamus. *Psychological Review, 79,* 433–453.

Nisbett, R. E. (1993). Violence and U.S. regional culture. *American Psychologist, 48,* 441–449.

Norcross, J. C., Prochaska, J. O., & Gallagher, K. M. (1989). Clinical psychologists in the 1980s: 2. Theory, research, and practice. *Clinical Psychologist, 42,* 45–52.

Norris, J. (1989). Normative influence effects on sexual arousal to nonviolent sexually explicit material. *Journal of Applied Social Psychology, 19,* 341–352.

Noton, D., & Stark, L. (1971, June). Eye movements and visual perception. *Scientific American,* pp. 35–44.

Novak, M. A., & Suomi, S. J. (1988). Psychological well-being of primates in captivity. *American Psychologist, 43,* 765–773.

Nowicki, S., Jr., & Duke, M. (1989, June). *Noverbal skills scale for children developed.* Paper presented at the American Psychological Society's first convention.

Nuechterlein, K. H., & Holroyd, J. C. (1980). Biofeedback in the treatment of tension headache: Current status. *Archives of General Psychiatry, 37,* 866–873.

Nurmi, J. E. (1991). Cross-cultural differences in self-serving bias: Responses to the attributional style questionnaire by American and Finnish students. *Journal of Social Psychology, 132,* 69–76.

Oetting, E. R., & Beauvais, F. (1990). Adolescent drug use: Findings of national and local surveys. *Journal of Consulting and Clinical Psychology, 58,* 385–394.

Ogur, B. (1986). Long day's journey into night: Women and prescription drug abuse. *Women and Health, 11,* 99–115.

Olds, J. (1955). Physiological mechanisms of reward. *Nebraska Symposium on Motivation, 3,* 73–139.

Olds, J. (1969). The central nervous system and the reinforcement of behavior. *American Psychologist, 24,* 114–132.

Olds, J., & Milner, P. (1954). Positive reinforcement produced by electrical stimulation of septal area and other regions of rat brain. *Journal of Comparative and Physiological Psychology, 47,* 419–427.

O'Leary, A. (1990). Stress, emotion, and human immune function. *Psychological Bulletin, 108,* 363–382.

O'Leary, K. D., Barling, J., Arias, I., Rosenbaum, A., Malone, J., & Tyree, A. (1989). Prevalence and stability of physical aggression between spouses: A longitudinal analysis. *Journal of Consulting and Clinical Psychology, 57,* 263–268.

Oliver, M. B., & Hyde, J. S. (1993). Gender differences in sexuality: A meta-analysis. *Psychological Bulletin, 114,* 29–51.

O'Regan, J. K. (1992). Solving the "real" mysteries of visual perception: The world as an outside memory. *Canadian Journal of Psychology, 46,* 461–488.

Ornstein, R. E. (1976). A science of consciousness. In P. R. Lee, R. E. Ornstein, D. Galin, A. Deikman, & C. T. Tart (Eds.), *Symposium on consciousness* (San Francisco, 1974). New York: Viking Press.

Ornstein, R. E. (1977). *The psychology of consciousness* (2nd ed.). New York: Harcourt Brace Jovanovich.

Ottati, V., Fishbein, M., & Middlestadt, S. E. (1988). Determinants of voters' beliefs about the candidates' stands on the issues: The role of evaluative bias heuristics and the candidates' expressed message. *Journal of Personality and Social Psychology, 55,* 517–529.

Owens, M. E., Bliss, E. L., Koester, P., & Jeppsen, E. A. (1989). Phobias and hypnotizability: A reexamination. *The International Journal of Clinical and Experimental Hypnosis, 37,* 207–216.

Pagano, R. W., Rose, R. M., Stivers, R. M., & Warrenburg, S. (1976). Sleep during transcendental meditation. *Science, 191,* 308–310.

Paikoff, R. L., & Brooks-Gunn, J. (1991). Do parent-child relationships change during puberty? *Psychological Bulletin, 110,* 47–66.

Paivio, A. (1971). *Imagery and verbal processes.* New York: Holt, Rinehart & Winston.

Palinkas, L. A., Russell, J., Downs, M. A., & Petterson, J. S. (1992). Ethnic differences in stress, coping, and depressive symptoms after the Exxon Valdez oil spill. *Journal of Nervous and Mental Disease, 180,* 287–295.

Pantin, H. M., & Carver, C. S. (1982). Induced competence and the bystander effect. *Journal of Applied Social Psychology, 12,* 100–111.

Papini, M. R., & Bitterman, M. E. (1990). The role of contingency in classical conditioning. *Psychological Review, 97,* 396–403.

Parke, R. D., & O'Leary, S. E. (1976). Father-mother-infant interaction in the newborn period: Some findings, some observations, and some unresolved issues. In K. Riegel & J. Meacham (Eds.), *The developing individual in a changing world: Vol. 2. Social and environmental issues.* The Hague, Netherlands: Mouton.

Parker, D. E. (1980, November). The vestibular apparatus. *Scientific American,* pp. 118–135.

Parker, G., Roy, K., Hadzi-Pavlovic, D., & Pedic, F. (1992). Psychotic (delusional) depression: A meta-analysis of physical treatments. *Journal of Affective Disorders, 24,* 17–24.

Patrick, C. J., & Iacono, W. G. (1989). Psychopathy, threat, and polygraph test accuracy. *Journal of Applied Psychology, 74,* 347–355.

Pavlov, I. P. (1927). *Conditioned reflexes.* London: Oxford University Press.

Payne, J. W., Bettman, J. R., & Johnson, E. J. (1992). Behavioral decision research: A constructive processing perspective. *Annual Review of Psychology, 43,* 87–132.

Pearlson, C. (1991). Electroconvulsive therapy. *General Hospital Psychiatry, 13,* 128–137.

Pedersen, D. M., & Wheeler, J. (1983). The Müller-Lyer illusion among Navajos. *Journal of Social Psychology, 121,* 3–6.

Pedersen, N. L., Plomin, R., Nesselroade, J. R., & McClearn, G. E. (1992). A quantitative genetic analysis of cognitive abilities during the second half of the life span. *Psychological Science, 3,* 346–353.

Peele, S. (1984). The cultural context of psychological approaches to alcoholism: Can we control the effects of alcohol? *American Psychologist, 39,* 1337–1351.

Pellizzer, G., & Georgopoulos, A. P. (1993). Mental rotation of the intended direction of movement. *Current Directions in Psychological Science, 2,* 12–17.

Penfield, W. W. (1958). *The excitable cortex in conscious man.* Springfield, IL: Charles C Thomas.

Penfield, W. W., & Jasper, H. (1954). *Epilepsy and the functional anatomy of the human brain.* Boston: Little, Brown.

Penfield, W. W., & Mathieson, G. (1957). Memory: Autopsy findings and comments on the role of hippocampus in experiential recall. *Archives of Neurology, 31,* 145–154.

Penfield, W. W., & Milner, B. (1958). Memory deficit produced by bilateral lesions in the hippocampal zone. *Archives of Neurological Psychiatry, 79,* 475–497.

Penfield, W. W., & Perot, P. (1963). The brain's record of auditory and visual experience. *Brain, 86,* 595–696.

Persky, H. (1978). Plasma testosterone level and sexual behavior of couples. *Archives of Sexual Behavior, 9,* 157–173.

Pesut, D. J. (1990). Creative thinking as a self-regulatory metacognitive process: A model for education, training, and further research. *Journal of Creative Behavior, 24,* 105–110.

Peterson, C., & Seligman, M. E. P. (1984). Causal explanations as a risk factor for depression: Theory and evidence. *Psychological Review, 91,* 347–374.

Peterson, J. L., & Marin, G. (1988). Issues in the prevention of AIDS among black and Hispanic men. *American Psychologist, 43,* 871–877.

Peterson, L. R., & Peterson, M. J. (1959). Short-term retention of individual verbal items. *Journal of Experimental Psychology, 58,* 193–198.

Petty, R. E., & Cacioppo, J. T. (1981). *Attitudes and persuasion: Classic and contemporary approaches.* Dubuque, IA: Wm. C. Brown.

Petty, R. E., and Cacioppo, J. T. (1985). The elaboration likelihood model of persuasion. In L. Berkowitz (Ed.), *Advances in experimental social psychology* (Vol. 19). New York: Academic Press.

Petty, R. E., Schumann, D. W., Richman, S. A., & Strathman, A. J. (1993). Positive mood and persuasion: Different roles for affect under high- and low-elaboration conditions. *Journal of Personality and Social Psychology, 64,* 5–20.

Pfister, H. P., & Muir, J. L. (1992). Prenatal exposure to predictable and unpredictable novelty stress and oxytocin treatment affects offspring development and behavior in rats. *International Journal of Neuroscience, 62,* 227–241.

Phares, V. (1992). Where's poppa? *American Psychologist, 47,* 656–664.

Piaget, J. (1932). *The moral judgment of the child.* London: Routledge & Kegan Paul.

Piaget, J. (1963). The attainment of invariants and reversible operations in the development of thinking. *Social Research, 30,* 283–299.

Pickens, R. W., Svikis, D. S., McGue, M., Lykken, D. T., Heston, L. L., & Clayton, P. J. (1991). Heterogeneity in the inheritance of alcoholism. *Archives of General Psychiatry, 48,* 19–28.

Pike, K. M., & Rodin, J. (1991). Mothers, daughters, and disordered eating. *Journal of Abnormal Psychology, 100,* 198–204.

Pion, G. M., Bramblett, J. P., Jr., & Wicherski, M. (1987). *Preliminary report: 1985 doctorate employment survey.* Washington, DC: American Psychological Association.

Pirenne, M. H. (1967). *Vision and the eye.* London: Science Paperbacks.

Pitman, R. K., Orr, S. P., Forgue, D. F., Altman, B., de Jong, J. B., & Herz, L. R. (1990). Psychophysiologic responses to combat imagery of Vietnam veterans with posttraumatic stress disorder versus other anxiety disorders. *Journal of Abnormal Psychology, 99,* 49–54.

Pittman, T. S., & Heller, J. F. (1987). Social motivation. *Annual Review of Psychology, 38,* 461–490.

Plomin, R. (1989). Environment and genes: Determinants of behavior. *American Psychologist, 44,* 105–111.

Plomin, R., Corley, R., DeFries, J. C., & Fulker, D. W. (1990). Individual differences in television viewing in early childhood: Nature as well as nurture. *Psychological Science, 1,* 371–377.

Plomin, R., & Neiderhiser, J. (1991). Quantitative genetics, molecular genetics, and intelligence. *Intelligence, 15,* 369–387.

Plotkin, W. B. (1980). The role of attributions of responsibility in the facilitation of unusual experiential states during alpha training: An analysis of the biofeedback placebo effect. *Journal of Abnormal Psychology, 89,* 67–78.

Plutchik, R. (1980). *Emotion: A psychoevolutionary synthesis.* New York: Harper & Row.

Pollatsek, A., Rayner, K., & Balota, D. (1986). Inferences about eye movement control from the perceptual span in reading. *Perception and Psychophysics, 2,* 123–130.

Pomerleau, A., Bolduc, D., Malcuit, G., & Cossette, L. (1990). Pink or blue: Environmental gender stereotypes in the first two years of life. *Sex Roles, 22,* 359–367.

Powell, D. A., Milligan, W. L., & Furchtgott, E. (1980). Peripheral autonomic changes accompanying learning and reaction time performance in older people. *Journal of Gerontology, 35,* 57–65.

Powell, K. E., Spain, K. G., Christenson, G. M., & Mollenkamp, M. P. (1986). The status of the 1990 objectives for physical fitness and exercise. *Public Health Reports, 101,* 15–21.

Powers, P. C., & Geen, R. G. (1972). Effects of the behavior and the perceived arousal of a model on instrumental aggression. *Journal of Personality and Social Psychology, 23,* 175–184.

Powers, S. I., Hauser, S. T., & Kilner, L. A. (1989). Adolescent mental health. *American Psychologist, 44,* 200–208.

Powley, T. L. (1977). The ventromedial hypothalamic syndrome, satiety, and a cephalic phase hypothesis. *Psychological Review, 84,* 89–126.

Pratkanis, A. R., Greenwald, A. G., Leippe, M. R., & Baumgardner, M. H. (1988). In search of reliable persuasion effects: 3. The sleeper effect is dead—Long live the sleep effect. *Journal of Personality and Social Psychology, 54,* 203–218.

Premack, D. (1962). Reversibility of the reinforcement relation. *Science, 136,* 255–257.

Premack, D. (1965). Reinforcement theory. In D. Levine (Ed.), *Nebraska Symposium on Motivation* (Vol. 13, pp. 123–180). Lincoln: University of Nebraska Press.

Premack, D. (1971). Language in chimpanzee? *Science, 172,* 808–822.

Prentice-Dunn, S., & Rogers, R. W. (1984). Effects of deindividuating situational cues and aggressive models on subjective deindividuation and aggression. *Journal of Personality and Social Psychology, 39,* 104–113.

Presser, H. B. (1989). Some economic complexities of child care provided by grandmothers. *Journal of Marriage and the Family, 51,* 581–591.

Preti, G., Cutler, W. B., Garcia, C. R., Huggins, G. R., & Lawley, H. (1986). Human axillary secretions influence women's menstrual cycles: The role of donor extract of females. *Hormones and Behavior, 20,* 474–482.

Price, D. D., et al. (1984). A psychophysical analysis of acupuncture analgesia. *Pain, 19,* 27–42.

Prinz, R. N., Vitiello, M. V., Raskind, M. A., & Thorpy, M. J. (1990). Geriatrics: Sleep disorders and aging. *New England Journal of Medicine, 323,* 520–526.

Proshansky, H. M., & O'Hanlon, T. (1977). Environmental psychology: Origins and development. In D. Stokols (Ed.), *Perspectives on environment and behavior: Theory, research, and application.* New York: Plenum Press.

Puffer, S. M. (1987). Prosocial behavior, noncompliant behavior, and work performance among commission salespeople. *Journal of Applied Psychology, 72,* 615–621.

Putnam, W. H. (1979). Hypnosis and distortions in eyewitness memory. *International Journal of Clinical and Experimental Hypnosis, 27,* 437–448.

Quigley, B., Gaes, G. G., & Tedeschi, J. T. (1989). Does asking make a difference? Effects of initiator, possible gain, and risk on attributed altruism. *Journal of Social Psychology, 129,* 259–267.

Quilitch, H. R., & Risley, T. R. (1973). The effects of play materials on social play. *Journal of Applied Behavior Analysis, 6,* 573–578.

Quinsey, V. L. Chaplin, T. C., & Upfold, D. (1984). Sexual arousal to nonsexual violence and sadomasochism themes among rapist and non-sex-offenders. *Journal of Consulting and Clinical Psychology, 52,* 651.

Rabizadeh, S., et al. (1993). Induction of Apoptosis by the low affinity NGF receptor. *Science, 261,* 345–348.

Rafaeli, A. (1989). When clerks meet customers: A test of variables related to emotional expressions on the job. *Journal of Applied Psychology, 74,* 385–393.

Ragins, B. R., & Sundstrom, E. (1989). Gender and power in organizations: A longitudinal perspective. *Psychological Bulletin, 105,* 51–88.

Rahe, R. H. (1989). Recent life change stress and psychological depression. In T. W. Miller (Ed.), *Stressful life events.* Madison, WI: International Universities Press.

Raisman, G., Morris, R. J., & Zhou, C. F. (1987). Specificity in the reinnervation of adult hippocampus by embryonic hippocampal transplants. In F. J. Seil, E. Herbert, & B. M. Carlson (Eds.), *Progress in brain research* (Vol. 71, pp. 325–333). New York: Elsevier Press.

Ramachandran, V. S. (1993). Filling in gaps in perception: Part II. Scotomas and phantom limbs. *Current Directions in Psychological Science, 2,* 56–65.

Rapee, R. (1986). Differential response to hyperventilation in panic disorder and generalized anxiety disorder. *Journal of Abnormal Psychology, 95,* 24–28.

Rappaport, J., (1987). Terms of empowerment/exemplars of prevention: Toward a theory for community psychology. *American Journal of Community Psychology, 2,* 121–148.

Raps, C. S., Reinhard, K. E., Peterson, C., Abramson, L. Y., & Seligman, M. E. P. (1982). Attributional style among depressed patients. *Journal of Abnormal Psychology, 91,* 102–108.

Ravussin, E., Lillioja, S., Knowler, W. C., Christin, L., Freymond, D., Abbott, W. G. H., Boyce, V., Howard, B. V., & Bogardus, C. (1988). Reduced rate of energy expenditure as a risk factor for body-weight gain. *New England Journal of Medicine, 318,* 467–472.

Ray, O. (1983). *Drugs, society, and human behavior* (3rd ed.). St. Louis: Mosby.

Rayner, K. (1993). Eye movements in reading: Recent developments. *Current Directions in Psychological Science, 2,* 81–85.

Rayner, K., & Fisher, D. L. (1987). Letter processing during eye fixations in visual search. *Perception and Psychophysics, 1,* 87–100.

Rayner, K., & Pollatsek, A. (1992). Eye movements and scene perception. *Canadian Journal of Psychology, 46,* 342–376.

Raz, S., & Raz, N. (1990). Structural brain abnormalities in the major psychoses: A quantitative review of the evidence from computerized imaging. *Psychological Bulletin, 208,* 93–108.

Ree, M. J., & Earles, J. A. (1992). Intelligence is the best predictor of job performance. *Current Directions in Psychological Science, 1,* 86–89.

Ree, M. J., & Earles, J. A. (1993). g is to psychology what carbon is to chemistry: 1. A reply to Sternberg and Wagner, McClelland, and Calfee. *Current Directions in Psychological Science, 2,* 11–12.

Reed, C. F. (1984). Terrestrial passage theory of the moon illusion. *Journal of Experimental Psychology: General, 113,* 489–516.

Reed, T. E., & Jensen, A. R. (1992). Conduction velocity in a brain nerve pathway of normal adults correlates with intelligence level. *Intelligence, 16,* 259–262.

Reiger, D. A., Boyd, J. H., Burke, J. D., Rae, D. S., Myers, J. K., Kramer, M., Robins, L. N., George, L. K., Karno, M., & Locke, B. Z. (1988). One-month prevalence of mental disorders in the United States. *Archives of General Psychiatry, 45,* 977–986.

Reis, H. T., & Shaver, P. (1988). Intimacy as an interpersonal process. In S. Duck (Ed.), *Handbook of personal relationships: Theory, relationships, and interventions.* Chichester, England: Wiley.

Reis, S. M. (1989). Reflections on policy affecting the education of gifted and talented students. *American Psychologist, 44,* 399–408.

Reisenzein, R. (1983). The Schachter theory of emotion: Two decades later. *Psychological Bulletin, 94,* 239–264.

Repa, B. K. (1988). Is there life after partnership? *ABA Journal, 74,* 70–75.

Repetti, R. L., Matthews, K. A., & Waldron, I. (1989). Employment and women's health. *American Psychologist, 44,* 1394–1401.

Reppucci, N. D., & Haugaard, J. J. (1989). Prevention of child sexual abuse. *American Psychologist, 44,* 1266–1275.

Rescorla, R. A. (1977). Pavlovian 2nd-order conditioning: Some implications for instrumental behavior. In H. Davis & H. Herwit (Eds.), *Pavlovian-operant interactions.* Hillsdale, NJ: Erlbaum.

Rescorla, R. A. (1978). Some implications of a cognitive perspective on Pavlovian conditioning. In S. H. Hulse, H. Fowler, & W. Honig (Eds.), *Cognitive process in animal behavior.* Hillsdale, NJ: Erlbaum.

Rescorla, R. A. (1988). Pavlovian conditioning: It's not what you think it is. *American Psychologist, 43,* 151–160.

Resnick, S. M. (1992). Positron emission tomography in psychiatric illness. *Psychological Science, 1,* 92–98.

Restle, F. (1970). Moon illusion explained on the basis of relative size. *Science, 167,* 1092–1096.

Rhodes, N., & Wood, W. (1992). Self-esteem and intelligence affect influenceability: The mediating role of message reception. *Psychological Bulletin, 111,* 156–171.

Rice, R. W., McFarlin, D. B. & Bennett, D. E. (1989). Standards of comparison and job satisfaction. *Journal of Applied Psychology, 74,* 591–598.

Richardson, J. L., Dwyer, K., McGuigan, K., Hansen, W. B., Dent, C., Johnson, C. A., Sussman, S. Y., Brannon, B., & Flay, B. (1989). Substance use among eighth-grade students who take care of themselves after school. *Pediatrics, 84,* 556–566.

Richardson, J. T. E., & Zucco, G. M. (1989). Cognition and olfaction: A review. *Psychological Bulletin, 105,* 352–360.

Richardson-Klavehn, A., & Bjork, R. A. (1988). Measures of memory. *Annual Review of Psychology, 39,* 475–544.

Richman, A. L., Miller, P. M., & LeVine, R. A. (1992). Cultural and educational variations in maternal responsiveness. *Developmental Psychology, 28,* 614–621.

Riger, S. (1992). Epistemological debates, feminist voices. *American Psychologist, 47,* 730–740.

Riley, W. T., Treiber, F. A., & Woods, M. G. (1989). Anger and hostility in depression. *Journal of Nervous and Mental Disease, 177,* 668–669.

Ring, K., Wallston, K., & Corey, M. (1970). Mode of debriefing as a factor affecting subjective reaction to a Milgram-type obedience experiment: An ethical inquiry. *Representative Research in Social Psychology, 1,* 67–88.

Rips, L. J. (1990). Reasoning. *Annual Review of Psychology, 41,* 321–353.

Ritter, J. M., & Langlois, J. H. (1988). The role of physical attractiveness in the observation of adult-child interactions: Eye of the beholder or behavioral reality? *Developmental Psychology, 24,* 254–263.

Robberson, M. R., & Rogers, R. W. (1988). Beyond fear appeals: Negative and positive persuasive appeals to health and self-esteem. *Journal of Applied Social Psychology, 18,* 277–287.

Robbins, M., & Meyer, D. (1970). Motivational control of retrograde amnesia. *Journal of Experimental Psychology, 84,* 220–225.

Roberts, G. W. (1988). Immunocytochemistry of neurofibrillary tangles in dementia pugilistica and alzheimer's disease: Evidence for common genesis. *Lancet, II* 1456–1457.

Roberts, T. A. (1991). Gender and the influence of evaluations on self-assessments in achievement settings. *Psychological Bulletin, 109,* 297–308.

Robinson, L. A., Berman, J. S., & Neimeyer, R. A. (1990). Psychotherapy for the treatment of depression: A comprehensive review of controlled outcome research. *Psychological Bulletin, 108,* 30–49.

Rodgers, J. L. (1988). Birth order, SAT, and confluence: Spurious correlations and no causality. *American Psychologist, 43,* 476–477.

Rodin, J. (1981). Current status of the internal-external hypothesis for obesity: What went wrong? *American Psychologist, 36,* 361–372.

Rodin, J. (1986). Aging and health: Effects of the sense of control. *Science, 233,* 1271–1276.

Rodin, J., & Ickovics, J. R. (1990). Women's health. *American Psychologist, 45,* 1018–1034.

Rodin, J., & Salovey, P. (1989). Health psychology. *Annual Review of Psychology, 40,* 533–581.

Rodman, H., Pratto, D. J., & Nelson, R. S. (1985). Child care arrangements and children's functioning: A comparison of self-care and adult-care children. *Developmental Psychology, 21,* 413–418.

Rodman, H., Pratto, D. J., & Nelson, R. S. (1988). Toward a definition of self-care children: A commentary on Steinberg (1986). *Developmental Psychology, 24,* 292–294.

Roehrs, T., Timms, V., Zwyghuizen-Doorenbos, A., & Roth, T. (1989). Sleep extension in sleepy and alert normals. *Sleep, 12,* 449–457.

Roffwarg, H. P., Muzio, J. N., & Dement, W. C. (1966). Ontogenetic development of the human sleep-dream cycle: The prime role of "dreaming sleep" in early life may be in the development of the central nervous system. *Science, 152,* 604–619.

Rogers, C. R. (1951). *Client-centered therapy.* Boston: Houghton Mifflin.

Rogoff, B., & Morelli, G. (1989). Perspectives on children's development form cultural psychology. *American Psychologist, 44,* 343–348.

Romano, S. T., & Bordieri, J. E. (1989). Physical attractiveness stereotypes and students' perceptions of college professors. *Psychological Reports, 64,* 1099–1102.

Rosch, E. (1973). Natural categories. *Cognitive Psychology, 4,* 328–350.

Rosch, E. (1978). Principles of categorization. In E. Rosch & B. B. Lloyd (Eds.), *Cognition and categorization* (pp. 27–48). Hillsdale, NJ: Erlbaum.

Rose, S. D. (1991). The development and practice of group treatment. In M. Hersen, A. E. Kazdin, & A. S. Bellack (Eds.), *The clinical psychology handbook* (2nd ed.). New York: Pergamon Press.

Rosenberg, H. (1993). Prediction of controlled drinking by alcoholics and problem drinkers. *Psychological Bulletin, 113,* 129–139.

Rosenstock, I. M., & Kirscht, J. P. (1979). Why people seek health care. In G. C. Stone, F. Cohen, & N. E. Adler (Eds.), *Health psychology—A handbook.* San Francisco: Jossey-Bass.

Rosenthal, D. (1970). *Genetic theory in abnormal behavior.* New York: McGraw-Hill.

Rosenthal, R., & DePaulo, B. M. (1979). Sex differences in accommodation in nonverbal communication. In R. Rosenthal (Ed.), *Skill in nonverbal communication.* Cambridge, MA: Oelgeschlager, Gunn & Hain.

Rosenthal, R., & Rubin, D. (1982). Further meta-analytic procedures for assessing cognitive gender differences. *Journal of Educational Psychology, 74,* 708–712.

Ross, H. S., & Lollis, S. P. (1987). Communication within infant social games. *Developmental Psychology, 2,* 241–248.

Ross, H. S., & Taylor, H. (1989). Do boys prefer daddy or his physical style of play? *Sex Roles, 20,* 23–26.

Ross, J. G., Saavedra, P. J., Shur, G. H., Winters, F., & Felner, R. D. (1992). The effectiveness of an after-school program for primary grade latchkey students on precursors of substance abuse. *Journal of Community Psychology* (OSAP Special Issue), 22–38.

Ross, L., Bierbrauer, G., & Hoffman, S. (1976). The role of attribution processes in conformity and dissent. *American Psychologist, 31,* 148–157.

Roth, J. D., & Kosslyn, S. M. (1988). Construction of the third dimension in mental imagery. *Cognitive Psychology, 20,* 344–361.

Rothbart, M. K., Taylor, S. B., & Tucker, D. M. (1989). Right-sided facial asymmetry in infant emotional expression. *Neuropsychologia, 27,* 675–687.

Rotter, J. B. (1966). Generalized expectancies for internal versus external control of reinforcement. *Psychological Monographs, 80*(1, Whole No. 609).

Rotter, J. B. (1990). Internal versus external control of reinforcement. *American Psychologist, 45,* 489–493.

Rowland, K. F. (1977). Environmental events predicting death for the elderly. *Psychological Bulletin, 84,* 349–372.

Roy, A., Segal, N. L., Ceterwall, B. S., & Robinette, C. D. (1991). Suicide in twins. *Archives of General Psychiatry, 48,* 29–32.

Ruback, R. B., & Pandey, J. (1991). Crowding, perceived control, and relative power: An analysis of households in India. *Journal of Applied Social Psychology, 21,* 315–344.

Rubin, R. T., Villanueva-Meyer, J., Ananth, J., Trajmar, P. G., & Mena, I. (1992). Regional xenon 133 cerebral blood flow and cerebral technetium 99m HMPAO uptake in unmedicated patients with obsessive-compulsive disorder and matched normal control subjects. *Archives of General Psychiatry, 49,* 695–702.

Rumbaugh, D. M., Gill, T. V., & Von Glaserfeld, E. D. (1973). Reading and sentence completion by a chimpanzee (PAN). *Science, 182,* 731–733.

Rumbaugh, D. M., & Savage-Rumbaugh, S. (1978). Chimpanzee language research: Status and potential. *Behavior Research Methods and Instrumentation, 10,* 119–131.

Rumbaugh, D. M., Savage-Rumbaugh, S., & Hegel, M. T. (1987). Summation in the chimpanzee (Pan troglodytes). *Journal of Experimental Psychology: Animal Behavior Processes, 13,* 107–115.

Russell, J. A. (1991). Culture and the categorization of emotions. *Psychological Bulletin, 110,* 426–450.

Russo, N. F., & Denmark, F. L. (1987). Contributions of women to psychology. *Annual Review of Psychology, 38,* 279–299.

Rustemli, A. (1991). Crowding effects of density and interpersonal distance. *Journal of Social Psychology, 132,* 51–58.

Ryan, R. M., Mims, V., & Koestner, R. (1983). Relation of reward contingency and interpersonal context to intrinsic motivation: A review and test using cognitive evaluation theory. *Journal of Personality and Social Psychology, 45,* 736–750.

Sadock, V. (1980). Special areas of interest. In H. Kaplan, A. Freeman, & B. Sadock (Eds.), *Comprehensive textbook of psychiatry* (Vol. 3). Baltimore: Williams & Wilkins.

Sakitt, B., & Long, G. M. (1979). Cones determine subjective offset of a stimulus but rods determine total persistence. *Vision Research, 19,* 1439–1443.

Salminen, S., & Glad, T. (1992). The role of gender in helping behavior. *The Journal of Social Psychology, 132,* 131–133.

Salt, R. E. (1991). Affectionate touch between fathers and preadolescent sons. *Journal of Marriage and the Family, 53,* 545–554.

Salzberg, H. C., & DePiano, F. A. (1980). Hypnotizability and task motivating suggestions: A further look at how they affect performance. *International Journal of Clinical and Experimental Hypnosis, 28,* 261–271.

Sandahl, C., & Ronnberg, S. (1990). Brief group psychotherapy in relapse prevention for alcohol dependent patients. *International Journal of Group Psychotherapy, 40,* 453–476.

Sande, G. N., Goethals, G. R., & Radloff, C. E. (1988). Perceiving one's own traits and others': The multifaceted self. *Journal of Personality and Social Psychology, 54,* 13–20.

Sanders, G. S., & Simmons, W. L. (1983). Use of hypnosis to enhance eyewitness accuracy: Does it work? *Journal of Applied Psychology, 68,* 70–77.

Sanders, R. J. (1985). Teaching apes to ape language: Explaining the imitative and nonimitative signing of a chimpanzee (Pan troglodytes). *Journal of Comparative Psychology, 99,* 197–210.

Sarason, I. G., & Sarason, B. R. (1987). *Abnormal psychology: The problem of maladaptive behavior* (5th ed.). Englewood Cliffs, NJ: Prentice-Hall.

Sartorious, N. (1982). Epidemiology and mental health policy. In M. O. Wagenfeld, P. V. Lemkau, & B. Justice (Eds.), *Public mental health: Perspectives and prospects.* Beverly Hills, CA: Sage Publications.

Sattler, J. M. (1992). *Assessment of children: Revised and updated* (3rd ed.). San Diego: Jerome M. Sattler.

Savage-Rumbaugh, S. (1987). A new look at ape language: Comprehension of vocal speech and syntax. In R. A. Dienstbier & D. W. Leger (Eds.), *Comparative perspectives in modern psychology.* Lincoln: University of Nebraska Press.

Savage-Rumbaugh, S., Pate, J. L., Lawson, J., Smith, S. T., & Rosenbaum, S. (1983). Can a chimpanzee make a statement? *Journal of Experimental Psychology: General, 112,* 457–492.

Sawicki, S. (1988). Effective crisis intervention. *Adolescence, 23,* 83–88.

Scarr, S. (1992). Developmental theories for the 1990s: Development and individual differences. *Child Development, 63,* 1–19.

Scarr, S., & Eisenberg, M. (1993). Child care research: Issues, perspectives, and results. *Annual Review of Psychology, 44,* 613–644.

Scarr, S., Phillips, D., & McCartney, K. (1990). Facts, fantasies, and the future of child care in the United States. *Psychological Science, 1,* 26–35.

Scarr, S., & Weinberg, R. A. (1983). The Minnesota adoption studies: Genetic differences and malleability. *Child Development, 54,* 260–267.

Schachter, S., Goldman, R., & Gordon, A. (1968). Effects of fear, food deprivation, and obesity on eating. *Journal of Personality and Social Psychology, 10,* 91–97.

Schachter, S., & Singer, J. E. (1962). Cognitive, social, and physiological determinants of emotional state. *Psychological Review, 69,* 379–399.

Schacter, D. L. (1992). Understanding implicit memory. *American Psychologist, 47,* 559–569.

Schacter, D. L., Kihlstrom, J. F., Kihlstrom, L. C., & Berren, M. B. (1989). Autobiographical memory in a case of multiple personality disorder. *Journal of Abnormal Psychology, 98,* 508–514.

Schaie, K. W. (1993). Ageist language in psychological research. *American Psychologist, 48,* 49–51.

Schaie, K. W., & Willis, S. L. (1986). *Adult development and aging* (2nd ed.). Boston: Little, Brown.

Scheier, M. F., & Carver, C. S. (1993). On the power of positive thinking: The benefits of being optimistic. *Current Directions in Psychological Science, 2,* 26–30.

Scherer, D. G., & Reppucci, N. D. (1988). Adolescents' capacities to provide voluntary informed consent. *Law and Human Behavior, 12,* 123–141.

Schiff, M., Duyme, M., Dumaret, A., & Tomkiewicz, S. (1982). How much could we boost scholastic achievement and IQ scores? A direct answer from a French adoption study. *Cognition, 12,* 165–196.

Schindler, P. J., Moely, B. E., & Frank, A. L. (1987). Time in day care and social participation of young children. *Development Psychology, 2,* 255–261.

Schmidt, D. F., & Boland, S. M. (1986). Structure of perceptions of older adults: Evidence for multiple stereotypes. *Psychology and Aging, 1,* 255–260.

Schmidt, F. L., & Hunter, J. E. (1992). Development of a causal model of processes determining job performance. *Current Directions in Psychological Science, 1,* 89–92.

Schmidt, F. L., Ones, D. S., & Hunter, J. E. (1992). Personnel selection. *Annual Review of Psychology, 43,* 627–670.

Schmidt, S. R. (1991). Can we have a distinctive theory of memory? *Memory and Cognition, 19,* 523–542.

Schneider, W., & Detweiler, M. (1987). A connectionist/control, architecture, and working memory. In G. H. Bower (Ed.), *The psychology of learning and motivation.* San Diego: Academic Press.

Schuman, M. (1980). The psychophysiological model of meditation and altered states of consciousness: A critical review. In J. M. Davidson & R. J. Davidson. (Eds.), *The psychobiology of consciousness.* New York: Plenum Press.

Schutte, N. S., Malouff, J. M., Post-Gorden, J. C., & Rodasta, A. L. (1988). Effects of playing videogames on children's aggressive and other behaviors. *Journal of Applied Social Psychology, 18,* 454–460.

Schwartz, J. C., & Shaver, P. (1987). Emotions and emotion knowledge in interpersonal relations. *Advances in Personal Relationships, 1,* 197–241.

Schwartz, P. (1983). Length of day-care attendance and attachment behavior in eighteen-month-old infants. *Child Development, 54,* 1073–1078.

Schwartzman, A. E., Gold, D., Andres, D., Arbuckle, T. Y., & Chaikelson, J. (1987). Stability of intelligence: A 40-year follow-up. *Canadian Journal of Psychology, 41,* 244–256.

Schwarz, L. M., Foa, U. G., & Foa, E. B. (1983). Multichannel non-verbal communication: Evidence for combinatory rules. *Journal of Personality and Social Psychology, 45,* 274–281.

Schweickert, R., & Boruff, B. (1986). Short-term memory capacity: Magic number or magic spell? *Journal of Experimental Psychology: Learning, Memory, and Cognition, 12,* 419–425.

Seeman, J. (1989). Toward a model of positive health. *American Psycholgist, 44,* 1099–1109.

Segal, L. (1991). Brief therapy: The MRI approach. In A. S. Gurman & D. P. Kniskern (Eds.), *Handbook of family therapy* (Vol. 2). New York: Brunner/Mazel.

Seif, M. N., & Atkins, A. L. (1979). Some defensive and cognitive aspects of phobias. *Journal of Abnormal Psychology, 88,* 42–51.

Sejnowski, T. J., Koch, C., & Churchland, P. S. (1988). Computational neuroscience. *Science, 241* 1299–1306.

Seligman, M. E. P. (1975). *Helplessness.* San Francisco: Freeman.

Seligman, M. E. P. (1976). *Learned helplessness and depression in animals and humans.* Morristown, NJ: General Learning Press.

Seligman, M. E. P. (1988, August). *Learned helplessness.* G. Stanley Hall lecture at the American Psychological Association convention, Atlanta.

Seligman, M. E. P. (1991). *Learned optimism.* New York: Knopf.

Selkoe, D. J. (1992, September). Aging brain, aging mind. *Scientific American,* pp. 135–142.

Selye, H. (1956). *The stress of life.* New York: McGraw-Hill.

Selye, H. (1976). *Stress in health and disease.* London: Butterworth.

Sengel, R. A., & Lovallo, W. R. (1983). Effects of cueing on immediate and recent memory in schizophrenics. *Journal of Nervous and Mental Disease, 171,* 426–430.

Shamir, B. (1992). Attribution of influence and charisma to the leader: The romance of leadership revisited. *Journal of Applied Social Psychology, 22,* 386–407.

Shanab, M. E., & Yahya, K. A. (1978). A cross-cultural study of obedience. *Bulletin of the Psychonomic Society, 11,* 267–269.

Shatz, C. J. (1992, September). The developing brain. *Scientific American,* pp. 61–67.

Shatz, M., & Gelman, R. (1973). The development of communication skills: Modifications in the speech of young children as a function of listener. *Monographs of the Society for Research in Child Development, 38*(2, Serial No. 152).

Shaver, P. R., Schwartz, J., Kirson, D., & O'Connor, C. (1987). Emotion knowledge: Further exploration of a prototype approach. *Journal of Personality and Social Psychology, 52,* 1061–1086.

Shaywitz, S. E., Escobar, M. D., Shaywitz, B. A., Fletcher, J. M., & Makuch, R. (1992). Evidence that dyslexia may represent the lower tail of a normal distribution of reading ability. *New England Journal of Medicine, 326,* 145–150.

Shedler, J., & Block, J. (1990). Adolescent drug use and psychological health. *American Psychologist, 45,* 612–630.

Shepard, S., & Metzler, D. (1988). Mental rotation: Effects of dimensionality of objects and type of task. *Journal of Experimental Psychology: Human Perception and Performance, 14,* 3–11.

Shepperd, J. A. (1993). Productivity loss in performance groups: A motivation analysis. *Psychological Bulletin, 113,* 67–81.

Sheridan, M. S. (1985). Things that go beep in the night: Home monitoring for apnea. *Health and Social Work,* 63–70.

Sherman, M., & Key, C. B. (1932). The intelligence of isolated mountain children. *Child Development, 3,* 279–290.

Shimamura, A. P., & Squire, L. R. (1986). Memory and metamemory: A study of the feeling-of-knowing phenomenon in amnesic patients. *Journal of Experimental Psychology: Learning, Memory, and Cognition, 12,* 452–460.

Shimberg, M. E. (1929). An investigation into the validity of norms with special reference to urban and rural groups. *Archives of Psychology, 104,* 1–62.

Shisslak, C. M., Crago, M., Neal, M. E. & Swain (1987). Primary prevention of eating disorders. *Journal of Consulting and Clinical Psychology, 55,* 660–667.

Shneidman, E. (1989). The Indian summer of life: A preliminary study of septuagenarians. *American Psychologist, 44,* 684–694.

Shore, J. H., Vollmer, W. M., & Tatum, E. L. (1989). Community patterns of posttraumatic stress disorders. *Journal of Nervous and Mental Disease, 177,* 681–685.

Shotland, R. L., & Heinold, W. D. (1985). Interpersonal relations and group processes: Bystander response to arterial bleeding—Helping skills, the decision-making process, and differentiating the helping response. *Journal of Personality and Social Psychology, 49,* 347–456.

Shute, V. J., Pellegrino, J. W., Hubert, L., & Reynolds, R. W. (1983). The relationship between androgen levels and human spatial abilities. *Bulletin of the Psychonomic Society, 21,* 465–468.

Siegel, E. F. (1979). Control of phantom limb pain by hypnosis. *American Journal of Clinical Hypnosis, 21,* 285–286.

Siegel, J. M. (1990). Stressful life events and use of physician services among the elderly: The moderating role of pet ownership. *Journal of Personality and Social Psychology, 58,* 1081–1086.

Siegel, S. (1988). State dependent learning and morphine tolerance. *Behavioral Neuroscience, 102,* 228–232.

Silverman, L. H. (1983). The subliminal psychodynamic activation method: Overview and comprehensive listing of studies. In J. Masling (Ed.), *Empirical studies of psychoanalytic theories* (Vol. 1, pp. 69–100). Hillsboro, NJ: Erlbaum.

Simon, H. A. (1992). What is an "explanation" of behavior? *Psychological Science, 3,* 150–161.

Simonton, D. K. (1988). Age and outstanding achievement: What do we know after a century of research? *Psychological Bulletin, 104,* 251–267.

Simpson, J. A. (1990). Influence of attachment styles on romantic relationships. *Journal of Personality and Social Psychology, 59,* 971–980.

Singer, D. G., & Singer, J. L. (1990). *The house of make-believe.* Cambridge, MA: Harvard University Press.

Singer, L. M., Brodzinsky, D. M., Ramsay, D., Steir, M., & Waters, E. (1985). Mother-infant attachment in adoptive families. *Child Development, 56,* 1543–1551.

Skinner, B. F. (1948). Superstition in the pigeon. *Journal of Experimental Psychology, 38,* 168–172.

Skinner, B. F. (1988, June). Skinner joins aversives debate. *APA Monitor,* p. 22.

Skinner, B. F. (1989). The origins of cognitive thought. *American Psychologist, 44,* 13–18.

Skinner, B. F. (1990). Can psychology be a science of mind? *American Psychologist, 45,* 1206–1210.

Slaikeu, K. A. (1990). *Crisis intervention* (2nd ed.). Boston: Allyn and Bacon.

Slobin, D. I. (1975). On the nature of talk to children. In E. H. Lenneberg & E. Lenneberg (Eds.), *Foundations of language development: A multidisciplinary approach* (Vol. 1). New York: Academic Press.

Smith, C. A. (1989). Dimensions of appraisal and physiological response in emotion. *Journal of Personality and Social Psychology, 56,* 339–353.

Smith, E. P., & Davidson, W. S., II (1992). Mentoring and the development of African-American graduate students. *Journal of College Student Development, 33,* 531–539.

Smith, M. C. (1983). Hypnotic memory enhancement of witnesses: Does it work? *Psychological Bulletin, 94,* 387–407.

Smith, M. L., Glass, G. V., & Miller, T. I. (1980). *The benefits of psychotherapy.* Baltimore: Johns Hopkins University Press.

Smyser, A. A. (1982). Hospices: Their humanistic and economic value. *American Psychologist, 37,* 1260–1262.

Snowden, L. R. (1987). The peculiar successes of community psychology: Service delivery to ethnic minorities and the poor. *American Journal of Community Psychology, 5,* 575–586.

Snowden, L. R., & Cheung, F. K. (1990). Use of inpatient mental health services by members of ethnic minority groups. *American Psychologist, 45,* 347–355.

Snyder, C. R., & Higgins, R. L. (1988). Excuses: Their effective role in the negotiation of reality. *Psychological Bulletin, 104,* 23–35.

Snyder, D. K., Wills, R. M., & Grady-Fletcher, A. (1991). Long-term effectiveness of behavioral versus insight-oriented marital therapy: A 4-year follow-up study. *Journal of Consulting and Clinical Psychology, 59,* 138–141.

Snyder, S. H. (1980). Brain peptides as neurotransmitters. *Science, 209,* 976–983.

Snyderman, M., & Rothman, S. (1987). Survey of expert opinion on intelligence and aptitude testing. *American Psychologist, 42,* 137–144.

Sobal, J., & Stunkard, A. J. (1989). Socioeconomic status and obesity: A review of the literature. *Psychological Bulletin, 105,* 260–275.

Sobell, M. B., & Sobell, L. C. (1982). Controlled drinking: A concept coming of age. In K. R., Blanstein & J. Polivy (Eds.), *Self-control and self-modification of emotional behavior.* New York: Plenum Press.

Sogon, S., & Masutani, M. (1989). Identification of emotion from body movements: A cross-cultural study of Americans and Japanese. *Psychological Reports, 65,* 35–46.

Solso, R. L. (1979). *Cognitive psychology.* New York: Harcourt Brace Jovanich.

Somer, E. (1990). Brief simultaneous couple hypnotherapy with a rape victim and her spouse: A brief communication. *The International Journal of Clinical and Experimental Hypnosis, 38,* 1–5.

Sorce, J. F., & Emde, R. N. (1981). Mother's presence is not enough: Effect of emotional availability on infant exploration. *Developmental Psychology, 17,* 737–745.

Sorce, J. F., Emde, R. N., Campos, J., & Klinnert, M. D. (1985). Maternal emotional signaling: Its effect on the visual cliff behavior of 1-year-olds. *Developmental Psychology, 21,* 195–200.

Spangler, W. D. (1992). Validity of questionnaire and TAT measures of need for achievement: Two meta-analyses. *Psychological Bulletin, 112,* (1), 140–154.

Spanos, N. P., Lush, N. I., & Gwynn, M. I. (1989). Cognitive skill-training enhancement of hypnotizability: Generalization effects and trance logic responding. *Journal of Personality and Social Psychology, 56,* 795–804.

Sperling, G. (1960). The information available in brief visual presentations. *Psychological Monographs, 15,* 201–293.

Sperry, R. W. (1985). Consciousness, personal identity, and the divided brain. In D. F. Benson & E. Zaidel (Eds.), *The dual brain: Hemispheric specialization in humans* (pp. 11–26). New York: Guilford.

Speth, C., & Brown, R. (1990). Effects of college students' learning styles and gender on their test preparation strategies. *Applied Cognitive Psychology, 4,* 189–202.

Sporer, S. L. (1993). Eyewitness identification accuracy, confidence, and decision times in simultaneous and sequential lineups. *Journal of Applied Psychology, 78,* 22–33.

Sprecher, S., Aron, A., Hatfield, E., Cortese, A., Potapova, E., & Levitskaya, A. (1992, July). *Love: American style, Russian style, and Japanese style.* Paper presented at the Sixth International Conference on Personal Relationships; Orono, Maine.

Sprecher, S., McKinney, K., & Orbuch, T. L. (1987). Has the double standard disappeared? An experimental test. *Social Psychology Quarterly, 50,* 24–31.

Spring, B., Chiodo, J., & Bowen, D. J. (1987). Carbohydrates, tryptophan, and behavior: A methodological review. *Psychological Bulletin, 102,* 234–256.

Squire, L. R. (1987). *Memory and brain.* New York: Oxford University Press.

Sroufe, L. A., & Waters, E. (1977). Attachment as an organizational construct. *Child Development, 48,* 1184–1199.

Stagner, R. (1988). *A history of psychological theories.* New York: Macmillan.

Standing, L. (1973). Learning 10,000 pictures. *Quarterly Journal of Experimental Psychology, 25,* 207–222.

Standing, L., Conezio, J., & Haber, R. N. (1970). Perception and memory for pictures: Single trial learning of 2500 visual stimuli. *Psychonomic Science, 19,* 73–74.

Starkey, P. (1992). The early development of numerical reasoning. *Cognition, 43,* 93–126.

Stasson, M., & Fishbein, M. (1990). The relation between perceived risk and preventive action: A within-subject analysis of perceived driving risk and intentions to wear seatbelts. *Journal of Applied Social Psychology, 20,* 1541–1557.

Staszewski, J. J. (1987). The psychological reality of retrieval structures: An investigation of expert knowledge (Doctoral dissertation, Cornell University, 1987). *Dissertation Abstracts International, 48,* 2168B.

Staszewski, J. J. (1988). Skilled memory and expert mental calculation. In M. T. H. Chi, R. Glaser, & M. J. Farr (Eds.), *The nature of expertise.* Hillsdale, NJ: Erlbaum.

Steblay, N. M. (1987). Helping behavior in rural and urban environments: A meta-analysis. *Psychological Bulletin, 102,* 346–356.

Steele, C. M. (1975). Name-calling and compliance. *Journal of Personality and Social Psychology, 31,* 261–269.

Steele, C. M., & Josephs, R. A. (1990). Alcohol myopia. *American Psychologist, 45,* 921–933.

Stein, M. I. (1974). *Stimulating creativity.* New York: Academic Press.

Steinberg, L., Dornbusch, S. M., & Brown, B. B. (1992). Ethnic difference in adolescent achievement. *American Psychologist, 47,* 723–729.

Steiner, D. D., & Rain, J. S. (1989). Immediate and delayed primacy and recency effects in performance evaluation. *Journal of Applied Psychology, 74,* 136–142.

Steiner, I. D. (1982). Heuristic models of groupthink. In M. Brandstatter, J. H. Davis, & G. Stocker-Kreichgauer (Eds.), *Group decision making.* New York: Academic Press.

Stephan, C. W., & Langlois, J. H. (1984). Baby beautiful: Adult attributions of infant competence as a function of infant attractiveness. *Child Development, 55,* 576–585.

Stephenson, J. S. (1985). *Death, grief, and mourning: individual and social realities.* New York: Macmillan.

Sternberg, R. J. (1984). The Kaufman Assessment Battery for Children: An information-processing analysis and critique. *Journal of Special Education, 18,* 269–279.

Sternberg, R. J. (1985). *Beyond IQ.* Cambridge, England: Cambridge University Press.

Sternberg, R. J. (1986a). *Intelligence applied: Understanding and increasing your intellectual skills.* New York: Harcourt Brace Jovanovich.

Sternberg, R. J. (1986b). A triangular theory of love. *Psychological Review, 93,* 119–135.

Sternberg, R. J., & Detterman, D. L. (Eds.). (1986). *What is intelligence? Contemporary viewpoints on its nature and definition.* Norword, NJ: Ablex Publishing.

Sternberg, R. J., & Wagner, R. K. (1993). The g-ocentric view of intelligence and job performance is wrong. *Current Directions in Psychological Science, 2,* 1–4.

Stets, J. E., & Pirog-Good, M. A. (1989). Sexual aggression and control in dating relationships. *Journal of Applied Social Psychology, 19,* 1392–1412.

Stimpson, D., Jensen, L., & Neff, W. (1992). Cross-cultural gender differences in preference for a caring morality. *Journal of Social Psychology, 132,* 317–322.

Stitzer, M. L. (1988). Drug abuse in methadone patients reduced when rewards/punishments clear. *Alcohol, Drug Abuse, and Mental Health, 14,* 1.

Stivers, C. (1988). Adolescent suicide: An overview. *Marriage and Family Review, 12,* 135–142.

Stone, M. H. (1980). *The borderline syndromes.* New York: McGraw-Hill.

Strayer, D.L, & Kramer, A. R. (1990). Attentional requirements of automatic and controlled processing. *Journal of Experimental Psychology: Learning, Memory, and Cognition, 16,* 67–82.

Streissguth, A. P., Barr, H. M., & Martin, D. C. (1983). Maternal alcohol use and neonatal habituation assessed with the Brazelton Scale. *Child Development, 54,* 1109–1118.

Streissguth, A. P., Barr, H. M., Sampson, P. D., Darby, B. L., & Martin, D. C. (1989). IQ at age 4 in relation to maternal alcohol use and smoking during pregnancy. *Developmental Psychology, 25,* 3–11.

Stricker, G. (1992). The relationship of research to clinical practice. *American Psychologist, 47,* 543–549.

Strickland, B. R. (1988). Clinical psychology comes of age. *American Psychologist, 43,* 104–107.

Strickland, B. R. (1989). Internal-external control expectancies: From contingency to creativity. *American Psychologist, 44,* 1–12.

Strickland, B. R. (1992). Women and depression. *Psychological Science, 1,* 132–135.

Striegel-Moore, R. H., Silberstein, L. R., & Rodin, J. (1986). Toward an understanding of risk factors for bulimia. *American Psychologist, 41,* 246–263.

Striegel-Moore, R. H., Silberstein, L. R., & Robin, J. (1993). The social self in bulimia nervosa: Public self-consciousness, social anxiety, and perceived fraudulence. *Journal of Abnormal Psychology, 102,* 297–303.

Stroop, J. R. (1935). Studies of interference in serial verbal reactions. *Journal of Experimental Psychology, 18,* 643–662.

Strughold, H. (1924). Ueber die Dichte und Schwellen der Smerzpunkete der Epidermis in der verschiedenen Korperregionen. *Z. Biol., 80,* 367–380.

Stuart, E. W., Shimp, T. A., & Engle, R. W. (1987). Classical conditioning of consumer attitudes: Four experiments in an advertising context. *Journal of Consumer Research, 14,* 334–349.

Stunkard, A., Coll, M., Lundquist, S., & Meyers, A. (1980). Obesity and eating style. *Archives of General Psychiatry, 37,* 1127–1129.

Suarez, E. C., & Williams, R. B. (1989). Situational determinants of cardiovascular and emotional reactivity in high and low hostile men. *Psychosomatic Medicine, 51*, 404–418.

Suddath, R. L., Christinson, G. W., Torrey, E. F., Casanova, M. F., & Weinberger, D. R. (1990). Anatomical abnormalities in the brains of monozygotic twins discordant for schizophrenia. *New England Journal of Medicine, 322*, 789–794.

Sue, S. (1988). Psychotherapeutic services for ethnic minorities. *American Psychologist, 43*, 301–308.

Sue, S. (1991). Ethnicity and culture in psychological research and practice. In J. D. Goodchilds (Ed.), *Psychological perspectives on human diversity in America*. Washington, DC: American Psychological Association.

Suedfeld, P. (1990). Restricted environmental stimulation and smoking cessation: A 15-year progress report. *International Journal of the Addictions, 25*, 861–888.

Sugarman, D. B., & Hotaling, G. T. (1989). Violent men in intimate relationships: An analysis of risk markers. *Journal of Applied Social Psychology, 19*, 1034–1048.

Suls, J., & Wan, C. K. (1989a). Effects of sensory and procedural information on coping with stressful medical procedures and pain: A meta-analysis. *Journal of Consulting and Clinical Psychology, 57*, 372–379.

Suls, J., & Wan, C. K. (1989b). The relation between Type A behavior and chronic emotional distress: A meta-analysis. *Journal of Personality and Social Psychology, 57*, 503–512.

Sutker, P. B., & Allain, A. N. (1988). Issues in personality conceptualizations of addictive behaviors. *Journal of Consulting and Clinical Psychology, 56*, 172–182.

Swets, J. A. (1992). The science of choosing the right decision threshold in high-stakes diagnostics. *American Psychologist, 47*, 522–532.

Swim, J., Borgida, E., Maruyama, G., & Myers, D. G. (1989). Joan McKay versus John McKay: Do gender stereotypes bias evaluations? *Psychological Bulletin, 105*, 409–429.

Szucko, J. J., & Kleinmuntz, B. (1981). Statistical versus clinical lie detection. *American Psychologist, 36*, 488–496.

Szymanski, K., & Harkins, S. G. (1987). Social loafing and self-evaluation with a social standard. *Journal of Personality and Social Psychology, 53*, 891–897.

Tagiuri, R. (1968). Person perception. In G. Lindzey & E. Aronson (Eds.), *The handbook of social psychology*. Reading, MA: Addison-Wesley.

Taylor, S. E., Kemeny, M. E., Aspinwall, L. G., Schneider, S. G., Rodriguez, R., & Herbert, M. (1992). Optimism, coping, psychological distress, and high-risk sexual behavior among men at risk for acquired immunodeficiency syndrome (AIDS). *Journal of Personality and Social Psychology, 63*, 460–473.

Taylor, S. H. (1990). Health psychology. *American Psychologist, 45*, 40–50.

Teevan, R. C., & McGhee, P. E. (1972). Childhood development of fear of failure motivation. *Journal of Personality and Social Psychology, 21*, 345–348.

Tellegen, A., Lykken, D. J., Bouchard, T. J., Jr., Wilcox, K. J., Segal, N. L., & Rich, S. (1988). Personality similarity in twins reared apart and together. *Journal of Personality and Social Psychology, 54*, 1031–1039.

Tennen, H., & Affleck, G. (1990). Blaming others for threatening events. *Psychological Bulletin, 108*, 209–232.

Tennov, D. (1981). *Love and limerance*. Briarcliff Manor, NY: Stein & Day.

Terrace, H. S. (1979, November). How Nim Chimpski changed my mind. *Psychology Today*, pp. 65–76.

Terrace, H. S. (1980). *Nim*. New York: Knopf.

Terrace, H. S. (1985). In the beginning was the "name." *American Psychologist, 40*, 1011–1028.

Teske, J. A. (1988). Seeing her looking at you: Acquaintance and variation in the judgment of gaze depth. *American Journal of Psychology, 101*, 239–257.

Theorell, T., Svensson, J., Knox, S., Waller, D., & Alvarez, M. (1986). Young men with high blood pressure report few recent life events. *Journal of Psychosomatic Research, 30*, 243–249.

Thompson, R. F. (1991). Are memory traces localized or distributed? *Neuropsychologia, 29*, 571–582.

Thorkildsen, T. A. (1989). Justice in the classroom: The student's view. *Child Development, 60*, 323–334.

Tice, D. M., & Baumeister, R. F. (1985). Masculinity inhibits helping in emergencies: Personality does predict the bystander effect. *Journal of Personality and Social Psychology, 49*, 420–428.

Tilley, A., & Warren, P. (1983). Retrieval from semantic memory at different times of day. *Journal of Experimental Psychology: Learning, Memory, and Cognition, 9*, 718–724.

Timberlake, W., & Farmer-Dougan, V. A. (1991). Reinforcement in applied settings: Figuring out ahead of time what will work. *Psychological Bulletin, 110*, 379–391.

Titchener, E. B. (1898). *A primer of psychology*. New York: Macmillan.

Tjosvold, D. (1987). Participation: A close look at its dynamics. *Journal of Management, 13*, 739–750.

Tjosvold, D., & Chia, L. C. (1989). Conflict between managers and workers: The role of cooperation and competition. *Journal of Social Psychology, 129*, 235–247.

Travis, C. B. (1988). *Women and health psychology: Biomedical issues*. Hillsdale, NJ: Erlbaum.

Treisman, A. M. (1969). Strategies and models of selective attention. *Psychological Review, 76*, 282–295.

Trickett, P. K., & Putnam, F. W. (1993). Impact of child sexual abuse on females: Toward a developmental, psychobiological integration. *Psychological Science, 4*, 81–87.

Trickett, P. K., & Susman, E. J. (1988). Parental perceptions of child-rearing practices in physically abusive and nonabusive families. *Developmental Psychology, 24*, 270–276.

Trites, D., Galbraith, F. D., Sturdavent, M., & Leckwart, J. F. (1970). Influence of nursing-unit design on the activities and subjective feelings of nursing personnel. *Environment and Behavior, 2*, 203–234.

Tronick, E. Z., & Cohn, J. F. (1989). Infant-mother face-to-face interaction: Age and gender differences in coordination and the occurrence of miscoordination. *Child Development, 60*, 85–92.

Tsai, M., & Uemura, A. (1988). Asian Americans: The struggles, the conflicts, and the successes. In P. Bronstein & K. Quina (Eds.), *Teaching a psychology of people*. Washington, DC: American Psychological Association.

Tsuang, M. T., & Faraone, S. V. (1990). *The genetics of mood disorders*. Baltimore: Johns Hopkins University Press.

Tsuang, M. T., & Vandermey, R. (1980). *Genes and the mind*. New York: Oxford University Press.

Tulving, E. (1972). Episodic and semantic memory. In E. Tulving & W. Donaldson (Eds.), *Organization and memory*. New York: Academic Press.

Tulving, E. (1991). Memory research is not a zero-sum game. *American Psychologist, 46*, 41–42.

Tulving, E. (1993). What is episodic memory? *Current Directions in Psychological Science, 2*, 67–70.

Turk, D. C. (1978). Cognitive behavioral techniques on the management of pain. In J. P. Foreyt & D. J. Rathgen (Eds.), *Cognitive behavior therapy: Research and application*. New York: Plenum Press.

Turk, D. C., Meichenbaum, D., & Genest, M. (1983). *Pain and behavioral medicine: A cognitive-behavioral perspective*. New York: Guilford.

Turkheimer, E. (1991). Individual and group differences in adoption studies of IQ. *Psychological Bulletin, 110*, 392–405.

Turner, S. M., Beidel, D. C., & Nathan, R. S. (1985). Biological factors in obsessive-compulsive disorders. *Psychological Bulletin, 97*, 430–450.

Turner, T. J., & Ortony, A. (1992). Basic emotions: Can conflicting criteria converge? *Psychological Review, 99*, 566–571.

Turrisi, R., & Jaccard, J. (1991). Judgment processes relevant to drunk driving. *Journal of Applied Social Psychology, 21*, 89–118.

Tversky, A., & Kahneman, D. (1973). Availability: A heuristic for judging frequency and probability. *Cognitive Psychology, 4*, 207–232.

Tybout, A. M., & Scott, C. A. (1983). Availability of well-defined internal knowledge and the attitude formation process: Information aggregation versus self-perception. *Journal of Personality and Social Psychology, 44*, 474–491.

Umberson, D., Wortman, C. B., & Kessler, R. C. (1992). Widowhood and depression: Explaining long-term gender differences in vulnerability. *Journal of Health and Social Behavior, 33*, 10–24.

U.S. Bureau of the Census. *See* Bureau of the Census.

U.S. Department of Health and Human Services (1986). *Suicide*. Rockville, MD: National Institute of Mental Health.

U.S. Department of Health and Human Services (1988). *Facts from the 1987 national high school senior survey*. Rockville, MD: Alcohol, Drug Abuse, and Mental Health Administration.

U.S. Department of Health and Human Services (1989a, May). Drug use by high school seniors lowest since 1975. *ADAMHA News*, p. 10.

U.S. Department of Health and Human Services (1989b). *Illicit drug use in U.S. shows steep drop—Except cocaine addiction*. Rockville, MD: Alcohol, Drug Abuse, and Mental Health Administration.

U.S. Department of Health and Human Services (1989c). *Latest ADAMHA research on AIDS reported at Montreal conference*. Rockville, MD: Alcohol, Drug Abuse, and Mental Health Administration.

U.S. Department of Health and Human Services (1989d). *Reducing the health consequences of smoking: 25 years of progress—A report of the Surgeon General*. (DHHS Publication No. [CDC] 89-8411). Washington, DC: Centers for Disease Control, Center for Chronic Disease Prevention and Health Promotion, Office on Smoking and Health.

U.S. Department of Health and Human Services (1992). *Identifying the needs of drug-affected children: Public policy issues*. Rockville, MD: Office for Substance Abuse Prevention.

Usdin, G., & Hofling, C. K. (1978). *Aging: The process and the people*. New York: Brunner/Mazel.

Vaillant, G. E., & Milofsky, E. S. (1982). The etiology of alcoholism: A prospective view. *American Psychologist, 37*, 494–503.

Valins, S. (1966). Cognitive effects of false heart-rate feedback. *Journal of Personality and Social Psychology, 4*, 400–408.

Valins, S., & Baum, A. (1973). Residential group size, social interaction, and crowding. *Environment and Behavior, 5*, 421–435.

Vandell, D. L., Henderson, V. K., & Wilson, K. S. (1988). A longitudinal study of children with day-care experiences of varying quality. *Child Development, 59*, 1286–1292.

Vandell, D. L., & Ramanan, J. (1991). Children of the national longitudinal survey of youth: Choices in after-school care and child development. *Developmental Psychology, 27,* 637–643.

Vernon, P. (1979). *Intelligence: Heredity and environment.* San Francisco: Freeman.

Vernon, P. (1991). Studying intelligence the hard way. *Intelligence, 15,* 389–395.

Vernon, P., & Mori, M. (1992). Intelligence, reaction times, and peripheral nerve conduction velocity. *Intelligence, 16,* 273–288.

Vitiello, M. V. (1989). *Unraveling sleep disorders of the aged.* Paper presented at the annual meeting of the Association of Professional Sleep Societies, Washington, DC.

Von Senden, M. (1932). *Raum- und Gaestaltauffassung bei operierten: Blindgeborernin vor und nach der Operation.* Leipzig, Germany: Barth.

Vroom, V. H. (1964). *Work and motivation.* New York: Wiley.

Vroom, V. H. (1974). A new look at managerial decision making. *Organizational Dynamics, 5,* 66–80.

Vroom, V. H., & Yetton, P. W. (1973). *Leadership and decision-making.* Pittsburgh: University of Pittsburgh Press.

Waid, W. M. (1976). Skin conductance response to both signaled and unsignaled noxious stimulation predicts level of socialization. *Journal of Personality and Social Psychology, 34,* 923–929.

Walk, R. D., & Gibson, E. J. (1961). A comparative and analytical study of visual depth perception. *Psychological Monographs, 75*(15).

Walker, E., Downey, G., & Bergman, A. (1989). The effects of parental psychopathology and maltreatment on child behavior: A test of the diathesis-stress model. *Child Development, 60,* 15–24.

Walker, E., & Emory, E. (1983). Infants at risk for psychopathology: Offspring of schizophrenic parents. *Child Development, 54,* 1269–1285.

Walker, E., Hoppes, E., Mednick, S., Emory, E., & Schulsinger, F. (1983). Environmental factors related to schizophrenia in psychophysiologically labile high-risk males. *Journal of Abnormal Psychology, 90,* 313–320.

Walker, E. A., Katon, W. J., Hansom, J., Harrop-Griffiths, J., Holm, L., Jones, M. L., Hickok, L., & Jemelka, R. P. (1992). Medical and psychiatric symptoms in women with childhood sexual abuse. *Psychosomatic Medicine, 54,* 658–664.

Walker, L. E. A. (1989). Psychology and violence against women. *American Psychologist, 44,* 695–702.

Walker-Andrews, A. S. (1986). Intermodal perception of expressive behaviors: Relation of eye and voice? *Developmental Psychology, 22,* 373–377.

Wallace, R. K., & Benson, H. (1972). The physiology of meditation. In *Altered states of awareness: Readings from Scientific American.* San Francisco: Freeman.

Wallerstein, J. S., & Blakeslee, J. (1989). *Second chances.* New York: Ticknor & Fields.

Walton, G. E., & Bower, T. G. R. (1993). Newborns form "prototypes" in less than 1 minute. *Psychological Science, 4,* 203–205.

Wandersman, A. H., & Hallman, W. K. (1993). Are people acting irrationally? *American Psychologist, 48,* 681–686.

Warchol, M. E., Lambert, P. R. Goldstein, B. J., Forge, A., Corwin, J. T. (1993). Regenerative proliferation in inner ear sensory epithelia from adult guinea pigs and humans. *Science, 259,* 1619–1622.

Washton, A. M. (1989). *Cocaine addiction.* New York: Norton.

Watkins, M. J. (1990). Mediationism and the obfuscation of memory. *American Psychologist, 45,* 328–335.

Watson, J. B. (1924). *Behaviorism.* Chicago: University of Chicago Press.

Watson, J. B. (1930). *Behaviorism* (2nd ed.). Chicago: University of Chicago Press.

Watson, J. B., & Rayner, R. (1920). Conditioned emotional reaction. *Journal of Experimental Psychology, 3,* 1–14.

Weary, G., Harvey, J. H., Schwieger, P., Olson, C. T., Perloff, E., & Pritchard, S. (1982). Self-presentation and the moderation of self-serving biases. *Social Cognition, 1,* 140–159.

Weaver, C. A., III (1993). Do you need a "flash" to form a flashbulb memory? *Journal of Experimental Psychology: General, 122,* 39–46.

Webb, W. B. (1975). *Sleep: The gentle tyrant.* Englewood Cliffs, NJ: Prentice-Hall.

Webb, W. B., & Agnew, H. W., Jr. (1974). Sleep and waking in a time-free environment. *Aerospace Medicine, 45,* 617–622.

Webb, W. B., & Agnew, H. W., Jr. (1975). The effects on subsequent sleep of an acute restriction of sleep length. *Psychophysiology, 12,* 367–370.

Wechsler, D. (1958). *The measurement and appraisal of adult intelligence* (4th ed.). Baltimore: Williams & Wilkins.

Weidner, G., Friend, R., Ficarrotto, T. J., & Mendell, N. R. (1989). Hostility and cardiovascular reactivity to stress in women and men. *Psychosomatic Medicine, 51,* 36–45.

Weingartner, H. (1977). Human state-dependent learning. In B. T. Ho, D. Richards, & D. L. Chute (Eds.), *Drug discrimination and state-dependent learning.* New York: Academic Press.

Weingartner, H., Adefris, W., Eich, J. E., & Murphy, D. L. (1976). Encoding-imagery specificity in alcohol state-dependent learning. *Journal of Experimental Psychology, 2,* 83–87.

Weinraub, M., & Wolf, B. (1983). Effects of stress and social supports on mother-child interactions in single- and two-parent families. *Child Development, 54,* 1297–1311.

Weins, A. N., & Menustik, C. E. (1983). Treatment outcome and patient characteristics in an aversion therapy program for alcoholism. *American Psychologist, 38,* 1089–1096.

Weintraub, S. (1987). Risk factors in schizophrenia: The Stony Brook high-risk project. *Schizophrenia Bulletin, 13,* 439–443.

Weissman, M. M., Gammon, G. D., John, K., Merikangas, K. R., Warner, V., Prusoff, B. A., & Sholomskas, D. (1987). Children of depressed parents. *Archives of General Psychiatry, 44,* 847–849.

Wells, G. L. (1993). What do we know about eyewitness identification? *American Psychologist, 48,* 553–571.

Wells, R. A., & Phelps, P. A. (1990). The brief psychotherapies: A selective overview. In R. A. Wells & V. J. Giannetti (Eds.), *Handbook of the brief psychotherapies.* New York: Plenum Press.

Werler, M. M., Mitchell, A. A., & Shapiro, M. B. (1989). The relation of aspirin use during the first trimester of pregnancy to congenital cardiac defects. *New England Journal of Medicine, 321,* 1639–1642.

West, M. A. (1980). Meditation and the EEG. *Psychological Medicine, 10,* 369–375.

West, M. A. (1982). Meditation and self-awareness: Physiological and phenomenological approaches. In G. Underwood (Ed.), *Aspects of consciousness: Vol. 3. Awareness and self-Awareness.* London: Academic Press.

Wexler, B. E., & Cicchetti, D. V. (1992). The outpatient treatment of depression. *Journal of Nervous and Mental Disease, 180,* 277–286.

White, J. R., Case, D. A., McWhirter, D., & Mattison, A. M. (1990). Enhanced sexual behavior in exercising men. *Archives of Sexual Behavior, 19,* 193–195.

White, M. J., & Gerstein, L. H. (1987). Helping: The influence of anticipated social sanctions and self-monitoring. *Journal of Personality, 55,* 41–45.

White, N. M., & Milner, P. M. (1992). The psychobiology of reinforcers. *Annual Review of Psychology, 43,* 443–471.

Whorf, B. L. (1956). *Language, thought, and reality: Selected writings of Benjamin Lee Whorf* (J. B. Carroll, Ed.). New York: Wiley.

Widiger, T. A., Frances, A. J., Pincus, H. A., Davis, W. W., & First, M. B. (1991). Toward an empirical classification for the *DSM-IV. Journal of Abnormal Psychology, 100,* 280–288.

Widom, C. S. (1989). Does violence beget violence? A critical examination of the literature. *Psychological Bulletin, 106,* 3–28.

Wiebe, D. J. (1991). Hardiness and stress moderation: A test of proposed mechanisms. *Journal of Personality and Social Psychology, 60,* 89–99.

Wiggins, J. S., & Trapnell, P. D. (1992). Personality structure: The return of the Big Five. In S. R. Briggs, R. Hogan, & W. H. Jones (Eds.), *Handbook of personality psychology.* Orlando, FL: Academic Press.

Wilder, D. A., & Thompson, J. E. (1980). Intergroup contact with independent manipulations of in-group and out-group interaction. *Journal of Personality and Social Psychology, 38,* 589–603.

Willerman, L., Schultz, R., Rutledge, J. N., & Bigler, E. D. (1992). Hemisphere size symmetry predicts relative verbal and nonverbal intelligence differently in the sexes: An MRI study of structure-function relations. *Intelligence, 16,* 315–328.

Williams, C. D. (1959). Case report: The elimination of tantrum behavior by extinction procedures. *Journal of Abnormal and Social Psychology, 59,* 269.

Williams, K. D., & Karau, S. J. (1991). Social loafing and social compensation: The effects of expectations of co-worker performance. *Journal of Personality and Social Psychology, 61,* 570–581.

Williams, K. J., Harkins, S., & Latané, B. (1981). Identifiability as a deterrent to social loafing: Two cheering experiments. *Journal of Personality and Social Psychology, 40,* 303–311.

Williams, K. J., Suls, J., Alliger, G. M., Learner, S. M., & Wan, C. K. (1991). Multiple role juggling and daily mood states in working mothers: An experience sampling study. *Journal of Applied Psychology, 76,* 664–674.

Williams, R. L. (1989). *The trusting heart: Great news about Type A behavior.* New York: Random House.

Williams, S. L., Kinney, P. J., & Falbo, J. (1989). Generalization of therapeutic changes in agoraphobia: The role of perceived self-efficacy. *Journal of Consulting and Clinical Psychology, 57,* 436–442.

Wilson, D., Mundy-Castle, A., & Panditji, L. (1990). Birth order and intellectual development among Zimbabwean children. *Journal of Social Psychology, 130,* 409–411.

Wilson, E. O. (1975). *Sociobiology: A new synthesis.* Cambridge, MA: Harvard University Press.

Wilson, G. T. (1987). Cognitive studies in alcoholism. *Journal of Consulting and Clinical Psychology, 55,* 325–331.

Wilson, M. N. (1989). Child development in the context of the black extended family. *American Psychologist, 44,* 380–385.

Wilson, R. S. (1983). The Louisville twin study: Developmental synchronies in behavior. *Child Development, 54,* 298–315.

Windmiller, M. (1980). Introduction. In M. Windmiller, N. Lambert, & E. Turiel (Eds.), *Moral development and socialization.* Boston: Allyn and Bacon.

Wing, L. (Ed.). (1976). *Early childhood autism* (2nd ed.). New York: Pergamon Press.

Wing, R. R., Epstein, L. H., Nowalk, M. P., & Lamparski, D. M. (1986). Behavioral self-regulation in the treatment of patients with diabetes mellitus. *Psychological Bulletin, 99,* 78–89.

Wise, R. A., & Bozarth, M. A. (1987). A psychomotor stimulant theory of addiction. *Psychological Review, 94,* 469–492.

Witt, L. A., & Nye, L. G. (1992). Gender and the relationship between perceived fairness of pay or promotion and job satisfaction. *Journal of Applied Psychology, 77,* 910–917.

Wittrock, M. C. (1987, August 29). *The teaching of comprehension.* Thorndike Award Address at American Psychological Association annual meeting, New York.

Wolfe, D. A., Edwards, B., Manion, I. & Koverola, C. (1988). Early intervention for parents at risk of child abuse and neglect: A preliminary investigation. *Journal of Consulting and Clinical Psychology, 56,* 40–47.

Wolpe, J. (1958). *Psychotherapy by reciprocal inhibition.* Stanford, CA: Stanford University Press.

Wood, J. M., Bootzin, R. R., Rosenhan, D., Nolen-Hoeksema, S., & Jourden, F. (1992). Effects of the 1989 San Francisco earthquake on frequency and content of nightmares. *Journal of Abnormal Psychology, 101,* 219–224.

Wood, W., Wong, F. Y., & Chachere, J. G. (1991). Effects of media violence on viewers' aggression in unconstrained social interaction. *Psychological Bulletin, 109,* 371–383.

Woodhead, M. (1988). When psychology informs public policy: The case of early childhood intervention. *American Psychologist, 6,* 443–454.

Woodward, W. R. (1982). The "discovery" of social behaviorism and social learning theory, 1870–1980. *American Psychologist, 37,* 396–410.

Woolfolk, R. L., & McNulty, T. F. (1983). Relaxation treatment for insomnia: A component analysis. *Journal of Consulting and Clinical Psychology, 51,* 495–503.

Worchel, S., Hardy, T. W., & Hurley, R. (1976). The effects of commercial interruption of violent and nonviolent films on viewers' subsequent aggression. *Journal of Experimental Social Psychology, 12,* 220–232.

Worell, J. (1978) Sex roles and psychological well-being: Perspectives on methodology. *Journal of Consulting and Clinical Psychology, 46,* 777–791.

Wundt, W. (1896). *Grundress er psychologie.* Leipzig, Germany: Engleman.

Wynn, K. (1992). Addition and subtraction by human infants. *Letters to Nature, 358,* 749–750.

Wynne, L. C., Cole, R. E., & Perkins, P. (1987). University of Rochester child and family study: Risk research in progress. *Schizophrenia Bulletin, 13,* 463–467.

Wyszecki, G., & Stiles, W. S. (1967). *Color science: Concepts and methods, quantitative data, and formulas.* New York: Wiley.

Yerkes, R. M., & Dodson, J. D. (1908). The relation of strength of stimulus to rapidity of habit formation. *Journal of Comparative Neurology and Psychology, 18,* 459–482.

Yoken, C., & Berman, J. S. (1984). Does paying a fee for psychotherapy alter the effectiveness of treatment? *Journal of Consulting and Clinical Psychology, 52,* 254–260.

Young, A. W., & Ellis, A. W. (1981). Asymmetry of cerebral hemispheric function in normal and poor readers. *Psychological Bulletin, 89,* 183–190.

Young, S. N., Smith, S., Pihl, R. O., & Ervin, F. R. (1985). Tryptophan depletion causes a rapid lowering of mood in normal males. *Psychopharmacology, 87,* 173–177.

Young, T. J. (1991). Suicide and homicide among Native Americans: Anomie or social learning? *Psychological Reports, 68,* 1137–1138.

Yuille, J. C. (1993). We must study forensic eyewitnesses to know about them. *American Psychologist, 48,* 572–573.

Yuille, J. C., & Cutshall, J. L. (1986). A case study of eyewitness memory of a crime. *Journal of Applied Psychology, 71,* 291–301.

Yussen, S. R. (1977). Characteristics of moral dilemmas written by adolescents. *Developmental Psychology, 13,* 162–163.

Zaccaro, S. J. (1984). Social loafing: The role of task attractiveness. *Personality and Social Psychology Bulletin, 10,* 99–106.

Zaidel, E. (1983). A response to Gazzaniga: Language in the right hemisphere, convergent perspectives. *American Psychologist, 38,* 542–546.

Zajonc, R. B. (1965). Social facilitation. *Science, 149,* 269–274.

Zajonc, R. B. (1986). The decline and rise of scholastic aptitude scores: A prediction derived from the confluence model. *American Psychologist, 41,* 862–867.

Zajonc, R. B., & Markus, G. B. (1975). Birth order and intellectual development. *Psychological Review, 82,* 74–88.

Zajonc, R. B., Murphy, S. T., & Inglehart, M. (1989). Feeling and facial efference: Implications of the vascular theory of emotion. *Psychological Review, 96,* 395–416.

Zakay, D., Hayduk, L. A., & Tsal, Y. (1992). Personal space and distance misperception: Implications of a novel observation. *Bulletin of the Psychonomic Society, 30,* 33–35.

Zangwill, O. L., & Blakemore, C. (1972). Dyslexia: Reversal of eye movements during reading. *Neuropsychologia, 10,* 371–373.

Zaragoza, M. S., & McCloskey, M. (1989). Misleading postevent information and the memory impairment hypothesis: Comment on Belli and reply to Tversky and Tuchin. *Journal of Experimental Psychology: General, 118,* 92–99.

Zeig, J. K., & Gilligan, S. G. (1990). *Brief therapy myths, methods, and metaphors.* New York: Brunner/Mazel.

Zepelin, H. (1986). REM sleep and the timing of self-awakenings. *Bulletin of the Psychonomic Society, 24,* 254–256.

Zigler, E. F. (1987). Formal schooling for four-year-olds? No. *American Psychologist, 42,* 254–260.

Zigler, E. F., & Hodapp, R. M. (1991). Behavioral functioning in individuals with mental retardation. *Annual Review of Psychology, 42,* 29–50.

Zins, J. E., & Barnett, D. W. (1983). The Kaufman Assessment Battery for Children and school achievement: A validity study. *Journal of Psychoeducational Assessment, 1,* 235–241.

Zitrin, C. M. (1981). Combined pharmacological and psychological treatment of phobias. In M. Navissakalian & D. H. Barlow (Eds.), *Phobias: Psychological and pharmacological treatments.* New York: Guilford.

Zola-Morgan, S., Squire, L. R., & Mishkin, M. (1982). The neuroanatomy of amnesia: Amygdala-hippocampus versus temporal stem. *Science, 218,* 1337–1339.

Zuber, J. A., Crott, H. W., & Werner, J. (1992). Choice shift and group polarization: An analysis of the status of arguments and social decision schemes. *Journal of Personality and Social Psychology, 62,* 50–61.

Zuckerman, M. (1969). Variables affecting deprivation results and hallucinations, reported sensations, and images. In J. P. Zubek (Ed.), *Sensory deprivation.* New York: Appleton-Century-Crofts.

Zuckerman, M. (1990). Some dubious premises in research and theory on racial differences. *American Psychologist, 45,* 1297–1303.

Abnormal behavior Behavior characterized as atypical, socially unacceptable, distressing, maladaptive, or the result of distorted cognitions.

Abnormal psychology The field of psychology concerned with the assessment, treatment, and prevention of maladaptive behavior.

Accommodation According to Jean Piaget, the process by which new concepts and experiences modify existing cognitive structures and behaviors.

Action potential An all-or-none electrical current sent down the axon of a neuron, initiated by a rapid reversal of the electrical balance of the cell membrane. Also known as a *spike discharge*.

Actor-observer effect The tendency for people to attribute the behavior of others to dispositional causes but to attribute their own behavior to situational causes.

Addictive drug A drug that causes a compulsive physiological need and that, when withheld, produces withdrawal symptoms.

Adolescence [add-oh-LESS-since] The period extending from the onset of puberty to early adulthood.

Affect A person's emotional responses.

Afferent neurons Neurons that send messages to the spinal cord and brain.

Age regression The ability, sometimes induced by hypnosis, to "return" to an earlier time in one's life and to report events that occurred at that time.

Ageism Prejudice against the elderly and the discrimination that follows from it.

Aggression Any behavior designed to harm another person or thing.

Agonists Chemicals that mimic the actions of a neurotransmitter, usually by occupying receptor sites.

Agoraphobia [AG-or-uh-FOE-bee-uh] An anxiety disorder characterized by fear and avoidance of being alone or in public places from which escape might be difficult or embarrassing.

Alcoholic A problem drinker who also has both a physiological and a psychological need to consume alcohol and to experience its effects.

Algorithms [AL-go-rith-ums] Simple, specific, exhaustive procedures that provide a solution to a problem after a step-by-step analysis.

All-or-none The principle by which a neuron will fire either at full strength or not at all.

Allele Each member of a pair of genes that occupies the same genetic locus on a chromosome.

Altered state of consciousness A pattern of functioning that is dramatically different from that of ordinary awareness and responsiveness.

Altruistic acts [ahl-true-ISS-tick] Behaviors that benefit other people and for which there is no discernible extrinsic reward, recognition, or appreciation.

Alzheimer's disease [ALTZ-hy-merz] A chronic and progressive disorder of the brain that is a major cause of degenerative dementia; it may be a group of related disorders tied together loosely under one name.

Amnesia The inability to remember events from the past, usually because of physiological trauma; typically involves loss of memory for all events within a specific period.

Anal stage Freud's second stage of personality development, from about age 2 to about age 3, during which children learn to control the immediate gratification they obtain through defecation and to become responsive to the demands of society.

Androgynous Having some typically male and some typically female characteristics apparent in one individual.

Anorexia nervosa [an-uh-REX-see-uh ner-VOH-suh] An eating disorder characterized by an intense fear of becoming obese, dramatic weight loss, concern about weight, disturbances in body image, and an obstinate and willful refusal to eat.

Antagonists Chemicals that oppose the actions of a neurotransmitter, usually by preventing the neurotransmitter from occupying a receptor site.

Anterograde amnesia Loss of memory for events and experiences occurring after the amnesia-causing event.

Antisocial personality disorder A personality disorder characterized by egocentricity, by behavior that is irresponsible and that violates the rights of other people—lying, theft, delinquency, and other violations of societal rules—and by a lack of guilt feelings, an inability to understand other people, and a lack of fear of punishment.

Anxiety A generalized feeling of fear and apprehension that might be related to a particular event or object and is often accompanied by increased physiological arousal.

Approach-approach conflict The conflict that results from having to choose between two equally attractive alternatives or goals.

Approach-avoidance conflict The conflict that results from having to choose an alternative or goal that has both attractive and repellent aspects.

Archetypes [AR-ki-types] In Jung's theory, emotionally charged ideas and images that have rich meaning and symbolism and are contained within the collective unconscious.

Assessment The process of evaluating individual differences among human beings by using tests and direct observation of behavior.

Assimilation According to Jean Piaget, the process by which new concepts and experiences are incorporated into existing mental frameworks so as to be used in a meaningful way.

Attitudes Lasting patterns of feelings, beliefs, and behavior tendencies toward other people, ideas, or objects which are based in our experiences, shape our future behavior, are evaluative in nature, and serve certain functions.

Attribution The process by which someone infers other people's motives and intentions from observing their behavior and deciding whether the causes of the behavior are *dispositional* (internal) or *situational* (external).

Autonomic nervous system [au-toe-NOM-ick] The part of the peripheral nervous system that controls the vital and automatic processes of the body, such as the heart rate, digestive processes, blood pressure, and regulation of internal organs.

Aversive counterconditioning A counterconditioning technique that pairs an aversive or noxious stimulus with a stimulus that elicits undesirable behavior so the subject will adopt a new, desirable behavior in response to the original stimulus.

Avoidance-avoidance conflict The conflict that results from having to choose between two equally distasteful alternatives or goals.

Babinski reflex A reflex in which an infant projects its toes outward and up when the soles of its feet are touched.

Backward search A heuristic procedure in which a problem solver starts at the end of a problem and systematically works in reverse steps to discover the subparts necessary to achieve a solution.

Balance theory An attitude theory stating that people prefer to hold consistent beliefs and try to avoid incompatible beliefs.

Behavior therapy A therapy, based on the application of learning principles to human behavior, that focuses on changing overt behaviors rather than on understanding subjective feelings, unconscious processes, or motivations. Also known as *behavior modification*.

Behaviorism The school of psychological thought that rejects the study of the contents of consciousness and focuses on describing and measuring only what is observable directly or through assessment instruments.

Biofeedback The general technique by which individuals can monitor and learn to control the involuntary activity of some of the body's organs and functions.

Biological perspective The school of psychological thought that examines psychological issues based on how heredity and biological structures affect mental processes and behavior, focusing on how physical mechanisms affect emotions, feelings, thoughts, desires, and sensory experiences. Also known as the *neuroscience perspective.*

Bipolar disorders Mood disorders characterized by vacillation between two extremes: mania and depression. Originally known as *manic-depressive disorders.*

Body language The communication of information through body positions and gestures.

Bonding A special process of emotional attachment suggested to occur between parents and babies in the minutes and hours immediately after birth.

Brain The part of the central nervous system that regulates, monitors, processes, and guides other nervous system activity; located in the skull.

Brainstorming A technique for problem solving that involves considering all possible solutions without making prior evaluative judgments.

Brief intermittent therapy A therapeutic approach that focuses on identifying the client's current problem and solving it with the most effective treatment as quickly as possible. Also known as *brief therapy.*

Bulimia nervosa [boo-LEE-me-uh ner-VOH-suh] An eating disorder characterized by repeated episodes of binge eating (and a fear of not being able to stop eating) followed by purging.

Burnout A state of emotional and physical exhaustion, lowered productivity, and feelings of isolation, often caused by work-related pressures.

Bystander apathy The unwillingness of witnesses to an event to help; an effect that increases when there are more observers.

Case study A method of interviewing subjects to gain information about their background, including data on such things as childhood, family, education, and social and sexual interactions.

Catatonic type [CAT-uh-TONN-ick] A major type of schizophrenia, characterized by displays of excited or violent motor activity or by stupor (in which the individual is mute, negative, and basically unresponsive).

Central nervous system One of the two major parts of the nervous system, consisting of the brain and spinal cord.

Child abuse Physical, emotional, or sexual mistreatment of children.

Chromosomes Strands of DNA in the nuclei of cells that occur in pairs and carry genetic information.

Chunks Manageable and meaningful units of information that allow for groupings to be easily encoded, stored, and retrieved.

Classical conditioning A conditioning process in which an originally neutral stimulus, by repeated pairing with a stimulus that normally elicits a response, comes to elicit a similar or even identical response. Also known as *Pavlovian conditioning.*

Client-centered therapy An insight therapy, developed by Carl Rogers, that seeks to help people evaluate the world and themselves from their own perspective by providing a nondirective environment and unconditional positive regard for the client. Also known as *person-centered therapy.*

Clinical psychologists Mental health practitioners who view behavior and mental processes from a psychological perspective and who use their knowledge to treat persons with serious emotional or behavioral problems or to do research into the causes of behavior.

Cognitive dissonance [COG-nuh-tiv DIS-uh-nins] A state in which individuals feel uncomfortable because they hold two or more thoughts, attitudes, or behaviors that are inconsistent with one another.

Cognitive psychology The school of psychological thought that focuses on the mental processes and activities involved in perception, memory, learning, and thinking; the study of the overlapping fields of learning, memory perception, and thought that emphasizes encoding, storage, analysis, recall, reconstruction, elaboration, and memory of events.

Cognitive theory An explanation of behavior that emphasizes the role of thought and individual choices regarding life goals and the means of achieving them.

Collective unconscious In Jung's theory, a storehouse (collection) of primitive ideas and images in the unconscious that are inherited from our ancestors.

Community psychology The branch of psychology that seeks to reach out to society to provide services such as community mental health centers and especially to effect social change through empowerment of individuals, planning, prevention, early intervention, research, and evaluation.

Concepts Classifications of objects or ideas that distinguish them from others on the basis of some common properties or features.

Concordance rate The percentage of occasions when two groups or individuals show the same trait.

Concrete operations stage Piaget's third stage of intellectual development (lasting from approximately age 6 or 7 to age 11 or 12), during which the child develops the ability to understand constant factors in the environment, rules, and higher-order symbolism.

Conditioned response The response elicited by a conditioned stimulus.

Conditioned stimulus A neutral stimulus that, through repeated association with an unconditioned stimulus, becomes capable of eliciting a conditioned response.

Conditioning A systematic procedure through which associations and responses to specific stimuli are learned.

Conflict The emotional state or condition in which a person has to make difficult decisions about two or more competing motives, behaviors, or impulses.

Conscious Freud's first level of awareness, consisting of the thoughts, feelings, and actions of which people are aware.

Consciousness The general state of being aware of and responsive to events in the environment and to our own mental processes.

Conservation The ability to recognize that something that changed in some way (such as the "shape" of liquid in a container) still has the same weight, substance, or volume.

Conservative focusing A hypothesis-testing strategy that involves the elimination of alternative possibilities from a narrow range of options.

Consolidation [kon-SOL-ih-DAY-shun] The evolution of a temporary neural circuit into a more permanent circuit.

Control group In an experiment, the comparison group—the group of subjects tested on the dependent variable in the same way as the experimental group but for whom the independent variable is not manipulated; the group of subjects that does not receive the treatment under investigation.

Convergent thinking The process by which possible options are selectively narrowed until they converge (come together) into one answer.

Conversion disorders Somatoform disorders characterized by the loss or alteration of physical functioning for no apparent physiological reason.

Convolutions Characteristic folds in tissues of the cerebral hemispheres and overlying cortex in human beings.

Coping skills The techniques people use to deal with stress and changing situations.

Coping The process by which a person takes some action to manage environmental and internal demands that cause or might cause stress and that will tax the individual's inner resources.

Correlation coefficient A number that expresses the degree and direction of a relationship between two variables, ranging from −1 (a perfect negative correlation) to +1 (a perfect positive correlation).

Counterconditioning   A process of reconditioning in which a person is taught a new, more adaptive response to a familiar stimulus.

Creativity   A process of thought and problem solving, generally considered to include originality, novelty, and appropriateness.

Crowding   The perception that one's space is too restricted.

Debriefing   The process of providing the participants in a study, at the end of the project, with information about the exact nature of the research, its hypothesis, and its methods.

Decay   The loss of information from memory as a result of the passage of time and disuse.

Decentration   The process, beginning at about age 2, of changing from a totally self-oriented point of view to one that recognizes other people's feelings, ideas, and viewpoints.

Decision making   The assessment of and choosing among alternatives.

Declarative memory   Memory for specific facts.

Deep structure   The organization of a sentence that is closest to its underlying meaning.

Defense mechanism   A largely unconscious way of reducing anxiety by distorting perceptions of reality.

Deindividuation   The process by which individuals in a group lose their sense of self-awareness and concern with evaluation.

Delusions   False beliefs, inconsistent with reality, held in spite of evidence to the contrary.

Demand characteristics   The elements of a study situation that might clue a subject as to the purpose of the study and might thereby elicit specific behavior from the subject.

Dementias   Impairments in mental functioning and global cognitive abilities of long-standing duration in otherwise alert individuals, causing memory loss and related symptoms.

Denial   A defense mechanism by which people refuse to accept the true source of their anxiety. .

Dependent variable   The variable in a controlled experiment that is expected to change because of the manipulation of the independent variable.

Depressive disorders   A general category of mood disorders in which people show extreme and persistent sadness, despair, and loss of interest in life's usual activities.

Descriptive statistics   A general set of procedures used to summarize, condense, and describe samples of data.

Deviation IQ   A standard IQ test score that has the same mean and standard deviation at all ages.

Diabetes mellitus   A condition in which too little insulin is produced, causing sugar to be insufficiently transported into body cells.

Diffusion of responsibility   The feeling of individual members of a group that they cannot be held responsible for the group's actions.

Discrimination   Behavior targeted at individuals or groups, with the aim of holding them apart and treating them differently.

Disorganized type   A major type of schizophrenia, characterized by frequent incoherence, absence of systematized delusions, and blunted, inappropriate, or silly affect.

Dissociative amnesia   A dissociative disorder characterized by the sudden and extensive inability to recall important personal information, usually of a traumatic or stressful nature.

Dissociative disorders   Disorders characterized by a sudden but temporary alteration in consciousness, identity, sensory/motor behavior, or memory.

Dissociative identity disorder   Often called *multiple personality,* a dissociative disorder characterized by the existence within an individual of two or more distinct personalities, each of which is dominant at particular times and directs the individual's behavior at those times.

Divergent thinking   The production of new information from known information or the generation of logical possibilities.

Double bind   A situation in which an individual is given two different and inconsistent messages.

Double-blind technique   A research technique in which neither the experimenter nor the subjects know who is in the control or the experimental group.

Down syndrome   A human genetic defect in which more than two whole chromosomes are present for the 21st pair; usually accompanied by characteristic physical abnormalities and mental retardation.

Dream analysis   A psychoanalytic technique in which a patient's dreams are interpreted and used to gain insight into the individual's unconscious motivations.

Dream   A state of consciousness that occurs largely during REM sleep and is usually accompanied by vivid visual, tactile, and auditory imagery.

Drive theory   An explanation of behavior emphasizing internal factors that energize organisms to seek, attain, reestablish, balance, or maintain some goal that helps with survival.

Drive   An internal aroused condition that directs an organism to satisfy physiological needs.

Drug   Any chemical substance that alters normal biological processes.

Eating disorders   Psychological disorders characterized by gross disturbances in eating behavior and in the way individuals respond to food.

Eclecticism   [ek-LECK-ti-sizm] A combination of theories, facts, or techniques. In clinical and counseling psychology, eclecticism is the practice of using whatever therapeutic techniques are appropriate for an individual client rather than relying exclusively on the techniques of one school of psychology.

Efferent neurons   Neurons that send messages from the brain and spinal cord to other structures in the body.

Ego analysts   Psychoanalytic practitioners who assume that the ego has greater control over behavior than Freud suggested and who are more concerned with reality testing and control over the environment than with unconscious motivations and processes. Also known as *ego psychologists.*

Ego   In Freud's theory, the part of personality that seeks to satisfy the id and superego in accordance with reality.

Egocentrism   [ee-go-SENT-rism] The inability to perceive a situation or event except in relation to oneself. Also known as *self-centeredness.*

Elaboration likelihood model   A theory of attitude change suggesting that there are two routes to persuasion: central, which focuses on thoughtful, elaborative considerations; and peripheral, which focuses on less careful, more emotional, and even superficial considerations.

Elaborative rehearsal   Rehearsal involving repetition (often in long-term memory) in which the stimulus may be associated with other events and be further processed.

Electroconvulsive shock therapy (ECT)   [eel-ECK-tro-con-VUL-siv] A treatment for severe mental illness in which a brief application of electricity to the head is used to produce a generalized seizure. Also known as *shock treatment.*

Electroencephalogram (EEG)   [eel-ECK-tro-en-SEFF-uh-low-gram] A record of electrical brain-wave patterns obtained through electrodes placed on the scalp.

Embryo   [EM-bree-o] The human organism from the 5th through the 49th day after conception.

Emotion   A subjective response, usually accompanied by a physiological change, that is interpreted by the individual, then readies the individual for some action that is associated with a change in behavior.

Empowerment   Facilitating the development of skills, knowledge, and motivation in individuals so they can act for themselves and gain control over their own lives.

Encoding   The process by which information is put into memory, through transduction of an experience into electrochemical energy for neural representations.

Encounter groups   Groups of people who meet together to learn more about their feelings, behavior, and interactions.

Endocrine glands   [END-oh-krin] Ductless glands that secrete hormones directly into the bloodstream.

Environmental psychology   The study of how physical settings affect human behavior and how human behavior affects the environment.

Episodic memory [ep-ih-SAH-dick] Memory for specific events, objects, and situations.

Erectile dysfunction In men, the inability to attain or maintain an erection of sufficient strength to allow sexual intercourse.

Ergonomics The study of the fit between people, their anatomy or physiology, and the demands of a particular task or piece of equipment, and the environment in which the task occurs.

Excitement phase The first phase of the sexual response cycle, during which there are initial increases in heart rate, blood pressure, and respiration.

Expectancy theories Explanations of behavior that focus on the expectation of success and the need for achievement as energizing factors for human beings.

Experiment A procedure in which a researcher systematically manipulates some variables to describe objectively the relationship between the variables of concern and the resulting behavior; well-designed experiments permit inferences about cause and effect and test hypotheses.

Experimental group In an experiment, the group of subjects for whom the independent variable is manipulated and who receive the treatment under investigation.

Extinction [Egg-STINCK-shun] In classical conditioning, the process of reducing the likelihood of a conditioned response to a conditioned stimulus by withholding the unconditioned stimulus; in operant conditioning, the process by which the probability of an organism's emitting a conditioned response is reduced when reinforcement no longer follows the response.

Extrinsic rewards [ecks-TRINZ-ick] Rewards that come from the external environment.

Factor analysis A statistical procedure designed to discover the mutually independent elements (factors) in any set of data.

Factor theory approach to intelligence Theories of intelligence based on factor analysis, including those of Spearman and Thurstone.

Family therapy Therapy in which two or more people who are committed to one another's well-being are treated at once, in an effort to change the ways in which they interact.

Fetus The human organism from the 49th day after conception until birth.

Fixation An excessive attachment to some person or object that was appropriate only at an earlier stage of development.

Fixed-interval schedule A reinforcement schedule in which a reinforcer (reward) is delivered after a specified interval of time, provided that the required response has occurred at least once after the interval.

Fixed-ratio schedule A reinforcement schedule in which a reinforcer (reward) is delivered after a specified number of responses has occurred.

Formal operations stage Piaget's fourth and final stage of intellectual development (beginning at about age 12), during which the individual can think hypothetically, can consider all future possibilities, and is capable of deductive logic.

Fraternal twins Double births resulting from the release of two ova that are fertilized by two sperm; fraternal twins are no more or less genetically similar than nontwin siblings.

Free association A psychoanalytic technique in which a person reports to the therapist his or her thoughts and feelings as they occur, regardless of how trivial, illogical, or objectionable their content may appear.

Free-floating anxiety Persistent anxiety not clearly related to any specific object or situation, accompanied by a sense of impending doom.

Frequency distribution A chart or array, usually arranged from the highest to the lowest score, showing the number of instances of each obtained score.

Frequency polygons Graphs of frequency distributions that show the number of instances of obtained scores, usually with the data points connected by straight lines.

Frustration-aggression hypothesis The view that frustration of goal-directed behavior leads to aggression.

Frustration The emotional state or condition that results when a goal—work, family, or personal—is thwarted or blocked.

Fulfillment In Rogers's personality theory, an inborn tendency directing people toward actualizing their inherited nature and thus attaining their potential.

Functional fixedness The inability to see that an object can have a function other than the one normally associated with it.

Functionalism The school of psychological thought (an outgrowth of structuralism) that was concerned with how and why the conscious mind works; its main aim was to know how the contents of consciousness functioned and worked together.

Fundamental attribution error The tendency to attribute other people's behavior to dispositional (internal) causes rather than situational (external) causes.

Gender differences Differences between males and females in behavior or mental processes.

Gender identity A person's sense of being male or female.

Gender role stereotyping Typical beliefs of society concerning the patterns of behavior expected, regulated, and reinforced based on gender.

Gender roles The full range of behaviors generally associated with one's gender; they help people establish who they are. Also known as *sex roles*.

Gender schema theory The theory that children and adolescents use gender as an organizing theme to classify and understand their perceptions about the world.

Generalized anxiety disorders Anxiety disorders characterized by persistent anxiety for at least 6 months, occurring more days than not sometimes with problems in motor tension, autonomic hyperactivity, apprehension, and concentration.

Genes The units of heredity transmission carried in chromosomes and consisting of DNA and protein.

Genetics The study of heredity, the biological transmission of traits and characteristics from parents to offspring.

Genital stage [JEN-it-ul] Freud's last stage of personality development, from the onset of puberty through adulthood, during which the sexual conflicts of childhood resurface at puberty and are often resolved during adolescence.

Gestalt psychology [gesh-TALT] The school of psychological thought that argued that behavior cannot be studied in parts but must be viewed as a whole; the focus was on the unity of perception and thinking; also an insight therapy that emphasizes the importance of a person's being aware of current feelings and situations.

Grammar The linguistic description of how a language functions, especially the rules and patterns used for generating appropriate and comprehensible sentences.

Grasping reflex A reflex in which an infant grasps vigorously any object touching its palm or fingers or placed in its hand.

Group polarization The exaggeration of individuals' preexisting attitudes as a result of group discussion.

Group therapy The treatment of emotional and behavioral problems, or any psychotherapeutic process, in which several people meet as a group with a therapist.

Group A number of individuals who are loosely or cohesively related and who share some common characteristics and goals.

Groupthink The phenomenon of people in a group reinforcing one another and seeking concurrence and group cohesiveness, rather than effectively evaluating choices and reasoning.

Hallucinations [ha-LOOSE-in-AY-shuns] Compelling perceptual (visual, tactile, olfactory, or auditory) experiences without a real physical stimulus.

Halo effect The tendency to let one of an individual's characteristics influence the evaluation of other characteristics.

Hawthorne effect The finding, based on early research studies at the Hawthorne industrial plant, that people behave differently (usually better) when they know they are being observed.

Health psychology Psychological subfield concerned with the use of psychological ideas and principles in health enhancement, illness prevention, diagnosis and treatment of disease, and rehabilitation processes.

Heuristics   [hyoo-RISS-ticks] Sets of selective strategies that act as guidelines for discovery-oriented problem solving but are not strict rules.

Higher-order conditioning   The process by which a neutral stimulus takes on conditioned properties through pairing with a conditioned stimulus.

Hormones   Endocrine gland chemicals that regulate the activities of specific organs or cells.

Human participants   Individuals who participate in experiments and whose behavior is observed for research data collection. Also known as *subjects*.

Humanistic psychology   The school of psychological thought that emphasizes the uniqueness of the human experience and the idea that human beings have free will to determine their destiny; an explanation of behavior that emphasizes the role of human qualities such as dignity, individual choice, and self-worth.

Hypnosis   An altered state of consciousness brought about by procedures that induce a trance.

Hypochondriasis   [hy-po-kon-DRY-a-sis] A somatoform disorder characterized by an inordinate preoccupation with health and illness, coupled with excessive anxiety about disease.

Hypoglycemia   [hi-po-gly-SEE-me-uh] Very low blood sugar levels resulting from the overproduction of insulin.

Hypothesis   A tentative statement or idea expressing a causal relationship between two events or variables that are to be evaluated in a research study.

Id   In Freud's theory, the source of instinctual energy, which works mainly on the pleasure principle.

Ideal self   The self that a person would ideally like to be.

Identical twins   Double births resulting from the splitting of a zygote into two identical cells, which then separate and develop independently; identical twins have exactly the same genetic makeup.

Imagery   A cognitive process in which a mental picture of a sensory event is created.

Impression formation   The process by which people use the behavior and appearance of others to infer their internal states and intentions.

Independent variable   The variable in a controlled experiment that is directly and purposefully manipulated by the experimenter to see how the variables under study will be affected.

Industrial/organizational (I/O) psychology   The study of how individual behavior is affected by the work environment, coworkers, and organizational practices.

Inferential statistics   Procedures used to reach conclusions (generalizations) about larger populations from a small sample of data with a minimal degree of error.

Informed consent   The signature of human participants on a document that indicates they understand the nature of their participation in the upcoming research and have been fully informed about the general nature of the research, its goals, and its methods.

Insight therapy   A therapy that attempts to discover relationships between unconscious motivations and current abnormal behavior in order to change that behavior.

Insomnia   Prolonged inability to sleep.

Insulin   A hormone produced by the pancreas that facilitates the transport of sugar from the blood into body cells, where it is metabolized.

Intelligence   According to Wechsler, "the aggregate or global capacity of the individual to act purposefully, to think rationally, and to deal effectively with the environment."

Interference   The suppression or confusion of one bit of information with another that was received either earlier or later.

Interpersonal attraction   The tendency of one person to evaluate another person (or a symbol or image of another person) in a positive way.

Interpretation   In Freud's theory, the technique of providing a context, meaning, or cause of a specific idea, feeling, or set of behaviors; the process of tying a set of behaviors to its unconscious determinant.

Interview   A series of open-ended questions used to gather detailed information about a person.

Intrinsically motivated behaviors   [in-TRINZ-ick-lee] Behaviors that a person engages in in order to feel more competent, satisfied, and self-determined.

Introspection   The description and analysis by a person of what he or she is thinking and feeling. Also known as *self-examination*.

Labor   The process in which the uterus contracts to open the cervix so the fetus can descend through the birth canal to the outside world.

Latency stage   [LAY-ten-see] Freud's fourth stage of personality development, from about age 7 until puberty, during which sexual urges are inactive.

Latent content   The deeper meaning of a dream, usually involving symbolism, hidden content, and repressed or obscured ideas and wishes.

Latent learning   Learning that occurs in the absence of any direct reinforcement and that is not necessarily demonstrated in any observable behavior, though it has the potential to be exhibited.

Lateralization   The localization of a particular brain function primarily in one hemisphere.

Learned helplessness   The behavior of giving up or not responding, exhibited by subjects exposed to negative consequences or punishment over which they have no control.

Learning   A relatively permanent change in an organism that occurs as a result of experiences in the environment.

Libido   [lih-BEE-doe] In Freud's theory, the instinctual (and usually sexual) life force that, working on the pleasure principle and seeking immediate gratification, energizes the id.

Linguistics   [ling-wist-icks] The study of language, including speech sounds, meaning, and grammar.

Logic   The procedure we use to reach a valid conclusion.

Long-term memory   The memory storage system that keeps a relatively permanent record of information.

Lucid dream   A dream in which people are aware of their dreaming while it is happening.

Mainstreaming   The administrative practice of placing exceptional children in regular classroom settings with the support of special education services.

Maintenance rehearsal   The repetitive review of information (usually in short-term memory) with little or no interpretation.

Major depressive disorder   A depressive disorder characterized by loss of interest in almost all of life's usual activities, as evidenced by a sad, hopeless, or discouraged mood on a day-to-day basis; sleep disturbance; loss of appetite; loss of energy; and feelings of unworthiness and guilt.

Manifest content   The overt story line, characters, and setting of a dream—the obvious, clearly discernible events of the dream.

Mean   A measure of central tendency calculated by dividing the sum of the scores by the number of scores. Also known as the *arithmetic average*.

Means-end analysis   A heuristic procedure in which efforts are made to move the problem solver closer to a solution by finding intervening steps (subgoals) and making changes that will bring about the solution as efficiently as possible.

Measure of central tendency   An index of the average, or typical, value of a distribution of scores.

Median   A measure of central tendency, the point at which 50 percent of all observations occur above and 50 percent below.

Mediation theory   The theory that people can create or discover a connection between previously unconnected things.

Meditation   A state of consciousness induced by a variety of techniques and characterized by concentration, restriction of sensory stimuli, and deep relaxation to produce a sense of detachment.

Memory span   The brief and limited number of items that can be easily reproduced after presentation in short-term memory, usually confined to a chunk of information.

Memory   The ability to remember past events, images, ideas, or previously learned information or skills; the storage system that allows for retention and retrieval of learned information.

Mental retardation   Below-average intellectual functioning, as measured on an IQ test, accompanied by substantial limitations in present functioning that originated during childhood.

Mode A measure of central tendency, the most frequently observed data point.

Model A perspective or approach derived from data in one field, used to help describe data in another field.

Morality A system of learned attitudes about social practices, institutions, and individual behavior used to evaluate situations and behavior as being right or wrong, good or bad.

Moro reflex A reflex in which an infant stretches out its arms and legs and cries when there is a loud noise or abrupt change in the environment.

Morphemes [MORE-feems] The basic units of meaning in a language.

Motivation Any condition, although usually an internal one, that appears by inference to initiate, activate, or maintain an organism's goal-directed behavior.

Motive A specific internal condition, usually involving some sort of arousal, that directs an organism's behavior toward a goal.

Naturalistic observation Careful and objective observation of events from a distance, without observer intervention.

Nature An individual's genetically inherited characteristics.

Need for achievement A social need that directs people to strive constantly for excellence and success.

Need A physiological condition arising from an imbalance and usually accompanied by arousal.

Negative instance A stimulus that is not an example of the concept under study.

Negative reinforcement Removal of an aversive stimulus after a particular response to increase the likelihood that the response will recur.

Neo-Freudians Personality theorists who have proposed variations on the basic ideas of Freud, usually attributing a greater influence to cultural and interpersonal factors than did Freud.

Nervous system The structures and organs that act as the communication system for the body, allowing all behavior and mental processes to take place.

Neuromodulators [NEW-roh-MOD-u-lay-torz] Chemical substances that function to increase or decrease the sensitivity of widely distributed neurons to the specific effects of neurotransmitters.

Neuron [NEW-ron] The basic unit (a single cell) of the nervous system, comprising dendrites, which receive neural signals; a cell body, which generates electrical signals; and an axon, which transmits neural signals. Also known as *nerve cell*.

Neurotransmitters [NEW-roh-TRANS-mitt-erz] Chemicals that reside in the axon terminal within synaptic vesicles and that, when released, move across the synaptic space and bind to the dendrites of the next cell.

Nondirective therapy A form of therapy in which the client determines the direction of therapy while the therapist remains permissive, almost passive, and accepts totally the client's feelings and behavior.

Nonverbal communication Information provided by cues or actions that involve movements of the body, especially the face, and sometimes the vocal cords.

Normal curve A bell-shaped curve, drawn as a frequency polygon, that depicts the approximately expected distribution of scores when a sample is drawn from a large population. Also known as *normal distribution*.

Norms The scores and corresponding percentile ranks of a large and representative sample of subjects from the population for which the test was designed.

NREM (no rapid eye movement) sleep Four distinct stages of sleep during which no rapid eye movements occur.

Nurture An individual's experiences in the environment.

Obedience The process by which a person complies with the orders of another person or group of people.

Observational learning theory The theory that organisms learn new responses by observing the behavior of a model and then imitating it. Also known as *social learning theory*.

Obsessive-compulsive disorders [ob-SESS-iv kom-PULS-iv] Anxiety disorders characterized by persistent and uncontrollable thoughts and irrational beliefs that cause the performance of intrusive and inappropriate compulsive rituals that interfere with daily life.

Oedipus complex [ED-i-pus] Occurring during the phallic stage, feelings of rivalry with the parent of the same sex and love of the parent of the opposite sex, ultimately resolved through identification with the parent of the same sex; *Electra complex* is this process specifically in girls.

Operant conditioning [OP-er-ant] A conditioning procedure in which the probability that an organism will emit a response is increased or decreased by the subsequent delivery of a reinforcer or punisher. Also known as *instrumental conditioning*.

Operational definition The set of methods or procedures used to define a variable; a definition based on a set of concrete steps used to define a variable.

Oral stage Freud's first stage of personality development, from birth to about age 2, during which infants obtain gratification primarily through the mouth.

Orgasm phase The third phase of the sexual response cycle, during which autonomic nervous system activity reaches its peak, and muscle contractions occur throughout the body, but especially in the genital area, in spasms.

Paranoid type [PAIR-uh-noid] A major type of schizophrenia, characterized by delusions and hallucinations of persecution or grandeur (or both), and sometimes irrational jealousy.

Parasympathetic nervous system [PAIR-uh-sim-puh-THET-ick] The part of the peripheral nervous system that controls the ongoing maintenance processes of the body, such as the heart rate, digestive processes, and blood pressure.

Percentile score A score indicating what percentage of the test population would obtain a lower score.

Performance appraisal The process by which a supervisor periodically evaluates the performance of a subordinate.

Peripheral nervous system [puh-RIF-er-al] The part of the nervous system that carries information to and from the central nervous system through a network of spinal and cranial nerves.

Personal space The area around an individual that is considered private and around which the person feels an invisible boundary.

Personality disorders Disorders characterized by inflexible and long-standing maladaptive ways of dealing with the environment, which typically cause stress and social or occupational problems.

Personality A set of relatively enduring behavioral characteristics and internal predispositions that describe how a person reacts to the environment.

Phallic stage [FAL-ick] Freud's third stage of personality development, from about age 4 to about age 7, during which children obtain gratification primarily from the genitals.

Phenylketonuria (PKU) [fee-nil-key-ton-NYEW-ree-uh] A human genetic disorder that prevents an individual from processing the amino acid phenylalanine.

Phobic disorder An anxiety disorder characterized by excessive, irrational, and unreasonable fear and subsequent attempted avoidance of specific objects or situations, acknowledged by the person as unreasonable.

Phonemes [FOE-neems] The basic units of sound that compose the words in a language.

Placebo effect [pluh-SEE-bo] A nonspecific therapeutic change that occurs as a result of a person's expectations of change rather than as a direct result of any specific treatment.

Placenta [pluh-SENT-uh] A group of blood vessels and membranes in the uterus connected to the fetus by the umbilical cord and serving as the mechanism for the exchange of nutrients and waste products.

Plateau phase The second phase of the sexual response cycle, during which the sexual partners are preparing for orgasm. Autonomic nervous system activity increases and there is further vasoconstriction.

Positive instance A stimulus that is an example of the concept under study.

Positive reinforcement Presentation of a rewarding or pleasant stimulus after a particular response to increase the likelihood that the response will recur.

Posttraumatic stress disorder A category of mental disorders that becomes evident after a person has undergone the stress of some type of disaster; common symptoms include vivid, intrusive recollections or reexperiences of the traumatic event and occasional lapses of normal consciousness.

Preconscious Freud's second level of awareness, consisting of the mental activities of which people gain awareness by attending to them.

Prejudice A negative evaluation of an entire group of people that is typically based on unfavorable (and often wrong) ideas about the group.

Premature ejaculation The inability of a man to delay ejaculation long enough to satisfy his sexual partner in at least half of his sexual encounters.

Preoperational stage Piaget's second stage of intellectual development (lasting from about age 2 to age 6 or 7), during which initial symbolic thought is developed.

Pressure The emotional state or condition resulting from others' real or imagined expectations for success or for specific behaviors or results; the feelings that result from coercion.

Prevalence The percentage of a population displaying a disorder during any specified period.

Primacy effect The more accurate recall of items that were presented first.

Primary erectile dysfunction The inability of a man *ever* to have attained an erection of sufficient strength for sexual intercourse.

Primary orgasmic dysfunction The inability of a woman *ever* to achieve orgasm through any means of sexual stimulation.

Primary punisher Any stimulus or event that follows a particular response and that by its delivery or removal acts naturally (without learning) to decrease the likelihood that the response will recur.

Primary reinforcer Any stimulus or event that follows a particular response and that, by its mere delivery (if pleasant) or removal (if unpleasant), acts naturally (without learning) to increase the likelihood that the response will recur.

Privacy The result of the process of limiting the access of other people by controlling the boundaries between those people and oneself.

Proactive interference [pro-AK-tiv] The decrease in accurate recall of particular information as a result of previous information interfering with its recall. Also known as *proactive inhibition.*

Problem solving The behavior of individuals when confronted with a situation or task that requires some insight or some unknown elements to be ascertained to deal with it.

Procedural memory Memory for the perceptual, motor, and cognitive skills required to complete a task.

Projection A defense mechanism by which people attribute their own undesirable traits to other people or objects.

Projective tests Personality-assessing devices or instruments by which examinees are shown a standard set of ambiguous stimuli and asked to respond in an unrestricted manner.

Prosocial behavior An act that benefits someone else or society but that generally offers no obvious benefit to the person performing it and that might even involve some personal risk or sacrifice.

Psychiatrists Physicians (medical doctors) who have completed a residency specializing in the study of behavior and the treatment of patients with emotional and physical disorders.

Psychic determinism [SIE-kick] A psychoanalytic assumption that everything a person feels, thinks, and does has a purpose and that all behaviors are caused by past events.

Psychoactive drug [SIE-koh-AK-tiv] A drug that alters behavior, thought, or emotions by altering biochemical reactions in the nervous system, thereby affecting consciousness.

Psychoanalysis [SIE-ko-uh-NAL-uh-sis] A lengthy therapy developed by Freud that aims at uncovering conflicts and unconscious impulses through special techniques, including free association, dream analysis, and transference.

Psychoanalysts Psychiatrists or occasionally nonmedical practitioners who have studied the technique of psychoanalysis and use it in treating people with emotional problems.

Psychoanalytic approach [SIE-ko-an-uh-LIT-ick] The school of psychological thought developed by Freud, who was interested in how personality develops. His approach focused on the unconscious and on how it directs day-to-day behavior. Also known as *psychoanalysis.*

Psychodrama [SIE-ko-dram-a] A group therapy procedure in which members act out their situations, feelings, and roles.

Psychodynamically based therapies [SIE-ko-die-NAM-ick-lee] Therapies based loosely on Freud's theory of psychoanalysis, using a part of the approach but rejecting some elements of Freud's theory.

Psycholinguistics The study of how language is acquired, perceived, understood, and produced.

Psychological dependence A compelling desire to use a drug, along with an inability to inhibit that desire.

Psychologists Individuals with advanced training who study behavior and use behavioral principles in scientific research or in applied settings for the treatment of emotional problems.

Psychology The science of behavior and mental processes.

Psychoneuroimmunology (PNI) [sie-ko-NEW-ro-IM-you-NOLL-oh-gee] The study of how psychological processes and the nervous system affect and in turn are affected by the body's natural defense system, the immune system.

Psychostimulant A drug that in low to moderate doses increases alertness, reduces fatigue, and elevates mood.

Psychotherapy [SIE-ko-THAIR-uh-pee] The treatment of emotional or behavioral problems through psychological techniques.

Psychotic [sie-KOT-ick] Suffering from a gross impairment in reality testing that interferes with the ability to meet the ordinary demands of life.

Puberty [PEW-burr-tee] The period during which the reproductive system matures; it begins with an increase in sex hormone production and occurs at (and signals) the end of childhood.

Punishment The process of presenting an undesirable or noxious stimulus or removing a desirable stimulus to decrease the probability that a particular preceding response will recur.

Questionnaire A printed form with questions, usually given to a large group of people; used by researchers to gather a substantial amount of data in a short time. Also known as a *survey.*

Range A measure of variability that describes the spread of scores in a distribution, calculated by subtracting the lowest score from the highest score.

Rape Forcible sexual assault of an unwilling partner, usually a woman.

Rational-emotive therapy A cognitive behavior therapy that emphasizes the importance of logical, rational thought processes.

Rationalization A defense mechanism by which people reinterpret undesirable feelings or behaviors in terms that make them appear acceptable.

Raw score An examinee's score on a test which has not been transformed or converted in any way.

Reaction formation A defense mechanism by which people behave in a manner opposite to their true but anxiety-provoking feelings.

Reasoning The process by which we generate and evaluate situations and reach conclusions.

Recency effect The more accurate recall of items presented last.

Reflexes Involuntary, automatic behaviors in response to stimuli, which occur without prior learning and usually show little variability from instance to instance.

Refractory period The recovery period of a neuron after it fires, during which time it cannot fire again; this period allows the neuron to reestablish electrical balance with its surroundings.

Rehearsal The process of repeatedly verbalizing, thinking about, or otherwise acting on information in order to keep the information in memory.

Reinforcer Any event that increases the probability of a recurrence of the response that preceded it.

Reliability The ability of a test to yield the same score for the same individual through repeated testings.

REM (rapid eye movement) sleep A stage of sleep characterized by high-frequency, low-voltage brain-wave activity, rapid and systematic eye movements, and dreams.

Representative sample A sample of individuals who match the population with whom they are to be compared, with regard to key variables such as socioeconomic status and age.

Repression A defense mechanism by which people block anxiety-provoking feelings from conscious awareness and push them into the unconscious.

Residual type A schizophrenic disorder characterized by inappropriate affect, illogical thinking, or eccentric behavior but with the patient generally in touch with reality.

Resistance In psychoanalysis, an unwillingness to cooperate by which a patient signals a reluctance to provide the therapist with information or to help the therapist understand or interpret a situation.

Resolution phase The fourth phase of the sexual response cycle, during which the body naturally returns after orgasm to its resting, or normal, state.

Retrieval The process by which stored information is recovered from memory.

Retroactive interference [RET-ro-AK-tiv] The decrease in accurate recall of information as a result of the subsequent presentation of different information. Also known as *retroactive inhibition*.

Retrograde amnesia [RET-ro-grade] Loss of memory for events and experiences occurring in a period preceding the amnesia-causing event.

Role A set of behaviors expected from a certain category of individuals; a person's roles may change depending on the group within which the person finds himself or herself.

Rooting reflex A reflex in which an infant turns its head toward a mild stimulus applied to its lips or cheeks.

Sample A group of subjects or participants who are assumed to be representative of the population about which an inference is being made.

Schema [SKEEM-uh] A conceptual framework that organizes information and makes sense of the world by laying out a structure in which events can be encoded.

Schizophrenia [SKIT-soh-FREN-ia] A group of disorders characterized by a lack of reality testing and by deterioration of social and intellectual functioning and beginning before age 45 and lasting at least 6 months. People diagnosed as schizophrenic often show serious personality disintegration with significant changes in thought, mood, perception, and behavior.

Secondary erectile dysfunction The inability of a man to achieve an erection in 25 percent or more of his sexual attempts.

Secondary orgasmic dysfunction A woman's inability to achieve orgasm in a given situation, even though she has achieved orgasm in the past by one technique or another. Also known as *situational orgasmic dysfunction*.

Secondary punisher A neutral stimulus with no intrinsic value to the organism that acquires punishment value through repeated pairing with a punishing stimulus.

Secondary reinforcer A neutral stimulus that has no intrinsic value to an organism but that acquires reinforcement value through repeated pairing with a reinforcing stimulus.

Secondary sex characteristics The physical features of a person's gender identity that are not directly involved with reproduction but that help distinguish men from women.

Sedative-hypnotic A class of drugs that relax and calm people and that, in higher doses, induce sleep.

Self-actualization The process of realizing one's uniquely human potential for good; the process of achieving everything that one is capable of achieving.

Self-efficacy A person's belief about whether he or she can successfully engage in and execute a specific behavior.

Self-fulfilling prophecy The unwitting creation by a researcher of a situation that leads to specific prophesied results.

Self-monitoring An assessment procedure in which a person systematically counts and records the frequency and duration of specific behaviors in him- or herself.

Self-perception theory An approach to attitude formation in which people are assumed to infer their attitudes on the basis of observations of their own behavior.

Self-perceptions People's attitudes toward and beliefs about themselves, largely formed during childhood and adolescence and often a reflection of other people's perceived attitudes.

Self-serving bias People's tendency to evaluate their own behavior as worthwhile, regardless of the situation.

Self In Rogers's theory of personality, the perceptions individuals have of themselves and of their relationships to other people and to various aspects of life.

Semantic memory Memory for ideas, rules, and general concepts about the world.

Semantics The study of the meaning of language components.

Sensorimotor stage The first of Piaget's four stages of intellectual development (covering roughly the first 2 years of life), during which the child begins to interact with the environment and the rudiments of intelligence are established.

Sensory memory The mechanism that performs initial encoding and brief storage of stimuli. Also known as the *sensory register*.

Separation anxiety In children from 8 to 15 months, the fear response displayed when the mother or caregiver is absent.

Sexual deviations Sexual practices directed toward objects rather than people, sexual encounters involving real or simulated suffering or humiliation, or sexual activities with a nonconsenting partner. Also known as *paraphilias*.

Sexual dysfunction The inability to obtain satisfaction from sexual behavior, often accompanied by the inability to experience orgasm.

Shaping The gradual training of an organism to give the proper responses by selectively reinforcing behaviors as they approach the desired response.

Short-term memory The memory storage system that temporarily holds current or recently acquired information for immediate or short-term use.

Shyness Extreme anxiety in individuals who are socially reticent and often overly concerned with how they appear to others, often leading to avoidance of social situations.

Significant difference A statistically determined likelihood that a behavior has not occurred because of chance alone.

Skinner box Named (by others) for its developer, B. F. Skinner, a box that contains a responding mechanism (usually a lever) capable of delivering a consequence, often a reinforcer, to an organism.

Sleep A nonwaking state of consciousness characterized by general unresponsiveness to the environment and general physical immobility.

Social cognition The thought process of making sense of events, people, ourselves, and the world in general through analyzing and interpreting them.

Social facilitation A change in performance that occurs when people believe they are in the presence of other people.

Social influence The way in which one or more people alter the attitudes or behavior of others.

Social loafing The decrease in productivity that occurs when an individual works in a group instead of alone.

Social need An aroused condition that directs people toward establishing feelings about themselves and others and toward establishing or maintaining relationships.

Social phobia [FOE-bee-uh] An anxiety disorder characterized by fear of, and desire to avoid, situations in which the person might be exposed to scrutiny by others and might behave in an embarrassing or humiliating way.

Social psychology The study of how individuals influence and are influenced by the thoughts, feelings, and behaviors of other individuals.

Social support The availability of comfort, recognition, approval, and encouragement from other people, including friends, family, members of organizations, and coworkers.

Sociobiology The theory that even day-to-day behaviors are determined by the process of natural selection—that social behaviors that contribute to the survival of a species are passed on through the genes from one generation to the next and account for the mechanisms that have evolved to produce behaviors such as altruism.

Somatic nervous system [so-MAT-ick] The part of the peripheral nervous system that carries information to skeletal muscles and thereby affects bodily movement; this part of the nervous system controls voluntary, conscious sensory and motor functions.

Somatization disorders Somatoform disorders characterized by recurrent and multiple complaints of several years' duration for which medical attention has been ineffective.

Somatoform disorders [so-MAT-oh-form] Disorders characterized by real physical symptoms not under voluntary control and for which no evident physical cause exists.

Specific phobia An anxiety disorder characterized by irrational and persistent fear of an object or situation, along with a compelling desire to avoid it.

Spinal cord The portion of the central nervous system that is contained within the spinal column and that transmits and receives signals from the senses to the brain, controls reflexive responses, and conveys signals from the brain to the muscles and glands.

Spinal cord The portion of the central nervous system that is contained within the spinal column and that transmits and receives signals from the senses to the brain, controls reflexive responses, and conveys signals from the brain to the muscles and glands.

Split-brain patients Persons whose *corpus callosum*—which normally connects the two cerebral hemispheres—has been surgically severed.

Spontaneous recovery The recurrence of an extinguished conditioned response following a rest period.

Standard deviation A descriptive statistic that measures the variability of data from the mean of the sample.

Standard score A score that expresses an individual's position relative to the mean, based on the standard deviation.

Standardization The process of developing a uniform procedure for administering and scoring a test, and for establishing norms.

State-dependent learning The tendency to recall information learned in a particular physiological state most accurately when one is again in that physiological state.

Statistics The branch of mathematics that deals with collecting, classifying, and analyzing data.

Stereotypes Fixed, overly simple (and often wrong) ideas, usually about traits, attitudes, and behaviors attributed to groups of people.

Stimulus discrimination The process by which an organism learns to respond only to a specific reinforced stimulus.

Stimulus generalization The occurrence of a conditioned response to a stimulus that is similar but not identical to the original conditioned stimulus.

Storage The process of maintaining information in memory.

Stress inoculation [in-OK-you-LAY-shun] The procedure of giving people realistic warnings, recommendations, and reassurances to help them prepare for and cope with impending dangers or losses.

Stress A nonspecific, often global, response by an organism to real or imagined demands made on it (a person must appraise a situation as stressful for it to be stressful).

Stressor A stimulus that affects an organism in physically or psychologically injurious ways and elicits feelings such as anxiety, tension, and physiological arousal.

Structuralism The school of psychological thought that considered immediate, conscious experience the proper subject matter of psychology.

Subgoal analysis A heuristic procedure in which a task is broken down into smaller, more manageable parts.

Sublimation [sub-li-MAY-shun] A defense mechanism by which people redirect socially unacceptable impulses into acceptable ones.

Substance abusers People who overuse drugs and rely on them to deal with stress and anxiety.

Sucking reflex A reflex in which an infant makes sucking motions when presented with a stimulus to the lips, such as a nipple.

Superego [super-EE-go] In Freud's theory, the moral aspect of mental functioning, comprising the ego ideal (what a person would ideally like to be) and the conscience, and taught by parents and society.

Superstitious behavior Behavior learned through coincidental association with reinforcement.

Surface structure The organization of a sentence that is closest to its written or spoken form.

Sympathetic nervous system The part of the autonomic nervous system that responds to emergency situations; active only occasionally, it calls up bodily resources as needed for major energy expenditures.

Symptom substitution The appearance of one symptom to replace another that has been eliminated by treatment.

Synapse [SIN-apps] The juncture of the axon terminals of one neuron and the receptor site of another including the microscopically small space between them.

Syntax [SIN-tacks] The study of how groups of words are related and how they are arranged in phrases and sentences.

Systematic desensitization A counterconditioning procedure in which a person first learns deep relaxation and then imagines a series of progressively fearful situations; with each successive experience, the person learns relaxation rather than fear as a new response to a formerly fearful stimulus.

Teratogens [ter-AT-oh-jen] Substances that can produce developmental malformations in a fetus.

Territorial behavior Behavior involved in establishing, maintaining, personalizing, and defending a delineated space.

Thanatology The study of the psychological and medical aspects of death and dying.

Theory A collection of interrelated ideas and facts put forward to explain and predict behavior and mental processes.

Time-out A punishment procedure in which a person is physically removed from a desired or reinforcing situation to decrease the likelihood that an undesired behavior will recur.

Token economy An operant conditioning environment in which patients who engage in appropriate behavior receive tokens that they can exchange for desirable items or activities.

Tolerance A progressive insensitivity to repeated use of a specific drug in the same dosage and at the same frequency of use.

Trait Any readily identifiable stable behavior that characterizes the way in which an individual differs from other individuals.

Transference A psychoanalytic procedure in which a therapist becomes the object of a patient's emotional attitudes about an important person in the patient's life, such as a parent.

Transformational grammar An approach to the study of language that assumes that each surface structure of a sentence has a deep structure associated with it.

Type A behavior Behavior characterized by competitiveness, impatience, hostility, and always striving to do more in less time.

Type B behavior Behavior characterized by more calmness, more patience, and less hurrying than that of Type A individuals.

Types Broad collections of traits loosely tied together and interrelated; see Trait.

Unconditioned response The unlearned or involuntary response to an unconditioned stimulus.

Unconditioned stimulus A stimulus that normally produces an involuntary, measurable response.

Unconscious motivation A psychoanalytic assumption that behavior is determined by desires, goals, and internal states, buried deep within the unconscious, of which an individual is unaware.

Unconscious Freud's third level of awareness, consisting of the mental activities beyond people's normal awareness.

Undifferentiated type A schizophrenic disorder characterized by a mixture of symptoms and which does not allow for clear diagnoses to meet criteria of other diagnostic categories.

Validity The ability of a test to measure only what it is supposed to measure.

Variability A measure of the extent to which scores differ from one another and especially the extent to which they differ from the mean.

Variable-interval schedule A reinforcement schedule in which a reinforcer (reward) is delivered after predetermined but varying intervals of time, provided that the required response has occurred at least once after each interval.

Variable-ratio schedule A reinforcement schedule in which a reinforcer (reward) is delivered after a predetermined but variable number of responses has occurred.

Variable A condition or a characteristic of a situation or person that is subject to change (that varies) across situations or individuals.

Vasoconstriction In the sexual response cycle, a constriction of the blood vessels, particularly in the genital area.

Vulnerability A person's diminished ability to deal with demanding life events. The extent to which people are easily impaired by an event and thus respond maladaptively to the external or internal demands being placed on them.

Withdrawal symptoms A variety of physiological reactions that occur when an addictive drug is no longer administered to an addict.

Working memory A new conception of short-term memory that focuses on the central processing capacities of this type of memory and views it as a holding place for information while other information is being processed and directed for further processing.

Working through The gradual, often repeated, slow process in therapy of interpretation, resistance to interpretation, and transference.

Zygote A fertilized egg.